Magill's
Cinema
Annual
2017

Magill's Cinema Annual 2017

36th Edition
A Survey of the films of 2016

Brian Tallerico, Editor

A VideoHound® Reference

A Cengage Company

Farmington Hills, Mich • San Francisco • New York • Waterville, Maine
Meriden, Conn • Mason, Ohio • Chicago

Magill's Cinema Annual 2017

Brian Tallerico, Editor

Senior Project Editor: Michael J. Tyrkus

Editorial: Laura Avery, Margaret Mazurkiewicz

Editorial Support Services: Wayne Fong

Composition and Electronic Prepress: Gary Leach, Gary Oudersluys, Evi Seoud

Manufacturing: Rita Wimberley

For product information and technology assistance, contact us at
Gale Customer Support, 1-800-877-4253.
For permission to use material from this text or product,
submit all requests online at **www.cengage.com/permissions.**
Further permissions questions can be emailed to
permissionrequest@cengage.com

While every effort has been made to ensure the reliability of the information presented in this publication, Gale, a Cengage Company, does not guarantee the accuracy of the data contained herein. Gale accepts no payment for listing; and inclusion in the publication of any organization, agency, institution, publication, service, or individual does not imply endorsement of the editors or publisher. Errors brought to the attention of the publisher and verified to the satisfaction of the publisher will be corrected in future editions.

EDITORIAL DATA PRIVACY POLICY: Does this product contain information about you as an individual? If so, for more information about our editorial data privacy policies, please see our Privacy Statement at www.gale.cengage.com.

Gale, a Cengage Company
27500 Drake Rd.
Farmington Hills, MI, 48331-3535

ISBN-13: 978-1-4103-2415-3

ISSN: 0739-2141

This title is also available as an e-book.
ISBN-13: 978-1-4103-3462-6
Contact your Gale sales representative for ordering information.

Printed in Merxico
1 2 3 4 5 6 7 21 20 19 18 17

Contents

Preface

Magill's Cinema Annual 2017 continues the fine film reference tradition that defines the VideoHound® series of entertainment industry products published by Gale. The thirty-sixth annual volume in a series that developed from the twenty-one-volume core set, *Magill's Survey of Cinema,* the *Annual* was formerly published by Salem Press. Gale's twentieth volume, as with the previous Salem volumes, contains essay-reviews of significant domestic and foreign films released in the United States during the preceding year.

The *Magill's* editorial staff at Gale, Cengage Learning, comprising the VideoHound® team and a host of *Magill's* contributors, continues to provide the enhancements that were added to the *Annual* when Gale acquired the line. These features include:

- More essay-length reviews of significant films released during the year
- Obituaries and book review sections
- Trivia and "fun facts" about the reviewed movies, their stars, the crew, and production
- Quotes and dialogue "soundbites" from reviewed movies, or from stars and crew about the film
- More complete award and nomination listings, including the American Academy Awards®, the Golden Globes, and others (see the User's Guide for more information on awards coverage)
- Box office grosses, including year-end and other significant totals
- Publicity taglines featured in film reviews and advertisements

In addition to these elements, *Magill's Cinema Annual 2017* still features:

- An obituaries section profiling major contributors to the film industry who died in 2016
- An annotated list of selected film books published in 2016
- Nine indexes: Director, Screenwriter, Cinematographer, Editor, Art Director, Music Director, Performer, Subject, and Title (now cumulative)

COMPILATION METHODS

The *Magill's* editorial staff reviews a variety of entertainment industry publications, including trade magazines and newspapers, as well as online sources, on a daily and weekly basis to select significant films for review in *Magill's Cinema Annual. Magill's* staff and other contributing reviewers, including film scholars and university faculty, write the reviews included in the *Annual.*

MAGILL'S CINEMA ANNUAL: A VIDEOHOUND® REFERENCE

The *Magill's Survey of Cinema* series, now supplemented by the *Annual,* is the recipient of the Reference Book of the Year Award in Fine Arts by the American Library Association. Gale, an award-winning publisher of reference products, is proud to offer *Magill's Cinema Annual* as part of its popular VideoHound® product line, which includes *VideoHound®'s Golden Movie Retriever* and *The Video Source Book.* Other Gale film-related products include the four-volume *International Dictionary of Films and Filmmakers, Women Filmmakers & Their Films,* the *Contemporary Theatre, Film, and Television* series, and the four-volume *Schirmer Encyclopedia of Film.*

ACKNOWLEDGMENTS

The writing staff of *Magill's Cinema Annual 2017,* which consists of publishing professionals, freelance writers, and paid film critics, has given their all to this year's remarkable edition. Together, we work to create a comprehensive, critical view of the year in film. The staff continues to impress with their knowledge, dedication, and abilities, as they analyze film not merely from the standpoint of a viewer but as experts in their field. They bring a wide variety of backgrounds and personalities together to support one purpose.

Magill's Cinema Annual 2017 was truly a collaboratively created work and would be nothing without the support of the writers assigned to it and the friends and family who so completely back its editor in every capacity. The editor would like to thank a professional support structure that includes Chaz Ebert, Matt Zoller Seitz, Hank Sartin, Bill Moller, and many more, along with the constant support of his loving wife Lauren and the daily inspiration of his three beautiful sons Lucas, Miles, and Noah. They make all work both possible and worthwhile.

We at *Magill's* look forward to another exciting year in film and preparing the next edition of *Magill's Cinema Annual.* As always, we invite your comments, questions, and suggestions. Please direct them to:

Editor, *Magill's Cinema Annual*
Gale, a Cengage Company
27500 Drake Road
Farmington Hills, MI 48331-3535
Phone: (248) 699-4253
Toll-Free: (800) 347-GALE (4253)
Fax: (248) 699-8865

The Year in Film 2016: An Introduction

The year 2016 began with a call for more diversity in cinema, reflected in the campaign #OscarsSoWhite, and ended with a creative world honestly concerned about its future with the moves of a presidential administration that seems more eager to control art and free speech than any in generations. It's a tense time to be an artist, and not just because healthcare for this notoriously low-income profession is being threatened but because actual free speech feels like it's at risk, captured in events like Asghar Farhadi's inability to attend the Academy Awards, even though he was not only a nominee but a former winner. Against this backdrop of political dissent and social upheaval, people kept going to the movies, although the sense that they were looking for something familiar and safe as opposed to something challenging and risk-taking was palpable if one looked at the box office. While the blockbusters of 2016 will go down as some of the most creatively bankrupt in history, voices from the fringe, like Barry Jenkins, Jim Jarmusch, Pablo Larrain, Kenneth Lonergan, and Damien Chazelle, gave film lovers a reason to be optimistic.

As for the business that we call show, rarely has the Hollywood-to-multiplex pipeline felt more like a product and less like an artistic venture than it did in 2016. In particular, the summer blockbuster season will be forever recognized as one of the worst in history, highlighted by week after week of sequels that no one asked for (such as *Now You See Me 2, Independence Day: Resurgence, Jason Bourne*) and producing almost nothing of quality. Looking at the films that were financially successful in 2016 could lead a film fan to serious depression. The entire top ten of the year was either animated, a sequel, or based on successful source material. In fact, it took until December for original projects to be met with box office success as Best Picture nominees *Hidden Figures* and *La La Land* both cracked the top 20 of the year (although in the last two positions on that list). If one wonders why they make so many sequels and animated films, ask them to look at the top ten of 2016, which contained no less than five sequels, and four animated projects (five if you include the heavily-CGI *The Jungle Book*).

Of the major financial windfalls of 2016, perhaps none will have the impact of February's stunning hit, *Deadpool,* the highest-grossing R-rated film of all time. *Deadpool* proved that the long-thought rule that comic book films had to be PG-13 was false, out-grossing more reliable men in tights flicks like *Batman v Superman: Dawn of Justice, Suicide Squad,* and *Doctor Strange.* After years of trying to get the project off the ground, Ryan Reynolds finally got the star vehicle he long deserved in the massive hit film, a work that was so successful it popped up during awards season, landing a Golden Globe nomination for Best Picture (Comedy or Musical) and a Producers Guild of America nomination. It was the bright spot in a relatively dire year for the superhero genre.

As is increasingly the case, animated and family films dominated the box office. The most successful was Disney/Pixar's *Finding Dory*, but hundreds of millions of dollars were earned by films like *The Secret Life of Pets, The Jungle Book, Zootopia, Sing*, and *Moana* as well. In fact, all five of those films grossed more than $240 million. If one ever wonders why there are so many animated films and movies based on superheroes, it's because they are the ones making money in the modern era and 2016 did nothing to change that.

So, what did change in 2016? The most notable story of the year was the way the industry responded to accusations of whitewashing that sprung up after the #OscarSoWhite campaign in January and February. It really started at Sundance with the world premiere of Nate Parker's *The Birth of a Nation*, a film that went from a highly coveted production (netting the biggest deal in Sundance history from Fox Searchlight) to cinematic poison when the story of its writer/director/star's trial for rape when he was in college surfaced. It was one thing that Parker infused his true story with an untrue subplot that turned his character into an avenger of raped slaves but then Parker woefully mishandled the publicity tour, refusing to display an ounce of remorse until it was too late.

Luckily, other filmmakers stepped up and 2016 will be remembered as a year in which diversity was well reflected in its best films. Not only did Denzel Washington deliver his best-directed film to date in *Fences*, but he earned Oscar nominations for himself and his supporting actress, Viola Davis. Arguably the biggest box office surprise of the year came late, in the true story of three African-American women who were foundational in the formative years of NASA, *Hidden Figures*. The film was a box office success, and even earned Oscar nominations for Best Picture and Best Supporting Actress.

However, the best film of 2016 was also a story of diversity, Barry Jenkins' *Moonlight*. Based loosely on an unproduced play by Tarrell McCraney, *Moonlight* is the three-part story of a young, black, gay man in Miami, the kind of person who feels he's so unseen that he could literally disappear into the ocean. Both lyrical and realistic at the same time, *Moonlight* is one of 2016's true masterpieces, driven by the year's best ensemble, including Naomie Harris, Mahershala Ali, Trevante Rhodes, Andre Holland, and more.

Moonlight shared much of the awards season spotlight with two other films: Kenneth Lonergan's *Manchester by the Sea* and Damien Chazelle's *La La Land*. The trio dominated most of the critics groups awards, and Chazelle's was poised to be the year's biggest Oscar winner after landing a record-tying 14 nominations. A love letter to the dreamers of Los Angeles, *La La Land* was one of those rare films that not only had critics raving but made a fortune at the box office. It is one of the few films from 2016 that will certainly be remembered, even if it's by those who thought it was overrated. *Manchester by the Sea*, on the other hand, was a year-long critical darling from its Sundance premiere through its Oscar nominations, including nods for Best Picture, Best Actor, Best Supporting Actress, and Best Director.

Other notable critical darlings of 2016 include Jim Jarmusch's *Paterson*, Maren Ade's *Toni Erdmann*, Park Chan-wook's *The Handmaiden*, Pablo Larrain's *Jackie*, David Mackenzie's *Hell or High Water*, Denis Villeneuve's *Arrival*, and a film nearly a quarter-century in production, Martin Scorsese's *Silence*.

In the end, the film story of 2016 was overshadowed by events in the real world, including the election of the most divisive president in generations. The film story of 2017 will be a more interesting year as Hollywood responds to President Trump and the issues raised by his presidency. In fact, we may look back on 2016 as one of the last predictable, normal film years, and the end of an era.

Brian Tallerico
Chicago, Illinois

Contributing Reviewers

Nick Allen
Professional Film Critic

Abbey Bender
Freelance Reviewer

David L. Boxerbaum
Freelance Reviewer

Tom Burns
Freelance Reviewer

Dave Canfield
Professional Film Critic

Erik Childress
Professional Film Critic

Mark Dujsik
Professional Film Critic

Don Lewis
Professional Film Critic

Jacob Oller
Freelance Reviewer

Locke Peterseim
Professional Film Critic

Matt Pais
Professional Film Critic

Josh Ralske
Freelance Reviewer

Brent Simon
Professional Film Critic

Michael Snydel
Freelance Reviewer

Peter Sobczynski
Professional Film Critic

Collin Souter
Professional Film Critic

Scout Tafoya
Freelance Reviewer

Brian Tallerico
Professional Film Critic

User's Guide

ALPHABETIZATION

Film titles and reviews are arranged on a word-by-word basis, including articles and prepositions. English leading articles (A, An, The) are ignored, as are foreign leading articles (El, Il, La, Las, Le, Les, Los). Other considerations:

- Acronyms appear alphabetically as if regular words.

- Common abbreviations in titles file as if they are spelled out, so *Mr. Death* will be found as if it was spelled *Mister Death.*

- Proper names in titles are alphabetized beginning with the individual's first name, for instance, *Gloria* will be found under "G."

- Titles with numbers, for instance, *200 Cigarettes,* are alphabetized as if the numbers were spelled out, in this case, "Two-Hundred." When numeric titles gather in close proximity to each other, the titles will be arranged in a low-to-high numeric sequence.

SPECIAL SECTIONS

The following sections that are designed to enhance the reader's examination of film are arranged alphabetically; they include:

- *List of Awards.* An annual list of awards bestowed upon the year's films by the following: Academy of Motion Picture Arts and Sciences, British Academy of Film and Television Arts Awards, Directors Guild of America Awards, Golden Globe Awards, Golden Raspberry Awards, Independent Spirit Awards, the Screen Actors Guild Awards, and the Writer's Guild Awards.

- *Obituaries.* Profiles major contributors to the film industry who died in 2016.

- *Selected Film Books of 2016.* An annotated list of selected film books published in 2016.

INDEXES

Film titles and artists are separated into nine indexes, allowing the reader to effectively approach a film from any one of several directions, including not only its credits but its subject matter.

- *Director, Screenwriter, Cinematographer, Editor, Art Director, Music Director,* and *Performer* indexes are arranged alphabetically according to artists appearing in this volume, followed by a list of the films on which they worked. In the *Performer* index, a (V) beside a movie title indicates voice-only work and an (N) beside a movie title indicates work as narrator.
- *Subject Index.* Films may be categorized under several of the subject terms arranged alphabetically in this section.
- *Title Index.* The title index is a cumulative alphabetical list of films covered in the thirty-six volumes of the *Magill's Cinema Annual,* including the films covered in this volume. Films reviewed in past volumes are cited with the year in which the film appeared in the *Annual;* films reviewed in this volume are cited with the film title and this year's edition in boldface. Original and alternate titles are cross-referenced to the American release title in the Title Index. Titles of retrospective films are followed by the year, in brackets, of their original release.

SAMPLE REVIEW

Each *Magill's* review contains up to sixteen items of information. A fictionalized composite sample review containing all the elements of information that may be included in a full-length review follows the outline on the facing page. The circled number following each element in the sample review designates an item of information that is explained in the outline.

1. **Title:** Film title as it was released in the United States.

2. **Foreign or alternate title(s):** The film's original title or titles as released outside the United States, or alternate film title or titles. Foreign and alternate titles also appear in the Title Index to facilitate user access.

3. **Taglines:** Up to ten publicity taglines for the film from advertisements or reviews.

4. **Box office information:** Year-end or other box office domestic revenues for the film.

5. **Film review:** A signed review of the film, including an analytic overview of the film and its critical reception.

6. **Reviewer byline:** The name of the reviewer who wrote the full-length review. A complete list of this volume's contributors appears in the "Contributing Reviewers" section which follows the Introduction.

7. **Principal characters:** Listings of the film's principal characters and the names of the actors who play them in the film.

8. **Country of origin:** The film's country or countries of origin and the languages featured in the film.

9. **Release date:** The year of the film's first general release.

10. **Production information:** This section typically includes the name(s) of the film's producer(s), production company, and distributor; director(s); screenwriter(s); cinematographer(s); editor(s); art director(s); production designer(s); music composer(s); and other credits such as visual effects, sound, costume design, and song(s) and songwriter(s).

11. **MPAA rating:** The film's rating by the Motion Picture Association of America. If there is no rating given, the line will read, "Unrated."

12. **Running time:** The film's running time in minutes.

13. **Reviews:** A list of brief citations of major newspaper and journal reviews of the film, including author, publication title, and date of review.

14. **Film quotes:** Memorable dialogue directly from the film, attributed to the character who spoke it, or comment from cast or crew members or reviewers about the film.

15. **Film trivia:** Interesting tidbits about the film, its cast, or production crew.

16. **Awards information:** Awards won by the film, followed by category and name of winning cast or crew member. Listings of the film's nominations follow the wins on a separate line for each award. Awards are arranged alphabetically. Information is listed for films that won or were nominated for the following awards: American Academy Awards®, British Academy of Film and Television Arts Awards, Directors Guild of America Awards, Golden Globe Awards, Golden Raspberry Awards, Independent Spirit Awards, the Screen Actors Guild Awards, and the Writers Guild of America Awards.

THE GUMP DIARIES ①

(Los Diarios del Gump) ②

Love means never having to say you're stupid.
—Movie tagline ③

Box Office: $10 million ④

In writer/director Robert Zemeckis' *Back to the Future* trilogy (1985, 1989, 1990), Marty McFly (Michael J. Fox) and his scientist sidekick Doc Brown (Christopher Lloyd) journey backward and forward in time, attempting to smooth over some rough spots in their personal histories in order to remain true to their individual destinies. Throughout their time-travel adventures, Doc Brown insists that neither he nor Marty influence any major historical events, believing that to do so would result in catastrophic changes in humankind's ultimate destiny. By the end of the trilogy, however, Doc Brown has revised his thinking and tells Marty that, "Your future hasn't been written yet. No one's has. Your future is whatever you make it. So make it a good one."

In *Forrest Gump*, Zemeckis once again explores the theme of personal destiny and how an individual's life affects and is affected by his historical time period. This time, however, Zemeckis and screenwriter Eric Roth chronicle the life of a character who does nothing but meddle in the historical events of his time without even trying to do so. By the film's conclusion, however, it has become apparent that Zemeckis' main concern is something more than merely having fun with four decades of American history. In the process of re-creating significant moments in time, he has captured on celluloid something eternal and timeless—the soul of humanity personified by a nondescript simpleton from the deep South.

The film begins following the flight of a seemingly insignificant feather as it floats down from the sky and brushes against various objects and people before finally coming to rest at the feet of Forrest Gump (Tom Hanks). Forrest, who is sitting on a bus-stop bench, reaches down and picks up the feather, smooths it out, then opens his traveling case and carefully places the feather between the pages of his favorite book, *Curious George*.

In this simple but hauntingly beautiful opening scene, the filmmakers illustrate the film's principal concern: Is life a series of random events over which a person has no control, or is there an underlying order to things that leads to the fulfillment of an individual's destiny? The rest of the film is a humorous and moving attempt to prove that, underlying the random, chaotic events that make up a person's life, there exists a benign and simple order.

Forrest sits on the bench throughout most of the film, talking about various events of his life to others who happen to sit down next to him. It does not take long, however, for the audience to realize that Forrest's seemingly random chatter to a parade of strangers has a perfect chronological order to it. He tells his first story after looking down at the feet of his first bench partner and observing, "Mama always said that you can tell a lot about a person by the shoes they wear." Then, in a voice-over narration, Forrest begins the story of his life, first by telling about the first pair of shoes he can remember wearing.

The action shifts to the mid-1950s with Forrest as a young boy (Michael Humphreys) being fitted with leg braces to correct a curvature in his spine. Despite this traumatic handicap, Forrest remains unaffected, thanks to his mother (Sally Field) who reminds him on more than one occasion that he is no different from anyone else. Although this and most of Mrs. Gump's other words of advice are in the form of hackneyed cliches, Forrest, whose intelligence quotient is below normal, sincerely believes every one of them, namely because he instinctively knows they are sincere expressions of his mother's love and fierce devotion. ⑤

John Byline ⑥

CREDITS ⑦

Forrest Gump: Tom Hanks
Forrest's Mother: Sally Field
Young Forrest: Michael Humphreys
Origin: United States ⑧
Language: English, Spanish
Released: 1994 ⑨
Production: Liz Heller, John Manulis; New Line Cinema; released by Island Pictures ⑩
Directed by: Robert Zemeckis
Written by: Eric Roth
Cinematography by: David Phillips
Music by: Graeme Revell
Editing: Dana Congdon
Production Design: Danny Nowak
Sound: David Sarnoff
Costumes: David Robinson
MPAA rating: R ⑪
Running time: 102 minutes ⑫

REVIEWS ⑬

Doe, Jane. *Los Angeles Times.* July 6, 1994.
Doe, John. *Entertainment Weekly.* July 15, 1994.
Reviewer, Paul. *Hollywood Reporter.* June 29, 1994.
Writer, Zach. *New York Times Online.* July 15, 1994.

QUOTES ⑭

Forrest Gump (Tom Hanks): "The state of existence may be likened unto a receptacle containing cocoa-based confections, in that one may never predict that which one may receive."

TRIVIA ⑮

Hanks was the first actor since Spencer Tracy to win back-to-back Oscars® for Best Actor. Hanks received the award in 1993 for his performance in *Philadelphia.* Tracy won Oscars® in 1937 for *Captains Courageous* and in 1938 for *Boys Town.*

AWARDS ⑯

Academy Awards 1994: Film, Actor (Hanks), Special Effects, Cinematography

Nomination:

Golden Globes 1994: Film, Actor (Hanks), Supporting Actress (Field), Music.

A

THE ACCOUNTANT

Calculate your choices.
—Movie tagline

Box Office: $86.3 Million

When a jigsaw puzzle is nearly completed in *The Accountant*, a problem arises that makes a satisfaction-stymied boy erupt in in a wailing tantrum—and the film itself eventually made many viewers know just how he felt. The production had gradually and rather intriguingly provided the audience with the many pieces of its story, challenging them to have fun fitting things together and perhaps see the big picture before it is finally revealed to them. Unfortunately, an attempt to ultimately make everything mesh in this already far-fetched but moderately entertaining film results in quite a mess, making one feel like howling with disappointment.

There is a joke about a doctor's simple, surefire cure for the insomnia of an accountant's wife: "Roll over, and ask him about his job." That this film's titular character works at ZZZ Accounting is yet another wink toward the commonly-held perception that details of what the profession entails could help a person catch forty. However, *The Accountant* had already belied that soporific-sounding signage in its first moments, reassuring moviegoers with an initial startling sight that the film itself would not be a snooze: a freshly-dispatched batch of unfortunates with blood seeping from kill shots to their craniums. Many more holes would violently ventilate many more heads before the production's own end, so viewers were not made to follow suit and enter into their own long slumber during *The Accountant*'s

protracted running time of over two hours. Fortunately, no one was aiming to do anything to their brains but tease them.

The film's puzzle-like nature then meaningfully manifests itself with the aforementioned actual one, and the single missing piece that so frustrates the youngster obviously references the internationally-recognized symbol for the problem with which he unmistakably struggles: autism. Director Gavin O'Connor insisted that great pains were taken to take issues seriously of those born with the condition and their loved ones. The film sets out to forge a fond bond between viewers and its protagonist by showing him first as a beleaguered boy. A more severely-afflicted girl movingly rises to the occasion and lifts the key piece from the floor and hands it to him, enabling him to succeed. The puzzle piece depicts the spot upon a triumphant Muhammad Ali's chest beneath which that underdog-turned-indomitable champion's heart fiercely beat. Thus, what the girl extends empathetically is also emblematic.

One's compassion intensifies after the boy's well-meaning but woefully-misguided military father—significantly, a specialist in psychological warfare—messes up this and his younger son with the brutal instilling and relentless honing of martial arts self-defense skills so formidable that no one would ever mess with them twice. The killing machine that this poor kid grows up to be (now played by Ben Affleck with an appropriate lack of expressiveness-for once) says he enjoys incongruity, and there is a lot to appreciate here. On the one hand, Christian Wolff is an affectless, bespectacled accountant in a nondescript Illinois strip mall who utilizes savant math skills (rare outside of cinematic autistics) to gently and kindly finagle tax deductions for seniors. On the other, he can suddenly ditch those glasses and brawnily burst forth from stiff suits like some double-identified comic book avenger (complete with a secret treasure-trove lair) to make deadly deductions, subtracting souls from the list of the living with unparalleled sharpshooting and pencak silat prowess while dealing with the repercussions of high-risk—but high-reward—work for far-less-wholesome folk worldwide. Upon learning that this apparently monotonous-jobbed CPA continually changes both his location and his name, the latter adopted from famous mathematicians like author (and supposed fellow Aspie) Lewis Carroll, moviegoers did, to borrow from Wonderland's Alice, grow "curiouser and curiouser." When Chris endures the self-inflicted agony of blaring music and bright strobes to maintain his toughness, the character's duality is represented by his face being half illuminated and half in shadow. He rolls a bar on his legs to create tough scar tissue, but already painfully evident is the emotional scarring from both his father's ill-advised regimen and his frazzled mother's desertion that was largely due to her disapproval of it.

Has he become hardened through and through? The film provides an answer when this socially-hamstrung fellow who discloses a yearning for interaction soon perceptibly enjoys some with Dana Cummings (the adorable Anna Kendrick), a financial-discrepancy-finding junior accountant at the robotics firm where Chris takes a consulting job on the up-and-up to throw off authorities looking into the downside of his career. That he is mired in lonely isolation is emphasized throughout the film by glimpsing him through windowpanes or visually cordoning him off within door frames. It is pleasing to watch Chris and Dana bonding and ever-so-faintly flirting amidst the findings, seeing him experience unfamiliar, simultaneous exhilaration within a conference room which he has covered with calculations as in *A Beautiful Mind* (2001)—togetherness in their own gleeful, glassed-in geekdom. It is therefore not surprising that Chris cannot simply leave town when these shared insights put her in the sights of knowledge-nullifying assassins, and he rousingly transitioning from pocket protector mode to that in which he chivalrously protects damsels in distress.

One noggin here is nullified against a bathroom sink, and while *The Accountant* does not quite include everything but the kitchen one, it starts to feel that way as the film follows numerous story strands involving numerous characters and their reassessment-inducing backstories that are traced back numerous times to numerous periods in the past. The plotline involving Ray King (J.K. Simmons), director of the Treasury Department's Financial Crimes Enforcement Division,

and the department analyst (Cynthia Addai-Robinson) that he blackmails into identifying and finding the mysterious, elusive accountant includes a scene with exposition so long-winded that one began to wonder if an entirely different season might be encountered upon exiting the multiplex. "How did everything go so wrong so fast?" is what CEO of Living Robotics Lamar Blackburn (John Lithgow) surmises an amputee here is thinking, but viewers did not have to ponder that much about the film after as an effort was made to tie everything together so preposterously. They found themselves gawking in as much disbelief as villainous Lamar does at the film's closed-circuit-captured, cockamamie contrivance of a climax, which features the painfully-far-fetched filial reunion between Chris and the lead assassin gunning for him, who coincidentally turns out to be his long-lost brother Braxton (Jon Bernthal). Lamar's roar of "What is this?!" took the words right out of moviegoers' mouths.

The Accountant's reveals that Chris selflessly funnels the millions that bad guys pay him into the very facility that still offers those with autism the chance his father had denied him, and that his prime beneficiary there, the mercifully-assuaging girl at the outset, was the indispensable computer voice that has skillfully guided him and provided tips to the good guys. Screenwriter Bill Dubuque is also responsible for *The Judge* (2014), and this film warns that judging too hastily might lead to an inaccurate assessment—of both the neurodivergent and neurotypical. Everyone is imperfect and struggling to somehow find a way in which they are able to make some kind of mark, "to leave something behind," as the closing song states. Unfortunately for *The Accountant*, that largely ended up being exasperation.

David L. Boxerbaum

CREDITS

Christian Wolff: Ben Affleck
Dana Cummings: Anna Kendrick
Ray King: J.K. Simmons
Brax: Jon Bernthal
Francis Silverberg: Jeffrey Tambor
Origin: United States
Language: English
Released: 2016
Production: Lynette Howard Taylor, Mark Williams; released by Electric City Entertainment, Warner Brothers Inc., Zero Gravity Management
Directed by: Gavin O'Connor
Written by: Bill Dubuque
Cinematography by: Seamus McGarvey
Music by: Mark Isham

Sound: Mark A. Mangini
Music Supervisor: Gabe Hilfer
Editing: Richard Pearson
Art Direction: John Collins
Costumes: Nancy Steiner
Production Design: Keith P. Cunningham
MPAA rating: R
Running time: 128 minutes

REVIEWS

Anderson, John. *Wall Street Journal.* October 13, 2016.
Burr, Ty. *Boston Globe.* October 13, 2016.
Debruge, Peter. *Variety.* October 12, 2016.
Greenblatt, Leah. *Entertainment Weekly.* October 12, 2016.
Holden, Stephen. *New York Times.* October 13, 2016.
Hornaday, Ann. *Washington Post.* October 13, 2016.
McCarthy. Todd. *Hollywood Reporter.* October 12, 2016.
Phillips, Michael. *Chicago Tribune.* October 13, 2016.
Roeper, Richard. *Chicago Sun-Times.* October 12, 2016.
Travers, Peter. *Rolling Stone.* October 13, 2016.

QUOTES

Ray King: "I spent my whole life only recognizing my lucky breaks after they were gone."

TRIVIA

Anna Kendrick's character was based on her mother, an accountant who reviewed the script and explained the math to her daughter.

ALICE THROUGH THE LOOKING GLASS

It's time for a little madness.
—Movie tagline

Box Office: $77 Million

One of the most beloved passages in Lewis Carroll's 1871 nonsense classic *Through the Looking Glass, and What Alice Found There* is the poem entitled "The Walrus and the Carpenter," and thus contemporary caretakers of Carrolliana might begin their assessment of this adaptation by borrowing from the tusked of the two: The time has come to talk of many things, and, alas, few of them are good.

As the hammer-carrying other half of that oyster-devouring duo had asserted, "It seems a shame to play them such a trick." However, that is unfortunately what this production perpetrated upon devotees of the book. In Carroll's work, Alice had noticed a number of chess

pieces amidst the cinders of the fireplace after crossing over into Looking-Glass House, and the story told here has essentially tossed most everything else in as well and put a match to it. In their stead are such things as fiery feminism, supposedly burning backstory questions finally and far-from-enthrallingly answered, and the imparting during maudlin moments of messages about life, love, and family expected to warm all hearts within proximity. Add time, both tiresomely travelled and personified as half-man, half-mechanical martinet with some screws loose, and any hope that this film directed by James Bobin might closely mirror Carroll's clever fun were reduced to ashes.

In Carroll's *Alice's Adventures in Wonderland* (1865), Hatter had famously confounded the girl as well as readers when he offered up a riddle to which he could not provide an answer. The author was hounded for decades by fans who bemoaned being stuck in a quandary and begged that he finally provide them with relieved release. As to why Disney chose to produce a sequel to its live-action *Alice in Wonderland* (2010), no one was mystified for even a minute: it earned more than $1 billion worldwide, despite mixed reviews. Those responsible for that film felt they had improved upon something that had not been deemed deficient during the previous 145 years, including psychological seriousness and the supposedly suspenseful, focused pursuit of an ostensibly thrilling goal. This "grounding" of Carroll's work, as that film's director Tim Burton referred to it, also involved burying a great deal of the source material, which included both *Alice* and *Through the Looking Glass*, the author's gratefully received (if somewhat less-lauded) follow-up.

Calling this adaptation *Alice Through the Looking Glass* is even more of a big-screen bait and switch. There is no dreaming, marvelously curious and imaginative seven-year-old Alice passing through a mirror into an oddly populated, delightfully nonsensical neighborhood, which she traverses as if it were a chess board so that she can ultimately be crowned a queen. Moviegoers ardent about the book felt as if they had been rooked, or were mere pawns of the dollar-making dynamo that is Disney. Like its own six-years-hence Alice antecedent, this cinematic sequel was scripted by Linda Woolverton, who seems to have been most inspired by the title of *Through the Looking Glass's* eighth chapter, "It's My Own Invention," and the first line of the White Knight's song sung therein: "I'll tell thee everything I can." The things the Knight had devised did not work out very well, and the same goes here for those of Woolverton. This underwhelming time in garishly hued "Underland" involves turning Alice into a psychological sleuth who provides viewers with more than they ever wanted to know about things they could not have cared less about, and the hammering of empowering messages about striving for the seemingly impossible and overcoming unfair, sexist treatment of the fair sex. "You can't just make things the way you want, Alice" the character's properly conventional mum says here. "Every woman has to face that." Not so for adapter Woolverton, who makes *Looking Glass* clearly reflect her own now-familiar view.

It seems sadly apropos that this film begins with fortune-hunting pirates unabashedly out to seize someone else's treasure and make it their own. One gets a sinking feeling from the start, with a twenty-something Alice (a rather wan Mia Wasikowska) shown to in every sense be the competent captain of her own ship. The men surrounding her fear that all is lost, but intensely intrepid Alice will have none of it. Despite being buffeted by siege and storm, she literally takes things into her own hands and ultimately (as well as inspiringly, it was hoped) prevails. Soon after, the broad expanse of a map depicting every continent and ocean is spread out before her, as if to visually convey Alice's undauntedly progressive belief that the whole world is open to her. Last time, Woolverton invented a framing story in which Alice, unsurely teetering on the edge of being befittingly but unbearably bridled to monied, toothy twit Hamish (Leo Bill), tumbles down a rabbit hole and comes up firmly convinced of her "muchness" and the inadvisability of a stiflingly stuffy betrothal. Here, she is caught once again in a Victorian vice and dreading the loss of her independence, forced by a vengeful Hamish to choose between dutifully retaining either her family homestead or the cherished, bequeathed boat upon which she can continue to thrillingly and fulfilling explore new horizons. At the behest of blue butterfly Absolem (the late, great Alan Rickman, to whom the film is dedicated), Alice escapes through the looking glass and soon after lands with a thud amidst old friends, most notably the White Queen (an airy, hand-fluttering Anne Hathaway), comical if creepy Tweedledee and Tweedledum (Matt Lucas), and the silky, smiling Cheshire Cat (Stephen Fry).

Unfortunately, Alice is not the only thing that falls flat. Where Woolverton previously tasked her with putting an end to the colossal, fire-breathing Jabberwocky and thus the tyranny of the equally monstrous, big-headed Red Queen (Helena Bonham Carter), the problems faced here are smaller and more mundane: Alice's self-determination and Mommy issues; the deleterious doldrums of the Hatter (Johnny Depp, much more distractingly affected, if still intermittently affecting), brought on because no one will believe that his estranged daddy and other supposedly dead family members might be alive; and the White Queen's childhood lie about mere crumbs that greatly altered the life, personality, and appearance of her sister, the Red Queen.

While the latter still demands the removal of heads, here there is also a restorative pursuit into the past to uncover and prevent what caused the painful memories nagging within noggins. No need to resort to Valium with valiant Alice on hand: boldly refusing to be turned back by Time himself (a mugging Sacha Baron Cohen, accented to convey Germanic precision), she pilfers the "chronosphere" by which she soon finds herself transported. Audiences? Not so much.

The heroine's repetitive crisscrossing of the ocean of time (how convenient she has expertly helmed her ship!) never results in gripping drama but had some viewers wanting to get hold of some Dramamine. Also, the building up of Alice as a shrewd, loyal, and resolute role model is undermined by her coming off instead as foolhardy, selfish, and reckless when she helps her old friend "no matter what" despite Time stressing that the past can be learned from but not altered—and no one may have a future if she proceeds. That seems crazy, and, speaking of which, Woolverton purposefully shoehorns in an insane asylum interlude about the outrageous treatment of some women who were diagnosed as psychologically abnormal simply because their conduct failed to conform to suitably proper norms. The last word of a major character is unsurprisingly Alice's emphatic "woman."

The ending of this $170 million-budgeted production, which only grossed a quarter of its predecessor's take amidst poor reviews, adheres to Disney norms, sodden with heartwarming healing. Lines from the closing song by Pink might double as Carroll's cheeky mockery from the Great Beyond, that singularly crafty crafter of verse, referring to "this madness, colorful charade/No one can be just like me anyway!" Now that is not nonsense.

David L. Boxerbaum

CREDITS

Hatter Tarrant Hightopp: Johnny Depp
Alice Kingsleigh: Mia Wasikowska
Iracebeth: Helena Bonham Carter
Mirana: Anne Hathaway
Time: Sacha Baron Cohen
Origin: United States
Language: English
Released: 2016
Production: Tim Burton, Joe Roth, Jennifer Todd, Suzanne Todd; released by Walt Disney Pictures
Directed by: James Bobin
Written by: Linda Woolverton
Cinematography by: Stuart Dryburgh

Music by: Danny Elfman
Editing: Andrew Weisblum
Art Direction: Todd Cherniawsky; Niall Moroney
Costumes: Colleen Atwood
Production Design: Dan Hennah
MPAA rating: PG
Running time: 113 minutes

REVIEWS

Barker, Andrew. *Variety*. May 10, 2016.
Burr, Ty. *Boston Globe*. May 26, 2016.
Chang, Justin. *Los Angeles Times*. May 26, 2016.
Greenblatt, Leah. *Entertainment Weekly*. May 10, 2016.
Holden, Stephen. *New York Times*. May 26, 2016.
Linden, Sheri. *Hollywood Reporter*. May 10, 2016.
Roeper, Richard. *Chicago Sun-Times*. May 25, 2016.
Travers, Peter. *Rolling Stone*. May 26, 2016.
Truitt, Brian. *USA Today*. May 26, 2016.
Walsh, Katie. *Chicago Tribune*. May 26, 2016.

QUOTES

Alice Kingsleigh: "I learned that I may not be able to change history but I can learn from it."

TRIVIA

This was Alan Rickman's last film; he passed away four months before the film's release.

AWARDS

Nominations:

Golden Raspberries 2016: Worst Remake/Sequel, Worst Support. Actor (Depp)

ALLEGIANT
(The Divergent Series: Allegiant)

Break the boundaries of your world.
—Movie tagline

The truth lies beyond.
—Movie tagline

Escape the world you know.
—Movie tagline

What makes us different ties us together.
—Movie tagline

Box Office: $66.1 Million

The third entry (and, apparently, the last one that will have a theatrical release, with the fourth and final installment currently planned to air on television) in the

series that began with *Divergent* (2014), *Allegiant* continues the series' trend of expanding its dystopian world of a future Chicago where people are divided into castes based on their primary personality characteristics. The first movie set up these "factions," although its central conflict—between one group that wanted to change which faction was in charge and characters who wanted to keep the power structure as it already was— was politically confused, to say the least. *Insurgent* (2015), the second installment, delved into the workings of the world slightly better, while presenting a simple chase plot. It felt like a minor improvement over the abundant exposition and conspiracy story of the first movie.

Each of these movies, then, has been very different from the others in terms of plot, purpose, and philosophy. (In the last regard, consider how no central character in the first movie even considered the possibility that the faction system was a bad thing, compared the second, in which the whole point was to eliminate it.) That makes it difficult to gauge whether this series is improving or simply throwing the audience off-kilter. Either way, *Allegiant*, which begins with the faction system having been ended, is almost a complete realignment of the series' focus, if only on a superficial level.

With the revelation—at the end of the previous movie—that the walled-off section of Chicago is essentially a laboratory in which the people are the subjects of an experiment, the entire plot thread of the factions and a revolution against the system basically has become meaningless. There is relatively little of those elements in the screenplay, adapted from Veronica Roth's novel by Noah Oppenheim, Adam Cooper, and Bill Collage. (All three are newcomers to the series; indeed, none of the entries has shared a single screenwriting credit with the others, which might partially account for the distinct feeling of each movie.)

Instead, the movie possesses a new central locale, a new aesthetic, and a new threat. Even with all of the new material, though, this installment, directed by Robert Schwentke (returning after directing the previous movie), ultimately rehashes a familiar story. Outwardly, the movie may have the appearance of being different. Underneath that surface, though, what is here is essentially the same as before.

The story begins shortly after the end of the previous movie, with the citywide broadcast of a message from one of the founders of the experiment. Tris (Shailene Woodley), who opened the box containing the message, wants to go beyond the city walls. Evelyn (Naomi Watts), the mother of Tris' love interest Four (Theo James), has become the de facto leader of Chicago, and she wants to start a faction-free society without any interference from the founders.

Tris and Four—along with the heroine's brother Caleb (Ansel Elgort), the self-serving Peter (Miles Teller), and Christina (Zoë Kravitz)—escape over the wall and find their way to the headquarters of the Bureau of Genetic Welfare, which has been overseeing the Chicago experiment. David (Jeff Daniels), the director of the bureau, explains that the world went to war over genetic tampering. Tris is the first subject of various experiments across the country to be genetically "pure." While Tris learns that the system of the world outside the wall is also based on arbitrary divisions, Four, having joined the bureau's military arm, discovers that the bureau is capturing children from the wasteland.

That wasteland is one of the movie's more effective visual elements. It looks akin to Mars—a vast, rusty red desert, which does not seem of this planet and within which blood-red water flows after raining down from the sky. After two movies set primarily among urban decay, the shift is drastic and refreshing, and the same can be said of the headquarters of the bureau. Built on the ruins of O'Hare International Airport, the central part of the edifice, a towering white spire, floats above the ground with rings shaped like a double helix encircling it. These sights are exceptions, though, since most of the movie's visual effects are either tacky (gelatinous bubbles and ooze-based showers that, respectively, protect and clean the movie's central characters after they are exposed to the toxic environment of the wasteland) or generic (assorted flying vehicles, which also look cheap on a few occasions).

There is not much of a central conflict here, since the story is apparently building to the series' ultimate one—between those who believe that the genetically "pure" are superior to people are genetically "damaged" and those who would rather stop treating people differently based on assorted labels. If it sounds similar to the previous movie's conflict, it pretty much is, albeit with vague genetic distinctions replacing the series' former distinctions of personality characteristics. If there is a greater point to this (the most obvious one would be about society changing terminology and/or targets in order to recycle prejudice), it is left unexplored. *Allegiant* is too busy establishing these new aspects of the series' world, as well as the rules that accompany them, to explore anything beneath the movie's new surface.

Mark Dujsik

CREDITS

Tris: Shailene Woodley
Four: Theo James
Peter: Miles Teller
David: Jeff Daniels
Johanna Reyes: Octavia Spencer
Evelyn: Naomi Watts
Christina: Zoë Kravitz
Origin: United States
Language: English
Released: 2016
Production: Lucy Fisher, Pouya Shahbazian, Douglas Wick; Red Wagon Entertainment; released by Lionsgate
Directed by: Robert Schwentke
Written by: Noah Oppenheim; Adam Cooper; Bill Collage
Cinematography by: Florian Ballhaus
Music by: Joseph Trapanese
Sound: Matthew Wood
Music Supervisor: Randall Poster
Editing: Stuart Levy
Art Direction: Alan Hook
Costumes: Marlene Stewart
Production Design: Alec (Alexander) Hammond
MPAA rating: PG-13
Running time: 120 minutes

REVIEWS

Andersen, Soren. *Seattle Times*. March 17, 2016.
Berardinelli, James. *ReelViews*. March 18, 2016.
Catsoulis, Jeannette. *New York Times*. March 17, 2016.
Ebiri, Bilge. *Village Voice*. March 18, 2016.
Hassenger, Jesse. *The A.V. Club*. March 17, 2016.
Johanson, MaryAnn. *Flick Philosopher*. March 10, 2016.
Koplinski, Chuck. *News-Gazette*. March 17, 2016.
Phillips, Michael. *Chicago Tribune*. March 16, 2016.
Turan, Kenneth. *Los Angeles Times*. March 17, 2016.
Wloszczyna, Susan. *RogerEbert.com*. March 18, 2016.

QUOTES

Tris: "EVERYONE is worth saving."

TRIVIA

Drones are supposed to be controlled with one's left hand. However, Chris is the only character who controls her drones with her right hand. This is due to Zoe Kravitz being left-handed.

AWARDS

Nominations:

Golden Raspberries 2016: Worst Actress (Watts)

ALLIED

Nothing is as it seems.
—Movie tagline

Box Office: $40 Million

A lone man parachutes into the middle of a desert. His mission is uncertain. His allies are unknown. So begins Robert Zemeckis' venture into classical filmmaking circa World War II, when attachment was a commodity too expensive for those fighting it. Throughout his career, the director has remained on the cutting edge of innovation, experimenting with not just grandiose special effects in both the living and animated world but also within the sleight of hand of filmmaking itself. In terms of examining his career it is easy to expect certain gimmicks in the way he presents each scene but never at the sacrifice of the story itself.

Max Vatan (Brad Pitt) is that man in the desert, picked up and delivered into Morocco. He is provided money, documentation, a weapon, and a wedding ring. A French resistance fighter, Marianne Beausejour (Marion Cotillard), is to pose as his wife for the explicit purpose of assassinating a German ambassador. Success is their mission. Survival is a luxury. As spies, the pair must walk their own tightrope of putting up a convincing front of a loving couple while not succumbing to the smiles, flattery, and touch of another human being. They are constantly testing and preparing each other for the big day (unfortunately there are no lessons in how to say "bonjourno"), keeping their distance until a moment of passion overcomes them on perhaps their last day on Earth.

Miraculously though the plan goes off without a hitch and with a previously uncertain future now gifted upon them, Max and Marianne give in to what they felt on the battlefield and marry each other. Though the war wages on around them they build a life together, most memorably as she gives birth in the middle of a bombing campaign. After a year of bliss, Max is called before his Special Ops superiors and informed that his wife may be a German agent. Despite his clear doubt, he is ordered to run an operation that will either expose her or clear her name. If proven a traitor, he is to execute her himself. But what if it is all just another intelligence game to test his own loyalty?

The screenplay by Steven Knight is playing with a full deck of genres and moods here. Instead of playing Three Card Monte or haphazardly shuffling them the way Max is required to prove his own skills, Zemeckis plays it relatively straight. Using the intrigue of the war and the exotic settings as scenery, the focus is put on the burgeoning relationship the way certain romance tales for adults became classics over time. It is no coincidence that one of the film's central locations is Casablanca and within the hands of a director who has subverted the concepts of time travel and the boundaries of animation one can be certain that *Allied* will find a way to cross paths with that doomed romance eventually.

Their first hurdle to extending their passionate sandstorm embrace is accomplishing their mission in a sequence that arrives very comfortably to a craftsman like Zemeckis. Waiting for the minutes on a clock to change have rarely felt as wrenchingly endless as they do here; more effective for its near real-time editing which is called back beautifully in a later scene as Max waits for a phone to ring. The elemental foundation of deception amongst spies translates naturally to the jealousy and one's concept of self-identification when giving themselves over to another human being body and soul. Pitt has been down this road before to more hyperbolic effect in *Mr. and Mrs. Smith* (2005), another spy-tinged examination of marriage that, like this film, featured behind-the-scenes innuendo about his co-star that eventually bled into the actor's personal life. If *The Walk* was Zemeckis' inward look at his own career and *Flight* (2012) was Denzel Washington's, then perhaps *Allied* is Pitt's.

His performance in this WWII tale is a low-key one, a distance from the macho bravado of his Nazi-scalping Lieutenant in *Inglourious Basterds* (2009) and his no-nonsense tank commander in *Fury* (2014). Pitt is practically a walking propaganda poster for his good looks, an image that Hitler may have even used if he wasn't so quintessentially all-American. Behind those eyes though initially are a coldness that has bared witness to likely some truly awful experiences that he may ready to finally be done with on this final suicide mission. That momentary respite of love and trust through wedded bliss and the creation of new life then becomes a personal journey through the horrors of his own past and a body count that continues to rise because of his uncertainty. "In Casablanca, the roof is where husbands go after they've made love to their wives," Max is told early on as potentially a suggestion of his only way out of the commitment to that very uncertainty.

With Pitt, the conscientious observer to his own fate, Cotillard must walk the more delicate line of suspicion. From her first scenes, there is clear connection to the manipulation that Marianne is peddling to Max; aware of his trust issues but also the flaws in his own attempts to do the same. As we begin to see her through his eyes, the femme fatale turns to a domestication that may still be nothing but a façade. Cotillard's ability to make an audience, along with Max, want to believe she is on the right side emboldens the film's climax when everything comes into focus and an unexpected emotional stake in its closing moments is earned rather than contrived.

Max and Marianne are victims of fate. Attraction cannot always be controlled whether it stems from genuine feelings or consistent proximity to a reciprocating force. On the surface, the most identifying trait of Zemeckis' work is Alan Silvestri's signature score which calls back to the melancholic strands of *Cast Away* (2000) where the lone man and the island were as literal as they were metaphorical. *Allied* does not burrow as deep as that film's examination of man and time but it recalls the type of filmmaking that those of a certain age would be happy to include in their hypothetical list of limited assets if stranded themselves. The filmmakers' reentry into "R"-rated filmmaking (something that took a 32-year hiatus between *Used Cars* [1980] and *Flight*) shows an interest in exploring not just the MPAA staples of achieving such ratings but more adult subject matter that includes a return to less razzmatazz storytelling.

The tightrope of innocence is a staple of Zemeckis' career, whether it be youthful or moral complexity of growing into flawed adults. His characters explore and grapple with it and he has never been afraid to playfully challenge their wherewithal and delight in our reaction to their dilemmas. These are protagonists who join politics to receive graft, ward off incestuous advances, or continue succumbing to their own peculiar vices in the name of heroism. Sometimes they are oblivious to their effect on the world such as Forrest Gump and that is part of the everlasting power to Zemeckis' craft. His affinity for the eternal power of film is evident in his clear appreciation for *Casablanca* (1942). Including his willingness to offer a counterpoint to its Hollywood fantasy. Just as Michael Curtiz' film climaxed with bittersweet parting and betrayals, Allied also brings its lovers to an airstrip to confront their fate. Rick and Ilsa had Paris. Max and Marianne had London. Moviegoers are fortunate enough to have both.

Erik Childress

CREDITS

Max Vatan: Brad Pitt
Marianne Beausejour: Marion Cotillard
Bridget Vatan: Lizzy Caplan
Frank Heslop: Jared Harris
Guy Sangster: Matthew Goode
Origin: United States
Language: English
Released: 2016
Production: Graham King, Steve Starkey, Robert Zemeckis; released by GK Films, Huahua Media, Imagemovers, Paramount Pictures Corp.
Directed by: Robert Zemeckis
Written by: Steven Knight
Cinematography by: Don Burgess
Music by: Alan Silvestri

Sound: Bjorn Ole Schroeder; Randy Thom
Editing: Mick Audsley; Jeremiah O'Driscoll
Art Direction: Jason Knox-Johnston
Costumes: Joanna Johnston
Production Design: Gary Freeman
MPAA rating: R
Running time: 124 minutes

REVIEWS

Berardinelli, James. *ReelViews*. November 22, 2016.
Dowd, A.A. *The A.V. Club*. November 22, 2016.
Erbland, Kate. *IndieWire*. November 21, 2016.
Lane, Anthony. *New Yorker*. November 28, 2016.
Larsen, Josh. *Larsen On Film*. November 25, 2016.
McGranaghan, Mike. *Aisle Seat*. November 27, 2016.
Nusair, David. *Reel Film Reviews*. November 24, 2016.
Phillips, Michael. *Chicago Tribune*. November 21, 2016.
Scott, A.O. *New York Times*. November 22, 2016.
Walsh, Katie. *Tribune News Service*. November 22, 2016.

QUOTES

Max Vatan: "We are married, why would we laugh?"

TRIVIA

The costumes for the film were inspired by *Casablanca* (1942) and *Now, Voyager*.

AWARDS

Nominations:
Oscars 2016: Costume Des.
British Acad. 2016: Costume Des. (B&W)

ALMOST CHRISTMAS

Five days together? Oh joy.
—Movie tagline

Box Office: $42 Million

Christmas movies thrive on family dysfunction. When it works, such as in *Home for the Holidays* (1987), it can be sublime. But it takes more than a great cast and a lot of shouting to convey holiday spirit and family bonds as true remedies for the way families drive each other crazy. *Almost Christmas* relies too much on the cast and the volume level to become a Holiday favorite, but it does the familiar routine well enough, and includes enough genuine spirit and family bonding to entertain.

Recently widowed, Walter Meyers (Danny Glover) has decided to gather his four adult children, their spouses, and his grandchildren together for the holidays.

Everyone has been shaken by the death of family matriarch Grace and the kids are up to their necks in life issues, including, but not limited to: New, sometimes-troubled marriages; the challenges of parenting single; college drama; and even drug dependency. Walter himself lives a simple life, volunteering at the local homeless shelter and trying to master the art of Grace's sweet potato pie recipe, which he just seems unable to replicate.

As the kids come home, they bring all the drama with them, which is increased exponentially by the simultaneous arrival of Grace's sister, their Aunt May (Mo'Nique), a lusty diva with seemingly few boundaries. Walter's oldest son Christian (Romany Malco) is running for Congress and gets home first with wife, kids, and Andy Brooks (John Michael Higgins) his campaign manager in tow. Walters oldest daughter Cheryl (Kimberly Elise) comes with husband Lonnie (JB Smoove) an arrogant professional basketball player. Middle child Rachel (Gabrielle Union) is a financially strapped single mom in law school determined to do it all on her own. Too bad she keeps running into the helpful old school chum Malachi (Omar Epps). Youngest sibling Evan (Jessie Usher), a celebrated college football player is also a secret drug addict. Soon, the family itself is straining under the weight of everyone's problems, short-sightedness, and selfish ambitions. May is determined to do all the cooking, even though the end results leave a lot to be desired. Rachel and Cheryl reignite their old family feud like only two sisters can. Christian neglects his wife and kids, and Evan is soon looking for somewhere to score a little peace and quiet.

The film has way too many characters and subplots and takes itself too seriously by trying to tie up all the clichéd loose ends. Suffice to say that the family draws together by story's end. Some of it, especially the bits involving the families shared grief work well. But too much of it seems forced. The film is at its strongest when it keeps things simple. There are a lot of pratfalls and some gross-out humor. The film is almost like an embarrassing uncle who thinks his jokes will go over better the louder they are. But enough of the gags work, especially ones that involve the irreverent Aunt May, that the movie can be appreciated if never revisited.

The younger cast members here have the least interesting job. To a one, their characters exist to give the older actors like Mo'Nique and Danny Glover the opportunity to steal scenes. The film even offers up legendary soul singer Gladys Knight in a small role as Dorothy, the director of the homeless shelter. The older cast is more than up for the small challenge of bringing their broadly-outlined characters to life. Glover reminds one exactly why he has consistently been counted among the finer actors of his generation. This is small stuff for

him but he treats it enthusiastically, even though, sadly underused as he is these days, he has come to be associated of late with exactly this sort of simplistic role.

Mo'Nique has the best role in the film. Like the other characters, Aunt May hovers somewhere between being a real human being and a cliché, but she has the added virtue of being there primarily to make viewers laugh. Comedian Mo'Nique is amply qualified to do just that. She might almost make *Almost Christmas* worth sitting through again for viewers who are reminded of the Aunt Mays in their own families.

This sort of nostalgic appeal is exactly the sort of comforting validation many viewers want from pop culture. It seems to distill emotions, remind them of the familiar, and impart meaning to it. There's nothing wrong with that, per se. There are no uncalculated moments in *Almost Christmas*. Watching it is a bit like unwrapping yet another nice but unnecessary present when something more was hoped for.

Dave Canfield

CREDITS

Aunt May: Mo'Nique
Rachel: Gabrielle Union
Cheryl: Kimberly Elise
Malachi: Omar Epps
Walter: Danny Glover
Brooks: John Michael Higgins
Christian: Romany Malco
Origin: United States
Language: English
Released: 2016
Production: William Packer; released by Perfect World Pictures, Universal Pictures Inc., Will Packer Productions
Directed by: David E. Talbert
Written by: David E. Talbert
Cinematography by: Larry Blanford
Music by: John Paesano
Sound: Wayne Lemmer; Derek Vanderhorst
Music Supervisor: Julia Michels
Editing: Troy Takaki
Art Direction: Gentry L. Akens, II
Production Design: Wynn Thomas
MPAA rating: PG-13
Running time: 111 minutes

REVIEWS

Anderson, Melissa. *Village Voice.* November 9, 2016.
Coggan, Devan. *Entertainment Weekly.* November 10, 2016.
Donato, Matt. *We Got This Covered.* November 12, 2016.
Gleiberman, Owen. *Variety.* November 9, 2016.
Guzman, Rafer. *Newsday.* November 10, 2016.

Hartl, John. *Seattle Times*. November 9, 2016.
Kenny, Glenn. *New York Times*. November 10, 2016.
Orndorf, Brian. *Blu-ray.com*. November 10, 2016.
Rothkopf, Joshua. *Time Out*. November 15, 2016.
Tucker, Rebecca. *Globe and Mail*. November 11, 2016.

TRIVIA

All of Young Fly's tattoos were edited out of the movie.

AMERICAN HONEY

Box Office: $663,246

American Honey begins with a dumpster dive and ends with something like a baptism. British director Andrea Arnold's first film set in America fills its languid two hour and forty-three-minute runtime with oddly romantic, hazy shots of red state environments. One could argue that nothing much happens in *American Honey*: it's a road movie (that most American of genres) that follows a group of scrappy teenagers running a suspect door-to-door magazine sales operation. At the center of the narrative is Star (Sasha Lane), a girl from a broken home, taking care of two young children and being harassed by their father, and desperate to find something better. When she sees Jake (Shia LaBeouf), all rat tail and sleazy swagger, and his crew by a local K-Mart, she instantly becomes intrigued, and soon enough she's off to join his "mag crew" (the fate of the children and the bulk of Star's background are conveniently brushed aside).

Once on the road, there's a lot of pot smoking and swaying to Top 40 music. *American Honey*, at times, feels like a more naturalistic, less aggressive answer to Harmony Korine's neon-drenched *Spring Breakers* (2012). Upon release, much was made of Arnold's decision to cast a variety of non-actors. Lane, who the director spotted sunbathing at the beach, proves to be an excellent find. Star could read as a cliché "trailer trash" role, built on little more than swagger and short shorts, but Lane imbues her with a potent mix of stoicism and innocence. Her face has a softness that at times makes her look even younger than she is, but she is constantly seen fending for herself and confronting both Jake and mag crew magnate Krystal (Riley Keough). Star may at times appear soft, but there's a steeliness at her core, and Arnold is determined to show this side of her often. In one pivotal scene, Star, frustrated with Jake's constant posturing, hitches a ride and briefly runs off with a group of middle-aged men clad in cowboy hats. Ages of unfortunate cinematic tradition within a sexist society set up some dicey expectations for this scene. It's hard to watch Star go off with a group of older men without assuming they may be predators. Surprisingly, they aren't. Once she arrives at their place, she asks for hard liquor, which she drinks with abandon, and at one point she even pushes one of the men into the swimming pool. Tense to watch though the scene may be, Star maintains a level of control, and even makes a big sale. The proceedings only become explicitly dangerous once Jake shows up, brandishing a gun. Impressively, Arnold does not paint her young protagonist as a victim here where again and again throughout the film it would be easy to do so.

Arnold finds room for touches of the pastoral in this setting of ragtag youth. Early on, Star dreamily rocks on a swing, surrounded by trees. The scene would not be out of place in a 19th century painting. Lens flares are frequent, and while this aesthetic, filled with splotches of woozy light, is often considered the stuff of indie film cliché, here it's interestingly subverted by being turned on a group of rebellious young adult drifters—in other words, the type of characters who don't usually have a light shining on them, in any sense. These characters may be scoffed at, called trashy or worse, but they have had to grow up fast and learn how to scam as a means of survival. Krystal is a particularly compelling figure in this sense. She can't be much older than her early twenties, but she is the de facto leader of the group, issuing no-nonsense commands in a southern drawl. While the cast of *American Honey* largely consists of heretofore unknowns, Keough's presence adds a bit of all American mythos—she is, of course, the granddaughter of none other than Elvis Presley, and her seductive stare and pout inevitably recall her famous forbearer. Her character has a commanding confidence that suggests she's had to fend for herself for far longer than most people her age. Early on she establishes a bond with Star over the two of them being from the south, "two real American honeys," but she quickly shows her dominant side. In a scene memorable for its over the top imagery, Krystal lectures Star about the fact that she hasn't been bringing in enough money. Krystal stands confidently, wearing a skimpy Confederate flag bikini with the tags still on while she has Jake rub tanning oil on her legs.

It's an image of such exaggerated southern fried tackiness it makes perfect sense that it was shot by someone from another country. *American Honey*, with an outsider's eye, recasts all the parts of American culture we might cast off as sparkling and sensually suggestive (if not always fully sensual, it's hard to get past Jake's hair or that flag bikini). Arnold is attuned to the mythic qualities of the road movie, and works to remodel the form from a feminine perspective. It's an admirable goal, and while Lane makes for a fine road trip protagonist, and Keough a convincing bad girl boss, there are some frustrating moments. Star, despite Lane's strong performance, sometimes feels like a bit of a blank slate. Her past is shadowy, and it's often difficult to tell how she feels or what she wants to do. Jake, while confident and wily, has something of a predatory quality, and though it's telegraphed from their very first meeting that he and Star will embark on a relationship of sorts, one often gets the sense that she's too good for him. Jake pulls a gun and fools around, Star on the other hand, traipses through the film with a blend of good humor and hard-won toughness. In a late, polarizing scene, Star gives a truck driver a hand job in exchange for money. It's tense and frustrating to watch—as though the bad outcomes expected during the earlier scene with the cowboy hat clad men have belatedly come true. In this scene, Star becomes a victim, though she tries to talk her way through the situation. In such a long film, a scene of female sexual subjugation feels superfluous—it's as if Arnold thought she had to add some requisite victimization to link the film back to how blue collar women have too often been portrayed.

American Honey is at its best when it captures its scrappy characters in a more loving light. By just allowing her characters to be misfits, and presenting them with a hazy glow, Arnold dignifies those who typically get left behind.

Abbey Bender

CREDITS

Star: Sasha Lane
Jake: Shia LaBeouf
Krystal: Riley Keough
Corey: McCaul Lombardi
Pagan: Arielle Holmes
Origin: United States
Language: English
Released: 2016
Production: Thomas Benski, Lars Knudsen, Lucas Ochoa, Pouya Shahbazian, Jay Van Hoy, Alice Weinberg; released by British Film Institute, Film 4, Maven Pictures, Parts&Labor, Protagonist Pictures, Pulse Films
Directed by: Andrea Arnold
Written by: Andrea Arnold
Cinematography by: Robbie Ryan
Sound: Nicolas Becker
Editing: Joe Bini
Art Direction: Lance Mitchell
Costumes: Alex Bovaird
Production Design: Kelly McGehee
MPAA rating: R
Running time: 163 minutes

REVIEWS

Bradshaw, Peter. *The Guardian.* May 14, 2016.
Edelstein, David. *Vulture.* September 30, 2016.
Fear, David. *Rolling Stone.* September 30, 2016.
Hassenger, Jesse. *The A.V. Club.* September 29, 2016.
King, Danny. *Village Voice.* September 28, 2016.
Lodge, Guy. *Variety.* May 14, 2016.
Morgenstern, Joe. *Wall Street Journal.* September 29, 2016.
Scott, A.O. *New York Times.* September 29, 2016.
Shone, Tom. *Newsweek.* October 14, 2016.
Sims, David. *Atlantic.* September 29, 2016.

QUOTES

Pagan: "You know what Darth Vader looks like beneath that mask? He's a skeleton. Just like the rest of us."

TRIVIA

The movie was filmed in chronological order and a lot of the dialogue was improvised.

AWARDS

Nominations:

Ind. Spirit 2017: Actor—Supporting (LaBeouf), Actress (Lane), Actress—Supporting (Keough), Cinematog., Director (Arnold), Film

AMERICAN PASTORAL

A radically ordinary story.
—Movie tagline

Box Office: $544,098

Hollywood has a tumultuous relationship with one of the world's most acclaimed and influential novelists, the singular Philip Roth. The Pulitzer Prize-winning novelist is one of the most beloved in modern history, but films based on his works have struggled, often notably. In fact, one of the few generally agreed-upon quality adaptations of his material came earlier in 2016 with James Schamus' directorial debut, *Indignation*. While that film was premiering at Sundance, the conversation turned to the long-awaited adaptation of arguably Roth's most famous book, the one that won him a Pulitzer, 1997's *American Pastoral*. One of Roth's most ambitious and time-spanning novels, the book was almost immediately wooed by Hollywood (as all successful books are) but just as quickly earned the dreaded appellation of "unfilmable." It was too long, too complex, and too driven by character's internal dramas to work in the external medium of film.

For over a decade, the adaptation lingered in development hell, as directors were attached and then dropped out, including Phillip Noyce and Fisher Stevens. In his introduction to the film at the premiere at the Toronto International Film Festival, Ewan McGregor commented on how, after being cast in the film as several directors came and went, he began to worry that the film wouldn't get made if he didn't take the reins and direct it himself. Perhaps he should have asked himself why so many other directors kept jumping ship on this complicated project and taken the hint.

American Pastoral opens at the 40-year reunion of Weequahic High School in New Jersey, keeping the structure of the book, which sees the bulk of the narrative through the eyes of a classmate of the protagonist. Immediately, something is off. It's the kind of structure that fits the fiction, and adds to the thematic density of the novel, but is something of a burden in film, not just for the reason that it requires some awful old-person makeup. Said prosthetics are on the face of Jerry Levov (Rupert Evans), who runs into the story's narrator, a Roth regular, Nathan Zuckerman (David Strathairn), and informs him of the fall of the golden boy of Weequahic, Jerry's brother, Seymour "The Swede" Levov (McGregor). Yes, *American Pastoral* is a flashback told to another character related to the audience. The degree of removal may work in fiction but starts the film on an awkward, clunky note from which it doesn't really recover.

The Swede was one of those people who seemed to have it all. He was an All-American icon, the handsome young athlete who looked like the world would open up and give him everything he wanted. Of course, that did not happen and Roth's vision is that of a changing country during the Vietnam War and the counter-culture movement as much as it is a family saga. Before the fall, The Swede married his high school sweetheart, Dawn Dwyer (Jennifer Connelly), a gorgeous beauty queen. The football star and the beauty queen, what could go wrong?

Seymour also joined the family business, working with his father, Lou (Peter Riegert), and the Levovs had a daughter named Merry (Dakota Fanning), settling into life on a gorgeous farm estate. She would ride horses, the mother would make a happy home, and dad would bring home the bacon. The seeds of eventual disruption start with a stuttering problem for Merry, as well as an unnatural relationship with her father, and arguable jealousy of her mother. Merry is pushed away by her father to help with that dynamic and the film seems to draw a line from those early issues to her later radicalization during the Vietnam War.

As she gets older, Merry joins in the chorus of young voices furious over the international conflict. She goes to New York City to protest, and fights with her father

about the War. After one such fight, the local post office in their small town of Old Rimrock gets blown up by a bomb, killing the owner. Merry disappears. Was she responsible? As Jerry deals with issues of civil rights at his glovemaking business, as well as the mental decline of his wife after the disappearance of their daughter, he also obsesses over where to find Merry. When a young lady named Rita Cohen (Valorie Curry) claims to have knowledge of Merry's location, The Swede follows her down a counter culture rabbit hole, seeing the dark side and eventual fate of a young lady forever warped by an America that certainly did not open up its arms and embrace her.

Philip Roth's *American Pastoral* takes place across several decades, incorporating complex elements like civil rights and the Vietnam War into a family saga. As such, it requires hundreds of pages and dozens of characters to convey its story, and arguably could have never worked in a standard film running time. Condensing Roth's vision into a film required someone who truly understood how to make these kind of epic, time-spanning pieces effective in another medium, and neither writer John Romano nor McGregor were that person. They stumble in their Cliffs Notes version of the source material, hitting highlights from the novel in a clunky, insincere manner, as if they're rushing through the book, skipping a chapter here or a subplot there.

Ignoring the concept that *American Pastoral* proves yet again that not all excellent works in one medium are going to work in another, McGregor makes other first-time director mistakes along the way. He's simply not very good with actors, drawing exaggerated performances from Connelly and Fanning, who never come off as believable, a fatal flaw in the film. *American Pastoral* needs to be about the deconstruction of "All American" archetypes like Dawn's beauty queen, but she's a two-dimensional character in the film, reduced to her major beats instead of given any depth at all. It's a bit more forgivable that Merry becomes a non-character, as the book is at least in part about how The Swede doesn't understand her, but Fanning is still ineffective. And there are scenes, especially one with Curry in a hotel room and everything related to Uzo Aduba's character (an employee of The Swede's), during which one can almost see the actors struggling and reaching for a strong directorial hand that never comes.

Even the period details are superficial, often reducing characters and scenes to popular songs on the soundtrack and costumes that look more like a '60s party in the '10s than something legitimately time-specific. That's really the key to why *American Pastoral* is such a broad failure—none of it feels real. The performances, the setting, the themes—they all reflect an obligation more than a passion to adapt a book that so many people loved. There's an egocentric fallacy that pervades Hollywood that nothing is truly "unfilmable." *American Pastoral* is solid proof otherwise.

Brian Tallerico

CREDITS

Swede Levov: Ewan McGregor
Dawn Levov: Jennifer Connelly
Merry Levov: Dakota Fanning
Lou Levov: Peter Riegert
Jerry Levov: Rupert Evans
Origin: United States
Language: English
Released: 2016
Production: Andre Lamal, Gary Lucchesi, Tom Rosenberg; released by Lakeshore Entertainment
Directed by: Ewan McGregor
Written by: John Romano
Cinematography by: Martin Ruhe
Music by: Alexandre Desplat
Sound: Christopher S. Aud
Music Supervisor: Eric Craig; Brian McNelis
Editing: Melissa Kent
Art Direction: Gregory A. Weimerskirch
Costumes: Lindsay McKay
Production Design: Daniel B. Clancy
MPAA rating: R
Running time: 108 minutes

REVIEWS

Adams, Sam. *The Wrap*. October 21, 2016.
Barker, Andrew. *Variety*. September 13, 2016.
Burr, Ty. *Boston Globe*. October 27, 2016.
Cole, Jake. *Slant Magazine*. October 17, 2016.
Dowd, A.A. *The A.V. Club*. October 26, 2016.
Goble, Blake. *Consequence of Sound*. October 21, 2016.
Hornaday, Ann. *Washington Post*. October 20, 2016.
Kenny, Glenn. *RogerEbert.com*. October 21, 2016.
LaSalle, Mick. *San Francisco Chronicle*. October 20, 2016.
Nicholson, Ben. *CineVue*. September 13, 2016.

TRIVIA

This film was Ewan McGregor's feature directorial debut.

THE ANGRY BIRDS MOVIE
(Angry Birds)

Why so angry?
—Movie tagline

Box Office: $107.5 Million

The mighty eagle of legend, storied protector of Bird Island and its inhabitants, emerges from his cave and steps on to the rock ledge above the Lake of Wisdom, where the movie's two comic sidekicks just had been swimming—performing a water ballet in which the two birds spit water back and forth between their mouths. The eagle takes in the sight of his realm, spreads his majestic wings, and proceeds to urinate into the lake.

This gag of literal toilet humor is the funniest one in *The Angry Birds Movie*, although it is not because of the golden stream on display or the gurgling sound of one, steady flow of fluid pouring into a standing body of another liquid. No, the joke works because directors Clay Kaytlis and Fergal Reilly focus the audience's attention on the reaction of the sidekicks—their frozen faces of confusion slowly morphing into visages of disgust. It is undeniably a gross joke, yet the timing of the bit distances its scatological implications just enough that the humor comes from the characters' reactions, not what causes them.

There is a point to the inordinate amount of time this piece already has spent on a potty joke, and it is that even the most effective moment of humor here eventually suffers from one of the movie's more stifling tendencies. Like so many of the jokes here, the post-swim-in-a-toilet gag goes on too long past the point it is amusing.

This tendency of drawing out jokes, situations, and entire plot threads beyond even their minor effectiveness is likely the result of the fact that there is not much to this material. The screenplay by Jon Vitti is based on the popular video game series, in which players control the trajectory of a slingshot loaded with an assortment of birds. The goal of a given level is to kill the green pigs that populate it, either by direct hits or by crushing them by way of toppling structures made of wood, stone, metal, etc. The games are cartoonish physics simulators without need for a story (although one is told in each of the games via static art).

The movie's story follows Red (voice of Jason Sudeikis), a cardinal with anger issues. Among his fellow, flightless birds, he is a loner, who has built a house on the beach outside the village. None of the other birds miss him, probably because he is prone to outbursts such as the one in the opening sequence, in which he insults and attacks a father who is upset that Red is late for a gig as a clown at a kid's "hatch-day" party. Red ends up in court after the incident, and he is sentenced to mandatory anger management classes.

This eventually leads to the movie's central plot, which sees the green pigs from Piggy Island, led by Leonard (voice of Bill Hader), arriving on Bird Island with a scheme to earn the birds' trust (in part, by giving them the slingshot that will be the pigs' undoing) and steal their eggs. Only Red suspects that the outsiders are up to no good, so he seeks the aid of Mighty Eagle (voice of Peter Dinklage) with the help of his sidekicks Chuck (voice of Josh Gad)—a speedy canary—and Bomb (voice of Danny McBride)—a bulbous bird that looks and explodes like his namesake.

With a vocal cast populated with an assortment of comic actors (including Maya Rudolph, Keegan-Michael Key, and Kate McKinnon, as well as Sean Penn providing grunts for a bulky bird, in what must be the easiest paycheck a big-name actor has ever received), most of the jokes here feel as if Kaytlis and Reilly simply relied on the cast's ability to improvise dialogue within a given situation. The trio invents lyrics to a ballad about Mighty Eagle to play to his massive ego. The sidekicks imagine—and obnoxiously vocalize—what the eagle's battle cry might be. There are puns galore (such as Red using the words "pluck" and "flock" as a replacement for a word that starts with first letter of the latter and ends with the final three letters of the former), and sexual innuendo is rampant and somewhat creepy in a movie primarily aimed at kids.

Even more unsettling, though, is the movie's ultimate lesson. All of the randomly assembled, repetitively jokey material of the first two acts eventually leads to a climax that finally resembles the game upon which *The Angry Birds Movie* is based. The birds realize the pigs are bad, and Red orchestrates an avian invasion of Piggy Island. As in the game, the birds launch themselves into pigs' city, and each one has a special power that results in a lot of destruction. (A toucan acts like a boomerang, and a chicken shoots fireballs out of its derriere.) The sequence is not only rushed but also emblematic of an unfortunate message: Anger is good and necessary.

Mark Dujsik

CREDITS

Voice of Red: Jason Sudeikis
Voice of Chuck: Josh Gad
Voice of Bomb: Danny McBride
Voice of Matilda: Maya Rudolph
Voice of Leonard: Bill Hader
Voice of Mighty Eagle: Peter Dinklage
Voice of Terence: Sean Penn
Origin: United States
Language: English
Released: 2016
Production: John Cohen, Catherine Winder; released by Columbia Pictures, Rovio Entertainment Oy

Directed by: Clay Kaytis; Fergal Reilly
Written by: Jon Vitti
Music by: Heitor Pereira
Sound: Tom Myers
Music Supervisor: Manish Raval; Tom Wolfe
Editing: Kent Beyda
Art Direction: Peter Oswald
Production Design: Peter Oswald
MPAA rating: PG
Running time: 97 minutes

REVIEWS

Berardinelli, James. *ReelViews*. May 21, 2016.
Goble, Blake. *Consequence of Sound*. May 17, 2016.
Hassenger, Jesse. *The A.V. Club*. May 19, 2016.
Henderson, Eric. *Slant*. May 17, 2016.
Kenny, Glenn. *New York Times*. May 19, 2016.
Macdonald, Moira. *Seattle Times*. May 19, 2016.
Orndorf, Brian. *Blu-ray.com*. May 19, 2016.
VanDerWerff, Todd. *Vox*. May 22, 2016.
Wloszczyna, Susan. *RogerEbert.com*. May 20, 2016.
Wright, Anders. *San Diego Union-Tribune*. May 19, 2016.

QUOTES

Red: "Something about those pigs isn't kosher."

TRIVIA

The character of Terence says no actual words in the film. He hums, grunts, and sings.

ANTHROPOID

Resistance has a code name.
   —Movie tagline

Box Office: $2.9 Million

Based on the true tale of the Czechoslovakian assassination of German SS officer Reinhard Heydrich, *Anthropoid* is a solidly-acted, moderately engaging action drama that on a fundamental level misjudges what is most interesting about its story, and thus loses its way during a plodding, poorly plotted finale. After premiering at the Karlovy Vary Film Festival in July, the movie was given a modest release in mid-August by Bleecker Street, during which it grossed nearly $3 million in theaters.

Unfolding over a six-month period beginning in December 1941, the film's story centers on Josef Gabcik (Cillian Murphy) and Jan Kubis (Jamie Dornan), two operatives of the London-based government-in-exile of Czechoslovakia, which during World War II was overrun and occupied by Nazi Germany. After parachuting in behind enemy lines, the pair make their way to Prague. Along the way they have to murder a fellow resistance fighter turned traitor in order to protect their anonymity.

Josef and Jan's top-secret mission, unbeknownst initially even to other Czech resistance fighters, is to assassinate Reinhard Heydrich (Detlef Bothe), the well-protected Nazi third-in-command behind Adolf Hitler and Heinrich Himmler, and the main architect behind the Third Reich's genocidal "Final Solution." The pair's initial contact is nowhere to be found, but Josef and Jan eventually meet up with another member of the Czech resistance, "Uncle" Jan Zelenka-Hajsky (Toby Jones), and are taken to a safe-house. As they continue to conduct reconnaissance research for their plot, Josef and Jan become involved with Lenka (Anna Geislerova) and Marie (Charlotte Le Bon), respectively.

While the women are game if cautious quasi-participants in the scheme, Josef and Jan's male peers in the resistance voice more doubts. These are less rooted in moral quandary than the knowledge that German reprisals will be brutal regardless of whether or not they are successful in their attempt. Their ambivalence is therefore a matter of simple math: is the death of one unambiguously monstrous man worth the lives of hundreds or thousands of innocent people? Eventually these concerns are swept aside, and Josef and Jan proceed with their efforts, triggering predictable fallout.

There are a few small moments of expertly crafted edginess, especially early on, in *Anthropoid*, which takes its title from the real name of the Czech resistance's assassination operation. When Marie first brings Lenka to meet Josef and Jan at a bar, and thus create the appearance of romantic pairs, Josef reacts strongly to the women's fashionable dressiness, pointing out that standing out and getting noticed in public very much increases their physical risk. As he seethes, and nearby German officers gaze curiously in the group's direction, Josef says, "This little scene needs an ending," and instructs Lenka to slap him—thus giving the impression of a romantic rebuke. It is a wonderful, well-constructed scene that brims with smart details about occupied life during wartime.

After a very engaging first 40 to 45 minutes, though, there are two elements that combine to weigh down *Anthropoid*. One of these factors is perhaps unavoidable, given the international nature of modern-day film financing and the fact that this production was backed by money from three different countries. Director Sean Ellis and/or the producers seem to feel they are making an action movie—or at least pandering to an action-hungry audience. So the film's third act becomes a very claustrophobic and repetitive shootout between avenging

German soldiers and Josef, Jan, and their Czech comrades. This may be factually accurate, but it is wholly inert on a dramatic level. Whereas the messy, chaotic assassination sequence itself—given a jumbled energy by editor Richard Mettler—communicates a genuine, spontaneous tension, the film's much brawnier final third communicates only tedium, devolving as it does into a seemingly endless spray of bullets and shouting.

Most problematically, though, Josef and Jan feel somewhat disconnected from the rest of the sociopolitical struggle faced by their fellow countrymen and women—a fact that is underscored when Lenka assertively challenges the notion that Josef and Jan have placed the women around them in a dangerous situation for which they are not prepared or emotionally steeled. That reaction is fine, honestly—it rings true. But the moment that follows it, as well as other scenes, feel like a missed opportunity for Ellis and co-screenwriter Anthony Frewin to dig further into the psyches of Josef and Jan. The latter is portrayed as emotionally distraught over having to put his lethal training into actual action, but the bolder, braver, and more interesting film would have played up the duo's collective isolation more—underscoring how there could still be a fierce commitment to their cause while at the same time a burgeoning recognition of the palpable sense that there was perhaps no longer a place for them in their homeland.

What *Anthropoid* most has going for it is a series of well-calibrated performances that elevate its script. Murphy has the intensity of a true believer without over-dialing his emotions in a manner that would come across as hackneyed. Dornan, best known for *50 Shades of Grey* (2015), here delivers a nuanced and very palpably inwardly reflected turn.

Stylistically, Ellis has some successes sprinkled in amongst a few misses. Working as his own cinematographer, he deploys a depressed yet earthy color palette, heavy on browns and mustard yellows, that evokes a time and place of subjugation, paranoia and fear. Ellis also makes good use of various historic Prague exteriors, lending the movie an easy and effective production value that meshes nicely with the budget-conscious work of production designer Morgan Kennedy. Other choices, however, like the heavy use of Robin Foster's overly affected score, give off a hackneyed vibe, undercutting the movie's effectiveness.

Overall, *Anthropoid* will appeal to fans of historical dramas. It is unfortunate, though, that the movie is less invested in its characters' backstories and psychological motivations than their ultimate demise. Last-stand gunfights may provide narrative finality, but they are not always inherently the most interesting aspects of a story.

Brent Simon

CREDITS

Josef Gabcik: Cillian Murphy
Jan Kubis: Jamie Dornan
Lenka Fafkova: Anna Geislerova
Jan Zelenka-Hajsky: Toby Jones
Marie Kovarnikova: Charlotte Le Bon
Origin: United States
Language: English
Released: 2016
Production: Mickey Liddell, Pete Shilaimon, Sean Ellis;
 released by 22h22, LD Entertainment, Lucky Man Films
Directed by: Sean Ellis
Written by: Sean Ellis; Anthony Frewin
Cinematography by: Sean Ellis
Music by: Robin Foster
Sound: James Mather
Editing: Richard Mettler
Art Direction: Radek Hanák
Costumes: Josef Cechota
Production Design: Morgan Kennedy
MPAA rating: R
Running time: 120 minutes

REVIEWS

Cordova, Randy. *Arizona Republic.* August 11, 2016.
Debruge, Peter. *Variety.* July 1, 2016.
Graham, Adam. *Detroit News.* August 11, 2016.
Kenny, Glenn. *RogerEbert.com.* August 12, 2016.
Keough, Peter. *Boston Globe.* August 11, 2016.
Kompanek, Christopher. *Washington Post.* August 11, 2016.
Linden, Sheri. *Los Angeles Times.* August 11, 2016.
Morgenstern, Joe. *Wall Street Journal.* August 11, 2016.
Verniere, James. *Boston Herald.* August 12, 2016.
Wright, Anders. *San Diego Union-Tribune.* August 12, 2016.

QUOTES

Josef Gabcik: [to Lenka and Marie] "You're gonna get
 yourselves noticed and that gets us noticed ... and if we all
 get noticed we all get killed."

TRIVIA

Anthropoid means "resembling a human being in form."

APRIL AND THE EXTRAORDINARY WORLD

(Avril et le Monde Truqué)

Box Office: $295,488

Considering that it is a form of cinematic storytelling in which virtually anything can happen and the only limits are in the imaginations of the filmmakers, it is kind of a shame that so many animated films of recent years have been so unadventurous. Oh sure, Pixar still comes up with gems from time to time like *Inside Out* (2015) and there are occasional knockouts like *Paranorman* (2012) and *Kubo and the Two Strings* (2016), but for the most part, too many animated films of recent years tend to follow the same dramatic lines and feel as if they are more interested in generating toy sales than in telling a compelling story in a visually interesting manner. By comparison, the French import *April and the Extraordinary World* goes gloriously against the grain by coming up with a wildly imaginative storyline that aims to dazzle the minds as well as the eyes of viewers and does so beautifully and the result is a film that more than lives up to the superlative in its title.

Based on the graphic novel by Jacques Tardi, the film presents viewers with an alternate history in which technological advances stopped during the Industrial Revolution and everything is still being run by such seemingly archaic methods as coal and steam. As we discover in the opening scene, Napoleon III had employed genial scientist Gustave (Jean Rochefort) to develop a serum to help create an army of invincible super-soldiers—although the serum failed to achieve its stated purpose, the animals that it was tested on in the lab did develop the power of speech. After a lab disaster that destroys the laboratory and allows two strange creatures to escape, the great scientific minds of the world begin to mysteriously vanish, along with the technological advances that they might have created.

The movie jumps ahead to 1931 and finds April (Marion Cotillard), the granddaughter of Gustave, being pursued by the relentless police inspector Pizoni (Bouli Lanners), who is convinced that she and her parents, who are working with Gustave to perfect that troublesome serum, know what is behind the disappearances. This results in April being orphaned and when we see her again in 1941, she is living in a pollution-choked Paris with the aging Darwin (Philippe Katerine), a talking cat that was the result of Gustave's original experiments. While still being followed by the now-disgraced Pizoni, who is convinced that April's parents are still alive and know what is behind the disappearances of the scientists, April continues the work of her parents and her grandfather. Before long, she—aided by Darwin and Julius (Tod Fennell), a young thief and police informant—makes a number of incredible discoveries that send them off on a search to find her parents and uncover exactly what has become of the great scientific minds of the world and what that means for the future of mankind.

As visualized by co-directors Christian Desires and Franck Ekinci, *April and the Extraordinary World* offers viewers a steampunk aesthetic that yields up one fascinating visual after another. With Europe having completely decimated their forests (and currently waging war in America in hopes of gaining their timber resources), the Paris on display here is a smog-choked nightmare in which one practically needs a mask in order to walk the streets. As for the technology that they have been able to cultivate, it has branched off in intriguing ways to make up for the lack of any great advances—there are blimps that move with bicycle power, mechanical rats that serve as spying devices, and elaborate variations to the railroad industry. In the most eye-catching detail, we learn that a second Eiffel Tower has been erected next to the original to serve as part of a cable car system that can rush people from Paris to London in a mere 84 hours. Everything is supposed to be dirty and grimy and run down, of course, but there is so much ingenuity to the various creations and other visual indicators of this alternate reality that viewers may want to pause the film from time to time just to be able to better drink it all in.

And yet, *April and the Extraordinary World* is more than a mere visual extravaganza. In terms of its depth and gravity and its refusal to dumb things down so as not to confuse younger viewers, it may remind some viewers of the works of the great Hayao Miyazaki. Like many of Miyazaki's films, it contains a strong message about the importance of conserving the environment but at the same time—and this is the tricky part—it also artfully illustrates the ways in which technological advances have actually had a salutary effect on the environment as well. This is not simply a message movie, however; it is also a bright and high-spirited adventure with a lot of humor and excitement to it and, in April, one of the more entertaining and inspiring animated heroines to come along in a while—some may suggest that a female lead is not the right move for a children's movie because of the fear that boys will not be interested but it is hard to think that even the most cootie-fearing among them would not find her an absolute delight. Watching her and faithful Darwin in the midst of their fantastic adventure, it may dawn on some people that Desires and Ekinci have actually given audiences a better, albeit ersatz, screen version of the beloved comic book character Tin Tin than Steven Spielberg was able to do with a gazillion dollars behind him.

April and the Extraordinary World only steps slightly wrong during the final act as the eventual revelation as to what is behind the disappearing scientists proves to be a little on the silly side. However, the rest of the film is so strong and engaging that even that is eminently forgivable. Alas, despite being one of the best animated films of 2016, not many people were able to catch it during its initial American theatrical release as it was largely relegated to art houses playing subtitled prints of the French-language version. However, an English-dubbed version has been made available for the DVD in which Cotillard, who does double duty on both versions, is joined by the likes of Susan Sarandon, Tony Hale, and Paul Giamatti. Regardless of which version one watches, this is a film for viewers of all ages to treasure.

Peter Sobczynski

CREDITS

April: Marion Cotillard
Darwin: Philippe Katerine
Pops: Jean Rochefort
Paul: Olivier Gourmet
Julius: Marc-André Grondin
Pizoni: Bouli Lanners
Origin: United States
Language: French
Released: 2016
Production: Eric Beckman, Michel Dutheil, Sophia Harvey, David Jesteadt, Marc Jousset, Franck Ekinci; released by Je Suis Bien Content, Jouror Distribution, Kaibou Productions, Need Productions, Proximus SA, Radio Television Belge Francophone, StudioCanal S.A., Tchack, arte France Cinema
Directed by: Christian Desmares; Franck Ekinci
Written by: Franck Ekinci; Benjamin Legrand
Music by: Valentin Hadjadj
Editing: Nazim Meslem
MPAA rating: PG
Running time: 105 minutes

REVIEWS

Burr, Ty. *Boston Globe.* April 7, 2016.
Connelly, Sherilyn. *Village Voice.* March 22, 2016.
Debruge, Peter. *Variety.* March 17, 2016.
Ivanov, Oleg. *Slant Magazine.* March 21, 2016.
Kenny, Glenn. *New York Times.* March 24, 2016.
Merry, Stephanie. *Washington Post.* April 7, 2016.
Mintzer, Jordan. *Hollywood Reporter.* July 8, 2015.
Robinson, Tasha. *The Verge.* March 29, 2016.
Savlov, Marc. *Austin Chronicle.* April 7, 2016.
Turan, Kenneth. *Los Angeles Times.* March 31, 2016.

TRIVIA

The film is based on a graphic novel by Jacques Tardi, who was also a graphic designer on the film.

ARRIVAL

Why are they here?
—Movie tagline

Box Office: $95.8 Million

It took just under three years for Denis Villeneuve to become one of the most popular and talked about directors in North America. The French Canadian's brutalist direction has struck a chord with both audiences and critics. 2010's *Incendies*, 2013's *Prisoners*, and 2015's *Sicario* each drew their fare share of criticism for their heavy-handed approach to drama, but audiences went in droves just the same. He steadily gained support from critics for his astounding visuals, which were praised even as his screenplays were criticized. Like other visually dynamic directors (he fittingly brings to mind Ridley Scott, whose own *Blade Runner* [1982] will receive a Villeneuve-directed sequel), the subtext and biographical links that critics look for in auteurs are buried a little deeper. There is very little linking all of his movies beyond his unfailingly precise eye. *Arrival*, his latest, feels related to *Sicario* and *Incendies* in its portrait of a woman overwhelmed by governments moving at the speed of sound, but its outlook is considerably different. Based on a short story by Ted Chiang, this is a film about accepting life, no matter how compromised it becomes, and seeing beauty even in despair. Usually, it's only Villeneuve's camera that does that.

Louise Banks (Amy Adams) is a professor of linguistics at a quiet college dealing with tragedy. She gets up and goes to teach her class every day with the sound of her daughter Hannah's voice echoing in her memory. Hannah (played at different ages by Jadyn Malone, Abigail Pniowsky, and Julia Scarlett Dan) died of a rare form of cancer and that tragedy lines Louise's face. It's in the way she sighs before teaching every day, the way her eyes never search for contact among her peers and students. Then something happens that pulls her from her isolation. Alien spacecraft have landed in 12 different parts of the world and the earth is in a collective state of crisis. China looks ready to start firing serious weaponry in the direction of the closest spacecraft. The US military has sprung into action and attempted to make contact with the pilots of the ships. The crafts are enormous and shaped like avocados and do not look as though they would provide easy access, but there are holes on the underside of the crafts and the military have started sending men up there. The issue is they have not been able to work out what the aliens (nicknamed heptapods, because they look like hands with seven fingers) are telling them. Their language is unlike any spoken or written on Earth, but plainly has a design—they write in a kind of temporary ink secreted from their fingers, and their sentences are presented as circular symbols of some kind. It would take an expert to decode them. Enter Louise Banks.

Louise is recruited by Colonel Weber (Forest Whitaker) of the US military to come to the ship in American airspace and help the effort to make contact.

She and Dr. Ian Donnelly (Jeremy Renner) are put in charge of decoding their language, which involves photographing and then deciphering their symbols as they are written on a barrier between the heptapods and the people. It takes them weeks but they uncover that the purpose of the heptapod visit is to offer a gift of some kind. This gift will apparently be of use not just to humans but also to the heptapods themselves. In 3000 years, there will arise a problem on the planet the heptapods call home, and it will be up to the humans to help save them. Louise and Ian are still missing crucial gaps in the language when some soldiers under Weber's command take matter into their own hands and plant explosives in the alien spaceship. The Chinese, under the command of the understandably frightened General Shang (Tzi Ma), are ready to start firing missiles. Louise and Ian have their time cut into next to nothing to understand what the heptapods are after before an intergalactic war is potentially ignited.

Arrival's many virtues mostly cover up its biggest flaws. There are a handful of truly risible pieces of dialogue meant as shorthand that come off as ham-fisted in the extreme. The most intriguing portion of the film should have been the minutiae of translating the heptapod language, but unfortunately screenwriter Eric Heisserer and Villeneuve did not actually work out what that might look like. The film has too little interest in its ostensible subject matter, language, to spend much time elaborating on its finer points. So the fascinating process by which humans learn to talk to aliens is left to a montage in the middle of the movie, the laziest and most enervating device in modern cinema. When Louise can suddenly speak their language in the final stretch of the movie, it feels like a leap into overt fantasy, instead of gentle science fiction, the film had until then resisted.

That montage speaks to an imbalance in the center of the film with regard to Villeneuve's form. He and editor Joe Walker rather eloquently ricochet between major life events in Louise's life for the first act of *Arrival*, hinting that the fluid chronology will wind up paying thematic dividends, which it does. But by ignoring this strategy for all but the most important seconds of the second and most of the third act, Villeneuve has no choice but to focus exclusively on the present, about which he does not care enough to get the exact details right. That editing, which calls to mind time travel sci-fi touchstones like Chris Marker's *La Jetée* (1962) and Alain Resnais' *Je t'aime, je t'aime* (1968), in which memory and the future are like a deck of cards waiting to be shuffled. Sticking to this editing strategy would have cut out the hokey nature of its worst passages. It also would have done more to showcase the excellent work of cinematographer Bradford Young. Young relies on shallow focus to a large degree, not just to isolate

Louise in a world and a timeline rushing past her, but to force us to pay attention to little details that will only become fully apparent when the third act closes, turning the film much more melancholy in hindsight. His shallow compositions and his reliance on harsh, claustrophobic lighting, counterpointed by haunting darkness, pull the viewer gently forward in the narrative. Like Jóhann Jóhannsson's haunting score, the photography is pleasing and ominous in equal measure. Together, they help Walker and Villeneuve's rhythm remain focused and ambling, all the better to play with big, frightening themes and ideas.

Young's landscape photography is just as wonderful as his interior shots, but if he and Villeneuve had stuck to the alienating device of presenting everything without comment from the script, it would have showcased Louise's mental state even more acutely. The degree to which Villeneuve feels the need to spell things out for his audience undermines the care he took to achieve atmospheric perfection. That same tendency also hamstrung *Incendies* and *Sicario*, proving that Villeneuve's refusal to edit the material given to him remains his Achilles' heel.

Fortunately, the film has a major ace up its sleeve in the third act. When the alien's gift is revealed, so too is a secret that Villeneuve has been keeping from us the whole time. It turns every decision Louise makes into a heartbreaking refusal to flee from life's most cruel gestures. Hannah's fate is both unspeakably cruel but also just part of life's design, as it must be for all people. Amy Adams' work as Louise is spectacular because she has to play off all-consuming sadness as sternness and bravery. She makes a woman torn about by guilt and sorrow seem like she's a career woman with garden variety doubts about her life choices. What *Arrival* ultimately wants us to think about is whether or not we would want to change any portion of our lives if we had the choice. Would we tempt fate by redesigning the saddest and most gut-wrenching events to better suit our emotional needs, even if they meant missing out on some of the most spectacular and life changing sensations? Louise has to ask what losing Hannah means played against the prospect of never having her in her life. If Villeneuve had made this a little more broadly the theme of the movie, instead of burying it under admittedly quite impressive artifice and gamesmanship, he might have achieved an even stronger moment of catharsis than the one he lands upon. *Arrival* proves that the clinical hand responsible for the stomach churning theatrics of *Sicario* and *Prisoners* could find real emotion under all the reveals and reversals. What he has not yet found is the willingness to let a film's ideas and his first rate images speak for themselves.

Scout Tafoya

CREDITS

Louise Banks: Amy Adams
Ian Donnelly: Jeremy Renner
Colonel Weber: Forest Whitaker
Agent Halpern: Michael Stuhlbarg
Captain Marks: Mark O'Brien
Hannah: Jadyn Malone, Abigail Pniowsky, Julia Scarlett Dan
Origin: United States
Language: English
Released: 2016
Production: Dan Levine, Shawn Levy, David Linde, Aaron Ryder; released by 21 Laps Entertainment, FilmNation Entertainment, Lava Bear Films, Xenolinguistics
Directed by: Denis Villeneuve
Written by: Eric Heisserer
Cinematography by: Bradford Young
Music by: Johann Johannsson
Sound: Sylvain Bellemare
Editing: Joe Walker
Art Direction: Isabelle Guay
Costumes: Renee April
Production Design: Patrice Vermette
MPAA rating: PG-13
Running time: 116 minutes

REVIEWS

Bradshaw Peter. *The Guardian.* September 1, 2016.
Burr, Ty. *Boston Globe.* November 10, 2016.
Collin, Robbie. *The Telegraph.* September 1, 2016.
Dowd, A.A. *The A.V. Club.* November 9, 2016.
Duralde, Alonso. *The Wrap.* September 1, 2016.
Ebiri, Bilge. *Village Voice.* November 7, 2016.
Kiang, Jessica. *The Playlist.* September 1, 2016.
Mac, Sam C. *Slant.* November 8, 2016.
Turan, Kenneth. *Los Angeles Times.* November 10, 2016.
Zacharek, Stephanie. *Time.* September 1, 2016.

QUOTES

Dr. Louise Banks: "You can understand communication and still end up single."

TRIVIA

The original name for the film was *Story of Your Life.* However, test audiences did not like the title, so it was changed.

AWARDS

Oscars 2016: Sound FX Editing
British Acad. 2016: Sound
Writers Guild 2016: Adapt. Screenplay
Nominations:
Oscars 2016: Adapt. Screenplay, Director (Villeneuve), Film, Film Editing, Production Design

British Acad. 2016: Actress (Adams), Adapt. Screenplay, Cinematog., Director (Villeneuve), Film, Film Editing, Orig. Score, Visual FX

Directors Guild 2016: Director (Villeneuve)

Golden Globes 2017: Actress—Drama (Adams), Score

Screen Actors Guild 2016: Actress (Adams)

ASSASSIN'S CREED

> *Your destiny is in your blood.*
> —Movie tagline

Box Office: $53.9 Million

Video game adaptations have never been awards contenders, points of cultural interest, or the recipient of more than a modest cult following. They are an orphaned subgenre for a few reasons. They typically rely too heavily on plot points that were never meant to work narratively. The story of any video game popular enough to warrant adaptation is ordinarily connective tissue meant to do little more than establish the actions taken by a player. If they are more complex than that, they are frequently far too complex for their own good, filled with byzantine mythologies that would need whole movies unto themselves before anything like satisfying developments might occur. Then there's the issue of replicating game play. How do you render cinematically something that only worked because of the thrill of control?

Tolerance for this mode of storytelling has varied from minimal to non-existent over the years so when it was announced that Michael Fassbender, Marion Cotillard, and director Justin Kurzel would all be reuniting after their apocalyptically portentous *Macbeth* adaptation from 2015 to adapt the video game series *Assassin's Creed* there was reason to hope. Though *Macbeth* was by no means a critical darling, the performances were transfixing, and the film's mesmeric, heavy metal-inspired images (courtesy of wunderkind cinematographer Adam Arkapaw, who returned to lens *Assassin's Creed*) lent the bard's most popular tragedy an air of edgy, contemplative doom. It was a completely unique telling of Shakespeare, so maybe these were the right people to finally rescue the video game movie from ignominy. Unfortunately, Kurzel and co. have let the game's complex web of juvenile ideas get in the way of their spectacle. Not even a prestige cast worth drooling over can save this film from itself.

The film begins and will frequently return to 1492 Spain, where a secret brotherhood of assassins convenes to ordain their latest member, Aguilar de Nerha (Michael Fassbender), who will lead the group in their most important mission: save Ahmed the outcast prince of Granada (Kemaal Deen-Ellis) from the Knights Templar, who want to use him as leverage. They think the prince's father, Sultan Muhammad XII (Khalid Abdalla), knows the location of a mythic stone called the Apple of Eden, supposedly host to the genetic code for free will. They hope that the threat of violence against Prince Ahmed will coerce him into giving up its location. Only the Assassins stand in the way of the Knights Templar gaining control of the Apple.

Assassin's Creed then jumps forward hundreds of years to the childhood home of Callum Lynch (Angus Brown). Callum lives with his mother Mary (Essie Davis) and father Joseph (Brian Gleeson) in Baja until the day he comes home and finds his mother dead, apparently by his father's hand. Joseph offers a cryptic warning to his son before allowing him to escape, just as a fleet of SUVs pulls up to their hideaway to take Joseph away. Callum goes on the run for thirty years (when grown to manhood he'll also be played by Fassbender), finally ending up on death row for the many crimes he committed while living on the fringes of society. Just before losing consciousness, he notices an odd sight at his execution: a woman he's never met before (Marion Cotillard) eying him very intently. To his considerable surprise, he wakes from his execution and sees her staring at him once again. Her name is Sofia Rikkin and she's a scientist dedicated to finding the Apple of Eden, like the Knights Templar before her. The group she works for her, Abstergo, run by her father (Jeremy Irons), is the modern incarnation of the Knights Templar, and they have never given up their quest for control of free will. Sofia tells Callum she means to use it for peaceful means, but her father and the head of their order (Charlotte Rampling) clearly mean to use it for some form of world domination. Regardless, Callum is the heart of their plan.

Abstergo have created a machine called the animus, which reads the bloodline of anyone who is hooked up to it, and allows subjects to regress to past lives. Callum is the last descendant of Aguilar the assassin, and if Sofia can get him to relive his final days, they can discover where he hid the Apple of Eden. It turns out that Aguilar, not the sultan, was the last person known to possess it. Callum must live through his ancestor's chaotic last days while Abstergo records the events he sees as Aguilar. Naturally Callum figures out that they're using him for dastardly means, and the other captives at Abstergo certainly don't mind telling him they don't like that he's leading the scientists right to the object that the assassins have kept hidden for hundreds of years. Callum is not sure he cares one way or the other by whom he's being used, especially when he discovers the murderous father he still loathes (now played by Brendan Gleeson) is being held in Abstergo's headquarters as well.

Assassin's Creed may be a thorny tangle of nonsense, narratively speaking, and one hardly worth understanding at that, but it's not without virtue. Arkapaw's images are frequently stunning and the pace and spatial arrangement are both commendable. The cast is superb and watching them commit so doggedly to something so completely nonsensical is as entertaining as any of Kurzel's finely if busily choreographed fight sequences. He relishes the opportunity to turn most of the film's flashbacks into extended chase sequences that visually ape the style of video games. They have a certain visceral quality, complete with parkour and close-quarter martial arts, but they're not enough to justify the film's daffy mythology. The business surrounding the Apple of Eden makes no sense and Sofia and her father's repeatedly calling their work "science" implies that either the film wants her to seem not just villainous but impossibly dumb, or the screenwriters simply do not know what the word means. She is, after all, just looking for an object that supposedly contains genetic coding, which is also a completely unsupportable idea even by the low standards of movie McGuffins. The only scientific practice the film can lay claim to is the inner workings of the animus, which, tellingly is almost treated like a holy object. There's something compelling about it in theory, which puts Callum through something akin to an imagined labour process (complete with epidural), but instead of creating life he is manifesting death. However, the film does nothing with that potentially interesting symbol, just as it introduces several characters it can't support and plot threads that lead nowhere. *Assassin's Creed* is an entertaining and honest mess, but an absolute mess it remains.

Scout Tafoya

CREDITS

Cal Lynch/Aguilar de Nerha: Michael Fassbender
Sofia: Marion Cotillard
Rikkin: Jeremy Irons
Joseph Lynch: Brendan Gleeson
Ellen Kaye: Charlotte Rampling
Callum: Angus Brown
Origin: United States
Language: English
Released: 2016
Production: Jean-Julien Baronnet, Patrick Crowley, Gerard Guillemot, Frank Marshall, Conor McCaughan, Arnon Milchan, Michael Fassbender; released by Regency Enterprises, Ubisoft Entertainment S.A.
Directed by: Justin Kurzel
Written by: Michael Lesslie; Adam Cooper; Bill Collage
Cinematography by: Adam Arkapaw

Music by: Jed Kurzel
Sound: Frank Kruse
Music Supervisor: Lucy Bright
Editing: Christopher Tellefsen
Art Direction: Marc Homes
Costumes: Timothy Everest; Sammy Sheldon
Production Design: Andy Nicholson
MPAA rating: PG-13
Running time: 115 minutes

REVIEWS

Collin, Robbie. *The Telegraph.* December 19, 2016.
Dyer, James. *Empire.* December 20, 2016.
Feeney, Mark. *Boston Globe.* December 21, 2016.
Fujishima, Kenji. *Playlist.* December 19, 2016.
Grierson, Tim. *Screen International.* December 19, 2016.
Hassenger, Jesse. *The A.V. Club.* December 19, 2016.
Riccio, Aaron. *Slant Magazine.* December 19, 2016.
Scherstuhl, Alan. *Village Voice.* December 19, 2016.
Walsh, Katie. *Los Angeles Times.* December 20, 2016.
Zacharek, Stephanie. *Time.* December 19, 2016.

QUOTES

Callum Lynch: "We work in the dark to serve the light. We are assassins."

TRIVIA

Around 80% of the film, including stunts, extras, and locations, were shot without using CGI.

AUTHOR: THE JT LEROY STORY

Master Piece. Master Mind.
     —Movie tagline

Box Office: $85,999

The documentary is the most pliant of narrative forms, allowing filmmakers to create their own rules with open boundaries by combining oral history, memory, biography, cultural journalism, and emotional inquiry. That elasticity is sometimes counterproductive or even a burden, underscoring the sense that many directors require the discipline and structure.

The filmmaker Jeff Feuerzeig is a deft and subtle portraitist, as he demonstrated in his exemplary documentary, *The Devil and Daniel Johnston* (2005), about the precarious divide between genius and breakdown regarding a talented musician. The director's new film, *Author: The JT Leroy Story,* tracking the rise and fall underpinning a literary phenomenon, is alternately thrilling, riveting, sad, and maddeningly incomplete. The director's absence of judgment and remarkable sensitivity at capturing the emotional complexities of his protagonist is deeply admirable even as it exposes the more problematic aspects of his telling.

For all of his stylistic fluency and his intelligent and impressive command of the frequently extraordinary material, Feuerzeig has made a work vague and underreported that is too narrowly rendered and one-sided to really achieve any lift. The central artist, the Brooklyn-born, San Francisco-based Laura Albert, emerges as an emphatically interesting writer of originality and raw talent though a deeply damaged individual. *Author* is a serious work with troubling implications, and the filmmaker's probing of those issues provides a vitality and often disarmingly fresh angle on a story more than a decade old. The absence of an alternate perspectives or contradictory voices negates the filmmaker's natural sympathy, yielding an imbalance between form and content that proves deeply frustrating.

Like Orson Welles's great *F for Fake* (1973), illusion is the movie's organizing principle. "A created thing is never invented and it is never true," reads the quotation attributed to the master Italian fabulist, Federico Fellini. "It is always and ever itself." Winona Ryder, one of the many actors, filmmakers, fashion artists, and musicians entrapped by the deceit, proves all too typical of those enraptured by the *idea* of Leroy more than a tangible presence. "You are an inspiration," she says.

Feuerzeig moves dexterously in time and space intertwining the wrenching details of Albert's troubled childhood against the dizzying speed and alarming ease her literary doppelganger took flight. Feuerzeig frames Albert in a recurrent medium close up against a stylized backdrop of an oversized book of text. He is unapologetic and direct presenting his subject, rarely if ever challenging her version of events. His tactic leaves wholly open the question of whether she is a fraud, a pathological liar, afflicted by multiple personality disorder or a preternaturally skilled performer who intuitively grasped cynical truths about the susceptibility governing culture, the internet, marketing, and the capricious nature of celebrity.

Albert endured a horribly difficult childhood, sexually molested by a family acquaintance at the age of three, an intimate witness to the breakup of her parents' marriage. Dealing with weight and body issues as a young girl, she was mercilessly taunted and bullied at school and was twice institutionalized. Emancipated from her parents, she was eventually raised in a group home. Her vulnerability is revealed in a series of plaintive, wrenching family photographs, and home movies

capturing a young girl streaked in sorrow, pain, and loneliness. (It is uncanny the visual connections between these peripheral images and Asia Argento's movie adaptation, *The Heart is Deceitful Among All Things* [2004], taken from LeRoy's same-titled short story collection [2001].)

The persona of "Terminator," a sexually fluid 15-year old child of a West Virginia truck stop prostitute, evolves from Albert's feverish conversations to a San Francisco suicide prevention hotline. She is overtaken by the power and control. The Leroy construct was her private dollhouse. Her manipulation allowed her the freedom to orchestrate everything to her own very specific ends. "I ordered and controlled the universe," she said.

Albert becomes ever more fearless and brazen in enlarging the scope of her invention, cultivating a series of literary patrons like the novelist Dennis Cooper and obtaining a prominent agent that results in a book deal. She wields the phone like a scalpel, perfecting a soft voice that veers between a hushed whisper and a manic glee. In *Author*, many of the most revealing passages emerge in the phone conversations that Albert meticulously recorded, a typical one involving the actor and musician Tom Waits marveling at her "wet narrative voice," and how every other established writer feels stodgy or dull by comparison. (Late in the film there's an exchange involving Courtney Love and cocaine that has to he heard to be believed.)

"I lived in fantasy," she says. Part of the fascination is how others were all too willing to indulge in the make believe. Albert enlisted her own conspirators, her husband, a musician named Geoff Knoop and most importantly, her sister-in-law, Savannah, a slim-hipped blonde with a buzz cut and exceptionally soft, androgynous features who slipped astonishingly gracefully into the public role of LeRoy. Albert was the master ventriloquist who continued to vocalize the part, in her phone calls. Savannah is the other part of the calculation, and it is striking how immaculate she is, adopting the same speaking rhythm, but with a remarkable sense of the spectacle or theater of the absurd, like a public reading in Rome where Savannah, posing as LeRoy, stops, pauses, and dives under a table to complete the performance, to a deafening applause.

LeRoy becomes a kind of Voltaire's *Candide* (1759), or the equivalent of Woody Allen's *Zelig* (1982). As the role took on ever greater heights of fancy and possibility, LeRoy, with Albert and her husband are swept into a peculiar and feverish existence, given a sympathetic, protective talk by Bono at a U2 concert, or being whisked into the protective, surreal world of public ritual and adulation, courted by off-Hollywood figures like director Gus Van Sant, reveling in the ecstatic heights of the international premiere at Cannes of Argento's movie adaptation.

The unmasking was always inevitable, and the start of the unraveling, whether subconsciously a confession or not, was no doubt instigated when Albert tells the rock singer Billy Corgan, during a private moment, "JT was an accident." Eventually, several more skeptical articles, originally in *New York Magazine* and then conclusively, in a series of investigations by reporters at the *New York Times*, revealed the extent of the literary fraudulence. The filmmaker Marjorie Sturm provides a much harsher and less forgiving view of Albert in her own documentary, *The Cult of JT LeRoy* (2015).

The film *Author* is not really a story about deception. The movie's most significant theme is seduction. Laura Albert longed to be a part of something, to feel wanted, and she created the avenue. The film certainly holds attention, but only up to a point. The missing material undercuts so much, leaving a half-formed impression. Not having access to Savannah or Geoff, Albert's husband, is especially problematic. Feuerzeig is caught in the middle, avid to make a particular kind of film though deprived of the necessary material and resources.

The last part hints at a better film, a reckoning about Albert, her talent, and the very nature of truth, creativity, and perspective. JT LeRoy was more than a passing fad, and his writing, imagery, and voice, of the Southern Neon gothic, permeates any number of recent films, haunting the movies of Harmony Korine, Ryan Gosling's directing debut, *Lost River* (2014), and the nonfiction hybrid films of Italian filmmaker Roberto Minervini, such as *Stop the Pounding Heart* (2013) and *The Other Side* (2014). *Author* is often lively and audacious. It disappointingly settles rather than truly takes off.

Patrick Z. McGavin

CREDITS

Herself: Laura Albert
Himself: Bruce Benderson
Himself: Dennis Cooper
Himself: Panio Gianopoulos
Herself: Winona Ryder
Origin: United States
Language: English
Released: 2016
Production: Jim Czarnecki, Brett Ratner, Molly Thompson; released by A&E Indiefilms, Fancy Film Post Services, RatPac Documentary Films
Directed by: Jeff Feuerzeig
Written by: Jeff Feuerzeig
Cinematography by: Richard Henkels
Music by: Walter Werzowa
Editing: Michelle M. Witten
MPAA rating: R
Running time: 110 minutes

REVIEWS

Baumbgarten, Marjorie. *Austin Chronicle*. September 14, 2016.
Chang, Justin. *Los Angeles Times*. September 8, 2016.
Cheshire, Godfrey. *RogerEbert.com*. September 9, 2016.
Ebiri, Bilge. *New York Magazine*. July 22, 2016.
Greenblatt, Leah. *Entertainment Weekly*. September 7, 2016.
Kohn, Eric. *IndieWire*. July 22, 2016.
Lewis, David. *San Francisco Chronicle*. September 8, 2016.
Merry, Stephanie. *Washington Post*. September 15, 2016.
Rothkopf, Joshua. *Time Out New York*. September 6, 2016.
Scott, A.O. *New York Times*. September 8, 2016.

AWARDS

Nominations:

Writers Guild 2016: Documentary Screenplay

B

BAD MOMS

Party like a mother.
—Movie tagline

Box Office: $113.2 Million

It is borderline impossible to imagine that anyone would think it is the ideal choice to have a movie about the specific and numerous challenges, frustrations, and satisfactions of motherhood written by men. Right away, *Bad Moms* reeks with the recognition that it comes from writers-directors Jon Lucas and Scott Moore, who wrote the first (and, contrary to popular belief, worst) installment in the, cough, trilogy launched by 2009's *The Hangover*. Their latest is a cartoon of suburban domesticity, trapped within a simplistic perspective of life and people, and relationships as binary, pretending it contains dimension because it shows that strong people suffer and struggling people fight. It is also, not most importantly but importantly, not funny.

Serving as an extremely questionable surrogate for overworked moms everywhere, Mila Kunis stars as Amy, who is beautiful and thin and never looks less than great despite, as she indicates in lazily conceived voiceover, always running late and feeling like the world's worst mom. As written and performed by Kunis, Amy has no interior reality, no sharp edges that might make her seem off-putting, or her experience vivid and difficult in ways that a little change of perspective could not fix. That limited detail also applies to her husband (David Walton), an inattentive bozo who laughs at her carrying a lot of grocery bags without offering to help. Their relationship exists in a vacuum of regret, having sparked from a pregnancy that turned into a marriage at 20 and

now, many years and two pre-teen kids later, barely seems to have anything left to save.

Too bad that Kunis barely makes an effort to sell Amy's curiosity about the divorce's impact on the children, or her scars after years of emotional decay and loneliness. When she finally decides that her terrible, cheating husband and lame, young boss (Clark Duke) and stacked plate of responsibilities are too much, it should turn into something that feels dramatic and even heavy: a pot boiling over, seams popping, the duties of a woman juggling a lot of roles at once exploding into self-interest. Instead, it is a feeble stab at comedy that feels anxious and stale, from Amy lashing out at the clichéd, uptight PTA president (Christina Applegate in a part that already felt dry in *Bad Teacher* [2011]) to the montage, predictably set to Icona Pop's overused "I Love It," of Amy and her new, likewise unhappy mom friends Carla (Kathryn Hahn) and Kiki (Kristen Bell) cutting loose in the supermarket. As if these moms could not possibly think of anywhere else to separate from social convention and decide to take a night to just be independent people who need to give themselves a break.

Of course, when they do, the joke, if there even is a joke, is that they are partying with the sloppy recklessness typically attributed to guys, a behavior presented not as liberating but unnatural. Well, first their bar exploits find Amy so cognitively lost down the hole of motherhood that she is unable to engage with men without mentioning Tupperware and diarrhea and trying to get a stain out of a shirt. Inevitably this changes with Jessie (Jay Hernandez), a widower frequently ogled by the moms at the kids' school and created as a flawless dreamboat out of a romance novel. This being a thinly conceived studio comedy overloaded with musical cues,

Bad Moms has no interest in the baggage that might emerge when Amy and Jessie merged their lives, only the hot sex that comes from their bodies. The demands of their lives will remind no one of NBC's excellent *Parenthood* (2010-2015) as, like *The Hangover*, *Bad Moms* creates only insultingly one-sided significant others for its main characters.

Speaking of that story of dudes gone wild: Kiki is the female version of Ed Helms' character, whipped by an overbearing husband who cannot handle the kids himself. Carla, the loose cannon in the Zach Galifiankis role, is a single mom, so naturally she has to be presented as promiscuous and unhinged. (That makes Kunis, the leader, the female version of Bradley Cooper, even though, unlike in the guys' movie, these women are never allowed to do anything that causes real damage.) Most of the male-female interactions unfold as a battle, rarely a team effort, and the punchline is that the filmmakers think they have landed on empowerment by staging a moms-only public confession ripped straight from the *Mean Girls* (2004) gymnasium.

The defense, assumedly, is that *Bad Moms* is not meant to be an in-depth look at parenthood. It attempts to be an escape about escape, removing the religious elements of the even lousier *Moms' Night Out* (2014) and elevating family friendly shenanigans to cheap gags like Carla using Kiki's hooded sweatshirt to demonstrate what to do with an uncircumcised penis. Only in the realization that perfection is unattainable and a support system is mandatory does it feel like the film is (albeit generically) opening up these moms to a different, more stable frame of mind. As for laughs, well, it is oddly amusing when Kiki says her daughter killed the neighbor's ferret on purpose, and NFL star J.J. Watt gets a chuckle or two as the middle school soccer coach who just wants to make enough money to feed his cats and fill his Prius.

That achieves very little, though. Lucas and Moore never develop any sense of place; the film is set in the Chicago area, but the filmmakers pay no more attention to that than they do to their one-dimensional characters. That results in minimal momentum or contemporary awareness of a society that still has a long way to go toward gender equality and parental expectations and judgments, and the issues are far more than bake sales and piano recitals. Moms deserve a credible presentation as heroes, not a phony salute, but comedy and truth come from specificity, and *Bad Moms* is an anonymous shrug in the direction of something it does not actually care to understand.

Certainly, there is something potent and potentially wickedly funny to be said about the impulses that push parents to do it all, and the basic limitations of time and human capability that blur the line between selfishness and necessary self-maintenance. There is unfunny tragedy in Amy's husband being asked to name three good things about her and merely listing two foods that she cooks. Shame that *Bad Moms* hardly can be bothered to create its own surface, much less scratch beneath it.

Matt Pais

CREDITS

Amy: Mila Kunis
Carla: Kathryn Hahn
Kiki: Kristen Bell
Gwendolyn: Christina Applegate
Stacy: Jada Pinkett Smith
Origin: United States
Language: English
Released: 2016
Production: Bill Block, Suzanne Todd; released by Block Entertainment, STX Entertainment
Directed by: Jon Lucas; Scott Moore
Written by: Jon Lucas; Scott Moore
Cinematography by: Jim Denault
Music by: Christopher Lennertz
Sound: Kami Asgar
Music Supervisor: Jason Markey; Julia Michels
Editing: Emma E. Hickox; James Thomas
Costumes: Julia Caston
Production Design: Marcia Hinds
MPAA rating: R
Running time: 100 minutes

REVIEWS

Dargis, Manohla. *New York Times.* July 28, 2016.
Duralde, Alonso. *TheWrap.* July 28, 2016.
Erbland, Kate. *IndieWire.* July 28, 2016.
Frosch, Jon. *Hollywood Reporter.* July 28, 2016.
Hassenger, Jesse. *The A.V. Club.* July 27, 2016.
Lemire, Christy. *RogerEbert.com.* July 28, 2016.
Nicholson, Amy. *MTV News.* July 29, 2016.
Olsen, Mark. *Los Angeles Times.* July 28, 2016.
Phillips, Michael. *Chicago Tribune.* July 28, 2016.
Stevens, Dana. *Slate.* July 28, 2016.

QUOTES

Carla: "My kid still watches *Sesame Street* and he doesn't get it."

TRIVIA

The main actresses are all real-life mothers.

BAD SANTA 2

Wilder. Drunker. Badder.
—Movie tagline

Box Office: $17.7 Million

Way back in the cinema of 2005, Terry Zwigoff's *Bad Santa* stood out because it was crotchety, alone, and hilarious. It was not only a bizarre character for Billy Bob Thornton, it was its own naughty force, however cult-viewing driven, featuring a character who would more likely be found in a dumpster than the center of his own movie. Whatever one thought of it, the movie earned its reputation because it was indeed groundbreaking, bringing about spiritual spin-offs like *Bad Teacher* (2011), *Bad Grandpa* (2013), and more.

The legacy comes full circle and then up its own ass with *Bad Santa 2*, a depressed and depressing piece of sequel cynicism that could not possibly have been made be-cause there was more story to tell. For the cult members who watched the original film and bought the various unrated DVD versions, this film merely seeks to add more to characters who have already said enough, especially as excessive use of the word "f***" loses its charm a few minutes into the movie.

The misadventures in this sequel are hardly inspired, placing the hero of ill behavior on another mission of misanthtopy. After getting fired from a valet driver gig (distracted by a breastfeeding woman, while drunk), Willie Sokes (Billy Bob Thornton) sticks his head in the ov-en and then tries to hang himself from a ceiling, his Raymond Chandler-on-depressants voiceover cluing the viewer into a suicide note. He is saved by accident by a friend (meaning someone that he despises)—the young Thurman (Brett Kelly), a hopelessly naive young man meant by the script to dance on the line of naiveté and mental deficiency. Thurman brings out the softest side of Willie, as when Thornton's character tries to help Thurman lose her virginity by hiring a prosti-tute (played by Octavia Spencer) in the film's first act.

But when his old friend Marcus (Tony Cox) shows up offering another job, involving Willie using his super skills to crack a safe inside a Chicago charity shelter, Willie puts his antihe-ro Santa suit back on. Also work-ing this job is Willie's estranged mother Sunny (Kathy Bates). Their plan is to infiltrate the shelter's mass of hired Santa Claus performers until they can break into the office of Regent Hastings (Ryan Hansen), who has around three million in the safe. The original plan is also to split the money evenly, which as the blunt back-stabbing as the story goes, does not happen.

Though *Bad Santa 2* is unmistakably laughless, it earns a heartbeat when Willie faces possibly abandoning Kelly's Thurman in a laundromat, like an animal who traveled to Chicago (played here poorly by Toronto) wearing only shorts and a sandwich shop polo. The scene plays without words, and gives the movie the dimension it lacks while dangling with naughty jokes.

If *Bad Santa* fans appreciate these films in the way that modern multi-plex audiences get their fill from caped crusaders, they might be barely amused by the shenani-gans that lead up to the night of attempted robbery. Cuss words are savored, Willie starts a rela-tionship with Regent's jilted wife Diane (Christina Hen-dricks), and woos her (in an alley, and later behind a dumpster). The introverted morality of the now-franchise steers the movie towards a shrugging conclu-sion, including double-crosses and a showdown with his mother at a Santa convention.

Thornton is hardly a salesman in the role, his character's indifference the result of Thor-noton's own transparent lack of interest in this venture. He provides the character with no bite, despite the blood alcohol level in his words and actions. Thornton volleys performance charisma to Bates, who could most be ac-cused of having fun with such a ridiculous role, adding a little pep and glee into vibrator jokes or moments of malevolence.

Instead of taking on the project with the pizazz of *Mean Girls* (2004), Waters takes on the minimal piece of fan amusement as a hired gig, dumping most of the action in a drab apartment, where forgettable banter is volleyed and the misadventures of these charac-ters proved the only life source. The production values err on the side of cancelled sitcom, with no energy coming from editing or the lifeless, clean digital cinematography.

By its own standards, which it sets early into the film regardless of one having seen the original or not, the shocking factor plays it safe. Even the derogatory stuff runs flat, with millions of jokes aimed at Marcus involving his short height, or Thurman's boyish naivete constantly leer-ing on mental illness. Trying to find its place in a world that villainies political correctness or laughs at safe spaces, *Bad Santa 2* has little to offer the world but gauche cynicism. The now-franchise's once-charming title id for the worst of humanity becomes a shill for a sequel rottener than his impulses.

Nick Allen

CREDITS

Willie Soke: Billy Bob Thornton
Sunny Soke: Kathy Bates
Marcus Skidmore: Tony Cox
Diane Hastings: Christina Hendricks
Thurman Merman: Brett Kelly
Origin: United States
Language: English
Released: 2016
Production: Andrew Gunn, Geyer Kosinski; released by Broad Green Pictures, Ingenious Media Partners, Miramax LLC

Directed by: Mark Waters
Written by: Johnny Rosenthal; Shauna Cross
Cinematography by: Theo van de Sande
Music by: Lyle Workman
Music Supervisor: Tracy McKnight
Editing: Travis Sittard
Art Direction: Jean-Pierre Paquet
Costumes: Mario Davignon
Production Design: Isabelle Guay
MPAA rating: R
Running time: 92 minutes

REVIEWS

Dowd, A.A. *The A.V. Club.* November 22, 2016.
Jones, J.R. *Chicago Reader.* December 1, 2016.
Kenigsberg, Ben. *New York Times.* November 22, 2016.
Kenny, Glenn. *RogerEbert.com.* November 23, 2016.
Lowe, Justin. *Hollywood Reporter.* November 16, 2016.
Nicholson, Amy. *MTV.* November 23, 2016.
Semley, John. *Globe and Mail.* November 22, 2016.
Tobias, Scott. *NPR.* November 23, 2016.
Walsh, Katie. *Los Angeles Times.* November 22, 2016.
Wolfe, April. *LA Weekly.* December 1, 2016.

QUOTES

Willie: "I travelled all the way across the USA to rob a … charity?"

TRIVIA

Willie says his birthday is August 4. This is actually Billy Bob Thornton's birthday.

BARBERSHOP: THE NEXT CUT

Everybody's back for a fresh cut.
—Movie tagline

Box Office: $54 Million

Twelve years after the first sequel (and eleven years after the series' spin-off movie *Beauty Shop* [2005]), *Barbershop: The Next Cut* returns to the local barbershop on Chicago's South Side with an unexpected purpose.

The previous movies were pure comedies, with *Barbershop* (2002) teetering between a hang-out movie, in which a group of barbers and local residents in the shop simply cut hair and talked without a filter about whatever topic might come up in conversation, and a broad situation comedy (The subplot involving a stolen ATM comes to mind.) The balance in *Barbershop 2:*

Back in Business (2004) tipped more toward the latter, as a plot about a rival shop put the store's fate in jeopardy.

Calvin's (Ice Cube) barbershop is once again on the brink of closing up its South Side location, although, this time, it is the owner's decision. There are no falling revenues, loan sharks to repay, or big, chain franchises with which to contend in this installment. Calvin simply has had enough of the rise of gang violence in his neighborhood. It is a rarity that more than a couple of days go by without him hearing about another shooting. His son Jalen (Michael Rainey Jr.) is in high school now, and Calvin worries that his son could either become a victim in the crossfire or, as a result of those normal growing pains that come when a son is able to score against his father in a pick-up game of basketball on the driveway, join a gang himself. The only option, as Calvin sees it, is to shut down the current shop and move his business and family to the North Side.

A lot has changed for this community—both locally and along broader racial lines—in the period of more than a decade since the last time these characters appeared on screen, and with that change comes a more serious tone than the one in the prior movies. It also means that screenwriters Kenya Barris and Tracy Oliver (both are new to the series, as is director Malcolm D. Lee) have a lot of catch-up to play. The United States has witnessed the election and re-election of its first African-American president. A string of questionable killings of black people across the country has put the spotlight on potential systemic or systematic racism in institutions of power, bringing with it three words that Calvin shouts, seemingly as a way to shield himself from gang members he thinks might harm him, in the early moments of the movie: black lives matter.

The threat, it turns out, is a joke perpetrated by Eddie (Cedric the Entertainer), the senior staff member of the barbershop, whose no-nonsense way with words continues here. (He insists that Barak Obama has more than a few women on the side and gets into an argument over his old-fashioned views of the role of women in society.) As with the previous installments, the movie is at its best when it allows these characters to talk freely and honestly about a range of topics.

Some of the old characters return in brief roles (Anthony Anderson's J.D. has another scheme involving a food truck) or cameos (Troy Garity's Isaac appears to get his hair cut). Of most importance to the plot, Sean Patrick Thomas' Jimmy, who now works in the mayor's office, arrives at his old stomping grounds with news that there are plans to put up a police enclosure within the neighborhood, which Calvin and everyone else in the shop believe would reduce business. This subplot, of course, is redundant, since Calvin already has a good motivation to leave the neighborhood, and the screenplay never addresses the political angle this external complication brings.

The new characters include Rashad (Common), who has married the previously relationship-weary Terri (Eve), and Angie (Regina Hall), who has opened a beauty salon connected to Calvin's shop. The addition of women into the mix promises some pushback against the male-dominated conversation of the previous two movies. After offering some thoughts on the outlandish expectations men have toward women's physical attributes, though, Draya (Nicki Minaj) comes between Rashad and Terri's marriage over the course of a forced subplot, while Bree (Margot Bingham) mainly serves as an object of desire for the nerdy Jerrod (Lamorne Morris).

Another side plot, which follows Jalen and Rashad's son Kenny (Diallo Thompson) as they gradually become more and more involved in a local gang, is more in line with the movie's ultimate purpose. Calvin and the rest of the shop's employees arrange a 48-hour ceasefire between the neighborhood's rival gangs. The plan is to use the barbershop as a place where anyone can come during that time to discuss the issue of the city's rising murder rate in recent years.

Instead of seeing the "straight talk" about popular culture and history that highlighted the earlier movies being transferred to this issue, though, the movie seems complacent to rest on its good intentions. The central argument is that this problem exists. Whatever may have caused and may be causing this violence are left unexplored. The solution, Calvin and his crew argue, is for the people of the neighborhood to take back the neighborhood on their own.

It is an optimistic sentiment and one that resonates, if only because it is coming from the second sequel in a series that has never approached something of such significance. Unfortunately, *Barbershop: The Next Cut* falls back into its old habits of having the external complications and unnecessary subplots overwhelm the real heart of the material—ordinary people talking freely about what matters to them. In this case, the subject matter is far too important for it to be overshadowed in the ways it is here.

Mark Dujsik

CREDITS

Calvin: Ice Cube
Eddie: Cedric the Entertainer
Angie: Regina Hall
Jimmy: Sean Patrick Thomas

Terri: Eve
Origin: United States
Language: English
Released: 2016
Production: Robert Teitel, George Tillman, Jr., Ice Cube; released by Cube Vision, Metro-Goldwyn-Mayer Inc.
Directed by: Malcolm Lee
Written by: Kenya Barris; Tracy Oliver
Cinematography by: Greg Gardiner
Music by: Stanley Clarke
Music Supervisor: Stephanie Diaz-Matos; Gabe Hilfer
Editing: Paul Millspaugh
Art Direction: Gentry L. Akens, II
Costumes: Danielle Hollowell
MPAA rating: PG-13
Running time: 111 minutes

REVIEWS

Anderson, Melissa. *Village Voice.* April 13, 2016.
Henderson, Eric. *Slant Magazine.* April 14, 2016.
Henderson, Odie. *RogerEbert.com.* April 15, 2016.
Olsen, Mark. *Los Angeles Times.* April 14, 2016.
Orndorf, Brian. *Blu-ray.com.* April 15, 2016.
Scott, A.O. *New York Times.* April 14, 2016.
Terry, Josh. *Deseret News.* April 16, 2016.
Walsh, Katie. *Chicago Tribune.* April 14, 2016.
Zacharek, Stephanie. *Time.* April 15, 2016.
Zilberman, Alan. *Washington Post.* April 14, 2016.

QUOTES

Bree: "Look at Prince. Dude be rockin' stilettos and can still get it."

TRIVIA

Although the film deals with the gang situation in Chicago, it was filmed in Atlanta.

BATMAN VS. SUPERMAN: DAWN OF JUSTICE

Who will win?
—Movie tagline

Box Office: $330.3 Million

Zack Snyder's *Man of Steel* (2013) was critically derided and generally disliked by audiences, but it made a fortune, and so DC and Warner Bros. quickly put a follow-up into production, again hiring Snyder to make superheroes as little fun as conceivably possible. And the modern rule of major sequels is "more, More, MORE," so Snyder's take on Superman had to, of course, be joined by another iteration of Batman. Why not throw in Wonder Woman while we're at it? Epic in running time and yet rather small in terms of ambition, *Batman vs. Superman: Dawn of Justice* became a dividing line between critics and audiences. After a vast majority of those who get paid to write about movies panned the flick, fans of the film even petitioned to shut down Rotten Tomatoes in perhaps the most definitive case of "Shoot the Messenger" in the modern internet age. Once all the drama subsided, the film could be adequately judged, and while it's certainly not good, it's at least a step up from Snyder's execrable last Superman film. It's cluttered and flat, but there are some decent performances and at least a few ideas that allow for a slight uptick in hope as to where this franchise is going.

One of the most interesting aspects of *Dawn of Justice* is how the film seems to address criticisms of *Man of Steel*. That film ended in a city-destroying showdown between Superman (Henry Cavill) and General Zod (Michael Shannon) that left fans of the character wondering where their peace-seeking hero had gone. Superman doesn't kill people. And he certainly doesn't allow hundreds to die as collateral damage. The destruction of Metropolis has become controversial between the two films, and Bruce Wayne sees Superman's actions as reprehensible, especially when the billionaire is closely tied to a survivor of that day's destruction. Superman doesn't particularly like Batman's form of heroism either and seeks to expose him through Clark Kent's work at the Daily Planet.

Meanwhile, Lex Luthor (Jesse Eisenberg) is planning … something. He's trying to import Kryptonite, under the auspices of keeping Kryptonians like Superman under control, but he also gains access to Zod's body and a Kryptonian scout ship. What exactly Luthor is planning and why we should care is one of the biggest weaknesses of Dawn of Justice. Eisenberg makes some interesting choices, playing Luthor as something more akin to his leading role in *The Social Network* (2010) that a traditional villain, but Snyder has no idea what to do with him. He's an uninteresting villain, there just to make things go boom in the final act and to bring Kryptonite into the narrative. Batman eventually tries to get his hands on some to stop the out-of-control Superman.

With all this pressure around him, Superman goes into hiding, forcing Luthor to kidnap his mother, Martha Kent (Diane Lane), to bring him out of hiding. He tells Superman that he has to kill Batman to save his mom. Superman tries to explain how Luthor has been pitting the two heroes against each other to Batman but the Dark Knight subdues the Man of Steel in one of the film's few entertaining action sequences. Just before Batman is about to kill Superman with a Kryptonite-poisoned spear, Superman implores him to "save Martha," which sends Batman spiraling into his own memories because that was the name of his mother too, a woman that Bruce Wayne always regrets not saving. Yes, the two heroes bond over a shared maternal name. Batman snaps out of his rage, rescues Martha Kent, and Superman goes to confront Lex Luthor.

Luthor unleashes a creature built from the DNA of Zod's body to, well, destroy things (as every DC movie has to end with citywide destruction) and Wonder Woman (Gal Gadot) joins the duo to stop him. In the final battle, Superman defeats the creature but is felled by the battle. The city mourns the loss of the Man of Steel, but the final moments hint that his death may be short-lived.

Zack Snyder's biggest problem as a filmmaker could be traced back to the success of Christopher Nolan's Dark Knight trilogy. While those films are undeniably superior to anything Snyder has ever delivered, they set a tone for DC/Batman adaptations that led to these flicks that take themselves way too seriously. Snyder's biggest problem is that he repeats himself over and over again. Every theme, every concept, even most of his visual compositions—if you like it the first time, know that you'll see it again. There's not a single subtle moment in this film, nothing open to interpretation or even designed to provoke conversation after the film is over. In that sense, it is purposefully disposable and forgettable, something that thinks it's deep but could not be more shallow.

Still, this is a slight step up from *Man of Steel* for a few reasons. First, one of the huge problems with both films is that Cavill is the most boring actor to ever play a superhero. He's flat and uninteresting, and it's sad that a whole generation will consider Superman to be this un-charismatic. *Dawn of Justice* splits superhero time and Affleck has a square-jawed take on Batman that actually works. He's never going to be compared to Christian Bale, or even Michael Keaton, but he's superior to Val Kilmer and George Clooney in the history of the character. Gadot cuts a striking figure as Wonder Woman, and her standalone film in 2017 could be interesting. Eisenberg is at least trying to have some fun, and the supporting cast is strong all around. They keep this thing from being as tedious as the last film or as boring as DC's other 2016 entry, *Suicide Squad*.

Tech elements are also stronger than the last film, strengthened by Larry Fong's moody cinematography and a strong score by Hans Zimmer and Junkie XL. Again, when compared to utter garbage like *Man of Steel* and *Suicide Squad*, *Batman vs. Superman: Dawn of Justice* feels like a masterpiece. It's only when one considers the wasted potential or compares it to the best of the Marvel Cinematic Universe that it really falters. Forget the Rotten Tomatoes petition campaign or any of the behind-the-scenes stories about the film's production. Forget even the fact that it made almost $1 billion worldwide. History will judge the film on its own disappointing merits, if it remembers it at all.

Brian Tallerico

CREDITS

Bruce Wayne/Batman: Ben Affleck

Clark Kent/Superman: Henry Cavill

Lois Lane: Amy Adams

Lex Luthor: Jesse Eisenberg

Martha Kent: Diane Lane

Diana Prince/Wonder Woman: Gal Gadot

Origin: United States

Language: English

Released: 2016

Production: Charles Roven, Deborah Snyder; DC Entertainment; released by Warner Bros. Entertainment Inc.

Directed by: Zack Snyder

Written by: Chris Terrio; David S. Goyer

Cinematography by: Larry Fong

Music by: Junkie XL; Hans Zimmer

Sound: Scott Hecker

Editing: David Brenner

Art Direction: Troy Sizemore

Costumes: Michael Wilkinson

Production Design: Patrick Tatopoulos

MPAA rating: PG-13

Running time: 151 minutes

REVIEWS

Burr, Ty. *Boston Globe.* March 23, 2016.

Dowd, A.A. *The A.V. Club.* March 23, 2016.

Ebiri, Bilge. *Village Voice.* March 22, 2016.

Kohn, Eric. *IndieWire.* March 22, 2016.

Lane, Anthony. *New Yorker.* March 28, 2016.

McWeeny, Drew. *Hitfix.* March 23, 2016.

Nashawaty, Chris. *Entertainment Weekly.* March 22, 2016.

O'Hehir, Andrew. *Salon.com.* March 23, 2016.

Roffman, Michael. *Consequence of Sound.* March 22, 2016.

Seitz, Matt Zoller. *RogerEbert.com.* March 22, 2016.

QUOTES

Batman: "You're not brave, men are brave. You say that you want to help people, but you can't feel their pain, their mortality. It's time you learn what it means to be a man."

TRIVIA

In this film, Batman wears a voice modulator in his suit to electronically alter his voice. After the casting of Ben Affleck in the role, this was an idea that had been suggested by his friend, director Kevin Smith, as he felt Affleck's natural speaking voice was too high-pitched for Batman.

AWARDS

Golden Raspberries 2016: Worst Director (Snyder), Worst Screenplay, Worst Sequel/Prequel, Worst Support. Actor (Eisenberg)

Nominations:

Golden Raspberries 2016: Worst Actor (Affleck), Worst Picture, Worst Support. Actor (Cavill)

A BEAUTIFUL PLANET

Experience Earth like never before.
—Movie tagline

Box Office: $8.7 Million

A Beautiful Planet is a 49-minute documentary made partly by amateur filmmakers, but like previous, annually released IMAX-produced shorts, it is a fine piece of blockbuster filmmaking. Similar to *Avatar* (James Cameron, 2009) or *Gravity* (Alfonso Cuaron, 2013), it offers viewers experiences that can only be seen in large-scope storytelling, this one coming with the budget of NASA trips to the International Space Station. Its lead characters and cinematographers are the astronauts who share with moviegoers their workday, in and out of the office, and the endlessly fascinating view they have outside their window.

Treating its title very broadly, director Toni Myers' massive short goes in many different directions. It wants to be about the formation of the planet, its current state, and careening future. On top of this, it also focuses on daily life for various astronauts in the International Space Station, which does provide a metaphor for actress Jennifer Lawrence's narration: "A truly awesome example of what we can achieve when we work together." The overall package is a bit scattered editorially, but it does serve a greater purpose: to share excitement about the Earth, and further stoke any interests in not destroying it.

The footage captured is, of course, spectacular. Wide overhead shots of entire planetary regions take precedence over talking head interviews. As Myers shows viewers the world in day and night, the voices of astronauts point out how the light of South Korea at night dies at its border with North Korea. In daytime satellite views, Earth is shown nakedly in its land formations, with Africa's vastly depleting greens, or a dry, carved out California. These satellite images are seamlessly mixed with animated excavations into the Milky Way and beyond. A success in its poignancy and awe, *A Beautiful Planet* leaves viewers with the possibility of life elsewhere on another planet called Kepler-186f, 490 light years away from Earth.

A Beautiful Planet has a curiosity as a type of NASA PR moment, like an exercise in providing the most accessible piece of educational entertainment possible within 49 minutes. It is constantly bidding for a viewer's awe, as when mixing astronauts talking about their daily lives up above (washing their hair, trying to make espresso, exercising, all of them fascinating anti-gravity feats) with their observations on the world below. There is a special joy to be found within this documentary of people floating, smiling through their passion and workspace; a sensation enhanced with giggly talking-head interviews and candid moments, including the likes of Italian astronaut Samantha Cristoforetti and NASA's Terry Virts and Kjell Lindgren.

One can also hear the producing too, as when the narration frames global warming as something that will directly affect the lemurs' habitat (already a subject of their own IMAX short, *Island of Lemurs: Madagascar*, directed by David Douglas), or using New Orleans as a loaded example of a city that will flood from a rise in the sea-level. Thankfully, while the text remains focused on more immediate examples, almost child-like in trying to connect with viewers, the stakes remain expansive and unquestionable.

Lawrence's guiding voiceover is perhaps too soothing. Her voice is kind to the ear as always, but her personality is minimized. Instead of inspiring a sense of awe, her job here is more about conveying information, with a name to put on the poster in the process. It brings to mind Leonardo DiCaprio's similar voiceover work for Myers' previous *Hubble 3D* IMAX doc from 2010, which sounded as instructional as his exposition moments from the first half of Christopher Nolan's *Inception* (2010). Other films with a similar focus on nature, such as 2014's *Bears* (Alastair Fothergill, Keith Scholey), prove that charisma need not be snuffed while giving viewers a full-balanced meal (as that movie did with animated voice work from the invaluable John C. Reilly).

There is a difference between reading that there are an estimated hundred billion galaxies and to feeling like one has seen them, while understanding one is just a grain of sand among it all. *A Beautiful Planet* achieves this unique sensation with a perspective that alternates between a massive and minute scope. A new precedent for annual IMAX documentaries, the film is a blockbuster experience of the God's-eye view.

Nick Allen

CREDITS

Narrator: Jennifer Lawrence
Himself: Terry Virts
Origin: United States
Language: English
Released: 2016
Production: Judy Carroll; released by Imax Corp., The Walt Disney Studios
Directed by: Toni Myers
Cinematography by: James Neihouse
Music by: Micky Erbe; Maribeth Solomon
MPAA rating: G
Running time: 45 minutes

REVIEWS

Anderson, Soren. *Seattle Times.* April 28, 2016.
Condes, Yvonne. *Common Sense Media.* April 29, 2016.
Eagan, Daniel. *Film Journal International.* April 27, 2016.
Howell, Peter. *Toronto Star.* April 28, 2016.
Jaworowski, Ken. *New York Times.* April 28, 2016.
McCahill, Michael. *The Guardian.* May 26, 2016.
Morgenstern, Joe. *Wall Street Journal.* April 28, 2016.
Strohman, Donald. *The Young Folks.* May 2, 2016.
Tobias, Scott. *Variety.* April 28, 2016.
Wolfe, April. *L.A. Weekly.* April 29, 2016.

BEN-HUR

Brother against brother. Slave against empire.
—Movie tagline

Box Office: $26.4 Million

Right away, the latest incarnation of the story of Judah Ben-Hur opens itself up to possible ridicule and eye-rolling from people who see a lot of movies. It opens with the unmistakable voice of Morgan Freeman giving a voice-over narration, heaping on a lot of exposition to the audience about the Romans, Judah (Jack Huston), and his adopted brother, Messala Severus (Toby Kebbell). Freeman is, of course, a great actor whose presence could easily bring integrity to just about any project, but having him narrate anything at this point should only be done so if the filmmakers are trying to get the audience to laugh in recognition of hearing Freeman narrate yet another film. After famously being the voice of authority and calm in *The Shawshank Redemption* (1994) and *An Inconvenient Truth* (2006) and many more films, having Freeman narrate anything has become a punchline of sorts. Freeman has actually parodied himself narrating on the Academy Awards telecast, so even he is in on the joke.

That is the problem in a nutshell with the latest *Ben-Hur*, a story that has been made into a film least three times now, first with *Ben-Hur: A Tale of the Christ* (1925) and then again most famously with William Wyler's *Ben-Hur* (1959), which won eleven Academy Awards, including Best Picture and boasted an unprecedented chariot race scene that set the bar for action scenes in American cinema for decades to come. There was also the TV mini-series *Ben-Hur* (2010). The very idea of remaking a film with that kind of pedigree seems foolish and this latest version only makes that point clearer with a big, messy, emotionally barren and badly written film that never makes a case for its existence. It is so desperate to be relevant that not only does Morgan Freeman narrate, but it also had a 3-D release.

For the most part, the story remains the same. Judah Ben-Hur gets wrongly accused of an assassination attempt on the Romans. His adopted brother Messala, now a Roman soldier who is trying to live down his Grandfather's name and become his own person, has an unbreakable alliance with the Romans, who have enslaved and persecuted thousands and are now taking over Jerusalem, where the Messala grew up in the House of Hur. Messala condemns his own brother to the Galleys where, for five years, he is a prisoner on a war ship, rowing endlessly across oceans. During a battle, the ship capsizes and Judah breaks free of the shackles on his feet. In this version, rather than saving the life of a high-ranking official, he washes ashore on Jerusalem and is taken in by Ilderim (Morgan Freeman), who would have turned him in if Judah did not express much interest in his horses.

Judah has every reason to believe his mother Naomi (Ayelet Zurur), sister Tirzah (Sofia Black-D'Elia), and wife Esther (Nazanin Boniadi) have been killed by the Romans, but a traitor among them seeks out Judah to inform him that his family is still alive. Meanwhile, Ilderim has Judah training day after day to get back into the game of chariot racing so that he can compete in the big Circus against his own brother. Throughout his life, Judah has meaningful run-ins with Jesus of Nazareth (Rodrigo Santoro), who appears among the people as just another citizen, but his words and actions are starting to have a strong impact. Never mind that, though, because the film really wants to get to the big chariot race, which appears to be the only reason for this film's very existence.

The chariot race scene here has been modernized with shaky-cam, 3-D horses, and Morgan Freeman yelling "Good move, Judah! Good move!" The scenes leading up to it, in which Judah practices his racing technique while hearing Ilderim feed him wisdom about racing, feels like a bad sports movie training sequence from a Jerry Bruckheimer production. Director Timur Bekmambetov directs the chariot race scene as though it were an outtake from a *The Fast and the Furious* movie, but almost never gives a clear view of what is happening.

The same holds true for the other big action set piece at the battle at the Ionian Sea. He is too overly concerned with close-ups and over-editing that these scenes never achieve any kind of suspense because the viewer is trying to figure out what just happened. The score has also been cranked up. Part of the genius of the 1959 version was its lack of score.

Taking nearly four hours to tell a story may not be fashionable these days, but there is something to be said for taking the time to put everything into context so that when Jesus does appear at the end of the film, it feels organic and justified. That is not the case here. This is one of those productions where Jesus looks more like a Los Angeles masseuse than the Son of God. While the film does deserve notice for having Jesus appear to be more like an average citizen in the early scenes, the role of Jesus feels wedged into the narrative like an afterthought, as though the studio had trepidations about just how faithful they wanted to be to the story, lest it should prolong the chariot race. There is also not much in the way of momentum regarding the fate of Judah's family and wife. Everything about it feels like an overly convenient plot contrivance rather than a lesson in empathy and devotion.

Clearly, Bekmambetov—the director of *Wanted* (2008) and *Abraham Lincoln: Vampire Hunter* (2012)—has no interest in presenting this as anything more than pure spectacle. The performances are mostly wooden and the use of shaky-cam even during the most banal of dialogue scenes is completely overdone. *Ben-Hur* is an empty studio product packaged as a summer blockbuster in hopes of bringing in teenagers, Biblical scholars, and church-goers in mid-August and giving them nothing in return (in 3-D, no less). It did not pan out that way. This epic story, rich with purpose and thematic weight, pandered to the lowest common denominator and ended the summer of 2016 with a resounding thud.

Collin Souter

CREDITS

Judah Ben-Hur: Jack Huston
Ilderim: Morgan Freeman
Messala: Toby Kebbell
Jesus: Rodrigo Santoro
Esther: Nazanin Boniadi
Naomi Ben-Hur: Ayelet Zurer
Origin: United States
Language: English
Released: 2016
Production: Mark Burnett, Sean Daniel, Duncan Henderson, Joni Levin; released by LightWorkers Media, Metro-Goldwyn-Mayer Inc., Paramount Pictures Corp., Sean Daniel Co.

Directed by: Timur Bekmambetov
Written by: Keith R. Clarke; John Ridley
Cinematography by: Oliver Wood
Music by: Marco Beltrami
Sound: Aaron Glascock
Editing: Dody Dorn; Richard-Francis Bruce; Bob Murawski
Art Direction: Felix Lariviere-Charron
Costumes: Varvara Avdyushko
Production Design: Naomi Shohan
MPAA rating: PG-13
Running time: 125 minutes

REVIEWS

Anderson, Soren. *Seattle Times*. August 18, 2016.
Braun, Liz. *Toronto Sun*. August 18, 2016.
Barnard, Lina. *Toronto Star*. August 19, 2016.
Holden, Stephen. *New York Times*. August 18, 2016.
Kenny, Glenn. *RogerEbert.com*. August 19, 2016.
LaSalle, Mick. *San Francisco Chronicle*. August 21, 2016.
Lumenick, Lou. *New York Post*. August 18, 2016.
Phillips, Michael. *Chicago Tribune*. August 18, 2016.
Turan, Kenneth. *Los Angeles Times*. August 18, 2016.
Whitty, Stephen. *Newark Star Ledger*. August 17, 2016.

QUOTES

Judah Ben-Hur: [to Dismas] "How many Romans do you even know? Have you ever had a conversation with a single one in your life? Don't spit your hate for all when you don't even know one."

TRIVIA

Director Timur Bekmambetov wanted the chariot circus be built for real, with as little computer-generated imagery as possible. He wanted the chariot race to look realistic.

THE BFG

The world is more giant than you can imagine.
—Movie tagline

Box Office: $55.4 Million

The story of *The BFG*'s release in 2016 is one of the more unfortunate stories of that year. Directed by Steven Spielberg and based on a beloved book by Roald Dahl, the film had many earmarks of being a summer hit. It had awe-inspiring special effects and it was the final screenplay credit for Melissa Matheson, the scribe who wrote *The Black Stallion* (1979) and *E.T. The Extra-Terrestrial* (1982). Mark Rylance had just won the Academy Award for Best Supporting Actor in Spielberg's most previous film, *Bridge of Spies* (2015) and the trailer promised a return to Spielberg's more whimsical, kid-friendly side which had not been seen since *The Adventures of TinTin* (2011), or, some would say, *Hook* (1991). A story of kids existing in the same world as giants seemed to be a sure enough bet, since fantasy films showed little sign of being unpopular anytime soon. And the popularity of the title, both for young and old alike, seemed to be a good enough lure for all ages to buy a ticket. Having the Disney logo above the title should also have had some appeal.

It did not pan out that way. *The BFG* opened to mixed reviews and a dismal box office performance and when watching the film, it is not hard to see why. Spielberg and Matheson remained loyal to the source material, almost to a fault. *The BFG*, the book, is filled with whimsy and magic, but it is hardly a page-turner. It is incredibly disjointed and almost every page has a new word for the reader to learn ("snozzcumbers" and "razztwizzler" are just two examples). Only in the final third does a real story actually begin to take shape with the two main characters solving a problem together. It starts out with an intriguing idea for a kids' story, but then goes off on tangents and flights of fancy that are charming enough in the moment, but hardly resonate later on. The film suffers those same problems and it is unlikely that the viewer will feel anything Spielberg so clearly wants the viewer to feel. To make matters worse, its title seemed confusing to those unfamiliar with the book.

The story centers on a 10-year-old girl named Sophie (Ruby Barnhill) who lives in an orphanage in the middle of London. Late one night, while having as bout of insomnia, she walks among the sleeping children with her orange cat. Outside, a giant, shadowy figure roams the streets, camouflaging itself in the shadows so as not to be seen by ordinary folk. The Giant (Mark Rylance) opens a window to the orphanage, reaches in and picks up Sophie. He tucks her away in one of his bags and then runs far, far away into Giantland (which is exactly what it sounds like). At first, Sophie is afraid that the Giant will want to eat her, but this is a different sort of giant. A Big, Friendly Giant. So, she nicknames him The BFG. The BFG has an old, wisened face and talks in a kind of broken English, hence the crazy wordplay from the book that Dahl has always been known for.

Throughout the BFG's home are jars full of what appear to be potions. They are, in fact, dreams. Every night, the BFG catches dreams in a net and blows them into little children's minds while they sleep. There are other giants in the land with names like Fleshlumpeater (Jemaine Clement), Bonecrusher (Daniel Bacon), and Bloodbottler (Bill Hader), but they are not nearly as nice. In fact, they often torment the BFG. These other giants race off at night to go and eat humans (or as they call them, "human beans"). The BFG will not have any part of that and soon, he and Sophie figure out an elaborate plan to get the giants to stop eating humans once and for all, but the plan involves the Queen of England (Penelope Wilton) and a vast army of soldiers.

That part of the story takes *The BFG* to a different kind of narrative territory, one that feels rather jarring, but in a strange way, refreshing. Once Sophie ends up in Giantland, the film takes way too long to figure out what it wants to accomplish there. The scenes between the nine giants tormenting the BFG go on way too long and the relationship between Sophie and the BFG lacks the magic that Spielberg has always been known for, going back to *E.T. The Extra-Terrestrial*. But once the story finally gets to the Queen of England, the film suddenly becomes more engaging and frequently funny. It might be too little too late for some viewers, but one thing is for certain: It is technical wizardry at its finest. Spielberg and his team have spared no expense at creating elaborate special effects shots that will have even the most knowledgeable film watcher asking themselves, "how did they do that?"

The special effects and Ryland's wonderful motion-capture performance were the two things audiences and critics could agree on as being the film's big strengths. Spielberg, though, in trying to stay true to Dahl's voice, ended up making a film that feels like a cross between Terry Gilliam (the part of him that goes off into narrative tangents at the expense of good storytelling) and Robert Zemeckis (who never met a challenging special effects shot he did not like), but little more. There have been better adaptations of Dahl's work, including the original *Willy Wonka and the Chocolate Factory* (1971), the Tim Burton remake *Charlie and the Chocolate Factory* (2005), which some would say is more faithful than the original, Danny Devito's *Matilda* (1996), and Nicolas Roeg's *The Witches* (1990). *The BFG* is a successful adaption in that it only stays true to the book, page for page, but it lacks certain elements to make it a successful film (while containing way too many fart gags).

The BFG is a mess, but not an unwatchable mess. Spielberg's technical skill has not dissipated with age and he still knows how to get good performances from young actors (newcomer Barnhill is very charming). In spite of its shortcomings, it is still sad to see a project like this fail. Spielberg and Dahl have captured the imaginations of young people for so many decades that the failure of *The BFG* signals another changing of the times. A Dahl book now looks too antiquated and out of touch with what young people are into these days. It is now up to parents, teachers, and librarians to keep these books alive because Hollywood will most likely look on this as a cautionary tale on adapting a book that came out over 40 years ago. Hopefully not, but *The BFG* turned out to be Spielberg's biggest commercial failure since *1941* (1979). Such notoriety is bound to sting for a while, but

then again, Spielberg always has at least four more films in the pipeline and Dahl always has groups of new fans somewhere in the world.

Collin Souter

CREDITS

BFG: Mark Rylance
Sophie: Ruby Barnhill
The Queen: Penelope Wilton
Fleshlumpeater: Jemaine Clement
Mary: Rebecca Hall
Bloodbottler: Bill Hader
Bonecruncher: Daniel Bacon
Origin: United States
Language: English
Released: 2016
Production: Frank Marshall, Sam Mercer, Steven Spielberg; released by Amblin Partners LLC, Walt Disney Pictures
Directed by: Steven Spielberg
Written by: Melissa Mathison
Cinematography by: Janusz Kaminski
Music by: John Williams
Sound: Richard Hymns
Editing: Michael Kahn
Art Direction: Todd Cherniawsky; Grant Van Der Slagt
Costumes: Joanna Johnston
Production Design: Rick Carter; Robert Stromberg
MPAA rating: PG
Running time: 117 minutes

REVIEWS

Braun, Liz. *Toronto Sun.* June 30, 2016.
Burr, Ty. *Boston Globe.* June 30, 2016.
Chang, Justin. *Los Angeles Times.* June 30, 2016.
Hornaday, Ann. *Washington Post.* June 30, 2016.
MacDonald. Moira. *Seattle Times.* June 30, 2016.
Phillips, Michael. *Chicago Tribune.* June 29, 2016.
Scott, A.O. *New York Times.* June 30, 2016.
Seitz, Matt Zoller. *Roger Ebert.com.* June 30, 2016.
Shoemaker, Allison. *Consequence of Sound.* June 28, 2016.
Sims, David, *The Atlantic.* July 1, 2016.

QUOTES

Sophie: "Why did you take me?
The BFG: "Because I hears your lonely heart, in all the secret whisperings of the world."

TRIVIA

"The BFG" (1982) was Roald Dahl's own favorite of all his stories.

BILLY LYNN'S LONG HALFTIME WALK

Box Office: $1.7 Million

Billy Lynn's Long Halftime Walk marks the second film in a row in which Ang Lee has brought a novel to the screen with an extreme cinematic style that wound up dominating the entire project. This time around, Lee has not only gone the 3-D route again but has upped the stakes by shooting it with 4K resolution and at an astonishing frame rate of 120 fps (compared to the 24 fps employed by conventional films) in order to give the film so much visual clarity that the effect on viewers is said to be virtually immersive. Alas, these innovations on display are so forward-thinking that there are literally only two theaters in the U.S. that are currently capable of presenting it exactly as intended with other theaters projecting it with a more conventional fps rate. This lack of proper presentation may disappoint Lee but he proves to be equally disappointing here by giving viewers both a deeply dubious technological achievement and, more distressingly, a film that is an absurdly over-scaled and wildly implausible drama that misses the mark so often that most people will likely come out of it not so much entranced by the future of cinema as befuddled.

Based on a 2012 novel by Ben Fountain, the film takes place over the course of Thanksgiving Day 2004 (with plenty of flashbacks to other times scattered throughout), and is centered on Billy Lynn (Joe Alwyn), a boyish-looking soldier fighting in Iraq who becomes a media sensation when he is caught on camera rushing into enemy fire in order to rescue his grievously wounded sergeant, Shroom (Vin Diesel). With Billy now the face of America's involvement in Iraq, he and his platoon, Bravo Squad, have been sent home for a two-week publicity tour that will culminate with them appearing at a nationally televised Turkey Day football game in Dallas as the guests of the team's smarmy owner (Steve Martin) and, as they only gradually discover, taking part in a garish halftime show alongside Destiny's Child. (Neither the group nor the NFL had anything to do with the film, leading to ersatz substitutions that are decidedly at odds with the ultra-realistic presentation.) While all of this is going on, a motormouth agent (Chris Tucker) is cynically trying to package the Bravo Squad story into a feature film that promises to earn them all a lot of money.

Although the tour and game are meant to be a sort of reward before he and the rest of Bravo Squad ships back out for another tour of duty, Billy is feeling increasingly disconnected. Although a simple and sweet country boy at heart, he is nevertheless fully aware that the incident that he is being celebrated for was actually a horrible event that has been cynically repackaged by the military and the media in order to gain public favor for the unpopular war. His older sister (Kristen Stewart), who feels guilty for being indirectly responsible for him enlisting in the Army in the first place, senses his disenchantment during a tense visit home and urges him to seek an honorable discharge and to see a doctor about the possibility that he is suffering from PTSD. On a brighter side, he catches the eye (and possibly other things) of one of the team's cheerleaders (Makenzie Leigh) and falls instantly in love for maybe the first time in his life, though her attraction seems to be less about him than in having a guy who is fighting overseas. As the game goes on, Billy is increasingly overwhelmed by both the sensorial overload of the day as well as the memories of the experiences for which he is being celebrated.

Having been unable to view *Billy Lynn's Long Halftime Walk* in Lee's preferred format, it is impossible to fully discern its effectiveness. (That said, reviews from those who did were not encouraging, suggesting that it looks like trying to watch a movie on an HDTV screen where someone forgot to turn off the motion smoothing setting.) However, considering how remarkably ugly the 2-D version is from a visual standpoint, it is difficult to believe that the extra bells and whistles could have possibly improved things. The film was shot by John Toll, a great cinematographer, but too many scenes feature looming close-ups of the faces of the actor that are so tight that they practically obscure everything else going on. The only sequence that actually demonstrates any real visual skill is the entire halftime sequence, where Toll properly captures the combination of tackiness and bombast that is part and parcel with such ceremonies—this was presumably the sequence that convinced Lee to employ this particular presentation and indeed, it is the only time that the film really comes to life.

Even if viewers are able to somehow overlook the questionable technical achievements, they are still left with a film that is equally unsuccessful on a dramatic scale as well. Presumably one of the key points of the story was to show through Billy's eyes how the lines between contemporary American combat and entertainment have blurred to the point where both now require equal measures of bombast and easily defined heroes, villains and mission objectives in order to succeed with the public. That aspect never really comes across, however, because the combat stuff is never particularly convincing and the showbiz satire involving the Tucker and Martin characters is exceptionally heavy-handed. The only scenes that really work are the ones featuring Kristen Stewart—they are as clumsily written as everything else, but she cuts through both the artifice of the screenplay and the overblown visual style with a directness that is genuinely affecting.

Ang Lee is, of course, a wonderful filmmaker—his best works (such as *Sense & Sensibility* [1995], *Crouching Tiger, Hidden Dragon* [2000], and his wildly misunderstood comic book epic *Hulk* [2003]) leave moviegoers feeling absolutely exhilarated and his lesser efforts generally have the good grace to be ambitious failures—but *Billy Lynn's Long Halftime Walk* is the kind of baffling misfire that most great visionary filmmakers stumble into at some point in their careers. Perhaps after the visual innovations of films like *Crouching Tiger, Hidden Dragon*, *Hulk* and *Life of Pi* (2012), he was looking for a new challenge but he could not have come up with a more off-putting combination of narrative and technology if he tried.

Peter Sobczynski

CREDITS

Billy Lynn: Joe Alwyn
Kathryn: Kristen Stewart
Albert: Chris Tucker
Dime: Garrett Hedlund
Shroom: Vin Diesel
Origin: United States
Language: English
Released: 2016
Production: Stephen Cornwell, Marc Platt, Rhodri Thomas, Ang Lee; released by Bona Film Group Ltd., Film 4, Marc Platt Productions, Studio 8, The Ink Factory, TriStar Productions, Tristar Pictures Inc.
Directed by: Ang Lee
Written by: Jean-Christophe Castelli
Cinematography by: John Toll
Music by: Jeff Danna; Mychael Danna
Editing: Tim Squyres
Costumes: Joseph G. Aulisi
Production Design: Mark Friedberg
MPAA rating: R
Running time: 113 minutes

REVIEWS

Burr, Ty. *Boston Globe*. November 17, 2016.
Callahan, Dan. *TheWrap*. October 14, 2016.
Chang, Justin. *Los Angeles Times*. November 10, 2016.
Gleiberman, Owen. *Variety*. October 16, 2016.
Merry, Stephanie. *Washington Post*. November 17, 2016.
Rooney, David. *Hollywood Reporter*. October 16, 2016.
Scott, A.O. *New York Times*. November 10, 2016.
Stevens, Dana. *Slate*. November 10, 2016.
White, Armond. *Out Magazine*. November 15, 2016.
Zacharek, Stephanie. *Time*. November 15, 2016.

QUOTES

Norm Oglesby: "Your story, Billy, no longer belongs to you. It's America's story now."

TRIVIA

This was the first film to be shot using a 120-frame rate.

THE BIRTH OF A NATION

Box Office: $15.8 Million

Nate Parker's directorial debut became one of the most interesting film stories of 2016, and not entirely for what was up on the screen. From the minute it was announced as a part of the U.S. Dramatic Competition slate for the Sundance Film Festival in January, the film had that ephemeral thing the industry often calls buzz. It wasn't just that Parker had chosen to reclaim the title of the 1915 D. W. Griffith film that was controversially recognized for its early filmmaking skills but also rightfully loathed for its blatant racism and help in forming the Ku Klux Klan. The film was also coming on the waves of a call for diversity in the industry, and greater recognition of the filmmaking skills of people of color. Just before the film's premiere, a remarkably Caucasian slate of Oscar nominees had been announced, even leading to a social media campaign called #OscarsSoWhite. When Parker's film landed in Park City, it almost literally exploded. The standing ovation after its conclusion was one of the loudest in festival history and Fox Searchlight broke a Sundance record by paying $17.5 million for the film.

Between the Sundance Film Festival in January and the next time the film played—at the Toronto International Film Festival in September—storm clouds moved in on *The Birth of a Nation*. In fact, rumors started to swirl of controversy in Parker's past just before the film won the Audience Award and Grand Jury Prize at Sundance on the last weekend of the festival. It was revealed that Parker and his co-writer Jean McGianni Celestin had been accused of rape when they were sophomores at Penn State University. Parker was acquitted but Celestin was convicted and received a prison sentence. There was also some controversy regarding Parker's behavior after the accusation—threatening and publicly shaming the victim—and whether or not he would have been acquitted under today's legal standards. Perhaps most damningly in the court of public opinion, Parker did not handle the issue well in the press. He first seemed downright aggravated it even came up and never wavered from an unapologetic tone that could have salvaged the film's public image. He claimed to not even know that the victim had killed herself in 2012, something that made him seem cold and indifferent, regardless of his guilt.

All of this off-screen drama might have been easier to ignore if Parker had not chosen to essentially make his debut film about a man whose anger over the rape of female slaves spurs him to action. Yes, a man accused of rape made a film about a rape avenger, a fictional element which Parker added to the true history of his subject matter. Too many of the reports about the controversy surrounded this film oddly ignored that aspect of the narrative, often pointing out that another assault charge against Casey Affleck failed to deafen the buzz around Oscar nominee *Manchester by the Sea* (2016), but it was the aspect of *Birth of a Nation* that felt like an apology or a revision of history that left the worst taste in people's mouths.

If it's possible to put all of this aside, *The Birth of a Nation* is actually a solid directorial debut, and an even better acting showcase for its star. The hype at Sundance was overblown, but there is still some strong filmmaking going on here, and Parker finds a way to convey the charisma and inspirational power of Nat Turner. This is a story that too many people don't yet know, and Parker's film artistically allows a way to bring it to viewers, even if some of his historical alterations are regrettable. His filmmaking inexperience often shows—as does his love for Mel Gibson's *Braveheart* (1995)—but there's a passion and an energy to this drama that's laudable.

The Birth of a Nation opens with a young Nat Turner deep in the woods of Virginia in the early 1800s. Immediately, Parker portrays Turner not as an average hero but a prophesied savior of his people, as the young man is taken to a ceremony where he is told he shall be a leader. The man repeats the same phrase: "We should listen to him. We should listen to him. We should listen to him." The effect is two-fold in that Parker the filmmaker is clearly trying to implore modern audiences to do the same: Don't forget this story. We should listen to him. With his debut feature, he tries to reclaim history that has somewhat been lost, and the sheer passion of the filmmaking allows one to easily overlook most of the freshman director's rookie mistakes.

Turner was taught to read by his slave owner, unlike most slaves, and his master's wife only allowed him to read one book—the Holy Bible. Consequently, Turner became a Man of God, preaching to fellow slaves in the field and teaching them lessons from The Good Book. After marrying a fellow slave (Aja Naomi King), Turner's master was convinced to let the young man travel to preach to other slaves in the region. The idea on the part of slave owners was to use Turner to help keep slaves in line. Teach them the word of God as a way to control their behavior. If they fled, God would punish them. Misbehave and risk God's wrath. Let's just say that the plan backfired.

Touring the area as a preacher for hire, Turner saw the full scope of the atrocities of slavery. Parker does not shy away from the horror, showing a little girl being paraded across a porch on a leash, a man having his teeth knocked out with a chisel so he can be forced to eat to keep working, and the aforementioned rape. Turner's wife is beaten at one point to a degree that she's unrecognizable. A preacher may have been sent out, but a rebel returns.

In 1831, Nat Turner led a slave rebellion. While the actual action of the final act looks a bit too much like Gibson's Oscar winner, Parker's passion for the material never wanes. We see the rage simmer inside him, spurred on not only by what he saw around him but how the Bible taught him his own value. It's not a particularly showy performance, as it easily could have been. It's grounded and mesmerizing. However, it's also one of those performances that steals so much focus from the rest of the cast that the director's rookie status becomes an issue. He clearly does not have a veteran's skill with supporting players. While Hammer is good, everyone else ranges from caricature to forgettable. While Parker never loses the complexity of Turner, the world around him feels two-dimensional.

Parker was wise to hire veterans for his technical team, including cinematographer Elliot Davis, who brings a balance between the lyrical and the realistic that keeps the film visually striking. The camerawork here is fluid and poetic while also never shying away from the horror or the bloodshed. Henry Jackman's score is strong as well.

The Birth of a Nation did not perform at the box office the way that Fox Searchlight certainly thought it would after that Sundance standing ovation. And that festival turned out to be the peak for the film in terms of awards as well, as the flick earned zero Oscar nominations. Would its fate have been different without Nate Parker's real-life drama dominating the conversation around it? Maybe not. It's still a film that falls short of greatness no matter how you feel about the division between art and artist. Perhaps the most interesting question is whether or not Nate Parker will be given a major film like it to direct again. How will people respond when he makes a follow-up? There's enough filmmaking skill here to hope that he does, but his unapologetic press tour and problematic handling of his past may mean that a sophomore effort will never happen.

Brian Tallerico

CREDITS

Nat Turner: Nate Parker

Samuel Turner: Armie Hammer
Elizabeth Turner: Penelope Ann Miller
Raymond Cobb: Jackie Earle Haley
Reverend Zalthall: Mark Boone, Jr.
Origin: United States
Language: English
Released: 2016
Production: Jason Michael Berman, Aaron L. Gilbert, Preston L. Holmes, Kevin Turen, Nate Parker; released by Argent Pictures, Bron Studios, Creative Wealth Media Finance, Follow Through Productions, Hit 55 Ventures, Infinity United Entertainment, Juniper Productions, Mandalay Pictures L.L.C., Novofam Productions, Oster Media, Phantom Four, Point Made Films, Tiny Giant Entertainment
Directed by: Nate Parker
Written by: Nate Parker
Cinematography by: Elliot Davis
Music by: Henry Jackman
Sound: Craig Henighan; Mac Smith
Editing: Steven Rosenblum
Costumes: Francine Jamison-Tanchuck
Production Design: Geoffrey Kirkland
MPAA rating: R
Running time: 120 minutes

REVIEWS

Berardinelli, James. *ReelViews*. October 6, 2016.
Chang, Justin. *Variety*. January 26, 2016.
Dowd, A.A. *The A.V. Club*. October 6, 2016.
Ebiri, Bilge. *New York Magazine*. January 26, 2016.
Fischer, Russ. *Playlist*. January 27, 2016.
Gerber, Justin. *Consequence of Sound*. January 26, 2016.
Kohn, Eric. *IndieWire*. January 26, 2016.
Raup, Jordan. *The Film Stage*. January 26, 2016.
Roeper, Richard. *Chicago Sun-Times*. October 5, 2016.
Whitty, Stephen. *New York Daily News*. October 5, 2016.

QUOTES

Bridget: "To watch a strong man broken down is a terrible thing."

TRIVIA

The film was shot in 27 days.

BLAIR WITCH

There's something evil hiding in the woods.
—Movie tagline

Box Office: $20.7 Million

The phenomenon that was Daniel Myrick and Eduardo Sanchez's *The Blair Witch Project* (1999) was seen as a landmark for creating both a new sub-genre of horror that would be copied for years to come but also in viral marketing. It was sold as a true incident that was then molded into a feature film consisting of the "found footage" recorded by the missing documentarians. Thus, the horror that audiences could pay to experience promised to be more visceral and disturbing than mere blood and guts. Divided as moviegoers may have been, there are still many who praised the film's sense of mystery, dread, and skillfully orchestrated shocks. Seventeen years and one poorly-conceived sequel later, a new pair of filmmakers--no stranger to the medium--have attempted to reboot the mythology in an all-too-familiar tale that has more in common with its mediocre copycats.

Heather Donahue went missing twenty years ago, but a video uploaded by Burkittsville locals, Lane (Wes Robinson) and Talia (Valorie Curry) have given Heather's brother, James (James Allen McCune) new evidence that she is still alive in the Black Hills woods. Lisa (Lisa Arlington), another film student, wants to make her own documentary on the search for Heather and they are joined by friends Peter (Brandon Jones) and Ashley (Corbin Reid).

Equipped with everything from GPS to drone cameras, the six of them head off first to the location where the new video was actually found. After their first night of camping, the symbolic stick figures that once plagued Heather's crew have multiplied. Only now realizing this may have been a bad idea, they decide to head out despite the objections of Lane and Talia who have already demonstrated they know more about the Blair Witch than their counterparts. As darkness overcomes them and every piece of equipment—aside from their cameras—failing, the amateurs become acutely aware that they may not be alone.

Amateurish is not a word many would associate with the actual filmmakers behind this sequel/reboot. Director Adam Wingard and writer Simon Barrett may have been associated with the often subpar *V/H/S* (2012) anthology series but had put the found footage gimmick behind them to craft *You're Next* (2011) and *The Guest* (2014), two thrillers solid enough to raise expectations they would not just fall back on old routines. There may be a couple decent set pieces—particularly a climactic one involving a claustrophobic dirt tunnel—but they amount to about six minutes of a narrative that is frustratingly familiar and lacking in the true atmosphere of classic horror.

Everything in this movie is just a gathering of noise from the proximity feedback on the walkie talkies to the death metal heard driving in. A haunted house has a "BOO!" around every corner and it is the cheapest and easiest device available to anyone who just wants to catch another off-guard. Every rollercoaster enthusiast will say that the ride up the hill is more terrifying than the drop and every horror fan has been on this ride before. The burden on Wingard and Barrett, clear students of the genre, is to justify why it is worth boarding again. Has a new loop been installed? Maybe a couple fresh dips? The answer with each ensuing scene though is that not only is it just the same old ride but the sense of dread and surprise that made it so terrifying the first time is also gone and there is an overwhelming sense of stale familiarity.

When Joe Berlinger, was tasked with expanding the mythology (and capitalizing on the first film's success) with *Book of Shadows: Blair Witch 2* (2000) the film was an unmitigated disaster. It lapsed into the familiar trappings of supernatural horror but also felt like a discomforting antithesis to the director's *Paradise Lost* (1996) which documented the case of the West Memphis Three. To see that same filmmaker absolve his victimized protagonists with a "devil made me do it" defense was truly disheartening. Putting aside all that in the years since its release, there may be a small grasp of appreciation that it did not just resort to repeating the setup and outcome of its unique successful predecessor. This *Blair Witch* does not just fail in this regard but aggravatingly takes the most frightening piece of its mythology—its infamous final shot—and inverts its effectiveness by changing the very reason for its existence.

Blair Witch may exist in a world where other found footage films have not yet gained popularity, but Wingard and Barrett have contributed to that world, and it is disappointing to watch them waste their shot at commentary on the phenomenon. Since 1999, the sub-genre of horror has had far more lowlights than high ones. But the ones that have worked such as *Cloverfield* (2008), *Diary of the Dead* (2008), *Afflicted* (2013), and the upcoming *Found Footage 3-D* (2017) did so by either finding a fresh perspective from a technical standpoint or a meta commentary on their very existence. This is no different than the *Paranormal Activity* films where it is just people waiting for something to jump in front of the camera. Except here it is the frequency of characters literally running into people who are just standing still.

In true what goes around, comes around fashion, trick marketing played a part in this film as well when the hype of "a new beginning for horror films" and "a nightmare of classic proportions" was attached to the new Wingard/Barrett collaboration known as *The Woods*. It was months later at the San Diego Comicon that the film's actual title was revealed to be *Blair Witch*. In this case, the more generic title was far more appropriate.

Erik Childress

CREDITS

James: James Allen McCune
Lisa: Callie Hernandez
Ashley: Corbin Reid
Peter: Brandon Scott
Lane: Wes Robinson
Talia: Valorie Curry
Origin: United States
Language: English
Released: 2016
Production: Jess Calder, Keith Calder, Roy Lee, Steven Schneider; released by Lionsgate, Room 101, Snoot Entertainment, Vertigo Entertainment
Directed by: Adam Wingard
Written by: Simon Barrett
Cinematography by: Robby Baumgartner
Music by: Adam Wingard
Sound: Andy Hay
Editing: Louis Cioffi
Art Direction: Sheila Haley
Costumes: Katia Stano
Production Design: Thomas S. Hammock
MPAA rating: R
Running time: 89 minutes

REVIEWS

Berardinelli, James. *ReelViews*. September 16, 2016.
Burr, Ty. *Boston Globe*. September 15, 2016.
Douglas, Edward. *New York Daily News*. September 16, 2016.
Gingold, Michael. *Time Out*. September 16, 2016.
Johanson, MaryAnn. *Time Out*. September 14, 2016.
Larsen, Josh. *LarsenOnFilm*. September 16, 2016.
McGranaghan, Mike. *Aisle Seat*. September 16, 2016.
McWeeny, Drew. *HitFix*. September 19, 2016.
Scott, A.O.. *New York Times*. September 15, 2016.
Vonder Haar, Pete. *Houston Press*. October 15, 2016.

QUOTES

Ashley: "There's something out there."

TRIVIA

Unlike The Blair Witch Project (1999), this movie is completely scripted.

BLEED FOR THIS

This is what the greatest comeback in sports history looks like.
—Movie tagline

Box Office: $5 Million

The final moment in the biopic *Bleed For This* is not a freeze-frame shot of triumphant boxer Vinny Pazienza (Miles Teller) at the center of the ring, surrounded by his people and hoisting his gloved fist in the air with a smile on his face and blood dripping down his cheeks. That would make sense, but instead, the film closes with an interview segment in which Pazienza explains to a reporter that "it's as simple as that." Meaning, his story happened because there is no other way it could have happened. Pazienza is a boxer and has no idea how to be anything else. He is like an animal in that sense. A very well-trained animal who was born and bred for one thing. Simple as that. As a bio-pic, the film adheres to this philosophy as well, though one can see director Ben Younger trying anything he can to separate his project from the usual fare of underdog-overcoming-adversity. Closing with an interview segment is part of that struggle.

At the start of the film, in 1988, Vinny is already an established boxer in his weight class. The film depicts his training and fight with Roger Mayweather (Peter Quillin). His father, Angelo (Ciarán Hinds), is part of his entourage while the rest of his family watches on TV from Vinny's home in Providence, RI, including his mother, Louise (Katey Sagal). After the fight, Vinny enlists the help of a new trainer to help him become a better boxer and maybe move him into a new weight class. Of course, the trainer, Kevin Rooney (Aaron Eckhart), is a hard-nosed alcoholic with a gravelly voice who sees potential in Vinny to do better, but never lets him off the hook. Vinny's managers and father insist that Vinny should retire and get married, but he has no choice but to stay in the game as long as possible. He cannot be talked out of it.

Then comes the life-changing moment that almost cost Vinny his life. One day while out driving, Vinny's car collided with another, leaving him with a broken neck and with a small chance of ever walking again. Vinny awakens in a hospital with a neck brace, unable to move. He insists on any treatment or surgery necessary to make him walk again so he can fight. His doctors tell him the chances are slim. They go ahead with a surgery that puts his head in a halo for months, during which time Vinny must stay home and recuperate. He cannot abide with a life like this, so he descends into the basement and attempts weight lifting, starting with just the plain, metal bar. He tells Kevin that he must continue training, even though it is deemed too dangerous for someone in his condition. They secretly train in the basement for a couple months before his father finds out and cannot believe his eyes.

Younger wisely takes his time getting to the car crash. The drama involving Mayweather and Vinny getting back into training makes the tragic moment all the more startling. If someone were to go into this film without knowing the story, it would indeed be a surprise moment and a time when one would least expect it in a film like this. The relationship between Vinny and Kevin is able to breathe a bit more even if it is filled with clichés. Younger is able to put Vinny's situation in context just long enough before the viewer grows tired of his cockiness and emptiness. In that sense, the car crash is almost a relief. Once it happens, though, the film becomes a by-the-numbers tale of a once-great champion overcoming great physical odds to achieve the impossible.

The film is really a showcase for Teller, who is delving into his first major true-life character that requires a physical transformation and an accent. He pulls it off well enough and it is hard not to watch him struggling with the limitations of the halo and not feel a bit of claustrophobia and unthinkable pain, particularly during the scene in which he has it removed without anesthesia. Ekhart has the right look for the part and will be unrecognizable to anyone who has no idea he is even in the film. It becomes hard to criticize a performance as being a bit of a cliché when it is about a real person, but that is what Ekhart's performance feels like a few too many times. Hinds has the more memorable performance as Vinny's father, who is always in his son's corner, but who has demons of his own to deal with.

Bleed For This has all the technical aspects right. The cinematography, editing, and sound design are all used to right effect. At one point during the final match with Roberto Duran (Edwin Rodriguez) in Vegas, Younger drops out all the crowd noise and just goes with the sound of the punches. One wishes he would attempt this sort of thing more often. Of course, he is trying to echo Scorsese's *Raging Bull* (1981). Unfortunately, *Bleed For This* is not memorable enough to be more than just another boxing movie. It is nowhere near as messy and poorly executed as the Duran bio-pic *Hands of Stone* (2016) from the same year, but it lacks the nuance and beauty of *Creed* (2015) from the year before. This one falls in the middle mainly for adhering a little too much with Vinny's credo of "it's as simple as that."

Collin Souter

CREDITS

Vinny Pazienza: Miles Teller
Kevin Rooney: Aaron Eckhart
Louise Pazienza: Katey Sagal
Angelo Pazienza: Ciaran Hinds
Lou Duva: Ted Levine
Origin: United States

Language: English

Released: 2016

Production: Bruce Cohen, Noah Kraft, Pamela Thur, Emma Tillinger Koskoff, Chad A. Verdi, Ben Younger; released by Bruce Cohen Productions, Sikelia Productions, Verdi Productions, Younger Than You

Directed by: Ben Younger

Written by: Ben Younger

Cinematography by: Larkin Seiple

Music by: Julia Holter

Music Supervisor: Susan Jacobs; Michelle Verdi

Editing: Zachary Stuart-Pontier

Costumes: Melissa Vargas

Production Design: Kay Lee

MPAA rating: R

Running time: 117 minutes

REVIEWS

Anderson, Soren. *Seattle Times*. November 17, 2016.

Dowd, A.A. *The A.V. Club*. November 17, 2016.

Goodykoontz, Bill. *Arizona Republic*. November 17, 2016.

Graham, Adam. *Detroit News*. November 18, 2016.

Gronvall, Andrea. *Chicago Reader*. November 17, 2016.

Guzman, Rafer. *Newsday*. November 17, 2016.

Howell, Peter. *Toronto Star*. November 17, 2016.

Kenny, Glenn. *New York Times*. November 17, 2016.

Seitz, Matt Zoller. *RogerEbert.com*. November 17, 2016.

Verniere, James. *Boston Herald*. November 18, 2016.

QUOTES

Vinny Pazienza: "I know exactly how to give up. You know what scares me Kev? Is that is easy."

TRIVIA

Miles Teller trained with boxing trainer Darrell Foster, who trained fighters such as Sugar Ray Leonard and helped Will Smith become Muhammad Ali for the 2001 film, *Ali*.

BLOOD FATHER

A father makes his own justice.
—Movie tagline

There was a time when an R-rated action movie in which Mel Gibson plays a criminal father trying to protect his daughter would have played at multiplexes around the world and been one of the biggest box office hits in the world that year. Oh, what a few audio recordings can do to a career. Films in which Gibson starred after his angry voice mails surfaced barely got released, including works like *Get the Gringo* (2012), and it appeared he may be relegated to minor roles like his near-

cameo in *The Expendables 3* (2014). 2016 changed everything. While his Oscar-nominated work on *Hacksaw Ridge* (2016) got the box office and the headlines, and will be the film to catapult him back to the A-list, that war drama should lead viewers back to a smaller film from earlier in the year that barely got released at all, but is actually the superior work, Jean-Francoise Richet's *Blood Father*. Premiering at the Cannes Film Festival in May, Lionsgate barely released the film stateside in August, although it found an audience on VOD and made some money overseas.

Lydia (Erin Moriarty) is dating a drug dealer named Jonah (Diego Luna). In the film's opening scenes, she's riding shotgun with the scumbag as he's about to pull a robbery. She thinks it will just be a simple smash and grab, but it turns out to be a vengeance killing, Jonah's planning to murder a family who stole money from his gang. He ties up one of the victims and tells Lydia that she has to pull the trigger. She refuses, shooting Jonah in the neck instead, and fleeing the scene. She's in serious trouble, and there's only one person she can call, her estranged, convict father, who will know what to do.

John (Mel Gibson) is an ex-convict living in a makeshift community of mobile homes and trying to stay as straight as possible. He did seven years in prison, which would be enough trauma for anyone, but he also regularly has to fend off the demons of alcoholism, with the help of a local sponsor/friend (William H. Macy). He answers Lydia's call, bringing her in and realizing that she's a drug addict and an alcoholic too. There's a subtext in that not only could protecting Lydia make him a better father but force him to deal with his issues as well, and give his life purpose.

Of course, it's not long before the Mexican cartel who was funding Jonah's gang come looking for Lydia, but Richet's film does not play out as predictably or generically as one might expect. He maintains a brutal realism to the action of the piece, such as when hired killers descend on John's trailer park, blasting it with high-powered weapons. John and Lydia are forced to flee, tracking down a former mentor of John's named Preacher (Michael Parks), who first agrees to help but betrays the father and daughter pair in pursuit of the reward on her head. Again, a chase scene ensues that feels blunt and brutal instead of standard Hollywood fare. Finally, John and Lydia learn that Jonah survived the shooting and has been spearheading the pursuit of John and Lydia. It is also revealed that Jonah stole from the cartel in the first place, trying to kill the family in the opening scenes to cover his tracks. In the final scenes, John sacrifices himself for his daughter's safety, giving meaning to a life that once looked like it would have no purpose left.

Mel Gibson has always excelled at characters living on the edge of sanity. Two of his most notable roles in *Mad Max* (1979) and *Lethal Weapon* (1987), and their subsequent sequels, were so definitive that they became genre archetypes for these kind of characters. It makes sense that he would return to this well as a way to help revitalize his career, although one has to admire his willingness to do so in such a brutal, R-rated way. Nothing about *Blood Father* feels designed by an actor looking to gain favor with the public. It's not pandering or simplistic. For the first time in years, one can see the acting ability that made Mel Gibson a star, that balance between sanity and heroism that proved so charismatic. He's very good here, and one hopes that the success garnered by *Hacksaw Ridge* leads to more films like *Blood Father* in its wake, and that it brings audiences back to find this solid genre pic who missed it the first time.

Brian Tallerico

CREDITS

Link: Mel Gibson
Lydia: Erin Moriarty
Jonah: Diego Luna
Preacher: Michael Parks
Kirby: William H. Macy
Origin: United States
Language: English
Released: 2016
Production: Chris Briggs, Pascal Caucheteux, Sebastien Lemercier, Peter Craig; released by Why Not Productions, Wild Bunch S.A.
Directed by: Jean-Francois Richet
Written by: Peter Craig; Andrea Berloff
Cinematography by: Robert Gantz
Music by: Sven Faulconer
Sound: Victor Ray Ennis
Music Supervisor: Bruce Gilbert
Editing: Steven Rosenblum
Art Direction: Billy W. Ray
Costumes: Terry Anderson
Production Design: Robb Wilson King
MPAA rating: R
Running time: 88 minutes

REVIEWS

Bowen, Chuck. *Slant Magazine*. August 10, 2016.
Dargis, Manohla. *New York Times*. August 25, 2016.
Duralde, Alonso. *TheWrap*. July 3, 2016.
Jagernauth, Kevin. *The Playlist*. August 5, 2016.
Kenny, Glenn. *RogerEbert.com*. August 12, 2016.
Kohn, Eric. *IndieWire*. May 21, 2016.
Mecca, Dan. *The Film Stage*. August 10, 2016.
Murray, Noel. *Los Angeles Times*. August 11, 2016.
Nashawaty, Chris. *Entertainment Weekly*. August 11, 2016.
Vishnevetsky, Ignatiy. *The A.V. Club*. August 10, 2016.

QUOTES

Kirby: "I'm sorry, Johnny. I did my best."

TRIVIA

Mel Gibson's character lives in a mobile home in both this movie and in the Lethal Weapon series.

BOO! A MADEA HALLOWEEN

(Tyler Perry's Boo! A Madea Halloween)

Witch, please.
—Movie tagline

Box Office: $73.2 Million

By now, most people have heard that the chief inspiration for *Boo! A Madea Halloween*, the latest film featuring the insanely popular character created and performed by cinematic one-man band Tyler Perry, came not from Perry himself but from a throwaway gag that comedian Chris Rock made in his own film *Top Five* (2014) where his character went to a movie theater where audiences were lined up around the block to see the ersatz film. As the story goes, studio executives liked the idea and asked Perry to come up with a real project along those lines and, after some initial resistance, he eventually acquiesced. As befitting the holiday, the end result is a film that proves to be a real trick-or-treat situation—a treat for Perry, whose film pulled in more at the box office in its opening weekend than *Top Five* managed to gross during its entire theatrical run and a trick of the cruelest kind to anyone hoping for a movie that might supply them with laughs, chills or anything other than a massive headache from trying to process it's increasingly bewildering blend of hard-sell slapstick, harder-sell sanctimony and the kind of technical crudity that not even its alleged six-day shooting schedule can completely explain.

What passes for a plot this time around finds Madea—accompanied by grumpy brother Joe (Perry again), prescription-pothead cousin Bam (Cassi Davis), and weirdo friend Hattie (Patrice Lovely)—summoned to the home of nephew Brian (Perry for the hat trick), who is just about to leave town on last-minute business in order to prevent his spoiled and bratty teen daughter Tiffany (Diamond White) and her more reluctant friend Aday (Liza Koshy) from sneaking out to attend a Halloween bash thrown by the rowdy local fraternity—of course, there is no indication of an actual college anywhere in the vicinity, but never mind. When the girls do sneak out, Madea and the others storm the party to retrieve them and, failing that, call the police and get it shut down. Aghast that his soiree has been scuttled, uber-bro frat president Jonathan (Yousef Erakat) gathers his brother to get revenge on Madea by scaring the crap out of her with a series of elaborate pranks involving everything from dressing up as killer clowns and zombies to employing a computer expert pledge to "hack" the plumbing. After the requisite shrieking and screaming, Madea learns the truth and figures out an equally elaborate way to get back at her tormentors—alas, without the use of the chainsaw that proved to be a central image of the film's ad campaign.

Although he has been quite prolific in the world of television in the last few years, *Boo! A Madea Halloween* is Perry's first big-screen project since *The Single Moms Club* (2014) but it quickly becomes evident that he has not used any of that time to hone his filmmaking skills in any discernible manner. As with his previous Madea-centered projects, he offers up a bizarre blend of piety and ribaldry in which moments of high melodrama are uneasily juxtaposed with jokes in which Madea flies off the handle at people or reminisces about her days as a stripper. Since the dramatic stakes are a little lower in comparison to some of his previous efforts because of its holiday theme, the clash between the two different tones is not quite as jarring as it has been in the past but those who have not already developed a taste for his narrative style (not to mention his tendency to direct his actors as if they were on stage playing to the rafters and beyond) are likely to find nearly all of it unendurable. Take the film's lowest point, the scene in which Madea, Bam, Hattie, and Joe talk about the virtues of corporeal punishment to the milquetoast Brian, who prefers a gentler approach. First of all, the entire premise of the scene—old people talking about the importance of beating one's kids in order to get them to show respect—is not particularly funny in and of itself, especially when we get the allegedly humorous details of how Brian was thrown off the roof of a house once as punishment by Joe and wound up with a pencil jammed in his testicle. That is bad enough but Perry lets the scene go on forever as each of the performers tries to out-mug the other, a gambit that can work on the stage but which is deadly dull on film, and by the time it finally comes to a merciful end, you will swear that you have seen Bela Tarr

films that were shorter and which had funnier punchlines to boot.

As for Madea, it has been three years since her last go around in the similarly holiday-themed *A Madea Christmas* (2013) but absence has not made the heart grow fonder in this particular case. As usual, she is strident, annoying, and almost aggressively unfunny in the way that she pummels her way into each of her scenes and goes off into several minutes of uninspired improve while the other actors do little more than just stand there and struggle to get a word or two in here and there. This may seem to be the height of humor to some (and indeed, the audience I saw it with seemed to be delighted with her antics throughout) but other will quickly grow tired of the character and her schtick. Oddly enough, Perry himself seems to be just as disenchanted with the character himself—he is clearly going through the performance motions this time around and even includes a number of jokes that go out of their way to undercut whatever tenuous strands of believability the character might have, including a couple of instances where other characters claim that she is really a man. Maybe Perry will one day be inspired to make a movie about a performer who becomes thoroughly sick and tired of the character that brought him fame and fortune in the first place and who yearns to do something else—*Madea's Stardust Memories*, if you will. If nothing else, maybe Chris Rock will be able to borrow something from it to use in his next film as a way of completing the circle.

Peter Sobczynski

CREDITS

Madea/Joe/Brian: Tyler Perry
Aunt Bam: Cassi Davis
Hattie: Patrice Lovely
Rain: Bella Thorne
Jonathan: Yousef Erakat
Origin: United States
Language: English
Released: 2016
Production: Ozzie Areu, Will Areu, Tyler Perry; released by The Tyler Perry Company Inc.
Directed by: Tyler Perry
Written by: Tyler Perry
Cinematography by: Richard J. Vialet
Music by: Elvin Ross
Sound: Michael D. Wilhoit
Music Supervisor: Joel C. High
Editing: Larry Sexton
Costumes: Shirley Inget

MPAA rating: PG-13
Running time: 103 minutes

REVIEWS

Callahan, Dan. *The Wrap*. October 20, 2016.
Gleiberman, Owen. *Variety*. October 21, 2016.
Goble, Blake. *Consequence of Sound*. October 23, 2016.
Graham, Adam. *Detroit News*. October 21, 2016.
Hessenger, Jesse. *The A.V. Club*. October 21, 2016.
Kenny, Glenn. *New York Times*. October 21, 2016.
Myers, Kimber. *Los Angeles Times*. October 21, 2016.
Orndorf, Bryan. *Blu-ray.com*. October 21, 2016.
Scheck, Frank. *Hollywood Reporter*. October 21, 2016.
Thompson, Luke Y. *Forbes*. October 21, 2016.

TRIVIA

The film was shot in six days.

AWARDS

Nominations:

Golden Globes 2016: Worst Director (Perry)
Golden Raspberries 2016: Worst Actress (Perry)

BORN TO BE BLUE

Box Office: $830,129

Chet Baker will always be fascinating to a certain audience. Robustly handsome, unconventionally but undeniably talented, his bruised confidence hiding behind a shy, genial exterior, he was like a problem that begged to be fixed. Like James Dean, to whom Baker was compared, the Oklahoma-born singer and horn player presented an affable challenge to everyone he met. He seemed so small behind his handsome eyes and square jaw, and everyone seemed to want to draw out the fire inside his soul. Bruce Weber tried and mostly succeeded when he shot Baker in the final year of his life for the unspeakably beautiful documentary *Let's Get Lost* (1988). It was that film that prompted Ethan Hawke's lifelong fascination with the troubled Baker. Director Robert Budreau is similarly obsessed by Baker, having directed the short film *The Deaths of Chet Baker* in 2009, starring Stephen McHattie. Both Budreau and Hawke are plainly enamored of the quiet hellraiser and while they understand his appeal and essence, they come up short in attempting to capture the lightning that was Chet Baker in a bottle or a biopic.

In Budreau's film, Baker (Hawke) is a beautiful mess, always appearing to be on the verge of blowing away on the breeze. We meet him in an Italian jail, serving time thanks to his heroin addiction. An off-screen Dino De Laurentiis bails him out to star in the movie version of his own life, which will never be completed or released. On the set of the film where he plays himself, Baker falls for his on-screen love interest Jane (Carmen Ejogo), who tolerates his sexism and flirtations with death long enough to become drawn to his mystifying chemistry and soft touch. He's nearly killed by drug dealers on their first date, but she stands by his side. Together they move back to Baker's hometown where he works at filling stations while he gets acclimated to new dentures. His father (played by McHattie in a nod to Budreau's earlier film) wastes no time reminding Chet what a hash he's made of his life and the family name. Spurred by the joint disapproval of Jane's father (Eugene Clark) who refuses to sign off on their marriage plans, and that of his own angry father, Baker finally moves toward reclaiming his dignity.

Baker seeks out his long-suffering friend and manager Dick Bock (Callum Keith Rennie) for help getting back on his feet. It's a long uphill climb as Bock struggles to find a place for the disgraced Chet in an ever-changing music scene. Baker plays as a session musician for other acts, and even paints and drywalls the studio to make a show for his parole officer (Tony Nappo), who wants him to get a real job. None of that will do when there's a light at the end of the tunnel in the form of playing the legendary Birdland once more. Between staying a step ahead of his parole officer, wooing an increasingly worried Jane, getting his chops back with his new teeth and increasingly frayed nerves, and trying to stay off heroin, which caused his first fall from grace, Baker has more demons than he knows what to do with. Unfortunately, Budreau and Hawke don't think a modern audience can handle the ugly truth about Baker and end on too high a note than can be called honest.

The most peculiar aspect of *Born To Be Blue* is its compulsive need to invent obstacles while at the same time pairing down the truth of Baker's life to fit an imaginary mold of biographical cinematic storytelling. It may have been more practical to create one fictitious woman for Baker to play against instead of trying to do service to the several women he tormented over the course of his too-short life. Jane feels so focus-grouped she barely exists. She wants to stay with Baker despite his raging addiction and self-destructive behavior but declines his numerous marriage proposals. Her acting career never goes anywhere but her disappointments can never be as fully realized as Baker's because it isn't her story. It can't be—she's not real. So she watches idly from the corner of the stages of his life, wearing a look of pained anticipation while he regains his self-confidence at the apparent expense of her career and their relationship; Budreau does not do nearly enough work to flesh out of either of those conflicts. Baker's soft emotional abuse, as much a part of his legend as his ragged-yet-dulcet singing voice, isn't portrayed as insidiously subtle as it was in reality. More productive would have been focusing on the moments where the musician was most alone, like his jail time or the moments where he has to decide whether to shoot up or stay clean. The juxtaposition of Chet Baker the lover and Chet Baker the tempestuous outcast, breaking windows and walking into the ocean whenever he meets a problem he doesn't like, feels like considerably less than the truth. *Born To Be Blue* behaves all too frequently like the rote Hollywood movie-within-a-movie it ostensibly criticizes for its flamboyant fakery. That kind of melodramatic filmmaking may not be honest about its characters' struggles but it does not want for personality or confidence, both of which elude Budreau and his misty-eyed hero worship.

While the film misfires substantively, it has many textural delights. Steve Cosens, a very fine cinematographer, really outdoes himself capturing Hawke's Baker in tableaux that find his weathered heart. Shots of Baker playing trumpet in the ocean or sitting cross-legged by himself in a studio, cigarette gently billowing smoke in the air above him, are truly marvelous. Letting Hawke simply exist as Baker, while the sound of the trumpet carries the editing, places much closer to the man than the dialogue. Hawke's performance itself is also a minor marvel. He already has the jazz icon's movie star looks, so it was only a matter of taking his usual brio and verve down to a whisper. Baker's singing voice sounded like addiction itself and that Hawke comes remotely close to achieving that effect is no mean feat. Ultimately Hawke and Budreau have to settle for an appealing, cagey shade of the man who so captivated them.

Scout Tafoya

CREDITS

Chet Baker: Ethan Hawke
Jane/Elaine: Carmen Ejogo
Dick: Callum Keith Rennie
Dad: Stephen McHattie
Mom: Janet-Laine Green
Origin: Canada, United States, United Kingdom
Language: English
Released: 2015
Production: Leonard Farlinger, Jennifer Jonas, Jake Seal, Robert Budreau; released by Productivity Media
Directed by: Robert Budreau
Written by: Robert Budreau

Cinematography by: Steve Cosens
Music by: David Braid; Todor Kobakov; Steve London
Music Supervisor: David Hayman
Editing: David Freeman
Art Direction: Joel Richardson
Production Design: Aidan Leroux
MPAA rating: R
Running time: 97 minutes

REVIEWS

Barker, Andrew. *Variety.* September 15, 2015.
Beardsworth, Liz. *Empire.* July 31, 2016.
Bowen, Chuck. *Slant.* March 22, 2016.
Di Nunzio, Miriam. *Chicago Sun-Times.* March 31, 2016.
Lee, Benjamin. *The Guardian.* September 18, 2015.
Murray, Noel. *Los Angeles Times.* March 24, 2016.
O'Malley, Sheila. *RogerEbert.com.* March 25, 2016.
Padua, Pat. *Washington Post.* March 31, 2016.
Roffman, Michael. *Consequence of Sound.* March 24, 2016.
Vishnevetsky, Ignatiy. *The A.V. Club.* March 23, 2016.

TRIVIA

Ethan Hawke wore prosthetic teeth to get the teeth gap in the beginning of the film.

THE BOSS

Watch your assets.
   —Movie tagline

Box Office: $23.6 Million

Even though Melissa McCarthy has never been a cast member of *Saturday Night Live*, despite making some truly memorable appearances as a host, possibly the best way to describe her movie *The Boss*, is to call it an "SNL Movie." As a genre, SNL Movies were a staple of the 1990s. Producer Lorne Michaels would take a popular character from the sketch comedy show and try to construct a movie around it.

While there were a few successes—the most memorable being 1980's *The Blues Brothers* and 1992's *Wayne's World*—the vast majority of SNL movies were critical and popular disappointments. Movies like *The Coneheads* (1993), *It's Pat* (1994), *A Night at the Roxbury* (1998), and *Superstar* (1999) all failed because they were never able to translate their inspired core characters into the world of narrative film.

The Boss suffers the exact same fate. McCarthy apparently used to perform her "Michelle Darnell" character while appearing in the LA comedy troupe The Groundlings, and the character, in and of itself, is funny, engaging, and entertaining. Unfortunately, like most

SNL movies, there's just not much of a movie around her.

The fault for this probably lies at the feet of McCarthy and her husband Ben Falcone, who co-wrote and directed *The Boss* (he held the same duties on the similarly underwhelming *Tammy* [2014]). They were obviously so enamored with the character of Michelle Darnell herself that they thought her very presence could elevate even the weakest premise into a passible big-screen comedy. They were wrong. Because, even though Darnell is a wickedly funny character, movies need a mixture of character and story to land with audiences, and *The Boss* has one of the thinnest, most disposable plots in recent memory.

As the movie opens, Michelle Darnell is one of the richest women in the world. She's a bloodthirsty, ego-centric tycoon, who gives financial seminars to auditorium audiences, and routinely abuses her single-mom assistant Claire (Kristen Bell). The opening scenes with Darnell are among the funniest in the movie, beautifully satirizing the oblivious excesses of America's 1

. When McCarthy allows Darnell to be caustic and unrelenting, she's hilarious. The problem is when, for "story" purposes, the movie decides that Darnell needs to have a heart.

Suddenly, Darnell is arrested on charges of insider trading and heads to a minimum security prison, in the finest tradition of Martha Stewart. Regrettably, when she's released, all of her assets are gone, she's marginalized by her former partner (and lover) Renault (an over-the-top Peter Dinklage), and finds herself with nothing. So, she shows up on good-hearted Claire's doorstep, which forces Claire and her daughter Rachel (Ella Anderson) to take Michelle in. After a brief period of wallowing, Michelle soon plans her financial comeback by taking over Rachel's Girl Scout troop and monetizing Claire's ability to bake inexplicably delicious brownies.

And that is, largely, the entire story. It reads more like the plot of an episode of a Disney Channel sitcom than an actual feature film. The thin premise sets up several comedic set pieces for Darnell—swearing in front of kids, sparing with a helicopter mom (Annie Mumolo), trying to pull off a wacky heist, participating in a Girl Scout battle royale that feels flat-out plagiarized from the *Anchorman* movies—but none of them land. There are individual moments and lines that elicit laughs, but the rest just feels so ephemeral and forgettable that McCarthy's energetic performance gets washed out in the overall blandness.

Which is a shame because the cast is fairly strong. Kristen Bell is an excellent straight-woman for McCarthy to play against. Her awkward flirting with Tyler Labine works better than it should. And Dinklage seems to think he's in a much broader comedy than Falcone

delivered, but it's hard to fault his efforts. He's trying to give some life to *The Boss*, which it resists for its entire run time.

In the end, *The Boss* is barely a movie. It's a collection of sketches strung together by a series of contrivances. Even the sad flashbacks where we learn about Darnell's hard childhood cannot actually convince viewers that this film contains an actual story. Because *The Boss* isn't a story. It's simply a character vehicle that isn't strong enough or funny enough to make us forgive its shortcomings.

Tom Burns

CREDITS

Michelle Darnell: Melissa McCarthy
Claire: Kristen Bell
Renault: Peter Dinklage
Rachel: Ella Anderson
Mike Beals: Tyler Labine
Origin: United States
Language: English
Released: 2016
Production: Will Ferrell, Adam McKay, Melissa McCarthy, Ben Falcone; released by Gary Sanchez Productions, Universal Pictures Inc.
Directed by: Ben Falcone
Written by: Melissa McCarthy; Ben Falcone; Steve Mallory
Cinematography by: Julio Macat
Music by: Christopher Lennertz
Sound: Andrew DeCristofaro; Becky Sullivan
Editing: Craig Alpert; Rusty Smith
Costumes: Wendy Chuck
MPAA rating: R
Running time: 99 minutes

REVIEWS

Dargis, Manohla. *New York Times.* April 7, 2016.
Eichel, Molly. *Philadelphia Inquirer.* April 7, 2016.
Greenblatt, Leah. *Entertainment Weekly.* April 8, 2016.
Hassenger, Jesse. *The A.V. Club.* April 6, 2016.
Kohn, Eric. *IndieWire.* April 6, 2016.
Lewis, David. *San Francisco Chronicle.* April 7, 2016.
Robinson, Tasha. *The Verge.* April 26, 2016.
Russo, Tom. *Boston Globe.* April 7, 2016.
Stewart, Sara. *New York Post.* April 7, 2016.
Travers, Peter. *Rolling Stone.* April 7, 2016.

QUOTES

Michelle Darnell: "I am amazed that the United Center is even still standing because I crushed it tonight!"
Tito: "You crushed it like velvet!"

THE BOY

Every child needs to feel loved.
—Movie tagline

Box Office: $35.8 Million

Even the most devoted fans of the genre will probably admit that most horror movies, especially those of more recent vintage, are largely exercises in nonsense that arrive in theaters with perilously low expectations that, more often than not, they fail to meet. However, what keeps fans coming back for more, even when they pretty much know that the film in question is going to be the pits, is the hope that something of interest—an effectively staged scare sequence, an eccentric performance, or an especially screw-loose plot twist—will cut through the boredom and liven things up a bit. *The Boy* is a perfect example of this. For the most part, it is a tedious and quite silly stab at slow-burn horror that never quite manages to catch fire, but toward the end tosses viewers a screwball that is so bizarre and audacious that it almost—*almost*—makes up for the rest of it.

Greta (Lauren Cohan of *The Walking Dead*) is an American woman who has chosen to flee an abusive former boyfriend by going off to England and finds herself applying for a job in a remote Gothic manor in the countryside to care for Brahms, the eight-year-old son of the aging Mr. and Mrs. Heelshire (Jim Norton and Diana Hardcastle) while they go on an extended holiday. The gig pays well but there are a couple of drawbacks—the house is so isolated that there is no Wi-Fi, the only other person in the immediate vicinity appears to be hunky deliveryman Malcolm (Rupert Evans), and Brahms turns out to be an exceptionally creepy-looking, life-size doll that the couple have doted on as if it were their own flesh & blood since their real son died in a fire 20 years earlier. One would think that all of this would set off a number of red flags amongst most semi-sentient human beings but Greta inexplicably agrees to the gig and settles in to care for Brahms, working from a long list of rules that she is expected to obey.

Before long, strange things begin to happen. Pieces of clothing mysteriously vanish. Even more disturbingly, Brahms occasionally seems to be moving of his own accord. Greta soon finds herself beginning to believe that Brahms may not be that inanimate of an object after all. Malcolm thinks this is nonsense but eventually reveals that the real Brahms was not exactly a sweet little kid and may have had something to do with the brutal death of a playmate just before his own demise. Could the mysterious goings-on involve the spirit of Brahms inhabiting the doll? Could the weirdness be the work of Malcolm, who does have a key to the place and seems to come and go as he pleases, or of Greta's ex (Ben Robson), who has learned of her whereabouts?

Eerie-looking dolls have long been a staple of horror movies but few have tried to milk the uneasiness that many feel towards them to this degree. Utilized in small doses, a properly deployed doll can inspire authentic shivers, but when one is placed at the center of a full-length film, the fear has a tendency to dissipate into silliness, especially when we are treated to endless scenes in which we see Greta gamely going about her duties of caring for her porcelain-based charge. Perhaps recognizing the limited returns of Brahms as a figure of fear, director William Brent Ball (whose previous films have included the terrible *Stay Alive* [2006] and the infamously awful *The Devil Inside* [2012]) and debuting screenwriter Stacey Menear try to goose things further by deploying any number of the hoariest horror clichés imaginable—several "BOO!" moments that turn out to be dreams, a central setting that strives to do for remote country manors what the Overlook did for remote Colorado hotels, and a shower scene that appears to be little more than an excuse to have Cohan clad in nothing more than a towel for the next ten minutes. None of these work particularly well and only add to the tedium of the enterprise.

Then, of course, there is that aforementioned plot twist that occurs fairly late in the proceedings. No details will be revealed here but, suffice to say, it is ridiculous and implausible, even by the standards of the narrative that this film asks viewers to accept. But it is undeniably effective and most viewers probably will not see it coming, if only because they are rational people would could not believe that anyone would dare present something so goofy as the climax to this story. Unfortunately, the film then proceeds to squander its one bit of genuine invention by dragging on for another ten or so increasingly lackluster minutes that seem to be going out of their way to nullify any possible audience goodwill that it might have engendered. Ironically, this is the exact opposite of what happened with *The Devil Inside*, in which Bell presented one of the dumbest plot twists of all time and then ended things right then and there, thereby ensuring rage and annoyance amongst viewers over its sheer stupidity.

To be fair, *The Boy* is better than *The Devil Inside* (though there are few films not directed by Tommy Wiseau that could not make that claim) and it does have a couple of virtues. Although few would consider it to be a great performance by any means, Cohan certainly commits to her part instead of simply succumbing to the silliness. The house itself—apparently a combination of a couple of different locations and sets—looks pretty fantastic and when things get dull, which is often, one can simply pause the film and marvel at the details. As a half-hour installment of an anthology show or movie, *The Boy* might have worked as a cheerfully simple-minded genre piece with an effective big twist but at three times that length, it just becomes both too absurd and too boring for its own good.

Peter Sobczynski

CREDITS

Greta Evans: Lauren Cohan
Malcolm: Rupert Evans
James: James Russell
Mr. Heelshire: Jim Norton
Mrs. Heelshire: Diana Hardcastle
Origin: United States
Language: English
Released: 2016
Production: Matt Berenson, Roy Lee, Gary Lucchesi, Tom Rosenberg, Jim Wedaa; released by Huayi Brothers Media Group, Lakeshore Entertainment
Directed by: William Brent Bell
Written by: Stacey Menear
Cinematography by: Daniel Pearl
Music by: Bear McCreary
Sound: Craig Mann
Music Supervisor: Eric Craig
Editing: Brian Berdan
Art Direction: James Steuart
Costumes: Jori Woodman
Production Design: John Willett
MPAA rating: PG-13
Running time: 97 minutes

REVIEWS

Cook, Linda. *Quad City Times.* January 28, 2016.
Genzlinger, Neil. *New York Times.* January 23, 2016.
Kang, Inkoo. *The Wrap.* January 23, 2016.
Lemire, Christy. *RogerEbert.com.* January 23, 2016.
Leydon, Joe. *Variety.* January 21, 2016.
Nordine, Michael. *L.A. Weekly.* January 25, 2016.
Orndorf, Brian. *Blu-Ray.com.* January 22, 2016.
Rife, Katie. *The A.V. Club.* January 21, 2016.
Scholz, Pablo. *Clarin.* February 7, 2016.
Tsai, Martin. *Los Angeles Times.* January 22, 2016.

QUOTES

Greta Evans: "You wouldn't hurt me, would you, Brahms?"

TRIVIA

Lauren Cohan plays an American nanny traveling to the United Kingdom for her job as a babysitter. Cohan is an American-born citizen but has a British accent after spending her adolescence in the UK, so she hid her accent.

THE BOY AND THE BEAST
(Bakemono no ko)

Box Office: $490,643

This action-packed but gentle-hearted anime fantasy is exactly what viewers have come to expect from writer/director Momuro Hosoda. *The Boy and the Beast* is far from original in plot or characterization but it takes what makes certain things so well-loved by fans of anime very seriously. It is a film that believes in itself but, more importantly, in the audience that will find it funny, heart-warming, inspiring, and most of all respectful of the powerful themes of self-identification and true spiritual enlightenment.

Ren is nine years old and grieving the loss of his mother. Refusing to live with his guardians, who in turn shun his absent father, he runs away to live in the streets of Shibuya. With only his instincts to help him avoid capture by the child-welfare authorities, he steals food and sleeps in alleys, torn up by his bitterness and anger.

Meanwhile, in the Beast Kingdom, the lord of all beasts has decided to retire and accept his reincarnation as a deity. Deciding to host a duel to crown his successor, he names two warriors: Iozen, an outwardly calm but judgmental figure, and Kumatetsu, a gifted fighter, but lazy and eternally angry loner. As each fighter is guided by the lord of all beasts on how best to train, Kumatetsu is encouraged to find a young disciple that he can support and inspire.

During a secret excursion to Tokyo, Kumatetsu stumbles across Ren and, impulsively, against the wishes of his companion Tatara, offers to make the boy his disciple. Ren hates the idea but his curiosity leads him to covertly follow the pair back to the Beast Kingdom, a mythical land populated entirely by sentient animals, where he witnesses an impromptu street battle between Iozen and Kumatetsu. Moved by Kumatetsu's unwillingness to give up, despite his being clearly outmatched, Ren comes out of hiding and cheers him on. Though Kumatetsu is badly beaten, Ren becomes his disciple.

Renamed Kyuta, he is nonetheless, a poor pupil in the hands of a poor teacher. The two constantly fight, almost to the point of blows. But Ren blossoms as he realizes he can learn by imitating Kumatetsu's movements during household chores. Eight years pass during which Kyuta becomes a respected kendo instructor, always wishing he could win the respect of his harsh teacher. Indeed, Kumatetsu has used his relationship with the boy to create followers for himself, including Jiromaru, the younger son of his rival, Iozen. Soon Kumatetsu is so busy that he fails to notice Kyuta has left, departed for the human world, in search of his birth father.

His time back in the human world affords Kyuta the time to meet and befriend a young woman named Kaede, who begins tutoring him. He also tracks down his father who is overjoyed to see him. But the pressure of his human world resentment toward his birth family, and his alienation in the Beast Kingdom, leaves him vulnerable to a dark void within himself that threatens to completely consume him, except for the gift of a small bracelet, a gift from Kaede, which he is told, has always had the power to calm her in anxious times.

In the Beast Kingdom the day of the duel has come, and Kumatetsu, weakened by his increased loneliness, is almost beaten, until Kyuta once again reveals himself. As Kumatetsu is declared the new lord of all beasts, Iozen's elder son, Ichirohiko, is revealed as having been a human all along; adopted on the streets by Iozen just as Ren was by Kumatetsu. Ichirohiko, who has been secretly consumed by his own void within, lashes out at Kumatetsu, seriously injuring him. Kyuta, driven to rage, is only able to control the urge to kill Ichirohiko through the calming power of Kaede's gift.

Chasing Ichirohiko to the human world, Kyuta is confronted by Kaede, who refuses to leave his side. When Ichirohiko attacks, Kyuta releases his own void to absorb the destructive force in an act of self-sacrifice. Kumatetsu, observing the battle, uses his privilege as the new lord to reincarnate, taking on the form of a sword that can only be handled by the heart, filling Kyuta's void, and allowing him to defeat Ichirohiko without killing him. Ichirohiko realizes that, like Ren, he is simply a human raised by beasts and is finally able to accept himself and his dual identity. Later Ren, who has laid aside his Beast Kingdom name, celebrates with Kaede and is finally able to reconcile with his human father, keeping Kumatetsu in his heart.

This is the fourth full-length feature film from Mamuro Hosoda, but the first solely credited to him as director and writer. His three previous features, *The Girl Who Leapt Through Time* (2006), *Summer Wars* (2009), and *Wolf Children* (2012), all acknowledge co-credit or sole writing credit to Satoko Okudera. This is the main reason to withhold judgement about Hosoda's place in the anime pantheon, despite how fashionable it is to hail him as the new Hayao Miyazaki. Whereas Miyazaki has often adapted the work of others, he generally works alone in crafting his screenplays. The result has been what many critics regard as the single greatest body of work any individual in animation has ever produced.

That said, Hosoda's work is consistently amazing. He has a grasp of where anime is headed in terms of jaw-dropping visuals and overall aesthetic, and he also seems to be interested, like Miyazaki, in the silence. As much glee and boyish enthusiasm as viewers might sense during action sequences or moments of broad slapstick humor in his films, there is always something intimate about Hosoda's work. The backgrounds teem with meaningful detail, giving the impression that these are wholly realized worlds where at any moment the camera might simply choose to follow one of the seemingly endless narrative threads. "Boy" might replace "Beauty" in the film's play on the classic Victor Hugo tale, but beauty is all around.

The narrative, too, looks like nothing special at first glance. A viewer could certainly be excused for feeling it a little thread worn. But even here Hosoda shows the desire to at least attempt some originality. The title of the film *The Boy and The Beast* implies two characters at work but Ren is actually the singular figure of the narrative with Kumatetsu standing in for Ren's own need to balance out his nature. Rather than tell a simple story in which Kumatetsu simply becomes a tamed father figure, Hosoda tells a story that includes Ren's natural human father as well. In fact, Ren's excursion back out into the human world in an effort to find identity is so prominent many critics have pointed out Kumatetsu could be a figment of Ren's imagination. But Hosoda treats Ren's citizenship in both worlds with equal seriousness and this is the point. The question is not whether the beast world is real but who Ren will become. In its own small way, this film tells a similar story to *The Jungle Book* while having the courage and the vision to go beyond the jungle. Comparisons to Tarzan are also inevitable. Hosoda has done an excellent job of using familiar elements in ways that remind the viewer how timeless those elements and stories are.

Dave Canfield

CREDITS

Kyuta (young): Luci Christian
Kyuta (teen): Eric Vale
Kumatetsu: John Swasey
Kaede: Bryn Apprill
Chico: Monica Rial
Origin: United States
Language: Japanese

Released: 2016

Production: Atsushi Chiba, Takuya Ito, Genki Kawamura, Yuichiro Sato; released by Chukyo TV Broadcasting Co., D.N. Dream Partners, DENTSU Inc., Fukuoka Broadcasting Corporation, Hiroshima Telecasting Co., Ltd., Kadokawa Corp., Miyagi Television Broadcasting Company Ltd., Nippon Television Network Corp., Sapporo Television Broadcasting Co., Ltd., Shizuoka Daiichi Television Corp., Studio Chizu, Toho Company Ltd., Video Audio Project, Yomiuri Telecasting Corp.

Directed by: Mamoru Hosoda

Written by: Mamoru Hosoda

Music by: Masakatsu Takagi

Costumes: Daisuke Iga

MPAA rating: PG-13

Running time: 119 minutes

REVIEWS

Connelly, Sherilyn. *Village Voice*. March 1, 2016.

DeBruge, Peter. *Variety*. September 24, 2015.

Keogh, Tom. *Seattle Times*. March 3, 2016.

Marsh, James. *South China Morning Post*. April 6, 2016.

McIndoe, Ross. *The Skinny*. February 29, 2016.

Pavlov, Marc. *Austin Chronicle*. March 3, 2016.

Solomon, Charles. *Los Angeles Times*. December 3, 2015.

Webster, Andy. *New York Times*. March 3, 2016.

Whittaker, Richard. *Austin Chronicle*. February 29, 2016.

Young, Neil. *Hollywood Reporter*. February 29, 2016.

BRIDGET JONES'S BABY

We're going to need bigger pants.
—Movie tagline

Box Office: $24.2 Million

An intriguing study in the crackerjack execution of a sometimes hacky, leaky premise, *Bridget Jones's Baby* makes hay out of a predictably contrived romantic quandary, reacquainting audiences with the endearing klutziness and many of the other qualities which first caused them to fall for Renée Zellweger. The result is an amiable, comfortably digested movie, at total peace with its ramshackle charm and lack of ambition.

Perhaps not surprisingly after a layoff of more than a decade, the *Bridget Jones* films have seen franchise fatigue set in. *Bridget Jones's Diary* (2001) grossed a cumulative $282 million, while *Bridget Jones: The Edge of Reason* (2004) raked in a cumulative $263 million. Still, while grossing only a modest $24 million during its stateside theatrical engagement, this third installment made a robust $182 million overall, owing to still-strong $158 million overseas haul. For those keeping track, that is over $750 million in theatrical box office against a combined budget of around $100—a huge return on investment.

Based on characters created by Helen Fielding and co-written by Emma Thompson, Dan Mazer,and Fielding herself, *Bridget Jones's Baby* is undeniably a critical bounce-back from the savaged second movie in the series (which scored only 27 percent fresh on Rotten Tomatoes), in large part because of the buoyant contributions of director Sharon Maguire, who also helmed the well-received first film. But there is no denying that *Bridget Jones's Baby* also feels more than a bit like warmed-over wish fulfillment, a movie that studiously avoids substantively delving into any number of the interesting sociopolitical gender and age issues which it raises.

The story centers on Zellweger's title character, a perpetually frazzled professional whose "singleton" existence fits her a bit differently in her 40s than it did in her 30s. At a music festival, one of Bridget's friends challenges her to sleep with the first man she meets; after a pratfall in the mud, Bridget is helped by a handsome stranger, who turns out to be an American billionaire, Jack Qwant (Patrick Dempsey), who is the inventor of a dating site which uses a special algorithm to match couples. Later that night, after accidentally entering his tent, Bridget reconnects with Jack, and the two make love.

As would happen, Bridget has also recently reconnected with ex-paramour Mark Darcy (Colin Firth), who is in the process of divorcing his wife. They too have sex, so when Bridget finds out some time later that she is pregnant, she is uncertain as to whom the father might be. After deciding to keep the baby, she then winds her way toward the big delivery date, with Mark and Jack both remaining a part of her life.

Most of the problems with *Bridget Jones's Baby* can be traced to its screenplay, and small sins and failures of both commission and omission. Bridget is a television news producer, but the movie seems to hold no small amount of condescension for her occupation, basically utilizing it as the set-up for a lot of screw-ups and pratfalls, both metaphorically and literally. If there were some sense of honest contrast between Bridget's steely professional competence and the unsettled nature of her personal life, the character might feel more grounded and realistic, and the comedy more relatable. Instead, while Thompson (who co-stars as Bridget's obstetrician, Dr. Rawlings) and her co-writers have some understandable fun at the expense of the click-bait, ratings-obsessed trashiness of modern journalism (particularly via Bridget's brash new boss Alice, well by played Kate O'Flynn), almost everything about Bridget's professional life seems forced and unnatural.

The screenplay rushes through some subplots and narrative turns (Bridget's thinly sketched relationship with her mother seems to represent an especially glaring missed opportunity), but belabors others, grinding them down into a fine dust of tedium that serves as the starchy binder of the two-hour-plus movie. Most damningly, though, *Bridget Jones's Baby* lacks genuine tension, making Mark and especially Jack for the most part eager partners in Bridget's impending motherhood. A bit of stock characterization (after all, it is not their names in the movie's title) is to be expected, but what about Bridget's conflicted feelings over these men—and specifically not their prospects as life partners, but their engagement with possible fatherhood? Delving into these complicated thoughts would have given this comedy some much-needed real-world heft.

On a technical level, *Bridget Jones's Baby* does not so much thrill or innovate as much as simply accrue credit for striking all the expected and desired emotional keys. If its song choices (Sister Sledge's "We Are Family" and Joe Cocker and Jennifer Warnes' "Up Where We Belong") are staggeringly generic, that is precisely the point. This movie labors not to solicit thought but basically to register memories of other entertainment and roughly analogous life moments.

Thankfully, Maguire and editor Melanie Ann Oliver have a flair for locating and conveying the emotional truth of Bridget's antics. This means that the desperation or desire or confusion she feels often connects on a subordinate level, whether or not the particular scenario feels manufactured. Cinematographer Andrew Dunn lights his frames brightly, and keeps the action centered in unfussy fashion.

If the screenplay generally fails to dazzle, the performers at least gamely work to give individual scenes piecemeal lift. In particular, Firth's excellent comic timing is put to fantastic use; in both standard cutaways and fleeting in-scene reactions, his work is a master-level class on conveying a roiling inner life, whether it is Mark being mistaken for Jack's lover at a parenting class or mentally calculating the (diminishing?) odds of his paternity.

In her first film in more than six years, meanwhile, Zellweger slips back into the character of Bridget like an old glove. She has a clear affinity for her foibles, and channels them in a way that is winning rather than exasperating. We have all known someone like Bridget in real life—a person led by their heart but still caught up in their own head. At their core, that is what makes these movies generally work. And Zellweger has the ability to breathe full-bodied life into those traits, in a way that keeps an audience rooting for Bridget's happiness.

That viewers never much doubt it is coming matters not one whit.

Brent Simon

CREDITS

Bridget Jones: Renee Zellweger
Mark Darcy: Colin Firth
Jack: Patrick Dempsey
Dr. Rawlings: Emma Thompson
Bridget's Mum: Gemma Jones
Bridget's Dad: Jim Broadbent
Origin: United States
Language: English
Released: 2016
Production: Tim Bevan, Eric Fellner, Debra Hayward; released by Miramax, StudioCanal, Universal Pictures Inc., Working Title Films Ltd.
Directed by: Sharon Maguire
Written by: Emma Thompson; Helen Fielding; Dan Mazer
Cinematography by: Andrew Dunn
Music by: Craig Armstrong
Sound: Glenn Freemantle
Music Supervisor: Nick Angel
Editing: Melanie Oliver
Art Direction: David Hindle
Costumes: Steven Noble
Production Design: John Paul Kelly
MPAA rating: R
Running time: 123 minutes

REVIEWS

Felperin, Leslie. *Hollywood Reporter.* September 16, 2016.
Graham, Adam. *Detroit News.* September 16, 2016.
Hornaday, Ann. *Washington Post.* September 15, 2016.
Lane, Anthony. *New Yorker.* September 26, 2016.
Lockerby, Loey. *Kansas City Star.* September 16, 2016.
Lybarger, Dan. *Arkansas Democrat-Gazette.* September 16, 2016.
Morgenstern, Joe. *Wall Street Journal.* September 15, 2016.
Stevens, Dana. *Slate.* September 15, 2016.
Verniere, James. *Boston Herald.* September 16, 2016.
Vincent, Mal. *Virginian-Pilot.* September 16, 2016.

QUOTES

Mark: "Well, I can always find time to save the world. And Bridget, you're my world."

TRIVIA

Three different endings were filmed for the movie; none of the cast members knew which was used, until the film was released to theaters.

THE BRONZE

There's no place like third.
—Movie tagline

Box Office: $615,816

The Bronze tries to transplant the crude humor associated with bro movies to the traditionally feminine world of gymnastics and only intermittently succeeds in being funny. The perfectly fussily named former gymnast Hope Ann Greggory (Melissa Rauch, who also co-wrote the screenplay) won the bronze medal in the 2004 Olympics and since a career-ending injury has lived at home in Amherst, Ohio with her father, whiling away her days with drugs, petty theft, and junk food. Hope is a bad girl resting on the laurels of having briefly been America's sweetheart, and the film could easily be more of a melodrama. There's a lot of sadness at the core of *The Bronze*: Hope's mother died when she was a baby, and her meek, working-class father (Gary Cole) seems like a nice guy who just isn't equipped to deal with his loud, immature daughter (to be fair, few people would be up to this task including, perhaps, the audience). Essentially, the film is a dirty comedy that uses crushed dreams as fodder for creatively expletive-laced rants. There are occasional moments of pathos but on the whole it is unpleasant, courting audiences who laugh upon seeing a gymnast flub a move they practiced for years.

After Hope's coach commits suicide, she receives a letter claiming that she will receive $500,000 on the condition that she coach current rising gymnastic star Maggie Townsend (Haley Lu Richardson). Hope, of course, is none too pleased but she begins to coach her, making sure to take every opportunity to curse at her. Maggie is the daughter of a single mom (Cecily Strong) who works as a school janitor, and she considers Hope her idol. Even when Hope is outwardly rude to Maggie, the girl still seems enthusiastic, and her earnestness and continued willingness to work with the older gymnast, even given her egregious behavior, almost becomes difficult to watch. It is jarring, then, that after Hope leads Maggie to victory, Maggie announces in a TV interview that she is going to leave Hope for a competing coach, Lance Tucker (Sebastian Stan).

The Bronze is not terribly concerned with coherent character development: Hope ends up softening a bit and the film's ending is oddly sweet, but there are one too many dirty set pieces, and the bad behavior from which Hope eventually reforms becomes grating early on. In one particularly cringe-inducing moment, Hope gives Maggie a marijuana-spiked smoothie to drink right before an important day at the gym. Maggie, unaware that she is under the influence, completely embarrasses herself in a scene that is meant to provoke laughter but really reveals Hope's cruelty as not just annoying but abusive. Unbelievably, Maggie decides to continue working with Hope, who slowly starts to get her act together and ultimately coach Maggie to a gold medal. Early on Hope complains, "I'm not a coach, I'm a star," but be-

ing a coach ends up giving her purpose. We eventually find out that the letter promising a financial reward for coaching was a ploy cooked up by Hope's father in an attempt to get his daughter out of the house and doing something productive. When Hope finds out about this, for once, her anger toward her father is justified. Prior to learning the truth about the terms around her coaching, the marijuana-smoothie-debacle serves as a wakeup call. Hope starts waking up early and strictly guiding her charge to victory. Maggie is considerably more prim than Hope, and the film mines their obvious differences for some of its funniest moments. At one point, Hope introduces a secret handshake, a crude gesture that Maggie is at first embarrassed by but soon embraces. After hearing many of Hope's swears at the gym, Maggie finally drops an expletive of her own upon messing up a move. "It makes me so proud to hear you curse normal," Hope says, in a rare moment of subversive sweetness. With her exaggerated Midwestern snarl and refusal to wear anything other than baggy Olympic tracksuits, Hope is an annoying character by design, but she gradually becomes something like an aggressive yet occasionally endearing older sister to Maggie.

With its small budget and production by the Duplass brothers, *The Bronze* could potentially be a small and quirky indie comedy but it strives for broad, gross-out gender-swapped humor more in the vein of *Bridesmaids* (2011). Rauch embodies the washed up antiheroine with a tight lipped smile, and unfashionable (but amusingly gymnast-accurate) poufy bangs. *The Bronze* wants to show that a petite blonde can be just as dirty as any man, and ultimately relies too heavily on crude shtick (culminating in an absurd naked gymnastic sex scene) to get a point across which should already be obvious.

Abbey Bender

CREDITS

Hope Annabelle Gregory: Melissa Rauch
Stan Greggory: Gary Cole
Ben Lawfort: Thomas Middleditch
Lance Tucker: Sebastian Stan
Maggie Townsend: Haley Lu Richardson
Origin: United States
Language: English
Released: 2015
Production: Stephanie Langhoff
Directed by: Bryan Buckley
Written by: Melissa Rauch; Winston Rauch
Cinematography by: Scott Henriksen
Music by: Andrew Feltenstein; John Nau; Randall Poster

Music Supervisor: Marguerite Phillips
Editing: Jay Nelson
Art Direction: Deborah Marsh
Costumes: Michelle Martini
Production Design: David Skinner
MPAA rating: R
Running time: 200 minutes

REVIEWS

Debruge, Peter. *Variety.* January 23, 2015.
Dziemianowicz, Joe. *New York Daily News.* March 16, 2016.
Genzlinger, Neil. *New York Times.* March 17, 2016.
Goldberg, Matt. *Collider.* March 18, 2016.
Hassenger, Jesse. *The A.V. Club.* March 16, 2016.
Hunt, Drew. *Slant.* March 14, 2016.
Kenny, Glenn. *RogerEbert.com.* March 18, 2016.
Lapin, Andrew. *NPR.* March 17, 2016.
McCarthy, Todd. *Hollywood Reporter.* January 23, 2015.
Merry, Stephanie. *Washington Post.* March 17, 2016.

QUOTES

Ben: "Pretty strict diet."
Hope: "That's nothing. I once ate nothing but watermelon juice for a month. I had to reteach my jaw how to chew."

TRIVIA

The Olympics are only implied during the film. The word "Olympics" and the Olympic symbol are not in the film due to strict control by the Olympic Committee.

THE BROTHERS GRIMSBY

(Grimsby)

One secret agent. One complete idiot.
—Movie tagline

Box Office: $6.9 Million

There is no greater detriment to a magician than an audience fully aware of the contents of their bag of tricks. While this is a metaphor frequently applied to filmmakers who achieve either a peak of artistic or commercial viability, the best ones discover new methods and directions to further their craft. The bad ones just forego innovation to do the same thing only bigger, louder, and flashier. No quicker decline may have befallen any other comedic mind than Sacha Baron Cohen, whose attempts at keeping ahead of the drawn line in the sand amidst an increasingly politically correct culture have now just become desperate and, frankly, sad.

Nobby Butcher (Cohen) has not seen his brother in nearly 30 years. In that time, he has become an irresponsible drinker and amassed a brood of eleven who live in his childhood home, where he preserves his sibling's bedroom in the hopes he will one day come back. Sebastian (Mark Strong) is too busy working for MI-6 to go home again, particularly when he comes upon information that philanthropist Rhonda George (Penelope Cruz) has become a target for assassination. Somehow, one of Nobby's friends realizes that Sebastian will be at the forthcoming conference and the brothers are reunited, causing the operation to go south.

Busting up Sebastian's mission as well as his ankle in the process, Nobby brings him home as a safe haven. His handlers, now believing he has turned against them, have activated the assassin Chilcott (Sam Hazeldine) to hunt him down. Despite assistance from his handler (Isla Fisher) within the agency, Sebastian remains with this train wreck under great personal risk just long enough to give him an excuse to stay. Nobby and his family become every bit a target as he is. As this allows plenty of time for flashbacks back to happier childhood times it also sets up the opportunity for the crudest and most humiliating jokes imaginable that run the gamut of nether-region poison retraction to infecting Daniel Radcliffe with HIV. And this is all within the first half hour.

Gags like that are revolting enough to give the liberal minded a panic attack even before it is announced the next stop on their journey is an extended trip to South Africa. Of course in the right hands of gifted satirists, even the most out-of-bounds jokes can have purpose. Jokes about race, the handicapped, and homophobia can be about confronting the very fruit that has been deemed forbidden by the comedy police and providing context against the fears of insensitivity. Too often, this feels like a child pushing boundaries to see what he can get away with.

Cohen used to know better. *The Ali G Show*, while occasionally being a more obnoxious version of the kind of "gotcha" journalism that made Michael Moore a household name, nevertheless gave rise to his most recognized contribution to the world of satire. Kazakh journalist Borat Sagdiyev got his own film in 2006 and while full of outrageous and daringly tasteless humor was a welcome exposé of racism and other entitlements of hatred in a country that has too often convinced itself it has moved beyond such things. It was a lightning in a bottle that Cohen tried to repeat in *Bruno* (2009) and *The Dictator* (2012), leaving audiences to discover that even though the satiric elements were relatively the same, there was no longer a bottle and the bolts were ten times as destructive but each one less bright by half. By Cohen's measure, if in one movie penises are blacked out to hysterical effect then he may as well exponentially increase the full-frontal humor until such "graphic nudity" loses any shock value or purpose.

"You managed to do in three seconds what Voldemort failed to do in eight movies," serves as one of the film's few funny lines as a reaction to possibly the film's most pointlessly cruel gag. Since everyone knows timing is everything in comedy, the failure of hiring a hack action director like Louis Leterrier looms throughout. The helmer of the first two *Transporter* films, Marvel's reboot of *The Incredible Hulk* (2008), and one of the most contemptible films in terms of plotting, motivation, and protagonist likability—*Now You See Me* (2013) —the closest Leterrier has come to a successful joke was his remake of *Clash of the Titans* (2010). He may be in his comfort zone designing *Hardcore Henry*-like (2016) action sequences with editing left to be desired, but he may be the one person less qualified than Cohen at this point to handle jokes about pedophiles in LegoLand and elephant orgies.

From the heights of *The In-Laws* (1979) to the depths of *Bad Company* (2002) and *Central Intelligence* (2016), only John Le Carre has plumbed the premise of ordinary citizen teaming up with covert agents more. But never has it been more scattershot than it is here. A plot that barely registers through 76 minutes with a backstory that desperately tries to add some humanity into the absent chemistry between Cohen and Strong, who comes up woefully short in creating the kind of send-up of James Bond or Jason Bourne that contemporaries such as Jean Dujardin, Colin Firth, and Jude Law have pulled off with winking grace.

Erik Childress

CREDITS

Nobby: Sacha Baron Cohen
Sebastian: Mark Strong
Jodie Figgis: Isla Fisher
Rhonda George: Penelope Cruz

Dawn Grobham: Rebel Wilson
Origin: Australia, United Kingdom
Language: English
Released: 2016
Production: Nira Park, Sacha Baron Cohen; Sony Pictures Entertainment Inc.; released by Columbia Pictures
Directed by: Louis Leterrier
Written by: Sacha Baron Cohen; Phil Johnston; Peter Baynham
Cinematography by: Oliver Wood
Music by: David Buckley; Erran Baron Cohen
Sound: Julian Slater
Editing: Jonathon Amos; Evan Henke; James Thomas
Art Direction: Stuart Kearns
Costumes: Paco Delgado
Production Design: Kave Quinn
MPAA rating: R
Running time: 83 minutes

REVIEWS

Berardinelli, James. *ReelViews*. March 15, 2016.
Dargis, Manohla. *New York Times*. March 10, 2016.
Douglas, Edward. *Den of Geek*. March 10, 2016.
Ebiri, Bilge. *Village Voice*. March 15, 2016.
Kenny, Glenn. *RogerEbert.com*. March 11, 2016.
Lodge, Guy. *Variety*. February 22, 2016.
McGranaghan, Mike. *Aisle Seat*. March 11, 2016.
Nusair, David. *Reel Film Reviews*. March 14, 2016.
Orndorf, Brian. *Blu-ray.com*. March 11, 2016.
Singer, Matt. *Screen Crush*. March 10, 2016.

QUOTES

Agent Sebastian Grimsby: "Nobby, meet the head of the biggest crime syndicate in the world."
Norman "Nobby" Grimsby: "What, she runs FIFA?"

TRIVIA

The big banner outside the Trawler Hotel pub in Grimsby read: "WELCOME HOME GRIMSBY'S VERY OWN SPY! SHH!"

C

CAFÉ SOCIETY

Anyone who is anyone will be seen at Café Society.
—Movie tagline

Box Office: $11.1 Million

Woody Allen continues his film-a-year pace with the same results even his most loyal fans have come to expect for roughly the last two decades. For every *Vicky Cristina Barcelona* (2008) or *Midnight in Paris* (2011), cinema will be forced to endure a few films of the caliber of *Magic in the Moonlight* (2014) or, most regrettably, *Whatever Works* (2009). If his latest venture falls somewhere in the middle of his recent output—neither loathsome nor particularly memorable—one could argue it's not as bad as it could have been. And the visual style here, capturing Golden Era Hollywood in all its bright blue skies and stylish fashion choices, at least allows one to be visually distracted as Allen the writer goes through the motions yet again.

Joining a long line of stand-ins for the writer/director, Jesse Eisenberg stars here as Bobby Dorfman, the youngest son of a New York City Jewish family in the 1930s. He has a sister named Evelyn (Sari Lennick), who is starting a family in NYC with her intellectual husband Leonard (Stephen Kunken), and he has a mobster brother named Ben (Corey Stoll), who is, well, doing poorly-defined mobster things. His parents, Rose (Jeannie Berlin) and Marty (Ken Stott), are supportive, but the impression is definitely given that Bobby is adrift, falling into less classical archetypes than his siblings and uncertain of his next move. Time for a trip to the City of Angels!

Bobby has an uncle in Hollywood named Phil Stern (Steve Carell), a titan in the industry as one of its most powerful agents. Bobby offers to work for him, running menial errands for the power player, who barely pays attention his jittery nephew. As his uncle is ignoring him, Bobby gets closer to Phil's secretary Vonnie (Kristen Stewart), who has been helping the young man get acclimated in Hollywood. Seeing that Vonnie is a special girl, Bobby falls in love with her, but knows that she's also carrying on an affair with a married man. Of course, that married man is Uncle Phil.

After a failed attempt to get Phil to leave his wife, Vonnie chooses to go with Bobby in this bizarre love triangle. Before they can live happily ever after in the California sun, Phil changes his mind, claiming he's going to get divorced and marry Vonnie. Confronted with a choice between a rich, stable future with a powerful agent or a more uncertain one with a young man who has no clear career path, Vonnie goes with Phil.

Bobby returns to New York City, heartbroken. There, he teams with his gangster brother to open a nightclub, which soon becomes the hottest place in town. It's there that Bobby meets the gorgeous Veronica Hayes (Blake Lively), and the two get married, starting a family together. In Allen's final act, he paints a picture of two people settling for what may look like happy, successful partnerships on the outside, but the lingering questions about what could have been between Bobby and Vonnie remain.

A product of Allen's later years in life, *Café Society* has a wistful, almost melancholic tone that's kind of rare for the filmmaker. He's not exactly casting WWII-era Hollywood and New York City in glowing, nostalgic light—the film has a notably cynical streak, especially in its final act—but this is definitely the product of an older filmmaker, someone who has seen romance dissipate and families fall apart. Allen's narration of the piece, with a voice that sounds more aged than he has in recent years, adds a sense of memory and arguably even autobiographical tone.

As for performance, the film again falls on the higher side of Allen's recent mediocre product, certainly outpacing something like *Irrational Man* (2015) but unlikely to be included in anyone's career-spanning, pre-speech clip reel down the road. Carell feels a bit miscast (and the part was originally going to be played by Bruce Willis, which could have added some much-needed heat to a very cool production) and Eisenberg can do this kind of Allen impression in his sleep, but Stewart yet again steals an arthouse movie. Since *The Twilight Saga* ended, she's made a habit of that, earning raves in films like *Clouds of Sils Maria* (2015), *Certain Women* (2016), and *Personal Shopper* (2017). This is further evidence that she's one of the most intriguing actresses of her generation. And Lively does similarly strong work in a very small role. In fact, Stewart and Lively are so much more intriguing than their male counterparts that it starts to become a flaw in the film—why would either settle for Bobby?

Ultimately, the key asset of *Café Society* is the visual work by expert cinematographer Vittorio Storaro. The masterful D.P. behind such classics as *Apocalypse Now* (1979) and *The Last Emperor* (1987) brings a unique visual palette to a filmmaker not exactly known for his compositions, especially since the turn of the century. Whether he's shooting poolside in Los Angeles or in the clubs of '30s New York City, Storaro finds a way to make *Café Society* pop. If only its creator could bring the same energy to every annual project.

Brian Tallerico

CREDITS

Bobby: Jesse Eisenberg
Vonnie: Kristen Stewart
Phil Stern: Steve Carell
Rose: Jeannie Berlin
Veronica: Blake Lively
Steve: Paul Schneider
Origin: United States
Language: English
Released: 2016
Production: Letty Aronson, Stephen Tenenbaum, Edward Walson; released by FilmNation Entertainment, Gravier Productions, Perdido Productions

Directed by: Woody Allen
Written by: Woody Allen
Cinematography by: Vittorio Storaro
Music Supervisor: Stewart Lerman
Editing: Alisa Lepselter
Art Direction: Michael E. Goldman; Douglas Huszti
Costumes: Suzy Benzinger
Production Design: Santo Loquasto
MPAA rating: PG-13
Running time: 96 minutes

REVIEWS

Dowd, A.A. *The A.V. Club.* July 13, 2016.
Ebiri, Bilge. *Village Voice.* July 12, 2016.
Gleiberman, Owen. *Variety.* May 11, 2016.
Kenny, Glenn. *RogerEbert.com.* July 14, 2016.
Kiang, Jessica. *The Playlist.* May 11, 2016.
Kohn, Eric. *IndieWire.* May 11, 2016.
Lane, Anthony. *New Yorker.* July 4, 2016.
Morgenstern, Joe. *Wall Street Journal.* July 14, 2016.
Robinson, Tasha. *The Verge.* July 22, 2016.
Scott, A.O. *New York Times.* July 14, 2016.

QUOTES

Steve: "Love is not rational. You fall in love, you lose control."

TRIVIA

"Cafe society" is a phrase created in 1915 by Maury Henry Biddle Paul to describe the "beautiful people" who socialized and threw parties in high-profile cafés and restaurants in New York, Paris, and London.

CAMERAPERSON

Box Office: $102,033

Kirsten Johnson has spent her life filming other people. In doing so, she has developed an understanding of the role that the camera plays in human dynamics. No matter how hard a documentary filmmaker may try to minimize it, the camera is a factor in any filmed interaction. Human behavior changes when it's on camera, even if it's only sometimes subconsciously. And what the cameraperson chooses to film, or chooses not to film, is an essential part of the process and the eventual product. No documentary is completely "true," as everything is filtered through the camera and the person holding it. Consequently, when Johnson chose to make her first autobiographical film, she used the tools of her life to do so—the camera and the footage it captured.

Instead of telling her life story chronologically or even personally, Johnson assembles her film like a collage, showing scenes, most often cut from the final product, from films she's worked on in the past, including *Citizenfour* (2014), *A Place at the Table* (2012), *The Invisible War* (2012), *No Woman, No Cry* (2010), *Throw Down Your Heart* (2008), and *Darfur Now* (2007). At first, the assemblage of moments that Johnson filmed feels random, but a rhythm and thematic purpose soon comes clear. She will include footage of a Bosnian shepherd, move to people praying in a foreign land, and, eventually, incorporate home movies, some from her childhood and some more recent, including those of her mother, who is deeply afflicted with Alzheimer's Disease. In her structure, Johnson draws lines and parallels from lives that would not seem to otherwise have them. And yet she makes connections that feel organic and emotional instead of literal.

Cameraperson has remarkable emotional power—especially in footage of war-torn countries or Johnson's own issues with her mother—but it becomes something even greater than an autobiographical documentary when one considers the greater implications of its structure. Kirsten Johnson chose to tell the story of her life not through those who know her or footage of herself, but through footage of who and what she shot in her profession. It is not that old dictum that "you are what you do" but the fascinating concept that the camera is merely an extension of the person holding it. What better way to tell Kirsten Johnson's story than through the camera she held so much of her life?

Some of *Cameraperson* feels random. She cuts from a young woman speaking of her decision to terminate her pregnancy to something that does not feel at all related—and yet it is because the same person filmed it. The same person chose the angle and chose to include it in this film. And so every piece of footage, no matter how much they may seem different in tone and substance, shares the commonality of the title of the film—the cameraperson. Johnson's film has a breathtaking cumulative power, especially as she either starts to make more literal connections or else the viewer just gets accustomed to the style—it's hard to say.

We remember our life in fragments of memory—a glimpse of childhood, a vision of our parents at a younger age, a memory of a trip somewhere. Film has never been able to capture that fragmented aspect of human existence as well as it is in *Cameraperson*. We don't remember things in the linear fashion of traditional autobiographical filmmaking, and what we do remember may not make the most perfect sense from memory to memory.

Johnson also finds time to address something that's clearly at the core of who she is—the question about what role a documentarian plays in ethics. What images should a cameraperson capture? Are there things that are not permissible? When should they intervene in the human story going on in front of them? Are there rules to being a cameraperson? Are there rules to being a human being in a war-torn or struggling part of the world? Through the clips she chooses, many of them related to women's issues, it becomes clear that these are questions with which Johnson has struggled, but there are no easy answers. Choices are made in filmmaking, as they are in life, about what to focus on and what to care about.

Obviously, *Cameraperson* is a special film. After waves of acclaim at Sundance and other film festivals, it received a modest release, barely making a dent at the box office (although that's typical for even the best documentaries, especially one this unusual). However, *Cameraperson* ended up on dozens of top ten lists, and has already been given a lavish Blu-ray release by the esteemed Criterion Collection, who recognizes the most important films ever made. *Cameraperson* deserves inclusion in that conversation.

Brian Tallerico

CREDITS

Herself: Kirsten Johnson
Himself: Roger Phenix
Origin: United States
Language: English
Released: 2016
Production: Marilyn Ness, Kirsten Johnson; released by Big Mouth Publications, Fork Films
Directed by: Kirsten Johnson
Cinematography by: Kirsten Johnson
Editing: Nels Bangerter
MPAA rating: Unrated
Running time: 102 minutes

REVIEWS

Chang, Justin. *Los Angeles Times*. September 22, 2016.
D'Angelo, Mike. *The A.V. Club*. September 7, 2016.
Ebiri, Bilge. *Village Voice*. September 6, 2016.
Hornaday, Ann. *Washington Post*. October 13, 2016.
Hunter, Allan. *Screen International*. August 28, 2016.
Schager, Nick. *Variety*. August 28, 2016.
Schindel, Daniel. *Film Stage*. August 28, 2016.
Scott, A.O. *New York Times*. September 8, 2016.
Seitz, Matt Zoller. *RogerEbert.com*. September 8, 2016.
Walsh, Katie. *Playlist*. August 28, 2016.

AWARDS

Nominations:

Ind. Spirit 2017: Feature Doc.

CAPTAIN AMERICA: CIVIL WAR

Whose side are you on?
—Movie tagline

Box Office: $408 Million

When *Captain America: The First Avenger* was released in 2011, few could have expected that it would kick off the most creatively successfully (and one of the most commercially successful) film trilogies in Marvel Comics history. Before *The First Avenger*'s release, it was feared that the character would be too jingoistic to appeal to international audiences, particularly after years of unpopular American foreign policy. Fortunately for Marvel, the film was a success, thanks largely to Joe Johnston's workman directorial hand. (He'd previously proven his penchant for WWII-era superheroes with the box-office disappointment *The Rocketeer* [1991].)

However, what no one could have expected was that *The First Avenger* would be followed by two sequels that were arguably better than fan-favorite Joss Whedon's Avengers movies or that such powerhouse sequels could be delivered by Anthony and Joe Russo, two directors best known for their television work and the low-key heist comedy *Welcome to Collinwood* (2002). The Russos are now responsible for two-thirds of the "Captain America Trilogy," a trio of films that took one of Marvel's most earnest and problematic characters and made him a movie star.

Not that the Russos did everything on their own. Due credit has to go to Chris Evans, who could have stumbled with Cap's "Aw shucks" patriotism, but instead has continued to find ways to make Steve Rogers charismatic, yet principled. The Russos' Captain America movies don't present a Pollyanna view of the world. They are decidedly more concerned with shadowy conspiracies, corruption, and the price of being a hero, but Evans' optimism makes their stories so much more digestible and entertaining than DC Comics' dour, nihilistic deconstructions of their core heroes.

The other thing that the Russos have going for them is that, particularly in their third film, *Captain America: Civil War*, Marvel Comics has allowed them to play with all of their toys. One could easily argue that *Civil War* is more of an Avengers movie than a Captain America movie simply because of the sheer number of superheroes present in the story.

While fanboys have made a big deal that the next Avengers movies (*Infinity War*) will include a monumental team-up of almost every character from Marvel's cinematic universe, *Civil War* is clearly that film's precursor, almost acting as a test case for whether or not you can actually have 12-plus heroes in a scene without los-

ing focus. (Not surprisingly, the Russos nabbed the directing job for *Infinity War* based on their track record with their Captain America films.)

Regardless of whether it's an Avengers or a Captain America movie, *Civil War* works. Frankly, it works better than it should. A film with so much on its agenda should feel overpacked and sluggish. And yet, while there are moments where the narrative flies off on unnecessary tangents, for the most part, the Russos keep things cohesive, light, and surprisingly character-driven throughout. This is particularly noteworthy after the underwhelming mess that was *Avengers: Age of Ultron* (2015), which spent entirely too much time trying to make audiences care about The Vision's incoherent origin story, among other missteps.

Civil War is loosely based on an existing Marvel storyline, a great premise with one of the lamest, cop-out endings in modern comic book history, but screenwriters Christopher Markus and Stephen McFeely thankfully only used the bones of the narrative to construct their own story about the consequences of being a superhero. As the film opens, a small team of the Avengers—Captain America, Black Widow (Scarlett Johansson), Scarlet Witch (Elizabeth Olsen), and the Falcon (Anthony Mackie)—are trying to stop terrorists from stealing a biological weapon in Africa. In the ensuing firefight, several innocent bystanders are killed, inspiring several world governments to call for regulations and accountability for the world's superhuman population.

When the United Nations is in session to approve the regulations (known as the Sokovia Accords), a bomb is detonated, killing many of the dignitaries. The attack is quickly blamed on Captain America's former best friend James "Bucky" Barnes (Sebastian Stan), who, in the previous film, it was discovered had been unwittingly transformed into a brainwashed cyborg assassin known as The Winter Solider. Captain America is skeptical of the accusations—as is the audience, who is introduced to a former military man Helmut Zemo (Daniel Brühl), who seems to be pulling strings in the background and trying to uncover the secrets of the Soviet program that created The Winter Soldier.

However, Cap's suspicions are not enough to convince U.S. Secretary of State Thaddeus Ross or Tony Stark (Robert Downey Jr., a.k.a. Iron Man). While sympathetic to Captain America's plight, the man inside of Iron Man informs Cap that Bucky will be arrested and that all superheroes, including the Captain, must sign the Sokovia Accords or else they'll be considered international criminals. (The script smartly uses Stark's guilt from the events of the last Avengers film as the driving force to cast him as an antagonist in Civil War—an antagonist with a point of view that might win over audience members as being more pragmatic and sensible than Cap's approach.)

This all leads to an international manhunt. Captain America refuses to sign, hoping to find Bucky before the authorities do, and his decision splits the Avengers community right down the middle. Some immediately agree with Iron Man's desire to follow the rule of law (War Machine, Vision, Black Widow), while others pledge their support to Captain America's desire to work unencumbered by international agendas (Falcon, Hawkeye, Scarlet Witch)

What follows are a series of bravura action sequences that are expertly staged by the Russos, even if some might complain that they are relatively low-stakes. We all know that Iron Man isn't going to kill or maim Captain America, so their battles are more about delaying each other in the most spectacular ways possible and griping about hurt feelings.

That said, the battles are entertaining. There's a cracking escape scene in Vienna, where the Winter Soldier flees from the new-to-the-Marvel-movie-universe hero Black Panther (Chadwick Boseman), which truly shows off how good the Russos are at blending stunt work and CGI effects. And, of course, the centerpiece of the film is the huge, sustained battle royale between the two Civil War factions at the Leipzig Airport that's going to stand as the gold-standard for superhero action sequences for a long time. Again, the stakes are low, but, after countless Marvel movies where the heroes have fought anonymous aliens, robots, or sinister white men in suits, superheroes fighting superheroes is probably the most engaging match-up that Marvel has accomplished so far.

The sequence isn't without its faults. Many have complained that Marvel movies have lackluster visuals and scores and it's a valid complaint. Henry Jackman's orchestral arraignments are forgettable to a fault and Trent Opaloch's cinematography frames the action sequences well, but never really delivers any particularly stirring visual imagery. These films succeed more as superhero delivery systems than anything else and one wishes that the Marvel studio complex could find a way to make their hero stories less dogmatic to the comic books and more cinematic in nature.

That being said, the Russos are really good at delivering superhero content. Two of the film's biggest tangents involve introducing two "new" characters to the current Marvel cinematic universe: Black Panther and Spider-Man (Tom Holland). While both heroes could fairly easily be excised from the story, their additions ultimately work due to some inspired casting and better-than-average writing. Are they superfluous? Yes, but they're not boring, which makes them palatable to the audience.

Captain America: Civil War is a strong, engaging superhero story that deserves credit for thinking harder about its characters than most summer blockbusters usually do. There's a moment in the third act when Tony Stark's motivation for chasing the Winter Solider shifts from political to personal reasons that is legitimately thrilling because it makes so much sense on a character level. And that's an experience that is fairly atypical in a superhero movie. The Russo Brothers have now directed two of the most interesting movies in Marvel's canon. Hopefully, they can continue to push the studio to make their films more focused and memorable on a cinematic level and leave the fanboy pandering behind them.

Tom Burns

CREDITS

Steve Rogers/Captain America: Chris Evans
Tony Stark/Iron Man: Robert Downey, Jr.
Natasha Romanoff/Black Widow: Scarlett Johansson
Bucky Barnes/Winter Soldier: Sebastian Stan
Sam Wilson/Falcon: Anthony Mackie
Origin: United States
Language: English, German, Xhosa, Russian, Romanian
Released: 2016
Production: Kevin Feige; released by Marvel Studios
Directed by: Anthony Russo; Joe Russo
Written by: Christopher Markus; Stephen McFeely
Cinematography by: Trent Opaloch
Music by: Henry Jackman
Sound: Daniel Laurie; Shannon Mills
Editing: Jeffrey Ford; Matthew Schmidt
Art Direction: Greg Berry
Costumes: Judianna Makovsky
Production Design: Owen Paterson
MPAA rating: PG-13
Running time: 147 minutes

REVIEWS

Bouie, Jamelle. *Slate*. May 5, 2016.
Burr, Ty. *Boston Globe*. May 4, 2016.
Collin, Robbie. *The Telegraph*. April 20, 2016.
Farley, Jordan. *Total Film*. April 13, 2016.
Fischer, Russ. *The Playlist*. April 13, 2016.
Hornaday, Ann. *Washington Post*. May 4, 2016.
Jolin, Dan. *Empire*. April 13, 2016.
McWeeny, Drew. *Hitfix*. April 18, 2016.
Nashawaty, Chris. *Entertainment Weekly*. April 27, 2016.
Persall, Steve. *Tampa Bay Times*. May 4, 2016.

QUOTES

Black Panther: "Move, Captain. I won't ask a second time."

CAPTAIN FANTASTIC

He prepared them for everything except the outside world.
—Movie tagline

Box Office: $5.9 Million

With so much madness and attention given to wasteful, meaningless lifestyles in modern society, it's often the dream of many to simply check out for a while and get back to basics. Be it unplugging from social media for a time or taking a camping trip in which "roughing it" is the primary objective, most Americans often tinker with the idea of getting off the grid for a bit to recharge. Ben (Viggo Mortensen) the lead character in Matt Ross' wonderful sophomore effort *Captain Fantastic*, takes this notion a step further as he's moved his entire family of six into the wilds of the Pacific Northwest where they spend their time exercising, reading philosophy, and obtaining food from gardening and hunting. For entertainment, they rock-climb, debate philosophical notions, and play their own instruments. In many ways, their existence seems to be an idealistic one, but, at its core, the basis for the family's wild lifestyle is all about "sticking it to the man" by becoming highly intelligent, resourceful, and physically above average. Sadly, as Ben knows, these are all ideals that do not really take up top spots in modern America. So, therefore, having his children become smarter, faster, and stronger than average American kids is truly an act of rebellion. Yet as *Captain Fantastic* shows viewers, an idealized, book-learned life may make one able to switch between being a Maoist one day and a Leninist the next, but it doesn't make one able to fit in socially in a world of unaligned values.

Captain Fantastic opens with Ben's family covered in black mud, skulking in the woods. Suddenly, a deer comes into a meadow, and, before long, it's hunted and killed with only a hunting knife and bare hands. As is soon revealed, the kill is a rite of passage for Ben's eldest son Bo, and Ben christens him with the blood of his kill as Bo shows respect for the fallen beast by eating its organs raw. Ben and his brood grow their own food, sleep in handmade tents and forts, and are home-schooled (as it were) by Ben himself who shows how proud of a Papa he is as he beams at one of his pre-teen sons reading Dostoyevsky's *The Brothers Karamazov* by campfire. This almost secretive, idealistic world is dragged into the light as Ben's wife and mother of his children, Leslie (Trin Miller), dies after a long illness back in "the real world."

This escalates the dramatic tension as obviously not everyone is in favor of the way Ben has chosen to live his life and raise his children, especially Leslie's now grieving parents Jack and Abigail (solidly played by Frank Langella and Ann Dowd) who directly accuse Ben of contributing to Leslie's death. However, while Leslie may have been a bit more practical than Ben, she was also heavily in favor of the life they chose, so the challenges for the audience is expertly drawn out throughout the film and it becomes easy to see both sides of the argument for and against Ben's (and Leslie's) life choices. The film is well-balanced in this sense, which makes for stimulating viewing.

Perhaps the best segment of the film takes place as Ben and his kids travel to Leslie's funeral even though they have been forbidden to do so by the well-to-do and litigious Jack. On their way, the family makes a stop at a cousin's house, where a prototypical modern family of four lives happily content in a suburban existence. While heads of households Harper and Dave (Kathryn Hahn and Steve Zahn) try to do right by their grieving relatives by offering shelter and serving a sustainably raised, organic dinner for them, the cracks between two very different lifestyles are immediately thrust to the fore. Harper and Dave's children are disengaged creeps who can't seem to survive without a video game in their hand but this is sadly "normal" in America, so immediately Ben's kids seem like freaky outcasts. But again, this sets up a challenge for viewers, as it's clear the typical life of a suburban family ends up being a low-effort existence meant only to beget more stereotypical suburbanite families. Ben's kids are so smart and self-sufficient, they literally have no place in this modern world. And thus *Captain Fantastic* adds another important and well-balanced angle to the film in that one questions what is "the right way" to lead a life and raise a family.

Captain Fantastic is indeed a fantastic film and the way writer/director Matt Ross (perhaps best known for his role as the Bill Gates-esque Gavin Belson on HBO's comedy series *Silicon Valley*) handles such a range of topics, emotions, and styles so seamlessly is beyond impressive. *Captain Fantastic* is at once a family drama, a comedy, a treatise on life, love and death as well as a socially conscious film. And although it often teeters to the edge of becoming too much for its two-hour runtime, Ross manages to keep it all on course throughout.

Don R. Lewis

CREDITS

Ben: Viggo Mortensen
Jack: Frank Langella
Harper: Kathryn Hahn

Ellen: Missi Pyle
Dave: Steve Zahn
Origin: United States
Language: English
Released: 2016
Production: released by Electric City Entertainment, ShivHans Pictures
Directed by: Matt Ross
Written by: Matt Ross
Cinematography by: Stephane Fontaine
Music by: Alex Somers
Music Supervisor: Chris Douridas
Editing: Joseph Krings
Art Direction: Erick Donaldson
Costumes: Courtney Hoffman
Production Design: Russell Barnes
MPAA rating: R
Running time: 118 minutes

REVIEWS

Duralde, Alonso. *The Wrap.* January 27, 2016.
Greenblatt, Leah. *Entertainment Weekly.* July 7, 2016.
Hornaday, Ann. *Washington Post.* July 14, 2016.
Kaufman, Anthony. *Screen International.* January 26, 2016.
Kohn, Eric. *IndieWire.* July 7, 2016.
O'Malley, Sheila. *RogerEbert.com.* July 8, 2016.
Persall, Steve. *Tampa Bay Times.* July 26, 2016.
Suzanne-Meyer, Dominick. *Consequence of Sound.* July 7, 2016.
Travers, Peter, *Rolling Stone.* July 7, 2016.
Watson, Keith. *Slant Magazine.* July 15, 2016.

QUOTES

Rellian: "What kind of crazy person celebrates Noam Chomsky's birthday like it's some kind of official holiday? Why can't we celebrate Christmas like the rest of the entire world?"

Ben: "You would prefer to celebrate a magical fictitious elf, instead of a living humanitarian who's done so much to promote human rights and understanding?"

TRIVIA

George MacKay did yoga for three to four hours a day so he could do the advanced poses he did in the film, stating it was the hardest part of the shoot for him.

AWARDS

Nominations:

Oscars 2016: Actor (Mortensen)
British Acad. 2016: Actor (Mortensen)
Golden Globes 2017: Actor—Drama (Mortensen)
Ind. Spirit 2017: Actor (Mortensen)
Screen Actors Guild 2016: Actor (Mortensen), Cast

CEMETERY OF SPLENDOR
(Rak ti Khon Khaen)

Box Office: $51,950

The supremely gifted Thai director Apichatpong Weersethakul is a force of nature who seemingly exists in his own beguiling world as a very intuitive maker of images that draws on experimental and abstract theories yielding mysterious, haunting, and very original works of art.

Weersethakul's artisanal way of working and personal signature is like no other practicing filmmaker. Known more colloquially as "Joe," he studied filmmaking and painting at the school of the Art Institute of Chicago. He is a superstar on the international film festival circuit. He has directed six features, and co-directed another film. He has also made dozens of shorts, video essays, and art installation pieces.

His opaque works are the purest distillations of "slow cinema," intoxicating, sensual, and enigmatic movies infused with a painterly beauty and marked by their own very distinct rhythms. At their best, his movies offer a continuously open, adventurous, and exciting way of watching, thinking, and dreaming about what the medium is capable of.

The director's new work, *Cemetery of Splendor*, is like much of his output concerned with the fantastic and dreamy, inviting a submission to its slow and hypnotic beauty as it continually disrupts conventional ideas about narrative. His cinema is about posing questions more than providing answers, and what it all means and how the pieces all fit together floats and whirls inside the viewer's head.

Weersethakul is a magic realist who constructs his entrancing and strange works out of folk tales, anecdotes, memories, and ethnography. He tethers to the fantastic and sometimes otherworldly imagery very concrete ideas about love, thwarted desire, and regret. Central to his art is a very literary idea of the "transmogrification," or a radical or profound physical transformation, like his breakthrough third feature, *Tropical Malady* (2004). That movie utilized an allusive two-part structure about the erotically playful relationship of a soldier and an ice cream truck driver that evolves into a tale of obsession as the driver plunges deep into the interior of the jungle in search of the soldier who has assumed the shape of a ghost tiger.

His fifth feature, *Uncle Boonmee Who Can Recall his Past Lives* (2010), won the Palme d'Or for best film at the Cannes Film festival. The story of the protagonist ruminating on his past as contemplates his own death is also an eerie and devastating "ghost story," dramatically playing off recovered visions of his dead wife or the altered form of his son. In Weersethakul's cinema, ghosts are not spectral or specially conjured ectoplasms that frighten or unhinge but rather emanations that dance back and forth between spiritual and material domains, like the ghost of Hamlet's father.

Autobiographical underpinnings also shade much of his work. His fourth feature, *Syndromes and a Century* (2006), told the story of how his parents met working as doctors at a rural medical clinic. His movies have a ravishing sense of the physical and natural wonder with their contrast of light, air, and landscape. The Thai equivalent of the pastoral is the director's trademark, the lush and verdant northeast jungle his recurring backdrop.

The new movie has a two-part structure and is set in the director's native Khon Kaen, a village in northeastern Thailand in the region of Isan. The premise verges on the science fiction. The story is set around a former elementary school converted into an army hospital facility designed for the unusual care of a group of soldiers who have fallen prey to a peculiar "sleeping sickness," a coma-like state of suspended animation.

Jenjira (Weersethakul regular Jenjira Pongpas Widner) turns up as a volunteer aid worker at the clinic who helps administer care and emotional comfort in different capacities, as a reader, or more tenderly, as a masseuse who swabs their bodies with ointments and soap and water. She is preternaturally serene and patient despite her own significant physical disability, a deformed right leg that is shorter that requires her to move around on crutches and wear a specially fitted shoe.

She develops a special affection with a handsome young soldier named Itt (Banlop Lomnoi), a Southerner with no attendant family or friends to call upon. Their shared kinship appears natural and clear after Itt suddenly revives at the moment of a graceful encounter between them. The third member of the unusual emotional triangle is Keng (Jarinpattra Rueangram), a medium who says she is able to read the desires and feelings of the somnolent soldiers and convey their thoughts to loved ones.

Weersethakul is a wry and observant humorist, and the presence of Keng leads to some dryly funny and touching moments. "I heard he has a mistress. Can you ask where he keeps her?" asks one of the wives as she stands over her husband. Keng tells Jenjira complains to Jenjira at another time: "They keep asking for lottery numbers. I don't see the future."

Jenjira is increasingly drawn into the soldier's emotional life. Married to an American expatriate (Richard Abramson) she met on the internet, Jenjira lights a prayer offering for Itt at a Buddhist temple. In a terrific scene, the two goddess statues poised atop the shrine materialize in human shape (played by Sjittraporn Wongsrikeaw and Bhattaratorn Skenraigul). In the cinema of Weersethakul, ghosts or spirits that take sentient form are invariably a dramatic rupture.

The goddesses offer a rationale for the soldiers' condition, suggesting they are never likely to recover because of the ground they now inhabit is a former royal cemetery for kings who died in a bloody war thousands of years earlier. "The spirits of the kings are drawing on the soldiers' energy to fight their battles," one of the princesses says.

The first part concludes with the most beautiful and poetically sustained visual passage in the film, a nearly 10-minute collage that invokes the extraordinary closing movement of Michelangelo Antonioni's *L'eclisse* (1962) as the camera retraces the physical spaces and architecture of its young lovers. In haunting and powerful images framed by ideas of solitude, Weersethakul strings together a succession of images: an overhead fan, a park street light, a billboard advertising a photography wedding studio, and another overhead shot of a labyrinth of escalators inside a movie theater complex that bleeds into a long dissolve of the interior of the clinic.

The use of light and composition is masterly, the subtle and intricate gradation of color capturing behavior, action, movement, and passing of time. The moment crystallizes Weersethakul's particular talent for infusing heightened sensation and feeling from the random or seemingly ordinary of objects. Itt moves in and out of consciousness though in the moments when he is awake, his senses are heightened. At the hospital, the doctors have installed special neon fluorescent pylons and hung them over each bed. The space is now aglow, the subtly altered patterns and colors giving way to infinite possibilities.

If much of the first movement unfolds almost entirely within interiors, the second half is more enigmatic, lilting, and strange as the imagery turns even more associative and free form, seemingly unconcerned with linear or segmented narrative. In the plein air, or "open air," the two women move through the landscape, punctuated by musical interludes, like a park roundelay as a group of men and women abruptly switch place among the benches.

Weersethakul at his most liberated is his most entrancing as the narrative line becomes ever more complicated, even diffuse, as Keng becomes the stand-in or conduit for the sleep-stricken Itt. Trying to parse all the meanings is less important than submitting to the strangeness and power of the moment. Weersethakul turns cinema into music, violating order and motion in favor of a mélange of moods, feelings, and actions.

As a movie, *Cemetery of Splendor* is meant to savor. The biggest complaint is the movie signifies more of a continuation than an advancement of the director's art. The cinematographer Diego Garcia, working with for the first time, invests every image with a clarity though power and texture. The movie is demanding but never punishing. The film does what the form is meant: it moves, slowly certainly at times, but always with confidence, energy, and a sense of mystery.

Jenjira Pongpas Widner has appeared in every one of the director's films since *Blissfully Yours* (2002). Her lack of technique is just right. (Her reaction to one of the princesses when she says they are dead is brilliant.) His actors, almost all of them nonprofessional, are direct, plain, and impossible to forget. They take the strange and unaccountable and make it deeply, recognizably human.

Patrick Z. McGavin

CREDITS

Jenjira: Jenjira Pongpas
Itt: Banlop Lomnoi
Keng: Jarinpattra Rueangram
Nurse Tet: Petcharat Chaiburi
The Mediator: Tuwatchai Buawat
Origin: Thailand, United Kingdom, Germany, France, Malaysia, South Korea, United States, Mexico, Norway
Language: English, Thai
Released: 2015
Production: Charles de Meaux, Simon Field, Hans W. Geissendorfer, Keith Griffiths, Michael Weber, Apichatpong Weerasethakul; released by Kick the Machine
Directed by: Apichatpong Weerasethakul
Written by: Apichatpong Weerasethakul
Cinematography by: Diego Garcia
Editing: Lee Chatametikool
Art Direction: Pichan Muangduang
MPAA rating: Unrated
Running time: 122 minutes

REVIEWS

Anderson, Melissa. *Village Voice*. March 1, 2016.
Chang, Justin. *Variety*. May 20, 2015.
Cooper, Julia. *Globe and Mail*. March 10, 2016.
Ehrlich, David. *Time Out New York*. September 18, 2015.
Johnson, G. Allen. *San Francisco Chronicle*. March 24, 2016.
Kenny, Glenn. *New York Times*. March 3, 2016.
Lattimer, James. *Slant Magazine*. September 21, 2015.
Lindsen, Sheri. *Los Angeles Times*. March 10, 2016.
Mintzer, Jordan. *Hollywood Reporter*. May 20, 2015.
O'Malley, Sheila. *RogerEbert.com*. March 4, 2016.

QUOTES

Sign post: Hunger for Heaven will lead you to Hell.

CENTRAL INTELLIGENCE

Saving the world takes a little Hart and a big Johnson.
  —Movie tagline

Box Office: $127.4 Million

Central Intelligence is the story of two high school acquaintances becoming best friends later in life, as they find a type of partner in their quest to control their narrative. An opening sequence at a pep rally shows just how opposite their experiences are in these so-called formative years: Calvin (Kevin Hart, playing a 17-year-old with the help of very amusing special effects) is being praised by the entire school for being everyone's favorite peer, only to be interrupted by the public humiliation of Robert Weirdicht (Dwayne Johnson, with his face digitally placed on the body of an obese young man). Calvin cuts through the chorus laughing at a traumatized, naked Robert by giving the victim his letterman jacket. It proves to be a friendly gesture more permanent than the identities created in high school, one of many ways in which *Central Intelligence* has some striking, genuine things to say about maturity.

Two decades later, on the eve of their high school reunion, life is much different for Calvin. His status as a king of high school has meant nothing in the real world, where he works an unfulfilling accounting job and lives in the suburbs with his high school sweetheart. He receives a random Facebook friend request from a Bob Stone (whose mostly blank profile includes a love for unicorns, cinnamon pancakes, and guns), only to reveal himself as Robert from the past, a footnote resurrected. When the two meet for drinks, Robert reveals his new form, as jacked-up as he used to be overweight, with a big smile on his face and a big bear hug to give Calvin. Bob still considers Calvin royalty, especially because of how Calvin gave him the letterman jacket. When Calvin and Bob are accosted by a couple of ruffians in a bar, an otherwise peaceful Bob displays his immediate fighting reflexes, switching Bob's decades-later awe for Calvin "The Golden Jet" Joyner to Calvin's own confusion about who Bob has become.

It is a shame when the movie takes its full form as an action-comedy, with Bob revealed to be a CIA agent who has become an enemy of the state when key information for nuclear codes goes missing. Calvin is used by Bob for his accounting expertise, with Bob saying that an evil force called "The Black Badger" is trying to sell nuclear codes in an auction, while the CIA thinks that Bob is the Badger, and that he killed his former partner (played by Aaron Paul). The plot is too sloppy to ever legitimize *Central Intelligence* as a decent action-comedy, leaving the script to feign genre as it drags the viewer through scant action thrills in the process.

For the ever-so-charismatic Johnson, it is far and away one of his best characters, as if primed to bolster his strengths and polish his weaknesses. While his action implementation leaves more to be desired, it plays into his comedic timing, allowing him to play a type of innocent man-child ("I'm big into 'corns," he says when talking about unicorns) that any audience member would want to befriend. And for any time that Johnson's line delivery can be rocky, he can fall back on Bob's established awkwardness, the character's own muscly presence not guaranteeing one of smooth social skills.

A lack of inspiration for the action-comedy can be found in its lazy casting, which shows that putting Hart and Johnson together was a fleeting great idea by the film's producers. Amy Ryan plays the head CIA figure tracking down Bob and trying to use Calvin's confusion against Bob. She has an icy presence that grossly underestimates her ability for either comedy or even multi-dimensional performance. Even smaller parts come with a shrug, as Jason Bateman plays the modern day version of the WASP-y bully that humiliated Bob in the opening scene, but decades later without a change of perspective (recalling similar notes, but with much less power, as he did when playing a former bully in Joel Edgerton's *The Gift* [2015]). Extremely talented comedians Melissa McCarthy and Kumail Nanjiani are brought in for single scenes each, providing little to the story than more disappointment with their isolated, minuscule screen time.

Central Intelligence is the kind of event film that raises its own standards in some elements, in which the other lesser components drag the movie down. It has the charisma to be the next great buddy action-comedy, but Thurber fails to find his footing within the genre. Hart and Johnson orchestrate a few laugh-out-loud moments, with Hart's neuroses and Johnson's lethal teddy bear presence on display. But the sequences that Thurber engineers with standard Hollywood cutting and sporadically inspired hand-to-hand combat create little momentum for the story, despite working with Arnold Schwarzenegger's action hero apparent, Johnson. An escape scene from Calvin's office setting bestows a couple of surprises, namely with how characters hit each other, but the movie runs out of gas.

Bob's declared appreciation for *Sixteen Candles* (1984) is no throwaway reference; there are moments in which Thurber's film can relate to viewers as expansively as Hughes' high school movies do, but with the story of two men trying to understand what *The Breakfast Club*

taught in 1985. An impressive comedic and emotional foundation only takes this set-up so far, as Hughes' work countered so brilliantly, but as Thurber accepts with a disappointing shrug. Though the movie merits an audience with a historic buddy casting that will hopefully be used one day to full effect by a better writer/director, *Central Intelligence* is a story with identity issues of its own.

Nick Allen

CREDITS

Bob Stone: Dwayne "The Rock" Johnson
Calvin Joyner: Kevin Hart
Agent Pamela Harris: Amy Ryan
Maggie: Danielle Nicolet
Trevor: Jason Bateman
Origin: United States
Language: English
Released: 2016
Production: Peter Principato, Scott Stuber, Paul Young; released by Bluegrass Films, New Line Cinema L.L.C.
Directed by: Rawson Marshall Thurber
Written by: Rawson Marshall Thurber; Ike Barinholtz; David Stassen
Cinematography by: Barry Peterson
Music by: Ludwig Goransson; Theodore Shapiro
Sound: Tammy Fearing
Editing: Brian Scott Olds; Michael L. Sale
Costumes: Carol Ramsey
Production Design: Stephen J. Lineweaver
MPAA rating: PG-13
Running time: 107 minutes

REVIEWS

Bahr, Lindsey. *Associated Press*. June 16, 2016.
Brody, Richard. *New Yorker*. June 27, 2016.
Catsoulis, Jeannette. *New York Times*. June 16, 2016.
Chang, Justin. *Los Angeles Times*. June 16, 2016.
Ebiri, Bilge. *Village Voice*. June 17, 2016.
MacDonald, Moira. *Seattle Times*. June 16, 2016.
Merry, Stephanie. *Washington Post*. June 16, 2016.
Vishnevetsky, Ignatiy. *The A.V. Club*. June 16, 2016.
Willmore, Alison. *Buzzfeed News*. June 17, 2016.
Zacharek, Stephanie. *Time*. June 23, 2016.

QUOTES

Bob Stone: "You're like a snack-sized Denzel."

TRIVIA

Dwayne Johnson is one-foot, one-inch taller than Kevin Hart and weighs over 100 pounds more.

CERTAIN WOMEN

Box Office: $1 Million

Kelly Reichardt is one of the only true poets working in American cinema. From her debut *River of Grass* (1994), she's been observing the inner lives of American drifters with more acuity and tenderness than any one of her contemporaries. In her films *Wendy & Lucy* (2008), *Night Moves* (2013), and most especially in her latest, *Certain Women*, she's been able to show the profound movement of the human heart into darkness in the simplest actions. A character looks at his hands in *Night Moves* and we see him consider the entirety of his life in a few seconds. The personal becomes enormous in fitful bursts, mostly hidden behind blank expressions. *Certain Women*, based on the writings of Maile Meloy, might be Reichardt's most complete and beautiful film to date, thanks in part to its structure. It ricochets between three stories, with little echoes of each appearing throughout. In splitting her focus, Reichardt pays even more careful attention to the behavior of her characters because she has less time to arrive at her conclusions. The result is a lot of heartbreak every few minutes and one unforgettable movie.

In the first segment, Laura Wells (Laura Dern) is a lawyer having an affair with a married man named Ryan Lewis (James LeGros). After leaving their usual spot one afternoon she returns to the office to find her least favorite client, Fuller (Jared Harris) waiting for her. He's been pestering her relentlessly over a case she's told him time and again is unwinnable. A workplace accident left him with greatly diminished brain power, and, because he took an initial settlement from his bosses, he now has no grounds for a negligence suit. When he is not blaming everyone in creation for his lot in life, he's trying to get Laura to spend time with him so he can get to know her better, as he can't stand his own wife. Laura attempts to wash her hands of Fuller, but a little while after learning he can't press forward with his lawsuit, he breaks into a county office looking for the records affiliated with his case and takes a security guard hostage. Laura volunteers to go talk to him and winds up having to relive the months they spent working on the case through every testimony she uncovers in the files.

In the second storyline, Ryan's wife Gina (Michelle Williams) is enduring the last day of a family vacation. She and Ryan barely get along these days and their daughter Guthrie (Sara Rodier) resents her mother's attempts to force the family to spend time together. Guthrie's naturally put out when Gina adds one stop to their itinerary before going home. Gina and Ryan are planning a construction project and want to use sandstone for a significant part of it. The only place they know

where to get some is the front lawn of an acquaintance named Albert (Rene Auberjonois) who's losing his memory in his old age. Gina has to talk Albert into letting them take the stone from his property during one of his moments of lucidity, but even if they do manage, both Ryan and Gina plainly feel incredibly guilty about asking a dying man for what little he has left in life.

The third and final piece of the puzzle focuses on a nameless Rancher (Lily Gladstone) working a horse farm in a little town called Belfry, MT. Bored and lonely, she sets out one night looking for something to do and sees people driving into a community college. Intrigued, she goes in and discovers a class on law related to public school teaching. She learns nothing during from the class itself but is taken with Beth (Kristen Stewart), the tired woman instructing. Beth took the job before she realized how far away Belfry was from her hometown of Livingston, MT and it takes her four hours to drive there. She hates the job and wants to quit to focus on her work at a law firm but can't find anyone to take over for her. The Rancher does not know how to help her but as long as Beth is going to be coming into her orbit, she's going to show up for every class just to watch her teach and go out to a local diner afterwards for small talk. When Beth does not appear one night, the Rancher gets in her truck and makes the four-hour drive to Livingston. The only setback is that she has not quite worked out what she's going to do when she gets there.

Certain Women does many things right, but its most astonishing feat is understanding the ways in which loneliness manifests itself, how it can creep into any sort of circumstance. Reichardt perfectly captures the deeply troubling and affecting ways in which we combat isolation; the searching looks in the eyes of those who feel truly alone, even when feet away from your spouse or friends. We know exactly why The Rancher gets that look of puppyish glee in her eyes when she sits across from Beth at the diner because we're intimately acquainted with her daily routine. Reichardt shows the monotony of feeding and caring for horses not just to illustrate what the Rancher does when waiting to see Beth again, but also to illustrate what time apart from purpose, especially newly found, looks and feels like. Fuller's insane overreaction to losing his chances at regaining his dignity with his lawsuit makes perfect sense because we see what he can't help but express to Laura, a woman he ostensibly wants to impress. His mood flips from murderous rage to uncontrollable melancholy in no time at all, thanks in part to the accident that left him unable to read. He just wants someone to tell him everything is going to be OK. Gina looks at her husband and daughter and sees nothing she can relate to. She sees only that they lack the skills necessary to understand and care for her. She sees more of herself in the blank stare Albert gives her from his window as she takes the sandstone off his front lawn. Michelle Williams and Rene Auberjonois manage to communicate years of woe in those few seconds they share together. Albert has been abandoned and Gina looks like she wonders if she will be too. The film's piercing gaze at the agony of having no one reflect your humanity back at you is unforgettable, as are Reichardt's haunting compositions of the unforgiving Montana landscape. As the Rancher says when Beth asks her if she knows anyone who can take over her class: "I don't know anyone."

Scout Tafoya

CREDITS

Laura: Laura Dern
Elizabeth Travis: Kristen Stewart
Gina: Michelle Williams
Ryan: James LeGros
Fuller: Jared Harris
The Rancher: Lily Gladstone
Origin: United States
Language: English
Released: 2016
Production: Neil Kopp, Vincent Savino, Anish Savjani; released by Film Science, Stage 6 Films
Directed by: Kelly Reichardt
Written by: Kelly Reichardt
Cinematography by: Christopher Blauvelt
Music by: Jeff Grace
Sound: Casey Langfelder
Editing: Kelly Reichardt
Art Direction: Kat Uhlmansiek
Costumes: April Napier
Production Design: Anthony Gasparro
MPAA rating: R
Running time: 107 minutes

REVIEWS

Burr, Ty. *Boston Globe*. October 20, 2016.
Chang, Justin. *Los Angeles Times*. October 13, 2016.
Dowd, A.A. *The A.V. Club*. October 12, 2016.
Hornaday, Ann. *Washington Post*. October 20, 2016.
Kaufman, Anthony. *Screen International*. January 26, 2016.
Murray, Noel. *The Playlist*. January 26, 2016.
Phillips, Michael. *Chicago Tribune*. October 20, 2016.
Raup, Jordan. *The Film Stage*. January 26, 2016.
Tallerico, Brian. *RogerEbert.com*. October 14, 2016.
Wolfe, April. *Village Voice*. October 13, 2016.

TRIVIA

Reichardt revealed that one of the reasons she chose to shoot on film was because snow appears "flat" in other formats.

AWARDS

Nominations:

Ind. Spirit 2017: Actress—Supporting (Gladstone), Director (Reichardt)

THE CHOICE

Let your heart decide.
    —Movie tagline

Box Office: $18.7 Million

On the narrow, tilted spectrum of Nicholas Sparks' movies, *The Choice* inspires what almost amounts to a rare recommendation with an asterisk. This remains corny, manipulative, formulaic garbage, but it is enhanced by star chemistry and a tangible sense of romance.

In the film's sun-drenched, minority-free coastal North Carolina setting, Travis (Benjamin Walker) is just a typical ladies' man veterinarian with a heart of gold, not counting his propensity to play loud music at night and wield his smirking confidence like a battering ram. At first, it is more than enough to get under the skin of his new neighbor, Gabby (Teresa Palmer), who has exactly the movie version of initial loathing that suggests an inevitable softening. She quickly sees her charming annoyance's softer side when his dog impregnates her dog and Gabby needs Travis' help. Of course, he is also the kind of playboy who jokingly but sincerely says things like, "There's nothing cuter than puppies in a basket," so this bad boy clearly exists in the sort of PG-13-rated universe where heartbreakers are really just waiting for the right person to come along.

There is never any doubt that the right person is Gabby, even though Travis long has had an on-again, off-again relationship with Monica (Alexandra Daddario), the kind of throwaway character destined to say something like "You'll never look at me the way you look at her." Meanwhile, Travis' sister (Maggie Grace) and friends exist only to comment on his love life, which does not take particularly long to trend in the direction of his new neighbor. That means the invitation to a boat party and a very deliberate observation from director Ross Katz's camera of how Gabby looks in a bikini. This prompts Travis to inform his dog, "Might be in trouble, boy."

It might all seem like pure hokum, a copy of a copy of Sparks' fondness (seen most recently in 2015's *The*

Longest Ride and 2014's *The Best of Me*) for predictable, contrived, tragedy-laced stories about a white man and a white woman separated by class differences that may or may not actually matter. Except Walker, in what might have been a breakout role if anyone took Sparks movies seriously at this point, and Palmer (who deserves more starring roles as well) build the foundation of a relationship that is no less than the entire crux of the movie. And they do so with only mild conflict until the whopper of a third act representing some of the worst of the author's need for terrible things to happen out of nowhere (for the record, Bryan Sipe wrote the script). *The Choice* seeks only to put two people in the same place and observe the degree to which they will break through barriers of varying size to be together for most of its running time. Gabby has a boyfriend (Tom Welling), though that he is a doctor who is a bit more refined than Travis seems especially unnecessary considering the latter's lucrative line of work.

It is no small achievement that Walker and Palmer so naturally establish a progressing dynamic between Travis and Gabby, who realize that once it is clear that change is on the way, people can either go with the tide or get swept underneath it, especially when that means discovering a feeling that simply cannot be suppressed. They transition from animosity to genuine spark without losing the sense of excitement. Instead, it is as if the world has opened up and revealed itself to them more clearly than they might have imagined seeing it before.

That makes it all the more exasperating when *The Choice,* for no identifiable reason, turns into an issue-driven euthanasia drama. Certainly no viewer expects this when Travis notes in the film's embarrassing opening voiceover, "Now, pay attention. 'Cause I'm about to tell you the secret to life. You ready? The whole damn thing is about decisions. Little, seemingly insignificant decisions that clear the road for monster-truck, life-altering ones. You see, every path we take leads to another choice, and some choices will change everything. Every damn moment for the rest of your life hangs on them. And, boy, do I got a choice I gotta make." Nothing about this is insightful in the least, and it suggests only, say, that he will have to decide between two women. Not that he will sit and ponder whether or not his wife will reach the 90-day point of a coma, at which her doctor (her ex-fiancée, which seems like a major conflict of interest breaking HIPAA) says she will become unlikely to wake up and should then follow through on a DNR document Travis accurately recognizes was meant for much later in life.

If *The Choice* really had dared to engage the terrifying and painful day-to-day of living in doubt while a loved one lies in the hospital, perhaps it would have become a deeper exploration of love. The story would open up into not just a document of the tingle-inducing early days but the devastating possibilities of the long-term. That would involve hard truths about impact on children and spouses, though, along with jobs and finances and much more. This is a movie in which Gabby says she believes in the moon and the stars and Travis does not run screaming in the opposite direction. Cutesiness is par for the course, but it's worth repeating how a rich sense of actual connection can transcend that. Sitting on the water, under the moon with the right person, looks irresistible in almost any movie, even if, a steamy kitchen scene aside, the presentation at times feels like true love for kids. "You bother me," Travis tells Gabby with a smile. They delight in the idea of bothering each other forever because once you feel a certain way, that itch is not going to go away, or scratch itself.

Matt Pais

CREDITS

Travis: Benjamin Walker
Gabby: Teresa Palmer
Steph: Maggie Grace
Monica: Alexandra Daddario
Shep: Tom Wilkinson
Origin: United States
Language: English
Released: 2016
Production: Theresa Park, Peter Safran, Nicholas Sparks; released by Safran Co.
Directed by: Ross Katz
Written by: Bryan Sipe
Cinematography by: Alar Kivilo
Music by: Marcelo Zarvos
Sound: Steven Iba
Music Supervisor: Marguerite Phillips
Editing: Lucy Donaldson; Joe Klotz
Costumes: Alex Bovaird
Production Design: Mark Garner
MPAA rating: PG-13
Running time: 111 minutes

REVIEWS

Dowd, A.A. *The A.V. Club.* February. 4, 2016.
Eichel, Molly. *Philadelphia Enquirer.* February 5, 2016.
Goldstein, Gary. *Los Angeles Times.* February 4, 2016.
Lewis, David. *San Francisco Chronicle.* February 4, 2016.
Moore, Roger. *Movie Nation.* February 4, 2016.
Roeper, Richard. *Chicago Sun-Times.* February 4, 2016.
Russo, Tom. *Boston Globe.* February 4, 2016.

Savlov, Marc. *Austin Chronicle*. February 10, 2016.
Snydel, Michael. *Film Stage*. February 5, 2016.
Worthington, Clint. *Consequence of Sound*. February 9, 2016.

QUOTES

Travis: "Why do you make it so hard for me to flirt with you?"
Gabby: "Because if I made it easy you wouldn't flirt with me anymore."

TRIVIA

This film is Nicholas Sparks' eleventh book made into a movie.

CITY OF GOLD

Discover the world, one meal at a time.
—Movie tagline

Box Office: $611,702

Much like the subject of the film of Laura Gabbert's *City of Gold*, *Los Angeles Times* food critic Jonathan Gold, the film itself is an understated wealth of insightful, inspiring, and whimsical looks at life, culture, music, and most of all, food. Like an amazing, nearly mind-altering meal discovered at a tiny, out-of-the-way location, *City of Gold* is indeed a film about the life and loves of its subject, but also touches upon the relevance of informed criticism to all art forms, the importance of educated and qualified people sharing information and pushing oneself to look outside their normal, day-to-day existence to discover something new. In many ways, *City of Gold* mimics Gold's passions as it comes across like a meal with a wild variety of flavors melded together to became a complete whole.

The subject of food critics and the havoc they can wreak if served a bad meal has been well-covered over the years in films like *Big Night* (1996), *Ratatouille* (2007), and *Chef* (2014), and, typically, the critic is portrayed as a food snob. Egomaniacal and snooty, the food critic in film has become quite the cliché. Jonathan Gold is pretty much the antithesis of any food critic seen onscreen to date. Schlubby and shy, he never comes off condescending or arrogant. Another twist on Gold's food critic persona is that rather than hit up the newest, hippest, and fanciest eateries on his Los Angeles home turf, Gold prefers to scour the ethnically diverse city to find the tiniest mom and pop eateries that lie off the beaten path. Rather than the glitz and glamour of a high-priced, new-fangled restaurant, one might typically find Gold hunkered down at a strip-mall taco shop.

As a result, Gold's writing has not only earned him diehard fans who love both his writing style and yen for great food, it also garnered him a 2007 Pulitzer Prize for writing, which the Pulitzer committee said was for "his zestful, wide ranging restaurant reviews, expressing the delight of an erudite eater." As if the award of a Pulitzer for writing about food wasn't odd enough, Gold has also morphed into a sort of ethnographic and cultural historian whose reviews obviously cover food but also trace the rich history of migration and immigration of diverse cultures into Los Angeles. Like the field collector of music, Alan Lomax, Gold seeks to try out the wide variety of foods available to him (and, anyone really) and inform readers what the recipes reflect and what they mean in terms of flavor, region, and cultural background. By inviting people to try new things (as Lomax did when encouraging people to listen to small, regional music by recording it and cataloguing it for posterity) Gold is the rare critic who has a way with words that might make one consider a delicacy like deer penis or boar tongue whereas before, it might seem more like a dare to try such things.

City of Gold opens with Gold driving around L.A. in his beat-up truck talking about a major passion of his, tacos. Not fancy arugula tacos spiced with truffle oil expunged from a rare spore in Germany. No, he's searching for straight-up, homemade tacos with recipes passed down through generations. The film is buffered by interviews with several well-known chefs who comment about finding a small, out-of-the-way eatery that they can't wait to tell friends about only to look over and see a review from Gold already on the wall, a best kept secret no more. Other chefs marvel at how a regular Caucasian, Jewish guy like Gold can know as much if not more about the cuisine they specialize in than them. Of course, this becomes a bit of an issue in the film as there's really no balance to the subject, *City of Gold* is basically a love letter to Jonathan Gold and that's o.k.

As a way to insert some balance and conflict into the film, a lengthy section dives into how the role of criticism has changed with the democratization of opinions via the Internet. Anyone can write a movie review on Amazon or an album review on iTunes and it can resonate. Anyone can review a restaurant on Yelp no matter how unqualified they really are and those opinions have grown to matter, sometimes more than those of actual skilled and paid critics. There seems to be an idea growing that specialized, educated critics have some kind of agenda and are snobs. There's still value in a person educated on the subject of which they're criticizing having their opinion count a little more than someone who just has an uninformed, off-the-cuff opinion, and a Wi-Fi signal.

City of Gold is a wonderful documentary because of the way it introduces a subject who is not well-known and chronicles their intriguing story. Gold is an interesting, odd character, who, after being a dedicated cellist discovered punk rock and L.A. gansta rap and began chronicling local bands and musical movements. In fact, many tip the cap to him in terms of bringing artists like Snoop Dog and Dr. Dre to the fore during his time as a music critic at Rolling Stone. Yet eventually, Gold found his zone, which is food writing and anyone who reads his work is honestly better for it.

Don R. Lewis

CREDITS

Origin: United States
Language: English
Released: 2016
Directed by: Laura Gabbert
Written by: Laura Gabbert
Cinematography by: Jerry Henry; Goro Toshima
Music by: Bobby Johnston
MPAA rating: R
Running time: 96 minutes

REVIEWS

Cheshire, Godfrey. *RogerEbert.com*. March 14, 2016.
First, Devra. *Boston Globe*. March 24, 2016.
Harvey, Dennis. *Variety*. January 20, 2016.
Ivanov, Oleg. *Slant Magazine*. March 7, 2016.
Izzo, Christina. *Time Out New York*. March 10, 2016.
Kang, Inkoo. *TheWrap*. March 8, 2016.
Nicholson, Amy. *Village Voice*. February 1, 2015.
Oller, Jacob. *Film Stage*. March 10, 2016.
Scott, A.O. *New York Times*. March 10, 2016.
Shah, Ibad. *IndieWire*. February 9, 2015.

TRIVIA

Jonathan Gold played the cello while he studied at UCLA.

THE CLUB
(El Club)

Box Office: $52,761

At the start of *The Club*, a man with a death-haunted look turns up at a modestly appointed yellow beach house that juts above a sandy ridge in the coastal Chilean town of La Boca. The director, Pablo Larraín, and the cinematographer, Sergio Armstrong, zero in tightly on the man's grizzled face to expose a mask of pain and sorrow.

The man, a disgraced priest named Lazcano (Jose Soza), appears frozen in time—the widescreen image amplifies the loss of status. The moment is further jolted by the sudden appearance of another stranger, first heard from inside the house and now perched outside a hill. The man, a local fisherman named Sandokan (Roberto Farias), shouts in graphic detail accusations of sexual and violent abuse he endured as a young child under the tutelage of the priest.

Violence soon erupts and sets in motion a story that works most effectively as a forensic and moral investigation into the complicated and contradictory nature of punishment. The setting—a sanctuary or safe house where four damaged men and a fallen woman live—sternly calls to attention how the sins of the past float over the present. It is a kind of eternal loop of passivity and denial that ensnares both the perpetrators and the victims alike.

The early scenes, captured without dialogue, establish the seemingly innocuous daily rhythms. The inhabitants of the beach house are glimpsed in their solitary activity or group movements. The older men convey little sense of excitement or interest as their movements are marked almost entirely by isolation and self-containment. Their lone sense of joy appears to come from the training they participate in with a greyhound that performs in the local dog racing circuit. Even that thrill is furtive and discrete and shown from a curious remove—the men watch the action through binoculars from a nearby hilltop.

The "club" is more accurately a prison, as bitterly described by one of the group. The men are defrocked or excommunicated priests suffering in purgatory and doing penance for their various sins or misdeeds. Their highly regimented lives and personal actions are overseen by the sister, Monica (Antonia Zegers, the director's wife). As laid down by her the rules of conduct are deeply regulated—the restricted times the men are permitted into the town, strict refusal of social interaction, and the rules forbidding self-flagellation or masturbation.

"You and I are condemned to be dishonest bodies," Father Vidal (Alfredo Castro), a sad and circumspect man, informs his interlocutor, a Jesuit named Father Garcia (Marcelo Alonso). The new priest is sent by the Vatican to investigate the circumstances of the violent action. The presence of Garcia, a crisis counselor who claims to represent a "new church," is openly resented by the men who think he is there to absolve the church of any culpability and also to find a rationale to close the club down.

The interviews, staged in two-shots and often in cramped spaces, forms the crux of the film as the confrontational format allows the director to reveal the particulars of the priests' transgressions. The absence of any easy moral outrage is both bracing and disturbing. These sequences make up the strongest parts of the film as the tension and byplay ratchet off each other, their startling self-justification and perverse denial played in sharp contrast with the loftier ambitions and piety of Garcia.

Father Vidal idealizes his sexual attractiveness to the young as the purest distillation of God's love. Father Ortega (Alejandro Goic) insists he acted out of a deeper egalitarian impulse and desire for social justice in facilitating a black market by forcing poor young women to give up their children to wealthy couples. Father Silva (Jaime Vadell), who served as an army chaplain for 35 years, claims himself a pawn of Auguste Pinochet's vindictive military class. Father Ramirez (Alejandro Sieveking) is the most enigmatic member, his failings mostly unknown, the man a blank slate as his mind is ruptured by dementia.

Sandokan is the movie's true tragic figure, a slippery and strange man who hovers over the proceedings. He is a stark reminder and tragic emblem of the moral failure wrought by these men. Those sins of the past have ruptured his state of consciousness, the man trapped between states of grace and despair. He has little sense of balance or the emotional display of feelings. In the most disquieting scene of the film, he proves himself incapable of carrying out a normal outlet for his sexual expression—the only way he achieves satisfaction is by having the woman mimic the same predatory habits.

Born in Santiago in 1976, three years after the dictator Pinochet seized power, Larraín has been drawn to the corrupting nature of authoritarianism with its attendant cruelty, extreme social inequity, and lack of political or intellectual freedom. The Club fits squarely into the moral and artistic terrain Larraín has addressed—directly and more obliquely—in his preceding loose trilogy: *Tony Manero* (2008), *Post Mortem* (2010), and *No* (2012).

Those films pulsed with anger, sadness, and pessimism. The best of the three, *No*—funny, profane, and more freewheeling—was by far the most liberating, in tone and style, based on the remarkable true story of a progressive advertising campaign deployed to remove Pinochet democratically from power. For better and worse, this film is more direct, punishing, and grim.

The movie is blunt and sporadically powerful but also mechanical and too determined in its plot and architecture to fully work as a drama. For a movie that pivots on emotional or personal aspects of discovery, the movie works toward a perceived conclusion rather than adequately illuminate human behavior or action. The filmmaker retains his anger at the institutional abuses and cover up of the Catholic Church. Too often the personal is swallowed up.

Larraín wrote the script in collaboration with Guillermo Calderon and Daniel Villalobos. The director is a skilled visual stylist, but he works too hard to achieve a formal look that subverts the emotional authenticity of the scene. The interrogations between Garcia and the priests are marred by the too fussy design—the edges of the frame deliberately blurred by a scrim of grime. It is unfortunately delivered here, moving from an eerie restraint to an aggrieved sense of violation that packs a wallop.

Larraín works in some very powerful and complex ideas, about moral inquiry and the nature of good and evil. Unfortunately, his best ideas suffer from a reliance on symbolism—Sandokan imagined as a Christ martyr, like the moment he drags a chair through the streets. Conceptually, the daring of *The Club* is that how it implicates the viewer without release in deeply uncomfortable proximity to a particular brand of horror. The drama is both too explicit and at times insufficiently shaped and developed.

The movie turns ugly in the last moments in a series of overlapping violent reprisals and vigilante movements carried out in a perverse bid at closure. The filmmakers lack the courage of their own convictions. The ending is a grubby and annihilating fate that denies a more complex portrait of the consequences of pain and suffering.

Patrick Z. McGavin

CREDITS

Padre Vidal: Alfredo Castro
Sandokan: Robert Farias
Hermana Monica: Antonia Zegers
Padre Garcia: Marcelo Alonso
Padre Silva: Jaime Vadell
Origin: United States
Language: Spanish
Released: 2016
Production: Juan de Dios Larrain, Pablo Larrain; released by Fabula
Directed by: Pablo Larrain
Written by: Pablo Larrain; Guillermo Calderon; Daniel Villalobos
Cinematography by: Sergio Armstrong
Music by: Carlos Cabezas
Editing: Sebastian Sepulveda
Art Direction: Estefania Larrain
Costumes: Estefania Larrain

Production Design: Estefania Larrain
MPAA rating: Unrated
Running time: 98 minutes

REVIEWS

Abele, Robert. *Los Angeles Times.* February 11, 2016.
Ebiri, Bilge. *Vulture.* February 9, 2016.
Dowd, A.A. *The A.V. Club.* February 3, 2016.
Foundas, Scott. *Variety.* February 9, 2015.
Keough, Peter. *Boston Globe.* February 18, 2016.
Kiang, Jessica. *Playlist.* December 10, 2015.
O'Sullivan, Michael. *Washington Post.* February 18, 2016.
Savlov, Marc. *Austin Chronicle.* March 9, 2016.
Scott, A.O. *New York Times.* February 5, 2016.
Sullivan, Kevin P. *Entertainment Weekly.* February 10, 2016.

TRIVIA

The film was Chile's entry for Best Foreign Language Film at the 88th Academy Awards, but was not nominated.

AWARDS

Nominations:
Golden Globes 2016: Foreign Film

COLLATERAL BEAUTY

We are all connected.
—Movie tagline

Box Office: $30.9 Million

At once mawkish and militant about its mission to deliver capital-F feelings, *Collateral Beauty* is so wrapped up in smug, self-satisfied notions of it being a thinking person's tearjerker that it never stops to untangle its narrative and truly get down into the bones of the characters in which it is asking viewers to emotionally invest. Starring Will Smith as a bereaved and somewhat mentally unstable advertising executive unwittingly being steered by worried friends, this heavily plotted, overly manipulative drama is a Hollywood studio-stamped imitation of life—glossy, and at times pretty to look at, but nourishing for neither the mind nor the soul.

Clocking in at only 94 minutes but feeling much, much longer, *Collateral Beauty* opened wide against *Rogue One: A Star Wars Story* on December 16, and in addition to suffering the slings and arrows of ignominious critical shaming, took a financial bath in theaters, limping to just over $7 million in its opening weekend—the lowest opening of Smith's career. In the end, it struggled to even match the underwhelming $35 million domestic

gross of *Concussion* (2015), Smith's Christmas effort the previous year.

It is usually a fool's game to analyze a film in comparison to alternate versions of its telling that did not materialize, but in the case of *Collateral Beauty* it is not only instructive, but somewhat illuminating. Scripted by Allan Loeb, the film was originally set up with Alfonso Gomez-Rejon as its director and Hugh Jackman as its star, before both individually departed for other projects, the former citing creative differences. That pairing seems intriguing. Everything about *Collateral Beauty* as realized, though, comes across as soft and fuzzy—it is a movie that feels constructed of felt pieces and rounded corners, with any jagged, recognizably human contours of anguish and misery sanded down into more comfortable, audience-friendly expressions of sadness.

Gomez-Rejon, coming off of the fresh, funky *Me and Earl and the Dying Girl* (2015), likely envisioned something a little more idiosyncratic, if still swollen with feeling, in Loeb's source material. Whatever one thinks of Frankel, who has made some good movies, he remains a pliable and less immediately distinctive voice than Gomez-Rejon—an infinitely more relaxing and less risk-averse selection for a studio looking to crank out four-quadrant commercial pablum. Smith, too, over dials the earnestness and pitiableness when compared to what one can reasonably imagine from Jackman—he pantomimes hollowness, which still occasionally emotionally connects, courtesy of Smith's enormously expressive visage and personality. But it is showy and slightly off-putting nonetheless, in a role that, owing to the failings of an overwritten script, definitively requires less rather than more.

Collateral Beauty centers on Howard Inlet (Smith), the CEO of an advertising firm who, two years after the death of his daughter, is still locked in a state of willfully exclusionary grief. He comes to work, but doesn't speak to anyone—instead spending his time constructing domino chains. At home he writes letters addressed to Time, Death, and Love—abstractions that Howard, presented as a gifted communicator and savant, has previously identified as the three basic animating preoccupations of human life.

With Howard's firm floundering, a trio of his longtime friends and colleagues—Whit Yardsham (Ed Norton), Claire Wilson (Kate Winslet), and Simon Scott (Michael Peña)—devise a last-ditch plan to save their jobs and the company, facilitating a friendly takeover bid by helping to publicly spotlight Howard's mental competency, or lack thereof. Specifically, amending an idea from Whit based on an old commercial, the group hires three actors—Aimee (Keira Knightley), Brigitte

(Helen Mirren), and Raffi (Jacob Latimore)—who are looking to fund their own low-budget theatrical production to portray the aforementioned ideas in a series of staged public interactions with Howard. The plan is that a private investigator (Ann Dowd) will then record these scenes and digitally erase evidence of the actors, leaving Howard's friends with the sort of digital evidence of his devolved mental proficiency that will force a sale of the company. Parallel to all this, Howard finally starts taking small proactive steps for self-betterment, attending a peer grief counseling group led by Madeleine (Naomie Harris).

Collateral Beauty is rather bafflingly constructed, seemingly in reverse-engineered fashion. In addition to its narrative hook and the attraction of a lot of supporting roles capable of being "cast up" and filled with stars in a New York-based production (as much a consideration in studio non-genre green-lighting these days as any legitimately creative note), it clearly has a few big notecard moments that could fool someone giving it just a quick glance into thinking it had something interesting to say about loss and grief.

At its core, though, *Collateral Beauty* peddles a conceit that is dubious at best, and morally reckless at worst—that sometimes, in order to help people you love, you have to first do them great harm. This is dumb, on its face. It is not that no one involved in making the movie grasped this point; the film pays lip service to Whit and Claire and Simon's distress throughout, and features a penultimate scene that attempts to wring crocodile tears from their pangs of regret. But Frankel does not stage any of these feelings in an honest way, and Loeb's screenplay is less interested in grappling with human complexity than it is in working extra-hard to set up a "twist" ending that falls completely flat. Additionally, Loeb's stab at love-death-time parallelism with Howard's friends (divorced parent Whit grapples with his daughter's anger, cancer survivor Simon suffers a setback, and Claire yearns for children but worries her biological window may be closing) also comes across as ham-fisted and phony, wasting time that could be devoted to more substantively exploring its other characters.

Collateral Beauty suffers from the added misfortune of arriving in the same theatrical release window as *Manchester by the Sea* (2016), another movie about an emotionally shattered man who retreats from the world and shuts out those who sincerely care about him and might help him climb up the steep cliffside of grief. Everything about writer-director Kenneth Lonergan's film has a weighted authenticity; it is somber without being suffocating, and lined with small, flinty moments of dark humor rooted in pathos. *Manchester by the Sea* is about learning to cope with the scars of the past without

letting them completely define and destroy you—about the utilitarian value of psychological boundaries, but also some of their limits, and expiration date. *Collateral Beauty* unfolds in the same space, but is about nothing so much as cattle-prodding an audience toward a wading pool marked "empathy."

As mentioned, Smith achieves a few moments of connection, but also feels in large measure miscast. The rest of the actors for the most part acquit themselves—Mirren in particular has fun, giving Brigitte a slightly self-centered buoyancy that is amusing. But for the most part they are mere pawns on *Collateral Beauty*'s board—ironically, they are all playing ideas rather than real characters. It is fitting for a movie that thinks it is playing chess, but is in fact not even adept at checkers.

Brent Simon

CREDITS

Howard: Will Smith
Whit: Edward Norton
Claire: Kate Winslet
Simon: Michael Pena
Brigitte: Helen Mirren
Madeleine: Naomie Harris
Amy: Keira Knightley
Origin: United States
Language: English
Released: 2016
Production: Anthony Bregman, Bard Dorros, Kevin Scott Frakes, Michael Sugar, Allan Loeb; released by New Line Cinema L.L.C.
Directed by: David Frankel
Written by: Allan Loeb
Cinematography by: Maryse Alberti
Music by: Theodore Shapiro
Sound: Lidia Tamplenizza
Music Supervisor: Julia Michels; Dana Sano
Editing: Andrew Marcus
Art Direction: Scott Dougan
Costumes: Leah Katznelson
Production Design: Beth Mickle
MPAA rating: PG-13
Running time: 97 minutes

REVIEWS

Brody, Richard. *New Yorker*. December 16, 2016.
Chang, Justin. *Los Angeles Times*. December 15, 2016.
Gleiberman, Owen. *Variety*. December 13, 2016.
LaSalle, Mick. *San Francisco Chronicle*. December 15, 2016.
Lawson, Richard. *Vanity Fair*. December 15, 2016.

Morgenstern, Joe. *Wall Street Journal.* December 15, 2016.
Rooney, David. *Hollywood Reporter.* December 13, 2016.
Russo, Tom. *Boston Globe.* December 15, 2016.
Scherstuhl, Alan. *Village Voice.* December 13, 2016.
Ward, Sarah. *Screen International.* December 13, 2016.

QUOTES

Brigitte: "Who won? You or the porcelain?"

TRIVIA

Hugh Jackman was supposed to star in the film but when scheduling conflicts arose, he was replaced by Will Smith.

COMPADRES

Sort of armed. Kind of dangerous.
—Movie tagline

Box Office: $3.1 Million

Action-comedy *Compadres* commits the unpardonable movie sin of being simply boring. Some mildly funny moments and decently staged action are not enough to overcome the sense that everything this movie does has been done before in better films. If director Enrique Begne had paid more attention to the Hollywood blockbusters he wants to emulate he might have noticed a need for likable characters and clear plotting. But this muddled and confusing mess is only interested in being a crossover vehicle for popular Mexican comedian Omar Chaparro. The shame is that Chaparro, a decent actor, could probably hold his own with better material. Watching him try to breathe life into this material is discouraging.

Garza (Omar Chaparro), a former cop, is looking for revenge on gangster Santos (Erick Elias), who kidnapped his girlfriend Maria (Aislinn Derbez) and framed Garza for the crime that put him in prison. Garza enlists the aid of his former boss Coronado (Jose Sefami) to help him locate Santos and find out about "the accountant," a former Santos associate responsible for stealing $10 million from the kingpin. But the accountant turns out to be Vic (Joey Morgan), a mouthy 17-year-old hacker who is too dumb to realize the danger of his situation. Soon, the two are on the run looking for a way to get Santos and the money before he gets them.

The plot makes it sound like *Compadres* is a straightforward "Buddy Cop" movie. If it were satisfied to be only that the film would at least have the questionable virtue of misplaced self-confidence. But Begne and his two co-writers, Ted Perkins and Gabriel Ripstein, spend the first thirty minutes creating a complex and clichéd backstory for the Garza character. He has the "you need to settle down" discussion with a friend, is informed that his girlfriend is pregnant, loses his partner by going in without backup, and has his girlfriend kidnapped by the bad guy. What follows is predictable in the extreme.

When not rooted in fart jokes and other scatology, the comedy is almost always the result of predictable, and thus largely unfunny, violence. Begne seems to have no idea how to film these kinds of moments for maximum payoff. One gag involving a severed finger and a touchscreen is a good example. The finger is barely visible at any point, only referenced in the dialogue. Thus, a visual gag becomes almost expository. Viewers are unlikely to see anything here for the first time but this is especially true of the way violence is used. Whether for laughs or emotional impact it comes across as flat and derivative. The film also has a major problem in the way it treats female characters. Every woman in this film is presented breasts forward, in peril, or ready for whatever groping the scene requires.

Omar Chaparro, a well-known Mexican comedian, is fine as Garza, but the role plays like a poor man's George Clooney. His good looks and decent acting are no help for his co-star Joey Morgan, who is a non-presence onscreen. Never mind that Morgan is dealing with bad material, he barely registers here. The part calls for a gifted physical comedian and Morgan lacks the chops to make the most of it. Eric Roberts and Kevin Pollak both pop up in minor roles, which is a mystery since literally anyone could have played their parts. *Compadres* must have been sold to them on the basis of it being a payday or a breakout hit for the lead. This is not a film they should put on their resume. More fun is Efren Ramirez, still best known as Pedro from *Napoleon Dynamite* (2004). He has fun with his role as a sadistic but bumbling hitman saddled with a brainless brute of a partner whose weapon of choice is a flamethrower.

The music used in the film is all over the map, and almost none of it seems right. But that fits neatly into the overall impression *Compadres* makes. The end result is almost as if someone took a light-hearted, reasonably entertaining, buddy cop movie and tried to spice it up to look bigger than it has any right to be. All those moments that worked are now buried deep under all the other things that clearly do not. Viewers live in an age where choices are unlimited. It is easy enough to imagine *Compadres* ending up on TV and becoming the focus of someone's drowsy Saturday afternoon or late night, provided they have trouble finding the remote or fall asleep soon after they tune in to it.

Dave Canfield

CREDITS

Garza: Omar Chaparro
Vic: Joey Morgan
Santos: Erick Elias
Maria: Aislinn Derbez
Guasa: Hector Jimenez
Origin: United States
Language: English
Released: 2016
Directed by: Enrique Begne
Written by: Enrique Begne; Ted Perkins; Gabriel Ripstein
Cinematography by: Federico Barbabosa
Music by: Joan Valent
MPAA rating: R
Running time: 101 minutes

REVIEWS

Barco, Uriel. *Garuyo*. April 1, 2016.
Cordova, Randy. *Arizona Republic*. April 21, 2016.
Genzlinger, Neil. *New York Times*. April 21, 2016.
Kenny, Glenn. *RogerEbert.com*. April 22, 2016.
Kupecki, Josh. *Austin Chronicle*. April 21, 2016.
Molina, Eduardo. *Reforma*. April 11, 2016.
Rodriguez, Sofia Ochoa. *En Filme*. April 1, 2016.
Ruelas, Cuauhtemoc. *Tijuaneo*. April 7, 2016.
Ruiz, Adrian. *Excelsior*. April 1, 2016.
Santos, Rafael Rosales. *Konexion*. April 1, 2016.

TRIVIA

Some of the movie was filmed at a real-life strip club in Mexicali.

THE CONJURING 2

The next true story from the case files of Ed and Lorraine Warren.
—Movie tagline

Box Office: $102.4 Million

While jump scares can be an incredibly effective way to scare someone, it's really kind of cheap. And while *The Conjuring 2* (2016) certainly offers up more craft and scare tactics than hiding in a room to get a cheap scare out of someone, the film lacks the assured, steady filmmaking of its predecessor *The Conjuring* (2013), opting for sneaky jump scares, out-of-place characters and that murky, black CGI that is apparently 2016's version of the overused "found footage" gimmick.

The Conjuring 2, like its predecessor, is based on real life paranormal investigators Ed and Lorraine Warren (Patrick Wilson and Vera Farmiga). The film opens three years after the events that occurred in the book and film *The Amityville Horror* (1979, and again in the forgettable 2005 remake), where their findings at that house haunting have launched them into celebrity status. Or, better, submerged them in a fish bowl-type existence where they guest on ubiquitous 1970s TV talk-shows paired with a person who thinks they are quacks. The constant arguing and defense of both their character and profession is wearing on the Warrens, and they both decide that while they will continue to study the paranormal, they will no longer take on cases in person. Since this would make for a pretty boring movie, they will, of course, be sucked into the fray once again.

Enter the Hodgson family, who live in Northern England. Matriarch Peggy (Frances O'Connor) is a single mother of four, and already facing difficulties trying to make ends meet due to a deadbeat dad situation. Things quickly turn worse as her youngest daughter Janet (Madison Wolfe) starts speaking to herself at all hours of the night in a raspy, possessive man's voice as well as sleepwalking. The plot thickens as Janet soon begins seeing a ghostly figure who seems intent to let the Hodgsons know they're in his house by sneaking up to her and shouting "my house!" which is an effective way to scare someone but not a particularly clever one. From here, *The Conjuring 2* begins a storyline that, depending on your attitude about it, can be seen as an homage to other, better haunting/possession films or as simply ripping them off.

For instance, after Janet starts getting the wits scared out of her, Peggy slowly comes around to the idea something might truly be amiss. This is shown by furniture moving around the house on its own, a la the first act of *Poltergeist*(1982, and again in the needless remake in 2015). Naturally, Peggy phones the police and they too encounter the inexplicable but are honest in the fact that, well, they cannot do much for what appears to be a haunting. Reliably, the Warrens, who are back home in the States and experiencing some weird demon presences of their own, are forced back into action to rescue Janet and the downtrodden Hodgson family.

No sooner have the Warrens arrived in Jolly Old England when Janet's possession symptoms worsen both in terms of the physical and the film continues its echoing of other, better horror films. Crosses on walls slowly spin upside down, people are thrown from furniture and the kitchen gets destroyed. And again, these are all effective horror moments that evoke scares very well but when creating a sequel to the truly frightening *The Conjuring*, especially when James Wan is at the helm for both, one expects more.

The Conjuring succeeded by utilizing a scary haunted house set up which also featured a terrifying looking doll. Yet Wan ratchets up the action—particularly in the second half of the film—by utilizing the camera as almost a literal vehicle taking viewers through a haunted house. Wan would slowly guide us down hallways where we knew something off-putting lurked but the steadiness and control of not only the visual medium but the audience caught in that gaze, was masterful. It was impossible to look away. In *The Conjuring 2* the tricks are more of the jump-scare variety and also focus on a mysterious demon who's terrorizing Lorraine Warren but who also looks a lot like Marilyn Manson in nun attire.

Don R. Lewis

CREDITS

Ed Warren: Patrick Wilson
Lorraine Warren: Vera Farmiga
Janet Hodgson: Madison Wolfe
Peggy Hodgson: Frances O'Connor
Margaret Hodgson: Lauren Esposito
Origin: United States
Language: English
Released: 2016
Production: Rob Cowan, Peter Safran, James Wan; released by New Line Cinema L.L.C.
Directed by: James Wan
Written by: James Wan; Carey Hayes; Chad Hayes; David Leslie Johnson
Cinematography by: Don Burgess
Music by: Joseph Bishara
Sound: Joe Dzuban
Music Supervisor: Dana Sano
Editing: Kirk Morri
Costumes: Kristin Burke
Production Design: Julie Berghoff
MPAA rating: R
Running time: 134 minutes

REVIEWS

Andersen, Soren. *Seattle Times.* June 9, 2016.
Chang, Justin. *Los Angeles Times.* June 9, 2016.
Conterio, Martyn. *CineVue.* June 15, 2016.
Douglas, Edward. *New York Daily News.* June 7, 2016.
Ebiri, Bilge. *Village Voice.* June 7, 2016.
Linden, Sheri. *The Hollywood Reporter.* June 2, 2016.
McWeeny, Drew. *Hitfix.* June 9, 2016.
Robinson, Tasha. *The Verge.* June 3, 2016.
Roffman, Michael. *Consequence of Sound.* June 2, 2016.
Whitney, Erin. *ScreenCrush.* June 9, 2016.

QUOTES

Lorraine Warren: "After everything we've seen, there isn't much that rattles either of us anymore. But this one ... this one still haunts me."

TRIVIA

A priest was brought in to bless the set on the first day of shooting.

CRIMINAL

The CIA's last hope is in the mind of a criminal.
—Movie tagline

Box Office: $14.7 Million

Director Ariel Vromen's *Criminal* is the worst kind of genre movie—it's a genre movie that's too embarrassed to admit that it's a genre movie. On one hand, you can sympathize with the director's delusions of grandeur. His last movie, 2012's *The Iceman*, while not a huge success, did attract some positive critical attention, largely thanks to Michael Shannon's lead performance. Similarly, *Criminal* has an impressive ensemble made up of Hollywood stalwarts (Kevin Costner, Tommy Lee Jones, Gary Oldman) and up-and-comers (Gal Gadot, Ryan Reynolds). That's a solid cast for any movie, so perhaps that's why Vromen thought that his thriller was more than just a silly, pulpy action flick. Unfortunately for Vromen, he was wrong.

There is a profound silliness at the heart of *Criminal*, a movie that's ostensibly about brain-swapping, and the film's greatest flaw is its inability to recognize it. This is a story that screams out to be treated as a fable. It's a story that requires big, broad strokes and gleeful leaps in logic, if it wants its audience to come along for the ride. But Vromen seems hell-bent on stripping *Criminal* of any of the naturally fantastical (i.e. fun) elements that one would expect to accompany its profoundly giggle-worthy plot.

This movie is no character study or grounded thriller. *Criminal* is a direct cousin to John Woo's *Face/Off* (1997), a film, for better or worse, that largely embraced its inner insanity and ran with it. Did no one tell Vromen that *Criminal* was written by Douglas Cook and David Weisberg, two of the writers responsible for Michael Bay's *The Rock* (1996)? While this may sound like cinephile blasphemy, Vromen's final product probably would have been a lot more creatively honest if he'd erred on the side of Woo and Bay more often. It would have suited the material better than his plodding attempts at realism.

The ideas behind *Criminal* are pure comic book fodder, the kind of storytelling usually found in a science fiction film. (Not because they are without value or inferior, but simply because sci-fi has a long history of playing with allegories.) However, Vromen approaches his material with the dour stoicism of a Jason Bourne film, which seems at odds with the film's main plot device.

Criminal is ostensibly about a brain transfer (even if it tries to dress it up in some pseudo-science). CIA operative Bill Pope (an uncredited Ryan Reynolds) is killed on duty while he's in the middle of a time-sensitive operation. An anarchist billionaire Xavier Heimdahl (Jordi Mollà) had hired a hacker named The Dutchman (an engaging, though under-utilized Michael Pitt) to create a way to hijack the U.S. government's nuclear arsenal. Bill Pope had stashed The Dutchman away and gathered enough money to pay him off, but he was killed by Heimdahl's goons before he could reveal to his bosses where everything was.

Thus, Pope's boss, Quaker Wells (Gary Oldman) decides that the solution to his problem is brain-swapping. (Obviously.) They dress it up in less-laughable terms, but, basically, Wells contacts a scientist, Dr. Micah Franks (a barely-there Tommy Lee Jones), who is working on a way to transplant memories from one mammalian brain to another. Even though they are years away from human testing, Franks and Wells decide to try out the procedure on a death row inmate, Jerico Stewart (Kevin Costner). The idea is that, if the procedure works, Bill Pope's memories will appear in Jerico's brain and help them find The Dutchman. If it does not work, fortunately, Jerico is just a violent death row inmate with a brain abnormality that prevents him from feeling empathy, so who cares if he lives or dies?

It's a normal movie trope that the person receiving the transplant also gets memories from the person who donated the organ. This time, the memories are the actual thing that got transplanted, which, admittedly, is a spin on the cliché. However, the results are just as predictable. Jerico escapes after the procedure and finds himself inexplicably drawn to Bill Pope's family—Pope's wife (Gal Gadot) and daughter. Some of Pope's memories and impulses also return, which makes Jerico a target of the CIA and Heimdahl, and forces Jerico to start acting altruistically, which greatly confuses him. Predictably, Jerico eventually makes a choice to continue Pope's work, finding The Dutchman and trying to save the world. (It should be noted that this is Ryan Reynold's second consecutive brain-swapping movie after 2015's *SelfLess*.)

Kevin Costner's performance is the best thing in *Criminal*, even though it feels like he should be acting in a different movie. Costner seems to be relishing playing a wholly unlikeable character, a true dead-eyed sociopath, who finds himself unexpectedly learning to care about things. That's a really complex character to play—almost a version of *Flowers to Algernon* where Charlie is imbued with empathy rather than intelligence—and Costner attacks it fearlessly. The problem is that, as was previously mentioned, this movie is not a character study. It's a CIA spy thriller with a "we need to save the world" plotline, and Costner's character clashes tonally with all the chases and cyber-nonsense. It gets especially uncomfortable when Vromen, realizing that Costner is no Matt Damon, replaces Bourne-style action with gratuitous violence. Perhaps he thought that was a way to make the movie seem more dynamic, while staying true to Jerico's death-row origins, but it's just another tonal misstep that makes one wonder about the audience for this film.

Had Vromen turned *Criminal* into a straight sci-fi Frankenstein allegory, he might have found a pulpy, hardboiled tone that worked for the material. But, unfortunately, just like the premise's unbelievable surgery, the film just grafts together a bunch of disparate elements, a procedure that is not nearly as successful as theoretical brain-swapping, apparently.

Tom Burns

CREDITS

Jericho Stewart: Kevin Costner
Quaker Wells: Gary Oldman
Dr. Franks: Tommy Lee Jones
Bill Pope: Ryan Reynolds
Xavier Heimdahl: Jordi Molla
Origin: United States
Language: English
Released: 2016
Production: Chris Bender, Christa Campbell, Boaz Davidson, Mark Gill, Lati Grobman, Matthew O'Toole, Trevor Short, JC Spink, John Thompson; released by Benderspink, Lionsgate
Directed by: Ariel Vromen
Written by: Douglas Cook; David Weisberg
Cinematography by: Dana Gonzales
Music by: Keith Power; Brian Tyler
Sound: Kris Casavant
Music Supervisor: Selena Arizanovic
Editing: Danny Rafic
Art Direction: Grant Armstrong
Costumes: Jill Taylor

Production Design: Jon Henson
MPAA rating: R
Running time: 113 minutes

REVIEWS

Andersen, Soren. *Seattle Times*. April 21, 2016.
Genzlinger, Neil. *New York Times*. April 14, 2016.
Keough, Peter. *Boston Globe*. April 14, 2016.
LaSalle, Mick. *San Francisco Chronicle*. April 13, 2016.
Moore, Roger. *Movie Nation*. April 13, 2016.
Rea, Steven. *Philadelphia Inquirer*. April 15, 2016.
Stewart, Sara. *New York Post*. April 14, 2016.

Turan, Kenneth. *Los Angeles Times*. April 14, 2016.
Vishnevetsky, Ignatiy. *The A.V. Club*. April 13, 2016.
Walsh, Katie. *Chicago Tribune*. April 14, 2016.

QUOTES

Jericho Stewart: [still standing after being shot with a tranquilizer] "You're gonna need another one."

TRIVIA

The medical-operation sequence featured a prosthetic dummy as a stand-in for Ryan Reynolds. It was much cheaper to create that instead of having Reynolds for two days of work.

D

THE DARKNESS

Evil comes home.
—Movie tagline

Box Office: $10.7 Million

Producer Jason Blum is the secret auteur behind almost everything he throws himself behind, under the auspices of his Blumhouse production company. Ever since he and director Oren Peli made it big with *Paranormal Activity* in 2007 and its many sequels, they have built themselves a formidable reputation, complete with house style and pet themes. The haunted house movies they have put their stamp on—*Insidious* (2010), *The Lords of Salem* (2012), *Dark Skies* (2013), *Oculus* (2013), *Sinister* (2012), etc.—are all at the mercy of how much will a director can exert over their mid-budget spook shows. Rob Zombie and Scott Derrickson faired better working with Blumhouse than the likes of James Wan, Mike Flanagan and Scott Stewart, because they have intense visual styles. Zombie cannot point a camera at something without making it personal, while Wan and Flanagan do not have a visual style strong enough to withstand Blum's insistence on clean action, tidy houses and tight budgets. *The Darkness,* the latest of the Blumhouse ghost stories, makes a test subject out of Australian director Greg McLean, and how strong his personality remains while under the tight restrictions imposed by his producers.

The Taylor family vacation is coming to an end. Last stop: The Grand Canyon. Peter and Bronny (Kevin Bacon and Radha Mitchell) are trying to enjoy some last minute leisure time with their married friends Gary and Joy (Matt Walsh and Jennifer Morrison) while their children hike the trails last minute. Eldest daughter Stephanie (Lucy Fry) resents the extra care her parents ask her to take of her autistic brother Michael (David Mazouz), which makes it easy for him to run off and fall into a crevasse while she's not looking. While he's down there he discovers something he decides he would like to take home with him as a souvenir: five stones with strange carvings on them.

Back home, the supernatural trouble starts quietly and the Taylors have problems enough already that the presence of angry spirits goes unnoticed at first. Peter and Bronny—he's a former philanderer, she's a recovering alcoholic—are having intimacy, trust and communication problems, compounded by Peter's newest co-worker (Trian Long Smith) appearing ready to be more than just office mates. Stephanie has body image issues that have morphed into bulimia, something her parents are split on how to handle. And then there are the strange smells and sounds that keep cropping up all over their too-perfect house. When Michael starts acting out in ways more peculiar than Bronny's used to seeing and he blames it on an imaginary friend named Jenny she starts to worry. When inky handprints appear on every surface in the house, Michael starts behaving violently towards house cats, and the neighbor's dog won't stop barking, everyone slowly admits there might be a bigger problem than even all the domestic squabbling.

Peter and Bronny are at their wit's end when Peter's boss Simon (Paul Reiser) introduces the couple to his partner Wendy (Ming-Na Wen). Wendy has her own supernatural story to share but Simon doesn't let her tell it, despite Bronny's urging. It's only after Michael has burned a part of his wall up, Bronny's returned to her drinking and coyotes have started appearing on the property that Peter asks for help and Simon confesses that he believes more in the uncanny than he let on. Years ago Simon and Wendy's son was sick and he sought the help of a spiritualist named Teresa, who cured the boy with a remedy that sounds like magic. Peter calls Teresa, who arrives with her translator granddaughter Gloria, prepared to do battle with an Anasazi spirit called 'the darkness' that has taken over the Taylor house.

From the first shots of painted red canyons, its clear that McLean is in there after all, and this isn't strictly a paycheck. The unforgivable Aussie landscapes he made come alive with unspeakable terror in his earliest horror outings *Wolf Creek* (2005) and *Rogue* (2007) are mirrored in the imposing canyons where Michael meets with the cursed stones. McLean may ultimately not do anything with those spooky cliffs, but they act as a signature all the same. Devices like low-lighting faces and occasional bouts of handheld camera are part and parcel of his approach to horror. He builds up believably mundane foundations so that when the walls start to crumble, you know what's at stake and who's capable of withstanding catastrophe. The Taylors are already at their wit's end just getting through an average day; when real trouble rears its head, they all but fall apart in an instant. McLean's handwriting can be found in the unforced charisma and chemistry of these characters, how lived-in and believable a family unit they are. Peter rejecting his co-worker's harmless advances because he knows where they'll lead or Bronny and Stephanie doing their make-up together, that's the kind of grace note that acts as a counter balance to the horrific elements and McLean's been practicing them since *Wolf Creek* in 2005. Bacon, Mitchell, Smith and Reiser all rise beautifully to the occasion, convincing as basically good people pushed into odd corners by fate.

It's when Jason Blum's pen hits this film's canvas that things get dicey. The house is too clean and new, right out of a real estate brochure, as they have been in most of his haunted house movies since *Paranormal Activity*. The insistence on telling a ghost story instead of giving McLean a freer hand to invent leads the director and his two co-writers Shayne Armstrong and Shane Krause into some preposterous corners. As good as they are at finding the levity and tension in realistic conversation, they are all quite poor at explaining a haunting. Relying both on outdated Native American mysticism that borders on ugliness and some troubling material about autistic children being especially prone to hauntings, the movie's plot outline feels 40 years old. The scares themselves are of the jump-and-bang variety, and though McLean's use of dark handprints is visually compelling, it does not hide the fact that he's using the

same strategy the whole film. *The Darkness* works well in spite of its perfunctory plotting and tired ideas about the business of scaring audiences because McLean's voice can be heard over the din of things going bump in the night. He cares about his human characters and gives them space to exist without judgment, and that's a rare quality in modern horror.

Scout Tafoya

CREDITS

Joy Carter: Jennifer (Jenny) Morrison
Bronny Taylor: Radha Mitchell
Peter Taylor: Kevin Bacon
Wendy: Ming Na
Stephanie Taylor: Lucy Fry
Origin: United States
Language: English
Released: 2016
Production: Jason Blum, Matthew Kaplan, Bianca Martino, Greg McLean
Directed by: Greg McLean
Written by: Greg McLean; Shayne Armstrong; Shane Krause
Cinematography by: Toby Oliver
Music by: Johnny Klimek
Sound: Paul Pirola
Editing: Sean Lahiff
Art Direction: Hunter Brown
Costumes: Nicola Dunn
Production Design: Melanie Jones
MPAA rating: PG-13
Running time: 92 minutes

REVIEWS

Bowen, Chuck. *Slant*. May 13, 2016.
Davis, Steve. *Austin Chronicle*. May 18, 2016.
DeFore, John. *Hollywood Reporter*. May 14, 2016.
Douglas, Edward. *New York Daily News*. May 13, 2016.
Dowd, A.A. *The A.V. Club*. May 13, 2016.
Hoffman, Jordan. *Guardian*. May 13, 2016.
Moore, Roger. *Movie Nation*. May 17, 2016.
Murray, Noel. *Los Angeles Times*. May 13, 2016.
Sobczynski, Peter. *RogerEbert.com*. May 13, 2016.
Tobias, Scott. *Variety*. May 17, 2016.

QUOTES

Stephanie Taylor: "Will you tell Michael to stay out of my room ... he keeps leaving dirty hand prints everywhere."

TRIVIA

Kevin Bacon and Jennifer Morrison previously worked together in *Stir of Echoes* (1999).

DE PALMA

Being a director is being a watcher.
—Movie tagline

Box Office: $165,237

Brian De Palma never thought he would become a filmmaker. Born to an orthopedic surgeon and raised in Philadelphia, he originally enrolled at Columbia as a physics student. There's a certain logic to De Palma's background being in computers and intellectual sciences like physics because his films have such a fine sense of detail and craftsmanship. When the young man saw *Citizen Kane* (1941) and *Vertigo* (1958), he became fascinated with film, enrolling at Sarah Lawrence College to become a theater student there. He met drama teacher Wilford Leach there, and the two co-directed a movie called *The Wedding Party* (filmed in 1963 but not released until 1969), which happened to co-star a young friend of theirs named Robert De Niro. If this introduction sounds rather biographical, it fits the tone of Noah Baumbach's simply-titled *De Palma*, a film that is little more than an interview that covers the entire career of its title subject, but oh what a fascinating interview it is.

The structure of *De Palma* becomes almost lyrical in its repetition. The director of such classic and beloved films as *Blow Out* (1980), *Dressed to Kill* (1980), *The Untouchables* (1987), and *Mission: Impossible* (1996) shares an anecdote about the production of nearly one of his films, followed or preceded by a clip. Clips-stories, clips-stories, repeat for two hours. Baumbach interviews no one else. There are not the traditional talking-head interludes with filmmakers inspired by De Palma or collaborators of his actors or writers. Some may bemoan the lack of a "complete picture" of De Palma's career, but Baumbach's laser focus achieves something unique in terms of the biographical documentary—it focuses so heavily on craft that it becomes more about filmmaking than a director's personality or other issues related to his life. It's a perfect tone to strike for a filmmaker who dedicated his life to his craft.

What is likely to be of most interest to De Palma fans, who will know many of the stories behind the more popular films of the director, is the early material, including anecdotes about early films like *Murder a la Mod* (1969) and *Hi, Mom!* (1970), along with details about the tumultuous production of *Get to Know Your Rabbit* (1972). Things started to change for De Palma with the release of *Sisters* (1973) and future cult hit *Phantom of the Paradise* (1974), but the real breakthrough came with an adaptation of Stephen King's hit novel *Carrie* (1976). De Palma's discussion of how he

maintained control over that project is one of the most interesting chapters of the film.

From here, *De Palma* runs a rollercoaster through the filmmaker's up-and-down career, including the controversies behind violent films like *Dressed to Kill* and *Scarface* (1983). De Palma clearly still loves the films of his that he considered a success, and even gets a bit defensive about films widely considered failures, such as 1990's *Bonfire of the Vanities*. The interview goes up all the way through his current, rocky era, but skims a couple late-career entries like *Mission to Mars* (2000) rather quickly.

If Baumbach's approach has a flaw it's in how much control he cedes to De Palma, almost as if he's not actually asking questions, just bringing up a film title and letting the director tell stories. Consequently, issues of De Palma's career, including regular accusations of misogyny in his work, are almost entirely ignored. And De Palma seems to retreat a bit when faced with the relative disappointment of his last two decades of output. Again, these omissions are forgivable for how much emphasis it allows De Palma to place on his career, but those coming to the film with reservations about the way he treats women will find no answers here, and neither will those wondering if and how he's past his prime.

Brian De Palma is often criticized for how openly he cribs from other filmmakers, most notably the bulk of Alfred Hitchcock's most popular films. The idea that how De Palma interprets Hitchcock's work for his own thrillers as easy is naïve, and an opinion that seems to be correcting itself over the last few decades, as films like *Blow Out*, his masterpiece, have been placed on pedestals next to some of the best thrillers of all time. De Palma is the kind of filmmaker whose career will be studied and appreciated for decades to come, probably even more so after he's gone. At that time, it will be nice to have this film-length interview to serve as a window into a career that film history is only now beginning to fully appreciate.

Brian Tallerico

CREDITS

Himself: Brian De Palma

Origin: United States

Language: English

Released: 2016

Production: Noah Baumbach, Jake Paltrow

Directed by: Noah Baumbach; Jake Paltrow

Cinematography by: Jake Paltrow
MPAA rating: R
Running time: 107 minutes

REVIEWS

Bowen, Chuck. *Slant Magazine*. June 2, 2016.
Burr, Ty. *Boston Globe*. June 16, 2016.
Ehrlich, David. *IndieWire*. June 14, 2016.
Goble, Blake. *Consequence of Sound*. June 8, 2016.
Goodykoontz, Bill. *Arizona Republic*. June 16, 2016.
Kiang, Jessica. *The Playlist*. September 12, 2015.
McWeeny, Drew. *Hitfix*. June 9, 2016.
Phillips, Michael. *Chicago Tribune*. June 16, 2016.
Rothkopf, Joshua. *Time Out New York*. June 8, 2016.
Sobczynski, Peter. *RogerEbert.com*. June 10, 2016.

QUOTES

Brian De Palma: "Holy mackerel."

TRIVIA

The documentary was filmed for one week in 2010. Brian De Palma wore the same shirt every day for continuity's sake.

DEADPOOL

With great power comes great irresponsibility.
    —Movie tagline

Wait 'til you get a load of me.
    —Movie tagline

Justice has a new face.
    —Movie tagline

Box Office: $363 Million

Comic book fans have often complained about the loyalty of movie adaptations to their beloved superheroes, but with *Deadpool*, they have little to complain about, at least in terms of how the character himself is portrayed. Ryan Reynolds, who plays Deadpool, was a fan of the comic book, and he plays the title character with such infectious enthusiasm that the irreverent wisecracking killer seems the role he was born to play. Of course, he's played the role before, in *X-Men Origins: Wolverine* (2009), but that misbegotten movie put a muzzle on the "Merc with a Mouth." *Deadpool* lets him loose. The movie itself may not have merited the heights of fanboy adulation it received, but it is a fun ride, for the most part, and Reynolds deserves a lot of the credit for that.

Deadpool isn't the first movie to have a main character who persistently breaks the fourth wall, turning to the camera and addressing the audience directly.

Heck, the film directly references *Ferris Bueller's Day Off* in its post-credit stinger, one of its funnier bits. It's obviously not the first movie to engage in self-referential humor involving its plot machinations, its tropes, even its intellectual property and its cast. After all, where would the oeuvre of Mike Myers be without that kind of humor? Deadpool is, at his core, pretty much *Ace Ventura: Pet Detective* (1994), but more of a violent sociopath. Even looking solely at mainstream superhero films, *Deadpool* comes well after Marvel's *Guardians of the Galaxy* (2014), which engaged in its own playful undercutting of genre expectations. *Deadpool* is more profane and bloody than one might expect, but it doesn't truly subvert the superhero film, like *Guardians* director James Gunn's *Super* (2010). Completely driven by Ryan Reynolds' jubilantly cynical chatterbox performance as the titular superhero, it's raucous, sophomoric fun that gets to have its cake and eat it, too, but knows better than to really sink its teeth into the corporate hand that feeds it. And a satire without teeth isn't really satire at all.

The opening credit sequence feels subversively forthright, listing superhero movie tropes ("The hot chick, the comic relief, a CGI character" etc.) instead of the names of the cast and crew, streaming across a cartoonish depiction of a particular moment of mayhem to come. It's a bold way to start the film, announcing that the filmmakers are aware of every cliché propagated by the genre, but it also sets up the disappointment of realizing that *Deadpool* does little to subvert those clichés, other than incessantly commenting on them.

The opening segment jumps back and forth in time, showing Deadpool in a bloody, brutal gun battle with the henchmen of the film's "British villain" (one of the aforementioned clichés), Ajax (Ed Skrein), and flashing back to his pre-Deadpool days as Wade Wilson, who became a low-rent mercenary after being dishonorably discharged from a seemingly very eventful military career. Wade takes odd jobs, and hangs out at a scuzzy mercenary bar run by Weasel (T.J. Miller), also known as "the comic relief." Miller's more laid-back sarcastic stoner style is both amusing and endearing, and he plays off Reynolds beautifully, something the filmmakers clearly recognize, as he has a larger role than would otherwise be justified. At the bar, Wade runs into Vanessa (Morena Baccarin), a prostitute nearly as sharp and cynical as himself. Like Miller, Baccarin coolly manages to hold her own against Reynolds' over-the-top antics. Thanks in part to her performance, Vanessa just barely manages to transcend that "hot chick" label.

Just as Wade and Vanessa seem on the path to perfect happiness together (there's no reference to their unseemly jobs once their romance begins), Wade gets a diagnosis of terminal cancer of everything. Faced with the possibility of a slow, painful death, he considers leaving Vanessa to spare her that misery. Instead, he sneaks off and reluctantly takes a sinister offer from an oily recruiter (Jed Rees), who promises to cure his illness, and transform him into a super soldier. Thus, he ends up in the hands of the sadistic Ajax and his superstrong henchwoman Angel Dust (the estimable Gina Carano). Not only does it turn out that the transformation into a superhuman is extremely painful and disfiguring, but Ajax's plans for Wade involve turning him into a slave, not a soldier. Things only get worse for Wade when he finds out Ajax's real name is Francis. But Wade escapes, of course, and finds himself hideously scarred from head to toe, but with increased strength, reflexes, and healing ability. Once he decides he can't go back to Vanessa in this horrifying state, he decides to track down Ajax and force him to make him "hot" again.

And so, he dons a red suit (to hide his wounds from his enemies) and mask, and becomes Deadpool. It's a curious pivotal plot point that Wade pretty much returns to his former life hanging out with Weasel and killing thugs, but that vanity won't allow him even to let Vanessa know he's still alive. For someone so cocksure, Wade/Deadpool is surprisingly low on self-esteem, not to mention shallow.

Deadpool's plan for revenge is by turns thwarted and abetted by two X-Men from Dr. Xavier's school, the metal giant Colossus (that "CGI character," voiced by Stefan Kapicic) and Negasonic Teenage Warhead, a goth-like teen girl with explosive abilities, played by Brianna Hildebrand with just the right degree of sullen lack of interest to get Deadpool's goat. Colossus, with his earnest, heavily accented chastising of Deadpool for his behavior and language, also plays well off the near-sociopathic antihero. While the movie's nearly nonstop stream of inside jokes is pretty hit-and-miss, they land a good one about the filmmakers not being able to afford the film rights for more than two X-Men.

While Tim Miller is a first-time feature director from the world of special effects, he keeps things bopping along, and films the bloody action in refreshingly coherent style, despite its sometimes Rube Goldberg-esque complexity. Screenwriters Rhett Reese and Paul Wernick have done this kind of genre parody before, with comparably solid results, with *Zombieland* (2009).

While *Deadpool* doesn't really break new ground or have anything particularly profound or even interesting to say about the superhero genre, it's still a broadly entertaining movie, thanks to its well-choreographed action, but especially due to its cast. Both Reynolds and the supporting cast make these characters feel surprisingly lived in, like their lives and relationships extend beyond what we see onscreen. Reynolds is the film's

white-hot glowing center, but each of the supporting players, from Miller to Baccarin to Skrein to Leslie Uggams, who plays Deadpool's caustic Ikea-obsessed roommate, Blind Al, plays off him in their own unique way. The film's biggest twist is that the humanity of those relationships generates not only a surprising amount of warmth, but some of its biggest laughs.

Josh Ralske

CREDITS

Deadpool/Wade: Ryan Reynolds
Dopinder: Karan Soni
Ajax: Ed Skrein
Warlord: Michael Benyaer
Gavin Merchant: Kyle Cassie
Voice of Colossus: Stefan Kapicic
Origin: Canada, United States
Language: English
Released: 2016
Production: Simon Kinberg, Lauren Shuler Donner, Ryan Reynolds; released by Donners' Company, Marvel Entertainment L.L.C.
Directed by: Tim Miller
Written by: Rhett Reese; Paul Wernick
Cinematography by: Ken Seng
Music by: Junkie XL
Sound: Jim Brookshire; Wayne Lemmer
Music Supervisor: John Houlihan
Editing: Julian Clarke
Costumes: Angus Strathie
Production Design: Sean Haworth
MPAA rating: R
Running time: 108 minutes

REVIEWS

Baumgarten, Marjorie. *Austin Chronicle.* February 12, 2016.
Chang, Justin. *Variety.* February 6, 2016.
Dargis, Manohla. *New York Times.* February 11, 2016.
Dowd, A.A. *The A.V. Club.* February 8, 2016.
Edelstein, David. *Vulture.* February 11, 2016.
Fujishima, Kenji. *Slant Magazine.* February 7, 2016.
McCarthy, Todd. *Hollywood Reporter.* February 12, 2016.
Robinson, Tasha. *The Verge.* February 7, 2016.
Singer, Matt. *Screencrush.* February 7, 2016.
Turan, Kenneth. *Los Angeles Times.* February 11, 2016.

QUOTES

Colossus: "You will come talk with Professor Xavier."
Deadpool: "McAvoy or Stewart? These timelines can get so confusing."

It took eight hours to apply Ryan Reynolds' body makeup. He was unable to sit or lie down once it was on.

AWARDS

Nominations:

Golden Globes 2017: Actor—Mus./Comedy (Reynolds), Film—Mus./Comedy
Writers Guild 2016: Adapt. Screenplay

DEEPWATER HORIZON

When faced with our darkest hour, hope is not a tactic.
—Movie tagline

Box Office: $61.4 Million

Director Peter Berg cements himself as a master orchestrator of cinematic spectacle with *Deepwater Horizon*, a true-life disaster movie with an unexpected emotional wallop. It is as visceral an experience as one could want from a blockbuster, in which the viewer is tethered to characters and follows them through a harrowing journey to survival. Whether one knows the results of this story is not an issue, as Berg's film speaks for itself as a documentation of the heroism that comes through tragedy.

A key part to the film's success is its casting, which has Mark Wahlberg playing the viewer's surrogate. His character, Mike Williams, even explains to his daughter in the opening scenes what he does as an oil rig worker, a clear piece of exposition done charismatically through Wahlberg's affable presence, while allusions to monsters in the water create a sense of something bigger than just his oil rig work place. His daughter's fascination with dinosaurs and fossils then makes him a type of beast handler, a fitting idea for what his place of employment, the Deepwater Horizon, means.

This script from Matthew Michael Carnahan and Matthew Sand (adapted from the New York Times article by Stephanie Saul and David Rohde) clues us into the lives of other characters, who do not get the same amount of time but are told poignantly enough: Andrea Fleytas (Gina Rodriguez) is a younger member of the oil rig fighting to command respect from her more experienced co-workers, just like the baby-faced Caleb Holloway (Dylan O'Brien); Kurt Russell's gruff Jimmy Harrell is a captain of sorts on the enterprise who has seen it all, but soon heading into retirement. The characterizations are familiar, yet the performances provide enough depth to make these narrative recreations of real-life people memorable.

The Deepwater Horizon rig itself, as it did in real-life within its horrifying chapter of American history (beginning a spill that lasted 87 days and spilled 200 million gallons of oil into the ocean) becomes a vivid symbol of corporate disregard for the well-being of the working class. As people like Mike and Jimmy point out to the figureheads of BP (including one played by John Malkovich, boasting an incredible Louisiana accent) hundreds of pieces of equipment on the rig are out of date, and the drill itself has reached a point underwater that it could unleash apocalyptic pressure. Sure enough, as the arrogance and greed of BP forces the rig to find out, men and women like Mike and Gina find their lives at stake when the rig explodes, setting the story into its main event and the occasion in which Berg's directing shines.

Berg has created a very potent tragedy of a disaster movie, in which the dread of watching what will happen to the rig is as thick as the resulting fear in watching people try to escape it. It is a chaotic experience with a great sense of detail and texture, a comprehensive picture of a lethal environment of untold amounts of glass, steel, and fire that could attack human beings at any second. The details are vivid, like broken glass tearing into Jimmy's naked body as he was in the shower during the first explosion, or the hell streams of oil blowing into a person's face. For the amount of black and gray that constitute such an environment, Berg and his editors Gabriel Fleming and Colby Parker Jr. service the tension with a terror that is as visually clear as it feels inescapable.

A key part of Berg's success for its second-half climax is that the story never feels like it comes from an outsider's perspective, in spite of the movie's grandiosity. Along with moments spent following around Wahlberg's Mike and his coworkers on the rig, Berg provides space and time to people on different parts of the rig, creating an emotional sense that his mass amount of characters are more than extras. The job lingo is there too, with various pressure tests and capacities discussed extensively, challenging the infantile inklings from a script that starts off with heavy exposition. As Berg did with his previous foray into men facing their physical limits, *Lone Survivor* (2013), he creates an inclusive image for his audience of a specific group of people whose livelihoods depend on their bodies.

That inclusivity further makes the film's respect for the true events more impressive, in which the heavy emotions of the movie do not require its true-life context to be primarily involving. Nor does the story shy away from the human factors of very real greed in the story, with Malkovich's BP figurehead showing how such avarice and apathy can be destructive, but that empathy was not entirely lost in the events. Berg cunningly refuses to turn *Deepwater Horizon* into a blaring, one-note attack on an already villainous enterprise, and his narrative is far more interesting because of it.

One of the most immediate comparisons for a film like *Deepwater Horizon* is James Cameron's 1997 epic *Titanic*; as Cameron's historic iceberg lay dormant and sinister in the freezing waters, so does the faulty pipe and burgeoning oil in Berg's film. *Deepwater Horizon* is like a testosterone version of Cameron's historic piece of Americans cinema, with man vs. nature as much as man vs. man, this time with the tragedy of a selfish industry affecting the lives of blue collar workers. Berg's film is able to stand apart from many other projects and their directors, however, with the compassionate filmmaking that motivates such an impressive enterprise.

Nick Allen

CREDITS

Mike Williams: Mark Wahlberg
Jimmy Harrell: Kurt Russell
Vidrine: John Malkovich
Andrea Fleytas: Gina Rodriguez
Caleb Holloway: Dylan O'Brien
Felicia Williams: Kate Hudson
Origin: United States
Language: English
Released: 2016
Production: Lorenzo di Bonaventura, Mark Vahradian, David Womark; released by Participant Media L.L.C., Summit Entertainment
Directed by: Peter Berg
Written by: Matthew Michael Carnahan; Matthew Sand
Cinematography by: Enrique Chediak
Music by: Steve Jablonsky
Sound: Wylie Stateman
Editing: Gabriel Fleming; Colby Parker, Jr.
Art Direction: Marc Fisichella
Costumes: Kasia Walicka-Maimone
Production Design: Chris Seagers
MPAA rating: PG-13
Running time: 107 minutes

REVIEWS

Bahr, Lindsey. *Associated Press*. September 29, 2016.
Ebiri, Bilge. *Village Voice*. September 23, 2016.
Greenblatt, Leah. *Entertainment Weekly*. September 29, 2016.
Hornaday, Ann. *Washington Post*. September 29, 2016.
Lane, Anthony. *New Yorker*. October 3, 2016.
Onion, Rebecca. *Slate*. September 28, 2016.
Scott, A.O. *New York Times*. September 29, 2016.

Tobias, Scott. *NPR*. September 29, 2016.
Vishnevetsky, Ignatiy. *The A.V. Club*. September 29, 2016.
Zacharek, Stephanie. *Time*. September 30, 2016.

QUOTES

Andrea Fleytas: "I don't want to die! I don't want to die!"
Mike Williams: "You're not going to die. Trust me."

TRIVIA

Kate Hudson published a picture with her stepfather Kurt Russell on Instagram and mentioned that this movie would be her first time working with him.

AWARDS

Nominations:

Oscars 2016: Sound FX Editing, Visual FX
British Acad. 2016: Sound

DEMOLITION

LIFE: Some Disassembly Required.
   —Movie tagline

Box Office: $1.9 Million

Everyone grieves in different ways. There's no "right" way to do it, especially when it comes to a major loss, and it's widely accepted to just let people do their own thing and come to grips with the reality of death in whatever way that best suits them. That is, provided they do not start making really bad and/or harmful decisions that affect themselves or those close to them. Wealthy investment banker Davis (Jake Gyllenhaal) does exactly that last part in the interesting and odd film *Demolition*.

As *Demolition* opens, Davis and his lovely wife Julia (Heather Lind) are driving and engaging in a steadily heating argument. The fight comes to a close in a surprising way that leaves Julia dead and sends Davis into an odd state of disconnectedness. While a state of disconnection following the loss of one's wife is not anything new, it's what Davis chooses to disconnect from and then connect into that has everyone concerned about his well-being.

For starters, Davis begins obsessively writing to a vending machine company in regards to some candy he tried to buy that ended up stuck in their machine. At first, the letters seem to be an aggrieved way for Davis to let off some seriously pressurized steam, but soon they take on an epistolary quality as he begins oddly opening up about the life he's led up to this point. While this is clearly a way for the film's screenwriter, Bryan Sipe, to fill in some character traits through straight-up exposition, it's a clever way to do so and it works. As the letter writing increases in quantity and release of information, Davis proceeds to kind of go *Jerry Maguire* (1996) on his wealthy investors, dropping on them some truth and honesty never seen before in the investment banking world. This causes his boss (who is also his father-in-law) Phil (Chris Cooper) to get more than a little worried about his protégé, who, as the film moves along, we find out was not always so well-liked. In fact, the feeling is mutual and everyone—especially Davis—soon realizes he has been given a second chance to lead a life that had nearly escaped him. This is where things get dicey.

Demolition deals with tough situations facing intriguing characters, and, as noted, it definitely gives one pause and reflection after it ends. But the kind of nagging darkness that almost clouds the entire film and subsequent thoughts about it is that Davis, who was admittedly living a lie in a loveless marriage and career he despised, gets a new lease on life when his wife meets an untimely end. While, yes, this is great for Davis, one cannot help the nagging suspicion that it's really pretty unfair for everyone else. As *Demolition* progresses, Davis takes a new approach at this do-over life and this presents an internal conflict because the changes he makes are interesting and positive for him but the way he's behaving is pretty disgusting seeing as a woman much loved by her family and friends is dead. But alas, therein lies the rub as grief and loss is processed differently by everyone.

In another surprising turn of events, lonely pothead Karen (Naomi Watts), who works for the vending machine company Davis has been writing, soon enters his life by calling him, ostensibly to follow-up on the letters. Yet it soon becomes clear she too is seeking a new lease on a lousy life and the letters Davis has written have seemingly helped her realize this. Just as Davis' decision to shake things up in an extreme (and rather cold-hearted way) Karen's awkward arrival and where the film goes from there requires a pretty big suspension of disbelief. Again, while many times the film appears to not really be working it comes together in the end and almost manages to be uplifting if not altogether really weird.

Much of that success is owed to Gyllenhaal who, while he remains a young man possessing the kind of good looks one only ever sees in movie stars, still manages to pull off an "everyman" quality. This is a trait he's really honed well through roles in a wide variety of films like the heartfelt boxing film *Southpaw* (2015), the criminally under seen *Moonlight Mile* (2002), and even more intense roles like the leads in *Jarhead* (2005) and

Nightcrawler (2014). *Demolition* also marks the latest film from director Jean-Marc Vallée, whose previous efforts were films that reeked of Oscar bait such as the Reese Witherspoon-starrer *Wild* (2014) and the film that nabbed Matthew McConaughey and Jared Leto acting Oscars, *Dallas Buyers Club* (2013). *Demolition* is a smaller, more contemplative film than Vallée's previous work, and it's nice to see him working from a smaller perspective in an equally morally ambiguous film.

Don R. Lewis

CREDITS

Davis: Jake Gyllenhaal
Karen: Naomi Watts
Phil: Chris Cooper
Chris: Judah Lewis
Carl: C.J. Wilson
Origin: United States
Language: English
Released: 2015
Production: Lianne Halfon, Sidney Kimmel, Thad Luckinbill, Trent Luckinbill, John Malkovich, Molly Smith, Russell Smith; released by Black Label Media, Right of Way Films
Directed by: Jean-Marc Vallee
Written by: Bryan Sipe
Cinematography by: Yves Belanger
Sound: Martin Pinsonnault
Music Supervisor: Susan Jacobs
Editing: Jay M. Glen
Art Direction: Javiera Varas
Costumes: Leah Katznelson
Production Design: John Paino
MPAA rating: R
Running time: 100 minutes

REVIEWS

Baumgarten, Marjorie. *Austin Chronicle.* April 6, 2016.
Burr, Ty. *Boston Globe.* April 7, 2016.
Ebiri, Bilge. *Village Voice.* April 7, 2016.
Ellwood, Gregory. *Hitfix.* September 11, 2016.
Erbland, Kate. *IndieWire.* September 10, 2016.
Holden, Stephen. *New York Times.* April 7, 2016.
Kurchak, Sarah. *Consequence of Sound.* April 7, 2016.
Persall, Steve. *Tampa Bay Times.* April 7, 2016.
Rodriguez, Rene. *Miami Herald.* April 7, 2016.
Roeper, Richard. *Chicago Sun-Times.* April 7, 2016.

QUOTES

Chris: "A bulldozer. You know you can buy almost anything on eBay. I just hope it comes with a manual."

Chris Cooper, who plays Jake Gyllenhaal's father-in-law in this film played the role of his father in *October Sky* (1999).

DEMON

Box Office: $104,038

When a film is this disturbing there is a tendency to file it under the horror genre and move on. But Marcin Wrona's *Demon* is, like its namesake, mercurial, wanting attention, and willing to do what it takes to get it. A closer look reveals a mean streak of dark humor and surprising sadness that deals with a chilling reality. Before World War II, Poland had 3.5 million Jews in its borders. It was a thriving community, one of the very largest in Europe. Today, it is home to a scant 3,200. The central question the film shrieks, laughs, and cries into the modern day is whether the past can be shoved aside simply for the sake of the comfortable future. Viewers should prepare to have a film knocking about in their heads for a while.

Peter (Itay Tiran) and Zaneta (Agnieszka Zulewska) have been given a wedding gift, a plot of land to build a home on, by her wealthy Father (Andrzej Grabowski). As the wedding looms, the groom begins to work the ground only to stumble into a pile of human remains clearly left over from the war. Deeply aware of Poland's role in the Final Solution, Peter is disquieted but decides to keep the secret to himself so that plans for the wedding can proceed. Soon, however, he begins acting strangely, not just unlike himself, but like someone else entirely.

The day of the wedding comes, and though the day-long event starts off fine, the father and other elders of the town are soon taken aback by Peter's bizarre behavior, concerned it will blemish not only the ceremony and celebration but the reputation of the town. In fact, it soon becomes apparent that no one in the town is concerned about anything else. Not even after an old man recognizes the strange language Peter has been speaking is Yiddish and that the groom has been taken over by a dybbuk, a demonic being angry at the callous hearts of those dancing on the graves of their martyred ancestors.

Demon is adapted from a play by Piotr Rowicki and though the story is easy to imagine taking place on a stage it is powerfully rendered for the screen. Wrona and his co-writer Pawel Maslona provide a screenplay so rich in theme it becomes almost impossible to identify a single dominant idea. This is a story concerned with politics, religion, and social caste, but without sacrificing one to shoe horn in another. Everything fits. One of the

genius conceits of *Demon* is that no one in the town is named. Characters are referred to by their social identity. Father, Doctor, Teacher, Aunt, etc. The end result is the emergence of a sort of every-community, a multifaceted but deeply flawed jewel valued far beyond its true worth.

Itay Tiran is inspired as the groom driven to increasingly frenzied physical states of possession. His performance ranks among the best in possession based cinema. Worth noting is the absence of CGI in his transformation. A small bit of makeup, otherwise Tiran is doing this alone. He is assisted by Wrona, who seems especially able to inspire the requisite madness in the rest of the cast who grow increasingly wild in their celebrations. This is laugh-out-loud funny at times, as when one guest says, "We must forget what we didn't see here." But at others the film assumes the heartbreak of Zaneta. Agnieszka Zulewska gives the bride a sympathetic edge without letting her completely off the hook. The films tragic ending hints at absurdist notions but her performance keeps the story grounded in what exactly is at stake.

The look of the film is rich and earthy. Across this palette, Wrona and his cinematographer Pawel Flis seem to move in full and effortless command of mood and atmosphere. Early scenes are almost pastoral, but as Peter descends into spiritual chaos the camera whips through his wild dancing and the threat of the supernatural like a dervish at one moment and like a tiger staring down a victim the next. Special effects are used sparingly and very effectively. This is sustained and virtuoso command of film's visual language. The word elegant is apropos, but at times the dirt and grime and sweat is so palpable, as if the screen itself were ready to open up and pour it on the viewer.

Worth noting is the tragic death of Marcin Wrona just as his film was hitting the festival circuit. Certainly a filmmaker who belonged on the world stage, he showed a breathtaking craft here. *Demon* is a most unusual ghost/possession story as much about why society is not afraid enough of its ghosts when they unexpectedly yell "Boo" from shared history.

Dave Canfield

CREDITS

Piotr: Itay Tiran
Zaneta: Agnieszka Zulewska
Ojciec: Andrzej Grabowski
Jasny: Tomasz Schuchardt
Gabryjelska: Katarzyna Herman
Origin: United States
Language: English

Released: 2016
Production: Marcin Wrona; released by Telewizja Polska S.A.
Directed by: Marcin Wrona
Written by: Marcin Wrona; Pawel Maslona
Cinematography by: Pawel Flis
Music by: Marcin Macuk; Krzysztof Penderecki
Editing: Piotr Kmiecik
Production Design: Anna Wunderlich
MPAA rating: R
Running time: 94 minutes

REVIEWS

Bittencourt, Ela. *Film Comment Magazine.* September 26, 2016.

Borders, Meredith. *Birth.Movies.Death.* July 18, 2016.

Jenkins, Mark. *NPR.* September 8, 2016.

Oberman, J. *Tablet.* September 14, 2016.

Orndorf, Brian. *Blu-ray.com.* September 21, 2016.

Rothkopf, Joshua. *Time Out.* September 6, 2016.

Savlov, Marc. *Austin Chronicle.* September 29, 2016.

Singer, Matt. *ScreenCrush.* August 29, 2016.

Webster, Andy. *New York Times.* August 31, 2016. .

Zilberman, Alan. *Washington Post.* September 15, 2016.

TRIVIA

Director Marcin Wrona killed himself during the Gdynia Polish Film Festival, where *Demon* was shown in competition.

DENIAL

> *When one man put the Holocaust on trial, she
> was forced to defend history.*
> —Movie tagline

Box Office: $4 Million

Anyone who has seen Claude Lanzmann's essential nine-hour documentary *Shoah* (1985), in which Holocaust survivors and officers following orders recount their horrific experiences at Auschwitz and other Nazi death camps, knows that it would be unthinkable to imagine people wanting to make up such stories. The emotions conjured up, the guilt of those who carried through unspeakable acts, and the details of the experiences are too vivid and too raw to be just an act. Yet there are people out there called "Holocaust deniers" who hold true to that theory and abide by it, no matter how wrong-headed. Chief among them is David Irving, a man who went so far as to publish a book on how the Holocaust never could have happened because of the lack of documentation. He even tried to sue renowned historian Deborah Lipstadt for her book, which took

Irving's theories to task and successfully shot them down. Irving sued her for libel because of her estimation of him as a liar.

Mitch Jackson's film *Denial* is about that case. Lipstadt (Rachel Weisz), a history professor in Atlanta, Georgia, had her book *Denying the Holocaust: The Growing Assault on Trust and Money* published in 1994. While on a book tour, in which she proclaims that she will never engage in a discussion with someone who denies the Holocaust, Irving (Timothy Spall) shows up and sabotages her moment by making a spectacle of himself and giving away his books for free. A couple years later, he sues her in London for libel in an effort to discredit her work. It is important that he sues her in London (where he lives) and not in America. The way their laws work, she now has to prove he is wrong for his findings. She ends up hiring none other than Anthony Julius (Andrew Scott), nicknamed "the junkyard dog" because of his handling of Princess Diana's divorce. Joining him as an expert witness and historian is Richard Rampton (Tom Wilkinson).

The film becomes a procedural in which Lipstadt has to cope with some unsettling ideas as to how her council will proceed in court, such as being told that she will not be testifying on her own behalf because the case is not about her, but about proving Irving had lied. Also, and most troubling, is that no Holocaust survivors will testify either, for fear of Irving making a mockery of them in court, which would not be unheard of given his history. Lipstadt raises money to fund her defense team, but a group of friends in the Jewish community advise to just settle the case and not go through with the trial. But Lipstadt holds true to her beliefs and travels to Auschwitz with her legal team and collect evidence in the ruins and mass graves. The unfortunate questions still come up: "How do we prove what this is?" In order to go against a denier, they have to think like one, the mindset of which goes against all logic.

The trial spans four years and it is not hard to figure out from watching the film which way the judge will sway. Irving is presented as one would expect, a villain who goes out of his way to show how lovely he can be with his young daughter when lawyers come to visit. There is nary a trace of historical background that would account for his point of view, which is indefensible, of course, but often can be fascinating to see when investigating its roots. Here, he exists to be the bad guy and nothing more. The simplicity of the screenplay does not end there. *Denial* is loaded, perhaps inevitably, with speeches about the ugliness of Holocaust deniers and references to Lipstadt and Irving being a modern day David and Goliath. Following almost every courtroom scene, Lipstadt's legal council is seen patting themselves on the back for a job well done, following with "Cheers!"

Even Julius is heard saying "That was the most boring trial ever." It is all too easy and that is the way it looks to the viewer of this film as well. Other than a German language barrier, there is really no accounting for why it took four years for the process of such a trial (one would have to read Lipstadt's book *Denial: Holocaust History on Trial* to get all the real details).

Weisz does her best, but she is often saddled with a script that repeatedly makes her look like someone without much in the way of common sense, such as when she is told to vary her route when jogging. She reacts with skepticism. Neither her nor the Irving character are given much of a background as to why their fight seems worth fighting so hard for. *Denial* misses an opportunity to expound on why a backwards mindset can be so frightening when one realizes that this person does not see themselves as a monster or a criminal. In Jackson's film, complexities take a backseat to heightened emotions, long shots of Lipstadt jogging to relieve stress and intense speechifying where Howard Shore's score swells as a character gets closer and closer to their obvious point. Still, seeing Spall and Wilkinson battle each other in the courtroom is a pleasure to watch. Their performances here are the highlight of the film.

Denial was released at a time when most films of this type get released: The end of September/beginning of October is when studios start releasing a huge amount of well-meaning films based on true stories, but *Denial's* release date has an interesting subtext. Here is a film in which a fully qualified, professional female historian has to go against a man who likes to pick fights and speak half-truths to any person of low intelligence who will listen. And she has to do it on a national stage. The parallels to the American election of 2016 make *Denial* a slightly more interesting entry into the "based-on-a-true-story" form of awards bait that studios tend to release at this time. It does not make it a great film by any stretch, but it does offer at least a springboard for another discussion altogether.

Collin Souter

CREDITS

Deborah Lipstadt: Rachel Weisz
Richard Rampton: Tom Wilkinson
David Irving: Timothy Spall
Anthony Julius: Andrew Scott
James Libson: Jack Lowden
Origin: United States
Language: English
Released: 2016
Production: Gary Foster, Russ Krasnoff; released by BBC Films, Krasnoff / Foster Entertainment, Participant Media L.L.C., Shoebox Films

Directed by: Mick Jackson
Written by: David Hare
Cinematography by: Haris Zambarloukos
Music by: Howard Shore
Music Supervisor: Maggie Rodford
Editing: Justine Wright
Art Direction: Christina Moore
Costumes: Odile Dicks-Mireaux
Production Design: Andrew McAlpine
MPAA rating: PG-13
Running time: 110 minutes

REVIEWS

Gilbert, Sophie. *The Atlantic.* September 29, 2016.
Hassenger, Jesse. *The A.V. Club.* September 29, 2016.
Howell, Peter. *Toronto Star.* October 6, 2016.
Jones, J.R. *Chicago Reader.* October 6, 2016.
Keough, Peter. *Boston Globe.* October 6, 2016.
Merry, Stephanie. *Washington Post.* October 6, 2016.
Puig, Claudia. *The Wrap.* September 12, 2016.
Scherstuhl, Alan. *Village Voice.* September 29, 2016.
Turan, Kenneth,. *Los Angeles Times.* September 29, 2016.
Wloszczyna, Susan. *RogerEbert.com.* September 30, 2016.

QUOTES

Richard Rampton: "They're a strange thing consciences. Trouble is, what feels best isn't necessarily what works best."

TRIVIA

The courtroom scenes' dialogue is taken verbatim from the trail records.

DESIERTO

From the Visionary Filmmakers That Brought You GRAVITY.
—Movie tagline

Box Office: $2 Million

Film, to borrow the title of Amos Vogel's landmark cultural study, truly is a subversive art. Half a century ago, the Poles, Czechs, and Hungarians repeatedly found innovative ways to express through the subjective, the nightmare, or the parable the quotidian horrors of living under totalitarian political regimes.

Film is also a dissident art. In the West, during a similar historical period, in movies like *Easy Rider* (1969), *Five Easy Pieces* (1970), *McCabe and Mrs. Miller* (1971), and *Scarecrow* (1973), the freedom and open American terrain proved illusory and deeper representation of violence and disillusion. The second feature of the young director Jonás Cuarón, *Desierto* is a peculiar hybrid poised between a stripped down exploitation B-movie and politically urgent allegory.

Jonás Cuarón is the son of the great filmmaker Alfonso Cuarón, a filmmaker who has moved nimbly between his personal Mexican films like *Y tu mamá también* (2001) and bracing, intelligent studio projects such as *Children of Men* (2006). Jonás Cuarón contributed to the script of his father's existential action movie, *Gravity* (2013). This new film is another study of survival unfolding in a terrifying and deeply hostile environment. The more abstract power and wonder of *Gravity* is replaced here by a more annihilating sense of disruption and despair as the protagonists come into opposition with a dark, self-appointed avenger.

Cuarón has a fine sense of tension, anxiety, and release, aided by the observant work of his superb cinematographer, Damian Garcia, working in a much different register than the plaintive black and white of *Güeros* (2014). This movie is shaped by dissonance. The expressive widescreen framing and the director's sharp use of the vast and expansive landscape is a frightening harbinger of violation. "Leaving is a form of dying," are the first words spoken on the soundtrack.

As the sun comes up, a pickup truck moves through the deserted stretch of land. The cargo is ferrying 14 refugees for a border incursion inside the United States when the truck breaks down. One of the passengers, Moises (Gael Garcia Bernal), mechanically knowledgeable and the most intrepid member of the party, informs the smugglers the engine is beyond repair. With little choice, the two leaders of the operation command the migrants to complete the dangerous mission on foot.

The greatest threat to their safety is not institutional, like the customs or border agents but a psychotic and racist vigilante hunter rather unsubtly named Sam (Jeffrey Dean Morgan). He roams the same badlands, in his Confederate flag-festooned truck, accompanied by his German shepherd, Tracker. Inevitably their paths cross. During a terrifying sequence the sadist Sam, a highly skilled sniper who's perched atop a rock, kills more than half the party with his frighteningly accurate, high-powered assault rifle. Unlike *Gravity*, the deaths here are visceral and cold-blooded, the vulnerable men and women desperate for shelter are open targets.

Cuarón, who also edited the film, intensifies the anguish and pain by altering the perspective, swiftly adopting the frightening perspective of the prey under siege or the cold, calculating perspective of the shooter as he studies his targets through the analytical frame of his long range scope. The sound is equally horrifying, either the stray bullets that smash off the desert terrain or the obscene rupture of bone or flesh violated. "Welcome to the land of the free," Sam says. The French

musician Yoann Lemoine, known as Woodkid, designed the ominous and unnerving soundtrack.

The ambush is the first of the movie's three dominant movements. Bernal's Moises is the leader of the survivors who were dislodged from the first wave of the migrant party. Sam quickly becomes aware of their existence and the group frantically seeks to evade his murderous rage. In the second section Cuarón varies the spatial relationships that alters the geographical dynamic, the terrifying horizontal line now dissolved by the scrub, ravines, crevices, and angular rock formations. The terror remains heightened, the horrifying threat of the long-range sniper is now deepened by the implacable, ferocious activities of the dog, which has been programmed to maim and kill with an even greater ruthlessness.

Night provides some valuable cover but the next morning, the group, now reduced to just Moises and a young woman named Adela (Alondra Hidalgo), must continually adapt to the circumstances and find a way to undermine the increasingly depraved killer. In *Desierto*, action displaces character. Bernal is a terrific actor who is blessed with the versatility and natural talent to go any number of ways. Cuarón slows the action enough to allow some nuance of character that breaks up the frantic rhythm and grants some plausibility and emotional believability to that quest.

The movie antecedents are clearly the original iteration of *The Most Dangerous Game* (1932) and Cornel Wilde's *The Naked Prey* (1966). The other significant comparison appears to be Robert Harmon's notorious *The Hitcher* (1986), in its expressive use of landscapes. This movie is not animated by the same psychosexual devices of that film. With his craggy lines, Morgan embodies the part. As genre, *Desierto* is very effective filmmaking. As psychology, the movie is more problematic and undeveloped internally. Sam is divested of any psychological acuity or interest. Who or what is he, a serial killer, a warped patriot or drunken fool?

He functions as pure id whose murderous act develops out of some fixation to protect something inherently clean or pure. Cuarón refuses to individualize the other migrants, making their deaths more symbolic than emotionally significant. The movie's dominant strength is its greatest liability. It is too lean and purposeful for its own good. The movie is very unsettling though overexplicit in its implications. The movie needed a greater profusion of ideas and thematic complexity to play off the action. *Desierto* often showcases a striking presence behind the camera. Jonás Cuarón, who wrote the script with Mateo Garcia, is not his strongest, muting some of the enthusiasm. *Desierto* is imperfect, for sure, though it is distinctive and that counts for something.

Patrick Z. McGavin

CREDITS

Moises: Gael Garcia Bernal
Sam: Jeffrey Dean Morgan
Adela: Alondra Hidalgo
Mechas: Diego Catano
Lobo: Marco Perez
Origin: United States
Language: Spanish, English
Released: 2016
Production: Alfonso Cuaron, Carlos Cuaron, Alex Garcia, Charles Gillibert, Jonas Cuaron; released by CG Cinema, Esperanto Kino, Itaca Films
Directed by: Jonas Cuaron
Written by: Jonas Cuaron; Mateo Garcia
Cinematography by: Damian Garcia
Music by: Woodkid
Sound: Sergio Diaz
Music Supervisor: Raphael Hamburger
Editing: Jonas Cuaron
Costumes: Andrea Manuel
Production Design: Alejandro Garcia
MPAA rating: R
Running time: 94 minutes

REVIEWS

Anderson, John. *Wall Street Journal.* October 13, 2016.
Chang, Justin. *Variety.* March 15, 2016.
Douglas, Edward. *New York Daily News.* October 12, 2016.
Kohn, Eric. *IndieWire.* October 13, 2016.
McCarthy, Todd. *Hollywood Reporter.* March 15, 2016.
Nashawaty, Chris. *Entertainment Weekly.* October 13, 2016.
Reed, Rex. *New York Observer.* October 12, 2016.
Vishnevetsky, Ignatiy. *The A.V. Club.* October 12, 2016.
Walsh, Katie. *Los Angeles Times.* October 13, 2016.
Zilberman, Alan. *Washington Post.* October 13, 2016.

TRIVIA

The entire film was shot outdoors.

DHEEPAN

Box Office: $248,392

Jacques Audiard's *Dheepan* fits naturally into the wider patterns of the French director's work, concerned with the hypnotic, terrifying rhythms, and textures of the criminal underworld. This material is colored in a different register, given a topical relevance examining the repercussions of a distant civil war and the displacement of three refugees.

Audiard wants desperately to breathe new life into received forms. He grooves on the idiosyncratic and violent impulses of the New American Cinema of the 1970s, especially the films of Martin Scorsese. One of his earlier films, *The Beat that My Heart Skipped* (2005), imaginatively reworked, in a French context, James Toback's feverish and propulsive *Fingers* (1978). The original idea for *Dheepan* was to make a revenge film in the style of Sam Peckinpah's *Straw Dogs* (1971).

Audiard is beholden to his material, for better or worse. What is undeniable is all of his films have a beautiful and exciting visual style. He is a nervy sensualist who uses the camera expressively, even voluptuously, to create heightened emotional states of expression—the hallucinatory prison murder scene in *A Prophet* (2009), or the devastating maritime work accident in *Rust and Bone* (2012), the glancing use of a reverse angle shot and water imagery heightening the sense of violent foreboding.

As a director, Audiard is at his best drawing out his characters' tragic vulnerability and need for escape and wonder. In his films, violence is not just the inevitable consequence; it defines the natural order. Adapted from stories of the American writer Craig Davidson, *Rust and Bone* was part of a very recognizable strain of modern European cinema as a social realist portrait of the economically marginalized, suggesting the influence of the movie's producers, the Belgian filmmakers Luc and Jean-Pierre Dardenne (*Rosetta* [1998], *Two Days, One Night* [2014]). Some of the other hallmarks of the Dardennes' early works, the use of nonprofessional actors and a regional location, also figure into the narrative strategies.

Audiard's new film is a synthesis of his earlier and nearer work. Montesquieu's 18th century picaresque *Persian Letters* (1721) is the dominant literary influence on the material. Audiard said the French writer and philosopher was concerned with what it meant to be human. Audiard wrote the script with his normal collaborator, Thomas Bidegain and the writer Noé Debré. The movie won the most important prize in international cinema, the Palme d'Or, for best film, at the Cannes Film festival, in a professional jury presided over the Coen Brothers.

Since his breakthrough second feature *A Self-Made Hero* (1996), Audiard has been drawn to stories challenging myth. Like much of the director's work, *Dhee-*

pan fixates on identity and authenticity. That quest is necessary for survival and freedom. The chilling opening sequence showing the bodies of the war dead laid out on a makeshift pyre and torched establishes the frantic and despairing mood.

Sivadhasan (Antonythasan Jesuthasan), a skilled and decorated, high-ranking Tamil rebel, who has probably experienced and committed various atrocities of war, slips out of his military uniform into civilian clothes, the first act of stripping away his past life. A haunted and defeated man, he fought on the losing side of the Sri Lankan civil war, and watched his wife and children perish in the conflict.

At a refugee camp, he assumes the identity of a dead man, Dheepan, fabricating a new family, his "wife," Yalini (Kalieaswari Srinivasan), and nine-year old "daughter," Illayaal (Claudine Vinasithamby). The scene of Yalini walking through the throngs of dazed, orphan children trying to find a suitable match is absolutely harrowing. Believing she is headed to England, where she has a cousin, Yalini learns instead she is being resettled in France.

Through a sympathetic interpreter (Nathan Anthonypillai), Dheepan attains his political asylum, convincing the French customs authorities he was the victim of government torture and political reprisals. So begins the new life for this makeshift family in the forlorn stretch of Le Pré Saint-Germain, a nondescript suburb in northeastern Paris. Audiard said his initial impulse was to make a film about the culturally invisible. Here, the family lives in plain sight, ostracized and alienated from any social order, afraid of any missteps or actions that might reveal their falsehoods.

Audiard is principally a genre director interesting in using color, movement, and form to deepen inner conflict. Because the adults barely speak or understand French, *Dheepan* has a fascinating correlation with Audiard's earlier film, *Read My Lips* (2001), about a deaf-mute woman (Emmanuelle Devos) caught up in a dangerous love affair. The new work is also about those stranded on the outside, unable to communicate. *Dheepan* is ostensibly a *banlieue* film, part of a class of contemporary French films depicting the socially restricted lives of the mostly black, poor or primarily Muslim immigrants who inhabit the ring of high rises on the outskirts of Paris.

At Le Pré, Dheepan has taken a job as a caretaker at the housing projects, a fortified block of apartment buildings broken into two distinct zones, including the central operation for the thriving drug trade. Audiard is an imagist who forsakes narrative line to document circumstance and existence. (One of the most striking images is a welder piercing a stainless steel object.) The whole movie is about breaking through barriers.

Mood, theme, and ideas are constantly free floating, like the insidious way violence always hovers around the main characters, like Illayaal reacting badly at her school playground of being left out of a group activity. Audiard is good at using humor, like a revealing exchange between the central couple, Dheepan mystified at the French, their customs and their humor, and Yalini telling him, amusingly, "even in Tamil, you are not funny."

Yalini has little use for the way women are shabbily treated at the projects, but she makes concessions, like wearing a head covering, to ease the tension. She takes a job preparing food for Mr. Habib (Faouzi Bensaïdi), a former drug lord, now incapacitated, whose high level apartment is used as a center of operations for the new boss, Brahim (Vincent Rottiers). In some of the strongest scenes in the film, Yalini engages in her own flirtatious banter with the young man, feeling liberated and unconstrained. Aware he is unable to understand her Tamil, she opens up and reveals the truth about her background.

The two worlds eventually collapse, and a fight over control of the drug trade leads to a robbery and eventually war between the factions that inevitably ensnares Dheepan and Yalini. If the movie *Dheepan* never quite ascends to the lyrical and fantastic heights of *A Prophet*, the movie represents a more concentrated and effective fusing of genre and social realist aesthetic than *Rust and Bone*. While Antonythasan lacks the technical depth of a trained actor, his brooding, handsome face projects a weary depth and achieves a quiet sorrow.

Audiard's devotion to the cinema of Martin Scorsese is probably overdone, particularly in the violent climax that is staged and directed in the precise manner of Travis Bickle's bloodbath at the finale of *Taxi Driver* (1976). *Dheepan* is a sad, painterly, and evocative work of people desperate to claim their dignity and honor. Flawed as it is from time to time, the movie captures something unassailable, a work of its time.

Patrick Z. McGavin

CREDITS

Dheepan: Jesuthasan Antonythasan
Yalini: Kalieaswari Srinivasan
Illayaal: Claudine Vinasithamby
Brahim: Vincent Rottiers
Youssouf: Marc Zinga
Origin: United States
Language: Tamil, French, English
Released: 2016

Production: released by Page 114, Why Not Productions
Directed by: Jacques Audiard
Written by: Jacques Audiard; Thomas Bidegain; Noe Debre
Cinematography by: Eponine Momenceau
Music by: Nicolas Jaar
Sound: Valerie Deloof
Music Supervisor: Frederic Junqua
Editing: Juliette Welfing
Art Direction: Helena Klotz
Costumes: Chattoune
Production Design: Michel Barthelemy
MPAA rating: R
Running time: 115 minutes

REVIEWS

Baumgarten, Marjorie. *Austin Chronicle.* June 22, 2016.
Chang, Justin. *Los Angeles Times.* May 12, 2016.
Ebiri, Bilge. *Village Voice.* May 4, 2016.
Foundas, Scott. *Variety.* May 23, 2015.
Hornaday, Ann. *Washington Post.* June 9, 2016.
Morgenstern, Joe. *Wall Street Journal.* May 12, 2016.
Nehme, Farran Smith. *New York Post.* May 5, 2016.
Rainer, Peter. *Christian Science Monitor.* May 6, 2016.
Rea, Stephen. *Philadelphia Inquirer.* May 27, 2016.
Scott, A.O. *New York Times.* May 5, 2016.

TRIVIA

This was the first film in the Tamil language and with Tamil lead actors to win the Palme d'Or.

AWARDS

Nominations:

British Acad. 2016: Foreign Film

DIRTY GRANDPA

Naughty is relative.
—Movie tagline

Box Office: $35.5 Million

Dirty Grandpa is a failure on almost every level possible, but, fair or unfair, more than anything, it feels like a particularly heinous misstep for Robert De Niro. He does not deserve the lion's share of the blame—writer John Philips and director Dan Mazer probably had the most direct hand in crafting this disposable shrug of a movie—however, it is next to impossible to watch *Dirty Grandpa* and not have an overwhelming urge to ask De Niro, "Did you really not save any of the *Meet the Parents* money?" Because there can be no coherent creative reason why anyone would choose to be in this film,

which means that De Niro's choice to take the titular role was both premeditated and wildly misjudged.

On a surface level, one might be able to see why De Niro would gravitate toward a raunchy comedy like this. Many of his peers, later in their careers, reinvented themselves by playing up the crudest, most exaggerated caricatures of what it means to be an "old man." De Niro previously dipped his toe in this arena with *Last Vegas,* (2013) but the best, relatively recent example of that transformation done well was probably 1993's *Grumpy Old Men.* Make no mistake, *Grumpy Old Men* was no revolutionary comedy, but it did reinvigorate the screen images of Jack Lemmon, Walter Matthau, and Burgess Meredith as caustic elderly icons, with Meredith, in particular, embracing a level of well-crafted, self-aware smuttiness that *Dirty Grandpa* could only aspire to.

Unfortunately, *Dirty Grandpa* is no *Grumpy Old Men.* It's no *Last Vegas* or *The Bucket List* (2007). It's not even *Bad Grandpa,* (2013), which was a movie from the crew behind *Jackass* that somehow dwarfs *Dirty Grandpa* in terms of human characters, plot, and emotion. Because, at its core, *Dirty Grandpa* is not a "dirty" movie; it's just a lazy movie, a spectacularly lazy movie with a plot cribbed from a 1986 ski-school sex comedy.

The true shame of *Dirty Grandpa* is that every single person involved with the film is slumming it. De Niro, obviously, but even Zac Efron has shown able comedic chops in *Neighbors* (2014) and earlier films. Aubrey Plaza, Jason Mantzoukas, Danny Glover, Adam Pally—everyone in *Dirty Grandpa* has appeared in other, better films before. So, beyond an easy paycheck, it's a mystery why any or all of them gravitated toward this film. The plot feels like something out of a *Simpsons* movie parody or a straight-to-Netflix Adam Sandler comedy, only with even less commitment to quality.

Efron's Jason is a young, tightly wound wannabe corporate attorney, with an even higher-strung fiancée, who reconnects with his grandfather Dick (De Niro) after the death of his grandmother. The once-close Jason and Dick had become estranged years earlier—seemingly only because Jason became such an uptight square—but his grandmother's passing fills Jason with enough regret to agree to drive brash, loud-mouthed Dick to Boca Raton, Florida (where dirty grandpas roam free, one imagines).

Dick cannot believe that Jason abandoned his dreams of becoming a globe-trotting photographer—every banker or lawyer has secret dreams of becoming an artist in hacky comedies like these—and Jason is not used to seeing his grandfather as such a sexually predatory beast. Dick has not had sex in years, due to his wife's cancer, so he's making up for lost time, but the filmmakers are seemingly only able to express that repressed side of Dick with cheap double-entendres and masturbation jokes. Because this is a very lazy movie, the road trip, of course, encounters some complications. On the road, Jason and Dick unexpectedly run into Shadia (Zoey Deutch), the bohemian co-ed former love of Jason's life, and Lenore (Aubrey Plaza), Shadia's inexplicable horndog best friend who finds herself lusting after the old man.

It is to Plaza's great credit that she is, apparently, the only actor in the movie who decided to inject any life into her character. Her Lenore is a foul-mouthed, hypersexualized battering ram. Yes, she might chew the scenery with her line reads, but, in a comedy this inert, you just want to hand her a MVP trophy for actually trying.

What follows is not really a plot, but is more like a pastiche of other, earlier sex comedies that the screenwriter saw on late night TV. Of course, Dick and Jason get diverted to Spring Break. Jason gets caught in compromising positions when he finally lets his hair down. Jason flirts with Shadia. Dick goes wild, but proves that his old-school lack of political correctness endears him to everyone, which is such a hackneyed, unearned device.

Jason and Dick bond. Jason rethinks his wedding. There is nothing wrong with a good raunchy sex comedy, but *Dirty Grandpa* brings absolutely nothing new to the table. One has to wonder what De Niro saw in the role, because Dick is no convention-shattering, stereotype-defying icon of aging. He's just a sad, dirty grandpa with nothing much of substance to leave to his descendants.

Tom Burns

CREDITS

Dick Kelly: Robert De Niro
Jason Kelly: Zac Efron
Shadia: Zoey Deutch
Lenore: Aubrey Plaza
Tan Pam: Jason Mantzoukas
Meredith: Julianne Hough
Origin: United States
Language: English
Released: 2016
Production: Jason Barrett, Bill Block, Barry Josephson, Michael Simkin; released by Lionsgate
Directed by: Dan Mazer
Written by: John Phillips
Cinematography by: Eric Alan Edwards
Music by: Michael Andrews
Music Supervisor: Kier Lehman
Editing: Anne McCabe
Art Direction: Jeremy Woolsey

Costumes: Christie Wittenborn
Production Design: William Arnold
MPAA rating: R
Running time: 102 minutes

REVIEWS

Greenblatt, Leah. *Entertainment Weekly.* January 22, 2016.
Hassenger, Jesse. *The A.V. Club.* January 22, 2016.
Jagernauth, Kevin. *The Playlist.* January 21, 2016.
Johnston, Trevor. *Time Out London.* January 25, 2016.
Kupecki, Josh. *Austin Chronicle.* January 27, 2016.
Rapold, Nicolas. *New York Times.* January 23, 2016.
Scheck, Frank. *Hollywood Reporter.* January 21, 2016.
Singer, Matt. *ScreenCrush.* January 22, 2016.
Walsh, Katie. *Los Angeles Times.* January 22, 2016.
Whitty, Stephen. *New York Daily News.* January 22, 2016.

QUOTES

Lenore: "I like your pull-out couch."
Dick Kelly: "Yeah? Well, I got news for ya. That's the only thing that's gonna be pulling out tonight."

TRIVIA

Zac Efron performed all of his own nude scenes except for the embarrassing beach sequence.

AWARDS

Nominations:

Golden Raspberries 2016: Worst Actor (De Niro), Worst Picture, Worst Support. Actress (Hough), Worst Support. Actress (Plaza)

THE DISAPPOINTMENTS ROOM

Some mysteries should not be unlocked.
—Movie tagline

Box Office: $2.4 Million

Aptly titled, this unimaginative supernatural thriller is unlikely to leave a mark on the memory of anyone who sees it. It wants the viewer to invest in whether or not its heroine is the victim of a haunting or retreating back into mental illness. But the payoff is so predictable and weak that whatever virtues the film has simply fade into the background like a ghost.

In need of a change following the death of a newborn, Dana (Kate Beckinsale), her husband David (Mel Raido), and their young son Lucas (Duncan Joiner), head out to the country in search of peace. Their new fixer-upper house is perfect. It's exactly the sort of run-down mansion seen in most haunted house movies these days—just run-down enough to be quaint and full of ample space for new dreams and nightmares. As Kate tries gamely to recover from the emotional breakdown following her infant daughter's death she begins hearing and seeing things that cause her to question her sanity. But those same things lead her to a hidden door in the attic, solidly locked and a box of keys. Further research reveals the presence of a disappointments room, a place where deformed or disabled children would be kept out of sight to protect the reputation of their families. This disappointments room was used by the evil Judge Blacker (Gerald McRaney) to hide his poor deformed daughter. Soon, the spirits of both seem to be dogging her every move threatening not only her but the safety of her own family.

Director D.J. Caruso works from a script by Wentworth Miller, for at least part of the time. There are plenty of indications that major fixes went on during filming. Those who still mourn the loss of creative talent that resulted in his excellent neo-noir debut, *The Salton Sea* (2002) will have absolutely no reason to watch this. Before the story falls apart in the last act, Caruso and cinematographer Rogier Stoffers manage to create some atmosphere around the time-worn situations and thin characters sketched out in Miller's script but none of it seems particularly inspired.

Miller had previously written the screenplay for the middling thriller *Stoker* (2013), which also suffered from predictability, but at least that film benefited greatly from excellent performances and the evocative direction of Chan-wook Park. No such luck here. Wentworth litters his second screenplay with unnecessary subplots and predictable scenes. Lucas Till shows up as a handyman with designs on Dana in a bit of repeated business that goes nowhere. The requisite scene involving a character looking through old newspaper clippings and talking to a local historian has no real payoff either. Neither do revelations that Dana has been secretly drinking. In short, it quickly becomes apparent that the characters are only here to fill time in between scares that never materialize. Not even when doors slam shut, ominous hounds lurk or phantom children scurry about.

Performances are fine throughout given the material everyone has to work with. Kate Beckinsale makes two or three of these kinds of films a year these days, which is a shame given that she long ago proved she has solid acting chops. Even just this year she displayed substantial charm Whit Stillman's *Love and Friendship* (2016). Mel Raido tries to invest David with as much energy as possible but the character itself is still two-dimensional.

Special effects here might provide some scares for someone young enough to have never seen a horror film before. There is some gore piled on at the end in an apparent attempt to distract viewers who might notice the large number of narrative loose ends that hang like cheap movie cobwebs. But the ghosts, the locked room that screams leave-me-the-hell-alone and the flashbacks into the homes troubled past all feel like leftovers.

Cinema is rife with haunting stories of heroines who may or may not be mad. The recently re-appreciated *Let's Scare Jessica To Death* (1973), *The Haunting* (1963), and various adaptations of Henry James' *The Turn of the Screw* including the excellent *The Innocents* (1961), are a few of the better ones. But there are scores of tired made-for-TV movies that seem to start with the idea that all they have to do to create a worthwhile film is throw an attractive women in emotional distress into the path of a ghost with some business to finish. This whole film feels like unfinished business.

The last word on *The Disappointments Room* involves a bit of irony. The project languished on Relativity Media shelves for more than a year after completion due to that company's slide toward bankruptcy. The fact of its release now could hardly feel more perfunctory.

Dave Canfield

CREDITS

Dana: Kate Beckinsale
David: Mel Raido
Ben: Lucas Till
Lucas: Duncan Joiner
Judge Blacker: Gerald McRaney
Origin: United States
Language: English
Released: 2016
Production: Sam Englebardt, William D. Johnson, Geyer Kosinski, Vincent Newman; released by Demarest Films, Media Talent Group, Relativity Media
Directed by: D.J. Caruso
Written by: D.J. Caruso; Wentworth Miller
Cinematography by: Rogier Stoffers
Music by: Brian Tyler
Music Supervisor: Bob Bowen
Editing: Vince Filippone
Art Direction: Kevin Hardison
Costumes: Marian Toy
Production Design: Tom Southwell
MPAA rating: R
Running time: 92 minutes

REVIEWS

Abele, Robert. *TheWrap.* September 9, 2016.
Barnes, Daniel. *Sacramento News & Review.* September 15, 2016.

Estrada, Erick. *Cinegarage.* December 20, 2016.
Farber, Stephen. *Hollywood Reporter.* September 9, 2016.
Granger, Susan. *SSG Syndicate.* September 10, 2016.
Holub, Christian. *Entertainment Weekly.* September 9, 2016.
Leydon, Joe. *Variety.* September 12, 2016.
Orndorf, Brian. *Blu-ray.com.* September 9, 2016.
Savlov, Marc. *Austin Chronicle.* September 15, 2016.
Walsh, Katie. *Los Angeles Times.* September 12, 2016.

TRIVIA

The film was written by Wentworth Miller, who had a small role in "Underworld," which also starred Kate Beckinsale.

DISORDER
(Maryland)

Box Office: $39,687

A story of a damaged man and his deepening relationship to the beautiful woman he is assigned to protect, the coolly intelligent French movie *Disorder* is an evasive thriller deliberately playing against itself. The movie is trying something different, eschewing easy closure or emotional access to its characters.

This is the second film written and directed by the very gifted young French director Alice Winocour. Her excellent debut, *Augustine* (2012), a 19th century period drama about a progressive neurologist who becomes emotionally attached to a young woman who suffers from unexplained seizures, revealed a natural and intuitive ability with actors and the rare talent for dramatizing the ineffable. Winocour also helped write the lively and quietly devastating coming of age film *Mustang* (2015), the Academy Award-nominated Turkish feature by Deniz Gamze Ergüven.

The subject of her first film was emotional and sexual instability, and the complicated way men and women negotiate traditional roles. The new film is united with that work through theme and ideas. In *Augustine,* Winocour and her talented cinematographer, Georges Lechaptois, extensively deployed the handheld camera to convey the central character's inner torment. Lechaptois also shot the new film, and the ink dark and impressionistic palette suggests a near pervasive sense of breakdown.

Winocour merges content and form pretty seamlessly, in her use of the subjective underlying the narrative importance of surveillance, manifested in the constant presence of security cameras and video monitors. *Disorder* is clearly meant to subvert the normal rhythms of the thriller. Time is almost never compressed or elided though agonizingly extended and pushed to its furthest duration. Instead of carefully mapping out the architecture of her story, Winocour underplays the expositional or emotional detail, allowing the accretion of action and behavior to take hold and making the viewer intuit what it actually means.

Vincent Loreau (Matthias Schoenaerts), a Special Forces soldier in an elite French unit, returns from a tour in Afghanistan clearly suffering symptoms, hearing loss and extreme isolation, consistent with post-traumatic stress disorder. Winocour refuses to fill out the character. He stays hidden and deeply guarded, about himself and his past. His physical grace and power offsets his asocial personal traits, the monosyllabic speaking patterns or his refusal to make eye contact. The stark and foreboding tattoos inscribed on his chest say everything.

The movie's French title, *Maryland,* refers to the name of an upscale-gated villa on the French Riviera. Through his friend, Denis (Paul Hamy), Vincent is part of a security detail made up of former military personnel working a party for a politically connected and wealthy Lebanese businessman named Imad Whalid (Percy Kemp). The party sequence is pivotal to the conception of the lead character and in introducing the deeper discordant tones. The ostentatious display of wealth, symbolized by a collection of expensive Chanel handbags or the sight of a beautiful bejeweled woman in a knockout red dress, only accentuates Vincent's social alienation.

Every scene pivots on some form of conflict, either real or perceived, like Vincent's exchange with a brusque and self-satisfied guest or the hard and unforgiving way he rips into a block of ice. He has a brusque, forward momentum and the natural intelligence to sense something amiss, captured in the in the slightly ominous overheard conversations about money, client states and dealmakers. His competence, professionalism and discretion catches the attention of the financier, who rewards Vincent with a lucrative follow up job watching over the man's wife, Jesse (Diane Kruger) and young son, Ali (Zaïd Errougui-Demonsant), during a business trip.

Winocour has an elliptical feel for story and character. She makes her points with a glancing sureness, revealing essential and necessary qualities about Vincent obliquely. She upends a primary supposition about those who experience combat, that one can inflict damage and pain without being permanently damaged in return. Increasingly the story of *Disorder* turns on the fine distinction between his inner tumult, his almost preternatural feeling of impending harm against his clients and actual threats that materialize against the woman and her son.

In the movie's big set piece, Winocour reveals a talent for action when following a quiet and reflective moment at the beach, masked assailants set upon the three as they sit inside their car. Winocour builds to an impressive tension and release, her slow burn rhythms fraught with an eerie sense of violation that suddenly accelerates into hand-to-hand combat. The musician Mike Lévy, known as Gesaffelstein, scored the jagged, atonal music, an aural counterpoint to Vincent's restlessness and unease.

Winocour's use of space is involving, the camera tight on bodies and faces, generating a feeling of dread in the seconds preceding the attack inside the car. Every time the film settles into a recognizable form, Winocour disrupts expectations. That unpredictability acquires a texture and depth and helps glide over the one striking implausibility about the film regarding Jesse, the film suggests, is so sheltered and blissfully unaware her husband is an arms merchant. It leads to a great sequence at the villa, now abandoned, with Jesse and her son closer to prisoners than inhabitants of the space. Denis turns up, at the insistence of Vincent for back up, and his ease and flirtatious banter with Jesse is such a contrast with Vincent that he becomes unhinged with jealousy.

Winocour dangles various plot devices, like some supposedly incriminating documents Walid left behind, to satisfy the genre requirements. On a central level, this is anti-entertainment, a work designed to frustrate and leave a great many questions unanswered. The actors fill in the gaps and supply the tension, a volatility that brings the material together. Schoenaerts is not just a presence. He is a great actor, with his relentless focus and drive, like the way he studies every frame of the video surveillance. He brings a kinetic physical power to the part, but it is the wounding part, the vulnerability and fear, that testifies to his range and command. When he lets everything out, pummeling one of the home invaders, the moment is shocking.

Kruger is a little more interesting in her French or German roles. In English, she always feels a bit mannered and decorative (an exception was her exceptional work on the FX cable series, *The Bridge*). The limitations of her character, as designed and written, prevent *Disorder* from being a great film. Like Schoenaerts, she is beautiful and her gift with language gives her naturalness that is not made up or manufactured. The enigmatic question of their relationship, down to the ambiguous coda, is part of Winocour's disruptive strategy. It leaves a

sting. *Disorder* is further proof of a dynamic and significant new talent.

Patrick Z. McGavin

CREDITS

Vincent: Matthias Schoenaerts
Jessie: Diane Kruger
Denis: Paul Hamy
Tom: Victor Pontecorvo
Ali: Zaïd Errougui-Demonsant
Origin: United States
Language: French
Released: 2016
Production: Emilie Tisne; released by Darius Films, Dharamsala
Directed by: Alice Winocour
Written by: Alice Winocour
Cinematography by: Georges Lechaptois
Music by: Mike Levy
Sound: Gwennole Le Borgne
Editing: Julien Lacheray
Costumes: Pascaline Chavanne
Production Design: Samuel Deshors
MPAA rating: Unrated
Running time: 98 minutes

REVIEWS

Chang, Justin. *Los Angeles Times*. August 18, 2016.
Cordova, Randy. *Arizona Republic*. August 25, 2016.
Ehrlich, David. *Indiewire*. August 11, 2016.
Gray, Christopher. *Slant Magazine*. August 5, 2016.
Lodge, Guy. *Variety*. May 20, 2015.
O'Malley, Sheila. *RogerEbert.com*. August 12, 2016.
Romney, Jonathan. *Screen International*. May 20, 2015.
Scott, A.O. *New York Times*. August 11, 2016.
Vishnevetsky, Ignatiy. *The A.V. Club*. August 11, 2016.
Wolfe, April. *Village Voice*. August 9, 2016.

TRIVIA

The producers planned on getting a dog who was not trained for films in order to save money. But every time the dog saw the camera, he would run away.

DOCTOR STRANGE

The impossibilities are endless.
—Movie tagline

Box Office: $231.9 Million

The Marvel Cinematic Universe has built up a tremendous cache of good will amongst its fans and even the casual observers who have never picked up a comic book in their lives. Thanks to the success of *Iron Man* (2008) the movies have been able to transition away from the most recognized heroes and take chances on lesser-known properties such as *Guardians of the Galaxy* (2014) and *Ant-Man* (2015). All the while, their rival, DC Comics, have stumbled through bringing their catalog to life since Christopher Nolan put his final stamp on Batman, and relying on a filmmaker like Zack Snyder who does not appear to even like Superman. Each side have their loyal defenders, sometimes to a fault, and while Marvel can afford to take the kind of risks that DC cannot it does not mean that they are without flaws. Scott Derrickson's *Doctor Strange* is, in many ways, a perfect example of this, proving that it takes more than just a few trippy visuals to create an origin story worthy of a follow-up.

Stephen Strange (Benedict Cumberbatch) is a brilliant neurosurgeon. Just ask him. It has brought him great wealth and privilege. But on the road to one of those privileges, he crashes his car, leaving him without the use of his prized hands. Exhausting all options and his fortune, the Doctor hears of a potential solution in Nepal. Led to the Kamar-Taj compound by Karl Mordo (Chiwetel Elijofor), Strange meets the Ancient One (Tilda Swinton, in the film's most interesting human persona), who is about to give him a fast lesson in the worldly dimensions unseen to Muggle eyes and not listed in any of the books to which he has dedicated his life.

With the words "Teach me," Strange—after a brief delay—puts the audience on the path to learn all about magical spells and interdimensional travel. Master Wong (Benedict Wong) resides over the mystical library, including the books under lock and key that were already violated by former pupil, Kaecilius (Mads Mikkelsen), who also killed Wong's predecessor. Strange learns of the Sanctums, a series of buildings in three of Earth's largest cities designed to protect the planet from other dimensions. His advanced learning draws comparison to the villain who seeks to bend the laws of time and space and summon the powerful Dormammu in a quest for immortality. Unless the Doctor and his trusty cloak can negotiate a truce in time.

Comic books have a built-in degree of disbelief suspension. In colorful paper, just about anything can be translated to the imagination. Bitten by a radioactive spider or radiated with gamma-infused anger makes a certain scientific sense when viewed on a comic book page. Magic, on the other hand, is a tricky venture, especially when captured as broadly as it is here. For *Doctor Strange*, powers are nothing but special effects, and if there is one thing that modern audiences have seen all before it is that.

Derrickson may think he is playing with images a bit out of the norm for a Marvel film but his two perceived innovations are just riffs on past ones. Strange's initial trip into the astral-projected void is little more than a Terry Gilliam cartoon drawn by computers. The film's biggest crutch though could be considered Christopher Nolan's contribution to the Marvel Universe since it is stolen wholesale from *Inception* (2010). Minus the originality and excitement of how the magicians (or the dreamers) can utilize the bending of the physical world to their advantage, it is merely just a collection of changing backdrops with nary an ounce of the visceral charge or relaxed understanding of how Joseph Gordon-Levitt could maneuver on the walls and ceiling to fight his adversaries.

The philosophies of the screenplay by Derrickson, Jon Spaihts, and C. Robert Cargill are as store-bought fortune cookie as they come. If they truly wanted to go outside the norm of Marvel expectations, they would have expanded on the concept of one's soul existing outside of the body than on the bland fighting techniques that usually involve its mystics circling up a mid-air charge of electric fireballs and pushing them at their foe. Its climax may be subversive enough to not come down to another fistfight, but it is still reminiscent of someone who really liked the central gimmick of *Edge of Tomorrow* (2014) and thought they could make it their own. In that, *Doctor Strange* really is not any different at all.

Marvel stories are not going away anytime soon. As Strange says, "This is how things are now. You and me trapped in this moment endlessly," and there is something wonderful in knowing that these films are playing out like one great big mini-series with separate chapters before coming together as wholes like in the Avengers films or the terrific *Captain America: Civil War* (2016). Cumberbatch's Strange has nowhere near the charisma of Robert Downey Jr's arrogant Tony Stark, leaving the actor to be a more watered-down version of his treasured incarnation as Sherlock Holmes on TV. The always-interesting Chiwetel Elijofor will likely be given more to do in future chapters. Hopefully at least more than Rachel McAdams gets to do in chapter one as Strange's colleague and former lover. When a red piece of cloth infuses the most personality in a world of geniuses and magicians it is time to really look inward and determine where the soul is in just another overstuffed CGI construction project.

Erik Childress

CREDITS

Dr. Stephen Strange: Benedict Cumberbatch
Mordo: Chiwetel Ejiofor
Christine Palmer: Rachel McAdams
Wong: Benedict Wong
Kaecilius: Mads Mikkelsen
The Ancient One: Tilda Swinton
Origin: United States
Language: English
Released: 2016
Production: Kevin Feige; released by Marvel Studios
Directed by: Scott Derrickson
Written by: Scott Derrickson; Jon Spaihts; C. Robert Cargill
Cinematography by: Ben Davis
Music by: Michael Giacchino
Sound: Daniel Laurie; Shannon Mills
Music Supervisor: Dave Jordan
Editing: Sabrina Plisco; Wyatt Smith
Art Direction: Ray Chan
Costumes: Alexandra Byrne
Production Design: Charles Wood
MPAA rating: PG-13
Running time: 115 minutes

REVIEWS

Berardinelli, James. *ReelViews.* November 3, 2016.
Chang, Justin. *Los Angeles Times.* November 3, 2016.
Edelstein, David. *New York Magazine/Vulture.* November 3, 2016.
Johanson, MaryAnn. *Flick Filosopher.* October 27, 2016.
Leitsch, Will. *New Republic.* November 4, 2016.
McGranaghan, Mike. *Aisle Seat.* November 8, 2016.
Minow, Nell. *Beliefnet.* November 3, 2016.
Ranson, Kevin A.. *MovieCrypt.com.* December 6, 2016.
Tobias, Scott. *NPR.* July 21, 2016.
Villarreal, Phil. *ABC Tucson.* November 4, 2016.

QUOTES

The Ancient One: "Arrogance and fear still keep you from learning the simplest and most significant lesson of all."
Dr. Stephen Strange: "Which is?"
The Ancient One: "It's not about you."

TRIVIA

The creators of Doctor Strange, Stan Lee and Steve Ditko, based his appearance on actor Vincent Price.

AWARDS

Nominations:
Oscars 2016: Visual FX
British Acad. 2016: Makeup, Production Design, Visual FX

DON'T BREATHE

This house looked like an easy target. Until they found what was inside.
—Movie tagline

Box Office: $89.2 Million

One of the most effective thrillers of the year is not without its third-act issues, but *Don't Breathe* is far too exciting to be rendered less than must-see by that. Director/writer Fede Alvarez and co-writer Rodo Sayagues make good on the promise hinted at so strongly in their *Evil Dead* (2013) remake and very nearly create a masterpiece of suspense here, thwarted mainly by a temptation to excess that draws their characters away from the moral ambiguity that powers the story until then.

Rocky (Jane Levy), Money (Daniel Zovatto), and Alex (Dylan Minnette) are three young people who use the info they cull from Alex's dads security company to plot a string of upscale home robberies. When they have trouble making money off the stolen goods, Money insists they pull one big heist that will let them move out of town and start anew. Rocky wants to get her little sister away from her lowlife mother and abusive boyfriend. Alex is not so secretly in love with Rocky. But Alex is uneasy. The mark is an Army vet sitting on $300,000 from an insurance settlement, money received after his daughter died in a car accident that was the fault of a teen from a wealthy family. While casing the neighborhood and the vet's house, Alex discovers the man is blind and has a ferocious dog. What seemed like an easy score now seems too cruel and dangerous.

After some argument, Money convinces them to proceed that night. They drug the dog and find a way into the unusually secure house where a search for the cash turns up only a locked door. Convinced the cash is behind the door but unable to open it, Money pulls out a gun, horrifying Alex, who tells the group their crime is now considered a felony. Before Alex can convince everyone to leave, Money shoots off the lock using a soda bottle as a silencer. The noise, though muffled wakes the old man who then subdues Money and kills him with his own gun.

From this moment on, the film plays a tense game of cat and mouse as Rocky and Alex attempt to hide their existence from The Blind Man who uses all his other senses to intuit there must be someone else in the house. After he opens the locked door and checks on his money, Rocky waits for him to start searching the rest of the house and steals the cash. As her and Alex look for a way out, they encounter a young woman chained up in the basement and realize she is the one who killed The Blind Man's daughter. Too late, The Blind Man has discovered their presence, unleashed his now-conscious attack dog, and what follows is an absolutely breathtaking series of confrontations.

Don't Breathe has been described as a reversal of the classic suspense film *Wait Until Dark* (1967), with the blind character as villain. The description fits. Just as Alan Arkin created a terrifying psychotic with the character of Roat, actor Stephan Lang is unforgettable as The Blind Man, a sightless but hardly helpless mentally ill veteran determined to protect the fortune, and the secrets, hidden in his house. But the similarities between the two projects mostly end there. Alvarez and his Production Designer Naaman Marshall start their story with a robbery in a tony suburban home before they introduce The Blind Man's abandoned inner city neighborhood full of urban rot and decay. This telescoping in towards madness and chaos continues into The Blind Man's home, a moldering multi-floored hovel that will likely have viewers remembering the great death houses of American genre cinema: *The Texas Chainsaw Massacre* (1974), *The People Under The Stairs* (1991), or *The Silence of The Lambs* (1991). The house is the central figure in an endlessly inventive series of set pieces set up by a screenplay that has the characters racing through tight corridors, playing hide and seek in the dark, fending off animal attack, and ending up in standoffs in hidden rooms. To be sure the house and its neighborhood are characters themselves here but also metaphors for the inner state of the human characters and even the state of the society they live in, where everything from the economy to simple human relationships have broken down.

Alvarez and his cinematographer Pedro Luque squeeze every last ounce of suspense out of their shot compositions. Though roughly 3/4 of the film takes place in the dimly lit house, action sequences remain visible and visceral. Violence too is photographed with a raw power and it must be noted that the trio of editors credited, Eric L. Beason, Louise Ford, and Gardner Gould, must surely have helped create the dynamic flow that keeps viewers on the edges of the seats throughout. Of further note is the stylistic and sprawling score. Bangs and knocks and otherworldly noises share space along with effective but more conventionally rendered orchestral pieces and neither approach draws attention to itself. This is supportive craft that ably underscores the emotional weight earned by all the other filmmaking expertise behind the story.

The cast is more than up for the demands of the screenplay. Performances are fine during action sequences. And when they have a chance to be still and converse, Jane Levy and Dylan Minnette invest their characters with intelligence and strength. Rocky is genuinely worried about the wellbeing of her sister. Alex is a dumb kid, in over his head and making dangerously bad decisions. Neither is perfectly likable of course but both remain empathetic as the crisis brings out their heroic sides. The Blind Man quickly becomes a larger than life figure in the film, able to match the would-be thieves at every step. Stephen Lang is a respected actor with a long sheet of solid credits but rarely has he been used as well as he is in *Don't Breathe*. Known mainly for playing military types and authority figures, Lang's Blind Man spends most of the film as a complex figure despite the outrageous violence he perpetrates. Beaten down by one tragedy at a time, Lang makes it easy to see the good man who teetered over the edge into darkness. The actor is smart enough to maintain some of that complexity when a third act reveal about his character threatens to remove any and all audience empathy.

But by then Alvarez and Sayagues dive headfirst into genre overkill giving The Blind Man a backstory that takes a disturbing and visually disgusting turn that goes far beyond kidnapping. As such, *Don't Breathe* almost becomes a mere monster movie, albeit an absolutely thrilling one, missing out on many possible and more compelling narrative payoffs though Alvarez does successfully and rather neatly set the story up for a well-earned and most welcome sequel. Most filmmakers would do this haphazardly these days but Fede Alvarez is well on his way to proving he is not most filmmakers.

Dave Canfield

CREDITS

The Blind Man: Stephen Lang
Rocky: Jane Levy
Alex: Dylan Minnette
Money: Daniel Zovatto
Diddy: Emma Bercovici
Origin: United States
Language: English
Released: 2016
Production: Sam Raimi, Fede Alvarez; released by Ghost House Pictures, Screen Gems, Stage 6 Films
Directed by: Fede Alvarez
Written by: Fede Alvarez; Rodo Sayagues
Cinematography by: Pedro Luque
Music by: Roque Banos
Sound: Jonathan Miller
Editing: Eric L. Beason; Louise Ford; Gardner Gould
Art Direction: Adrien Asztalos
Costumes: Carlos Rosario

Production Design: Naaman Marshall
MPAA rating: R
Running time: 88 minutes

REVIEWS

Carlson, Marten. *Consequence of Sound*. March 15, 2016.
Crump, Andy. *Paste Magazine*. September 1, 2016.
Diones, Bruce. *New Yorker*. September 25, 2016.
Dowd. A.A. *The A.V. Club*. August 25, 2016.
Harvey, Dennis. *Variety*. March 14, 2016.
Kohn, Eric. *IndieWire*. March 16, 2016.
McDonagh, Maitland. *Film Journal International*. August 25, 2016.
Newman, Kim. *Empire Magazine*. August 18, 2016.
Russo, Tom. *Boston Globe*. August 25, 2016.
Weinberg, Scott. *Nerdist*. August 26, 2016.

QUOTES

Money: "Just because he's blind doesn't mean he's a saint, bro."

TRIVIA

The dog was played by three different dogs: Athos, Astor, and Nomad.

THE DRESSMAKER

Revenge is back in fashion.
—Movie tagline

Box Office: $2 Million

The good news about *The Dressmaker* is that it contains both a nifty and attention-grabbing opening moment and an equally compelling bit just before the final fade out. The bad news is that practically everything else in between is pretty much a total botch—a bizarre tonal mismatch that cannot decide whether it wants to be an overheated revenge drama, a campy spoof of overheated revenge dramas, an inspiring work about a woman who comes to a small and repressed town and inspires everyone through her unique gifts, or a serious story about a wronged woman trying to come to terms with her tragic past and therefore switches approaches practically from scene to scene. The end result is a film that is as baffling as it is bad, all the more so because of the shocking array of talent that was somehow convinced to sign up for a project that does none of them proud.

Set in 1951, the film opens as a bus arrives in the distant Australian backwater with the highly appropriate name of Dungatar and disgorges a femme fatale type who immediately lights up a cigarette and mutters "I'm back, you bastards." This is Myrtle "Tilly" Dunnage (Kate Winslet) and her return home sends the rest of the town into a tizzy—understandable because the last time anyone saw her; she was being shipped away as a child after being accused of murdering a classmate. Hav-

ing lived in Spain, London, and Paris and becoming an expert dressmaker in the interim, she has returned determined to prove herself innocent of the crime. However, this will be tricky because she has few memories of what happened that day, her mother, "Mad" Molly (Judy Davis) seems to be in the throes of senility (or at least a highly selective variation of it) and most everyone else—especially town power broker Even Pettyman (Shane Bourne), whose son was the one who was killed, and the unfortunately named Miss Harridene (Kerry Fox), the cruel and abusive teacher who said that she saw Tilly hitting the boy with a brick—is still convinced of her guilt. About the only people that Tilly has in her corner are friendly cross-dressing policeman Sgt. Farrat (Hugo Weaving) and hunky football player Teddy (Liam Hemsworth).

The key weapon in her arsenal is her trusty Singer 201K2 and with it, she hits upon the plan of creating gorgeous haute couture designs for the women of Dungatar (not that they necessarily have anyplace to wear them) in the hopes of getting close enough to them in the process to glean information that might help her case. This may seem an unlikely approach but after the womenfolk get a load of the makeover she whips up for the formerly frumpy Gertrude (Sarah Snook) to help her gain the confidence to win the boy of her dreams, she has them lining up at her door while inspiring the anti-Tilly forces to import their own designer, albeit a fairly talentless one, to combat her influence. As the town grows chicer, Tilly begins to make discoveries that shed new light on what really happened on that day long ago but also finds that her opponents are as determined as ever to lay the blame on her. Meanwhile, the hunky Teddy tries to convince Tilly that Dungatar is far beneath her and that the two of them should just leave. Just when everything seems to be going Tilly's way at last, there is a tragic turn of events that leads to a drastic increase in the local body count as she finally gets her vengeance on all of those that wronged her.

The film was based on a 2000 novel by Rosalie Ham and having seen the end result, one can only hope for the sake of Ham's reputation that director Jocelyn Moorhouse (marking her first time in the director's chair since *A Thousand Acres* [1997]) and co-writer P.J. Hogan have made total hash of the source material. The film was presumably intended to be a darkly funny revenge story of a woman righting the wrongs done to her along the lines of *The Bride Wore Black* (1968) or *The Girl Most Likely To...* (1973) but if that was case, then something went horribly wrong along the way. For one thing, while the majority of the townspeople are meant to be terrible people, the film presents them in such garishly caricatured terms that they seem more cartoonish than truly hateful—for all of its presumably feminist leanings, the treatment of many of the female characters is so cruel that comes fairly close to outright misogyny. At other times, it wants us to forget about Tilly's elaborate revenge plot and genuinely feel for her need for closure about the incident that changed her life—ironically for the better, as one character eventually points out—and those moments of sincerity jar uneasily with the more outrageous stuff. If that weren't enough, the film also tosses in material that is so grotesque and off-base that you simply have to wonder what Moorehouse and Hogan could have possibly been thinking. At one point, we see Pettyman drug his troubled wife and rape her while she is unconscious in a moment that is, astonishingly enough, placed in the middle of an ostensibly comedic montage and which is presumably meant to inspire laughs. At another, a character is murdered in a manner so gory—especially considering the bloodless nature of the rest of the story to that point—that even though they are deserving of it, it still comes across as more tasteless than cathartic.

What is almost as frustrating as the film's inability to find and maintain a consistent tone is the way in which it wastes the talents of the fairly incredible array of actresses that appear in it. Kate Winslet is one of those rare actresses who is never less than eminently watchable and she is the closest thing that it has to a saving grace, even though she is ultimately unable to make heads or tails out of the material. (It should also be noted that while she looks absolutely smashing throughout, she nevertheless looks about a decade older than the other characters who are supposed to be around the same age.) Casting the great Judy Davis as her dotty mother sounds like a sure-fire move but her character turns out to be a disappointingly clichéd creation and there is only one scene—in which she loudly reacts to a screening of *Sunset Boulevard* (1950)—in which she gets to truly shine. There are other gifted actresses on display here in smaller roles, such as Sarah Snook (who you should have seen in the nifty sci-fi mind-bender *Predestination* [2014]), Kerry Fox (the star of Jane Campion's *An Angel at My Table* [1990]), and Julia Blake (who was the elderly woman getting a chance to love again in the heartbreaking *Innocence* [2000]), but not even they can do much with their one-note characters. That said, they still come off better than the guys—Hemsworth does little more than smile and take off his shirt while Weaving, despite his considerable efforts, is stuck with a role in which no one ever decided whether it was supposed to be campy or tragic.

Even by the standards of the Australian film industry, which has long valued strange and bizarre films about strange and bizarre people doing strange and bizarre things, *The Dressmaker* is absolutely inexplicable and not in a good way. Alternately overheated and undercooked, it lurches about from incident to incident without any sort of coherent rhyme or reason but aside from the killer opening and closing moments, none of it works on any of the multiple levels that it is trying to hit. If it had just picked one approach and stuck with it, it might have had a chance of working, especially with the level of talent involved. After all, considering that it is all about a dressmaker, one might have thought that it would have heard about the joys of Simplicity.

Peter Sobczynski

CREDITS

Myrtle "Tilly" Dunnage: Kate Winslet
Teddy McSwiney: Liam Hemsworth
Sergeant Farrat: Hugo Weaving
Gertrude "Trudy" Pratt: Sarah Snook
Molly Dunnage: Judy Davis
Origin: United States
Language: English
Released: 2016
Production: Sue Maslin; released by Ingenious Senior Film Fund, Screen Australia
Directed by: Jocelyn Moorhouse
Written by: Jocelyn Moorhouse
Cinematography by: Donald McAlpine
Music by: David Hirschfelder
Sound: Glenn Newnham
Music Supervisor: Kate Dean
Editing: Jill Bilcock
Art Direction: Lucinda Thomson
Costumes: Marion Boyce; Margot Wilson
Production Design: Roger Ford
MPAA rating: R
Running time: 119 minutes

REVIEWS

Abele, Robert. *Los Angeles Times*. September 21, 2016.
Bender, Abbey. *Village Voice*. September 22, 2016.
Chang, Justin. *Variety*. September 14, 2015.
Fresch, Jon. *Hollywood Reporter*. September 14, 2015.
Hornaday, Ann. *Washington Post*. September 22, 2016.
Lapin, Andrew. *NPR*. September 22, 2016.
Russo, Tom. *Boston Globe*. September 22, 2016.
Scott, A.O. *New York Times*. September 22, 2016.
Verniere, James. *Boston Herald*. September 23, 2016.
Whitty, Stephen. *New York Daily News*. September 20, 2016.

QUOTES

Teddy McSwiney: "I reckon you came home for one of two things, revenge or ... me ...."

TRIVIA

Tilly's sewing machine is a Singer 201K2. They were sturdy and expensive, costing about six months' wages for a working woman. They are still considered one of the best sewing machines by professional dressmakers and tailors.

E

EDDIE THE EAGLE

(Eddie the Eagle: Alles ist Möglich)

Inspired by a dream come true.
　—Movie tagline

Win or lose, always aim high
　—Movie tagline

Box Office: $15.8 Million

Dexter Fletcher's underdog tale *Eddie the Eagle* is a taste test for how long a film can be of the unofficial "feel-good" variety before it just feels rotten. As if cinema had an emotional breakdown and cannot handle nuance or stress, it wants to be feel-good within every cell of its existence. With character construction, dialogue, soundtrack choices, and its direct plot, the film takes on this designation to the point of gimmick, which only tests the bounds to which this albeit curious story can be accepted as human.

The script, from Sean Macaulay and Simon Kelton does offer a lean nature that makes the story more palatable. It does not clutter up its straight-to-the-point narrative while making grand statements about following one's dreams. From the opening credits, it paints the picture of title character Eddie Edwards as an underdog to root for, presented as a young boy (played by Tom Costello) with giant glasses who dreams of being an Olympian. His clumsiness makes for slapstick scenarios, like a javelin breaking a window, as met with the frown of his crusty father Terry (Keith Allen), but supported by his much warmer mother Janette (Jo Hartley). In the opening credits, a montage shows Eddie placing broken glasses—not medals—into a tin he has reserved for awards, and shows him running away from home to join the Olympics. It is all very quaint and extremely written; precise but to the point that no life escapes from it.

Years later, Eddie's dreams of becoming an Olympian lead him to Germany, where he (now played by a tedious Taron Egerton) decides to become Great Britain's first Olympic ski jumper since 1928. Working on a set of practice slopes where the other teams want nothing to do with him, he is a self-motivating ski jumper with no experience until he comes across the former Olympian Bronson Peary (Hugh Jackman in his most suave, Hugh Jackman-est role yet), an American who was once one of the greats, but spends his time drinking and quietly wallowing. Of course, the two are at odds with each other at first, with Bronson only eventually becoming Eddie's coach. And Bronson has his own demons as well, his advice to Eddie about eschewing hubris reflecting back on his own relationship with his coach, Warren Sharp (Christopher Walken). Eddie breaks through to Bronson, and receives his guidance about how to properly ski jump, as Eddie chases his goal of simply becoming an Olympian.

The script takes on a direct nature as it moves to Eddie's dream of becoming a ski jumper, despite not having the decades of practice behind it, which condenses his goals and characters to a single place in Germany, and the unruly coach who becomes an inspiration. Usual inspirations of family and love interests are left to the side, and the script becomes focused on watching Eddie try and fail and try again. Fletcher treats the movie with a light irony, using an 80s soundtrack for an air of goofiness but tacky choices ("You Make My Dreams Come True" by Hall & Oates is used without any inspiration).

Thankfully, as the story is dragged by its easily recognizable script components about underdogs and their dreams, the real life narrative of the movie intervenes to create an interesting twist. When Eddie's dream of becoming an Olympian looks like a gimmick when compared to the many other, far better ski jumpers at the Olympics, the story forces Eddie to confront his image as a novelty. For a movie that treats him in the exact same way, Eddie then has to prove he has more than his comical stubbornness, and it makes for an unexpected climax.

However, this third act only highlights an idea that nags this story, of someone whose idea of skill is twisted with a need for attention, one that this story essentially glamorizes in its canonization of him. *Eddie the Eagle* is a case of story of how dumb luck helped one person reach his dream of being listed as an Olympian, who was lucky to find a coach who needed Eddie just as much as Eddie needed him, and was then able to nail his last big jump without dying in the process. This is an interesting element to add to the skill story, sure, but it does not make for the most inspirational skill saga, nor does it make a giant hero out of its title character. Eddie becomes a fluke, which is how the British Olympic team saw him during and after his brief time, and that attitude does not transition into the story's tone. Worst of all, this element of dumb luck requires a type of nuance that the film is often deaf to, proving only able to make huge turns with its plot, as in the third act, instead of smaller, more exact pivots.

Fletcher's way of filming the ski jumping proves essential to adding energy to the movie, especially as training montages only make the story seem more wholesale. Brilliantly, *Eddie the Eagle* includes the audience into the visual drama of the speed and height that come with ski jumping. Throughout Eddie's arc the camera provides a growing sense of perspective, with POV shots of skis zooming down the slope, or close-ups of Eddie's face as he's about to hit a jump. Especially when it comes to botched landings, the visual gaps are closed by CGI, a glaring difference from the visceral, unexpected surges that *Eddie the Eagle* can offer. Its best visuals in creating the stakes of ski jumping involve stunt work, who provide viewers with that rush of wanting to see a jumper, flying high in the air, land as gracefully as possible.

The most disturbing takeaway from *Eddie the Eagle* is that by treating life as a cliché, it wants to use such exaggerations as a gimmick itself, as if the characters themselves know they are just instruments for the desired feel-good air. This inescapable attitude when thinking about the film reduces its emotional effect greatly, not to mention sours its chances to be light entertainment. *Eddie the Eagle* is a key example of how safety within storytelling can easily erase its human quality, and that when it comes to even the lightest of amusement, some element of emotional texture is vital.

Nick Allen

CREDITS

Eddie Edwards: Taron Egerton
Bronson Peary: Hugh Jackman
Janette: Jo Hartley
Terry: Keith Allen
Matti Nykanen: Edvin Endresen
Origin: Germany, United Kingdom, United States
Language: English, German
Released: 2016
Production: Adam Bohling, Rupert Maconick, David Reid, Valerie Van Galder, Matthew Vaughn; released by Marv Films
Directed by: Dexter Fletcher
Written by: Sean Macaulay; Simon Kelton
Cinematography by: George Richmond
Music by: Matthew Margeson
Sound: Danny Sheehan
Editing: Martin Walsh
Art Direction: Tim Blake
Production Design: Mike Gunn
MPAA rating: PG-13
Running time: 106 minutes

REVIEWS

Braun, Liz. *Toronto Sun.* February 25, 2016.
Burr, Ty. *Boston Globe.* February 25, 2016.
Ebiri, Bilge. *New York Magazine/Vulture.* February 28, 2016.
Genzlinger, Neil. *New York Times.* February 25, 2016.
Hornaday, Ann. *Washington Post.* February 25, 2016.
Lemire, Christy. *RogerEbert.com.* February 25, 2016.
MacDonald, Moira. *Seattle Times.* February 25, 2016.
Morgenstern, Joe. *Wall Street Journal.* February 26, 2016.
Pickett, Leah. *Chicago Reader.* February 25, 2016.
Taylor, Kate. *Globe and Mail.* February 26, 2016.

QUOTES

Eddie Edwards: "Any tips then?"
Bronson Peary: "Don't die?"

Producer Matthew Vaughn said: "Whoever invted ski jumping was insane. There's no logical reason for doing it."

THE EDGE OF SEVENTEEN

You're only young once ... is it over yet?
—Movie tagline

Box Office: $14.4 Million

The Edge of Seventeen, writer/director Kelly Fremon Craig's debut film, is a blunt and honest look at and appreciation of the troubled times of a teenage girl. It is something of rarity, in that it presents a female protagonist who is flawed but instantly sympathetic, intelligent, and witty but also a bit hypocritical, and a loner, who believes that status is by choice but does not understand what that choice means when she actually wants to make a connection with another person.

Hailee Steinfeld's Nadine, in other words, is a full-blooded character, not a phony construct or shallow stereotype of the supposedly "typical" teenage girl. She is not simply looking to become popular, since she rejects that notion, or win over the affections of a boy in school. While Nadine does fantasize about one guy in particular, it is of secondary, tertiary, or even lesser concern for Craig's examination of this character. Nadine's awkwardness with that boy and another one, whose intentions are comparatively purer than the first guy, are symptoms of a more significant problem from which she is suffering.

She has difficulty connecting with people. Craig knows that is not the root of the problem, either. The film peels away at the layers of this character, and the very fact that there are layers to the character is a quality to appreciate. That Craig does so with plenty of humor and considerable understanding is even more admirable.

Nadine's life up until the start of the story proper comes through a brief prologue. She was always uncertain of herself, even as a child. A routine battle with her mother Mona (Kyra Sedgwick) was getting out of the car to go to school in the morning. Her father (Eric Keenleyside), Nadine explains in a momentary break from the sardonic tone of her narration into pleasant nostalgia, would serve as the intermediary between mother and daughter. She stayed to herself back then, too, although she made a single friend, with whom she remained close ever since they bonded over a caterpillar. The girl's name is Krista (played in the present by Haley Lu Richardson), and she remains Nadine's sole friend.

Nadine's father, the only person other than Krista who really understood her, died after having heart attack in front of her three years ago. Craig's screenplay does not announce the psychological repercussions of this event, although it does offer more than enough information to comprehend them.

A few details emerge. She tells her favorite teacher/rival Mr. Bruner (Woody Harrelson), who is as willing to give back the insults that Nadine throws her way, that she was unable to complete a homework assignment because of a death in the family. It is, of course, an excuse for not doing the work, yet if there is one thing of which Nadine seems incapable, it is maliciously lying. There must be some truth to the statement, just as there is truth to her revealing to Erwin (Hayden Szeto), the boy who has an obvious crush on her, that she saw a psychiatrist and was prescribed medication for depression after her father's death. That she neither still sees the psychiatrist nor takes the pills regularly is just enough information, without Craig resorting to armchair psychoanalysis. Those details do not even include Nadine's insecurity about her appearance and personality or, as she puts it, the dread that came with her realization that she is going to have to live the rest of her life as herself.

Although it may sound depressing, this description is somewhat a mischaracterization of the entirety of the film. It is simply intended to highlight the subtlety with which Craig reveals the genuine pain behind this character, who does all that she can to hide it. The film's tone is primarily comic, driven by a combination of a series of uncomfortable situations and what amounts to a running commentary of Nadine's cynical worldview. (The hypocritical part of her character comes when she complains about the way her generation uses social media to write their every thought; Nadine simply says it, with or without anyone requesting her thoughts).

The story's conflict arises when Krista begins dating Nadine's older—but still in high school—brother Darian (Blake Jenner), whom Nadine resents for being seen as "perfect" to their mother and pretty much everyone else. (Without prompting, a stranger at a party tells Nadine that she sees them akin to the mismatched pairing of Arnold Schwarzenegger and Danny DeVito in *Twins* [1988]). Nadine gives her best friend an ultimatum: Stop seeing Darian, or their friendship is finished. Krista refuses to make such a choice, and despite her friend's objection to being made to choose, Nadine, ending the friendship, still is clearly hurt that Krista did not choose her.

This detail—of Nadine hearing what she wants to hear—is yet another example of the film's specificity in regards to the character. Expecting the worst to happen to her, she puts herself in situations in which the worst is inevitable. It is a testament to Steinfeld's seemingly effortless performance, which is precise in pinpointing how Nadine uses humor as a defense mechanism while still remaining funny, that Nadine is as immediately and consistently engaging as she is. Craig neither makes excuses for Nadine's attitude nor judges the character's behavior. (A terrible "date" with Nick [Alexander Calvert], the boy to whom she is attracted, is the closest the film comes to "punishing" her, but the scene is too discomforting to be seen in that light). Nadine may be selfish in certain respects, yet her gradual realization of that quality is part of her development.

Craig, essentially, does not make a joke of Nadine, although the filmmaker does rightly observe the sometimes absurd ways in which her protagonist nearly makes a joke of herself. If there is a lesson to be taken from *The Edge of Seventeen*, it is that surviving one's life as a teenager is a challenge at which nobody succeeds because, thankfully, everyone grows out of it eventually.

Mark Dujsik

CREDITS

Nadine: Hailee Steinfeld
Krista: Haley Lu Richardson
Darian: Blake Jenner
Mona: Kyra Sedgwick
Mr. Bruner: Woody Harrelson
Origin: United States
Language: English
Released: 2016
Production: Julie Ansell, James L. Brooks, Richard Sakai, Kelly Fremon Craig; released by Gracie Films, STX Entertainment
Directed by: Kelly Fremon Craig
Written by: Kelly Fremon Craig
Cinematography by: Doug Emmett
Music by: Atli Orvarsson
Sound: Erin Oakley
Music Supervisor: Jason Markey
Editing: Tracey Wadmore-Smith
Art Direction: John Alvarez
Costumes: Carla Hetland
Production Design: William Arnold
MPAA rating: R
Running time: 104 minutes

REVIEWS

Bahr, Lindsey. *Associated Press*. November 17, 2016.
Chang, Justin. *Los Angeles Times*. November 17, 2016.
Gray, Christopher. *Slant*. October 23, 2016.
Grierson, Tim. *Screen Daily*. September 17, 2016.
Holden, Stephen. *New York Times*. November 17, 2016.

Hornaday, Ann. *Washington Post*. November 17, 2016.
Larsen, Josh. *LarsenOnFilm*. November 26, 2016.
Waldman, Katy. *Slate*. November 18, 2016.
Wolfe, April. *Village Voice*. November 16, 2016.
Zacharek, Stephanie. *Time*. November 18, 2016.

QUOTES

Nadine: "There are two types of people in the world: The people who naturally excel at life. And the people who hope all those people die in a big explosion."

TRIVIA

This was Kelly Fremon Craig's directorial debut.

AWARDS

Nominations:
Golden Globes 2017: Actress—Mus./Comedy (Steinfeld)

ELLE

Box Office: $1.9 Million

For over 45 years, Paul Verhoeven has been shocking and entertaining audiences, both in his homeland of the Netherlands and in Hollywood. During roughly that same period of time, French actress Isabelle Huppert has been challenging and provoking audiences around the world with a series of brave, edgy, and oftentimes brilliant performances in which she has thrown herself heedlessly into the kind of potentially troublesome roles that many actresses would not even dream of pursuing. With his fondness for narratives centering on complex female characters and hers for working with directors who are constantly challenging both themselves and the actors working for them, it was perhaps inevitable that these two would eventually collaborate on a project at some point. However, it is unlikely that anyone could have predicted an end result as stunning as *Elle*, a cinematic provocation so intense and daring that even devoted fans of both Verhoeven and Huppert may find themselves utterly blindsided by what the two have in store for them this time around.

Huppert stars as Michele Leblanc, the head of a video game company that specializes in elaborate fantasy productions suffused with violent and oftentimes highly sexual imagery. As the film opens, she is attacked in her well-appointed home by a black-clad masked intruder who brutally rapes her—her cat bearing witness to the entire incident—before taking off. Her immediate reaction to this gross intrusion of her home and person will no doubt come as a surprise to many people—she sweeps up the mess made during the attack, orders in dinner and then takes a bath whose purpose as a symbol of purification is short-circuited by a shot of a few drops of blood seeping through the bubbles. The next day, she gets a medical checkup and buys herself a small axe and pepper spray for protection. Although she eventually tells a couple of people at dinner that night—a bit of information relayed with about the same level of import as the recitation of the menu specials—she refuses to contact the police about what happened, instead electing to try to suss out the identity of her attacker herself.

This decision may seem baffling to some, but as the film begins to fill in the details of her life, the inexplicable becomes at least somewhat understandable. From a practical standpoint, Michele is not inclined to go to the cops because of an incident when she was a child when her father went on a murderous rampage and insinuations were made during the investigation that she was involved as well that continue to dog her decades later. Beyond that, Michele is a woman for whom every personal and professional relationship is complicated—her adult-age son (Jonas Bloquet) is a doofus who can barely hold a job in a fast-food restaurant but who expects her to pay for an expensive apartment for him, his decidedly trashy girlfriend (Alice Issaz) and the upcoming baby that only he believes is actually his, her ex-husband (Charles Berling) is a pretentious writer who is now dating a young yoga instructor and begging her to buy his idea for a video game, her mother (Judith Magre) is a self-absorbed monster currently "dating" a guy half her age, her staff at the video-game company loathe her and channel their attitudes towards her into their overtly misogynistic work and she is sleeping with the husband (Christian Berkel) of her best friend/business partner (Anne Consigny)—and the only way that she knows how to deal with them is by exerting total control over each situation. By figuring out the identity of her assailant, she can regain the control that she momentarily lost during that attack. There is also the suggestion—outrageous as it may be—that the attack was actually a bit of a turn-on for her that she wants to replicate, albeit on her own terms.

Elle has all the trappings of a standard revenge fantasy about a woman getting back at her attacker, but whatever expectations one might have about such a narrative are gleefully subverted in every possible manner. Instead of having a sweet and good-natured woman as its center in order to make her defilement all the more tragic in the eyes of viewers, it is centered around one who consciously refuses to succumb to any of the usual tenets of victimhood, and whose caustic and oftentimes cruel manner of dealing with everyone in her orbit, whether they deserve it (such as her smarmy ex, whose car she deliberately smashes and who she "accidentally"

zaps with Mace) or not (such as the yoga instructor that her ex is now seeing) makes her come across as anything but conventionally sympathetic. In regards to her plan to find her attacker on her own, it is not so much borne out of a desire for revenge—she seems more involved with the sushi order that she calls in after being attacked for the first time than with the attack itself—and more out of a wish to turn the tables on her attacker by taking charge of their shared situation and forcing him to lose control. This is a character who is perfectly willing to be harsh, cutting, and dismissive to everyone around her and to use her considerable sexual charisma to twist people around to get exactly what she wants.

In other words, she is a character who seems to have been tailor-made for Isabelle Huppert, one of the best and most fearless actress working today. It is therefore astonishing to learn that Verhoeven originally intended to shoot this film in the United States with an American actress as Michele and relocated it to France when he was unable to find a suitable person to play the role. This turned out to be a blessing because after watching the film, it is impossible to imagine anyone even daring to take on the part, let alone pulling it off to the degree that Huppert has done here. This part is a high-wire act of the riskiest order—even the slightest misstep could transform the entire endeavor into a grisly and unsightly mess—but Huppert never once steps wrong. In many ways, her character is a monster but she makes her such a captivating and compelling character throughout that she effortlessly brings viewers over to her side even while refusing to smooth over Michele's rougher and pricklier aspects in an attempt to engender audience sympathy—even when she reveals the dark secret about her father, a moment that might otherwise be the very thing that would allow viewers to finally like and understand Michele, she does it in such a way as to deflate those sympathies and even suggest that this revelation is nothing more than a coldly considered and executed gambit. Because Huppert has given so many brilliant performances over the years, it would be impossible to flat-out state that this is her finest screen work to date but there is no question that in the annals of cinema history, this is one of the performances that she will be remembered for the most (and the one that earned her first Oscar nomination).

As for Verhoeven, whose most gripping works, including *The 4th Man* (1983), *Basic Instinct* (1992), *Showgirls* (1995), and *Black Book* (2006), have told stories revolving around powerful women running roughshod over comparatively weak and decidedly overmatched men, *Elle* is also a triumphant career high-water mark. Having stumbled a bit with his previous effort, *Tricked* (2012), something about this material, adapted by David Birke from the novel by Philippe Di-jan, clearly resonated with him. While Michele may suffer from the occasional loss of control that only furthers her desire to seize it back, Verhoeven has an exceptionally firm grasp on every aspect of the proceedings in the way that he takes all the expected elements of a standard rape-revenge narrative and then blows them apart while at the same time expertly juggling a number of subplots that might have bogged down a lesser filmmaker. Even more surprising—though perhaps not so much to those familiar with the director's oeuvre—is just how funny the whole thing is. Verhoeven spikes the material with doses of jet-black comedy that manages to provoke and amuse at the same time; the best example being an acidly amusing Christmas party that Michele hosts for most of the people in her life that develops in ways that would have had Luis Bunuel swooning with delight.

Transgressive, formally exquisite and shockingly entertaining in equal measure, *Elle* is an absolute triumph and one of the finest and most audacious films of 2016. At an age when most directors are content to either repeat past triumphs or hit the Lifetime Achievement Award circuit, Verhoeven has come up with what may prove to be his best and most lasting work—one that is utterly unique and original while at the same time fitting in perfectly with the rest of his filmography. Because it deals with edgy material in a bold and frank manner without trying to dial things down in order to reach a wider and softer audience, *Elle* may prove to be too much for viewers who are more sensitive or who like their stories and characters to be warmer and friendlier. And yet, while the film may not be for everybody, anyone who watches it will certainly never forget it.

Peter Sobczynski

CREDITS

Michele Leblanc: Isabelle Huppert
Patrick: Laurent Lafitte
Anna: Anne Consigny
Richard Leblanc: Charles Berling
Rebecca: Virginie Efira
Origin: United States
Language: French
Released: 2016
Production: Saïd Ben Saïd, Michel Merkt; released by Entre Chien et Loup, France 2 Cinema, SBS Productions, Twenty Twenty Vision Filmproduktion GmbH
Directed by: Paul Verhoeven
Written by: David Birke
Cinematography by: Stephane Fontaine
Music by: Anne Dudley
Sound: Alexis Place

Music Supervisor: Elise Luguern
Editing: Jobter Burg
Costumes: Nathalie Raoul
Production Design: Laurent Ott
MPAA rating: R
Running time: 130 minutes

REVIEWS

Hoffman, Jordan. *Vanity Fair.* November 10, 2016.
Hornaday, Ann. *Washington Post.* November 17, 2016.
Lane, Anthony. *New Yorker.* November 14, 2016.
Lodge, Guy. *Variety.* May 22, 2016.
Mintzer, Jordan. *Hollywood Reporter.* May 22, 2016.
Reed, Rex. *New York Observer.* November 19, 2016.
Scott, A.O. *New York Times.* November 10, 2016.
Stevens, Dana. *Slate.* November 11, 2016.
Taylor, Ella. *NPR.* November 10, 2016.
Zacharek, Stephanie. *Time.* November 10, 2016.

TRIVIA

Before production began, Paul Verhoeven went to an institute to learn French so he'd be able to communicate with the cast and crew.

AWARDS

Golden Globes 2017: Actress—Drama (Huppert), Foreign Film
Ind. Spirit 2017: Actress (Huppert)
Nominations:
Oscars 2016: Actress (Huppert)

ELVIS & NIXON

The true story you won't quite believe.
　—Movie tagline

Box Office: $1Million

The most requested photograph among the millions in the National Archives is not one of the many indelible images of WWII or Martin Luther King's March on Washington. It is, in fact, a picture in the White House of the 37th President of the United States shaking hands with the King of Rock 'N' Roll. Leaders of State rubbing elbows with celebrity endorsers and contributors is hardly uncommon nowadays. Yet so many have stared into this enigma of a photograph and wondered how these seeming opposites came to have a meeting in the Oval Office. One attempt was made by Allan Arkush in the made-for-cable mockumentary, *Elvis Meets Nixon* (1997), but Liza Johnson's film is interested in more than just an iconic image and the presumed absurdity behind it. She may not quite get through the granulation of these two men's framework but it is often an entertaining trip through the "lost weekend."

Sitting alone in his Graceland mansion, Elvis Presley (Michael Shannon) watches multiple images of civil and political unrest with a little of Dr. Strangelove's exaggeration thrown in for good measure. A fuse is lit and he ventures without his entourage to not ask, but tell the government what he can do for his country. When his independent trip to the airport does not go as planned, he calls in friend Jerry Schilling (Alex Pettyfer) who has left the Memphis Mafia lifestyle for a movie studio gig and a pending marriage proposal. Elvis convinces him to join him on a trip to Washington DC that takes him through the levels of administration (including a scene with Shannon's *Killer Joe* playwright, Tracy Letts) where he hopes to deliver a handwritten letter to none other than Richard Nixon (Kevin Spacey).

The President's staff, headlined by Egil Krogh (Colin Hanks) and Dwight Chapin (Evan Peters), see this as an opportunity for their unpopular boss to connect with young folk. Not wanting to limit voter pandering, Krogh suggests that "everybody loves Elvis" though Nixon sees it as a waste of time. H.R. Haldeman (portrayed in one scene by Tate Donovan) famously wrote "Are you kidding me?" in the liner of the official request. Feeling rebuffed by both the White House and the level of loyalty represented by joining entourage member Sonny West (Johnny Knoxville), Elvis takes his quest for a badge to be a "federal agent at large" elsewhere until the call finally comes through for the historic meeting that was only supposed to take five minutes.

Those expecting a more chatty one-on-one affair along the lines of the more theatrical *Frost/Nixon* (2008) may grow restless wading through a hour-plus setup to get to the main event which is given less than 20 minutes of screen time. This allows ample opportunity for Johnson and the screenwriters (Joey and Hanala Sagal and actor Cary Elwes with his first writing credit) to lay the groundwork for the inner discontent that may allow the King to connect with the President on a more personal level. At least in Elvis' case, they mostly succeed.

Michael Shannon does not set out to do a blatant impersonation of the legend, instead allowing the costume and the hair do that for him. There is a funny scene where a pair of impersonators mistake him for one of their own rather than the genuine article, but the further we get away from the idolized version from our memory the easier it is for Shannon to get at the man within. Similar to what Bruce Campbell did in the role of an older Elvis in *Bubba Ho-Tep* (2003), Shannon plays him half amusingly oblivious to the rules of aver-

age society (let alone the Secret Service) and the other half keenly aware of how his own celebrity has left him a lonely man.

Spacey's Nixon, on the other hand, is mostly played as a comic foil. Some momentary dialogue is snuck into his scenes about not having the look or feel of a Kennedy all his life as if quickly providing a crash course to anyone yet to see Oliver Stone's *Nixon* (1995). It does not cheapen Elvis' psychological profile one bit though it would have been nice to see a more evenly concentrated treatment of the icons sharing the title name. Too often does the film shift focus to Pettyfer's Schilling, who not only was an adviser on the film and wrote the book "Me and a Guy Named Elvis: My Lifelong Friendship with Elvis Presley" but was actually there with him that weekend. Insight is one thing. Offering a window into Presley's deep need for a genuine friend is another. But interrupting the flow of the show we came to see to in order to care whether or not Schilling makes a flight on time to meet his future fiancé's parents is a pointless, if ironic, juxtaposition of one of Elvis' people caring more about their own needs than his.

As the film's tagline playfully suggests "the two most famous recording artists in history" do get to take center stage with the often very funny interplay of Shannon's sincere offers to fix this country and Spacey's reactive moments of silent disbelief in what he's hearing. The final act approaches the revisionist absurdity of Andrew Fleming's *Dick* (1999) though in this case truth may indeed be stranger than fiction. The personal touch that Schilling's involvement brings to the story is most welcome even if the insertion of his importance to it is a distraction once too often. Johnson's film may only go about halfway to seriously digging into the dynamic of this meeting but it is still an entertaining window into a photograph that may be holding on to the mystery of its 500 other words no matter how many eyes come upon it.

Erik Childress

CREDITS

Elvis: Michael Shannon
President Richard M. Nixon: Kevin Spacey
Jerry: Alex Pettyfer
Sonny: Johnny Knoxville
Krogh: Colin Hanks
Origin: United States
Language: English
Released: 2016
Production: Cassian Elwes, Holly Wiersma; released by Amazon Studios

Directed by: Liza Johnson
Written by: Joey Sagal; Hanala Sagal; Cary Elwes
Cinematography by: Terry Stacey
Music by: Ed Shearmur
Sound: Gene Park
Music Supervisor: Robin Urdang
Editing: Sabine Hoffman; Michael Taylor
Art Direction: Kristin Lekki
Production Design: Mara Lepere-Schloop
MPAA rating: R
Running time: 86 minutes

REVIEWS

Brody, Richard. *New Yorker.* April 24, 2016.
Burr, Ty. *Boston Globe.* April 21, 2016.
Campbell, Christopher. *About.com.* April 21, 2016.
Dargis, Manohla. *New York Times.* April 21, 2016.
Hornaday, Ann. *Washington Post.* April 21, 2016.
Minow, Nell. *Beliefnet.* April 21, 2016.
Phillips, Michael. *Chicago Tribune.* April 20, 2016.
Robinson, Tasha. *The Verge.* April 22, 2016.
Rothkopf, Joshua. *Time Out.* April 22, 2016.
Snider, Eric D. *EricDSnider.com.* April 20, 2016.

QUOTES

Sonny: "Some snacks. Nice ones."

TRIVIA

With Jerry Schilling presenting Elvis Presley's side of the story
and Bud Krogh offering the White House version, the
producers knew they had the makings of a great film.

EMBRACE OF THE SERPENT

(El abrazo de la serpiente)

Box Office: $1.3 Million

Based on the true stories of Theodor Koch-Grunberg and Richard Evan Schulte, two scientists who undertook separate journeys to the Amazon, 40 years apart, *Embrace of the Serpent* is as winding as the Amazon river itself, using its characters to explore the length and breadth of themes suggested by its primary image, that of a python giving birth and feeding. It's a grotesque but somehow beautiful metaphor which evokes not only the danger and mystery of the dense jungle through which the characters must pass but the cycle of life and death—the old giving way to the new—and that lays out the foundation for intense tragedy and transcendent spiritual revelation.

The opening shot is a pan which moves past an image of gently stirring river water up to a reflection in that water of an Amazonian native, deep in thought, and finally the actual native looking up in surprise, encountering something unexpected, and possibly threatening. The film then reveals that the threat is a white explorer, Von Martius (Jan Bijvoet), deeply in need of tribal medical attention that only the native, with his knowledge of the jungle's healing herbs, can offer. The native, Karamakate (Nilbio Torres), is hesitant to help. The white men have already come once before and destroyed his people and plundered the sacred jungle. Desperate, Von Martius tells Karamakate that a remnant of his tribe survives and he will lead the native back to them if he will help him.

Columbian director Ciro Guerra then turns his narrative 40 years into the future to capture the encounter between an older Karamakate (Antonio Bolivar) and a new explorer Evan (Brionne Davis), who has read Von Martius' writings, and is driven to find out if the rare jungle flower that supposedly saved his life really exists. As the pair set off on the new journey the questions that immediately arise are many. Who is Karamakate all these years later? Can either of them be trusted to forge genuine bonds given the troubled cultural collisions of the past?

Guerro turns his third feature film into an inner and outer travelogue. The black and white cinematography of David Gallego suggests a dreamscape, a peek back at ghosted memories. It would have been interesting to have photographed the film in color but the end result would likely have been far more nightmarish and intense, and, for the most part, Guerro has a more muted and hypnotic visual goal in mind. At times, it trips him up. The film is a little light on narrative, choosing instead to concentrate on the scenery and in exploring the brokenness of all participants.

Casting is expert. Jan Bijvoet is a visual force utilizing his unique gaunt physicality and piercing eyes to great effect. Brionne Davis is enigmatic as the quieter modern explorer Evan, who later emerges as a darker more troubled character. But the natives themselves, almost all locals with no previous acting experience, lift this film into exactly the sort of otherworld that is associated with the Amazon in the minds of film lovers.

When the film does introduce other characters, it does so in almost haphazard fashion, but they are all linked in the way they represent the past by which Karamakate is haunted. There is the missionary school holding the barest remnants of his former tribe. In a heartbreaking scene, he gathers a group of these repatriated children aside, having rescued them, momentarily, from the monk who was whipping them. He urges them not to forget their origins. Clearly it is too little too late.

There are also a scant few tribal members scattered to the fringes of the jungle eking out an existence. The forests have been desecrated by Columbians and White men seeking rubber trees and a mutilated native, a symbol of the forest, begs for death when he discovers that Karamakate has destroyed his harvest in anger. In one bizarre sequence, Evan and Karamakate find themselves held captive by a Columbian who has lost his mind and assumed the role of messiah for another lost tribal remnant. The violent encounter almost plunges the film into full horror mode and in the end is distracting, especially since the film has already explored the effects of religious colonialism by this point.

Likewise the end of the film has an abrupt tonal shift that while, perhaps, hinted at by the psychotropic nature of the ritual that precedes it, is still pretty jarring when it occurs. Full-color lightscapes ala the end of Kubrick's *2001: A Space Odyssey* (1968) or perhaps more aptly Ken Russell's *Altered States* (1980), take over the screen, signaling a transcendental mystical experience which awakens Evan out of his 21st-century blind spot and leaving him aware of his connection to the past, present, and future that connects him to Von Martius and the past and future fate of the tribes and forest.

The first Columbian film nominated for an Academy Award, *Embrace of the Serpent* calls immediately to mind Werner Herzog's *Aguirre: the Wrath of God* (1972). It uses the form of film to explore the ways in which the jungle, and in this case time itself, invites madness even as it clearly shows a way to escape, for those who will become one with it.

Dave Canfield

CREDITS

Young Karamakate: Nilbio Torres
Theo: Jan Bijvoet
Old Karamakate: Antonio Bolivar
Evan: Brionne Davis
Manduca: Yauenku Migue
Origin: Argentina, Colombia, Venezuela
Language: Spanish, Portuguese, German, Catalan, Latin
Released: 2015
Production: Cristina Gallego
Directed by: Ciro Guerra
Written by: Ciro Guerra; Jacques Toulemonde Vidal
Cinematography by: David Gallego
Music by: Nascuy Linares
Sound: Carlos Garcia

Music Supervisor: Carlos Garcia
Editing: Etienne Boussac
Costumes: Catherine Rodriguez
Production Design: Angelica Perea
MPAA rating: Unrated
Running time: 125 minutes

REVIEWS

Anderson, Soren. *Seattle Times*. March 10, 2016.
Brody, Richard. *New Yorker*. February 12, 2016.
Chang, Justin. *Variety*. October 21, 2015.
Garrett, Stephen. *New York Observer*. February 19, 2016.
Holden, Stephen. *New York Times*. February 16, 2016.
Ignatiy, Vishnevetsky. *The A.V. Club*. February 16, 2016.
Kearney, Ryan. *New Republic*. February 17, 2016.
Nehme, Farran Smith. *New York Post*. February 18, 2016.
Scherstuhl, Alan. *Village Voice*. February 16, 2016.
Turan, Kenneth. *Los Angeles Times*. February 18, 2016.

QUOTES

Young Karamakate: "Knowledge belongs to all. You do not understand that. You are just a white man."

TRIVIA

The indigenous languages spoken in the movie are Cubeo, Wanano, Tikuna, and Uitoto.

AWARDS

Nominations:

Oscars 2015: Foreign Film
Ind. Spirit 2016: Foreign Film

EQUITY

On Wall Street, all players are not created equal.
—Movie tagline

Box Office: $1.6 Million

Equity is a standard Wall Street thriller, but its female protagonists set it apart in the genre. The traditionally male-dominated, corruption-fueled world of finance certainly would benefit from a more nuanced female perspective. While *Equity* strives to level the playing field, it ultimately is not as compelling as audiences might hope. Protagonist Naomi Bishop (Anna Gunn), a senior investment banker who deals with IPOs, has the kind of intense stare and soft yet commanding voice that quickly make clear her seriousness and ambition. Gunn convincingly embodies the role of a woman who has coiled anger hiding just below the surface of her polished, professional exterior. Sometimes the film is a bit overdetermined in showing the release of her considerable tensions—in an early scene, she violently hits a punching bag at the gym; in a late scene she has an outburst over the number of chips in a chocolate chip cookie she is given.

Naomi is unquestionably successful, but all that success is undergirded by stress—and who can blame her, really? Naomi constantly needs to prove herself after running into professional setbacks, and the bulk of the film finds her handling the IPO for (a very timely) ultra-encrypted social media platform called Cachet. Cachet's founder has the long hair and sweatshirt audiences have come to expect from entrepreneurial tech bros, and Naomi, meanwhile brings no-nonsense determination to every boardroom meeting. Of course, there's more to *Equity* than just IPOs, and the plot thickens as it pits two equally powerful, successful women against one another. Samantha Ryan (Alysia Reiner), Naomi's old college classmate, is now working as a public attorney and investigating Naomi's broker boyfriend, Michael Connor (generic Brit James Purefoy), who may be involved in insider trading. There are a lot of tense dinners in which one character tries shrewdly to extract information from another, but one gets the sense that all this might be just a bit more engaging if it was not ultimately all about business.

At times, *Equity* feels more like a television show than a film. The pacing and aesthetic (tastefully appointed modern apartments, largely drab lighting) all suggest a procedural, and the film does start to sag when it comes to Michael's character and Naomi's easily anticipated outbursts. *Equity* is written, directed, and produced by women, something that is all too rare and deserves commendation. It's frustrating, then, when we literally see a character reading an article with the headline "Why Women Still Can't Have it All" on her phone. Do women still struggle in male-dominated fields, and face a variety of obstacles that their male peers have the luxury of not thinking about? One would be a fool to say no. Yet the appearance of the headline on the phone is frustratingly obvious, and serves as the most basic and cheap form of exposition.

More effective is an early scene in which Naomi tells Michael she bought her diamond earrings herself. She's a woman who works hard and treats herself—and these assets are often frowned upon in a patriarchal society. Released in the summer of 2016, *Equity* plays differently after the unfortunate election results than it might have before them. The corporate feminism of "breaking the glass ceiling" has been in full force for much of the year, pre-November 8th, and though the phrase itself is never uttered in the film, it was likely on the writer's mind. Without a female president, one could argue that films like *Equity*, which prioritize female characters and present them with grit and determination, are even more important.

Something rare happens in *Equity*: more than once, the protagonists explicitly say they like money. Considering that everyone, regardless of gender, likes money, saying it seems gauche, and the sense of obvious exposition can be felt. The film's final line, cribbed from an earlier speech by Naomi and spoken by Samantha as she interviews for a corporate position, is "Money doesn't have to be a dirty word. We can like that too." It's a winking thesis statement, a gender-swapped reworking of the iconic "Greed is good" line from *Wall Street* (1987).

Equity, while competent and assured at best and annoyingly obvious at worst, remains the kind of film that Hollywood needs more of. Ideally it can serve as a template for more nuanced and intellectually provocative depictions of women at work. If more women-created stories of professional women follow in the footsteps of *Equity*, the awkwardly expository treatment of ambition will have all been worthwhile.

Abbey Bender

CREDITS

Naomi Bishop: Anna Gunn
Michael Connor: James Purefoy
Erin Manning: Sarah Megan Thomas
Samantha: Alysia Reiner
Benji Akers: Craig Bierko
Origin: United States
Language: English
Released: 2016
Production: Sarah Megan Thomas, Alysia Reiner; released by Broad Street Pictures
Directed by: Meera Menon
Written by: Amy Fox
Cinematography by: Eric Lin
Music by: Samuel Jones; Alexis Marsh
Sound: Rich Bologna
Music Supervisor: Abe Bradshaw
Editing: Andrew Hafitz
Art Direction: Rory Bruen
Costumes: Teresa Binder-Westby
Production Design: Diane Lederman
MPAA rating: R
Running time: 100 minutes

REVIEWS

Ehrlich, David. *IndieWire.* July 29, 2016.
Felperin, Leslie. *Hollywood Reporter.* January 27, 2016.

Hoffman, Jordan. *The Guardian*. January 28, 2016.
Hornaday, Ann. *Washington Post*. August 11, 2016.
Lodge, Guy. *Variety*. January 27, 2016.
Robinson, Tasha. *The Verge*. July 29, 2016.
Rowe, Amy. *New York Daily News*. July 27, 2016.
Scott, A.O. *New York Times*. July 28, 2016.
Vishnevetsky, Ignatiy. *The A.V. Club*. July 28, 2016.
Zacharek, Stephanie. *Time*. July 28, 2016.

QUOTES

Michael Connor: "You know what's weird about the whole privacy thing?"

Naomi Bishop: "What?"

Michael Connor: "Half the world is paranoid and the other half's password is 'password'."

TRIVIA

This is the first woman-driven Wall Street film.

EVERYBODY WANTS SOME!!

Here for a good time, not a long time.
    —Movie tagline

Box Office: $3.4 Million

It does not matter that Hollywood continues to trend toward movies focusing on the extreme and impossible. Writer-director Richard Linklater has built his career on the natural and universal, to the degree that in his movies the specifics of what happens frequently take a backseat to how they feel. In his best work, a situation experienced by all, to an extent, seems like it is being captured exactly as the people watching remember it happening to them.

That is just part of the beauty of *Everybody Wants Some!!*, Linklater's "spiritual sequel" to 1993's *Dazed and Confused*, which shifts from the last day of high school to a few days before classes begin at a Texas college, leaving intact the essential feeling of giddy beginnings and delayed endings. It is August 1980, and freshman pitcher Jake (Blake Jenner) arrives at the adjoining houses where the school's renowned baseball team lives. The fridge primarily contains beer and Miracle Whip; the ceiling threatens to cave in. This is a version of paradise, though, as laid-back as laid-back gets, an entire season and varying perceptions of an entire life waiting ahead, specific plans merely problems for tomorrow. For the three days and change until class begins, the team, led by arrogant star McReynolds (Tyler Hoechlin) and charmingly upbeat Finn (Glen Powell), favors drinking

over thinking, and cares not for the coach's rule about bringing alcohol in the house and girls upstairs. Big things mean little, and little things mean a lot. Cue the competition for gnarliest bong hit and largest tolerance for pain during rounds of knuckle flicking.

What might seem aimless and free of stakes, however, crystallizes into what Linklater never achieved in the wildly overrated *Boyhood* (2014): the innocent power of individual and group experience, small lessons and smaller decisions, accumulating into something that may only take on resonance years later. Like 2015's *Magic Mike: XXL*, another infectious movie about camaraderie and identity, the seeming plotlessness of *Everybody Wants Some!!* taps into something beautiful about life as a distillation of time. (Arguably Linklater's favorite subject.) Finn recognizes that he will not play baseball forever, but it does not turn into a serious discussion about the future. "You gotta appreciate it while it lasts," Willoughby tells him. Linklater is so attuned to both the union of and separation between present and future, with a casual approach toward trying on different personas that almost turns posing as a disco fan/philosopher/punk fiend/astrology expert, all in the name of getting laid, into a pure and noble pursuit.

It is a testament to the streak of goodness that informs *Everybody Wants Some!!*, which, unlike its spiritual sibling, has hazing but no bullies. The few conflicts vanish soon after they appear (a fight between McReynolds and Jay [Juston Street] resolves simply with Jay, a hot-headed pitcher, telling McReynolds "Good hit," and the latter saying, "We're cool"). There would be no reason to paste some kind of phony rivalry or threat of expulsion onto this period, and Linklater knows the difference between a quietly electric slice of hope and just wandering around, drama-free. The guys test their abilities with women and the universe (one sequence involves Willoughby hilariously failing to get others to read his mind), and the significance comes from the friends who share in the experience, however innocuous it may seem.

The optimism, underscored by uncertainty, is both contagious and effortless, as each cast member interacts exactly according to how long the characters have known each other and what is or is not building between new friends. Finn is the closest thing to Matthew McConaughey's standout character in *Dazed and Confused*, and Powell brings a similar yet unique charisma, informed by enthusiasm rather than a shred of something that teeters on pathetic. This is undoubtedly an ensemble piece, though, and incidental scenes take on weight even as they are lighter than air, like the guys all stuffed into a car, rapping along to the Sugar Hill Gang's "Rapper's Delight." The joy on their faces, the freedom in the moment, elevates what Linklater captures far beyond coming-of-age or nostalgia.

Like these characters, the relaxed, observant *Everybody Wants Some!!*, which earns its exclamation points through sensation rather than force, has possibilities running through its veins, but never in a way that feels naïve or obvious. In the long term, certain things may seem out of reach for college students, whether they really are or not. In a shorter window, it sometimes seems anything can happen, especially with the right feeling and the right people. Life is full of discovery, but that does not happen on its own, as Jake realizes with Beverly (Zoey Deutch) in the movie's most substantive yet thankfully underplayed romantic subplot. *Everybody Wants Some!!* appreciates it all while it lasts, and no one watching will want it to end.

Matt Pais

CREDITS

Jake: Blake Jenner
Jay: Juston Street
Roper: Ryan Guzman
McReynolds: Tyler Hoechlin
Willoughby: Wyatt Russell
Finnegan: Glen Powell
Origin: United States
Language: English
Released: 2016
Production: Megan Ellison, Ginger Sledge, Richard Linklater; released by Annapurna Pictures, Paramount Pictures Corp.
Directed by: Richard Linklater
Written by: Richard Linklater
Cinematography by: Shane F. Kelly
Sound: Tom Hammond
Music Supervisor: Randall Poster
Editing: Sandra Adair
Art Direction: Rodney Becker
Costumes: Kari Perkins
Production Design: Bruce Curtis
MPAA rating: R
Running time: 117 minutes

REVIEWS

Burr, Ty. *Boston Globe*. March 31, 2016.
Chang, Justin. *Variety*. March 11, 2016.
Dowd, A.A. *The A.V. Club*. March 29, 2016.
Kols, Dan. *Slate*. March 31, 2016.
Lund, Carson. *Slant Magazine*. March 30, 2016.
Moore, Roger. *Movie Nation*. April 14, 2016.
Olsen, Mark. *Los Angeles Times*. March 30, 2016.

Phillips, Michael. *Chicago Tribune*. March 31, 2016.
Roeper, Richard. *Chicago Sun-Times*. March 31, 2016.
Rodriguez, Rene. *Miami Herald*. April 7, 2016.

QUOTES

Finnegan: "That just went from cute to restraining order."

TRIVIA

According to Richard Linklater, this film is a continuation of *Boyhood* (2014).

EYE IN THE SKY

The longer you watch, the less clearly you see.
 —Movie tagline

Box Office: $18.7 Million

It is not uncommon for films exploring moral quandaries to themselves get a little lost in confusion. After all, as with real-world gray-area issues, not being 100% sure of what is the "right choice" (or, more often, facing a complete lack of right choices) can leave filmmakers with mixed and unsatisfying creative results. There is some of that at work in the geo-political thriller *Eye in the Sky*, from director Gavin Hood and screenwriter Guy Hibbert. Luckily, the film's subject matter (the use of remote surveillance and firepower in civilian environments), its narrative approach (a microcosm of politics and ethics juxtaposing individual lives against global concerns), and its reliable cast (including Helen Mirren, Alan Rickman, Aaron Paul, and Barkhad Abdi) keep *Eye in the Sky* solidly on the side of flawed but compelling "message" cinema.

Neither Hood nor Hibbert are new to exploring murky moral territory during wartime—Hood's filmography includes *Rendition* (2007) and *Ender's Game* (2013), and Hibbert wrote *Five Minutes of Heaven* (2009). With *Eye in the Sky*, they focus on one short moment in the ongoing War on Terror (the film unfolds mostly in real time) in one small place: a home in Nairobi, Kenya where terrorist bombers are rendezvousing even as civilians go about their daily lives on the busy street outside.

Watching over it all are a ground-level local informant (Abdi); a U.S. pilot operating a predator drone over Nairobi from an Air Force base in Las Vegas (Paul); the steely, determined British Colonel Powell in London (Mirren); her military superior (Rickman); and various British and American politicians, diplomats, and legal advisors spread across the globe from China and Singapore to Hawaii and Washington, D.C. The original plan is to capture a female British national assisting the militant Islamic terrorist group Al-Shabaab, but when minute cameras inside the house spy the terrorists assembling suicide bomber vests, Powell's mission takes on lethal immediacy.

The main complication: An innocent pre-teen girl (Aisha Takow) has set up her bread stand next to the terrorist's meeting house, well within the blast range of a potential drone strike from above. Powell wants an instant attack to prevent a suicide bombing that could murder up to a hundred people, but Paul's drone operator, Watts—a low-ranking "warrior" who has only remotely operated surveillance missions while sitting thousands of miles away from the war zone—has understandable qualms about pulling the trigger to launch a Hellfire Missile that will likely kill the young girl. Meanwhile Rickman's Lieutenant General Benson runs interference between the invested political and military parties on both sides of the Atlantic, most of whom are busy "referring up" the final decision to someone else. (The performances are uniformly sturdy, as to be expected from actors of this caliber; this was Rickman's final on-screen role before his passing.)

Hood and Hibbert waste no time milking this set up for every drop of emotional manipulation, ginned-up suspense, and socio-political propaganda they can fit in, but while *Eye in the Sky* is stylistically subdued, even flat, all the film's mechanisms, no matter how obvious, work for the most part. Grounding their story with genuine elements (the British national is based on the real Samantha Lewthwaite, Al-Shabaab claimed responsibility for a 2013 shopping mall attack in Kenya that killed 67, and the United States does operate regular and controversial drone surveillance and strikes in African nations and civilian collateral damage does occur), the filmmakers continually slam the granular human cost of war up against global security interests and then stir the resulting moral, ethical, and legal issues and their surrounding layers of authority and accountability.

The main characters are all given small, perfunctory humanizing touches to offset their military stances (Powell loves her dog, Benson bought the wrong doll for his granddaughter, Watts joined the Air Force to pay off student debts); while Washington legal counsels use a "point system for collateral damage" to do cold, logical risk assessment on the operation—not to determine military costs, but rather political and public relations fallout. (Watts is exhorted to ensure the drone video does not end up on YouTube.)

Mostly playing out as a drawing-room stage drama with video monitors, in addition to prosecuting the moral calculations of warfare, *Eye in the Sky* also hits secondary notes about the long-distance voyeuristic nature of modern life—whether it is waging a video-game war from a chair in front of a counsel with joystick in hand, or the ways in which that same global communication technology allows audiences to peer into other countries and cultures from the comfort of the art house or home-theater couch.

Eye in the Sky does often lurch awkwardly from the political to the thriller. It is always a risk with a film like this that those viewers seeking political and moral discourse will be annoyed by edge-of-seat action-suspense scenes—no matter how viscerally effective they are on screen (and they are) and the horrific points they want to make about the cost of war, those sequences feel jarringly shoehorned in. Likewise, more casual viewers looking for an entertaining spy thriller will certainly be frustrated by the film's heavier hand-wringing around its message. But while *Eye in the Sky* does not perfectly synthesize all its thematic and creative complexities into a fully cohesive experience, it does a good enough job holding both the audience's attention and conscience while raising painful questions it cannot fully answer.

Locke Peterseim

CREDITS

Colonle Katherine Powell: Helen Mirren
Steve Watts: Aaron Paul
Lieutenant General Frank Benson: Alan Rickman
Jama Farah: Barkhad Abdi
Brian Woodale: Jeremy Northam
Origin: United Kingdom
Language: English
Released: 2015
Directed by: Gavin Hood
Written by: Guy Hibbert; Mark Kilian
Cinematography by: Haris Zambarloukos
Music by: Paul Hepker
Sound: William R. Dean
Music Supervisor: Nick Angel
Editing: Megan Gill
Art Direction: Patrick O'Connor
Costumes: Ruy Filipe
Production Design: Johnny Breedt
MPAA rating: R
Running time: 102 minutes

REVIEWS

Burr, Ty. *Boston Globe.* March 17, 2016.
Holden, Stephen. *New York Times.* March 10, 2016.
Hornaday, Ann. *Washington Post.* March 17, 2016.
Lee, Benjamin. *Guardian.* September 12, 2015.

Macdonald, Moira. *Seattle Times.* March 18, 2016.
Nordine, Michael. *Village Voice.* March 9, 2016.
O'Hehir, Andrew. *Salon.* March 11, 2016.
Robey, Tim. *The Telegraph.* September 12, 2015.
Savlov, Marc. *Austin Chronicle.* March 23, 2016.
Wheeler, Brad. *Globe and Mail.* March 24, 2016.

QUOTES

Lt. General Frank Benson: "Never tell a soldier that he does not know the cost of war."

TRIVIA

This was Alan Rickman's final live-action film role.

THE EYES OF MY MOTHER

Box Office: $27,099

With *The Eyes of My Mother*, Nicolas Pesce has created a visually unnerving feature film debut. He couples his disturbing images with a story that seems scant, almost too scant despite his uncanny knack for finding beauty in the grotesque. But what makes *The Eyes of My Mother* work so well lies exactly in what it leaves out of its narrative, a simple explanation as to why its mentally ill protagonist, a young woman named Francisca, does the awful things she does. Instead, the film almost seems to beg the viewer to allow some room for empathy despite a lack of understanding. *The Eyes of My Mother* is a very special film indeed.

Young Francisca (Olivia Boand) lives with her mother (Dianna Agostini) and father (Paul Nazak) on a small farm. Her mother, a former surgeon, has taken it upon herself to teach Francisca anatomy and basic surgery technique by having her practice on already-dead farm animals. One afternoon, a young salesman, Charlie (Will Brill) appears at the screen door, asking to use the restroom. Misgivings come too late and Francisca's mother finds herself fighting for her life as the apparently psychotic stranger forces her into the next room. During the resultant scuffle, Charlie kills the woman but is wounded himself and winds up captive in the barn when Francisca's father returns home. After helping her father bury mother in the backyard, Francisca, who has no other friends, forms a strange relationship with Charlie. Removing his eyes and vocal cords she becomes both his caretaker and torturer. Time passes. Francisca's father dies and she preserves his remains in a bathtub, continuing a relationship with him after death. Later, Charlie tries to escape and Francisca kills him.

More time has passed and an adult Francisca (Kika Magalhaes), desperate to end her isolation, goes into town where she meets Kimiko (Clara Wong), a Japanese student at a bar. The pair arrive at Francisca's home but Francisca is unable to go through with the encounter. As she tries to explain herself, Francisca nonchalantly describes her parent's deaths, frightening Kimiko who tries to leave. Francisca murders Kimiko.

Sometime later, Francisca is hiking in the woods near her home and hitches a ride with Lucy (Flora Diaz), a young mother with baby in tow. Seeing another way to end her isolation, Francisca grabs the child and runs home, stabbing the hysterical Lucy when she follows. Time passes and we see that Francisca has raised the child as her own, naming him Antonio. One day Antonio enters the forbidden barn and finds his mother captive there. Lucy escapes, leading the police back to Francisca's home, where she is killed.

Near the beginning of the film, Pesce gives the viewer everything they really need to understand what his film is about. A conversation between Francisca and her mother about the story of St. Francis of Assisi is key. His life in the wild, his sudden sense of calling confirmed for him by the appearance of stigmata on his own body, and the lesser known fact that he died of an eye ailment that also causes psychosis leads her mother to note "loneliness can do strange things to the mind." Viewers see that it has already affected Francisca, who seizes the moment to run her finger across a crown of thorns until she draws a drop of blood. Pesce has found a perfect muse in the arresting screen presence of Kika Magalhaes, who is able to use her thin, wide-eyed physicality to portray exactly the sort of wounded-ness needed to lift her character believably past simple judgement.

This is not for the faint-hearted. Pesce offers his triptych narrative up largely without dialogue, leaving the viewer plenty of time to weigh the words and the nature of the relationships onscreen. But what will have even more impact are the visuals. In a time when Martin Scorsese has recently noted that films no longer create meaningful images, *The Eyes of My Mother* is almost all about its images, and powerful images they are indeed. Zach Kuperstein's black-and-white photography creates a stunning backdrop, almost lyrical in presentation. An impromptu kitchen table lesson in bovine eye anatomy takes on the appearance of a demented Norman Rockwell tableau.

All of these are brought to life by careful composition. It is clear Pesce believes his characters deserve no less than these considerations. Viewers will either want to unpack the effects of the trauma at the center of the film or walk away in confusion or maybe disgust. But there is far more to this film than art house pretension.

Dave Canfield

CREDITS

Francisca: Kika Magalhaes
Mother: Diana Agostini
Young Francisca: Olivia Bond
Charlie: Will Brill
Father: Paul Nazak
Origin: United States
Language: English, Portuguese
Released: 2016
Production: Max Born, Jacob Wasserman, Schuyler Weiss; released by Borderline Presents, Tandem Pictures
Directed by: Nicolas Pesce
Written by: Nicolas Pesce
Cinematography by: Zach Kuperstein
Music by: Ariel Loh
Sound: Michael Kurihara
Editing: Nicolas Pesce; Connor Sullivan
Art Direction: Caroline Keenan Russell
Costumes: Whitney Anne Adams
Production Design: Sam Hensen
MPAA rating: R
Running time: 76 minutes

REVIEWS

Catsoulis, Jeannette. *New York Times.* December 1, 2016.
Dowd, A.A. *The A.V. Club.* December 1, 2016.
Hertz, Barry. *Globe and Mail.* December 16, 2016.
Lane, Anthony. *New Yorker.* November 28, 2016.
Lodge, Guy. *Variety.* February 4, 2016.
McDonagh, Maitland. *Film Journal International.* November 30, 2016.
O'Sullivan, Michael. *Washington Post.* December 1, 2016.
Robinson, Tasha. *The Verge.* December 6, 2016.
Rothkopf, Joshua. *Time Out.* November 23, 2016.
Wolfe, April. *Village Voice.* November 29, 2016.

QUOTES

Francisca: "Go placidly amid the noise and haste, and remember what peace there may be in silence. And whether or not it is clear to you, the universe is unfolding as it should."

TRIVIA

The show that Francisca's father keeps watching on TV is *Bonanza.*

AWARDS

Nominations:
Ind. Spirit 2017: Cinematog.

F

THE FAMILY FANG

Box Office: $262,921

The Family Fang is Jason Bateman's second artistic statement as a director so far, having made his debut with the spelling bee cussing comedy *Bad Words* in 2013. In comparison, this indie drama is a huge departure of taste and tone, focused family and art, with a script driven by character far more than a naughty joke. It is not long into his latest film, however, in which while Bateman establishes a maturity of his own, he is still missing a distinct artistry compared to other whimsical, domestic directors he wants to parallel. Even with a whimsical script about a family of performance artists, he manages to package it without a hint of the characters' own abrasiveness.

The title clan is an odd bunch, appropriately so. As led by patriarch Caleb (Christopher Walken in present day, Jason Butler Harner in flashback), the Fangs are essentially a quartet of performance artists, who seek to confront public crowds with bizarre situations and make horrified viewers into the art. Their stunts often involve using the violated innocence of their children, Baxter and Annie, while Caleb and wife Camille (Maryann Plunkett in present day, Kathryn Hahn in the past) in help create a scene, with one of the adults filming. In the film's opening scene, a young Baxter robs a bank where Caleb pretends to be a security guard, but a woman (Camille) is shot in the process. The moment is lightened when Baxter breaks character, saying that the blood tastes like syrup, while the family leave the scene with bank customers and employees even more disturbed.

Decades later, Baxter and Annie have become artists, but not like their parents. In fact, their history of performance art, with questionable agency even as people involved in the stunt, has led them away from most of the world and to a special brother and sister bond. Baxter (Bateman) is a struggling writer with only one book to his name, working on a new novel about siblings who escape a dark hole. Meanwhile, his sister Annie (Nicole Kidman) is at a low point with her career as a famous actress, especially as she seemingly has no control over getting the roles that she wants or not doing petty nude scenes.

With these interesting characters in place, David Lindsay-Abaire's script (adapting Kevin Wilson's 2011 novel) frames a great chunk of the family as a mystery. After a reunion maybe 30 minutes into the film, the parents and their middle-aged children are divided over doing one more stunt (involving fake free coupons for a sandwich shop). When the stunt goes wrong, Caleb storms off with Camille. It is revealed not long after that their car was found abandoned with blood all over it, appearing like they have been murdered. This causes the brother and sister to explore what could have happened, while investigating the family's pasts through recordings of their stunts. When they find a lead about a second family, Baxter and Camille set off to understand what other realities their Andy Kaufman-esque parents could have disappeared to.

The film's strongest attribute is its cast, who create full characters across the short board for a film that can often be considered a chamber piece with flash backs. As director, Bateman creates a vivid idea of a family; the intense, extreme nature of Walken is a striking opposite to the mother character, who has an intensity about art that she does not bring into arrogant leadership. Bateman the actor and Kidman complement each other as very close siblings, going through similar crisis on vastly different artistic scales. As it seeks to provide the most detailed portrait possible of this mysterious family, *The Family Fang* becomes an achievement in family chemistry acting, their bond is bizarre but deep.

Unexpectedly, *The Family Fang* becomes one of the ideologically busiest movies of the year, and dialogue proves to be its toughest feat. Art is constantly on its mind, how people discuss or how they live it, along with the endless question of what defines good art. Sometimes told with documentary inserts about the family, juxtaposed within the much more intimate narrative that Bateman constructs, *The Family Fang* can hit too hard on the head. A glaring example is when Bateman visualizes the debate inherent in the Fang's art by showing two art critics arguing with each other about the credibility of their performances. Throughout the story, Lindsay-Abaire's script tries to cover exposition and conversation at once, and the effect is often only as good as the film's wit to portray them.

Like its recurring harp and music box theme composed by a more-whimsical-than-usual Carter Burwell, *The Family Fang* can be distinctly graceful, especially in how it creates a very intimate lifelong experience with a family. As Annie and Baxter piece together their lives, looking back upon family dinners at home where they seemed to be the only people n world, the movie achieves a warmth albeit with characters that are meant to be as discordant as possible. Cinematographer Ken Seng articulates the feeling of being in the Fang clan with delicate negative space, never resisting the chance to visualize a main character's isolation by placing them inside a door frame.

The irony about Bateman's film is that while it discusses provocative art in such detail, *The Family Fang* has very little teeth of its own. While attempting to make his proclamation as a serious director, he aims for his style to be recognizable, especially to other post-2000's indies, not distinguished. For as much that is said about how "great art leaves scorched earth," Bateman does not provoke his audience; he offers them a tame conversation.

Nick Allen

CREDITS

Annie Fang: Nicole Kidman
Baxter Fang: Jason Bateman
Caleb Fang: Christopher Walken
Camille Fang: Maryann Plunkett
Suzanne Crosby: Marin Ireland
Origin: United States
Language: English
Released: 2016
Production: James Garavente, Riva Marker, Per Saari, Daniela Taplin Lundberg, Leslie Urdang, Dean Vanech, Nicole Kidman, Jason Bateman; released by Aggregate Films, Red Crown productions
Directed by: Jason Bateman
Written by: David Lindsay-Abaire
Cinematography by: Ken Seng
Music by: Carter Burwell
Sound: Benjamin Cheah
Music Supervisor: Christopher Mollere
Editing: Robert Frazen
Art Direction: Elise G. Viola
Costumes: Amy Westcott
Production Design: Beth Mickle
MPAA rating: R
Running time: 105 minutes

REVIEWS

Bahr, Lindsay. *Associated Press*. April 28, 2016.
Chang, Justin. *Variety*. September 14, 2015.
Dargis, Manohla. *New York Times*. April 28, 2016.
Graham, Adam. *Detroit News*. May 6, 2016.
Hassenger, Jesse. *The A.V. Club*. April 28, 2016.
Kenny, Glenn. *RogerEbert.com*. April 29, 2016.
Merry, Stephanie. *Washington Post*. May 5, 2016.
Rooney, David. *Hollywood Reporter*. September 14, 2015.
Rothkopf, Joshua. *Time Out*. April 25, 2016.
Scherstuhl, Alan. *Village Voice*. April 26, 2016.

QUOTES

Baxter Fang: "Don't be afraid. Own the moment. If you're in control then the chaos will happen around you and not to you."

TRIVIA

Kevin Wilson, who wrote the novel upon which the film is based, works as a professor at Sewanee.

FANTASTIC BEASTS AND WHERE TO FIND THEM

Explore a new era of J.K. Rowling's wizarding world.
—Movie tagline

Box Office: $232.8 Million

There are two narratives competing in *Fantastic Beasts and Where to Find Them*, screenwriter J.K. Rowling's return to the world of witchcraft and wizardry that developed over the course of her seven *Harry Potter* books (and a couple of spin-offs, including the textbook from which this film gets its title and hero), which were, in turn, adapted into eight movies. This story takes place before the father of "The Boy Who Lived" was even a twinkle in his own father's eye, so the connections to the previous books and films are entirely composed of broad concepts, a world in which witches and wizards must hide their magical abilities from non-magical folks, and the thematic concerns that run through Rowling's tales.

The good news is that each of the two, main narrative threads work quite well on their own. One concerns itself with the sense of discovery and wonder that is a cornerstone of Rowling's work, while the other uncovers the darker side of this world, where prejudice, resentment, and repression fester. The disappointing news is that the narratives do not form a convincing, cohesive whole on account of the distinct differences in tone and function. Rowling's screenplay eventually forces the two threads together in an action-oriented climax that ultimately seems to be setting up the future of this new series.

The film is doing a lot with only the minimum of a guiding purpose. It is a strange and sometimes strained beginning to a new storyline, as well as an introduction to a new hero, within Rowling's world, yet the film's setting, cast of characters, menagerie of magical creatures, and even its overreaching ambition keep it just engaging enough.

The hero is Newt Scamander (Eddie Redmayne), a quiet and socially awkward expert on the eponymous subjects. He has come to New York City, with an enchanted suitcase filled with unusual animals, from London in order to return a formerly captured phoenix to its natural habitat of the desert of Arizona.

The year is 1926, and if anything, at least the film's re-creation of the era—complete with such wizarding-world touches as a speakeasy populated by elves and goblins—offers a different aesthetic than the previous movies. The political connections within Rowling's screenplay are more contemporary for the period, too, instead of the sort of broad allegory that came with the *Potter* books and films. Here, a dark wizard named Gellert Grindelwald (played in the briefest of cameos by Johnny Depp) has been wreaking havoc in Europe and sowing conflict between magical folk and "muggles"— or, as they are called among witches and wizards in the United States, "no-majs."

Within this specific story, those prejudices and that distrust come from a subplot involving Graves (Colin Farrell), an official of the magical government of the U.S., seeking a powerful wizard within an anti-witch organization run by Mary Lou Barebone (Samantha Morton). Her adopted son Credence (Ezra Miller) wants to be part of the wizarding world, and he and Graves conspire in the shadows, behind the backs of the abusive Mary Lou and the government, to uncover the identity of the secret witch or wizard. This side of the story is full of foreboding and dread. Rowling and director David Yates (who helmed the final four *Potter* films) communicate much about the fear and oppressive nature of this semi-religious cult with a twisted nursery rhyme that one of Mary Lou's adopted daughters sings—detailing the various and violent ways with which witches should be dealt.

Newt's adventure, on the other end of the spectrum, is rather light and comic. Some of his creatures escape into the city after a mishap in which he and Jacob Kowalski (Dan Fogler), a no-maj cannery worker who wants to open a bakery, accidentally switch cases. An incident involving a kleptomaniacal platypus-like creature alerts Tina Goldstein (Katherine Waterston), a disgraced Auror (akin to a magical police officer) with the government, to Newt's illegal possession of magical creatures. She and her mind-reading sister Queenie (Alison Sudol) eventually join Newt and Jacob on their hunt for the other escaped animals.

Until the climactic showdown with a swirling cloud of black mist and electricity (an image that has run its course over the past few years and has become a cliché this year), the film's action sequences mostly consist of amusing encounters with Newt's creatures in the city. The nimble platypus-thing steals from a window display at a department store, leading to plenty of destruction. Newt attempts to lure a giant rhinoceros-hippopotamus hybrid that is in heat with pheromones, grunts, and a sort of modern dance display, until the hapless Jacob inadvertently douses himself in the alluring scent (while the implications of this scene are discomforting, James Newton Howard's bouncy score keeps them at bay). A snake with the head of a bird can increase its mass to fit any available space, and the quartet must find a way to contain it. A significant diversion from the tone comes with an eerie scene in which Newt and Tina must escape an execution chamber.

The supporting cast is likeable, especially with Fogler and Sudol providing some charming comic relief, and Redmayne's decidedly self-conscious and internalized Newt is a dramatic shift from the heroes that one may have come to expect from this series. The character is a passive one, who is more worried about saving his creatures than about saving the day, and while the primary hook of his character (that he is a guardian of these animals) provides one truly imaginative sequence (a tour of Newt's massive shelter within the deceptively small walls of his suitcase), it is disappointing that the film's finale relies on the light-show quality of wand duels.

Where Newt's adventures will go from here is uncertain, although that uncertainty is not necessarily a negative. *Fantastic Beasts and Where to Find Them* has the unenviable double-duty of telling its own story and establishing the foundation for a larger narrative. The results are enjoyable, albeit shaky.

Mark Dujsik

CREDITS

Newt Scamander: Eddie Redmayne
Porpentina Goldstein: Katherine Waterston
Queenie Goldstein: Alison Sudol
Jacob Kowalski: Dan Fogler
Percival Graves: Colin Farrell
Origin: United States
Language: English
Released: 2016
Production: David Heyman, Steve Kloves, Lionel Wigram, J. K. Rowling; released by Heyday Films, Warner Bros. Entertainment Inc.
Directed by: David Yates
Written by: J.K. Rowling
Cinematography by: Philippe Rousselot
Music by: James Newton Howard
Sound: Glenn Freemantle
Music Supervisor: Karen Elliott
Editing: Mark Day
Art Direction: David Allday
Costumes: Colleen Atwood
Production Design: Stuart Craig; James Hambidge
MPAA rating: PG-13
Running time: 133 minutes

REVIEWS

Chang, Justin. *Los Angeles Times.* November 17, 2016.
Dargis, Manohla. *New York Times.* November 17, 2016.
Ebiri, Bilge. *Village Voice.* November 16, 2016.
Gire, Dann. *Daily Herald.* November 16, 2016.
Johanson, MaryAnn. *Flick Filosopher.* November 17, 2016.
Noveck, Jocelyn. *Associated Press.* November 15, 2016.
Orndorf, Brian. *Blu-ray.com.* November 17, 2016.
Phillips, Michael. *Chicago Tribune.* November 15, 2016.
Putman, Dustin. *TheFilmFile.com.* November 16, 2016.
Vishnevetsky, Ignatiy. *The A.V. Club.* November 17, 2016.

QUOTES

Newt Scamander: "My philosophy is if you worry, you suffer twice."

TRIVIA

The cast members were required to attend a wand boot-camp in order to learn how to use a wand properly.

AWARDS

Oscars 2016: Costume Des.
British Acad. 2016: Production Design
Nominations:
Oscars 2016: Production Design
British Acad. 2016: Costume Des., Sound, Visual FX

FENCES

Box Office: $57.6 Million

There are as many motivating passions among actors who make the transition behind the camera as there are philosophies of acting. Sometimes they are merely interested in leveraging celebrity star power to fund a passion project, and sometimes fairly clear thematic through-lines come into focus. For Denzel Washington, as much as he might eschew discussing it publicly, or even outright deny it, it is clear that his interest in directing lies in telling unique stories about social mobility within the African-American community.

That was a component of his directorial debut, *Antwone Fisher* (2002), and it was also integral to *The Great Debaters* (2007). Washington's third film behind the camera, and the first not based on a true story, is *Fences*, a straightforward, emotionally direct adaption of playwright August Wilson's Pulitzer Prize-winning stageplay of the same name. Washington first came to *Fences* by way of a 2010 Broadway revival in which he starred, and for which both he and costar Viola Davis earned Tony awards.

Written in 1983, this 1950s-set work is part of Wilson's 10-play "Pittsburgh Cycle," about the African-American experience growing up in the urban Pennsylvania city. Socioeconomic struggle and the shifting landscape of race relations are the backdrop for what is essentially a generously apportioned character study, and look at the corrosive effects of pridefulness, bitterness, and obstinance on one man's extended family.

Fences centers on Troy Maxson, a 53-year-old garbage collector struggling to reconcile his broken personal dreams of a professional baseball career with a family life that is at once tidy and settled on the surface and somewhat jumbled underneath. Troy has a loving wife, Rose (Davis), and a teenage son, Cory (Jovan Adepo), as well as a loyal friend and coworker, Bono (Stephen Henderson), who hangs on his every word.

And there are many, many words. By turns charming, angry, funny, resentful, and deluded, Troy is a mile-a-minute talker, scarcely pausing to take a breath, no matter the company. He immediately dominates any physical space into which he steps, and everyone in his life accommodates his loquaciousness, giving him wide berth. Among the most frequent targets for Troy's barbed derision are his adult son from a previous relationship, Lyons (Russell Hornsby), whom he ceaselessly hectors about his decision to pursue music as a career. The figure he seemingly saves the most compassion for is his brother Gabe (Mykelti Williamson), a World War II veteran left with diminished mental capacity by a traumatic brain injury, who now possessively carries around a trumpet around the neighborhood, getting chased by children.

The title is both literal and metaphorical; in handyman fashion, Troy is constructing a wall around the backside of the Maxson property—a task he can never quite seem to finish. As the story unwinds, details about dark family secrets come out—typically shared in an open and candid way which feels refreshing, divorced from any satisfied deliverance of a twist—and natural flash points of tension arise. Among the former are revelations that Troy spent the $3,000 government disability payout Gabe received from the Army to purchase a house for himself and Rose, and also that he has spent time in prison for a violent act. Among the bigger points of ongoing contention is Cory's desire to play high school football, as a means to earn a college scholarship. Troy, though, is vehemently opposed to this, certain in knee-jerk fashion that his son will gain no material advantage but instead only suffer the discrimination that he felt kept him out of major league baseball. This and other hurdles, over the course of several years, will challenge the family's ability to stay together.

At the core of the strong critical praise that *Fences* received are its performances, and there is no doubt that the movie, which reunites five cast members from the aforementioned 2010 production, is an actor's showcase. Washington has long, meaty, philosophically-tinged monologues throughout (a cheekier alternate title for the film could be *According to Troy*), all of which he delivers with relish. His easygoing magnetism fits the character of Troy hand-in-glove, and longtime fans of the actor will not be disappointed; it is a robust performance that feels priced by the pound.

The film really hangs on its other performers, though, who by nature of the material have to carve out fully realized, three-dimensional characters who live in Troy's shadow. Adepo is wonderful as Cory, layering his portrayal with small manifestations of the frustration a kid feels when they have to rely on one parent to run interference for them on even the most reasonable requests of piecemeal freedom and social allowance. As the affable Bono, however, Henderson has probably the most difficult role. He has to spend most of his time reacting, but also elucidate why Bono is so enamored with Troy, and devoted to their friendship. He delivers a warm, wonderful performance.

Justifiably lauded by critics groups and other awards voting bodies, meanwhile, Davis is strong and steely; her turn as Rose is magnetic, and not merely for the memorable third-act speech in which she goes to bat for her own hopes and dreams. She makes clear Rose's love for Troy, but also the weight of the sacrifices which she has made, and continues to make, on behalf of him, and their relationship.

Owing to its roots, *Fences* is a work of considerable speechifying; there is not a music cue in the film's first 45 minutes, and its opening 35-plus minutes is basically a series of monologues by Troy, punctuated with brief replies from Rose, Bono, and Lyons. Washington embraces, particularly as a director, the Shakespearean grandiosity of Wilson's tale—so much so that it is easy to envision not too radically different a version of this screenplay being performed in black-box theaters, perhaps splitting stage time with a production of the thematically similar *King Lear*.

Some of this works quite well (there is a reason that Wilson won the Pulitzer for his work, obviously), but other elements come across as somewhat hammy, and do not translate to the medium of film. When, late in the film, a thunderstorm arrives in the middle of the night, and Troy opens his window and starts yelling at Death, one could be forgiven for thinking "Important metaphor!" might start flashing on the bottom of the screen. Also, the character of Gabe is at best symbolic and at worst wince-inducing and retrograde, lingering in the background of multiple scenes like a piece of human furniture and quoting Bible verses that serve as a meta-commentary.

From a narrative standpoint, the most interesting part of *Fences* actually occurs late in the film. If forgiveness is giving up all hope of a different past, it is in this portion of the movie that first Rose, and then other family members, have to grapple with what it is they truly love and have learned from their spouse/father, and what life lessons he has taught them in the negative. They have to learn to forgive, in other words.

There is the potential for a heavenly grace and centeredness to blossom in *Fences*'s final reel. The problem is that Troy is such a complete, blunt force of nature, personality-wise, that he wears out his welcome a bit, and this conclusion feels rushed, and not quite fully realized. Washington, working from a screenplay completed by Wilson himself before his death in 2005, feels too reverential by one-third. A slight reframing of the material—opening it up to take us outside of the Maxson house, and/or spending more time with Cory or even Lyons, to better understand their relationships with their father, in both their similarities and differences—would perhaps have given *Fences* more dramatic punch, and resonance. As is, it feels overlong in first two acts, and too tightly boxed.

The film's technical credits, from Charlotte Bruus Christensen's cinematography to Hughes Winborne's editing, are spare and streamlined, keeping the focus on the text. David Gropman's production design is the standout element from this bunch, communicating both the era in broad strokes and the modest resources of the Maxson household more specifically.

Bound to a specific time and place but also seeded with enough timeless elements to give it allegorical heft, Wilson's work is widely cited as marrying the personal and social in unique and engaging fashion, and this adaptation of *Fences* in large measure also achieves this union. Years hence, however, Washington's film will be remembered less for anything to do with its story, and more just for its acting.

Brent Simon

CREDITS

Troy Maxson: Denzel Washington
Rose Maxson: Viola Davis
Bono: Stephen Henderson
Cory: Jovan Adepo
Lyons: Russell Hornsby
Origin: United States
Language: English
Released: 2016
Production: Todd Black, Scott Rudin, Denzel Washington; released by Bron Studios, MACRO, Paramount Pictures Corp., Scott Rudin Productions
Directed by: Denzel Washington
Written by: August Wilson
Cinematography by: Charlotte Bruus Christensen
Music by: Marcelo Zarvos
Sound: Per Hallberg
Editing: Hughes Winborne
Art Direction: Karen Gropman; Gregory A. Weimerskirch

Costumes: Sharen Davis
Production Design: David Gropman
MPAA rating: PG-13
Running time: 139 minutes

REVIEWS

Churnin, Nancy. *Dallas Morning News*. December 28, 2016.
Gleiberman, Owen. *Variety*. November 22, 2016.
McCarthy, Todd. *Hollywood Reporter*. November 22, 2016.
Morgenstern, Joe. *Wall Street Journal*. December 15, 2016.
Phillips, Michael. *Chicago Tribune*. December 19, 2016.
Scott, A.O. *New York Times*. December 15, 2016.
Truitt, Brian. *USA Today*. December 15, 2016.
Turan, Kenneth. *Los Angeles Times*. December 15, 2016.
Vincent, Mal. *Virginian-Pilot*. December 23, 2016.
Wilkinson, Alissa. *Vox.com*. December 29, 2016.

AWARDS

Oscars 2016: Actress—Supporting (Davis)
British Acad. 2016: Actress—Supporting (Davis)
Golden Globes 2017: Actress—Supporting (Davis)
Screen Actors Guild 2016: Actor (Washington), Actress (Davis)

Nominations:

Oscars 2016: Actor (Washington), Adapt. Screenplay, Film
Golden Globes 2017: Actor—Drama (Washington)
Screen Actors Guild 2016: Cast
Writers Guild 2016: Adapt. Score

THE 5th WAVE

Protect your own.
—Movie tagline

Box Office: $34.9 Million

Now that *Twilight*, *The Hunger Games*, and the *Divergent* series have proven the commercial cinematic viability of Young Adult fantasy book series, there must now be the inevitable imitators and wannabes of the genre. The formulas have been starting to look rather obvious in light of these successes. The stories must have a hero or heroine that once had a normal life, but then gets thrown into extraordinary circumstances. Often, there is a family member who gets caught up in the plot and who has to be rescued, usually as a way to put the hero to the test to see if they have the courage it takes to be a "chosen one." And, of course, the story needs at least two possible love interests so that the faithful readers can debate the hero's romantic fate. Whether it be vampires, apocalyptic visions, Greek mythology, or deadly game shows, it really does not matter the setting or concept as long as the stories meet these narrative needs.

The 5th Wave, based on the novel by Rick Yancey, follows this formula so closely that it almost begins to feel like a parody, right down to the voiceover narration from the heroine, in this case a teenage girl named Cassie Sullivan (Chloe Grace Moretz), talking about how "Before all this, I was a normal teenager" and how "Hope makes us human"; right down to the manner in which the family members are separated during a crucial moment that sets up the second act; right down to the ponderous, emo rock song that closes the film as the final moments set up what is obviously supposed to be a franchise, but probably never will be. *The 5th Wave* never misses a cliché.

Its concept of choice is the alien invasion and its aftermath. Cassie, at the start of the film, finds herself in an abandoned gas station where she meets a man who may be armed. On instinct, she ends up killing him. The film then flashes back to before the invasion when Cassie was a simple high school girl with simple high school crushes, namely on Ben Parish (Nick Robinson), who does not notice her advances. She has both parents and a little brother named Sam (Zackary Arthur). The invasion of the aliens (or "the others") happens quite suddenly. The power goes out, cell phones stop working, and cars are no longer mobile. The alien ships flying over the earth look too much like the alien ships in *District 9* (2009) to be menacing or even interesting. The "first wave" involves the power going out. The "second wave" involves actual tsunamis, earthquakes, and tidal waves engulfing every major metropolitan area.

The "third wave" is a bird flu epidemic. Cassie's mom (Maggie Siff) happens to be a nurse treating patients with the virus. She contracts it and dies herself. In spite of other automobiles no longer functioning, the military shows up in armored vehicles and school buses to take civilians to a safe haven. The children, of course, must be separated so that they will be out of harm's way. Cassie and Sam reluctantly board the school bus while their father, Oliver (Ron Livingston), stays at the military barracks. When Sam insists he cannot leave without his prized stuffed animal, Cassie gets off the bus to quickly retrieve it, but of course she is too late and the bus takes off without her. When Cassie makes her way back to the barracks, the discussion between the civilians and the top military personnel, Colonel Vosch (Liev Schreiber), gets so heated that everyone ends up dead from a gunshot wound.

Cassie is now on her own with a few firearms, some snacks, and a sleeping bag. Sam gets whisked off to another military facility where he, Ben and several other teens and pre-teens get screened and trained to be soldiers. The "fourth wave" has to do with "the others" taking human form. One can only see the aliens with special glasses. Meanwhile, Cassie endures a gunshot wound to her leg during a random shoot-out with a stranger. She awakens and finds herself in a house with a mysterious, hunky doctor named Evan Walker (Alex Roe), who treats the wound while treating her and the young women in the audience to a shot of him bathing shirtless. The remainder of the plot has Cassie trying to make her way to the training facility to rescue her little brother. Joining Sam and Ben is a random new recruit named Ringer (Maika Monroe), a no-nonsense soldier who puts the men in their place, yet has plenty of time on her hands to apply just the right of goth looking eyeshadow and who provides Ben with some unnecessary romantic tension.

The viewer has the "yeah, we already figured that out" moment when Ben (appropriately nicknamed "Zombie") learns what the "fifth wave" is really all about and preaches it to his squad. It will be very obvious to anyone who has watched a lot of movies over the past 20 years that when Schreiber appears on screen, he usually plays a character who cannot be trusted. His mere presence in a film like this should arouse immediate suspicion that nothing is as it seems. He does nothing with his performance that he has not already done a dozen times. Moretz tries her best, but the material is beneath her. Clearly, her agent tried to convince her that she could be the next Jennifer Lawrence if she were to take this role. Monroe's performance as Ringer is so over-cooked and one-note that whatever progressive virtues she was supposed to embody have pretty much been muted.

The obvious nature of the story is only part of the problem with *The 5th Wave*. Its derivativeness with the science fiction also has major problems. Every kid or teenager gets a small device stuck behind their neck so they can be marked as a human and not be confused as an "other." The actual "others" have taken over human host bodies so as to blend in. The obvious references to *Invasion of the Body Snatchers* (1956) and John Carpenter's *They Live* (1988) have a way of aligning with the clichés of the piece as a whole. Furthermore, the disaster-movie element in the first act—the tsunamis and tidal waves—have been so poorly constructed and look unbearably fake that the film even fails to entertain on even the lowest of levels.

Basically, *The 5th Wave* has most of the production value, but none of the scope or ambition of a *Hunger Games* film. It exists to cash in on its successes, while using the *Divergent* playbook as an easy route to a storyline that has nothing in the way of freshness. Sony Pictures clearly thought this would get a franchise going, much in the same way they tried to cling to the *Spider-*

Man series by churning out bad films that had neither the wit nor style of its predecessors. Even the film's director, J Blakeson, appears to have no interest in putting his real name on it. *The 5th Wave* came out in January and barely made anyone's radar. While it tried to pass itself off as a film about hope, its chief aspiration was to have the teenage audience debate whether or they were Team Evan or Team Ben. Neither choice is very interesting.

Collin Souter

CREDITS

Cassie Sullivan: Chloe Grace Moretz
Lizbeth: Gabriela Lopez
Ben Parish/Zombie: Nick Robinson
Oliver Sullivan: Ron Livingston
Lisa Sullivan: Maggie Siff
Sam Sullivan: Zackary Arthur
Origin: United States
Language: English
Released: 2016
Production: Tim Headington, Graham King, Tobey Maguire, Matthew Plouffe; released by Columbia Pictures Industries Inc., GK Films
Directed by: J. Blakeson
Written by: Susannah Grant; Akiva Goldsman; Jeff Pinkner
Cinematography by: Enrique Chediak
Music by: Henry Jackman
Sound: Richard King
Editing: Paul Rubell
Art Direction: Julian Ashby
Costumes: Sharen Davis
Production Design: Jon Billington
MPAA rating: PG-13
Running time: 112 minutes

REVIEWS

Anderson, Soren. *Seattle Times*. January 21, 2016.
Barnard, Linda. *Toronto Star*. January 21, 2016.
Davis, Steve. *Austin Chronicle*. January 28, 2016.
Guzman, Rafer. *Newsday*. January 23, 2016.
Lane, Anthony. *New Yorker*. January 25, 2016.
O'Malley, Sheila. *RogerEbert.com*. January 22, 2016.
Phillips, Michael. *Chicago Tribune*. January 22, 2016.
Pickett, Leah. *Chicago Reader*. January 28, 2016.
Verniere, James. *Boston Herald*. January 22, 2016.
Whitty, Stepehen. *Star-Ledger*. January 22, 2016.

QUOTES

Cassie: [narrating] The Others see our hope as a weakness; as a delusion. But they're wrong. It's our hope that lets us survive. That lets us bend, but remain unbroken. It's our hope that will let us win one day. It's our hope that makes us human."

TRIVIA

Chloe Grace Moretz said she read the book the film is based on three times.

FIFTY SHADES OF BLACK

Once you go black, you never go gray.
—Movie tagline

Box Office: $11.7 Million

The famous Jean-Luc Godard quote goes, "Instead of writing criticism, I [now] film it." Fewer multiplex comedians take this to heart more than Marlon Wayans. His newest point of interest is the camp phenomenon *Fifty Shades of Grey* (2015), which launched a film franchise and turned author E.L. James' revamped "Twilight" fan-fiction into a multi-million dollar brand. Wayans' criticism is on-point like Godard's *Goodbye to Language* (2014), but at his own terms. "Who wrote this, a third grader?" He asks, while holding a jumbo-size version of the book. "This is fucking terrible!"

Keeping with Wayans' family spoof film traditions, *Fifty Shades of Black* takes the structure of *Fifty Shades of Grey* and refurnishes it, albeit with pop culture references that date the movie down to its first showing, and R-rated racial and sexual humor that employ brash stereotypes as cultural imagery, in which ethnic casting plays as key a part as the jokes delivered at a rapid pace. The story is unabashedly recognizable to *Fifty Shades of Grey*, as if playing in a bizarro world. A mysterious and sexually eccentric billionaire (Marlon Wayans' Christian Black) is entranced by a virginal college student (Kali Hawk's Hannah Steale, a sharp take on Dakota Johnson's Anastasia Steele) to the point of wooing her into a contract that allows for a dominant/submissive relationship. To re-quote Wayans' Black, it is a terrible excuse of a story, a thread the original failed to hang anything on, or to create tension, of the dramatic or erotic variety. *Fifty Shades of Black* seems to comment upon this by turning the new story into a group of frank sexual sequences into which they try more than just whips and paddles, but engage in gross sexuality *Fifty Shades of Grey* is comparatively too prudish for: butt plugs, oral sex with pencils, and various bodily functions and much more that appear in this mix. Within Wayans' brand of comedy, these sequences run like hit-and-miss crude rants, even if a very specific reference "Big Brother Almighty!" of Spike Lee's *School Daze* (1988) or the "rushing or dragging" scene from

Damien Chazelle's *Whiplash* (2014) (but with an instructional Florence Henderson in bed)—brings a zany charm. Enjoyment of *Fifty Shades of Black* does boil down to matters of taste, regarding an audience's vacation from it.

Aside from turning the pasty *Fifty Shades of Grey* into *Fifty Shades of Black*, the film proves a great opportunity for Wayans, who remains a high-voltage actor in the bedroom, as exemplified in his rampaging love-making scenes with the ghost from *Paranormal Activity* (2007) or the doll from *The Conjuring* (2013) in *A Haunted House* and *A Haunted House 2* (2014), respectively. Though he may never get his comedic due performing in raunchy racial comedies that are barely screened for critics, Wayans is as valuable and charismatic a comedian as any multiplex star, unafraid to hurl himself into full physical bursts to get even a chuckle, here complementing the original story's sociopathic sexuality with that of a grade-A clown. A highlight includes him flashing back to a *Magic Mike*-like parody, in which his well-defined torso is on display, along with a vivid shamelessness that punctuates falling into the crowd and being crushed by an overweight woman with a micro-penis joke. *Fifty Shades of Black* is a circus inside Wayans' wheelhouse, with commentary a surprising souvenir.

Wayans' performance is driven by a refreshingly feminist response to the Christian Grey fantasy. Black is shown as physically vulnerable in spite of the power he projects with his sexual interests and his words; many jokes end with emasculation or with Black's perfect physical specimen revealed to be sexually incompetent and anti-virile (punchlines that Wayans savors with each abrupt ejaculation). Unfortunately, the film still slacks on giving Hawk her own fortified character; it's her game quality for the sexual shenanigans that *Fifty Shades of Black* can most show off. Taken on her own, Hawk's version of the sexually naive Steale is a set of flat virginity jokes.

Fifty Shades of Grey had a fair amount of faux-classiness as the Goldschläger of erotic mainstream movies, which Tiddes recreates with visual footnotes, like rhyming the large, shadowed conference table where the two first meet their contractual agreement, or the city skyline apartment view that provides a type of class in between sexual moments. A score from Jim Dooley keeps things buoyant, and editing can sometimes find its punchline in either an abrupt cut or extensive physical act, whether it's a character failing to open a door or the many sex acts that match Wayans' banshee bed moments.

Fifty Shades of Black can be undone by its fleeting attributes, but is far more enjoyable than watching *Fifty Shades of Grey* a second time. Though its box office total of $21 million is considerably less than the source's

$571 million, Tiddes' movie is a victory for the whole Wayans filmmaking attitude, a project that destroys the incognizant vanity of a campy blockbuster with the unexpected consciousness of trash.

Nick Allen

CREDITS

Christian: Marlon Wayans
Hannah: Kali Hawk
Gary: Fred Willard
Ron: Mike Epps
Eli: Affion Crockett
Claire: Jane Seymour
Origin: United States
Language: English
Released: 2016
Production: Marlon Wayans, Rick Alvarez; released by IM Global
Directed by: Michael Tiddes
Written by: Marlon Wayans; Rick Alvarez
Cinematography by: David Ortkiese
Music by: Jim Dooley
Sound: Craig Mann
Music Supervisor: David Schulhof; Trygge Toven
Editing: Lawrence Jordan
Costumes: Ariyela Wald-Cohain
Production Design: Ermanno Di Febo-Orsini
MPAA rating: R
Running time: 92 minutes

REVIEWS

Duralde, Alonso. *TheWrap.* January 29, 2016.
Holub, Christian. *Entertainment Weekly.* January 31, 2016.
Huddleston, Tom. *Time Out.* March 7, 2016.
LeVoit, Violet. *AllMovie.* January 29, 2016.
Jones, J. R. *Chicago Reader.* February 4, 2016.
Lemire, Christy. *RogerEbert.com.* January 29, 2016.
Rife, Katie. *The A.V. Club.* January 29, 2016.
Tobias, Scott. *Variety.* January 29, 2016.
Tsai, Martin. *Los Angeles Times.* January 29, 2016.
Webster, Andy. *New York Times.* January 29, 2016.

QUOTES

Hannah Steele: (after Christian buys cable ties and tape) "If I didn't know better, I might mistake you for a serial killer."

TRIVIA

This was the last film appearance by Florence Henderson who passed away ten months after the movie's release.

AWARDS

Nominations:

Golden Raspberries 2016: Worst Remake/Sequel, Worst Support. Actress (Seymour)

FINDING DORY

An unforgettable journey she probably won't remember.
—Movie tagline

Box Office: $486.3 Million

Finding Nemo (2003) begins, appropriately enough, with a fish fishing for compliments from the missus about his choice of deep-sea digs, repeatedly exclaiming "Wow" while purposefully marveling at their new top-notch view upon the bottom. During first-run showings of the now-classic Disney/Pixar production and countless subsequent viewings over the thirteen years leading up to the spawning of this sequel, those taking in the superior sights laid out before them have routinely gone on to echo the opening's appreciative exclamations, often thrilled enough to surpass the character's thrice. "Did your man deliver, or what?" clownfish Marlin (Albert Brooks) had then asked his wife Coral (Elizabeth Perkins), and *Nemo*'s fervent fans were eager for an answer as to whether the man most responsible for that film, writer-director Andrew Stanton, had delivered with his eagerly-anticipated follow-up, or (gulp) what? While Coral had gazed at the beauty off the edge of the Great Barrier Reef and concluded that the "drop off is desirable," moviegoers spoiled by the truly-entrancing first film were prepared to offer up a harsher assessment of any decline that they observed. Happily, while this film now focusing on a fish that keeps forgetting ironically keeps recalling too many elements of *Nemo*, it also features sufficient loveliness and laugh-inducing aquatic antics, along with a depth of feeling that had many viewers adding their own saltwater to the proceedings.

Since the aforementioned couple's conversation had ended abruptly with Coral and all but one of her ready-to-hatch eggs going down the hatch of a barracuda, it may seem highly inappropriate to say that the depiction of Dory as a small fry at the outset here is so cute that one could just eat her up. Nevertheless, diminutive Dory is indeed quite adorably voiced (by Sloane Murray), but the presentation is about as devastating as she is darling. Previously, as Marlin's scene-stealing sidekick in *Nemo*, the blue tang had largely been a chipperly-determined, chuckle-inducing ichthyological idiosyncrasy. However, this reintroduction of the character not only steals one's heart but also makes it sink with the strength and swiftness of the film's oft-mentioned undertow, as what had

been flashes of silly-sounding quirkiness is made quite sobering. Dory's short-term memory loss problem is revealed to have been a lifelong struggle, and parents, particularly those of special-needs children, found themselves unexpectedly relating quite profoundly to a couple of fish forebears who are as palpably filled with trepidation as they are with love. It is quite touching to watch Charlie (Eugene Levy) and Jenny (Diane Keaton) struggle to make their memory tricks stick, potentially safeguarding their particularly-at-risk offspring.

Unfortunately, things soon do not go swimmingly. As this piteous pipsqueak version of the film's protagonist is shown to have remained lost and alone for years within such voluminous and potentially dangerous environs (dwarfing her further through the use of long shots only intensifies the impression of peril), forlornly asking for help until she can no longer clearly recall what she needed it for, viewers were in need of the comic relief previously provided by this character that was now identified by Stanton as being fundamentally tragic. After showing when Dory (now so engagingly voiced by Ellen DeGeneres) finally and fatefully bumped into more-panicked-than-usual papa Marlin and set out with him to get Nemo back from a scuba diving snatcher, the film jumps ahead a year to reveal that Dory (now residing with amusing aptness in a hollow brain coral near kith-like-kin Marlin and Nemo) is starting to get back her memory in fleeting, intriguing flashes. Things she sees and hears remind her of things from the past, and with the initiation of a trek across the Pacific to try and reunite two generations of a family, things also started sounding rather familiar to fans of *Nemo*. A specific example: Marlin's harsh, hurtful words spoken in anger to Dory early on that he did not really mean are inescapably reminiscent of Nemo's "I hate you!" to his protective-to-the-point-of-smothering dad. Such things gradually started to pile up like the reef's calcified coral remains, and the repetitiousness related to the spotlighting here of Dory and her condition gradually got almost as old as the Great Barrier's ancient accumulations.

Stanton posited that Dory's "optimism and helpful nature are a defense. It is an unconscious armor she presents in hopes others won't tire of her challenge and ditch her." Similarly, he not only seems to have counted on her ingratiating personality's ability to compensate for what might have eventually become grating to the point of alienating audiences, but also that the fizzy, frenetic, and increasingly far-fetched fun of the proceedings on the way to the wholly-expected happy ending would keep its heavier moments from weighing too much on the minds of moviegoers. Indeed, when things head east instead of west this time and a child pursues a parent instead of that also being the other way around, those watching enjoyed being reeled in by all the comedic chaos as Dory and devoted pals Marlin and Nemo try to locate Charlie and Jenny at their suddenly-recalled last known address: The Marine Life Institute in Morro Bay, California. (A Sea World-type setting was jettisoned from an early draft of the script and replaced with this fictionalized version of the environmentally-empathetic Monterrey Bay Aquarium after the 2013 documentary *Blackfish* gave a black eye to the theme park.) The conscientious conservationists at the Institute are dedicated to "Rescue, Rehabilitation, and Release," three things that Dory needs and receives here before the end of all the stressful striving to put her troubled mind at rest (at least, as much as is possible with her) and reconnect with her biological blue tang clan.

"Newsflash: Nobody's fine," asserts curmudgeonly MLI resident Hank (a terrific Ed O'Neill), a seven-armed octopus who conversely yearns for separation instead of unification and is the film's ultra-slippery break out star in more than one sense. Similar to mind-like-a-steel-sieve Dory, who finds that her inability to recall potential risks or previous failure is actually the enviable key to her unusual can-do tenacity (her journey is also very much about self-discovery, hence the title), Hank is an extraordinary-capable escape artist despite having lost an arm. These characters are present to make an uplifting point: deficits need not destine one for defeat. Speaking of destiny, there is also the whale shark by that name (Kaitlin Olson) who is profoundly nearsighted, beluga whale Bailey (Ty Burrell) fears his echolocation skills are compromised, Nemo (now Hayden Rolence) has his malformed fin), and Becky the loon seems loony. Despite their inauspicious imperfections, each character is indispensable, and through cooperative coalescence, success is made possible.

Quite colorful in a different way than these characters (and at times more profoundly captivating) are the myriad, multitextured components of the reef, its pristine, sunlight-infused beauty contrasted with the murkier coastal kelp forest that is shamefully studded with man's detrimental detritus. (Perhaps too much of an inside joke was the way-out public address presence of Sigourney Weaver, referring to the use of her voice in various nature presentations.) However, amidst the signs of dispiriting ecological change is a lovely, heartening example of constancy in which Dory is guided home by evidence of her parents' unflagging devotion. Inside theaters, as within Bailey's body, it was blubber, blubber, blubber.

Since inspired masterwork *Finding Nemo* had grossed $943.3 million worldwide, it is hard to fathom why it took so long to make this $200 million-budgeted sequel, which broke the $1 billion mark amidst warm, if less rapturous, reviews. *Finding Dory* ends as *Nemo* had begun, with a contented appraisal from the drop off.

"Unforgettable," Dory declares. Not quite, as far as this more modestly-impressive charmer is concerned, but there thankfully was no precipitous falling-off here beyond the topographical.

David L. Boxerbaum

CREDITS

Voice of Dory: Ellen DeGeneres
Voice of Marlin: Albert Brooks
Voice of Hank: Ed O'Neill
Voice of Destiny: Kaitlin Olson
Voice of Nemo: Hayden Rolence
Origin: United States
Language: English
Released: 2016
Production: Lindsey Collins; released by Pixar Animation Studios, Walt Disney Pictures
Directed by: Andrew Stanton; Angus MacLane
Written by: Andrew Stanton; Victoria Strouse
Cinematography by: Jeremy Lasky
Music by: Thomas Newman
Sound: Steve Slanec
Editing: Axel Geddes
Art Direction: Don Shank
Production Design: Steve Pilcher
MPAA rating: PG
Running time: 97 minutes

REVIEWS

Ebiri, Bilge. *Village Voice.* June 15, 2016.
Feeney, Mark. *Boston Globe.* June 16, 2016.
Gleiberman, Owen. *Variety.* June 10, 2016.
Hornaday, Ann. *Washington Post.* June 16, 2016.
McCarthy, Todd. *Hollywood Reporter.* June 10, 2016.
Morgenstern, Joe. *Wall Street Journal.* June 16, 2016.
Nashawaty, Chris. *Entertainment Weekly.* June 10, 2016.
Phillips, Michael. *Chicago Tribune.* June 15, 2016.
Rainer, Peter. *Christian Science Monitor.* June 17, 2016.
Roeper, Richard. *Chicago Sun-Times.* June 15, 2016.

QUOTES

Young Dory: "I like sand. Sand is squishy."

TRIVIA

Dory is the most liked character on Facebook from any Disney or Pixar film, with more than 25 million likes.

AWARDS

Nominations:
British Acad. 2016: Animated Film

THE FINEST HOURS

We all live or we all die.
    —Movie tagline

Box Office: $27.5 Million

Based on a true story of the incredible rescue of 32 people, earnest and predictable period piece action drama *The Finest Hours* is not a big, special effects extravaganza or water-soaked disaster movie like *Poseidon* (2006) or *San Andreas* (2015). It is instead meant to be a more intimately scaled human story that just happens to also feature huge waves and boats being torn apart. The chief problem, though, is that there is no sense of proper space or scale to the movie, so its action is all generic, confusing, and utterly pointless—unless one merely enjoys watching actors get wet and yell in the wind and rain, in which case, hey, this is definitely the movie for you.

Opening in 1951, *The Finest Hours* spends its first 15 minutes trying to get viewers to emotionally invest in a romance between Bernard Webber (Chris Pine) and Miriam (Holliday Grainger), with only mediocre success. The film is set in Massachusetts, where Webber is an employee of the United States Coast Guard, conducting rescues and emergency operations at sea. After a vicious storm literally splits two oil tankers in half, all the rescue personnel from the larger city of Boston are deployed to try to save the SS Fort Mercer (which is never seen in the movie). This leaves a much smaller, undermanned outpost presided over by Chief Warrant Officer Daniel Cluff (Eric Bana) to try to find and save the SS Pendleton, whose hull has broken off, leaving it without a captain.

Cluff commands Webber to do this, so Webber enlists the support of Richard Livesey (Ben Foster), Andrew Fitzgerald (Kyle Gallner), and Ervin Maske (John Magaro), and undertakes a rescue operation in an 35-foot motor-operated life boat. In the middle of this raging storm, it is a supremely risky move which older colleagues regard as a suicide mission, and urge Webber to avoid.

Meanwhile, on the SS Pendleton, chief engineer Ray Sybert (Casey Affleck), a quiet man respected for his knowledge if not particularly liked or even well known, tries to rally the remaining crew members to pitch the sinking tanker up on a shoal, where they can hope for help. With choppy ocean waters rendering their lifeboats unsafe, Sybert convinces the crew that this is their last, best hope at survival. In the end, through the convergence of bravery, skill and considerable luck on the ends of both Webber and Sybert, almost all the men are saved.

One of the easiest and most frequent pre-release comparisons for *The Finest Hours* was *The Perfect Storm* (2000), which grossed more than $328 million worldwide. But that film had compelling characters plus a director, Wolfgang Petersen, who was able to balance human emotion with enormous special effects and smart, classic editorial technique. On a very basic level, *The Finest Hours* struggles to effectively build tension. The stakes are clearly high for its characters, but the movie never taps into a believable sense of danger and imperilment that an audience can get lost in.

An assertive sound mix injects *The Finest Hours* with subjectivity, and definitely helps convey to viewers a sense of being battered by the weather. But the film's sensory assault is immediately overwhelmed by Carter Burwell's overproduced, too-loud score. This robs and bleeds the movie of what most makes it potentially special—its experiential quality. Instead of inducing a feeling of actually being there, pounded by waves or desperately trying to plug a leaking tanker wall, the movie just keeps poking viewers, reminding them that this situation was surely intense.

The sly subversion present in director Craig Gillespie's early work—the underrated *Lars and the Real Girl* (2007), and even wildly different genre efforts like *Mr. Woodcock* (2007) and *Fright Night* (2011)—is perhaps understandably absent here, but replaced with a plodding, workmanlike touch that, while not bad, lacks any discernible personality. Most problematically for *The Finest Hours*, there is not a clear sense of the spatial relationships in the movie. Consequently, because of the way Gillespie and editor Tatiana Riegel cut scenes, the action and rescue sequences are essentially just a jumbled blur of things being tossed back and forth in the ocean.

In terms of the performances, Pine is cast against type as a somewhat mopey guy who is totally uncertain of himself in both his personal life and work. It is understandable and easy to see why he would enjoy the challenge of playing such a subdued character. Sometimes this counterintuitive casting choice works, and sometimes it does not (Pine's accent wavers, blowing in and out like the wind). It is also worth noting that Affleck, unlike a lot of his peers in the same age range, is an actor who derives his level of engagement not from dialogue but instead moments of pause and/or quiet reflection. To that end, he is perfectly cast as Ray, a strong-but-silent type; he gives the movie an anchoring presence, though occasionally overplaying these moments of tranquility just a bit, for dramatic effect.

It must be stressed that *The Finest Hours* is not actively bad, so if one deeply enjoys formulaic true-life stories of cookie-cutter emotional uplift, there are far worse ways to spend 105 minutes. Also, if grading on a curve, the film sidesteps some potential pitfalls that one might have expected prior to viewing. It does not, for instance, take cloying character shortcuts and simply depict all these men as just "of the sea," and doing what they love; by varying degrees, Webber, Sybert, and the other men are unsettled by circumstances, even before the storm is at its worst and the stakes are heightened to life and death.

Unfortunately, screenwriters Scott Silver, Paul Tamasy, and Eric Johnson fumble badly in their depiction of Miriam, going to unrealistic lengths to establish her as a progressive character, in an effort to underscore her love story with Webber. They have Miriam get into an argument with Cluff, and just generally behave in a manner far out of step with 1950s conventions. This would be fine if it seemed natural, but it comes across as extraordinarily contrived. Her behavior is even actively commented upon by multiple other characters (one literally says, "Miriam, none of the other girls do this"), which only serves to highlight how blatantly emotionally manipulative it is. Awash in disposable spectacle, *The Finest Hours* is most suitable for maritime lovers or hardcore fans of Pine and Affleck. But it unfortunately does not live up to its title.

Brent Simon

CREDITS

Bernie Webber: Chris Pine
Ray Sybert: Casey Affleck
Richard Livesey: Ben Foster
Daniel Cluff: Eric Bana
Miriam Webber: Holliday Grainger
Andy Fitzgerald: Kyle Gallner
Origin: United States
Language: English
Released: 2016
Production: Dorothy Aufiero, James Whitaker; released by Walt Disney Pictures
Directed by: Craig Gillespie
Written by: Scott Silver; Paul Tamasy; Eric Johnson
Cinematography by: Javier Aguirresarobe
Music by: Carter Burwell
Editing: Tatiana S. Riegel
Art Direction: William Ladd (Bill) Skinner
Costumes: Louise Frogley
Production Design: Michael Corenblith
MPAA rating: PG-13
Running time: 117 minutes

REVIEWS

Andersen, Soren. *Seattle Times.* January 28, 2016.
Barker, Andrew. *Variety.* January 18, 2016.
Burr, Ty. *Boston Globe.* January 28, 2016.
LaSalle, Mick. *San Francisco Chronicle.* January 28, 2016.
Linden, Sheri. *Hollywood Reporter.* January 18, 2016.
Morgenstern, Joe. *Wall Street Journal.* January 28, 2016.

Phillips, Michael. *Chicago Tribune.* January 27, 2016.
Rainer, Peter. *Christian Science Monitor.* January 29, 2016.
Savlov, Marc. *Austin Chronicle.* January 29, 2016.

QUOTES

Andy Fitzgerald: "Please tell me we are taking this boat to a bigger boat."

TRIVIA

Post-production lasted more than a year; the film required nearly 1,000 visual-effects shots.

THE FIRST MONDAY IN MAY

Box Office: $527,474

No doubt fueled in at least some part by the success of the screen version of *The Devil Wears Prada* (2006), the last decade or so has seen a pronounced uptick in documentaries dealing with some aspect of the fashion industry, usually focusing either on the designers who create the outfits or the tastemakers whose opinions in large part determine whether they sell or not. For the most part, these films-including *Valentino: The Last Emperor* (2008), *The September Issue* (2009), and *Dior and I* (2014)—have been superficially entertaining at best but too fawning towards their subjects to satisfy anyone other than the most hard-core of fashionistas. At first glance, *The First Monday in May* would seem to offer a little more substance than its predecessors but it eventually proves itself to be just as shallow and simple-minded, if not more so.

The subject of the film is the annual charity ball thrown by New York's Metropolitan Museum of Art on the titular date as a fundraiser for their Costume Institute. Under the auspices of curator Andrew Bolton and *Vogue* editor Anna Wintour, the event has become what one observer breathlessly describes as "The Super Bowl of Fashion" as the biggest names in entertainment, fashion, and politics turn up on the red carpet in jaw-dropping outfits from some of the most notable designers. The film covers the development of the 2015 edition, "China—Through the Looking Glass," an ambitious exhibit that plans to chart China's cultural influence on fashion throughout history. Over the course of eight months, Bolton, along with artistic director Wong Kar-wai, works to put on a spectacular show while sidestepping the potential cultural pitfalls involving colonialism, Orientalism, and cultural appropriation. Meanwhile, Wintour and her formidable crew tackle the even more fraught-with-portent task of figuring out which A-list celebrities should receive one of the coveted invites ("Josh Hartnett—what has he done lately?") and trying to figure out where to seat them all. There is much consternation, for example, when it turns out that Rihanna, who is scheduled to be the evening's entertainment, travels with a non-negotiable entourage large and expensive enough to send the budget spiraling completely out of control.

As *The First Monday in May* goes about its meandering way, it becomes apparent that director Andrew Rossi is juggling three different narrative threads throughout but cannot get a fix on any of them. The film opens with the question of whether fashion should be considered a legitimate work of artistic expression along the lines of painting or sculpture—the question is an interesting one but after paying a little bit of lip service to it early on, the idea is summarily dropped and never returned to in any substantial manner. (It might have been interesting to examine some of the fashions worn by the gala guests in order to explore whatever artistic concepts they might have been harboring.) Likewise, the stuff about cultural appropriation and the worries of a show dedicated to Chinese art and fashion being put on by a non-Asian crowd also gets short shrift as well. In one especially frustrating moment, an Asian journalist more or less poses this question to Wintour in an interview but she dodges it and is then caught making a catty remark about it afterwards in a way that suggests that Rossi is totally on Wintour's side on the issue. Then there is the stuff about the actual staging of the gala but since it is evident that Rossi is not going to show anything that might show it in a bad light, there is nothing particularly interesting about these scenes as well unless one gets inordinately excited at endless shots of people worriedly consulting increasingly elaborate seating charts.

In fact, the only time that Rossi seems to have any real interest in the proceedings comes during the elongated finale chronicling the Met Ball itself and that is only because it is at that point that he officially abandons any sort of intellectual or sociological pretext in order to offer up the sight of dozens of famous faces arriving in outfits ranging from the stylish to the cringe-inducing (what is that thing atop Sarah Jessica Parker's head?) with all the breathlessly vapid enthusiasm of a typical red carpet ceremony. Although it might have been interesting to get some of the arrivals thoughts on the fashion-as-art question, it appears that Rossi wasn't allowed to actually speak to any of them, perhaps so as not to conflict with the Vogue camera crew, led by Andre Leon Talley, lobbing softball suck-up questions to the likes of Jennifer Lopez and Kim Kardashian. (There is a momentary crisis when George and Amal Clooney arrive and commit the heresy of ignoring them entirely.) When he can find the time, Rossi also deigns to show

little bits of the completed exhibition but it says a lot about where his priorities are that there is probably just as much, if not more, footage devoted to Justin Bieber capering about like a twerp than to the artifacts on display.

In the end, *The First Monday in May* is little more than a 90-minute informercial for *Vogue* and Anna Wintour—you almost expect an ad rate card to be included among the special features on the Blu-ray—that has precious little to say about art, fashion, Asian culture, or any of the things that it initially professes to take an interest in. If all that one wants from a film like this is just to see beautiful people in fancy outfits, it will probably suffice but anyone hoping for anything more substantial than that is going to be disappointed. Face it, when Rihanna—whose entourage difficulties were evidently settled—appears during the gala to sing *Bitch Better Have My Money* for the well-heeled throngs, it is the closest that the movie ever gets to an actual message.

Peter Sobczynski

CREDITS

Herself: Anna Wintour
Himself: Andrew Bolton
Himself: John Galliano
Himself: Karl Lagerfeld
Himself: Jean-Paul Gaultier
Origin: United States
Language: English
Released: 2016
Production: Fabiola Beracasa, Skot Bright, Dawn Ostroff, Sylvana Ward Durrett; released by Conde Nast Entertainment, MediaWeaver Entertainment, Relativity Studios
Directed by: Andrew Rossi
Cinematography by: Andrew Rossi; Bryan Sarkinen
Music by: Ian Hultquist; Sofia Hultquist
Editing: Andrew Rossi; Chad Beck; Andrew Coffman
MPAA rating: PG-13
Running time: 90 minutes

REVIEWS

Bender, Abbey. *Village Voice*. April 13, 2016.
Dillard, Clayton. *Slant Magazine*. April 13, 2016.
Howell, Peter. *Toronto Star*. April 21, 2016.
Kenny, Glenn. *New York Times*. April 14, 2016.
Kohn, Eric. *IndieWire*. April 13, 2016.
Merry, Stephanie. *Washington Post*. April 14, 2016.
Murray, Noel. *Los Angeles Times*. April 14, 2016.
Orndorf, Brian. *Blu-ray.com*. April 13, 2016.

Schafer, Nick. *Variety.* April 13, 2106.

Scheck, Frank. *Hollywood Reporter.* April 13, 2016.

QUOTES

Kar-Wai Wong: "When there is too many things to see, you see nothing."

THE FITS

Box Office: $166,425

In one of the most lilting moments of *The Fits*, the central character Toni (Royal Hightower), a wide-eyed, inquisitive, and beautiful young dreamer, moves through the terraced, enclosed overhang pass she uses as a training space with a gorgeous precision. The camera on her back, she begins by working through her traditional athletic movements before breaking into a more lyrical and ecstatic form of dance and self-expression, the moment a private reverie.

This is just one of many touching, piercing moments aglow in this wondrous, small miracle of a movie directed, produced, and written by the very gifted new filmmaker Anna Rose Holmer. This accomplished and alive first narrative feature is like a short story, self-contained, compact, and filled with moments of startling intimacy and grace. It's also infused with a strangeness and mystery through its entwining of realist and magic realist underpinnings. Holmer wrote the script with Lisa Kjerulff and Saela Davis, the movie's editor, the glancing, elliptical structure has a wondrous unity.

Right from the start, Holmer eschews standard exposition and plunges right into the story with its evocative opening image, a close up of the 11-year old Toni performing sit-ups inside the boxing club at the recreational center located on the West End of Cincinnati where virtually all the action unfolds. The moment immediately crystallizes the direct, private sensations of the young girl. Working with the very gifted cinematographer Paul Yee, Holmer composes in deep focus with Toni occupying the foreground, the middle space catching two boxers sparring in a ring and in the deep background a third boxer working with a rope.

Holmer came up as an electrician, cinematographer and she has a great eye. She also has a background in documentary, explaining her vivid sense of place. She conjures a world, a milieu of backstage action, camaraderie, discipline, and toughness. Toni idolizes her older brother Jermaine (Da'Sean Minor), her entry point to the highly ritualistic club. As the only girl inside the boxing club, she is taken seriously and respected by the older boys. Holmer refuses to romanticize the sport or downplay the inherent violence, like a montage that shows the pain and the privation, a boy who takes a violent punch the stomach, his wind knocked from him, another boy with a busted nose or a third whose face plunges hard into the canvas.

Toni lives inside her head, keeping her thoughts and feelings closed off, and moving to her own rhythm, like the way she walks down a hallway. The architecture of the recreation center, with its windows and lines, naturally creates divisions and separations. Holmer emphasizes the young girl's isolation at the start, beautifully captured by a diagonally slanted window that reveals her plaintive and open face she stares into the adjacent dance room where a group of older girls go through their own elaborately worked out routines. The sequence, quiet and forceful and marked by a melancholy, is the first of the movie's dramatic ruptures as Toni realizes her identity and need for personal expression is part of a greater desire to belong.

Her attention, focus, and drive shift from the boxing club to the dance group, an electric and joyous group called the Lionesses who bring a lively and raucous energy to their rehearsals, especially the three older teenagers who establish the social order of the group. The group is a perennial city champion and they are preparing for a new competition. Rapt and fascinated, Toni now studies these girls, the movements, the way they bend and twirl their bodies or flail their arms or strut. She is not the most natural or technically accomplished, but Toni has conviction and style and she moves with a furious abandon.

The movie is just 72 minutes long, and the story is more anecdotal and open ended than carefully mapped out. Holmer has a very observant style, aided by the terrific camerawork and lively colors deployed by Yee. Not a moment is wasted or overdone, and every shot carries a physical charge. When the movie does move outside the recreational center, like two key scenes set on the floor of an emptied out swimming pool, *The Fits* reaches a higher level visually and its dramatic use of space.

The other significant narrative rupture explains the film's title and introduces a knotty and mysterious emotional register as various members of the dance troupe, beginning with the older girls, suddenly experience a series of terrifying convulsions, inexplicable seizures in which they lose control of their bodies and are subject to a form of ecstasy. The local officials launch an investigation to determine the source, perhaps connected to the contaminated water.

These episodes, stark and strange and deeply unsettling, point out one of the ineluctable mysteries and entrancing qualities of the larger film, an inquiry into consciousness and being. Toni also "fits," between worlds, the one of her brother and her new vocational art, and the training scene on the overpass illustrates the dynamic beautifully, a young girl caught in extremes and working out her own self-actualization.

The movie is, nominally, a coming of age story, though *The Fits* more expressively limns a world rarely explored, even in independent cinema, the inner life of a young girl of color. Her developing confidence and self-assertion, evident in a funny and lyrical scene when she self-pierces her own ears, is glorious to take in. The camerawork, darting and quick and alert to the pull and sweep of Toni's movements, feel intuitive and natural and never ostentatious. Some of the loveliest scenes of the film are the most naturalistic, featuring Toni in the moment, nervous, active, and newly emboldened or interacting with two other new recruits, Beezy (Alexis Neblett, delightful) and Maia (Lauren Gibson).

Adults are peripheral to the action of the movie, and the young actors really hold the center. This is Hightower's first time acting in a film, and she is a discovery. It is an emotionally muted and interior performance, but deeply expressive in other ways, her taut body outlining a sharp and ready physical presence, her face complex and moving. Even when her identity shifts another time, in the form of her dazzling new dance outfit, she never surrenders her dynamic individualism. As the older brother Jermaine, Minor is also a revelation in his natural, easy, and graceful manner, watchful and protective of Toni though sufficiently open to her need for new adventures.

The co-writer Saela Davis is also the editor, and the cutting rhythm is imaginative, creating echoes and a sense of movement, color, and shape that is absolutely entrancing. The movie ends on a transporting moment, with its magic realist incursions of flight a thrilling and deeply felt expression of the adolescent's urge for freedom and anarchy. The thrill is contagious.

Patrick Z. McGavin

CREDITS

Toni: Royalty Hightower
Beezy: Alexis Neblett
Legs: Makyla Burnam
Jermaine: Da'Sean Minor
Maia: Lauren Gibson
Origin: United States
Language: English
Released: 2016
Production: Lisa Kjerulff, Anna Rose Holmer
Directed by: Anna Rose Holmer
Written by: Anna Rose Holmer

Cinematography by: Paul Yee
Music by: Danny Bensi; Saunder Jurriaans
Music Supervisor: Annie Pearlman
Editing: Saela Davis
Costumes: Zachary Sheets
Production Design: Charlotte Royer
MPAA rating: Unrated
Running time: 72 minutes

REVIEWS

Burr, Ty. *Boston Globe.* July 21, 2016.
Dargis, Manohla. *New York Times.* June 2, 2016.
Ebiri, Bilge. *Village Voice.* June 1, 2016.
Hornaday, Ann. *Washington Post.* June 23, 2016.
Lewis, David. *San Francisco Chronicle.* June 16, 2016.
Morgenstern, Joe. *Wall Street Journal.* June 2, 2016.
Murray, Noel. *The A.V. Club.* June 1, 2016.
O'Malley, Sheila. *RogerEbert.com.* June 3, 2016.
Schager, Nick. *Variety.* January 29, 2016.
Turan, Kenneth. *Los Angeles Times.* June 9, 2016.

TRIVIA

The film was funded entirely through grants.

AWARDS

Nominations:
Ind. Spirit 2017: First Feature

FLORENCE FOSTER JENKINS

The inspiring true story of the world's worst singer.
  —Movie tagline

Box Office: $27.4 Million

"Like a bird I am singing, like a bird, like a bird!"

The above lyrics sounded even more erroneous than they are emphatic when emanating from soprano Florence Foster Jenkins, so much so that it seemed a wonder that the Audubon Society never filed a class-action suit for musical misrepresentation or defamation on behalf of winged warblers worldwide. Critics often made only aptly-odious ornithological comparisons, likening the ludicrously-deluded diva to so many variously-ailing varieties that she singlehandedly represented an entire ailing aviary. Her voice swooped around like a bird hunting for notes it rarely found. The Audubon website does note birds that display such sorry "singing skills" that one cannot help but laugh—and find them endearing.

"To each other," it charitably opines, "they probably sound like some bird version of Pavarotti," but one cannot go so far as to say that Jenkins ever sounded that way to members of her own species. Nevertheless, those responsible for this rewarding film starring an ironically pitch-perfect, potentially Oscar-bound Meryl Streep (who did all her own singing) clearly hoped that, after first cheekily chortling at Jenkins as so many understandably had, her kind might ultimately come to feel kindly towards her.

Since the film opens with a snippet of Hamlet, one might put the question screenwriter Nicholas Martin surely pondered when addressing the life of this oft-cited "the World's Worst Singer" as follows: To belittle or not to belittle? While the film's advertising used that epithet, it is also specified that this would be an "inspiring story," gradually lifting up this woman who admittedly deserves that putdown and placing her onto a seemingly-improbable pedestal as an example: an appalling yet appealing patron saint of persistence and panache. Unexpectedly enviable is the blindered bliss with which this enigmatic eccentric, a former child piano prodigy who suffered a career-aborting hand injury, presses on to somehow spread the joys of music, stalwartly civic-minded as she writes personal checks to support the arts and also raises funds for all sorts of good causes through a slew of New York City social organization like her own Verdi Club, performing only to like-minded, loyal friends. Jenkins is presented as heroically indomitable in the face of incurable, pitifully-debilitating syphilis, contracted from an ex-husband she had married with disastrous youthful impetuousness. Jenkins is lauded here for her unwitting delights, providing a singular, selfless salve to World War II-era Americans who were weary, anguished and anxious as Good and Evil remained locked in a fight to the death overseas. The film wants to know: how can anyone now fail to feel charitably towards this personal pain-transcending (if peculiar)—patriot?

Jenkins so sang her heart out that it is made understandable how no one close to her could bear to break it with the truth. (One also recognizes here that those who stood to gain financially from the well-to-do, well-connected socialite also did not want to potentially hurt their own social aspirations or pocketbook.) She inadvertently provided people with what they increasingly wanted from her, but not what she so wanted to be giving them and seemed sure that she was. Jenkins' operatic obliviousness (possibly the result of her health struggle) was, as one critic had put it, "innocently uproarious": who could it hurt? The answer turned out to be Jenkins, who in October of 1944 paid—unanticipatedly dearly—to rent out celebrated Carnegie Hall for her first performance open to the general public,

and thus also the first for which Bayfield could not protectively screen out the "mockers and scoffers." Critics such as the New York Post's Earl Wilson (Christian McKay) eschewed polite, evasive euphemisms and instead cut to the heart of the matter on principal, and audience laughter was unrestrained. Jenkins' eyes were agonizingly opened wide for the first time (her concert disconcertment is conveyed through the use of canted angle point-of-view shots), and her resulting mortification shut them for the last time the following month at the age of 76.

As if to make amends, this critically-praised production, which notes Jenkins' superstitious terror of things that are sharp-edged or pointed, is mercifully neither. Yes, in this fairly-faithful, time-compressing, foreshadowing-filled film as in life, she grabs audiences with aural assaults that sorely try one's ossicles while also tickling the funny bone. However, to utilize the title of a 1987 Stephen Frears film, his latest hopes that something emitted with equal passion but far fewer decibels might also prick up your ears. The other half of her quite-uncommon common law marital relationship, St. Clair Bayfield (Hugh Grant, possibly at his best ever) soothingly recites Shakespeare's Sonnet 116, which recognizes sublimity in unswerving devotion. (Jenkins and Bayfield, assessed as a less-than-stellar actors, were birds of a feather.) Unavoidably amidst amusement, the film continually offers up serious appreciation of her fervent, focused musical pursuits, as well as how, like the rope handlers who strain offstage to keep fleshy Florence aloft as the Angel of Inspiration, Bayfield's constancy has him endlessly struggling to keep her spirits up, palpably dreading a potentially-devastating thud back down to earth. Unlike those ropes (and by Bayfield's own admission here), their circumstances were rather knotty and he perhaps naughty, secretly enjoying younger girlfriend (and future wife) Kathleen (Rebecca Ferguson) in a separate apartment paid for by Jenkins. Bayfield rationalizes having this morally-debatable sexual outlet on the side because syphilis precluded intimacy with Jenkins.

In one scene, the arm of illustrious conductor Arturo Toscanini (John Kavanagh) is not outstretched while leading an orchestra but in request of a handout from apparently-easy musical-minded mark Jenkins. Increasingly, the movie itself is also quite a maestro, eliciting a well-orchestrated response from those sitting before it. Jenkins' fey, fidgety keyboard accompanist Cosmé McMoon (a humorous Simon Helberg, an accomplished pianist) is initially so aghast when Florence raises her voice in song that his eyebrows quite comically soar as well. In private, he subsequently nearly busts a gut giggling, but it is shown how he comes to admire her gutsiness. Even more calculated is the film's creation of a wholly-fictional character to guide viewers from bemusement and amusement to an affectionate "Bravo!": brassy broad Agnes Stark (a thoroughly-enjoyable Nina Arianda) goes from doubled-over derision to standing up for a reeling Jenkins and turning the tide in her favor at Carnegie Hall. Florence may be somewhere wishing that this reel support had been real, but this posthumous purposefulness likely garnered her more sincere fans than could ever be shoehorned into that august venue.

Camille Saint-Saëns' lovely *Le Cygne* (*The Swan*), heard early on, is repeated late in the film as Jenkins is fading fast. Music lovers likely noted that this famous piece has long been used for the short ballet *The Dying Swan*, in which an agonizingly-wounded creature can fight no more and perishes. Its inclusion seemingly imparts that something of estimable grandeur is succumbing here. Just before, Jenkins hallucinates herself singing perfectly (the way she may have always sounded to herself) and finally achieving nothing but approbation—a dreamer until the very end. Comfortingly to both her and moviegoers, she follows that dream out death's door with a smile. It has been her bittersweet swan song, and, as she bows in her aforementioned, appropriately white-winged costume, there is a final, affecting fade to black. Some tears were shed in theaters, and Jenkins would surely appreciate they no longer resulted from laughter.

David L. Boxerbaum

CREDITS

Florence Foster Jenkins: Meryl Streep
St. Clair Bayfield: Hugh Grant
Cosme McMoon: Simon Helberg
Kathleen: Rebecca Ferguson
Agnes Stark: Nina Arianda
Phineas Stark: Stanley Townsend
Origin: United States
Language: English
Released: 2016
Production: Michael Kuhn, Tracey Seaward; released by BBC Films, Pathé Pictures, Qwerty Films
Directed by: Stephen Frears
Written by: Nicholas Martin
Cinematography by: Danny Cohen
Music by: Alexandre Desplat
Sound: Becki Ponting
Music Supervisor: Karen Elliott
Editing: Valerio Bonelli
Art Direction: Patrick Rolfe
Costumes: Consolata Boyle
Production Design: Alan MacDonald
MPAA rating: PG-13
Running time: 111 minutes

REVIEWS

Burr, Ty. *Boston Globe*. August 11, 2016.
Dalton, Stephen. *Hollywood Reporter*. April 13, 2016.
Genzlinger, Neil. *New York Times*. August 11, 2016.
Greenblatt, Leah. *Entertainment Weekly*. August 11, 2016.
Hornaday, Ann. *Washington Post*. August 11, 2016.
Lane, Anthony. *New Yorker*. August 15, 2016.
Lodge, Guy. *Variety*. April 13, 2016.
Morgenstern, Joe. *Wall Street Journal*. August 11, 2016.
Rainer, Peter. *Christian Science Monitor*. August 12, 2016.
Travers, Peter. *Rolling Stone*. August 11, 2016.

QUOTES

Florence Foster Jenkins: "People may say I couldn't sing, but no one can ever say I didn't sing."

TRIVIA

Influential singer David Bowie had Florence Foster Jenkins' original recording in his record collection.

AWARDS

British Acad. 2016: Makeup
Nominations:
Oscars 2016: Actress (Streep), Costume Des.
British Acad. 2016: Actor—Supporting (Grant), Actress (Streep), Costume Des.
Golden Globes 2017: Actor—Mus./Comedy (Grant), Actor—Supporting (Helberg), Actress—Mus./Comedy (Streep), Film—Mus./Comedy
Screen Actors Guild 2016: Actor—Supporting (Grant)

THE FOREST

Stay on the path.
—Movie tagline

Box Office: $12.7 Million

Nobody sets out to make something unmemorable. People spend months and years working on films that they hope will be remembered fondly by a mass audience. Even if it's just a genre film that follows many genre conventions, there always exists a hope that a piece of work will resonate with audiences that have paid admission. How strange that there are so many movies that fail to meet that singular expectation. With so many talented writers, producers, and directors out there, how is it that a movie as bland and conventional as *The Forest* can still manage to get through the system and onto America's movie screens? The answer, of course, is in the question. The fewer chances a movie takes, the more likely it will get nationwide promotion for a big Friday release. *The Forest* seems to be written, produced, and directed by the committee to release forgettable January movies in the actual month of January.

It tells the story of Sara (Natalie Dormer), a typically bland, white, female horror movie victim whose twin sister Jess has gone missing in Japan. She had last been seen going into a mystical forest where most people commit suicide. Undeterred by such silly sounding ghost stories, Sara makes her way to Japan to search for Jess. When she arrives, she is served sushi that still slithers on the plate and has the usual nightmares of running through forests late at night and encountering little girls whose mouths open freakishly wide. She also meets a hunky expatriate named Aidan (Taylor Kinney), who writes for an Australian travel magazine and who speaks fluent Japanese. When she explains her predicament to him in a bar the night before she ventures into the forest, he takes an interest and wants to write about it.

When Sara first goes to the forest, she enters a cabin where a woman explains to her that the forest should not be entered into lightly. At first, Sara believes Jess might be in the cabin when the woman mistakenly recognizes her in a picture. She keeps corpses in the basement, but she does not have Jess. At least three times Sara is told to stay on the path. Aidan is also aware of the legend of the suicide forest and cautions Sara to never enter. But she must. Her twin sister remains alive. She just knows it. So, Aidan recruits an acquaintance of his named Michi (Yukiyoshi Ozawa), who is an expert field guide for the forest. "If you have sadness in your heart, they will use that against you," she is told. Michi also tells her that people often see things in the forest that are not really there.

In spite of everyone repeatedly warning her, one of the first things Sara, Michi, and Aidan do is go off the path and into the unknown. It's not long before they find a dead body dangling from a tree, which Michi has to cut down. Later on, they find Jess's tent and clothes hanging on a clothesline. Sara wants to stay overnight despite every warning not to. Aidan decides to stay with her. The rest of the film finds the three of them wandering through the forest and having many false scares and hallucinations as Sara must decipher between reality and illusion and whether or not she can really trust Aidan and/or Michi. It is all but a guarantee that the viewer will be way ahead of her.

That pretty much goes for the entire film. Once the audience gets told that not everything in the forest will be real, there exists little reason to be scared of anything. If a character looks down and sees maggots coming out

of her veins after being cut by a branch, she will freak out and try to cut them out of her wrists. The viewer will be left wondering why she fails to remember that key rule that was told to her by at least two people. Furthermore, all plot twists feel null and void once it has been established that people go crazy in the forest. It also feels like a bit of a cheat when, in the third act, Michi recruits an entire search party to go into the forest to search for Sara who has now officially gone missing. So, basically, nobody should ever go into the forest unless accompanied by cops and investigators, which begs the question as to why these guys were not brought in to search for Jess in the first place.

Nevertheless, the film cannot exist without the false jump-out-and-scare moments that remain the cornerstone of modern day PG-13 horror. The movie labors under the notion that Japanese girls and women with old, wrinkled, weathered faces are the stuff of nightmares. Is this the essence of the sadness that lurks within Sara's heart that the forest can use against her? Director Jason Zada (making his feature debut) and screenwriters Nick Antosca, Sarah Cornwell, and Ben Ketai throw out the usual Macguffins at the audience that by the time the film ends and comes to its rather predictable conclusion, the viewer is left with little to be scared of and even less to ponder.

Maybe Zada has been saddled with a lame script and just jumped at the chance to direct a feature film for a major studio. Maybe nobody could have made this any better. Technically, there are some nice color schemes going on with the lighting. Cinematographer Mattias Troelstrup clearly favors bits of solid colors in dark spaces and the forest itself has a nice texture to it that give the greens a more ominous feel to them. That is not enough, however, to make *The Forest* stand out as anything more than the standard slumber party horror film that inexperienced viewers will watch simply because they need a time killer and the parents approve of the PG-13 rating. One could program an entire film festival consisting of January horror films like *The Forest*. The idea of sitting through that festival sounds scarier than anything on screen here.

Collin Souter

CREDITS

Sara/Jess Price: Natalie Dormer
Rob: Eoin Macken
Valerie: Stephanie Vogt
Mayumi: Noriko Sakura
Aiden: Taylor Kinney
Origin: United States

Language: English

Released: 2016

Production: David S. Goyer, David Linde, Tory Metzger; released by Lava Bear Films

Directed by: Jason Zada

Written by: Nick Antosca; Sarah Cornwell; Ben Ketai

Cinematography by: Mattias Troelstrup

Music by: Bear McCreary

Sound: Kelly Cabral

Editing: Jim Flynn

Costumes: Bojana Nikitovic

Production Design: Kevin Phipps

MPAA rating: PG-13

Running time: 93 minutes

REVIEWS

Barnard, Linda. *Toronto Star.* January 8, 2016.

Clarke, Cath. *Time Out.* February 22, 2016.

Cruz, Lenika. *The Atlantic.* January 21, 2016.

Dujsik, Mark. *RogerEbert.com.* January 8, 2016.

Ebiri, Bilge. *New York Magazine.* January 10, 2016.

Goldstein, Gary. *Los Angeles Tim.* January 8, 2016.

LaSalle, Mick. *San Francisco Chronicle.* January 8, 2016.

Schager, Nick. *Playlist.* January 9, 2016.

Smith, Kyle. *New York Post.* January 8, 2016.

QUOTES

Sara: "I don't know if this forest made you psycho or you were always this crazy."

TRIVIA

The Japanese guide's name, Michi, translates as "path" in Japanese.

FREE STATE OF JONES

Based on the incredible true story.
—Movie tagline

Box Office: $20.8 Million

There is an intentionally jarring moment in *Free State of Jones* in which the action moves from the past of 1863 to the more recent past of 1948. The 85-year jump is the first sign that writer/director Gary Ross has much more on his mind than a straightforward biographical and/or historical account of Newton Knight and his armed resistance against Confederate forces during the American Civil War. Knight's story has become something of a legend, partially because of poor or conflicting contemporary records and partially because of the inherently political nature of the history of the American South.

The facts of Knight's resistance, with a group of Confederate Army deserters and runaway slaves in Jones County, Mississippi, is not in doubt, although the extent to which it occurred—whether or not the county did secede from the larger secessionist entity known as the Confederate States of America—is historically unclear. Ross' screenplay presupposes the rebellion and the institution of the eponymous "Free State of Jones" were as far-reaching and real as the most generous accounts of the legend. The film also insists that such moves had little impact in the face of history's natural, circular motion, which always revolves around the status quo at varying distances.

The status quo here is systemic prejudice, which is still a depressingly timely subject in 2016. By the end of the film, one has a sense that Ross' story could have continued beyond its final chronological point—a time of segregation and laws against interracial marriage based on a "purity" standard of a person's genealogy—to even the present day. The only thing that stops the film from proceeding further is the story's connection to Knight, whose progeny indeed did, a few generations after him, become involved in a legal battle by the state of Mississippi against the marriage of Knight's great-grandson on the basis of the great-grandson's ancestry. The point is painfully clear: racism does not end, it simply takes new forms by adopting different language and instituting different legislation.

It takes a while to get to that conclusion, since Ross' screenplay is still beholden to a somewhat rigid biographical template. That is another issue that keeps the film from reaching the emotional and thematic heights it could have. Apart from the peaks into the future, the story always belongs to Newton (Matthew McConaughey), a medic with the Confederate Army. He becomes disillusioned with the Confederacy and the war when his nephew Daniel (Jacob Lofland) is killed in battle, despite Newton's best efforts to find the boy safe passage through the trenches and past the sharpshooters on the battlefield.

After returning his nephew's body home to Jones County, Newton remains, trying to protect the women and children from a group of Confederate officers who seize the farmers' crops for the war effort. To flee arrest and inevitable hanging for desertion, Newton hides in the local swampland with runaway slaves and, later, other disenchanted deserters. He befriends Moses (Mahershala Ali), one of those runaways, and falls in love with Rachel (Gugu Mbatha-Raw), a house slave on a local plantation who brings supplies to the fugitives. Their romantic relationship is of central concern to the prejudicial prosecution eight decades later, as the state questions whether Davis Knight (Brian Lee Franklin) is the great-grandson of Rachel or Newton's wife Serena (Keri Russell).

There is no denying that the stories of Moses and Rachel are not only more intriguing within the context of this era but also more significant to the ultimate point Ross makes here. In fairness to the film, it does not dismiss or otherwise diminish the experiences of those characters, although the perspective from which the audience observes those experiences is almost exclusively Newton's. It also takes the length of the film's first and second act before the experience of either of those characters, or the freed slaves they come to represent, comes closer to being the film's central point.

Until then, the film is a fine dramatization of a relatively unknown piece of history. The plotting, in which Newton and his group work to undermine the local Confederate military officials, becomes a routine revenge story, and Newton's proclamations of forming a solidary community based on principles of equality and freedom are not enough to make the character anything more than a mouthpiece for those principles (McConaughey's steely, quiet performance is more befitting an icon than a man). Ross includes text and archival photographs that establish the progress of the war and Reconstruction, as well as the changing political and social atmosphere.

The scenes involving Reconstruction, though, quickly rise above the safe historical and biographical approach, finally moving toward the purpose of those scenes set in a Mississippi courtroom in 1948. The film's history lesson suddenly becomes one that is directly tied to politics. The old ways of slavery have been undone by the Thirteenth Amendment, so the plantation owners, given a second chance by the United States government after they pledge an oath, simply find a new word to replace "slave" for the workers they need.

Ross and cinematographer Benoît Delhomme repeat the motif of a certain shot here three times: first as slaves work the fields, second as a freed man tills his own land for the first time in the South, and third as a repetition of the first shot. This time, though, the workers have become technically legal "apprentices" to men who still prefer to be called "masters." The "apprentices" even live in the same field houses as the slaves of only a few years before.

The Reconstruction-era section of the film is its most effective and powerful, especially during a sequence in which Moses finally becomes the central subject—walking across the wide expanse of the county looking to register freedmen to vote for the first time. The progress here is slow and uncertain, particularly with the rise of the Ku Klux Klan.

Thusly, the film ties its two time periods together: the uneasy progression of Reconstruction leading to the same prejudice and racism 85 years later, under a different name but with the same goal. *Free State of Jones* may be more ambitious in its thematic and political aims than its story, with its limited perspective, allows. Even then, though, the film serves as a timely, unfortunate reminder that the actions of today will one day be the unjust history of tomorrow.

Mark Dujsik

CREDITS

Newton Knight: Matthew McConaughey
Rachel: Gugu Mbatha-Raw
Moses: Mahershala Ali
Serena: Keri Russell
Jasper Collins: Christopher Berry
Origin: United States
Language: English
Released: 2016
Production: Jon Kilik, Scott Stuber, Gary Ross; released by Bluegrass Films, Vendian Entertainment
Directed by: Gary Ross
Written by: Gary Ross
Cinematography by: Benoit Delhomme
Music by: Nicholas Britell
Sound: Paul Hsu
Music Supervisor: Jason Markey
Editing: Pamela Martin; Juliette Welfing
Art Direction: Dan Webster
Costumes: Louise Frogley
Production Design: Philip Messina
MPAA rating: R
Running time: 139 minutes

REVIEWS

Burr, Ty. *Boston Globe.* June 23, 2016.
Cheshire, Godfrey. *RogerEbert.com.* June 24, 2016.
Cole, Jake. *Slant Magazine.* June 22, 2016.
Ebiri, Bilge. *Village Voice.* June 22, 2016.
Jones. J.R. *Chicago Reader.* June 30, 2016.
LaSalle, Mick. *San Francisco Chronicle.* June 23, 2016.
Phillips, Michael. *Chicago Tribune.* June 23, 2016.
Scott, A.O. *New York Times.* June 23, 2016.
Toppman, Lawrence. *Charlotte Observer.* June 22, 2016.
Zacharek, Stephanie. *Time.* June 23, 2016.

QUOTES

Newton Knight: "No man ought to tell another man what he's gotta live for or what he's got to die for."

TRIVIA

Victoria Bynum, the author of the book *The Free State of Jones: Mississippi's Longest Civil War,* makes a cameo as a hospital nurse in the film.

G

GENIUS

Max Perkins discovered Ernest Hemingway and F. Scott Fitzgerald. But he never met anyone like Thomas Wolfe.
—Movie tagline

Box Office: $1.4 Million

"Good? No. But it's unique." That's the warning given to Max Perkins (Colin Firth) as a giant, unruly manuscript is dropped on his desk like a ton of bricks. The book, *O Lost*, is by then-unknown Thomas Wolfe (Jude Law). It will become *Look Homeward Angel* when Perkins is through with the book and its dashing, guileless author. As he reads the book, read in his unconscious in Wolfe's honeyed Southern drawl, he sees something in the woolly prose, the asymmetrical turns of phrase, the specificity of description. And when he finishes his first read of the novel, the title of the movie, *Genius*, appears next to Perkins' head on a crowded train, just in case anyone in the audience wasn't clear what he thought of Wolfe's work. First-time director Michael Grandage's film, with its faded auburn-and-ash color palette and heavy doses of borrowed poetry, wants very much to aspire to its title, but it cannot even manage "unique." Maybe if everyone would stop explaining away the subtext whenever there's a lull, the audience might get a chance to form an opinion of these people the movie didn't form for them first.

When we meet Wolfe, he's smoking in the rain, stamping his feet impatiently over a half dozen dead cigarettes on the wet ground below him. *O Lost* has been rejected by every publisher in New York City so when Perkins tells him he's going to be published Wolfe

all but breaks down. Defeat has exhausted his body, but not his spirit. He runs home to tell his lover and patron Aline Bernstein (Nicole Kidman) the good news before heading back to Perkins' home to begin work. After meeting Perkins' wife Louise (Laura Linney) and their five daughters, they get to work editing Wolfe's behemoth. Grandage elides the editorial process, having found no way to render it cinematically. One day they're going to start, the next day they're agonizing over a title, and on day three it's sitting on bookshelves. Bernstein resents the increasingly central role Perkins takes in Wolfe's life and worries that he's co-opting her lover's talent and using him as one more notch in his belt. She fears Perkins is only interested in adding Wolfe to his stable of money making geniuses like F. Scott Fitzgerald (Guy Pearce) and Ernest Hemingway (Dominic West), both on hand to give historically accurate accounts of their mental health to act as warnings for Wolfe's future.

An indeterminate amount of time passes before Max and Tom meet each other again following the publication of *Look Homeward Angel*. Wolfe approaches Perkins with three crates full of hastily scrawled prose that make up his next masterpiece *Of Time and the River*. As the film is exclusively focused on the relationship between these two men, we don't see the creation of the novel, just the comedy reaction shot when the buckets of pages are carried into the Scribner's offices that morning. Writing and inspiration tellingly don't interest Grandage. Perkins is excited but cautious of the challenge of taming not just Wolfe's prose but Wolfe himself. They have many soul-searching, overly obvious discussions about the nature of writing that all try to justify the film's lack of personality. Perkins wants Wolfe to simplify, to cut out his lengthy tangents and descriptors. The movie does the same, leaving out everything that might have actually been interesting about these two men or their long-suffering partners. Their hysterical devotion to their work makes their personal lives suffer, and eventually takes its toll on their friendship.

Genius is the latest in a long line of dubiously motivated biopics that transpire over a manageably short period of time in an effort to skirt the form's allergy to satisfactory narratives, and presumably to save money on casting and sets. Well-intentioned bores like *Ray* (2004) and *A Beautiful Mind* (2001) could never be entirely satisfactory as drama or history because they have to ignore or invent one to stay true to the other. Life stories are not tidy but movies that win Academy Awards have to be so their creators cut and paste and fabricate to extract meaning and dramatic purpose where there was none to be found. Lately films like *Miles Ahead* (2016), *Born To Be Blue* (2016), *The Imitation Game* (2014), and *Get On Up!* (2014) have tried to bury the dramatic limitations of the long form biopic by shrinking the focus to just a couple incidents and times. They may Ping-Pong around their subject's timeline, but only to stencil the same few thematic concerns. The worst example of this kind of opportunistic filmmaking is the staggeringly awful *Nina* (2016), whose deliriously stupid excesses at least have moments of delicious high camp. *Genius* is a close second and an absolute snooze. It has nothing to offer but a sort of dictionary definition of this self-serving, utterly artificial truncated biopic. It's a veritable "what not to do" filmmaker field guide.

Grandage and his editor Chris Dickens commit so many unpardonable trespasses against taste it's difficult to know where to begin. The score is dreadful; dripping with chipper jazz to mimic the spark of creation (there's even a truly embarrassing touristic scene where Wolfe takes Perkins to listen to jazz for the first time). Every actor in this movie has pitched their performance in a different register and they clang together like pots and pans. Law's dopily grandiloquent Wolfe runs and stomps around like Robin Williams in *The Fisher King* (1991), trying to make a meal of a meager ration of eccentricities where a personality ought to be. Colin Firth's gone drier than ever to play the joyless Perkins, sounding like a doctor trying not to betray how catastrophic a diagnosis he's about to deliver. Nicole Kidman falls into her easiest register, frigid, distant, and shrill, which would slightly be more tolerable if the film also did not take pains to point out that she's the only Jewish character in the movie. Laura Linney is the only one who tried to ensure her performance would make tonal sense, sticking it out in the middle of all this scenery chewing with slightly cold rationalism and good humor.

The script never takes a second to discuss anything that is not about the "incredibly important historical work" being done. All feelings are spelled out in the broadest possible language as frequently as possible. Bernstein berates Perkins on the day of *Look Homeward Angel's* release thusly: "We should give Mr. Perkins all of the credit. After all he's the genius who made your dream come true. He's the one who shaped that massive collection of words into a marketable best seller, putting it into the eager hands of readers everywhere." Not only does that artlessly explain one of the film's central conflicts for the audience, it manages to sound like nothing a human being would ever say. When Perkins has to choose between editing *Of Time and the River* and going on vacation with his family, the kind of cheap ultimatum movies pull all the time, he snaps at Louise: "I get a writer like Tom once in a lifetime." Unfortunately, we get ten or twelve movies like this a year now; they're just usually less awful.

Scout Tafoya

CREDITS

Aline Bernstein: Nicole Kidman
Thomas Wolfe: Jude Law
Max Perkins: Colin Firth
F. Scott Fitzgerald: Guy Pearce
Louise Perkins: Laura Linney
Origin: United States
Language: English
Released: 2016
Production: James Bierman, Michael Grandage, John Logan
Directed by: Michael Grandage
Written by: John Logan
Cinematography by: Ben Davis
Music by: Adam Cork
Sound: Ian Wilson
Music Supervisor: Karen Elliott
Editing: Chris Dickens
Art Direction: Patrick Rolfe
Production Design: Mark Digby; Jane Petrie
MPAA rating: PG-13
Running time: 104 minutes

REVIEWS

Chang, Justin. *Los Angeles Times.* June 9, 2016.
Edelstein, David. *New York Magazine.* June 16, 2016.
Goodykoontz, Bill. *Arizona Republic.* June 16, 2016.
Greenblatt, Leah. *Entertainment Weekly.* June 8, 2016.
Lumenick, Lou. *New York Post.* June 9, 2016.
Phillips, Michael. *Chicago Tribune.* June 16, 2016.
Rainer, Peter. *Christian Science Monitor.* June 10, 2016.

Russo, Tom. *Boston Globe.* June 16, 2016.

Scott, A.O. *New York Times.* June 9, 2016.

Wilson, Calvin. *St. Louis Post-Dispatch.* June 16, 2016.

QUOTES

Aline Bernstein: "I don't exist anymore. I've been edited."

TRIVIA

Colin Firth keeps his hat on during the entire film until the end when he reads Thomas' posthumous letter, when he takes it off in respect.

GHOSTBUSTERS

Who you gonna call?
—Movie tagline

Box Office: $128.3 Million

The Paul Feig-directed, all-female reboot of Ivan Reitman's beloved 1984 comedy became one of the major movie talking points of 2016, a film so divisive that it feels like some message boards will literally never stop talking about it. Hardcore fans of the original, most of them men, felt like Feig and his cast were desecrating something sacred when they rebooted *Ghostbusters* without the original cast and with switched genders. In fact, the response to the very existence of *Ghostbusters* clearly influenced the final product, as the film often makes meta-references to troll culture, judging things before you see it, and those who doubted the cast and creators of this film. The tragedy is that the final film is neither as good as it could have been nor as bad as its sight-unseen haters might have people believe. The sheer talent of the cast, especially one particular member in it, keeps it humming, but Feig seems distracted by the issues surrounding the film, never finding the comic timing he did in superior works like *Bridesmaids* (2011), *The Heat* (2013), and *Spy* (2015).

Abby Yates (Melissa McCarthy) and Erin Gilbert (Kristen Wiig) are old friends and former colleagues, who once published a book on the existence of the paranormal. Erin does not like to talk about that book too much, trying to put it behind her and lead a traditional life as an educator at Columbia University. Abby has not yet given up on the cause and continues to study the paranormal with the help of an eccentric engineer named Jillian Holtzmann (Kate McKinnon). When Erin discovers the book is back in print, threatening her chance at tenure, she begs Abby to take it out of print. Abby agrees but only if her old partner will join her on one final investigation into the other side.

Of course, Yates, Gilbert, and Holtzmann stumble upon an actual ghost, but few people believe them, even with video proof. A recurring theme in *Ghostbusters* is that of people denying what's really happening, using the Internet to create their own versions of what happened. The mayor (Andy Garcia) and his lackey (Cecily Strong) keep trying to paint the Ghostbusters as kooks, to the point that they put the city in danger. Feig's not-to-subtle inference that Internet culture is dangerous drains the film of some of its fun factor, leaving a bitter taste as to how the movie was treated by morons instead of just being a joyous comedy in its own right.

Because what is the villain of *Ghostbusters* other than an Internet troll? Rowan North (Neil Casey) is a mad scientist who has been bullied and ignored for too long and plans to bring about the end of the world, breaking down the barrier between the real world and the supernatural one. As his efforts are allowing supernatural activity to erupt all over town, the trio of scientists get a fourth—MTA worker Patty Tolan (Leslie Jones)—and a "himbo" receptionist (Chris Hemsworth) before officially branding themselves as "Ghostbusters," even getting a hearse-based vehicle like the original group, proton packs, and a visit from Slimer.

Feig and his talented cast work best when they are allowed to play characters caught in unpredictable but genuine situations, whether it's the romantic dealings of *Bridesmaids* or even the realism brought to McCarthy's character in *Spy*. The biggest problem with *Ghostbusters* is how much Feig allows his cast members to become cogs in the plot machine. Wiig and McCarthy, in particular, do little more than push the plot forward, rarely given anything interesting in terms of character or chances to improvise. One can feel the pressure that Feig was under to write a story that lived up to the standards set by fans of the original, but let's just say storytelling is not his strong suit. No one remembers the plot of *The Heat* or *Spy*. They remember the characters and jokes—and *Ghostbusters* is too full of plot to have time for characters and jokes.

Having said that, one performer nearly single-handedly saves the film by refusing to get smothered by the relatively-bland plot: Kate McKinnon. The Emmy-winning star of *Saturday Night Live* injects each line delivery with a wink and a smile, bringing so much unique energy to her character that clearly wasn't even there on the page. She paints Holtzmann as a brilliant oddball, not just the smartest person in the room, but the weirdest too, and she's the only performer who really makes an impact, although it's worth noting that Jones does just fine in her first major film role. The worst thing about the movie in terms of performance is the cameos from the original cast members, all of which feel forced.

Forced is a good word for a lot of *Ghostbusters* (especially when it comes to the awful CGI special effects, which look like an homage to what was possible back in the era of the original film). As painful as it is to say it, it feels like the Internet outrage had its desired impact on the final film, distracting the cast and creator from the reasons they wanted to make it in the first place. *Ghostbusters* just isn't fun enough. Sure, there are far worse mainstream Hollywood comedies, especially in the dire Summer of 2016, but it's hard not to call a "just OK" *Ghostbusters* something of a disappointment given the quality of the original and the talents of the people rebooting it. Maybe the third time's the charm for this franchise. If they do go back to this well again, and there's every reason to believe they will, given the cyclical nature of Hollywood, here's the first and only piece of advice: Ignore the Trolls.

Brian Tallerico

CREDITS

Abby Yates: Melissa McCarthy
Erin Gilbert: Kristen Wiig
Jillian Holtzmann: Kate McKinnon
Patty Tolan: Leslie Jones
Kevin: Chris Hemsworth
Origin: United States
Language: English
Released: 2016
Production: Amy Pascal, Ivan Reitman; released by Columbia Pictures, Feigco Entertainment, Ghostcorps, LStar Capital, Montecito Picture Company L.L.C., Pascal Pictures, Village Roadshow Pictures
Directed by: Paul Feig
Written by: Paul Feig; Katie Dippold
Cinematography by: Robert Yeoman
Music by: Theodore Shapiro
Sound: Andrew DeCristofaro
Music Supervisor: Erica Weis
Editing: Melissa Bretherton; Brent White
Art Direction: Beat Frutiger
Costumes: Jeffrey Kurland
Production Design: Jefferson Sage
MPAA rating: PG-13
Running time: 116 minutes

REVIEWS

Dargis, Manohla. *New York Times.* July 10, 2016.
Grierson, Tim. *Screen International.* July 10, 2016.
Hassenger, Jesse. *The A.V. Club.* July 11, 2016.
Lane, Anthony. *New Yorker.* July 18, 2016.
Nicholson, Amy. *MTV News.* July 14, 2016.
Pile, Jonathan. *Empire.* July 10, 2016.
Raup, Jordan. *Film Stage.* July 10, 2016.
Stevens, Dana. *Slate.* July 14, 2016.
Stewart, Sara. *New York Post.* July 14, 2016.
Wloszczyna, Susan. *RogerEbert.com.* July 14, 2016.

QUOTES

Patty Tolan: [as a ghost leaves on the subway] "I guess he's going to Queens—he's going to be the third scariest thing on that train."

TRIVIA

Harold Ramis could not make a cameo like his costars from the original *Ghostbusters* due to his death in 2014, but there is a bust of him just outside of Erin's university office near the beginning of the film.

THE GIRL ON THE TRAIN

What you can see can hurt you.
—Movie tagline

Box Office: $75.4 Million

When it made its transformation from the page to the screen, Gillian Flynn's enormously popular novel *Gone Girl* was fortunate to attract the talents of one of America's best filmmakers in David Fincher. Considering how slavishly it tried to follow in the footsteps of *Gone Girl* in print, with its combination of steamy sex, gory violence, and increasingly implausible plot developments, one might have hoped that the film version of *The Girl on the Train* might have done the same by hiring another director who was equally adept at transforming something of dubious literary merit into a worthy piece of cinema. Alas, the directing gig somehow landed in the lap of Tate Taylor, whose biggest film made a lot of money while displaying no discernible cinematic style.

The title character is Rachel Watson (Emily Blunt), a divorcee who takes the train into New York every day for work. Well, that is what she tells people but the truth is that she is a full-blown alcoholic who lost her job more than a year ago because of her drinking problem. The real reason that she takes the train every day is so that she keep an eye on two particular points of interest. One is the house where she used to live when she was married to Tom (Justin Theroux), who now resides there with new wife Anna (Rebecca Ferguson) and their infant daughter. During their marriage, Rachel, who hit the bottle after repeated failures to conceive, began acting out in horrible ways that she would then forget due to convenient blackouts. Since the divorce, Rachel has been bothering Tom and Anna—constantly calling and texting, lurking about outside and even one time sneaking into the home and picking up the baby while Anna was asleep on the couch. The other is a house a couple of doors down inhabited by Scott (Luke Evans) and Megan (Haley Bennett), a young and seemingly happy couple upon whom she projects her romantic dreams as she passes by on the train every day.

That abruptly changes one day when Rachel sees Megan on her back deck embracing a man who is definitely not Scott. The next morning, she wakes up with no memory of the previous evening, blood on her hands and clothes, hearing the news that Megan has gone missing. Rachel is convinced that the mysterious other man had something to do with Megan's disappearance but to the cynical Detective Riley (Allison Janney), she looks more like a suspect than a witness. Unable to get the police to believe her, Rachel begins to dig around for information herself but does it in such a way that both Megan's hunky shrink (Edgar Ramirez) and Scott find themselves being accused of being involved with the disappearance. Nevertheless, she presses on while trying for once to stop guzzling vodka by the gallon and winds up making a number of shocking discoveries, not just about Megan and her whereabouts, but what she herself may or may not have done on that fateful night.

In bringing the book to the screen, Taylor and screenwriter Erin Cressida Wilson have largely stuck to what was on the page—the key change has been to transplant the action from England to New York. In print, Hawkins conveyed the story in a slick and eminently readable manner that allowed readers to overlook its essential stupidity until they were done. Since Taylor and Wilson have failed to come up with a cinematic equivalent to Hawkins' prose stylings, moviegoers cannot easily ignore the failings that they were able to previously dismiss. The story is a mess that tries to bring together three separate narrative lines while deploying a complex structure that weaves flashbacks in and out of the narrative. Now, a skilled filmmaker might have the ability to juggle all of these balls in the air—Fincher managed to handle a similarly convoluted narrative in *Gone Girl* without much of a problem—but the screenplay quickly devolves into a mass of contrivances and sloppy plotting.

A problematic carryover from the book to the screen is the highly dubious sexual politics on display throughout. If one tries hard enough, the story can theoretically be read as a quasi-feminist tome that illustrates how women can have their seemingly perfect lives manipulated in ways big and small by the men in their lives. Fine, except the three main female characters here are hardly anyone's idea of exemplars of the pro-woman agenda. Rachel is a drunken, self-pitying mess whose attempts to finally assert herself by trying to solve Megan's disappearance on her own only wind up with several other people, herself included, becoming prime suspects. Megan is an outwardly strong but inwardly weak creature who appears to be perfectly willing to sleep with anyone in her zip code with the sole exception of her husband. Anna is a terrible wife and mother who fondly recalls the days when she was the other woman causing the end of Rachel's marriage and complaining that she simply doesn't have the time or energy to take care of her own child. If a man had written this stuff, it would have been derided as retrograde sexist garbage.

Perhaps worst of all, *The Girl on the Train* wastes the talents of its lead actresses—Blunt has never been less interesting than she is here, Ferguson demonstrates none of the fire that electrified audiences when she turned up in *Mission: Impossible: Rogue Nation* (2015) and current It Girl Bennett seems to have been cast solely for her vague resemblance to *Gone Girl* star Rosamund Pike. Far from being the top-notch thriller that it promised to be, the end result is such a complete mess that those who read and loved the book will be outraged at how badly it has been handled while those unfamiliar with it will spend most of their time wondering what all the fuss could have possibly been about in the first place.

Peter Sobczynski

CREDITS

Rachel: Emily Blunt
Megan: Haley Bennett
Anna: Rebecca Ferguson
Tom: Justin Theroux
Scott: Luke Evans
Origin: United States
Language: English
Released: 2016
Production: Jared LeBoff, Marc Platt; released by Amblin Partners LLC, DreamWorks SKG, Marc Platt Productions, Reliance Entertainment, Storyteller Distribution
Directed by: Tate Taylor
Written by: Erin Cressida Wilson
Cinematography by: Charlotte Bruus Christensen
Music by: Danny Elfman
Sound: Paul Urmson
Music Supervisor: Jonathan Karp
Editing: Andrew Buckland; Michael McCusker
Art Direction: Deborah Jensen
Costumes: Michelle Matland
Production Design: Kevin Thompson
MPAA rating: R
Running time: 112 minutes

REVIEWS

Burr, Ty. *Boston Globe*. October 6, 2016.

Chang, Justin. *Los Angeles Times*. October 6, 2016.

Dargis, Manohla. *New York Times*. October 5, 2016.

Gleiberman, Owen. *Variety*. October 3, 2016.

Grey, Christopher. *Slant*. October 4, 2016.

Lawson, Richard. *Vanity Fair*. October 4, 2016.

McCarthy, Todd. *Hollywood Reporter*. October 3, 2016.

Nordine, Michael. *Village Voice*. October 4, 2016.

Waldman, Katy. *Slate*. October 6, 2016.

Zacharek, Stephanie. *Time*. October 3, 2016.

QUOTES

Rachel: "I need to remember."

TRIVIA

The book this film is based on is set in England. For the film, the location was changed to New York but Rachel speaks with Emily Blunt's natural British accent.

AWARDS

Nominations:

British Acad. 2016: Actress (Blunt)
Screen Actors Guild 2016: Actress (Blunt)

GOAT

Cruelty. Brutality. Fraternity.
—Movie tagline

Box Office: $23,020

Featuring a former child star doing very adult things, a surprising supporting performance by James Franco, and a consideration of how identity develops and disappears within groups during college, *Goat* almost asks to be seen as a male *Spring Breakers* (2013). Both movies even open on partying, nameless characters making sounds, inaudible to viewers, in a spirit of celebration. Yet, where the latter captures debauchery with curiosity and a lack of judgment, the former presents a far more menacing and isolating, animal enthusiasm. Consequently, there is less discovery in its assessment of power and violence, and only degrees of impact in its indictment of how interpersonal bonds are not without self-interest.

Though he clearly looks up to Brett (Nick Jonas, promising in his first serious film role), Brad (Ben Schnetzer) initially does not seem interested in following in his older brother's path and joining the Phi Sigma Mu fraternity at the fictional Brookman University.

Then, an attack happens. After leaving a party, Brad generously agrees to give a stranger a ride, not realizing the guy will then say, "Let me get my boy" and force Brad to drive and drive and keep driving until something innocent begins to feel ominous at best, sinister at worst. Soon, Brad has been beaten up and had his car stolen. It is no surprise that suddenly a network of guys—brothers, whose slogan begins with "All my strength is in my union"—with whom to feel safe sounds pretty good. That Chance (Gus Halper), one of the house members, praises Brad's ability to take a punch is not insignificant, both regarding the soon-to-be-pledging young man's plan and the film's presentation of desirable traits of masculinity.

Much of that, as Brad enters the pledgeship process along with his roommate, Finch (Danny Flaherty), and other 18- and 19-year-olds willing to submit to varying forms of physical and emotional abuse, comes from the suppression of vulnerability. Which, of course, is not phrased in those terms. "Don't be a pussy," Chance tells Brad after telling him that they are blowing off class to go to a bar. "Do you think I'm a pussy?" Brad asks Brett earlier, in sheepish disbelief that he did not fight back against his assailants. "I'm a faggot, and nobody likes me," Finch is forced to say on camera as part of hell week, during which drinking hot sauce is one of the lighter activities to which the oppressed recruits are subjected. To those who went through the fraternity system themselves, this progression may feel familiar and authentically intense. To those who have not, *Goat* may seem terribly upsetting, as any benefits to participation explode in the context of escalating, cruel hazing at the hands of pledgemaster Dixon (Jake Picking).

Writers Andrew Neel (who also directed), David Gordon Green and Mike Roberts, adapting the real Brad Land's memoir, underplay any legitimate camaraderie in Phi Sig, as it is called in casual conversation. Brad wants to join because he is sick of feeling scared, but there is little sense of strong bonds among the brothers. In one scene, Chance insults the bulk of the group behind their backs, telling Brett that only the two of them are going places, and a later attempt at sincerity seems false. This presentation does not seem like a close read of this group, though, as much as evidence of how under-conceived *Goat* comes to feel. What else is going on in these characters' lives? The film maintains unjust narrowness to the world of the fraternity, as if the guys are as obsessed as, say, Miles Teller's ambitious drummer in *Whiplash* (2014). While the tormented pledges will put themselves through extreme circumstances to gain acceptance, and most of the brothers (Brett excepted) undoubtedly delight in passing down the abuses they previously endured, the presentation of the day-to-day lives and thoughts of college students does not ring true.

As a result, the vision of how identity is created (Dixon had a cigarette put out on his ass in front of a sorority, fueling his eventual meanness) or destroyed in these settings feels shallow and one-sided, pain without payoff.

That is not to say that the portrait of peer pressure and community feels less than pulsing. Schnetzer convincingly displays Brad's determination through unease, even as he takes selfies of his bruised face, one after being pummeled by enemies, one after being hurt by so-called friends. The sequence in which he drunkenly tells a young woman he loves her, causing her to end their hookup because they barely know each other, effectively reiterates that no matter what physical pain a college man can withstand, that has no bearing on his emotional preparation for intimate relationships (or Brad's lingering post-traumatic stress). Every instance of posturing or weakening here seems perceptive, as does the way certain things matter so much at a particular time and age. And when Mitch (Franco), a legend in the house who is now a dad and could be a future version of a bro from *Neighbors* (2014), toasts, "To the greatest group of gentlemen the civilized world has ever known," it is clear that he believes it, but also that the sentiment has little to give it weight. Even in a small role, Franco imbues Mitch with a clear perspective just from the way he says "Maybe" when someone asks if he's "the craziest motherf**ker" to come through the house. Mitch is happy to have the label and to return to the days of binge drinking, even if it means falling asleep with vomit on his shoulder, and his cell ringing, assumedly his wife.

No one needs a movie to condone this behavior. Yet there is judgment in the cautionary tale and in the less than unpredictable move toward tragedy. Of course, *Goat* is based on a true story, and very well may be an accurate depiction of one young man's experience. But Neel does not get close enough to enough of his characters to turn them into real people with complicated feelings and desires. (The view of male sexuality, both with and without the influence of porn, also fails to go beyond stereotypes and clichés). What he captures is like the multiple slapping wars he chronicles: forceful enough to hurt, minor enough to fade.

Matt Pais

CREDITS

Brad: Ben Schnetzer
Brett: Nick Jonas
Will: Danny Flaherty
Leah: Virginia Gardner
Origin: United States
Language: English

Released: 2016
Production: James Franco, David Hinojosa, Christine Vachon; released by Fresh Jade, Killer Films, Rabbit Bandini Productions
Directed by: Andrew Neel
Written by: Andrew Neel; David Gordon Green; Mike Roberts
Cinematography by: Ethan Palmer
Music by: Arjan Miranda
Music Supervisor: Josh Kessler
Editing: Brad Turner
Costumes: Sarah Mae Burton
Production Design: Akin McKenzie
MPAA rating: R
Running time: 96 minutes

REVIEWS

Bakare, Lanre. *Guardian*. January 27, 2016.
Debruge, Peter. *Variety*. January 27, 2016.
Duralde, Alonso. *TheWrap*. January 27, 2016.
Gerber, Justin. *Consequence of Sound*. January 29, 2016.
Jones, Oliver. *New York Observer*. September 14, 2016.
Kaufman, Anthony. *Screen International*. January 29, 2016.
Kohn, Eric. *IndieWire*. January 28, 2016.
Murray, Noel. *PlayList*. January 27, 2016.
Raup, Jordan. *Film Stage*. January 27, 2016.
Rooney, David. *Hollywood Reporter*. January 27, 2016.

TRIVIA

The film was based on the true story and memoir by Brad Land.

GOD'S NOT DEAD 2

Box Office: $20.8 Million

Objectivity plays an important part when coming into a film that is designed to test one's way of thinking. As the social climate divides itself between facts and feelings, it has been become increasingly difficult to have level-headed discussion, especially when the word "faith" often halts any potentially fascinating philosophical and theological talk in its tracks. The Christian version of an Almighty being has been put on trial for centuries, but instead of attempting to extol the virtues in such a belief, *God's Not Dead 2* continues to preach to a jury that has already made up its mind before a single piece of evidence is presented.

Grace Wesley (Melissa Joan Hart) is a devout Christian whose first name reflects the blessing of sinners while sharing a surname with the founder of the Methodist Church. She is also a high school history teacher, who, while teaching a lesson about the non-violent fights of Gandhi and Martin Luther King, makes a not off-handed comparison to Jesus Christ and his Sermon on the Mount. As if programmed to report such terrorist-like behavior, many of her students begin texting their parents and Grace soon finds herself on the receiving end of discipline by the overreactive Principal Kinney (Robin Givens) and the School Board. Suspension of her career aside, it is also revealed that charges will be filed against her for violating the separation of church and state.

In her corner is Defense Attorney Tom Endler (Jesse Metcalfe), a non-Christian whose initial legal strategy seems to have been derived from watching *A Few Good Men* (1992) where Demi Moore began research for their case with "I've got medical reports and Chinese food. I say we eat first." Also supporting her is Brooke (Hayley Orrantia), the grieving student who injected the idea of Jesus into the lesson a day after Grace offered up Christ as the answer to all her fears and doubts. Against them is apparently the entire world, represented in court by Pete Kane (Ray Wise), who is determined to use this case to "prove once and for all that God is dead."

From the outset, Grace and her father (Pat Boone) are portrayed as soft-spoken sad sacks who enter every room as if they just carried the history of Christianity on their backs before conversing. "In this day and age people seem to forget that the most basic human right of all is the right to have known Jesus," says Dad. Firmly beset as underdogs from the beginning, it only takes a threat to their livelihood and an applied pressure by a two-dimensional villain to understand that this will not be a complex, subtle examination of faith. After all, as one character states, "That's the thing about atheism. It doesn't take away the pain. It takes away the hope."

One of the few things in favor of this second cinematic attempt to defend Christianity is that it has reduced the number of personal subplots involving existential crises. The dopey, accident-prone Reverend Dave (David A.R. White) is back to conveniently be put on the jury, and there is a reporter with cancer using the trial to regain her faith. But this slightly more focused narrative does nothing to uncloud the hypocrisy and questionable ethics of its centerpiece. The defense is run by an incompetently-written attorney who takes a full hour to figure out that Christ has merit as a historical figure in the lesson Grace was teaching. Not only that but he never even thought to call the one witness who started the Jesus argument to begin with. Metcalfe's Tom would rather press a black woman on the stand about Dr. King's faith-tinged Mountaintop speech, which she claims to know only to recant faster than Peter before the cock crowed.

One must also wonder just what kind of remedial educators this school has when even Grace's history relay capper involves identifying one of the most quoted lines from the Declaration of Independence. She also has to be told the rules of jury selection as if she were a scientifically-challenged character in a 1950s science-fiction film. Using the greatest hits as the filmmakers often do, there is nothing in court other than the breakdown of Christ's actual existence by an expert witness that rises above the level of common knowledge. Ray Wise's Pete Kane loudly proclaims "the future of our Republic" depends on the anti-Christian side winning and even tells his rival in court, "I hate what people like your client stand for and what they're doing to our society." That client may have once portrayed a teenage witch on TV but to cast the actor whose most recognizable turns involved killing both Officer Murphy in *Robocop* (1987) as well as Laura Palmer in *Twin Peaks* and then playing none other than Satan on television's *Reaper* as the man now determined to add God to his hitlist feels like stacking the cinematic deck on one particular side.

God's Not Dead 2 may not end as egregiously as the first film—killing off its biggest non-believer while the mass advocates celebrate at the concert of a Christian band without an ounce of soul—but it will never be confused with the intricacies of *Inherit the Wind* (1960). Each side is argued with such a firm extreme that the undecided will remain as such while the wall between faith and everything else is plastered with an extra layer of bricks. The hymnal strains of a self-congratulatory resurrection against the government is too similar to that of the real-life Kim Davis who used the name of God to deny people different than her the right to be married. Grace Wesley may not emerge from her courthouse as a song from Survivor plays, but somewhere in the background one can almost see the filmmakers in the background raising their arms in triumph.

Erik Childress

CREDITS

Catherine Thawley: Maria Canals-Barrera
Walter Wesley: Pat Boone
Principal Kinney: Robin Givens
Grace Wesley: Melissa Joan Hart
School attorney: Brad Heller
Origin: United States
Language: English
Released: 2016
Production: Russell Wolfe, Elizabeth Travis, Brittany Lefebvre, Michael Scott, David A. R. White; released by Pure Flix Entertainment L.L.C.

Directed by: Harold Cronk
Written by: Chuck Konzelman; Cary Solomon
Cinematography by: Brian Shanley
Music by: Will Musser
Editing: Vance Null
Costumes: Cami Nemanich
Production Design: Mitchell Crisp
MPAA rating: PG
Running time: 120 minutes

REVIEWS

Bibbiani, William. *CraveOnline*. April 1, 2016.
Bradshaw, Peter. *Guardian*. April 28, 2016.
Cooper, Jackie K. *Huffington Post*. April 1, 2016.
Mayer, Dominick. *Consequence of Sound*. April 1, 2016.
McGranaghan, Mike. *Aisle Seat*. April 1, 2016.
Rizov, Vadim. *The A.V. Club*. April 1, 2016.
Schager, Nick. *Variety*. April 1, 2016.
Thompson, Luke Y. *Forbes*. March 31, 2016.
Villarreal, Phil. *New Yorker*. April 1, 2016.
Wilkinson, Alissa. *Flavorwire*. April 8, 2016.

QUOTES

Grace Wesley: "I am not going to be afraid to say the name Jesus."

TRIVIA

Walter (Pat Boone) tells Grace he's 81, but she corrects him and say's he's 82. In real life, Pat Boone was 82 at the time.

GODS OF EGYPT

The journey of a lifetime begins.
—Movie tagline

Box Office: $31.2 Million

When the fantasy epic *Gods of Egypt* opened in the United States, it received a tepid reaction from moviegoers and an avalanche of bad reviews from critics that derided as nothing more than two agonizing hours of CGI silliness. In response, director Alex Proyas took to social media to defend his film and, more importantly, excoriate the critical community (who had, it should be noted, rallied around him over such films as *The Crow* [1994] and the cult favorite *Dark City* [1998]) as "deranged idiots," "less than worthless," and "misguided." As it turns out, neither side of this particular argument has much ground to stand on. Proyas is wrong because, speaking honestly, his film is kind of terrible—a silly stab at epic filmmaking that is constantly undermined by miscast actors, a meandering

screenplay, and an avalanche of cartoony special effects that are more ridiculous than exciting. On the other hand, the critical pile-up on this particular film seems equally silly in hindsight because while it is indeed a bad film, it is one that nevertheless has a certain charm to it that cannot be denied—unlike most of the tiresome fantasy films of late that try to bludgeon you with elaborate visuals that seem untouched by human hands, this is one whose heart is in the right place, even if its brain is clearly off on an extended holiday.

As the film opens, Osiris (Bryan Brown) is preparing to turn over control of his kingdom where gods and mortals coexist in peace, the lush and fertile part of Egypt including the Nile given to him by his father, the god Ra, over to his son Horus (Nikolaj Coster-Waldau, when the coronation ceremony is rudely interrupted by the arrival of black sheep brother Set (Gerard Butler), who has been languishing in the desert lands that Ra gave him to rule. Right then and there, he kills his father, removes Horus's eyes—the source of his incredible powers—before exiling him to the desert and enslaves the population. Among the newly enslaved are adorably cynical thief Bek (Brandon Thwaites) and his lovely wife Zaya (Courtney Eaton), who still fervently believes that Horus will return one day to save them by defeating Set. The only way he can do this, however, is if he gets his eyes back. Luckily, Zaya just happens to work for Urshu (Rufus Sewell), Set's personal architect and the man who designed the elaborately protect pyramid where the peepers in question are being held, and a plan is hatched where she will steal the blueprints to the pyramid, Bek will steal the eyeballs and return them to Horus and Horus lay the proverbial smackdown upon his uncle and retake his kingdom.

The break-in goes fine at first but Bek is only able to grab one of the eyeballs before everything goes sideways and to make matters worse, Zaya is killed when she and Bek try to escape the clutches of Set and Urshu. As she begins her long journey through the underworld to the afterlife, Bek finds Horus, in the midst of a pity party that has already gone on for a year, and makes him a proposal—he will help Horus retrieve the other eye and gain back his godlike powers if Horus will then use them to return Zaya to the living. With Set's men in pursuit, the two set off on a long and arduous journey that will see them doing battle with a couple of nasty goddesses astride giant flying snakes, matching wits to decipher the riddle of the Sphinx and even encountering Ra (Geoffrey Rush), who spends his days flying through the skies on what appears to be a ginormous spaceship. As it turns out, these are all but minor concerns for Horus—the thing that has him really upset is that it turns out that his beloved, the goddess Hathor (Elodie Yung), took up with Set as soon as he was exiled and even when she immediately returns to him, he finds it difficult to believe anything she says or does in the wake of this apparent betrayal.

Right from its opening moments, it is pretty easy to see that with *Gods of Egypt*, Proyas and screenwriters Matt Sazama and Burk Sharpless are clearly trying to make a modern-day version of one of those old Ray Harryhausen epics like *Jason and the Argonauts* (1963) and the various *Sinbad* movies that have entranced generations of moviegoers with their stalwart heroes, cheesy heroines, narratives driven by cherry-picked bits of ancient mythology surrounded by utter silliness, and, most importantly, elaborate stop-motion visual effects set pieces that were so thrilling and entertaining to behold that viewers were willing to forgive all the other nonsense in order to get to them. This time around, however, the nonsense is pretty thick—our heroes are not particularly interesting or likable, the storyline meanders endlessly before coming to a moral (Gods, even though they are technically your inferiors, treat mortals nicely and they will be nice to you!) that seems a little dubious considering that the humans are the least interesting aspect of the film, and the performances mostly run the gamut from the forgettable to the awful—and the visual effects are CGI sludge that will dazzle very few viewers along the way. And even if you can somehow work your way around all of these missteps, there is still the unavoidable fact that this is a film set in ancient Egypt in which the key roles, save for the presence of Chadwick Boseman as the God of Wisdom, are populated by French, English, Swedish, and Australian actors. (This whitewashing caused such a furor after the release of its first trailer that Proyas and the studio basically offered a public apology for the casting more than three months before its release.)

And yet, as bad as *Gods of Egypt* is by most critical standards, it does have a certain mutant charm that may not quite elevate it to something that is actually worth seeing but which may come as a relief to those who are forced to sit through it for whatever reason. Unlike a lot of big-screen epics of late, this is a film that never takes itself especially seriously for the most part and after watching a slew of half-baked fantasy epics that present themselves with the kind of solemnity usually reserved for the most turgid of Biblical sagas—films like the lame *Clash of the Titans* (2010) remake or the more recent *Warcraft* (2016)—it is kind of refreshing to see one that can barely keep a straight face. Similarly, the visual effects are fairly terrible throughout (and presumably look even worse when presented in the majesty of 3-D) to the point where the stuff in the foreground oftentimes fails to match what is going but every once in a while, an arresting image—the notion of the gods bleeding gold or Rush up in the cosmos—does emerge from the mire. And even those who consider Gerard Butler's name

in the credits to be more of a warning than a virtue will have to admit that he, among all the actors, is the one who most clearly understands what Proyas is going for here and as a result presents us with a scenery-chewing turn for the ages that actually fits the character to a T—if someone is playing a character who is a surly god with persistent fertility problems, you really need an actor who starts off going over the top and then proceeds on from there.

All things considered, *Gods of Egypt* is a mess through and through and anyone going to see it hoping for some of the singular filmmaking genius in *The Crow* or *Dark City* will be sorely disappointed with what he has offered up this time around. On the other hand, the sheer silliness of the entire venture does have a certain charm to it and, despite a couple of hundred dull points, it is never entirely boring. Most people probably will have no interest in seeing the sequel that is laboriously set up during the final moments (including some of the actors) but if they are stuck in a situation where they are more or less forced to watch it, they will find that for an admittedly awful film, it does go down easily enough.

Peter Sobczynski

CREDITS

Bek: Brenton Thwaites
Zaya: Courtney Eaton
Horus: Nikolaj Coster-Waldau
Set: Gerard Butler
Isis: Rachael Blake
Origin: United States
Language: English
Released: 2016
Production: Basil Iwanyk, Alex Proyas; released by Mystery Clock Cinema, Summit Entertainment, Thunder Road Pictures
Directed by: Alex Proyas
Written by: Matt Sazama; Burk Sharpless
Cinematography by: Peter Menzies, Jr.
Music by: Marco Beltrami
Sound: Wayne Pashley
Editing: Richard Learoyd
Costumes: Liz Keogh
Production Design: Owen Paterson; Ian Gracie
MPAA rating: PG-13
Running time: 127 minutes

REVIEWS

Chang, Justin. *Variety*. February 25, 2016.
Dargis, Manohla. *New York Times*. February 25, 2016.
Davis, Steve. *Austin Chronicle*. March 3, 2016.

Duralde, Alonso. *The Wrap*. February 25, 2016.

Ebiri, Bilge. *New York Magazine/Vulture*. February 27, 2016.

Howell, Peter. *Toronto Star*. February 25, 2016.

Leitch, Will. *New Republic*. February 26, 2016.

Scheck, Frank. *Hollywood Reporter*. February 25, 2016.

Sims, David. *Atlantic*. February 27, 2016.

Tobias, Scott. *NPR*. February 25, 2016.

QUOTES

Set: [to Hathor] "I tore the wings off my wife. Imagine what I'll do to YOU...."

TRIVIA

The staff-like weapon some of the gods wield in the film is called a "was scepter," and was associated with people of power in ancient Egypt, specifically gods and pharaohs.

AWARDS

Nominations:

Golden Raspberries 2016: Worst Director (Proyas), Worst Picture, Worst Screenplay

GREEN ROOM

One way in. No way out.
—Movie tagline

Box Office: $3.2 Million

The gruesomely effective thriller *Green Room* opens with the introduction of a struggling punk rock band on a tour that has landed them hungover and stranded in the middle of a cornfield in their gas-free tour van. For most groups in that situation, that would be the low point—the moment when the members begin thinking of chucking it all in and looking into the executive training program at Bloomingdale's. Unfortunately for these guys, this is nowhere near the low point as their tour from hell eventually lands them in a literal hell from which they must fight if they hope to survive. This is the situation dreamed up by writer/director Jeremy Saulnier and it results in one of the most brutally effective films of its type to come along in many a moon. This is a work that is so dark and twisted and unabashedly nasty, in fact, that even those with a taste for intense cinema will come out of it feeling as brutally worked over as the increasingly hapless characters on the screen.

The band in question is the Ain't Rights and on the tail end of a tour marked by long trips to gigs where they play for largely disinterested audiences for little pay, the four members—Pat (Anton Yelchin), Sam (Alia Shawkat), Tiger (Callum Turner), and Reece (Joe Cole)—are just about ready to pack it in when they get

an offer to do a show at a remote skinhead club hidden deep in the woods of Oregon that is run by white supremacists. Desperate for money, they agree to the show but are so appalled at the crowd they are playing for that they kick off their set with a blatantly antagonistic cover of the Dead Kennedy's tune "Nazi Punks Fuck Off," a move that does not exactly endear them to their audience. Once they leave the stage, the plan is to get the hell out of there as quickly as possible but that falls apart when they open the wrong door and happen upon several skinheads, one of whom has just had a knife shoved into her head.

They, along with Amber (Imogen Poots), the dead girl's best friend, are herded into the backstage green room and told to wait—they are assured that the cops are coming and that everything will be straightened out. In reality, the skinhead leader, Darcy (Patrick Stewart), has been summoned and determines that there can be no witnesses. Eventually, the band realizes that the cops are not coming and barricade themselves in the room while searching for some means of escape. From that point on, the film is a relentless siege that finds Darcy's men viciously attacking the band with all sorts of weaponry from their well-stocked arsenal—not to mention a couple of hungry dogs for gruesome good measure. At the same time, after the grotesque results of their initial confrontation, the group begins to pull itself together and give as good as they get with Amber proving to be a surprisingly resourceful leader in their hoped-for flight to safety.

In creating the follow-up to his acclaimed revenge drama *Blue Ruin* (2013), Saulnier has given viewers a film that owes a tip of the cap to such classic violent siege thrillers as *Straw Dogs* (1971) and *Assault on Precinct 13* (1976), two unapologetically grisly films that were not afraid to make viewers squirm with their brutal intensity and their unwillingness to let them off the hook with the kind of cathartic violence that would have them leaving the theater cheering. Right from the start, he creates an undeniable atmosphere of dread and unease, aided in no small part by the contributions of director of photography Sean Porter, editor Julia Bloch and, especially, the incredible work of production designer Ryan Warren Smith, whose vision of the club will seem both frightening and frighteningly familiar to any music fan worth their salt. After the slow burn first act, Saulnier manages to continually turn the screws with one grisly set piece after another that are all the more effective because they feel as offhand and chaotic as such a struggle might be like in real life. From that point, the film never lets up and Saulnier puts viewers through such an unceasing array of horrors and grisly imagery that it may frankly be too much for some of them to take.

At the same time, *Green Room* does have some

subtler aspects to it that work well within the overall intensity of the piece that might wind up getting overlooked by some in the wake of all the nastiness on display. While the film is not a comedy by any stretch of the imagination—everything from the basic situation to the gore is presented in a refreshingly direct and irony-free manner—there are some moments of quiet and genuine wit to be had in Saulnier's screenplay ranging from the bland announcements about upcoming activities that Darcy makes to his followers to Pat's decidedly uninspiring pep talk to his friends when the chips are down and the blood is flowing. The punk rock soundtrack proves to be a bracing one that mirrors the energy and edginess of the on-screen material without seeming to be too obvious about it. Most significantly, there are a number of excellent performances contributed from the gifted cast. As the not-exactly-heroic Pat, Yelchin gives arguably the most compelling and galvanizing performance of what would prove to be a career cut short far too soon. As Amber, who first seems as fragile as a puff of smoke before pulling herself together into a portrait of furious vengeance, Poots is a knockout throughout as she proves to be more cunning, vicious, and deadly than an entire roadhouse full of neo-Nazi skinheads. That said, the film is pretty much stolen completely by Stewart as Darcy—clearly reveling in a chance to play a bad guy for the ages, he takes a low-key approach to the role that ends up standing out amidst the rest of the chaos and becomes especially terrifying when he goes about suggesting the most monstrous things in a way that makes them sound, at least for the moment, entirely reasonable under the circumstances.

If there is a complaint that one could lodge against *Green Room*, it is that some might find it to be a bit of a regression following the marvelously constructed narrative of *Blue Ruin*—while that one contained numerous dramatic and psychological nuances throughout its running time that left you shaken and thinking afterward, this one is far less complex and only interested in leaving you shaken. That is probably true but while *Blue Ruin* is probably the better film of the two in the long run in that it gives you more to savor once the end credits have run, *Green Room* makes for the more unforgettable viewing experience. It may ultimately be a one-note thriller, especially in comparison to its predecessor, but oh, what a note it is.

Peter Sobczynski

CREDITS

Pat: Anton Yelchin
Reece: Joe Cole
Sam: Alia Shawkat
Daniel: Mark Webber
Gabe: Macon Blair
Origin: United States
Language: English
Released: 2015
Production: Neil Kopp, Victor Moyers, Anish Savjani; released by Broad Green Pictures, Film Science
Directed by: Jeremy Saulnier
Written by: Jeremy Saulnier
Cinematography by: Sean Porter
Music by: Brooke Blair; Will Blair
Sound: Roland Vajs
Music Supervisor: Lauren Marie Mikus
Editing: Julia Bloch
Art Direction: Benjamin Hayden
Costumes: Amanda Needham
Production Design: Ryan Warren Smith
MPAA rating: R
Running time: 95 minutes

REVIEWS

Abele, Robert. *Los Angeles Times.* April 14, 2016.
Ebiri, Bilge. *Village Voice.* April 14, 2016.
Felperin, Leslie. *Hollywood Reporter.* May 18, 2015.
Lodge, Guy. *Variety.* May 18, 2015.
Lund, Carson. *Slant.* April 11, 2016.
O'Hehir, Andrew. salon.com. April 13, 2016.
Reed, Rex. *New York Observer.* April 21, 2016.
Scott, A.O. *New York Times.* April 14, 2016.
Sragow, Michael. *Film Comment.* April 14, 2016.
Tobias, Scott. *NPR.* April 14, 2016.

QUOTES

Reece: "You can't keep us here; you gotta let us go."
Gabe: "We're not keeping you here, you're just staying."

TRIVIA

The stance of the person holding the machete in the poster references The Clash's *London Calling* album cover which features Paul Simonon smashing his bass.

H

HACKSAW RIDGE

One of the greatest heroes in American history never fired a bullet.
—Movie tagline

Box Office: $66.6 Million

Mel Gibson's first directorial effort in a decade, and first since audio recordings of his anger management issues became part of his legacy, ended up being one of the biggest surprises of 2016, leading some to conclude that Gibson's career has been resurrected. The film was a sizable hit at the box office, making over $150 million worldwide, but it was the way it unexpectedly became a part of awards season that was the most surprising, indicating that Gibson was being accepted back into a circle of Hollywood that had once evicted him for his bad behavior. *Hacksaw Ridge* even earned six Oscar nominations, including ones for Best Picture, Best Actor, and, most surprisingly, Best Director. Not only was the return to glory for Gibson unexpected but *Hacksaw Ridge* is not exactly groundbreaking filmmaking. It's a solid war drama, strengthened greatly by a fantastic lead performance that deserved its accolades, but it's also a film that struggles against its filmmaker's propensity for violence. It is a film about a pacifist that fetishizes bloodshed to exaggerated degrees. That makes it pretty fascinating from a critical standpoint, but also arguably ineffective filmmaking in the sense that one wonders if the peaceful man whose story it tells would even want to sit through it.

Said man is Desmond Doss (Andrew Garfield), who grew up near Lynchburg, Virginia with a supportive mother (Rachel Griffiths) and an alcoholic father (Hugo Weaving), dealing with a heavy degree of PTSD from his time in World War I. In childhood, Desmond has an incident in which he almost accidentally kills his brother, leading to a formative lesson about the power of the commandment "Thou shalt not kill." He also saves a man after a car accident, meeting a nurse named Dorothy (Teresa Palmer), with whom he falls in love. These early scenes are easily the worst in the film, an outsider's view of Norman Rockwell's America, in which Weaving and Griffiths are forced to play caricatures and the whole thing has the feeling of famous people playing dress-up. The period details are wrong, the costumes look too perfect, and one worries that the whole film is going to have this exaggerated air of falsity to it.

Hacksaw Ridge improves greatly after Desmond is moved to sign up for the Army to fight in World War II. He will enlist as a conscientious objector, working as a medic in the field, but never even carrying a weapon, much less shooting one. The second act of Gibson's film consists of the difficulties Doss faced in basic training from fellow soldiers who considered him weak, or even worse, a liability on the battle field. One such man is Doss' commander, Sergeant Howell, played with unexpected gravity by Vince Vaughn. Howell and Captain Glover (Sam Worthington) work to get Doss dismissed, and his fellow soldiers go as far as beating the young man, but Doss refuses to drop out of the Army. Those who object even get Doss arrested for insubordination. Dorothy tries to convince him to plead guilty, but Desmond's father comes to his rescue in the courtroom. The charges are dropped, Desmond and Dorothy are married, and Desmond ships out.

The young man is assigned to the 77th Infantry

Division, which is shipping out to fight in the notoriously deadly Battle of Okinawa. Doss finds himself relieving the 96th Infantry Division, who were trying to hold the cliff at Maeda Escarpment, which was referred to as Hacksaw Ridge. Given the advantage held by the Japanese, the battle has been brutal, with men being pushed off the ridge on a daily basis, and casualties mounting. However, the 77th rushes in and the battle that ensues is intense and terrifying. Doss saves dozens of men in the fight, even rigging up a pulley system to take the injured to safety. As portrayed in the film, Doss' heroism is inspirational, giving the remaining men the will to win the battle. In the end, Doss saved over 75 soldiers in the Battle of Okinawa, and never fired a weapon. He received the first Medal of Honor given to a conscientious objector.

When the bloodshed of *Hacksaw Ridge* unfolds it does so with a never-before-seen degree of brutality for a major Hollywood war picture. Long gone are the days when the opening scenes of Steven Spielberg's *Saving Private Ryan* (1998) could shock viewers with the ugliness of war. Perhaps knowing this, and wanting to convey the awfulness of that day, Gibson turns the volume up to eleven in his war scenes. In one of the first moments, a man is using another dead man's torso as a human shield. Body parts fly, people scream, explosions happen everywhere—it is truly a vision of war as Hell, which it undeniably is, but it also has the air of artifice in its over-the-top intensity. The action of *Hacksaw Ridge* is when the film comes most to life, hinting how much Gibson, a director never shy of combat, really comes alive during this kind of filmmaking. One would not want a vision of *Hacksaw Ridge* that softpedals the ugliness of what Doss survived that day, but one would also not want a *Call of Duty* video game version of the truth, and Gibson veers into the latter lane a few times here.

What truly anchors *Hacksaw Ridge* and keeps Gibson's more extremist tendencies in check is the work from Andrew Garfield, an actor who did a one-two punch of accomplished drama in 2016 with this film and Martin Scorsese's *Silence*. He is so fully committed to the role that we lose sight of the actor and start to believe we're actually watching the life of Desmond Doss. The way he balances both Doss' unwavering commitment and desire to protect and serve his country is remarkable. He does not portray Doss as a saint, as so many other actors would, capturing his insecurities and uncertainties alongside his heroism. It's a great performance from one of the best actors of his generation, made even more powerful by the counterpart to it in Scorsese's film. Vaughn is also good, but this is Garfield's film through and through, and he deserves all the acclaim received for it, even if the Oscar was always more

likely to go elsewhere (Casey Affleck for *Manchester by the Sea* [2016] or Denzel Washington for *Fences* [2016]).

It's actually not often that Hollywood exiles are allowed back into the inner circle. Once an A-lister embarrasses his circle of friends and respected colleagues, he has a tendency to shrink off into history. Mel Gibson refused to do that. After a few years of licking his wounds, and taking small but interesting roles in films like *Blood Father*, earlier in 2016, he came shrieking back into the spotlight. It seems likely that he won't be going away again any time soon.

Brian Tallerico

CREDITS

Desmond Doss: Andrew Garfield
Sgt. Howell: Vince Vaughn
Capt. Glover: Sam Worthington
Smitty: Luke Bracey
Tom Doss: Hugo Weaving
Origin: United States
Language: English
Released: 2016
Production: Terry Benedict, Paul Currie, Bruce Davey, William D. Johnson, Bill Mechanic, Brian Oliver, David Permut; released by Cosmos Filmed Entertainment, Cross Creek Pictures, Demarest Media, IM Global, Icon Productions, Kilburn Media, Pandemonium, Permut Presentations, Vendian Entertainment, Windy Hill Pictures
Directed by: Mel Gibson
Written by: Robert Schenkkan; Andrew Knight
Cinematography by: Simon Duggan
Music by: Rupert Gregson-Williams
Sound: Robert Mackenzie
Editing: John Gilbert
Art Direction: Mark Robins
Costumes: Lizzy Gardiner
Production Design: Barry Robison
MPAA rating: R
Running time: 139 minutes

REVIEWS

Collin, Robbie. *The Telegraph.* September 10, 2016.
Ebiri, Bilge. *Village Voice.* November 2, 2016.
Edelstein, David. *New York Magazine.* November 2, 2016.
Gleiberman, Owen. *Variety.* September 4, 2016.
Greenblatt, Leah. *Entertainment Weekly.* November 3, 2016.
Lane, Anthony. *New Yorker.* October 31, 2016.
Roeper, Richard. *Chicago Sun-Times.* November 2, 2016.
Rooney, David. *Hollywood Reporter.* September 4, 2016.
Scott, A.O. *New York Times.* November 2, 2016.
Zacharek, Stephanie. *Time.* September 10, 2016.

Desmond Doss: "With the world so set on tearing itself apart, it don't seem like such a bad thing to me to want to put a little bit of it back together."

TRIVIA

It took 19 days to shoot the battle scenes.

AWARDS

Oscars 2016: Film Editing
British Acad. 2016: Film Editing
Nominations:
Oscars 2016: Actor (Garfield), Director (Gibson), Film, Sound FX Editing
British Acad. 2016: Actor (Garfield), Adapt. Screenplay, Makeup, Sound
Golden Globes 2017: Actor—Drama (Garfield), Director (Gibson), Film—Drama
Screen Actors Guild 2016: Actor (Garfield)

HAIL, CAESAR!

Box Office: $30.5 Million

Joel and Ethan Coen's latest comedy is a perfectly tuned slice of life on a major studio backlot in the '50s, a film that intertwines multiple plotlines, settings, and characters all under the Coen's deeply intellectual and hysterical understanding of the way Hollywood used to work. Some of it may be exaggerated and silly, but this is a studio comedy by outsiders, a film that feels nothing like what a major company like Universal would typically release nationwide, and that feels, in itself, like a bit of outsider rebellion. Who else could make a movie about a pregnant actress, an actor kidnapped by Communists, a rising Western star, and the tinsel town gossip scene, and get this many talented actors and actresses to star in it much less producers to pay for it? The Coens are as distinct as anyone working in film today. At a time when so many filmmakers feel interchangeable, no one else could make a Coen film.

It is 1951 and the Hollywood studio system is going strong. Eddie Mannix (a perfectly cast Josh Brolin) works as the fixer behind the scenes for Capitol Pictures. He makes sure their stars don't get in trouble and that productions stay on budget and get done on time. *Hail, Caesar!* is about a particularly rough stretch for Mr. Mannix, forced to put out several fires in his unique job, all of which reflect, at least somewhat, the Coens dual affection for old Hollywood and relative distaste for a studio system that valued actors and faces over writers and actual creative voices. It's no coincidence that Man-

nix is being wooed by the Lockheed Corporation, makers of the atomic bomb—less risk, more reward.

The first issue that Mannix has to keep from rival gossip columnists Thora and Thessaly Thacker (both played delightfully by Tilda Swinton) is the pregnancy of the unmarried swimming movie star DeeAnna Moran (Scarlett Johansson). Mannix will put the baby in foster care and then DeeAnna can adopt the baby, without anyone knowing it was hers all along, but they still need to find Moran a man.

Meanwhile, the star of the film within a film that gives its name, *Hail, Caesar! A Tale of the Christ*, Baird Whitlock (George Clooney) is kidnapped. He awakens in a beachside mansion to a group of conversational intellectuals known as "The Future." It turns out these men are Communists, demanding $100,000 from the studio for the return of Whitlock. The actor joins in on discussion of economics and politics and becomes swayed by their Communist worldviews. At least partially, the Coens seem to be portraying actors as malleable objects—people who read lines and can be easily swayed or confused. There's something ironic about the writer/directors gathering their biggest, most A-list cast in pursuit of such a theme.

At the same time as the Whitlock kidnapping and the Moran pregnancy drama, Capitol is working to turn Western movie star Hobie Doyle (Alden Ehrenreich) into a household name. They move him from his Western milieu to a period drama directed by the legendary Laurence Laurentz (Ralph Fiennes). In a hysterical scene, Doyle's lack of range and period veracity becomes an issue, almost leading to Laurentz replacing him, but Doyle is the "next big thing" for Capitol and no one gets in the way of that. He even gets set up with another star, Carlotta Valdez (Veronica Osorio), and the two attend a premiere of one of Doyle's Westerns. Doyle is initially disappointed that the tone of his scene in the film has changed but comes to terms with it when the audience responds positively. Again, actors are easily persuaded.

A musical movie star named Burt Gurney (Channing Tatum), who arguably steals the entire film with a full musical number called "No Dames," about a group of seamen headed out to a female-less world on the water, is the go-between for The Future and Capitol Pictures. Doyle spots Gurney with the briefcase of money meant for the ransom and follows him to the Malibu home, but finds only Whitlock inside. The Communists have escaped.

In 1951, the studio system was starting to fall apart, and the Coens know as much about film history as anyone making movies in the '10s. Their films have long referenced classic cinema (perhaps no more than their Preston Sturges riff in *O Brother, Where Art Thou?* [2000]) but *Hail, Caesar!* is their densest film to date in this regard, a mirror reflection of how much the Coens know about the period. They exaggerate just the right details for comedic effect, but never puncture the genuine atmosphere of the overall piece (and the film justly earned a Production Design Academy Award nomination). *Hail, Caesar!* exists in a fascinating place as both nostalgia and parody. The Coens love old Hollywood, but know how to mock it intellectually as well. As much as we like to remember the Golden Era of Hollywood for its great films, it was also filled with garbage movies and selfish people as well. There's something here about how Hollywood was dealing with silly actors while Communism and the Nuclear Bomb were becoming actual concerns.

The cast here is uniformly fantastic, something that critics have been able to say about Coen films for decades now, but this one is particularly star-studded. Even very minor roles like the ones filled out by Tatum, Swinton, Johannsson, Fiennes, and Jonah Hill work. And the major ones are even better. Clooney has been a Coen staple for years, arguably getting their sense of humor better than any other actor. Ehrenreich is the real find here, ironically playing a young man who the studio is trying to turn into a star because he's going to be a star himself. (He was recently cast as young Han Solo, and already has a habit of stealing films he's in, including *Rules Don't Apply* [2016] and *The Yellow Birds* [2017].)

The various subplots of *Hail, Caesar!* sometimes get lost in the Coen's expansive vision, and the lack of throughline or "big laughs" could throw off some viewers looking for a more traditional comedy. It also feels like something of a mistake was made with Brolin's Mannix, in making him arguably the least interesting character in the film. It was likely purposeful, in that the "actors" like Doyle, Whitlock, and Gurney should be more charismatic than the man who protects them, but it's a slight misstep. There are no "major" missteps in *Hail, Caesar!* While it may not be their best film, a "just good" Coen brothers film is still a gift to cinephiles.

Brian Tallerico

CREDITS

Eddie Mannix: Josh Brolin
Baird Whitlock: George Clooney
Hobie Doyle: Alden Ehrenreich
Laurence Laurentz: Ralph Fiennes
DeeAnna Moran: Scarlett Johansson
Origin: United States
Language: English

Released: 2016
Production: Tim Bevan, Eric Fellner, Ethan Coen, Joel Coen; released by Working Title Films Ltd.
Directed by: Ethan Coen; Joel Coen
Written by: Ethan Coen; Joel Coen; Carter Burwell
Cinematography by: Roger Deakins
Editing: Ethan Coen; Joel Coen
Art Direction: Dawn Swiderski
Costumes: Mary Zophres
Production Design: Jess Gonchor
MPAA rating: PG-13
Running time: 106 minutes

REVIEWS

Brody, Richard. *New Yorker*. February 5, 2016.
Chang, Justin. *Variety*. February 3, 2016.
Dargis, Manohla. *New York Times*. February 4, 2016.
Ehrlich, David. *Slate*. February 3, 2016.
Kenny, Glenn. *RogerEbert.com*. February 3, 2016.
McWeeny, Drew. *Hitfix*. February 3, 2016.
O'Hehir, Andrew. *Salon.com*. February 4, 2016.
Robinson, Tasha. *The Verge*. February 4, 2016.
Singer, Matt. *ScreenCrush*. February 3, 2016.
Snydel, Michael. *Film Stage*. February 3, 2016.

AWARDS

Nominations:

Oscars 2016: Production Design
British Acad. 2016: Production Design

THE HANDMAIDEN
(Ah-ga-ssi)

Box Office: $2 Million

Acclaimed Korean auteur Park Chan-wook delivers what is perhaps his most accomplished work to date with this riveting thriller based on Sarah Waters' *Fingersmith*. Park transplants the action of the Victorian era novel to Korea under Japanese colonial rule, and amplifies some of the more lascivious aspects of the narrative to create an entrancing vision of gender and class roles. In Park's world, social standing is ripped away, revealing a base of primal needs that propel the characters from one double cross to another. It is a dizzying film, a movie that defies description and must be experienced. It's also one of the best foreign films of 2016.

Count Fujiwara (Ha Jung-woo) is a con man. One day, he travels to a poor Korean district in Japanese-occupied Korea to find a pickpocket, stumbling upon Sook-Hee (Kim Tae-ri), who is very good at what she does. Fujiwara convinces her to become the handmaiden to the mysterious Japanese heiress Lady Hideko (Kim Min-hee), befriending her to such a degree that she can introduce Hideko to Fujiwara, who will marry the millionaire, commit her, and steal her fortune. Sook-Hee takes on the name Tamako and begins her employment in Hideko's unique mansion, run by the vicious Uncle Kouzuki (Cho Jin-woong). It's not long before Sook-Hee falls in love with Hideko, and the two have explicit sex. Caring more for Hideko, Sook-Hee expresses reluctance to go through with the plan, but Fujiwara forces her to do so, and the Count and the Heiress are married, consummating their relationship. With the inheritance theirs, the trio travels to the asylum but the tables are turned and Sook-Hee is taken away, Fujiwara having betrayed his partner to keep the fortune entirely for himself.

The plot description above would be enough for most normal movies but it's just the first-third of *The Handmaiden*. Park flips the tables and starts over at this point, revealing different angles on the story and different motivations. We learn that Hideko knew a lot more than suspected in the first act. With some background, it is revealed that Hideko knows how to read, being forced by Kouzuki to read aloud his massive library of erotica to wealthy guests who then bid on the books (although are really just there for the cheap thrill of a pretty girl reading them). Fujiwara attends one of these readings, meeting with Hideko and telling her of his plan to get a poor handmaiden to be committed in Hideko's place so the two can run off together. Hideko originally goes along with the plan, but her feelings for Sook-Hee are genuine, and she works to turn the tables on Fujiwara.

In the final act of this brilliant film, Sook-Hee escapes from the asylum courtesy of a piece of jewelry given to her by Hideko. As the two heroines run off together, the two men of this tale are left miserable and alone in Kouzuki's basement of erotic torture and sexual deviancy. It's not a stretch at all to say that Park has made a feminist erotic thriller, in which the men are generally worthless, convinced they are in control of the women around them but unable to dictate their passions, eventually being left with only each other.

Park Chan-wook's career is filled with thrillers built on secrets and double crosses, including beloved films like *Oldboy* (2003), *Lady Vengeance* (2005), *Thirst* (2009), and *Stoker* (2013). He's one of the most consistently interesting filmmakers of the last two decades, always finding new ways to tell his stories, and *The Handmaiden* is his most lavish, technically impressive film to date. It maintains all of the period details of

a Merchant/Ivory production with some of the best costume design and art direction of the year, but it also contains atypically modern sensibilities for a period piece. None of this contains the typical stuffiness of a piece about heiresses and counts—to such a degree that Park almost seems to be deconstructing the period drama to show the heat and humanity underneath the ornate costumes.

It helps that Park is working again with his regular cinematographer Chung Chung-hoon, who delivers a gorgeous film, whether it's in the fields outside the mansion or in is darker chambers of its basement. Chung is a master of light and shadow, and his work here is some of his best, whether it's the playful way he chooses angles on his leads to represent power roles or the way he glides his camera down the mysterious halls of this film's setting.

Park rarely gets enough credit for the way he works with actors, and the same can be said for the praise around *The Handmaiden*, which accurately lavished acclaim on the twists and turns of the screenplay and the gorgeous look of the film, but barely mentioned performance. All four of the leads here are phenomenal, playing text and subtext brilliantly, alternating motivations and desires from scene to scene while never feeling like mere cogs in Park's densely plotted machine. All four are memorable but the two women get the best parts, and they do not strike a false note in roles that could have felt exploitative or even pornographic. Their passion is believable and so their victory feels rewarding.

Perhaps due to the extreme subject matter of *The Handmaiden*, Korea chose to submit the good-not-great noir drama *Age of Shadows* (2016) for the Oscar for Best Foreign Language Film instead, leaving them out of the Oscar race altogether. Would *The Handmaiden* have made the cut? Given the near-universal acclaim, one has to assume it would have at least been considered (and should have been in the conversation for Best Adapted Screenplay and Best Art Direction as well, two categories it WON from the Chicago Film Critics Association, who also nominated it for Best Picture of the Year). Regardless, *The Handmaiden*, like Park Chan-wook films before it, will find a loyal, devoted audience through word of mouth and over time. Films this good always do.

Brian Tallerico

CREDITS

Count Fujiwara: Jung-woo Ha
Uncle Kouzuki: Jin-woong Jo
Origin: United States

Language: Japanese, Korean
Released: 2016
Production: Chan-wook Park; released by Moho Film
Directed by: Chan-wook Park
Written by: Chan-wook Park
Cinematography by: Chung-hoon Chung
Music by: Yeong-wook Jo
Editing: Sang-Beom Kim
Costumes: Sang-gyeong Jo
Production Design: Seong-hie Ryu
MPAA rating: Unrated
Running time: 144 minutes

REVIEWS

Bowen, Chuck. *Slant*. October 12, 2016.
Chang, Justin. *Los Angeles Times*. October 20, 2016.
Dargis, Manohla. *New York Times*. October 20, 2016.
Douglas, Edward. *New York Daily News*. October 21, 2016.
Dowd, A.A. *The A.V. Club*. October 26, 2016.
Kiang, Jessica. *Playlist*. May 21, 2016.
Lane, Anthony. *New Yorker*. October 17, 2016.
Lee, Maggie. *Variety*. May 21, 2016.
Roeper, Richard. *Chicago Sun-Times*. October 27, 2016.
Seitz, Matt Zoller. *RogerEbert.com*. October 21, 2016.

QUOTES

Lady Hideko: "You can even curse at me or steal things from me. But please don't lie to me. Understand?"

TRIVIA

The director described the Lady Hideko as a white cat, elegant and distanced.

HANDS OF STONE

No mas. No surrender.
—Movie tagline

Box Office: $4.7 Million

In *Hands of Stone*, the career of Panamanian boxer Roberto Durán is defined primarily by other people, while his life is defined by his desire to answer to no one. This biographical movie's interpretation of Durán is one that presents a man whose career is his life, meaning that his life, then, is not his own.

The movie, a co-production of Panama and the United States, is, like its version of Durán, caught between those two worlds. Writer/director Jonathan Jakubowicz essentially neuters his central character's outlook on the world in order to make it more palatable for American audiences. The filmmaker makes it clear that Durán is a man whose nationality and political views drive him, yet his heritage and that political outlook are obstacles for him to overcome.

Instead of approaching Durán as someone who is defiant and outspoken, Jakubowicz turns the character's most defining characteristics into his most significant character flaw. The Durán of the movie is not rebellious. He is stubborn.

Whether or not this is or ever was true about the real man is irrelevant, because the most important thing that matters here is whether or not the characterization works in terms of drama. It does not.

Outside of the ring, Durán is a one-note personality—a man who could have everything he possibly could want yet whose inability to play by anyone else's rules keep him from achieving happiness or even feeling content. In terms of his career, the story of the movie's Durán is framed by his relationships with two American characters: first, his trainer and, later, his most famous opponent.

Jakubowicz's screenplay begins, not with Durán (played by Edgar Ramírez), but with Ray Arcel (Robert De Niro), the boxer's American trainer who immediately puts the central character's story in the context of Ray's history. Roberto, Ray says in the opening voice-over narration, was the best pugilist he ever trained. The statement is not only a way for Jakubowicz to establish the audience's expectations for what defines Durán but also a method of lower their expectations for the story that follows.

Essentially, Durán does not need to be a fully formed character—or even one whose life away from the boxing ring possesses more than generic significance—so long as he fulfills Ray's initial promise. The most crucial moment of the character's political life comes early in the movie, as a young Roberto (David Arosemena) witnesses the events of and following Martyrs' Day, in which police and the United States Army fought against protestors of United States control of the Panama Canal, in 1964. The movie offers little context for the event or its fallout, except that it angers Roberto—an anger with the U.S. government that continues for the rest of the movie.

Jakubowicz is more generous with Ray's back story. He is a former professional trainer who was unofficially exiled from the boxing world because of his attempts to legitimize the sport and, indirectly, remove the mafia's influence from it. John Turturro appears in a few scenes as the mob boss who once tried to kill Ray, meaning that the trainer is risking his life to help Roberto escape the slums of Panama (Ellen Barkin plays Ray's stereotypically concerned but vaguely supportive wife).

For his part, Roberto comes across as a spoiled upstart, who does not appreciate Ray's sacrifices and eventually cannot handle the fame, as well as the money, that comes with his success. His relationship with his wife Felicidad (Ana de Armas) primarily serves as a way to show this fall. The couple's early, passionate romance turns sour once Roberto gains fame and wealth.

As Roberto rises through the lightweight ranks in routine boxing scenes (they exist to move the story forward; they do not, though, offer more than a simple notion of how Roberto fights), his primary competition comes into focus: the, at the time, undefeated welterweight champion Sugar Ray Leonard (played by a charismatic Usher Raymond IV in the movie's most effective performance). The most fascinating element of this rivalry takes place outside the ring, as Jakubowicz suggests that Roberto gives birth to the concept of a fighter trash-talking his opponent. Roberto uses it to give himself a psychological edge against the clean-cut, mild-mannered Sugar Ray. Roberto goes after his opponent's wife (Jurnee Smollett-Bell) in public. He uses weigh-ins and press conferences as opportunities to throw more insults.

Eventually, Jakubowicz rationalizes Roberto's behavior as a specific tactic for the matches. Before that, though, the more intriguing angle of Roberto's actions is, not the behavior itself, but how Sugar Ray responds to it. The movie's focus is so scattershot and so distancing from its central character that a supporting player's moral dilemma—whether to respond to Roberto's actions in kind or to rise above them—is more involving than whatever is happening to that central character.

Hands of Stone wants to present a critical portrait of Durán—one that avoids turning him into a perfect hero. That is a fine approach, although it is misguided here. The movie's approach to this biography is to see its subject from other people's perceptions of him. It is Durán's story told second-hand and told in such a way that he becomes neither a legend nor a person but a cliché.

Mark Dujsik

CREDITS

Roberto Duran: Edgar Ramirez
Ray Arcel: Robert De Niro
Sugar Ray Leonard: Usher Raymond
Carlos Eleta: Ruben Blades
Felicidad Iglesias: Ana de Armas
Origin: United States
Language: English
Released: 2016

Production: Carlos Garcia de Paredes, Claudine Jakubowicz, Jay Weisleder, Jonathan Jakubowicz; released by Epicentral Studios, Fuego Films
Directed by: Jonathan Jakubowicz
Written by: Jonathan Jakubowicz
Cinematography by: Miguel Ioann Littin Menz
Music by: Angelo Milli
Sound: Paula Fairfield
Music Supervisor: Lynn Fainchtein
Editing: Ethan Maniquis
Art Direction: Lisa Vasconcellos
Costumes: Bina Daigeler
Production Design: Tomas Voth
MPAA rating: R
Running time: 111 minutes

REVIEWS

Berardinelli, James. *ReelViews.* August 27, 2016.
Covert, Colin. *Minnesota Star Tribune.* August 26, 2016.
Kenny, Glenn. *New York Times.* August 25, 2016.
Merry, Stephanie. *Washington Post.* August 25, 2016.
Orndorf, Brian. *Blu-ray.com.* August 26, 2016.
Phillips, Michael. *Chicago Tribune.* August 25, 2016.
Tobias, Scott. *NPR.* August 25, 2016.
Truitt, Brian. *USA Today.* August 26, 2016.
Vishnevetsky, Ignatiy. *The A.V. Club.* August 25, 2016.
Zacharek, Stephanie. *Time.* August 23, 2016.

TRIVIA

Ray Arcel became the first trainer to be admitted to the International Boxing Hall of Fame in 1991.

HARDCORE HENRY

First they made him dangerous. Then they made him mad.
—Movie tagline

Box Office: $9.3 Million

Strap a camera onto the face of the lead actor and surround him with stunts, physical trauma, and explosions. What sounds like it could be a fun action movie experiment ends up as a textbook example of why more is not more. *Hardcore Henry* is a gimmick masquerading as a movie that hammers away at one visual note like a twelve-year-old fingering through the rote motions of leveling up in a bad video game.

The character of Henry, or rather Henry's visual point-of-view, is introduced as he floats in a sensory deprivation tank, which is then emptied, leaving him with no memory and unable to speak. A scientist named

Estelle (Haley Bennett), claiming to be his wife, quickly walks him through the process of having an arm and a leg replaced with cybernetic limbs. The lab is attacked by an armed group led by a vicious telekinetic named Akan (Danila Kozlovsky), who claims Henry is his property. Fleeing the scene in an escape pod, Henry and Estelle crash land onto a Moscow highway, Estelle is abducted and Henry is rescued by a mysterious figure named Jimmy (Sharlto Copley). After explaining that Henry's cybernetic limbs and other implants are running out of power Jimmy is killed in another attack only to show up again soon afterward to help Henry get to a place he can charge up. Henry spends the rest of the film fending off attackers, racing around looking for Estelle, and finally unravels the mystery of his own origins in a climactic series of battles with Akan and his men.

The overall skeleton of *Hardcore Henry* is built using first-person shooter video game aesthetics. This is all *Hardcore Henry* is built on. Characters float in and out of Henry's line of sight, to provide bits of mostly weak comic relief, or explain some plot point. But as soon as they fulfill that purpose they get whisked back off the screen so the mayhem can continue. The truly surprising thing is how little entertainment appeal all the attempted adrenaline pumping generates. Every once in a while, viewers might wonder how a particular stunt was pulled off, but all writer/director Ilya Naishuller ultimately brings to the table is an impossible-to-maintain, feature-length attempt at adrenaline rush. What worked to create a viral action music video for his band Biting Elbows a few years ago collapses under its own weight.

Tellingly, the character of Henry himself is played by no less than a dozen actors and stunt men none of whom are credited for the role on the IMDB. To top that off, the screenplay invents a reason for Henry to be mute. The end result is a faceless, voiceless stand-in for the viewer who is likely to care less about anything that gets thrown at him/them and this film throws it all; boobs, dogs, flamethrowers, more boobs, and way too many obnoxious close-ups of other actors. The sense of seamy meanness is on ample display in the way that film abuses not only Henry's body but the bodies of everyone around him. *Hardcore Henry* is pretty inventive in the way it keeps violence flowing across the eye but the film is hardly witty enough to stand up to examination alongside truly great non-stop action comedies like *Shoot 'Em Up* (2007). It also lacks the visual style and panache that make the films in the Crank franchise so interesting to watch.

The special effects beg observation only due to the fact that they are on constant display and of wildly varying quality. In an age when the public was less savvy about special effects, there would have been room for a little wonder during a well-executed early sequence where Henry and Estelle escape pod their way through the clouds but only a little, and very few sequences in the film work as well as that one. Distracting CGI explosions, fire, and smoke all work against suspension of disbelief. Of course, *Hardcore Henry* overreaches visually because it has to in support of its main reason for being; the providing of a nonstop, almost unmoored, sense of adventure to its audience. But the irony is palpable. There is no real sense of adventure anywhere in this film, only ersatz images of it that never generate enough emotional power to get off the screen.

Coply, a gifted South African character actor whose nuanced performance in the breakout hit sci-fi actioner *District 9* (2009) blew audiences away, is called on to step into several character roles here including but not limited to a perpetually stoned hippie, a South African soldier, and a homeless man, all named Jimmy. But these are only characters in the broadest possible sense. Ostensibly they reflect the psyche of one man, a Wizard of Oz-type character behind the curtain of reality Henry is exploring, but in reality they are a thinly disguised excuses for hammy stereotypes and expository dialogue.

Hardcore Henry starts with a slow motion credits sequence, which is really all about letting the viewer in on visual details of punches, gunshots, and stabbings. On a cinematic level, it looks cool for the fanboys. Nothing wrong with that particularly. But, like the rest of the film, the images just float by and disappear, out of sight, out of mind. Viewers more apt to think about the experience later are probably of the kind that are simply trying to remember what they were doing before they hoisted that twentieth brew.

Dave Canfield

CREDITS

Jimmy: Sharlto Copley
Akan: Danila Kozlovsky
Estelle: Haley Bennett
Henry's father: Tim Roth
Henry/Slick Dmitry: Andrei Dementiev
Origin: United States
Language: English, Russian
Released: 2015
Production: Timur Bekmambetov, Ekaterina Kononenko, Inga Vainshtein, Ilya Naishuller; released by Bazelevs Production
Directed by: Ilya Naishuller
Written by: Ilya Naishuller
Cinematography by: Chris W. Johnson; Pasha Kapinos; Vsevolod Kaptur; Fedor Lyass

Music by: Darya Charusha
Sound: Kami Asgar; Sean McCormack
Music Supervisor: Mary Ramos
Editing: Steve Mirkovich
Costumes: Anna Kudevich
MPAA rating: R
Running time: 90 minutes

REVIEWS

Abele, Robert. *Los Angeles Times.* April 7, 2016.

Derakhshani, Tirdad. *Philadelphia Enquirer.* April 7, 2016.

Diones, Bruce. *New Yorker.* April 18, 2016.

Harvey, Dennis. *Variety.* September 20, 2015.

Kenny, Glenn. *New York Times.* April 7, 2016.

Lemire, Christy. *ChristyLemire.com.* April 9, 2016.

Lickona, Matthew. *San Diego Reader.* April 7, 2016.

Nashawaty, Chris. *Entertainment Weekly.* April 7, 2016.

O'Sullivan, Michael. *Washington Post.* April 7, 2016.

Wheeler, Brad. *Globe and Mail.* April 8, 2016.

QUOTES

Jimmy: "Like my father always said, a grenade a day keeps the enemy at bay."

TRIVIA

The film was shot almost entirely with GoPro Hero3 Black Edition cameras.

HELL OR HIGH WATER

Justice isn't a crime.
—Movie tagline

Box Office: $27 Million

When audiences first meet Tanner and Toby Howard (Ben Foster and Chris Pine), they are pulling a bank job with big black sweatshirts and ski masks, looking husky, anonymous, and imposing. They do not look like heroes. When they take the masks and the sweats off and they are left in their denim and cowboy boots, their unkempt hair stuck to their faces like a stain; they just look sad and overwhelmed. Director David Mackenzie very purposely takes away any hint that he's rhapsodizing these men and their outlaw lifestyle. These are just regular guys with bad luck and dumb ideas. Their uniforms as criminals are as unflattering as the many waitresses and casino employees they encounter. They are lonely, melancholy men whose only real hope is leaving something behind for the people they will abandon when death comes for them. And in the brutal, bleached Southern landscape of *Hell or High Water,* death is never far away.

Tanner and Toby have led very different lives. Tanner was a screw-up who wound up in jail with knowledge of guns and robberies after killing his dad. Toby got married and had children, but his wife (Marin Ireland) left him, leaving him free to hole up on the family farm and care for his mother while she wasted away. With no money to take care of a reverse mortgage, their farm will be seized by Texas Midlands Bank now that mom has passed away. Toby, the brains of the operation, comes up with an ingenious scheme to not just get the farm back, but put one over on the greedy bankers out to ruin his life. Toby and Tanner are going to rob every branch of the Texas Midlands Bank in the South, launder it at casinos to make it look like winnings, then buy the farm back. To sweeten the deal, Toby's just discovered oil on the property, and if he can sell to the right interests that's enough revenue to keep his family in the black for the rest of their lives. Of course, Toby doesn't know from bank robberies, so Tanner jumps into the fray with him to make sure he lives long enough to make restitution and take care of their land and his family.

There's a slight snag in their plan in the form of Texas ranger Marcus Hamilton (Jeff Bridges). Days away from retirement, Hamilton takes the Midlands robberies as a way to get out of the office to stave off boredom, bringing his ornery partner Alberto (Gil Birmingham) with him. When he realizes he's dealing with something more than garden variety armed robbery, he gets a reinvigoration of purpose. He figures out what the Howard boys are up to and sets out to stop them, even if it means sitting outside branches of the Texas Midlands Bank for days on end waiting for them to show. Alberto brings his own unique cultural perspective. The banks and the government they serve took all this land from the native population and now their foreclosing on all of the property sold to every poor family in the South who cannot afford to live on this hijacked property. It's almost enough to make the rangers respect the brothers but no one stays a hero for long.

Hell or High Water is one of the finest action movies in recent memory. Mackenzie films the shoot-outs and car chases—and the film has plenty—with clarity and momentum. His camera rides through dying Southern towns with a vicious, exhaust-spewing purpose that recalls George Miller's *Mad Max* movies, with which *Hell or High Water* shares a fabulously desolate setting and heroes driven by a less-than-righteous cause to do harm. Mackenzie's sure hand at the helm, tracking and making stylish use of differing focal lengths to expound on the relentless landscape and oppressive heat that surrounds the Howards on their quest to settle accounts. He's been a reliable director for many, many years but until now was never given the chance to flex his muscles across expanses like these in quite the same way. He gets remarkable work from his cast as well. Jeff Bridges basically directs himself these days, though his Marcus Hamilton is one of his most lovably violent coots yet. His words come out like a sticky jumble of crackerjacks, his codger witticisms endlessly endearing and hilarious. Gil Birmingham is the perfect, stoic foil to Bridges' unchained eccentricity, mining laughs, but also pathos, from sideways glances and underplayed responses. Chris Pine, so handsome and charming in J.J. Abrams' *Star Trek* movies, tries world-weariness on like his Fu-Manchu mustache and it fits him better than expected. Those soulful eyes do a lot of the work, but as an actor he's mastered the personal purgatory between having promise and losing hope. Ben Foster, as usual, just about steals the film. The blonde bolt of lightning has made psychopaths like Tanner his stock in trade, but rarely does he manage to come off so effortlessly winning as he does here. His go-for-broke folksy bluster is hilarious and his arrogant but protective care for Toby is most affecting. This is one of his best performances and he's chalked up quite a few great ones.

If *Hell or High Water* has a weakness, it's the script by actor-turned scribe Taylor Sheridan. Maybe it was all that time spent on the set of *Sons of Anarchy*, where he played Deputy Chief David Hale, but his turns of phrase too frequently border on the insultingly obvious and clichéd. Sheridan has an exhausting tendency to spell out his messages in black and white, which is not only an enervating exercise in monotony, it takes away from how keen his ear is for good, unforced dialogue. Alberto's monologue about banks at the first act break might as well be delivered through a bullhorn with the word "message" painted on the side. It's no less embarrassing than Hamilton's repeated use of tired Native American jokes made at Alberto's expense, but at least you can forgive bad jokes coming from a man who looks 100 years old if the sun hits him right. Mackenzie still produced a home run even though he left the worst of Sheridan's too-proud prose in the final cut, which makes him look more heroic than any of his characters.

Scout Tafoya

CREDITS

Marcus Hamilton: Jeff Bridges
Toby Howard: Chris Pine
Tanner Howard: Ben Foster
Old Man: Buck Taylor
Alberto Parker: Gil Birmingham
Origin: United States
Language: English
Released: 2016

Production: Peter Berg, Carla Hacken, Sidney Kimmel, Julie Yorn; released by Film 44, OddLot Entertainment, Sidney Kimmel Entertainment
Directed by: David Mackenzie
Written by: Taylor Sheridan
Cinematography by: Giles Nuttgens
Music by: Nick Cave; Warren Ellis
Sound: Frank Gaeta
Editing: Jake Roberts
Art Direction: Steve Cooper
Costumes: Malgosia Turzanska
Production Design: Tom Duffield
MPAA rating: R
Running time: 102 minutes

REVIEWS

Abele, Robert. *TheWrap*. August 11, 2016.
Addiego, Walter. *San Francisco Chronicle*. August 11, 2016.
Dowd, A.A. *The A.V. Club*. August 11, 2016.
Edelstein, David. *New York Magazine*. August 11, 2016.
Gleiberman, Owen. *Variety*. May 20, 2016.
Nashawaty, Chris. *Entertainment Weekly*. August 11, 2016.
Rea, Steven. *Philadelphia Inquirer*. August 19, 2016.
Roeper, Richard. *Chicago Sun-Times*. August 11, 2016.
Whipp, Glenn. *Los Angeles Times*. August 11, 2016.
Zacharek, Stephanie. *Time*. August 18, 2016.

QUOTES

Tanner Howard: "Why is it always the sweet ones that are such devils when you get them revved up?"

TRIVIA

Although set in Texas, the movie was filmed in New Mexico.

AWARDS

Ind. Spirit 2017: Actor—Supporting (Foster)
Nominations:
Oscars 2016: Actor—Supporting (Bridges), Film, Film Editing, Orig. Screenplay
British Acad. 2016: Actor—Supporting (Bridges), Cinematog., Orig. Screenplay
Golden Globes 2017: Actor—Supporting (Bridges), Film—Drama, Screenplay
Ind. Spirit 2017: Film Editing, Screenplay
Screen Actors Guild 2016: Actor—Supporting (Bridges)
Writers Guild 2016: Orig. Screenplay

HELLO, MY NAME IS DORIS

She's not ready to act her age
—Movie tagline

Box Office: $14.4 Million

Doris (Sally Field) is a woman in her sixties who lives alone, in the house left behind by her recently deceased mother. She's an outsider of all sorts, from the way she takes a ferry into her work in New York City each evening, to the young employees at her company that surround her with generations between them. She has friends at home, and a brother who lives with his family (Stephen Root), but in more than just her marital status, Doris is single.

Five minutes into the film, she meets someone special. In a meet-cute that has a simple touch, she's scrunched next to a younger man named John in an elevator (Max Greenfield), who has a pleasant way about him, along with a casual handsomeness. In the office, he is amused by her in return, the way she wears reading glasses over her regular glasses, or has an eccentric wardrobe that would be thrift store gold, if it did not already come directly from Doris' closet. With Doris psychologically struggling to put herself back in action after her mother's funeral, (and attending inspirational talks built on the catch phrase *I'm Possible*) she becomes fixated on John as a workplace Prince Charming, and finds ways to pursue him.

Co-written and directed by Michael Showalter, the co-writer of the expert romantic comedy spoof *They Came Together* (David Wain, 2014), the film follows Doris as she tries to get the attention of John, and then ultimately woo him. It initially starts with a few amusing bits, like when she has him inflate her cubicle's medicine ball chair, which has sexual overtones that Showalter doesn't ham up, but lets the pumping of air and bouncing of Doris provide the comedy. Things get a bit more extreme however, as Doris even goes so far as to create a faux-Facebook profile, stalk him online to learn about him, and then show up at the concert of his favorite band, which then lets her snuggle socially into his circle of friends.

However much it may be packaged as a romantic comedy, *Hello, My Name is Doris* is far more a character piece, with Showalter and co-writer Laura Terruso (based on her 2011 short film, *Doris & the Intern*) focusing on how her life is changed by getting to know John, his friends, and a world outside of her mother's home. The movie has an old soul to it as well, which functions as a charm along with its gender reversal of the usual May-December romance, in which a young man is now the target of an older woman's interest. The movie covers a lot of comedic and dramatic territory within its 95-minute running time, but its flat visual style can make the film drag.

Showalter tells the story mostly from Doris' perspective, which is shown in a few flat comedy bits that have a tendency to daydream. But the progressively wild nature of her story (going to a rock concert, making hip young friends who adore her, and even spending time alone with John) feels to be more the contrivance of Showalter than Doris. Though his intentions are noble in presenting a world that accepts his character, it smooths over social gaps and makes contrived characters and even interactions of those outside Doris' head. As Doris is placed deeper into her social fantasy, the film progressively becomes the unintentional kind of cringe comedy, in which the machinations feel more desperate than revealing to the story.

Greenfield's John, especially, whose bright smile and kind eyes are a nice counter to Doris' disheveled gawking gaze, is written to be a bit too naive–accepting a friend request from a rogue profile, about not getting many of Doris' hints until the end–all to serve a quaint purpose. The tone of the film becomes a fantasy that is too high, even for comedy's sake. *Hello, My Name is Doris* might have felt more believable if it all proved to be a dream.

Though weak as a director, Showalter does have the gift of Field, whose selectivity with roles makes *Hello, My Name is Doris* a special event in more ways than one, and a vehicle for the actress that offers amusement even when it runs thin. She is a very game player for Showalter's dark comedy, creating an image of a woman who transitions from complete enigma to connecting with others, while opening up to the new opportunities that life gives her. When the movie later puts Doris back to the reality of her hoarding, Field provides a full image of her character's emotional delicacy, screaming and lashing out, all with the same ease of an earlier solo dancing scene. Proving her skill yet again albeit with a movie that will not stand out in her filmography, the two-time Oscar-winning actress can do it all.

Nick Allen

CREDITS

Doris Miller: Sally Field

John Fremont: Max Greenfield

Brooklyn: Beth Behrs

Cynthia: Wendi McLendon-Covey

Todd: Stephen (Steve) Root

Origin: United States

Language: English

Released: 2015

Production: Kevin Mann, Riva Marker, Jordana Mollick, Daniel Crown, Daniela Taplin Lundberg; Haven Entertainment; released by Red Crown productions

Directed by: Michael Showalter

Written by: Michael Showalter; Laura Terruso

Cinematography by: Brian Burgoyne
Music by: Brian H. Kim
Sound: Tom Paul
Music Supervisor: Andrew Gowan
Editing: Robert Nassau
Art Direction: Eve McCarney
Costumes: Rebecca Gregg
Production Design: Melanie Jones
MPAA rating: R
Running time: 95 minutes

REVIEWS

Brody, Richard. *New Yorker.* March 7, 2016.
Dargis, Manohla. *New York Times.* March 10, 2016.
Duralde, Alonso. *TheWrap.* March 9, 2016.
Eichel, Molly. *Philadelphia Inquirer.* March 18, 2016.
Hornaday, Ann. *Washington Post.* March 17, 2016.
Jones, J.R. *Chicago Reader.* March 17, 2016.
Kohn, Eric. *IndieWire.* January 14, 2016.
MacDonald, Moira. *Seattle Times.* March 17, 2016.
Rife, Katie. *The A.V. Club.* March 10, 2016.
Walsh, Katie. *Tribune News Service.* March 9, 2016.

QUOTES

John: "You're a baller, Doris. Straight up!"

TRIVIA

When the film was released, Sally Field was exactly twice Max Greenfield's age.

HIDDEN FIGURES

Meet the women you don't know, behind the mission you do.
—Movie tagline

Box Office: $135.5 Million

History is full of great stories still waiting to be told by Hollywood filmmakers. And yet, a common response to Theodore Melfi's massive hit and Oscar nominee *Hidden Figures* was understandably, "How did I not know this story earlier?" The film has no answers as to why no one tackled this heartwarming, inspirational, and dramatically rewarding tale before 2016, but the wait may have been worth it, because it's hard to imagine too many people doing a better job than the cast and crew assembled here. This is an old-fashioned crowd-pleaser, filled with strong actors doing strong work, in pursuit of an entertaining night at the movies, and if you walk out inspired and educated, all the better. This kind of filmmaking is often written off as it does not fit

the modern auteurist vision of cinema in which everything has to be defiantly unique, but there's something to be said for a film this solidly well-made. It's a lot harder than it looks.

Hidden Figures, adapted from the book of the same name by Margo Lee Shetterly by Melfi and Allison Schroeder, opens with a scene that's something of a microcosm of the rest of the film. It is 1961 and mathematician Katherine Goble (Taraji P. Henson), engineer Mary Jackson (Janelle Monae), and supervisor Dorothy Vaughan (Octavia Spencer) are broken down on the side of the road. Not only do they have to work together to fix a vehicle to get them to their destination (as they will work together to get astronauts home) but they face skepticism, gender bias, and racism from the local cop who looks suspiciously at their NASA IDs.

The three women work at the Langley Research Center in Hampton, Virginia, from where Goble becomes the first African-American woman assigned to work on the American space program, under increased pressure since the announcement that the Russians have launched a satellite into orbit. Al Harrison (Kevin Costner) is single-minded about getting a man into orbit, and he will use whoever it takes to do so. His career drive allows him to look past Katherine's race and gender, but those factors make her job much harder. For example, she has to run to a segregated bathroom in another building whenever she has to use it. And she seems ignored or dismissed by most of colleagues.

Meanwhile, Mary discovers a flaw in the heat shields, which leads her to work harder to get her engineering degree, despite segregated school laws that make that difficult. She is forced to go to court to convince a judge to allow her to attend night classes at an all-white school. At the same time, Dorothy faces institutional racism, embodied in the form of a supervisor named Vivian (Kirsten Dunst), who is really an amalgamation of several real people, but serves the film's dramatic purposes well.

As Dorothy faces obstacles to her leadership and Mary strives for greater educational opportunities, Katherine's story takes front and center. As arrangements for John Glenn's launch are being made, Katherine is left out of the process, fired after she's deemed to have served her purpose. Of course, on Glenn's return to the planet, a warning light leads NASA to run to Katherine, who knows what to do to bring Glenn home safely.

Hidden Figures is the story of the three women who overcame institutional racism to make the planet a better place through the advancement of our space program. It's no exaggeration to call them heroes, and cinema does not have enough stories of black female heroes, something it feels like the world needs in 2016 as much as it ever did. This is a story that is intrinsically moving, just based on the facts of the narrative.

However, it's also a story that could have easily been screwed up, turned into manipulative pablum like *The Help* (2011), or worse, but Melfi avoids melodrama and trusts his cast. In the end, *Hidden Figures* is an old-fashioned ensemble piece, a film in which a director and his team cast well, trust their story, and doesn't do much to screw it up from there. They trust their ensemble and their audience, and Melfi knows his job is really just to not get in the way of what works here.

To that end, the cast is phenomenal. Octavia Spencer walked away with the Oscar nomination for Best Supporting Actress, but it really feels like a nomination designed to represent the entire ensemble more than anything else, an ensemble that unexpectedly won the Screen Actors Guild Award for Best Ensemble. Henson is fantastic, Monae is going to be a breakout star, and Costner hasn't been this good in years. Only a slightly caricature-ish Jim Parsons stands out negatively, but he fades into the background in the second half.

Hidden Figures is a simple film, but that does not make it any less effective. If anything, this kind of moviemaking is too often dismissed as being simple or easy. If it was, there would be more movies like *Hidden Figures* in the market. Maybe it took so long for this true story to come to the screen because no one could figure out how to do it this well.

Brian Tallerico

CREDITS

Katherine G. Johnson: Taraji P. Henson
Dorothy Vaughan: Octavia Spencer
Mary Jackson: Janelle Monáe
Al Harrison: Kevin Costner
Vivian Mitchell: Kirsten Dunst
Paul Stafford: Jim Parsons
Origin: United States
Language: English
Released: 2017
Production: Peter Chernin, Donna Gigliotti, Jenno Topping, Pharrell Williams, Theodore (Ted) Melfi; released by Chernin Entertainment, Fox 2000 Pictures, Levantine Films
Directed by: Theodore (Ted) Melfi
Written by: Theodore (Ted) Melfi; Allison Schroeder
Cinematography by: Mandy Walker
Music by: Benjamin Wallfisch; Pharrell Williams; Hans Zimmer
Sound: Wayne Lemmer; Derek Vanderhorst
Editing: Peter Teschner
Art Direction: Jeremy Woolsey

Costumes: Renee Ehrlich Kalfus
Production Design: Wynn Thomas
MPAA rating: PG
Running time: 127 minutes

REVIEWS

Brody, Richard. *The New Yorker*. December 26, 2016.
Henderson, Odie. *RogerEbert.com*. December 21, 2016.
Hornaday, Ann. *Washington Post*. December 22, 2016.
Nicholson, Amy. *MTV News*. January 8, 2017.
Perez, Rodrigo. *Playlist*. December 11, 2016.
Rainer, Peter. *Christian Science Monitor*. January 6, 2017.
Roeper, Richard. *Chicago Sun-Times*. December 21, 2016.
Scherstuhl, Alan. *Village Voice*. December 21, 2016.
Turan, Kenneth. *Los Angeles Times*. December 22, 2016.
Zacharek, Stephanie. *Time*. December 23, 2016.

QUOTES

Mary Jackson: "Every time we get a chance to get ahead they move the finish line. Every time."

TRIVIA

The colors used on the sets helped set the film's mood. "Cold" sets at NASA were filmed in sterile whites, grays, and silvers were contrasted against the "warm" sets of Kevin Costner's office and the ladies' homes.

AWARDS

Screen Actors Guild 2017: Cast

Nominations:

Oscars 2016: Actor—Supporting (Spencer), Adapt. Screenplay, Film
British Acad. 2016: Adapt. Screenplay
Golden Globes 2017: Actress—Supporting (Spencer), Score
Screen Actors Guild 2016: Actress—Supporting (Spencer)
Writers Guild 2016: Adapt. Screenplay

HIGH-RISE

Leave the real world behind.
   —Movie tagline

Box Office: $346,472

In 1975, science-fiction New Wave writer J.G. Ballard released his futuristic book *High-Rise* and it immediately became an attractive property to turn into a film. Soon after the book was released, art house auteur Nicolas Roeg was attached to direct, but that project never came to fruition. For decades, the main sticking point in terms of adapting the book to the screen was how to handle Ballard's graphic depictions of sex, violence, and rape. While certainly 1970's cinema was no stranger to the aforementioned themes with Stanley Kubrick's *A Clockwork Orange* having bowed in 1971, the project eventually dwindled and died in terms of becoming a film.

Over four decades later, British director Ben Wheatley (*Kill List* [2011], *Sightseers* [2012]) got a crack at the beloved novel, with his most high-profile cast and largest budget to date. The resulting film does not defy the theory that this source material was too difficult to successfully adapt. While Wheatley's movie almost coolly revels in its deranged depictions of a wealthy group of hi-tech apartment owners gone dog-eat-dog mad, it is also thoroughly confusing in terms of story, motivation, and resolution.

The plot of *High-Rise* concerns wealthy young professional Robert Laing (Tom Hiddelston), a recently-widowed doctor who has bought an upper floor apartment in a state of the art "tower block" style space in a futuristic, dystopian-looking London. While the film cold-opens with Laing living like an apocalypse survivor, dressed in rags and eating what he can find (including household pets), the film soon flashes back three months, before the end of civilization. Thus, viewers know how things are going to end and the journey to how they got so bad is the thrust of Wheatley's film.

As Laing settles into his apartment, he meets a menagerie of wealthy, narcissistic party animals. There's the sultry Charlotte (Sienna Miller) and the rowdy, ne'er do-well Wilder (Luke Evans), who flaunts his overtly sexual impulses in front of the entire building, including his seemingly clueless and pregnant wife Helen (Elisabeth Moss). Viewers also meet the architectural mastermind behind the high-rise in the subdued but quirky Royal (Jeremy Irons). Characters come and go and they all seem to be updated versions of the self-absorbed, rich dolts in Jean Renoir's classic *Rules of the Game* (1939). Yet even the word "updated" is suspect here as Wheatley has chosen to set the entire film in the same era as the book, the late-1970s. As such, all the "futuristic" accouterments in the apartment look like cast-offs from a B-level science-fiction movie of that same era. As the mental health of the building's tenants begin to deteriorate, the "fancy" electronic equipment, designed to make life easier, also begins to malfunction.

As each night of overindulgent, adulterous party-going blends into the next, petty jealousies and a mini-revolt against the established hierarchy cause the apartment dwellers to also fall apart and slowly begin attacking one another. Literally. Ultra-violence, rape, and all sorts of depravity traipse nonchalantly across the screen and for sheer, Id-inspired ugliness, you can barely

do better than *High-Rise*. But without a clear message or point of view the film becomes a bizarre case study in bratty rich people one-upping each other in terms of cruelty.

By far the best parts of the film are the scenery, production design, and camera work. Wheatley's go-to Director of Photography Laurie Rose is the real standout here as his use of near-psychedelic colors and epic underwater photography paint each scene with a finely-skilled brush. There's also some truly spectacular exterior shots of the tower and surrounding landscape that are clearly CGI but rendered so well as to look, and feel, real. The aforementioned, cutting-edge accouterments in the apartment are also clever and cool. Despite the detailed design element, watching a group of rich people devolve into lecherous and dangerous monsters gets old very quickly.

It feels appropriate here to hearken back to the previously mentioned *A Clockwork Orange* as Wheatley is clearly taking his cues from that film. *High-Rise* features cold, distant performances and one shocking scene after another. Yet whereas *A Clockwork Orange* uses contrapuntal sound and music as well as an unreliable narrator to great effect, *High-Rise* seems content to just get down to the gluttonous nitty-gritty without establishing any sort of moral ground. Kubrick's classic makes viewers at once scared and intrigued by Alex (Malcolm McDowell) and his Droogs, cautiously wondering what they might do next. In *High-Rise*, the plot unfolds in a pretty straightforward way even though it's a downward spiral. Every character behaves like a spoiled child, and, in the end, the film feels like a glorified bourgeois steel cage match where the "winner" is revealed in the opening scene.

Don R. Lewis

CREDITS

Laing: Tom Hiddleston
Royal: Jeremy Irons
Charlotte: Sienna Miller
Wilder: Luke Evans
Helen: Elisabeth (Elissabeth, Elizabeth, Liz) Moss
Origin: United States
Language: English
Released: 2016
Production: Jeremy Thomas; released by HanWay Films, Recorded Picture Company
Directed by: Ben Wheatley
Written by: Amy Jump
Cinematography by: Laurie Rose
Music by: Clint Mansell

Sound: Martin Pavey
Music Supervisor: Ian Neil
Editing: Ben Wheatley; Amy Jump
Art Direction: Nigel Pollock
Costumes: Odile Dicks-Mireaux
Production Design: Mark Tildesley
MPAA rating: R
Running time: 119 minutes

REVIEWS

Anderson, Melissa. *Village Voice.* May 10, 2016.
Barnes, Henry. *The Guardian.* September 16, 2016.
DeBruge, Peter. *Variety.* September 16, 2016.
Hertz, Barry. *The Globe and Mail.* May 19, 2016.
Kenny, Glenn. *RogerEbert.com.* May 12. 2016.
Kurchak, Sarah. *Consequence of Sound.* May 10, 2016.
McWeeny, Drew. *Hitfix.* September 24, 2016.
Mobarak, Jared. *The Film Stage.* May 9, 2016.
Pierce, Nev. *Empire.* March 14, 2016.
Robinson, Tasha. *The Verge.* April 29, 2016.

QUOTES

Nathan Steele: "Looks like the rot's set in."

TRIVIA

In a majority of the scenes, a character is smoking.

THE HOLLARS

Box Office: $1 Million

There comes a point in a seemingly well-intentioned, humanist comedy where the viewer has to ask, "Is it really well-intentioned?" A film consisting of a family where the mother is undergoing brain surgery, the father is facing bankruptcy for his business, one son dealing with divorce, and another son facing fatherhood has the makings for something heartwarming, full of wisdom and with a message on togetherness and the importance of family support. But something feels off about *The Hollars*, a quirky indie comedy about this very family and their problems. Actually, everything feels way off. The humanism within the humor feels strangely inhuman, as if the human who wrote the film (James C. Strause) forgot how real humans actually behave. The feeling of it being well-intentioned is overshadowed by having all the men take center stage while the women in the film have all the real problems.

John Krasinski stars in the film as John Hollar, an aspiring artist who lives in New York with his pregnant girlfriend, Rebecca (Anna Kendrick). They get a call that John's mother, Sally (Margo Martindale), is about to undergo surgery due to a newly discovered brain tumor. He immediately flies to the middle-America hometown where he grew up and stays with his father, Don (Richard Jenkins) and brother, Ron (Sharlto Copley). The surgery will be in a few days and, for now, there is almost always someone at Sally's bedside keeping her company. Don has a business that is going down the tubes, financially, and is dealing with his employees no longer showing up for work because they have not been paid in a long time. Ron has moved back home after a divorce. His ex-wife Stacey (Ashley Dyke) now lives with a pastor named Dan (Josh Groban), who calmly puts up with Ron's unpredictable behavior whenever he comes by to see his two daughters.

John has been dealing with general unhappiness with his life as a struggling artist. He lives with his girlfriend who has enough money from her family to afford an apartment downtown while he tries to find himself. John's mother confesses, perhaps via a drug-induced state, that she often regrets marrying Don, which only adds to the angst John feels about marriage to Rebecca. To make matters worse, one of the nurses John sees regularly at the hospital is Jason (Charlie Day), who is now married to John's high school sweetheart, Gwen (Mary Elizabeth Winstead). Jason reluctantly invites John over for dinner at their house at the request of Gwen who has not seen John in many years and wants to catch up. John accepts and finds himself in an awkward situation in which Gwen still feels a strong attraction to him and acts on it.

This moment in the film is where the screenplay starts making drastically wrong turns. First of all, why would any husband actually go through with asking John to come to their house, knowing full well his wife has a history with him? It would be so much easier to just say to the wife that he asked and John declined. End of story. Secondly, why would John even accept this unwanted invitation? It would be so easy to just decline. End of story. Finally, why does Gwen need this dinner gathering to express her feelings to John? She could simply wait outside the hospital for him to come out and maybe fake a run-in. End of story. This is something Roger Ebert used to call "the Idiot Plot," in which characters' actions make no sense and a simple problem could be solved with a line or two of dialogue and everyone could move on, but because the screenwriter wants to prolong the situation for comedic or dramatic effect, the audience is forced to impatiently go along with whatever stupid decisions the seemingly smart and grounded characters make. The fact that Gwen never appears in the film again and John's interaction with her has no effect on him only makes the scene that much more infuriating.

But then, nothing seems to have much of effect on John until the end, and he is supposed to be the narrative throughline. His problems are the least interesting in the film. Screenwriter Strouse has written this kind of material before with the charming *People Places Things* (2015), in which a single dad had to try dating again after a divorce while seeing his two young daughters on weekends. Copley's character is an echo of that, though nowhere nearly as likeable as Jemaine Clement. Copley's appearance, ticks, and mannerisms make it really hard to believe he could ever get married and start a family with any intelligent and beautiful woman. When he meets his mother's Asian doctor (Randall Park), one of his first questions is "What kind of martial arts do you know?" His decision to sneak into his wife's house late at night so he can sleep in the same bed with his two girls is another symptom of the screenplay's endless supply of Idiot Plots.

Krasinski directed the film and he seems to be using the same playbook that another respected television actor, Zach Braff, used on his feature debut, *Garden State* (2004). Krasinski even has a slo-mo shot of him on an airplane at the beginning of his film. He also underscores just about every scene in the film with an indie rock song. But where Braff's film had a main character worthy of the audience's sympathies, Krasinski's film feels empty and overly concerned with a character who should be secondary to Sally and/or Don. There are a few nice comedic touches that Krasinski gets right as a director and he is not going out of his way to show off any visual flair. The actors all do the best they can with the material, but the material is the main problem here. In the end, the male journey through the possible death of a mother, the pregnancy of a girlfriend, and the pressures of marriage should amount to more than just "well, now I'm happy."

Collin Souter

CREDITS

Sally Hollar: Margo Martindale
Ron Hollar: Sharlto Copley
Don Hollar: Richard Jenkins
John Hollar: John Krasinski
Rebecca: Anna Kendrick
Origin: United States
Language: English
Released: 2016
Production: Ben Nearn, Tom Rice, Allyson Seeger, John Krasinski; released by Fancy Film Post Services, Sunday Night, Sycamore Pictures

Directed by: John Krasinski
Written by: James C. Strouse
Cinematography by: Eric Alan Edwards
Music by: Josh Ritter
Sound: Perry Robertson
Editing: Heather Persons
Costumes: Caroline Eselin
Production Design: Daniel B. Clancy
MPAA rating: PG-13
Running time: 88 minutes

REVIEWS

Bender, Abbey. *Village Voice*. August 24, 2016.
Duralde, Alonso. *The Wrap*. August 25, 2016.
Dziemianowicz, Joe. *New York Daily News*. August 26, 2016.
Genzlinger, Neil. *New York Times*. August 25, 2016.
Goldstein, Gary. *Los Angeles Times*. August 25, 2016.
Hassenger, Jesse. *The A.V. Club*. August 25, 2016.
Mayer, Dominick. *Consequence of Sound*. August 25, 2016.
Seitz, Matt Zoller. *RogerEbert.com*. August 26, 2016.
Smith, Kyle. *New York Post*. August 25, 2016.
Walsh, Katie. *Tribune News Service*. August 23, 2016.

TRIVIA

Filming took about 17 hours for the airport scenes, but only about ten minutes ended up on screen.

A HOLOGRAM FOR THE KING

Box Office: $4.2 Million

A decade ago, a collaboration between Tom Hanks (America's golden boy, the safest movie star in the world), Tom Tykwer (Germany's zany enfant terrible director), and Dave Eggers (the literary wunderkind and famous bleeding heart) would have seemed if not impossible then highly unlikely. And yet here in 2016 is just such a bizarre and surprisingly effective melding of those minds. Tykwer has adapted Eggers' 2012 novel *A Hologram for the King* with Hanks as put-upon fallen capitalist Alan Clay. Tykwer takes to Eggers' style—bittersweet levity laced with the arsenic of the past—like a fish to water. He takes great pleasure dreaming up clever ways to dramatize Clay's neuroses, paranoia, and regret and he loves throwing in near-subliminal flashbacks to his former glories and failures. He falls into a handful of traps that plague studio filmmakers of his generation, like racially iffy casting and too-obvious dramatic payoffs and visual metaphors, but he shows that even saddled with the biggest dramatic actor on earth he can still be himself. In fact, Hanks may ultimately have helped Tykwer's filmmaking stay grounded.

Alan Clay (Hanks) has been sent to Saudi Arabia on a mission, one self-imposed and one handed to him by corporate. Officially, he's got to sell the king on new software technology, but, as is so frequently the case when Americans go abroad in dramedies like this, he's really there to rediscover his sense of self. He's paying for his daughter's (Tracey Fairaway) college singlehandedly after a messy divorce and he's still stinging from letting his last clients down; a screw up that cost hundreds of people their livelihoods. He finds his new surroundings to be most unforgiving. His team is overworked and underfunded, working doggedly in an un-air-conditioned tent with no Wi-Fi. Alan's chauffeur/sidekick Yousef (Alexander Black) is a goon who insists on finding meaning in every incident that befalls the hapless American businessman. Clay ricochets between two women, insatiable power player Hanne (Sidse Babett Knudsen) and the gentle physician with a troubled lovelife Zahra (Sarita Choudhury), though he's acutely aware he doesn't have enough charm or appetite to woo them. Compounding everything, the king refuses to arrive so that Alan can demonstrate his wares. All this stress manifests itself physically in the form of a cyst on Alan's back, which may be cancerous and needs to be treated with invasive surgery. Everything seems to be conspiring against Alan's success in Saudi Arabia. He's going to need a massive outlook overhaul if he's going to leave in one piece.

Tykwer's stylistic playbook has been honed, sanded, sharpened, and focused since his 1998 film, *Run Lola Run,* lit up the international arthouse scene. His images, courtesy of his longtime crack cinematographer Frank Griebe, still buzz with intimacy, isolation, and agoraphobia. Their framing and lighting turn all Tykwer's heroes into lone figures of romantic alienation, something like Anton Corbijn's photographs of post-punk stars. His editing remains deeply ironic, postmodern, and breathless, like a comic strip seen from the window of a speeding car. His preferred female character remains crimson-haired, willful, and dangerous, and his worldview remains multifaceted and international. The cast is rounded out by actors of every nationality, which makes decisions like casting New Yorker Alexander Black as Saudi Arabian Yousef a little peculiar, but the color blindness at least has precedent. Ever since Tykwer hooked up with the Wachowski siblings for their jointly authored, sprawling adaptation of David Mitchell's *Cloud Atlas,* his progressive multicultural attitude took on something like fluidity. Actors (including Hanks) repeatedly and obviously play against type, gender, and ethnicity in *Cloud Atlas* (2012) to demonstrate the essential humanity of the diverse players. Charitably, you could say a handful of the choices in *A Hologram for the King* follow the same optimistic schematic, but it's equally possible Tykwer just did not care about precise representation. Luckily, the film has enough style and heart to overcome the issue, for the most part. Just as Tykwer turned the spy thriller on its ear in 2009's *The International,* the application of his excitingly nervous filmmaking grammar to what might be called the exotic rediscovery genre (seen in movies like *Eat Pray Love* [2010] and *Under The Tuscan Sun* [2003]) at least makes the expected narrative arc look fresh.

The edit gives one the impression of being on a tilt-a-whirl, and fourth-wall breaking asides like Hanks dreaming himself into a kind of music video for a rewritten version of the Talking Heads' "Once In A Lifetime" are the kind of thing that only someone like Tykwer would try. It's the mix of earnestness and fantasy, like the cartoon tangents that recur in *Run Lola Run* and make a brief appearance on Alan Clay's hotel TV, that make them uniquely Tykwer's. Everything here walks a fine line between playful and outright silly, and the danger is always that they're too broad and ridiculous to take seriously. The risks he takes tonally are part of his narrative strategy and help us understand the plight of his characters; every precariously balanced element could come crashing down at any moment. In the same way Tykwer's little-seen 2010 film *3* begins with a man literally talking to an angel, so much of *A Hologram for the King* is difficult to accept unless one is willing to give in to the mood of pervasive optimism hiding below the morbid nature of Alan Clay's many predicaments. There are, however, real emotional coups that need no grain of salt to enjoy, such as a scene of scuba diving that is so sublime it would singlehandedly justify the movie's existence.

It helps in no small measure that Alan is played by Tom Hanks. Not just because Hanks is playing to type and quite well, but because in his decades-long career he became the symbol of romantic reinvention and the embracing of life's mysteries. Twice he's been lost to sea (first in the remarkable *Joe Versus The Volcano* [1990] and then again in *Castaway* [2000]), only to return to life with renewed fervor. *A Hologram for the King* trades in on Hanks' reputation as the man who can't help but love life, the one who always illustrates the glory of the American way. The performance isn't exactly risky, even if he does swim with topless women and appear nearly nude himself in a handful of shower scenes, but it is at least honest. Very thin, too closely shaved, tired, and routinely hung-over, Alan Clay is proof that Hanks is willing to sacrifice a little of his natural charisma to bring a film down to earth.

Scout Tafoya

CREDITS

Alan: Tom Hanks
Yousef: Alexander Black
Zahra: Sarita Choudhury
Hanne: Sidse Babett Knudsen
Kit: Tracey Fairaway
Origin: United States
Language: English, Arabic
Released: 2016
Production: Stefan Arndt, Gary Goetzman, Tim O'Hair, Uwe Schott, Arcadiy Golubovich; released by The Playtone Co., X Filme
Directed by: Tom Tykwer
Written by: Tom Tykwer
Cinematography by: Frank Griebe
Music by: Tom Tykwer; Johnny Klimek
Sound: Frank Kruse
Editing: Alexander Berner
Art Direction: Kai Koch
Costumes: Pierre-Yves Gayraud
Production Design: Uli Hanisch
MPAA rating: R
Running time: 98 minutes

REVIEWS

Ebiri, Bilge. *Village Voice*. April 20, 2016.
Grierson, Tim. *Screen International*. April 20, 2016.
LaSalle, Mick. *San Francisco Chronicle*. April 21, 2016.
Linden, Sheri. *Hollywood Reporter*. April 20, 2016.
Reed, Rex. *New York Observer*. April 21, 2016.
Robinson, Tasha. *The Verge*. April 26, 2016.
Russo, Tom. *Boston Globe*. April 21, 2016.
Smith, Kyle. *New York Post*. April 27, 2016.
Turan, Kenneth. *Los Angeles Times*. April 21, 2016.
Uhlich, Keith. *The A.V. Club*. April 20, 2016.

TRIVIA

Tom Hanks gave a positive review about Dave Eggers' source novel in 2012.

HOW TO BE SINGLE

Welcome to the party.
—Movie tagline

Box Office: $46.8 Million

Perhaps self-awareness and obliviousness can be two sides of the same coin. At least, that is how it seems in *How to Be Single*, a movie savvy enough to include a funny visual joke in which two women attempt to race through a thorough, multi-step, pre-work hangover cure only to arrive on the job three and a half hours late and a completely sincere, dopily earnest shot of one of those women sticking her head out the window of a New York City cab to the tune of Taylor Swift's "Welcome to New York." If there were a mid-20s, self-discovery-focused update of 2000's *Not Another Teen Movie*, it would feature that exact scene. Yes, with the character inevitably bumping her head on the side of the bridge or something.

Throughout the uneven *How to Be Single*, Alice (Dakota Johnson) is likewise a blend of assured and adrift, clarity and doubt sharing the revolving door that is being new on the job, newly single, or just living in a place that never rests at an age that begs to be satisfied. That often happens alongside Robin (Rebel Wilson), a colleague who becomes an instant best friend after Alice begins work as a paralegal. She is never tasked with any responsibility, and she seems to have minimal daily ambition; her professional life serves only to introduce Robin, who is both a complete rehash of Wilson's usual, big-personality comic relief and an always-welcome example of a sex-positive woman presented without judgment. Though far from a responsible decision-maker (certainly a fair presentation of many professionals at that age, going out on weeknights and waking up not entirely remembering what happened the night before), Robin lives confidently and without feeling a need for a partner. She is single and happy, a female characterization that seems so simple it would be easy to forget how rare it is.

Telling her long-term boyfriend, Josh (Nicholas Braun), that they are bored, not happy, and she needs to know herself better before fully committing, Alice thinks she wants to be single. But timing does what timing does and flips good intentions into a lesson: She tests the waters, tries reconnecting, and he is not interested, no longer sure he wants the same things. "You mean, like me?" she asks. Johnson needs a lot more time to develop as a comic actress, but she sells the tight shot on Alice's face as Josh asserts, his offense sounding like defense, that he's not an idiot and he'll pass on running back to her. Johnson also gets another nice moment with the spontaneous way she plays a throwaway line and makes it land: "I don't know why I always talk myself out of doing the things I really want to do."

Meanwhile, in a likable subplot that sort of fits, Alice's sister, Meg (Leslie Mann), a delivery room doctor sure she does not want kids, instead decides to go the sperm donor route only to then meet the perfect guy (Jake Lacy, in many ways reprising his role from 2014's superior *Obvious Child*). In the other plotline, which runs like an afterthought to everything else, Lucy (Alison Brie) copes with being hopelessly obvious in her formulaic efforts to find love while being progressively charmed by Tom (Anders Holm), a bartender very proud of himself for being honest about his disinterest in commitment. He even designs his apartment to ensure women cannot stay for breakfast or even hydrate properly, prompting his new friend/agenda-free hookup Alice to suggest that he's a sociopath. It is one of the movie's few risky yet perceptive points that this recognition does not necessarily make Tom less sexually appealing to her.

For what it is worth, the film also does not set up an onslaught of predictable, inevitable pairings. It treats relationships like what they are: two people in the same place for an endless number of reasons, weighing the past, present and future consciously or unconsciously and determining how long they want to stay in that place together. Tangentially, that involves David (Damon Wayans Jr.), a widower whom Alice starts dating; and George (Jason Mantzoukas), who does not have the same playboy swagger as Tom but may be the one for Lucy anyway. *How to Be Single* allows for characters who possess traits that actually exist in reality and decisions that are necessary when the way everything will turn out is not abundantly clear to everyone involved.

Like the dating world itself, though, director Christian Ditter's overly perky romantic comedy is nothing if not a mixed bag. It is empowering and annoying, endearing and misguided, constantly alternating between difficult truths and cheap lunges at spinning drama into comedy by ending scenes with jokes and pop music cues. Most of the former comes thanks to Mann, who avoids anything cutesy as Meg progressively softens after telling a child, "You're not that cute, and I am not falling for it." Later, when Meg shares her plan to conceive with her sister, Mann layers subtle overcompensation into her excitement as she exclaims, "There's no strings attached at all, nothing!" It sets up her soon asking, "If this was a bad idea, would you tell me?" Mann is a gifted actress who has not received a shred of the credit she deserves.

More often, though, *How to Be Single*, a long way from something as specific and insightful as 2013's *Frances Ha,* frustrates with its inconsistency and occasionally wide-eyed embrace of clichés. (That includes the nice guy who turns out to be a cad and the ladies' man who wants to settle down. Better to say as little as possible about Alice stating in voiceover, "This story isn't about relationships; it's about all those times in life when maybe, just maybe, our real life is happening.") While it is admirable to give a character a chance to really try to know herself and figure out the rest later (meanwhile making some distinctions between wants and needs), please do not present that in the context of something as painfully trite as a young woman finally having time to sit on her windowsill and read Cheryl Strayed's *Wild.*

Thankfully the movie has some found moments like Lucy's character accidentally almost drinking a candle, but *How to Be Single* mistakes a troublesome quantity of mediocre for a fitting amount of wobbling. Being refreshingly frank yet open-minded about the potentially lonely comedown from the party only goes so far when phony, sitcom-level sequences, several literally taken from *Friends*, ultimately do a lot more to kill the buzz.

Matt Pais

CREDITS

Alice: Dakota Johnson
Rebel Wilson: Rebel Wilson
Meg: Leslie Mann
David: Damon Wayans, Jr.
Tom: Anders Holm
Origin: United States
Language: English
Released: 2016
Production: Drew Barrymore, Nancy Juvonen, John Rickard, Dana Fox; released by Flower Films, New Line Cinema L.L.C.
Directed by: Christian Ditter
Written by: Abby Kohn; Marc Silverstein; Dana Fox
Cinematography by: Christian Rein
Music by: Fil Eisler
Sound: Robert Eng
Music Supervisor: Season Kent
Editing: Tia Nolan
Costumes: Leah Katznelson
Production Design: Steve Saklad
MPAA rating: R
Running time: 110 minutes

REVIEWS

Eichel, Molly. *Philadelphia Enquirer.* February 11, 2016.
Greenblatt, Leah. *Entertainment Weekly.* February 11, 2016.
Jones, Kimberley. *Austin Chronicle.* February 17, 2016.
Keough, Peter. *Boston Globe.* February 11, 2016.
Lemire, Christy. *RogerEbert.com.* February 12, 2016.
Moore, Roger. *Movie Nation.* February 11, 2016.
Rife, Katie. *The A.V. Club.* Feb. 10, 2016.
Roeper, Richard. *Chicago Sun-Times.* February 11, 2016.
Smith, Adam. *Empire.* February 22, 2016.
Whitty, Stephen. *New York Daily News.* February 11, 2016.

QUOTES

Tom: "Marriage! The end of spontaneous sex, travelling by yourself, and buying whatever you want without having to ask permission. Right?"

TRIVIA

The movie is based on the novel of the same name by Liz Tuccillo.

HUNT FOR THE WILDERPEOPLE

Nature just got gangster.
—Movie tagline

Box Office: $5.2 Million

Some films need to be seen by everyone with a beating heart. *Hunt for the Wilderpeople* falls into that rare category. It is as wild as the New Zealand outback in which it takes place, but also as spacious. That is important. Everyone in this film is running away from or toward something and everyone changes course before they get to the end of their journey. Along the way, they come of age, reflect on a long life, fight off wild animals and wilder men, and go on one heck of an entertaining adventure.

Fifteen-year-old New Zealander Ricky Baker (Julian Dennison) is a handful. He breaks stuff. Steals stuff. Burns stuff and spits. Now in the by-the-book hands of maniacal Child Protective Services Officer Paula (Rachel House), he has one last chance to stay out of a juvenile detention center. He can try to make a go of one final foster home on the edge of the outback. Bella (Rima Te Wiata), his new foster mother, is dotty and doting. Her husband Hec (Sam Neill) is a grumpy old fart. At first, Ricky tries to run away.

But when a tragedy leaves Hec and Ricky with only each other and their dogs for company, Child Services sends word they will be coming to collect Ricky. Angry at Hec, who wants him to leave, Ricky runs away. But before he disappears into the bush he burns a dummy to throw the adult world off the trail, inadvertently burning down the family barn. Hec takes off after him and Paula, convinced that Hec has become mentally deranged, launches a nationwide manhunt for the pair. With no choice left but to run, Hec and Ricky find themselves fast becoming legends as they run into one odd person and one dangerous situation after another, leading to an inevitable showdown between them and authorities.

Taika Waititi directed the 2014 breakout hit *What We Do In The Shadows*, a laugh-out-loud mockumentary about four vampires trying to share a flat and find their place in present day New Zealand. So the constant humor in *Hunt for the Wilderpeople* should hardly come as a surprise. The film is based on the novel *Wild Pork and Watercress* by Barry Crump and is adapted solely by Waititi, who finds a near equal balance of humor, heart, and action in the story. But he also brings a winsome visual style and a command of the film medium that allows him to use tools like voiceover effectively, something that is harder than it looks. His use of special effects in the film, including the staging of a giant boar fight, is handled perfectly, never distractingly. He also cleverly divides the film into chapters that are titled in a way that speak to the inner life of the characters. A lot of people write and direct their films but few do both this well.

The film is expertly cast. Rima Te Wiata is so endearing as the cock-eyed optimist Bella. Her barreling determination to make Ricky feel welcome never feels less than completely authentic. Everyone has known a Bella; the kind of person you only miss after they are gone. Sam Neill has left his mark in so many wonderful films that his excellent performance here can hardly be a surprise. But his grizzled appearance and aged annoyance are tailor made to the character of Hec, and a perfect counterpoint to the energy Bella brings.

But the real find here is in young Julian Dennison. He communicates so much and so well with just his face that dialogue seems like an afterthought. His acting is a foundation here that he builds on virtually every time he opens his mouth. It is easy to believe Ricky is a young man of exceptional imagination who has been through hard, hard times.

In fact, the film has no shortage of memorable and entertaining characters. Paula, who repeats the phrase "No child left behind" like a hypnotized party guest is a great caricature of everyone's worst government employee nightmare. At one point, Hec and Ricky, holed up in a remote cabin are found out by a trio of doofus hunters. At another, the pair runs into Psycho Sam (Rhys Darby), a hermit-like bush dweller, completely out of his mind, but willing to help them in their fight against Paula and her government cronies. Even the young girl on horseback and her starstruck dad come off as colorful and important parts of the overall story.

Most surprising of all is the graceful way Waititi comes to the story's end. To be sure, said path involves guns, car crashes, youthful rebellion, and a little time in jail, but, despite the rambunctiousness, Waititi is more intent on showing how a little enthusiasm and hope can go a long way to save us from ourselves. This is a film full of beautiful people. They may not always look like it on the outside, but it's their beauty on the inside that takes them on life's adventures.

Dave Canfield

CREDITS

Hec: Sam Neill
Ricky: Julian Dennison
Bella: Rima Te Wiata
Paula: Rachel House
Kahu: Tioreore Ngatai-Melbourne
Origin: United States
Language: English

Released: 2016

Production: Carthew Neal, Matthew Noonan, Leanne Saunders; released by Defender Films

Directed by: Taika Waititi

Written by: Taika Waititi

Cinematography by: Lachlan Milne

Music by: Lukasz Pawel Buda; Samuel Scott; Conrad Wedde

Editing: Tom Eagles; Yana Gorskaya; Luke Haigh

Art Direction: Jon Lithgow

Costumes: Kristin Seth

Production Design: Neville Stevenson

MPAA rating: PG-13

Running time: 101 minutes

REVIEWS

Barnard, Linda. *Toronto Star*. June 24, 2016.
Bartlett, James. *Film Ireland Magazine*. October 5, 2016.
Dargis, Manhola. *New York Times*. June 23, 2016.
Hornaday, Ann. *Washington Post*. June 30, 2016.
Huddleston, Tom. *Time Out*. September 13, 2016.
Lickona, Matthew. *San Diego Reader*. July 14, 2016.
Long, Tom. *Detroit News*. July 14, 2016.
McCarthy. *Hollywood Reporter*. June 14, 2016.
Schager, Nick. *Village Voice*. April 20, 2016.
Turan, Kenneth. *Los Angeles Times*. June 23, 2016.

QUOTES

Officer Andy: "We're offering ten thousand dollars to anyone who can capture them, dead or alive. Oh. Alive. They should be alive."

TRIVIA

The uncle is portrayed as someone illiterate; in real life Sam Neill has a BA in English literature.

THE HUNTSMAN: WINTER'S WAR

The story before Snow White.
—Movie tagline

Box Office: $48.4 Million

While 2016 witnessed the premiere of many big-budget sequels, *The Huntsman: Winter's War* might qualify as the most unusual sequel of the year—and the most unnecessary. While 2012's *Snow White and the Huntsman* was definitely a profitable international hit, it didn't exactly light the world on fire. Director Rupert Sanders' revisionist take on the Snow White fable was a fairly workman-like summer movie. It did its job. Critics didn't hate it. Audiences didn't love it. *Snow White*

and the Huntsman was the definition of a "fine" movie. A decent way to spend 90 minutes in a theatre, but you would forget 90

of the film on your walk to the car. That's why, when it was announced that Universal had greenlit the production of a sequel, focused on Chris Hemsworth's Huntsman character, it was surprising to say the least.

Snow White and the Huntsman was a new riff on a classic legend. Disney, in particular, has shown the box office potential of creating live-action versions of previously animated fables. A big-budget Snow White action movie with Kristen Stewart and Charlize Theron makes sense. A Huntsman movie does not.

More than anything, *The Huntsman: Winter's War* feels like a film assembled by a committee. One can imagine that they looked at the disparate pieces surrounding their moderate Snow White success and convinced themselves they could build a franchise out of them. They realized that they had the star of *Thor* (2011) under contract, they could bring back Theron following her *Mad Max: Fury Road* (2015) success, and they could mine the backlist of Grimm's Fairy Tales to provide suitably mythic trappings. Unfortunately, what the screenwriters—Evan Spiliotopoulos and Craig Mazin—forgot, as they assembled their franchise Jenga pieces, was to actually write a story.

Admittedly, the Snow White screenwriters had it much easier. They could always ape the structure of the classic Snow White fable in their action-movie adaptation. But there is no Huntsman fable, so instead, the screenwriters just threw together a fairy tale mishmash and hoped that it would actually resemble a hero's journey. (Spoiler alert: It does not.)

The end result is a movie that nakedly tries to rip-off the *Snow Queen* source material that Disney used as the inspiration for their mega-hit *Frozen* (2013), while, at the same time, having the audacity to function as both a prequel and a sequel to *Snow White and the Huntsman*. But, as *Winter's War* proves, there simply isn't enough mythical meat to turn the Huntsman into a franchise.

The film opens on a dark riff on the Elsa/Anna dynamic from *Frozen*. In the prequel portion of the film, Freya (Emily Blunt), the younger sister of the sinister Queen Ravenna (Charlize Theron), is pregnant with the daughter of a married nobleman. But, after her newborn daughter is murdered under mysterious circumstances, Freya's rage causes her to "Let It Go" and she unleashes an explosion of previously untapped ice magic, transforming her into a powerful Snow Queen.

Beside herself with grief and a broken heart, Freya begins abducting children and training them to become her "huntsmen," a.k.a. her hard-hearted soldiers who will overthrow kingdoms in her honor. This is where we meet Eric, Chris Hemsworth's character from the previous film, and we learn that, while he worked for Freya, he fell head over heels for his fellow huntsman Sara (Jessica Chastain). But cold-hearted Freya can't deal with two of her henchmen being in love, so she murders Sara in front of Eric's eyes and banishes him into the wilderness.

The opening of *Winter's War* really speaks to director Cedric Nicolas-Troyan's weaknesses as a filmmaker. His prior resume involves a lot of visual effects work and second-unit directing, but, despite his obvious technical prowess, storytelling and character development apparently does not fall into his skill set

He has the luxury of having an absurdly talented cast in this film and he squanders them completely. Hemsworth and Chastain have no chemistry, and the great Emily Blunt, in particular, looks about as lost and vacant as Natalie Portman did in George Lucas' *Star Wars* prequels. Everything about her performance and the scenes that Nicolas-Troyan builds around her telegraphs a lack of depth. Blunt constantly looks like she's looking for something, anything to focus her eyes on, and the director never gives her anything suitable to play off.

Cut to the sequel portion of the film. We learn that, following the events of the first film, Snow White (now the queen) has fallen ill and her husband William (Sam Claflin) blames Queen Ravenna's Magic Mirror. However, as William's soldiers were transporting the Mirror away from their castle for storage, it went missing. William enlists Eric's help in finding the Mirror, teaming him up with two of the dwarves from the previous film, Nion (Nick Frost) and Gryff (Rob Brydon). It turns out that Ravenna's essence still exists within the Mirror, Freya wants the Mirror to bolster her powers, and, surprise surprise, Sara is still alive, fully believing that Eric abandoned her all those years ago. (Freya's magic visions are to blame.)

Spiliotopoulos and Mazin try to weave all of these plotlines into a satisfying whole, but they simply can't manage. Hemsworth's Eric is not an engaging enough protagonist to hold our attention throughout the film's relentlessly over-done CGI battle sequences, scenes that make the worst moments of Peter Jackson's Hobbit films look downright gritty and realistic in comparison. The story just isn't there. No one changes. Nothing feels earned or honest. It's artifice masquerading as mythology.

The "artificial" feel of the film might be its biggest flaw. It feels generic, like a franchise-in-a-box starter pack and it looks painfully unreal. While so many summer blockbusters over-rely on CGI imagery, *The Huntsman: Winter's War* makes you feel the claustrophobia of the green-screen set in almost every scene. The film does not feel like a cinematic experience. It feels like

something a technician could drag onto a flash drive, toss into his pocket, and accidentally throw into the wash without realizing what he had done.

The Huntsman: Winter's War is both a fairy tale and a sequel that no one really wanted. Fortunately, it's forgettable enough that audiences won't have to worry about another unnecessary chapter in this story making its way to the multiplex next summer.

Tom Burns

CREDITS

The Huntsman/Eric: Chris Hemsworth
Ravenna: Charlize Theron
Sara: Jessica Chastain
Queen Freya: Emily Blunt
Nion: Nick Frost
Origin: United States
Language: English
Released: 2016
Production: Joe Roth; released by Roth Films, Universal Pictures Inc.
Directed by: Cedric Nicolas-Troyan
Written by: Evan Spiliotopoulos; Craig Mazin
Cinematography by: Phedon Papamichael
Music by: James Newton Howard
Editing: Conrad Buff, IV
Art Direction: Frank Walsh
Costumes: Colleen Atwood
Production Design: Dominic Watkins
MPAA rating: PG-13
Running time: 123 minutes

REVIEWS

Collin, Robbie. *The Telegraph*. April 18, 2016.
Hassenger, Jesse. *The A.V. Club*. April 20, 2016.
Macdonald, Moira. *The Seattle Times*. April 21, 2016.
McWeeny, Drew. *Hitfix*. April 20, 2016.
Moore, Caitlin. *Washington Post*. April 21, 2016.
Rea, Steven. *Philadelphia Inquirer*. April 22, 2016.
Russo, Tom. *Boston Globe*. April 21, 2016.
Truitt, Brian. *USA Today*. April 21, 2016.
Walsh, Katie. *Chicago Tribune*. April 21, 2016.
Zwecker, Bill. *Chicago Sun-Times*. April 21, 2016.

QUOTES

Sara: "We blind ourselves to the truth because we are weak, because we hope. But there's no hope for love. Love ends in betrayal. Aye and always."

TRIVIA

The film was loosely based on the Hans Christian Anderson fairy tale *The Snow Queen*.

I

I, DANIEL BLAKE

Few working directors have a style, theme, or aesthetic as immediately recognizable as the left-wing British filmmaker Ken Loach. Since his groundbreaking BBC documentaries of a half-century ago (like the great, sobering *Cathy Come Home* [1966]), Loach has specialized in movies drawn to the emotional plight of the socially marginalized or disenfranchised.

Given his early training and background, Loach has always favored a direct address style. His films also meditate on history. Two of his strongest works, *Land and Freedom* (1995) and *The Wind that Shakes the Barley* (2006), deal with devastating 20th century civil wars in Spain and Ireland, for instance. His movies are of a piece, but they are not all the same. His weakest or less inspired work tends toward the didactic. His best films, like his masterpiece *Kes* (1969), featuring a riotously funny soccer match, or *Riff-Raff* (1971), with its hilarious interplay among construction workers, or the delirious fantasy of *Looking for Eric* (2009), operate in a much different emotional register and carry a sly ebullience, wit, and self-reflexive humor.

Loach is also an underrated visual stylist. His documentary realist design appears fairly unadorned and invisible. A closer examination shows how worked out and complex his technique has become. Working with great cinematographers, like Chris Menges or Barry Ackroyd, Loach has developed a breathless concision and speed compositionally. Even the framing is lesser work is impeccable. That formal talent synchronizes wonderfully with Loach's greatest talent, his skill with actors. Actors love Loach because of the freedom, values, and depth of feeling: the monologues that sing and soar, or the arias of anger, defiance, and dramatic self-assertion.

Loach's most significant collaborator has been the scenarist Paul Laverty, a lawyer and natural muckraker. Laverty has written almost all of the director's films since *Carla's Song* (1996). Laverty is a wildly uneven talent. He is more of a sensationalist than Loach. At his worst, he weighs his stories down with melodrama. He is also a chameleon who knows how to throw the rhythm off. *The Angels' Share* (2011) begins as one very specific kind of a "Loach film," and then becomes something quite different.

Loach's new film, *I, Daniel Blake*, is his strongest film since *The Wind that Shakes the Barley*. Significantly, both films won the most distinguished prize in international cinema, the Palme d'Or, for best film at the Cannes Film festival. The new movie is marred in the final third by some highly questionable plot movements. Fortunately the rest of the film is strong enough to overcome that lapse. The acting is sensational, the tone and mood emotionally persuasive, and the urgency and tenacity of its ideals prove heartbreakingly relevant.

Loach also has a great eye for unorthodox casting. The English stand-up comedian Dave Johns, in his first film part, is mesmerizing as the eponymous 59-year-old carpenter from Newcastle, the economically depressed region in northeast England adversely impacted by government austerity policies and privatization of public services. Loach has long used the cinema to denounce the severe political, class, and social stratification of British culture that has deepened the vast social inequality. Daniel leads a hardscrabble life and the early scenes lay out his restricted, boxed in existence.

Daniel experiences the vicissitudes of a draconian and irresponsible social system, trapped by a catch-22 that proves especially crippling. A widower who lives very modestly, Daniel suffered a serious heart attack on a job and his doctor has ordered him to avoid work. Applying for a social safety benefit called the Employment and Support Allowance, his case is originally approved only for Dan to be suddenly deprived of further benefits on the basis of a seemingly arbitrarily designed eligibility test. The social services center deems his healthy enough to seek work. As he waits out a complex appeals process, his only recourse is to apply for a provisional claim that mandates he actively seek work, with corresponding proof.

Daniel is twice handcuffed, by an authoritarian system and the imperatives of the new economy. *I, Daniel Blake* is a painful study of human obsolescence in the digital age. With little formal education, Daniel must adapt to the alien surroundings and learn on the fly how to use the new technology to complete the standardized forms necessary to carry out his appeal. Even the most straightforward of digital tasks completely flummoxes him. Daniel takes a class that teaches how to compose curriculum vitae, until the mounting frustration and anger crystallize his disgust and pain and he ends up drawing out the form in longhand.

Daniel is a deeply humane and decent man, a point dramatically underscored when he intervenes on behalf of Katie Morgan (Hayley Squires), a single mother of two young children and recently arrived from London, who is also unfairly punished by the Byzantine rules at the social service agency. He develops an immediate (platonic) connection with the woman. Their rapport and shared experiences are the nerviest, strongest sequences of the film.

In these middle sections, the movie achieves a raw, uninflected power. *I, Daniel Blake* gives definition and shape to those accustomed to the shadows. The movie dramatizes powerlessness and fear, an underpinning of shame and loss of control, to devastating effect. In the most remarkable passage of the film, Katie goes to a food bank and suffers a breakdown. She has forsaken eating for herself, sacrificing in order to take care of her children. Having sudden access to food, she reveals the depth of her vulnerability, shaming herself in the process. It is a shocking moment, but a painfully realistic one and Loach, tenderly, tragically, never exploits her misery.

That is why a significant narrative mistake in a third-act plot movement that signals Katie's deepening desperation, and Daniel's attendant heartbreak, feels particularly disingenuous. The bad judgment does not completely invalidate what came before it. The action detracts significantly from the range of expression and precision of the telling, a patently false action in a movie otherwise sharply rooted in emotional realistic behavior.

Thanks to the subtlety and depth of Johns' performance, the movie recovers. He has a comic's natural pathos, his dark humor and absurdity the only natural response to the bureaucratic skullduggery and lack of institutional accountability that permanently damns those to misfortune. Even as Daniel and Katie are ground down by the machinations, their humanity, dignity, and grace somehow endure. Johns has the natural exasperation down perfectly. With her tight face and defiance, Squires is also a force of nature.

Other than the one dramatic misstep, *I, Daniel Blake* is a sharp and diamond-hard shaped work. The movie feels lived in and authentic, like Daniel's interactions with his younger neighbors that underline the observational grace. The fluid camerawork by Robbie Ryan is vibrant, expressive, and deeply attuned to the actors' actions. This is a serious work with tragic undertones. The movie is never solemn or pretentious. Even the welfare and social service workers are treated honestly and bracingly though never condescendingly. The movie gives voice and shape to those most desperately in need. Daniel Blake demands to be seen for his own worth and intrinsic value. The movie makes it impossible to look away.

Patrick Z. McGavin

CREDITS

Daniel: Dave Johns
Katie: Hayley Squires
Sheila: Sharon Percy
Daisy: Briana Shann
Dylan: Dylan McKiernan
Origin: United States
Language: English
Released: 2016
Production: Rebecca O'Brien; released by Sixteen Films, Why Not Productions, Wild Bunch
Directed by: Ken Loach
Written by: Paul Laverty
Cinematography by: Robbie Ryan
Music by: George Fenton
Editing: Jonathan Morris
Costumes: Jo Slater
Production Design: Fergus Clegg; Linda Wilson
MPAA rating: R
Running time: 100 minutes

REVIEWS

Abele, Robert. *Los Angeles Times*. December 22, 2016.
Bradshaw, Peter. *The Guardian*. May 21, 2016.
D'Angelo, Mike. *The A.V. Club*. December 19, 2016.

Douglas, Edward. *New York Daily News.* December 29, 2016.

Gleiberman, Owen. *Variety.* May 21, 2016.

Holden, Stephen. *New York Times.* December 22, 2016.

Kohn, Eric. *IndieWire.* May 21, 2016.

Lemire, Christy. *RogerEbert.com.* January 5, 2017.

Nashawaty, Chris. *Entertainment Weekly.* January 5, 2017.

Rooney, David. *Hollywood Reporter.* May 21, 2016.

QUOTES

Job center floor manager: "There's a special number if you've been diagnosed as dyslexic."

Daniel: "Right, can you give us that 'coz with computers, I'm dyslexic."

Job center floor manager: "You'll find it online, sir."

TRIVIA

The film was shot in chronological order.

AWARDS

Nominations:

British Acad. 2016: Actress—Supporting (Squires), Director (Loach), Film, Orig. Screenplay

I SAW THE LIGHT

The story of Hank Williams.
—Movie tagline

Box Office: $1.6 Million

Hank Williams is one of the few truly immortal figures in Country music, so talented and important that his legacy survived years of posthumous revision by his first wife Audrey Williams. Audrey pushed Hank to stardom, acted as his de facto manager, and through her love, emotional abuse, and infidelity, inspired some of the greatest songs ever written. Without Audrey, Hank Williams would never have written "Your Cheatin' Heart," but he was also so happy to be rid of her that, when they divorced, he staged his next wedding to Billie Jean Jones as a public event, akin to a concert. When Hank died, Audrey kept on managing him. She renamed their son Hank Williams Jr., and started managing his music career, is rumored to have paid Jones for the legal right to call herself Hank's widow, and produced a movie, *Your Cheatin' Heart* (1964) that revised the story of their life together. Colin Escott's *Hank Williams: The Biography* set the record straight and it's from that book that Marc Abraham's movie *I Saw The Light* draws its version of Williams' life. Like too many biopics, it is far too cowed by Williams' legacy as the most important country musician who ever lived to be much of a drama.

The script hits every major event in Williams' life with the obviousness audiences will have come to expect from mid-budget biographies of this stripe.

We meet Williams (Tom Hiddleston) mid-song, bathed in a heavenly golden glow, looking more god than man. Then the film proceeds to gently if unconvincingly humanize him. He marries sweetheart Audrey Mae Sheppard (Elizabeth Olsen) at a gas station, becoming a half-hearted father to Sheppard's daughter Lycretia (played as a toddler by Tabitha Faith and Ellie Foco as a pre-adolescent). He tries to turn his regionally popular radio program into a national sensation with the help of his gargoyle-esque stage mother Lillie (Cherry Jones), who does not care for the encroaching presence of Audrey. Audrey also thinks she knows what is best for Hank's career, and it conveniently involves her singing with him during broadcasts. People, including the station managers and the members of Hank's band, find Audrey's voice to be a blight on Hank's recordings. Her atonal wailing threatens to derail him, but when cooler heads tell Hank he needs to fire his wife from the band, she threatens to leave him. Not helping their marriage are Hank and Audrey's mutually wandering eyes. By the time Hank's music has gotten much traction in the public conscious, Audrey and Hank have broken up and gotten back together, had a son, and can not stand each other for more than a few months at a time.

Hank's professional life is organized around his one goal: playing the Grand Ole Opry, a country institution. Making it to the opry would make Williams a sensation and grant him the approval he so craved in his private life. He signs with Fred Rose (Bradley Whitford) and agrees to let him manage his career and a handful of Rose's canny decisions do eventually launch him to the national stage. The issue is that Williams' relationships, as well as the drugs he takes to handle his Spina bifida, and the alcohol he uses to medicate his depression and disappointment constantly threaten to derail his progress. Williams cannot handle fame anymore than he can his own id and libido. He meets two women—Billie Jean Jones (Maddie Hasson) and Bobbie Jett (Wrenn Schmidt)—at roughly the same time, marrying one and impregnating the latter. Before he can work out the steps towards late onset maturity he is killed in a car accident on his way to a concert.

The events of *I Saw The Light* are schematically shapeless except in their inexorable pull towards Williams' death. There are far too many moments where Williams prophetically explains something important to him in a way completely inorganic to the character created by the film and the mood of the piece. This did not have to be an issue except that director Marc Abrahams keeps trying to force an importance and shape to a life that was only important after Williams' death, because his art rendered him legendary. His marriages and substance abuse problems informed the songs, so they must be important to the story of Williams. Except they do not play half as compellingly as cinema because Abraham, like too many before him, expect his hero going through these events to carry the film, instead of the other way around. On top of that, Abraham adds not one but two kinds of narration to the story to keep it on track, as if the events did not speak for themselves.

Stylistically, the movie is only about one third as strong as it needs to be to get by on facts alone. Abraham, a prolific producer, has only directed one other film, the forgettable *Flash of Genius* (2008), also based on a true story. He has almost found a visual and dramatic language to make these stories come to life as more than filmed encyclopedia entries. He has a way with space that is very appealing and to which it is easy to become accustomed. His script is entirely too obvious, but he finds a lot of wonderful moments that are more compelling than more flashy historical moments. It is much less interesting watching Williams show off an embryonic version of "Your Cheatin' Heart" than it is to see him giggling like a child at the newly installed electric garage door in his house. The film's strongest moments are the ones that can't be proved, that Abrahams likely invented, like the garage door or when Audrey and Hank harmonize together while singing Hank Jr. to sleep. The whole endeavor needed more confidence in its invention, and what little it has is mostly courtesy of veteran cinematographer Dante Spinotti, who helps each of Abraham's environments and liberties with the truth feel not just necessary but vital. Spinotti creates a moody and realistic portrait of the American south that Williams haunted, each beam of light from the sky or the stage etching his destiny into history books. The sundry streets and backwaters come to arresting, beautifully expressive life through Spinotti's lighting. Performers, all of them adequately suited to their roles, look nearly divine through Spinotti's lens even though Abraham tries as hard as he can to bring them down to earth by focusing on their foibles and weaknesses. Williams' story will always be too thorny and important to ever be captured in a fiction film as long as filmmakers remain awed by his legacy.

Scout Tafoya

CREDITS

Hank Williams: Tom Hiddleston
Audrey Williams: Elizabeth Olsen
Fred Rose: Bradley Whitford
Lillie Jones: Cherry Jones
Billie Jean Jones: Maddie Hasson

James Dolan: David Krumholtz
Origin: United States
Language: English
Released: 2015
Production: Aaron L. Gilbert, Brett Ratner, G. Marq Roswell, Marc Abraham; RatPac Entertainment; released by Bron Studios
Directed by: Marc Abraham
Written by: Marc Abraham
Cinematography by: Dante Spinotti
Music by: Aaron Zigman
Music Supervisor: Carter Little
Editing: Alan Heim; Merideth Boswell
Art Direction: Rob Simons
Costumes: Lahly Poore
MPAA rating: R
Running time: 123 minutes

REVIEWS

Barker, Andrew. *Variety*. September 11, 2015.
Dargis, Manohla. *New York Times*. March 24, 2016.
Erbland, Kate. *IndieWire*. March 23, 2016.
Halligan, Fionnuala. *Screen Daily*. September 12, 2015.
Huddleston, Tom. *Time Out London*. September 12, 2015.
Keough, Peter. *Boston Globe*. March 31, 2016.
Murray, Noel. *IndieWire*. September 11, 2015.
Roeper, Richard. *Chicago Sun Times*. March 30, 2016.
Scherstuhl, Alan. *Village Voice*. March 22, 2016.
Turan, Kenneth. *LA Times*. March 24, 2016.

QUOTES

Hank Williams: "What is it with me? Every woman in my life has kids. Every one of 'em. Before I even get to 'em."
Bobbie Jett: "You're obviously very attractive to mothers, Hank."

TRIVIA

Tom Hiddleston was 35 years old when he made the film; Hank Williams died at the age of 29.

ICE AGE: COLLISION COURSE

One small step. One giant mess.
—Movie tagline

Box Office: $64 Million

Why are they still releasing *Ice Age* movies in theatres? The answer is probably purely financial. (2012's *Ice Age: Continental Drift* grossed over $870 million at the international box office.) But the franchise feels cheaper than ever. Blue Sky Studios never exactly set the animation world on fire with their work on the *Ice Age* movies, but, at this point, their efforts just reek of complacency and laziness. *Ice Age: Collison Course* looks like a movie that your child would discover five menus down on the "Acceptable Family Movies" menu on Netflix. Everything about it seems to suggest that it's a straight-to-streaming rip-off of another, better movie. Alas, *Ice Age: Collison Course* is, in fact, a first-run movie, even though it rarely lives up to even that meager of a label.

To say that the story of *Ice Age: Collison Course* is thin would be the understatement of the year. If you want an easy way to recognize how non-existent the story is, consider how much screen time is given to Scrat, the franchise's saber-toothed squirrel/Wile E. Coyote surrogate. Scrat started off as a fun slapstick aside in the first movie, but he's since progressed to become the filmmakers' go-to distraction to keep the audiences from realizing that the screenwriters only composed 55 minutes' worth of story for the feature film. The interminably long Scrat interludes in *Collison Course* are reminiscent of Disney's *Cinderella* (1950) in a way. Yes, *Cinderella* was beautifully animated and bolstered with catchy songs, but the story was so barely there that Disney supplemented the story with about 20 minutes of cat-and-mouse nonsense.

Ice Age: Collison Course does not come close to matching the technical virtuosity of *Cinderella*, but it similarly thinks that it can gloss over its plot-holes with wacky animal hijinks. Unfortunately, the whole movie is not much more than those animal hijinks mixed with some of the hackiest sitcom storytelling in recent memory. The writers of *The Big Bang Theory* would blush at the dusty plot devices that director Mike Thurmeier tries to get away with in *Collison Course*, and the audience should too.

The film opens with Scrat setting off the film's ticking clock. In his relentless, eternal pursuit of an acorn, Scrat discovered an ancient underground alien space ship (no, really), turns it on, and sends it shooting out into the cosmos. As Scrat screams through outer space, the flying saucer inadvertently sends a series of planet-killing asteroids hurtling towards Earth.

Meanwhile, the *Ice Age* gang of inexplicably chummy prehistorical animals are dealing with broad personal issues that would not provide enough story for a single episode of *Modern Family*. Wooly mammoth Manny (Ray Romano) and his wife Ellie (Queen Latifah) are preparing themselves for their daughter Peaches' upcoming marriage to the irresponsible Julian (Adam Devine). Take that in for a moment. A movie about

anthropomorphic mammoths has a wedding anxiety storyline. (Sigh.) Sloth Sid (John Leguizamo) is dealing with a recent heartbreak, and saber-toothed tiger Diego (Dennis Leary) and his mate Shira (Jennifer Lopez) have decided they want to start a family, but children are terrified of them, because, well, they are big scary tigers. Unfortunately, the script tries to update these clichéd plotlines with interjecting them with a lot of "current" humor, i.e. jokes about hashtags and the like. The results aren't pretty.

Eventually, the animal realize that Scrat's asteroids are going to destroy the planet, so they journey to the site of previous asteroid crashes, the fabled Geotopia, where Manny and friends meet an immortal race of animals led by the Shangri Llama. (Sigh.) One of Manny's travelling buddies, Buck, a one-eyed weasel of some sort (voiced with aplomb by Simon Pegg, the only voice actor who appears to be trying), realizes that they can use Geotopia's magnetic meteor fragments to help repel the incoming asteroids, but it would mean that the citizens of Geotopia have to give up their immortality in return.

The "conflicts" are pure sitcom fodder. Diego learns to be comfortable around children, Sid finds new love, Manny realizes that he has to let his daughter grow up. It's unsettlingly how painfully conventional every story beat is when you realize that the movie is all about talking animals trying to prevent extinction-level events.

But the *Ice Age* sequels have rarely exhibited any stakes, on story or on character levels. While the first film did spin together a somewhat engaging tale about disparate animals banding together to survive a global climate change, the resulting films have just devolved into loud, farting, burping mess, offering audiences a master class in the law of diminishing returns.

Audiences did not flock to see *Ice Age: Collison Course* in the same way they did with *Continental Drift*. (This film made less than half of what its predecessor earned internationally.) While that's a sign that people are becoming less and less amused with *Ice Age*'s tired antics, it still represented over $400 million in box office receipts. And, regrettably, the *Ice Age* films offer up such a pervasive sense of cheapness that the existing profit margins might mean this franchise is not quite yet dead and buried.

Tom Burns

CREDITS

Manny: Ray Romano
Sid: John Leguizamo
Diego: Denis Leary

Ellie: Queen Latifah

Shira: Jennifer Lopez

Julian: Adam DeVine

Origin: United States

Language: English

Released: 2016

Production: Lori Forte; released by Blue Sky Studios Inc., Twentieth Century Fox Animation

Directed by: Michael Thurmeier

Written by: Michael J. Wilson; Michael Berg; Yoni Brenner

Cinematography by: Renato Falcao

Music by: John Debney

Sound: Michael Silvers

Music Supervisor: John Houlihan

Editing: James Palumbo

Art Direction: Michael Knapp

MPAA rating: PG

Running time: 94 minutes

REVIEWS

Bradshaw, Peter. *The Guardian*. July 18, 2016.

Derakhshani, Tirdad. *Philadelphia Inquirer*. July 21, 2016.

Dowd, A.A. *The A.V. Club*. July 20, 2016.

Hazelton, John. *Screen International*. Jun 22, 2016.

Mirchandani, Raakhee. *New York Daily News*. July 20, 2016.

Moore, Roger. *Movie Nation*. July 27, 2016.

Rechtshaffen, Michael. *Hollywood Reporter*. Jun 20, 2016.

Russo, Tom. *Boston Globe*. July 21, 2016.

Stewart, Sara. *New York Post*. July 21, 2016.

Wloszczyna, Susan. *RogerEbert.com*. July 20, 2016.

QUOTES

Sid: "Everybody has somebody and all I've got is my boyish good looks and this Mariachi band."

TRIVIA

Not including spin-offs, this film makes *Ice Age* the first computer-animated theatrical franchise to feature five installments.

IN A VALLEY OF VIOLENCE

> *Keep your finger on the trigger.*
> —Movie tagline

Box Office: $53,647

Having made a fairly solid name for himself with slow-burn indie horror films like *The House of the Devil* (2009), *The Innkeepers* (2011), and *The Sacrament* (2013), writer/director Ti West has taken a hard right turn away from horror genre filmmaking for his latest effort *In a Valley of Violence*. With his newest film, West has gone Western and upped the ante in terms of star power by casting Ethan Hawke and John Travolta as his leads. The resulting adventure is enjoyable, and fans of West's will feel his directorial style at work in his ability to draw out a scene with a distinctive pleasure-delay characteristic that he's honed beautifully thus far in his career.

In a Valley of Violence opens with plains drifter named Paul (Hawke) trotting through middle of nowhere America with his trusty dog Abby. Silent and stoic, Hawke's Paul fits the classic western hero archetype almost to the point of cliché, but West deftly lets us get to know the character a bit better via banter with Abby. Yet *In a Valley of Violence* is more than a tale of a man and his dog, there's a valley ahead and it's full of violence as Paul, and the audience, soon find out.

Looking to rest up before continuing their long journey to Mexico, Paul and Abby stumble into the po-dunk town of Denton, which seems the kind of place that may have once been prosperous but is now one step away from a ghost town. No sooner has Paul bellied up to the bar for a well-deserved drink, then *In a Valley of Violence* swipes a few pages from classic Westerns like *Shane* (1953) or *High Noon* (1952) when Paul is forced into action due to nothing he's really said or done. In short, Paul get's messed with by some local bullies and before he knows it, he's smack dab in the middle of a fight. And as is the case in most fights with bullies, this one does not end well for anyone involved. As audiences discovered in *John Wick* (2014), it's not wise to come between a sociopath trying to go straight and his dog and here, the results here are equally violent and chaotic.

As noted, the film oftentimes comes across as a Tarantino knock-off yet it still manages to pull together its own sense of style. One way *In a Valley of Violence* echoes Tarantino is in it's characters chattiness. Every scene is loaded with wordiness, yet the witty banter between characters has a different vibe and reason than Tarantino's in that, here, the chatting is much more practical. Characters here share realistic and usually strikingly funny observations that capture the moment perfectly. This use of dialogue also comes off a bit like a screwball comedy. *In a Valley of Violence* is very much a pastiche of styles and influences, most notably the aforementioned slapstick/screwball comedy but there's also touches of horror as well as classic Western and revenge film motifs. All these disparate parts come together as a whole by the time the film ends.

In a Valley of Violence isn't all male posturing and Taissa Farmiga as lonely hotel proprietor Mary-Anne provides some solid female presence in the film. Mary-Anne becomes attracted to the strong and silent Paul and sees him as a way to get out of one-horse-town

Denton. But as many archetypal Western film females have learned over the years, men like Paul tend to be loners who prefer to ramble on without any attachments. Yet here, the doe-eyed Farmiga brings a feeling of independence and strength to her character rather than falling into a classic female victim of neediness as is usually the case in classic Westerns.

Also excellent is John Travolta as Denton's put-upon town Marshal. Since it's his cocky, dimwitted son Gilly (an outstanding James Ransone) who not only kicks off the chain reaction of violence and payback but perpetuates and exacerbates every issue that befalls the cast of characters, the Marshal must play father, lawman, and advocate for common sense and keeping the peace. That's a lot of hats to wear, and the Marshal has more than a little trouble keeping them from disarray.

With so many plates spinning style-wise (classic Western, slapstick, revenge) it's kind of a wonder that *In a Valley of Violence* works as well as it does. Many films that have a collision of styles often times get almost segregated in their own inconsistencies. But West manages to pull it all off somehow and that's due to his slow moving, tense plot, clever insights from characters and an excellent cast which also includes terrific character actors Larry Fessenden, Toby Huss, and Karen Gillan. There's also great tension and striking scenes of violence that thankfully punctuate the payoffs that take place throughout the film. *In a Valley of Violence* is indeed a solid throwback Western that also manages to feel new and timely.

Don R. Lewis

CREDITS

Paul: Ethan Hawke
Marshal: John Travolta
Mary Anne: Taissa Farmiga
Gilly: James Ransone
Ellen: Karen Gillan
Origin: United States
Language: English
Released: 2016
Production: Jason Blum, Jacob Jaffke, Peter Phok, Ti West; released by Blumhouse Productions
Directed by: Ti West
Written by: Ti West
Cinematography by: Eric Robbins
Music by: Jeff Grace
Editing: Ti West
Art Direction: RA Arancio-Parrain
Costumes: Malgosia Turzanska
Production Design: Jade Healy

MPAA rating: R
Running time: 104 minutes

REVIEWS

Andersen, Soren. *Seattle Times*. October 20, 2016.
Bowen, Chuck. *Slant Magazine*. October 17, 2016.
Catsoulis, Jeannette. *New York Times*. October 20, 2016.
Ehrlich, David. *IndieWire*. June 15, 2016.
Fragoso, Sam. *TheWrap*. October 19, 2016.
O'Malley, Sheila. *RogerEbert.com*. October 21, 2016.
Rowe, Amy. *New York Daily News*. October 19, 2016.
Savlov, Marc. *Austin Chronicle*. October 19, 2016.
Wolfe, April. *Village Voice*. October 22, 2016.
Zacharek, Stephanie. *Time*. October 27, 2016.

TRIVIA

This is John Travolta's first western.

INDEPENDENCE DAY: RESURGENCE

Humanity's last stand.
—Movie tagline

Box Office: $103.1 Million

The world may not have been ready for the alien invasion of 1996, but movie audiences certainly were. That summer, Roland Emmerich and Dean Devlin's blockbuster film was a callback to the post-Atomic era of the 1950s when science fiction warned us that outside beings were intent of our destruction. *Independence Day* was the biggest hit of the year and helped usher in a crest of an impending wave of disaster films, where big casts ran away from meteors, comets, volcanoes, and every temperature of weather imaginable. Emmerich himself has ridden that wave for the bulk of his career following his success with the likes of *Godzilla* (1998), *The Day After Tomorrow* (2004), and *2012* (2009) until there were practically no more landmarks, cities or countries to destroy. Nevertheless, 20 years later somebody thought it was a good idea to mine this territory well past the statute of moviegoer limitations on nostalgia and hold its very fans in contempt for anything they liked about it in the first place.

Presented in an alternate timeline from our own, the world has utilized the alien technology our heroes brought down in 1996 to create early warning systems included on bases on both the Earth's moon and Mars. Jake Morrison (Liam Hemsworth) is a hotshot pilot in Earth Space Defense who lost his parents in the original attack. His former friend and now rival, Dylan (Jessie Usher), is the son of Captain Steven Hiller (Will Smith's hero from the first film who is now deceased once the actor chose not to return for the sequel.) David Levinson (Jeff Goldblum), now working as a researcher at Area 51, is brought to Africa to check out a downed alien ship and discovers that a distress call was sent back through the galaxy in case their mission was a failure.

A more prescient warning comes courtesy of those that retained a psychic link to the aliens after direct contact with them. Former President Whitmore (Bill Pullman) is a shell of his former self kept out of the public view and Dr. Okun (Brent Spiner) wakes out of a 20-year coma, both having visions that either translate to a large spherical object or a hula hoop given some of the Hudsucker-like drawings. When conflicting hypotheses within the scientific and military communities confuse benevolence with an outright threat, the battle begins once again with a Queen Commander beset on drilling into the Earth's core. Some will fight. Others will run. But all will be lost within a film that dooms itself to failure at every layer of the process.

The first film wore its reference points on its sleeve proudly, and even through its more ludicrous machinations, such as hacking alien hardware with a man-made computer virus, it still maintained the sense of fun it so clearly tried to grasp. It takes not even ten minutes for the sequel to work backwards with more annoying introductions than any Transformers film and heroics that are more likely to draw a hand over the eyes rather than a wiped brow. Once the stakes are finally established, there is never a sense that anything is really going to be different. Aliens arrive, there is division on their purpose and then they attack. All that is left to do is to marvel at how the rest of the film feels like a fan edit of the original; a fan who managed to chop over a half hour out with no sense of story structure, purpose, or vision.

"That is definitely bigger than the last one," Levinson—and his dad (Judd Hirsch)—say in regards to the spacecraft 3,000 miles in diameter that not a single radar could detect. It is the only indication that Emmerich and his four co-scripters have in growing this sequel into the kind of behemoth that audiences want to come back to. This slow reverse in gravity takes on a two-fold complex as characters returning to Earth in a mooncraft can casually observe cars, airplanes, and buildings slowly sucked into the atmosphere without the slightest fear of being caught in the crossfire. Only when gravity reverses itself do any of them plot to finally turn the wheel. Though managing to take out a few of the contractually-obligated returnees, Hirsch as Levinson Sr. is given a reprieve after outrunning—in just his speedy fishing boat—a debris-laden tidal wave that makes the climaxes of *The Abyss* (1989) and *Deep Impact* (1997) look like splashes in a swimming pool.

There is not a single person in front of the camera here that gives the slightest mannerism that any of them want to be here. Not the returning cast nor the next generation of alien fighters or the least of which Robert Loggia who, in his final film appearance, sits silent in a wheelchair beset with Alzheimer's Disease with a sad, symbolic irony. Twenty years ago, the mixture of homeland destruction with top-of-the-line special effects was enough to draw people's cheers. The technology is even more advanced now and science fiction ideas are as strong as they have ever been. None of this applies to *Resurgence*, which follows the same attack-run-repel structure of the first film and exists in a timeline of actual reality where audiences have basically seen it all and then some. Many such films may owe themselves to the chord that *Independence Day* struck in July of 1996 but few have felt as empty and disenfranchised as its sequel. A more proper title than "Resurgence" would have been "Regression."

Erik Childress

CREDITS

Jake Morrison: Liam Hemsworth
David Levinson: Jeff Goldblum
Dylan Hiller: Jessie T. Usher
President Whitmore: Bill Pullman
Patricia Whitmore: Maika Monroe
President Lanford: Sela Ward
Origin: United States
Language: English
Released: 2016
Production: Dean Devlin, Harald Kloser, Roland Emmerich; released by Centropolis Entertainment Inc., Twentieth Century Fox Film Corp.
Directed by: Roland Emmerich
Written by: Roland Emmerich; James A. Woods; Nicolas Wright; James Vanderbilt; Dean Devlin
Cinematography by: Markus Forderer
Music by: Harald Kloser; Thomas Wander
Sound: Paul N.J. Ottosson
Editing: Adam Wolfe
Art Direction: Patrick M. Sullivan, Jr.
Costumes: Lisy Christl
Production Design: Barry Chusid
MPAA rating: PG-13
Running time: 120 minutes

REVIEWS

Berardinelli, James. *ReelViews*. June 26, 2016.
Bibbiani, William. *CraveOnline*. June 24, 2016.
Douglas, Edward. *Den of Geek*. June 23, 2016.

Harkness, Alistair. *Scotsman.* July 4, 2016.

Johanson, MaryAnn. *Flick Filosopher.* June 29, 2016.

Lane, Anthony. *New Yorker.* June 27, 2016.

Mayer, Dominick. *Consequence of Sound.* June 24, 2016.

Ranson, Kevin A. *MovieCrypt.com.* July 8, 2016.

Snider, Eric D. *EricDSnider.com.* September 9, 2016.

Turan, Kenneth. *Los Angeles Times.* June 24, 2016.

QUOTES

Dylan Hiller: "It's the Fourth of July, let's show 'em some fireworks."

TRIVIA

The Earth Space Defense Program in the film has space stations located on Earth, the Moon, Mars, and Rhea, which is the second-largest moon of Saturn.

AWARDS

Nominations:

Golden Raspberries 2016: Worst Director (Emmerich), Worst Picture, Worst Screenplay, Worst Sequel/Prequel

INDIGNATION

Based on the novel by Philip Roth.
—Movie tagline

Box Office: $3.4 Million

Philip Roth is a brilliant prose stylist whose deft social portraiture, ribald humor, and emphatic moral inquiries on sex and identity are supple, comic, and enthralling. They cut deep. Roth's novels, with their complex social and historical concerns, idiosyncratic structures, and complex use of the narrator protagonist, especially the Zuckerman books, are exceptionally hard to pull off as films.

Seven of his novels or story collections have now been adapted, and the bulk are deeply unsatisfying, from Larry Pierce's version of *Goodbye, Columbus* (1971) to Ewan McGregor's strained and deeply unfortunate *American Pastoral* (2016). So much has to go right in accurately capturing the language, manners, and the milieu. Some very talented directors have failed the writer spectacularly, like Robert Benton's *The Human Stain* (2003), with Anthony Hopkins as the tormented black man passing as a Jew, or Barry Levinson's *The Humbling* (2015), with the egregiously wrong Al Pacino as a washed-up Shakespearean actor.

The most exacting and thrilling Roth adaptation, Alex Ross Perry's superb *Listen Up Philip* (2014) braids together, very loosely, strands of Roth's *The Ghost Writer* (1979) with William Gaddis' novel, *The Recognitions* (1955), in charting the fractious relationship between an ascendant young writer and the celebrated now blocked novelist. The movie has the solidity and density of the novel fused with the radical technique of film, like the narrator whose descriptive analysis colors the complex psychological portraits of the characters.

An adaptation of Roth's same-titled novel (2008), his 29th book, *Indignation* marks the directing debut of James Schamus, a writer, producer, and former art-house film distributor. As a creative talent, Schamus is best known for his long and distinguished partnership with Ang Lee, including *The Ice Storm* (1997), from the novel by Rick Moody. The movie adaptation *Indignation* is a lucid, intelligent, and mostly successful translation of a vital piece of contemporary literature. The tone and form are novelistic, varied slightly from Roth's formal architecture though retaining most of the particulars of the story. Set in 1951, the film is permeated by a kind of primal fear and national trauma of the Korean War.

Schamus has employed an interesting circular structure, a kind of double prologue that intertwines two different framing stories in binding the two lead characters. The first is a flash forward that reveals a character in a care facility studying the flower-shaped patterns of the wallpaper and the second is a combat sequence as a North Korean soldier pursues an American infantryman inside a bunker that ends with the sound of gunfire.

The proper story begins with the funeral of Goldberg, and introduces the protagonist, Marcus Messner (Logan Lerman), who also narrates. He is bright, studious, and ambitious son of a kosher Newark butcher who is deeply relieved at the prospect of leaving home to attend college, in the Midwest, at the (fictional) Winesburg College, in Ohio. As the dutiful only child, Marcus has dealt with the burden of expectations. Now he feels suffocated by their demands, particularly his overbearing and irrational father (Danny Burstein) and his increasingly wound-up mother, (Linda Emond).

At the pastoral Midwestern college, Marcus quickly discovers a new set of social conditions and deeply regimental and conservative customs he must negotiate. The most galling for this atheist Jew is the compulsory weekly chapel attendance. The learning and intellectual fervor is deeply exciting. Marcus insists on his own autonomy, rejecting an offer to join a Jewish fraternity. He takes a job at the library.

The women are also intoxicating, and he quickly falls for the blonde, beautiful, and elusive Olivia Hutton (Sarah Gadon). The sight of her legs angled and free says everything. Marcus works up the nerve to ask her out. Their date, which begins nervously at the town's only French restaurant, ends with the two parked in the car Marcus has borrowed from his roommate. The deeply intimate sexual moment the two share rapidly unhinges him. Marcus is unable to process emotionally the implications of Olivia's provocation. Rather than feeling exhilarated, Marcus is ripped apart by the shame and jealousy, and it creates an awkward rift. The confusion carries over to his other relationships with his roommates, and he eventually transfers into an austere single space.

That incident yields the most spellbinding passage in the film, a voluble and sustained 16-minute verbal joust that plays out between Marcus and Caudwell (Tracy Letts), the censorious college dean who has summoned him to account for his behavior. The scene is taken almost verbatim from the book, though Schamus alters the order slightly. In the novel, the scene takes up about 30 pages. The deft camerawork of Christopher Blauvelt accentuates the acrimony and fury. The staging and cutting are sharp and vigorous, developing a horrifying anger and dread.

Caudwell makes a series of bristling inferences, charging Marcus with being obstinate, selfish, and unable to compromise, and most damaging, trying to conceal or deny his religion. In turn, Caudwell is affronted by Marcus repeated habit of breaking up the conversation by calling him "sir," and his deference to the militant Marxist philosopher Bertrand Russell and his highly polemical essay, *Why I Am Not a Christian* (1927). Letts is not only a terrific actor; he is a Pulitzer-winning playwright, for *August: Osage County* (2008). He has a writer's knowledge of rhythm and speed. He uses his height ominously, pivoting to stand directly behind Marcus or strategically using his hands to drive home his points. Defensive though scared, Marcus valiantly counters the dean until the duet becomes simply too much. He literally comes apart and violently vomits inside the dean's immaculately adorned office.

Like the novel, *Indignation* is a mystery about fate, circumstance, and chance. The double framing device Schamus utilizes contrasts Marcus and Olivia in particularly interesting ways, probing the very question of existence and consciousness. Marcus awakens in the hospital to discover Olivia back in his life. A subsequent visit by his mother, who learns some intimate details about the vulnerable, damaged Olivia, leads to her emotionally blackmailing Marcus. The key late passage from the book is the movie's leitmotif, "the terrible, the incomprehensible way one's most banal, incidental, even comical choices achieve the most disproportionate result."

Olivia vanishes late in the story, and her fate is enigmatic and unresolved, all the more so by the multiple ways to read the opening and closing images. Roth reveals the circumstances of Marcus about one-fourth into the book. Schamus is more ambiguous, though traces and clues are stitched throughout. Like many late period Roth novels, the action is more compressed. Schamus is good on elisions and interpretation. He also makes some judicious cuts. If there is a weakness to the film, the final scenes are rushed and feel too hurried over. What is missing from the movie is hallucinatory climax, the blinding snowstorm, and reckless display of male sexual entitlement.

The actors are sensational. Lerman is quite good at locating the deeply vulnerable though recognizable strain brought about by his social and sexual estrangement, the essential confusion and disruption of assimilation. A regular in the films of David Cronenberg, Gadon combines a sexual bravado with something harder and more difficult to grasp. The hard fluctuations of her character are heartbreaking.

Schamus has not completely solved the structural and formal problems of adapting Roth. A perfect Philip Roth adaptation is likely impossible to achieve. This is as good as to be expected. *Indignation* is subtle, cryptic, and beautifully made.

Patrick Z. McGavin

CREDITS

Marcus: Logan Lerman
Olivia: Sarah Gadon
Dean Caldwell: Tracy Letts
Esther: Linda Emond
Max Messner: Danny Burstein
Origin: United States
Language: English
Released: 2016
Production: Anthony Bregman, Rodrigo Teixeira, James Schamus; released by Bing Feng Bao Entertainment, Likely Story, RT Features
Directed by: James Schamus
Written by: James Schamus
Cinematography by: Christopher Blauvelt
Music by: Jay Wadley
Sound: Lewis Goldstein
Editing: Andrew Marcus
Art Direction: Derek Wang
Costumes: Amy Roth
Production Design: Inbal Weinberg
MPAA rating: R
Running time: 110 minutes

REVIEWS

Baumgarten, Marjorie. *Austin Chronicle*. August 10, 2016.
Edelstein, David. *New York Magazine*. July 28, 2016.
Holden, Stephen. *New York Times*. July 28, 2016.
LaSalle, Mick. *San Francisco Chronicle*. August 4, 2016.
Macdonald, Moira. *Seattle Times*. August 11, 2016.
Morgenstern, Joe. *Wall Street Journal*. July 28, 2016.
Phillips, Michael. *Chicago Tribune*. August 4, 2016.
Rooney, David. *Hollywood Reporter*. January 27, 2016.
Turan, Kenneth. *Los Angeles Times*. July 28, 2016.
Zuckerman, Esther. *The A.V Club*. July 28, 2016.

QUOTES

Max Messner: "I don't care what it suggests, Dean Caldwell, I will not be condemned on the basis of no evidence."

TRIVIA

This film is the directorial debut of James Schamus.

INFERNO

Every clue will take him deeper.
   —Movie tagline

Box Office: $34.3 Million

In the opening moments of *Inferno*, the screen version of the Dan Brown bestseller, erstwhile Harvard symbologist Robert Langdon (Tom Hanks) wakes up in a hospital in Florence, Italy, with no memory of who he is or how he got there but with occasional furtive visions of the tortures of Hell itself. Most moviegoers will be able to sympathize because while many of them probably went to see the previous films based on Brown's books focusing on Langdon, *The Da Vinci Code* (2006) and *Angels & Demons* (2009), it is unlikely that they actually remember much of anything about those deeply dopey movies except for the most excruciatingly silly moments. If they are lucky, amnesia will strike them again as soon as the film ends so that they quickly and blessedly forget having endured a film so alternately laughable and logy that it almost makes its predecessors seem borderline competent by comparison.

This time around, Langdon has barely woken up in that hospital room with a head wound received during an attack he cannot recall when he barely escapes another attack on his life with the aid of Dr. Sienna Brooks (Felicity Jones), a brilliant British prodigy who is familiar with Langdon and his work. It eventually transpires that billionaire bioengineer Benjamin Zobrist (Ben Foster), despairing that the world is heading towards imminent self-destruction through overpopulation, has taken it

upon himself to solve the problem by devising a virus that, once unleashed, will swiftly kill off at least half the world's population and give the planet a new lease on life. Although Zobrist kills himself in order to ensure that he will not reveal the location of the virus if he is captured before it is set off, he has inexplicably created a series of clues designed to point to the hiding place that are based around references to the works of Dante Alighieri, specifically in Botticelli's painting of Dante's depiction of Hell laid out in *The Divine Comedy*.

Despite being sufficiently rattled in the noggin from the earlier attack so as to be unable to remember the word "coffee," Langdon is able to look at a copy of the painting that was found on him and not only suss out all the differences between it and the original but immediately grasp what they mean. From there, he and Sienna are off to follow where the clues lead in an attempt to find the virus before it goes off, even though his injury means that he is still occasionally plagued with visions that suggest that Dante's Inferno has sprung to life all around him. Meanwhile, they are being pursued by representatives of the World Health Organization, who are apparently convinced that Langdon is in cahoots with Zobrist and his followers. Also in pursuit is another shadowy organization run by Harry Sims (Irrfan Khan) that is somehow involved with the goings-on and needs to find Langdon as well. Further perils along the way occur in the form of a rogue agent (Omar Sy) who wants to acquire the virus himself in order to sell it to the highest bidder and an assassin (Ana Ularu) who failed to kill Langdon in that opening hospital ambush and is determined to finish her job.

Like its predecessors, *Inferno* is a film that offers viewers the chance to experience a mystery-thriller that contains no real mystery to speak of and no actual thrills. Part of the fun in a story like this for viewers is to be able to play along and see if they can tease out and decipher the clues before the characters do. However, unless they happen to be a Dante scholar, there is no way that most viewers will be able to penetrate any of the clues for themselves and therefore have to sit there passively while having everything spelled out to them at excruciating length in seemingly endless spouts of raw, untreated exposition that explains, sort of, but never edifies. The explanations also help to diminish the thriller aspect as well by constantly forcing the characters to pause in the middle of what is, after all, a race against time to prevent the murder of half the people on the planet, to once again spell out this, that, and the other thing. That said, the action isn't exactly of the nail-biting variety even when the characters stop yakking and make with the running and jumping and whatnot as director Ron Howard (also returning to the Langdon fold for the third time) stages the scenes with all the verve of someone who clearly has no burning interest in telling this particular story but who knows that, in the wake of a couple of recent flops, he needs to make a film that is all but guaranteed to be a hit at the box office. (That said, the film wound up coming in a surprising second in its opening weekend, falling behind the second weekend of *Boo! A Madea Halloween* [2016].)

To be fair, many of the other problems with the film—the lumpy dialogue, the paper-thin characters, the increasingly nonsensical plot developments, and the absolute lack of anything that might be mistaken for a sense of humor—come straight from the original source material and to change them in any fundamental ways might alienate the audiences that made huge hits out of *The Da Vinci Code* and *Angels & Demons*. As a result, blockbuster screenwriter David Koepp merely translates the material to the screen instead of trying to make it work in cinematic terms and when he does veer significantly from the original text, it is to take the one mildly interesting element on hand and replace it with the usual action film foolishness. As Langdon, the always-affable Tom Hanks does his best to make something out of the material but even he cannot disguise the fact that this is little more than a cash grab for him. Having survived the earlier films, he knows how to cruise through this nonsense with a minimum of fuss but his fellow co-stars appear stymied throughout by the increasingly ludicrous that they struggle in vain to transform into something vaguely plausible.

The problem with *Inferno* is not that it is a stupid film—although it is as dumb as can be from beginning to end—but that it is a stupid film that has somehow convinced itself that it is actually smart just because it tosses around a couple of Dante references. For all its stabs at being a film designed to challenge the mind while setting the heart racing, it is little more than the contemporary equivalent of one of those alternately dopey and draggy international thrillers that were all the rage in the Seventies that allowed the likes of George Kennedy, Sophia Loren, and Anthony Quinn (or Raf Vallone, if Quinn was unavailable) to pick grocery money with little effort outside of trying to make sense of the impenetrable plots. Amusingly, it begins with a voice on the soundtrack invoking the supposed inscription at the entrance to Hell cited by Dante in *The Divine Comedy*—"Abandon all hope, ye who enter here." Too bad no one thought to post those same words outside of theaters showing *Inferno* to warn unsuspecting moviegoers that they were about to spend eternity—or at least an eternity-feeling two hours—trapped in cinematic Hell.

Peter Sobczynski

CREDITS

Robert Langdon: Tom Hanks
Sienna Brooks: Felicity Jones
Christoph Bouchard: Omar Sy
Harry Sims: Irrfan Khan
Elizabeth Sinskey: Sidse Babett Knudsen
Origin: United States
Language: English
Released: 2016
Production: Brian Grazer, Ron Howard; released by Columbia Pictures, Imagine Entertainment, LStar Capital, Mid Atlantic Films
Directed by: Ron Howard
Written by: David Koepp
Cinematography by: Salvatore Totino
Music by: Hans Zimmer
Sound: Daniel Pagan
Editing: Tom Elkins; Daniel P. Hanley
Art Direction: Phil Sims
Costumes: Julian Day
Production Design: Peter Wenham
MPAA rating: PG-13
Running time: 121 minutes

REVIEWS

Burr, Ty. *Boston Globe*. October 27, 2016.
Cole, Jake. *Slant Magazine*. October 26, 2016.
Dargis, Manohla. *New York Times*. October 27, 2016.
Ebiri, Bilge. *Village Voice*. October 28, 2016.
Felperin, Leslie. *Hollywood Reporter*. October 9, 2016.
Harkness, Alistair. *Scotsman*. October 14, 2016.
Lodge, Guy. *Variety*. October 9, 2016.
O'Sullivan, Michael. *Washington Post*. October 27, 2016.
Solomons, Jason. *TheWrap*. October 10, 2016.
Turan, Kenneth. *Los Angeles Times*. October 27, 2016.

QUOTES

Robert Langdon: "The greatest sins in human history were committed in the name of love."

TRIVIA

The film is the sixth time Hans Zimmer has collaborated with Ron Howard.

THE INFILTRATOR

The true story of one man against the biggest drug cartel in history.
—Movie tagline

Box Office: $15.4 Million

Brad Furman's *The Infiltrator* is the ultimate contradictory text. Slick and impersonal, the movie is fast, sensationalized, and amateurish with all sides playing against the middle until it all collapses into banality and obviousness. It is a strange mix, too seriously intended to work as trash though its disreputable tone and crazy texture often make it strangely watchable.

The storytelling is inherently ridiculous, constantly introducing threads and ideas and rarely following up. The rhythm is choppy and bloated. Despite that, the movie commands a certain respect because the actors are sensational even when the material seriously undermines their ambition or attempts to work out something interesting. Furman is not really able to shape or conceive the material visually or give it propulsive lift the best thrillers achieve more realistically. He redeems himself, somewhat, with his excellent casting instincts. He lets his actors go and they certainly get lost.

The movie is based on the memoir of Robert Mazur, a federal customs agent and accounting specialist who deftly impersonated a corrupt businessman in order to insinuate himself inside the complex financial network of Pablo Escobar's notorious Medellin drug cartel. Bryan Cranston plays the central character, completing the beautiful irony of a career resurgence made possible by his remarkable work as the criminal drug mastermind on the great cable series, *Breaking Bad*. Cranston is versatile, a chameleon blessed with a face that goes either way. He has a dark switch, and he adopts his off-kilter, handsome looks to often very interesting ends. He excels at playing men who are hidden or constantly switching perspective.

The film is set during the height of the drug wars ravaging Miami in 1986, at the moment the Dade County coroner's office is renting out refrigerators from Burger King in order to properly store the dead. The movie is not binary politically, reducing everything to a story of good men pursuing bad people. It is more complex and layered. That turns out not entirely in the movie's favor. Furman never quite acknowledges the deeper structural flaw, the virtual absence of surprise or narrative discovery. Every significant scene feels too familiar or previously played out to achieve the necessary feeling of exhilaration or wonder.

The opening illustrates the dilemma. Mazur's undercover operative is introduced working a drug transaction at a bowling alley. The sting operation nearly kills him when his wire malfunctions and burns a hole into his chest. Brian DePalma wove in a much more tense and harrowing sequence from a nearly identical scenario in his masterful *Blow Out* (1981). The sequence underlines how the lack of originality is not just nagging, but a constant reminder of the wider failure of imagination. It is a work that reacts rather than asserts its own identity.

The double life weighs on Mazur psychologically in his effort at normalcy or sense of balance at home with his wife, Evelyn (Juliet Aubrey), or in his navigating the office politics of his demanding superior, Tischler (Amy Ryan). His competence and instincts set him apart. Turning down a chance to retire, that near death experience brings a clarity and deeper realization that interdiction is not sufficient response. The only way to unravel the business is circumventing the financial underpinning of the operation.

Another agency undercover operative, Emir Abreu (John Leguizamo), nervy, street smart, and savvy though ostracized by his peers because of his flamboyant tactics, provides the initial entry point through his connection to a low level Escobar-connected drug courier. Mazur seizes the opportunity to reinvent himself as Bob Musella, a preternaturally amoral New Jersey businessman whose great talent is grafting illegal profits into legitimate business concerns. His acumen allows ever-greater accessibility to Escobar's hierarchal financial structure.

The situations are not terribly original, but the movie capably captures the fear, danger and mounting paranoia as this ostensibly rational, free thinking operative must continually protect his identity and maintain his emotional equilibrium in dealing with people who by default are psychopaths. Musella nearly sabotages the operation when he turns down an opportunity for sex with a stripper arranged by his new clients. Instantly realizing his mistake, he blurts out staying faithful to his fiancée. Tischler arranges for a new agent, Kathy (Diane Kruger), an analyst with no field experience, to play the part.

The movie's best parts are the interplay between these opposite forces, the agents poised and giddy and operating in a realm beyond their abilities matching wits and cool against their opposite figures, ruthless and exotic underworld characters like Javier Ospina (Yul Vazquez), an epicene and fastidious gangster whose sexual play for Musella nearly unravels him. Abreu also has a fantastic sequence where his actual identity is threatened by his reliance on an unstable informant (Juan Cely). *The Infiltrator* is at its most effective in animating the stark moral consequences of the dangerous culture, of people drawn to the excitement and danger but also coping against the constant anxiousness and dread of being found out.

The adaptation, by Ellen Furman Brown, expands the central story to introduce several connective threads, like the rise and fall of the Bank of Credit and Commerce International (BCCI), a politically connected financial concern that facilitated all manner of patently illegal operations by the CIA and other foreign agencies. The movie becomes more dependent on plot and incident, and some of the more unsavory though fascinating characters, like Dominic (Joe Gilgun), a furloughed convict who helps and protects Mazur.

The more diffuse the plot turns, the more Furman proves himself unable to successfully merge all the disparate parts. Shuttling from Miami to New York and Paris, *The Infiltrator* turns increasingly incoherent as the actions, motivations and double crosses prove increasingly difficult to disentangle, a menacing figure now trailing the lead agent, an assassination carried out by executioners on motorcycle, the unexplained (and deeply homophobic) killing inside a Paris burlesque club or another ritualistic, voodoo-inflected killing never again alluded.

Furman needed to push more freely the notion, expressed beautifully in Shakespeare's great line, from *As You Like It* (1623), "All the world's a stage, all the men and women merely players." The movie's dominant theme is subterfuge, the ease of discomfort of people slipping in and out of masks. Only once, in a frightening moment where Mazur's opposite identities are brought together at a restaurant with his actual wife, *The Infiltrator* makes plain the sorrow and anguish of people forced to step outside their true selves and reveal something ugly and brutal in order to achieve the larger means.

The movie is also more about results than process. As a result, *The Infiltrator* ultimately fails because it never truly considers the moral or personal ramifications of what is being carried out, eliding over the Stockholm Syndrome, for instance, of being caught up in the ease and privilege of the criminal life when the fake couple are accepted into the intimate sphere of the top Escobar lieutenant, Roberto Alcaino (Benjamin Bratt) and his wife, Gloria (Elena Anaya). The pumped-up ending only accentuates the false veneer. Rather than sad, the gung-ho conclusion is markedly jubilant, satisfaction at a job well done instead of a reckoning of the personal damage wrought.

Patrick Z. McGavin

CREDITS

Robert Mazur: Bryan Cranston
Kathy Ertz: Diane Kruger
Emir Abreu: John Leguizamo
Roberto Alcaino: Benjamin Bratt
Javier Ospina: Yul Vazquez
Origin: United States
Language: English

Released: 2016
Production: Miriam Segal; released by Good Films
Directed by: Brad Furman
Written by: Ellen Brown Furman
Cinematography by: Joshua Reis
Music by: Chris Hajian
Music Supervisor: Seth C. Harris
Editing: Luis Carballar; Jeff McEvoy; David Rosenbloom
Art Direction: Karen Wakefield
Costumes: Dinah Collin
Production Design: Crispian Sallis
MPAA rating: R
Running time: 127 minutes

REVIEWS

Chang, Justin. *Los Angeles Times*. July 12, 2016.
Gleiberman, Owen. *Variety*. July 6, 2016.
Holden, Stephen. *New York Times*. July 12, 2016.
LaSalle, Mick. *San Francisco Chronicle*. July 13, 2016.
Morgenstern, Joe. *Wall Street Journal*. July 12, 2016.
Phillips, Michael. *Chicago Tribune*. July 13, 2016.
Rainer, Peter. *Christian Science Monitor*. July 13, 2016.
Rea, Stephen. *Philadelphia Inquirer*. July 13, 2016.
Roeper, Richard. *Chicago Sun-Times*. July 12, 2016.
Roeper, Richard. *Chicago Sun-Times*. July 12, 2016.

QUOTES

Robert Mazur: "Roberto, I am glad you are here. But there is a part of me that wishes you hadn't taken that risk."
Roberto Alcaino: Without family or friends, what kinda world will it be? There will be no reason to be alive. Hmm? It's a good day."

TRIVIA

Mazur's sting led to more than 100 criminal indictments and the collapse of the world's seventh largest private bank in 1991, when the Bank of Credit and Commerce International forfeited $550 million in U.S. assets after pleading guilty to fraud, larceny, and money-laundering.

THE INNOCENTS
(Les innocentes)

Box Office: $1 Million

Anne Fontaine's latest film takes what one of its characters calls "an indescribable nightmare" and uses it to examine the ways that faith can be tested, refined, and ultimately vindicated, despite the presence of evil in the world. It calls to mind other great movies in which nuns react to the presence of nonbelievers in their midst, but unlike the visually grand technicolor spectacle of *Black Narcissus* (1947) or the charming and sentimental *Lilies of the Field* (1963), *The Innocents* takes place in the bleakest and coldest environment possible, made more frigid by wounded human hearts, full of doubt and fear. This is a powerful testimony to the idea of a God who is bigger than the broken creation over which he presides, especially in the way he speaks through those who doubt his existence.

It is Warsaw, Poland in 1945 when French Red Cross student Mathilde (Lou de Laâge) is approached by Maria (Agata Buzek), a Polish nun who pleads for her to venture to the convent. At first, she resists, but she finds herself compelled to make the dangerous trek after she sees the nun in prayer outside the surgical room. On arriving at the convent, she finds herself presiding over a dangerous breech birth. She manages to deliver the baby but is surprised to discover she is an unwelcome guest and has to beg the nuns, and the especially cold Mother Superior (Agata Kulesza), for permission to return and check in on her patient.

When she does return, the baby is gone, supposedly taken away to live with the mother's family. Mathilde's suspicion about the situation is confirmed when she also discovers that one of the nuns is pregnant. A conversation with a Sister Maria reveals that there are seven other pregnant nuns, the result of savage invasion of the convent by Russian soldiers who raped the women repeatedly. Horrified, Mathilde begs to bring other Red Cross workers in to help but is denied. The Mother Superior will only allow her to continue caring for the women if she keeps their secret.

Mathilde keeps the secret and becomes absolutely committed to her mission, even at the expense of her work back at the surgical camp. Soon, she realizes the difficulty of what she has agreed to do. The convent is in a severe crisis of faith. Many of the women are afraid to be seen or touched, thinking such exposure a sin, and during one of her increasingly dangerous treks to the convent Mathilde is nearly raped herself at a surprise Soviet check point. It forms a delicate bond between her and the sisters that grows as Mathilde watches the care they give one another and the earnest inward searching of their hearts as they sort through why God has allowed this to happen. That bond grows even more when Mathilde is able to trick another group of Soviet Soldiers into leaving the convent.

But the Mother Superior, who has been riddled by syphilis, grows increasingly desperate to preserve the convent and its secret as the babies are born in quick succession and makes a desperate tragic decision that, when discovered by Mathilde and the nuns, leads the sisters to the very edge of hopelessness. Only by accept-

ing the truth and bringing it out into the light are they able to imagine a healing solution, one that expands the love they have for one another out into the war-torn world around them, outside the cocooned existence of the convent itself.

The film credits five writers. They are, Pascal Bonitzer (adaptation and dialogue), Anne Fontaine (adaptation and dialogue), Sabrina B. Karine (dialogue), Alice Vial and Sabrina B. Karine (screenplay), and Philippe Maynial (creator of original concept). For all of that input, the film tells, in many ways, a very simple, powerful story. Dialogue is often kept at bay while the film searches character's eyes and watches them go about their daily business. The screenplay provides incident but not at the expense of letting the characters convince viewers of their motivations through simple actions.

The performances are outstanding. Lou de Laage imbues Mathilde with both a headstrong sense of purpose and the humility to question her own materialistic understanding of life. Agata Buzek brings the questioning character of Maria to life without making her own struggle with faith post attack seem rote. She is a person who has witnessed something that has shaken her to the core and she must learn to recognize what she sees in the mirror and beyond again. A less-skilled actor than Agata Kulesza would simply have highlighted the bitterness of Mere Abesse, but Kulesza finds the humanity, the vulnerability that leads to Abesse' downfall. She becomes an example of how personal tragedy can override belief if it is not faced head on. To turn from it, and by extension turn away from the way it shapes understanding of faith, can lead a person to do unnecessary and even evil things in the name of God.

Dave Canfield

CREDITS

Mathilde Beaulieu: Lou de Laâge
Maria: Agata Buzek
Mere Abesse: Agata Kulesza
Samuel: Vincent Macaigne
Irena: Joanna Kulig
Origin: United States
Language: French, Polish, Russian
Released: 2016
Production: Eric Altmayer, Nicolas Altmayer; released by Aeroplan Film, France 2 Cinema, Mandarin Cinema, Mars Films, Scope Pictures
Directed by: Anne Fontaine
Written by: Anne Fontaine; Pascal Bonitzer
Cinematography by: Caroline Champetier
Music by: Gregoire Hetzel

Editing: Annette Dutertre
Art Direction: Anna Pabisiak
Costumes: Katarzyna Lewinska
Production Design: Joanna Macha
MPAA rating: PG-13
Running time: 115 minutes

REVIEWS

Brait, Ellen. *Globe and Mail.* July 14, 2016.
Burr, Ty. *Boston Globe.* July 14, 2016.
Chang, Justin. *Variety.* June 28, 2016.
Demara, Bruce. *Toronto Star.* July 14, 2016.
Goodykuntz, Bill. *Arizona Republic.* July 29, 2016.
Lickona, Matthew. *San Diego Reader.* August 4, 2016.
MacDonald, Moira. *Seattle Times.* July 28, 2016.
O'Hehir, Andrew. *Salon.com.* July 1, 2016.
Turan, Kenneth. *Los Angeles Times.* June 30, 2016.
Wolfe, April. *Village Voice.* June 29, 2016.

TRIVIA

Anne Fontaine originally met with Agata Kulesza because she was an admirer of her work, but told her that she did not wish to cast her as the Mother Superior since she thought her too sexy for the role. Kulesza asked if she could wear a veil and read for Fontaine. Once she did, Fontaine decided to give her the part.

THE INVITATION

> *There is no darkness. Just reunion.*
> —Movie tagline

Box Office: $231,737

Grief became a surprisingly common subject matter in 2016 films, including major works like *Arrival* and *Manchester by the Sea.* It was also the focus of a lesser-seen but fantastic horror/drama from earlier in the year, Karyn Kusama's *The Invitation*, which premiered at the SXSW Film Festival in early 2015 but was not released theatrically for over a year. The independent film and TV veteran director brings a craftsman's eye to this story of two very different reactions to unimaginable pain. The film has echoes of Roman Polanski's '70s horror in its examination of paranoia and the horrors that men and women can convince one another to perpetrate. With striking performances and a terrifying final act, *The Invitation* is the kind of film that builds a cult following over the years and will someday be appreciated alongside the other already-considered-great films about grief from this year.

Once-married Will (Logan Marshall Green) and Eden (Tammy Blanchard) have been dealt unfathomable emotional grief by life—the loss of their child. Since their son Ty's death, their lives have gone in different directions, and Will is surprised to receive an invitation to a dinner party at Eden's house. It will be the first time he's seen her in years, and he brings his new girlfriend Kira (Emayatzy Corinealdi) to the event, which also features a number of the couple's old friends. It's a happy reunion of sorts, but something dangerous hangs in the air. Eden seems too together given how her marriage to Will ended. And then there's the mysterious David (Michiel Huisman), her new husband, who Eden met in a grief-support group. It does not help that Will hits a coyote on the way to the party and has to mercy kill it. Let's just say—not a good sign that the night will go well.

The tension rises as Will meets two people at the party who are not part of the reunion core group of friends. First, there's Sadie (Lindsay Burdge), a free-spirited young woman who Eden and David met in Mexico and now lives with the couple. To say she seems on the verge of being entirely unhinged would be an understatement. There's a striking moment when Will sees her making screaming, pained faces in the mirror. What's her story? Will's suspicions continue to rise, but they don't really gain a foundation until the arrival of Pruitt (John Carroll Lynch), another friend of Eden's from the grief support group. Could this group be a cult? When Will notices that David has locked the front door, he begins to really suspect the worst.

Of course, for the bulk of *The Invitation*, no one believes Will, and there's an interesting commentary embedded in the scenario about how grief can impact perception. Perhaps Will is just being paranoid. Just because Eden is dealing with her grief in a completely different manner might not make her dangerous, right? In fact, perhaps her new group has the answers that Will has yet to find in his life. The bulk of *The Invitation* is really a series of questions. What happened to Choi, the guest who told his girlfriend he was close to the party but never arrived? What is Sadie up to exactly? Do Eden and David have malicious intent? When another guest leaves and it looks like Pruitt tries to stop her, Will's suspicion builds. Kusama brilliantly keeps slowing turning up the dial on the burner underneath viewer's seats. To be blunt, there's little movie if Will is wrong about the night being dangerous and so viewers know a climax is inevitable, but the exact shape and form things will take keep viewers on the edge of their seats until the jaw-dropping final minutes of the film.

With the knowledge that audiences will be aware that a climactic ending is likely, Kusama and cinematographer Barry Shore expertly used confined spaces to give the film an increasingly claustrophobic tension. Reminiscent of Roman Polanski's paranoia-filled horror films like *The Tenant* (1976) and *Rosemary's Baby* (1968), Kusama's work here uses mundane spaces like hallways and fancy kitchens in a way that makes them feel confined and foreboding. The director also works well with her ensemble, especially Green and the always-effective Lynch. It's easy to believe that these people have known each other a long time and Green and Blanchard convincingly sell their shared tragic past in just a few scenes.

That past really becomes the foundation for why *The Invitation* works overall. It is, ultimately, a horror film but it is one that is built on relatable human tragedy and the all-too-shared feeling of grief. It is a film about two people dealing with the most awful day of their lives in completely different ways, and how one cannot force someone to process grief in the way they think it should be processed. While it may be a shared human emotion, it is also something deeply personal, and something that must be carried and lived with instead of washed away by a cult or a perceived solution. As 2016 proved, filmmakers willing to dissect grief in personal, interesting ways can also make for great art.

Brian Tallerico

CREDITS

Will: Logan Marshall-Green
Eden: Tammy Blanchard
David: Michiel Huisman
Gina: Michelle Krusiec
Ty: Aiden Lovekamp
Origin: United States
Language: English
Released: 2016
Directed by: Karyn Kusama
Written by: Phil Hay; Matt Manfredi
Cinematography by: Bobby Shore
Music by: Theodore Shapiro
MPAA rating: Unrated
Running time: 100 minutes

REVIEWS

Chang, Justin. *Variety*. April 7, 2016.
Dargis, Manohla. *New York Times*. April 7, 2016.
Garnett, Abby. *Village Voice*. April 5, 2016.
Keough, Peter. *Boston Globe*. April 13, 2016.
Macdonald, Moira. *Seattle Times*. April 7, 2016.
Nashawaty, Chris. *Entertainment Weekly*. April 8, 2016.
Phillips, Michael. *Chicago Tribune*. April 14, 2016.
Rife, Katie. *Los Angeles Times*. April 8, 2016.

Suzanne-Mayer, Dominick. *Consequence of Sound*. April 7, 2016.
Wloszczyna, Susan. *RogerEbert.com*. April 8, 2016.

QUOTES

David: "Each one of us is on a journey and we feel it's important to be on this journey with the people you love."

TRIVIA

The film was independently produced, so the director and writers had complete creative control.

IP MAN 3
(Yip Man 3)

Box Office: $2.7 Million

Over the course of three films, Donnie Yen has portrayed Ip Man, the master teacher of the Wing Chun school of Chinese martial arts, whose claim to international fame was his role as a teacher of Bruce Lee. The films—all of which were directed by Wilson Yip and co-written by Edmond Wong and Tai-Li Chan (with Lai-yin Leung joining the screenwriting team for this third entry)—cleverly have skirted around the draw of Ip's most famous student. The first two entries only mention Lee in the coda (*Ip Man* [2008]) or show him in the epilogue as a young boy interested in learning from Ip (*Ip Man 2* [2010]).

In *Ip Man 3*, Lee (played by Kwok-Kwan Chan) arrives at the beginning of the film under his birth name. For an international audience, the telltale sign of the young man's identity is the way he thumbs his nose as a way of showing confidence. He again requests the master's training, and Ip tests the young man's speed by flicking cigarettes at him. Lee proceeds to kick them in slow motion. With the test complete and Ip impressed but critical, the master shows his own speed by being halfway to the door of his schoolroom before Lee turns his head at the sound of movement from the chair in which Ip had been sitting. When Ip opens the door to the room, Lee takes it as a sign of rejection and leaves. His disappointment might also be a reflection of the audience's own.

What has been fascinating about this series is the way it defies expectations in terms of what an audience might expect to see from Ip's story. For example, Lee may be a constant in the films, but he is never more than a momentary presence. The film's ending suggests that, if it were to happen, a fourth entry in the series might focus on the relationship between teacher and student, but then again, the finale of the second film felt that way, too. Even in this installment, when Lee appears again, it is not even as a fighter but, instead, as a dancer.

The films also take biographical elements of Ip's life and alter them in such a way that engenders a more action-oriented story (The first film's depiction of Ip's life during the Second Sino-Japanese War was changed dramatically so that he essentially had to fight for survival). Even then, though, the changes and the action remain faithful to the spirit of the man.

Much of that success rests on Yen, whose performances in each of these films have a sense of totality in regards to that spirit. This is a man who encounters people with a polite smile, brushing off compliments to his personality and abilities with a sense of modesty that is wholly sincere. He never angers, even as forces of local, national, and even international corruption and oppression work against everything in which he believes. The most Yen's face displays during a fight is a sense of determination and focus. At some points during combat, he even turns his head away from his opponent, as if his skills are extrasensory: He does not need to look at a combatant to determine what moves he must make to counter the attacks.

Throughout these films, there is an almost preternatural sense of calm to Yen's performance. Nothing that has happened to Ip has broken that veneer. There is a moment in this film, though, that finally does. When that moment happens, the impact is all the greater because of the impassiveness that Yen has cultivated in his performance until then.

The story of this installment is the most cluttered of the series' tales. There is about three movies' worth of material within the plot, which begins with Ip once again confronting corruption in Hong Kong. This time, it is 1959, and the threat surrounds Frank (Mike Tyson), an American property developer who does not shy away from criminal activity to expand his reach. He has assigned his right-hand heavy Ma King-Sang (Patrick Tam) to force a local school, which Ip's son Ching (Wang Yan Shi) attends, to sell the building to Frank. Ip volunteers to oversee a security detail for the school.

Meanwhile, Cheung Tin-Chi (Max Zhang), an upstart student of the Wing Chun tradition, wants to open a new school for martial arts and is willing to help Ma to do so. Inevitably, there is a popularity contest between Cheung and Ip's schools in the public eye, and that leads to a final fight between the two men to prove whose abilities are stronger.

These two plotlines result in a series of fights between Ip and an assortment of combatants—individually and in groups. Once again, they serve as a showcase for Yen's physical prowess and as a way to further define Ip's character (Woo-Ping Yuen seamlessly takes over choreography duties from Sammo Hung, who choreographed the first two films). Also once again, Yip, along with cinematographer Kenny Tse and editor Ka-Fai Cheung (the latter also returning to the series for a third time), shoots and cuts the action sequences with respect for the physicality on display. It is especially true during the climactic fight between the evenly matched Ip and Cheung.

All of this is to be expected from the series by now, but the screenplay offers a third storyline that puts Ip's character to the test and places the course of his life until this point in a critical, self-reflective context. His wife Cheung Wing-sing (Lynn Hung) is diagnosed with cancer, and their relationship, which is already under heavy strain on account of Ip's drive to help those who need it, takes priority in his life and within the film.

The question raised by this section—if Ip's dedication to the martial arts and strangers has been worth the price of neglecting his wife—adds a level of depth to a man whose life and actions have been treated as the stuff of uncritical legend. *Ip Man 3* takes perhaps the series' most significant step toward presenting the legend as a man.

Mark Dujsik

CREDITS

Ip Man: Donnie Yen
Cheung Wing-sing: Lynn Hung
Cheung Tin-chi: Jin Zhang
Frank: Mike Tyson
Ma King-Sang: Patrick Tam
Origin: United States
Language: Chinese, English
Released: 2016
Production: Bak-Ming Wong
Directed by: Wilson (Wai-Shun) Yip
Written by: Lai-Yin Leung; Chan Tai-Li; Edmond Wong
Cinematography by: Kenny Tse
Music by: Kenji Kawai
Editing: Ka-Fai Cheung
Costumes: Pik-kwan Lee
Production Design: Kenneth Mak
MPAA rating: PG-13
Running time: 105 minutes

REVIEWS

Abrams, Simon. *Village Voice.* January 19, 2016.
Fujishima, Kenji. *Paste Magazine.* January 18, 2016.
Henderson, Odie. *RogerEbert.com.* January 22, 2016.
Jenkins, Mark. *Washington Post.* January 21, 2016.
Lee, Maggie. *Variety.* January 28, 2016.
Mac, Sam C. *Slant Magazine.* January 19, 2016.
Macnab, Geoffrey. *Independent.* January 14, 2016.
Murray, Noel. *The A.V. Club.* January 21, 2016.
Rabin, Nathan. *Globe and Mail.* January 22, 2016.
Rechtshaffen, Michael. *Los Angeles Times.* January 21, 2016.

QUOTES

Cheung Wing-sing: "Why'd God make women pretty but dumb? They're pretty, so men will like them. They're dumb, so they will like men."

TRIVIA

Donnie Yen studied Mike Tyson's past boxing matches to help prepare for their fight scenes.

J

JACK REACHER: NEVER GO BACK

Never give in. Never give up.
—Movie tagline

Box Office: $58.7 Million

The film incarnation of Lee Child's Jack Reacher character arrived into theaters in 2012 on a rocky foundation. Just as Tom Cruise had been plagued by fans of the vampire Lestat—not to mention author Anne Rice herself—that he was too short to play the towering character, so went the same complaints over him cast as the 6'5" one-man army from Child's hit books. Then, on the week of its release, a horrific tragedy occurred at Sandy Hook Elementary School that made the opening scene—a seemingly random sniper attack—hard to reconcile as entertainment. Alas, Cruise and director Christopher McQuarrie still managed to make it work with a combination of fierce fights and chases that complimented the genuine starpower invested in a character who stood out for his deductive intellect as well as his brawn. This was a character worth another go-round. Unfortunately, the greater mystery this time is how everyone involved forgot what kept Reacher from just being another generic punch-thrower.

Reacher (Cruise) continues living off the land as a drifter and involving himself in circumstances that call for justice. After his latest takedown of a human trafficking ring, he marks a return to his old stomping grounds to meet with Susan Turner (Cobie Smulders), who saved him from arrest and commands his former unit. When he arrives, it is discovered she has been arrested herself for espionage related to the deaths of two

soldiers in Afghanistan. Colonel Sam Morgan (Holt McCallany) notices Jack doing some snooping around Turner's lawyer. Soon after, he is being tailed by goons, the lawyer is killed and Reacher is framed for it.

More assassins show up to ensure Turner never goes to trial, but Reacher beats them to her and breaks her out of prison in the process. The two of them head off the grid in hopes of clearing her name, but another case of a more personal nature interferes. A paternity suit has been filed against Reacher. Despite having no knowledge—or proof—of having a child, the information is strong enough for their adversaries to go after the 15-year-old Samantha (Danika Yarosh). More out of a sense of duty than direct parenting, Reacher and Turner decide to give them a military escort to her private school. Except Samantha's careless naivete in tracking devices put them all in even greater danger.

The contrast between the two Reacher films is rather striking. The first can certainly be classified as an action picture but was also every bit an investigative exercise. Jack Reacher was not just a constantly-hunted defense machine like the memory-challenged Jason Bourne. His memory is spot-on, able to breakdown the facts with the efficiency of Sherlock Holmes. Seeing things his inferiors would miss in any given situation there was something to fall back upon in the downtime between fighting suspects and outrunning the leaders of the investigation. *Never Go Back* is all about the running and then occasionally the fighting. Though Reacher makes the proclamation to "stop running and start hunting," there are barely enough revelations to even classify this as a mystery, and every new finding is either something printed out or phoned in that saves Reacher the trouble of exploiting his unique thinking talents for the audience.

Never Go Back may have been able to get away with this approach of literally going back on the character's standout traits if the macho bravado surpassed or equaled its predecessor. There are certainly a few bone breaks and proof that a car window is no detriment to Reacher's muscle, but none of them scream further than routine necessities. The five-against-one street fight of the original may have felt superfluous but it was beautifully staged with a clever tone. Same goes for the screeching-tire, engine-revving car chase of the original. The old cliché of sequels forcing in children for its heroes to deal with is distractingly in play here, which offers nothing to Reacher's character.

Cruise and his *The Last Samurai* (2003) collaborator, Edward Zwick, probably had one shot (no pun intended) to maintain interest in this character as a franchise staple. That is likely gone now as this barely qualifies as camouflage for a collection of recent solo acts with guns and fists. Matt Damon's Bourne gave way to Ben Affleck's *The Accountant* (2016). Jack Reacher may have even paved the way for Keanu Reeves' *John Wick* (2014), though that was more likely Tom Hanks' Michael Sullivan in *Road to Perdition* (2002). Lee Child's version of the character could just as easily have influenced David Mamet to create Val Kilmer's *Spartan* (2004). It is circumspect why of out of the twenty books that Reacher appears in (with a 21st hitting shelves when the film reached theaters) that this story was chosen to be the next best evolution of a character looking to stand out in a crowded field. When Reacher is asked "When'd you get back?" and answers "Not sure I ever did," it is the most accurate deduction he gets to make in the entire film.

Erik Childress

CREDITS

Jack Reacher: Tom Cruise
Turner: Cobie Smulders
Espin: Aldis Hodge
Samantha: Danika Yarosh
The Hunter: Patrick Heusinger
Origin: United States
Language: English
Released: 2016
Production: released by Paramount Pictures Corp., Skydance Media
Directed by: Edward Zwick
Written by: Edward Zwick; Richard Wenk; Marshall Herskovitz
Cinematography by: Oliver Wood

Music by: Henry Jackman
Sound: Mark P. Stoeckinger
Editing: Billy Weber
Art Direction: Peter Borck
Costumes: Lisa Lovaas
Production Design: Clay A. Griffith
MPAA rating: PG-13
Running time: 118 minutes

REVIEWS

Bell, Josh. *Las Vegas Weekly*. October 20, 2016.
Berardinelli, James. *ReelViews*. October 20, 2016.
Dargis, Manohla. *New York Times*. October 20, 2016.
Ebiri, Bilge. *Village Voice*. October 21, 2016.
Minow, Nell. *Beliefnet*. October 21, 2016.
Nusair, David. *Reel Film Reviews*. November 21, 2016.
Orndorf, Brian. *Blu-ray.com*. October 21, 2016.
Roten, Robert. *Laramie Movie Scope*. November 1, 2016.
Snider, Eric D.. *EricDSnider.com*. October 26, 2016.
Vonder Haar, Pete. *Houston Press*. October 27, 2016.

QUOTES

Jack Reacher: "If it were up to me, I'd just kill ya."

TRIVIA

Cobie Smulders trained for eight weeks in martial arts to prepare for her role.

JACKIE

I want them to see what they have done to Jack.
   —Movie tagline

Box Office: $13.5 Million

"And how would you like him to be remembered Mrs. Kennedy?" In the first exchange of Pablo Larrain's mesmerizing *Jackie*, the issues of legacy and versions of history have already been raised, and those are the beats to which this ambitious director will return throughout his film. It will be the recurring theme of this excellent drama, about the weeks after the assassination of John F. Kennedy, but also about something greater—about a woman dealing with not only grief in the glare of an international spotlight but the realization that she's writing the final chapter of a crucial American chapter in history. How will JFK be remembered? How will Jackie? Larrain and writer Noah Oppenheim's vision of Jackie Kennedy (Natalie Portman, giving a career-best performance) is as a woman keenly aware of public perception, but also trying to manage her own deep pain at losing a partner loved by the entire world.

Jackie jumps back and forth between several key arenas in the weeks following JFK's death. It's main structure spins off an interview between Jackie and a reporter (Billy Crudup) a week after the assassination, during which Jackie discusses many of the themes of the film and Larrain and Oppenheim capture a woman in great control of her image. She tells the journalist what she will allow him to print in his story. She asks him as many questions as he asks her. *Jackie* jumps to the minutes shortly after the assassination, including startling footage of the car speeding down an empty freeway (which would have been cleared for the motorcade) and Jackie wiping her husband's blood off her face. Larrain and Oppenheim have much more ambitious goals than any sort of "then this happened" biopic, making a film that feels like it's structured emotionally as much as it is historically.

Jackie also features scenes about the planning of JFK's funeral, and the procession that Jackie insisted accompany it, no matter the protestations from Bobby Kennedy (Peter Sarsgaard) or Lyndon Baines Johnson (John Carroll Lynch). In one of the film's most interesting narratives, Jackie discusses religion and philosophy with a priest (John Hurt, fantastic in one of his final roles). Everything about this film is finely-tuned to such a degree that Portman's performance changes slightly depending on to whom she's speaking, and Larrain and cinematographer Stéphane Fontaine balance their filmmaking style as well, shooting much of the film in extreme close-up when Jackie is feeling insecure or pulling back when she's more confident. It's a rare film in which performance and cinematography work together in such perfect conjunction to amplify a director's themes.

Larrain and Oppenheim return regularly to a segment that Jackie filmed for national television (co-starring Greta Gerwig), and it's not merely designed to show the First Lady in a happier time, but to emphasize how much she recognized her place in the history of the White House and America. She restored much of the physical legacy of the White House, bringing back antiques and furniture that had been put in storage. And, when her husband died, she recognized that this Kennedy Chapter of American history was heading into its final passage. How would JFK be remembered? So, there's a lot of discussion of processions, funeral arrangements, and legacy. (Arguably too much as Oppenheim could have made the same points a few less times.) This version of Jackie refuses to allow the final image of her husband to be slumped in the back seat of the motorcade, his brains splattered against the car.

At the same time, Jackie is dealing with unimaginable grief as a wife and now-single mother. And this is where Portman's Oscar-nominated performance really becomes remarkable—in the way she balances the multiple personalities of Jackie Kennedy. She changes her personal dynamics depending on to whom she's speaking, as much of a politician as her husband in that regard. Portman's performance, while staying true to Jackie's unique accent and speaking cadence, never feels like an imitation. It's the rare biopic performance that seems to work from the inside out instead of the other way around. Most biopics depend on what happened to their subject matter, often presenting history in a chronological, dry fashion, and turning their historical figures into mere passengers of their life's greatest moments. *Jackie* works as well in its non-historical moments—such as in the scenes with Portman and Hurt—as it does in the major beats that we know about from our history books.

One could say that *Jackie* is as remarkable for what it isn't as for what is. While the structure could have easily been disjointed and hard-to-follow, Larrain's masterful control as a director keeps it from becoming so. While it could have felt like an invasion of privacy for a woman still held in incredibly high esteem by the American public, one never feels like Jackie's grief is being used manipulatively. And while Natalie Portman's performance could have been showy and gimmicky, it never is, allowing the greater themes of the film to work through her fantastic work. For the record, everyone here is very good, including underrated work by Hurt, Sarsgaard, and Crudup, who did not get enough critical attention in Portman's wake.

Some critics thought *Jackie* was a bit too cold and calculated, but that's because of the deliberate personification of a Jackie Kennedy in complete control and entirely self-aware. Yes, the film lacks the manipulative emotions that other directors would have brought to the story of the widow of one of our greatest Presidents. That movie would have been easy. It might have produced a few tears, and maybe even more Oscar nominations. But it would have dissipated quickly in movie history. Much as Jackie Kennedy herself recognized the lasting power of what she was doing, this film her about feels like one that will be discussed and appreciated for decades to come.

Brian Tallerico

CREDITS

Jackie Kennedy: Natalie Portman
Bobby Kennedy: Peter Sarsgaard
Nancy Tuckerman: Greta Gerwig
The Journalist: Billy Crudup
The Priest: John Hurt
Origin: United States

Language: English

Released: 2016

Production: Darren Aronofsky, Scott Franklin, Ari Handel, Juan de Dios Larrain, Mickey Liddell; released by Jackie Productions (II), Why Not Productions

Directed by: Pablo Larrain

Written by: Noah Oppenheim

Cinematography by: Stephane Fontaine

Music by: Mica Levi

Music Supervisor: Bridget Samuels

Editing: Sebastian Sepulveda

Art Direction: Halina Gebarowicz

Costumes: Madeline Fontaine

Production Design: Jean Rabasse

MPAA rating: R

Running time: 100 minutes

REVIEWS

Burr, Ty. *Boston Globe.* December 7, 2016.

Dargis, Manohla. *New York Times.* December 1, 2016.

Dowd, A.A. *The A.V. Club.* November 30, 2016.

Kiang, Jessica. *Playlist.* September 16, 2016.

Lang, Nico. *Salon.com.* December 4, 2016.

Lodge, Guy. *Variety.* September 16, 2016.

Romney, Jonathan. *Screen International.* September 16, 2016.

Shoemaker, Allison. *Consequence of Sound.* November 30, 2016.

Tobias, Scott. *NPR.* December 20, 2016.

Turan, Kenneth. *Los Angeles Times.* December 1, 2016.

QUOTES

Jackie Kennedy: "I never wanted fame. I just became a Kennedy."

TRIVIA

Caspar Phillipson was dubbed by the real John F. Kennedy in the only scene he had the opportunity to speak.

AWARDS

British Acad. 2016: Costume Des.

Nominations:

Oscars 2016: Actress (Portman), Costume Des., Orig. Score

British Acad. 2016: Actress (Portman), Orig. Score

Golden Globes 2017: Actress—Drama (Portman)

Ind. Spirit 2017: Actress (Portman), Director (Larrain), Film, Film Editing

Screen Actors Guild 2016: Actress (Portman)

JANE GOT A GUN

She turned to her past to protect her family.
—Movie tagline

Box Office: $1.5 Million

The western is one of those genres that has to struggle for a resurgence in popularity. So few get made and those that do either have poor distribution or become box office duds. For every *The Hateful 8* (2015) or *Bone Tomahawk* (2015), there is a *The Lone Ranger* (2013) or a *A Million Ways to Die in the West* (2014). Like musicals, westerns are often a tough sell, but they remain revered by cinephiles and filmmakers who want to stretch out stylistically. The genre has a way of bringing out the best in cinematographers eager to light every night scene through lanterns while taking advantage of the wide open vistas of the bare American landscape for the daytime scenes. But what was once a thriving and noble American genre has now become such a troublesome niche of the film world that it's a wonder any get made at all anymore.

Jane Got A Gun was one of those troubled western projects that never could catch a break. It seemed like such a simple and typical western film. When watching it, there exist little signs of strain or messiness that plagued the project, but there is also little sign of passion for the material. The film went through a few directors, all of whom walked off the film during preproduction. Gavin O'Connor stepped in to direct, but halted production so he could make changes to the script. The cast also became a revolving door of A-list players who eventually declined, forcing co-writer Joel Edgerton to step in for the lead role he had no intention of playing. Once the film got finished, its distributor, Relativity, filed for bankruptcy, but not before it released the film from its clutches. The Weinstien Company, who have a long and sordid history of burying their films, eventually released the $28 million film on a few screens with little fanfare.

It seems that only the film's star and producer, Natalie Portman, remained the constant champion that got the film off the ground and completed. She stars in the film as Jane Hammond, a woman with a husband named Bill, or "Ham" (Noah Emmerich), and a five-year old child. They live out on a remote ranch somewhere in New Mexico. The year is 1871. One day, Ham comes home wounded from bullets and barely able to walk. As Jane tends to his wounds, he warns her "the Bishop boys are coming," meaning a band of outlaws headed by John Bishop (Ewan McGregor), with whom both of them have a past. Knowing the Bishop Boys are on the hunt for her and her child, she enlists the help of a gunslinger from her past by the name of Dan Frost (Joel Edgerton), who is reluctant to take the job.

His reluctance has to do with the fact that they has a romantic past that had deep roots. Through flashbacks, the story goes that he had to leave her out of necessity, but promised he would return. When three years went by and he never showed up, she ended up with Ham and started a new life. A tragedy brought Jane and Ham together and she has been with him out of necessity ever since. At the time she married him, she believed that Dan was dead. During those three years apart, though, he tried desperately to find her, showing her picture to everyone he met. Once he did find her, she had already given birth to her daughter with her new husband, signalling the end of their relationship for good. Now, Dan and Ham are under the same roof with Jane, who tends to her husband while relying on a tormented former lover's good will to protect them.

Jane and Ham's backstory is told through flashbacks, which seem to get just as much screen time as the present day stuff. While they do provide enough context as well as a few twists toward the end, they also have the feel of a western as written by Nicholas Sparks. Flashbacks involving them talking about future plans, about him finding her with Ham and all the other backstory elements have a pedestrian feel to them and slow down whatever forward momentum the film might have had. One never gets the sense that these two really belong together or that there existed any strong chemistry between them. It almost feels like the flashbacks exist to fill screen time when a five- or ten-minute prologue at the beginning of the film would have sufficed. Plus, Jane's story in her time between these two men, is muddled and unconvincing.

Portman and Edgarton try to make it work, but they just don't seem to click together. Portman seems miscast and Edgarton never quite gels as a leading man type. Both are fine actors who, perhaps just through circumstance surrounding the production, find themselves at odds with the material. McGregor does fine as John Bishop, but it is a villain that the western has seen many times before. While the film does offer a solid showdown sequence in the third act, it feels like it should be in a better film. O'Connor has an assured hand for a western and the film looks terrific, but it misses the kind of emotional punch he so expertly brought to the screen with films like *Miracle* (2004) and *Warrior* (2011). *Jane Got A Gun* has many elements to comprise a good western, but through bad luck and misfortune, never had a chance at being one of the more memorable of the small amount of westerns released in its day.

Collin Souter

CREDITS

Jane Hammond: Natalie Portman
Dan Frost: Joel Edgerton
Colin McCann: Ewan McGregor
Fitchum: Rodrigo Santoro
Bill Hammond: Noah Emmerich
Origin: United States
Language: English
Released: 2016
Production: Terry Dougas, Aleen Keshishian, Scott LaStaiti, Mary Regency Boies, Zack Schiller, Scott Steindorff, Natalie Portman; released by Handsomecharlie Films, Straight Up Films
Directed by: Gavin O'Connor
Written by: Joel Edgerton; Brian Duffield; Anthony Tambakis
Cinematography by: Mandy Walker
Music by: Marcello De Francisci; Lisa Gerrard
Sound: Christopher Eakins
Music Supervisor: Andy Ross
Editing: Alan Cody
Costumes: Terry Anderson; Catherine George
Production Design: Tim Grimes; James Oberlander
MPAA rating: R

REVIEWS

Baumgarten, Marjorie. *Austin Chronicle.* February 4, 2016.
Guzman, Rafer. *Newsday.* January 29, 2016.
Hassenger, Jesse. *The A.V. Club.* January 30. 2016.
Huddleston, Tom. *Time Out.* April 19, 2016.
Kenny, Glenn. *New York Times.* January 29, 2016.
Lane, Anthony. *New Yorker.* January 25, 2016.
Nordine, Michael. *Village Voice.* February 3, 2016.
Perez, Rodrigo. *The Playlist.* January 30, 2016.
Rechtshaffen, Michael. *Los Angeles Times.* January 30, 2016.
Sobczynski, Peter. *RogerEbert.com.* January 29, 2016.

QUOTES

Jane Hammond: [sarcastically to her wounded husband] "If them bullets don't kill you, and this storm you somehow brought upon us don't kill you, goes without saying... I will kill you."

TRIVIA

Lynne Ramsay dropped the project after a standoff with producer Scott Steindorff. She was replaced less than a day later by Gavin O'Connor.

JASON BOURNE

You know his name.
—Movie tagline

Box Office: $162.4 Million

When *The Bourne Identity* (2002) was released in 2002, it had the good fortune to come out at a time when action films in general and spy thrillers in particular were not exactly thriving as genres. The idea of combining the insanely complex plotting of the Robert Ludlum novel with a hyperkinetic visual style and the intriguing casting of Matt Damon as the amnesiac ass-kicked proved to be an inspired one. Things got even better when Paul Greengrass stepped in to replace Doug Liman as director of the follow-up *The Bourne Supremacy* (2004), adding genuine emotional stakes to the previously established thrills that continued on through the next installment, the even-better *The Bourne Ultimatum* (2007). Best of all, Greengrass and Damon clearly realized that they could not do much more with the franchise without drifting into self-parody and announced that they were calling it quits.

Needless to say, Universal Pictures was not quite as willing to put the Bourne saga to bed and miss out on the millions that it was generating and, after failing to lure Greengrass and Damon back into the fold with insane amounts of money, they decided to forge ahead with a new film set in the same universe but with a whole new cast of characters dodging bullets and uncovering vast governmental conspiracies. The resulting film, *The Bourne Legacy* (2012), certainly had plenty of talent involved with it. It was directed and co-written by Tony Gilroy (who worked on the scripts for the previous films in the franchise and directed the acclaimed *Michael Clayton* [2007]) and included such strong actors as Jeremy Renner, Edward Norton, and Rachel Weisz—but the whole thing, for all the huffing and puffing involved, just seemed labored. Undaunted, Universal once again reached out to Greengrass and Damon and this time were able to persuade them both to return to the series for another go-around. Alas, the only thing that the ensuing film, *Jason Bourne*, manages to do is prove that their initial instincts to end the franchise were sound because this revival is a tired and noisy drag that pretty much fails to justify its existence as anything other than a naked cash grab.

Having successfully gone into hiding after helping to expose some of the CIA's dirtiest secrets, Jason Bourne (Damon) has been eking out a quiet living off the grid as a bare-knuckle boxer in the outskirts of Greece when he is contacted by former CIA analyst Nicky Parsons (Julia Stiles), who has also left the agency and is working for a Wikileaks-type group based out of Iceland. As it turns out, she has uncovered a whole new slew of dirty agency secrets that involve both Bourne and his father (Gregg Henry) and implicate new CIA director Robert Dewey (Tommy Lee Jones) in a number of illegal activities. Desperate to retrieve both the incriminating evidence and the agency's own Rogue One, Dewey, with the help of ambitious cyber operations head Heather Lee (Alicia Vikander) begins tracking Bourne

via satellite feeds, data traces, and an assassin known as The Asset (Vincent Cassel), who, perhaps inevitably, has his own past with Bourne. The pursuit takes Bourne from Berlin to Beirut, before finally landing him in Las Vegas, where Dewey is attending a technology convention where he will be debating (and later murdering) an Internet entrepreneur (Riz Ahmed) who has developed a program that Dewey, who secretly financed it, plans to use to as the key component of all-powerful mass surveillance program dubbed Iron Hand.

It all sounds fabulously complex in theory but it only takes a few minutes of watching *Jason Bourne* to realize that it has virtually nothing fresh or original to offer moviegoers. The screenplay by Greengrass and Christopher Rouse feels less like a fully fleshed-out story than it does narrative water-treading that is content to rehash past glories instead of striking off in new directions. Sure, it pays lip service to such hot-button issues as government intrusion into civil liberties, Internet privacy, and corporate greed but it is not about any of those things per se—they are just things used to fill in the blanks in the otherwise boilerplate dialogue that has been designed solely to get the various characters from point A to point B and set up the action set-pieces that have grown to dominate the proceedings. Those action scenes also come up short as well, especially in comparison to the earlier films. In those, the herky-jerky approach to shooting the action sequences was a genuinely inspired approach that felt different from other such scenes in actions films of the time and also helped to subtly place viewers within the fractured mindset of Bourne himself. This time around, the bloom is off the rose and the various brawls and chases look as hackneyed and derivative as the very scenes that they were creatively rebelling against when they first started out. The nadir is easily the extended Vegas climax that finds Bourne hurtling down the strip in a car chase that is so overblown in the consequence-free destruction that is wrought during it that it feels at times as if Greengrass simply went home for the day and that John Landis took over for a bit.

Despite having an uncommonly good cast, *Jason Bourne* also pretty much fails to inspire any creative sparks from the actors as well. At one time, the sight of Matt Damon, at the time thought of as being associated with more cerebral films than the usual action fodder, unexpectedly holding his own during the complicated action beast was genuinely exciting and provocative. This time around, he is just going through the motions and seems vaguely embarrassed to have gone against his initial instincts by deigning to appear in something so trivial. In one of her first films since winning the Oscar for *The Danish Girl* (2015), Alicia Vikander is similarly wasted—all she gets to do for the most part is stare at computer screens and CCTV monitors while reciting utility-grade dialogue without even trying to put any kind of distinct spin on it. That said, the contributions from Damon and Vikander seem highly focused and committed when compared to the paean to sheer laziness that is the performance by Tommy Lee Jones, whose contempt for the proceedings is palpable every time he appears on the screen.

The most depressing aspect about the film, other than the film itself, is that audiences did not seem to mind such laziness and it went on to pull in over $400 million worldwide, the kind of money that all but ensures that another film will almost certainly be forthcoming. This time, however, one can only hope that Greengrass and Damon have finally realized that they were right all along and will leave the room when Universal tries to get them to sign on for another one.

Peter Sobczynski

CREDITS

Jason Bourne: Matt Damon
CIA Director Robert Dewey: Tommy Lee Jones
Heather Lee: Alicia Vikander
Asset: Vincent Cassel
Nicky Parsons: Julia Stiles
Aaron Kalloor: Riz Ahmed
Origin: United States
Language: English
Released: 2016
Production: Gregory Goodman, Frank Marshall, Ben Smith, Jeffrey M. Weiner, Matt Damon, Paul Greengrass; released by Universal Pictures Inc.
Directed by: Paul Greengrass
Written by: Paul Greengrass; Christopher Rouse
Cinematography by: Barry Ackroyd
Music by: David Buckley; John Powell
Sound: Oliver Tarney
Editing: Christopher Rouse
Art Direction: Paul Inglis
Costumes: Mark Bridges
Production Design: Paul Kirby
MPAA rating: PG-13
Running time: 123 minutes

REVIEWS

Burr, Ty. *Boston Globe*. July 28, 2016.
Cole, Jake. *Slant*. July 27, 2016.
Debruge, Peter. *Variety*. July 26, 2016.
Ebiri, Bilge. *Village Voice*. July 26, 2016.
Klimek, Chris. *NPR*. July 28, 2016.
McCarthy, Todd. *Hollywood Reporter*. July 26, 2016.

Orndorf, Brian. *Blu-ray.com*. July 28, 2016.
Scott, A.O. *New York Times*. July 27, 2016.
Turan, Kenneth. *Los Angeles Times*. July 28, 2016.
Zacharek, Stephanie. *Time*. July 28, 2016.

QUOTES

CIA Director Robert Dewey: [Jason, who has a gun pointed at Dewey, says he's trying not to be a killer] "How's that working out for you?"

TRIVIA

The car-chase sequence ended up wrecking 170 vehicles.

JULIETA

Box Office: $1.3 Million

Modern melodrama often comes under unfair fire due to the unforgiving taste of American audiences and the preponderance of sloppy, half-hearted novel adaptations for the screen. Writer/Director Pedro Almodóvar continues to keep this heightened subgenre alive with his vivid tale of family in the wake of a daughter's disappearance, *Julieta*.

The film's lead, Julieta, the harrowed mother of Antía (various actresses across the film's timeline), is played by Emma Suárez and Adriana Ugarte as modern-day and past, younger versions of herself, respectively. Her story begins slowly, with the majority of the film told in flashback. Ugarte is more than up for the task, her deep eyes conveying hurt and joy with equal luminescence. Julieta runs into an old friend of her daughter's (Michelle Jenner) who tells her that Antía is living in Switzerland and has three children. It becomes understood that Antía and Julieta are estranged, but the raw impact spurs the central mystery of the film. As Julieta writes a cathartic, unsent, autobiographical letter to her daughter, their family history unfolds vibrantly before us.

Almodóvar's bright primary colors—on wallpapers and dresses, on traditional tattoos and architecture—underscores his intensely emotional drama, drama that can sometimes bleed (like his bold colors) into excess. *Julieta* dabbles in gaudy symbolism that only sometimes fits into the loud world Almodóvar's crafted, like when a stag runs astride the train upon which Julieta meets her partner (and Antía's father) Xoan (Daniel Grao). However, the deliberate dialogue and genuine romantic tension between Xoan and Julieta add weight to the possibly flighty story. An achingly lingered shot tracking their prone bodies as they share a train car focus on feet, legs, and curious eyes. The quiet moments allow Almodóvar to go big when he wants and drive the film with more urgency than some of his most meaty twists.

As the characters age into a relationship filled with complex love and family issues like the cyclical invalidity of its women, including Xoan's ex-wife, Julieta's mother, and at times, Julieta herself and the doomed machismo of its men. While the women bear their emotions as typical "chicas Almodóvar," stalwart women with fleshed-out professional and love lives, the men lack much of the nuance. Though the characters represent people along different paths of grief and using different coping mechanisms to handle it, some, like Julieta's father (Joaquín Notario), cannot escape their generic bindings to transcend the more hokey material. This is not a criticism of the actors—they simply do not have the time because of how much plot is crammed into the film's tight 99 minutes.

After a tragic loss, Julieta sinks into depression and Antía must care for her. The girl grows up fast as Julieta succumbs to loss, the two women reflecting consequences of despair like a broken mirror. The continued refusal to reflect dour emotion in the color scheme surrounding it emphasizes that sadness even more, a gorgeous reminder that life goes on taunting its characters in every frame. When Antía must dry her mother's hair after helping her from the bath, she covers her whole head with the towel. When this motherly duty is done and the towel lifted, Ugarte has transformed into Suárez, aged by her daughter's maturity in the film's most strikingly effective visual moment. The aging and anti-aging makeup and hairstyles allow this transition between flashback and renewed reality the punch needed to remind us of the life we've seen her live.

This life has taken an unforeseen toll on those around Julieta. When the film's central mystery is addressed (but never explained, leaving it a tantalizing bit of speculation), the thematic grief clicks perfectly into the dramatic framework. A few cheesy pieces of plot progression bridge the gaps between a plot whose unknowns are also its most succulent delights, but they are well worth the treacle. As Julieta rides towards a Byzantine plot with the promise of a cathartic reunion, one where the past may be understood, though not forgiven. Redemption comes in shared emotional survival and the ability to keep moving forward - something Almodóvar accentuates in his dramas so that the lives of his viewers seem more manageable and optimistic than before.

Jacob Oller

CREDITS

Julieta, older: Emma Suarez
Julieta, younger: Adriana Ugarte
Xoan: Daniel Grao

Ava: Inma Cuesta
Lorenzo: Dario Grandinetti
Origin: United States
Language: Spanish
Released: 2016
Production: Agustin Almodovar, Esther Garcia; released by El Deseo
Directed by: Pedro Almodovar
Written by: Pedro Almodovar
Cinematography by: Jean-Claude Larrieu
Music by: Alberto Iglesias
Editing: Jose Salcedo
Art Direction: Carlos Bodelón
Costumes: Sonia Grande
Production Design: Antxon Gomez
MPAA rating: R
Running time: 99 minutes

REVIEWS

Bailey, Jason. *Flavorwire*. October 15, 2016.
Cheshire, Godfrey. *RogerEbert.com*. December 22, 2016.
Ebiri, Bilge. *Village Voice*. May 18, 2016.
Felperin, Leslie. *Hollywood Reporter*. April 8, 2016.
Halligan, Fionnuala. *Screen International*. April 8, 2016.
Kiang, Jessica. *Playlist*. May 17, 2016.
Lane, Anthony. *New Yorker*. December 12, 2016.
Phipps, Keith. *Uproxx*. December 23, 2016.
Scott, A.O. *New York Times*. December 20, 2016.
Soghomonian, Talia. *Collider*. May 19, 2016.

TRIVIA

The color red is featured in almost every shot.

AWARDS

Nominations:

British Acad. 2016: Foreign Film

THE JUNGLE BOOK

The legend will never be the same.
—Movie tagline

Box Office: $364 Million

Early on in *The Jungle Book*, panther Bagheera (voiced with gruff gravitas by Sir Ben Kingsley) instructs young Mowgli (newcomer Neel Sethi) to show the utmost respect for those who have created everything within the boy's surroundings. "The mountains, the trees, the birds in the trees," the black cat enumerates while bowing along with this "man-cub" who has been integrated into, but is not of, the wilderness. Bagheera then notes a single exception: "But they did not make you." While the jungle generators to whom he refers are the elephants who majestically pass by, shrouded in both myth and mist, his words could also be used to describe the hugely-talented special effects artists responsible for filling most of every frame with computer-generated flora and fauna that look as real as Neel. Aside from mere glimpses of a protoplasm-possessing infant Mowgli, his father, and a few inhabitants of the man-village, the film's living, breathing, loinclothed lead is its only on-screen portrayer devoid of pixels.

However, far more here has been successfully synthesized beyond live-action shots of Sethi and the amazingly-lifelike virtual virtuosity around him. Director Jon Favreau aimed to merge the determinedly-lighthearted, G-rated, and tune-filled Disney whimsy that he and so many others fondly recall from the 1967 cartoon classic (the last produced by Walt) with some darker, deeper, and more dramatic aspects of the Rudyard Kipling tales that have sparked imaginations since the 1890s. Not only would this age-old story be put forth using cutting-edge technology (extensions of that used for 2012's *Life of Pi*, 2014's *Dawn of the Planet of the Apes*, and, especially, 2013's *Gravity*), but the venerable material would also be mixed with potentially-impactful up-to-date messages: valuing a person's non-pigeonholed and fully-expressed "special" self; the benefits of community cohesiveness and peaceful coexistence; and finding creative means by which we can rescue that which we have unconscionably—or sometimes unconsciously—put at risk in the environment. For Sethi's CGI creature costars, vocal talent had to be chosen that might best imbue what would ultimately be viewed. The movie resulting from all this melding is a PG production that endeavors to be both touching and intensely gripping, sometimes heartwarming and at other moments making one's blood run fairly cold. With dashes of humor and two beloved tunes (plus a third over its end credits) that aim to offset any upset, this hybrid successfully appeals to all but the youngest family members who might wet themselves from worry. Made on a budget of $175 million, critically-lauded *The Jungle Book* grossed nearly $1 billion worldwide.

While a sequence less than five minutes in conveys the Indian jungle's transition from its rainy season to one of withering drought, viewers should have already sensed that change was in the air. After a throwback Disney castle logo at the outset that was hand painted on cels, shot in Technicolor, and aims to simulate Uncle Walt's once-highly-innovative multiplane camera, a shot moves forward past an antiquatedly-animated jungle and ultimately to a stunningly-photorealistic, 3D depiction of the Seoni one has to see to believe. Adult ears nostalgi-cally noticed that music from the 1967 opening is immediately recalled in composer John Denby's scoring of this introductory homage. This first shot recalls that of *Bambi* (1942), which, along with other in-house classics right up to 1994's *The Lion King* (of which there are numerous echoes throughout) has instructed Favreau as to how Walt successfully combined both delightful and dicey elements—even death.

Mowgli appears to be trying to avoid his own in the film's highly-kinetic and compelling opening scene. The boy appears to be the terror-stricken quarry of a red-hot pursuit as he hotfoots it through the jungle, scrambles up a tree and then leaps through the canopy, successfully negotiating along branches like a hellishly-hurried but admirably-agile high-wire performer—a Flying Wallenda of the wilds. The drama of Mowgli's seemingly-high-stakes sprinting is another early signal that change from 1967 is afoot. While the film largely honors Disney's many divergences from the source material, this latest Mouse House metamorphosis has resulted in some entirely-new twists. For example, the lame-from-birth Shere Khan in Kipling now bears a deformity caused by Mowgli's fire-wielding dad, who the beast murders here along with the lad's beloved adoptive wolf father. Let mutual revenge begin!

"How Fear Came" is the title of one of the Mowgli stories in Kipling's dual-volumed *Jungle Book* (both of which also include other, unrelated short works), and it comes quite often throughout a film. Of course, the aforementioned tiger is what triggers the apprehension, first and foremost. No offense to the late, great George Sanders and his purr-fect pipes, but Idris Elba's Shere Khan so thoroughly convinced viewers that he is both made of, and out for, flesh-and-blood that he must be rated tops in terms of trepidation. He first sinisterly slinks on the scene when a menagerie gathers en masse to cooperatively quaff from a drought-diminished watering hole (Kipling's "water truce"), emerging from a location-shoot-mimicking sun flare as if to convey that this predator is as oppressive as said orb's parching rays. This gathering, which commences after Ikki the Porcupine (who is voiced by Garry Shandling, to whom the film was dedicated upon his sudden death) acts like a quilled town crier, also affords the folks at MPC an opportunity to show off an amazing array of their artistry.

Viewers jumped when Shere Khan soon and suddenly did the same out of nowhere at Mowgli—and this time the boy's suspenseful evasion involves no playing around. The cat's brutal (but, cognizant of the kiddies, bloodless) dispatching of wolf leader Akela (Giancarlo Esposito), Mowglis' pawed pa, is as alarmingly precipitous as the cliff from which he then viciously hurls assassinated Akela for a fate-sealing exclamation point.

"Have I got your attention now?" the usurper then growls at the boy's wolf mother Raksha (Lupita Nyong'o, as palpably warm as Elba's Khan is cold) and the rest of the pack, almost sounding like a striped stand-in for the much-better-intentioned Favreau.

More sources of fright follow. Particularly noteworthy is gender-reassigned Kaa (a seductive Scarlett Johansson), here a huge, mesmerizing murderess of a snake who eerily emerges for a literally-eye-opening reveal of Mowgli's origins within one of her pernicious peepers—all the while with another eye toward his demise. There is also the rampaging, cave-in-inducing pursuit of the boy by Weta Digitals' now-colossal King Louie (Christopher Walken), who sings how he wants to be like Mowgli until, burning with frustration because he cannot obtain the secret of man's "red flower" (i.e. fire), he then wants the kid to no longer be. What ceased to be ages ago is the Gigantopithecus, an ape ancestor who appears here in lieu of 1967's Louie, a character that does not exist in Kipling's books.

As previously mentioned concerning the film's first scene but also in its furious and fiery climactic showdown, Mowgli exhibits an impressive ability to balance. Favreau does the same throughout. However, the inclusion of "I Wanna Be Like You" and "The Bare Necessities" creates two noticeable, if only mildly consequential, wobbles. The director said their excision would have left fans of the earlier film feeling as disappointed as Rolling Stones concertgoers who waited in vain to hear the band's long-loved greatest hits. While some viewers might very well have complained, the presence of these memorable Disney ditties in an action/adventure version of *The Jungle Book* causes a potentially-problematic unsteadiness of tone. For family viewing, perhaps Favreau felt, for example, that Walken's rendition, although newly-sinister, might somewhat temper the hirsute character's hair-raising temper tantrum that follows.

The King's initial emergence from the shadows intentionally recalls that of Marlon Brando's Colonel Kurtz in *Apocalypse Now* (1979), another ominous antagonist of a leader encountered after a river journey. Here, that trip involves the recreation of the iconic image of Mowgli atop the belly of Balloo (a perfectly-cast Bill Murray), who offers up a version of his character's song that (like Walken's) pales in comparison to the original, yet it offers some enjoyably-breezy ballast. On the whole, Murray's chuckle-inducing performance does just that.

The Mowgli of Kipling's stories is certainly a kid who becomes filled with anxiety, the term "man-cub" emphasizing the seemingly-irreconcilable, discombobulating duality of his identity. "I am two Mowgli's," he la-ments while growing into a teen torn between the animals he has considered family for as long as he can remember and the utterly-foreign folk with whom he seems destined by DNA to rejoin—both of which at different points painfully cast him out. Favreau's Mowgli is not (or, at least, not yet—sequels are planned) an adolescent beset by gnawing angst, but simply a bummed-out wolf wannabe not so much howling as kvetching about having no choice in leaving his jungle home in order to avoid losing his life instead. A striking shot seems to visually underscore how Mowgli is betwixt and between, his future suddenly very much up in the air. At the exact moment Bagheera discloses to Mowgli that they are headed for the protection of the man-village, the boy is seen dangling from a tree branch he is using to traverse a symbolically-demarcating gorge, temporarily and precariously possessing footing on neither side.

By the end here, however, Mowgli is blithely reclining upon another branch and sticking with the critter compadres who stuck with him against Shere Khan after everyone appropriately recites in unison from Kipling's "Law of the Jungle": "For the strength of the Pack is the Wolf, and the strength of the Wolf is the Pack." This constructive coming together is satisfying to behold as the real world increasingly seems to be falling apart. Kipling's page-turners have long intrigued us about how a boy could possibly fit in amidst the surprisingly-articulate animals of an adventure-filled Indian jungle, all of which the author's father and others illustrated with the utmost realism. Now, thanks to some new-fangled "tricks," Favreau and company have piqued our curiosity on the subject in an additional sense as the fascinatingly-fused images of each astonishingly-artistic frame flicker by.

David L. Boxerbaum

CREDITS

Mowgli: Neel Sethi

Voice of Baloo: Bill Murray

Voice of Bagheera: Ben Kingsley

Voice of Shere Khan: Idris Elba

Voice of Raksha: Lupita Nyong'o

Origin: United States

Language: English

Released: 2016

Production: Brigham Taylor, Jon Favreau; released by Fairview Entertainment, The Moving Picture Co.

Directed by: Jon Favreau

Written by: Justin Marks

Cinematography by: Bill Pope

Music by: John Debney
Sound: Christopher Boyes; Frank E. Eulner
Editing: Mark Livolsi
Art Direction: Andrew L. Jones
Costumes: Laura Jean Shannon
Production Design: Christopher Glass
MPAA rating: PG
Running time: 106 minutes

REVIEWS

Barker, Andrew. *Variety*. April 3, 2016.
Burr, Ty. *Boston Globe*. April 14, 2016.
Dargis, Manohla. *New York Times*. April 14, 2016.
Ebiri, Bilge. *Village Voice*. April 12, 2016.
Hornaday, Ann. *Washington Post*. April 14, 2016.
Lane, Anthony. *New Yorker*. April 18, 2016.
McCarthy, Todd. *Hollywood Reporter*. April 3, 2016.

Morgenstern, Joe. *Wall Street Journal*. April 14, 2016.
Nashawaty, Chris. *Entertainment Weekly*. April 12, 2016.
Phillips, Michael. *Chicago Tribune*. April 14, 2016.

QUOTES

Shere Khan: [to Mowgli] "Did you think I would let you grow old?"

TRIVIA

The film was released in India on April 8, a week ahead of its U.S. debut, in order to honor the Indian environment of the movie.

AWARDS

Oscars 2016: Visual FX
British Acad. 2016: Visual FX

K

KATE PLAYS CHRISTINE

A nonfiction psychological thriller.
—Movie tagline

Box Office: $25,564

Actress Kate Lyn Sheil receives an odd assignment from director Robert Greene in *Kate Plays Christine*. Greene wants her to prepare for the role of late journalist Christine Chubbuck as if she were going to play her in a movie. On July 15th, 1974, Chubbuck looked into a camera and said these famous last words "In keeping with Channel 40's policy of bringing you the latest in blood and guts, and in living color, you are going to see another first--attempted suicide." She then produced a pistol and shot herself in the head. She had been a TV journalist in Sarasota, FL, and a lonely one by all accounts. When she did this the roar that followed was a dull one. It should have changed the way we think about television, news, and the cruel expectations we place on working women, to name just a few. It did none of those things. Greene wants to know why and what if anything we can learn from Chubbuck today. So he has Sheil attempt to become Chubbuck, to go where she went and do what she did, to not so much research a life but give a living performance of empathy. If it's unclear how much control Greene or Sheil have over this woman's haunted legacy, themselves and their instruments, that is very much by design. *Kate Plays Christine* has more on its mind than simple questions or simple answers.

Robert Greene is unlike any other documentarian working today. When he isn't directing, he writes eloquently and furiously about the state of non-fiction

film for many different outlets. He warns and decries the traps many documentarians fall into. The one thing he hates above all else is safety. He shies away from expected theory and practice like talking head interviews or heavy handed music on the soundtrack telling you how to feel. He dislikes movies that act as fact-delivery systems; that rig the game emotionally to force you to draw one conclusion about the material presented. But the most effective way he's combatted the malaise that's fallen over the international non-fiction scene is through the movies he himself directs. His debut, the introspective, incidental national self-portrait *Owning The Weather* (2009) introduced his gently psychedelic aesthetic. A very public fan of *2001: A Space Odyssey* (1967), Greene plainly saw a form of non-fiction filmmaking that was unique, proudly aberrant, emotional and searing. By disobeying all the unwritten rules of documentary he's been resuscitating his beloved form, with each new film like a shock from a pair of defibrillators.

Greene's next films, the beautiful community portraits 2010's *Kati with an I* and 2012's *Fake It So Real* simmer with intimacy. He gets closer to his subjects—a girl on the verge of graduating high school and a team of regional wrestlers—than seems possible. Scenes of his heroine crying in *Kati with an I* as she decides whether to go to college or stay in town to be with her boyfriend are stunning revelations and a Rosetta stone for his later work. His camera treats her with the compassion of both a character and a human being. It's astonishing and feels unprecedented. In 2014's *Actress* he followed Brandy Burre's attempt at a comeback after taking time away from her career to raise children. Here, he directly and deliberately challenges expectations of conventional non-fiction by creating phantom versions of the housewife life she's trying to escape to recommit to her art. She acts out a fantasy of the life from which she needs fantasy to escape. As beautiful as *Actress* is, it was only a warm-up for the mind games to come.

It's not hyperbole to say that the spectacular and troubling *Kate Plays Christine* is the culmination of Greene's obsession with the thin line between performance and real behavior, where lives become movies and vice versa. Like Greene's other protagonists, Kate Lyn Sheil is performing and she isn't. She is herself, she is playing the character of an actress playing a role, and deeply, distantly, she's also playing Christine Chubbuck. The look on her face as she retraces the steps once tread by Chubbuck looks entirely too riddled with fear and trepidation to be part of the version of herself she plays. She's filled with doubt and unease in her task. She meets a few of the people who knew Christine, listens to them talk about what kind of woman she was, how she placed too much faith in a co-worker's attention, etc. She even buys a gun from the same shop Christine bought the weapon she used to take her life. What she learns about Christine starts to creep into her expression, affecting her willingness to delve further into this woman's psyche. Christine was lonely, lived with her mother, and if there was hope of improving her life or moving on to bigger and better things, no one around her let on. She was treated like a sympathy-hire at the TV station at which she worked. Sheil, a major figure in the American independent film scene, also has major studio credits and so is keenly aware how the "system" treats women. Her growing discomfort with becoming Christine is externalized as she starts to feel what Christine went through. When Greene finally stages Christine's suicide, with Sheil tanned, wigged, and dressed exactly like her inspiration, the effect is beyond eerie. It's almost unearthly.

Kate Plays Christine asks dozens of questions, each more nagging and fascinating than the last. Its identity crisis drama is relayed in nearly surreal terms. We're only privy to Sheil's thoughts as she sparingly voices them and by how clearly her magnificently emotive face shows contempt and melancholy. She has one of the greatest faces in American cinema, her small eyes projecting seas of trauma, and few people play inscrutable or existentially exhausted as well as she. Greene, ever sly and patient, does little else but observe Sheil as the full extent of the maddening life that suffocated Christine becomes clear. In so doing he makes his audience complicit in this slightly morbid, if wholly sympathetic chameleon act. Sheil's trips to the tanning bed and the gun store are so casually shot by cinematographer Sean Price Williams, it isn't until much later that we realize we've been watching her prepare for a furious séance. Sheil isn't just

invoking the spirit of Chubbuck by donning her clothes, speaking to her surviving co-workers and absorbing her pain, she's preparing to vomit Christine's damaged spirit back at us like Linda Blair in *The Exorcist*. To project this hurt back on the same public who watched Christine on TV week after week. The public watched this very likely depressed woman between reports of murder and the country's growing discontent and saw nothing and nobody. She was just a face on a screen to her audience and her friends alike—a talking head—and Greene and Sheil give her depth again, taking her out of the two dimensional screen in which her death is forever trapped.

Christine's suicide was, for years, a synecdoche for the country's incredibly frayed and irresponsible history of both televised sensationalism. Even as a symbol, she was rendered more simply than she was. In all these years her legacy was allowed to rest as what M.R. James would call a warning to the curious. She inspired incredulity and sick fascination and her last words have become a prediction, but it took 40 years before much in the way of a public investigation into her humanity took place. Greene's film, as well as Antonio Campos' fiction take on the same story *Christine* (2016) starring Rebecca Hall, look for answers about her, and not what she stood for, in diametrically opposed forms. They search for the ragged mass of smothered feelings under the histrionic public treatment of her act. A woman who was unhappy in her life, who had her inferiority reinforced by everyone around her, has been a dog-eared page in a book of historical oddities for too long. By meticulously and mundanely creating this woman from scratch, Sheil and Greene want us to see how ordinary her upsets and defeats were, to see ourselves in Christine's quiet misery. To see the cruel irony that she used to speak to an audience every day but never felt like anyone heard her. As Greene peers closer and closer at Sheil's transformation, she chafes at his attention, feeling all too sharply what Christine went through when she had to deliver news about the world she'd never see without affect or emotion. Christine's broadcasts were records of her withering on the inside. Sheil wears that slow internal death around her just as she does her wig and clothes. She becomes Christine, but she also becomes the voice Christine never found; a voice of righteousness and anger and devastation.

Scout Tafoya

CREDITS

herself: Kate Lyn Sheil
himself: Steve Zurk
himself: David Mackey

himself: Michael Ray Davis
himself: Holland Hayes
Origin: United States
Language: English
Released: 2016
Production: Susan Bedusa, Douglas Tirola; released by 4th Row Films, Faliro House Productions, Prewar Cinema Productions
Directed by: Robert Greene
Written by: Robert Greene
Cinematography by: Sean Price Williams
Music by: Keegan DeWitt
Editing: Robert Greene
Art Direction: Jerry Eller
Costumes: Hannah Kittell
Production Design: John Dickson
MPAA rating: Unrated
Running time: 112 minutes

REVIEWS

Bowen, Chuck. *Slant Magazine.* August 15, 2016.

Brody, Richard. *New Yorker.* August 22, 2016.

Dowd, A.A. *The A.V. Club.* August 23, 2016.

Grozdanovic, Nikola. *The Playlist.* January 30, 2016.

Kohn, Eric. *IndieWire.* January 30, 2016.

Lodge, Guy. *Variety.* January 30, 2016.

O'Hehir, Andrew. *Salon.com.* August 24, 2016.

Rooney, David. *Hollywood Reporter.* August 22, 2016.

Rothkopf, Joshua. *Time Out New York.* August 25, 2016. .

Seitz, Matt Zoller. *RogerEbert.com.* August 24, 2016.

KEANU

Wait 'til you get a load of meow.
—Movie tagline

Box Office: $20.6 Million

Keanu is a good-natured mélange of over the top gangster movie tropes and the kind of smart and silly banter with which fans of *Key and Peele* are familiar. While the film never reaches the highs of the Comedy Central show's finest sketches, with their incisive and hilarious takes on racial issues, it offers some funny set pieces and allows Jordan Peele and Keegan-Michael Key a chance to enact cinematic fantasies. Their show featured many film references, and with the raining bullets, tense hostage scenes, and crime kingpins on display here, it's clear they know and love that which they are parodying. The setup is undeniably ridiculous. Rell (Peele) and Clarence (Key) are cousins with opposing personalities. Rell is a despondent stoner living in a messy apartment covered with movie posters, while Clar-

ence is an uptight married man wearing boat shoes and driving a SUV. In the opening scene, we see a killing spree at a drug-processing facility. In this tableau, which could be ripped from any generic action movie, there's an incongruous presence--an adorable kitten that darts through the bloodbath and manages to escape, ending up on Rell's doorstep. Rell is immediately cheered up by the presence of the sweet creature and names him Keanu. Given the cat's sketchy provenance, it's no surprise that Keanu goes missing shortly after Rell has made him his own and introduced him to Clarence. The two men go out to a movie and when they come back Rell's apartment is in total disarray with no Keanu in sight. This sets Rell and Clarence on their increasingly convoluted journey into the criminal underworld. They first demand answers from Hulka (Will Forte, trying too hard), Rell's next-door neighbor and drug dealer, and find out that the break-in was the doing of the Blips, a local gang. Rell and Clarence go to the strip club where the gang meets, hoping to get Keanu back. Rell and Clarence's infiltration of the gang provides some of the film's strongest comedic moments. The two men banter about the appropriate use of the "n-word" while at the strip club and both adopt exaggerated "gangsta" personas complete with the ridiculous nicknames of "Tectonic" and "Shark Tank." The theme of passing and expressing various forms of black masculinity was a running theme on *Key and Peele*, handled with nuance. In *Keanu*, everything is more broad, and while the comedians' self-aware handling of a cliché version of blackness is still very funny, it isn't quite as dynamic as it is when distilled to a short sketch. As Rell and Clarence fall in deeper and deeper with the gang and the body count rises, the film begins to feel a bit too long though there's humor to be found along the way.

While *Keanu* is mostly enjoyable, the problems it has feel quite common to the circumstances under which it was made. Cinematic efforts from sketch comedy teams often feel thin and not as funny as their source material. In order to succeed, a comedy sketch must be condensed and pack a punch. Key and Peele are highly charismatic performers, and the parts of *Keanu* that drift away from their characters, or focus too heavily on plotting (or, in some cases, comically exaggerated violence) are not as strong as simply watching the two men shoot the breeze. Early on, Rell takes amusingly intricate photographs of Keanu posed in different settings from his favorite films. It seems that in the film, Key and Peele are creating their own highly referential fantasy tableaus to play around in. They use a macho cinematic framework as a means of both embracing the cheesy fun of genre conventions and critiquing them. *Keanu*'s whole plot is one big joke: all this action and violence for the sake of a cute kitten. Rell and Clarence are regular guys who find themselves caught up in a situation straight out of a movie. The need to act tough in such ridiculous circumstances makes for an amusing commentary on the fragility of masculinity. An ongoing joke is Clarence's enthusiasm for George Michael. Rather than just make this affinity into a throwaway gay panic joke, the film features an extended scene in which some of the Blips turn on the music in Clarence's car, unexpectedly releasing a torrent of George Michael, in all his 80s glory. At first Clarence panics--he fears he's going to be found out as not tough enough, not black enough. But he lays on his exaggerated macho persona, talking about the musician as though he were black ("He's light skinned") and before too long all the gang members are singing along. *Keanu* is keenly aware that much of masculinity is an act, and delights in playfully poking holes in racial stereotypes.

Abbey Bender

CREDITS

Rell Williams/Oil Dresden: Jordan Peele
Clarence Goobril/Smoke Dresden: Keegan Michael Key
Hi-C: Tiffany Haddish
Cheddar: Method Man
Trunk: Darrell Britt-Gibson
Origin: United States
Language: English
Released: 2016
Production: Joel Zadak, Peter Principato, Paul Young, Jordan Peele, Keegan Michael Key; released by New Line Cinema L.L.C.
Directed by: Peter Atencio
Written by: Jordan Peele; Alex Rubens
Cinematography by: Jas Shelton
Music by: Steve Jablonsky; Nathan Whitehead
Sound: Michael Babcock; Jon Michaels
Music Supervisor: JoJo Villanueva
Editing: Nicholas Monsour
Art Direction: Erin Cochran
Costumes: Abby O'Sullivan
Production Design: Aaron Osborne
MPAA rating: R
Running time: 100 minutes

REVIEWS

Bastien, Angelica Jade. *Roger Ebert.com.* April 29, 2016.
Chang, Justin. *Variety.* March 13, 2016.
Dargis, Manhola. *New York Times.* April 28, 2016.
DeFore, John. *Hollywood Reporter.* Match 13, 2016.
Dowd, A.A. *The A.V. Club.* April 28, 2016.

Edelstein, David. *Vulture.* April 29, 2016.
Ide, Wendy. *Guardian.* July 17, 2016.
Sims, David. *Atlantic.* April 29, 2016.
Tobias, Scott. *NPR.* April 28, 2016.
Zacharek, Stephanie. *The Times.* April 29, 2016.

QUOTES

Clarence Goobril: "Wordness to the turdness."

TRIVIA

The character played by Method Man is named Cheddar. For his role on the television show *The Wire* he played a character named Cheese.

KEEPING UP WITH THE JONESES

Every couple needs a little action.
—Movie tagline

Box Office: $14.9 Million

Jeff and Karen Gaffney (Zach Galifianakis and Isla Fisher) are living the American Dream in their suburban cul-de-sac. He works in human relations trying to solve employee grievances at a local tech company. She is an interior designer currently working on her client's bathroom. When they send their kid away for the summer, their attention begins to shift to their new neighbors. Tim and Natalie Jones (Jon Hamm and Gal Gadot) are an impossibly attractive and interesting couple that would be the envy of anyone whose anecdotal excitement consists of a trip to Kinko's. His stories as a world traveler would put Professor McBragg to shame and her skills at throwing sharp objects might be a red flag if her long legs were not already a distraction.

Karen is not so easily duped and begins following Natalie, albeit not very conspicuously. When she realizes that the Joneses may be keeping an eye on them as well, further discoveries blow all their covers and the truth comes out that they are actually CIA operatives. Something hinky is going on with Jeff's computer at work, punctuated by the fact that his internet access attracts everyone there to use it. Quickly determining that Jeff is not the prime suspect, the spies-turned-lovers find themselves forced into involving the suburbanites into their plan to foiling the real bad guys.

The prospect of an absurdist John le Carre tale where an ordinary citizen gets thrust into the world of international espionage would be a tasty opportunity for satire if the well had not been gone to so many times before. Arthur Hiller's *The In-Laws* (1979) may be the gold standard but the premise extends as far back as Bob Hope's *My Favorite Blonde* (1942) and *My Favorite Spy* (1951) up through Hitchcock's *North by Northwest* (1959) and continued with variations as high as Joe Dante's *The 'Burbs* (1989) and as low as the recent *Central Intelligence* (2016). Michael LeSieur's screenplay for Joneses was never going to win points on originality but its familiarity makes it even more forgettable.

The boredom represented in the suburbs has been such a fallback cliché in movies that those who enjoy quiet and free parking would be justified in strongly worded op-eds defending their perceived bubble-like existence. A little of that seeps into the contrasts between the couples, only the film never finds time to really make a case for either of their positives or negatives. What becomes lost is a burgeoning empathy between the two men wishing not for the economic or global freedom of the other but to inherit the goodness and strength of their counterpart. Hamm is a natural comic actor but it is in these moments where he can shine so brightly that the film's myriad of flaws stand out so much more.

Zach Galifianakis has never quite found his footing beyond his stand-up routines and the brilliance of his recurring *Between Two Ferns* interview show but he can turn it down just enough to create a sympathetic figure on occasion. The late appearance by his *The Comedians of Comedy* (2005) touring partner, Patton Oswalt, who has been so good in dramatic roles like *Big Fan* (2009) and *Young Adult* (2011), is alternatively turned so far up in volume that it just falls flat right when the film needed a boost in energy. Isla Fisher is doing her best to accentuate the absurdity on the page by injecting as much physical comedy as her director will let her get away with. Exploring that male dynamic further would have really left the women in a lurch as neither generate any kind of rapport thanks in large part to Gal Gadot who has yet to prove there is anything beyond her slinky frame and blank stare of hardened sexiness.

Greg Mottola has done some wonderful work in his career with outlandish comic premises. His combination of favorite slacker man-children Simon Pegg and Nick Frost on a road trip with an alien in *Paul* (2011) was much funnier than it might sound. With *Superbad* (2007) he helped take the stale all-night teenage quest for booze and babes into a poignant and even dark film about leaving comfort zones behind. That sense of danger is one of the many things missing from Keeping Up with the Joneses. Never do the stakes feel large or outrageous enough to register as anything but loud reminders that the Joneses are polar opposites to the Gaffneys and a good many of the funnier premises that laid the groundwork for this to be so easily lost in the shuffle. Not that it needed any help falling well behind the pack.

Erik Childress

CREDITS

Jeff Gaffney: Zach Galifianakis
Tim Jones: Jon Hamm
Karen Gaffney: Isla Fisher
Nataline Jones: Gal Gadot
Scorpion: Patton Oswalt
Origin: United States
Language: English
Released: 2016
Production: Laurie MacDonald, Walter F. Parkes; released by Fox 2000 Pictures, Parkes+MacDonald Image Nation
Directed by: Greg Mottola
Written by: Michael LeSieur
Cinematography by: Andrew Dunn
Music by: Jake Monaco
Sound: Lewis Goldstein
Editing: David Rennie
Art Direction: Jeremy Woolsey
Costumes: Ruth E. Carter
Production Design: Mark Ricker
MPAA rating: PG-13
Running time: 105 minutes

REVIEWS

Brody, Richard. *New Yorker*. October 24, 2016.
Duralde, Alonso. *TheWrap*. October 18, 2016.
Gonzalez, Ed. *Slant Magazine*. October 18, 2016.
Judy, Jim. *Screen It!*. October 21, 2016.
Lapin, Andrew. *NPR*. October 20, 2016.
Lybarger, Dan. *Arkansas Democrat-Gazette*. November 14, 2016.
Nusair, David. *Reel Film Reviews*. November 7, 2016.
Rife, Katie. *The A.V. Club*. October 20, 2016.
Rothkopf, Joshua. *Time Out*. October 22, 2016.
Russo, Tom. *Boston Globe*. October 20, 2016.

QUOTES

Natalie Jones: "The first rule of being a spy is not to be in love with your partner."

TRIVIA

The interiors of the villian's penthouse were built in a complex of buildings that once housed an ice-cream distributor.

KEVIN HART: WHAT NOW?

The comedy event of the year.
—Movie tagline

Box Office: $23.6 Million

Kevin Hart is an all-time comedian who could kill in a room of silence; he does not need the laughs of others to prove his brilliance. The success of his film career has paralleled that of his stand-up, which has been documented by feature-length documentaries that play in multiplexes, essentially making him one of the few modern comedians to make stand-up blockbusters. But at the core of this success is a selfish idea of comedy, which becomes hugely on display in his latest stand-up film, *Kevin Hart: What Now?*. In it, his comic charisma involving his short stature and easy emasculation leads to an ugly Napoleonic complex, proving his desperate need to be the funniest guy in the room, or in this case, a sold-out football stadium.

The premise of *Kevin Hart: What Now?* is that things are even bigger than his previous stand-up feature, 2013's *Kevin Hart: Let Me Explain*. Whereas that earlier documentary featured him selling out New York City's Madison Square Garden, a type of honor for comedians achieved by only a few, now he is telling jokes to 53,000 fans on the scale of Philadelphia's Lincoln Financial Field, home of the NFL's Philadelphia Eagles.

The movie starts on very rough note with an opening sequence titled "Casino," with story credit going to Hart, as directed by Tim Story of Hart's *Think Like a Man* (2012) and *Ride Along* (2014) films. From its stylized, James Bond-like opening sequence that features his name constantly in the lyrics, it becomes a display less of a playful character but his ego. This carries over into the shabby sequence, which features Halle Berry (as a love interest) playing into the high-energy, confrontational humor that excels on Hart's fake reality series show, BET's *Real Husbands of Hollywood*, but feels forced here. Ed Helms even makes a brief cameo as a casino bartender, who serves a cringingly named "Kevin Hartini" to one person, while providing the title star a can of the movie's huge sponsor, Miller Lite. All of this marketing and weak entertainment adds to a narcissism that deflates any chance at humor, leading to an action climax in which Hart dispatches bad guys to save a briefcase full of money for his show that night. Director Story continues his laziness with the action genre (as seen in *Ride Along 2* [2016]) with grotesque editing during Hart's brief moments of hand-to-hand combat.

Eventually, *Kevin Hart: What Now?* parts with this tedious introduction and begins the main event, directed by Leslie Small, with animation showing Hart being launched from under the stage into a sky of white light. No longer a secret agent, he's now Kevin Hart the Comedian, with a gold chain, gold watch, gold bracelet, and gold microphone to declare to his audience a type of royalty. Cameras that move throughout the stadium, on cranes and drone machines, paint a thorough picture of a sold-out facility. A strong part of Hart's image is his background as a hustling comedian in Philadelphia, which makes *Kevin Hart: What Now?* all the more special for the achievement it documents. It is this spirit that dissipates from this point, especially as the event film becomes more akin to someone throwing their own birthday party.

Kevin Hart: What Now? registers as isolating quickly into his routine, in which he tells an expansive, overly-written joke involving his long driveway at his mansion, which then evolves into jokes about his son being emasculated by his private school education. Other familiar themes from his previous stand-up specials come into play, like overly aggressive wild animals, his crazy dad, and thugs that speak macho gibberish—all played with animation from Hart, but with the connection to his audience progressively weakened by the non-relatable context of his success. His narrative as a comedic presence has drastically changed for the worse, as in how one bit involves Hart being accosted by a fan while on the toilet in the airport, but the core of the joke is that he does not want to use public toilets. Hart loses his ability to be a comic of the people, and instead becomes a comic for his narcissism.

That very isolating factor of the film can be seen in its coverage of the audience, which wants to savor the scope of a sold-out football stadium, but is a bit delusional as to a viewers' involvement. Roughly half of the B-roll involves viewers who are far away from the stage, watching monitors of Hart's performance. More often than not they are not laughing. It further drives the idea that Hart would rather fill an audience than make all of them feel involved, going for personal size instead of the intimate experience of making someone laugh.

Whereas his previous stand-up film *Kevin Hart: Let Me Explain* ended with him walking into a ray of light, *Kevin Hart: What Now?* ends on a similarly sanctimonious note. After flying away from the venue in a helicopter with Halle Berry in tow, Hart mentions that the mission continues: "I think it's time we show the world how funny Kevin Hart can be." Aside from the grotesque third-person usage, it is a fitting closer to how Hart views his comedy as a type of service, that his jokes might even bring people together in laughter, but by means of primarily raising himself and his brand above all else. Hart has done incredible things in a career that can be charted day-by-day, deal-by-deal with hard work, but this latest installment brings him down to a new low. It is his first stand-up film yet in which one does not at all wish they were there for the real deal.

Nick Allen

CREDITS

Himself: Kevin Hart
Herself: Halle Berry
Himself: Don Cheadle
Bartender: Ed Helms
Victor: David Meunier
Origin: United States
Language: English
Released: 2016
Production: Jeff Clanagan, Dana Riddick, Leland "Pookey" Wigington; released by Hartbeat Productions, Universal Pictures Inc.
Directed by: Leslie Small
Written by: Kevin Hart; Joey Wells; Harry Ratchford
Cinematography by: Cameron Barnett
Sound: Kami Asgar; Sean McCormack
Music Supervisor: Todd Bozung
Editing: Guy Harding
Art Direction: Nicolas Plotquin
Costumes: Olivia Miles
Production Design: Bruce Ryan
MPAA rating: R
Running time: 96 minutes

REVIEWS

DeFore, John. *Hollywood Reporter*. October 12, 2016.
Derakhshani, Tirdad. *Philadelphia Inquirer*. October 13, 2016.
Guzman, Rafer. *Newsday*. October 13, 2016.
Henderson, Odie. *RogerEbert.com*. October 14, 2016.
Jones, J.R. *Chicago Reader*. October 20, 2016.
Kenny, Glenn. *New York Times*. October 13, 2016.
Semley, John. *Globe and Mail*. October 14, 2016.
Scherstuhl, Alan. *Village Voice*. October 13, 2016.
Walsh, Katie. *Tribune News Service*. October 12, 2016.
Zacharek, Stephanie. *Time*. October 13, 2016.

TRIVIA

Kevin Hart said this film is his last standup special because he wanted to end his specials at the peak of his career.

KNIGHT OF CUPS
(Vitez se peharom)

Box Office: $566,006

As observers of the works of Terrence Malick can attest, his unique cinematic style has in recent years moved beyond the already tenuous grasp on conventional narrative structure displayed in films like *Badlands* (1973), *Days of Heaven* (1978), *The Thin Red Line* (1998), and *The New World* (2005) to such increasingly enigmatic efforts as *The Tree of Life* (2011) and *To the Wonder* (2013). This is especially true in regards to his latest work, the long-awaited *Knight of Cups*, a film destined to leave even his most ardent fans scratching their heads in utter confusion immediately after watching it for the first time and detractors once again screaming about how this particular emperor has once again been caught starkers. And yet, as muddled and bizarre as it may seem at first glance, there is something truly striking about it and those willing to mull it over for a while and perhaps give it a second viewing are liable to finally come away from it thinking that they have indeed encountered greatness, albeit the kind of greatness that you might not necessarily recommend to any close friends or loved ones unless you know their moviegoing tastes really well.

So what exactly is *Knight of Cups* about anyway? Put simply, this is not the kind of film that lends itself well to a one or two paragraph summary. Following a recitation of the opening lines of *The Pilgrim's Progress* by Sir John Gielgud and a view of the aurora borealis as seen from the vastness of space, we are introduced to Rick (Christian Bale), who recounts the tale of a knight who was sent out West by his father in search of treasure and while on that quest, he was served a mysterious and intoxicating brew that caused him to forget everything— his quest, his family, and his self—and to spend the rest of his days as though lost in a daze. As it turns out, Rick himself is pretty much the contemporary analogue of that knight—years earlier, he ventured to the West— Los Angeles, to be exact—to become a screenwriter and while he has clearly done well for himself, he too finds himself spiritually and emotionally adrift, alienated from his family—his broken-down father (Brian Dennehy) and his volatile brother (Wes Bentley) and the ever-present spirit of another brother whose suicide years earlier fractured the bonds of those left behind—and from himself. Nothing gets to him—not even an earthquake or what has to be one of the oddest movie industry shindig ever captured on film. (The guest list includes, however fleetingly, Antonio Banderas, Joe Manganiello, Ryan O'Neal, Fabio, Jason Clarke, Nick Kroll, Thomas Lennon, Joe La Truglio, and the proverbial many, many more.)

As for that intoxicating brew that has helped to keep him drifting unmoored through his own existence, that is represented in the form of a number of alluring women who drift in and out of his life, seemingly at random. There is Della (Imogen Poots), who looks like the ultimate Manic Pixie Dream Girl but who may be wiser than she appears to be at first glance. There is Helen (Freida Pinto), a model that he meets at a party, Karen (Teresa Palmer), a good-natured stripper with whom he spends a few idyllic days taking in the deliberately artificial sights of the Vegas strip, Nancy (Cate Blanchett), the ex-wife with whom he had no children and who quickly grew tired of his extended malaise, Elizabeth (Natalie Portman), a married acquaintance whom he got pregnant and who is devastated by the guilt she feels, and Isabel (Isabel Lucas), a beautiful blonde who he spots at the beach and whose golden beauty holds out the promise/curse of the future and all it holds. There are other women who pop up from time to time to further entice and distract him—one-night stands, party pickups, and even evidence of at least one threesome.

Although divided into sections (each titled, like the film itself, after a Tarot card) as a way of bringing superficial order to what might otherwise be chaos, *Knight of Cups* is as freeform as any film ever made by a major American filmmaker—with its collection of random imagery, non-linear narrative, and a preference for the visual over the verbal (there is precious little dialogue to be had in the film and of that, most of it comes in the form of voiceovers instead of two people simply talking to one another), the closest thing to compare it to are the latter-day efforts of Jean-Luc Godard like *Goodbye to Language* (2014) that have seen him attempting to rip apart the entire filmmaking apparatus and remake it into something that is both universal in scope and achingly personal in tone. Even if you didn't know going in that Malick was working more or less without a formal script—he would supply his actors with ideas and the odd line of dialogue and go from there—it would not take very long to realize that he was pushing his impressionistic filmmaking approach to unheard-of levels. Compared to this film, even such free-form experiments as *The Tree of Life* and *To the Wonder* feel like they came straight out of the Syd Field playbook by comparison.

In the case of virtually any other film that wasn't an explicitly experimental work, such an approach would be a recipe for disaster—the kind of thing that you might see only in an exceptionally broad Hollywood spoof of crazy artist types—but in *Knight of Cups*, it actually works kinds of beautifully once you settle in with its peculiar rhythms and refusal to follow the tenets of traditional narrative. As we follow Rick on his aimless path, we begin to get a true sense of his essential rootlessness and dissatisfaction towards an existence that most people would kill to have—a life that not even money, fame, and the company of some of the most beautiful women imaginable can provide significance. In much the same way that we are observing Rick as he goes through the motions of his life—studio meetings in which art and commerce do daily battle, Hollywood parties in which bullshit banalities flow as effortlessly as

the champagne, and his various assignations—Rick is experiencing them in a similarly detached manner that suggests a highly internal person who has managed to find himself in a world in which virtually everything is external. Malick beautifully captures this sense of ennui throughout and even though most moviegoers might not exactly relate to the specifics of Rick's existence, they will recognize that sense of long for some kind of place in the world. It may not be a sensation that they necessarily want to spend $10 to see on the big screen but it is there. Indeed, it is fascinating to watch Bale, usually one of the most controlled and focused of actors, playing a character as emotionally adrift as this one.

In regards to the women on display in the film, some have criticized Malick for presenting them as little more than ciphers who are asked to do little more than gambol around in flowing dresses while allowing Rick (and those of us in the audience) to drink in their undeniable beauty while denying them their own agency or, in a couple of cases, their own names—a charge that is ultimately unfair on a couple of counts. For one, Malick treats the women in the same way as he treats Rick—as incredibly attractive vehicles for his various themes instead of as fully developed characters—and therefore makes it a far more palatable playing field than if he were the wise sage and they were the pretty ciphers who have no existence outside of their connection to him. More importantly, and this is one of the many aspects of the film that are revealed on a second veiwing, they are not quite the gorgeous empty vessels they seem to be at first glance. The Blanchett and Portman characters, despite their brief screen time, are vividly etched portrayals of the potentially devastating results of falling into Rick's orbit and, to steal a phrase, the unbearable lightness of his being. The Pinto and Palmer characters—the model and the stripper—speak wisely and lucidly about their seemingly frivolous occupations and what they mean to them. Even the Poots character—who seems to be a walking (and skipping) cliché at first glance proves to be wiser than she seems, at one point correctly diagnosing Rick by observing "You aren't looking for love—you are looking for a love experience."

Trying to explain what *Knight of Cups* ultimately "means" is a foolhardy task at best because, like a great Bob Dylan song, it is the kind of thing that will mean different things to different people at different points in their lives and to try to nail it down to one specific explanation would be to reduce it somehow. What can be talked about is what an overwhelming sensorial experience it is to watch. Working again with cinematographer Emmanuel Lubezki, with whom Malick has collaborated since *The New World* and shooting in a variety of formats that include HD, 35mm, and 65mm, the two offers up a barrage of striking imagery throughout ranging from the overtly gorgeous to the intriguingly off-kilter. More than just a series of arresting imagery, they manage to take locations as familiar as Los Angeles and Hollywood parties and present them in a manner that forces viewers to look at it anew and perhaps to even find the beauty amidst the banal facades. All of this is driven by a score that incorporates the usual Malick musical suspects (Grieg, Chopin, and Part, among others), new music from Haran Townshend (who composed music for *To the Wonder*) and even a few contemporary dance beats for good measure. The end result is an oftentimes stunning audio-visual experience of the sort that is rarely seen these days.

Knight of Cups is a one-of-a-kind work by a one-of-a-kind filmmaker—one who combines the technical expertise of a veteran at the peak of his creative powers and the restless and inquisitive nature and riskiness of a newcomer with nothing to lose—that grows and grows in stature with every viewing. However, as most singular cinematic experiences go, it is clearly not for everyone and even Malick's most fervent supporters may come away from it thinking that his detractors may have a point after all. One almost hesitates to recommend it wholeheartedly to others because those who do not find themselves connecting to its strange and particular wavelength are almost certainly going to find it to be baffling at best and downright enraging at worst. That said, if you are one of those brave souls who enjoys watching films that are not afraid to push the boundaries of what art can say about the human condition and are willing to spend the time grappling with it afterwards, perhaps to the extent of giving it a second or third look, then *Knight of Cups* is something to watch and treasure.

Peter Sobczynski

CREDITS

Rick: Christian Bale
Nancy: Cate Blanchett
Elizabeth: Natalie Portman
Barry: Wes Bentley
Joseph: Brian Dennehy
Origin: United States
Language: English
Released: 2015
Production: Nicolas Gonda, Sarah Green, Ken Kao; Waypoint Entretainment; released by Dogwood Films
Directed by: Terrence Malick
Written by: Terrence Malick
Cinematography by: Emmanuel Lubezki
Music by: Hanan Townshend
Sound: Joel Dougherty

Music Supervisor: Lauren Marie Mikus
Editing: A.J. Edwards; Keith Fraase; Geoffrey Richman; Mark Yoshikawa
Art Direction: Ruth De Jong
Costumes: Jacqueline West
Production Design: Jack Fisk
MPAA rating: R
Running time: 118 minutes

REVIEWS

Brody, Richard. *New Yorker*. March 9, 2016.
Chang, Justin. *Variety*. February 8, 2015.
Ebiri, Bilge. *Village Voice*. March 1, 2016.
Hornaday, Ann. *Washington Post*. March 10, 2016.
Jenkins, Mark. *NPR*. March 4, 2016.
Lane, Anthony. *New Yorker*. March 7, 2016.
McCarthy, Todd. *Hollywood Reporter*. February 8, 2015.
Reed, Rex. *New York Observer*. March 3, 2016.
Scott, A.O. *New York Times*. March 3, 2016.
Turan, Kenneth. *Los Angeles Times*. March 3, 2016.

QUOTES

Della: "You don't want love, you want a love experience."

TRIVIA

In tarot cards, if the Knight of Cups is upright, it represents adventures and change.

KRISHA

Box Office: $144,822

Trey Edward Shults' directorial debut *Krisha* opens with a slow fade in and zoom on lead actress Krisha Fairchild, who stars in the titular role. The actress and character sharing the same name is not a coincidence, and is something Shults does throughout the film, which adds a real air of ease, familiarity, and voyeuristic discomfort. The camera holds in a medium shot, Fairchild's watery eyes staring directly into camera as loud, discordant, and frightening notes play in the background. The look on her face conveys sadness, pleading, or shame. Because of the eerie musical notes playing viewers are automatically led to believe this is a horror movie and Krisha is the source of horror. Most of this is correct. *Krisha* is also a pitch-black comedy, a family drama, and one of the most striking directorial debuts of the past decade. Yet, at its heart, *Krisha* is an intensely personal story of severe family dysfunction that pretty much everyone can relate to in some way.

After the unsettling and powerfully dramatic slow zoom in on Krisha, the film immediately dives headlong into another confidently bold scene. This time it's an 8-minute plus tracking shot of Krisha stressfully arriving in a suburban neighborhood and racing around nervously, looking for a house. The shot immediately draws viewers into the action from a first person point of view and this placement of the viewer in the driver's seat lasts the entire film. As a result, viewers feel like a silent partner to Krisha as she awkwardly enters the home of her sister and the stickiness of the strained relationships therein begin to bubble to the surface. From here on out, viewers are passengers on a tense, bumpy ride centered on a seemingly normal family forced to deal with the black sheep of the family in Krisha.

There are many wonderful things about *Krisha* and it's one of the best films of the year. From the dazzling camera work by Drew Daniels (the film is shot on 35mm but the camera movements, angles, and intimacy feel almost a like a digital video documentary or "Mumblecore" film) to the excellent, tense chemistry between the cast members this is a remarkable debut from a young filmmaker, one that will surely be difficult for young Shults to follow up on. Perhaps its biggest accomplishment is that throughout the film's tight, 80-minute run time one feels strapped in for a nerve-racking ride through someone else's family drama. The dread and tension rise through excellent sound design and the editing of Shults himself. He is indeed a triple-threat as writer/director and editor and his style and skill create an all new type of family drama.

Obviously, every family has their fair share of awkwardness or small contingencies of friends and enemies within any family gathering. But in *Krisha* one almost feels as though they are spying on a real life family in real life moments. Yet in actual real life one could choose to look away or go hide in another room (or, inside their cell phone), but here they are forced to confront what they are seeing. The discomfort is frequently palpable.

Also adding an air to the realness of the film is the fact *Krisha* is populated with mostly non-actors. While fans of indie film may recognize Bill Wise (*Boyhood* [2015]) or Chris Doubek (*A Teacher* [2013]) everyone else onscreen has yet to form a visual bond with audiences. Therefore it feels as though they could actually really be the characters they're portraying. Add to this the fact many of the characters and actors share the same name, including Krisha and her estranged son Trey (played by the Shults, making him a quadruple threat), and again the feeling of spying on someone else's weird, maladjusted family really takes hold.

As *Krisha* slowly unfolds, viewers are given just enough information to put together what the main source of pressure and stress is in this family; it's Krisha herself, as the title clearly indicates. Her constant inability to stay sober and, as a multitude of family members put it, "get her act together," at first seems like tensions formed from years past. However, as the film plays out, it soon becomes clear Krisha's dysfunction, self-medicating, and subversive (as well as outright) abuse of others has never gone away. It's who she is inside. This almost puzzle-piece style of storytelling is yet another brilliant stroke from Shults—he gives the audience just enough to piece together this story of Krisha's family but also leaves enough space for one to fill in the blanks, probably with personal stories or feelings about their own familial issues. Yet *Krisha* isn't all about figuring out what's gone wrong here, it's also visually brilliant in bringing one into the acts being perpetrated.

Through clever camera work and a haunting, almost antagonistic score, Shults creates a feeling of stress that washes over one like the first much needed stiff drink at a family gathering. Krisha sneaks around the house, trying to corner Trey to talk to him and attempt to heal their pain and the shots of her awkwardly lurking around every corner add to the uncomfortable voyeuristic approach that resonates throughout the entire film. By the time the films ends—ingeniously on the very same shot that opens the film—one feels almost as exhausted as the put-upon family they just infiltrated. While, like a Rorschach test everyone will walk away feeling something different (anger, confusion, disgust, thankfulness that their family isn't as screwed up as the one they just spent time with) it's hard not to be moved and afterward dropped into deep thought from the experience of having seen *Krisha*.

Don R. Lewis

CREDITS

Krisha: Krishna Fairchild
Alex: Alex Dobrenko
Olivia: Olivia Grace Applegate
Trey: Trey Edward Shults
Logan: Bryan Casserly
Origin: United States
Language: English
Released: 2015
Production: Justin R. Chan, Chase Joliet, Wilson Smith, Trey Edward Shults; released by Dogwood Films, Hoody Boy Productions
Directed by: Trey Edward Shults
Written by: Trey Edward Shults; Brian McOmber
Cinematography by: Drew Daniels
Sound: Tim Rakoczy
MPAA rating: R
Running time: 83 minutes

REVIEWS

Burr, Ty. *Boston Globe*. March 24, 2016.

Chang, Justin. *Variety*. March 31, 2016.

Dargis, Manohola. *New York Times*. March 17, 2016.

Keogh, Tom. *Seattle Times*. March 24, 2016.

Lang, Nico. *Consequence of Sound*. March 24, 2016.

Lattimer, James. *Slant*. March 14, 2016.

Linden, Sheri. *Hollywood Reporter*. February 26, 2016.

O'Malley, Sheila. *RogerEbert.com*. March 18, 2016.

O'Sullivan, Michael. *Washington Post*. March 24, 2016.

Phillips, Michael. *Chicago Tribune*. March 24, 2016.

TRIVIA

Several of the family members in the film are actually related.

KUBO AND THE TWO STRINGS

Be bold. Be brave. Be epic.
—Movie tagline

Box Office: $48 Million

"If you must blink, do it now." With these seven words, LAIKA, the company behind modern children's classics *Coraline* (2009), *Paranorman* (2012), and *The Boxtrolls* (2014), open what is possibly their most accomplished and impressive film to date, *Kubo and the Two Strings*. The tone is unmistakable—this is no casual adventure story to be watched while kids are concurrently looking at their Facebook feed. It is a complex parable designed to teach children about loss and legacy. It plays like a hybrid of *The Wizard of Oz* (1939) and classic Japanese literature, with visual influences inspired by art of the region. With phenomenal voice work, ambitious storytelling, and mesmerizing visuals, it's the best animated film of 2016 by some margin.

Kubo (voiced by Art Parkinson) lives with his ill mother Sariatu (Charlize Theron) in a cave atop a distant mountain inspired by the art of Hokusai, most well-known for the iconic The Great Wave of Kanagawa. Kubo has magical powers that can transform paper into origami when he plays his two-string guitar. This is a world in which magic lives alongside reality. Kubo's ability is not treated with wonder by the locals, as Japanese literature often features blends of the magical and the real; the natural and the supernatural. Kubo plays his shamisen in the town square, and relays the story of Hanzo, a notable warrior who also happens to be Kubo's missing father. But Kubo never finishes his tale. His mother tells him about how his grandfather tried to kill both of them, stealing Kubo's eye in the process, but it's telling that the young man has not written an ending to his family's legacy quite yet.

Kubo learns of an Obon festival, a ceremony in which people light lamps and attempt to speak to deceased loved ones. He travels there to try and speak to his father, disobeying an order from his mother to never stay out after dark. As the sun sets, he is confronted by his mother's sisters (both voiced in concurrently, creepy fashion by Rooney Mara), who want to take him to The Moon King (Ralph Fiennes), his grandfather, to get his other eye. In a terrifying showdown, the Sisters chase Kubo through the village, destroying it along the way. Sariatu leaps to protect Kubo, telling him to flee. He takes a lock of her hair as he is flown away by his mother's magic.

Kubo awakens in a snowy tundra, accompanied by a talking monkey who appears to be an embodiment of the wooden charm that his mother had told him to always carry. Monkey is also voiced by Charlize Theron, adding to the sense that it is not just another traveling companion, but actually his mother's magic and protection traveling with Kubo in his journey. Monkey tells Kubo that his mother is dead. They must find the three magical items from Kubo's story if they hope to save the child and defeat The Moon King. The next morning, they awaken to find one of Kubo's origami characters sprung to life, a "Little Hanzo" warrior who shows Kubo and Monkey the way. They are quickly joined by a Beetle (Matthew McConaughey) with no memory of his past but allegiance to Kubo and vague recollections of being Hanzo's apprentice.

A quest begins for the quartet (again, the *Wizard of Oz* parallels, especially with the way characters represent others in Kubo's real world are strong). First, they find an underground cave called the "Hall of Bones," where the "Sword Unbreakable" is sticking out of the skull of a giant skeleton. Deep in the middle of the Long Lake they find the "Breastplate Impenetrable," floating in a "Garden of Eyes," where people are paralyzed if they stare too long. The quest for the "Helmet Invulnerable" takes them to Kubo's final battle with the Moon King, a return to reality, and an understanding about how those we love are always with us, and never completely lost.

As with all LAIKA films, the design elements here never feel quickly-considered or designed, as they are in so many children's films, just to push the story forward. *Kubo and the Two Strings* is a gorgeous enough film to watch with the sound off, and received not only an Animated Film nomination from the Academy but a Visual Effects one as well, and many thought it should have been considered for Costume Design or Production Design. It looks beautiful, but that beauty serves the story, never once feeling flashy or showy. There's a depth of field and detail to the character design that's the best LAIKA has yet produced.

And the voice work may be the company's best as well. In particular, Theron strikes just the right note as both Kubo's mother and Monkey, differentiating the characters ever so slightly while imbuing both with the protectiveness the roles needed. McConaughey is enjoyable; Mara is terrifying; Fiennes has practically cornered the market on legendary villains who shall not be named.

Kubo and the Two Strings was seen as being too scary or challenging for some viewers, making less than $70 million worldwide, and less domestically than any LAIKA film to date. It's a shame and indicative of how much parents fail to trust their kids to take in and comprehend complex themes. Most of the fairy tales which culture have deemed timeless and essential have elements of fear and adult themes. To be blunt, scaring a kid is good for them as it teaches the lessons they'll need later in life. Parts of *Kubo* may be scary, but the conversations that emerge from it are essential. And young ones who see it at the right age could come away with a greater appreciation of the cultures it represents and the art of storytelling. In that sense, it's one of the most important films of 2016.

Brian Tallerico

CREDITS

Monkey: Charlize Theron
Kubo: Art Parkinson
Moon King: Ralph Fiennes
The Sisters: Rooney Mara
Hosato: George Takei
Beetle: Matthew McConaughey
Origin: United States
Language: English
Released: 2016
Production: Arianne Sutner, Travis Knight; released by Laika Entertainment L.L.C.
Directed by: Travis Knight
Written by: Marc Haimes; Chris Butler
Cinematography by: Frank Passingham
Music by: Dario Marianelli
Sound: Tim Chau
Music Supervisor: Sara Matarazzo
Editing: Christopher Murrie
Costumes: Deborah Cook
MPAA rating: PG
Running time: 101 minutes

REVIEWS

Adams, Sam. *The A.V. Club.* August 17, 2016.
Chang, Justin. *Los Angeles Times.* August 18, 2016.
Debruge, Peter. *Variety.* August 12, 2016.
Ebiri, Bilge. *Village Voice.* August 13, 2016.
Ehrlich, David. *IndieWire.* August 12, 2016.

Hasseger, Jesse. *The A.V. Club.* August 17, 2016.
Kenny, Glenn. *New York Times.* August 18, 2016.
Laffly, Tomris. *Time Out New York.* August 18, 2016.
Lemire, Christy. *RogerEbert.com.* August 18, 2016.
Rechtshaffen, Michael. *Hollywood Reporter.* August 12, 2016.

QUOTES

Beetle: "I'm either a samurai or a really bad hoarder. Either way, inside my thorax beats the heart of a warrior."

TRIVIA

The movie consists of more than 145,000 photographs turned into a stop-motion film.

AWARDS

British Acad. 2016: Animated Film
Nominations:
Oscars 2016: Animated Film, Visual FX
Golden Globes 2017: Animated Film

KUNG FU PANDA 3

Grab destiny by the rice dumplings.
—Movie tagline

Box Office: $143.5 Million

DreamWorks Animation has quietly moved into a very solid second place in terms of animated blockbuster films (after Disney/Pixar). The backbone of the Dream-Works animated cash cows have thus far been the *Shrek* films and spinoffs as well as the *Madagascar* films and their spawn. Judging on the success of the first two installments, *How to Train Your Dragon* is going to be around for many years to come as well. Yet arguably the most consistently solid animated film properties the studio puts forth are the *Kung Fu Panda* films, which always seem to deliver on not only making all ages laugh but also delivering potent messages about growing up and self-worth. *Kung Fu Panda 3* is another step in the evolution of a powerful franchise, as well as in the growth of the film's main character Po (Jack Black), the eponymous lovable mammal with martial arts expertise.

Throughout the *Kung Fu Panda* films (*Kung Fu Panda* [2008] and *Kung Fu Panda 2* [2011]) viewers have watched the classic hero's journey unfold through a once lazy Panda and his team of well-trained and ethnically representative animals called "The Furious Five": Tigress (Angelina Jolie), Monkey (Jackie Chan), Mantis (Seth Rogen), Crane (David Cross), and Viper (Lucy Liu). If these films have any major drawback it's that there are simply too many members in Po's posse. As a result, very little focus is shared on these other team members to the point of them falling from secondary to tertiary characters. Every fledgling superhero team needs a mentor, and here it's a red panda named Shifu (Dustin Hoffman) who remains the straight "man" throughout the zany antics provided by Po and his team.

The original *Kung Fu Panda* focused on Po as a slovenly panda being discovered and more or less forced to become "the chosen one" (here named the "Dragon Warrior") selected to bring peace to his homeland of Gongmen City, in the Valley of Peace, suddenly besieged by violence from Tai Lung (Ian McShane), a snow leopard bent on world domination. Call him a panda version of Luke Skywalker (*Star Wars* [1977]) or Neo (*The Matrix* [1999]) but this is Po's journey in that first film: to become what he thinks he cannot be and thus become accepted as such by his peers and skeptical trainer. The film introduces the aforementioned characters as well as Po's "father," a shop-owning goose named Mr. Ping (James Hong). This is the best running gag in all the films in that Po firmly believes this duck to be his father even though they're clearly very different species. The first film also introduces aged tortoise Oogway (Randall Duk Kim), who is a mentor to Shifu and his students before being dispatched from this mortal coil.

Kung Fu Panda 2 deals more with Po assimilating and being better accepted by the "Furious Five," but he begins to question who he really is deep down. While he continues to excel as a Kung Fu master, Po has yet to find the "inner peace" Shifu knows is holding him back. This is all brought about due to yet another megalomaniacal animal in search of world domination in Lord Shen (Gary Oldman), an angry peacock whose arrogance and tendency toward the dark side had him banished. Yet Shen reveals more about Po, giving him a Christ-like storyline about being abandoned mysteriously before being discovered in a basket by Mr. Ping. While by the end of that film, Lord Shen is defeated, Po temporarily overcomes his psychological loss of not knowing who his true parents are because he has Mr. Ping and the Furious Five. Still, existential angst lingers.

Although the *Kung Fu Panda* films are not doing anything new in terms of the hero's journey, where they succeed is in excellent characters and fantastic use of a variety of animations. The films also seem to be building towards something in the evolution of Po as a complete being and this trilogy-long plot development pays off here in the third installment.

Kung Fu Panda 3 once again finds the Valley of Peace a target for a psychotic animal who is trying to become supreme leader. This is rather ironic (as it was in the other films as well) because the Valley of Peace does not seem to have a designated ruler to overthrow. Still, this time around the bad guy is perhaps the greatest villain in Kai (J.K. Simmons), a yak who has just defeated Master Oogway in the spirit realm and stolen his Chi, along with the Chi of all the other great, deceased Kung Fu masters. Kai has stored these Chi in small jade amulets and returns to the mortal world to use them to defeat Po, since Oogway—before allowing himself to be defeated a la Obi-Wan Kenobi (Alec Guinness) in the original *Star Wars*—told Kai that he is the new Dragon Warrior.

Back in the real world, Po is up to his usual routine of overeating and being a Kung Fu master but he is shocked by the news that Shifu will no longer be his instructor. Adding more insult to injury, Shifu informs Po that he is now in charge of leading and training the Furious Five, which in many ways sets Po's struggle back to square one. Yet what has always been a sort of secret thread throughout all the films, one which came to a head in part two has to do with who Po's parents really are and the underlying stress and confusion of his "true self." While perhaps a bit too heady for younger viewers, this search for one's true self and eventual learning and loving of that self is an important and unique idea for viewers of all ages. Enter a strange panda visitor to Gongmen City in Li (Bryan Cranston) who, it is quickly revealed, is Po's father.

Thus *Kung Fu Panda 3* becomes about Po not only reconnecting with his true panda roots but also being tasked with training unskilled pandas in the art of self-defense to ward off Kai, who has the ability to reanimate the Chi of the defeated Kung Fu masters he stores in the jade amulets.

Like its predecessors, *Kung Fu Panda 3* is a fun film for the entire family. Yet it would be disingenuous to say the films are not growing a bit tiresome. As noted, the hero's journey is indeed a classic storytelling method and the *Kung Fu Panda* films render it well, but by the same token, savvy viewers know where it's going. With the amount of money these films bring in, *Kung Fu Panda 4* is likely, and it's pretty much a no-brainer to know that film will deliver a love interest to Po. *Kung Fu Panda 5* will introduce a baby panda to the couple and on and on march the sands of modern day tentpole moviemaking. At least these films are walking the well-trod roads with heart and creativity.

Don R. Lewis

CREDITS

Voice of Po: Jack Black
Voice of Li: Bryan Cranston
Voice of Shifu: Dustin Hoffman
Voice of Tigress: Angelina Jolie
Voice of Kai: J.K. Simmons

Origin: United States

Language: English, Mandarin Chinese

Released: 2016

Production: Melissa Cobb; released by DreamWorks Animation SKG Inc., Oriental DreamWorks Film & Television Technology Company Ltd.

Directed by: Alessandro Carloni; Jennifer Yuh

Written by: Jonathan Aibel; Glenn Berger

Music by: Hans Zimmer

Sound: Erik Aadahl; Ethan Van der Ryn

Art Direction: Max Boas

Production Design: Raymond Zibach

MPAA rating: PG

Running time: 95 minutes

REVIEWS

Andersen, Soren. *Seattle Times.* February 11, 2016.

Hartlaub, Peter. *San Francisco Chronicle.* January 28, 2016.

Moore, Roger. *Movie Nation.* February 1, 2016.

Morgenstern, Joe. *Wall Street Journal.* January 28, 2016.

Persall, Steve. *Tampa Bay Times.* January 27, 2016.

Pushkar, Katherine. *New York Daily News.* January 27, 2016.

Robery, Tim. *The Telegraph.* March 29, 2016.

Russo, Tom. *Boston Globe.* January 28, 2016.

Taylor, Kate. *Globe and Mail* (Toronto). February 14, 2016.

Zacharek, Stephanie. *Time.* February 9, 2016.

QUOTES

Li: "You have to come home with me."

Po: "What? To the secret village?"

Li: "Yes, son. You must rediscover what it is to be a panda. You have to learn how to live like a panda. Sleep like a panda. Eat like a panda. Those 103 dumplings? I was just warming up."

Po: "I always knew I wasn't eating up to my full potential."

TRIVIA

Kai's eyes were made green in accordance with Chinese legends of eyes of that color being synonymous with evil.

L

LA LA LAND

Here's to the fools who dream.
　—Movie tagline

Box Office: $135.2 Million

Mia and Sebastian are just two people in Los Angeles who have a dream. She (Emma Stone) wants to be an actress, to make all of the countless hours spent auditioning feel like they were worth something, especially after moving from the suburbs long ago; he (Ryan Gosling) wants to start a fried chicken music club with his skills as a jazz pianist, despite recently being pushed out of a place that became a tapas bar, and having one last gig playing Christmas songs for a forgettable restaurant. The two meet, they eventually fall in love, and they face what the world has planned for them artistically. Their stories are just a couple stars in the sky of a city that gives *Whiplash* (2014) writer/director Damien Chazelle's place its whimsical name. His exploration into their pursuits is a passionate one, even if it too often feels like he is playing the hits instead of taking art and music forward.

The film's first scene is one hell of a musical sequence, an explosion of color and choreography that rightfully gets viewers think beyond *Whiplash*. For "Another Day in the Sun," a group of Los Angeles commuters, donned in saturated clothes, dance and sing (in one take, up and down the freeway) about the dreams they had that now leave them gridlocked. It is a shot of adrenaline for both the ideas and the filmmaking dedication that follows, a melting pot of dancers (and different styles of dancers, like flamenco and stepping). But this scene also shows the limit to the story's creativity. The sequence proves to be Chazelle's most original contribu-

tion to the world of movie musicals, but has the feel of an iPhone commercial appropriating the filmmaking of Jacques Demy.

Aside from working with Hollywood nostalgia, Chazelle owes a strong amount of his success to his casting agent, who was able to get Ryan Gosling and Emma Stone back for the same movie. Their first pairing in *Crazy, Stupid, Love* (Glenn Ficarra, John Requa, 2011) helped make the movie seem more special than its script showed it be, so much that the collective charisma carried into Ruben Fleischer's boring bomb *Gangster Squad* (2013). In the likes of *La La Land*, their chemistry is essentially perfect, both of them calibrated with self-deprecating humor, expert comic timing, and unconscionable charm. Before they even step into the shoes of Ginger Rogers and Fred Astaire, they bring a massive movie star quality that is by all senses timeless.

Along with cinematographer Linus Sandgren, Chazelle and his crew labor to create the cinematic experience of past musicals beyond song and dance sequences. Wide angle lenses give a classic feel to the movie's polished view of Los Angeles, which is filled with saturated colors like bright yellows or reds, worn by characters to make them pop just right. The movie never resists a long take too, as it gets an energy from letting characters bantering. When it comes to musical performance, Gosling is given unbroken takes that rightfully display the skills he earned as a bonafide jazz pianist, covered with dramatic lighting in a moment that displays Chazelle's exciting fascination with raw talent.

It's most successful sequence is the song of playful courtship, "A Lovely Night," which plays up the fun tension between Mia and Sebastian. The two tap dance under a street light while a perfectly orange, purple, and blue sunset maintains the calmness of the film. With both actors singing and dancing, they achieve something that has natural beauty, the unprofessionalism working as honest but productive. (It recalls the sweetness in Woody Allen's *Everyone Says I Love You* [1996], which also preferred actors over professional singers.) The number is also the most immediately catchy song, a completely subjective type of experience but a fact crucial to connecting with such a film.

Nostalgia is a key piece to this enterprise, for better or worse. Chazelle is constantly working with references, so much that his filmmaking tests the definition of homage to reincorporating, as with a tracking shot of Sebastian and Mia in the following scene, walking past different film sets, as Gene Kelly and Debbie Reynolds did in *Singin' in the Rain* (1952). The movie can be a pastiche at times (mixing Demy colors with Busby Berkeley edits) earning its personality as an old soul, wanting to be patted on the back for refined taste and intense labor to recreate that old feeling. It's a polarizing mission for such a film, but for the first half of *La La Land* it is thoroughly warming.

Chazelle's heart gets the best of him in a following dequence that goes for a flat beauty, recalling the slick commercialism of the same aesthetics. After a projection of *Rebel Without a Cause* leaves them without a movie date, they venture to the famous planetarium from the film. Moving graciously throughout the landmark to Justin Hurwitz's gorgeous score, Mia touches a telescope (Sebastian then wipes it with a handkerchief) and the two sit down for a small kiss before they start to float. Eventually they dance as silhouettes among the stars to a full orchestral version of Sebastian's piano melody, and it's the kind of whimsy the movie believes in wholeheartedly. Aside from the boredom of seeing a musical use CGI, it reckons that floating became one of the year's most overdone visual metaphors, as seen in movies ranging from *The Witch* (2016) to *Tallulah* (2016). The people are perfect but the aesthetic is simple and could be used to sell handkerchiefs.

The old soul nature gets vocal into the second half, in which Mia and Sebastian stop singing, with Chazelle focusing them on their careers and exploring what he wants to say with these characters. Mia decides to write herself a part, so she pens a one-act play called "So Long, Boulder City," presumably about her experience of moving to LA. Mia asks if a play is too old-fashioned, which Chazelle uses as a gesture to break the previous squeaky-cleanness of his film: "Fuck 'em," Sebastian replies. And so too are Sebastian's dreams protected by the movie, of wanting to save jazz despite getting a gig with a rock/pop/funk pastiche, as led by John Legend.

Even though he is told by a musician of color (played by John Legend) that the revolution that will save jazz won't come from playing the old stuff. As Sebastian grapples with this idea, making money from his touring group but not for playing the music he loves, Chazelle fashions less of a critique of Sebastian's thinking than making him a martyr of Chazelle's ideals.

The climax of *La La Land* is an audition by Mia, one last shot at facing her artistic passion that has given so little back to her. Like Gosling's piano playing, it features her musical talent—singing—as presented in a long take, as she tells a story. Though the piece she sings is the movie's most dramatic moment ("Here's to the ones who dream; foolish as they may seem. Here's to the hearts that ache; here's to the mess we make"), it feels like a retread of the opening song, despite its potential to rally an army of dreamers to fight against the brutal enemy that is self-doubt. Stone's performance of the song has a hugeness to it, especially as the camera remains in a close-up on her face, spinning around her delicately.

Aside from the numerous past movies, it brings to mind Chazelle's previous innovations as a director or screenwriter: The sniper in *Grand Piano* (2013) that threatens to shoot Elijah Wood's concert pianist character for hitting one note, or the voice of J.K. Simmons' Oscar-winning *Whiplash* screaming at Teller's drummer to play perfectly. With *La La Land*, the characters are in a place of considerable less stakes. Chazelle's narrative suffers from the way it presents two artists who are already talented enough, and can sustain decent living spaces in the cutthroat world of Los Angeles, but it is just a matter of having their skills recognized. In comparison to the way in which a movie like *Whiplash* (which is even more of a masterpiece for what it does comparably with music) showed the growth of hard-earned skills, *La La Land* has far less of a crucial tension.

La La Land does center on the gift that Chazelle has, which he now shares with cinema in a promising career: his ear. Since his first film, *Guy and Madeline on a Park Bench* (2009, a lo-fi *La La Land*), which used real musicians in everyday settings for its musical numbers, Chazelle has been hip to how much music creates a personality for everyone person on-screen, and how the sounds they choose define them. This is beautiful shown in *La La Land*'s aforementioned opening scene, with each passing car listening to music that's completely different, spanning time and continent. And it is no coincidence that one of the movie's most romantic gestures—Sebastian laying on the car horn until Mia appears—relies on the communication of sound.

The film's technical successes often parallel the need for nostalgia to preserve the past, instead of being adventurous. In this way, *La La Land* struggles to be more than a thoughtful novelty; there is little to take away after its images have faded. Even the songs lack a consistent catchiness to become souvenirs, aside from Sebastian's piano melody that plays throughout the story. The impact of *La La Land* depends greatly on whether the songs remain stuck in your head, and occupy a happy in one's heart they do. But it took three viewings for this reviewer to have the opening song play on repeat in the brain long after the movie was over. *La La Land* often relies on the familiar, despite Chazelle's fresh voice.

Nick Allen

CREDITS

Sebastian: Ryan Gosling
Mia: Emma Stone
Keith: John Legend
Laura: Rosemarie DeWitt
Bill: J.K. Simmons
Origin: United States
Language: English
Released: 2016
Production: Fred Berger, Gary Gilbert, Jordan Horowitz, Marc Platt; released by Black Label Media, Gilbert Films, Impostor Pictures, Marc Platt Productions, Summit Entertainment
Directed by: Damien Chazelle
Written by: Damien Chazelle
Cinematography by: Linus Sandgren
Music by: Justin Hurwitz
Sound: Ai-Ling Lee
Music Supervisor: Steven Gizicki
Editing: Tom Cross
Art Direction: Austin Gorg
Costumes: Mary Zophres
Production Design: David Wasco
MPAA rating: PG-13
Running time: 128 minutes

REVIEWS

Brody, Richard. *New Yorker*. December 12, 2016.
Hornaday, Ann. *Washington Post*. December 15, 2016.
Jones, J.R. *Chicago Reader*. December 15, 2016.
Morgenstern, Joe. *Wall Street Journal*. December 15, 2016.
Nicholson, Amy. *MTV*. December 7, 2016.
Noveck, Jocelyn. *Associated Press*. December 8, 2016.
Phillips, Michael. *Chicago Tribune*. December 15, 2016.
Stevens, Dana. *Slate*. December 9, 2016.
Tallerico, Brian. *RogerEbert.com*. September 14, 2016.
Vishnevetsky, Ignatiy. *The A.V. Club*. December 30, 2016.

QUOTES

Bill: "You're fired."
Sebastian: "It's Christmas."
Bill: "Yeah, I see the decorations. Good luck in the new year."

TRIVIA

Ryan Gosling spent six days a week for two hours a day taking piano lessons to learn the music by heart.

AWARDS

Oscars 2016: Actress (Stone), Cinematog., Director (Chazelle), Orig. Score, Orig. Song Score and/or Adapt. ("City of Stars"), Production Design
British Acad. 2016: Actress (Stone), Cinematog., Director (Chazelle), Film, Orig. Score
Directors Guild 2016: Director (Chazelle)
Golden Globes 2017: Actor—Mus./Comedy (Gosling), Actress—Mus./Comedy (Stone), Director (Chazelle), Film—Mus./Comedy, Score, Screenplay, Song ("City of Stars")
Screen Actors Guild 2016: Actress (Stone)
Nominations:
Oscars 2016: Actor (Gosling), Costume Des., Film, Film Editing, Orig. Screenplay, Orig. Song Score and/or Adapt. ("Audition (The Fools Who Dream)"), Sound FX Editing
British Acad. 2016: Actor (Gosling), Costume Des., Film Editing, Orig. Screenplay, Production Design, Sound
Screen Actors Guild 2016: Actor (Gosling)
Writers Guild 2016: Orig. Screenplay

LAST DAYS IN THE DESERT

Rodrigo Garcia's drama is one of the more unique films in which someone plays Jesus Christ that cinema has yet produced. There have been dozens of movies about the early days of Christ and even more about his Crucifixion, but few that have tackled such a small chapter of his life and in such a humanizing manner. *Last Days in the Desert* isn't about the death of Christ or even the importance of life. It's a parable of many of the things he espoused, including empathy and sacrifice, but it's told in a daring, non-sermonizing way.

It's also not about Christ, the figure, but Yeshua, the man, played by Ewan McGregor. Yeshua is introduced in the desert, where he has been wandering for days, seeking meaning and acceptance of his purpose and fate. He too is searching, opening the film with

"Father, where are you?" Garcia will return over and over again to issues of fathers and sons. Yeshua's father just happens to be the "big one." As he seeks something he cannot even fully define in the desert in the days just before his crucifixion he speaks not only to himself but to an imagined version of Satan, also played by McGregor. While the idea of one actor playing Jesus and Satan, and having the two of them converse, may sound horrible on paper, Garcia and McGregor actually pull it off. These conversations are deeply philosophical without sounding overwritten, and, as crazy as it sounds, McGregor grounds both characters in something genuine and truthful, never turning either into the caricature they could have become.

Yeshua meets a family in the desert—a father (Ciaran Hinds), his wife (Ayelet Zurer), and his son (Tye Sheridan). Of course, the dynamic within this family becomes a parable for not only Christ's relationship with God but that of God and man. The son wants to leave the encampment, to travel to a bigger city, and start his life. His father refuses, suggesting that sacrificing to stay in the desert is the more valuable life to live. Why continue to suffer? The boy's mother is being killed by the desert conditions, but the father continues to refuse any alternative. Should Jesus "save" the boy and his mother from an abusive father? Convince him to do so himself? Or not intervene? Garcia walks a subtly fine line, capturing religious debates about freewill through story instead of directly. As Jesus, Father, and Son work together to perform tasks, one can easily extrapolate religious doctrine or philosophies about the roles of God and Man, but one can also appreciate Garcia's narrative directly.

Last Days in the Desert has a poetic aspect that's notably amplified by the cinematography of Emmanuel Lubezki, winner of the Oscar in his field for three years running (*Gravity* [2013]; *Birdman* [2014]; and *The Revenant* [2015]). As crazy as it may be to consider, this is actually some of Lubezki's best work for what's it's not more even than what it is. The temptation to get showy with the camerawork, to shoot the desert more like he did for Terence Malick's *The Tree of Life* (2010), must have been hard to ignore, but Lubezki's work rarely calls attention to itself. It's functional while also being graceful enough to add to the overall poetry of the piece.

As one can imagine given the simplicity of the film, a lot of the success here also rests on the shoulders of the small ensemble. Zurer, Hinds, and Sheridan are all excellent, but the film understandably belongs to McGregor, who gives not one, but two great performances. One of the best things about his work here is how subtly he distinguishes Jesus and Satan, often with an arched eyebrow or the gift of a different camera angle from Garcia and Lubezki. They will often shoot Yeshua from above, making him look small against the massive desert. And they shoot his demonic alter ego from below, making him giant against a black night sky.

Last Days in the Desert was a tough sell for any studio, and Broad Green never found a way to get it to even a small audience. Box office reporting sites don't report any income for the film at all. History will be kind to it, as viewers stumble upon it. One hopes that the masses who go see faith-based garbage like *Left Behind* (2014) and *War Room* (2015) could somehow make the journey to this subtle, delicate film, and discover that there are films that speak to religious issues that do not pander or talk down to their audiences.

Brian Tallerico

CREDITS

Jesus: Ewan McGregor

Father: Ciaran Hinds

Mother: Ayelet Zurer

Son: Tye Sheridan

Demonic woman: Susan Gray

Origin: United States

Language: English

Released: 2016

Production: Bonnie Curtis, Julie Lynn, Wicks Walker; released by Mockingbird Pictures

Directed by: Rodrigo Garcia

Written by: Rodrigo Garcia

Cinematography by: Emmanuel Lubezki

Music by: Danny Bensi; Saunder Jurriaans

Editing: Matt Maddox

Art Direction: John Demeo

Costumes: Judianna Makovsky

Production Design: Jeannine Oppewall

MPAA rating: PG-13

Running time: 98 minutes

REVIEWS

Ebiri, Bilge. *New York Magazine.* February 1, 2015.

Fujishima, Kenji. *Slant Magazine.* May 9, 2016.

Grierson, Tim. *Screen International.* May 9, 2016.

Hoffman, Jordan. *The Guardian.* February 1, 2015.

Holden, Stephen. *New York Times.* May 12, 2016.

Hornaday, Ann. *Washington Post.* May 12, 2016.

Perez, Rodrigo. *The Playlist.* February 1, 2015.

Raup, Jordan. *The Film Stage.* May 9, 2016.

Scherstuhl, Alan. *Village Voice.* May 10, 2016.

Suzanne-Mayer, Dominick. *Consequence of Sound.* May 13, 2016.

Ewan McGregor portrays both the characters of Jesus and Lucifer.

LAZER TEAM

Four unlikely heroes have to save the planet.
Whether we like it or not.
—Movie tagline

Box Office: $1.2

The growth of YouTube and its content creators in the past decade has led to a new wave in American independent cinema, involving homemade production companies who go from shorts to features, taking their fan bases with them. Previous examples that will go down as a part of this YouTube wave include RedLetterMedia.com's various films like 2010's *Feeding Frenzy* (directed by Jay Bauman and Mike Stoklasa) and 2016's *Space Cop* (also Bauman & Stoklasa) or Cinemassacre.com's James Rolfe funding and directing *Angry Video Game Nerd: The Movie* (2014). The latest, and possibly biggest effort of this movement yet is from Rooster Teeth Productions, known previously for their fanboy-friendly "Halo" footage comedy series "Red vs. Blue." With distribution through the website's subscription-only YouTube Red branch, *Lazer Team* aims to be a blockbuster event on an indie scale.

It is sad to report that *Lazer Team* manages to completely squander its underdog narrative, the one that fuels it on and off the screen. There is an inspired idea by having a quarter of dorky men attached to different pieces of an alien-fighting spacesuit, as happens here in the film five minutes in. But the execution of the story is disturbingly average, as if the opportunity and freedom from filmmakers meant they only wanted to churn out something without imagination.

The group of accidental heroes starts with Hagan (Burnie Burns), a disrespected small-town police officer introduced in the film by aiming a speed gun at an elderly woman crawling by him on a scooter. Hagan is a bit of a loser in the town, especially with a bad history of destroying the career of former friend Herman (Colton Dunn), who had his legs broken when Hagan did not block him during a football game years ago. One fateful night, Hagan busts a party that his daughter Mindy (Allie DeBerry) had been attending, and drags away her boyfriend Zach (Michael Jones). In route to the police station, Hagan sees two men shooting off fireworks illegally, who are revealed to be Herman and his simpleton friend Woody (Gavin Free). When there's an altercation between Hagan and Herman, a firework is accidentally fired into the air and hits a space ship, one

that has been carrying the special suit that will be used to fight alien lifeforms. Attached to Hagan's arm is a device that creates a giant shield; on Woody's head is a helmet that allows him telepathic powers and super intelligence; attached to Herman's legs are giant boots that allow him to run very fast. And Zach is given a giant laser on his arm, hence the name of the film after he makes it a famous hashtag.

As the film tells the viewer in an overlong opening sequence, one man, Alan Ritchson's Adam, has been training his whole life to work with this very suit. The arrival and subsequent battle for humanity has been known by government officials for years like an upcoming sports event. With the suit dispersed among the goofy quartet, Adam has to train them within four days. When that proves impossible for the physically and mentally inept bunch, they have to work together to win the battle for the world.

With story credit going to lead actor Burnie Burns, who shares script credits with Chris Demarais, Josh Flanagan, and director Matt Hullum, there is an aggravating lack of suspense to the story, despite all that is at stake. Added on top of the movie's pathetic imagery of wannabe macho men acting like boys, who put life or death significance on sports or treat the one female character as property, *Lazer Team* becomes an aggressively miserable experience, its inadequacies confronting viewers at every corner.

In its most basic failure, its jokes are simply never funny. With all the characters trying to out-ham each other, there proves no dynamic to the film, just an awkward desperation for everyone to be the top clown. Without this foundation of who the straight man is, there proves little chance. The jokes are often cheap, going for abrupt slapstick or a pitiful "fanboys will be fanboys" chuckle. Worse, many punchlines are delivered over ADR. Many films do that for the throwaway lines, but *Lazer Team* uses ADR for pieces meant to get the biggest laugh.

The movie is defined by a distinct laziness with imagination, despite its sci-fi set-up that requires aliens, special weapons, top secret military procedures and more. The outfits for the team, for example, are an extremely drab gray and white. The aliens themselves look like designs from 80s cartoons, with the cliché worm-like appearance and large black eyes, fittingly coming from a giant flying saucer that is exactly as is. Zombie alien soldiers thrown into the second act prove a wasted opportunity for an interesting genre niche, merely wear yellow contact lenses and growl in low voices.

Given the many shots of flaunted military vehicles, the amount of explosions and the often decent special effects, these shortcomings ring loudly as self-imposed. Surprisingly for an indie production, there's even a full credited orchestra for the film's music, which wants to hit all the same notes as a John Williams score, but forgets to have a memorable theme. Without even a hint of parody to its moldy production design, Hullum has made a movie that rivals Ed Wood's imagination for *Plan 9 from Outer Space*. But then again, Wood's film involved the viewer in one way or the other.

Lazer Team has a flop-in-progress aesthetic, with very little that is special to boast about. But the project was no failure by any means, thanks in part to the fan support it received long before cameras started rolling. With their background in YouTube videos and "Red vs. Blue," the film made a record for an Indiegogo campaign, hauling in $2.4 million in a single month from contributions, and boasted a whopping 535 extras for a throwaway crowd scene. Hullum's movie is F-grade entertainment by any other standards. But this movie was made in its own world, which seems to be the only reason why a sequel has been green-lit for the near future.

Nick Allen

CREDITS

Hagan: Burnie Burns
Woody: Gavin Free
Zach: Michael Jones
Herman: Colton Dunn
Mindy: Allie DeBerry
Origin: United States
Language: English
Released: 2016
Directed by: Matt Hullum
Written by: Burnie Burns; Matt Hullum; Chris Demarais; Josh Flanagan
Cinematography by: Philip Roy
Music by: Jeff Williams
MPAA rating: PG-13
Running time: 102 minutes

REVIEWS

Anderson, Soren. *Seattle Times*. January 29, 2016.
Connelly, Sherilyn. *Village Voice*. January 26, 2016.
D'Angelo, Mike. *The A.V. Club*. January 28, 2016.
Darling, Cary. *Fort Worth Star-Telegram/DFW.com*. January 28, 2016.
Fagerholm, Matt. *RogerEbert.com*. January 29, 2016.
Genzlinger, Neil. *New York Times*. January 28, 2016.
Harvey, Dennis. *Variety*. February 1, 2016.
LaSalle, Mick. *San Francisco Chronicle*. January 28, 2016.
O'Hehir, Andrew. *Salon.com*. January 28, 2016.
Wheeler, Brad. *Globe and Mail*. January 29, 2016.

QUOTES

Hagan: "One more word out of you...."
Zach: "You gonna what? You gonna double arrest me?"

TRIVIA

The movie occurs in 1977 and 2015.

THE LEGEND OF TARZAN

A new threat awaits.
—Movie tagline

Box Office: $126.6 Million

One thing becomes clear while watching *The Legend of Tarzan*: Nearly as much effort was expended in trying to redefine what the title character embodies as portrayer Alexander Skarsgård put into achieving the requisite (some sighing women said exquisite) definition of his body. Both exertions involved a daunting challenge. After his determined and protracted adherence to a willpower-testing diet and a muscle-punishing exercise program, the actor's physique, particularly his abdominals, wound up admirably toned. As for the film itself, an attempt to be as much a cut above previous Tarzan productions as Skarsgård is cut below was not completely successful.

The encircled letter R next to Tarzan's name on-screen at the outset is obviously a trademark, but one could not be blamed for imagining it to instead be a stigmatizing stamp denoting probable racism ahead. Increasingly, all things Tarzan have not only been deemed deserving of such a racist brand but have been succinctly summed up as one: a long line of mountingly—and perhaps insurmountably—problematic products beginning with Edgar Rice Burroughs' first story in 1912 that have frequently come to elicit outraged outbursts that exceed the character's own famous, formidable battle cry. The century-plus premise sure appears prejudiced today: despite the serious disadvantages of being orphaned in the African jungle and raised thereafter by apes, as well as being merely self-educated using books left behind by his bygone begetters, Tarzan--whose name means "White Skin"— apparently could not help but rise in spite of it all to be handsome, astute head and supremely-strong shoulders above the black native populace by virtue of his supposedly-superior Anglo-Saxon blood. Director David Yates declared that it was time to ditch Tarzan's bigoted baggage, recognizing it has not worn well and is no longer in style, anyway. However, it appears to have not been quite so simply set aside.

Still, in making a movie featuring action-adventure, amour, arresting aerial views of the African landscape, and the aforementioned abs, those responsible for this Tarzan tried with what appears to be the best of intentions to in some way also make amends. More than one cinematic adaptation from the 1930s and 1940s featured cringeworthy scenes in which equipment-toting, caricatured tribesmen, finding themselves weighed down as a result of the white man's burden, topple to their deaths from precipitous passes, and the reaction of the explorers amounts to an outrageous "all's well that ends well" as long as the supplies they did not look upon as expendable had been saved. However, in *The Legend of Tarzan*, black lives now contrastingly and, it was hoped, perhaps somewhat correctively do matter.

The classic Caucasian make-believe superman is tasked here with kicking out white colonialists, laudably besting the somewhat-factual forces of Belgian King Leopold II and halting the blithely-inhumane exploitation of those living within his erroneously-named Congo Free State who were punished—and then perished by the millions--if their forced labor was too slow in feeding Leopold's ravenous hunger for local resources. The film also attempts to honor George Washington Williams (Samuel L. Jackson), a real-life, remarkable African-American who crowned a remarkably-accomplished life by writing an open letter to the King that revealed to the world Leopold's carefully-concealed, odious atrocities. Williams is credited with coining the phrase "crimes against humanity," which, heartbreakingly, has yet to stop coming in handy.

What also seems regrettable is that, while most moviegoers would otherwise have not made Williams acquaintance, this historical figure of such remarkable character can only proceed, as he does here literally in one scene, by piggybacking upon a mere fictional character who is sadly known to multitudes more—and a strapping symbol of white supremacy, at that. Early on in the film, Williams must convince Tarzan (ironically dubbed "Africa's favorite son"), living respectably but restlessly in England now as the House of Lords' John Clayton III, Fifth Earl of Greystoke, to accept an invitation from Leopold to visit the Congo because it will only be through the white celebrity's validating involvement that Williams might be in a position to be heard about Leopold. Sadly, some things never change.

Yates purposefully paid homage to Williams as the "real hero," the actual indispensable man of the film, as it is he who is successful in getting Tarzan to return to Africa early and who writes that eye-opening letter partially intoned at the end, as well as intervening in between on multiple occasions to help out with well-aimed weaponry and wisdom painfully born of his own lamented role in this county's mistreatment of Native Americans. Yet one should not bother trying to find this impressive achiever deserving of his own film on posters for this one. Its purported hero is reduced to being the superhero's sidekick, cracking nuts when first seen and then continually cracking wise thereafter in a jarringly anachronistic, if sometimes mildly amusing, manner.

Williams certainly has more spark that his subdued brooder of a buddy, the epitome of the strong-silent type that some found intriguing and others found as bloodless as a victim of Skarsgård's HBO vampire. Bloodthirsty in a different sense is Leopold's evil envoy Leon Rom (Christoph Waltz), a real-life villain hiding within a misleadingly-white suit who casually (and symbolically) plucks an African flower and whose rosary is used to bring anything but comfort. (The Panama that Waltz sports may be new, but he performs in a manner that has become old hat.) It appears that Jane (Margot Robbie, brimming and bristling with 2016 agency) was wrong in calling the hippo "the most dangerous beast in Africa," and Tarzan chooses to shed both his civilized ways and clothes, releasing his carefully-caged animal within to defeat this Belgian one. However, Tarzan seems most palpably motivated to free kidnapped Jane than the enslaved Africans, whom the film bothers very little to differentiate. They cheer wildly as the Belgians are turned back for them, which likely caused countless real-life natives to turn over in the graves they entered for tragic lack of any such timely and definitive defeat.

Amidst a sometimes-confusing use of numerous origin-revealing flashbacks, CGI fauna that are less pleasing to the eye than in this year's *The Jungle Book* and periodically caused eyes to roll, and action during which vines are gripped far more tightly than were viewers, there is a singularly-striking moment in which Tarzan humbles himself in giving Chief Mbonga (Djimon Hounsou) something that had long been owed: an admission amounting to an apology amidst rain and mist representing a cleansing. Still mourning the loss of his own child in a miscarriage, Tarzan shows remorse for having exacted his own grief-fueled version of justice years before upon Mbonga's son, a mere boy with no idea that the ape upon which he all-too-successfully tried out his bow and arrow was Tarzan's beloved adoptive mother. "Where was your honor?" cries the chief. Tarzan finally and potently lets loose a painful acknowledgment: "I had none." Whether this symbolism-heavy expression of regret that diverges significantly from Burroughs now makes the character seem any less regrettable remains to be seen, and if this insertion of him into the past to liberate black Africans can liberate him from his own troubled past to the point where he is welcome in the future.

This $180 million effort to make that happen grossed $126.6 million domestically amidst mixed reviews. The makers of *The Legend of Tarzan* at least had their hearts in the right place, trying to signal with apparent sincerity that they, along with their titular titan, have come to see the light.

David L. Boxerbaum

CREDITS

John Clayton/Tarzan: Alexander Skarsgard
George Washington Williams: Samuel L. Jackson
Jane Clayton: Margot Robbie
Chief Mbonga: Djimon Hounsou
Leon Rom: Christoph Waltz
Origin: United States
Language: English
Released: 2016
Production: David Barron, Alan Riche, Jerry Weintraub; released by Dark Horse Entertainment, Jerry Weintraub Productions, Village Roadshow Pictures
Directed by: David Yates
Written by: Adam Cozad; Craig Brewer
Cinematography by: Henry Braham
Music by: Rupert Gregson-Williams
Sound: Glenn Freemantle
Editing: Mark Day
Art Direction: James Hambidge
Costumes: Ruth Myers
Production Design: Stuart Craig
MPAA rating: PG-13
Running time: 110 minutes

REVIEWS

Brody, Richard. *New Yorker*. July 5, 2016.
Burr, Ty. *Boston Globe*. June 29, 2016.
Dargis, Manohla. *New York Times*. June 30, 2016.
Debruge, Peter. *Variety*. June 29, 2016.
Greenblatt, Leah. *Entertainment Weekly*. June 29, 2016.
McCarthy, Todd. *Hollywood Reporter*. June 29, 2016.
Morgenstern, Joe. *Wall Street Journal*. June 30, 2016.
Rainer, Peter. *Christian Science Monitor*. July 1, 2016.
Roeper, Richard. *Chicago Sun-Times*. June 29, 2016.
Travers, Peter. *Rolling Stone*. June 30, 2016.

QUOTES

John Clayton: "The Tekes say an elephant's eyes speak the greatest language. Who else can make you feel so much without a word?"

TRIVIA

To get in shape for the role, Alexander Skarsgard spent four months training and also worked out during production.

THE LIGHT BETWEEN OCEANS

Love demands everything.
    —Movie tagline

Box Office: $12.5 Million

As a writer/director, young Derek Cianfrance announced his cinematic presence with his first feature, the darkly personal family drama *Blue Valentine* (2010). The film was heralded for the painfully honest performances of Ryan Gosling and Michelle Williams, as well as for the way Cianfrance combined highly stylized elements with harsh realism. Having studied at the University of Boulder under avant-garde master Stan Brakhage, Cianfrance isn't particularly experimental in his style but the man sure can tell a story visually. Cianfrance followed up *Blue Valentine* with the equally impressive *The Place Beyond the Pines* (2012) which was more of an action film but also dealt with what people, particularly men, will do to hold on to love. Now Cianfrance is back with the criminally underseen *The Light Between Oceans* (2016), which again sees the filmmaker taking on a very different genre, tone, and style, but still zeroing in on what men will do in the name of love.

The Light Between Oceans is a period piece focusing on a WWI soldier named Tom (Michael Fassbender), who has arrived home to Australia. He's also more than likely suffering from a strong case of Post-Traumatic Stress Disorder from the horrors he witnessed and inflicted in the war. Since such a designation wasn't around in 1918, Tom claims he just needs a little peace and quiet to pull himself together and a recent job opening as a lighthouse keeper on a small island off the coast seems just what the doctor ordered. Before embarking on a 3-month trial run wherein he will be almost completely alone, Tom immediately catches the eye of lovely local Isabel (Alicia Viklander), but, since he's still suffering from the trauma of war, he makes little effort to connect, at least at first.

Tom impresses with his initial stint of solitary lighthouse-keeping and earns the job permanently, but the more he sees Isabel on forays back to the mainland, the more he realizes no man is an island and he could really use some companionship. In a delicate epistolary sequence, Tom woos Isabel and before long, they are married. Isabel has a gift when it comes to drawing Tom out of his shell and together, their burgeoning marriage wanders to thoughts of a large family together. Almost as soon as this fairy tale romance begins to unfold, Isabel becomes pregnant, but sadly, the onscreen drama spirals horrifically from here on out.

On a dark and stormy night, Tom heads to late-night duty in the lighthouse, leaving a very pregnant Isabel alone. At nearly the moment he is across the island in the midst of a thundering storm, Isabel starts to feel severe pains in her stomach. Alone to deal with this increasingly scary situation, Isabel attempts to reach Tom. She fails and loses the baby. Obviously, this is devastating to the young couple, but, after a time, they try again. And, excruciatingly, fail. If there's one rather salty issue hampering *The Light Between Oceans*, it's the way the film almost takes on a lengthy and cruel bent when it comes to Isabel's suffering. Granted, that may also be a nod to Cianfrance's skill as he's extremely adept at sketching characters we care about and putting them through the wringer, but here it starts to feel a bit piled on.

Soon, it becomes clear Tom and Isabel are not to be parents and while it definitely hurts Isabel most, the couple carries on with their quiet island life. That is until one day a boat runs ashore and inside of it there's a dead man and a very alive baby. By this time (rather late in the film, really) Cianfrance has skillfully led the audience to really like and understand this couple, which makes the decision they must make about this newfound treasure feel particularly heart-wrenching. Isabel makes a compelling argument towards keeping the child, and after much consternation from Tom, he relents and the couple act as if the baby was their own. After all, Isabel was recently pregnant and no one knows she lost it, so the ruse is a rather simple one to pull off. But as always with Cianfrance, love comes at a heavy cost. Once again, an almost utopian life begins to form on the island. until one day in town, Tom and Isabel meet the bereaved Hannah (Rachel Weisz), who has recently lost her husband and daughter in an accident at sea. As the pressure of their lie begins to bear down on Tom, the audience also finds themselves stuck in a moral quandary involving the nature of parenthood, love and lies.

While certainly not a perfect film, *The Light Between Oceans* is very good. It's overlong and perhaps a bit too literal as in it feels like Cianfrance (who also adapted the source material) did not leave out any parts of the book. Still, Fassbender, Vikander, and Weisz all bring serious acting depth to their roles, and the story manages to feel quite personal even though it does get dragged out a bit. By the time the credits roll, one feels pretty emotionally drained, having lived a life with Tom and Isabel. It's also interesting to see Cianfrance again pivot stylistically by taking on a near epic period piece but still managing to keep his ideas of the difficulty of patriarchal love intact albeit in a very different way. Barely seen in the United States, *The Light Between Oceans* is well worth searching out.

Don R. Lewis

CREDITS

Tom Sherbourne: Michael Fassbender
Isabel Graysmark: Alicia Vikander
Hannah Roennfeldt: Rachel Weisz
Lucy-Grace: Florence Clery
Ralph Addicott: Jack Thompson
Origin: United States
Language: English
Released: 2016
Production: Jeffrey Clifford, David Heyman; released by Amblin Partners LLC, DreamWorks SKG, Heyday Films, LBO Productions, Participant Media L.L.C., Reliance Entertainment, Touchstone Pictures
Directed by: Derek Cianfrance
Written by: Derek Cianfrance
Cinematography by: Adam Arkapaw
Music by: Alexandre Desplat
Sound: Tony Volante
Editing: Jim Helton; Ron Patane
Art Direction: Sophie Nash
Costumes: Erin Benach
Production Design: Karen Murphy
MPAA rating: R
Running time: 133 minutes

REVIEWS

Bleasdale, John. *CineVue*. September 1, 2016.
Change, Justin. *Los Angeles Times*. September 1, 2016.
Collin, Robbie. *The Telegraph*. September 1, 2016.
Duralde, Alonso. *The Wrap*. August 30, 2016.
Greenblatt, Leah. *Entertainment Weekly*. August 31, 2016.
Holden, Stephen. *New York Times*. September 1, 2016.
Robinson, Tasha. *The Verge*. August 31, 2016.
Roeper, Richard. *Chicago Sun-Times*. August 30, 2016.
Whitney, Erin. *ScreenCrush*. August 31, 2016.
Wolfe, April. *Village Voice*. August 31, 2016.

QUOTES

Frank Roennfeldt: "You only have to forgive once. To resent, you have to do it all day, every day."

TRIVIA

During production, Michael Fassbender and Alicia Vikander were 37 and 25 years old respectively. In the novel the film was based on, Tom is 28 and Isabel is 19.

LIGHTS OUT

You were right to be afraid of the dark.
—Movie tagline

Box Office: $67.2 Million

In the short film created by David Sandberg that inspired this longer work, a woman gets ready for bed and turns the lights off, only to notice something in the shadows. Flip the switch back on and its gone. Turn it off and there it is again. She gets under the covers, hears some floorboards creaking and finally sees a hideous face by her nightstand as the lights go off one last time. That whole premise took less than three minutes. Sandberg may have lost the competition he entered but the film attracted a feature producer close to James Wan who already produced one spinoff from the prologue of *The Conjuring* (2013)—the creepy doll known as *Annabelle* (2014)—and saw potential in Sandberg's treatment for an extension of his short. As is often the case though, a singular idea is best left to brevity rather than stretching its thinness across a larger canvas.

For *Lights Out* to go from two-and-a-half minutes to 75, Sandberg needs to provide an array of new characters. This starts with the stepfather of Rebecca (Teresa Palmer), who is killed in his textile warehouse along with his assistant by the silhouette of the malevolent presence. Rebecca gets a little more life, fleshing out her story with boyfriend Bret (Alexander DiPersia), to whom she will not quite commit despite his insistence. She also has a much younger brother in Martin (Gabriel Bateman), who lives with their mom, Sophie (Maria Bello), whose depression is beginning to take hold again.

The horror of the unknown regularly wins the debate over what makes for the scariest villains. To fill in the additional 73 pages of a screenplay though, *Lights Out* provides an unabridged backstory to the being hiding in the shadows. Her name is Diana and she was a friend of Sophie's back in her institution days. She was burdened with Xeroderma Pigmentosum, a rare condition that made her skin sensitive to light. An experimental cure ended up killing her, and now she haunts Sophie all the live-long night. As long as the lights are off.

The next important step in any establishment of rules in the paranormal is the ability to follow them and cleverly find ways for its characters and their adversary to exploit them. This is one of the biggest failures of Eric Heisserer, a subpar screenwriter whose contributions to the remake of *A Nightmare on Elm Street* (2010) and the fanfic-like prequel of *The Thing* (2011) are amongst the greatest of genre sins of the new millennium. Here the rules appear to be simple. Lights on, you are safe. Lights off and Diana can get you. She can apparently still move throughout illuminated space—hence the creaks—but can only interact in the dark.

Heisserer's best innovation is to have Diana sabotage the power only to quickly solve that wrinkle by conveniently having portable black lights available to Rebecca and company. Plus, is holding the shadow figure at gunpoint really a viable solution? Sandberg does no service to the surrounding attacks by sporadically connecting the light switches to giant booms on the soundtrack to announce Diana's proximity. The boring overused tactic does nothing for an audience's expectation for dread other than preparing their ears for sudden Dolby Stereo.

The establishment of the relationship between Rebecca and Bret is easily the best and most natural moment in the whole film because it feels honest. But it also feels like a short film. Once it shifts into the growing family backstory and explaining evil there is less to draw our interest with the lights on. Young Gabriel Bateman's scared face too often looks like he is grossed out over a bad smell. More troubling is Maria Bello relying more on psychotic arrogance in the mother role right down to a moment that should elicit sympathy instead of shrugged indifference. Eliminating any ground rules can be fun for viewers who enjoy chaos or filmmakers who love to throw the kitchen sink at them without the need to be clever doing it. Anyone can do chaos just as easily as anyone can yell "BOO" behind your seat and shake you out of quiet concentration. *Lights Out* is stuck somewhere in the dark and is forgotten quicker than the two minutes it took to watch the short or the amount of time it takes to flip a switch.

Erik Childress

CREDITS

Rebecca: Teresa Palmer
Martin: Gabriel Bateman
Bret: Alexander DiPersia
Paul: Billy Burke
Sophie: Maria Bello
Origin: United States
Language: English
Released: 2016
Production: James Wan; released by Atomic Monster, Grey Matter Productions, New Line Cinema L.L.C., RatPac-Dune Entertainment, Warner Bros. Entertainment Inc.
Directed by: David F. Sandberg
Written by: Eric Heisserer
Cinematography by: Marc Spicer
Music by: Benjamin Wallfisch
Sound: William R. Dean
Editing: Michel Aller; Kirk M. Morri
Art Direction: Shannon Kemp
Costumes: Kristin M. Burke

Production Design: Jennifer Spence
MPAA rating: PG-13
Running time: 81 minutes

REVIEWS

Berardinelli, James. *ReelViews*. July 21, 2016.
Cerny, Alan. *ComingSoon.net*. July 22, 2016.
Chang, Justin. *Los Angeles Times*. July 21, 2016.
Edelstein, David. *New York Magazine/Vulture*. July 23, 2016.
Judy, Jim. *Screen It!*. July 22, 2016.
McGranaghan, Mike. *Aisle Seat*. July 22, 2016.
Nusair, David. *Reel Film Reviews*. July 27, 2016.
Phipps, Keith. *Uproxx*. July 21, 2016.
Roeper, Richard. *Chicago Sun-Times*. July 21, 2016.
Weinberg, Scott. *Nerdist*. July 28, 2016.

QUOTES

Sophie: "There's no you without me."

TRIVIA

The film made back its entire production budget on its opening day at the box office.

LION

The true story of a life lost and found.
—Movie tagline

Box Office: $38.5 Million

Upon perusing the highlights of Gath Davis' career as a director of commercials, one award-winner stands out that seems to have foreshadowed his helming of this film, which is his Oscar-nominated feature-length debut. (Davis is also known for directing episodes of top-notch *Top of the Lake* with Jane Campion.) *Lion* recounts a true story involving an Indian boy's fateful nighttime boarding of an empty, idle passenger train in search of a comfy place in which to address his drowsiness, after which he rose the next morning to find himself many miles from his home and beloved family—a wholly-accidental, thoroughly-frightening overnight relocation. Five years prior to this production, it almost seems as if it was presaged by a TV spot entitled "Nocturnal Migration" that Davis did for Tooheys, one of the brewing divisions of a company strikingly named (suspenseful drumroll) Lion.

This film that is its namesake winds up seeming a little too much like another well-made Davis advertisement in its second half, as it is shown that Saroo Brierley's return trip home twenty-five years later would not have been possible without the wondrous invention that is Google Earth. Even with the assistance of this technological marvel, attempting to pinpoint a location without accurate knowledge of its name and only minimal recollection of a few sites was like trying to find the proverbial needle in a haystack. *Lion*, particularly during its superior first half leading up to that successful stab in the dark, is equally triumphant in its own endeavor to pierce one's heart.

To a large extent, the reason for this is that said hearts are first note worthily warmed by the portrayal of Saroo by then-six-year-old Sunny Pawar, a newcomer who is an absolutely-beguiling natural with electrically-expressive eyes. *Lion* far from coincidentally begins with the first of many Google Earth-like extreme high angle aerial shots, these scanning India from the sky in 1986 until gradually descending to pinpoint pint-sized Saroo, a tactic that contrasts him with the big world in which he will soon find himself lost and very much alone. It is then established that he is actually far from alone with the introduction of a close-knit clan that will soon be ripped apart. This includes Guddu (promisingly-charismatic Abhishek Bharate), the twelve-year-old who puts a protective arm around the little brother who obviously idolizes him, and loving mother, Kalma (Priyanka Bose), whose security-bestowing smile imperfectly hides the pain of knowing that she has not been able to adequately provide for her children since her husband's desertion. After Saroo successfully pesters Guddu into taking him along when the latter leaves to do a week's-worth of physically-demanding manual labor in order to help support their family, the triumphant child is seen proudly perched upon the handle bars of his brother's bicycle. Viewers have thus quickly gone from a shot peering way down through the clouds toward Saroo to one that shows the child carefree and clearly on cloud nine, they wished that there was a way to prevent this utterly delighted and delightful child's imminent, precipitous plunge back down to earth.

It is after this that Saroo is jostled awake by the aforementioned train as it noisily hurtles ever farther from his home, but some pretty profound rattling is also being done here by Davis. The director aimed to shake moviegoers up with a powerful visual depiction of the poor kid's own alarm, keeping the camera level with Saroo's line of sight so that the jolt to his system and psyche might best be conveyed to viewers through their already-established emotional connection to this child now screaming in tears to be saved. Likewise, when nearly-scared-to-death Saroo is finally, mercifully able to emerge from his entombment days later and almost a thousand miles away, the overwhelmingly-chaotic crush of the crowd upon the platform in Kolkata (formerly Calcutta) is viewed as this small inadvertent sojourner does: a highly-imposing, nearly-impenetrable forest of adult legs. When his endless pleas for assistance go unanswered because Bengali and not his Hindi is understood there, the daunting nature of Saroo's dilemma deepened along with one's concern for him.

Both Saroo and his situation start to appear grimmer, grimier, and downright Dickensian, with acutely-vulnerable Saroo needing to summon every ounce of savvy, resilience, and resourcefulness he can muster as one of the tumultuously-teeming metropolis' multitude of street urchins trying desperately to avoid a dead end. Once again, Saroo is shown not to have been awakened by a nightmare but to one in a scene featuring the echoing footsteps of children scurrying even faster than the rats within a forbidding subway tunnel to escape encroaching adult hands that suddenly grab at them for some highly-questionable reasons from out of the shadows. Later, what seems at first to be help at long last does not last long, as things take yet another harrowing turn. Saroo finally winds up in an orphanage, where a troubled older boy is dragged off in the night with the chilling stipulation that he be brought back in the morning, doubtlessly after being made even more troubled. Through it all, viewers wholeheartedly pull for Saroo with a profound sense of urgency, and are intensely relieved when he becomes one of the lucky ones who winds up in contrastingly good hands, adopted by Sue Brierley (real-life adoptive mother Nicole Kidman) and her husband John (David Wenham), a patiently-nurturing, well-off Caucasian couple from Australia—almost 6,000 additional miles away from Saroo's loved ones. (Racial, cultural, and economic dissimilarities are never deeply addressed.)

Davis has Pawar hesitate briefly in a doorway before approaching the Breirleys expectantly waiting beyond, expressing Saroo's momentary uncertainty while momentously poised on the threshold of a new, very different, but wonderful life. However, that does not necessarily mean that he will then be able to simply shut the door on the old one and forget it. Unfortunately, that turned out to be impossible for many viewers, as well. In the film's production notes, producer Emile Sherman stated that the idea was to lead off with "letting the audience fully experience young Saroo's life in India" so that "the enormous power of this experience is then felt through the Australian section, and we fully appreciate his emotional pull back." However, one not only winds up feeling things empathetically but also in an emphatic way that no one responsible for *Lion* ever intended. The swimming, adult incarnation of Saroo (Oscar-nominated Dev Patel, with his unruly lion's mane of hair), who literally resurfaces here twenty years later, presents himself as a thoroughly-assuaged and happily assimilated Aussie, and yet he suddenly goes from identifying himself as "not really Indian" to "lost" when his senses overwhelmingly reconnect him with his homeland upon encountering the fried, sugar-soaked jalebi that had not

been on his tongue since he talked about them with Guddu in their last moments together.

Certainly less enthralling by comparison are other images that Saroo's mind also repetitively returns to for further preoccupied pondering, namely those of Google Earth. Watching Saroo incessantly stare at his computer while using the global mapping program is increasingly soporific, whereas the scene in which he looks lovingly at Sue as she reveals eye-opening, tear-inducing, theretofore-unknown details about why Saroo and his psychologically-scarred adopted brother, Mantosh (Divian Ladwa), mean the world to her and John, is quite compelling. (It is likely that this moving speech was largely responsible for Kidman's Oscar nomination.) Saroo's ferocious focus not only takes a toll on him but puts a strain on his relationships, including that with girlfriend, Lucy (Rooney Mara), who is supposed to represent a formidable pull toward the future that Saroo must reconcile with the one toward his past, but only the latter tug on his heart is truly palpable here. However, everyone, certainly including those watching, is gratified when the moment of discovery at long last arrives for this Google Earth gazer. It almost appears as if Saroo is using the hand cursor to caress his first view of the place he has yearned for since losing touch so long ago, and it is satisfying to watch the look in his eyes upon making this contact by computer proxy shift from incredulity to incredible joy.

Even more poignant is when the exhilarating elation that the resulting, long-awaited, cathartic cry-inducing reunion with his birth mother puts upon his face unmistakably mixes with soul-penetrating grief upon learning of Guddu's demise. In a wonderful profile done by *60 Minutes*, footage from which is utilized at the movie's end along with photos, the actual Saroo, choking up once again in recalling this thunderbolt revelation, explained: the member of his beloved family that he was closest to was not there. In the final scene, Guddu returns to Saroo's now-more-peaceful mind's eye in a vision featuring a close visual bracketing of these best buddies once again as they frolic upon train tracks that stretch out as the camera pulls back, symbolizing Saroo's extended journey.

Lion justly received positive reviews and six Oscar nomination, including the following beyond those already mentioned: Best Cinematography (Greig Fraser); Best Adapted Screenplay (Luke Davies); and Best Original Score (Volker Bertelmann, aka Hauschka, and Dustin O'Halloran). It turned out that Saroo had not only imperfectly remembered the name of his hometown but also his own (which is Sheru, Hindi for lion), and the film that adopted that English translation for its title is also imperfect. Yet, that mattered little when the climax came, and anyone whose cheeks remained dry has a heart akin to those stones with which indestructibly-loving Kalma selflessly and tirelessly struggled in order to provide.

David L. Boxerbaum

CREDITS

Saroo: Dev Patel
Lucy: Rooney Mara
Sue: Nicole Kidman
John: David Wenham
Young Saroo: Sunny Pawar
Origin: United States
Language: English
Released: 2016
Production: Iain Canning, Angie Fielder, Emile Sherman; released by Aquarius Films, Screen Australia, See Saw Films, Sunstar Entertainment, The Weinstein Co.
Directed by: Garth Davis
Written by: Luke Davies
Cinematography by: Greig Fraser
Music by: Volker Bertelmann; Dustin O'Halloran
Sound: Robert Mackenzie
Music Supervisor: Jemma Burns
Editing: Alexandre de Franceschi
Costumes: Cappi Ireland
Production Design: Chris Kennedy
MPAA rating: PG-13
Running time: 118 minutes

REVIEWS

Burr, Ty. *Boston Globe.* December 21, 2016.
Debruge, Peter. *Variety.* September 16, 2016.
Franich, Darren. *Entertainment Weekly.* November 21, 2016.
Lane, Anthony. *New Yorker.* November 21, 2016.
Merry, Stephanie. *Washington Post.* December 23, 2016.
Morgenstern, Joe. *Wall Street Journal.* November 23, 2016.
Roeper, Richard. *Chicago Sun-Times.* December 22, 2016.
Rooney, David. *Hollywood Reporter.* September 16, 2016.
Scott, A.O. *New York Times.* November 24, 2016.
Travers, Peter. *Rolling Stone.* November 22, 2016.

QUOTES

Dinner guests: "What paper trail?"
Saroo Brierley: "My mum could not read ... or write."
Dinner guests: "What did she do?"
Saroo Brierley: "A laborer. She carried rocks."

TRIVIA

The movie was partly filmed in Tasmania, which is a rare location for film sets. This film, with a crew of more than 300 people and international funding, marks the largest production to take place in Tasmania.

AWARDS

British Acad. 2016: Actor—Supporting (Patel), Adapt. Screenplay
Nominations:
Oscars 2016: Actor—Supporting (Patel), Actress—Supporting (Kidman), Adapt. Screenplay, Cinematog., Film, Orig. Score
British Acad. 2016: Actress—Supporting (Kidman), Cinematog., Orig. Score
Directors Guild 2016: Director (Davis)
Golden Globes 2017: Actor—Supporting (Patel), Actress—Supporting (Kidman), Film—Drama, Score
Screen Actors Guild 2016: Actor—Supporting (Patel), Actress—Supporting (Kidman)

LITTLE MEN

Be on each other's side.
—Movie tagline

Box Office: $702,537

Little Men was another film directed by Ira Sachs that received an all-too-quiet release. The film is the kind of family drama that never cries out to be noticed for any stylistic flourishes, but rather for what it knows about human beings and the truths that come out in sticky situations. Sachs puts his characters first and in a brisk, economical running time (in this case, 85 minutes), he is able to paint a larger portrait of a family and friendship with deep ties and a lot of history. It is quite an accomplishment every time around, and yet his films seem to fly under the radar for even the most devoted arthouse attendees. *Little Men* may not move mountains with its simple look at the lives of New Yorkers and their troubles, but it does achieve its goals with very little manipulation or corny sentiment.

The film tells the story of a family who move to Brooklyn after the death in the family. Brian Jardine (Greg Kinnear), a struggling stage actor, has just lost his father, who had an apartment in Brooklyn above a small clothing boutique. Brian's wife, Kathy (Jennifer Ehle), works as a psychotherapist and on her day off, visits the shop, which has not been doing well because of the changing neighborhood. They have a 13-year-old son named Jake (Theo Taplitz), a gifted artist who has no interest in moving to Brooklyn. On the day of the funeral (the same day they move to Brooklyn), Jake meets Tony (Michael Barbieri) and they become instant friends. Tony's mom, Leonor (Paulina Garcia), is struggling and on the verge of losing her store. Tony's father is, according to him, living in Africa and travelling the globe.

The two families become friends, but there eventually comes the complications involving the store and the apartment. Rent has gone up quite a bit in the last couple years and the Jardines have inherited his status as landlord. Leonor and her son have become like family to the late grandfather, but now that he is gone, they are faced with the fact that the store cannot remain open under the old lease. Brian and his sister Audrey (Talia Balsam) draw up a new lease, but even that is too much of a financial strain. The conflict causes a rift between Jake and Tony and soon, that rift affects the relationship between the two boys and their parents. They each vow to give their parents an interminable silent treatment until the matter is resolved.

Sachs is careful not to make anyone a real adversary here. Both families have something at stake, but it is the emotional toll the situation takes on everyone that is the center of the story. The key to the film's success lies in the casting. Kinnear is always a reliable everyman who has to keep everything grounded and he makes for an interesting through-line for the audience. His character clearly does not have all the answers, but the wisdom he can impart based on his non-success has value and Kinnear perfectly embodies that mixture of failure in his profession and success as a loving and understanding father. As Leonor, Garcia has the tough job of not playing the victim, but also using whatever sentimental value she can muster to help the Jardines see her side of the situation. Just when she is about to come off as unreasonable, she has a moment that earns the audience's empathy.

As for the two young newcomers, Taplitz and Barbieri have a natural chemistry and come off as real teenagers caught in the middle of a touchy conflict. Taplitz, playing the sensitive, quiet artist, has the right look and the right sense of early teenage awkwardness for the role. He always appears as though every situation is new to him because it forces him out of his shell. Barbieri plays the more outgoing of the two characters and his thick Brooklyn accent goes nicely with his confidence and cockiness. He also plays it beautifully in a moment when he asks a girl out and she declines, saying she prefers older men. It is a moment when Tony has to reckon with the idea that he remains a littler man than he thought.

Sachs strikes the right balance here as a director who clearly invests a lot in his screenplay while also making the smart choice to have moments of improv as the camera lingers on young teenagers while they talk among themselves. He recognizes that young people act differently when they are away from their parents and he is smart to just let the actors and the extras surrounding them just be themselves. One stand-out moment is a scene in which Tony learns an improv lesson in his acting class, a scene that clearly took on a life of its own as the camera just rolled. *Little Men* is in no way flashy and does not cry out to be heard like the characters in that scene, but the accomplishments are worth praising and the performances never appear to be coached out of the actors.

Collin Souter

CREDITS

Brian Jardine: Greg Kinnear
Kathy Jardine: Jennifer Ehle
Leonor Calvelli: Paulina Garcia
Hernan: Alfred Molina
Jake Jardine: Theo Taplitz
Tony Calvelli: Michael Barbieri
Origin: United States
Language: English
Released: 2016
Production: Lucas Joaquin, Christos V. Konstantakopoulos, Jim Lande, L.A. Teodosio, Ira Sachs; released by Charlie Guidance, Faliro House Productions, Race Point Films
Directed by: Ira Sachs
Written by: Ira Sachs; Mauricio Zacharias
Cinematography by: Óscar Durán
Music by: Dickon Hinchliffe
Editing: Mollie Goldstein; Affonso Goncalves
Art Direction: Ramsey Scott
Costumes: Eden Miller
Production Design: Alexandra Schaller
MPAA rating: PG
Running time: 85 minutes

REVIEWS

Burr, Ty. *Boston Globe.* September 1, 2016.
Hassenger, Jesse. *The A.V. Club.* August 4, 2016.
Jones, J.R. *Chicago Reader.* September 15, 2016.
Lane, Anthony. *New Yorker.* August 1, 2016.
LaSalle, Mick. *San Francisco Chronicle.* August 10, 2016.
Linden, Sheri. *Los Angeles Times.* August 10, 2016.
MacDonald, Moira. *Seattle Times.* August 18, 2016.
O'Malley, Sheila. *RogerEbert.com.* August 5, 2016.
Phillips, Michael. *Chicago Tribune.* September 1, 2016.
Stewart, Sara. *New York Post.* August 4, 2016.

TRIVIA

After the film premiered, Michael Barbieri was accepted at the Fiorello H. LaGuardia High School of Music & Art and Performing Arts in New York.

AWARDS

Nominations:

Ind. Spirit 2017: Actress—Supporting (Garcia), Screenplay

THE LITTLE PRINCE

Growing up isn't the problem ... forgetting is.
—Movie tagline

Box Office: $1.3 Million

After a somewhat troubled road to a domestic release, director Mark Osborne (*Kung Fu Panda* [2008]) finally found a home for his wonderful *The Little Prince* on home streaming service Netflix. The fact that the film was summarily dropped from theaters by Paramount a mere week before it was set to debut is alarming on many levels, but the biggest issue with that decision is that they let one of the very best animated films of the year slip off their plate. Alas, Paramount's boneheaded move is Netflix's gain, and the film will likely reach a larger audience in the end due to the decision, and it should have as big an audience as possible because *The Little Prince* is fantastic.

Based on the classic children's novella *The Little Prince* by Antoine de Saint-Exupéry the film eschews a straightforward adaptation, and instead wisely chooses to set the film in modern America with the source material playing out in an intriguing way. The film opens with the introduction of a young girl (who remains unnamed throughout the film) voiced by Mackenzie Foy (*Interstellar* [2014]) who is well on her way to being a Type-A personality workaholic. This is due to her mother (Rachel McAdams), who not only pushes her daughter to excel but who also has planned her life out for her down to the minute, literally. After failing to get into a popular private school by interview, the mother and daughter move to a new house near the school to circumvent the system and get her the best education available.

The house they move to is available because the neighboring house is a run-down mess owned by a seemingly crazy old aviator (Jeff Bridges), who keeps the house in ill-repair, all the while working on a dilapidated airplane in his backyard. Soon the aviator and the little girl strike up an unlikely friendship, which then dovetails in with the original story of *The Little Prince*. This is a clever stroke by screenwriters Irena Brignull and Bob Persichetti because they are able to envelop the poetic, allegorical tale told in the book into a modern story of societal pressures forcing kids to grow up sooner than they should. The aviator in the film turns out to be a grown up version of the protagonist in the book and the plot soon revolves around him and the little girl trying to find out what became of the little prince.

Director Osborne also ups the ante by really digging deep into a variety of animated styles to bring this film to life. He also did this in the original *Kung Fu Panda* by combining styles and mediums to show moments from the past juxtaposed with the modern. In *The Little Prince*, action that takes place in the "now" is animated with fairly standard, almost "Pixar-lite" CGI. Yet where the film really opens itself up creatively and artistically is when the aviator tells the tale of The Little Prince, taken straight from the book's pages. This animation is also CGI but it's wholly unique looking, almost a mix of wood-carved puppets and paper art. It's truly beautiful work and adds a more classic, whimsical feeling to the well-known story.

If *The Little Prince* stumbles, it's in the way the poetic, allegorical messages and lines from the original book are sometimes shoehorned into the plot. While this works in an almost impressionistic way it can be difficult to have enough time to dwell on and consider what is being said and shown before being brought back into the "now." The most popular quotes from the book are uttered by a small fox (here voiced by James Franco) and what the fox says in the film is indeed profound and deep. However, where *The Little Prince* succeeds in blending two times, styles, and types of film together it also tends to strip away some of the poignant, simple power of the original text.

Yet, this is but a mere quibble as *The Little Prince* is an animated film for everyone. For an ostensible "kids movie" *The Little Prince* really delves into some heavy, thought-provoking topics, including mortality, chasing one's dreams and even heavy hitting business and consumerism. The sheer beauty of the animation mixed with the truthfulness of the message of growing old and forgetting one's childlike joy is profound and everlasting. Plus, Jeff Bridges as the amicable aviator feels like an old friend who's retuned into one's life. *The Little Prince* is a must-see film and the fact it's so readily available is a rare opportunity for everyone to get on board with a lovely little film that needs more love and attention than most children's blockbusters deserve.

Don R. Lewis

CREDITS

The Aviator: Jeff Bridges
The Mother: Rachel McAdams
Mr. Prince: Paul Rudd
The Rose: Marion Cotillard
The Fox: James Franco
The Little Girl: Mackenzie Foy
Origin: United States
Language: English
Released: 2016
Production: Dimitri Rassam, Aton Soumache, Alexis Vonarb; released by ON Animation Studios, On Entertainment, Onyx Films, Orange Studio, Paramount Animation, Stop Frame Animations

Directed by: Mark Osborne
Written by: Irena Brignull; Bob Persichetti
Cinematography by: Kris Kapp
Music by: Joann Le Blanc; Richard Harvey; Hans Zimmer; Rebecca Delannet
Sound: Christopher Barnett
Music Supervisor: Astrid Gomez-Montoya
Editing: Carole Kravetz-Akyanian; Matt(hew) Landon
Production Design: Celine Desrumaux; Lou Romano
MPAA rating: PG
Running time: 108 minutes

REVIEWS

Bleasdale, John. *CineVue*. May 22, 2015.
Bowen, Chuck. *Slant*. March 15, 2016.
Ellwood, Gregory. *Hitfix*. June 4, 2015.
Felperin, Leslie. *Hollywood Reporter*. August 4, 2016.
Foundas, Scott. *Variety*. May 22, 2015.
Greenblatt, Leah. *Entertainment Weekly*. August 4, 2016.
Pulver, Andrew. *Guardian*. May 22, 2015.
Smith, Kyle. *New York Post*. August 4, 2016.
Solomon, Charles. *Los Angeles Times*. August 4, 2016.
Tallerico, Brian. *RogerEbert.com*. August 4, 2016.

QUOTES

The Little Prince: "If you love a flower that lives on a star, it is sweet to look at the sky at night. All the stars are a-bloom with flowers...."

TRIVIA

This is the first-ever animated feature film adaptation of Antoine de Saint-Exupery's *The Little Prince*.

LIVE BY NIGHT

The American Dream has a price.
—Movie tagline

Box Office: $10.3 Million

Ben Affleck, the actor, has had his strings of ups and downs with the projects he has chosen. Acclaim from working with actors' directors like Gus Van Sant, Roger Michell, and David Fincher. Less so with pyrotechnic craftsmen such as Michael Bay, John Woo, and Zack Snyder. Affleck is no dummy though, and when embarking on his own directorial career managed to take the best traits of his former helmsmen while knowing how to combine both when his stories called for it. Thus, Affleck, the director, has become one of the more fascinating and successful double-duty filmmakers of his time paying off with both recognition from audi-

ences as well as his peers for the Best Picture-winning, *Argo* (2012). For his follow-up, the director-actor-writer returns to the world of author Dennis Lehane who wrote his exceptional debut feature, *Gone Baby Gone* (2007). This time around, Affleck's eye is a bit too concentrated on the photogenic surroundings of his own character to allow the grimier aspects of this tale evolve into an epic that hums rather than sighs.

During Prohibition, Joe Coughlin (Affleck) went from an injured war veteran to a petty criminal. He robs a backroom poker game aided by inside gal, Emma Gould (Sienna Miller), who serves as mistress not only to Joe but Albert White (Robert Glenister), a rival mob boss. When Joe goes to jail he is protected by another boss, Maso Pescatore (Remo Girone) in exchange for favors from Coughlin's father, Thomas (Brendan Gleeson), a Captain in the Boston police. As one father figure falls to his guilt, Maso sends Joe to Florida to aid in the family Rum business with his friend, Dion (Chris Messina).

Down South, Joe's Empire begins to expand with help from Cuban revolutionary Graciela (Zoe Saldana), with whom he begins a love affair. Everyone wants a piece of the business, including a dunderhead from the Ku Klux Klan (Matthew Maher), robbing the local dives. This brings Joe to Police Chief Figgis (Chris Cooper), who shares a familial connection to the Klan's leader. He also has a daughter, Loretta (Elle Fanning), who goes from ingénue to a provocateur in both porn and religion that becomes an unwitting lynchpin to the fates of everyone involved.

Already there is an abundance of plot covering a vast landscape of thematic fire zones, but to what extent does it all work together as drama? For all the waters that Joe tips his toes in, he is not a particularly interesting protagonist, which poses a murky problem for Affleck the director. One could view Joe as a guidepost to the antagonists of America's growth; the good man who must be bad to navigate through them. But just how good? Joe may work with the Irish and the Italian but as his loyalties begin to shift towards Cuban immigrants and against the KKK, he veers dangerously into the cliché lane of a literal white knight who is photographed so well by the amazing Robert Richardson it's a wonder if he had help from the light of that halo.

Joe as a kind of walk-through-this-world-with-me anti-hero would have taken some of the heat off of Affleck, the actor, who could just give the best scenes to another impressively-assembled cast. Messina gets the meatiest moments as Joe's henchman, even if some of the comic bits, while amusing, feel out of place in a film with such a flat tone. Cooper and Gleeson also stand out in their too-few moments though it is impossible not to flashback to Cooper's arc in *American Beauty* (1999). As for the hopeful counterparts that challenge Joe on the female side, Zoe Saldana is as bland as always, letting a cigarette and her slinky dresses define the character. Sienna Miller lays it on a bit too thick as the hard-living moll that is supposed to define the titular mantra. The biggest disappointment may be the use of Elle Fanning though, who basically gets one scene each to define this character's downfall and hypocrisies and then is given a footnote farewell that feels like just a plot point to influence a final action by another.

Live By Night is unquestionably a beautiful film to look at with all the period details impeccably defined by its set decorators and costumers. By the time it is all over though it has all the gravitas of a photo booth at a theme park. This material was not designed to be a vacation stop where a larger thesis is forgotten about to engage in some well-staged shootouts and play dress-up. Affleck has earned his way into the director's chair. He balanced action, drama and even romance so well in the exciting *The Town* (2010), but this has the feel of Francis Ford Coppola's truncated cut of *The Godfather* (1972) that drew the ire of its producer Robert Evans. He wanted a film so authentic that you could "smell the spaghetti." Audiences for *Live By Night* may feel like they came down with a severe case of Hyposmia; possibly infected by those who put it all together.

Erik Childress

CREDITS

Joe Coughlin: Ben Affleck
Loretta Figgis: Elle Fanning
Thomas Coghlin: Brendan Gleeson
Dion Bartolo: Chris Messina
Emma Gould: Sienna Miller
Graciella Suarez: Zoe Saldana
Origin: United States
Language: English
Released: 2017
Production: Leonardo DiCaprio, Jennifer Davisson Killoran, Jennifer Todd, Ben Affleck; released by Appian Way, Pearl Street Films, Warner Bros. Entertainment Inc.
Directed by: Ben Affleck
Written by: Ben Affleck
Cinematography by: Robert Richardson
Music by: Harry Gregson-Williams
Sound: Erik Aadahl; Ethan Van der Ryn
Editing: William Goldenberg
Art Direction: Christa Munro; Bradley Rubin
Costumes: Jacqueline West
Production Design: Jess Gonchor

MPAA rating: R
Running time: 129 minutes

REVIEWS

Berardinelli, James. *ReelViews.* January 11, 2017.
Burr, Ty. *Boston Globe.* January 12, 2017.
Cline, Rich. *Contactmusic.com.* January 12, 2017.
Johanson, MaryAnn. *Flick Filosopher.* January 5, 2017.
Mayer, Dominick. *Consequence of Sound.* January 11, 2017.
McGranaghan, Mike. *Aisle Seat.* December 24, 2016.
Morgenstern, Joe. *Wall Street Journal.* January 2, 2017.
Roeper, Richard. *Chicago Sun-Times.* January 12, 2017.
Singer, Matt. *Screen Crush.* January 9, 2017.
Taylor, Kate. *Globe and Mail.* January 13, 2017.

QUOTES

Joe Coughlin: "You realize to be free in this life, breaking the rules meant nothing. You have to be strong enough to make your own."

TRIVIA

Leonardo DiCaprio produced the film, but had been up for the lead role.

LO AND BEHOLD: REVERIES OF THE CONNECTED WORLD

The human side of the digital revolution.
—Movie tagline

Box Office: $594,912

Not content to rest on his laurels as one of the most unique narrative filmmakers of his time, Werner Herzog has also made great strides to go down as one of the great creators of documentaries as well. Over just the past decade, he has taken his cameras to such far-flung locations as Antarctica (*Encounters at the End of the World* [2007]), the Chauvet caves of Southern France and the ancient paintings contained within (*Cave of Forgotten Dreams* [2010]), Siberian Taiga (*Happy People: A Year in the Taiga* [2010]), and the death row of a Texas prison (*Into the Abyss* [2011]) and come up with stories just as strange and engrossing as the ones in his one-of-a-kind dramas. For his latest effort, *Lo and Behold, Reveries of the Connected World*, he tackles a subject that most viewers may know of but may not know that much about—the Internet—and comes up with another fascinating and eminently watchable work that takes viewers on a journey through numerous facets of the topic at hand that illustrate, in his inimitably offbeat manner, how it came to infiltrate everyday lives to such a degree and speculate as to where it may be taking mankind in the future.

Broken up into ten short sections that each cover one aspect regarding the Internet and its influence, the film kicks off by taking viewers back to the very beginning with a tour of the halls of UCLA, where the birth of what would become known as the World Wide Web occurred on October 29, 1969. From that starting point, the film goes on to cover a wide range of topics that cover both the best things that the Internet has to offer (such as an online video game involving bio-molecular structures with the potential to help bring about genuine medical discoveries) to the worst (ranging from video game addiction to the horrifying story of a troubled young woman who died in a car accident and whose family was tormented when gory photos of the crash were posted online and inspired unimaginably cruel harassments from total strangers protected by anonymity).

In the later sections of the film, Herzog shifts focus from the past to the future and finds both the good and bad in what lies ahead. There is much talk about developments in robotics (including self-driving cars and robots learning to play soccer) and artificial intelligence that could eventually change the very nature of humanity in ways that include the possibilities of living on Mars and of merging with our ever-developing electronic environments to such a degree that the line between man and man-made becomes virtually non-existent. At the same time, however, having established just how quickly and completely the Internet has become integrated into contemporary society, it then illustrates just how easily it could all be brought down with potentially catastrophic results for all. Legendary hacker Kevin Mitnick turns up to discuss just how vulnerable the systems are to anyone who really puts their mind towards breaking into them—his recounting of how he was able to obtain important source code from Motorola in just a matter of minutes with only a couple of phone calls is both darkly humorous and totally terrifying. Not all the dangers are man-made either—Hurricane Sandy demonstrated how vulnerable the system was and a solar storm along the lines of the famous Carrington Event of 1859 could have the potential to knock the entire thing out and take the world back to a place where it was not too long ago but which now probably seems unimaginable to most people.

The film raises any number of questions about technology and how it relates to the world today but, as has been the case with most of his documentaries, Herzog is not especially interested in providing any sort of definitive answer to any of them. Here, he prefers to simply sit back and allow the participants to talk at length about their various obsessions, theories, and predictions as a way of giving viewers the equivalent of an especially intense college dorm bull session. Other than asking the occasional question of his subjects or making a pithy comment once in a while (the funniest of which has him going through the halls of UCLA and remarking "The corridors here look repulsive"), he stays out of the proceedings and even the interviews themselves are staged in the simplest and most direct talking head manner imaginable. (The one exception is the funeral-like tableau he utilizes to present the surviving family members of the aforementioned car crash victim, an overly self-conscious presentation that is the film's one real mistake.) However, it is easy enough to detect Herzog's own ambivalence towards the subject at hand and indeed, the section that he seems most comfortable with is one involving Green Bank, West Virginia, a town housing a telescope so large and powerful that the electromagnetic waves it attracts make it impossible to operate cell phones, making it both a mecca for those with an acute sensitivity to such things and a place that would be well-equipped to go on if the Internet were to one day be brought down somehow.

Compared to the lengths that he went through in order to produce some of his recent documentaries, *Lo and Behold, Reveries of the Connected World* may not seem quite as ambitious of an effort on Werner Herzog's part. And yet, even though his cameras do not go beyond some ordinary homes, offices, and hotel rooms, the scope and impact of what the people in those rooms have to say is so stimulating and thought-provoking that few viewers will notice or care. At one point in the film, an observer rues the fact that, due to the constant streams of information available at the click of a button, the art of deep critical thinking—the ability to take information and form one's own conclusions based on the material at hand—is one that is in danger of being lost completely before too long. Thankfully, that will not be the case for as long as people like Herzog continue to make films as absorbing and provocative as this one.

Peter Sobczynski

CREDITS

Himself: Elon Musk
Himself: Kevin D. Mitnick
Himself: Lawrence Krauss
Himself: Sebastian Thrun
Herself: Lucianne Walkowicz
Origin: United States
Language: English

Released: 2016

Production: Rupert Maconick, Werner Herzog; released by Saville Productions

Directed by: Werner Herzog

Written by: Werner Herzog

Cinematography by: Peter Zeitlinger

Editing: Marco Capalbo

MPAA rating: PG-13

Running time: 98 minutes

REVIEWS

Abele, Robert. *Los Angeles Times*. August 18, 2016.

Bowen, Chuck. *Slant*. June 15, 2016.

Chang, Justin. *Variety*. January 24, 2016.

Hillis, Aaron. *Village Voice*. August 17, 2016.

Hornaday, Ann. *Washington Post*. August 18, 2016.

Lane, Anthony. *New Yorker*. August 22, 2016.

McCarthy, Todd. *Hollywood Reporter*. January 24, 2016.

Morgenstern, Joe. *Wall Street Journal*. August 18, 2016.

Scott, A.O. *New York Times*. August 18, 2016. .

White, Armond. *National Review*. August 29, 2016.

QUOTES

Professor Leonard Kleinrock: "This machine is so ugly that it's beautiful."

TRIVIA

During the Catsouras interview, breakfast pastries were laid out for the crew. Cinematographer Peter Zeitlinger suggested it would be a more interesting shot if the food stayed in the frame.

THE LOBSTER

An unconventional love story by Yorgos Lanthimos.
        —Movie tagline

Box Office: $9 Million

A barbed shot at the institutionalization of romance (looking at you, Hallmark) and the coupling/marriage panic that more generally grips society, Greek-born director Yorgos Lanthimos's *The Lobster* exists at an intersection rarely visited in mainstream narrative filmmaking, where the emotionally brutal meets the willfully absurd. Co-written by Lanthimos and frequent collaborator Efthymis Filippou, the film uses a radically silly premise—that single people are given a month-and-a-half to find mates or suffer the consequences of a ritualized yet mysterious transformation—to satirically explore human desire, sadness and frailty.

After winning the Jury Prize at the 2015 Cannes Film Festival, *The Lobster* was bought by A24 Films, who gave the movie an early summer theatrical release in 2016, where it grossed over $9 million in its counter-programming run. Though certainly not for all tastes, this ultra-dry, shrewdly observant behavioral comedy, Lanthimos's first English-language effort, is a pleasingly singular and offbeat film—an intellectually adventurous affair which lovers of bold and original cinema should, at the very least, respect in piecemeal fashion.

One of the strongest things *The Lobster* has going for it is a rich, evocative, and thought-provoking world which operates with specific set of rules that is beyond the reproach of its audience. As with each of Lanthimos's previous two movies to receive Stateside distribution, *Dogtooth* (2010) and *Alps* (2012), the former of which was nominated for an Academy Award for best foreign language film, *The Lobster* requires audience buy-in on an elemental level.

Colin Farrell stars as David, a somewhat sad-sack man who, upon learning his wife is leaving him for another man, is promptly escorted to a countryside hotel. There, he and others will have 45 days to find a new partner with whom they share a distinguishing trait or else be transformed into an animal of their choosing, explains the hotel manager (Olivia Colman). Upon check-in, David chooses the titular creature, given their long lifespan and his love of the ocean. Among the many rules of the hotel (self-stimulation is strictly forbidden, but stimulation by the wait staff is required) are mandatory seminars with pantomimed plays to reinforce the benefits of coupling. Residents can also extend their stay on hunts where they tranquilize single people in the forest, earning an extra day for each quarry bagged.

The rest of the characters remain nameless, identified instead only in the end credits by blunt descriptors. In short order, David befriends Lisping Man (John C. Reilly) and Limping Man (Ben Whishaw), two other inhabitants whose physical afflictions seemingly augur a less successful chance at mating. As desperation over their circumstances set in, the Limping Man injures himself in order to couple with Nosebleed Woman (Jessica Barden), and start a family. Feeling utterly disconnected, David similarly forces a match with a Heartless Woman (Aggeliki Papoulia).

A little less than halfway into its two-hour runtime, *The Lobster* shifts gears. After his aforementioned coupling goes sideways, David escapes into the woods surrounding the hotel, where he joins up with a group of people who exist outside of this society and are working to undermine its mission of rehabilitation. The Loner Leader (Lea Seydoux) explains quite sternly that within their group romantic couplings are expressly forbidden and sexual acts punished, but David eventually develops feelings for a Shortsighted Woman (Rachel Weisz), and vice versa. Naturally, this creates new problems.

It is worth stressing that *The Lobster* is funny, albeit in a dark manner. There are various amusing set-ups (an advice panel for choosing the activities of one's last night as a human, for example), and the dialogue is barbed, full of hilarious bureaucratic asides delivered in straight-faced fashion. ("If you encounter any problems, tensions or arguing that you cannot resolve yourselves, you'll be assigned children—that usually helps, a lot," says the hotel manager.)

Violence is part of this world too, though. In addition to the group hunts of "loners," fetishistically presented in slow-motion, and the Lisping Man getting his hand placed in a toaster as punishment for masturbation, the Heartless Woman also callously kicks an animal to death. As in David Lynch's *Wild at Heart* (1990), Lanthimos seems to relish the idea that there is both darkness and humor in such circumstances, leaving viewers to grapple with the discomfort this can evoke.

As Guy Lodge correctly noted in his *Variety* review following the Cannes Film Festival premiere, *The Lobster* is a movie "in which nearly every scene requires bookmarking, to be intuitively cross-referenced at a later point." Lanthimos and Filippou carefully layer things, so that various scenes—of David absentmindedly playing with his dog, for instance—later register a more pronounced emotional impact.

One of the film's most gifted psychological insights is how intense loneliness can warp one's judgment and affect their ability to connect with other people, precisely during the time they most need companionship. While this rich paradox receives some consideration, one wishes it was explored in even greater depth and detail—it feels like a half-tapped vein. Part of the brilliance of *Eternal Sunshine of the Spotless Mind* (2004) was in how it plumbed the intense melancholy inherently attached to romantic love, by way of the process through which we mentally sort relationships that do not work out, or even bad moments in ones that do. Similarly, *The Lobster* is at its best when probing the sexual frustration ("That's awful, just awful," says David after a maid grinds her pelvis into his crotch for motivation, and then leaves) and depression of its characters, and how their newfound singledom casts long shadows of doubt and despair, informing their actions.

Lanthimos and Filippou, however, seem too eager to get outside out of the hotel. In exploring the on-the-lam group of loners, they establish an instrument for the examination of parallel reactionaries, no doubt. But this setting feels comparatively underdeveloped and is never

as interesting as the hotel, which, with its lack of a specific setting (a variety of actors speak in their native accents), serves as an allegorical weigh station for the vagaries of the human condition. Both the stagings and motivations of its characters feel less anchored, and the Loner Leader lacks the necessary dimension to give full-bodied life to the worldview they advocate.

As *The Lobster* winds its way toward a dark and unforgiving conclusion, then, it is not the bleakness itself—orchestrated by Lanthimos with a clinical precision, and making effective use of existent orchestrations which encompass both stabbing marionette strings of dread and mournful string melodies—that weighs the movie down. It is instead a more conventionally sludgy third act, burdened by a lack of insight into how these characters would function in opposition—even in such a heightened, absurd world. This creates an imbalance from which the film cannot escape, no matter its overarching imagination.

The Lobster continues to make the case for Farrell as a much more interesting character actor than movie star. Although he is the lead here, he is subservient to the story throughout—rendered appropriately mopey through a combination of his moustache and paunch—while still retaining a certain melancholic magnetism. Longtime Lanthimos collaborator Papoulia, meanwhile, makes a strong impression as the unsympathetic Heartless Woman; she cuts through her scenes like a knife, without regard for vanity. Seydoux and Weisz, though, struggle to breathe comparable subtlety or vitality into their characters.

Still, *The Lobster* is a one-of-a-kind film, with even its missteps registering as interesting. Loneliness lingers in the very ether of the film, never given cathartic release. Such frustrations seem a small price to pay for such an original work.

Brent Simon

CREDITS

David: Colin Farrell
Short-Sighted Woman: Rachel Weisz
Lisping Man: John C. Reilly
Hotel Manager: Olivia Colman
Loner Leader: Lea Seydoux
Origin: United States
Language: English, French
Released: 2016
Production: Ceci Dempsey, Ed Guiney, Lee Magiday, Yorgos Lanthimos; released by Film 4, Irish Film Board
Directed by: Yorgos Lanthimos
Written by: Yorgos Lanthimos; Efthymis Filippou

Cinematography by: Thimios Bakatakis
Sound: Johnnie Burn
Music Supervisor: Amy Ashworth
Editing: Yorgos Mavropsaridis
Costumes: Sarah Blenkinsop
Production Design: Jacqueline Abrahams
MPAA rating: R
Running time: 118 minutes

REVIEWS

Felperin, Leslie. *Hollywood Reporter*. May 15, 2015.
Fujishima, Kenji. *Slant*. September 27, 2015.
G'Sell, Eileen. *Salon*. May 20, 2016.
Katz, Anita. *San Francisco Examiner*. May 20, 2016. .
Lodge, Guy. *Variety*. May 15, 2015.
Marshall, Lee. *Screen Daily*. May 15, 2015.
Martin, Philip. *Arkansas Democrat-Gazette*. June 10, 2016.
Talu, Yonca. *Film Comment Magazine*. March 17, 2016.
Toppman, Lawrence. *Charlotte Observer*. May 31, 2016.
Wilson, Calvin. *St. Louis Post-Dispatch*. May 26, 2016.

QUOTES

Hotel manager: "Now have you thought of what animal you'd like to be if you end up alone?"

David: "Yes. A lobster."

Hotel manager: "Why a lobster?"

David: "Because lobsters live for over one hundred years, are blue-blooded like aristocrats, and stay fertile all their lives. I also like the sea very much."

TRIVIA

The movie was filmed almost entirely with natural light and no makeup.

AWARDS

Nominations:

Oscars 2016: Orig. Screenplay
Golden Globes 2017: Actor—Mus./Comedy (Farrell)

LONDON HAS FALLEN

Prepare for bloody hell.
        —Movie tagline

Box Office: $62.5 Million

Antoine Fuqua's *Olympus Has Fallen* (2013) was one of two competing "terrorists attack the White House" films that year. The other, Roland Emmerich's *White House Down* (2013) lost viewership after moviegoers may have decided they had all that they could

stomach from the first ugly, bloody go round. Since the former turned out to be enough of a hit though, a sequel was commissioned in the usual cynical attempt to leave no dollar left behind. If *Die Hard* (1988) could spin its genre-creating scenario through four sequels surely this was good enough for at least one. Despite changing directors—and even studios—no one seemed up to the task of forgetting everything that was so terrible about the first film. In fact they seemed to look upon the nature of one nauseating revolt countered by another as a virtuous agenda rather than entertainment.

In this continuation a few years after POTUS was taken hostage, the British Prime Minister has died after complications from surgery. President Asher (Aaron Eckhart) insists on attending services despite his secret service director Jacobs (Angela Bassett) trying to talk him out of these "last minute trips" as if her job never calls for such contingencies. Then again she may be watching the same movie where the Joint Security Committee talks about this gathering of world leaders being a "logistical nightmare." One newscaster goes so far to call it "the most protected event on Earth." Thankfully, Asher's friend and personal protection agent, Mike Banning (Gerard Butler), the man who saved him from the White House attack in the first film is on hand even if he has more to protect personally now with a pregnant wife (Radha Mitchell) on the homefront.

Sure enough there is not enough forewarning involved for British Intelligence to notice terrorists dressed as bobbies and the Queen's Guard. Coordinated attacks take out nearly every world leader and a number of recognizable tourist attractions just for good measure. When Banning gets away with the President and Jacobs, the bad guys become less coordinated trying to climb into their vehicle even after penetrating their bulletproof windows. Allowing them to escape should not please mastermind Aamir Barkawi (Alon Moni Aboutboul) who put everything into motion after a drone strike meant for him years earlier killed his family instead. He intends to capture Asher alive so his death can be broadcast as an example. Although the only example about to be set is by one Mike Banning.

"This man is responsible for more deaths than the plague," says Vice President Trumbull (Morgan Freeman) about their adversary. Whichever plague he is referring to is up for discussion but its body count is about to be surpassed by the one-man Delta Force. "How many you think died," Asher asks? "I don't know. A lot," says Banning before being put through a war zone on the abandoned streets of London that make the hellhole of *Escape from New York* (1981) seem like a vacation spot. Babak Najafi's sequel lacks not only the exploitation fun and satiric slant of John Carpenter's film but also the grungy panache of its anti-heroes. "I hate funerals" is the best quip Banning can muster after creating the need for so many new ones.

After 9/11 a new American hero was born in Jack Bauer, the counter-terrorism agent who always got the job done in 24 hours no matter who he had to kill, torture, or merely yell at. Butler's Banning is more in the mold of the Reagan-era action hero spilling blood to protect his country against all domestic and foreign evils. Only he is as sadistic as the tortuous avenger Butler played in *Law Abiding Citizen* (2009) opposite *White House Down*'s President, Jamie Foxx. When not shooting his way through any masked terrorist goon or drinking a glass of water in a single manly bound, Banning takes even greater pleasure stabbing eyes, chests, and necks with more knives than the combined supply of Michael Myers and Danny Trejo's Machete. Denying protective retribution against those that prey upon the innocent would certainly negate the good vs. bad nature inherent in these cinematic fantasies. But when our hero is advised to "stay alive" so he can see his kid only to receive follow-up counsel to "make those [bad people] pay" it is easy to suspect that the film's priorities are a tad out of whack.

Director Najafi does the bare minimum in creating any sort of suspense or thrills by simply lining up faceless masks for Butler to shoot like targets in a video game. The shoddy nature of the special effects suggests we are witnessing the propaganda of Third World filmmakers using a modded Commodore 64 to render its explosive carnage. Najafi does no favors to a cast this film does not deserve by making them less present than the dead bodies accumulated. Robert Forster has about as much screen time as he did in *Mulholland Drive* (2001). Jackie Earle Haley's big non-expositional moment is turning around so as not to witness what's going on around him. Poor Melissa Leo, whose first appearance suggests she is still traumatized by her hair-dragging ordeal when Olympus fell, has all of one line in the entire film. "Number six on the ten list," is the Oscar-winning actress' solo line in case you miss it. This is a film that begins with a terrorist saying that "vengeance must be profound and absolute" and then the American Vice President ends it by telling the nation that minding our own business in this dangerous world is "a bad idea and we have few good options, but the worst option is to do nothing." In the case of a sequel to *Olympus Has Fallen,* that would have actually been the best.

Erik Childress

CREDITS

Mike Banning: Gerard Butler
MI6 Jacquelin Marshall: Charlotte Riley

Speaker Trumbull: Morgan Freeman
Deputy Chief Mason: Jackie Earle Haley
Secretary of Defense Ruth McMillan: Melissa Leo
Origin: Bulgaria, United Kingdom, United States
Language: English
Released: 2016
Production: Mark Gill, Danny Lerner, Alan Siegel, Les Weldon, Gerard Butler; released by Millennium Films Inc.
Directed by: Babak Najafi
Written by: Creighton Rothenberger; Katrin Benedikt; Chad St. John; Christian Gudegast
Cinematography by: Ed Wild
Music by: Trevor Morris
Sound: Lee Walpole
Music Supervisor: Selena Arizanovic
Editing: Michael J. Duthie; Paul Martin Smith
Costumes: Stephanie Collie
Production Design: Joel Collins
MPAA rating: R

REVIEWS

Abele, Robert. *Los Angeles Times.* March 3, 2016.
Gonzalez, Ed. *Slant Magazine.* March 2, 2016.
Hunter, Rob. *Film School Rejects.* March 4, 2016.
Lemire, Christy. *ChristyLemire.com.* March 14, 2016.
Minow, Nell. *Beliefnet.* March 3, 2016.
Nicholson, Amy. *MTV.* March 5, 2016.
Pais, Matt. *RedEye.* March 2, 2016.
Phillips, Michael. *RedEye.* March 2, 2016.
Schager, Nick. *Playlist.* March 4, 2016.
Vishnevetsky, Ignatiy. *The A.V. Club.* March 2, 2016.

QUOTES

Mike Banning: "How was your vacation, sir?"
VP Trumbull: "Do you have any idea the joy a man experiences pulling a seven-pound king mackerel out of the waters around the bay?"
Mike Banning: "No, sir, I don't."
VP Trumbull: "Neither do I...."

TRIVIA

Due to scheduling conflicts, Morgan Freeman and Gerard Butler don't appear in the same scene together in person. The scene in the hallway at the White House uses body doubles, and doesn't show faces.

AWARDS

Nominations:
Golden Raspberries 2016: Worst Actor (Butler)

LOUDER THAN BOMBS

Break the silence.
—Movie tagline
Box Office: $163,807

The subtle and intricate family drama *Louder Than Bombs* is a superior demonstration of how the movies absorb other art forms in locating an invigorating, unexpected depth. This is a painstaking movie that floats in its own delicate and observant rhythms.

The film is the third feature and the first in English by the gifted Norwegian director Joachim Trier. He previously made the freewheeling and inventive comedy *Reprise* (2006) and the more mournful and emotionally unforgiving *Oslo, August 31st* (2011), in collaboration with Eskil Vogt, a talented writer and very fine director (*Blind* [2014]) in his own right.

The emotional tone the two filmmakers establish is crucial given the architecture of the story. The interlocking stories move deftly from character to character, negotiating time and space. The movie is never settled or complacent. If anything the ambition sometimes overwhelms the execution. The thematic concerns are concerned with memory and grief and how the past impinges on the present. Perspective and mood color everything. Too fine and exacting and the ideas feel suffocated or too dramatically explicit. Told at too far a remove, and it feels cold and impersonal and deprived of any inner conflict.

The movie has its own internal logic and mode of expression. Other narrative forms, particularly the novel, photography, theater, and reportage, are additional entry points to rethink the material. The beautiful and evocative opening image of a man reaching out and grasping the tiny hand of his newborn child conjures the deeply elemental and natural bond between parents and children.

The movie is a chamber drama about pain and loss. The core story is knotty and dark and marked by a pervasive sense of dread and anxiousness floating over the principal survivors. The movie animates the presence of an absence. Isabelle Reed (Isabelle Huppert), a brilliant and dedicated photographer who worked in conflict zones, is the subject of a major gallery exhibition three years after her death from injuries suffered in a car accident near her family's suburban Nyak, New York home.

Richard (David Strathairn), a correspondent and her colleague at the *New York Times*, is writing an accompanying essay. In the piece, Richard informs her husband Gene (Gabriel Byrne) the tribute essay is going to reveal Isabelle's death was a suicide. The couple's oldest son, Jonah (Jesse Eisenberg), has known the truth about his mother's death. The new father is a university sociology professor. The younger son, Conrad (Devin Druid), is a high school sophomore. He is emotionally cut off, sullen, and much harder to reach. He is also unaware of the precise circumstances of his mother's death. The imminent publication pressures Gene to come forward.

The film shares remarkable similarities with Erik Poppe's *1,000 Times Good Night* (2013), another Norwegian film, in English, about the ruptured family dynamics occasioned by a wife and mother (played by another French actress, Juliette Binoche) who is a war zone photographer. The Trier film is much riskier and bolder, particularly as a narrative.

The film meditates on the act of storytelling. The nonlinear fragmentation employs a wide range of subjective techniques such as flashbacks, shifting narrative tenses, daydreams, and hallucinations. The film also plays off echoes and discoveries, like each brother separately learning at crucial narrative points of an aspect of their parents' sexual behavior.

The narrative destabilization underlines the sudden abruptness of time, indicating how things move forward and backward, even sideways for a discursive, often telling detail. The technique yields some very disturbing and provocative moments, like in one detailed flashback of Isabelle relating a sexually explicit dream of her tryst with another man in a violent war zone as the cuckold Gene watches passively in a nearby car. The moment crystallizes Isabelle's disconnection from her husband and deepens her feeling of being unnecessary.

The sequence finds its parallel with Gene, eager to connect with younger son, tracking the teenager from the vantage of his car, and watching him as he sits alone at a park, going into café and then moving on to the cemetery where Isabelle is buried. The moment ends with Conrad collapsing. Later this sequence is replayed, this time from Conrad's perspective, with magic realist touches and a reference to Alfred Hitchcock's *Vertigo* (1958), allowing a greater subtlety and range to the character.

The fantasies and hallucinations are grounded in the psychologically acute and specific, achieving a jolt and flair that is both uncomfortable and unsparing. The alternate sequence from Conrad's point of view acknowledged his infatuation with his beautiful classmate (Ruby Jerins). In a stunning sequence at school, the girl, nervous and tentative, reads aloud passages from the novel the class is studying. Conrad transforms her speech into an elegy to his mother, altering the language, description, and meaning, like something out of J.G. Ballard's hallucinatory novel *Crash* (1973) into a tender, tragic visual reconstruction of his mother's end.

Back home to assist his father in the cataloguing Isabelle's vast professional archive for the museum retrospective, Jonah remains unmoored, fleeing his own adult responsibilities of fatherhood and finding emotional release by gravitating toward his former college girlfriend, Erin (Rachel Brosnahan). It's the weakest part of the script, depriving the same scope and fullness to his largely unseen wife and child. (Amy Ryan, who plays Conrad's English teacher and Gene's mistress, is also underutilized.)

The byplay between the brothers is strong and compelling as Jonah's protective and curious love for his brother underscores a shared grief, lingering and ever present. Conrad sublimates himself into his own private world, ostensibly living inside his own head and creating his own manifesto, a feverish and detailed private essay showing off his wealth of interests and obsessions that acknowledge innate curiosity and love of gadgets, forms and video games. Jonah is both fascinated and concerned. "You're not going to shoot up a school, or something," he says. Seeing the young woman of Conrad's joy, he is more direct. "Sit this one out," he advises him. "It is going to get better."

The movie's final movement is intricately staged, beautiful, and transcendent, filled with quiet moments of tenderness, grace, and bruised vulnerability. Everything is scaled and perfectly apportioned, like Gene's private encounter with the man who also loved Isabelle, setting up an ecstatic reverie of a young man eager to understand and connect with the object of his own waking dreams.

The acting is sensational. In French, Huppert is one of the two or three greatest actors alive, fearless and unbound and extraordinarily risky and rapt. In English, she tends to be more circumspect, and her speech is harder and less musical. Byrne conveys a wholly different kind of pain and sorrow. Eisenberg, with his natural bravado and entitlement, is also just right, going inside himself and quietly projecting his own pain and helplessness. Druid is the true revelation, commanding, confident, and alive to possibility. Jerins is also exceptionally, especially in their long sequence together walking home from a party.

The movie's title, named after compilation album (1987) by the great English band The Smiths, is deceiving. The movie is at its best by capturing something furtive and unspoken. The telling is never less than entrancing.

Patrick Z. McGavin

CREDITS

Gene: Gabriel Byrne
Isabelle: Isabelle Huppert
Jonah: Jesse Eisenberg
Conrad: Devin Druid
Hannah: Amy Ryan

Origin: United States
Language: French, English
Released: 2016
Production: Joshua Astrachan, Albert Berger, Alexandre Mallet-Guy, Thomas Robsahm, Marc Turtletaub, Ron Yerxa; released by Animal Kingdom, Motlys
Directed by: Joachim Trier
Written by: Joachim Trier; Eskil Vogt
Cinematography by: Jakob Ihre
Music by: Ola Flottum
Sound: Gisle Tveito
Editing: Olivier Bugge Coutte
Art Direction: Gonzalo Cordoba
Costumes: Emma Potter
Production Design: Molly Hughes
MPAA rating: R
Running time: 105 minutes

REVIEWS

Dowd, A.A. *The A.V. Club.* April 6, 2016.
Debruge, Peter. *Variety.* May 20, 2015.
Duralde, Alonso. *The Wrap.* April 10, 2016.
Ebiri, Bilge. *Village Voice.* April 10, 2016.
Edelstein, David. *New York Magazine.* April 7, 2016.
Linden, Sheri. *Los Angeles Times.* April 7, 2016.
Morgenstern, Joe. *Wall Street Journal.* April 7, 2016.
Rodriguez, Rene. *Miami Herald.* April 28, 2016.
Scott, A.O. *New York Times.* April 7, 2016.
Zacharek, Stephanie. *Time.* April 10, 2016.

QUOTES

Conrad: "There are days I'm invisible, I can do whatever I want. I must be careful not to lose that ability."

TRIVIA

The medieval Lord of the Rings-type of game that Conrad is seen playing is the Elder Scrolls Online.

LOVE & FRIENDSHIP

Opportunistic, devious, shrewd, calculating, cunning, unprincipled.
—Movie tagline

Box Office: $14 Million

An adaptation of one of the least well-known and most subversive Jane Austen works, *Lady Susan*, Whit Stillman's *Love & Friendship* is a nearly perfect melding of source material and adaptor. Just as Austen's work is an examination of the trials of class and gender, and the absurdity of social structure, Stillman's filmography is all about lovingly popping the bubbles of the entitled to expose them to the real world. It's not only their mutual passions, but their love of the sound and possibilities of the English language that makes these two such perfect bedfellows. Stillman writes dialogue that's dense, erudite, and irony-laden, and who could be better to tease out the humor and undercurrent of delicious nastiness in Austen's elastic prose.

Eschewing the usual passive romances of many Austen novels, the narrative centers on Lady Susan Vernon (Kate Beckinsale), a recent widower who's developed a reputation for seducing rich men after she was kicked out of the Manwaring estate for cavorting with the married Lord Manwaring (Lochlann O'Mearáin). Looking for a way back into high society and a suitable match for her daughter, Frederica (Morfydd Clark), Susan heads to Churchill, the country home of her brother-in-law. Her brother-in-law, Charles Vernon (an admirably dim Justin Edwards) receives her warmly, but his wife, Catherine (Emma Greenwell), and her brother, Reginald DeCourcy (Xavier Samuel) are less sure about her, having heard endless tales of her flirting abilities.

Within days, Reginald is enthralled with Susan, finding her to be beguilingly charming and deeply intelligent. He's decades younger than her, but he's already courting her despite the protests of Catherine and the rest of his family. But Susan has a masterplan that's ten steps ahead of every person on screen, orchestrating every move to secure an easy future for her and Frederica, who cleverly falls into the mold of a traditional Austen protagonist.

An epistolary novella on the page, Stillman presents the story episodically, but also affectionately draws attention to its original format in multiple ways. Every time the film comes to a new setting, Stillman presents a roll call of the inside players with static portraits of each character, and a cheeky caption that tells the audience something about their status or intelligence level. And nearly as often, Stillman will write out character's dialogue onscreen as they speak to emphasize the duality of the prose in terms of tone.

In general, Stillman's approach to the material is fully committed to emphasizing the comedy, drawing out the nasty and hilarious ways that her work poked fun at pomp and circumstance, but also making sure never to tip these characters into caricature. Rather, he treats the opportunity to showcase such complex and entertaining dialogue like a five-course feast, creating a film that relentlessly skewers every possible Austen archetype from the ivory tower buffoon to outmatched ingenues to the clueless hunks, all while still maintaining a thin veneer of civility.

The key to that balance is the cast, which is filled with Stillman regulars like Beckinsale and Chloë Sevigny alongside newcomers like Samuel, Edwards, and the previously unmentioned Tom Bennett, who tears into a Mr. Collins style role. Bennett falls into the grand cinematic tradition of Austen jesters like Melville Cooper, playing a wealthy dolt with such hypnotizing springboard energy that it's hard to decide whether to watch or look away.

And at the center is Beckinsale, who last worked with Stillman on *Last Days of Disco* (1998), and bares fangs sharper than any character in the *Underworld* series. She's an ideal partner for Stillman, bringing a cloaked venom to every line that complements Stillman's built world of egomaniacs and doofuses. Beckinsale makes Susan a schemer worthy of Lady Macbeth, planning her rise in society like a master thief while appearing to be the perfect model of humility. She hurtles into each new line, delivering each bon mot in such a roundabout turn of phrase that she's already moved on to the next subject by the time the listener realizes they are being insulted.

Alas, as quick as Stillman is with dialogue, his plain tendency as a visual stylist is the film's biggest weakness. *Love & Friendship* is filled with sumptuous production design and ornate costumes, but his camerawork is strictly utilitarian, and combined with the stop-start pacing, the film could use more establishing shots to feel less disjointed. Similarly, the last act of the film feels too crowded and loses some of the cleanness that makes the film so structurally appealing.

These are comparatively small nitpicks when placed against the success of the performances and Stillman's sense of control over the story. Austen is an author who's been adapted ad nauseam, but like Joe Wright's recent adaptation of *Pride & Prejudice* (2005), *Love & Friendship* is another welcome reminder that Austen's work can still feel vital and new on screen.

Michael Snydel

CREDITS

Lady Susan Vernon: Kate Beckinsale
Frederica Vernon: Morfydd Clark
Sir James Martin: Tom Bennett
Lady Lucy Manwaring: Jenn Murray
Lord Manwaring: Lochlann O'Mearain
　　Eimer Ni Mhaoldomhnaigh
Origin: United States
Language: English
Released: 2016
Production: Lauranne Bourrachot, Katie Holly, Whit Stillman; released by Blinder Films, Westerly Films
Directed by: Whit Stillman

Written by: Whit Stillman
Cinematography by: Richard Van Oosterhout
Music by: Benjamin Esdraffo
Sound: Ranko Paukovic
Editing: Sophie Corra
Art Direction: Louise Mathews; Bryan Tormey
Production Design: Anna Rackard
MPAA rating: PG
Running time: 92 minutes

REVIEWS

Cole, Jake. *Slant.* May 10, 2016.
D'Angelo, Mike. *The A.V. Club.* May 12, 2016.
Erbland, Kate. *IndieWire.* May 12, 2016.
Hornaday, Ann. *Washington Post.* May 19, 2016.
Lane, Anthony. *New Yorker.* May 23, 2016.
Murray, Noel. *IndieWire.* January 24, 2016.
Nehme, Farran Smith. *New York Post.* May 12, 2016.
Phillips, Michael. *Chicago Tribune.* May 16, 2016.
Scott, AO. *New York Times.* May 12, 2016.
Seitz, Matt Zoller. *Roger Ebert.* May 13, 2016.

QUOTES

Lady Susan Vernon: "Ah, mortality. Our mortality and that of others, but most particularly our own, is the hardest and most intractable hand life can deal us."

TRIVIA

Morrfyd Clark and Emma Greenwell, who play Fredrica and Catherine Vernon, were in another Austen adaption, *Pride and Prejudice and Zombies* (2016) as Georgiana and Caroline Bingley.

THE LOVERS & THE DESPOT

They were kidnapped by their biggest fan.
—Movie tagline

Box Office: $55,511

A bizarre, fascinating, true-life tale of commingled art, autocratic bullying, kidnapping, and more, *The Lovers and the Despot* unfolds against a sprawling geopolitical canvas that still holds intrigue and relevance today, telling the story of a famous South Korean filmmaker and actress abducted in the late 1970s by North Korean dictator-in-waiting Kim Jong-Il for the purpose of generating a higher quality of state-sanctioned propaganda.

In only skimming the surface of the volcanic psychological pressures facing its subjects both during their indentured servitude and following their escape, though, co-directors Robert Cannan and Ross Adam's documentary provides one moment of frustration for every two of engagement. It is a willfully demure work, flirting with deeper meaning but chiefly connecting in parallel fashion to the enigmatic and mysterious story it tells. After premiering at the Sundance Film Festival, *The Lovers and the Despot* was acquired by Magnolia Pictures, and given an autumnal stateside theatrical release. Despite generally positive critical response, the film failed to crack six figures at the domestic box office.

The lovers of the film's title are Choi Eun-Lee and her husband Shin Sang-ok, the undisputed power couple of South Korean cinema during its heyday of the 1960s and '70s. Choi was a popular and lauded actress equally at home in a variety of genres while Shin was respected as a prolific auteur. Their individual and shared successes, particularly at international film festivals, garnered the attention of their communist neighbors.

As the son of North Korean founder and dictator Kim Il-Sung, Kim Jong-Il lacked both his father's charisma and physical stature. Sensing the need to shore up his own power base in the interest of a looming hereditary transition of rule, the younger Kim, a major movie aficionado, sought to cultivate appeal through a cult of personality, while also propping up his country's reputation abroad. Deeming North Korean movies at the time too boring ("We're like nursery school and they're in college," he would say in recorded comments, decrying the prevalence of crying scenes), Kim hatched a plan to forcibly upgrade his nation's artistic bonafides.

In 1978, Choi was lured to Hong Kong with the promise of work in a film. Once there, she was kidnapped by North Korean agents, whisked back to Pyongyang, and held in captivity. When Shin went to Hong Kong searching for his ex-wife (by this time they were divorced), he immediately began to suspect her fate. Trusting in a former colleague who turned out to be a North Korean informant, Shin too was then kidnapped. Held separately for a period of years in order to erode and test their wills, Choi and Shin would eventually be reunited, and tasked with crafting films exalting the creative freedoms of North Korea. Photographed often in public, they would work diligently, cranking out 17 films—including North Korea's first love story—in a period of 27 months, before eventually slipping handlers during a trip abroad.

Choi and Shin would be granted asylum in the United States, the oddity of their story (and questions of its validity) fading when stacked up against the bigger and more colorful geopolitical villains of the time. Shin would go on to write and direct the kiddie-karate sequel *3 Ninjas Knuckle Up* (1995), of all things—a curiosity that could perhaps sustain its own dramatic retelling. The more intellectually spry and unconventional telling of this overall story would weave this peculiarity, and others details like it, into the fabric of a more rigorous examination of freedom and submission, exploring the after-effects of its subjects' detainment and forced ideological identification with their captors. But *The Lovers and the Despot* is not that movie.

The most interesting thing Cannan and Adam do is intercut clips from Shin's movies (mostly predating his kidnapping, but also including some from his North Korean filmography) into the narrative. Juxtaposing footage of a smiling Choi and the handsome, younger, rakish Shin does give *The Lovers and the Despot* an effective emotional spine.

Apart from this, though, the filmmakers eschew any sort of flashy visual or editorial style, opting instead for a more straightforward presentation. They build the movie around interview footage with Choi and, to a lesser extent, the pair's two adopted adult children. (Shin himself died in 2006.) While interviews with film critics like Pierre Rissent and other contemporaries of Shin familiar with his life and work provide a loose sense of the gossip circulating during the time of some of the events in question (it was a popular rumor at the time that either he and/or Choi in fact defected, of their own free will), they do not really deepen the narrative.

The authenticity of the story at the core of *The Lovers and the Despot* is lent credence by audiotapes of Kim allegedly recorded by Choi and Shin—recordings that offer unique insights into both his warped perspective and his sense of humor. (There may be no more hilarious movie line in 2016 than Kim's conversational ice-breaker of, "Look at me—aren't I small like a midget's turd?") Still, a greater breadth of opinion and deep-dive of why some doubt(ed) their claims would only enrich the film.

Choi, though, is an eloquent subject, and the subtitled translations of her candid musings have a bracing, cross-cultural punch. "I both missed him and hated him," she says in describing her pre-kidnapping estrangement from Shin. "That's how humans are."

She gives the film its heart, as her ruminations also shine an interesting light on the universal nature of cinema, and its power to shape perceptions of feelings. Describing her reunion with Shin, in which Kim brought the pair together at a party, Choi relates the emotionally disconnected and even deadened emotional state of an actress who for years had lived her life through the movies, and had now come to realize she was held hostage in a living play: "If this was a film, there would be tears." Instead, she feels only numbness, and shock.

The Lovers and the Despot presents an inherently intriguing story. So even if Cannan and Adam seem to shy away from taking a harder investigatory tack on the still-disputed nature of Choi's claims, or even really socio-politically framing them in a way that would offer their film greater mooring, it is still interesting, especially for cinephiles. It offers a glimpse of the sort of emotional prison which authoritarian-minded regimes encourage and inflict, as well as affecting lessons of resistance.

Brent Simon

CREDITS

Himself: Shin Sang-ok
Herself: Choi Eun-hee
Origin: United States
Language: Korean, English
Released: 2016
Production: Natasha Dack, Ross Adam, Robert Cannan; released by Hellflower Film, Submarine, The Documentary Company, Tigerlily Films
Directed by: Ross Adam; Robert Cannan
Written by: Ross Adam; Robert Cannan
Music by: Nathan Halpern
Music Supervisor: Connie Farr; Amine Ramer
Editing: Jim Hession
Art Direction: Sarah Delucchi
MPAA rating: Unrated
Running time: 98 minutes

REVIEWS

Anderson, Soren. *Seattle Times*. September 29, 2016.
Dargis, Manohla. *New York Times*. September 22, 2016.
Keough, Peter. *Boston Globe*. September 21, 2016.
Morgenstern, Joe. *Wall Street Journal*. September 22, 2016.
Padua, Pat. *Washington Post*. September 22, 2016.
Smith, Kyle. *New York Post*. September 22, 2016. .
Thompson, Luke Y. *Nerdist*. September 21, 2016.
Turan, Kenneth. *Los Angeles Times*. September 22, 2016.
White, Dave. *The Wrap*. September 22, 2016.
Zoller Seitz, Matt. *RogerEbert.com*. September 23, 2016.

LOVING

All love is created equal.
    —Movie tagline

Box Office: $7.7 Million

In the hands of another filmmaker, the story of Richard and Mildred Loving contains enormous rage. A couple told that its interracial relationship violates the law, supposedly created by God and enforced locally, would respond with justified anger at a system that in no way has been harmed by two people sharing their lives together. Racist police officers would make loud declarations about what they perceive as right and proper, and a teeming crowd would take outspoken sides of protest outside of a courtroom.

Loving is not that movie. Not even close. Written and directed by Jeff Nichols (who also glided rather than exploded earlier in the year with the sci-fi *Midnight Special* [2016]), this true story technically involves a major legal battle. Yet it dares to remove the pulsing energy that normally accompanies that sort of film. Instead, it thrives on narrow, muted intimacy, presenting the love between two people as the purest thing in the world, and bigoted, societal rejection of that relationship as unworthy of fueling drama. There are plenty of movies about people giving speeches to get what they want. This is a quiet snapshot of people who have what they want and will not complicate something that is not complicated. After all, there is nothing forced about that title. That is their name. That is their life, no matter what anyone says.

In no way is that presented as some kind of fantasy, either. The dynamic between Richard (Joel Edgerton), who is white, and Mildred (Ruth Negga), who is black, represents love not as burning fire but joint, consistent comfort. His hair so blond it's almost white, her demeanor perhaps the only softer disposition than his, what they have comes through on screen immediately as unshakeable ease. "I'm pregnant," she tells him in the opening scene. He laughs a little. "Good," he says. "That's real good." Their bond needs no additional background, and, it being 1958, they are used to the sideways looks they receive in the community. It does not matter. They have each other and know that rises above what others do not understand.

So when cops burst into their room in the middle of the night and say that the marriage certificate they obtained discreetly in D.C. is no good in Virginia, it begins an unexpectedly underplayed clash between tolerant and racist ideologies marked more by what it is not than what it is. Richard is more frustrated than furious at their arrest and eventual need to agree to not be in the state together for 25 years. Nichols, whose work frequently involves varying levels of loyalty, knows *Loving* does not need swelling music and intense reactions to depict the injustice here, and that, with a few movies every year about the nation's legacy of intolerance, the feeling comes through best when it exists among these specific people.

That means the sense that Mildred's father (Christopher Mann) knows the way this society works and has been beaten down by it, his words of consolation "It's all right, baby. It's all right," landing as resignation rather than comfort. It means showing love through the closeness in the hug between Richard and Mildred, and the subtly heartbreaking look on her face as they drive away from her family out of necessity, an inversion of the freedom suggested by an early sequence of cars racing. Of course, as these two determine to live as they will, they quickly execute a tense, late-night exchange to get Mildred back to Virginia because she always imagined Richard's mother (Sharon Blackwood) would deliver their baby. "You never should have married that girl," Richard's mom tells him after delivering her grandson. "I thought you liked her," he says. "I like a lot of people," she responds. "Doesn't mean you should have gone and done what you did. You knew better." All of this conflict is subdued, but that does not mean that it is not powerful, especially because of the contrast between a pair whose relationship seems so obvious to them and the people living in and perpetuating a prejudiced system that, to them, believe the obvious is that people like Richard and Mildred should not be together.

In a very different but no less effective performance than he gave Nichols in *Midnight Special,* Edgerton finds admirable earnestness in Richard, who is defined not by his quantity of words but his reliability, bordering on idealism. Nichols regular Michael Shannon reiterates his remarkable ability to feel new with every role, right down to the way he, as a reporter interviewing the Lovings, runs toward their house. Negga, however, delivers the film's most striking performance, with several moments a marvel of nearly imperceptible expressions appearing on her face. After spending years distanced from her family, Mildred's very happy to see her sister Garnet (Terri Abney), but as Mildred listens to Garnet speak, Negga wordlessly shows Mildred's isolation. This also sets up her seeing Martin Luther King Jr. leading a march on TV and saying it "might as well be halfway around the world." After writing a letter to Attorney General Robert Kennedy about their situation, she speaks by phone with Bernie Cohen (Nick Kroll, a long way from the lawyer he played on *The League* [2009-2015]), a lawyer from the American Civil Liberties Union. The manner in which her face changes after she says they cannot afford a lawyer and he says the ACLU will handle the fee is some of the year's most lovely, natural, humane acting.

Despite executing all of this affecting restraint, Nichols' characteristically observant style does not always succeed. Juxtaposing possible disasters at Richard's construction work site and a child running into the street suggests a visual restlessness not seen elsewhere in the film, and it should be considered that viewers get to know very little about the Lovings' children. About a decade passes, and the spectrum gets no bigger than the life Richard and Mildred inhabit, and sometimes it feels even smaller than that. Leaving out certain moments in their lives does not serve to deepen the feeling of repression and hiding, only obscure them as people.

Loving is about resilience in the face of external factors. Nichols is right to not include, for example, scenes in which the kids are being bullied at school, or an argument between Richard and Mildred stemming from the stress of their situation. In some ways minimizing race as a relevant factor between certain people without claiming it can be discarded entirely, the film is built around an almost hopeful distance from the injustices of the world, and the small but visible woes brought out by the performances do just enough to reflect hidden sorrow. Especially because Mildred progressively takes action, including participating in interviews when Richard has little interest in the cameras. Mildred has goodness in her but does not seem like a saint or a hero, and her involvement (and, to a lesser extent, Richard's) prevents any perception that they just expect everything will turn out fine.

If anything, it is more that they cannot believe this is even an issue, evidenced by Richard telling Bernie that the only thing he wants him to tell the justices is, "I love my wife." Ideally, this would be enough, and, eventually, it is, at least in terms of the Supreme Court ruling on the side of love and marriage as a fundamental right regardless of race. Needless to say, it would be many years until everyone in the country, no matter their sexuality, received that same permission, and the day in which no sideways glances are given has yet to come. Just as *Loving* springs from a specific point in history, it, like all art, arrives at one too, and it undeniably plays differently after the 2016 U.S. presidential election and the many hate crimes it inspired than it did before.

It is no secret that the United States long has dealt with racism; the degree to which so much unpleasantness wanted a chance to bubble over in the modern era arguably is news to many. No matter the year that the events take place, Nichols' film demonstrates that when a great deal of people see an issue as black and white, there are some that will engage, some that will fight, and some that will just do what they know to be right, making a world of their own. In 2016, that is inspiring, with an undercurrent of dread.

Matt Pais

CREDITS

Richard Loving: Joel Edgerton
Mildred Loving: Ruth Negga
Grey Villet: Michael Shannon

Sheriff Brooks: Marton Csokas
Bernie Cohen: Nick Kroll
Origin: United States
Language: English
Released: 2016
Production: Nancy Buirski, Ged Doherty, Colin Firth, Sarah Green, Peter Saraf, Marc Turtletaub; released by Big Beach Films, Raindog Films
Directed by: Jeff Nichols
Written by: Jeff Nichols
Cinematography by: Adam Stone
Music by: David Wingo
Sound: Will Files
Music Supervisor: Lauren Marie Mikus
Editing: Julie Monroe
Art Direction: Jonathan Guggenheim
Costumes: Erin Benach
Production Design: Chad Keith
MPAA rating: PG-13
Running time: 123 minutes

REVIEWS

Burr, Ty. *Boston Globe.* November 10, 2016.
Dargis, Manohla. *New York Times.* November 3, 2016.
Dowd, A.A. *The A.V. Club.* November 2, 2016.
Ebiri, Bilge. *Village Voice.* November 3 2016.
Nicholson, Amy. *MTV News.* November 10, 2016.
Phillips, Michael. *Chicago Tribune.* November 10, 2016.
Robinson, Tasha. *TheVerge.* September 9, 2016.
Stevens, Dana. *Slate.* November 3, 2016.
Tallerico, Brian. *RogerEbert.com.* September 11, 2016.
Turan, Kenneth. *Los Angeles Times.* November 3, 2016.

QUOTES

Mildred: "I know we have some enemies. But we have some friends, too."

TRIVIA

The film received a standing ovation at its premiere at the Cannes Film Festival in May of 2016.

AWARDS

Nominations:

Oscars 2016: Actress (Negga)
Golden Globes 2017: Actor—Drama (Edgerton), Actress—Drama (Negga)
Ind. Spirit 2017: Actress (Negga), Director (Nichols)
Writers Guild 2016: Orig. Screenplay

M

MAGGIE'S PLAN

Chapter Three: A Change of Heart.
—Movie tagline

Box Office: $3.3 Million

Maggie's Plan is a brisk romantic comedy centered around the amusingly interlocked love lives of Maggie (Greta Gerwig), John (Ethan Hawke), a scholar of "ficto-critical anthropology," and Georgette (Julianne Moore), his haughty wife. The film has a unique origin story: the screenplay was in part an adaptation of a then unpublished novel by Karen Rinaldi. There may not be opportunity for the book versus movie conversations that inevitably arise with cinematic adaptations, but the film does take delight in literary inspirations. Maggie, plucky and hoping to set people up, at times recalls a Jane Austen heroine. Director Rebecca Miller takes stylistic cues from the talky New York comedies of Woody Allen and with the pacing and bickering lovers coming and going the film shows a broad screwball influence. The effect is enjoyable in the moment, if ultimately a bit slight overall. Greta Gerwig, always an appealing, authentically quirky presence, is here cast in something of a transitional role: rather than be the recently graduated, scattered twentysomething, she now works in an administrative role at a university, and is seriously considering motherhood. Maggie begins the film single but sees this as no obstacle. She decides to enlist a college friend, Guy (Travis Fimmel), to be her sperm donor. The forthrightness with which the film presents this mode of motherhood, which not long ago might have been frowned upon, is admirable. Guy is a quick study, a

bearded hipster pickle entrepreneur (one wonders how these hipster clichés will play a few years from now). Inevitably, interpersonal complications ensue. Around the same time that Maggie is pursuing single motherhood, she and John, a professor at her university, begin a flirtatious rapport. They start with small talk, and soon enough John is asking her to read the novel he is writing. Audiences can likely predict that as soon as the novel gets read, an affair is imminent.

John is married with children, and the romantic tension between him and Maggie comes to a head, of course, on the same day Maggie attempts to inseminate herself with Guy's sperm. The timing is a little too perfect: John and Maggie end up having sex, in a sweet, suggestive seduction scene, featuring Maggie in a long, old-fashioned nightgown. The film then takes a gamble, jumping ahead three years without any explicit "a few years later" exposition. Maggie and John are now married and have a daughter, Lily. Maggie is an attentive mother, and the scenes of her and Lily, including one of them in the bath, have a coziness that seems a byproduct of a female writer-director. Tensions begin to arise in Maggie and John's relationship. John fits into the egotistical male writer mode, and as such doesn't treat Maggie as well as he should. Maggie becomes convinced that John should get back with his ex-wife and starts scheming about ways to bring them together. As Georgette, Julianne Moore hams it up with an exaggerated foreign accent that makes her performance seem too much like caricature. It also doesn't really seem likely that Maggie's plan would work, but the film asks us to suspend our disbelief and give in to its whimsical rhythms.

Maggie's Plan shares with Miller's earlier film *Personal Velocity* (2002) a sensitivity toward women at a critical point in their lives. The film is essentially a romantic comedy, but it finds Maggie at many points of stress, from new motherhood to divorce. Maggie's quirkiness feels unforced (thanks in large part to Gerwig's earnestness and slightly hesitant gestures) and she stands in obvious contrast to Georgette. The difference between the two women can be seen in how they are styled. Maggie wears long skirts, sweaters, and loafers, while Georgette has a tight bun and expensive looking fur vests. Maggie is classic and wholesome, while Georgette is an ice queen with the hauteur of a chic art gallery owner. The differences here may be too broadly telegraphed but are still mostly enjoyable to watch. The film also makes good use of Saturday Night Live alumni Bill Hader and Maya Rudolph in supporting roles that are comic but not too silly. There's a brief appearance by Wallace Shawn, whose presence seals the deal that this is a New York movie dealing with intellectuals. *Maggie's Plan* could easily present Maggie as a manic pixie dream girl or try too hard to be funny or quirky. Thankfully, it mostly avoids these pitfalls. With a charismatic cast and a classical setting, the film remains pleasant, with intermittent moments of comedy and poignancy.

Abbey Bender

CREDITS

Guy: Travis Fimmel
John: Ethan Hawke
Georgette: Julianne Moore
Felicia: Maya Rudolph
Maggie: Greta Gerwig
Tony: Bill Hader
Origin: United States
Language: English
Released: 2016
Production: Damon Cardasis, Rachael Horovitz, Rebecca Miller; released by Locomotive
Directed by: Rebecca Miller
Written by: Rebecca Miller
Cinematography by: Sam Levy
Music by: Michael Rohatyn
Sound: Marlena Grzaslewicz
Music Supervisor: Adam Horovitz
Editing: Sabine Hoffman
Art Direction: Brian Goodwin
Costumes: Malgosia Turzanska

Production Design: Alexandra Schaller
MPAA rating: R
Running time: 98 minutes

REVIEWS

DeFore, John. *Hollywood Reporter*. September 12, 2015.
Edelstein, David. *Vulture*. May 20, 2016.
Harvey, Dennis. *Variety*. September 12, 2015.
Hornaday, Ann. *Washington Post*. May 26, 2016.
Ide, Wendy. *The Guardian*. July 10, 2016.
Kohn, Eric. *IndieWire*. September 15, 2015.
Lemire, Christy. *Roger Ebert.com*. May 20, 2016.
Morgenstern, Joe. *Wall Street Journal*. May 19, 2016.
Scott, A.O. *New York Times*. May 19, 2016.
Stewart, Sara. *New York Post*. May 19, 2016.

QUOTES

Tony: "It's what keeps my wife in post-modern choreography and me in self-loathing."

TRIVIA

The language that Julianne Moore and her kids speak is Danish.

THE MAGNIFICENT SEVEN

Justice has a number.
—Movie tagline

Box Office: $93.4 Million

The sacrilege of remaking classics is a phenomenon that no Hollywood exorcist has been able to root out. The mere thought of crafting a new version of John Sturges' *The Magnificent Seven* (1960) is one of those high-echelon genre pictures that would constitute as an irredeemable heresy in some people's eyes if it were not for them to take a step back and realize that the Western itself was already a remake of Akira Kurosawa's all-timer, *The Seven Samurai* (1954). Improvement was never a primary factor in the announcement of this project. Put aside the skepticism of monetary motivation and instead focus on the potential fun just in the casting. Like with Steven Soderbergh's *Ocean's* trilogy and its forthcoming all-female continuation, just the speculation of getting an A-list crew together to occupy this iconic band of heroes suffocates some of the objections involved in messing with something unbroken. Though after years of attempting to create an old-fashioned moviestar-driven vehicle, the understudy-laden version makes it easy to revisit all the criticisms of its inception to begin with.

A signal to mark this version's commitment to diversity, the villain has been changed from Eli Wallach's Mexican bandido, Calvera, to Peter Sarsgaard's Caucasian landowner, Bartholomew Bogue. He demands restitution for the town of Rose Creek's attempt to undermine his power; killing some of the locals in exchange. Emma Cullen, the wife (Haley Bennett) of one of the slaughtered rides off in hopes of finding help in the form of protection or even revenge. She meets Sam Chisholm (Denzel Washington), a stoic black-outfitted warrant officer who agrees to put together a team upon learning the source of their troubles.

Chisholm's first recruit is Josh Faraday (Chris Pratt), a gambler with the kind of colorful personality enhanced by alcohol. Goodnight Robicheaux (Ethan Hawke) is a sharpshooter with PTSD issues from the Civil War who now takes to hustling takers on the knife skills of his cohort, Billy Rocks (Lee Byung-Hun). Also, joining the fray is Mexican outlaw Vasquez (Manuel Garcia-Rulfo), Comanche warrior Red Harvest (Martin Sensmeier), and legendary tracker Jack Horne (Vincent D'Onofrio) whose years of self-isolation may have taken a toll on his faculties. Once formed this seven-some repel Bogue's men for the time being before a final stand that makes Antietam seem like a snowball fight.

Fans of good old-fashioned showdowns are likely to delight in the film's climax, which is nicely pieced together and rather unrelenting. As fun as it may be as an observer rather than a participant, Fuqua's non-stop carnage is just as likely to shock those caught in-between the casually non-graphic violence of Western's "B"-movie era and the slaughter of *The Wild Bunch* (1969) or even *Saving Private Ryan* (1998). It is anyone's guess how this version managed to get by the MPAA with a mere "PG-13" rating given the amount of extras not just shot in the background but the bodies in the foreground receiving multiple bullet wounds, dynamited, tomahawked, or shot out of towers onto rooftops and on down. If 88 men is the official death tally of Arnold Schwarzenegger in *Commando* (1985), then you can imagine what seven men (plus a woman) can do to an army full of lockstep cowboys. By visual confirmation Fuqua has at least matched *Commando*'s numbers—and that is before they bring out the Gatling gun.

However fun may be defined by so much loss of make-believe life, it is important to consider how the remake gets itself there beyond the expected trappings of its source material. Going back to its inception in 2012 there was talk of this being a Tom Cruise vehicle with names such as Matt Damon, Kevin Costner, and Morgan Freeman rounding out the magnificence. That is a cast worthy of succession of Yul Brynner, Steve McQueen, Charles Bronson, and James Coburn to name just a few. Once the promise of such names fell off the table, the

project did not have the same allure. When the final pieces were put into place, it becomes abundantly clear that the film is missing a large dose of personality as well.

Denzel Washington is as charismatic a movie star of his time and as A-list as they come when compiling the best actors period. His approach to Chisholm however is a frustrating hybrid of grave stoicism. He may be paying tribute to the lack of an African-American presence of leadership from this period or simply that of Yul Brynner's original man in black. Washington looks bored throughout most of the film and only comes to life briefly when he is first reunited with his *Training Day* (2001) co-star in Hawke, who fares much better. Chris Pratt may be the current flavor of Hollywood thanks to major successes in *Guardians of the Galaxy* (2014) and *Jurassic World* (2015), but once again looks like an actor trying too hard to be ruggedly likable and goofy. D'Onofrio is far better as the underutilized mountain man. The most interesting of the lot turns out to be Sarsgaard's Pogue who appears to have taken a cue from Val Kilmer's Doc Holliday in *Tombstone* (1993), laced him with an evil, humorless streak and winds up commanding the screen in his too few moments.

This version of *The Magnificent Seven* is not a particularly bad film. It is beautifully shot by Mauro Fiore, the action is furious when it arrives and it will be hard for fans of the original not to receive a little charge when Elmer Bernstein's iconic score kicks in over the closing credits. The film's original composer, James Horner, tragically died in a plane crash before completion of filming but had already began to record arrangements, leaving portions of this score as a final memento to a great career. There is just a could-have-been aspect to a production that under a stronger filmmaker than Fuqua. It may have blended a giddier heehaw mentality with the brand of diverse emphasis on something and somebody for everyone that was eventually became of a remake that began as a potential event only to dissolve into just another variation on an old story.

Erik Childress

CREDITS

Chisolm: Denzel Washington
Josh Faraday: Chris Pratt
Goodnight Robicheaux: Ethan Hawke
Jack Horne: Vincent D'Onofrio
Billy Rocks: Byung-hun Lee
Vasquez: Manuel Garcia-Rulfo
Red Harvest: Martin Sensmeier
Origin: United States

Language: English

Released: 2016

Production: Roger Birnbaum, Todd Black; released by Columbia Pictures, Metro-Goldwyn-Mayer Pictures

Directed by: Antoine Fuqua

Written by: Richard Wenk; Nic Pizzolatto

Cinematography by: Mauro Fiore

Music by: Simon Franglen; James Horner

Sound: David Esparza; Mandell Winter

Editing: John Refoua

Art Direction: Leslie McDonald

Costumes: Sharen Davis

Production Design: Derek R. Hill

MPAA rating: PG-13

Running time: 133 minutes

REVIEWS

Berardinelli, James. *ReelViews*. September 22, 2016.

Burr, Ty. *Boston Globe*. September 22, 2016.

Dargis, Manohla. *New York Times*. September 22, 2016.

Erhlich, David. *IndieWire*. September 8, 2016.

Goodykoontz, Bill. *Arizona Republic*. September 22, 2016.

Gronvall, Andrea. *Chicago Reader*. September 22, 2016.

Hornaday, Ann. *Washington Post*. September 22, 2016.

Howell, Peter. *Toronto Star*. September 8, 2016.

Phillips, Michael. *Chicago Tribune*. September 22, 2016.

Rothkopf, Joshua. *Time Out*. September 10, 2016.

QUOTES

Emma Cullen: "Whatever they were in life, here, at the end, each man stood with courage and honor. They fought for the ones who couldn't fight for themselves, and the died for them, too. All to win something that didn't belong to them. It was magnificent."

TRIVIA

Out of 109 cast listed for the movie, only nine are women.

MANCHESTER BY THE SEA

Box Office: $46.9 Million

Kenneth Lonergan's masterful drama is about a deep well of grief that most people can barely even imagine. And yet it is not a film that wallows in that pain, exploiting it for manipulative tears. Instead, it is a film about living with grief, not getting past it as so many Hollywood dramas like to claim that people can, but actually living with it and finding a sliver of hope in a painful world. It is a perfectly calibrated family drama as

much about compassion for others as it is the pain of loss. Anchored by a breathtaking performance from Casey Affleck that won nearly every award given for Best Actor of 2016, *Manchester by the Sea* is about how we can pull others out of their darkest places just by being ourselves, and about a unique relationship between a man and his nephew that does just that for both of them.

Lee Chandler (Affleck) lives a solitary life as a handyman in Boston. In a wonderful series of vignettes, we see Lee going about his life, working on tenant's problems, taking out the trash, sitting alone in his nondescript apartment, etc. There does not appear to be much to the life of Lee Chandler outside of annoying tenants and the occasional barfight. Work, drink, sulk, fight—do it again the next day. Then he gets a life-changing phone call.

Lee's brother Joe (Kyle Chandler, seen in flashbacks) has passed away at a tragically young age. Joe was diagnosed with a heart condition years earlier, and so everyone in this circle knew that this day was coming sooner than it had any right to come, but the news is still shocking. It forces Lee to go back home and care for his nephew Patrick (Lucas Hedges, in a breakthrough, Oscar-nominated performance) while his brother's estate is being settled. Patrick's mother (Gretchen Mol) left years ago, and the bulk of *Manchester by the Sea* consists of Lee being forced into a guardian role of a confident teenager. Patrick wants to go about his busy life—two girlfriends and a band—while Lee freaks out when he's told that Joe wanted him to be the boy's guardian. He can't be a father again.

In a devastating flashback, cut perfectly to the news that Joe wanted Lee to care for Patrick, Lonergan reveals the source of Lee's pain, a night on which he made a horrendous mistake that cost him his family. It also becomes clearer why Lee's ex-wife Randi (Michelle Williams), who has moved on and re-married and even had a new child, isn't in Lee's life anymore. As Lee contemplates what to do about his new duty as Patrick's guardian, he comes closer to healing the wounds that opened when his family fell apart years earlier.

Affleck perfectly captures a man carrying so much grief than one can almost see the weight of it on his frame. His shoulders are slumped; his eyes are cast downward. He finds it difficult to interact with people, especially Randi, and there's a devastating scene in the final act when the two do encounter each other that's a master class in acting—and earned them both Oscar nominations. Watch the way they speak over each other (the lines were reportedly in columns in the script, indicating they should be said at the same time) and how the emotional walls come tumbling down. Affleck,

Williams, and Hedges are fantastic, and deserving of their awards, but it's a testament to Lonergan's direction that every performance here, even the most minor ones, feel genuine.

That directorial attention to detail extends to more than just performance. Few films of 2016 had a more believable, lived-in sense of place than *Manchester by the Sea*. Lonergan very purposefully opens and closes his film with shots of water, returning to it throughout the piece as well. Lee Chandler's grief may be bottomless, but the world keeps moving; water keeps flowing past these people as they go about their lives. And there are other beautiful details of setting, such as the crucifixes on the walls and the hockey on the TV sets. Alcohol also plays a central role, as it often does in this part of the world. Beer, God, and sports—it's the trifecta of everyday life, and it's these details that Lonergan understands more completely than most directors, giving Lee and Patrick such a believable world that they become three-dimensional within it. It is very easy to believe that Lee and Patrick Chandler exist before the beginning of this film and that their lives go on after it. Viewers are merely sharing one of their most important chapter with them.

This emphasis on setting allows Lonergan's emotional cues to feel organic instead of manipulative. Most films about death inevitably get to that moment in which it feels like heartstrings are being pulled, but *Manchester by the Sea* produces honest emotion instead of forced tears. Lonergan has always been able to find truth in human relationships, no more so than in his breakthrough Sundance hit *You Can Count on Me* (2000), 16 years before this film made waves at the same film festival.

How do people move on from the unimaginable? While a viewer experiences *Manchester by the Sea*, there is someone dealing with the death of a parent or a child. Maybe it was expected; maybe it was sudden. *Manchester by the Sea* captures both kinds of loss—the foretold death of a sick father and the unexpected death of a child—and how these events alter our trajectory. New priorities come into place. New decisions have to be made. But the world goes on. The backdrop doesn't change. And people like Lee Chandler eventually learn to manage their grief and find their way through the water yet again.

Brian Tallerico

CREDITS

Lee Chandler: Casey Affleck
Randi: Michelle Williams
Joe Chandler: Kyle Chandler
Patrick: Lucas Hedges
Elise: Gretchen Mol
Origin: United States
Language: English
Released: 2016
Production: Lauren Beck, Matt Damon, Chris Moore, Kimberly Steward, Kevin J. Walsh; released by B Story, Big Indie Pictures, CMP, Pearl Street Films, The Affleck/Middleton Project
Directed by: Kenneth Lonergan
Written by: Kenneth Lonergan
Cinematography by: Jody Lee Lipes
Music by: Lesley Barber
Sound: Jacob Ribicoff
Music Supervisor: Linda Cohen
Editing: Jennifer Lame
Art Direction: Jourdan Henderson
Costumes: Melissa Toth
Production Design: Ruth De Jong
MPAA rating: R
Running time: 137 minutes

REVIEWS

Chang, Justin. *Variety.* January 24, 2016.
Dowd, A.A. *The A.V. Club.* November 16, 2016.
Ebiri, Bilge. *New York Magazine.* January 24, 2016.
Nashawaty, Chris. *Entertainment Weekly.* November 17, 2016.
Phillips, Michael. *Chicago Tribune.* November 24, 2016.
Roeper, Richard. *Chicago Sun-Times.* November 24, 2016.
Seitz, Matt Zoller. *RogerEbert.com.* November 18, 2016.
Stevens, Dana. *Slate.* November 22, 2016.
Turan, Kenneth. *Los Angeles Times.* November 17, 2016.
Wolfe, April. *Village Voice.* November 16, 2016.

QUOTES

Patrick: "Who you're gonna shoot? You or me?"

TRIVIA

The town was called Manchester until 1989, when resident Edward Corley led a highly controversial campaign to formally change its name to Manchester-by-the-Sea. The action was passed by the state legislature that year.

AWARDS

Oscars 2016: Actor (Affleck), Orig. Screenplay
British Acad. 2016: Actor (Affleck), Orig. Screenplay
Golden Globes 2017: Actor—Drama (Affleck)
Ind. Spirit 2017: Actor (Affleck)
Nominations:
Oscars 2016: Actor—Supporting (Hedges), Actor—Supporting (Williams), Director (Lonergan), Film

British Acad. 2016: Actress—Supporting (Williams), Director (Lonergan), Film, Film Editing

Directors Guild 2016: Director (Lonergan)

Golden Globes 2017: Actress—Supporting (Williams), Director (Lonergan), Film—Drama, Screenplay

Ind. Spirit 2017: Actor—Supporting (Hedges), Film, Film Editing, Screenplay

Screen Actors Guild 2016: Actor (Affleck), Actor—Supporting (Hedges), Actress—Supporting (Williams), Cast

Writers Guild 2016: Orig. Screenplay

MASTERMINDS

What would you do with $17 million?
—Movie tagline

Box Office: $17.4 Million

The greatness of the original American comedy sprang from the electric daring of performance fused to elaborate visual gags. Character merged with incident in amplifying fear or vulnerability, like Charlie Chaplin caught inside the restricted space with the lion in *The Circus* (1928) or Buster Keaton, unflappable as the housing scaffolding bends poetically around his silhouette in *Steamboat Bill Jr.* (1928).

The coming of sound introduced a more verbal and screwball-inflected brand of humor. The animating principle was still speed and efficiency. The best comedy directors seamlessly linked performer and action, like Blake Edwards' *Pink Panther* films, with the incomparable Peter Sellers. Despite its television origins, *Saturday Night Live* quickly took hold in the consciousness, style and energy of American movies, as its early generation cast members, like John Belushi, in John Landis' *Animal House* (1978) or Bill Murray in Harold Ramis' *Stripes* (1981), tapped into a free spirited anarchy and freedom.

As Hollywood now plays primarily to foreign markets, the comedy has suffered significantly, turning ever more strained, coarse and manic. The dominant mode now is embarrassment and humiliation, best represented by films of the Farrelly Brothers. The early promise of *Kingpin* (1996) and *There's Something about Mary* (1998) suggested exquisite comic timing and iconoclastic undermined by a perverse imbalance toggling between the outré and sentimental that turned increasingly mean-spirited, shrill and misanthropic.

Of the comically inflected directors working actively at work, the Coen Brothers, Joel and Ethan, and Wes Anderson, are the rare filmmakers who frame their comic work through formal concerns of framing, color and movement. They use the film frame expressively, so the humor emerges in that buoyancy and wit. But they also control every aspect of their productions, from cinematography to production design and costume, their scripts grounded in character, situation and incident.

After the independent American comedy *Napoleon Dynamite* (2004) became a niche popular success (relative to budget), the director Jared Hess appeared to be another interesting and unpredictable comic sensibility with his funky and eccentric sense of character and incident. As a devout Mormon, he made faith central to his work, obvious in his fascination with and studies about outsiders, renegades or misunderstood eccentrics in his subsequent movies *Nacho Libre* (2006) and *Gentlemen Broncos* (2009). By the time of his virtually unwatchable *Don Verdean* (2015), Hess was adrift and scrambling for relevance.

The director's new film, *Masterminds*, is a comic burlesque filled with redneck humor, broad satire and sentimental flourishes. It works very hard to work up some excitement, but settles rather indiscriminately for the lowbrow standards of the current comedy. Desperation seems permanently suspended over the project, deadening the movie in particularly unpleasant ways. It is a bad film, not exactly offensive or unnecessarily cruel towards its character. It is enervated and flat, more a simulacrum of a comedy than an attempt to do something fresh or interesting.

The movie riffs on the actual, made-for-tabloid bizarre events surrounding the October 1997 cash robbery of more than $17 million from the Charlotte, North Carolina regional vault office of Loomis Fargo. The filmmakers deserve some credit for trying to invest new energy into the fact-based procedural. The movie is a shotgun marriage yoking together these different strands without ever figuring out a tone, style or consistent form. Three different writers worked on the credited script, but significantly not Hess, making this the first of his five features he has directed but not written. He is a hired hand who does not bring much personal investment or direct engagement with the material. The dominant artistic personality is Lorne Michaels, the *Saturday Night Live* impresario who is the movie's producer.

Masterminds is ostensibly a sketch movie, seemingly improved moment to moment, with an occasional funny bit (thanks largely to the *Saturday Night Live* performers who make up the ensemble) but with little discernable shape or rhythm. The plot more or less conforms to the actual events. The patsy at the center, David Ghantt (Zach Galifianakis), is a moon-faced schlub with a Dutch boy haircut that leaves little question of how the director perceives him. He is an armored car driver and vault supervisor who carries a torch for his former colleague, the playful and carnal Kelly Campbell (Kristen Wiig).

She is fired at the start for insubordination, but seems a cool (or cruel) enough customer to keep him permanently wrapped around her finger. The putative brains of the operation, Steve Chambers (Owen Wilson), concocts the astoundingly easy heist operation. In one of the more painful moments, a diner scene where he elaborates the details, Chambers insists on shielding his identity from his dim-witted collaborator Ghantt to protect his anonymity. The scene more accurately the talented actor's embarrassment at his agent for trapped in such a lousy movie.

The writers have a wide range to work in, but the sledgehammer approach is their preferred form of storytelling. Every beat in the heist is foreshadowed, like the apprentice who walks in halfway or underlining the main character's ineptitude, his failure to notice the incriminating video monitors or gets himself locked inside the armored car's vault. It only serves to underline how mechanical and joyless much of it feels.

Rather than celebrate the excitement and adrenalized sensation of such cool amorality, the movie goes to lengths to celebrate the amateurishness and stupidity of its characters. Believing Kelly is going to rendezvous with him, Ghantt absconds to Mexico, taking as much cash as humanly possible. Hiding out in plain sight, living in up in five-star resort hotels, he is like a craven and spoiled king unleashed. The action shuttle between his comic adventures on the lam and the upward mobility of Chambers and his family, using their ill-gotten gains to penetrate Charlotte's high society.

Wiig's Kelly is the crucial part of the puzzle, but it is part of the larger timidity and failure of nerve to either render her a true femme fatale or sympathetic character caught in over her head. If *Masterminds* develops any real tension or flair, it comes in the secondary figures, like the great Kate McKinnon as Ghannt's put-upon fiancée who gets a measure of revenge in a great department store confrontation with Campbell. Leslie Jones also breaks up the monotony as a rollicking and fearsome FBI special agent assigned to investigate the robbery. Jason Sudeikis, often at his best in small, isolated moments, also brings a more elevated touch and physical humor as a contract killer dispatched to Mexico to remove Ghantt from the equation. The supporting players only illustrate the deficiencies of the central characters.

Even in the more accomplished movies he is part of, like *Into the Wild* (2007) or *Birdman* (2014), Galifianakis is an acquired taste. He specializes too often in playing pity magnets, instead of characters, and Ghantt is part of that tradition. His naiveté about Kelly is more delusional than funny or sad. His broad playing, here including trying to eat a live tarantula or suffering a humiliating personal action inside a swimming pool, is a

bludgeoning quest for approval. Wiig is given little to do and never really breaks out. Wilson is just going through the motions.

The white trash humor is pretty gentle (unlike the treatment of say the three Mexican federal officers tracking Ghantt there, moving toward ugly racist caricature). The filmmakers contrive a way to bring all the central characters together, but the resulting sound and fury, car chases, slamming of doors and getting even rarely has felt so anticlimactic. *Masterminds* has too many conflicting sensibilities to really take flight. What is finally so disappointing is how such promising material ends up so flat and square.

Patrick Z. McGavin

CREDITS

David Ghantt: Zach Galifianakis
Steve: Owen Wilson
Kelly: Kristen Wiig
Jandice: Kate McKinnon
Detective: Leslie Jones
Mike McKinney: Jason Sudeikis
Origin: United States
Language: English
Released: 2016
Production: John Goldwyn, Lorne Michaels, Andrew Panay; released by Broadway Video Inc., Michaels-Goldwyn, Relativity Media
Directed by: Jared Hess
Written by: Chris Bowman; Hubbel Palmer; Emily Spivey
Cinematography by: Erik Alexander Wilson
Music by: Geoff Zanelli
Sound: Michael J. Benavente
Music Supervisor: Bob Bowen; Happy Walters
Editing: Keith Brachmann; David Rennie
Art Direction: Elliott Glick
Costumes: Sarah Edwards
Production Design: Clayton Hartley
MPAA rating: PG-13
Running time: 95 minutes

REVIEWS

Burr, Ty. *Boston Globe.* September 29, 2016.
Derakhshani, Tirdad. *Philadelphia Inquirer.* September 29, 2016.
Dowd, A.A. *The A.V. Club.* September 29, 2016.
Debruge, Peter. *Variety.* September 29, 2016.
Holub, Christian. *Entertainment Weekly.* September 29, 2016.
Kenny, Glenn. *New York Times.* September 29, 2016.
LaSalle, Mick. *San Francisco Chronicle.* September 29, 2016.
Rothkopf, Joshua. *Time Out New York.* September 29, 2016.

Seitz, Matt Zoler. *RogerEbert.com.* September 29, 2016.
Walsh, Katie. *Chicago Tribune.* September 29, 2016.

QUOTES
Detective: "Katie Candy Cane, is she a stripper?"

TRIVIA
The film was based on the 1997 Loomis Fargo Bank Robbery in Charlotte, North Carolina, where $17.3 million in cash was stolen.

MAX STEEL

Box Office: $3.8 Million

Based on a line of action figures, *Max Steel* presents yet another superhero origin story, albeit one that falls even below the standards of predictability and routine that have become the hallmarks of such tales. At its best, the movie is a repetitive, overly familiar bore—a generic story featuring all of the usual plot and character beats. At its worst, it is obnoxious and forced, with the presence of a woefully unfunny excuse for a comic sidekick pathetically serving as the movie's primary source of "fun."

Even the screenplay, written by Christopher Yost, seems unconvinced of the potential for this new cinematic superhero. By the time the movie offers up its version of a superhero, it is forced to rush through the resulting material. Until that point, Yost relies on slew of underdeveloped clichés to establish the main character, who eventually will don a silly suit of armor and occasionally show off super-powered feats of strength, as an average, if troubled, teenager.

The character's back story and exposition play out like a checklist of details that could make him relatable and sympathetic. Max McGrath (Ben Winchell) has returned to his childhood home (for reasons that are never quite made clear) after being away for a period of time (that is also sketchy) after the death of his father (Mike Doyle) Max's father died after Max's birth during an accident at the local scientific facility where his own father worked. Max and his mother, Molly (Maria Bello), are still grieving the loss, and now the teenager has to adjust to a new life in an old place that is filled with painful memories.

Out of that facility comes Steel (voice of Josh Brener), a flying, alien robot, which is about the size of a house pet, with wing-like extensions that move like arms and a sense of humor that is as annoying as it is constant. The robot is drawn to Max on account of the teen's sudden development of strange, inexplicable powers that allow him to absorb energy and then expel it

from himself in a way that looks like some sort of rippling liquid. Director Stewart Hendler basks in the effect of Max's powers without ever explaining them or offering a comprehension of why they might be useful (until, of course, they become convenient to resolve the showdown of the climax, by which point it is far too late for understanding).

In Max's life, they are mostly an inconvenience, since, as with any movie about a teenage boy struggling to figure out his place in the world, there is a love interest. She is Sofia (Ana Villafañe), whom Max meets when she hits him with her car on their way to school. They quickly develop an awkward, approaching-romantic relationship, only for Max to dismiss and ignore her as things become more complicated. (This is slightly better than Steel's response to her presence, which is to suggest that killing her might be for the best.) In the fashion of male fantasy, Sofia alternates between being slightly irritated and mildly amused by Max toying with her feelings, only to be waiting for him when everything is finished.

The plot follows the established motions of what has become a genre unto itself. Max discovers his powers. He hones them in a montage. He learns about some great threat (in this case, aliens like Steel that want to take over the world and try to do so by creating events that act like weather phenomena, leading to a particularly dark and incoherent action scene in which Max fights an alien), and he uses those powers to defeat the menace.

The villain is Max's father's business partner Miles Edwards (Andy Garcia, who appears visibly bored by the material), which is only a spoiler for anyone who has never before seen one of these movies. (Yost attempts a lame fake-out involving Molly, although the ruse only lasts for about five minutes.) What is strange here is that the powers Max develops are mostly useless. The final battle is between Max and Miles as they strike each other in matching armored suits that are, amusingly, color-coordinated to their roles here. (Max's armor is white with blue accents, and Miles' suit is black with red highlights.)

Everything about *Max Steel* is rote, even the inevitable suggestion that a sequel will be forthcoming. One can at least take comfort in the almost-near certainty that such an outcome will never come to pass.

Mark Dujsik

CREDITS
Max McGrath: Ben Winchell
Steel (voice): Josh Brener
Molly McGrath: Maria Bello
Dr. Miles Edwards: Andy Garcia

Sofia Martinez: Ana Villafane
Origin: United States
Language: English
Released: 2016
Production: Bill O'Dowd, Julia Pistor; released by Dolphin Entertainment, Mattel Entertainment, Open Road Films, Playground Productions
Directed by: Stewart Hendler
Written by: Christopher Yost
Cinematography by: Brett Pawlak
Music by: Nathan Lanier
Sound: Eric Offin
Editing: Michael Louis Hill
Art Direction: Richard Bloom
Costumes: Allison Leach
Production Design: William O. Hunter
MPAA rating: PG-13
Running time: 92 minutes

REVIEWS

Dowd, A.A. *The A.V. Club.* October 14, 2016.
Lane, Jim. *Sacramento News & Review.* October 20, 2016.
Lemire, Christy. *RogerEbert.com.* October 14, 2016.
Leydon, Joe. *Variety.* October 14, 2016.
Lui, John. *Straits Times.* October 26, 2016.
Murray, Noel. *Los Angeles Times.* October 14, 2016.
Orndorf, Brian. *Blu-ray.com.* October 14, 2016.
Scheck, Frank. *Hollywood Reporter.* October 14, 2016.
Welch, Alex. *IGN.* October 14, 2016.
Yaniz, Robert, Jr. *We Got This Covered.* October 16, 2016.

TRIVIA

Originally, the character of Sydney Gardner, Max's love interest from *Max Steel* (2013) was going to be in the film, but it was changed to Sofia Martinez.

ME BEFORE YOU

Box Office: $56.2 Million

Jojo Moyes' hit novel is adapted for the big screen by the author herself in this better-than-average weeper, a film that could have been another piece of Nichols Sparks sentimentality but is elevated greatly by a committed performance from its leading lady. It's still an imperfect film with a morally questionable final act, but to say it's better than most recent Sparks films (either the ones directly adapted from the king of the twisty romantic weeper or those inspired by him) would be an understatement.

Will Traynor (Sam Claflin) is introduced to viewers when he's on top of the world. He's young, handsome,

and rich. He's on the phone one day while crossing the street when he's hit by a motorcycle, paralyzing him for life. This lifechanging incident brings the lovely Louisa Clark (Emilia Clarke) into Will's world. Louisa is a delightful optimist, but she's left adrift after the café she's worked at for the last six years is forced to let her go. Looking for a new career path, she becomes a caregiver, finding a job taking care of Will.

At first, Will's understandable bitterness at the hand dealt him by life clashes with Louisa's naturally spunky attitude. Of course, this is a romance, so Louisa rather quickly breaks down the walls that Will has put up to emotionally protect himself from the rest of the world. Louisa soon learns that there's another reason that Will has not allowed anyone to get close—he's planning to kill himself. Much to the dismay of his parents (a well-cast Janet McTeer and Charles Dance), Will has given them six months before they have to take him to Switzerland for an assisted suicide. The pain and suffering of being in a wheelchair have just been too much for Will to bear, and he's ready to move on.

Naturally, Louisa makes it her goal to stop Will from shuffling off this mortal coil. She decides that seeing all the great things that the world has to offer, even from the vantage point of a wheelchair, will change Will's mind. They travel, have fun, fall in love, and do all the things that one expects from a movie like this one, but Will confesses that he's still going to go through with it. If anything, his time with Louisa has convinced him even more fully that he should end his life because he refuses to be an anchor around her future. She's furious, and gives him the cold shoulder, but eventually gives in to his wishes, and he leaves her enough money in his will to follow her dreams.

Yes, *Me Before You* ends with a suicide. And that's where any discussion of the film gets a little tricky. Some viewers, including several leaders of groups that work to make life better for physically disabled people, were concerned that Moyes' story could be an encouragement of suicide. There is arguably something a bit irresponsible about a film that advocates suicide for anyone, and the film even sparked protests around the world, including major ones in the UK and Australia. If one finds the very message of director Thea Sharrock's film offensive, any critical discussion of it falls away, and that's an understandable, relatable response to the film.

However, if one sees this purely as Will's choice and not a choice being advocated for others (which is the stance taken by its defenders), there are elements here that work. Most notably, Clarke proves that she can hold her own in projects other than the HBO hit *Game of Thrones*. She gives a likable, charming performance, and to say she's the best thing about the film would be a massive understatement. With a lesser actress in the role, this romantic drama could have quickly become an exaggerated mess, but Clarke knows not to overplay either Louisa's wide-eyed optimism or her heartbreaking romance. In a film without too many subtle beats narratively, she finds ways to make her character believable, which is no small feat. She also has strong chemistry with Claflin, which is essential for a romantic drama to be effective.

Served up as nice counterprogramming to a season of summer blockbusters that were mostly driven at men, *Me Before You* became a surprise hit, grossing over $55 million domestically on a $20 million budget, but that was merely a fraction of its overall success, as it brought in over $150 in foreign receipts. It's the kind of doomed love story that plays around the world, and works in multiple languages. And it's the kind of doomed love story that should lead to better roles for Emilia Clarke. It turns out the Sparks-inspired subgenre of romantic dramas may do some good after all.

Brian Tallerico

CREDITS

William Traynor: Sam Claflin
Louisa Clark: Emilia Clarke
Alicia: Vanessa Kirby
Josie Clarke: Samantha Spiro
Bernard Clark: Brendan Coyle
Origin: United States
Language: English
Released: 2016
Production: Alison Owen, Karen Rosenfelt; released by Metro-Goldwyn-Mayer Inc., New Line Cinema L.L.C.
Directed by: Thea Sharrock
Written by: Jojo Moyes
Cinematography by: Remi Adefarasin
Music by: Craig Armstrong
Music Supervisor: Karen Elliott
Editing: John Wilson
Art Direction: Nick Dent
Costumes: Jill Taylor
Production Design: Andrew McAlpine
MPAA rating: PG-13
Running time: 110 minutes

REVIEWS

Edelstein, David. *New York Magazine (Vulture).* June 5, 2016.
Ehrlich, David. *IndieWire.* June 7, 2016.
Gant, Charles. *Screen International.* May 24, 2016.
Linden, Sheri. *Hollywood Reporter.* May 24, 2016.
Myers, Kimber. *Playlist.* June 2, 2016.

Roeper, Richard. *Chicago Sun-Times.* June 2, 2016.
Shoemaker, Allison. *Consequence of Sound.* June 2, 2016.
Truitt, Brian. *USA Today.* June 2, 2016.
Wloszczyna, Susan. *RogerEbert.com.* June 2, 2016.
Zacharek, Stephanie. *Time.* June 2, 2016.

QUOTES

Will Traynor: "Live boldly. Push yourself. Don't settle."

TRIVIA

In the original book *Me Before You* Lou Clarke gets a tattoo of a bumble bee. Emilia Clarke's first tattoo was also of a bumble bee on her finger which she got after wrapping on the film.

MECHANIC: RESURRECTION

Revenge is a dangerous business.
—Movie tagline

Box Office: $21.2 Million

The illustrious journal known as *Boating Magazine* presumably does not have a section for film reviews but if they did, there is an excellent chance that they would give their Movie of the Year award for 2016 to *Mechanic: Resurrection*. It seems as if every other scene either involves people on a boat, people heading for boats, or blowing up boats. The film even manages to drag in a couple of U-Boats in the third act to add a little bit of international flavor. As it turns out, the onscreen flotilla proves to be the only remotely interesting thing about the film. A loose sequel to the 2011 film (itself a remake of a fairly decent 1972 Charles Bronson film of the same name) that was so instantly forgettable that even star Jason Statham may get it confused with several of the short-titled action throwaways that he has ground out over the last few years, it is so devoid of style, humor, energy, or even creative violence that it practically redefines the phrase "generic action thriller."

Having successfully faked his death at the end of the previous film, master assassin Arthur Bishop (Statham) has retired to Rio to spend his days living the good life on his boat. Through a series of events too convoluted to recount here, Bishop winds up becoming involved with Gina (Jessica Alba), an aid worker protecting victims of human trafficking who is being used as bait by Craine (Sam Hazeldine), an all-around bad guy with a really big boat who shares a murky past with him to boot. Craine wants Bishop to perform three kills for him—all designed to look like accidents and on a highly abbreviated schedule—and kidnaps Gina to force him to do his bidding. Determined to save the love of his life—whom he just met maybe a few days ago—Bishop sets out to off his targets in locations ranging from an impregnable island prison to a glass swimming pool dangling high over the streets of Sydney. By the time he reaches his third target, a weirdo arms dealer played by a soul-patched Tommy Lee Jones, Bishop begins to suspect that something is up and hits upon a plot to rescue Gina and take down Craine for good.

This is a film in which absolutely nothing happens. Oh sure, things happen—there are plenty of scenes of Bishop drilling things, mixing powders, or punching people in the face—but all of it is so random and disconnected that one could go into the editing room and rearrange all the footage and it would hardly make any difference. Aside from the assault on the high-rise swimming pool—a shameless knockoff of the Dubai sequence in *Mission:Impossible—Ghost Protocol* (2011) but still reasonably nifty—none of the action sequences have any spark of originality or energy to them and even when the film promises something a little more outlandish, it shies away at the last second. For example, during the sequence set on that impregnable prison island, Bishop is told that he will swim through shark-infested waters. At this point, after such a buildup, most viewers will no doubt be expecting a sequence where Bishop either has to swim through a lot of sharks or, even better, wind up getting into a fight with one of them. Instead, all the film provides is one lonely shark that happens to float in behind him without posing any semblance of a threat. This may boost sales of shark repellent but it certainly does not boost the excitement level.

The oddest thing about the film is that it has a somewhat more impressive cast than one might expect for a project with such low-rent origins and such a crummy script. The only explanation is that they all looked at it as a paid vacation to exotic locales like Bangkok, Thailand, and Bulgaria. Alba can be a first-rate charmer but all she gets to do here is walk around in a bikini and get slapped around by the bad guys who are holding her. And yet, her role is a meaty one when you compare it to what the film has in store for the great Michelle Yeoh. Having recruited one of the all-time female action icons, the film then wastes her on a couple of scenes in which she plays an old friend of Bishop who fails to deliver a single punch or kick at all. As for Tommy Lee Jones—who does not even turn up until the last half-hour—he is clearly just going through the motions but he is so obvious about it that his performance actually turns out to be kind of entertaining despite itself.

Of course, the only reason to even contemplate seeing *Mechanic: Resurrection* is the presence of Jason Statham. Among the current crop of action stars, he may be the best of the bunch—not only is he one of the few who actually looks convincing in fight scenes, he is a genuinely gifted actor as well, as he demonstrated with his brilliant self-parodying performance in *Spy* (2014)—but despite his presence in the hugely successful *Fast and the Furious* and *The Expendables* franchises, he has never quite had the breakthrough solo hit that he has long deserved. Instead, he has spent the last few years headlining a series of increasingly forgettable action films that play in theaters for a week or two and evidently do well enough on home video to inspire more.

Peter Sobczynski

CREDITS

Arthur Bishop: Jason Statham
Gina: Jessica Alba
Max Adams: Tommy Lee Jones
Mei: Michelle Yeoh
Riah Crain: Sam Hazeldine
Origin: United States
Language: English
Released: 2016
Production: William Chartoff, Robert Earl, John Thompson, David Winkler; released by Millennium Films Inc.
Directed by: Dennis Gansel
Written by: Philip Shelby; Tony Mosher
Cinematography by: Daniel Gottschalk
Music by: Mark Isham
Sound: Kris Casavant
Music Supervisor: Selena Arizanovic
Editing: Ueli Christen; Michael J. Duthie; Todd E. Miller
Art Direction: Aaron Haye
Costumes: Preyanan Suwannathda
Production Design: Sebastian T. Krawinkel
MPAA rating: R
Running time: 98 minutes

REVIEWS

Ashton, Will. *Playlist.* August 29, 2016.
Fischer, Russ. *TheWrap.* August 26, 2016.
Gleiberman, Owen. *Variety.* August 26, 2016.
Kenny, Glenn. *RogerEbert.com.* August 26, 2016.
Kupecki, Josh. *Austin Chronicle.* September 1, 2016.
Murray, Noel. *Los Angeles Times.* August 26, 2016.
Orndorf, Brian. *blu-ray.com.* August 26, 2016.
Scheck, Frank. *Hollywood Reporter.* August 26, 2016.
Webster, Andy. *New York Times.* August 26, 2016.
White, Stephen. *New York Daily News.* August 26, 2016.

The picture filmed on four continents and in six countries: Australia, Europe (Bulgaria), South America (Brazil), and Asia (Cambodia, Thailand, Malaysia).

THE MEDDLER

Box Office: $4.3 Million

Upon hearing the basic premise of *The Meddler*, most rational moviegoers could probably be forgiven for wanting to avoid it like the plague. After all, the uber-sitcommy concept of an adorably overbearing mother meddling in the lives of virtually everyone she comes across, ranging from her increasingly exasperated adult offspring to the guy at the Apple store trying to show her how to work her iPhone, sounds like the kind of hard-sell combination of wheezy whimsy and sticky sentiment that could send audiences off in search of the latest Michael Haneke joint in order to regain some kind of psychic balance to their systems. That would be understandable but it would also be a shame because the film somehow manages to transcend its potentially dubious concept thanks to a screenplay that manages to be funny, touching, and incisive without becoming cloying and a performance by Susan Sarandon that is one of the best things that she has done in years.

Sarandon plays Marnie Minervini, a woman who has recently relocated from Brooklyn to Los Angeles following the death of her husband in order to be closer to her only child, screenwriter Lori (Rose Byrne). Armed with a big heart, a generous inheritance, and no evident working knowledge of the meaning of the word "boundaries," she cheerfully inserts herself into every possible aspect of her daughter's life, ranging from showing up unannounced on her doorstep in the morning with bagels to trying to find her a new suitor after she gets dumped by her actor boyfriend. Even when Lori is off on her own, Marnie still keeps on top of her via an endless string of voicemails that she leaves on subjects ranging from the glories of Los Angeles to the new Beyonce song she heard on the radio. To be fair, Marnie's intrusions are done with the best possible intentions—she has just been hard-wired with one of those outsized and outgoing personalities—but even though even Lori finds it hard to stay mad at her for too long, it is obvious that she is getting more and more exasperated with her mother intruding in everything.

Eventually, Lori hits her limit and when she has to go out to New York for a few weeks for work, she decides that this would be an ideal time to finally establish some concrete boundaries with her mother. As she does with practically everything else, Marnie takes this news in stride and begins applying her desire to do good towards other people. When she discovers that the Apple Store employee (Jerrod Charmichael) who is always helping her operate her iPhone left law school, she not only encourages him to reapply but even goes so far as to drive him to his classes and help him study for his exams. She volunteers at a hospital and latches onto an old woman who seems to have no one else to visit her. When she learns that one of Lori's friends (Cecily Strong) cannot afford to give her girlfriend the wedding of their dreams, Marnie offers to help pay for it. She even accidentally wanders onto a movie location and winds up getting put on camera, an incident that also introduces her to Zipper (J.K. Simmons), a retired cop moonlighting as a security guard who becomes instantly smitten with her.

The Meddler was written and directed by Lorene Scafaria, whose previous effort was the underrated comedy-drama *Seeking a Friend for the End of the World* (2012). In interviews, she has admitted that the film was indeed inspired to a large extent with her relationship with her own mother. Even if one did not actually know that going in, they would probably surmise it fairly quickly because the film as a whole feels less like a heavily plotted narrative than it does a string of anecdotes that most viewers will be able to relate to on some basic level. Though their own personal relationships with their mothers may not exactly mirror what is shown here, a lot of the behavior will ring true. Instead of going for big and showy moments, Scafaria offers up scenes that are quieter and more nuanced and the film is all the better for it. This is not to say that it does not contain a number of big laughs as well—it certainly does—but for the most part, the laughs spring from the characters themselves and not just from the contrivances of the story. Likewise, when the story delves into more serious-minded waters, they are never overbearing and include a number of elements that will hit home with a lot of moviegoers.

Susan Sarandon is, of course, one of the best American actresses of her time but it is no secret that her output over the last few years, whether from a lack of strong material to choose from or for reasons that are otherwise impossible to understand, has been suspect at best and cringe-worthy at worst—a lot of VOD titles, some undistinguished television turns and an appearance in one of Adam Sandler's very worst films in *That's My Boy* (2012). Finally working with decent material for the first time in a while, she gives a lovely and utterly endearing performance as Marnie that provides her character with loads of wit and charm while at the same time suggesting a certain sadness beneath the sunshine and without shying away from the elements that might indeed make extended exposure to Marnie as much of a chore as it seems to Lori from time to time. Though the film is primarily a showcase for Sarandon, there are also nice turns from Byrne and Simmons, the latter getting to give a surprisingly gentle performance as the would-be suitor whose relationship with Marnie does not develop as expected.

The Meddler may not be as penetrating of a comedic exploration of parent-adult child relationships as, say, Albert Brooks's great *Mother* (1996) and those who do not find Marnie and her antics endearing (and there are a few that skirt that line) may well find it all to be fairly unendurable. For the most part, however, it is a funny and occasionally touching comedy-drama that deals with situations and emotions that most viewers will instantly recognize in a smart and entertaining manner. However, anyone watching it should make sure not to make any immediate plans after seeing it because the minute that it ends, they will almost certainly be seized with the urge to give their own mothers a call.

Peter Sobczynski

CREDITS

Marnie: Susan Sarandon
Lori: Rose Byrne
Zipper: J.K. Simmons
Freddy/Fredo: Jerrod Carmichael
Jillian: Cecily Strong
Origin: United States
Language: English
Released: 2015
Production: Paul Green, Joy Gorman; released by Anonymous Content, Stage 6 Films
Directed by: Lorene Scafaria
Written by: Lorene Scafaria
Cinematography by: Brett Pawlak
Music by: Jonathan Sadoff
Sound: Trevor Gates
Music Supervisor: Linda Cohen
Editing: Kayla Emter
Costumes: Annie Bloom
Production Design: Chris L. Spellman
MPAA rating: PG-13
Running time: 100 minutes

REVIEWS

Dargis, Manohla. *New York Times*. April 21, 2016.
Debruge, Peter. *Variety*. September 14, 2015.
Frosch, Jon. *Hollywood Reporter*. September 15, 2015.
Goldstein, Gary. *Los Angeles Times*. April 21, 2016.
Keough, Peter. *Boston Globe*. May 5, 2016.
Lawson, Richard. *Vanity Fair*. September 15, 2015.
Orndorf, Bryan. *Blu-ray.com*. May 4, 2016.
Reed, Rex. *New York Observer*. April 22, 2016.
Taylor, Ella. *NPR*. April 21, 2016.
Wolfe, April. *L.A. Weekly*. April 20, 2016.

QUOTES

Marnie: "I would kill my daughter if she died on a motorcycle."

TRIVIA

The house Marnie goes to babysit at is the house from the original *A Nightmare on Elm Street*.

MEET THE BLACKS

Just when you thought it was safe to move to Beverly Hills ...
    —Movie tagline

Box Office: $9 Million

Before the film even starts, *Meet the Blacks* establishes itself as an unabashed take-over of the *Purge* franchise, by mimicking the films' famous governmental warning about all crime is legal for 12 hours, an event that favors the rich and white citizens of America who can protect themselves. In the case of this legally unrelated film, the message is delivered by executive producer Snoop Dogg, dressed in a blonde wig and white face, talking about joining his white friends to kill poor black people during the purge. It is not the most shocking statement—the *Purge* movies directly deal with issues of race and class in their narratives—but it establishes the film's refreshing point of view. After three installments, this series that so anxiously deals with these narratives will finally now be treated from a minority's perspective, without a sense of self-consciousness. This is only one of many charms to be found in Deon Taylor's *Meet the Blacks*, a thoroughly silly racial commentary that succeeds with such standards.

The key ingredient to this story is actor Mike Epps, who from the very beginning gives the movie a laid back attitude and a quick wit. He plays Carl Black, a father who ran an infamously terrible wiring business in Chicago but was able to escape the city with his family. After fudging some financial details, he was able to purchase a fancy mansion in a white suburban development located in Beverly Hills, despite still technically being on welfare. His presence is a conflict from the very beginning: in his very first scene, he has a sharp exchange with a black security guard who does not believe he lives in the neighborhood. When he pulls into his driveway, he's confronted by a second black man, who also aggressively does not believe him.

While the family is still unpacking for the move, it's revealed to be Purge Night. The family, including young son Carl Jr. (Alex Henderson), older daughter Allie (Bresha Webb), and his wife Lorena (Zulay Henao), are more distressed about it than he is. Claiming that he has seen plenty of violence in Chicago, Carl laughs off the idea of the purge, especially living in a neighborhood where he assumes his neighbors will not try to attack. Soon enough, not long after the purge commences do people try to break into the house, including Allie's boyfriend Freezee (Andrew Bachelor, hilariously over-the-top) who tries to kill his girlfriend's patriarch.

If that detail sounds familiar to DeMonaco's franchise-starting 2013 film, it is not the only plot piece that *Meet the Blacks* uses, a script that essentially steals, not just directly reflects, big parts from DeMonaco's screenplay. The respective family members are in somewhat the same position as the original movie, like how the young, reclusive son plays with gadgets, or the high-school aged daughter is sneaking around with Freezee right when the purge starts. The movie cannot resist merely sexualizing Lorena, and it adds another family member to the mix, the wacky Cronut (Lil Duval) who constantly gets in the way of Carl but is still protected.

With these similar characters in place, the events themselves are highly reminiscent to *The Purge*, even echoing the low-budget affair of making the story about home invasion. In the case of this comedy, the attackers are more like set-pieces, with angry white neighbors (led by actor Gary Owen) or a Chicago bouncy house employee (Mike Tyson) popping up at various moments, creating hit-or-miss blasts of big performances, often ending with bursts of violence. Though the filmmaking is too choppy for smooth slapstick, the cartoonish nature is prominent with its library of sound effects, always keeping the horror-comedy light as it zips along.

While the film may lose some of its viewers, there is an ambitious silliness to the film that one has to admire. The movie does not have the pressure of other comedies display to create a decent story, characters, or to have a certain edge to its wit. *Meet the Blacks* is dedicated entirely to catharsis about its situation, which makes it one of the year's most irreverent films and at times one of its most ruthless. Its parody goes deeper than select jokes, especially in how its plot parodies how a black man from Chicago could finagle his way into Beverly Hills, and then find himself and his family hated by everyone in the process. There is thorough zaniness to the movie that wins in spite of its numerous flat jokes, and places it among a Zucker & Abrahams or Wayans-produced comedy.

To say that *Meet the Blacks* is a parody of *The Purge* is a huge understatement. It essentially borrows the original's blueprint and gives it a different, less-serious perspective. *The Purge* and *Meet the Blacks* are political, loaded with ideas about America as a melting pot of characters but still segregated within. But Taylor's comedy has the upper-hand. It answers to DeMonaco's self-righteousness with in-your-face non-political-correctness, while soaking up the very stereotypes DeMonaco films anxiously work against in order to wring them out. With such similarities but essential differences, *Meet the Blacks* could very well be considered the best *Purge* film yet.

Nick Allen

CREDITS

Carl Black: Mike Epps
The Stranger: Gary Owen
Lorena: Zulay Henao
Allie: Bresha Webb
Cronut: Lil Duval
Origin: United States
Language: English
Released: 2016
Directed by: Deon Taylor
Written by: Deon Taylor; Nicole DeMasi
Cinematography by: John T. Connor
Music by: RZA
MPAA rating: R
Running time: 94 minutes

REVIEWS

Angulo Chen, Sandie. *Common Sense Media*. April 8, 2016.
Hassenger, Jesse. *The A.V. Club*. April 3, 2016.
Hoffman, Jordan. *Guardian*. March 31, 2016.
Kojder, Robert. *FlickeringMyth.com*. April 1, 2016.
Lemire, Christy. *RogerEbert.com*. April 3, 2016.
Orndorf, Brian. *Blu-ray.com*. April 1, 2016.
Shotwell, James. *Substream Magazine*. April 4, 2016.
Snider, Eric D. *EricDSnider.com*. April 5, 2016.
Uhlich, Keith. *Hollywood Reporter*. April 1, 2016.
Williams, Kam. *Baret News*. April 4, 2016..

QUOTES

Carl Black: "We gotta make sure there're no more black people 'round here, 'cause they *will* snitch."

TRIVIA

In the beginning one of the scene you hear Mike Epps character say "45,47" making a reference to his lotto scene in the movie *All About The Benjamins*.

THE MERMAID
(Mei Ren Yu)

Box Office: $3.2 Million

The trouble with a lot of film fantasies of late is that they just aren't fun anymore. It seems as if even the most seemingly heedless of entertainments are now laced with darker and grittier moments to make everything seem "edgy." That is why a film like Stephen Chow's *The Mermaid* is such a refreshing delight—here is a film that takes its fantastical premise and is not afraid to present it in a cheerfully goofball manner throughout. Even when it gets a bit violent and gory at certain points, there is something about it that is so irresistible that only a churl could possibly emerge from a screening of it without a big, silly grin plastered on their face.

As the film opens, the greedy, womanizing real estate tycoon Liu Xuan (Deng Chao) has just purchased Green Gulf, a pristine ocean sanctuary that cannot legally be used for development. That is not going to stop Liu, of course, and he hires a marine biologist to chase all the marine life out of the area permanently using sonar devices whose blasts will cause them horrible pain. What Liu doesn't know is that Green Gulf is also the home to the world's last surviving mermaids and they are not willing to give up their home without a fight. The ingenious plan devised by their leader, Octopus (Show Lo) is to have one of their own, the lovely Shan (Jelly Lin), disguise herself as a normal human and head to dry land in order to track down, seduce, and assassinate Liu in order to stop the project and save their home.

When Liu and Shan first meet, he is not particularly attracted to her but after being burned by a colleague over his taste in women, he decides to ask Shan out on a date. At first, Shan uses this as an opportunity to finish her task but her numerous attempts fail in spectacularly funny fashion—the best of the bunch find Octopus trying to lend a hand, so to speak, while pretending to be a sushi chef but having his own tentacles chopped up by his unsuspecting fellow chefs—but before long, she finds that there is more to Liu than initially meets the eye and begins to fall in love with him. For his part, Liu finds her oddball nature to be a refreshing change from the gold diggers that he usually goes out with and finds himself smitten with her as well. Eventually, Shan's real nature is revealed and when Liu's corporate cronies go ahead with the plan to depopulate Green Gulf for good, he is forced to decide which is more important—the love of Shan or the money that he stands to make.

On paper, this sounds like the basis for a feature-length PSA on the importance of conserving the oceans delivered through a pleasant but relatively ordinary comedy/fantasy along the lines of *Splash* (1984) Of course, no one has ever accused Stephen Chow—whose previous films have included such audaciously eye-popping action/comedies as *The God of Cookery* (1996), *Shaolin Soccer* (2001), and *Kung-Fu Hustle* (2004)—of being ordinary and that is certainly the case here as he transforms the material into a wild slapstick comedy that still somehow manages to convey a heartfelt, ecological message. As with many of his films, the story is little more than a clothesline from which to hang his comedic set pieces but considering how hilariously conceived and executed those parts are, few will mind the lack of dramatic heft. (If the scene in which a police sketch artist attempts to properly capture Liu's description of Shan after discovering she is a mermaid does not turn out to be the single funniest scene of 2016, it will definitely be in the running.) The only time when the film steps wrong is in the final reels in which Chow tries to combine a certain degree of sincerity with a surprising amount of violence during the battle between the mermaids and their oppressors—the sudden shift in tone is too abrupt and does not quite pay off.

Some people have complained that *The Mermaid* is too outlandish for its own good and that the CGI effects looked somewhat tacky in comparison to most effects-heavy films of late. What they fail to realize is that Chow is not trying to make one of those slick, soulless, state-of-the-art blockbusters. As is the case with many of his other films, he is frankly trying to make a live-action comedy in which everything is presented in a bright, audacious, and highly stylized manner and in that regard, he has succeeded mightily. Even the less-than-perfect special effects work in this context—they give the film a sort of homey, hand-made feel that demonstrates a lot more personality that most fantasy spectaculars of late. Of course, the brightest special effect on display is Jelly Lin as the title character—in what is probably the most significant female role in the entire Chow oeuvre, she is an absolute delight throughout whether she is awkwardly flirting with Liu or even more awkwardly attempting to negotiate walking around on land on her trussed-up tail.

When *The Mermaid* debuted in China, it quickly became that country's all-time box-office hit. Despite this, not to mention the cult following that Chow developed in the U.S. through the domestic releases of *Shaolin Soccer* and *Kung-Fu Hustle*, when the film was released in America, it was mysteriously dumped in only a handful of theaters with so little advance word that many people did not realize that it was out unless they happened to stumble upon it while looking at their theater listings. Happily, the word did get out and it managed to stick around for a couple of weeks to allow Chow devotees to see it as it was meant to be seen—on the big screen and in 3-D to boot. (While not exactly necessary, Chow's use of 3-D is slightly more inventive than the norm.) Hopefully, more viewers will discover *The Mermaid* on home video and succumb to its peculiar but definite charms.

Peter Sobczynski

CREDITS

Shan: Jelly Lin
Liu Xuan: Chao Deng
Octopus: Zhixiang Luo
Li Ruolan: Yuqi Zhang
Uncle Rich: Hark Tsui
Origin: United States
Language: Mandarin Chinese
Released: 2016
Directed by: Stephen (Chiau) Chow
Written by: Stephen (Chiau) Chow; Hing-Ka Chan; Chi Keung Fung; Miu-Kei Ho; Ivy Kong; Si-Cheun Lee; Zhengyu Lu; Kan-Cheung (Sammy) Tsang
Cinematography by: Sung Fai Choi
Music by: Fuhua Huang; Wendy Zheng
MPAA rating: R
Running time: 94 minutes

REVIEWS

Bowen, Chuck. *Slate.* July 5, 2016.
Ebiri, Chuck. *New York Magazine/Vulture.* February 21, 2016.
Ehrlich, David. *Slate.* February 26, 2016.
Kenney, Glenn. *New York Times.* February 20, 2016.
Kerr, Elizabeth. *Hollywood Reporter.* February 23, 2016.
Lee, Maggie. *Variety.* February 23, 2016.
Morgenstern, Joe. *Wall Street Journal.* February 26, 2016.
Nordine, Michael. *Village Voice.* February 26, 2016.
Tsai, Martin. *Los Angeles Times.* February 22, 2016.
White, Armond. *National Review.* July 21, 2016.

TRIVIA

Shot in a glass production factory along with some external locations in Shenzhen.

MIDDLE SCHOOL: THE WORST YEARS OF MY LIFE

Box Office: $20 Million

The literary world is not unlike Hollywood in that once a successful first book spawns a series, imitators tend to follow. Take Greg Kinney's *Diary of a Wimpy Kid* books, for instance. Once struggling writers saw how much money could be made with simple stories of today's youth peppered with cartoon doodles in the margins, the formula became the norm. Out of the success of that series of books (and a trilogy of films) came *Dork Diaries, Timmy Failure,* and *Middle School: The Worst Years of My Life.* Previous generations have had to gravitate toward more fulfilling and realistic stories by authors such as Judy Blume and Beverly Cleary, and their audience was, for the most part, female. Today's youth, however, have volumes upon volumes of tales of oppressed suburban white boys, books that are more concerned with getting a laugh than with inspiring introspection from their young audience. They have little depth, but they do engage and the kids do read them. The success of these kinds of books is not hard to figure out.

Whether or not they work as films is another matter. The latest to make the jump to the big screen, *Middle School: The Worst Years of My Life,* tells the story of Rafe (Griffin Gluck), a 13-year-old who has been kicked out of two schools and is now on his last chance for an education that does not involve learning military drills. The middle school is run by Principal Dwight (Andrew Daly) who has pretty much outlawed any and all forms of creative thought and expression. He is obsessed with the upcoming standardized test, the BLAAR (a reference to the real-life and controversial PARCC assessment test), which is coming up. On his first day, Rafe is handed a list of about 30 school rules, many of which border on the absurd. Within his first few hours of school, Rafe has his notebook full of sketches seized and destroyed before his very eyes.

Frustrated with the rules at this school, Rafe and his best friend, Leo (Thomas Barbusca), plot to break every single rule this school has and do it in a grand fashion. They just have to do it in a covert manner by breaking in in the middle of the night. Over the next few weeks, the school is decorated completely in Post-It notes, the sprinkler system sprays colored paint, and Principal Dwight's hat mysteriously leaves him with pink hair. The students take notice and the unknown prankster becomes something of a folk hero. One girl, an AV club member and student council rep named Jeanne (Isabela Moner), learns of Rafe's identity and gets in on the game as well during morning announcements. Principal Dwight is not the film's only villain, though. At home, Rafe has to deal with his mother's (Lauren Graham) new idiotic boyfriend, Bear (Rob Riggle), whom Rafe and his little sister Georgia (Alexa Nisenson) despise.

This is a film for the undiscerning middle-school student who lives in the suburbs and who just wants a film to relate to and laugh at. Other than a couple lines of dialogue laced with double entendre, *Middle School* is fairly harmless and fits in with any other innocuous after-school comedy show aimed at a young audience looking to relax after a long day at school. For its target audience, it will be entertaining enough and will work as an adolescent fantasy where kids take over the school and only the cool adults (which are few and far between here) are allowed back in. Kids will be more forgiving of leaps in logic, like how Rafe is able to break into the school night after night. The film might also speak to those whose parents are no longer together and who have to deal with a new parental figure. And unlike the *Diary of a Wimpy Kid* movies, *Middle School* tries its best for an emotional payoff (via a surprising twist) that makes the film about something more than just revenge on the adult establishment. While the emotion does not quite ring true, the attempt is admirable for a film like this.

Unfortunately, Carr stops right there when it comes to any attempt at authenticity. *Middle School* was clearly created by someone who had never really set foot in a real school or talked to that many real kids. It falls into the trap of something that panders rather than enlightens. Even the homelife material falls flat as the character of Bear is an insufferable bonehead that no woman with half a brain would ever consider hanging around with, much less marry. But the film needs to pad itself out with more sight gags meant to humiliate more adults. Only Graham's character and the single likable teacher in the school, Mr. Teller (Adam Palley), get away with not being the adult butt of a joke. Still, these are two actors who deserve better roles in their careers. As for the young cast, they all have a certain level of charm, the stand-outs being Nisenson and Moner.

Middle School has its moments, but the momentum of the film is dampened by animated sequences meant to convey Rafe's active imagination. Other than a lesson involving food chains, they have little value here. The plot is pretty much lifted from Allan Moyle's high school drama, *Pump Up the Volume* (1990), only instead of a pirate radio station, it's the overnight pranks. For a film about the joys of breaking the rules, the film plays by virtually every rule about pandering to the youth of America in hopes of kickstarting a cheaply produced movie franchise: Make everything brightly lit, have the kids behave more like adults (and vice versa), pepper the soundtrack with anthemic, catchy hits and establish everything through voice-over from the overly good-looking wimpy kid.

Collin Souter

CREDITS

Rafe: Griffin Gluck
Jules: Lauren Graham
Georgia: Alexa Nisenson
Principal Dwight: Andrew Daly
Leo: Thomas Barbusca
Origin: United States
Language: English
Released: 2016
Production: Leopoldo Gout, Bill Robinson; released by CBS Films, James Patterson Entertainment, Participant Media L.L.C.
Directed by: Steve Carr
Written by: Chris Bowman; Hubbel Palmer; Kara Holden
Cinematography by: Julio Macat
Music by: Jeff Cardoni
Sound: Kelly Oxford
Music Supervisor: Dave Jordan; JoJo Villanueva
Editing: Wendy Greene Bricmont; Craig P. Herring
Art Direction: Alan Au
Costumes: Olivia Miles
Production Design: Perry Andelin Blake
MPAA rating: PG
Running time: 92 minutes

REVIEWS

Baumgarten, Marjorie. *Austin Chronicle.* October 7, 2016.
Dundas, Deborah. *Toronto Star.* October 7, 2016.
Duralde, Alonso. *The Wrap.* October 7, 2016.
Graham, Adam. *Detroit News.* October 7, 2016.
Hartlaub, Peter. *San Francisco Chronicle.* October 7, 2016.
Hassenger, Jesse. *The A.V. Club.* October 7, 2016.
Means, Sean. *Salt Lake Tribune.* October 6, 2016.
Watson, Keith. *Slant Magazine.* October 7, 2016.
Webster, Andy. *New York Times.* October 7, 2016.
Wheeler, Brad. *Globe and Mail.* October 7, 2016.

MIDNIGHT SPECIAL

He's not like us.
　　—Movie tagline

Box Office: $3.7 Million

Like Alton, its fantastical child protagonist, Jeff Nichols' *Midnight Special* is a total anomaly. At its heart, it's a genre movie, the kind of backroads Americana supernatural story that children of the 1980s would identify as "Spielbergian." There are definite shades of Spielberg, Robert Zemeckis, John Carpenter, and even John Landis in *Midnight Special,* but, make no mistake, this film is no throwback. While lesser films might have overindulged in period details to link it to its inspirations, devolving into a nostalgia-fest, *Midnight Special* instead chooses to draw from its predecessors and create something wholly new and visionary. There have been sci-fi-tinged movies like this before—a special child with unnerving abilities on the run from government agents—but few are as nimble and graceful as *Midnight Special*.

Possibly the most heartening thing about watching *Midnight Special* is realizing how much Nichols trusts his audience. He refuses to spoon-feed them revelations or exposition. As a director, he's content to allow his audience to twist in the wind when the moment calls for it. Because, like the best storytellers, he knows how effective that disorientation can be as a narrative device, particularly when he consistently pays off those untethered moments with so much grounded, honest humanity later.

The film introduces audiences to Roy Tomlin (Michael Shannon) and his best friend Lucas (Joel Edgerton, who brings so much to such a quiet role) as they hide out in a motel with an eight-year-old boy named Alton Meyer (Jaeden Lieberher). Their setup feels like a spiritual cousin of Clint Eastwood's *A Perfect World*. There's evidence to suggest a possible kidnapping, but the affectionate manner between Alton and his adult companions belies a much deeper, less sinister bond. However, sinister does enter the picture in the form of Pastor Calvin Meyer (Sam Shepard), the leader of a Texas-based religious cult known as The Ranch, who has attracted the attention of the FBI.

Young Alton, apparently, had been placed in the care of The Ranch (according to Meyer), and many in the congregation thought the boy was blessed with holy visions. The Ranch found themselves on the FBI's radar because, while "speaking in tongues," Alton reveal secret government codes—encrypted messages that the boy never should have been able to intercept. Thus, both the government and the cult are desperate to obtain Alton, while it becomes increasingly clear that Roy and Lucas just want to protect him.

It also is slowly revealed that there is something legitimately unusual about Alton. He appears to be photosensitive, he communes with light, shafts of brightness exude from his hands and eyes, and he has strange abilities. Also, much like Spielberg's *Close Encounters of the Third Kind* (1977), a secret date and location play a defining role in the story. Alton's revelations of codes and numbers seem to be leading him to a very specific place and time. Roy is determined to help him reach it, even as he fears for the boy's safety. Michael Shannon, so often cast as a villain, is a revelation as Roy. His fierce, yet gentle paternal instincts are perfectly tuned—

the way he looks at Alton believably conveys that Roy can and will protect the boy from anything. (Lieberher is a similarly gifted actor, especially for a boy his age.)

Roy and Lucas eventually reunite Alton with his mother Sarah (Kirsten Dunst), but the relentless hunt is beginning to take its toll on the boy. Alton looks drained yet remorseful after he causes a satellite to come crashing to Earth—it had been tracking them from space and needed to be stopped. After run-ins with Calvin's religious zealots and the FBI, Alton finds himself face-to-face with Agent Sevier (Adam Driver) from the FBI, who becomes a sympathetic ally to the boy and his protectors. Roy, Lucas, and Sarah race to get Alton to the time and place he feels compelled to visit: the Florida swamps.

While *Close Encounters* was interested in framing "First Contact" as an almost religious experience, *Midnight Special* is much more grounded in human emotion. For example, in *Close Encounters*, Richard Dreyfuss shrugged off his family with ease to gape at the alien landing, while in *Midnight Special*, one gets the impression that Michael Shannon would tear open the fabric of space and time to deliver his son to his ultimate destiny. (It feels unlikely that it's a coincidence that both characters are named Roy.) Yes, *Midnight Special* is reminiscent of movies like *Starman* (1984), but it is so much more performance and emotional driven than most of those genre classics of the '80s.

Much like Nichols' *Take Shelter* (2011), the ending of *Midnight Special* is both spectacular and ambiguous. Nichols does not create films that end with a period, instead choosing to end his narratives with an ellipsis. But, while *Take Shelter* offered an oppressive feeling of impending doom, *Midnight Special* is significantly more joyous and spectacular. Comparatively, *Take Shelter* was a meditation on the end of the word, while *Midnight Special* is Nichols' exploration of Shakespeare's declaration that "There are more things in heaven and Earth, Horatio / Than are dreamt of in your philosophy."

Nichols' steady hand as a screenwriter and director truly elevate *Midnight Special* above so many other 2016 films, as do the technical contributions of cinematographer Adam Stone and David Wingo's score. The textures of the film—both visually and aurally—are so precise and perfect, creating the atmosphere of a lonely highway urban legend somehow brought to life. One wonders why there can't be more genre pictures like *Midnight Special*. Because, with this film, Nichols proves that, when it takes itself and its storytelling seriously, science fiction can become something truly revelatory.

Tom Burns

CREDITS

Sevier: Adam Driver

Lucas: Joel Edgerton

Sarah Tomlin: Kirsten Dunst

Roy: Michael Shannon

Calvin Meyer: Sam Shepard

Origin: United States

Language: English

Released: 2016

Production: Sarah Green, Brian Kavanaugh-Jones; released by Warner Bros. Entertainment Inc.

Directed by: Jeff Nichols

Written by: Jeff Nichols

Cinematography by: Adam Stone

Music by: David Wingo

Sound: Will Files

Editing: Julie Monroe

Art Direction: Austin Gorg

Costumes: Erin Benach

Production Design: Chad Keith

MPAA rating: PG-13

Running time: 112 minutes

REVIEWS

Andersen, Soren. *Seattle Times.* March 31, 2016.

Debruge, Peter. *Variety.* February 12, 2016.

McWeeny, Drew. *Hitfix.* March 16, 2016.

Nashawaty, Chris. *Entertainment Weekly.* March 17, 2016.

Rea, Steven. *Philadelphia Inquirer.* March 31, 2016.

Roeper, Richard. *Chicago Sun-Times.* March 31, 2016.

Rooney, David. *Hollywood Reporter.* February 12, 2016.

Tallerico, Brian. *RogerEbert.com.* March 16, 2016.

Turan, Kenneth. *Los Angeles Times.* March 17, 2016.

Vishnevetsky, Ignatiy. *The A.V. Club.* March 16, 2016.

QUOTES

Sevier: "Is it too much to ask you to punch me in the face? No? Never mind."

TRIVIA

The film was shot in 40 days.

MIKE AND DAVE NEED WEDDING DATES

They needed hot dates. They got hot messes.
—Movie tagline

Box Office: $46 Million

Idiot characters doing idiotic things are nothing new in terms of cinema. In fact, these types of characters and plot devices could be considered as old as the classic French silent film *A Trip To The Moon* (1902) by Georges Méliès in which a group of pseudo-scientists shoot themselves out of an oversized gun-like device and crash land on the moon. Not too bright. While Charlie Chaplin and Buster Keaton certainly had panache and brilliant comedy skills, their characters were essentially morons trying to get by in life. Just mentioning *The Three Stooges* or *The Marx Brothers* really drives the point home. Dumb people doing dumb things onscreen is nothing movie goers have not experienced before.

Cut to "Modern America," where everything has to be bigger and better than anything that's come before. A burger has to have an extra patty and more bacon than ever seen before, and a soda has to be bigger than a human bladder. For many comedy films, that means more dumb people than just the previously established duo. Even as they get more and more ridiculous, these films find their audience largely out of a human need to laugh at doltish behavior to feel better about oneself, and the survival instinct common in memories of when we did dumb things and lived to tell the tale. *Mike and Dave Need Wedding Dates* is merely the latest entry in a long lineage of dumb movies about dumb people doing dumb things.

Mike and Dave Stangle (Adam Devine and Zac Efron, respectively) are two brothers who love a good wedding. Not because of the romance, commitment, and connections that occur therein, but rather because they know a wedding is a chance to drink copious amounts of alcohol in order to loosen up and rain down their particular brand of hard-partying craziness. This typically involves madcap antics, over-the-top dancing, and, of course, chasing girls. Mike and Dave are good-looking, funny guys, and although they feel they bring life and a certain *je ne sais quoi* to every party they attend, their father Burt (Stephen Root) could not disagree more. Nor can their little sister Jeanie (Sugar Lyn Beard), who is the person having the wedding indicated in the title of the film.

Burt and Jeanie tell Mike and Dave they need wedding dates, and not just any party girl they can find. They want the brothers to bring nice, respectable girls to the wedding in Hawaii so as not to embarrass the family. While at first indignant and hurt, Mike and Dave acquiesce to the wedding demands, and as morons are prone to do, they concoct a terrible idea and decide to place an ad on Craigslist looking for wedding dates with the promise of a free trip to Hawaii as the catch. Now is probably a good time to mention the entire plot of *Mike and Dave Need Wedding Dates* is based on a true story and while certainly liberties have been taken with what happens next, it is true their Craigslist post went viral and Mike and Dave achieved controversial notoriety for their real-life version of television reality show *The Bachelor*.

After many insufferable people attempt to woo the Brothers Stangle in order to get the free trip to Hawaii, it is eventually Alice (Anna Kendrick) and Tatiana (Aubrey Plaza) who manage to dupe the dopey brothers into thinking they are classy ladies who will make a good showing at the wedding. Yet viewers already know that Alice is a recently jilted bride (as well as burgeoning alcoholic) and Tatiana is some kind of sociopath who is not only hyper-focused on her own pleasure but also dead-set on helping Alice get "back on the horse" as the saying goes.

Thus we have four not very bright, self-absorbed people attempting to perpetuate a lie about not only their goals but also, who they really are, on their way to Hawaii where a near-montage of silly antics build toward the inevitable wedding disaster. All that being said, *Mike and Dave Need Wedding Dates* is mildly amusing once the actors get out of their own way and allow the film to work as an ensemble rather than Efron, Kendrick, and Plaza desperately trying to play against type as Adam Devine positions himself to be the next zany bonehead since Jack Black has apparently relinquished the throne.

Having crafted a career as a negative, always bored-looking girl with a hidden soft side on the television show *Parks and Recreation*, Plaza tries to go full floozy here to limited effect. Her choice of how to play Tatiana is funny because it quickly becomes clear this is a completely self-involved woman, but her character also comes off as borderline racist as she frequently appropriates hip-hop lingo and slang. Kendrick also tries to break free of her "aww shucks" Disney-esque personae earned from well-received roles in films like *In The Woods* (2014) and the *Pitch Perfect* films, but here it feels very forced. Efron continues to show he's more than just a pretty face (and, body) but Devine doesn't match him well because of his inability to play anything besides the frustrated, ranty "Adam Devine" character he honed on the television series *Workaholics*.

Mike and Dave Need Wedding Dates is not a terrible film and there's some funny moments, yet it suffers from an almost drawn-out and highly predictable storyline. Yes, there are some vaguely shocking comedy moments, but mostly the film is just four half-wits making really bad choices and then spending the rest of the scene reacting to said choices. It's a very familiar affair.

Don R. Lewis

CREDITS

Dave Stangle: Zac Efron
Alice: Anna Kendrick
Mike Stangle: Adam DeVine
Tatiana: Aubrey Plaza
Burt Stangle: Stephen (Steve) Root
Origin: United States
Language: English
Released: 2016
Production: Peter Chernin, Jenno Topping, Jonathan Levine; released by Chernin Entertainment, Twentieth Century Fox Film Corp.
Directed by: Jake Szymanski
Written by: Andrew Jay Cohen; Brendan O'Brien
Cinematography by: Matthew Clark
Music by: Jeff Cardoni
Sound: Donald Sylvester
Music Supervisor: John Houlihan
Editing: Lee Haxall; Jonathan Schwartz
Art Direction: Mark Garner; Caleb Mikler
Production Design: Tyler B. Robinson
MPAA rating: R
Running time: 98 minutes

REVIEWS

Abele, Robert. *The Wrap*. July 5, 2016.
Dargis, Manohla. *New York Times*. July 7, 2016.
Douglas, Edward. *New York Daily News*. July 5, 2016.
Ehrlich, David. *IndieWire*. July 5, 2016.
Eichel, Molly. *Philadelphia Inquirer*. July 7, 2016.
Greenblatt, Leah. *Entertainment Weekly*. July 7, 2016.
Grierson, Tim. *Screen International*. July 6, 2016.
Hoffman, Jordan. *Guardian*. July 5, 2016.
Travers, Peter. *Rolling Stone*. July 8, 2016.
Walsh, Katie. *Los Angeles Times*. July 7, 2016.

QUOTES

Tatiana: "The key to teaching children is repetition. You'd be surprised how stupid they are."

TRIVIA

The number of responses that Mike and Dave received to their advertisement on Craiglist seeking wedding dates was about 6,000.

MILES AHEAD

If you gonna tell a story, come with some attitude.
　—Movie tagline

Box Office: $2.6 Million

One of the most difficult aspects of the cinema is trying to make compelling or urgent drama from the act of artistic creativity. The poet, painter, or composer by their very nature is enigmatic, idiosyncratic, and highly particular and they frequently exist outside the range of traditional interpretation.

Jazz is an authentic and indigenous American art form though its elastic and hybrid nature, bringing together traditional and avant-garde musical idioms, makes it especially hard to pin down as a narrative form. Two of the best jazz features, Bertrand Tavernier's *'Round Midnight* (1986) and Clint Eastwood's *Bird* (1988), are exacting, poetic, and visually allusive works that excel as emphatic and striking portraits of an artist. Both films are especially fine at capturing that interior life, sorrow, contradictions, the ravages of addiction, and both pass between a reverie and lament.

Don Cheadle's *Miles Ahead*, about the singular and extraordinary American composer, bandleader, and trumpeter Miles Davis (1926-1991), works in a different register. At a certain level it is no less ambitious than the Tavernier or Eastwood films. The movie qualifies as Cheadle's *Citizen Kane*, given the breadth of his personal and artistic investment as director, co-writer, producer, and lead actor.

It is a leaner and faster film than any of its nearest predecessors. Right at the start you have to acknowledge that about half of the movie is bunk, an entertaining, stinging, and often riotously funny cloth of fiction. This is almost certainly the only film about a major American jazz artist that opens with a car chase and shootout. Cheadle understands the structural limitations of the standard film biography and has sought to avoid the trappings of a movie like *Ray* (2004), Taylor Hackford's more traditional, square rendering of the life of Ray Charles.

Myth has always been a central feature about Miles Davis, and in constructing a wholly invented framing story Cheadle has made a film more attuned to the spirit and ideas of the man than imposing a strict documentary verisimilitude. The life and art was extraordinary, a Julliard-trained classicist who first made his reputation as a trumpeter in Charlie Parker's famed quintet and broke off to produce such exhilarating and ravishing studio recordings, primarily at Columbia Records, as *Round About Midnight* (1957), *Kind of Blue* (1959), and *Sketches of Spain* (1960).

Structurally *Miles Ahead* is best appreciated as nonfiction informed by fictional techniques. The movie is really two different films playing off each other, one unfolding inside the man's head, a series of actions, memories, and incidents given a density of shape and color, and the other a frantic and screwball romp meant to capture the man at a particular time in his life. The syntax is like jazz, vibrant, disruptive, and atonal but also dynamic and unpredictable. One of the first images of the film is the fast-forward of a video image, illustrative of the jagged, impressionistic rhythms.

The title is taken from the same name of Davis' gorgeously lush sixth studio album (1957). The Miles presented early on is not all different from the Charles Foster Kane at the start of Orson Welles' *Citizen Kane* (1941), a ruined and physically decaying man trapped by his past. It's the late 1970s, and Miles is a wreck. His body pallid and skeletal, Miles is a live wire recluse living in the nocturnal shadows of his Upper West Side brownstone, fixing on his cocaine binges and free floating paranoia. His personality is still combative and lucid, like a funny early moment when he publicly bickers with a radio host about the cultural relevancy of his own art.

The movie is more about attitude, actions, and flavor than a real narrative. A story emerges with the appearance of a journalist, Dave Brill (Ewan McGregor), a writer for *Rolling Stone*, who contrives a way inside Miles' house and asks to interview him for a purported article explaining his absence. The music industry, particularly jazz, has long given rise to self-invented. Cheadle wrote the script with Steven Baigelman, and these sections bristle with feeling and verve as the panorama expands and the colorful and quixotic gallery of secondary characters fills up.

Everybody's a hustler and the motivations, rationale, or nature of being fluctuating moment to moment. Every character has a secret angle they are looking to exploit for personal gain, like a manager, Harper Hamilton (Michael Stuhlbarg) promoting his gifted young trumpeter, Junior (Keith Stanfield). Miles has been living off a special retainer from the Columbia label, and the executives there are naturally eager to get their hands on some new and fresh material. The plot turns on the discovery of a new session tape as barter, Brill as a way to deepen his hold over his subject or Hamilton as leverage with the studio.

It's a riff, funky, and pleasurable, a way to get into the heart of the film, the beauty, grace, and original power of Miles' art. The journalist who poses a constant stream of question is also a natural way to meditate on the past. The present filters out the past, flights of fancy, or the shards of memory that creates something far more tangible and expressive. Cheadle and the cinematographer, Roberto Schaefer, visually contrast the periods with style and elegance. The present is diamond sharp and hard, the past luscious and romantic, anti-nostalgia of pain, regret, and sorrow.

At Columbia offices, Miles walks into an elevator and sees the spellbinding cover art of *Someday My Prince Will Come* (1961), framed by the beautiful and haunting close up of his first wife, Frances Taylor (Emayatzy Corinealdi). These burnished, at times, emotionally devastating flashbacks are the emotional heart of the film and the parts that really sing and flourish. Lithe and regal, Taylor is exquisite, and the extraordinary Corinealdi gives the part an extraordinary sensuality and grace, like the moment Miles turns up at her Broadway dance audition and her combination of movement, grace and style is intoxicating.

The past is the movie's reckoning, as a fuller and deeper portrait of Miles emerges, naked, vulnerable, and unflinching, where his baser instincts, his violence and sexual betrayal are on full view. In one of the best scenes in the film, Miles, cold and steely eyed, phones Frances in London during a European tour. He cajoles and browbeats her, shaming her for her alleged indifference to him that reveals the depths of his manipulation and sexual hypocrisy.

Cheadle locates the charm, braggadocio, and self-absorption of Miles. He is one of the great American actors, evident from his remarkable work in three very different films: Carl Franklin's *Devil in a Blue Dress* (1995), Paul Thomas Anderson's *Boogie Nights* (1997), and Steven Soderberg's *Out of Sight* (1998). Cheadle is quick, explosive, and volatile, but every movement is always perfectly calibrated and his movements and line readings are always fluent, intense, and often quite funny and dramatically revealing. He goes either way, never halting or uncertain.

The flashback material is strong and observational, about the way Miles integrated his acts, but it is also direct and frightening about what it meant to be a black artist in America in that time, drawing on a notorious episode outside Birdland in 1959 when Miles was grievously wounded by police officers after being seen in the company of a beautiful white woman.

It is a deliberately jagged portrait, terrifying at times, especially in the cruelty Miles displayed against Frances. The lingering guilt and pain, explicit in his hallucinations and walking dreams, is made palpable. Moments of extreme tenderness, like Frances swabbing Miles wounds after his night in custody, is played against abject horror of Miles' demonic rage. Discontinuous and fragmented, Corinealdi moves between states of being, ethereal but also full bodied and vivid.

The framing material is a lark, funny, and outrageous and at times too absurd for its own good. It is marred at the end by a repetition of incident. The parts all come together in a perverse and beautiful climax at a boxing match that Cheadle imaginatively entwines three alternative time movements. The material should not that work this well, appearing too diffuse and scattered. On the one hand it seems far removed from the meaning and art of Miles Davis. Don Cheadle may not always adequately explain what made his art so singular. Cheadle moves to his own rhythm. *Miles Ahead* sharply conjures a man who was a thrilling, ugly, and titanic force of nature.

Patrick Z. McGavin

CREDITS

Miles Davis: Don Cheadle
Dave Braden: Ewan McGregor
Frances Taylor: Emayatzy Corinealdi
Junior: Keith Stanfield
Walter: Brian Bowman
Origin: United States
Language: English
Released: 2016
Directed by: Don Cheadle
Written by: Don Cheadle; Steven Baigelman
Cinematography by: Roberto Schaefer
Music by: Robert Glasper
MPAA rating: R
Running time: 100 minutes

REVIEWS

Bastien, Angelica Jade. *RogerEbert.com*. April 7, 2016.
Burr, Ty. *Boston Globe*. April 14, 2016.
D'Angelo, Mike. *The A.V. Club*. March 30, 2016.
Dargis, Manohla. *New York Times*. March 31, 2016.
Edelstein, David. *New York Magazine*. March 24, 2016.
Merry, Stephanie. *Washington Post*. April 7, 2016.
O'Hehir, Andrew. *Salon*. March 31, 2016.
Phillips, Michael. *Chicago Tribune*. April 7, 2016.
Scherstuhl, Alan. *Village Voice*. March 30, 2016.
Whitty, Stephen. *New York Daily News*. March 30, 2016.

QUOTES

Doorman: "Do you have a pass?"
Miles Davis: [points to his face] "You're looking at it."

TRIVIA

Originally titled *Kill The Trumpet Player*.

MIRACLES FROM HEAVEN

How do we explain the impossible?
—Movie tagline

Box Office: $61.7 Million

With the recent influx of religious-themed (almost exclusively Christianity of a certain, evangelical bent) movies that exist primarily to preach to the choir and proselytize those outside the chapel, there is reason for skepticism when a new movie of this brand is released. What sets *Miracles from Heaven* apart from the crop is that the movie's focus is primarily dramatic, not religious. This is first and foremost a story of characters struggling with ordinary, earth-bound problems: serious illness, finances, marital issues, and the fear of losing a loved one. Its hope and faith, surprisingly, are not in matters of the otherworldly but in the kindness of other people. The movie turns out to have a fairly humanist message, even as its characters ultimately appeal to a specific, divine higher power.

The screenplay by Randy Brown (adapted from Christy Beam's memoir of the same name) leaves room for doubt, compromise, and criticism in terms of matters of religious faith. While it may only be the result of comparison to similarly themed movies that have come out recently, this movie feels earnest in its purpose.

The story follows the Beam family, a clan of Texans with seemingly perfect lives. Christy (Jennifer Garner), her husband Kevin (Martin Henderson), and their three daughters—Abbie (Brighton Sharbino), Anna (Kylie Rogers), and Adelynn (Courtney Fansler)—live on a fairly sizeable ranch. Kevin has just opened the largest animal hospital in the state—a financial gamble that puts the family's livelihood at risk. They attend church services every Sunday morning and are happy to host the post-service barbeque at their home.

The 10-year-old Anna suddenly falls ill. She vomits regularly, and her abdomen is constantly distended. Early diagnoses that Anna is lactose intolerant or has acid reflux prove incorrect. Repeated trips to different doctors and the emergency room offer no insight into her condition.

After a frustrated Christy pushes one ER doctor into doing a more thorough diagnosis, a specialist (Bruce Altman) gives her and Kevin the terrible news: Anna suffers from pseudo-obstruction motility disorder. In layman's terms, her intestines are incapable of processing food. The best-case scenario is that she will need to be fed a liquid diet via a tube through her nose for the rest of her life. The other side of that diagnosis, though, is that Anna's lifespan will be drastically shortened. If she does not receive specialized care, she will die sooner rather than later.

The movie's religious elements come early, with the local minister (John Carroll Lynch) preaching about tests of faith after a Christian rock band performs at the Sunday service. These first-act moments do not engender much confidence in director Patricia Riggen's desire to

move beyond a limited view of this story. Patience is required.

It pays off once the story turns its focus to the family's fight for Anna's survival. Christy's faith is tested by a combination of her daughter's illness and a group of judgmental parishioners who insinuate that Anna's health crisis may be the result of some unspoken sin on the girl's part. She stops attending church and makes it her sole duty to find Anna proper treatment. Dr. Nurko (Eugenio Derbez), a renowned pediatrician at a children's hospital in Boston, seems to be the best answer, although his waiting list is long and only clears when a patient of his stops needing treatment.

Garner's performance is a key component of the movie's stronger points. Even when the screenplay seems ready to indulge in the melodramatic side of this scenario, Garner helps to keep it at bay with a genuinely felt, consistently sympathetic sense of desperation, hopelessness, and resilience in the face of those other two emotions. As the afflicted Anna, Rogers is also adept in her performance as a young girl whose primary concerns tragically shift from wanting to appear "normal" in front of her classmates to serious considerations of whether or not death would be better than the pain she is suffering.

There are times at which Brown's screenplay seems apologetic for the dire situation. An extended sequence involving Queen Latifah as a waitress, whom Christy and Anna meet at a restaurant in Boston, is frustrating in its comic approach (Latifah's natural charisma nearly saves it). A lengthy montage, in which Kevin tries to hold down the homestead while Anna and Christy tour the city and keep doctor appointments, skips over what appears to be the movie's entire purpose—to show this family's struggles with the effects of illness while maintaining a semblance of normalcy.

Matters of faith are discussed, although with unexpected infrequency. Christy is confronted by a journalist (Wayne Péré) whose daughter (Hannah Alligood) is in the same hospital room as Anna. Anna gives the girl her cross pendant as a gift, and the father disapproves. What could be an obvious moment of evangelization instead becomes a scene of commiseration between two parents who have more pressing concerns than a debate about religion. It is the human capacity for compassion, the movie argues, that is the real salvation here.

The story's most sensationalistic element is an out-of-left-field turn involving an accident in the third act that refocuses everything toward a religious experience. There is room for questioning the veracity of the possibility of some divine intervention here, yet Brown and Riggen still lay on the miracle angle rather thick. (Even when the movie makes a point of showing that it is people who are responsible for the good on display here, it cannot help but insist on the divine.) One supposes that is to be expected from a movie such as *Miracles from Heaven*, although it does not make it any less disappointing.

Mark Dujsik

CREDITS

Christy Beam: Jennifer Garner
Anna Beam: Kylie Rogers
Kevin Beam: Martin Henderson
Abbie Beam: Brighton Sharbino
Adelynn Beam: Courtney Fansler
Dr. Nurko: Eugenio Derbez
Angela: Queen Latifah
Pastor Scott: John Carroll Lynch
Origin: United States
Language: English
Released: 2016
Production: DeVon Franklin, T. D. Jakes, Joe Roth; released by Affirm Films, Tristar Pictures Inc.
Directed by: Patricia Riggen
Written by: Randy Brown
Cinematography by: Checco Varese
Music by: Carlo Siliotto
Sound: Odin Benitez
Editing: Emma E. Hickox
Art Direction: Doug Fick
Costumes: Mary Jane Fort
Production Design: David Sandefur
MPAA rating: PG
Running time: 109 minutes

REVIEWS

Berry, David. *National Post.* March 17, 2016.
Coyle, Jake. *Associated Press.* March 15, 2016.
Davis, Steve. *Austin Chronicle.* March 18, 2016.
Guzmán, Rafer. *Newsday.* March 15, 2016.
Jaworowski, Ken. *New York Times.* March 15, 2016.
Keough, Peter. *Boston Globe.* March 15, 2016.
Lemire, Christy. *RogerEbert.com.* March 18, 2016.
Lewis, David. *San Francisco Chronicle.* March 15, 2016.
Orndorf, Brian. *Blu-ray.com.* March 17, 2016.
Schaefer, Stephen. *Boston Herald.* March 16, 2016.

QUOTES

Christy Beam: [narrating] "As you can see, we now live as if every day is a miracle. Because for us, it is."

TRIVIA

Heaven in the movie didn't reflect heaven in Anna's actual life.

MISS PEREGRINE'S HOME FOR PECULIAR CHILDREN

Stay peculiar.
—Movie tagline

Box Office: $87.2 Million

From its publication in 2012, Ransom Riggs' bestselling YA fantasy novel *Miss Peregrine's Home for Peculiar Children* seemed tailor-made to be adapted by Tim Burton. The novel could not possibly be more in the iconic filmmaker's thematic wheelhouse. As it turns out, this thematic commonality is the central reason why the film ultimately does not quite work. The Burtonesque elements are so thoroughly baked into the original narrative that there was nothing for the director to bring to the material to make it his own. Although the end result is visually stronger than most of his recent work, one cannot shake the feeling while watching it that it is the kind of thing that Burton has done many times before and oftentimes better than here.

Jacob (Asa Butterfield) is an ordinary teenager living in an utterly depressing Florida suburb. He witnesses the death of his beloved grandfather (Terrence Stamp, apparently now set to take on all the roles for which Burton might have utilized Christopher Lee in the past) and is convinced that he saw a bizarre and frightening apparition as well. No one believes him, of course, and Jacob is eventually sent to a child psychologist (Allison Janney) to help him distinguish between fantasy and reality. Jacob knows what he saw, however, and when he stumbles upon a few other clues that remind him of the fantastic tales his grandfather used to tell him, some involving the mysterious orphanage where he used to live on a remote Welsh island, he convinces the doctor that it would be a good idea to travel to said island to achieve closure. Alas, when he gets there, he is saddened to discover that the place was destroyed by a bomb dropped during a German air raid in 1943 and all of the inhabitants were killed.

Appearances can be deceiving. When Jacob returns to the site of the orphanage later in the trip, it is standing tall and housing children with strange abilities. One can bring inanimate objects to life, another has a second mouth located in the back of her head, and the lovely Olive (Lauren McCrostie) is lighter than air, forced to wear lead boots to keep from floating away. All of these "peculiar children" are under the tutelage of Miss Peregrine (Eva Green), just as it must have been back in 1943. In fact, it is 1943, more or less—Miss Peregrine has created a time loop that keeps them permanently locked in the 24 hours preceding the fateful air raid. Miss Peregrine and her charges, known as peculiars, have been staying on the island so as to avoid the clutches of Barron (Samuel L. Jackson), a monstrous peculiar, and his band of grotesque followers, who have been hunting down peculiars and eating their eyeballs in the hopes of absorbing their powers and becoming immortal. As Barron gets closer, Jacob must get in touch with his own peculiarity in order to save the others and create a new time loop for them before they are all destroyed.

Miss Peregrine's Home for Peculiar Children owes a considerable debt of inspiration to both the *Harry Potter* and *X-Men* franchises and eventually winds up falling into the traps to which the former managed to avoid and the latter has, more often than not, succumbed. Burton and screenwriter Jane Goldman spend so much time setting up their premise and introducing the characters that by the time that is done, all of the actual dramatic conflict in the second half winds up being rushed through in such a way that those not familiar with the book are liable to come away confused. Save for Jacob's crush object Olive, the other peculiar children are given no development outside of their particular traits, and so it is hard to work up much rooting interest for them when they are threatened. Another problem is that as "big bad fantasy franchise villains" go, the one offered up here is not particularly inspired—he is introduced too late in the proceedings to have much of an impact, and it is never made completely clear what he hopes to gain from killing off the other peculiars.

Although Burton generally does not get the credit that he deserves for his work with actors, the performances here are unaccountably all over the map. The best one is turned in by Eva Green, who is a blast to watch as the fiercely protective Miss Peregrine. Among the younger actors, Lauren McCrostie is a standout as the lighter-than-air Olive. Among the veterans, Terrence Stamp makes the most of his few minutes of screen time. Most detrimentally, Asa Butterfield is curiously bland and uninteresting as Jacob, not the kind of qualities a film needs for the character who is meant to be at the center of a big new film franchise—he comes across less like a peculiar and more like someone in need of some chicken soup and a couple of days of bed rest. Somewhere in the middle of the extremes of Green and Butterfield is Samuel L. Jackson's turn as Barron—it may not be one of his better performances but he is one of the few actors around with enough force of personality to still stand out even as the avalanche of special effects set pieces in the final reels threaten to engulf everyone else.

And yet, as deeply flawed as it is as a whole, the film is still a stronger effort from Burton than such recent efforts as the ghastly *Alice in Wonderland* (2010), the unnecessary *Dark Shadows* (2012), and the ambitious-but-clunky *Big Eyes* (2014), even if there is the sense throughout that he is merely raiding his bag of tried-and-true tricks. Visually, the film is often wonderful—the orphanage setting is beautifully designed and there are any number of striking moments ranging from the sight of a peculiar whose power is the ability to project his dreams like a movie projector to the arrival of a skeleton army straight out of the works of Ray Harryhausen—and there are times here and there when he seems more engaged with the material he is working with than he has in a long time. Unfortunately, he can never quite figure out how to pull it all together in a completely satisfying and engaging manner. However, now that he has gotten all that annoying backstory out of the way, perhaps a sequel (such as the one hinted at in the final moments) will allow him to delve more fully into the other peculiars and make them into characters instead of caricatures. If that were to happen, this could be the rare film to inspire a sequel far more engaging than the original. Now *that* would be peculiar indeed.

Peter Sobczynski

CREDITS

Miss Peregrine: Eva Green
Jake: Asa Butterfield
Barron: Samuel L. Jackson
Franklin Portman: Chris O'Dowd
Dr. Golan: Allison Janney
Ornithologist: Rupert Everett
Origin: United States
Language: English
Released: 2016
Production: Peter Chernin, Jenno Topping; released by Twentieth Century Fox Film Corp.
Directed by: Tim Burton
Written by: Jane Goldman
Cinematography by: Bruno Delbonnel
Music by: Michael Higham; Matthew Margeson
Sound: Bjorn Ole Schroeder
Editing: Chris Lebenzon
Costumes: Colleen Atwood
Production Design: Gavin Bocquet
MPAA rating: PG-13
Running time: 127 minutes

REVIEWS

Chang, Justin. *Los Angeles Times*. September 29, 2016.
Dargis, Manohla. *New York Times*. September 29, 2016. .
Debruge, Peter. *Variety*. September 25, 2016.
Ehrlich, David. *IndieWire*. September 25, 2016.

Lawson, Richard. *Vanity Fair*. September 28, 2016.
O'Sullivan, Michael. *Washington Post*. September 29, 2016.
Packham, Chris. *Village Voice*. September 25, 2016.
Savlov, Marc. *Austin Chronicle*. September 29, 2016.
Truitt, Brian. *USA Today*. September 29, 2016.
Zacharek, Stephanie. *Time*. September 29, 2016.

QUOTES

Emma Bloom: "You don't have to make us feel safe ... because you've made us feel brave."

TRIVIA

The house where the children live, is an actual house. It's called "Torenhof," and can be found near Antwerp, Belgium.

MISS SLOANE

Make sure you surprise them.
—Movie tagline

Box Office: $3.5 Million

The year 2016 saw more than its fair share of political absurdities with a game-changing election that will be dissected, second-guessed, and theorized to death long after the current president's term has ended. It might very well be mentioned in the same conspiratorial breath as the JFK assassination, Watergate, and the War in Iraq. Throughout the year, it seemed that every month, the election cycle would take unprecedented turns that would cause one to comment, "this is like something out of a movie." Except it was real and there was no going back. The country had changed, the world had changed, and people's faith in the democratic system had most certainly changed. This is why films such as *Miss Sloane* almost seem quaint when looked at in the post-Election 2016 world. It feels like a film of a bygone political era and its release date (November 25, 2016) after the election results that shocked America, was most unfortunate.

In the film, Elizabeth Sloane (Jessica Chastain) is a high-powered, highly sought-after lobbyist who works for a firm that has been hired to lobby for the 2nd Amendment Rights activists. When Elizabeth walks into a room, everyone better be ready to answer her questions with well-researched facts. The worst thing anyone can say to her is "I don't know." She gets lured away from the firm by a campaign that will combat the hardcore 2nd Amendment Rights activists with the Hedon-Harris Bill, a gun control measure that needs a certain number of votes to pass. It will be up to Elizabeth and those in her crew to lobby for those votes by any means

necessary. For Elizabeth, it is not so much about the cause as it is about the need to win. She will protect her reputation as a winner of every battle, no matter what.

The film jumps back and forth in time between her lobbying efforts and her trial, in which she stands accused (for what, it is unclear until later). She constantly takes the fifth when it comes to questions about her job, but occasionally gives into her worst instincts by spouting off in defiance against her detractors, much to the chagrin of her only true ally, Rudolfo Schmidt (Mark Strong), who hired her for the job. She also makes use of one of her fact checkers, an all-knowing statistician named Esme Manucharian (Gugu Mbatha-Raw), who takes the fight for gun control very personally because of her past. Elizabeth is quick to exploit that on a national stage, without so much warning Esme that she is now a spokeswoman, a role that comes at a high price.

First-time screenwriter Jonathan Perera obviously studies the works of Aaron Sorkin and the like to deliver a dialogue heavy product that forces actors to speak their dialogue at a rapid rate, which sometimes works, sometimes not. He is smart not to give Elizabeth too much of a back-story. At one point, Adolfo asks her, "Were you ever normal? What were you like as a child?" The film never gives an answer as to who she really is or what happened to her family. To help compensate for the lack of a love life, Elizabeth employs male escorts, usually the same guy every time, but who is now no longer available. For now, she'll have to settle for Forde (Jake Lacy), a typical piece of eye candy who will, of course, play more than one role in her life. But Elizabeth, for all her bravado, confidence, and shamelessness, remains a mystery and it is probably better that way.

Miss Sloane is easy to watch, thanks in large part to Chastain and Mbatha-Raw, two actors who should have more screen time together in a better film. Chastain is clearly having a great time with this juicy role and one could certainly see the appeal for an actor of her strength. Mbatha-Raw is perhaps even better in the less showy role as the one who has to react to Elizabeth's unpredictable and, at times, deplorable behavior. The best stuff in the film belongs to them and their scenes together. Esme might be the one person who can peel away at Elizabeth's hardened exterior and find a human being underneath. As it happens, though, the audience feels a great deal of sympathy for Esme because the more she peels away those layers, the more one suspects she is being played.

Unfortunately, the movie does not really work in the end. It wants to paint a picture of lobbyists that will resonate with the current political climate, but never mind that it arrived too late. The outcome of this is just too unlikely to take seriously. Imagine the most absurd episode of *House of Cards* and realize that this is even more absurd than that. For all its good intentions and solid cast, director John Madden cannot save the script from itself in terms of what the audience is supposed to believe. The film wants to have it both ways, both as an important political thriller meant to get a national conversation going as well as a tale of conspiracy in which deals are made in a dark parking garage and a mechanical robot cockroach can help bring about someone's downfall. *Miss Sloane* could have done for lobbyists what *Nightcrawler* (2014) did for freelance video journalists. Instead, it disappears from view pretty quickly once it ends and the audience is left to go back into the real world in which absurdities know no end.

Collin Souter

CREDITS

Elizabeth Sloane: Jessica Chastain
Esme Manucharian: Gugu Mbatha-Raw
Pat Connors: Michael Stuhlbarg
Congressman Ron M. Sperling: John Lithgow
Rodolfo Schmidt: Mark Strong
Origin: United States
Language: English
Released: 2016
Production: Ben Browning, Kris Thykier, Ariel Zeitoun; released by Archery Pictures, Canal+ Group, Cine Plus, FilmNation Entertainment, France 2 Cinema, France Televisions Distribution S.A., Transfilm
Directed by: John Madden
Written by: Jonathan Perera
Cinematography by: Sebastian Blenkov
Music by: Max Richter
Sound: Francois Fayard
Editing: Alexander Berner
Art Direction: Mark Steel
Costumes: Georgina Yarhi
Production Design: Matthew Davies
MPAA rating: R
Running time: 132 minutes

REVIEWS

Braun, Liz. *Toronto Sun*. December 8, 2016.
Colburn, Randall. *Consequence of Sound*. December 6, 2016.
Covert, Colin. *Minneapolis Star Tribune*. December 8, 2016.
Graham, Adam. *Detroit News*. December 9, 2016.
Jones, J.R. *Chicago Reader*. December 8, 2016.
Katz, Anita. *San Francisco Examiner*. December 9, 2016.
McDonald, Moira. *Seattle Times*. December 8, 2016.

O'Malley, Sheila. *RogerEbert.com*. November 25, 2016.
Smith, Kyle. *New York Post*. December 7, 2016.
Verniere, James. *Boston Herald*. December 9, 2016.

QUOTES

Elizabeth Sloane: "Tonight, we'll leave them wanting more."

TRIVIA

Screenwriter Jonathan Perera was the only writer to work on the script. This is a rarity in the movie industry.

AWARDS

Nominations:

Golden Globes 2017: Actress—Drama (Chastain)

MOANA

The ocean is calling.
—Movie tagline

Box Office: $244.9 Million

Over the past decade, Disney has worked tirelessly to overhaul their extremely iconic (and profitable) princess "brand." Realizing that modern audiences were expressing concerns about lead female characters who only functioned as damsels in distress, the folks at Disney found themselves faced with a difficult proposition—how do they balance the classic elements of their popular princess mythology with the need to create more self-actualized, self-rescuing heroines? The results have been mixed. While most Disney fables are fairly engaging, new-wave princesses like Tiana from *The Princess and the Frog* (2009) and Merida from *Brave* (2012) delivered on the feminism side and not on the charisma side.

Things shifted with 2013's *Frozen*, a film that introduced two princesses, but re-contextualized them by making their narrative more of a sister story than a royalty story. The dynamic worked in a big way. *Frozen*, despite its flaws, was unmistakably entertaining, and the film was a massive success.

Moana is the first new Disney princess musical since *Frozen* and it functions as both a throwback to earlier Disney classics and as a worthy descendant of the *Frozen* legacy. It was directed by Ron Clements and John Musker, the filmmakers behind such Disney landmarks as *The Little Mermaid* (1989) and *Aladdin* (1992), and their confidence radiates through every frame of *Moana*. With Clements and Musker's knack for storytelling and Jared Bush's confident script, *Moana* offers a much stronger narrative than *Frozen*. It feels more like a legend passed down from generation to generation.

However, while *Frozen* had plot holes big enough to drive a Zamboni through, it is a more entertaining film than *Moana*. The South Pacific fable is stirring, smart, and amusing, but *Frozen* beats it through sheer showmanship. Its songs were stronger, its jokes were funnier. *Moana* may not be a backwards step for Disney, but audiences should expect a more subdued experience than *Frozen* offered.

One reason for this might be that this is Disney's first attempt to craft a movie out of the legends of indigenous peoples since *Pocahontas* (1995), an irresponsibly white-washed film that represents one of the lowest points in Disney's recent creative history. Fortunately, *Moana* seems to have learned from both *Frozen* and *Pocahontas*' examples (and mistakes). The title character in *Moana* does not need a white European to teach her about the "Colors of the Wind." Instead, she's an activated, three-dimensional character (wonderfully voiced by Auli'i Cravalho) who sets off to save her people because of her own social conscious, not because she wants to impress a boy. (The lack of a tacked-on romantic interest is one of the most refreshing aspects of the film.)

Moana is destined to become the chief of the island community of Motunui one day, but she feels conflicted about inheriting the responsibilities of her father Chief Tui (Temuera Morrison). From a young age, Moana has felt an urge to get out onto the ocean, beyond her island's protective reef, despite her father's stern warnings about the dangers of the open sea. What her father does not know is that the ocean itself befriended Moana at a young age, playfully interacting with her in a fashion that's reminiscent of the sentient water tentacles from James Cameron's *The Abyss* (1989).

However, Moana's island ennui is broken by the realization that her island and the surrounding ocean is starting to die. Her shamanistic grandmother Tala (Rachel House) explains that all their problems started when the bombastic demigod Maui decided to steal the stone "heart" of Te Fiti, an island goddess, to win himself even more praise from humanity. Following his theft, Maui was struck down by the lava monster Te Ka, and the demigod and the "heart" was never seen again. Moana's mission is clear—she needs to find the stone, find Maui, and convince Maui to return the heart to Te Fiti or else every island in the ocean is doomed.

There are a host of problems with the plan—Moana's lack of sailing ability, weird coconut pirate people, a whole realm of monsters—but the biggest problem might be that Maui doesn't want to do it. Moana finds the demigod trapped on an island and all he wants to do is find his long-lost magic fishhook and get back to

being a beloved deity. Maui is voiced by Dwayne Johnson and his performance is easily one of the highlights of the film. He imbues Maui with an impressive vocal swagger that truly sells the demigod as a vain, wounded egotist, who desperately wants the adoration of everyone around him. His introductory song "You're Welcome", one of many numbers composed by Hamilton's Lin-Manuel Miranda, is a big, brash, worthy addition to the Disney musical canon.

The music in *Moana* is one of its most memorable assets. While the musical numbers do not have the same infectious Broadway appeal as Robert Lopez and Kristen Anderson-Lopez's songs from *Frozen*, they do present a much wider range of motifs and emotions. The tribal island songs from Polynesian singer and composer Opetaia Foa'I give the film a tremendous sense of place and emotional heft. When those songs are mixed with Mark Mancina's musical score and Miranda's impressive character-driven showtunes, the result is something fairly magical. It feels both mythic and entertaining.

The first half of the film is stronger than the second half. There are some generic third-act conflicts that are too easily telegraphed and too predictable to take seriously, but, on a whole, *Moana* cares so much about its characters and their journey that it's hard to not feel the same way. It's an aspirational story at its heart and that kind of palpable ambition makes for great cinematic storytelling.

At one point in the film, Maui jokes, "If you wear a dress and have an animal sidekick, you're a princess." If he's right, *Moana* might represent Disney's best take on a "modern" princess yet. She's a figure of royalty who earned her status through hard work, restlessness, compassion, and empathy. Plus, she's not afraid to set off onto the ocean on her own, armed only with her wits and her steadfast belief that she has the power to bend mythological figures to her will, if the situation calls for it. If that's what's considered a "princess" these days, children around the world (and their parents) are very, very fortunate.

Tom Burns

CREDITS

Moana: Auli'i Cravalho
Maui: Dwayne "The Rock" Johnson
Gramma Tala: Rachel House
Chief Tui: Temuera Morrison
Tamatoa: Jemaine Clement
Origin: United States
Language: English
Released: 2016
Production: Osnat Shurer; released by Walt Disney Pictures

Directed by: Ron Clements
Written by: Jared Bush
Music by: Opetaia Foa'i; Mark Mancina; Lin-Manuel Miranda
Sound: Timothy Nielsen
Editing: Jeff Draheim
Production Design: Ian Gooding
MPAA rating: PG
Running time: 107 minutes

REVIEWS

Chang, Justin. *Los Angeles Times.* November 22, 2016.
Ebiri, Bilge. *Village Voice.* November 21, 2016.
Lemire, Christy. *RogerEbert.com.* November 22, 2016.
Mitori, Jody. *St. Louis Post-Dispatch.* November 22, 2016.
Parker, Andrew. *The Globe and Mail.* November 23, 2016.
Rechtshaffen, Michael. *Hollywood Reporter.* November 7, 2016.
Roeper, Richard. *Chicago Sun-Times.* November 21, 2016.
Savlov, Marc. *Austin Chronicle.* November 23, 2016.
Travers, Peter. *Rolling Stone.* November 23, 2016.

QUOTES

Moana: "I am not a princess."
Maui: "If you wear a dress and have an animal sidekick, you're a princess."

TRIVIA

Lin-Manuel Miranda was hired to write the music for the film before the Broadway stage musical *Hamilton* became a worldwide hit.

AWARDS

Nominations:

Oscars 2016: Animated Film, Orig. Song Score and/or Adapt. ("How Far I'll Go")
British Acad. 2016: Foreign Film
Golden Globes 2017: Animated Film, Song ("How Far I'll Go")

MONEY MONSTER

#FollowTheMoney
   —Movie tagline

Box Office: $41 Million

At last, eight years after the global financial collapse and six months after the exceptional, Oscar-nominated *The Big Short* (2015), a movie comes along to make the presses-stopping point that sometimes high-powered people make irresponsible decisions that may as well set the little guy's dollar on fire. In other groundbreaking news, according to *Money Monster*: Private information can be vulnerable on the Internet, loudmouth TV hosts are really obnoxious, and celebrities don't necessarily have spotless personal lives.

Yeesh. It is truly astonishing that this mediocre thriller, attempting to harness a country's economic frustration through one average person's revenge on a detached disseminator of bad advice, comes from director Jodie Foster, who previously showed such fearlessness in 2011's unusual *The Beaver.* Aside from pulling off the risky, difficult task of creating art so thought-provoking it allows viewers to separate Mel Gibson the actor from Mel Gibson the off-camera trainwreck, that film also dealt with challenging ideas regarding mental illness and family tension in daring ways. It remains one of the weirder, more sadly unseen movies of the decade.

Money Monster, on the other hand, has only delusions of impact rather than legitimate purpose. Lee Gates (George Clooney), the Jim Cramer-esque host of the titular financial guidance TV show, epitomizes the overproduced, hyperbolic shouting that long ago turned cable news programs like *Mad Money* (2005-) into self-parodies (and were amusingly sent up several years earlier on *Arrested Development* [2003]). Lee is all disingenuous flash, opening shows with ridiculous dance routines (backup dancers included, of course) and smarm that turns his good looks into a weapon. "Are you listening? Are you paying attention out there?" he asks as the movie begins. "Good, because it's about to get complicated."

No, it isn't. When Lee's director, Patty Fenn (Julia Roberts), asserts "We don't do gotcha journalism here," it could not be more predictable that the line is followed by, "Hell, we don't do journalism period," just to make sure there is no misunderstanding about the three-person group of writers' fish-in-a-barrel point of view. The presentation of an arrogant TV host deserving of falling a few rungs soon gets its push in the form of Kyle Budwell (Jack O'Connell), unofficially representing every victim of a stock, recently guaranteed by Lee, that plummeted due to an alleged glitch in its algorithm and cost investors $800 million. Kyle sneaks onto the set and at gunpoint forces Lee to put on a suicide vest, threatening to release the detonator if the cameras stop rolling. In theory, this might play out as a late but cathartic experience for anyone still wondering when and if, recession or not, the U.S. will return to a place where the middle class can prosper and feel like wealth is being accumulated, not drifting away, toward people who already have it.

In practice, *Money Monster* is all gums, feebly chomping on its issue with lines like, "I'm telling you, it's rigged. The whole goddamn thing. They're stealing the country out from under us." Foster tries to establish degrees of ambiguity regarding characters' likability, humanizing Kyle and Lee, but the result merely shifts the blame to the big, powerful executive making illegitimate moves with funds he takes from people who have no ability to fight back. That simplistic compromise not only prevents a thriller from having any real tension but it gives the obvious *Money Monster* the feeling of stalling, just as Patty is asked to do.

Meanwhile, there is the *Speed*-esque (1994) consideration of shooting the hostage and pretty one-dimensional performances from everyone involved, given only broad strokes to work with. A sequence in which Lee and Kyle compare lives on a scoreboard is particularly ridiculous, turning the former into a stereotypical, lonely phony and the latter into a generic, working-class victim. No better is when Lee attempts to save his life and Kyle's savings by encouraging everyone watching to buy the stock and increase the price, something the SEC probably would not find up to code. As for the awkward comic relief of Ron (Christopher Denham), an employee of the show testing out a new erectile cream to help Lee determine if he should endorse the stock, well, sometimes screenwriters need to fill time, so why not with a pointless little subplot that establishes a female employee (who works for product placement, someone notes) not shown working at all, just having sex with Ron.

Clearly, this is far from a worthy update of *Network* (1976). Even with such palpable unrest off the screen, the contrived *Money Monster* instantly feels irrelevant with its basic message about greed, human error, and media frivolousness. It counts as yet another example of Clooney, as producer and/or director and/or star of films like *The Ides of March* (2011), *Our Brand is Crisis* (2015) and *The Monuments Men* (2014), having good intentions but little recognition of how much actually is or is not being achieved.

In brief moments, *Money Monster* fairly recognizes that money can neither buy happiness nor should be taken as insignificant. It still carries power, and increasingly so as society pushes itself toward opposite spectrums, whose distance from each other speaks volumes and is both figurative and literal, emotional and geographical. The film tries to break down that wall, but its battering ram to the issue couldn't get through glass.

Matt Pais

CREDITS

Lee Gates: George Clooney
Patty Fenn: Julia Roberts
Kyle Budwell: Jack O'Connell
Walt Camby: Dominic West
Diane Lester: Caitriona Balfe
Origin: United States
Language: English, Korean, Icelandic
Released: 2016

Production: Lara Alameddine, Daniel Dubiecki, Grant Heslov, George Clooney; released by Tristar Pictures Inc.
Directed by: Jodie Foster
Written by: Jamie Linden; Alan DiFiore; Jim Kouf
Cinematography by: Matthew Libatique
Music by: Dominic Lewis
Sound: Chris Gridley
Editing: Matt Chesse
Art Direction: Deborah Jensen
Costumes: Susan Lyall
Production Design: Kevin Thompson
MPAA rating: R
Running time: 98 minutes

REVIEWS

Abele, Robert. *TheWrap.* May 12, 2016.
Anderson, Melissa. *Village Voice.* May 14, 2016.
Hassenger, Jesse. *The A.V. Club.* May 12, 2016.
Gray, Christopher. *Slant Magazine.* May 12, 2016.
Grierson, Tim. *Screen International.* May 12, 2016.
Kohn, Eric. *IndieWire.* May 12, 2016.
McCarthy, Todd. *Hollywood Reporter.* May 12, 2016.
Persall, Steve. *Tampa Bay Times.* May 12, 2016.
Roeper, Richard. *Chicago Sun-Times.* May 12, 2016.
Zacharek, Stephanie. *Time.* May 13, 2016.

QUOTES

Won Joon: "They're only calling it a glitch because nobody understands how the algo works. And if nobody can understand the math, then nobody has to explain the money."

TRIVIA

For scheduling reasons, Julia Roberts and George Clooney didn't work together a lot in the movie. Roberts shot all of her scenes with green screen on the monitors her character constantly watches.

A MONSTER CALLS

Stories are wild creatures.
—Movie tagline

Box Office: $3.7 Million

Juan Antonio Bayona's adaptation of Patrick Ness' hit Young Adult novel is well-intentioned and well-made but frustrating in its storytelling approach, one that constantly tells viewers what to think and feel instead of letting them come to those conclusions for themselves. The great fairy tales of literature and cinema leave something open to interpretation, provoking further dissection and discussion upon their conclusion. While the story of *A Monster Calls* is undeniably moving, it's all up there on the screen, leaving too little to take away from the experience.

Conor O'Malley (Lewis Macdougall) is going through the roughest period of his young life. His mother (Felicity Jones) is dying of cancer, meaning that he may soon have to go live with his strict grandmother (Sigourney Weaver). Meanwhile, he's being bullied at school and remains distant (both emotionally and physically) from his father (Toby Kebbell). Life sucks for Conor. And that's often when the supernatural intervenes.

One night at exactly 12:07am, Conor looks out his window to see a giant tree come to life and stomp to his window. The monster, voiced by Liam Neeson, grabs Conor and tells him how it's going to go—he will tell Conor three stories, after which Conor must tell him one. Of course, the stories are all parables for dealing with grief, loss, and the world that will be without his mother. *A Monster Calls* is the story of a young man coming to terms with devastating loss through the help of an aggressive, terrifying creature (so much so that the film earned a PG-13 rating, likely hurting its overall box office).

The first story the monster tells Conor is that of a prince whose girlfriend is murdered and his stepmother queen is accused of the crime. The prince tells the villagers that the queen is a witch and she must be overthrown, but the monster takes the queen and protects her. She was a witch, but she did not kill the girl. In fact, the prince did it himself to rally the people against his stepmother. Of course, Conor learns that life and death are not fair, and that people's motivations, including his grandmother's may not be as simple as they first seem.

The second story involves a man of science vs. a man of faith. An apothecary is run out of business by a parson who turns his congregation against the cures the former provided. When the parson's children get sick, he relents and turns to the apothecary for help, but the man refuses, letting the girls die. He may have been a greedy man but he could have saved lives if the parson had let him in the first place. There is belief in science as well as faith. And, again, life isn't fair, and will only hurt you if you deny the needs of another.

There's little purpose in spoiling the third story, but suffice it to say that it pushes Conor to finally share his own. It's a nightmare that actually opens the film, in which Conor's mother is on the edge of a massive cliff created by a earth-tearing quake. He tries to hold on to her, but she falls. The truth that Conor is forced to confront is that he lets her go. He has to let her go. We all do when death comes for a loved one.

Clearly, *A Monster Calls* has good intentions in the manner it confronts issues like death and fear in a way that doesn't talk down to children or worry too much about frightening them. Having said that, it's also a film notably lacking in subtlety. It's clearly designed in a way to reflect Guillermo Del Toro's *Pan's Labyrinth* (2006) (Bayona and Del Toro are regular collaborators and friends), but that film leaves room for both visual and narrative interpretation that Bayona's simply does not. Every story literally ends with a recap as to what Conor and the viewer is supposed to take away from it, and the film is often noisy when it should be graceful.

Despite the relative missed opportunity, there are things to like about Bayona's work (and his other superior films, *The Orphanage* [2007] and *The Impossible* [2012], are also worth seeking out). He has displayed skill with visual effects in the past, and that comes in handy here, especially when it comes to the design of the tree-monster, a creature that somehow feels both menacing and trustworthy. The duality of the creature is helped by Liam Neeson's voice work, which also strikes a balance that makes it sound like a stern father— someone willing to punish but also there to help.

A Monster Calls failed to find an audience in the United States (making less than $4 million from a lackluster campaign by Focus Features, who never really figured out how to get it to an audience) but did better in other markets, even earning several Goya Award nominations (Spain's equivalent to the Oscars). It's a film that had loyal fans, however, and they are likely to share it over the years, much like the Monster's stories, passing it down from friend to friend and generation to generation. In the end, that's how our most impactful stories endure, by sharing them.

Brian Tallerico

CREDITS

Grandma: Sigourney Weaver
Mum: Felicity Jones
Conor: Lewis MacDougall
The Monster: Liam Neeson
Dad: Toby Kebbell
Origin: United States
Language: English
Released: 2017
Production: Belen Atienza; released by A Monster Calls, Apaches Entertainment, La Trini, Participant Media L.L.C., River Road Entertainment
Directed by: Juan Antonio Bayona
Written by: Patrick Ness
Cinematography by: Oscar Faura

Music by: Fernando Velazquez
Sound: Oriol Tarrago
Editing: Jaume Marti; Bernat Vilaplana
Costumes: Steven Noble
Production Design: Eugenio Caballero
MPAA rating: PG-13
Running time: 108 minutes

REVIEWS

Bowen, Chuck. *Slant Magazine*. December 20, 2016.
Debruge, Peter. *Variety*. September 11, 2016.
Fuller, Graham. *Screen International*. September 10, 2016.
Genzlinger, Neil. *New York Times*. December 22, 2016.
Hertz, Barry. *The Globe and Mail*. January 5, 2017.
Kenny, Glenn. *RogerEbert.com*. December 22, 2016.
Kohn, Eric. *IndieWire*. September 10, 2016.
Roeper, Richard. *Chicago Sun-Times*. January 5, 2017.
Smith, Nigel M. *The Guardian*. September 11, 2016.
Stewart, Sara. *New York Post*. December 21, 2016.

QUOTES

The Monster: "Stories are wild animals ... if you let them loose, who knows what havoc they may wreak."

TRIVIA

The host of the ScreenJunkies Show, Hal Rudnick, claims he openly cried in a Chipotle thinking about this movie.

MOONLIGHT

This is the story of a lifetime.
—Movie tagline

Box Office: $22.1 Million

The location and cultivation of compassion for others with life experiences and circumstances different than your own is not the only measure of artistic achievement, but it is a valid one, and in this regard as well as others the sensitive, finely calibrated *Moonlight* is an overwhelming success.

Adapted by director Barry Jenkins from playwright Tarell Alvin McCraney's stage play *In Moonlight Black Boys Look Blue*, the film is a small, evocatively tender story writ large, tracking the difficult life of a young African-American grappling with questions of sexual identity. By investing in his lead character's humanity in non-flashy fashion, Jenkins locates a special grace—in the process delivering a ruminative, melancholic treatise about modern American masculinity and life on the margins.

After premiering at the Telluride Film Festival on September 2, distributor A24 Films used other festival presentations to build critical buzz and audience anticipation for a platform release strategy that would push *Moonlight* into eight-figure theatrical grosses and, eventually, a clutch of Academy Award nominations.

Set predominantly in Miami, *Moonlight* unfolds in three chapters over the course of roughly 16 years, focusing on Chiron (Alex Hibbert), a nine-year-old kid dubbed "Little" for his diminutive size and withdrawn personality. Chiron has a friend, Kevin (Jaden Piner), but mostly leads a fairly unmoored existence; his home life with his mother Paula (Naomie Harris) is particularly chaotic. After Chiron crosses paths with drug dealer Juan (Mahershala Ali), he begins to seek out both physical and psychological escape with Juan and his girlfriend, Teresa (Janelle Monáe). A surrogate father figure, Juan tries to instill lessons of black pride in Chiron ("We were first on this Earth, we're everywhere," he tells him), and even teaches him how to swim, but when Chiron finds out that Juan is selling drugs to his mother, whom he loathes for her unpredictability, he leaves, effectively severing the relationship.

The film's second chapter chronicles Chiron as a teenager (Ashton Sanders), during which his friendship with Kevin (Jharrel Jerome) becomes more complicated. Bullied by a classmate, Chiron is increasingly certain of his attraction to other boys—including his best friend. One night at the beach, while smoking a joint with Kevin, the pair kiss, and Kevin gives Chiron a handjob. Later, at school, a bully pressures Kevin into punching Chiron—an act which has devastating consequences.

In *Moonlight*'s third chapter, Chiron (Trevante Rhodes) has moved to Atlanta, and become a successful drug dealer. After an out-of-the-blue phone call from Kevin (André Holland), now a short-order cook, Chiron eventually travels back home to Miami to visit him. At the Cuban restaurant where he works, Kevin greets Chiron warmly, and prepares him an off-the-menu meal. They make small talk, avoiding the painful subject of their past and how and why they lost touch, until they no longer can.

Watching *Moonlight* for a second time, or merely pondering it in the context of the brutal 2016 presidential campaign and Donald Trump's Electoral College victory, it is hard not to find extra relevance and poignancy in this portrait of a marginalized "double minority" (in this case a person of color and a homosexual). It is not so much that Chiron is specifically failed by institutions as it is that the movie serves up a heartrending portrait of emotional and psychological unsettledness, and in doing so *Moonlight* takes on additional layers and levels of meaning. The fact that six different young actors portray its two central characters only further heightens its achievement and connection.

Jenkins' gifts as a director were readily apparent in his first narrative feature—so much so that it raises uncomfortable and troubling systemic questions about why it took so long for him to be able to marshal the resources for a follow-up. A shoe-gazing, San Francisco-set romance marked by wonderful naturalistic performances and a commitment to quotidian beauty, tenderness and hope, *Medicine for Melancholy* (2009) is the type of film—funny but socio-politically inquisitive, lightly sentimental without tipping over into treacle, and marked by a winning off-screen underdog story since it was made for only $15,000—that feels like it would be a Sundance Festival-minted hit had it been made by a Caucasian auteur instead of an African-American writer-director.

Though not as leavened with levity as its predecessor, *Moonlight* shares that film's fierce evocation of place; both movies are about the inner struggles of its characters as well as the complicated relationship(s) they have with the cities in which they live. Jenkins and Mc-Craney each grew up in public housing projects in Miami, and had mothers who struggled with drug addiction, but their simpatico relationship is evidenced in more than mere biography. There is an awareness and questioning of minority status and identity politics (a particularly big part of *Medicine for Melancholy*), as well as an uncommon overall sensitivity to character—even if, in both conversation and conflict, *Moonlight* rarely shifts into higher than third gear. It is instead a film largely about small moments.

Jenkins also paints a complex portrait of the role that drugs play in disadvantaged communities. Chiron is a drug dealer, true, but *Moonlight* is not a movie invested in turf wars or other violent, outwardly manifested conflict that so typically marks movies with these types of characters. Instead, *Moonlight* looks inward, and connects drugs to the escape they can provide, both for users (an early customer of Juan's, and later Chiron's mother) as well as those hedged in and shut out from other economic opportunities in society.

In his slow, careful pacing, Jenkins imbues his film with a carefully manicured, poetic stillness that belies the more hard-edged narrative components that might appear in a simple log-line. This exactitude is most prevalent in the script and Nat Sanders and Joi McMillon's skillful editing, but extends to *Moonlight*'s other technical elements as well. Working in widescreen CinemaScope, Jenkins and cinematographer James Laxton devise distinct looks and color palettes for each chapter, with the moody greenish-blue of its middle passage and the darker, almost purple tones of its finale contributing

to the film's fervent impressionism. Composer Nicholas Britell's beautiful, largely string-oriented classical score, processed to slow it down a few octaves, similarly abets a swelling plaintive feeling.

The film's performances are what one might characterize as "sneaky" good, as just when one is getting caught up in the work of a particular actor and feeling rooted, they are traded out for other iterations of the characters. They fit together like puzzle pieces or squares of a large quilt, though, all part of Jenkins' collagist sensibility. It is especially remarkable, then, to learn that Jenkins shot with Hibbert, Sanders, and Rhodes in two-week segments, and did not have the three meet with one another prior to production, wanting to avoid any sort of imitations or mimicry. They are the anchors of this film, though Ali and Harris also deliver fine performances—the former subtle and the latter more volatile, informed by Paula's embittered self-centeredness.

Eschewing overly plotted drama in favor of a wounded soulfulness, *Moonlight* is not a movie with the originality of a big narrative hook. But in a world, cinematic and otherwise, filled with so much bombast, its simplicity, emotional forthrightness, and even slight preciousness is not only refreshing but engaging. "At some point you have to decide for yourself who you're going to be," Juan tells Chiron early in the film. "You can't let anybody else make that decision for you." The quiet, swallowed heartbreak of *Moonlight* lies in how easily that important message is stamped out by poverty and close-mindedness. The hope of the film is found in its embrace of the maxim that one is never too old to change.

Brent Simon

CREDITS

Juan: Mahershala Ali
Terrence: Shariff Earp
Little: Alex Hibbert
Chiron: Ashton Sanders
Black: Trevante Rhodes
Paula: Naomie Harris
Origin: United States
Language: English
Released: 2016
Production: Dede Gardner, Jeremy Kleiner, Adele Romanski; released by A24, Plan B Entertainment
Directed by: Barry Jenkins
Written by: Barry Jenkins
Cinematography by: James Laxton
Music by: Nicholas Britell

Sound: Joshua Adeniji
Music Supervisor: Marguerite Phillips
Editing: Joi McMillon; Nat Sanders
Art Direction: Mabel Barba
Costumes: Caroline Eselin
Production Design: Hannah Beachler
MPAA rating: R
Running time: 111 minutes

REVIEWS

Burr, Ty. *Boston Globe.* November 2, 2016.
Debruge, Peter. *Variety.* July 1, 2016.
Graham, Adam. *Detroit News.* September 2, 2016.
Marks, Scott. *San Diego Reader.* November 3, 2016.
Rainer, Peter. *Christian Science Monitor.* October 28, 2016.
Scott, A.O. *New York Times.* November 11, 2016.
Smith, Michael. *Tulsa World.* November 17, 2016.
Tallerico, Brian. *RogerEbert.com.* September 13, 2016.
Wilson, Calvin. *St. Louis Post-Dispatch.* November 10, 2016.
Washington, Julie. *Cleveland Plain Dealer.* November 10, 2016.

QUOTES

Paula: "You ain't got to love me, but you gonna know that I love you."

TRIVIA

Like the character Chiron's mother, director Barry Jenkins' mother also suffered from addiction.

AWARDS

Oscars 2016: Actor—Supporting (Ali), Adapt. Screenplay, Film
Golden Globes 2017: Film—Drama
Ind. Spirit 2017: Cinematog., Director (Jenkins), Film, Film Editing, Screenplay
Screen Actors Guild 2016: Actor—Supporting (Ali)
Writers Guild 2016: Orig. Screenplay
Nominations:
Oscars 2016: Actress—Supporting (Harris), Cinematog., Director (Jenkins), Film Editing, Orig. Score
British Acad. 2016: Actress—Supporting (Harris), Film, Orig. Screenplay
Directors Guild 2016: Director (Jenkins)
Golden Globes 2017: Actor—Supporting (Ali), Actress—Supporting (Harris), Director (Jenkins), Score, Screenplay
Screen Actors Guild 2016: Actress—Supporting (Harris), Cast

MORRIS FROM AMERICA

Nothing rhymes with Germany.
—Movie tagline

Box Office: $91,151

A tight shot of a young man, his baby face younger than he feels, listening to this particular hip-hop song for the first time. A few feet away in the apartment, his dad, nodding his head more emphatically. Clearly, this session constitutes both bonding and a lesson. The kid, 13-year-old Morris (Markees Christmas), thinks the beat is too slow. "It's minimal," his father, Curtis (Craig Robinson), says. "There's a difference." Eventually he sends his son to his room for saying the track is boring; after a few minutes of the men fiddling with their phones separately, Curtis un-grounds Morris so they can go out together.

This is the remarkable opening of *Morris From America*, so efficiently demonstrating several kinds of loneliness. Curtis, a widower, knows how to separate a pressing absence of intensity and the milder recognition of it, like his expectations for the world have down-shifted, and he is handling it. In an impressive dramatic turn from the usually comedic Robinson, Curtis comes off as a man who has lived and hurt and recovered, never, except in that first sequence, transposing his own struggles to his son. He is a great father, always demonstrating that to be a man is to be honest, vulnerable, and resilient, and it is a tribute to the performance that this comes through so clearly. In total, *Morris From America* often feels both over-plotted and under-plotted, flirting with excellence, and landing on a pretty good try. Which is often as much as teenagers can hope for in a coming-of-age story that (mostly) prefers truth over fantasy.

These New Yorkers have moved to Heidelberg, Germany, where there appear to be no other black people in sight. Curtis speaks decent-enough German, having impulsively surprised his late wife there after only knowing her for three months, eventually missing his flight and not booking a new one, the ultimate in romantic travel audibles. Morris takes lessons from Inka (Carla Juri), who, because of Morris' fondness for hot chocolate with one marshmallow, challenges his endearing efforts to come off as a current badass and future hip-hop star. "One marshmallow's a gangster move," he says, Christmas always keeping the character likable instead of obnoxious. That image is a curious one, though, when considering how the story develops into a small, white presence floating temporarily in a darker, unknown world.

That presence is Katrin (Lina Keller), who is 15 and intrigued by Morris, who she assumes should dance (he does not), play basketball (he does not), and have a big dick (he does not know what to say about that). After an ill-advised prank that makes it seem as if her kindness was a mask for cruelty, Katrin brings Morris to her house so he can use her boombox to play a cassette his dad gave him, and she can show that she is a friend, not a bully. When she asks who is rapping on the tape, a less imaginative film might have Morris lie to her, but he tells her it is his dad, unashamed. Later, after saying that he has nothing to prove to anyone at a talent show, he signs up in hopes of impressing Katrin, only to have his freestyle cut off almost immediately by people in charge. They seem to prefer the show consist of performances less graphic than teenage descriptions of threesomes. But it shows the good instincts of writer-director Chad Hartigan that the talent show is not a culmination in the story but a bump in a life that has no particular map from which to work. He also knows how to put a pulse into a party, with a clear idea of how it feels to be young, what that leads you to do and, especially in Katrin's simultaneous encouragement and disrespect, what it leads others to do to you.

The filmmaker is not always in such control, though. Inka is more of a storytelling convenience than a legitimate character, and the movie struggles to detail Curtis' point of view while it tracks Morris' affections for Katrin. (Plus, despite being a striking image every time it is used on screen, a shot of Morris and Katrin sharing earbuds to listen to the same song has been done before. A lot.) For every few moments that feel really specific, there is one that seems vague.

Morris remains a remarkably sweet character (when Katrin invites him out, he asks Inka to teach him how to say "Thank you for the invitation" in German), and the way he first dances with a pillow on which he has placed Katrin's sweater, before taking things to a more sexual place, unfolds exactly as it should for this nice, horny, uncertain teen boy. He has a good sense of self and not much idea what to do with that; one of the best scenes comes when Curtis scolds him for rapping about things he has not experienced, angry not about explicit content but about its falseness. "Until you know shit, you need to rap about how you don't know shit." That kind of humility is rare in rap and an important lesson from a man who is never overprotective, only a source of guidance and trust. He is so supportive, in fact, that Morris thinks he is not in trouble for leaving town and getting stranded without money or a cell phone. He is, of course.

But that is youth: doing something that feels right, not knowing or not caring about the chance that it will cause a problem, suffering from it, and bouncing back. That Morris, absolutely killing his first full public freestyle, gets a truly unforgettable experience along the way is nothing less than beautiful. He is a kid, a young man, a voice in development, sharing it with others for the first time, inspired by someone who will exist longer in his mind than his life. This earnestness-free search for

authenticity helps *Morris From America* emerge from convention with a smile and a sting.

Matt Pais

CREDITS

Morris Gentry: Markees Christmas
Curtis Gentry: Craig Robinson
Inka: Carla Juri
Sven: Patrick Güldenberg
Katrin: Lina Keller
Origin: United States
Language: English
Released: 2016
Production: Martin Heisler, Sara Murphy, Adele Romanski, Gabriele Simon; released by Beachside Films, INDI Film GmbH, Lichtblick Media, Südwestrundfunk
Directed by: Chad Hartigan
Written by: Chad Hartigan
Cinematography by: Sean McElwee
Music by: Keegan DeWitt
Sound: Marvin Keil
Music Supervisor: Ruth Ersfeld; Laura Katz
Editing: Anne Fabini
Costumes: Nana Kolbinger
Production Design: Babett Klimmeck
MPAA rating: R
Running time: 91 minutes

REVIEWS

Bailey, Jason. *Flavorwire.* May 3, 2016.
Chang, Justin. *Variety.* January 31, 2016.
Ebiri, Bilge. *New York Magazine (Vulture).* January 31, 2016.
Fragoso, Sam. *Playlist.* January 31, 2016.
Grierson, Tim. *Paste.* January 28, 2016.
Halligan, Fionnuala. *Screen International.* January 31, 2016.
Kohn, Eric. *IndieWire.* January 31, 2016.
Moylan, Brian. *Guardian.* January 31, 2016.
Raup, Jordan. *Film Stage.* January 31, 2016.
Suzanne-Mayer, Dominick. *Consequence of Sound.* January 31, 2016.

TRIVIA

Craig Robinson learned conversational German to play his character.

AWARDS

Nominations:
Ind. Spirit 2017: Actress—Supporting (Robinson)

MOTHER'S DAY

Come celebrate the mother of all holidays.
    —Movie tagline

Box Office: $32.5 Million

M is for the mawkish things it gave us,

O is for one-dimensionality,

T is for being oh-so-terribly humorless,

H is for being unfailingly hackneyed,

E is for its emphatic sense of emptiness,

R is for our regret resultantly!

Put them all together and they spell "MOTHER," as in that old tear-jerking tune heard as the film's closing credits rolled. However, such things—and more--also spelled trouble for *Mother's Day*'s prospects. Critical reaction to this deeply unaffecting ode to "everyone's first love" tended toward hatred, and was often more humorous than the film itself: a "crapfest " (The Chicago Sun-Times); "A treacly cavalcade of horror" (The Atlantic); "The worst thing Hollywood has done to mums since *Psycho*" (The Telegraph). Even one of its stars, Jennifer Aniston, seems compelled at one point to break character and express her mortified recognition that everyone involved is tarnishing the silver screen: "This is all so stupid!" she forlornly declares. "What am I doing? I feel like such an idiot!" Similar if not identical words of discontent and self-recrimination ran through the minds of many ticket buyers as *Mother's Day* so poorly sang the praises of our all-too-often unsung heroines.

Although shot in Atlanta, this production is far from a peach. *Mother's Day* was 81-year-old director Garry Marshall's third and final invitation to a crowded and contrived celebration that most who attended wished they had declined. (He died three months after the film's release.) Following his disheartening *Valentine's Day* (2010) and *New Year's Eve* (2011), expectations have steadily dropped like the Times Square ball in that last fete's finale. Marshall quipped that he opted to focus on this latest holiday because he thought it "would make a better movie than Arbor Day," and while moviegoers were thus spared the cinematic equivalent of Dutch Elm Disease, nothing flourishes here either, let alone yields enjoyable filmic fruit.

As expected, Marshall presents a medley of matriarchs. Sandy (Aniston) is a struggling divorced mom of two young boys (Brandon Spink and Caleb Brown) whose expectation of reunification with ex Henry (Timothy Olyphant) turns out instead to be an ego-eviscerating notification: he has opted for Tina (Shay Mitchell), a much newer model who is stunning enough to be of the runway-strutting variety. Struggling to avoid being stunning are mothers Jesse (Kate Hudson) and her sister Gabi (Sarah Chalke), in the sense that both the former's marriage to an Indian-American doctor (Aasif Mandvi) and the latter's same-sex partnership with Max (Carmen Esposito) have remained convolutedly kept

secrets in order to avoid incurring the wrath of their sure-to-be-horrified bigoted begetters Flo and Earl (Margo Martindale and Robert Pine). Newest mom and bar waitress Kristin (Britt Robertson) keeps refusing to marry baby daddy/bartender Zack (Jack Whitehall), even though he comes off as quite a stand-up guy (if not much of a standup comedian), fearing potential rejection as a result of having been given up for adoption. Kristin knows who her birth mom is, and many viewers quickly thought they did as well. Thus, the eventual face-to-face moment of reckoning that follows the revelation is only startling for career-concentrating Miranda (Julia Roberts), a Home Shopping Network luminary who ironically hawks crystal jewelry that reveals one's mood while a purposefully plastered smile that is also for public consumption helps to conceal lingering feelings of loss. (Roberts did not look out of this world in a wig reused from her outer space Helix segment of 1999's Notting Hill.) Mr. Mom Bradley (Jason Sudeikis) runs an apparatus-filled gym but finds himself ill-equipped to be all things to his daughters (Jessi Case and Ella Anderson) while still mired in mourning for his Marine wife a year after her death in combat. While she did not emerge unscathed, portrayer Jennifer Garner, appearing only in a brief, schmaltzy video postcard, consequently had the best chance of doing so after Marshall and company took heavy fire.

Garner's character is seen performing karaoke in a mess hall, and that first word was only one of the four-letter ones that came to mind as the 118 minutes of this *Mother's Day* ticked by all too slowly. While the film may be as well-intentioned as voluptuous Tina, nothing here is as pleasingly well-developed as she is. Characterizations are generally as bare-boned as that chomped-on fried chicken appendage hanging from the mouth of Pine's Earl, half of the film's cartoonish Lone Star stereotype couple geographically gifted here with what is assumed to be a constellation's-worth of pigeonholing prejudices. Some important things obviously need to finally get through the thick skulls atop these rednecks, and an apparent fear that viewers would be equally slow on the uptake has resulted in the glaring insertion of clunky and often superfluous exposition, some of it ludicrously and lousily dubbed. For example, Kristin shows great promise as a ventriloquist when she announces her "abandonment issues" onscreen without moving a single muscle of her mouth.

However, the jaws of many a fellow moviegoer could plainly be seen dropping at how lame it all was. Cinematographer Charles Minsky noted that he tried to "open up the movie" to help ensure that it would "feel like a feature film, not a television show," but the script largely remained confined to musty sitcom material. No one's sides ached from guffawing in theaters showing *Mother's Day*, but some did hurt from repeatedly leaning against arm rests to share disgruntled disbelief. Jesse's Indian mother-in-law says Flo's thoughtless joking "sounds racist—and funny!": were we supposed to think the same? There was certainly no chance of doubling over without comedic cause a la the inexplicable response garnered in the film by Zack's all-too-feeble attempts at being funny. In a different—but no less fervent—sense than this forever-proposing (purported) comic, viewers were continually disappointed in their own desire to become engaged, their hopes steadily deflated like one scene's backyard party apparatus that promised fun. There was precious little to be had here, and while the actors enthused that merry mensch Marshall provided them with a memorably high time onset, most moviegoers will only remember feeling low after their own experience.

The much-mentioned Mother's Day parade never materializes, but what does pass by onscreen is a poor procession indeed, including: the given name of a mixed-race child resultantly possessing more pigment than his Caucasian mom is Tanner; someone else's offspring slides out of a vehicular vagina/womb wagon float; an already-mortified dad desperately averts a painfully predictable PA system price check on the tampons he is dutifully purchasing for his daughter; said father chooses to sing and bust a move with his children to a version of "The Humpty Dance" that mercifully does not mention gettin' busy in a Burger King bathroom or other lascivious hijinks, then has a great fall and busts a leg; and saccharine wisdom is dispensed by a clown, comparing his seemingly bottomless pocket that is endlessly stuffed with scarves to the bottomless, endless love of a mother for her children. Only the pocket is intriguingly deep. Bringing up the rear are all-too-tidy resolutions, especially longstanding narrowmindedness broadened in mere minutes, that were expected to make joyous teardrops fall all around. Instead, many in attendance rained on this parade.

Still, it was amazingly not a washout, as this $25-million film grossed more than $40 million worldwide. Late in the film, Miranda wants her viewers to listen up because Kristin has "something very special she'd like to say," and everyone responsible for *Mother's Day* presumably aimed to do the same. Unfortunately, the material devised to deliver a universally relatable message about the bond between children and the tireless, sometimes tiresome, but always very human beings who gave birth to them is itself lamentably barren. Producer Mike Karz fondly recalled brainstorming sessions in which "we sat around with the writers and threw out ideas." If only in a different sense they had.

David L. Boxerbaum

CREDITS

Sandy: Jennifer Aniston
Henry: Timothy Olyphant
Tina: Shay Mitchell
Mikey: Caleb Brown
Peter: Brandon Spink
Miranda Collins: Julia Roberts
Jesse: Kate Hudson
Origin: United States
Language: English
Released: 2016
Production: Brandt Andersen, Howard Burd, Daniel Diamond, Mark DiSalle, Mike Karz, Wayne Allan Rice; released by Open Road Films, Rice Films
Directed by: Garry Marshall
Written by: Anya Kochoff; Matthew Walker; Tom Hines
Cinematography by: Charles Minsky
Music by: John Debney
Sound: Terry Rodman
Music Supervisor: Julianne Jordan
Editing: Bruce Green; Robert Malina
Costumes: Marilyn Vance; Beverley Woods
Production Design: Missy Stewart
MPAA rating: PG-13
Running time: 118 minutes

REVIEWS

Barker, Andrew. *Variety.* April 28, 2016.
Chaney, Jen. *Washington Post.* April 28, 2016.
Chang, Justin. *Los Angeles Times.* April 28, 2016.
Collin, Robbie. *Telegraph.* June 9, 2016.
Frosch, Jon. *Hollywood Reporter.* April 28, 2016.
Highfill, Samantha. *Entertainment Weekly.* April 28, 2016.
Hoffman, Jordan. *Guardian.* April 28, 2016.
Kenny, Glenn. *New York Times.* April 28, 2016.
Keough, Peter. *Boston Globe.* April 28, 2016.
Morgenstern, Joe. *Wall Street Journal.* April 28, 2016.

QUOTES

Kristin: "I have abandonment issues!"

TRIVIA

This was director Garry Marshall's final film; he passed away shortly after the movie's release.

AWARDS

Nominations:

Golden Raspberries 2016: Worst Actress (Roberts), Worst Support. Actress (Hudson)

MOUNTAINS MAY DEPART

(Shan he gu ren)

Box Office: $82,913

Jia Zhang-ke is undeniably a master of cinematic language, but that language is, pointedly, not English. *Mountains May Depart* is typical of Jia's work in many ways. It is intimate in scale but epic in theme and scope. Its classic melodrama is played with touching subtlety, for the most part, and some degree of formal inventiveness, and it is all underscored with a dry wit. While his work is generally more self-contained, the ultimate failure of *Moutains May Depart* is not in conception, but in execution. Jia seems perfectly capable of handling the scope of his decades-long tale, but falters in some of the specifics in the third and final section. It's a thoughtful and sometimes beautiful work, but it's inconsistent. It doesn't have the formal cohesion and allegorical sharpness of his masterpiece, *The World* (2005), and it lacks the startling jolt of energy supplied by the reflexive genre elements in his previous film, the angry, violent *A Touch of Sin* (2014).

Like much of Jia's work, *Mountains May Depart* is set, initially, in his hometown of Fenyang. The film is split into three sections. The first takes place in 1999, and is presented in boxy Academy aspect ratio, reportedly chosen because it matched video party footage that Jia and his longtime cinematographer Yu Lik Wai shot at the time, which Jia seamlessly weaves into the film. The second section takes place in 2014, and here Jia expands to standard widescreen format. The third section, set in 2024 Perth, is shot in a very sleek wider format. The expanding palette both suggests both a wider, international world opening up to modern-day China, and the essential emptiness of that rootless life, as characters are dwarfed by the cold, sterile environments around them, sharply contrasting from the more primitive, homey charm of the opening sequence.

The film opens with a celebratory sequence, featuring Tao (Jia's wife and frequent collaborator, Zhao Tao) dancing joyously with a group of friends to the strains of the Pet Shop Boys' cover of the Village People's "Go West." The tune's understated irony suits the film's themes well, and Jia returns to it over the course of the film. His repetitive use of music here, in fact, reminds one of Hong Kong master Wong Kar-Wai's, as Jia also repeatedly uses Sally Yeh's plaintive Cantonese pop ballad, "Take Care," which takes on an important emotional component that runs throughout Jisheng's life, and throughout the film.

After the dance sequence, we see Tao on the streets of Fenyang, where she's asked about performing at a

New Year's party. It's the dawn of a new millennium, and the Chinese village is in a celebratory mood. The frame may be closed in, but there's a sense of something momentous in the air. This first segment begins with hopefulness and optimism, as Tao meets with her male friends, Liangzi (Liang Jin Dong), seemingly a salt-of-the-earth type who works in the local mine, and the slightly callow, successful Jinsheng (Zhang Yi), whom Liangzi jokingly calls "Boss Zhang." That joke isn't funny anymore as the rivalry between the two for Tao's affections becomes more overt. Jinsheng takes the pair for a spin in his late-model Volkswagen, and they're appropriately impressed, but he really wants Tao to himself. When his fortunate financial circumstances present the opportunity to buy the failing mine where Liangzi works, he offers to promote Liangzi if he'll clear his way with Tao, but when Liangzi angrily rejects his offer, Jinsheng fires him. The seemingly oblivious Tao, having difficulty choosing between her country's taciturn past, represented by Liangzi, and its internationally expanding capitalist future, represented by Jinsheng, wants everyone to remain friends, but when Jinsheng pushes to her make a choice, she agrees to marry him. When she attempts to deliver a wedding invitation to her longtime friend, Liangzi, he petulantly storms out, abandoning his home in his eagerness to rid himself of her.

Jia's class-based conflict might come off as pedantic (and okay, maybe it does a little) but that feeling is ameliorated by the richness of the performances and the depth of these characters. Tao's reasons for choosing Jinsheng over Liangzi are fairly inscrutable, but she doesn't seem to be in thrall to his expanding wealth, or enticed by the promise of, say, international travel. She may just find him more fun than the more introspective Liangzi. But there's a surprisingly rewarding emotional complexity to this section, and to the dourer section that follows.

2014 finds our trio in less happy circumstances. Jinsheng and Tao have a seven-year-old son (Rong Zishan), whom he's named Dollar, but they're divorced, and the wealthy Jinsheng, who has moved to Shanghai with his new wife, has full custody of the boy. The news gets worse. Liangzi, suffering from lung disease from his years in the mine, and without the means to get the medical care he needs, reluctantly returns to Fenyang with his new wife and child, in hopes of convincing Tao to lend him the money he needs. In a heartbreaking scene, they break into his old house, where he finds the ancient wedding invitation still lying on the counter, covered in dust.

For her part, Tao is now wealthy and runs a local gas station, but she's alone, and clearly questioning the choices she's made. When her elderly father unexpectedly dies, in another perfectly pitched and moving scene, she sends for Dollar, so that he can attend his grandfather's funeral. It's clear that he doesn't know his mother, and she's disappointed in the effects that his parents' cosmopolitan lifestyle has had on him. Still, the barest hint of a connection is made, in part over that Sally Yeh song. She overhears Dollar video-chatting with his stepmother, and learns that they plan to move to Australia. Rather than fight Jinsheng, she allows him to take Dollar away, presumably to a better life.

Jia's cinema is thoughtful and deliberately paced. At their best, his films gradually develop a surprising cumulative emotional and intellectual power, but their spell is a delicate one, and *Mountains May Depart* falters in the third section, set in Australia, partly because Jia chooses to shoot much of it in English, and neither the dialogue, nor Dong Zijian's performance as the alienated teen Dollar feel true. It's not that Dong's a bad actor, but his performance suffers because he's simply not convincing as a kid who grew up speaking English. Any subtlety to Zhang Yi's performance also goes out the window here, as his character has degenerated into a cliché of a bitter old capitalist, clinging to his collection of assault weapons (which, per the film, Australia has made legal again for some reason), his old language, and a perverse notion of personal freedom. Dollar is trapped, listless, rudderless, and longing for a connection to his native culture that he can't consciously remember. It is set in an antiseptically designed future Perth, where aside from some minor developments in electronics, and Jinsheng's absurd new mustache, not much seems to have changed in the world.

Dollar's aged but still vital Chinese teacher, Mia, played by Taiwanese film legend Sylvia Chan, offers him both a glimpse of the cosmopolitan, globalist existence he seems destined for, and a subconscious reminder of Tao, the mother he barely recalls. A contentious meeting between Dollar, Jinsheng, and Mia doesn't resonate the way it should. Mia and Dollar's relationship is fraught and unsettling, as it should be, but their story never quite feels genuine, and the film's power to engage its audience is further hampered by the absence of Tao, easily the film's most compelling character, for most of its final section. *Mountains May Depart* is a worthwhile addition to Jia's oeuvre, but it doesn't reach the heights of the director's best work.

Josh Ralske

CREDITS

Tao: Tao Zhao
Zhang Jinsheng: Yi Zhang
Liangzi: Jing Dong Liang
Dollar: Zijian Dong
Mia: Sylvia Chang

Origin: United States
Language: Chinese, Mandarin Chinese, English
Released: 2016
Production: Shozo Ichiyama, Nathanael Karmitz, Shiyu Liu, Zhong-lun Ren, Zhangke Jia; released by Office Kitano, arte France Cinema
Directed by: Zhangke Jia
Written by: Zhangke Jia
Cinematography by: Nelson Lik-wai Yu
Music by: Yoshihiro Hanno
Editing: Matthieu Laclau
MPAA rating: Unrated
Running time: 131 minutes

REVIEWS

Barsanti, Chris. *PopMatters*. February 12, 2016.
Burr, Ty. *The Boston Globe*. May 12, 2016.
Cheshire, Godfrey. *RogerEbert.com*. February 12, 2016.
Cole, Blake. *Slant*. September 29, 2015.
Dargis, Manohla. *New York Times*. February 11, 2016.
Foundas, Scott. *Variety*. May 24, 2015.
Lattimer, James. *The House Next Door*. May 23, 2015.
Rainer, Peter. *Christian Science Monitor*.
Tobias, Scott. *Village Voice*. February 9, 2016.
Vishnevetsky, Ignatov. *The A.V. Club*. February 11, 2016.

QUOTES

Mia: "The hardest thing about love is caring."

TRIVIA

Some sequences used in the 1999 segment were filmed in 2001.

MR. RIGHT

They make a killer couple.
—Movie tagline

Box Office: $34,694

Mr. Right is the kind of action-based romantic comedy that tries to incorporate so many elements of its two chosen genres, but fails miserably at connecting them to anything worthwhile. It goes out of its way to please both the women in the audience who paid good money to see a rom-com and the men in the audience who would rather skip the first half of the film and get right to the plot about the hitman. It must have seemed like a sure thing during production to cross-pollinate two commercially successful genres that would endear both target audience genders. The formula has worked in the past with such films as *Grosse Pointe Blank* (1998) and *Mr. & Mrs. Smith* (2005), to name just a couple. But clearly nobody involved in the production of *Mr. Right* went beyond the concept to go a little further in exploring their protagonists' quirks or inner conflicts.

They certainly have quirks, but they are a shallow pair. Martha (Anna Kendrick) gets introduced in the film as a child, who, when she is asked what she wants to be when she grows up, answers with "I'm a T-rex!" Flash-forward to present day and she still seems pretty immature as an adult. The film opens in typical rom-com fashion in which the main character finds her boyfriend cheating on her. She gets overly drunk with some friends and heads to a convenient store where she has the typical meet-cute with a mysterious man (Sam Rockwell) in which a mishap between them causes many boxes of condoms to come flying off the shelves. After some forced banter between the two, the man immediately asks her out on a date and she accepts.

The man, named Francis, remains a mystery to her, but he somehow charms her enough to keep seeing him. He gets introduced as a hitman who likes to wear a red clown nose just before he kills. The FBI has been on his trail for many years. The man in charge of the operation, Reynolds (Tim Roth), doesn't want to do a straightforward attack on him for fear of too many civilian casualties. He is that violent and that quick. There are also a group of thugs after Francis for killing one of their men who hired him to kill someone, but he killed the guy who hired him instead, which is typical of his behavior. Martha and Francis have a mostly steady relationship in which they play dangerous knife-throwing games. Eventually, of course, Martha learns of his double life and she gets caught up in the crossfire of all these men who are after him.

The main problem with the film is the casting of two very likeable actors who have no chemistry at all. Rockwell tries to come off as suave and irresistible, but instead comes off as charmless and hard to root for. He has never been able to pull off the leading man type of performance that makes women swoon or the men envious. His strength has always been in playing the outsider roles, the troubled and maybe quirky loners who cannot get out of the way of their own behavior. He gave a very funny and likeable performance in *The Way, Way Back* (2013) and it seems like he is trying to tap into that once again, but the material never suits him and he is never able to rise above it. His character comes off as a one-dimensional, smart-alecky killer with no qualms about what he does.

Kendrick has a different kind of problem. She can do the leading lady role and she can portray a convincing troubled soul, but she has been written into being an erratic, flighty caricature of someone who has no direction in life, no job to speak of, and no wants or needs other than to be someone's other half. The prologue that introduces her being a bit crazed and unpredictable serves nothing for her character other than to provide her with a lame punchline at the end of the film. She does the best she can with the banter that she has been given, but she and Rockwell look as though they want to break free of it and explore.

It would be bad enough to see these two trapped in a lame romantic comedy, but they are also victims of a pedestrian action film as well. *Mr. Right* never borrows from the best, but instead regurgitates all the stale action films that came before it as well. The slow motion shots that interrupt the action only make them that much more noticeable as being weak. The violence never escalates beyond excessive bullet wounds or grabbing someone's hand who is holding a gun and using it to kill someone else. The plot involving the thugs exists only so that there can be more violence in the third act. Roth's character has enough going on (certainly more than the two leads) that he could have made the third act entirely his own, but the script will not have it.

Mr. Right has the feel of being made by a committee of people who know all the modern day movie conventions, but have no clue how to go beyond them. Director Paco Cabezas clearly enjoys working off the screenplay by Max Landis, but the whole project feels like everyone taking the easy route toward a paycheck. The best that can be said about the endeavor is that it came and went quietly, so nobody had to fail on a grand scale and the title and poster art are just bland enough so as to go unnoticed by people looking for something to stream at home. But Rockwell and Kendrick have too much talent to warrant such a fate. They probably had a good enough time making the film and working with each other, but strangely enough, their good time does not make it any easier or fun to watch it.

Collin Souter

CREDITS

Mr. Right/Francis: Sam Rockwell
Martha McKay: Anna Kendrick
Hopper/Reynolds: Tim Roth
Von Cartigan: James Ransone
Richard Cartigan: Anson Mount
Origin: United States
Language: English
Released: 2016
Production: Bradley Gallo, Michael A. Helfant, Rick Jacobs, Lawrence Mattis; released by Circle of Confusion
Directed by: Paco Cabezas

Written by: Max Landis
Cinematography by: Daniel Aranyo
Music by: Aaron Zigman
Music Supervisor: Maureen Crowe; David A. Helfant
Editing: Tom Wilson
Costumes: Jillian Kreiner
Production Design: Mara Lepere-Schloop
MPAA rating: R
Running time: 90 minutes

REVIEWS

Braun, Liz. *Toronto Sun*. May 26, 2016.
Grozdanovic, Nikola. *Playlist*. September 18, 2015.
Jones, Oliver. *New York Observer*. April 26, 2016.
Lickona, Matthew. *San Diego Reader*. April 7, 2016.
MacDonald, Moira. *Seattle Times*. April 7, 2016.
Murray, Noel. *The A.V. Club*. April 7, 2016.
Padua, Pat. *Washington Post*. April 7, 2016.
Scherstuhl, Alan. *Village Voice*. April 8, 2016.
Seitz, Matt Zoller. *RogerEbert.com*. April 11, 2016.
Whitty, Stephen. *Newark Star-Ledger*. April 7, 2016.

QUOTES

Martha McKay: "'Cause humans just wanna put a name on something to make it feel safe, but really, what is a dinosaur other than a dragon?"

TRIVIA

Paco, who was thrown under the bridge by Johnny Moon, is Paco Cabezas, the director of this film.

MY BIG FAT GREEK WEDDING 2

People change. Greeks don't.
　—Movie tagline

Box Office: $59.7 Million

It was Marcus Aurelius (or Hannibal Lecter) who said that to analyze anything, one should ask, "What is this, fundamentally? What is its nature and substance, its reason for being?"

And so, viewers of *My Big Fat Greek Wedding 2* may ask why in the world was this film made? And why is its mediocracy—in fact, its very existence—so irritating?

The original *My Big Fat Greek Wedding* (like its sequel) was written by Nia Vardalos based on her stand-up comedy about her own oversized Greek family. Vardalos also starred as Toula Portokalos, a single 30-something whose life (both love- and otherwise) is stifled by her loving but loudly overbearing extended family.

When it arrived late in the middle of 2002, at first in a modest number of theaters then spreading, the sitcom-ish rom-com struck a chord with audiences—perhaps in part because it used a minority subculture to poke gentle "see, we're all the same" fun at family commonalities, and perhaps in part because in the wake of the 9-11 terrorist attacks, moviegoers were happy to embrace simple, familiar fam-com warmth.

And embrace it they did, to the sleeper-hit tune of $370 million at the worldwide box office against a $5 million budget, making *My Big Fat Greek Wedding* one of the most financially successful films in history. (Vardalos also napped an Oscar nomination for her original screenplay and went on to spin the film's success and her family tales into a short-lived sitcom.)

In the 14 years since, however, *My Big Fat Greek Wedding* has become primarily a cinematic footnote. A nice, amusing, money-maker that people once liked then promptly forgot about. It is hard to imagine a significant cadre of *MBFGW* hardcore fans dreaming of a sequel for over a decade. But somewhere someone on the production side convinced themselves that lightning could strike twice. And when a creative person hits that much unexpected success with one project and is unable to follow it up with anything to its equal, it is easy to understand their desire to go back to the ouzo well. Ultimately, this sequel seems to exist because its film-makers ran out of ways to say "no" to themselves.

So here is *My Big Fat Greek Wedding 2* with most of the original's cast returning (including John Corbett as Toula's husband, having a soft-focus dull-off with Vardalos; Michael Constantine and Lainie Kazan as her parents; and MVP Andrea Martin as her life-loving, camera-mugging aunt). Also returning are the same broad face-pulling slapstick, kid-safe winks about sex, and most of the cute-but-weak jokes about Windex, ouzo and "opa!" and the Greek etymology of all words. And, of course, weddings, marriage, and family. And more about family. And still more about family.

The *Greek Wedding* films obsess over family in the most pandering manner possible, usually acting as if just saying "family" a lot (or playing songs with "family" in their lyrics) counts as talking about it. Obviously these movies are not intended to be complicated, naturalistic probes into honest family dynamics, but instead *Greek Wedding 2*, like its predecessor, pretends to throw heavy "family problems" in front of its characters: Toula and Ian face an empty nest and a stale relationship when their daughter, played by Elena Kampouris, heads off to college while Toulas parents undergo a trumped-up, superficial marital crisis in their sunset years. Along the way, numerous contrived subplots spring up randomly, each hijacking the screen for a few minutes. But after batting its narrative conflicts around for a bit, the script seems to tire of them, quickly resolving each with a short, shallow heart-felt speech and a pop song montage and moving on.

Most egregious is a tossed-off, after-thought bit about one of Toula's relatives being a closeted homosexual. In the course of two scenes and maybe three minutes of screen time, they fret about it for a few seconds, then eventually tell their family, and everyone is completely accepting and has a laugh and some ouzo and all is fine. That is how all the film's conflicts, big and small, are resolved: Someone worries about something until suddenly they decide to no longer worry, and everyone hugs and smiles and "The end."

To be fair, perhaps Vardalos' feel-good intent is to be aspirational—maybe this is not how real families deal (or do not) with complicated interpersonal problems, but it would be nice if they did. Its string of one-note problem-solving platitudes aside, there is nothing aggressively awful about this film. (Though Vardalos is the driving creative force, the film is directed by Kirk Jones, whose primary task is getting all the numerous family members in frame.) But while it shares so much of the first film's jokes and themes, the only thing consistent about *My Big Fat Greek Wedding 2* is how unfocused, uninspired, and oddly impersonal it feels. (Not to mention mostly unfunny, except at the most bland-common-denominator level of pleasant smiles.

Usually when evaluating a creative work, it is not hard to tell if its failings are a result of laziness, contempt, or ineptitude. But it is hard to pin down which of those sins did in *My Big Fat Greek Wedding 2*. It's not just that its spin-the-wheel plot feels off—its entire reason for being is unclear. If the original film was driven by Vardalos' expression of her familial frustrations and affections, its sequel inoffensively serving up what she thought people liked about the first film. It feels wrapped in a listless desperation, constantly chasing after some vague idea of itself—as if it just showed up in the theater and is doing its best to fake knowing why it is here.

Released in March, *My Big Fat Greek Wedding 2* bombed with both audiences and critics, earning less than a quarter of its predecessor's worldwide box office despite a budget more than three times that of the original.

Locke Peterseim

CREDITS
Toula: Nia Vardalos
Ian: John Corbett
Nick: Louis Mandylor
Anna: Rita Wilson

Panos: Mark Margolis
Origin: Canada, United States
Language: English
Released: 2016
Production: Gary Goetzman, Tom Hanks, Nia Vardalos, Rita Wilson; Gold Circle Films, HBO Films; released by Universal Pictures Inc.
Directed by: Kirk Jones
Written by: Nia Vardalos
Cinematography by: Jim Denault
Music by: Christopher Lennertz
Sound: Martyn Zub
Music Supervisor: Deva Anderson
Editing: Mark Czyzewski
Costumes: Gersha Phillips
Production Design: Gregory P. Keen
MPAA rating: PG-13
Running time: 94 minutes

REVIEWS

Catsoulis, Jeannette. *New York Times*. March 24, 2016.
Ebiri, Bilge. *Village Voice*. March 22, 2016.
Ehrlich, David. *Slate*. March 24, 2016.
Hassenger, Jesse. *Onion A.V. Club*. March 23, 2016.
Keegan, Rebecca. *Los Angeles Times*. March 24, 2016.
LaSalle, Mick. *San Francisco Chronicle*. March 24, 2016.
Macdonald, Moira. *Seattle Times*. March 24, 2016.
Merry, Stephanie. *Washington Post*. March 24, 2016.
Russo, Tom. *Boston Globe*. March 24, 2016.
Taylor, Kate. *The Globe and Mail*. March 24, 2016.

QUOTES

Aunt Voula: "Stop trying to fix everything. You baby your parents because you can't parent your baby no more."

TRIVIA

The movie was filmed in Toronto, Canada's Greektown area.

MY BLIND BROTHER

Romantically challenged.
—Movie tagline

There are multiple ways that *My Blind Brother* could have strayed. There are flashes of those ways throughout the film, such as obvious jokes about blindness or the overtly situational humor of some scenes. And yet, in her debut feature, writer/director Sophie Goodhart mostly avoids the obvious and clearly would not dream of engaging in the distasteful. As broad as the overarching scenario may be, the filmmaker has made a film that

294

is first and foremost about characters. The situations are secondary to these people and complementary to their predicaments.

It has something akin to a sitcom setup: A man falls for a woman, only to see her end up dating his brother. Goodhart does not simply leave it there, though. There is a clear understanding of what drives these characters, and it is what each has to offer the other that provides the conflict—not an assortment of external and forced-upon obstacles. Most of those motives are shallow, and two of these characters are unrepentantly lazy, while the third is an unrepentant jerk. These, though, are not necessarily flaws in Goodhart's eyes. She treats their issues with respect, even though they might not always deserve it. In two cases, that respect is more than the characters give themselves.

Bill (Nick Kroll) is in a difficult situation. His brother Robbie (Adam Scott) is blind after a childhood accident, and while Robbie has become a local hero for the way he has overcome his handicap, Bill has not amounted to much of anything in comparison. He manages a print shop. He wishes he could watch television all day.

Robbie runs marathons and participates in other physical activities in order to raise money for charity. Bill is always at his brother's side during training and the actual event, yet he goes unacknowledged by Robbie. After a marathon that opens the film, Robbie gives a speech to the adoring crowd. He seems ready to thank his brother—pointing out how grateful he is for the person who has been next to him, talking in his ear, for the entire process. Bill looks on expectantly, and then Robbie thanks God. One suspects the build-up and the sudden twist might be an intentional slight against Bill.

Robbie is the kind of person to do such a thing and to do it in such a passive-aggressive way. One of Goodhart's more daring choices in the film is to make Robbie—who, by way of his condition, would seem to be the most sympathetic presence within the film—into the most overtly unsympathetic character here. He is a show-off, an egotist, a sexist, and, in general, a jerk. His charity work is not for any cause except himself. Robbie has videos of his appearances on the news, and he prides himself on his minor celebrity. Scott's performance relies too much on these negative qualities, which slightly undermines the eventual and rather sudden sympathy Goodhart attempts to elicit for the character during the climactic swim. (The revelation of how Robbie became blind, which is hinted at earlier in the film, comes too late.)

He is, in turn, a perfect foil for Bill, who possesses no career or personal aspirations of any kind. The only flash of him having ambition arrives with Rose (Jenny Slate), whom he meets at a bar after the marathon. They get along well together after a few drinks and return to the house where Bill lives with Robbie. The next morning, he jokes about getting her phone number, but she makes it clear that she is finished with him. Shortly thereafter, Rose starts helping Robbie to train for yet another physical endurance challenge for charity: swimming across a local lake. After a misunderstanding involving some whipped cream on Robbie's sleeve, Rose starts to date him. A confused Bill tries to undermine the relationship and to win Rose's affections without hurting his brother's feelings.

Rose's flaw is a co-dependent personality. Her most recent boyfriend was killed after being hit by a bus—while chasing her after she ended their relationship. For her, the incident has only solidified her feelings about relationships. She prevents herself from starting something with Bill, but in her new mindset of wanting to help others, Rose falls into an unintentional romance with Robbie. Her best friend/roommate Francie (Zoe Kazan) voices what Rose already knows, and the character is also here to serve as an ill-fitting fourth wheel during a double date.

Goodhart's comic approach is of putting these characters into seemingly innocent, mundane situations and allowing the characters' personality quirks to collide, as Robbie's sense of entitlement fuels Rose's need to stay with him, which adds to Bill's resentment of his brother and heightens his attempts to win over Rose. The filmmaker's comic sensibilities are of the increasingly uncomfortable variety, as the situations become more complicated and the characters' frustrations bring out the worst in each of them. Goodhart's tone is never judgmental, which is judicious in terms of allowing these characters to develop, although the move is, perhaps, too generous toward them, as well.

It is, though, better to err on the side of too much generosity than the alternative, especially since Kroll and Slate are more than effective at making these characters sympathetic. *My Blind Brother* understands and relates something deeper about this pair of characters that helps to soften their harder edges. They both have a desire to do the best that they can within the context of their flawed selves. The comedy comes out of how they fail, not by forcing them to do so. Goodhart knows the difference, and the comedy, the characters, and the film itself are stronger as a result.

Mark Dujsik

CREDITS

Robbie: Adam Scott
Bill: Nick Kroll
Rose: Jenny Slate

Francie: Zoe Kazan
Micia: Talia Tabin
Origin: United States
Language: English
Released: 2016
Production: Tyler Davidson, Tory Tunnell; released by Low Spark Films, Safehouse Pictures, Think Media Studios
Directed by: Sophie Goodhart
Written by: Sophie Goodhart
Cinematography by: Eric Lin
Music by: Ian Hultquist
Sound: Ian Stynes
Music Supervisor: Nick Bobetsky
Editing: Jennifer Lee
Costumes: Keri Lee Doris
Production Design: Lisa Myers
MPAA rating: R
Running time: 85 minutes

REVIEWS

Barker, Andrew. *Variety.* March 14, 2016.
Goldstein, Gary. *Los Angeles Times.* September 22, 2016.
Hassenger, Jesse. *The A.V. Club.* September 22, 2016.
Jones, Kimberley. *Austin Chronicle.* September 23, 2016.
Kenigsberg, Ben. *New York Times.* September 22, 2016.
Keogh, Tom. *Seattle Times.* September 22, 2016.
Mercer, Benjamin. *Brooklyn Magazine.* September 21, 2016.
Orndorf, Brian. *Blu-ray.com.* September 22, 2016.
VanDenburgh, Barbara. *Arizona Republic.* September 22, 2016.
Vonder Haar, Pete. *Village Voice.* September 22, 2016.

QUOTES

Robbie: "Most importantly, I ... I have just got to thank one individual who is next to me the whole time I am running down that road. Doubts? Sure, I have doubts. But, there is this voice, right next to you telling you that you can do it. I, of course, am taking about ... God."

TRIVIA

Jenny Slate, Adam Scott, and Nick Kroll all previously worked together on *Parks and Recreation*.

MY GOLDEN DAYS
(Trois souvenirs de ma jeunesse)

Box Office: $269,144

The superb French director Arnaud Desplechin originally caught the attention of English-language audiences with his second full-length feature, *My Sex Life ... or How I Got Into an Argument* (1996), a lyrical and audacious three-hour movie pivoting around the sexual and intellectual entanglements among a group of young French academics.

The movie premiered in the competition at the Cannes Film festival and positioned Desplechin as an impossibly gifted filmmaker who demonstrated a sharp flair for character, behavioral detail, and group dynamics. He used time rhapsodically and expressively through a freewheeling and generous visual style that was especially fluent, like his use of iris shots, collage, direct-camera address and flashbacks. His soundtracks are also memorably inventive, judiciously throwing together classical, American jazz, and French hip-hop.

Desplechin was at the forefront of a "new New Wave," in French cinema—with Olivier Assayas, Claire Denis, and Leos Carax—as a creator of modernist, self-reflexive movies that yoked together formative youth influences like cinema, rock and roll, and literature to a highly realistic milieu in producing intensely personal, exciting, and thrilling works of art.

For all of his excitement and natural abilities as a visual stylist, Desplechin also proved himself a remarkable director of actors, marked by generosity, freedom, and openness. He cultivated his own specific company of actors, the most prominent being the brilliant Mathieu Amalric. In *My Sex Life*, Amalric played the doctoral student Paul Dédalus with élan and vulnerability, perfecting a bruising and exacting mixture of ambition, precociousness, and envy.

The director's buoyant new movie, *My Golden Days*, is a lyrical and pungent work about memory and time that deftly negotiates the past to conjure the emotional wonder, abandon, and ecstasy of youth. The movie explores younger iterations of some of the key characters of *My Sex Life*. The title notwithstanding, the movie is colored by a darker and more circumspect register of melancholy and regret. It's a reverie, the past spilling out in multiple directions, so that everything is amorphous and sometimes hard to grasp.

Like much of the director's work, it makes for heartbreaking and enthralling viewing. The original French title, translated as *Three Stories from My Youth*, underlines the essential form and shape. The film is composed in three movements, or chapters. Working with the writer Julie Peyr, Desplechin wields a dovetailing and circular structure—the movie opens and closes with a man and woman in bed—emphasizing the story's pattern of repetition, echo, and the possibility of the double.

The specter of the doppelganger is the movie's central premise, acknowledged by the protagonist, Paul

Dédalus, a variant of Stephen Dedalus, the autobiographically drawn literary hero of James Joyce's landmark modernist novels, *A Portrait of the Artist as a Young Man* (1916) and *Ulysses* (1922).

Desplechin uses language and conversation as something joyous, ecstatic, and devastating. Most of the movie is in French, with some passages in Hebrew and Russian. The movie's framing device is Paul (Amalric), an anthropologist and ethnographer who has been working in Tajikistan, reflecting on his past as he prepares to return to Paris for a government position after a decade in exile. "I remember," Paul says.

The first two movements are elliptical, moving from the terrifying to the dramatic. In the first chapter, "Childhood," an 11-year-old Paul (Antoine Bui) is introduced during a violent confrontation with his emotionally unbalanced mother (Cecile Garcia-Fogel) atop the family stairwell that shatters any sense of idyll or comfort. The family, including his brother and sister and a passive and overmatched father (Olivier Rabourdin) unable to control his wife's self-destructive temperament, dances emotionally on a knife's edge. Paul gains sanctuary by fleeing to the home of his great-aunt Rose (Francoise Lebrun), an aesthete who pushes his innate and youthful curiosity and need for self-discovery. Paul is inquisitive and alert, but his early ardor does not shield him from pain and loss, and the first part ends with a bleak kicker.

On his return to Paris, Paul is detained by the authorities and questioned by a French intelligence operative (Andre Dussollier) that yields the second chapter, evocatively titled "Russia." Under interrogation Paul details a colorful and revealing episode in political theater he participated in. Now a confident teenager and thrill seeker, Paul (Quentin Dolmaire) is recruited into a dangerous mission by a high school classmate (Marc Zylberberg) to smuggle money and documents to Jewish refuseniks during a class trip to Minsk. Desplechin stages the scenes with speed and precision, building tension organically, like the way the two draw on instincts and cool aplomb to outsmart local police. Paul courageously gives up his passport to his opposite figure, a Russian Jewish teenage dissident and makes possible the boy's own freedom.

Questions of identity, fate, and circumstance swirl around Paul. "I don't know who I am," he admits. The centerpiece is the third and longest chapter, "Esther." Now on the cusp of young adulthood, Paul must negotiate the most difficult and complex of subjects by working through his deep and abiding emotional and sexual attraction to the beautiful, free-spirited, and dangerously unpredictable beauty Esther (Lou Roy-Lecollinet).

This is Desplechin's first time shooting one of his films digitally, this time working in collaboration with the excellent cinematographer Irina Lubtchansky. He wields the camera seductively, constructing movement through glancing and intricate choreography that maps a pattern of desire and flirtation. The camera floats and hovers over the characters, a visual correlative that sharply conveys the corresponding feelings, emotions, or attitudes underpinning the characters. One striking illustration occurs during their first encounter as Paul moves gracefully across the courtyard toward the suddenly alone and free Esther, who is both exceptionally composed and light, almost ethereal, and the intimate and active camera moves in rhythm.

The third movement takes up about three-quarters of the movie's running time. If the first two parts are bound by a tension and drama, the third is more open ended and expansive, playing off Desplechin's mastery of mood, tempo, and conflict. "Esther" is dense with character, incident, and action and Desplechin deftly merges tones and forms and his observational talent and ability to locate humor only deepens character and dramatic revelation, like Paul undergoing a physical thrashing by a couple of romantic rivals over the attention of Esther or working through the knotty complications of his own family life, a wayward brother (Raphael Cohen) with a crazy idea to rob a bank, his moody and unhappy sister (Lily Taieb), or displaced cousin (Theo Fernandez).

Desplechin works off a terrific idea, about the pain and torment of beautiful young people dealing with their first significant romantic fixation. The setup begins with a familiar trajectory of Paul's chase and pursuit of Esther, the youthful affair complicated by the demands of Paul's university education. The action oscillates between Roubaix (the director's native town) and Paris as Paul begins to orbit around a wider range of students and intellectual mentors.

Like most of Desplechin's films, the acting is sensational. Working with the director for the sixth time, Amalric is spectral, tough, mercurial, and still haunted by the memories and heartbreak. The two newcomers rise to the occasion. Dolmaire is a natural, intuitive performer whose ease and grace conceal an intensity and conviction. Roy-Lecollinet is also fearless and devastating, enticing and at times uncomfortably needy but always ready to her push herself emotionally or sexually.

The three-part structure reveals themes and ideas, meditating on identity and sexuality as it ponders the nature and consequence of freedom. The furtive gay love affair of Paul's great-aunt Rose with her Russian lover gives way to his quixotic stagecraft that ends with a wholly different kind of political rupture: the fall of the Berlin Wall and the collapse of the Soviet system. *My*

Golden Days is a memory piece, but it captures something vital, pure, and immediate.

Patrick Z. McGavin

CREDITS

Paul Dedalus (adolescent): Quentin Dolmaire
Esther: Lou Roy-Lecollinet
Paul Dedalus (adult): Mathieu Amalric
Irina: Dinara Drukarova
Jeanne Dedalus: Cecile Garcia-Fogel
Origin: France
Language: English, French
Released: 2015
Production: Pascal Caucheteux; released by Why Not Productions
Directed by: Arnaud Desplechin
Written by: Arnaud Desplechin; Julie Peyr
Cinematography by: Irina Lubtchansky
Music by: Gregoire Hetzel; Mike Kourtzer
Music Supervisor: Frederic Junqua

Editing: Laurence Briaud
Production Design: Toma Baqueni
MPAA rating: R
Running time: 123 minutes

REVIEWS

Chang, Justin. *Variety*. May 23, 2015.
Dargin, Manohla. *New York Times*. March 17, 2016.
Jones, Kimberly. *Austin Chronicle*. April 6, 2016.
Lane, Anthony. *New Yorker*. March 21, 2016.
Merry, Stephanie. *Washington Post*. March 31, 2016.
Morgenstern, Joe. *Wall Street Journal*. March 17, 2016.
Rainer, Peter. *Christian Science Monitor*. April 1, 2016.
Rea, Stephen. *Philadelphia Inquirer*. April 1, 2016.
Vishnevetsky, Ignatiy. *The A.V. Club*. March 16, 2016.
Zacharek, Stephanie. *Time*. March 22, 2016.

AWARDS

Nominations:

Ind. Spirit 2017: Foreign Film

N

NEIGHBORS 2: SORORITY RISING

There's a new war next door.
—Movie tagline

Box Office: $55.5 Million

Nicholas Stoller's *Neighbors* (2014) sounded like a one-joke movie. A loud, party-heavy fraternity moves into a suburban neighborhood next door to new parents and a war of wills commences, making each side miserable. The end result actually proved more clever than that, delving deeper into the fears of growing old and holding onto the youthful exuberance that once defined us while still managing to be raunchy and very funny. By its conclusion, it felt like a story that had been told without the need for a second dose of property line hi-jinks. However, the decree of massive hits dictates a sequel—*Neighbors 2: Sorority Rising*. To the credit of the five writers involved, they have again hit on a social matter that promises more than just repetition for a quick buck. Unfortunately, it has been presented in such a shockingly sloppy manner that it stifles the laughter and, more importantly, the message.

Upon the news that they are pregnant once again, Mac and Kelly Radner (Seth Rogen and Rose Byrne) decide to upgrade their living situation. Due to their ignorance in understanding the concept of escrow ("This is how the housing crisis happened," says their realtor) they have agreed to allow their perspective buyers a thirty-day inspection of the property. If anything is amiss, they will be forced into keeping two homes. Meanwhile, at the local college, Shelby (Chloe Grace Moretz) is stunned to hear of the restrictions placed on sororities and their party-throwing abilities while fraternities are given no such rules. Along with a couple of other pledges, Beth (Kiersey Clemons) and Nora (Beanie Feldstein), they decide to start their own sorority in the same house that the Radners waged war with before.

The former residents have now moved on from college or, at least, some of them. Mac's former nemesis, Teddy (Zac Efron), has not progressed past the retail phase of his life. So when a pair of his fraternal brothers pledge their love for one another and ask him to move out he runs back to the home that once embraced him. It is here where he meets Shelby, advises her how to start her new venture, and finds a gateway to a future that can now incorporate the glory days of his past. None of this is good news for the parents who learned last time how cool their present is and now find themselves in another war of attrition against a group of youths whom under different circumstances might even fight for their right to party.

This is a key flaw that was successfully avoided in the first film by creating an equality on both sides at least in regards to their fears of growing responsibilities. Antagonists may have been created by the central couple but it was partially due to a perceived betrayal and the ensuing antics then cleverly poked holes in their facades. The ladies of Rush Kappa Nu come off like entitled brats by comparison. They may be brats with a point, but quickly unlikable ones that are sorely lacking in the kind of intellectual fluctuation that made Teddy's fraternity so engaging. Clemons and Feldstein's sidekicks range from quietly unfunny to obnoxious, while Moretz as the ringleader comes off as annoyingly entitled.

Far more shocking than any of the expected vulgarity or how returning cast members are so good at selling jokes that would not fly in most mainstream conversations is just how sloppily so much of it has been put together. From the moment Shelby announces "it's on" the battle shifts into such a poorly edited montage of pranks that it first enforces the lack of basic decency on one side and then is forced into rediscovering its focus and pacing. Just how does that cop sequence offering commentary on racial brutality fit into the middle of anything? Already peppered with questionable distractions such as establishing Pete's newfound orientation and a regression from Teddy's reconciliation with Mac, there is a disassociation from everyone that becomes troubling. One sequence involving an elaborate attempt to use Mac and Kelly's cell phones against them is so frustratingly mangled as to the how, when, and where that the film never regains its momentum.

The shame of all this is that it bleeds into the ideas it is trying to both hammer home as well as satirize; a very fine line. Explorations of sexism (as well as reverse) are ironically lost in a screenplay that misses the mark on the most basic disproved debate that women can be as funny as men. Rose Byrne practically stole the show the first time, but while she has her moments here, she often feels like a reactive presence to the male chaos around her. Though there is a nice shift to Teddy and a sympathetic nudge to his insecurities (which Efron makes the most of), for there to be such an outright failure in providing equal dimension to Shelby feels too hypocritical to ignore. *Neighbors 2* does sneak in a good laugh here and there when it is not blatantly offering callbacks to airbags and a big party climax. However, for a vulgar comedy with very smart and funny people at the helm to hit the repeat button on the type of double-standard humor it calls out, flies in the face of the very progress it purports to champion.

Erik Childress

CREDITS

Mac Radner: Seth Rogen
Teddy Sanders: Zac Efron
Kelly Radner: Rose Byrne
Shelby: Chloe Grace Moretz
Beth: Kiersey Clemons
Nora: Beanie Feldstein
Jimmy: Ike Barinholtz
Origin: United States
Language: English
Released: 2016
Production: James Weaver, Seth Rogen, Evan Goldberg; released by Universal Pictures; Good Universe, Point Grey Pictures.

Directed by: Nicholas Stoller
Written by: Seth Rogen; Nicholas Stoller; Andrew Jay Cohen; Brendan O'Brien; Evan Goldberg
Cinematography by: Brandon Trost
Music by: Michael Andrews
Sound: Michael Babcock
Music Supervisor: Manish Raval
Editing: Zene Baker; Peck Prior; Michael A. Webber
Art Direction: Cate Bangs
Costumes: Leesa Evans
Production Design: Theresa Guleserian
MPAA rating: R
Running time: 92 minutes

REVIEWS

Berardinelli, James. *ReelViews.* May 20, 2016.
Brody, Richard. *New Yorker.* May 23, 2016.
Clarke, Cath. *Time Out.* May 20, 2016.
Duralde, Alonso. *The Wrap.* May 4, 2016.
Ehrlich, David. *IndieWire.* May 17, 2016.
Kenny, Glenn. *RogerEbert.com.* May 20, 2016.
Lapin, Andrew. *NPR.* May 20, 2016.
LaSalle, Mick. *San Francisco Chronicle.* May 19, 2016.
Lodge, Guy. *Variety.* May 4, 2016.
Roeper, Richard. *Chicago Sun-Times.* May 19, 2016.

QUOTES

Beth: "I'm a human woman! I need to watch this!"

TRIVIA

Selena Gomez appears in the trailer, but is only in the film briefly.

THE NEON DEMON

Beauty isn't everything. It's the only thing.
—Movie tagline

Box Office: $1.3 Million

The first words uttered in *The Neon Demon*, Nicolas Winding Refn's lurid and ultimately cringe-inducing exploration of the fashion world, are "Am I staring?" These words, spoken by Ruby (Jena Malone) a makeup artist to Jesse (Elle Fanning) a young, angelic model, are a kind of thesis for the film. With a sleazy, 1980s-inspired aesthetic, and many attractive, scantily clad bodies onscreen, Refn obviously wants us to stare. But then, cruelly, he also wants to punish us for doing so, using absurdly overwrought carnal imagery (spoiler alert: the models literally have cannibalistic impulses) to prove a flimsy argument about the fashion industry being fundamentally corrupt. That the fashion industry has long fetishized youth and trafficked in vapidity should come as no surprise to most people, but Refn paints the industry with such broad brushstrokes as to insult the intelligence of any viewers with even a passing interest in fashion. Jesse is naïve, with her wholesome snub-nosed look and soft voice reminiscent of a young Mariel Hemingway, so of course the first professional photographer she works with immediately asks her to take off all her clothes. Refn seems to think he's being subversive by presenting men in the fashion industry as predators, but it really feels more like the stuff of a particularly lurid Afterschool Special. The fashion world deserves exploration and mockery (*Zoolander* [2001] remains one of the best cinematic depictions of fashion's frivolities) but *The Neon Demon* casts everything in too ominous a light, meant to provoke with a nearly mechanical precision that ends up feeling tacky.

The film has its moments of aesthetic inspiration. The photoshoot sequences surrounded by troubling gender politics though they may be, have the look of an uncanny dream world. Models wear Kabuki-like makeup and pose in front of white backdrops that seem to go on forever. As evidenced by his earlier film *Drive* (2001) Refn has a vision of a lurid style, but it only works intermittently, and the characters are frequently left feeling hollow. Most of what we need to know about Jesse comes from her impassive, wide-eyed expression during photoshoots. Fanning is a talented actress, but she isn't given much to work with here--she's little more than a virginal blonde with a shadowy family history and a growing understanding of the power of her looks. Jesse is a good girl, and all of the other models are bad. She becomes a literal sacrificial lamb, and before that is subject to indignities as preposterous as a motel proprietor (Keanu Reeves) forcing her to fellate a knife. No one in the film can be trusted. Even the model agent (Christina Hendricks) who signs Jesse, and in a less mean-spirited film could become a mentor, is only present in one scene and eagerly tells the model to lie about her age. This comment is one of the film's precious few funny moments, "Always say you're nineteen, eighteen is too on the nose," the agent says. One of *The Neon Demon*'s chief flaws is the fact that the film itself is too on the nose (it's tagline could well be "Fashion! It's evil!") and this line suggests a touch of self-awareness. Refn obviously knows his film is over the top, but to what end? What is it really saying other than that fashion is fetishistic and frequently problematic? And do we really need all these things to be said, again? The film pays aesthetic homage to retro Italian horror and the creepy ambiance of David Lynch but in this day and age this style alone, while sometimes alluring, doesn't quite make up for such a flimsy argument about such a powerful industry.

Jean-Luc Godard once famously said of the violence in his film *Pierrot le Fou* (1965) "It's not blood, it's red." *The Neon Demon* has a similar philosophy, albeit applied far less effectively. The film aims to shock as blood spills from nubile bodies with increasing frequency. The blood becomes nothing more than red, a chic, powerful colorful snaking its way through so many fashionable images. Refn aims to both shock us with the violent eroticism of fashion imagery and desensitize us, but the violence is so outré it ultimately becomes a bit silly. At one point a model, angry that Jesse was chosen for a job over her, smashes a bathroom mirror in a fit of jealousy. Jesse runs in and promptly gashes her hand on a jagged edge. These models have a distorted view of themselves and experience severe pain amplified by a competitive environment. The broken mirror, the blood, the competition, it's all manifested in an extreme way here, but it's not nearly as shocking as Refn wants it to be. Rather, he's just embellishing what most women already know and presenting it as the ultimate provocation.

Abbey Bender

CREDITS

Jesse: Elle Fanning
Hank: Keanu Reeves
Dean: Karl Glusman
Ruby: Jena Malone
Gigi: Bella Heathcote
Sarah: Abbey Lee
Roberta Hoffmann: Christina Hendricks
Origin: United States
Language: English
Released: 2016
Production: Lene Borglum, Sidonie Dumas, Vincent Maraval, Nicolas Winding Refn; released by Bold Films, Vendian Entertainment
Directed by: Nicolas Winding Refn
Written by: Nicolas Winding Refn; Mary Laws; Polly Stenham
Cinematography by: Natasha Braier
Music by: Cliff Martinez
Editing: Matthew Newman
Costumes: Erin Benach
Production Design: Elliott Hostetter
MPAA rating: R
Running time: 118 minutes

REVIEWS

Abrams, Simon. *Roger Ebert.com*. June 24, 2016.
Dowd, A. A. *The A.V. Club*. June 23, 2016.
Gleiberman, Owen. *Variety*. May 19, 2016.
McCarthy, Todd. *Hollywood Reporter*. May 19, 2016.

Kenny, Glenn. *New York Times.* June 23, 2016.
Kohn, Eric. *IndieWire.* May 19, 2016.
Lawson, Richard. *Vanity Fair.* May 20, 2016.
O'Sullivan, Michael. *Washington Post.* June 23, 2016.
Soghomonian, Talia. *Collider.* June 24, 2016.
Zacharek, Stephanie. *Time.* May 20, 2016.

QUOTES

Jesse: "I can't sing, I can't dance, I can't write...no real talent. But I'm pretty, and I can make money off pretty."

TRIVIA

The film was striking with its use of color. Director Nicolas Winding Refn said he is colorblind.

NERUDA

A renowned poet. An unknown inspector. A legendary manhunt.
—Movie tagline

Box Office: $913,371

One of three films in 2016 by Chilean auteur Pablo Larraín, *Neruda* is the latest to attempt to revamp the cinematic understanding of the biopic alongside recent films like *Get On Up* (2014) and Larrain's own *Jackie* (2016). His second collaboration with Guillermo Calderón, who co-wrote the similarly structurally inventive *No* (2012), *Neruda* is a purposefully elusive and mythic retelling of the life of Nobel Prize-winning surrealist poet/Communist/politician Pablo Neruda (Luis Gnecco).

The film is less a recounting of a single man's considerable life than a portrait of Chilean political tumult shown through the existential cat-and-mouse chase between Neruda and pseudo-fictional police detective, Oscar Peluchonneau (Gael García Bernal). A microcosm of the film's approach to history, Peluchonneau is an invention, but also a symbol of the very real threat of racism in 1940s Chile.

Neruda begins in 1948 after he's been a Senator for a few years, and right at the time when President Gabriel Gonzalez Videla outlawed Communism in Chile. Forced into hiding and expelled from his political position, Neruda goes on the run with the help of Communist contacts in the country. Tucked away in hideouts, Neruda spends his days writing influential speeches to ignite the working class, going stir-crazy with his aristocratic wife, Delia del Carril (Mercedes Morán), and dreaming of his close pursuer, Peluchonneau, who's eternally one step behind.

True to Neruda's own enigmatic prose, the film is far less interested in historical specificities of Neruda's life than examining how his role as a writer took on a secondary life for the people around him, and how he views that pressure. The film shows him being embraced by the working class who find inspiration in his words and the artists and musicians who find beauty in his words while chaos is all around them. But it also acknowledges the deep ego and narcissism that comes with being a voice of the unspoken. He's lifted as a patron saint by others, but Larraín shows him to be more of an empathetic elite than one of the common people.

In Larraín's version of Neruda's life, romantic illusion takes priority over all social realities, and the obsession of almost being caught becomes the one reason for Neruda to continue living. Narrated first in the lilting voice of Neruda before switching over to Peluchonneau, the perspective is kept bleary to the point where there's constant ambiguity whether what's being said is an objective truth or the personal projections of Neruda or Peluchonneau.

That confusion surprisingly doesn't defuse the stakes, it's principal to understanding these characters, and how their turn to narrate is the time when they try to regain control of their own life. That's meant quite literally as well as figuratively as Peluchonneau and Neruda actively wrestle for control of their own story, and the upper hand in the chase. But it's also implicitly a discussion of the very nature of being a reader and writer with Peluchonneau being forced to submit to being told a story rather than knowing the ending.

Played with bumbling grace by Bernal, Peluchonneau is a deeply pathetic character, but the film finds a melancholy beauty in his constant failures. He's a police officer who's trying to bring pride to his family name, but he's deeply ashamed of his roots, and blissfully unaware of the larger political forces going on around him. His sole goal in life seems to be capturing Neruda, but Neruda has already wrote his future, and it's a fate that he has no control over.

This metatextual commentary isn't just in the structure, but in the fundamental visual rhythms. Compared to the elliptical flow of Larrain's *The Club* (2015), *Neruda* is violent, with jagged staccato editing that regularly throws the viewer into a place of instability. In a moment, Larraín and cinematographer Sergio Armstrong, will change color schemes, setups, and even move between indoor and outdoor settings in the middle of dialogue, but these flourishes nearly always feel earned, only further establishing the film as a place of irregular space and time, and unreliable narration.

Ultimately, *Neruda* can sometimes feel more like an exercise in dismantling structure and subverting expectation than a cohesive film. But like Larraín's other films, it has a deceptive emotional weight, and a final message that even the most insular personal stories can stand in for the experiences of thousands.

Michael Snydel

CREDITS

Óscar Peluchonneau: Gael Garcia Bernal
Pablo Neruda: Luis Gnecco
Delia del Carril: Mercedes Morán
Picasso: Emilio Gutierrez-Caba
Martinez: Diego Muñoz
Origin: United States
Language: French, Spanish
Released: 2016
Production: Renan Artukmac, Peter Danner, Fernanda Del Nido, Juan Pablo Garcia, Axel Kuschevatzky, Juan de Dios Larrain, Ignacio Rey, Gaston Rothschild, Jeff Skoll, Alex Zito; released by AZ Films, Casting del Sur, Fabula, Funny Balloons, Participant Media L.L.C., Reborn Production, Setembro Cine, Willie's Movies
Directed by: Pablo Larrain
Written by: Guillermo Calderon
Cinematography by: Sergio Armstrong
Music by: Federico Jusid
Sound: Miguel Hormazabal
Editing: Herve Schneid
Production Design: Estefania Larrain
MPAA rating: R
Running time: 107 minutes

REVIEWS

Chang, Justin. *Los Angeles Times*. December 15, 2016.
D'Angelo, Mike. *The A.V. Club*. December 15, 2016.
Kenny, Glenn. *Roger Ebert*. December 16, 2016.
Kiang, Jessica. *The Playlist*. May 13, 2016.
Kohn, Eric. *IndieWire*. May 13, 2016.
Lane, Anthony. *New Yorker*. January 2, 2017.
Lee, Benjamin. *Guardian*. May 14, 2016.
Marchini Camia, Giovanni. *The Film Stage*. May 16, 2016.
Puig, Claudia. *The Wrap*. December 14, 2016.
Weissberg, Jay. *Variety*. May 13, 2016.

TRIVIA

This film was Chile's official submission for the Best Foreign Language Film category of the 89th Academy Awards.

AWARDS

Nominations:
Golden Globes 2017: Foreign Film

NERVE

We dare you.
—Movie tagline
Box Office: $38.6 Million

Nerve has much more in common with the B-movies of the 1980s than the teen-starring and teen-driven schlock usually shoveled at its contemporary audience. The film places its leads in a game with a set of rules and objectives well-defined enough to satisfy the audience's need for coherency yet kept vague enough to be foreboding.

The first rule, like in many movies with kidnapped protagonists (or movies where a kidnap victim must be rescued), is no snitching. No police personnel can know about the game. Users sign into the titular app that allows them to choose between being a "watcher" or a "player." As an anonymous watcher, players pay a fee to spectate on the antics of other gamers, and the money has direct influence over the dares presented. One can "sponsor" a favorite player to, say, steal a motorcycle or do live karaoke in a diner. The players receive dares from their viewers with escalating monetary rewards attached to them. Players must keep completing dares to keep the money, as winner (most highly-viewed) takes all in Nerve. If a player bails or fails (as the game puts it), he or she gets nothing, like a more openly sadistic, morally-flipped *Willy Wonka & the Chocolate Factory*.

The game's real-life comparisons immediately seem associated with the boom of virtual reality video game fare, but the more accurate comparison would be to YouTube vlogger (video blogger) culture. Amassing a fan following through any means necessary, including prank videos, stunts, and oversharing, YouTubers that make money off their videos are always clamoring for the next big draw for their subscribers. Their questions are the same as many businesses: how can they please their virtual audience and how can they attract more viewers/customers? Commenters can ask for anything they want, hiding behind usernames and fake e-mails.

YouTube's most notorious prankster, accused of crossing the line when he convinced his girlfriend that their three-year old had died in an accident, earns a salary in the millions of dollars. Fame and money are not corruptors exclusive to the internet, but they are certainly easier to succumb to with it.

All this is to say that *Nerve* has a much more trenchant point to make than its often thin writing might lead one to believe, especially since the film insists on shoehorning Vee (Emma Roberts, utterly charming as her giggly shyness evolves into self-assuredness) into a tired high school coming-of-age B-plot. Vee is a bookworm who prefers the sidelines—literally at one point, taking pictures of the football team and cheerleading squad. Her adventurous best friend and gateway into Nerve is Sydney (Emily Meade, with the hidden vulnerability of the "cool girl"), who, on the cheerleading squad, flashes her breasts to the crowd on a Nerve dare. High school drama ensues, mostly to fill time, as love interests come and go and best friendships crumble only to be restored. This, along with a strange family plotline with her mother (Juliette Lewis, not really in the film), is filler to the fun.

The meat, the fun and flash, come from directors Henry Joost and Ariel Schulman. Their visual style grabs the internet with both hands and stretches it onto the big screen more successfully than anything but *Unfriended* (2014, and a film taking place entirely on a laptop monitor). Touch screens, text messages, phone calls, Facebook photo likes, and live-streaming video are the cinematic language in which Joost and Schulman are fluent. Paired with the neon underglow of Ian's (Dave Franco, perfectly cast) motorcycle and the variously lit sectors of New York he and Vee travel to after they are paired up by their Nerve viewers, this is a uniquely gorgeous and modern movie.

The stunts (including shoplifting, blindfolded driving, and climbig to great heights) are exciting, well-shot, and—if you happen to have a touch of acrophobia—will make your palms sweat. All the while, the grinning faces of these fearless twenty-somethings (playing high schoolers) are constant reminders of the inevitable crash that is waiting after all this escalation. It is exhilarating with a dash of smugness, an argument against peer pressure through action.

That said, the worst part of the film is the final twenty minutes. Rather than allowing Vee and Ian (the perfectly beautiful people that viewers would love to watch) to break free of the game by fighting within the established confines of the system—the grounding rule set that gives the film narrative weight—it brings in outside elements like hacking done by dull side characters. This falls into the same pit as the high school drama.

It doesn't fit with the principled logic of B-movies where, if a schlocky movie makes its restrictions clear from the beginning—like *Assault on Precinct 13* (1976, survive the night), *The Running Man* (1987, win the game), or *The Warriors* (1979, make it to Coney Island)—then the film reaches a more satisfying conclusion. It is better to be great at set goals even if they are relatively easy than to bring in too many elements and be great at some. In the end, *Nerve* does the latter.

Jacob Oller

CREDITS

Vee: Emma Roberts
Ian: Dave Franco
Sydney: Emily Meade
Tommy: Miles Heizer
Nancy: Juliette Lewis
Origin: United States
Language: English
Released: 2016
Production: Anthony Katagas, Allison Shearmur; released by Allison Shearmur Productions, Keep Your Head, Lionsgate
Directed by: Henry Joost; Ariel Schulman
Written by: Jessica Sharzer
Cinematography by: Michael Simmonds
Music by: Rob Simonsen
Music Supervisor: Meghan Currier
Editing: Madeleine Gavin; Jeff McEvoy
Art Direction: Marc Benacerraf
Costumes: Melissa Vargas
Production Design: Chris Trujillo
MPAA rating: PG-13
Running time: 96 minutes

REVIEWS

Burr, Ty. *Boston Globe.* July 28, 2016.
Dowd, A. A. *The A.V. Club.* July 28, 2016.
Ehrlich, David. *IndieWire.* July 26, 2016.
Henderson, Odie. *RogerEbert.com.* July 27, 2016.
Merry, Stephanie. *Washington Post.* July 27, 2016.
Nicholson, Amy. *MTV.* July 27, 2016.
Scherstuhl, Alan. *The Village Voice.* July 27, 2016.
Smith, Anna. *Time Out.* July 26, 2016.
Smith, Kyle. *New York Post.* July 28, 2016.
Willmore, Alison. *Buzzfeed.* August 2, 2016.

QUOTES

Nancy: [in nurses uniform, upset at what she sees on her cellphone] "Somebody is putting money in my account!"
Black patient in wheelchair: "White people problems."

TRIVIA

When Vee and Sydney say goodbye to each other, they touch their own noses. In the book, the characters learned sign language in order to secretly communicate.

THE NICE GUYS

They're not that nice.
—Movie tagline

Box Office: $36.3 Million

Shane Black's *The Nice Guys* opens with the old-fashioned Warner Brothers logo from the 1970s, the one with the rounded, white "W" and the orange and black background. A few years ago, David O. Russell did something similar with the opening of his film *American Hustle* (2013) by using the older Columbia Pictures logo. David Fincher, likewise, did so with the Paramount Pictures logo at the front of *Zodiac* (2007). There have been other clever ways of inserting a studio logo from yesteryear at the front of a film and the effect is one of nostalgia and affection for the time period in which the film is set, but also to put the viewer even more in the frame of mind for the times in which the story takes place. *The Nice Guys* takes place in 1977 and the film does a mostly good job of putting the viewer in that time period from the get-go.

The film is a comedic detective thriller that brings to mind *The Big Lebowski* (1998) and *Inherent Vice* (2014). It opens with a scene that cleverly puts an action scene in the background of another, slightly more mundane (but no less interesting) scene in which a boy is up in the middle of the night sneaking a peek at his father's porno magazine, at which point a car crashes through the house and goes right into a ravine. The boy investigates and finds a mostly naked woman sprawled out. Her last words to him: "How do you like my car, big boy?" Black, who wrote the screenplay as well as directed, then introduces the viewer to two investigators, of sorts: One named Jackson Healy (Russell Crowe), who often gets hired to look for older men who lure younger women into buying drugs and having sex with them. The other, Holland March (Ryan Gosling), an incompetent private investigator who gets the cases nobody else will waste time with, such as a woman who believes her husband has gone missing since his funeral.

March's wife has died and he is left with a thirteen-year-old daughter named Holly (Angourie Rice) to raise on his own. Both characters narrate the story at the start. March is investigating the death of the woman who died in the car crash, a porn star named Misty Mountains. This search leads him to a woman named Amelia (Margaret Qualley), who hired Healy to protect her. Amelia did a porno with Misty Mountains and does not want to be found. This brings Healy and March together for the first time as Healy insists March stop looking for her. Healy, who is more of a musclehead than a PI, gets paid a visit by two thugs who are looking for Amelia. That changes his mind about March and he decides to reverse his stance on the investigation and actually help March in any way he can.

The search leads them to (among other places) an air pollution protest group that Amelia once belonged to, in which many lie on the steps of the state capital building pretending to be dead while wearing gas masks. They also end up at a filmmaker's house, which has just burned down to the ground, but they investigate the rubble anyway and have a rather odd conversation with a young witness who knows a little too much for his age

about the pornography business. The big turning point of the film occurs when they go to a costume party (which March's young daughter attends by insisting she tag along). There they meet a couple other porno actors and come across more helpful artifacts that aid with the case later. Of course, the title of Misty Mountain's last film is "How Do You Like My Car, Big Boy?"

The plot here is secondary to the two leads and their chemistry together. *The Nice Guys* is a buddy comedy, through and through, but it is never as simple as "good cop/bad cop" or "uptight PI/wacky PI." Gosling's Holland March has confidence in what he does, but will never admit to his level of incompetence. He has no problem shooting a gun or taking a beating (he becomes like a human pinball in one sequence), but his scream when something horrifying happens is hilariously childlike. Crowe's Healy has a kind of swagger and world weariness about him, but not without a smile. There is never a point where they appear to dislike one another. The glue holding them together, though, is Holly, who is older than her years and often drives Holland around in their car, a sight that hardly ever gets mentioned as being unusual or dangerous. She just does it.

Black clearly enjoys playing with genre conventions and audiences expectations from those conventions. After all, this is the guy who wrote the love letter to old monster movies *The Monster Squad* (1987) and the big-budget in-joke comedy *The Last Action Hero* (1993), which probably would have turned out a whole lot better had he directed it. But *The Nice Guys* has more in common with his directorial debut, the underrated *Kiss Kiss Bang Bang* (2005), in which Robert Downey Jr. directly addressed the audience (via narration) as "clever filmgoers." Here, Black is a bit more subtle with his playfulness. This is still a film about films. It opens with a cheesy educational film that goes south quickly. It has fun skewering the porno industry and its practices as an art form. And its plot could not exist without the advent of 16mm film.

The Nice Guys works on many fronts. As a comedy, the laughs are pretty consistent, most of them coming through clever dialogue and ingenious sight gags. As a detective thriller, the story works in the same way other detective stories work in spite of their absurdities. It's pulpy fun, for the most part. As a buddy comedy, it works because the two actors—primarily known for their more serious roles—seem to be having the most fun they have ever had in a film. Unfortunately, as with *Kiss Kiss Bang Bang*, audiences expressed little interest in the pairing and *The Nice Guys* got generally ignored during the summer season. Too bad, because this is one buddy comedy where a sequel would have been most welcome.

Collin Souter

CREDITS

Holland March: Ryan Gosling
Jackson Healy: Russell Crowe
Holly March: Angourie Rice
John Boy: Matt Bomer
Amelia Kuttner: Margaret Qualley
Origin: United States
Language: English
Released: 2016
Production: Joel Silver; released by Warner Bros.; Misty Mountains, Nice Guys, Silver Pictures, Waypoint Entertainment
Directed by: Shane Black
Written by: Shane Black; Anthony Bagarozzi
Cinematography by: Philippe Rousselot
Music by: David Buckley; John Ottman
Sound: Oliver Tarney
Music Supervisor: Randall Poster
Editing: Joel Negron
Art Direction: David Utley
Costumes: Kym Barrett
Production Design: Richard Bridgland
MPAA rating: R
Running time: 116 minutes

REVIEWS

Edelstein, David. *New York Magazine.* May 20, 2016.
Hornaday, Ann. *Washington Post.* May 19, 2016.
Jones, J.R. *Chicago Reader.* May 19, 2016.
Jones, Kimberly. *Austin Chronicle.* May 19, 2016.
LaSalle, Mick. *San Francisco Chronicle.* May 19. 2016.
Lumenick, Lou. *New York Post.* May 19, 2016.
O'Hehir, Andrew. *Salon.com.* May 19. 2016.
Orr, Christopher. *The Atlantic.* May 21, 2016.
Rea, Stephen. *Philadelphia Enquirer.* May 19, 2016.
Scott, A.O. *New York Times.* May 19, 2016.

QUOTES

Holly: "You're the world's worst detectives."

TRIVIA

The mid-1970s Warner Brothers logo opens the film.

NINE LIVES

His life just got put on paws.
—Movie tagline

Box Office: $19.7 Million

Nine Lives is not so much a bad movie—though it is, to be sure, a very bad movie—as it is a thoroughly baffling one. In most cases, when one watches a movie, even a terrible one, they can usually get some sort of idea of what the filmmakers were trying to convey and the kind of audience that they were trying to reach. And yet, this film is so bizarre in so many ways that even those most basic concepts are virtually impossible to discern. It is so mystifying that, as awful as it is, instead of looking at it with boredom or anger—the ways that people might react to most bad movies—one is more likely to regard it with a certain morbid curiosity in regards to its ineptitude. After all, anyone can make an ordinary bad movie but to come up with an idea this ridiculously bad and then somehow convince a lot of talented people to sign up for it and a studio to release it to boot takes a certain kind of genius and/or nerve.

Two-time Oscar winner Kevin Spacey stars as Tom Brand, an insanely wealthy and powerful New York real estate developer who has already burned through one family thanks to his obsession with work and is well on the way with doing so again with his second—he rarely gets around to seeing devoted daughter Rebecca (Malina Weissman) and wife Lara (Jennifer Garner) is beginning to contemplate divorce. Rushing out to buy a last-minute birthday present for Rebecca—the cat she has long desired—the feline-hating Tom stumbles upon a weird pet shop run by the oddball Felix Perkins (played, perhaps inevitably, by Oscar-winning actor Christopher Walken). Alas, no sooner has Tom purchased a grumpy-looking fur ball by the name of Mr. Fuzzypants than he has an accident that puts his body into a coma but transplants his mind and soul into—you guessed it—the body of Mr. Fuzzypants. According to Perkins, a "cat whisperer" who is the only person who can understand Tom and knows what is really going on, the only way he can get back into his human body is to figure out how to reconcile with Lara, Rebecca, and David (Robbie Amell), the son from his first marriage, before he is trapped as a cat forever.

Yes, this sounds like a fairly stupid premise for a presumably family oriented film but, to be fair, it is not that much worse than the conceits behind any number of such films in the past—there was once a major motion picture about a place-kicking mule, for God's sake. What separates *Nine Lives* from the competition, however, is how it seems to deliberately go out of its way to alienate all potential audience members. Instead of spending time showing Tom attempting to reconnect with his family despite being housed in the form of an animal notorious for its generally anti-social tendencies, an enormous chunk of the blessedly brief screen time is dedicated to his desire to build the tallest building in

North America, the attempts by a slimy underling, Ian (Mark Consuelos), to sell the company out from under Tom while he lies comatose, and David searching for the right documents to save the company from being taken public. Unless *Barbarians at the Gate* has become a standard kindergarten textbook, there are precious few children who are going to have any interest in any of that material. As for anyone whose age is in the double digits, there is nothing here that will grab their interest either—even cat fanciers will be better served watching cat videos on YouTube than seeing the array of CGI-heavy simulations on display here—and the more adult-leaning material, which includes stuff about divorce, heavy drinking, euthanasia, and even a suicide attempt, seems insanely out of place. Considering that there are no fewer than five credited screenwriters involved with the screenplay, you would think that one of them might have suggested that some of the stuff they were coming up with was wildly inappropriate, but apparently that was not the case.

Kevin Spacey, Jennifer Garner. Christopher Walken. Director Barrry Sonnenfeld, who once specialized in offbeat fantasy-comedies that scored with kids and adults alike such as the *Addams Family* films and *Men in Black* (1997). These are smart people who have done fine work in the past and who will presumably continue to do so in the future—how then to explain their participation in this particular enterprise. Were they under the deluded impression that it was going to be some kind of hip and subversive take on empty-headed family-oriented vehicles? Did it in fact start out that way, only to get messed around with at some point during production? Did they all just figure that they would take the money and hold their noses in the belief that the final product would never see the inside of a multiplex? Spacey may have been swayed by the fact that most of his contributions would come in the form of a voiceover but he puts so little effort into those lines that it inspires a distancing effect that only adds to the weirdness. Walken presumably signed on after reading the script, realizing that whoever played the part would most likely end up doing a tired Christopher Walken impression and deciding that he could do a tired Walken impression as well as anyone else. As for Sonnenfeld, perhaps he wanted to see if he could possibly make a film that was more gruesomely conceived and executed than the infamous *Wild, Wild West* (1999).

Unless you have been dying to see a film that was essentially a mash-up of the worst elements of *Oh Heavenly Dog* (1980) and *The Hudsucker Proxy* (1994) lashed together with a visual style that would give even Tommy Wiseau pause, *Nine Lives* should prove to be a head scratcher for the ages. Even in a time that has given moviegoers the likes of both *Garfield* films, *Beverly Hills Chihuahua* (2007), and numerous vehicles for Alvin and the Chipmunks, this may be a new low for the not-exactly-robust subgenre of talking animal films. The central character of the film may be a cat but trust me, the film as a whole is 100% dog.

Peter Sobczynski

CREDITS

Tom Brand: Kevin Spacey
Lara Brand: Jennifer Garner
David Brand: Robbie Amell
Rebecca Brand: Malina Weissman
Felix Perkins: Christopher Walken
Ian Cox: Mark Consuelos
Origin: United States
Language: English
Released: 2016
Production: Lisa Ellzey; Trans Film; released by EuropaCorp S.A.
Directed by: Barry Sonnenfeld
Written by: Gwyn Lurie; Matt Allen; Caleb Wilson; Dan Antoniazzi; Ben Shiffrin
Cinematography by: Karl Walter Lindenlaub
Music by: Evgueni Galperine; Sacha Galperine
Sound: Janice Ierulli
Editing: Don Zimmerman
Art Direction: Jean-Andre Carriere
Costumes: Marylin Fitoussi
Production Design: Michael Wylie
MPAA rating: PG
Running time: 87 minutes

REVIEWS

Coggan, Devan. *Entertainment Weekly.* August 5, 2016.
DeFore, John. *Hollywood Reporter.* August 5, 2016.
Ehrlich, David. *IndieWire.* August 5, 2016.
Gleiberman, Owen. *Variety.* August 5, 2016.
Mendelson, Scott. *Forbes.* August 5, 2016.
Nicholson, Amy. *MTV.* August 5, 2016.
Orndorf, Brian. *Blu-Ray.com.* August 4, 2016.
Travers, Peter. *Rolling Stone.* August 5, 2016.
White, Dave. *TheWire.* August 5, 2016.
Wloszczyna, Susan. *RogerEbert.com.* August 5, 2016.

QUOTES

Tom Brand: [pawing at a tablet] "It's ironic, but I really could use a mouse right now."

TRIVIA

Around 70% of the film was computer generated.

THE 9th LIFE OF LOUIS DRAX

A mystery beyond reality.
—Movie tagline

Fantasy and reality merge in obnoxious and slightly discomforting ways in *The 9th Life of Louis Drax*, a movie about suffering characters that does not have much interest or sympathy for that suffering. Instead, the screenplay by Max Minghella (based on the novel by Liz Jensen) is more concerned with crafting a game in which elements of the fantastic and the realistic fight for the direction of the narrative, while director Alexandre Aja unsuccessfully attempts to juggle the disparate tones of those two modes.

The extremity of that shift is never more apparent than in the comparison of the prologue to the rest of the movie. In that introductory montage of the life story of the eponymous character, Aja plays a series of near-fatal mishaps and misadventures for broad comedy. The title character, played by Aiden Longworth at that character's present age, narrates how his life, since the time of his birth, has been marked by one disaster after another. An almost-deadly event appears, to him and everyone who knows his story, to be an annual occurrence.

There is his problematic birth by Caesarean section. There is the time a light fixture above his crib fell into said crib. He has been bitten by a poisonous spider and nearly electrocuted. By the occasion of his ninth birthday, when Louis's story proper begins in the movie, young Louis should have already died eight times, according to an assortment of doctors and his mother Natalie (Sarah Gadon), who tells her son that she hopes his "ninth life" will be a good one.

With the main character's dreamy intonation of his history and the whimsical score by Patrick Watson, this section presents Louis's dilemma as something strange, otherworldly, and almost magical, and Aja seems to play each accident as a punch line of sorts. Even the prologue's final moment, in which the boy falls over the side of a cliff in slow motion and with Louis's indifferent attitude about what is happening, is detached from the reality of the situation.

After being clinically dead for two hours, Louis ends up in a coma as a result of the accident. His father Peter (Aaron Paul) has gone missing. Natalie accuses her husband, from whom she has separated, of pushing Louis off the cliff. Dr. Allan Pascal (Jamie Dornan), a neurologist with unconventional methods of treatment, oversees Louis's care, and Dalton (Molly Parker), a tough-as-nails police detective, tries to discover what

happened during the birthday picnic that resulted in a nine-year-old boy falling from a cliff.

Reality mostly takes over as the investigation unfolds and Allan starts to become a little too close to the mother of his patient. In between those relatively grounded plots, though, Louis's backstory continues through a series of flashbacks, still narrated by the character in conversations with a mysterious creature, within the boy's mind. The picture of the kid is not a flattering one. He insults his psychiatrist (played by Oliver Platt), another quirky example of his profession. He intentionally stirs up trouble between his parents. He kills small animals, believing that he has a right to do so once his pet hamsters have reached the end of the animal's average lifespan. The character is insufferable and eerie—a spoiled, entitled kid with sociopathic tendencies.

The other characters are not much better. Dornan's performance as the conflicted doctor is far too bland, considering that his pursuit of Natalie both is highly unethical and comes across as rather predatory. Paul provides a heartfelt performance, although the story's machinations, which retain questions about his allegiance to his son, keep Peter at an arm's length in terms of sympathizing with him. Gadon's work is the most accomplished here, playing a woman who seems to be a constant victim but who approaches obstacles with poise. Natalie has a character arc, though, that is essentially the opposite of Peter's, leading to a similar result in regards to sympathy for her.

The central question is whether Louis possesses supernatural abilities of some kind or he is a normal child caught up in an extreme—but still realistic—situation. The scenes within Louis's mind could go either way, until a point (The third act of the movie involves psychic communication and what seems to be an instance of contacting the dead). Aja splits the difference: This situation is both real and fantasy.

Where this mystery goes—quite predictably after a certain point—is grave. The way Aja undermines it, even before the over-the-top climax, makes *The 9th Life of Louis Drax* an uncomfortable experience.

Mark Dujsik

CREDITS

Dr. Allan Pascal: Jamie Dornan
Natalie: Sarah Gadon
Peter: Aaron Paul
Louis Drax: Aiden Longworth
Dr. Perez: Oliver Platt
Dalton: Molly Parker

Violet Drax: Barbara Hershey
Origin: United States
Language: English
Released: 2016
Production: Timothy Bricknell, Shawn Williamson, Alexandre Aja, Max Minghella; released by Blank Tape; Brightlight Pictures, Miramax LLC
Directed by: Alexandre Aja
Written by: Max Minghella
Cinematography by: Maxime Alexandre
Music by: Patrick Watson
Sound: Michael O'Farrell
Editing: Baxter
Art Direction: Nigel Evans
Costumes: Carla Hetland
Production Design: Rachel O'Toole
MPAA rating: R
Running time: 108 minutes

REVIEWS

Abele, Robert. *Los Angeles Times*. September 1, 2016.
Ebiri, Bilge. *Village Voice*. September 2, 2016.
Fujishima, Kenji. *Paste*. September 3, 2016.
Genzlinger, Neil. *New York Times*. September 1, 2016.
Gonzalez, Ed. *Slant*. September 1, 2016.
Linden, Sheri. *Hollywood Reporter*. August 31, 2016.
Orndorf, Brian. *Blu-ray.com*. September 2, 2016.
Padua, Pat. *Washington Post*. September 2, 2016.
Rife, Katie. *The A.V. Club*. September 1, 2016.
Taylor, Kate. *Globe and Mail*. September 2, 2016.

TRIVIA

Jamie Dornan and Barbara Hershey both appeared on ABC's *Once Upon a Time,* but never in the same episodes.

NOCTURNAL ANIMALS

When you love someone you can't just throw it away.
—Movie tagline

Box Office: $10.7 Million

Nocturnal Animals opens with images of obese nude women dancing. As their flesh jiggles, we quickly realize we are watching a film (and a not particularly great one, at that) which chiefly aims to provoke. It turns out the nude women's images are part of an art installation, and the film, which unfolds via vignettes in both the art world and an imagined rural one, luxuriates in the lurid. This sophomore feature by suave fashion designer-cum-director Tom Ford, maintains the eye for style of his

2009 debut, *A Single Man*, but it unfortunately lacks that film's emotional pull.

The story here, based on Austin Wright's 1993 novel *Tony and Susan*, hints at psychological intrigue but never quite delivers. Amy Adams plays Susan, a high-powered art gallery owner in Los Angeles who receives a manuscript of a troubling, creepy, potentially semi-biographical novel from her ex-husband, Edward (Jake Gyllenhaal). The film alternates between the real world and the world of the novel—a reasonably compelling device with mixed results. Adams, a typically fine performer, is given a role that requires little more than pouting and hauteur. The alternating aesthetics of the real world and the imagined world of the novel frequently result in an atmosphere of confusion. Ford creates an environment that shifts abruptly from the sleek glamour of a *Vogue* photoshoot to the foreboding rural plains of *Deliverance* (1972). *Nocturnal Animals* feels a bit like two films in one, and perhaps the film as a whole would be better if Ford committed himself more fervently to one story or the other.

Edward's manuscript, which comes into Susan's life seemingly out of the blue, tells a disturbing story of a family on a road trip that goes horribly awry. The story is, essentially, a highly exaggerated retelling of the dramas of Edward's relationship with his ex-wife, with rape and murder thrown in as a means of conveying some sort of seething misogynistic fantasy. In addition to playing Edward, Gyllenhaal also plays the novel's protagonist, Tony. Having Gyllenhaal play both characters anchors Tony's experience in Edward's, and gives us a glance into the author's consciousness. In the flashbacks we see of Edward and Susan's early relationship, the two actors ably play more fresh-faced and idealistic versions of themselves. We see Gyllenhaal navigate various guises of masculinity, playing Edward as a sensitive creative type, and Tony as a capable father forced to attempt to protect himself and his family and fight off macho rural aggression. Unfortunately, Susan's avatar within Edward's novel, Laura (played by passable Amy Adams lookalike Isla Fisher) is given little more to do than play scared as a menacing southern gang takes on her and her family. The gang that terrorizes the fictionalized family feels too much like a cliché of grimy Texan masculinity. Brit Aaron Taylor-Johnson plays Ray, the leader of the gang, with a scenery chewing "yee-haw" accent and a mustache. A moment in which he sits on an outdoor toilet and shouts feels like a particularly egregious example of trashy southern posturing. Ray and his gang's rape and murder of Tony's wife and daughter leads to the entrance of a detective, Bobby Andes, played by Michael Shannon. Shannon's version of Texas masculinity feels more compelling and less cliché than Taylor-Johnson's. Shannon tends to bring an eccentric edge to his roles, and here, as a chain smoking, cowboy hatted figure, he adds some more mystery and intrigue not only to Edward's novel but to the film. Shannon's character feels like he stepped out of some old-timey saloon, and while he's out to help Tony, it seems he has a mysterious life of his own.

Mysterious lives and the impossibility of truly knowing another person's psyche may well be the guiding theme of *Nocturnal Animals*. This was expressed potently in the film noirs and Alfred Hitchcock films of the 1940s and 1950s, and both cinematic touchstones seem to be influences on Ford's world. The psychology of *Nocturnal Animals*, though, is somewhat flimsy. Edward wrote a disturbing book to process his failed marriage to Susan, but what do the sensationalized images of violence that color his imagined narrative really have to say about him, other than that he's been through emotional turmoil and feels resentment toward his ex-wife for having cheated on him? We would be able to glean these insights into Edward's embittered psyche without the fatalistic posturing of his novel. This is the chief issue of the film: Ford revels in lurid southern crime, yet the scenes do little to create suspense, and when we return to the art world from the world of the novel there's similarly little reprieve from the over-the-top. Being stylized is certainly not a bad thing, and Ford showed a keen eye for a cohesive aesthetic in the sunny yet moody and impressionistic 1960s world of *A Single Man*. In *Nocturnal Animals* the highly stylized art world becomes frankly a bit silly. All of the art that surrounds Susan is (intentionally?) bad. In one scene of art world small talk that edges into self parody, Susan encounters a lower level employee, Sage (Jena Malone) clad in a ridiculous "conceptual" designer outfit in front of a huge painting that simply reads "REVENGE." *Nocturnal Animals* doesn't explore the nuances of the art world so much as make it a backdrop for predictable drama.

Nocturnal Animals has a few things to recommend it, chief among them Shannon's hardboiled performance, a seductive score by Abel Korzeniowski, and the sight of Amy Adams in fabulous femme fatale makeup and an emerald dress that perfectly complements her red hair. But overall it feels a bit like a stylized ad for a fashion house: it's aesthetically intriguing, to an extent, but hollow. The thriller elements aren't all that thrilling and the sexual politics, from the opening images of nude obese women as a shorthand for provocative art to the seemingly inevitable rape in the novel, leave much to be desired. Ford revealed an eye for captivating atmospheres and nuance in *A Single Man* and one hopes he'll return to this more emotionally rich world for his next film. If not, he's still a pretty good fashion designer.

Abbey Bender

CREDITS

Susan Morrow: Amy Adams
Edward Sheffield/Tony Hastings: Jake Gyllenhaal
Bobby Andes: Michael Shannon
Ray Marcus: Aaron Taylor-Johnson
Laura Hastings: Isla Fisher
Sage: Jena Malone
Origin: United States
Language: English
Released: 2016
Production: Robert Salerno, Tom Ford; released by Fade to Black Productions, Focus Features L.L.C., Universal Pictures Inc.
Directed by: Tom Ford
Written by: Tom Ford
Cinematography by: Seamus McGarvey
Music by: Abel Korzeniowski
Sound: Lon Bender
Editing: Joan Sobel
Art Direction: Christopher Brown
Costumes: Arianne Phillips
Production Design: Shane Valentino
MPAA rating: R
Running time: 116 minutes

REVIEWS

Bradshaw, Peter. *Guardian.* November 3, 2016.
Dargis, Manohla. *New York Times.* November 17, 2016.
Gleiberman, Owen. *Variety.* September 2, 2016.
Goldberg, Matt. *Collider.* November 16, 2016.
Kenny, Glenn. *Roger Ebert.com.* November 18, 2016.
Orr, Christopher. *The Atlantic.* November 18, 2016.
Vishnevetsky, Ignatiy. *The A.V. Club.* November 17, 2016.
Rooney, David. *Hollywood Reporter.* September 2, 2016.
Whitty, Stephen. *New York Daily News.* November 15, 2016.
Zacharek, Stephanie. *Time.* September 2, 2016.

QUOTES

Bobby Andes: "It's gonna be rough on them out there, not knowing how it's gonna come. Maybe Ray gets killed, for resisting arrest, or coming at home late at night, might get shot by a burglar."

TRIVIA

After a bidding war in Cannes, the film was purchased by Focus Features for $20 million, the highest amount ever paid for a film at a festival.

AWARDS

Golden Globes 2017: Actor—Supporting (Taylor-Johnson)
Nominations:
Oscars 2016: Actor—Supporting (Shannon)

British Acad. 2016: Actor (Gyllenhaal), Actor—Supporting (Taylor-Johnson), Adapt. Screenplay, Cinematog., Director (Ford), Film Editing, Makeup, Orig. Score, Production Design

Golden Globes 2017: Director (Ford), Screenplay

Writers Guild 2016: Adapt. Screenplay

NORM OF THE NORTH

Bear to be different.
—Movie tagline

Box Office: $17.1 Million

Splash Entertainment, the production house responsible for the exceptionally chintzy *Norm of the North,* seems chiefly interested in producing content that will exclusively entertain toddlers. Even with that low a bar, their first theatrical release after almost a decade making TV programs cannot clear it. The animation looks cheap, the characters are inexpressive, and the jokes are recycled and will largely fly over the heads of the intended audience when it isn't traumatizing them with images of cuddly seals being eaten by killer whales. Take out the references to marketing, criminal law, dead languages, film production, and other adult concerns, and the film would not be long enough to fill one of Splash's usual half-hour television slots.

Norm (voiced by Rob Schneider) is a graceless polar bear with a pacifist streak. He can't hunt seals to save his life, and even if he could, he does not have the heart to kill and eat them. He would much rather do the Arctic Shake, a dance craze he started. The other bears don't accept Norm and his dancing, or his lack of killer instinct. Norm's problems grow exponentially when a real estate developer named Mr. Greene (voice of Ken Jeong) wants to start building luxury condos in the arctic. Mr. Greene's head of public relations Vera (voice of Heather Graham) is put in charge of shooting a commercial to help advertise the new developments but Norm and his lemming pals sabotage the shoot. All looks hopeless for Mr. Greene until he sees Norm in some of Vera's footage of her new arctic neighborhood and decides a polar bear would make a perfect mascot for the company.

When Norm realizes that his temporary solution to the problem of the developers cannot be solved just by chasing away advertisers, his sea bird friend Socrates (voice of Bill Nighy) tells him he could do more good by going to New York and seeing Mr. Greene in person. Norm hops on a boat bound for the Big Apple, and soon he's at Mr. Greene's offices. Vera thinks Norm is a man in a bear costume, which wins him the role of mascot when he accidentally crashes an audition. Things

get even more complicated for Norm when he discovers that Mr. Greene is holding Norm's grandfather (voice of Colm Meaney) hostage in his basement. This further incentivizes him to ruin Mr. Greene's campaign to put houses in the Arctic. Luckily, Vera's daughter Olympia (voice of Maya Kay) is just as invested in the future of the Arctic as Norm and comes up with a solution. If Norm can persuade Greene's chief investor (voice of Gabriel Iglesias) to pull funding from the project, he might put a stop to the development.

Norm of the North pretends its heart is in the right place. Its message about raising awareness for climate change is delivered hastily, vaguely, and unconvincingly. Lip service is paid to rising oceans but no facts or scientific analysis are ever hinted at, let alone unpacked. Such things may on their face seem too sophisticated for pre-school age children, but if writers Daniel Altiere, Steven Altiere, Malcolm T. Goldman, and Jamie Lissow thought kids would be able to make sense of the minutiae of public relations and the real estate business, why couldn't they have tried their hand at an actual concern or two? Every time the film seems in danger of educating its young audience, Norm starts dancing to one of a handful of pop songs that date the film more than its shoddy animation will.

Norm of the North commits many unpardonable sins, but the strangest is its bizarre fixation on death. There's the aforementioned seal murder, lemmings threatening to die every time Norm sits on them, a joke about tranquilizers only occasionally being lethal for humans, and Norm's life flashing before his eyes while the lemmings play like the orchestra on the deck of the Titanic during the film's climax. The film cannot bother spelling out the dangers of global warming, which is the only reason to have made its lead character a polar bear in the first place, but it can constantly bombard children with images and ideas regarding death in ways that feel flip and unearned. It's enough to make one wonder if the writers and director Trevor Wall expected their target demographic to laugh off all the morbid humor or really take something from the tone-deaf lessons about the fleeting nature of existence.

Since the 2001 blockbuster success of *Shrek,* it has become old hat for children's movies to traffic in jokes intended only for the parents in the room. *Norm of the North* does not do a great job of pandering to either age group. The kids may enjoy the sight of a polar bear dancing or the brightly colored, poorly rendered characters and environments he encounters, but they cannot possibly be expected to make sense of the Shakespearian actor in a bear suit who boasts that he smells like "sweet vermouth." It's tough to picture parents finding that joke funny or appropriate for their offspring. The scatological jokes peppering the film may be the only thing parents and kids could agree at least resemble something funny, even if the execution is wanting. Take the scenes where the lemmings pee in a fish tank. Like the rest of the movie, it goes on entirely too long to be funny or comfortable for any crowd to sit through. *Norm of the North* is ostensibly about charming Americans enough that they won't mind being lectured about an important issue. That it does not succeed at charming anyone should not be treated as a concern because the writers did not think up a lesson worth imparting to begin with.

Scout Tafoya

CREDITS

Voice of Norm: Rob Schneider

Voice of Vera: Heather Graham

Voice of Mr. Greene: Ken Jeong

Voice of Socrates: Bill Nighy

Voice of Grandfather: Colm Meaney

Voice of Chief Investor: Gabriel Iglesias

Voice of Olympia: Maya Kay

Origin: United States

Language: English

Released: 2016

Production: Nicolas Atlan, Ken Katsumoto, Steve Rosen, Liz Young, Mike Young; released by Liongate; Assemblage Entertainment, Splash Entertainment, Telegael

Directed by: Trevor Wall

Written by: Daniel Altiere; Steven Altiere; Malcolm T. Goldman; Jamie Lissow

Music by: Stephen McKeon

Sound: Trip Brock

MPAA rating: PG

Running time: 90 minutes

REVIEWS

Abele, Robert. *TheWrap*. January 14, 2016.

Coggan, Devan. *Entertainment Weekly*. January 15, 2016.

Dujsik, Mark. *RogerEbert.com*. January 15, 2016.

Ebiri, Bilge. *New York Magazine*. January 16, 2016.

Kenny, Glenn. *New York Times*. January 14, 2016.

Keough, Peter. *Boston Globe*. January 14, 2016.

Ordona, Michael. *San Francisco Chronicle*. January 14, 2016.

Rife, Katie. *The A.V. Club*. January 14, 2016.

Stewart, Sara. *New York Post*. January 14, 2016.

White, James. *Empire*. March 14, 2016.

QUOTES

Norm: [to the three lemmings] "Someone's coming. Act natural." [the lemmings start farting]

Norm: [in disgust] "Not THAT natural!"

TRIVIA

The film's production took six years, with multiple delays and rewrites.

NOW YOU SEE ME 2

You haven't seen anything yet.
—Movie tagline

Box Office: $65.1 Million

Original genre films absent any previous intellectual property connection are a rare enough commodity in Hollywood these days that when one becomes a hit, it only stands to reason that franchise capitalization is an immediate topic of conversation. Such was the case with *Now You See Me* (2013), a spry ensemble heist thriller which grossed over $350 million against a budget of only $75 million. Perhaps most importantly, though, the movie grossed two-thirds of that box office haul, or $234 million, by way of the booming international marketplace.

Frantically paced by director Jon Chu—replacing Louis Leterrier from the first film—*Now You See Me 2* expands the borders of its predecessor and serves up a cavalcade of colorful incidents and new characters, with much gusto. It therefore services the franchise-in-bloom in dutiful fashion, but also manages to make the case that some narratives should be closed loops.

A moderate critical punching bag (the movie rated only 35 percent fresh on Rotten Tomatoes), *Now You See Me 2* saw its domestic fortunes dip mightily, grossing only $65 million against the $118 million of its predecessor. But its foreign box office yield increased, to just shy of $270 million (including $97 million from China alone), guaranteeing a receptive audience for a third installment.

Most of the principal players from the first movie reprise their roles here. That means there is Danny Atlas (Jesse Eisenberg), the somewhat arrogant de-facto leader of the Four Horsemen; sardonic hypnotist and mentalist Merritt McKinney (Woody Harrelson); sleight-of-hand illusionist Jack Wilder (Dave Franco); and former FBI agent Dylan Rhodes (Mark Ruffalo), revealed at the end of the first film to be the son of a famed magician and escape artist, and working in service of the Four Horsemen the entire time. Absent is Henley Reeves, ostensibly due to Isla Fisher's real-life pregnancy; she is replaced in the mix by Lula May (Lizzy Caplan), a Four Horsemen devotee who talks her way into the group.

Set one year after the events of the first film, the sequel opens with magic debunker Thaddeus Bradley (Morgan Freeman) in prison, and the Horsemen still awaiting further instructions from the Eye, the clandestine society of magician-activists into which they have all been recruited. Danny is restless and Jack equally so, the latter tired of having to live in the shadows in order to keep up the public lie of his death. Dylan eventually gives the group its new assignment: to take down a corrupt businessman, Owen Case (Ben Lamb), who is launching a new smartphone which secretly vacuums up its users' private data.

The Horsemen hijack Owen's launch party but their plans go awry, quickly thrusting the group into a seemingly untenable situation. Captured by Merritt's twin brother Chase (also Harrelson), the Horsemen are blackmailed by Owen's former business partner, Walter Mabry (Daniel Radcliffe), who wants them to steal the data-mining device for him. Meanwhile, having been stripped of money, power, and reputation by the Horsemen in the first film, Arthur Tressler (Michael Caine) also has reason to root for their comeuppance. With Dylan's identity publicly outed, he becomes a fugitive from the law, and turns to Thaddeus for assistance in saving the Horsemen, even though Dylan still blames Thaddeus for the death of his father, Lionel Shrike, when he was still a boy.

If it sounds a bit convoluted, that is the point. *Now You See Me 2* is a movie that thrives on head-feints and reversals, obscured and muddied motivations. It is not just smoke and mirrors, but a smoke machine inside a mirrored funhouse. In order to appreciably enjoy the series, and in particular this second offering, one has to surrender to the idea that its characters are so enchanted by magic, bound by hidden fraternity and powered by curiosity that they will continue to act less out of self-interest or self-preservation than out of an intrepid inquisitiveness into what is happening to them. As much as anything, *Now You See Me 2* is selling the idea of mystery, more than the mystery of its actual storyline.

The film's Chinese marketplace performance was worth mentioning earlier for a couple reasons. The original *Now You See Me* did well in the Middle Kingdom; it was the movie's second-highest-grossing foreign territory, ahead of even the United Kingdom and behind only France. As a result, a Chinese production company, TIK Films, contributed to the sequel's funding. So when, early in *Now You See Me 2*, the Horsemen escape a stage show in a scramble and flee from a rooftop only to somehow end up literally in the semi-autonomous Southern Chinese port city of Macau ("Guys, I don't think we're in Chinatown—I think we're in China," says McKinney), well, it feels like a grand and silly, though not particularly well-concealed, metaphor for the tremendous influx of Asian capital into Hollywood filmmaking, and how it is shaping choices on even a granular narrative level.

To be clear, this pivot to the East is not the film's undoing. (Taiwanese actor and music superstar Jay Chou also appears as Li, a magic shop owner and member of the Eye, though one wishes he was given a bit more to do.) The core problem is that too many of the movie's big set pieces lack a practical mooring, and instead rely on overly slick CGI trickery.

Even when there is a simple, fun idea in Ed Solomon's script, Chu, editor Stan Salfas, and the rest of his below-the-line collaborators overdo things. The best example of this is a sequence in which the Horsemen, after stealing the chip containing Owen's data-mining device, have to collectively defeat a high-security vault and its vigilant guards by way of passing around a playing card. In its scrupulous presentation, what could be a scene of considerable tension instead becomes an over-choreographed parody of distraction. The result, specifically and more broadly, undermines any legitimate amazement and wonder at magicians' skill and artistry that an audience might feel.

This does not make *Now You See Me 2* terrible or boring. It merely makes it disappointing—sugary and facile and unabashedly populist when something more emotionally substantive would be more memorable. The first film worked because it took reconstituted elements of Steven Soderbergh's *Ocean's* franchise (the motley team, a heist), added magic, authoritative pursuit and a bit of mystery, and then frosted it liberally with a populist, Robin Hood-type message of sticking it to the elites.

Now You See Me 2 is an exercise in franchise management, moving pieces around a board to set the stage for a third installment. Its performances are fine, even if Caine and Freeman are on mannered paycheck-autopilot. Ruffalo brings a rakish charm to Dylan; Harrelson chews scenery particularly as evil twin Chase; and Radcliffe has a blast playing the unhinged Walter. For most viewers, that will be entertaining enough—a fine way to while away some time. But one will have a hard time remembering exactly what happened in this movie, and to whom, meaning that they will have to read a recap or two, and decide if they still care, before eventually catching *Now You See Me 3*.

Brent Simon

CREDITS

J. Daniel Atlas: Jesse Eisenberg
Dylan Rhodes: Mark Ruffalo
Merritt McKinney/Chase: Woody Harrelson
Jack Wilder: Dave Franco
Walter Mabry: Daniel Radcliffe

Owen Case: Ben Lamb
Arthur Tressler: Michael Caine
Li: Jay Chou
Lula May: Lizzy Caplan
Thaddeus Bradley: Morgan Freeman
Origin: United States
Language: English, Mandarin Chinese
Released: 2016
Production: Bobby Cohen, Alex Kurtzman, Roberto Orci; released by Lionsgate; Summit Entertainment
Directed by: Jon M. Chu
Written by: Edward Solomon
Cinematography by: Peter Deming
Music by: Brian Tyler
Sound: John Marquis; Nancy Nugent
Editing: Stan Salfas
Art Direction: Stuart Kearns
Costumes: Anna B. Sheppard
Production Design: Sharon Seymour
MPAA rating: PG-13
Running time: 115 minutes

REVIEWS

Catsoulis, Jeannette. *New York Times*. June 9, 2016.
Gleiberman, Owen. *Variety*. June 1, 2016.
Gonzalez, Ed. *Slant*. June 8, 2016.
Graham, Adam. *Detroit News*. June 9, 2016.
Linden, Sheri. *Hollywood Reporter*. June 1, 2016.
MacDonald, Moira. *Seattle Times*. June 9, 2016.
Persall, Steve. *Tampa Bay Times*. June 9, 2016.
Rea, Stephen. *Philadelphia Inquirer*. June 9, 2016.
Schaefer, Stephen. *Boston Herald*. June 10, 2016.
Williams, Cole. *Fort Worth Weekly*. June 9, 2016.

QUOTES

Walter Mabry: "Get your last words in quickly everybody!"

TRIVIA

Walter Mabry says he did some magic in school. The character is played by Daniel Radcliffe, who played wizard Harry Potter in that franchise.

O

OFFICE CHRISTMAS PARTY

Party like your job depends on it.
—Movie tagline

Box Office: $54.7 Million

Perhaps the most interesting thing about *Office Christmas Party*, 2016's R-rated holiday comedy from directors Will Speck and Josh Gordon, is that it feels like the movie should have been made years ago, because there's a finite number of truly organic set-ups for a raunchy Hollywood comedy. There are only so many situations where one can reasonably expect to see that much sex, drugs, and alcohol, so those premises are often hoarded like screenwriters' gold. *Animal House* (1978) wisely exploited its fraternity setting, *The Hangover* (2009) played off the pop culture reputation of bachelor parties, and *Office Christmas Party* builds its entire concept—and its wildly unoriginal title—around the well-known cultural trope of grown adults awkwardly trying to cut loose around their co-workers. How did it take Hollywood this long to bring this well-known workplace nightmare to the big screen?

The resulting film is not as subversive or wild as *Animal House* or *The Hangover*, but it does score laughs more often than it misses, largely due to its cast. The screenwriters (Justin Malen, Laura Solon, and Dan Mazer) craft some memorable situations and one-liners, but the movie's energy flags whenever they move away from the party setting. The titular party is the film's true reservoir of comedy. It gives the story structure and verve. But, unfortunately, when the filmmakers try to expand the movie's paper-thin plot beyond the workplace

rager, it simply stops working. Maybe the fact that the movie cannot sustain itself beyond the party speaks to the inherent thinness of the premise, but, despite its weak third act, *Office Christmas Party* does mine some legitimate laughs out of their vision of uninhibited workplace socializing gone wrong.

The office in question belongs to Zenotek, a technology company led by beleaguered CEO Carol Vanstone (Jennifer Aniston). As the film opens, due to flagging profits, Carol threatens to slash the staff and cancel the annual Christmas party of the Chicago branch of Zenotek, which is managed by Carol's irresponsible brother Clay (T.J. Miller). (The long-simmering resentment between the brother-sister pair is one of the movie's funnier running gags, entirely thanks to Miller and Aniston's comedic chemistry.) In response to Carol's threats, Clay, his chief technical officer Josh (Jason Bateman), and tech guru Tracey (Olivia Munn) come up with a plan to save their branch—they promise Carol that they can land rich financier Walter Davis (Courtney B. Vance) as a new client. Carol consents to the plan, despite her skepticism of her brother's ability to pull it off.

In order to win over Walter, Clay invites him to Zenotek's now-un-cancelled Christmas party and begins planning an overly elaborate celebration that makes both Josh and Mary from Human Resources (a scene-stealing Kate McKinnon) very, very nervous. After a slow start, things proceed to get exponentially more out of control as the night goes on. Walter accidentally ingests cocaine, which turns him into a party-crazed maniac. Clay's various debaucheries attract crowds from all over Chicago. And nervous developer Nate (Karan Soni) hires a prostitute to pose as his girlfriend at the party, to impress his nerdy co-workers, which brings the Zenotek gang into contact with Trina (Jillian Bell), the escort's unstable pimp. Things rapidly turn sexual, inebriated, and violent, especially after Carol realizes that Clay is actually throwing his forbidden holiday party. To quote Ron Burgundy, "That escalated quickly."

There's nothing particularly surprising about *Office Christmas Party*, which is a good and bad thing. That feeling of overall familiarity even extends to the film's better-than-average cast. The vast majority of them have been hired to play variations of characters they have already played before.

T.J. Miller is essentially playing a riff on his character from HBO's *Silicon Valley*, Jennifer Aniston is tapping into her *Horrible Bosses* (2011) and *We're the Millers* (2013) characters, and Jason Bateman continues to cash-in as Hollywood's go-to straight man, bringing the exact same energy that he brought to *Horrible Bosses* and *Identity Thief* (2013). Even Jillian Bell's character is not particularly far removed from her *22 Jump Street* (2014) drug dealer. The only character that truly feels "new" is Kate McKinnon's repressed HR rep Mary. Just like she did in 2016's *Ghostbusters*, McKinnon brings a fierce and unusual energy to *Office Christmas Party*, which makes it hard to take your eyes off her. She's clearly having the most fun of the cast, even if her character feels more like something from a *Saturday Night Live* skit than a feature-length film.

As mentioned, the movie loses steam in its final act, inventing an internet emergency that's too convoluted and low stakes to actually work as a satisfying conclusion. The audience came to see an office party (as promised in the title) and there's just not enough life beyond that party to justify leaving it behind. When it stays true to its premise, *Office Christmas Party* has a strong (though not particularly original) comedic energy, creating a familiar template that lets its skilled cast shine within its confines. However, when the movie expects viewers to start caring about the story or characters beyond that wild holiday mixer, the party is over.

Tom Burns

CREDITS

Josh Parker: Jason Bateman
Tracey Hughes: Olivia Munn
Clay Vanstone: T.J. Miller
Carol Vanstone: Jennifer Aniston
Mary: Kate McKinnon
Walter Davis: Courtney B. Vance
Origin: United States
Language: English

Released: 2016
Production: Guymon Casady, Daniel Rappaport, Scott Stuber; released by Bluegrass Films, Dreamworks L.L.C., Paramount Pictures Corp., Reliance Entertainment
Directed by: Josh Gordon; Will Speck
Written by: Justin Malen; Laura Solon; Dan Mazer
Cinematography by: Jeff Cutter
Music by: Theodore Shapiro
Sound: Elliott Koretz
Music Supervisor: Jonathan Karp
Editing: Jeff Groth; Evan Henke
Art Direction: Jami Primmer
Costumes: Karen Patch
Production Design: Andrew Laws
MPAA rating: R
Running time: 105 minutes

REVIEWS

Ashton, Will. *Playlist*. December 8, 2016.
Bradshaw, Peter. *The Guardian*. December 8, 2016.
Dowd, A.A. *The A.V. Club*. December 7, 2016.
Genzlinger, Neil. *New York Times*. December 8, 2016.
Greenblatt, Leah. *Entertainment Weekly*. December 7, 2016.
O'Sullivan, Michael. *Washington Post*. December 8, 2016.
Robey, Tim. *The Telegraph*. December 7, 2016.
Walsh, Katie. *Los Angeles Times*. December 8, 2016.
Winning, Josh. *Total Film*. December 7, 2016.
Wloszczyna, Susan. *RogerEbert.com*. December 9, 2016.

QUOTES

Mary: "I've got doughnuts! I've got jelly and sprinkles, but not cronuts because they're a bastard pastry."

TRIVIA

At the end of production on the film, furniture and props were donated to charity.

ONLY YESTERDAY
(Omohide poro poro)

Box Office: $453,243

It took a quarter-century to be released in the United States, but the wait was worth it for one of the legendary Studio Ghibli's best films, this heartfelt and moving drama about memory and regret. Written and directed by Isao Takahata, who co-founded Ghibli with the more-famous Hayao Miyazaki, and directed a few classics of his own, including *Grave of the Fireflies* (1988) and *The Tale of Princess Kaguya* (2013), *Only Yesterday* is one of the influential animation house's best films. It is proof that animation is a medium and not a genre, it is a form capable of much more than the family film branding often put upon it.

It is 1982, and Taeko is a 27-year-old single woman living in Tokyo. She needs to get away from her urban ennui, and decides to visit the elder brother of her brother-in-law in the countryside. There, she will help with the safflower harvest and reconnect with what matters to her. On a sleeper train to Yamagata, she flashes back to her childhood, 16 years earlier.

It is 1966, and Taeko is an 11-year-old girl, itching to see the world. The duality is purposeful. When we are young, we want nothing more than to leave. When we are old, we want nothing more than to find the comfort of home. *Only Yesterday* plays out in flashbacks during Taeko's trip to Yamagata, as her memories of childhood continue to influence her adult life to greater and greater degrees. It is a purposefully episodic film, one about how much of our value system and personality is formed in childhood, and how easy it is to lose sight of those things that matter as we get older. As Taeko says, voiced beautifully by Daisy Ridley of *Star Wars, Episode VII: The Force Awakens* (2016) in the dubbed version, "I didn't expect to bring my fifth-grade self along for the trip." We all bring along our fifith-grade selves everywhere.

One of many remarkable elements of *Only Yesterday* is the lack of melodrama or manipulation when it comes to Taeko's memories. Some seem insignificant. Not all are pleasant. In fact, many of them are sad, but formative, such as bullies in Taeko's school or her first period. She also remembers a father who was distant and unloving. Takahata's vision is complex enough to understand that it is not the best memories of youth or even the biggest moments that form us, but the cumulative power of it all. He's also too subtle to offer direct cause-and-effect storytelling. A large number of films about childhood draw lines from point A to point B—our protagonist behaves like this because of what happened in the past. Takahata's vision is much more complex, refusing to draw direct parallels.

It's also a beautiful film. Unlike a lot of Ghibli, there are no fantasy elements here, but *Only Yesterday* still stands as one of the company's most visually stunning works (which means it's one of the most visually stunning animated films ever). Miyazaki may be the more recognized name in the canon, but Takahata's work has a mesmerizing lyricism, finding beauty in the real. Taeko's memories have the air of something ephemeral, but never feel manipulative in that regard, and Takahata achieves lyricism without resorting to the typical techniques some directors use to do so. The score is lovely but underplayed, and the film feels more like a truthful drama than a traditional animated picture.

That's the thinking as to why *Only Yesterday* took 25 years to get released in the United States. No one knew how to market an animated film designed more for adults than kids. In Japan, this is not a problem, as animation long ago broke out of the family film designation, becoming something childless adults feel no compunction about seeing. However, this has not exactly happened in the United States, although one wonders why Disney didn't attempt to get this film to audiences during the wave of acclaim for Ghibli's *Princess Mononoke* (1997) and *Spirited Away* (2001), which won the Oscar for Best Animated Film.

Whatever the reason, stateside audiences should be grateful that *Only Yesterday* ever made it to the United States, and that this long-awaited chapter of Studio Ghibli can be finally be conveyed. There's no more important studio for animation in the history of cinema other than perhaps Disney, and *Only Yesterday* proves that the range of the company is even greater than we had previously known. And yet this is not just a minor chapter in the history of Studio Ghibli, as one could argue the also-long-delayed *Ocean Waves* (2016) was for the company. This is a top ten film for Ghibli, which means it's a film everyone must see.

Brian Tallerico

CREDITS

Taeko: Daisy Ridley
Toshio: Dev Patel
Young Taeko: Alison Fernandez
Tsuneko: Hope Levy
Aiko: Stephanie Sheh
Origin: United States
Language: Japanese, English, Hungarian
Released: 2016
Production: Toshio Suzuki; released by Nippon Television Network Corp., Studio Ghibli, Studiopolis, Tokuma Shoten
Directed by: Isao Takahata
Written by: Isao Takahata
Cinematography by: Hisao Shirai
Music by: Katsu Hoshi
Editing: Naoki Kaneko; Tomoko Kida; Yasutaka Mori; Takeshi Seyama
Art Direction: Kazuo Oga
MPAA rating: PG
Running time: 118 minutes

REVIEWS

Coggan, Devan. *Entertainment Weekly*. February 25, 2016.
Connelly, Sherilyn. *Village Voice*. December 30, 2015.
Ivanov, Oleg. *Slant*. December 28, 2015.

Jagernauth, Kevin. *The Playlist*. February 25, 2016.
Kenny, Glenn. *RogerEbert.com*. January 1, 2016.
Murray, Noel. *The A.V. Club*. February 24, 2016.
Rapold, Nicolas. *New York Times*. January 1, 2016.
Savlov, Marc. *Austin Chronicle*. February 24, 2016.
Snydel, Michael. *Film Stage*. February 23, 2016.
Turan, Kenneth. *Los Angeles Times*. February 25, 2016.

QUOTES

Hirota: "Rainy days, cloudy days, sunny days...which do you like?"

Taeko: "...cloudy days."

Hirota: "Oh, then we're alike."

TRIVIA

The film was a surprise box-office smash when first released in Japan; it was the highest-grossing domestic film in 1991, grossing ¥1.87 billion.

OTHER PEOPLE

Box Office: $91,441

It happens every year—a movie makes a big, splashy world premiere at a high-profile film festival, only in the ensuing months to completely disappear from awards consideration or even financial relevance, leaving festival attendees to wonder whether the entire experience was some sort of collective fever dream. One such casualty from 2016 is *Other People*, the semi-autobiographical feature film writing and directing debut of television comedy writer Chris Kelly.

A true, under-appreciated treasure, the movie is a note-perfect dramedy about the messy business of dying, and how the slow wind-down of a terminal illness in a loved one can bleed the energy of an entire family, in ways both heartbreaking yet also illuminating. Featuring strong performances from Jesse Plemons and Molly Shannon, *Other People* is not built around huge moments of revelation, but rather just smart, wholly motivated and entirely engaging relationship dynamics. In split distribution deals several weeks after the movie's debut at the Sundance Film Festival, Netflix acquired streaming rights to the movie, while Vertical Entertainment released it in a dozen theaters in September, where it grossed under $100,000.

Set over the course of 10-plus months, the film tells the story of David Mulcahey (Plemons), a struggling 29-year-old New York City comedy writer who returns home to Sacramento after his mother Joanne (Shannon), a second-grade teacher, is diagnosed with a rare form of cancer. Moving back in with his mom, his father Norman (Bradley Whitford), and his sisters Alexandra (Maude Apatow) and Rebeccah (Madisen Beaty), David grapples with re-acclimating to his hometown.

After struggling through chemotherapy, Joanne decides to cease treatment. She has a brief period of physical uptick, during which the family visits New York, before her health levels off and then begins to decline even more. David just wants his mom to die thinking he is doing okay, as he tells a friend, which explains part of the reason why he does not mention anything about breaking up with his boyfriend of five years, Paul (Zach Woods). His father's lingering difficulty accepting his homosexuality, 10 years after his coming out, also factors into his difficulty in being more open with his family about his personal life.

At the center of what makes *Other People* special is its script. The film avoids too many specific disease-related demarcations in its narrative, instead taking a more impressionistic approach, and filtering Joanne's condition through David's interactions with her, as well as free time he is able to have with family or friends. Kelly peppers his story with sharply observed supporting characters, and perfectly captures the awkwardness of running into old high school classmates as well as family interactions with people who do not really know what you do for a living. He has an eye and ear for the random background detail, too, whether that is a stranger standing too close at a bar or capturing the way a song (in this case Train's "Drops of Jupiter") can haunt you and take over a certain cycle of your life, being exasperating at one moment and genuinely cathartic in the next.

By the same token, Kelly, a veteran of *Saturday Night Live* and *Broad City*, is a gifted writer of winding jokes rooted in strongly character-based perspective. So little from the year in film approaches the idiosyncratic hilarity of David discussing with Paul both the thrill and shame of old teenage masturbatory habits. There is a distinctive personality to *Other People*—totally engaging without being affected or odd simply for the sake of novelty—that is lacking in most films examining a family dynamic.

Another big part of *Other People*'s appeal lies in its smart, unfussy performances. Shannon has an underrated strength as a dramatic actress, as previously showcased in *Year of the Dog* (2007). Here she never asks viewers to feel sorry for her character; she imbues Joanne with a grace and dignity, yes, but does not sacrifice her brassiness either, for the sake of some overly prim and proper vision of what a cancer patient is supposed to act like. This gives *Other People* more emotional resonance in small, organic, measurably human scenes, like where Joanne finds herself so weakened that she cannot effectively share a favorite anecdote about a student.

Plemons, meanwhile, is the film's anchor. His work as Todd Alquist on the fifth season of *Breaking Bad* was superlative, and required a certain stillness. David is a completely different character, obviously, but shares Todd's inward reflectiveness. As much as *Other People* is about Joanne's illness, it is also in substantive ways about returning to one's adolescent home and chafing at its fit as a young adult. Movies with this theme are common (and in fact *The Hollars* [2016], John Krasinski's sophomore directorial effort, tackled very similar subject matter this same year), but Plemons embodies the full spectrum of this struggle wonderfully. As David, he is by turns frustrated, bemused, nostalgic, and adrift. It is Plemons' best role and most fully realized movie performance to date.

Kelly is no slouch as a director, either. He wrote a funny screenplay, but also elicits strong performances from his actors. This is especially seen in some of the supporting players. Paul (the aforementioned Woods), David's friend Gabe (John Early), and Gabe's younger, flamboyant pre-teen brother Justin (J.J. Totah), to name but three, are all examples of Kelly delivering fully sketched-out, three-dimensional characters for roles with no more than two scenes apiece. Kelly and editor Patrick Colman find a great, very natural rhythm in these sequences and others, and composer Julian Wass' score beautifully contributes to the movie's wistful, lived-in vibe, without too forcefully steering viewers' emotions.

There is a saying, of course, that one cannot go home again. *Other People* belies that, dealing in very small and specific authenticity that translates universally, and serving as a rich reminder that we all have baggage from where we have been in life—and that we are usually richer and more interesting for it.

Brent Simon

CREDITS

David: Jesse Plemons
Joanne: Molly Shannon
Norman: Bradley Whitford
Alexandra: Maude Apatow
Rebeccah: Madisen Beaty
Origin: United States
Language: English
Released: 2016
Production: Sam Bisbee, Adam Scott, Naomi Scott; released by Gettin' Rad Productions, Park Pictures
Directed by: Chris Kelly

Written by: Chris Kelly
Cinematography by: Brian Burgoyne
Music by: Julian Wass
Sound: Ian Stynes
Music Supervisor: Chris Swanson
Editing: Patrick Colman
Art Direction: Leigh Poindexter
Costumes: Kerry Hennessy
Production Design: Tracy Dishman
MPAA rating: Unrated
Running time: 97 minutes

REVIEWS

Connelly, Randy. *San Francisco Weekly*. September 7, 2016.
DeFore, John. *Hollywood Reporter*. January 22, 2016.
Gold, Daniel M. *New York Times*. September 8, 2016.
Goodykoontz, Bill. *Arizona Republic*. September 8, 2016.
Jones, Kimberley. *Austin Chronicle*. September 16, 2016.
Lemire, Christy. *RogerEbert.com*. September 9, 2016.
Murray, Noel. *IndieWire*. January 22, 2016.
Roeper, Richard. *Chicago Sun Times*. September 8, 2016.
Smith, Kyle. *New York Post*. January 22, 2016.
Zilberman, Alan. *Washington Post*. September 8, 2016.

QUOTES

David: "This all just feels like...something that happens to other people."
Gabe: "Yeah well now, you're other people to other people."

TRIVIA

Molly Shannon replaced Sissy Spacek who was originally cast in the role of the mother but had to drop out due to her commitment to the second season of *Bloodline*.

AWARDS

Ind. Spirit 2017: Actress--Supporting (Shannon)
Nominations:
Ind. Spirit 2017: Actor (Plemons), First Feature, First Screenplay

THE OTHER SIDE OF THE DOOR

When they come back, they don't come alone.
—Movie tagline

Box Office: $3 Million

When a film is titled *The Other Side of the Door* and in that movie, when one person says, "Whatever you do, never open that door," it becomes quite clear that the film in question only exists so that strange and/or horrifying things can happen to everyone in the second and third act. The film ends up robbing itself of suspense with the title alone. Of course, the door will be opened, and, of course, bad things will happen. From the get-go, the film has a feeling of being an obligation to merely exist. A relatively cheaply made horror movie was needed on a particular weekend in the first quarter of the year to help make a solid bottom line for the studio. Said horror film met the criteria of being safe, indistinguishable, partially populated with kids, some of whom have creepy faces and who can open their mouths really wide, and with a cast of mostly unknowns.

The one distinction with *The Other Side of the Door* is that it takes place in Mumbai, India. It pretty much stops there because the main characters are still white Americans who decide at the start of the film to live their lives there, have a family and save themselves the hassle of commuting back and forth for years (they are usually there on business). Maria (Sarah Wayne Callies) and Michael (Jeremy Sisto) have their whole lives ahead of them, and six years after making that decision, their lives have been severely altered by tragedy. While still living in Mumbai, they have had two kids, one of whom, Oliver (Logan Creran), drowned in an auto accident in which his sister, Lucy (Sofia Rosinsky) and his mother survived. Now, Maria lives with the guilt of that tragedy and cannot let go of the memory of her child.

After Maria attempts suicide, her servant, Piki (Suchitra Pillai), has an idea for her: There is a forest in South India that has an abandoned temple. The line between the world of the dead and the living exists within this place. If she takes the ashes of her son and spreads them on the steps of this temple, she will be able to talk to him through the door of the temple and say her final goodbye. No matter what happens, she must not open the door. Perhaps her grief clouds her judgment, because she actually goes through with the act of digging up her son's dead body, burning it and taking the ashes with her in a little box. Once she gets there, she has to descend a dark staircase to get to the temple that is filled with creepy noises, bats, and ominous wind chimes.

Again, it comes as no surprise that she would hear the voice of her son coming through the other side of the door. They have a brief, emotional exchange that eventually leads to him being taken away. Unwilling to accept this as her final moment with the spiritual manifestation of her own flesh and blood, she opens the door and finds nothing. She returns home with a comforting sense of closure on the whole experience. She also sees Oliver in a spiritual form still lurking within the house. Their daughter finds a toy that had been buried with Oliver and the piano starts playing by

itself. Poor husband Michael has been kept in the dark about all of this.

The Other Side of the Door then dissolves into a usual parade of MacGuffins, cheap jump scares, and extended sequences of weirdness that turn out to be nightmares had by the main character. Everything happens as expected. Dark, shadowy figures appear hauntingly in otherwise bland, tranquil settings. The little girl gets possessed at some point. The dog starts making weird noises in the middle of the night. The film tries to get as much mileage as it can out of that toy tiger that used to belong to Oliver. Even the typical nightmare ghoul with no face and backwards, creaky limbs shows up to take a stab at scaring the audience who will likely be too jaded for this sort of thing. Just about everything on the Modern-Day Horror Movie checklist can be marked off, except for maybe the optional "found footage" style (although if this film worked hard enough, it could have incorporated that as well).

This is a shame because there are good performances here by Callies and Sisto and even Rosinsky, the little girl, has effective moments. Director and co-writer Johannes Roberts does an okay job of depicting the grief of a loved one early in the film and is smart to let that play out longer than other horror films would let it. In that sense, *The Other Side of the Door* has an almost old-fashioned approach by giving the audience time to get into the characters' heads before laying on the scares. At the same time, though, the film lacks any punch or wit that will make it memorable. Even when *The Conjuring* movies are playing by the rules of the haunted house genre tropes, they do so with a few laughs and an uncanny intelligence. Callies, as Maria, does a good enough job of being the victim, but she is saddled with a role that rarely asks her to do more than cry and look petrified, an all-too-common shortcoming for this genre.

The Other Side of the Door will be memorable for the wrong reasons, though. Its setting of India is a change of pace, but its depiction of the people as mere servants of the white people and ritual killers of their children is off-putting and unfortunate. The film also goes into an area in the third act that will be troublesome for many viewers (it involves the little girl and the family dog). There are all sorts of ways to treat a horror movie audience to some scares without insulting their intelligence or making them feel bad for the people on the screen or feel bad about themselves for buying a ticket. *The Other Side of the Door* could have been an interesting horror film about grief and the decay of the family unit. Instead, it is only about what is on the other side of that door.

Collin Souter

CREDITS

Maria: Sarah Wayne Callies

Michael: Jeremy Sisto

Lucy: Sofia Rosinsky

Oliver: Logan Creran

Piki: Suchitra Pillai

Origin: United States

Language: English

Released: 2016

Production: Rory Aitken, Alexandre Aja, Ben Pugh; released by 42, Fire Axe Pictures, Kriti Productions, TSG Entertainment

Directed by: Johannes Roberts

Written by: Johannes Roberts; Ernest Riera

Cinematography by: Maxime Alexandre

Music by: Joseph Bishara

Sound: James Mather

Editing: Baxter

Art Direction: Prashant Laharia

Costumes: Divya Gambhir; Nidhi Gambhir

Production Design: David Bryan

MPAA rating: R

Running time: 96 minutes

REVIEWS

Baumgarten, Marjorie. *Austin Chronicle.* March 10, 2016.

Bradshaw, Peter. *Guardian.* March 3, 2016.

Grierson, Tim. *Screen International.* March 4, 2016.

Holub, Christian. *Entertainment Weekly.* March 4, 2016.

Huddleston, Tom. *Time Out.* March 1, 2016.

Lemire, Christy. *RogerEbert.com.* March 4, 2016.

Lowe, Justin. *Hollywood Reporter.* February 29, 2016.

Moore, Roger. *Movie Nation.* March 10, 2016.

Newman, Kim. *Empire Magazine.* February 29, 2016.

White, Dave. *The Wrap.* February 23, 2016.

QUOTES

Piki: [speaking to Maria] "Did you think that you could bring back somebody from the world of the dead and they would be the same? Did you think there would be no consequences?"

TRIVIA

Mary Lambert, director of *Pet Sematary,* appears as Oliver's grandmother in a photo that Piki throws into a garbage bag.

OUIJA: ORIGIN OF EVIL

When you talk to the other side, you never know who will be listening.
—Movie tagline

Box Office: $35.1 Million

This sequel to the awful *Ouija* (2014) should have ghosted through cinemas like so many generally unwanted follow-ups. Instead, *Ouija: Origin of Evil* was a big hit with critics and audiences alike. The primary reason rests squarely on the shoulders of a rising talent, writer/director Mike Flanagan, who has amassed an impressive streak of surprisingly strong horror films and was clearly more than just a sequel director-for-hire here. This is a movie full of genuinely scary scenes that even achieves insight on the human condition. The end result falls somewhere between supernatural drama and monster movie, but that lack of clear genre definition just indicates how Flanagan is able to deal with time-worn material and make it seem fresh and frightening.

It is Los Angeles, 1967. Recent widower Alice Zander (Elizabeth Reaser) makes her living, assisted by her daughters Lina (Annalise Basso) and Doris (Lulu Wilson), holding fake séances in her suburban neighborhood, firm in the belief that the scam helps many of her customers find closure in tragedy. When Lina sneaks out to a late-night party, where the guests fool around with a Ouija board, she uses the story to defuse her angry mother, suggesting they incorporate one into their séances. After rigging the device to respond to her commands, Alice begins practicing with it, and, in the process, without realizing, contacts a spirit named Marcus, who uses the opportunity to possess her daughter Doris. She also forgets to say goodbye at the end of the session, leaving the door open for Marcus to further influence and control. The three rules of the Ouija are never to use the device alone, never use it in a graveyard, and to always say goodbye.

Doris is soon using the board by herself, contacting other spirits and producing work at school beyond her years. School Principal Father Tom (Henry Thomas) becomes concerned about her, but Alice is convinced they have come into contact with her late husband, the girl's father Roger, especially after a spirit leads Doris to a hole in the wall containing enough cash to save the family home from foreclosure. As Alice and Doris team up to give real spirit readings to bereaved customers, Lina is unconvinced, deeply disturbed by her mother's unwillingness to accept Roger's death and look beyond her grief to see what is really happening with Doris.

Father Thomas and Lina team up looking for proof that the spirit manifestations are of evil origin. They find written evidence of ghastly experiments performed in the basement and decide to perform an exorcism. Too late. Whatever is inside Doris lashes out, killing Lina's boyfriend, prompting Alice, Father Tom, and Lina to try burning the Ouija board in the basement furnace. They discover bones in the walls of the basement and draw the horrified conclusion that they have been operating the board in a graveyard the entire time. As old phonograph music and Doris' cries emanate from the hidden basement tomb, Father Tom crawls inside, only to be possessed himself, leading to a deadly confrontation.

Setting the story in the mid-sixties does more than turn this sequel into a prequel. It sets the story and the characters in a time that viewers might see as a little more innocent—even wide-eyed—and thus a little more dangerous for the characters as they get in over their heads. While the script flirts with the idea of a possible romance between Alice and Father Thomas, it stays centered on the Zander family and their complicated dynamic, keeping the sense of danger rooted in the threats that work to tear the family apart.

Casting adds to the easy suspension of disbelief. While Lulu Wilson is impressive as Doris, especially given her age and the amount of screen time she has, the film is blessed to have the ample chemistry provided by Elizabeth Reaser and Annalise Basso. They offer a solid backdrop and even a few standout mother-daughter moments in the midst of a lot of horror movie fright conventions. Henry Thomas, an underused actor in general, does solid work with a nice role as a priest struggling with his own grief and sense of calling. His character arc could have ended on a more interesting note, but his performance plays into the dark and desperate nature of the story being told.

Flanagan utilizes a blend of practical and CGI effects but wisely supports them with just the right lighting, sound, and shot composition. The transformation of Doris into a creature of possession is certainly unnerving despite CGI effects that might be less disturbing in the hands of someone who had less visual imagination. As it stands, comparisons to James Wan, who has a real knack for keeping things scary after his bogeys are seen, seem more than fair.

Mike Flanagan has been a roll. *Absentia* (2011), his first horror film, was effective enough that it warranted keeping an eye on what he did next. Viewers were then treated to the overly busy but effective and thematically complex *Oculus* (2013). Next came *Hush* (2016), a nail-biting home invasion thriller told largely from the point of view of its deaf protagonist. An as-of-yet-unreleased supernatural fantasy, *Before I Wake* has garnered some impressive reviews despite being stuck in distributor limbo. All of Flanagan's dark genre films deal with the general themes of isolation and fear of the unknown.

Oujia: Origin of Evil ends like many horror movies with a character imprisoned in a mental asylum unable to convince anyone of the true version of events. But even here, in well-worn territory, Flanagan looks into the stark despair of isolation and the constant invitation that state makes towards evil and whatever realm evil calls home. It simply becomes easier to fall asleep under

its spell than to keep fighting for a world that pretends to have all the answers merely to keep from confronting its own worst fears.

Dave Canfield

CREDITS

Lina Zander: Annalise Basso
Alice Zander: Elizabeth Reaser
Doris Zander: Lulu Wilson
Father Tom Hogan: Henry Thomas
Origin: United States
Language: English
Released: 2016
Production: Michael Bay, Jason Blum, Stephen Davis, Andrew Form, Brad Fuller, Brian Goldner; released by Allspark Pictures, Blumhouse Productions, DENTSU Inc., Hasbro, Intrepid Pictures, Platinum Dunes
Directed by: Mike Flanagan
Written by: Mike Flanagan; Jeff Howard
Cinematography by: Michael Fimognari
Music by: The Newton Brothers
Sound: Trevor Gates
Editing: Mike Flanagan
Costumes: Lynn Falconer
Production Design: Patricio M. Farrell
MPAA rating: PG-13
Running time: 99 minutes

REVIEWS

Erbland, Kate. *IndieWire*. October 24, 2016.
Genzlinger, Neil. *New York Times*. October 20, 2016.
Gonzalez, Ed. *Slant*. October 18, 2016.
Huddleston, Tom. *Time Out*. October 18, 2016.
Newman, Kim. *Screen International*. October 18, 2016.
Savlov, Marc. *Austin Chronicle*. October 20, 2016.
Scheck, Frank. *Hollywood Reporter*. October 19, 2016.
Scherstuhl, Alan. *Village Voice*. October 20, 2016.
Weinberg, Scott. *Nerdist*. October 21, 2016.
Wilson, Calvin. *St. Louis Dispatch*. October 20, 2016.

QUOTES

Alice Zander: [crying] "I just wanted to be able to talk to Daddy again. I just wanted you to be able to talk to Daddy."
Possessed Doris: "He's gone. He lives in the dark and the cold, and he screams, and screams, and screams...."

TRIVIA

This film is one of three movies directed by Mike Flanagan that was released in 2016, the others being *Hush* and *Before I Wake*.

OUR KIND OF TRAITOR

Who can you trust with the truth?
—Movie tagline

Box Office: $3.1 Million

Spy movies are a difficult proposition in the modern world. Exciting new technology does not have the impact it once did because so much of the world has the most incredible technology at their disposal anyway. Complex spy rings don't resonate because most of the incriminating information out there is uncovered online all the time and discussed to death on CNN before dinner. In short, imagination has been trumped by real life. Writer Hossein Amini and director Susanna White tried anyway by adapting a fairly recent novel by John le Carré, an author who's been at the forefront of spy literature since the 1960s. Le Carré worked for MI5, the British Security Service, spying on radicals for the government before resigning and becoming a full-time writer. The details of information gathering and the banality of top secret missions abroad ring true in *Our Kind of Traitor,* thanks to le Carré's detail-heavy foundation, but the film never finds the spark it needs to become truly exciting, nor does it commit to the ugly, boring nature of real-world spying.

English poetry lecturer Perry (Ewan McGregor) and his barrister wife Gail (Naomie Harris) are in Marrakech, Morocco trying to rekindle their romance. He slept with one of his students and Gail cannot seem to find it in her to let him touch her anymore. After a disappointing dinner, Gail leaves Perry alone at their hotel restaurant, and over walks Dima (Stellan Skarsgård), who invites Perry to have a drink and go to a party. At that party Perry has to talk himself out of another infidelity and then witnesses a mobster beating up a woman and breaks it up. Dima repays his heroism by inviting Perry and Gail to tennis and then to an even more lavish party that night. It's there that Dima confides in Perry that he needs help. The Prince, the new head of the Russian mafia (Grigoriy Dobrygin) wants Dima to turn over all the accounts he's managed over the years. Dima does not want to do this because the only member of the mob to do so thus far was murdered mere minutes later. Dima fears that the Prince will kill him and his whole family once he's in control of Dima's accounts, so he concocts a plan. If Perry will take some evidence to the UK and hand it over to MI6, they can work an immunity deal and offer asylum to the Russian mobster. Perry accepts, and days later he's in an airport interrogation room with an official named Hector (Damian Lewis).

Hector finds Dima's evidence compelling enough to bring it to his supervisor Billy Matlock (Mark Gatiss) because it implies ties between the Russian mob and British politician Aubrey Longrigg (Jeremy Northam). Hector has a longstanding grudge against Longrigg and wants him brought down. Unfortunately, Billy knows this only too well and thinks Hector's judgment is clouded by bias. Billy denies Hector further resources to investigate Dima's claims but Hector continues anyway. He lies to Perry that he's got the support of his government, and tells him and Gail to make contact with Dima in Paris, and follow him to Bern, Switzerland, where the Prince will take over his accounts. There they just have to distract the Prince's men long enough for Dima, his wife (Alicia von Rittberg), and children to escape to a safe house in the French Alps. Of course, once Dima and Perry discover that Hector is operating as a rogue agent, their confidence in the mission wanes considerably.

Everything about *Our Kind of Traitor* is just a little too tidy, a little too pretty, and a little too safe. The look of the film is truly wonderful, thanks to maverick cinematographer Anthony Dod Mantle, who has been turning digital photography into acrylic paint since the late '90s when he discovered its capacity for total conversion of environments into spaces of cinematic rebirth. Here, he turns one gorgeous location after another into an otherworldly negative of itself, his pale yellows, deep greens, and blinding blues always just beyond the faces of the cast. From the opening shot of a ballerina in suspended motion on a stage, it's clear that he's the primary voice behind the film's visual personality. White fights a little against his typically strange, alienating compositions in order to keep her spy story fixed to reality, but that proves a battle not worth winning. By rejecting the more abstract tendencies Mantle usually brings to his work behind the camera, White looks like she's fighting to keep the movie as ordinary as possible. And as good as Amini's screenplay is at maintaining le Carré's tone, the film plays like a James Bond film without as compelling a center and no sense of humor. It's tough to explain the constant location hopping and the host of gorgeous faces on display as anything other than a kind of paean, or worse, concession, to more famous film spy stories.

The performances range from good to workmanlike. Ewan McGregor strains too hard to act like a normal person, failing at ordinary things like lying to his wife about a black eye. He's too alien in his movie star pulchritude to play a teacher with a wandering eye. It makes even less sense thanks to the presence of the beautiful Naomie Harris as Gail, who is even more supernaturally beautiful than McGregor. Stellan Skarsgård acquits himself perfectly well as Dima, but there's never anything singular enough about his blustering performance to indicate why he was hired over an actual Russian-born actor. The suits fare much better, with Damian Lewis' slimy, prim Hector a truly loathsome sort of hero. He's hard to like but impossible not to watch. Mark Gatiss and Jeremy Northam, two underutilized actors, don't much to do in their cameo appearances but they bring titanic gravity to their slightly sinister colorlessness. They represent the central problem with *Our Kind of Traitor*. White does not trust that regular people in shabby places falling into compromising positions are always more interesting than beautiful people chasing bad guys in paradise.

Scout Tafoya

CREDITS

Perry: Ewan McGregor
Dima: Stellan Skarsgard
Hector: Damian Lewis
Gail: Naomie Harris
Aubrey: Jeremy Northam
Origin: United States
Language: English
Released: 2016
Production: Simon Cornwell, Stephen Cornwell, Gail Egan; released by Film 4, StudioCanal S.A.
Directed by: Susanna White
Written by: Hossein Amini
Cinematography by: Anthony Dod Mantle
Music by: Marcelo Zarvos

Sound: Lee Herrick
Music Supervisor: Kle Savidge
Editing: Tariq Anwar; Lucia Zucchetti
Art Direction: James Foster
Costumes: Julian Day
Production Design: Sarah Greenwood
MPAA rating: R
Running time: 108 minutes

REVIEWS

Dargis, Manohla. *New York Times*. June 30, 2016.
Debruge, Peter. *Variety*. May 5, 2016.
Felperin, Leslie. *Hollywood Reporter*. June 20, 2016.
Goldstein, Gary. *Los Angeles Times*. June 30, 2016.
Greenblatt, Leah. *Entertainment Weekly*. June 23, 2016.
Hassenger, Jesse. *The A.V. Club*. June 29, 2016.
Ivanov, Oleg. *Slant*. June 29, 2016.
Kenny, Glenn. *RogerEbert.com*. July 1, 2016.
Lane, Anthony. *New Yorker*. June 27, 2016.
Phillips, Michael. *Chicago Tribune*. June 30, 2016.

TRIVIA

The film used around 50 locations and about 90 film sets.

P

PAPA: HEMINGWAY IN CUBA

Hemingway's untold story.
—Movie tagline

Box Office: $1.1 Million

It is a known fact amongst those savvy to entertainment industry posturing that when the behind-the-scenes story of a movie's making becomes the focal point of persuasive audience solicitation, or indeed its entire advertising campaign, it is a tacit admission of narrative shortcomings—a misdirection designed to appeal to viewers' basest instincts of surface intrigue.

Assertively billed, alternately, as the first Hollywood movie shot in Cuba since the country's 1959 revolution and the feature directorial debut of prolific producer Bob Yari (thus ignoring straight-to-video *Mind Games* [1989]), *Papa: Hemingway in Cuba* is one such offering. Plodding, perfunctory, and alternately dramatically perplexing and unconvincing, the movie takes a sideways look at Ernest Hemingway. Lacking any of the understated style of its ostensible subject, however, the result is a special cocktail of dumb and boring for which even hardcore aficionados of the legendary author will have a hard time mustering much enthusiasm.

Set during the sunset of the 1950s, the film centers on Ed Myers (Giovanni Ribisi), a reporter for the (fictional) *Miami Globe* whose girlfriend Debbie Hunt (a miscast Minka Kelly) mails off a letter he wrote to his idol, Ernest Hemingway (Adrian Sparks). When Hemingway responds and invites Myers to visit him and his wife Mary (Joely Richardson) in Cuba, an unlikely friendship develops in which Hemingway helps Myers find his literary voice.

Naturally, *Papa* unfolds against the backdrop of the Cuban revolution, in which rebels allied with Fidel Castro are in the process of overthrowing President Fulgencio Batista's government. While depicted robustly, this historical underpinning lacks any political gravitas, and is instead mostly used as ballast for the assessments of hard-drinking manliness and self-reliance that Hemingway imparts to his young charge.

Yes, *Papa* deploys the increasingly familiar trope of assaying a famous subject through the eyes of a journalist only tangentially and/or briefly connected to him or her. In this case, this choice is in theory grounded in truth, since the movie is based on the memoir of the late Denne Bart Petitclerc, an American reporter and war correspondent who actually befriended Hemingway. But Petitclerc's self-adapted screenplay self-consciously reaches for brusque, masculinized truth, usually by way of tersely delivered platitudes ("The only value we have as human beings are the risks we are willing to take"). Some of these might sound better in the guise of more naturalistic conversation, but they are so awkwardly scattered throughout *Papa* that they come off as cheap motivational poster cliches.

As such, *Papa's* revelations or insights about Hemingway, as either the writer or a man, are scant and limited to what is obvious on the surface—that he is driven by a sense of adventure and intellectual curiosity, but also profoundly difficult to live with. Cue, between he and Mary, the sort of drunken arguments that occasionally make for good audition scenes for films within films, but rarely feel fresh or interestingly staged as real drama. Neither does *Papa* feel believably connected to the events unfolding around its characters ("Goddamn war!" Hemingway growls when Castro's rebels enact their overthrow). FBI surveillance of Hemingway (which really happened) and shootouts in which Myers and the celebrated author dodge gunfire (a more dubious invention) all come across as empty, risible, artificially inserted intrigue, propped up as they are by Mark Isham's emotionally goading score.

A producer of *Crash* somewhat known for his brash outsider status (Yari famously tried to sue his way into an Oscar after being denied a stage presence for that film's awards season run through Producers Guild of America arbitration), Yari seems to have absorbed no defining sense of authorial vision from any of the directors with whom he met and worked. Ergo, his film feels like a collection of scenes in search of some cohesive point.

It is not merely that *Papa* is dull, but it possesses no unifying visual scheme. Cinematographer Ernesto Melara captures some gorgeous sunsets, and there is the added cachet or trivia value of the movie having shot at the sprawling, cream-colored estate (now a museum) which was Hemingway's actual place of residence in Cuba. But while a languidly photographed backdrop could serve as counterpoint for the spare, tight prose of its titular subject, or a more tightly wound approach could complement it, Yari seems to vacillate between the two. Editor Glen Scantlebury's choices are similarly dissonant, seemingly suiting only the rhythms of expeditious escape from any given scene, and no greater purpose or master.

Yari's approach with actors seems equally haphazard, giving them wide berth rather than clear direction. Ribisi can (and does) easily channel world-weariness and a halting, inwardly-reflected uncertainty. So it is easy to feel his overwhelmed wonder at being thrust into a sort of master-class apprenticeship at the feet of his idol, even if it is a turn that does feel overly familiar from him. Sparks, meanwhile, seems frequently lost, delivering a dinner-theater-level performance that leans on obvious indicators.

Sometimes movies are a great way to learn about the past, and explore an era or figure that represents a viewer's blind spot. *Papa: Hemingway in Cuba*, however, offers up only two-dimensional characters and pat, pedestrian drama. It imparts no greater understanding of Hemingway than could be gleaned by skimming any random encyclopedia entry.

Brent Simon

CREDITS

Ed Myers: Giovanni Ribisi
Mary Hemingway: Joely Richardson
Ernest Hemingway: Adrian Sparks
Debbie Hunt: Minka Kelly
Evan Shipman: Shaun Toub
Origin: United States
Language: English
Released: 2016
Production: Amanda Harvey, Weezie Melancon, Michael Pacino, Bob Yari; released by Studio 2050, Sunstone Film Productions, Yari Film Group
Directed by: Bob Yari
Written by: Denne Bart Petitclerc
Cinematography by: Ernesto Melara
Music by: Mark Isham
Sound: Steven Iba
Music Supervisor: Michelle Kuznetsky
Editing: Glen Scantlebury
Costumes: Jane Anderson
Production Design: Aramís Balebona Recio
MPAA rating: R
Running time: 110 minutes

REVIEWS

Di Nunzio, Miriam. *Chicago Sun-Times.* April 29, 2016.
Keough, Peter. *Boston Globe.* April 28, 2016.
LaSalle, Mick. *San Francisco Chronicle.* April 28, 2016.
Leydon, Joe. *Variety.* April 27, 2016.
Long, Tom. *Detroit News.* April 29, 2016.
Lumenick, Lou. *New York Post.* April 28, 2016.
Merry, Stephanie. *Washington Post.* April 28, 2016.
Rea, Stephen. *Philadelphia Inquirer.* April 28, 2016.
Scherstuhl, Alan. *Village Voice.* April 27, 2016.
Verongos, Helen. *New York Times.* April 28, 2016.

TRIVIA

Mariel Hemingway, the granddaughter of Ernest Hemingway, appears in the birthday dinner scene.

PASSENGERS

Nothing happens by accident.
—Movie tagline

Box Office: $99 Million

The opening scenes of *Passengers* are so enormously promising that it seems as if it might actually turn out to be that rarest of cinematic birds—an intelligent, large-scale, and original science-fiction film that is not a sequel, remake, reboot, or adaptation of a previously established property. That feeling lasts for about 25 minutes or so, and then the film takes a disastrous turn for the worse with one of the ickiest plot developments imaginable, one that is made all the worse by its essential refusal to come to terms with just how grotesque it has become because of it. The end result is such a singularly unpleasant experience that most moviegoers will be not so much dazzled as they are dumbfounded as to what it was about it, other than the size of their paychecks, that could have possible induced co-stars Jennifer Lawrence and Chris Pratt and director Morton Tyldum—the latter making his follow-up to his Oscar-winning hit *The Imitation Game* (2014)—to sign on to do it despite presumably knowing full well just how completely and distastefully it goes off the rails.

In the not-too-distant future, colonizing other planets has become a big business. People are willing to leave their lives on Earth behind and place themselves in suspended animation for around 120 years to travel to a new home via spaceship. One such ship is the Avalon, and, as the film opens, it is about 30 years into its journey to the planet of Homestead II with over 5,000 passengers and crew sleeping away. An inadvertent collision with an asteroid causes a glitch that ends up awakening engineer Jim Preston (Pratt) 90 years too early. At first, he doesn't notice because he is on the groggy side, but he soon realizes that not only is he the only person awake on the ship, he cannot put himself back into hibernation and will therefore almost certainly die long before the ship reaches its destination and the others wake up. When he realizes that he cannot fix the problem, he tries to make the best of his situation by enjoying the ship's amenities, primarily the bar run by amiable robot mixologist Arthur (Michael Sheen), but after a year of this, the isolation and loneliness gets to Jim and he begins idly contemplating just ending it all.

As noted, these opening scenes are actually fairly compelling. Although the technological details may be somewhat different, the screenplay effectively taps the universal fear of compete isolation in ways that are both poignant and darkly humorous. Pratt is amiably goofy as he learns the way around the place where he will be spending the rest of his life, and touching as the full gravity of his situation begins to weigh heavier upon him. For his part, Tyldum sets everything up in a relatively clean and efficient manner, and the look is undeniably impressive. It is here that the film winds up going straight to hell at supersonic speed.

One day, while feeling especially sorry for himself, Jim literally stumbles upon the pod containing a young woman named Aurora Lane and since she looks just like Jennifer Lawrence, he is immediately besotted with her. After endlessly studying her video profile (she is a writer who plans to spend a year on Homestead II and return to Earth to write her story), he becomes convinced that she is the ideal woman for him and is crestfallen that she can be physically so near to him and yet so far away in all other respects. Well, not necessarily, as it turns

out. Using his engineering skills, Jim figures out a way in which he can override Aurora's pod and wake her up early as well. Sure, this means that he is dooming her as well to an existence that will end long before the ship arrives at Homestead II but hey, at least he will be able to spend the years with his dream girl. Besides, he is sure that she will eventually be okay with it, once she gets over the initial shock and he turns on the shaggy-dog charm to win her over. Just to be sure, he will not mention his part in her early revival at first, claiming instead that it was the same kind of mechanical error that woke him up.

To simply contemplate doing such a thing to Aurora—violating her person by waking her up without her consent and then trying to win her heart by lying about what he has done to her for largely selfish reasons—is pretty much beyond the pale, though perhaps somewhat understandable given the circumstances if it is assumed that the isolation has begun to drive Jim mad. To actually do all of that, however, is simply monstrous, a series of acts that one could liken to rape and murder without sounding overly hyperbolic. And yet it offers up a number of potentially intriguing narrative developments once Aurora inevitably discovers the truth about her revival. For Aurora now has to confront the fact that not only has Jim pretty much destroyed her life and hopes in order to satisfy his own selfish desires, she now, through no fault of her own, is forced to spend the rest of her life with the very person that ruined it. For Jim, not only does he have to face up the enormity of what he has done, he has to do so while feeling even more isolated than before. This could all be spun as poignant drama, jet-black comedy, or even as a flat-out horror film as Aurora's rejection finally sends Jim over the edge once and for all. Any of these approaches might work as long as the film is honest and upfront about Jim being a creep without trying to sugarcoat it in any way.

Not only does the film fail in this regard, it tries to insist that Jim really is a good guy after all and that no one—not even Aurora—should hold his tiny little slip in judgement against him in ways that are literally mind-boggling. When Aurora eventually learns the truth—Arthur accidentally lets it slip—it is at just the moment when Jim is about to propose marriage to her and when she stalks off in anger, the film lingers on him looking hurt and rejected. When she refuses to even listen to his self-serving explanations for why he took her life into his hands, he forces her to do so by commandeering the ship's sound system so that she has to hear him no matter how much she tries to avoid him (a moment that is meant to be heartbreaking but which is actually creepy beyond measure). When she has finally had enough and is about to bash his brains in with a crowbar for what he has done, he gives her a big puppy dog look while refusing to defend himself so that she looks like the cruel aggressor. The screenplay even contrives to wake up another character in one of the ship's deckhands (Laurence Fishburne), who ostensibly turns up to explain why many aspects of the ship have been malfunctioning and to supply a *deus ex machina* but whose real purpose is to essentially tell Aurora that yeah, Jim messed up and stuff but she should really get over it. And if all of that weren't enough, the screenplay even throws in a third act disaster that threatens the entire ship and forces Aurora to work with Jim in order to save everyone on board—a convenient twist that not only serves to distract from the real matter at hand with pyrotechnics and contrived heroics but seems intended to cause viewers to think "Well, if he didn't wake her up, she would have died— let's get him a present, preferably one that looks especially nice in a bathing suit."

Seemingly designed by and for guys who go onto Facebook who complain that women refuse to date them even though they insist that they are "nice guys," *Passengers* is arguably the worst film of 2016, not just for the atrocious things that it does but because of the number of ways in which the premise could have been transformed into something interesting had it landed in less idiotic hands. There are even aspects of the film that one can come away admiring, such as the score by Thomas Newman and the oftentimes ingenious visuals created by cinematographer Rodrigo Prieto and the army of visual effects technicians on duty (the most impressive of the bunch showing the effect that a sudden loss of gravity can have on a swimming pool and anyone unlucky enough to be in it at the wrong time). Sadly, not even these contributions can even come close to redeeming the monstrosity that is *Passengers*, a film that, if it were truly being honest with moviegoers (which was not the case, as the wildly misleading trailers and commercials proved), probably should have been called *Pig In Space*.

Peter Sobczynski

CREDITS

Aurora Lane: Jennifer Lawrence
Jim Preston: Chris Pratt
Arthur: Michael Sheen
Gus Mancuso: Laurence Fishburne
Captain Norris: Andy Garcia
Origin: United States
Language: English
Released: 2016
Production: Stephen Hamel, Michael Maher, Ori Marmur, Neal H. Moritz; released by Columbia Pictures

Directed by: Morten Tyldum
Written by: Jon Spaihts
Cinematography by: Rodrigo Prieto
Music by: Thomas Newman
Sound: Will Files
Editing: Maryann Brandon
Art Direction: David Lazan
Costumes: Jany Temime
Production Design: Guy Hendrix Dyas
MPAA rating: PG-13
Running time: 116 minutes

REVIEWS

Abele, Robert. *The Wrap*. December 15, 2016.
Bennett, Laura. *Slate*. December 20, 2016.
Ebiri, Bilge. *Village Voice*. December 15, 2016.
Gleiberman, Owen. *Variety*. December 15, 2016.
Grierson, Tim. *Popular Mechanics*. December 19, 2016.
Holden, Stephen. *New York Times*. December 20, 2016.
Hornaday, Ann. *Washington Post*. December 21, 2016.
Linden, Sheri. *Hollywood Reporter*. December 15, 2016.
Turan, Kenneth. *Los Angeles Times*. December 20, 2016.
Zacharek, Stephanie. *Time*. December 21, 2016.

QUOTES

Aurora: "If you live an ordinary life, all you'll have are ordinary stories."

TRIVIA

The symbols dot dot dot, dash dash dash, dot dot dot--morse code for S.O.S.--appear under the title on the movie poster.

AWARDS

Nominations:

Oscars 2016: Orig. Score, Production Design

PATERSON

If you ever left me I'd tear my heart out and never put it back.
—Movie tagline

Box Office: $1.7 Million

Jim Jarmusch's beautiful new drama is about seeing poetry in the mundanity of normal life. It is as delicate, nuanced, and ultimately moving as the poetry of William Carlos Williams, who inspired the film in the first place. Jarmusch's film washes over the viewers like the waterfalls to which the title character returns throughout the simple story of a bus driver and his book of poems.

Jarmusch envisions a world in which there is as much beauty in a box of matches or a morning kiss as there is in a romantic sonnet. On the surface, there's not much to *Paterson*. It is merely a relatively average week in the life of a New Jersey bus driver. And yet it has a remarkable cumulative power, like a collection of poems that may not seem connected but make a combined impact when you read the final stanza.

On one level, *Paterson* is about finding rhythms and patterns in life. And so it makes perfect sense that the film's title would refer both to its setting—Paterson, New Jersey—and the name of its title character, played perfectly by Adam Driver. Paterson has an ordinary, predictable life. Each day of the week we spend with him opens with a title card announcing the day ("Monday," "Tuesday," and so on). He wakes up next to his lovely girlfriend Laura (Golshifteh Farahani), kisses her on the check, puts on his watch, has his Cheerios, and walks to work. His routine at night is also not often dissimilar from day to day. It involves walking Marvin, their English Bulldog, and a stop at the local watering hole run by Doc (Barry Shabaka Henley). The days may be differentiated by conversations on the bus or at the bar, or a different poem that Paterson happens to be working on, but they are generally the same.

Into this familiar structure, Jarmusch introduces natural rhyming patterns, the kind that exist in everyday life but are often ignored as coincidence. For example, Paterson and Laura discuss a dream of having twins and then the theme of partners/twins is repeated throughout the film. First, he passes a pair of twins sitting on a bench on the way to work, and then partnerships become a recurring theme, referenced in things like the musicians Sam and Dave and the star-crossed lovers at the bar who have echoes of Romeo and Juliet. It starts to make sense that Paterson is inspired by the world around him to write poetry because we sense that Jarmusch sees that poetry in everyday life as well.

And yet *Paterson* is never an overly lyrical or pretentious film, even if Jarmusch does stop to project Paterson's poetic words over slow-motion shots of waterfalls—something that absolutely should not work but somehow it does. One of the reasons is that he never allows the poetry to overtake the realism. He's just as interested in conversations on Paterson's bus (including a clever one that reunites the young stars of *Moonrise Kingdom* (2010), Kara Hayward and Jared Gilman) or at Doc's bar between the forlorn Everett (William Jackson Harper) and his lost love Marie (Chasten Harmon). *Paterson* is as much about routine as it is poetry, and its brilliance is in how it blends the two, not merely placing the former on top. There is poetry IN the routine.

None of this would work without one of 2016's best performances courtesy of Adam Driver. His character is more of an observer than anything else, but Driver never feels like merely a watcher. He gives a wonderfully internal performance, always taking in everything around him. One of the best scenes of the year in any film comes courtesy of Sterling Jerins, as a girl who Paterson finds sitting alone. At first, he's concerned, but then he learns she's a poet too, and he wants to hear her poem, "Water Falls." Not only is it a great poem, Jerins plays it like she knows it's great, and Driver's joy at hearing something beautiful is palpable. His love for Laura, his interest in Doc's stories, his commitment to his job—Driver creates a fully-realized, three-dimensional character without any of the typical dramatic or manipulative screenwriting crutches usually given an actor. It's a breathtakingly good performance.

Jarmusch regularly breaks the mundane plot of *Paterson* for poetic interludes, literally putting his protagonist's words up on the screen in a handwritten font. Driver reads them as if he's coming up with them for the first time—poetry and film coming to life in the same moment. He writes them down in a journal, finding beauty in real life, just as his idol, William Carlos Williams, also from Paterson, did. Laura begs him to make copies, and the fact that he does not gives the film it's one dramatic thrust, but even that's not overplayed. Neither is Laura, a character who could have easily been a Manic Pixie Dream Girl, painting everything in her house and making cupcakes for a local bake sale.

Paterson is a great movie about cupcakes, dog walks, and bus rides. It's a miracle of a film not only for the beauty it captures but for how much it shouldn't work, based on that description alone. These are not the traditionally cinematic themes of great drama. And yet *Paterson* undeniably is a great drama. It may be the best film of its remarkably confident director's notable career. And, like the best poems, it will have a life far beyond its initial release, moving others to create film, write poetry, or just see the beauty of the world around them.

Brian Tallerico

CREDITS

Paterson: Adam Driver
Laura: Golshifteh Farahani
Doc: Barry (Shabaka) Henley
Method Man: Method Man
Everett: William Jackson Harper
Origin: United States
Language: English
Released: 2016

Production: Joshua Astrachan, Carter Logan; released by
    Amazon Studios, Animal Kingdom, Inkjet Productions, K5
    Film, Le Pacte
Directed by: Jim Jarmusch
Written by: Jim Jarmusch
Cinematography by: Frederick Elmes
Music by: Jim Jarmusch; Carter Logan; Squrl
Editing: Affonso Goncalves
Costumes: Catherine George
Production Design: Mark Friedberg
MPAA rating: R
Running time: 118 minutes

REVIEWS

Chang, Justin. *Los Angeles Times.* December 27, 2016.
Cole, Jake. *Slant.* September 23, 2016.
Dowd, A.A. *The A.V. Club.* December 21, 2016.
Ebiri, Bilge. *Village Voice.* December 27, 2016.
Grierson, Tim. *Screen International.* May 21, 2016.
Hornaday, Ann. *Washington Post.* January 5, 2017.
Kenny, Glenn. *RogerEbert.com.* December 27, 2016.
Kohn, Eric. *IndieWire.* May 21, 2016.
Wiegand, David. *San Francisco Chronicle.* January 5, 2017.
Zacharek, Stephanie. *Time.* December 28, 2016.

QUOTES

Paterson: "Morning, Donny."

Donny: "Ready to roll, Paterson?"

Paterson: "Yeah." [pause]

Paterson: "Everything OK?"

Donny: "Now that you ask, no, not really. My kid needs braces
    on her teeth, my car needs a transmission job, my wife
    wants me to take her to Florida but I'm behind on the
    mortgage payments, my uncle called from India and he
    needs money for my neice's wedding, and I got this strange
    rash on my back. You name it, brother. How 'bout you?"

Paterson: "I'm OK."

Donny: "OK, well, have a nice day."

Paterson: "OK, you too."

Donny: "Yeah, I doubt it."

TRIVIA

Director Jim Jarmusch wrote the poem that was read to
    Paterson by the little girl in the film.

PATRIOTS DAY

The inside story of the world's greatest manhunt.
    —Movie tagline

Box Office: $31.7 Million

In 2012, actor Mark Wahlberg gave an interview to *Men's Journal* in which he not only claimed that he was originally scheduled to fly on one of the hijacked planes that crashed into the World Trade Center on September 11, 2001, but that he would have been able to subdue the terrorists and save the day if he had been there. Many were offended by this bizarrely self-aggrandizing statement, and Wahlberg eventually apologized for it. But it must have sparked something in him because, over the next few years, he, in collaboration with director Peter Berg, has begun a cottage industry of producing and starring in films that take recent real-life tragedies and transforms them into highly dubious endeavors that allow Wahlberg to symbolically step in and save the day as much as possible—*Lone Survivor* (2013) recounted the bloody ambush of a group of Navy Seals in Afghanistan at the hands of Taliban soldiers and *Deepwater Horizon* (2016) chronicled the 2010 explosion of the offshore oil rig of the same name that precipitated the biggest oil spill in U.S. history. Both films were fairly terrible in the ways that they reduced complex events into simple-minded genre fare that allowed Wahlberg to play out his multi-million-dollar hero fantasies, but even they succeed in comparison to *Patriots Day*, the latest and most appalling Wahlberg/Berg rehash of a bloody and tragic piece of recent history to date. In bringing to the screen the events surrounding the April 15, 2013 bombing of the finish line of the Boston Marathon and its aftermath, the film clearly thinks that it is doing a service both to the victims of the blast and those who finally brought the attackers to justice, but it not only does the very opposite of that, it does so in such a grotesque and off-putting manner that the whole enterprise borders on the obscene.

The film offers a beat-by-beat look at the events beginning a few hours before the commencement of the marathon and the subsequent blast to the final firefight a few days later in the neighboring town of Watertown that led to the death of one bomber, Tamerlan Tsarnaev (Themo Melikdze), and the eventual capture of the other, his brother Dzohokhar (Alex Wolff). Although it utilizes the perspectives of a number of figures involved with the story, it is recounted mostly through the eyes of Tommy Saunders (Wahlberg), a Boston police sergeant whose last act as part of a suspension for insubordination before reinstatement found him working the finish line of the marathon just when the two bombs were detonated, killing three people and causing scores of injuries. A good thing he was there because he is the first to rush towards the blast and all but single-handedly guides the immediate rescue efforts. Once the FBI, led by Rick DeLauriers (Kevin Bacon), arrives and the formal investigation begins, Saunders is called back in to provide crucial information that leads to the discovery of the Tsarnaevs on security camera footage taken just before the blasts. Later on, Saunders happens to be the cop who takes the statement from Dun Meng (Jimmy O Lang), the man whom the Tsarnaevs carjacked in the hopes of getting to New York City to explode more bombs, and not only takes place in the ensuing gun battle but is the one to discover the boat that a wounded Dzohokhar was hiding out in.

Considering how important Saunders was to the key moments in the story, it seems odd that he is nowhere to be seen during the lengthy documentary segment tacked on to the end of the film featuring the real-life people whose stories were just dramatized. Actually, the reason for this is perfectly simple—"Tommy Saunders" is not a real person but a fictional construct devised by Berg and a small army of co-writers to reduce several actual individuals and their respective narratives into one as a way of streamlining the story. The use of composite or wholly fictional characters in historical narratives to help move the story along is nothing new of course and, when intelligently deployed, they can help add levels of emotional and dramatic interest that might not have otherwise existed had the stories in question stuck wholly to the historical record. Here, however, it is handled so ineptly that anyone with even the slightest connection to the actual events should be mortified at the lengths that the film goes to in order to allow Wahlberg to satisfy his heroic delusions—imagine how much less effective *Spotlight* (2015) would have been if it had been rewritten so that Michael Keaton wound up making every single discovery depicted.

Even if one can overlook the notion that he is somehow front and center for every key event as a simple narrative construct, it is impossible to ignore the way that it goes out of its way to make sure that virtually every single bit of heroism or intelligent police procedure springs solely from Saunders. During the rare moments when Saunders isn't dazzling everyone with his investigative skills, the other characters talk at length about how smart he is and about how much he truly cares. At the big cathartic finale at Fenway Park when the key players are saluted for their efforts to protect the city, it is Saunders that we see getting the extended pep talk from David Ortiz. Thanks to moments like these, *Patriots Day* becomes less a testament to the city of Boston than a testament to Wahlberg's incredible ego that just becomes gross after a while.

That said, Berg is not entirely blameless because there are plenty of directorial choices on his part that do not involve the Saunders character that are pretty much beyond the pale. One of the subplots involves a couple of newlyweds (Christopher O'Shea and Rachel Brosnahan) who were standing right by one of the bombs when

it went off and lost their legs as a result. In an especially questionable artistic move, Berg pictures them in bed together on the morning of the marathon by lingering almost entirely on their currently-attached legs. After the explosion, Berg milks maximum pathos out of the fact that the body of a young boy who was one of the three fatalities had to stay on the street during delays in collecting evidence but never even makes reference to the other two bombing deaths until a title card just before the closing credits. He constantly undercuts his attempts at verisimilitude with such off-base additions as blatant commercial plugs (especially for Dunkin Donuts and the Zac Brown Band), inappropriately jokey banter and a depiction of the Watertown gunfight that seems as if it was lifted from the climax of a *Mission: Impossible* film. And while Berg probably thinks that he has made an even-handed film about the events, he still makes time for a tacky and legally questionable sequence in which the widow of Tamerlan (Melissa Benoist)—a woman never charged with anything in connection with her husband's crimes and who has denied any prior knowledge of his actions—is interrogated at length by a mysterious FBI agent (Khandi Alexander) who grills her at length and then tells the other agents—and, more importantly, the viewers—that she obviously knew everything but that she will never admit it.

What makes *Patriots Day* especially sickening is that there are elements to it that are good enough to make one wonder what a film on the subject might have been like in saner and more sensitive hands. It is fairly well-done on a technical level, the score by Trent Reznor and Atticus Ross is an unexpected change from the kind of bombast that one might have otherwise expected, and the stuff involving the carjacking and kidnapping of Dun Meng is genuinely suspenseful. That said, the film never quite manages to answer the fundamental questions of why anyone would possibly want to see a film on this particular subject so soon after it happened or why anyone thought it would be a good idea to turn it into a tribute to the massive ego of its star/producer.

Peter Sobczynski

CREDITS

Tommy Saunders: Mark Wahlberg
Commissioner Ed Davis: John Goodman
Special Agent Richard DesLauriers: Kevin Bacon
Sergeant Jeffrey Pugliese: J.K. Simmons
Carol Saunders: Michelle Monaghan
Origin: United States
Language: English
Released: 2017

Production: Dorothy Aufiero, Dylan Clark, Stephen Levinson, Hutch Parker, Michael Radutzky, Scott Stuber, Mark Wahlberg; released by CBS Films, Closest to the Hole Productions

Directed by: Peter Berg

Written by: Peter Berg; Matt Cook; Joshua Zetumer

Cinematography by: Tobias A. Schliessler

Music by: Trent Reznor; Atticus Ross

Sound: Dror Mohar

Editing: Gabriel Fleming; Colby Parker, Jr.

Art Direction: Steve Cooper

Costumes: Virginia Johnson

Production Design: Tom Duffield

MPAA rating: R

Running time: 133 minutes

REVIEWS

Burr, Ty. *Boston Globe*. December 21, 2016.
Debruge, Peter. *Variety*. November 18, 2016.
Duralde, Alonso. *TheWrap*. November 18, 2016.
Fujishima, Kenji. *Paste*. December 29, 2016.
Kenny, Glenn. *New York Times*. December 20, 2016.
Linden, Sheri. *Hollywood Reporter*. November 18, 2016.
Reed, Rex. *New York Observer*. December 29, 2016.
Turan, Kenneth. *Los Angeles Times*. December 20, 2016.
White, Armond. *National Review*. January 10, 2017.
Wilkinson, Alissa. *Vox*. December 21, 2016.

QUOTES

Whiskey Steakhouse analyst: "He's got more porn than Osama bin Laden."

TRIVIA

The casting call for extras for the film resulted in a line stretching the entire quarter-mile length of Braintree Street in Allston, Massachusetts.

THE PERFECT MATCH

It's what everyone's looking for.
—Movie tagline

Box Office: $9.7 Million

In 2014, David Wain made a film called *They Came Together*, starring Paul Rudd and Amy Poehler. It was an outright parody of every romantic comedy cliché seen in the last 20 years of the genre. It contained many inspired moments of absurdity and was clearly made by people who watched countless innocuous rom-coms. Even the font in the opening credits was hilariously accurate. It would seem that following the release of the film, there could be no more predictable, blandly-lit, shallowly written romantic comedies with trite plot contrivances or superficial endings. Just like how *Airplane!* (1980) brought about the end of the *Airport* disaster movies of the '70s. They could not be taken seriously on any level anymore. Unfortunately, *They Came Together* had a limited theatrical release and went pretty much unnoticed. Given how badly it was marketed and how dead-on it was as a parody, many probably mistook it for an actual cliché-ridden romantic comedy.

So, the typical rom-com still exists and *The Perfect Match* is proof of that. It is exactly the film *They Came Together* had in mind, except it had not been made yet. Or had it? The film contains so many echoes of past rom-coms that it feels comprised of scenes from other films of its type, all of them bad. The fact that it took three people to write it boggles the mind. From the best friend characters to the sub-plots involving dead parents and work politics, *The Perfect Match* has a flair for the bland and conventional. The film opens with a song that repeats "It's our world / it's our rules...," which probably is meant to convey the difference between men and women, but instead it signals a willingness to succumb to "the rules" of bad genre tropes.

This one centers around Charlie (Terrence Jenkins), a confirmed bachelor, amateur photographer, and agent to up-and-coming YouTube stars. Charlie meets a girl named Dana (Layla Jama). They flirt, hook up, and go their separate ways, until they meet again at a dinner party thrown by one of Charlie's friends. They exchange awkward glances, but nothing comes of it. Charlie has brought a woman with him who will likely not be a serious significant other anytime soon, which prompts everyone to ask him, "When are you going to get serious and settle down?" Charlie's friends are exactly what one would expect from a film like this. Victor (Robert Christopher Riley) is marrying Ginger (Lauren London), and the cost of their wedding is taking a toll on their relationship. Rick (Donald Faison) and his wife, Pressy (Dascha Polanco), are trying to have a kid. And of course, there is Charlie's big sister, Sherry (Paula Patton), who is a therapist.

Charlie's friends challenge him to not just sleep with a woman, but hang with her until the wedding, just to see if he can. He accepts the challenge and immediately tries picking up a woman named Eva (Cassie Ventura) via a forced meet-cute. She turns him down, but then texts him later on, inviting him out for a burger. She heard his friends talking about the challenge and she says she is up for it. They start sleeping together with the provision that it remains casual and uncomplicated. All he has to do is keep his phone handy and await her messages. Meanwhile, Charlie's day job consists of pleasing his boss (Joe Pantoliano) and dealing with erratic diva clients who want more money than they deserve.

Not only does *The Perfect Match* eerily resemble every cliché parodied in *They Came Together*, it also echoes a popular *Saturday Night Live* character played by Cecily Strong, the One-Dimensional Female Character In A Male Driven Comedy, in which Strong blankly spouts out clichés of the kinds of women who show up in these films, such as "I don't just like salads. I like burgers. I sleep in a jersey." At one point in *The Perfect Match*, Charlie talks about his amateur photography with Eva. It is meant to deepen his character as something other than a high-rolling agent. Eva only says "I'm into lots of things." And then nothing. Screenwriters Brandon Broussard, Gary Hardwick, and Dana Verde make no attempt at fleshing out any of their characters beyond "I'm into lots of things." Everyone is simply a model for Charlie to take pictures of while they smile at him.

There is nothing particularly distinctive about Billie Woodruff's direction. No narrative gimmicks or visual flairs. The art direction cannot compensate for the lack of character development in the screenplay. Charlie lives in one of those houses that only a single person in a romantic comedy can afford. One look at his immaculate front doors and one begins to wonder how he is not the owner of the agency where he works. That becomes another problem. *The Perfect Match* focuses heavily on the politics of where Charlie works, but it never comes off as remotely interesting and the predictable dilemma in the third act, in which Charlie has to decide whether or not to tell a client he is getting screwed, becomes a stale imitation of *Jerry Maguire* (1996). Furthermore, Charlie's drunken, self-destructive stupor later on is unbearably forced and goes on way too long. Then again, the same could be said about everything else in the film.

Collin Souter

CREDITS

Charlie: Terrence Jenkins
Eva: Cassie Ventura
Sherry: Paula Patton
Rick: Donald Adeosun Faison
Karen: Kali Hawk
Origin: United States
Language: English
Released: 2016
Production: Douglas Shaffer, Yaneley Arty, Alex Avant, Otis Best, Johnson Chan, Shakim Compere, Terrence Jenkins; released by Codeblack Films
Directed by: Bille Woodruff

Written by: Brandon Broussard; Gary Hardwick; Dana Verde
Cinematography by: Tommy Maddox-Upshaw
Music by: Kurt Farquhar
Music Supervisor: Kier Lehman
Editing: Paula Patton; Michael Jablow
Costumes: Janelle Nicole Carothers
Production Design: Niko Vilaivongs
MPAA rating: R
Running time: 96 minutes

REVIEWS

Dunn, Patrick. *Detroit News*. March 11, 2016.
Duralde, Alonso. *The Wrap*. March 10, 2016.
Durgin, Teddy. *Screen It!* March 11, 2016.
Fink, Jim. *Film Stage*. March 12, 2016.
Gelb, Daniel. *AllMovie*. March 11, 2016.
Kenny, Glenn. *New York Times*. March 11, 2016.
Kickham, Dylan. *Entertainment Weekly*. March 12, 2016.
Lane, Jim. *Sacramento News & Review*. March 25, 2016.
O'Malley, Sheila. *RogerEbert.com*. March 10, 2016.
Tobias, Scott. *Variety*. March 11, 2016.

TRIVIA

Lauren London, Terrance Jenkins, and Brandy Norwood all appeared in the TV show *The Game*.

PETE'S DRAGON

Some secrets are too big to keep.
—Movie tagline

Box Office: $76.2 Million

Like any major conglomerate responsible for putting out entertainment, the Walt Disney company has weathered its share of storms for what some might call the exploitation or even manipulation of children. After all, many of their films aimed at an age of growth often wipe out any traces of parental units from childhood and put their characters in the capable arms of talking objects and catchy songs with life lessons. This is a good way to instill their brand of merchandising all the way through to adulthood. At first, David Lowery's *Pete's Dragon* appears to be just another cog in the company's remake train. It is gloriously not, and should be a future model as to how to properly render a live-action family film.

Unlike the family of sketchy vagrants that the young protagonist was on the run from in the 1977 film, Pete is comfortably on vacation with his mom and dad in this remake. That ends abruptly when a car accident (tastefully not done for shock value) leaves him alone in the woods. When he is rescued by a large green dragon, Pete (Oakes Fegley) names him Elliot after the lost puppy in his favorite storybook and an adventure begins with his new best friend. Despite surviving in the forest for six years together, the only other human who claims to have laid eyes on this creature is Meacham (Robert Redford), who tells stories to the local children about it.

Grace (Bryce Dallas Howard), Meacham's daughter, is the local park ranger. She has never quite opened herself up to believing his tall tales. At the lumberjack site run by her husband, Jack (Wes Bentley), and his brother, Gavin (Karl Urban), Grace's daughter, Natalie (Oona Laurence) spots Pete. After trying to remain undetected, along with his occasionally-invisible dragon, Pete is knocked out and awakens in a hospital. Unfamiliar with the environment he has all but forgotten, Grace offers to take him into their home while Elliot is now left alone to evade capture from a new set of witnesses determined to do more than pass down stories.

The story of a child and their surrogate best friend is certainly rooted in classic literature, but those themes are taken seriously here and rendered effectively. Gone are the forgettable songs from 1977. In their place are moments of silent expression (peppered by a lovely Daniel Hart score) between two friends of different languages. Elliot is not force-fed yukety-yuk dialogue to align him with animated counterparts such as Shrek, Olaf, or the Minions. He is a dragon. And the humans who bring him to life in such rich detail are keenly aware of how themes of communication have enriched the best of these stories.

Oakes Fegley is a true revelation as Pete. This is a performance entrenched in observance. At no point does Fegley go for mere wide-eyed reactions or become just another moppet with an infectious smile. In every scene, there is the sense that he is working things out in any given situation. That includes knowing when to be quiet and when to reach out to his new surroundings. David Lowery, known for *Ain't Them Bodies Saints* (2013), brings the same kind of lush imagery (along with cinematographer Bojan Bazelli) that he did to that minimalist fugitives-on-the-run indie. Although it may have been his *St. Nick* (2009) about a runaway brother and sister living in an abandoned house in the woods that suggested he may have been the filmmaker with the right skills to provide *Pete's Dragon* the magic touch that makes it fly.

However the decision was made, it is clear that Lowery was allowed to make the movie he wanted to instead of just being another yes man for a packaged corporate product. Every true filmmaker carries their influences close to their heart and while Lowery's output to date has weaved in and out of varying genres, it is

this film that concretely stamps his ability to communicate a fully-fleshed narrative and relationships through a minimal number of words. Drawing comparisons to Steven Spielberg's *E.T.* (1982) is a given, not the least of which being the shared name between that film's young protagonist and Disney's green dragon. What that film also shares is the bridge of communication between different species that so defined *The Black Stallion* (1979) before it and *The Iron Giant* (1999) afterwards. There is nothing cartoonish about the situations or the adversaries in *Pete's Dragon*. Playful sometimes but nothing to suggest that even with a giant, mythical creature on hand that this is a fable that foregoes real-world empathy for cinematic embellishment. As the film's hopeful final image washes over its audience they should recognize that Lowery has not only crafted a singular vision out of rehashed material but that it will live on alongside the short list of classic family films in an increasingly product-driven industry.

Erik Childress

CREDITS

Grace: Bryce Dallas Howard
Meacham: Robert Redford
Pete: Oakes Fegley
Natalie: Oona Laurence
Jack: Wes Bentley
Origin: United States
Language: English
Released: 2016
Production: James Whitaker; released by The Walt Disney Co.
Directed by: David Lowery
Written by: David Lowery; Toby Halbrooks
Cinematography by: Bojan Bazelli
Music by: Daniel Hart
Sound: Christopher Boyes
Editing: Lisa Zeno Churgin
Art Direction: Ken Turner
Costumes: Amanda Neale
Production Design: Jade Healy
MPAA rating: PG
Running time: 103 minutes

REVIEWS

Brody, Richard. *New Yorker.* April 22, 2016.
Dowd, A.A. *The A.V. Club.* August 11, 2016.
Edelstein, David. *New York Magazine/Vulture.* August 12, 2016.
Erhlich, David. *IndieWire.* July 27, 2016.
Kenny, Glenn. *New York Times.* August 11, 2016.
Nicholson, Amy. *MTV.* August 12, 2016.

Phillips, Michael. *The Verge*. August 11, 2016.
Seitz, Matt Zoller. *RogerEbert.com*. August 12, 2016.
Tobias, Scott. *NPR*. August 11, 2016.
Turan, Kenneth. *Los Angeles Times*. August 11, 2016.

QUOTES

Grace: [to Pete] "You're very brave, did you know that? You
might be the bravest boy I've ever met."

TRIVIA

The film takes place in 1977 and 1983.

POPSTAR: NEVER STOP NEVER STOPPING

Box Office: $9.6 Million

Justin Bieber unintentionally provides a sharp parody of himself. The world does not need a feature-length analysis of an obnoxious, unlikable dope or the shameless, unenlightening documentary that only works to establish him as a product. So it is something of a relief that *Popstar: Never Stop Never Stopping*, its title a nod to 2011's *Justin Bieber: Never Say Never* and the vapid effort to suggest inspiration in the story of someone who became rich and famous before finishing puberty, does not focus on indicting the widely despised singer. It also does not target the recent bulk of docs (also chronicling Katy Perry, One Direction, and other stars appealing to a particular demographic) claiming inside access only to suggest that record label executives have kept a close eye on what information is revealed. Rather, *Popstar: Never Stop Never Stopping* primarily seeks to create a hilarious comedy out of the financial excess and emotional thinness of pop music. While this could be taken places that actually say something about the state of society and pop culture, the film's commentary only goes as far as its laughter.

Making great use of the charm he pulls from innocence-driven idiocy, Andy Samberg stars as Conner, a singer of virtually nonexistent talent whose success has turned him into a gleeful, oblivious egomaniac. He posts videos on YouTube to note when he eats a taco or masturbates, these clips only serving as a break from his 16-part series of brushing his teeth. Conner wasn't always a one-man show; he broke out as part of the Style Boyz, who inspired rappers as revered as Nas with tracks like "Karate Guy," which, to put it mildly, does not quite provide lyricism on par with Nas. But after the group imploded due to personality differences, Lawrence (Akiva Schaffer) is now a farmer and Owen (Jorma Taccone) serves the thankless role of being Conner's DJ, which really just involves pressing play on an iPod. Can Conner's

sophomore solo album "Connquest" equal the heights of his debut, the extraordinarily titled "Thriller Also," and what will this immature goofball do if it fails?

Popstar: Never Stop Never Stopping comes from the comedic minds of The Lonely Island (co-writer Samberg, co-writer/co-director Taccone, co-writer/co-director Schaffer) and feels like it at every moment. Conner's hysterically awful song "Equal Rights," in which he speaks on behalf of gay marriage (after it has already been legalized) while constantly reiterating that he is not gay and ensuring the clarity of the message by randomly saying manly things like "sports" and "hot wings," strongly recalls The Lonely Island's "No Homo." The group is great at cheerfully identifying various forms of absurdity, and a spirit of unpredictability gives the film its best moments. This ranges from Ringo Starr adoring Conner's catchphrase "Doink de doink" to a verse Conner supplies to Claudia Cantrell (Emma Stone) that is just a random series of other attempted catchphrases to his own song that wonders why the world cares so much about the Mona Lisa, which he sees as "an overrated piece of shit." The comic extremes even find clever, honest pieces of emotion, like when Conner struggles to leave his house and get to the hospital (his turtle is sick) because of the swarming fans and photographers. Pop stars are people, too, and it is worth questioning how selfless certain supporters would ever be, even in a time of urgency.

If only Samberg, Taccone, and Schaffer were willing to explore more questions like that. *Popstar: Never Stop Never Stopping* never considers why these terrible songs connect so strongly with audiences, or how specifically Conner or his former bandmates have influenced the real stars who appear briefly to spout praise. Seeing A$AP Rocky delivering a verse as bad as Conner would be a lot funnier than Usher excitedly getting on stage to do the "Donkey Roll," a dance craze that sounds stranger than it actually is. The film chuckles at the shallowness of this world (and, to its credit, never feels nasty or condescending in pointing out stupidity), but it does not feel curious about what any of that means outside of some people's breathless lust for stardom or the stars themselves. That may be why it eventually settles into a narrative dangerously close to replicating the clichés it should be inverting. Give Trey Parker and Matt Stone a shot at this, and count on the statement about friendship and second chances not being so simplistic.

Its peaks, though, create the rare experience of laughing uncontrollably. Conner's manager (Tim Meadows) blew his chance at fame as the fourth member of a R&B group, foolishly advocating to call themselves Tony! Toni! Tone! Tone?; Conner employs someone to punch him in the crotch to help him maintain humility and someone who is shorter than him to stand nearby on red carpet and manipulate the perspective of the viewer; along with Adam Levine's hologram, he performs a song about how humble he is that includes lines like, "I don't complain when my private jet is subpar"; and Lawrence's solo career is shown to have stalled because his single was a list of things in his Jeep and, in a nutshell, listeners had other things in their Jeep and could not relate.

That this is presented as footage from a documentary hardly matters, except for a late moment when there are so many artists with so many camera crews in the same place that no one can tell into which camera to speak. The movie feels closer to *This is Spinal Tap* (1984) or MTV's "True Life" than to *Katy Perry: Part of Me* (2012). It might have been fruitful to see how Conner's handlers worked to adjust a documentary about him in the wake of his many, many questionable instincts. Instead, *Popstar: Never Stop Never Stopping* just smiles and laughs with them, closing with a song in which Conner and his pals think "What if a garbage man was actually smart?" qualifies as an incredible thought. Perhaps there's subtle brilliance in the depiction of the public mindlessly eating up stuff like that, and so many comedies far, far worse than this one.

Matt Pais

CREDITS

Conner: Andy Samberg
Owen: Jorma Taccone
Lawrence: Akiva Schaffer
Paula: Sarah Silverman
Harry: Tim Meadows
Origin: United States
Language: English
Released: 2016
Production: Judd Apatow, Rodney Rothman, Andy Samberg, Jorma Taccone, Akiva Schaffer; released by Apatow Productions, Universal Pictures Inc.
Directed by: Jorma Taccone; Akiva Schaffer
Written by: Andy Samberg; Jorma Taccone; Akiva Schaffer
Cinematography by: Brandon Trost
Music by: Matthew Compton
Editing: Craig Alpert; Jamie Gross; Stacey Schroeder
Production Design: Jon Billington
MPAA rating: R
Running time: 86 minutes

REVIEWS

Burr, Ty. *Boston Globe*. June 2, 2016.
Chang, Justin. *Los Angeles Times*. June 2, 2016.
Duralde, Alonso. *TheWrap*. June 1, 2016.
Greenblatt, Leah. *Entertainment Weekly*. June 2, 2016.
Hornaday, Ann. *Washington Post*. June 2, 2016.

McWeeny, Drew. *Hitfix*. June 9, 2016.
Persall, Steve. *Tampa Bay Times*. June 1, 2016.
Phillips, Michael. *Chicago Tribune*. June 2, 2016.
Truitt, Brian. *USA Today*. June 2, 2016.
Zacharek, Stephanie. *Time*. June 2, 2016.

QUOTES

Harry: "Conner, don't worry about it. You were up there for, like, ten seconds."
Conner: "Ten seconds is an eternity, Harry. It's a third of the way to Mars."
Harry: "Conner, we've talked about this. Thirty Seconds to Mars is the name of a band. It's not a fact."

TRIVIA

This movie is Andy Samberg and Judd Apatow's first collaboration.

PRIDE AND PREJUDICE AND ZOMBIES

Bloody lovely.
—Movie tagline

Box Office: $11 Million

Based on the best-selling novel, *Pride and Prejudice and Zombies* by Seth Grahame-Smith, and by extension Jane Austen's original novel, *Pride and Prejudice,* this film adaptation is every bit as clunky and occasionally entertaining as its source. "Piecemeal" is a more-than-fair description. There are moments that are genuinely clever, funny, etc., but, ironically, they are relentlessly trampled by a lifeless storyline that involves a zombie uprising against the upper classes which also tries to shoehorn in the more genteel romance of manners that has made Austen's original story the source of many adaptations in the past.

The film introduces the world it inhabits via a scene in which Jane Austen's Mr. Darcy, here a Colonel, travels to an English estate to investigate whether inhabitants have become infected with the zombie virus. After opening a small vial full of carrion flies at a luncheon, he locates the infected person, the family patriarch, and kills him. But he leaves too soon and the film reveals a small girl zombie, newly infected, devouring one of the servants upstairs.

The film also quickly introduces the Bennett Sisters, Elizabeth (Lily James), Jane (Bella Heathcote), Kitty (Suki Waterhouse), Lydia (Ellie Bamber), and Mary (Millie Brady)–all young woman who have been sent to China by their father, as is the custom, to be trained in the use of weapons and martial arts. Their mother, Mrs. Bennet (Sally Phillips), still holds out hope her daughters will marry into money and social standing, much to Elizabeth's disdain.

When the Bingleys next door throw a ball, Mrs. Bennett does her best to make sure the girls catch the eye of young Mr. Bingley (Douglas Booth), but Elizabeth, to her own surprise, becomes upset when she overhears Mr. Darcy say something disparaging about her and goes outside, only to be saved by Darcy from an approaching zombie horde that then attacks the party. After witnessing Elizabeth's fighting skills, Darcy falls for her immediately.

The film goes on to provide ample opportunities for flirtation and fighting, made almost bearable by the fun that Matt Smith has with the role of Parson Collins, whose clumsy attempts at wooing the sisters and general disdain of their zombie warrior lifestyle are at the heart of what could have made this film great. Sadly, his observations come and go unobserved by the rest of director/writer Burr Steers' screenplay which seems almost smarmy in its haphazardness.

Elizabeth eventually meets a soldier named Wickham (Jack Huston), who has his own dark history with Darcy, and who reveals an area to her where zombies have begun to gather and eat pig brains to keep from becoming completely savage. Torn between Wickham, who wants her help in stopping zombies, and Darcy, who has teamed with a notorious female zombie warrior Lady Catherine de Bourgh (Lena Headey) to escalate the conflict, Elizabeth and Darcy duel only to part company in mutual hatred.

In its last third, the film becomes messy in the extreme with characters trading alliances and swords with hardly a thought for the poor audience who will wonder how anyone thought they could continue caring. Going back to the observation of how smarmy it all feels, Wickham himself is revealed to have been infected all along while Darcy switches the pig brains the zombies have been eating to alleviate their savagery for human brains, which turn them back into a ravenous horde. Steers betrays the zombies in his story simply so the rest of the characters can continue to run around and clash swords, and eventually run off to find out that true love means never having to say you're an entitled war-mongering elitist. This ugly and mean-spirited turn plays as less the result of attempted satire than a desperate stab at justifying how badly conceived the whole story is.

Pride and Prejudice and Zombies is not a movie to hate any more than any bland adaptation of Jane Austen's charming story, but that a zombie movie can be as bland as any entry-level costume drama says a lot. The keyword is charm, something this film lacks almost entirely. Most adaptations of this story have worked well in the past specifically because they start by helping the viewer feel the romance of the bygone and genteel British way of life that creates the backdrop for the characters. *Pride and Prejudice and Zombies* treats its characters like simple clichés. There is never any hope of caring about what happens in their silly little world precisely because it seems so little. None of the values seem important enough to set the people here in motion.

Another real letdown here are the special effects. In the age of *The Walking Dead* TV series and the amazing practical effects work of any number of more cheaply made zombie films, the CGI effects here seem like animatics, at least in terms of impact on the viewer. There is not one CGI effect in this movie that benefits from not having been done practically. Action sequences suffer here too, for precisely the same reason. The actors, particularly the Bennett sisters, routinely defy simple physics in the dispatching of the undead and the sense of contrivance is heightened beyond bearing.

Oddly, the performances are fine. The actors are clearly having some fun and to them must go the lion's share of compliments. All do their level best to pay some sort of homage to the great story at the center of Jane Austen's timeless tale while also chopping, lopping, and dropping the flesh-eating hordes.

Pride and Prejudice is one of the most-written-about works of British literature in history for good reason. Since its first publication it has inspired insightful satirical observation on class distinctions and the question of what constitutes true honor in love. That was the whole point of Austen's work. Here, there is no point, no honor, and precious little creative love on display.

Dave Canfield

CREDITS

Elizabeth Bennet: Lily James
Mr. Darcy: Sam Riley
Jane Bennet: Bella Heathcote
Lydia Bennet: Ellie Bamber
Mary Bennet: Millie Brady
Origin: United States
Language: English
Released: 2016
Production: Marc Butan, Sean McKittrick, Brian Oliver, Natalie Portman, Annette Savitch, Allison Shearmur, Tyler Thompson; released by Cross Creek Pictures, Handsomecharlie Films
Directed by: Burr Steers
Written by: Burr Steers
Cinematography by: Remi Adefarasin
Music by: Fernando Velazquez

Sound: Martyn Zub
Music Supervisor: Laura Katz
Editing: Padraic McKinley
Art Direction: Steve Carter
Costumes: Julian Day
Production Design: David Warren
MPAA rating: PG-13
Running time: 107 minutes

REVIEWS

Bahr, Lindsay. *Associated Press*. February 3, 2016.
Dargis, Manohla. *New York Times*. February 5, 2016.
Hassenger, Jesse. *The A.V. Club*. February 4, 2016.
LaSalle, Mick. *San Francisco Chronicle*. February 4, 2016.
Kermode, Mark. *Observer*. February 14, 2016.
MacDonald, Moira. *Seattle Times*. February 4, 2016.
Marsh, James. *South China Morning Post*. April 6, 2016.
Mount, Paul. *Starburst*. February 25, 2016.
Stewart, Sara. *New York Post*. February 4, 2016.
Tobias, Scott. *NPR*. February 4, 2016.

QUOTES

Elizabeth Bennet: "Your abilities as a warrior are beyond reproach, Mr. Darcy. If only you were as good a friend."

TRIVIA

All the actresses playing the Bennet sisters did their own stunts for the film.

THE PURGE: ELECTION YEAR

Purge for your liberty.
—Movie tagline

Box Office: $79.2 Million

James DeMonaco's 2013 exploitation film *The Purge* proved an unexpected smash hit. The film's premise was that the US government legalized all violent crime for one night in order to prevent it during the other 364 days in a year. Once it established the premise, *The Purge* then confined its action to one house, playing out like a home invasion slasher film. The film's success at the box office allowed DeMonaco access to greater resources on his next go around, and fittingly 2014's *The Purge: Anarchy* ran with the idea of the Purge. Disparate characters, led by an enigmatic veteran (Frank Grillo), tried to survive Purge night, a bloody, neon free-for-all where all manner of creative carnage lies in wait around every corner. Both Purge night and Grillo's angry vet, now given a full name and a little shading, are back

in the third installment of the runaway hit franchise. DeMonaco has more of an axe to grind this time around and the title—*The Purge: Election Year*—is a dead giveaway. The trouble is he cannot seem to stay out of his own way. For every well-intentioned satirical jab at the American Far Right, there are a handful of risible stereotypes on display that place the supposedly progressive DeMonaco in the same ignorant camp as the people he means to skewer.

Leo Barnes (Grillo) has survived the events of *The Purge: Anarchy* and come out with a renewed sense of purpose. He's going to do something about the grizzly annual event if it kills him. He's chosen to throw in his lot with Senator Charlie Roan (Elizabeth Mitchell), who is running for President of the United States. She too has a Purge story of her own. Eighteen years before running for the highest office in the country, she watched helplessly while her family was slaughtered in their living room by an intruder on Purge night. She's running a single-issue platform: Abolish the Purge. The reigning political power in the country, called the New Founding Fathers of America, started the event 25 years prior and have profited from the deaths of low-income citizens ever since. They are not going to let Roan alter their plans now. The NFFA infiltrate her security team and hire a group of Blackwater-esque mercenaries, led by Earl Danzinger (Terry Serpico) to make sure she does not survive this year's Purge. Only Barnes, who's become the head of Roan's Secret Service detail, will be left standing by the marked Senator's side after the NFFA have made their first move. The two will have to work together if they want to make it through the night.

Complicating matters for the NFFA are the changing fortunes of a convenience store owner named Joe Dixon (Mykelti Williamson). He's sick of the annual murder festival because everyone always tries to loot his shop and the insurance company refuses to cover it unless he pays the inflated premium. Dixon's plan is to sit on his roof, along with his only other employee Marcos (Joseph Julian Soria), and shoot at any potential threat to his livelihood. This goes well until a group of school girls show up looking to get even with Joe for embarrassing them during an attempted shoplifting spree. Then, it's up to former hoodlum Laney Rucker (Betty Gabriel), who used to go by the name La Pequeña Muerte, to save Joe and Marcos. Laney typically runs a triage unit on Purge night, but she's known Joe for decades and when she hears someone is threatening his life, she springs into action.

It's during this rescue operation that Joe, Marcos, and Laney cross paths with Charlie Roan and Leo Barnes. They flee into the night, looking for someone who might be able to keep the Senator safe long enough for her to abolish the Purge once and for all. Their first thought is to hook up with anti-Purge activist Dante

Bishop (Edwin Hodge), who wants Roan to win but has a contingency plan of his own in case she does not make it through the night, a plan that worries the pacifist Roan deeply. From here on out, everyone's going to have blood on their hands, it's just a question of whose and how much.

The Purge: Election Year could not be more clearly a takedown of the kind of far-right political climate that led to the rise of Donald Trump. DeMonaco thinks he's got something to say, but it boils down to "only kill people who deserve it." Roan goes out of her way to tell Barnes not to kill people if he can help it, and even tries a nearly suicidal rescue mission to save someone she hates because she cannot stand the thought of people dying on her account. When Barnes murders dozens and dozens of people to keep her safe, the movie ultimately sides with him over Roan, because the film's ostensibly happy ending relies on how efficiently and viciously he can kill. And if the movie had just owned that position, it would not have felt quite like the betrayal of its best stretches. The parts where Joe Dixon, Roan, and the rest try to survive the most outlandish, costumed Purge revelers have a gleefully deranged quality, held over from *The Purge: Anarchy*, that makes for unscrupulous fun. That fun only lasts, however, until DeMonaco tries to make a point about America's race problem.

What finally undoes *The Purge: Election Year* is that DeMonaco wants very badly to have something worth saying about the current climate of police brutality, racist politicians, and the Black Lives Matter movement. He uses footage from the protests in Ferguson, MO against police violence, has an image of one of many t-shirts festooned with the name of a black man murdered by police, and his villain is a boardroom full of cranky, sexist, racist white men plotting to rig an election. Which is all perfectly fair game for satire, but he writes Joe Dixon as a stereotype that would have felt tired 40 years ago. He cannot give him a line of dialogue that does not sound stereotypical. And, worst of all, he makes him a tired mouthpiece for a kind of hollow unification. When Dante Bishop's guerillas have Barnes and Roan pinned down with guns, Dixon tries to calm them down by saying "I like black people but I ain't gonna let y'all shoot these white folks. These are our white people." Not only is that lame racially inflected writing, but it's a deeply unrealistic sentiment. Only a white liberal could possibly expect this dialogue to fly in a movie like *The Purge: Election Year*. This movie uses images culled from the aftermath of the very real murder of unarmed black men as window dressing, ostensibly exists as a stylized violence delivery system, and still wants to believe in a Utopian future, martyring black

characters along the way so a white character can make changes. It's too little and too much at the same time.

Scout Tafoya

CREDITS

Leo Barnes: Frank Grillo
Senator Charlie Roan: Elizabeth Mitchell
Joe Dixon: Mykelti Williamson
Dwayne "The Stranger" Bishop: Edwin Hodge
Marcos: Joseph Julian Soria
Origin: United States
Language: English
Released: 2016
Production: Michael Bay, Jason Blum, Andrew Form, Brad Fuller, Sebastien Lemercier; released by Blumhouse Productions, Platinum Dunes, Universal Pictures Inc., Why Not Productions
Directed by: James DeMonaco
Written by: James DeMonaco
Cinematography by: Jacques Jouffret
Music by: Nathan Whitehead
Sound: Lewis Goldstein
Editing: Todd E. Miller
Art Direction: David Blankenship
Costumes: Elisabeth Vastola
Production Design: Sharon Lomofsky
MPAA rating: R
Running time: 109 minutes

REVIEWS

Abrams, Simon. *RogerEbert.com*. June 30, 2016.
Chang, Justin. *Los Angeles Times*. June 30, 2016.
Ebiri, Bilge. *Village Voice*. July 1, 2016.
Fear, David. *Rolling Stone*. June 30, 2016.
Kohn, Eric. *IndieWire*. June 29, 2016.
McWeeny, Drew. *Hitfix*. July 13, 2016.
Nashawaty, Chris. *Entertainment Weekly*. June 29, 2016.
Nicholson, Amy. *MTV News*. July 14, 2016.
Phillips, Michael. *Chicago Tribune*. June 30, 2016.
Vishnevetsky, Ignatiy. *The A.V. Club*. June 29, 2016.

QUOTES

Uncle Sam: "We will now purge. We will torture you and violate your flesh. Remove your skin and share in your blood. This is the American way."

TRIVIA

The movie was filmed in Woonsocket, Rhode Island, and is the only *Purge* film not to take place in Los Angeles, California.

Q

QUEEN OF KATWE

One girl's triumphant path to becoming a chess champion.
—Movie tagline

Box Office: $8.9 Million

The year 2016 saw the release of two films in which kids from slum neighborhoods become chess champions. The films were released roughly six months apart, but the first of the two, *The Dark Horse* (2016), went mostly unnoticed in spite of a strong critical reception (it did not help that there was another film titled *Dark Horse* (2016) within a month of its release, which added confusion). That film came out of New Zealand and had been sitting on the shelf in the United States for a couple years before it was finally released. Then, in September, Disney and ESPN Films released Mira Nair's *Queen of Katwe*, which told a similar true story about a young chess prodigy. The main difference between the two films is the central character. *The Dark Horse* tells the story of a chess teacher's redemption whereas *Queen of Katwe* tells the story of a chess student's discovery of her talent for the game. The common trait between the two is the tried and true formula that exists in the storyline that has been played out time and time again. Both films, miraculously, overcome that burden and deliver something special while still adhering to the basic sports-movie formula.

The story of Phiona Mutesi (Madina Nalwanga), the titular Queen of Katwe, takes place in the slums of Kampala, Uganda, a most unlikely place to find a champion of anything. Phiona lives with her protective, domineering mother, Harriet (Lupita Nyong'o), and her two brothers, one a toddler, the other Mugabi Brian (Martin Kabanza), a middle child. The story starts in 2007 when Phiona was only 10 years old. She crosses paths with a minister named Robert Katende (David Oyelowo), who teaches a chess class to younger kids. Phiona takes a liking to the game and soon develops a passion for it. By 2008, after going through a few hurdles from chess organizations who have a bias against slum kids competing against the more affluent schools, Robert's young chess club play in a tournament at King's College.

Robert has his own set of challenges at home as a new father and having a less-than-ideal income. He tries getting a second job in a field that is less fulfilling, but with higher pay. Throughout the next few years, he takes Phiona, her brother Brian, and many of the other players through many tournaments, mentoring them and giving them a sense of hope for their lives. But it becomes clear that Phiona is becoming something of a prodigy. She wins often and cannot stand the thought of losing. She also learns to read from Robert's wife, Hope (Esther Tebandeke), who is a school teacher. Meanwhile, Phiona's mother struggles with letting Phiona go on long trips out of Kampala, fearing that her daughter might have set her sights too high for the future and that a life in Kampala as a street vender is still a strong possibility.

All of the elements are there for a crowd-pleasing true story of overcoming adversity and becoming an unlikely inspiration against all odds. After all, when a film presents itself as being a product of ESPN Films, it is clear this will not be a film about failure. Yet, *Queen of Katwe* succeeds in so many respects because Nair is so in tune with the environment and the country where the story takes place. She elevates the film to a level beyond just being another inspirational true story. Best known for her break-out film, *Salaam Bombay!* (1988), Nair has a deep understanding of the hardships and struggles of living in a slum. Of course, this being a Disney production, she has to go soft on the prostitution and political elements, but her eyes are trained on capturing the visual details while, most refreshing, letting the characters speak in their native tongue once in a while. Cinematographer Sean Bobbitt provides the film with a rich visual look in which the colors pop and the camera is not always in the most obvious of places.

The cast also shines, particularly newcomer Nalwanga, who successfully conveys Phiona's aging from a 10- year old to a 15 year old through not just her overall appearance, but her expressions and body language. It is a tough feat to pull off, but she manages to give a nuanced and memorable performance as a girl coming into her own over the course of five years. She is an actress to keep an eye on. Oyelowo continues to remind viewers why he is one of the best actors working today. The scene people will likely most remember of his is when he has to give a pep talk to his Chess Pioneers. It is a wonderful moment in which a teacher must inspire while also relating to his students' sense of self worth. As Phiona's headstrong mother, Nyong'o is careful not to give a one-note performance, as would normally be the case in a film like this. Her love of her children is evident even if she is not convinced that they are doing the right or realistic thing.

Even at 124 minutes, there are scenes in *Queen of Katwe* that feel rushed and truncated, but that is often a symptom of a film trying to cover a lot of ground in a timeline that spans years. The story does get more interesting and complex in the second half, particularly when Phiona has a hard time transitioning back to her chores in the slums after achieving great success and enjoying fine dining elsewhere. It is the side of a success story that often gets overlooked, the idea that success is intermittent and not always as easy as "rags-to-riches." By the film's end, the "riches" feel earned and the story achieves its epic quality. The final capper that Nair puts on the closing credits is a moving twist on the usual True Story template where the audience gets to see photographs of the real people that inspired the story. Nair goes a few steps further not just in the cast and subject intros, but also a final musical sequence that

makes *Queen of Katwe* not just an inspirational re-telling of Phiona's story, but a literal celebration of it.

Collin Souter

CREDITS

Phiona Mutesi: Madina Nalwanga
Robert Katende: David Oyelowo
Nakku Harriet: Lupita Nyong'o
Mugabi Brian: Martin Kabanza
Night: Taryn Kyaze
Origin: United States
Language: English
Released: 2016
Production: Lydia Dean Pilcher; released by ESPN Films, The Walt Disney Co., Walt Disney Pictures
Directed by: Mira Nair
Written by: William Wheeler
Cinematography by: Sean Bobbitt
Music by: Alex Heffes
Sound: Blake Leyh
Music Supervisor: Linda Cohen
Editing: Barry Alexander Brown
Costumes: Mobolaji Dawodu
Production Design: Stephanie Carroll
MPAA rating: PG
Running time: 124 minutes

REVIEWS

Burr, Ty. *Boston Globe*. September 22, 2016.
Goble, Blake. *Consequence of Sound*. September 21, 2016.
MacDonald, Moira. *Seattle Times*. September 22, 2016.
Merry, Stephanie. *Washington Post*. September 22, 2016.
Pickett, Leah. *Chicago Reader*. September 22, 2016.
Rife, Katie. *The A.V. Club*. September 22, 2016.
Scott, A.O. *New York Times*. September 22, 2016.
Slotek, Jim. *Toronto Sun*. September 23, 2016.
Stevens, Dana. *Slate*. September 23, 2016.
Stewart, Sara. *New York Post*. September 22, 2016.

QUOTES

Robert Katende: [speaking to Phiona] "Sometimes the place you are used to ... is not the place where you belong."

TRIVIA

Madina Nalwanga was selected to play the role of Phiona Mutesi after filmmakers searched for a relatively unknown actress to play the role.

R

RACE

The incredible true story of gold medal champion Jesse Owens.
—Movie tagline

Box Office: $19.2 Million

Against the backdrop of a delicate and complex discussion about a lack of diversity amongst 2016's Oscar nominees, *Race* released to theaters in late February—a solid drama about one of the United States' earliest African-American athletic heroes, legendary track and field athlete Jesse Owens, who won a record-breaking four gold medals at the 1936 Olympics in Berlin, Germany. With a market positioning that could scarcely seem better designed in fiction to capture the op-ed pages and imaginations of a stirred-up populace eager for greater variety on the big screen, the film nevertheless opened in sixth place the weekend of its bow—caught up in the undertow of *Deadpool*'s tremendous holdover success, but also bested by fellow debut openers *Risen* and *The Witch*, each of which grossed greater than $1,000 more per screen than *Race*.

Thus this good if slightly reductive film—an engaging, affecting and appropriately complex true-to-life telling of one man's struggle against considerable odds, and how it helped move a country's societal needle, if only slightly, further toward equality and respect for all—gets stung by time, waiting instead to be rediscovered. Directed by Stephen Hopkins, *Race* serves as a case study and cautionary tale, embodying as it does the marketplace difficulties inherent in both mid-budget dramas and material spotlighting compelling historical stories of notable persons of color and other historically marginalized groups.

Sometimes financial restrictions can bring a certain narrative clarity to a project, and that seems to be the case here, as out of necessity *Race* avoids the trap of more sprawling biopics and chooses instead to focus on the period leading up and including what is probably the defining moment of its subject's life. The film begins with Owens (Stephan James) enrolling at Ohio State University, where he is challenged by a tough-minded coach, Larry Snyder (Jason Sudeikis), who believes Owens has the natural speed to become a world champion. The first in his family to go to college, though, Owens also has a lot of other pressures and responsibilities that his white coach either does not know about (a young daughter with his fiancé, who remains at home) or cannot fully appreciate (the punishing effects of racial discrimination and harassment).

Parallel to Owens' collegiate competition and Olympic training are scenes showing discussions by the United States Olympic Committee about whether to even participate in the upcoming 1936 Olympics, given some of the disturbing rhetoric and news reports coming out of Germany from the recently elected Adolf Hitler. This conflict is embodied by Jeremiah Mahoney (William Hurt), who advocates boycotting the Olympic Games on moral principle, and Avery Brundage (Jeremy Irons), who argues that the confirmation of equality is best achieved by American athletes of mixed ethnicities and backgrounds participating in the Olympics, and winning.

Screenwriters Joe Shrapnel and Anna Waterhouse make an honest emotional investment in addressing both external political considerations like those above, as well as Owens' own inner pressures and uncertainties over his choice to participate abroad in the Olympics, at a time when African Americans in the United States still routinely faced overt discrimination and much worse. This deepens the movie's dramatic resonance, making it more than just a story about a heroic figure overcoming adversity to win an athletic competition, and thus strike a blow against prejudiced thinking. *Race* is about that, of course. But more broadly it is about the universality of honor, respect, hard work, friendship, and other enduring fundamental principles that should never go out of style.

Certainly, the film's stellar acting helps impart this message. The Canadian-born James, who was excellent in a small supporting role in *Selma* (2014), here delivers a career-making performance. He channels Owens' strong willpower and inherent decency. Meanwhile, Sudeikis, well known as a comedic actor, here makes a convincing case that he has considerable dramatic gifts as well. It helps that he has the proper face and mannerisms for a period piece like this, seeming to belong instantaneously and effortlessly to this era. But Sudeikis also communicates tough love while not taking the edge off of the unearned privilege Snyder's ethnicity has conferred upon him.

In other supporting performances, Irons is superb and forceful as Brundage—morally indignant over Nazi Germany's repugnant racial attitudes even as he gets drawn into a questionable business deal with Hitler's leadership. Quite good as well is Carice van Houten as the German filmmaker Leni Reifenstahl, tasked with chronicling the Olympics and wanting to deliver a lasting work of art while also juggling the demands of Hitler's propaganda minister Joseph Goebbels (a chilling, effective Barnaby Metschurat).

Shot mostly in Montreal, but also on location at Olympic Stadium in Berlin, where key events in the movie took place, *Race* does a good job of maximizing its production values. There is a nice sense of scope and scale here, but one that does not overwhelm the decidedly smaller, more intimately scaled contours of the human story at its core. Hopkins, an underrated director-for-hire seemingly banished to television ever since the critical and commercial belly-flop of *The Reaping* (2007), delivers with cinematographer Peter Levy and editor John Smith a good-looking movie that flirts with the subjectivity of competitive track and field but does not go overboard in this regard.

While true that it sprints through some rich subplots, *Race* artfully condenses an important historical event and significant part of Owens' amazing life,

chronicling each intertwined portion in engrossing fashion. It deserves a wider audience.

Brent Simon

CREDITS

Jesse Owens: Stephan James
Larry Snyder: Jason Sudeikis
Dave Albritton: Eli Goree
Ruth Solomon: Shanice Banton
Leni Riefenstahl: Carice van Houten
Origin: United States
Language: English
Released: 2016
Production: Karsten Brunig, Luc Dayan, Kate Garwood, Jean-Charles Levy, Nicolas Manuel, Louis-Philippe Rochon, Dominique Seguin, Stephen Hopkins
Directed by: Stephen Hopkins
Written by: Joe Shrapnel; Anna Waterhouse
Cinematography by: Peter Levy
Music by: Rachel Portman
Music Supervisor: George Acogny
Editing: John Smith
Costumes: Mario Davignon
Production Design: David Brisbin
MPAA rating: PG-13
Running time: 134 minutes

REVIEWS

Barker, Andrew. *Variety.* February 18, 2016.
Brody, Richard. *New Yorker.* February 22, 2016.
Graham, Adam. *Detroit News.* February 19, 2016.
Hicks, Tony. *San Jose Mercury News.* February 18, 2016.
Holden, Stephen. *New York Times.* February 18, 2016.
Katz, Anita. *San Francisco Examiner.* February 19, 2016.
Morgenstern, Joe. *Wall Street Journal.* February 18, 2016.
Slotek, Jim. *Toronto Sun.* February 18, 2016.
Tobias, Scott. *Village Voice.* February 19, 2016.
Zacharek, Stephanie. *Time.* February 19, 2016.

QUOTES

Jesse Owens: "In those ten seconds, there's no black or white, only fast or slow."

TRIVIA

There were ten children in Jesse Owens' family, of which he was the youngest.

RATCHET & CLANK

Ready to kick some asteroid!
—Movie tagline

Box Office: $8.8 Million

No sound effect is left unused in the cacophonous *Ratchet & Clank*, a wearying and truly wretched animated family film that treats captive viewers like a pinball, to be bounced around in haphazard fashion and subjected to a lot of stimulation. Based on the action-oriented PlayStation videogame series of the same name, this thinly-imagined effort is frenetic and derivative in equal measure. The result is a disposable mess that will grate on the nerves of adults and likely bore all but the smallest children. Released by Focus Features in late April up against *Keanu* and *Mother's Day*, *Ratchet & Clank* slotted seventh in its opening frame, stunningly bested even by fellow animated film *Zootopia* in its ninth weekend. Rightfully derided by critics and mostly ignored by audiences, it scratched out a meager $8.8 million in theaters.

The story centers on Ratchet (voiced by James Arnold Taylor), a Lombax on the planet Veldin who works as a mechanic under Grimroth Razz (voiced by John Goodman). Ratchet idolizes the Galactic Rangers—led by blowhard Captain Qwark (voiced by Jim Ward) and consisting of Cora (voiced by Bella Thorne), Brax (voiced by Vincent Tong), and tactical specialist Elaris (voiced by Rosario Dawson)—and dreams of joining their heroic ranks.

Presenting a threat to galactic peace is Chairman Drek (voiced by Paul Giamatti), a somewhat bumbling villain who chuckles gleefully while using a Death Star-esque weapon called the "De-Planetizer" to destroy the uninhabited planet Tenemule. Drek is assisted by Dr. Nefarious (voiced by Armin Shimerman), who builds a robot army for his master while also nursing even darker ambitions of his own.

A defective robot acquires Drek's future plans and escapes the clutches of Drek's bumbling lieutenant Victor Von Ion (voiced by Sylvester Stallone), eventually crash-landing on Veldin, where Ratchet takes him in and names him Clank (voiced by David Kaye). When Ratchet fails to impress the Galactic Rangers and team up with them, he then sets out with Clank to stop Drek, Dr. Nefarious, and other morally flexible parties who fall under their sway.

Co-written by director Kevin Munroe, Gerry Swallow, and T.J. Fixman (the latter of whom has experience writing for the franchise's videogame series), *Ratchet & Clank* expends a lot of energy establishing extraneous details for what boils down to very simplistic motivations. There are various rib-nudging title cards thrown in to set up scenes ("Cue bad guy speech in..."), a couple tired jokes at the expense of social media ("Hashtag Killing It! Hashtag Not a Mole!" says Qwark after striking a confidential sweetheart deal with Drek) and some things that the writers clearly think are clever

(a reference to the "Star Cracker Chamber"). But it is not particularly clear why adults would find relief in these asides, given the haphazard nature of their inclusion.

More problematically, while Ward gives a very energetic vocal performance that strikes a good balance between self-regard and "himbo" obliviousness, there is not a lot of internal consistency to the character of Captain Qwark; one minute he is proclaiming, "I'm not a sellout!" and the next he is enjoying chocolates and asking who will be massaging his feet. This capriciousness is obviously played for laughs, scene to scene, but it is problematic given that the movie's finale substantively hinges on an abrupt change-of-heart from Qwark, in which he sees the error of his ways, apologizes to Ratchet and helps him thwart Dr. Nefarious.

Other elements of that muddled climax also help illustrate the basic fact that *Ratchet & Clank* seems chiefly the product of at-odds studio executive notes about both tone and basic narrative direction. The movie ends with characters arguing about the quality of their one-liners—a weak stab at sophistication and deconstruction of genre that *Ratchet & Clank* does not earn. "You're no better than Nefarious," exclaims Ratchet in the middle of this battle, only to turn around literally less than a minute later and say to Qwark, "You're not like Nefarious!"

Ratchet & Clank, then, is basically a movie merely just to retain corporate control over intellectual property rights. There is less a cogent and involving narrative or even a unifying visual aesthetic to the film than seemingly one simple directive: "Fast and furious!" Munroe and cinematographer Anthony Di Ninno obligingly cram in as much unmotivated camera movement as possible, and Even Wise's score similarly assaults the senses.

While *Ratchet & Clank* is not short on color, you see the difference in animation quality relative to other mainstream releases in the lack of background detail—as well as in an over-reliance on gimmicky screen wipes, which the filmmakers deploy in an effort to paper over a tedious, uninspired story.

As a character, Ratchet never much connects; he comes across as a kind of cut-rate Crash Bandicoot, even though the performance of Taylor, best known for voicing Obi-Wan Kenobi in various *Star Wars: The Clone Wars* projects, admittedly imbues him with a lively energy. As mentioned, Ward's vocal performance is the other standout here, coasting wryly above the proceedings. The rest of the voice work in *Ratchet & Clank*, though, comes across as either overly broad or drab.

Immediately forgettable but still significantly irritating in the moment, *Ratchet & Clank* is a work which ranks as either a misfire or letdown across the creative spectrum. Perhaps most chilling is a mid-credits stinger featuring Dr. Nefarious reincarnated as a T-800-style robot. This threat of a sequel provokes the biggest emotional response in the entire film.

Brent Simon

CREDITS

Voice of Ratchet: James Arnold Taylor
Voice of Clank: David Kaye
Voice of Captain Qwark: Jim Ward
Voice of Elaris: Rosario Dawson
Voice of Chairman Drek: Paul Giamatti
Origin: United States
Language: English
Released: 2016
Production: Brad Foxhoven, Kim Dent Wilder, David Wohl; released by Gramercy Pictures
Directed by: Kevin Munroe; Jericca Cleland
Written by: Kevin Munroe; T.J. Fixman; Gerry Swallow
Cinematography by: Anthony Di Ninno
Music by: Evan Wise
Sound: Nelson Ferreira; J.R. Fountain
Editing: Braden Oberson
Production Design: James Wood Wilson
MPAA rating: PG
Running time: 94 minutes

REVIEWS

Abele, Robert. *The Wrap.* April 28, 2016.
Andersen, Soren. *Seattle Times.* April 28, 2016.
Dujsik, Mark. *Slant.* April 29, 2016.
Graham, Adam. *Detroit News.* April 29, 2016.
Kupecki, Josh. *Austin Chronicle.* May 6, 2016.
Lengel, Kerry. *Arizona Republic.* April 28, 2016.
Nolfi, Joey. *Entertainment Weekly.* April 29, 2016.
Riccio, Aaron. *Slant.* April 28, 2016.
Walsh, Katie. *Los Angeles Times.* April 28, 2016.
Webster, Andy. *New York Times.* April 28, 2016.

QUOTES

Qwark: "Prepare to be blown away by my epic humility."

TRIVIA

Ratchet and Clank were voice by the same actors who voice the characters in the games, except the original 2002 game, which is the only one in the series where Ratchet was voiced by another actor.

THE RED TURTLE
(La tortue rouge)

Box Office: $591,836

Animator-director Michael Dudok de Wit started out making short films, which caught the eyes of Studio Ghibli, the Japanese animation studio best known for feature-length films that delve into mysticism, dreamlike narratives, folk and fairy tales with films such as *Princess Mononoke* (1999), *Spirited Away* (2002), and *The Secret World of Arrietty* (2010). After viewing Dudok de Wit's short film *Father and Daughter* (2000), they offered to distribute it in Japan and invited him to make a feature length film for the studio. The offer obviously took Dudok de Wit by surprise, but he nonetheless delivered a film that fits right in with the Studio Ghibli aesthetic. *The Red Turtle* is a film untethered from convention, a genuine work of art that exists to celebrate and expound upon nature and its limitless beauties and horrors, with a dose of magic realism that feels right at home with this particular studio.

The story starts out simple enough. A nameless man washes ashore on a deserted island. He wears simple clothing that tells nothing about the time and place in which this story exists. The island has plenty to offer as far as pine trees, boulders, and caves that run deep. There are also plenty of curious crabs that keep watch over the man and observe everything he does. Naturally, among his first instincts is to find food, build a fire, and assemble a raft. This takes some time, but what else is there to do? Once the raft has been assembled, he takes it out to the endless ocean before him and, perhaps inevitably, it falls apart due to the heavy currents or a mysterious underwater creature crashing into it. Nature can be so cruel and unforgiving at times.

It is hard not to watch the first third of this film and not think of Robert Zemeckis' *Cast Away* (2000) or J.C. Chandor's *All Is Lost* (2013), two films in which a man (Tom Hanks and Robert Redford, respectively) washes ashore on an island or is stranded on a boat and filmed in a way that uses few words. Here, though, the film takes a left turn from what an audience would expect. The titular Red Turtle makes an appearance in the ocean just as the man's raft falls apart and knocks him out. Later, he discovers that the creature turns out to be a woman. Rather than try and explain her origins or reason for being, the film asks the viewer to accept this idea and move on. The man certainly has no problem doing so and, surprisingly, the film ends up telling a life story that goes beyond someone trying to get off an island.

The story feels as though it comes from some kind of ancient folklore or legend that has been passed down generations. The fact that Dudok de Wit conceived the story on the fly it as a means of making good on his deal with Studio Ghibli to deliver a feature film makes him a talent worth noticing. The 2-D animation is sparse in detail, but never to the point where it looks like there were corners cut. It has the right look for something that feels ancient in origin. Its visual simplicity works in its favor and the characters' emotions are always felt even when given just the slightest amount of expression by the animators. The color palette is limited, but it hardly matters because there is a clear dedication to the craft that goes beyond being nice to look at.

A big part of that has to do with the fact that the film is completely wordless, save for a few grunts from the characters in the third act. Dudok de Wit's choice to do away with dialogue makes the film all the more mesmerizing and a lovely feat of visual storytelling (and, of course, makes the film more marketable across the globe). It seems like an anomaly to make that choice until one considers that silent films have made a bit of a comeback of sorts in the past few years, not just with the Academy Award-winning *The Artist* (2011), but in animated films such as Sylvain Chomet's *The Illusionist* (2010) and Aardman Studios' *Shaun the Sheep* (2015). Of course, the opening sequence to Pixar's *Up* (2009) also comes to mind. *The Red Turtle*'s lack of dialogue gives the film a storybook feel to it that seems rare. Laurent Perez Del Mar's score, while slightly overdone at times, enhances this feeling greatly.

The film marks the first non-Japanese film from Studio Ghibli and is a monumental addition to their catalog. Dudok de Wit is a Dutch animator and much of the film was made in France. Only six animators from Studio Ghibli actually worked on the film. Nevertheless, it still earns a valuable place in the studio's impressive filmography and the storytelling capabilities of Dudok de Wit and co-screenwriter Pascale Ferran make them a good fit. It is not hard to see why world-renowned animator Hayao Miyazaki was so taken with this talented filmmaker. Here are two people who look beyond conventional wisdom and who can see the possibilities for all kinds of stories within their chosen artform. Folk and fairy tales never have to be over-explained. They just have to resonate with their themes and emotions. *The Red Turtle*. accomplishes that and more.

Collin Souter

CREDITS

Origin: United States
Language: English
Released: 2017
Production: Pascal Caucheteux, Vincent Maraval, Gregoire Sorlat, Toshio Suzuki, Isao Takahata; released by Belvision, CN4 Productions, Prima Linea Productions, Studio Ghibli, Why Not Productions, Wild Bunch, arte France Cinema
Directed by: Michael Dudok de Wit

Written by: Michael Dudok de Wit; Pascale Ferran
Music by: Laurent Perez Del Mar
Sound: Sébastien Marquilly
Editing: Céline Kélépikis
MPAA rating: PG
Running time: 80 minutes

REVIEWS

Abrams, Simon. *Village Voice*. November 16, 2016.
Brady, Tara. *Irish Times*. August 10, 2016.
Debruge, Peter. *Variety*. May 18, 2016.
Kohn, Eric. *IndieWire*. May 18, 2016.
Mac, Sam C. *Slant*. November 21, 2016.
Moreno, Ashley. *Austin Chronicle*. October 26, 2016.
Murray, Noel. *The A.V. Club*. November 16, 2016.
Nesselson, Lisa. *Screen International*. May 20, 2016.
Rogers, Nathaniel. *Film Experience*. November 7, 2016.
Turan, Kenneth. *Los Angeles Times*. November 17, 2016.

TRIVIA

This was the first non-Japanese film to be produced by Studio Ghibli.

AWARDS

Nominations:

Oscars 2017: Animated Film

REMEMBER

> *It's never too late for revenge.*
> —Movie tagline

Box Office: $1.1 Million

"The past isn't dead. It's not even past," the novelist William Faulkner famously wrote. The past has been the signature thematic and formal preoccupation of the filmmaker Atom Egoyan, especially in relation to the particulars of his background. Born in Cairo to artists of Armenian descent, Egoyan grew up in western Canada and came of age, artistically and intellectually, in the vibrant film, theater, and visual arts culture of downtown Toronto.

He stands with David Cronenberg and Guy Maddin as one of the major figures of English-language Canadian cinema. His early films—*Next of Kin* (1985), *Family Viewing* (1987) and *Speaking Parts* (1989)—fixated on identity, sexuality, and voyeurism. In his most autobiographical and formally ravishing work, *Calendar* (1993), Egoyan played the central character, a photographer whose marriage disintegrates as he carries out an assignment shooting Armenian churches.

Exotica (1994) and his two literary adaptations, *The Sweet Hereafter* (1997) and *Felicia's Journey* (1999), meditated on grief and mourning and ruminate on memory and time in fluidly shifting between past and present. His angriest film, *Ararat* (2003), addressed the specter of cultural annihilation, through a different kind of moral witness, the making of a film about the Ottoman Empire's World War I campaign to liquidate the Armenian population.

Where the Truth Lies (2005) marked a shift as Egoyan, attempting to widen his appeal, began to experiment with more popular forms. His visual style became even more fractured and baroque, the emotional extremes turn ever more pronounced in *Chloe* (2009) and *The Captive* (2014), in kinky and unruly work that toggled between the exploitive and the truly transgressive. Egoyan never deviated from his technique. His movies were often structured as roundelays and privileged nonlinear storytelling.

Even as his proudly took on genre material and sought to undermine it, Egoyan worked feverishly to find the right balance between his impulse as an artist and his desire to satisfy an audience. *Remember* is a canny work intended to dissolve those narrative and thematic boundaries. It is a thriller marked by retribution and the lust for revenge and a reckoning addressing the most profound subject of the 20th century. The movie is a road film negotiating both a moral and physical space, a heart of darkness where a grievous and horrible wrong stands to be corrected. "What you did is something you cannot apologize for," the protagonist tells one target.

In a deeply concentrated performance, Christopher Plummer plays Zev Guttman, a 90-year old German émigré and Auschwitz survivor now living in a specialized elder care facility in New York City. Suffering from dementia, his own memories have trapped him in a permanent past he is more easily capable of summoning. The death of his beloved wife, Ruth, from complications of cancer, seems only to further accentuate his cognitive disorder.

His wife's passing also liberates him to undergo his dangerous and existential quest to track down and kill the Auschwitz *Blockfuhrer*, or block leader, who was responsible for the massacre of his family. His friend Max Rosenbaum (Martin Landau), another survivor whose family perished in the death camps, is the architect of the plan. Bound in a wheelchair though sharp and furiously detailed, Max has procured intelligence the former SS officer has been living, incognito, under the name "Rudy Kurlander."

Max has tracked down four former German nationals who fit the age and description and are located in suburban Cleveland, Canada, rural Idaho, and California. Max provides cash and a detailed itinerary, in a form of an elaborately reported letter that Zev draws on to jolt his frayed memory. From the start, Guttman's mission is marked by intrigue and is constantly threatened by his own unraveling, the chance of being discovered by the authorities.

Guttman appears damaged and out of balance ("Sometimes I forget things," he tells a gun shop clerk in trying to acquire a weapon). There is also a method to his madness, a natural and single-minded purist at work. What he discovers at the other end of the road is a particularly dispiriting and bleak universe, of men who tried and failed to vanquish their own demons.

Remember plays out in a bleak succession of sterile hotel rooms, dispiriting tenements, and ramshackle and dilapidated houses in the middle of nowhere. Guttman finds a death-ravaged and haunted man (played by the great Swiss actor Bruno Ganz) who served in Rommel's Africa Korps. "I didn't care about the Jews," he protests. "What happened was shameful, but it was not me."

Working with his usual cinematographer Paul Sarossy, Egoyan eschews the more elaborate and ornate visual design in favor of a more stripped-down aesthetic. That simplicity creates some low-key and sharp passages, the camera tight on Guttman's face as the open road yields open landscapes and rolling hills. Egoyan gets into trouble when he works outside that reference frame, like a moment of Guttman in repose in the bathtub, the mist and water droplets conjured to evoke the horror of Auschwitz.

The most electrifying sequence is also the most problematic as Guttman's journey takes him into the American heartland on the outskirts of Boise. He discovers his subject died there months earlier. The man's son, John (Dean Norris), a drunken and embittered state trooper, has adopted his rancid racial and political theories. He proudly flies a swastika in his house and shows off a pristine SS uniform. The scene has a blistering and grotesque humor as Egoyan braids together the tension, disbelief, and horror with a mounting dread. The use of restricted space is sharply realized, made all the more potent by the horrifying sound of a shrieking dog (the only time the concentration camp parallels work dramatically).

Plummer worked previously with Egoyan on *Ararat*. He brings a remarkable physical intensity to the performance, shaded by a psychological subtlety of guilt, honor, and cunning. The scene inside the Idaho house reaches a pitched climax, a ruthless aspect that raises interesting revelations about character and identity that leads to the explosive and highly charged denouement that only further complicates matters of justice and honor. He brings a pathos and dignity and considerable physical presence to the role, marked by a restraint and psychological vulnerability.

The script, the first produced by Benjamin August, yokes together parts of Samuel Fuller's *White Dog* (1983), Christopher Nolan's *Memento* (2000), and Steven Spielberg's *Munich* (2005). The movie is best appreciated as a work of the imagination. Otherwise the mounting implausibly of the plot becomes too overwhelming to seriously entertain.

If Egoyan's work now operates more fully in the realm of pulp, his talent for the visceral helps mitigate the ridiculous and preposterous aspects. Even some of his best films are marred by the sometimes overly mechanical construction. By contrast this is a lean and unfussy piece of storytelling, direct in its power and authority. His frequent composer, Mychael Danna, also delivers a plaintive and melancholy score.

Any work about the Holocaust is ultimately about representation and the question of authenticity and perspective. Paradoxically Egoyan is at his best frequently when he is awkward. *Remember* often risks the ridiculous and the patently absurd. A good director and a great actor make it work.

Patrick Z. McGavin

CREDITS

Zev Guttman: Christopher Plummer
Paula: Kim Roberts
Cele: Amanda Smith
Max Rosenbaum: Martin Landau
Max's Aide: Sean Francis
Origin: United States
Language: English, German
Released: 2016
Directed by: Atom Egoyan
Written by: Benjamin August
Cinematography by: Paul Sarossy
Music by: Mychael Danna
MPAA rating: R
Running time: 95 minutes

REVIEWS

D'Angelo, Mike. *The A.V. Club*. March 9, 2017.
Genzlinger, Neil. *New York Times*. March 11, 2016.
Goodykoontz, Bill. *Arizona Republic*. March 24, 2015.
Keough, Peter. *Boston Globe*. March 17, 2016.
Kompanek, Christopher. *Washington Post*. March 17, 2016.
Rainer, Peter. *Christian Science Monitor*. March 18, 2016.
Reed, Rex. *New York Observer*. March 10, 2016.
Roeper, Richard. *Chicago Sun-Times*. April 7, 2016.
Romney, Jonathan. *Screen International*. September 19, 2015.
Whitty, Stephen. *New York Daily News*. March 9, 2016.

RIDE ALONG 2

The brothers-in-law are back.
—Movie tagline

Box Office: $91.2 Million

Director Tim Story's career narrative is one that exemplifies the flash of studio manu-facturing. By 2016, he has subsequently launched four franchises, with 2002's *Barbershop*, 2005's *Fantastic Four*, 2014's *Think Like a Man* and 2014's *Ride Along*, and driven three of them into the ground. Each second serving for those three films was bigger and worse than the first: 2007's *Fantastic Four: Rise of the Silver Surfer*, 2014's *Think Like a Man Too* and now *Ride Along 2* (it could then be argued that the *Barbershop* franchise flourished because he left the series after the first film). It is a telling statistic about the limits of his vision within Hollywood filmmaking, but also the system itself—a film can captivate an audience to the tune of a box-office success, but the re-manufacturing of its successful parts, whether comic book action, fraternal shenanigans, or Kevin Hart implementation, has zero guarantee of quality in even just the second round.

Ride Along 2, commissioned by the 2014 original film's massive box office success ($134.9 million domestic) is his latest bungle. The spark to pair spitfire Kevin Hart up with the grumpy Ice Cube has dwindled, as their poster-friendly chemistry proves com-pletely flat in this second adventure. Instead of becoming an event sequel boasting more stars and a wider scope, *Ride Along 2* further proves that big franchise installments can be profoundly minor events, especially if there is very little going on within.

In the film, Atlanta-based police officers Ben Barber (Hart) and James Payton (Cube) are searching for a hacker played by Ken Jeong, who has been cast here for his for his dorky, boyish physical comedy, at times even wearing a backpack to accentuate his smallness. (He is essentially doubling Hart; when the two debate *Star Wars* films in one throw-away moment, it's a Frick-and-Frack moment among many.) While in pursuit of Jeong's hack-er, the Atlanta cops team up with a Miami officer named Maya played by Olivia Munn, who exists to be the female body that the boys interact with the most, and a prize for Ice Cube by the end; in the history of token women characters in male pursuits, hers is forget-table and even worse, disposable. The action leads all of the people to Antonio Pope, a villain played by Ben-jamin Bratt, who shares the same anti-mojo as anyone else trying to hold together some sort of plot about malevolent shipments in freight yards.

Aside from lacking in rousing buddy cop repartee, the chemistry of Hart and Cube of-fers no interesting commentary on their contrasting foundations of masculinity. Hart is a rookie with more video game experience than that of on the field, a trait that matches his juvenile, screeching nature when the movie places him in violent sequences. This is all compared to the turgid, unamused Ice Cube, who volleys Hart's tiresome rants and hyperactivity with glares from behind always-adorned sunglasses. Early on, *Ride Along 2* reveals a major deficiency, in which Hart is plainly not that funny here; Cube is even less inspired proving how futile Hart's comic energy can be. Instead of taking their chemistry to a different level, the movie only adds a snappy nickname to their duo: "The Brothers-in-Law," relating in part to Ben's upcoming marriage to Ice Cube's sister, played by Tika Sumpter.

Story's vision with a buddy cop tale is barely serviceable, in that there are enough set pieces, seemingly changing every five minutes; from a shootout in a club to a chase through the backyards of Miami to a bikini store, *Ride Along 2* keeps itself busy from its absent inspiration. But any time Story stops for his dialogue, his flat camera coverage only adds more colossal dullness to the project, even if Hart is flailing to provide a sense of comic urgency to bored cinematography.

Yet for each growing set piece in which the bumbling Barber and destructive Payton convert Miami into a playground of bangs and booms, the energy of the film fully depletes around the midway point. As it builds to a climax featuring a big chase through a synonymous storage yard, the size of explosions proves to be provide Story's film its sole sense of spectacle. Many directors have their visions enhanced by the fleeting amusement of pyrotechnics, but Story's has his overshadowed, and defined, by them.

Nick Allen

CREDITS

James Payton: Ice Cube
Ben Barber: Kevin Hart
Angela Payton: Tika Sumpter
Antonio Pope: Benjamin Bratt
Maya: Olivia Munn
Origin: United States
Language: English
Released: 2016
Production: Matt Alvarez, Larry Brezner, William Packer, JC Spink, Ice Cube; released by Cube Vision, Universal Pictures Inc.

Directed by: Tim Story
Written by: Phil Hay; Matt Manfredi
Cinematography by: Mitchell Amundsen
Music by: Christopher Lennertz
Sound: Kami Asgar; Sean McCormack
Editing: Peter S. Elliot
Costumes: Olivia Miles
Production Design: Chris Cornwell
MPAA rating: PG-13
Running time: 102 minutes

REVIEWS

Chang, Justin. *Variety*. January 13, 2016.
Cohen, Sandy. *Associated Press*. January 14, 2016.
Derakhshani, Tirdad. *Philadelphia Inquirer*. January 15, 2016.
Duralde, Alonso. *TheWrap*. January 13, 2016.
Ebiri, Bilge. *New York Magazine/Vulture*. January 17, 2016.
MacDonald, Moira. *Seattle Times*. January 14, 2016.
Samoy, Kayla. *Arizona Republic*. January 14, 2016.
Scherstuhl, Alan. *Village Voice*. January 12, 2016.
Scott, A.O. *New York Times*. January 14, 2016.
Wilson, Calvin. *St. Louis Post-Dispatch*. January 14, 2016.

QUOTES

James Payton: [when Ben once again shoots someone out of nervousness] "Again?"
Ben Barber: "My nerves is bad, man! Oh, my God! He's a zombie! Headshot, Walking Dead!"

TRIVIA

The movie was shipped to some cinemas under the pseudonym *Winter's Bride*.

RISEN

Witness the manhunt that changed the course of human history.
—Movie tagline

Box Office: $36.9 Million

While *Risen* surpasses its simple designation as a "swords-and-sandals pic," it still takes some time for interest in the film to gel into immersion. And, while *Risen* certainly can be seen as agitprop for Christianity, the film is also a clever historical (fiction?) film mixed with healthy sides of mystery and political thriller.

Directed by Kevin Reynolds (best, or worst known for Kevin Costner flops *Robin Hood: Prince of Thieves* (1991) and *Waterworld* [1995]) *Risen* is a first-person narrative about Clavius (Joseph Fiennes), a Roman tribute who, for lack of a better description, is assigned to find out what has happened to the missing body of a crucified Nazarene named Yeshua (Cliff Curtis). But do not be fooled into thinking that the film is being coy with the names and events here. Rather, *Risen* is trying to remain historically accurate with names and based on the fact this missing Nazarene was crucified, buried in a sealed tomb where he soon, mysteriously went missing. Viewers quickly realize this is the story of Jesus Christ.

Clavius is a died-in-the-wool Roman solider with eyes on rising in the ranks. So, when Pontius Pilate (Peter Firth) summons him to his chambers while he is still covered in blood from a recent brutal battle, Calvius seems resigned, but immediately responds to the order to oversee the crucifixion of the pesky Yeshua. From here, Christ's resurrection unfolds through the eyes of Clavius, who is very much the unbeliever. While a simple tale of how one Roman soldier came to believe could have been told in a more straightforward fashion, *Risen* takes viewers on a kind of early-AD whodunit.

Fearing the body of Yeshua will be stolen by zealots, his tomb is sealed with a massive round stone, which is tied with thick ropes and sealed in wax. That's about as secure as it comes in early Roman times. Yet, sure enough, the body goes missing and Clavius is paired with Roman soldier newbie Lucius (Tom Felton, best known as Draco Malfoy in the *Harry Potter* films), and the two begin combing the desert to find out where the missing corpse has gone.

Throughout the film, there is a real sense of the political inner-workings between the Jews and Romans, and how they both had major concerns about this Yeshua fellow inspiring people in new ways. Yet the film never gets too heavy-handed in terms of who's to blame for the crucifixion of Jesus and the subsequent attempts to hush up (and kill) his new followers as say *The Passion of the Christ* (2004) does. Instead, Reynolds focuses on Clavius and his search for "the truth."

Granted, "the truth" here has a much bigger meaning than just finding out where this corpse has gone missing, and soon Clavius finds himself mixed in with the Twelve Apostles who themselves are having a tough time following Yeshua's simple commands of love and acceptance. How can they allow this brutal Roman warrior who has killed hundreds and was on-hand, looking into the eyes of their leader when he was crucified, to be in their presence and not retaliate? It's an interesting conundrum and personally the kind of open-ended question that has an answer in, yes, the basic tenets of Christianity.

While clearly *Risen* is on the side of Judeo-Christian ethics, the film never feels too on the nose in its messaging. Yeshua's followers do not pontificate or drop

pearls of wisdom to try and sway Clavius (and, the viewers) to their side but rather present them as twelve men who are simply blown away by how amazing and cool Yeshua appears to be. He loves unconditionally and makes people happy just by his being around. Who wouldn't want to be around someone like that? And in that sense, *Risen* is Christian propaganda of the highest order. Yet that idea has a rather negative connotation when paired with other Christian propaganda of our time such as *God's Not Dead* (2014) or the Kirk Cameron *Left Behind* films. Yet the fact a film as layered and solid as *Risen* is forced to contend with public phonies and filmmakers conforming Christianity for their own purposes shows just how sadly divisive such a topic has become.

Don R. Lewis

CREDITS

Clavius: Joseph Fiennes
Lucius: Tom Felton
Pilate: Peter Firth
Yeshua: Clifford Curtis
Mary Magdalene: Maria Botto
Origin: United States
Language: English
Released: 2016
Production: Patrick Aiello, Mickey Liddell, Pete Shilaimon; released by Affirm Films, LD Entertainment
Directed by: Kevin Reynolds
Written by: Kevin Reynolds; Paul Aiello
Cinematography by: Lorenzo Senatore
Music by: Rocque Banos
Editing: Steve Mirkovich
Costumes: Maurizio Millenotti
Production Design: Stefano Ortolani
MPAA rating: PG-13
Running time: 107 minutes

REVIEWS

Andersen, Soren. *Seattle Times.* February 18, 2016.
Catsoulis, Jeanette. *New York Times.* February 18, 2016.
Chang, Justin. *Variety.* February 18, 2016.
Henderson, Eric. *Slant.* February 18, 2016.
Hornaday, Ann, *Washington Post.* February 18, 2016.
Keough, Peter. *Boston Globe.* February 18, 2016.
LaSalle, Mich. *San Francisco Chronicle.* February 19, 2016.
Moore, Roger, *Movie Nation.* February 18, 2016.
Nordine, Michael. *Village Voice.* February 23, 2016.
Witty, Stephen. *New York Daily News.* February 18, 2016.

ROGUE ONE: A STAR WARS STORY

A rebellion built on hope.
—Movie tagline

Box Office: $529.5 Million

With the Disney-*Star Wars* deal in place and the first Disney-produced film, *Star Wars: The Force Awakens* (2015), released to an enthusiastic audience who made it the biggest money-maker of all time, it was clear that the franchise still had a vitality to it that would see it go into many different directions for the unforeseeable future. Like the Marvel Universe, the *Star Wars* Universe has limitless possibilities with a rich array of characters and settings, all of whom have an important back-story worth exploring. There will not only be numeric Episodes that tell large, operatic stories of fathers and sons, there would also be one-off adventure films that fill in the gaps between these episodes. These stories are meant to expand on legends and stories told in passing and are a chance for lifelong fans to write and direct a *Star Wars* movie that can have its own sensibilities without conflicting too much with the established style and substance of what came before.

Rogue One: A Star Wars Story is the first live-action spin-off film to tell a story that takes place between episodes and populated with characters who will never be seen again. While that may be true, the film still makes direct reference to future events and past characters, thereby earning the label *Episode 3.5* from many fans. Still, it is its own film in many other ways. It is darker, murkier, grungier, and more stylistically raw than other installments. It is bold in that in is the first one to do away with many of the tropes and standards audiences have come to expect from a *Star Wars* film. It is, indeed, a film that goes rogue with many of its choices. And yet, there still exists the spirit of hope and good triumphing over evil. Audiences can still cheer

during pivotal scenes and laugh at the right moments of levity. And it is still about parents and their offspring, in this case, a father and daughter. While the back-story may not be as deeply explored as that between Luke Skywalker and Darth Vader, it still shows that the *Star Wars* movies have a heart beating beneath the spectacle.

This film tells the story of how the Rebels acquired the plans to destroy the Death Star. It centers on Jyn Erso (Felicity Jones), the daughter of Galen Erso (Mads Mikkelson), who worked as a top scientist on the Death Star and who was in charge of devising its deadliest weapon, the ability to destroy an entire planet. He has since defected from the Empire and now lives as a humble farmer on a remote planet with his wife and child. He gets captured and taken back to the Death Star to complete his work and his daughter spends the next 20 years in hiding and under the care of Saw Gerrera (Forest Whitaker), a rebel extremist. As an adult, she lives in a prison labor camp. She gets busted out by Rebels who feel she might be useful in finding Galen Erso and assisting on finding out whether or not the Death Star has a weakness. She becomes the reluctant hero, eager to find her father or even her guardian, but not interested in fighting the greater fight.

Of course, it eventually comes down to her becoming a bigger player in the bigger picture. She joins up with those who will eventually become known as Rogue One. Cassian Andor (Diego Luna) is a hired assassin for the Rebellion who takes a long time before he trusts Jyn. Bodhi Rock (Riz Ahmed) is a fighter pilot responsible for getting the word out on the Death Star's weakness. The new droid, K-2SO (Alan Tadyk), is a lovably sarcastic, filterless creation that will say whatever he feels regardless of how others will react. The less memorable Baze Malbus (Wen Jiang) is pretty much just a soldier, a grunt with little to say. The most memorable human character, though, is Chirrut Îmwe (Donnie Yen), a blind Jedi-in-training (probably) who may never have completed his lessons, but can certainly handle himself in a fight. He has a smile that is full of wisdom and confidently declares through prayer, "I am one with the Force and the Force is with me."

There is a lot of exposition here. Many characters and many more planets and systems have to be established in the first half that it can be hard for viewers to keep track of where they are and who is who. This is compounded by a constant momentum to keep everything moving at a pace that gives the film a sense of urgency. It rarely takes time to breathe, which ends up costing the film. The characters are plentiful, but many of them will be forgotten as the story needs to keep moving forward toward the third act, which basically turns it into a heist film and a war film. Narratively, *Rogue One: A Star Wars Story* has some clunkiness and the second act, particularly the sequence in which an assassination has to be carried out in the rain. It bogs the film down a bit. However, it is hard to imagine a fan leaving the theater truly disappointed once this team of true Rebels goes through with their plan. It ends on one of the biggest high notes this series has ever seen.

It also accomplishes a technical feat not seen in any other film before, at least not to this degree. Two characters make a return here. The easy and obvious one is Darth Vader (Daniel Naprous and Spencer Wilding, voiced by James Earl Jones), who has a couple scenes, one of which contains an eye-rolling pun that does not suit him in the slightest. The trickier one is that of Grand Moff Tarkin, Vader's icy commander in charge of all Death Star operations. Here, Tarkin is played by Guy Henry, who acted as a stand-in for what would become a stunning special effect where it would appear that the late Peter Cushing himself came back to play one of his most iconic roles. It looks like Cushing. It sounds like Cushing. It looks mostly human, save for a few jerky moments. It takes a long time for the eyes to adjust to this idea.

The viewer will likely miss most of what these scenes are about because they will be so fixated on the notion that any actor can now be preserved for life and appear in any film long after they have passed away. This raises all kinds of ethical and moral questions about how far special effects have come and how far they should go. In this instance, there is a comfortable grey area in that the Cushing estate gave its blessing for this magic trick and it is merely resurrecting a role that Cushing played already and, by all accounts, did not regret playing. One would hope this technology does not fall into the wrong hands outside of the film industry and one also hopes that this does not become a habit for storytellers eager to bring back actors who have no say in what films they wish to appear. There was a science fiction film called *The Congress* (2014), in which Robin Wright Penn had her likeness preserved for all eternity so she could appear in action films for the rest of her life. It appears as though real life has caught up with that once absurd notion.

Still, it cannot be denied that *Rogue One: A Star Wars Story* attempted something bold and director Gareth Edwards and his team deserve credit for taking such a risk with something so precious to many people. His style suits this story. Just as he did with *Godzilla* (2014), Edwards is not interested in giving the audience a major spectacle to be wowed at every fifteen minutes. He makes the audience wait for the big moments so that they have more impact. Cinematographer Greig Fraser keeps the lighting low and the camera shaky when necessary without overdoing it. Editors John Gilroy, Colin Gouldie, and Jabez Olssen have the tricky job of editing

the final third of the film that resembles the trifecta of conflicts that took place in *Star Wars Episode III: Return of the Jedi* (1983) and they do a commendable job of keeping the audience zeroed in on every situation. Michael Giacchino's score (composed in four weeks after the original score by Alexandre Desplat got rejected) helps keep the spirit of *Star Wars* alive as the first score to not be composed by John Williams. It is a solid effort that, appropriately, strikes a nice balance between the scores of *Star Wars Episode III: Revenge of the Sith* (2005) and *Star Wars Episode IV: A New Hope* (1977).

Whatever its flaws, *Rogue One: A Star Wars Story* is a fun and welcome entry into the *Star Wars* saga. Even though it opens without the traditional opening scrawl (which might have fixed some of the narrative problems), even though it makes the odd choice of only naming *Rogue One* in its title and not the *A Star Wars Story* part and even though it pays fan service a little more than some would care for, the spirit is still there. The fact that Disney is taking chances on directors such as Edwards for this and Rian Johnson for *Episode VIII* bodes well for the future of the franchise. Even if one *Star Wars* movie every year for the next several years takes the event factor out of it, a solid entry in which actors can say dialogue without feeling embarrassed, planets look like tangible entities, and directors infuse their passion for this world into their distinct style and smart approach will always be a welcome form of escapism.

Collin Souter

CREDITS

Jyn Erso: Felicity Jones
Cassian Andor: Diego Luna
K-2SO: Alan Tudyk
Chirrut Îmwe: Donnie Yen
Orson Krennic: Ben Mendelsohn
Origin: United States
Language: English
Released: 2016
Production: Simon Emanuel, Kathleen Kennedy, Allison Shearmur; released by Allison Shearmur Productions, Lucasfilm Ltd., Stereo D, Walt Disney Studios Motion Pictures
Directed by: Gareth Edwards
Written by: Chris Weitz; Tony Gilroy
Cinematography by: Greig Fraser
Music by: Michael Giacchino
Sound: Christopher Scarabosio
Editing: John Gilroy; Colin Goudie; Jabez Olssen
Art Direction: Al Bullock

Costumes: David Crossman; Glyn Dillon
Production Design: Doug Chiang; Neil Lamont
MPAA rating: PG-13
Running time: 133 minutes

REVIEWS

Anderson, Soren. *Seattle Times*. December 13, 2016.

Burr, Ty. *Boston Globe*. December 13, 2016.

Edelstein, David. *New York Magazine*. December 14, 2016.

Goodykoontz, Bill. *Arizona Republic*. December 13, 2016.

Hornaday, Ann. *Washington Post*. December 13, 2016.

Pickett, Leah. *Chicago Reader*. December 15, 2016.

Seitz, Matt Zoller. *RogerEbert.com*. December 13, 2016.

Stewart, Sara. *New York Post*. December 13, 2016.

Vishnevetsky, Ignatiy. *The A.V. Club*. December 13, 2016.

Walsh, Katie. *Tribune News Service*. December 13, 2016.

QUOTES

Chirrut Imwe: "I'm one with the Force, and the Force is with me."

TRIVIA

This is the first Star Wars film in which no one mentions the name "Skywalker."

AWARDS

Nominations:

Oscars 2016: Visual FX
British Acad. 2016: Makeup, Visual FX

RULES DON'T APPLY

Box Office: $3.6 Million

For more than forty years, Warren Beatty has publicly toyed with the idea of making a film about billionaire businessman, film producer, and eventual recluse Howard Hughes. But despite the occasional announcements in the press that would inevitably come to naught, nothing ever came of it. Although he never officially abandoned it, the combination of the success of Martin Scorsese's own Hughes project *The Aviator* (2004) and Beatty's own retreat from the film industry following the tortured production and disastrous release of the insanely expensive romantic comedy debacle *Town & Country* (2001) suggested that it was headed for the same fate as such legendary non-starters as Stanley Kubrick's *Napoleon* and Francis Ford Coppola's *Megalopolis*—a much-discussed and wildly ambitious project from one of Hol-lywood's heaviest hitters that still never managed to get off the ground.

Therefore, it came as a shock a couple of years ago when it was announced that Beatty was ending his long sabbatical from filmmaking with his long-gestating Hughes project, which he would write, produce, and direct as well as appear in as Hughes himself. Of course, that may prove to be nothing compared to the shock of anyone sitting down to watch the finished film, *Rules Don't Apply*, expecting it to be a straightforward biopic along the lines of *The Aviator*. As the title suggests, what Beatty has given us is a deeply idiosyncratic work that freely mixes fact and fiction together into a film that is less a narrative about Hughes than a meditation on such subjects as the sexual revolution, the eternal battle between bold risk-taking individualists and an increasingly conservative corporate mindset, and an elegy for the waning days of the Golden Age of Hollywood in which Hughes figures from time to time. Although not without its flaws and foibles, the resulting film is an intriguing and oddly endearing work that ends up more or less being worth the wait.

The film is so unconcerned with coming across as a Hughes biopic that he does not even make an on-screen appearance until roughly a half-hour into the proceedings. For most of that opening segment, the central character is Marla Mabrey (Lily Collins), a wide-eyed innocent and reigning Apple Blossom Queen who has just arrived in Los Angeles with her mother (Annette Bening) in tow at the behest of Hughes, who has put her under contract and plans to shoot a screen test with her that could lead to fame and fortune. After a couple of weeks, however, Marla's enthusiasm begins to wane a bit—although she has been given a lovely house to stay in and a weekly paycheck, she still has not even met Hughes, let alone taken a screen test, and it seems that there are at least a couple dozen other starlets who are also being kept hanging in a similar manner. When she mentions this to her driver, Frank Forbes (Alden Ehrenreich), he admits that he too has been working for Hughes for a few weeks and also has yet to meet the man himself.

While awaiting the moment when they will each be allowed to finally meet the man that they hope will become the facilitator of their respective dreams—the ambitious Frank is putting together a real estate deal that he is hoping that Hughes will help finance—Frank and Marla develop an almost immediate attraction to each other, a situation that brings with it any number of complications. For one, Marla is the prototypical Good Girl of the era and has had it drummed into her that even the most benign form of premarital sexual activity would be a sin of the highest order. As for Frank, he is less concerned with the mores of the time but he is at the moment engaged to his girlfriend from the 7th grade (Taissa Farmiga). The biggest snag to any possible relationship, as Frank is constantly reminded by his smarmy superior (Matthew Broderick), is that Hughes strictly forbids any romances between his employees and his bevy of starlets and will fire anyone who disobeys this particular rule. The two try to keep their mutual attraction under wraps but it gets to be quite hard at times.

As for Hughes, when he finally does make an appearance, he is somewhere between the charming rogue who first captured the nation's imagination a couple of decades earlier with his wealth, ambition, and way with the ladies and the sad man who would become a total recluse and a prisoner of his own deep-seated psychological disorders. On the one hand, he can still turn on the charm when necessary, as he demonstrates when he finally meets face-to-face with both Marla and Frank. On the other hand, his problems with paranoia and obsession-compulsion are manifesting themselves in increasingly bizarre ways, ranging from bugging his first meeting with Marla and repeatedly playing the tape back afterwards to satisfying a craving for a recently deleted flavor of Baskin-Robbins' ice cream by buying up every remaining carton of it. From a professional standpoint, such behaviors have weakened him enough in the eyes of his business partners to inspire them to try to take control of his chief asset, TWA. From a personal perspective, however, he is still the biggest fish imaginable and his interactions with Marla and Frank end up irrevocably changing their relationships both with him and with each other.

Rules Don't Apply opens with a title card reading "Never check an interesting fact," a quote supposedly attributed to Hughes himself and a clear tipoff that the film is not going to follow the standard biopic template as the screenplay by Beatty mixes together fact, fiction, and overt anachronisms (starting with the fact that by the time that this film takes place, Hughes had long since sold off his interest in RKO) as a way to highlight the larger-than-life qualities that ultimately are of more importance to the story he wants to tell than a scrupulous hewing to the historical record. As was the case with the great *Melvin and Howard* (1980) (whose screenwriter, Bo Goldman, worked on the script for this film at one point and who received a co-credit for the story), the Howard Hughes presented here is less a person than an ultimately unpredictable force of nature who is rarely seen but who casts an unmistakable shadow over the real story being told.

Instead, Beatty is more interested in using Hughes and our collective knowledge of him as a way of easing

viewers into subjects that have captivated him as a filmmaker throughout his career—sex and power—and how they shifted irrevocably in America during the period covered here. Regarding the sexual hypocrisy of the time—when men could act as randy as they wanted but women could only be seen as saints or sluts—he chronicles the onset of the sexual revolution with the kind of glee one might expect from one of the most celebrated libertines of his time. (At one point, he has Hughes advising Frank to invest his money in a new thing called the birth control pill). When it comes to other kinds of power, however, his attitudes are a little more complex. On the one hand, he casts a disapproving eye on Hughes and the ways that he allowed his vast wealth and increasing paranoia to dominate both his own life and the lives of practically everyone in his employ. At the same time, Beatty also has some degree of sympathy for a time when power was wielded by individuals who went out and did things and not by faceless corporations who amassed their fortunes with the stroke of their pens. Beatty also demonstrates a nostalgia for the days of the Hollywood studio system that were coming to an end when he first arrived on the scene as an actor in the late '50s. (In one of the more amusing bits, Beatty pays homage to a time when virtually every film had to have a title song by having aspiring songwriter Marla pen a song entitled *Rules Don't Apply* that is heard several times throughout with a different underlying meaning each time.)

Some viewers might complain that the two young lovers at the center of the story are not nearly as colorful or interesting as someone like Hughes but that is how it is supposed to be—if they were too brash or bold, there is no way that Hughes would have taken them under his wing in the first place. This is not to say that the performances by Collins and Ehrenreich are lacking at all—Collins is very impressive as the initially reserved and skeptical ingénue who grows stronger and more confident as things progress and Ehrenreich is engaging as the young man who is instantly besotted by her but who proves to not possess the same kind of inner strength of conviction as she does. For his part, Beatty, in what is essentially the first supporting role in his long screen career, turns in one of the loosest and most entertaining performances of his career as Hughes, cannily deploying his own considerable star charisma (not to mention curiosity over his own long absence from the screen) to suggest the spell that Hughes himself cast over so many people and his equally considerable, if oftentimes underrated, acting skills to suggest the gradual inset of the eccentricities and paranoias that would soon overwhelm Hughes himself. To fill out the rest of the cast, Beatty has recruited a large cast of familiar faces in supporting roles—besides those previously mentioned, there are appearances from the likes of Candice Bergen, Martin Sheen, Haley Bennett, Paul Sorvino, Paul Schneider, Megan Hilty, E. Harris, Amy Madigan, Oliver Platt, Dabney Coleman, Steve Coogan, and Alec Baldwin (whose presence cannot help but evoke memories of *The Aviator*, in which he appeared in a small but pivotal role)—and all of them acquit themselves nicely.

Rules Don't Apply is not without its flaws—some of the editing seems a bit rough and haphazard and a five-year advance in the narrative is handled in an especially graceless manner, both of which give the distinct impression that Beatty shot enough material for a film with the same extended running time as *Reds* (1981) and then chose to reduce it to a more manageable size at the last minute without fully smoothing over the cuts—and anyone looking for a conventional film about Howard Hughes is likely to be at least somewhat put off by what Beatty has given them instead. And yet, there are so many wonderful things about it (including the glorious behind-the-scenes contributions from cinematographer Caleb Deschanel, production designer Jeannine Oppenwell, and costume designer Albert Wolsky that beautifully evoke both the period being depicted and the films that Hollywood cranked out during that time) that the problems can largely be forgotten or at least forgiven even as they make one long to see what a longer version of the film might have to offer. Unfortunately, since American audiences chose to largely ignore the film when it was released despite an avalanche of promotion (including an extended press tour from the usually reticent Beatty), it seems highly unlikely that such a thing will occur anytime soon. That said, this is a film made for the long run as opposed to the hot take and hopefully it will one day be rediscovered and justly celebrated as a compelling look at the life of one of the most fascinating celebrities of the 20th century as seen through eyes of another.

Peter Sobczynski

CREDITS

Howard Hughes: Warren Beatty
Marla Mabrey: Lily Collins
Frank Forbes: Alden Ehrenreich
Levar Mathis: Matthew Broderick
Bob Maheu: Alec Baldwin
Lucy Mabrey: Annette Bening
Origin: United States
Language: English
Released: 2016
Production: Steve Bing, Ron Burkle, Molly Conners, Frank Giustra, Sarah E. Johnson, William D. Johnson, Jonathan Mccoy, Arnon Milchan, Steven Mnuchin, Sybil Robson Orr, James Packer, Brett Ratner, Terry Semel, Jeffrey Soros, Christopher Woodrow, Warren Beatty; released by RatPac Entertainment, Regency Enterprises
Directed by: Warren Beatty
Written by: Warren Beatty
Cinematography by: Caleb Deschanel
Sound: David Giammarco
Editing: Robin Gonsalves; Leslie Jones; F. Brian Scofield; Billy Weber
Costumes: Albert Wolsky
Production Design: Jeannine Oppewall
MPAA rating: PG-13
Running time: 127 minutes

REVIEWS

Brody, Richard. *New Yorker.* November 21, 2016.
Debruge, Peter. *Variety.* November 11, 2016.
Holden, Stephen. *New York Times.* November 22, 2016.
Kohn, Eric. *IndieWire.* November 11, 2016.
McCarthy, Todd. *Hollywood Reporter.* November 11, 2016.
Merry, Stephanie. *Washington Post.* November 22, 2016.
Nordine, Michael. *Village Voice.* November 22, 2016.
Strauss, Bob. *Los Angeles Daily News.* November 11, 2016.
Turan, Kenneth. *Los Angeles Times.* November 22, 2016.
Zacharek, Stephanie. *Time.* November 25, 2016.

QUOTES

Frank Forbes: [from trailer] "You're an exception. Rules don't apply to you."

TRIVIA

Lily Collins and Annette Bening improvised most of the dialogue during the back seat-of-a-car sequence.

AWARDS

Nominations:
Golden Globes 2017: Actor—Mus./Comedy (Bening)

S

THE SALESMAN
(Forushande)

Box Office: $1.5 Million

The most interesting figure of the next generation of Iranian filmmakers, Asghar Farhadi stands apart, by style, temperament, and working methods, from the New Wave directors Abbas Kiarostami, Jafar Panahi, and Mohsen Makhmalbaf, who propelled the country's national cinema into wider international recognition. The great Kiarostami (1940-2016), in masterpieces from *Close-Up* (1990) to *The Wind Will Carry Us* (1999), experimented brilliantly with form and content in adroitly combining fiction and nonfiction techniques in typically working with nonprofessional actors and without a traditional script. Born in 1972, just seven years before the Islamic Revolution, Farhadi is not the radical modernist characteristic of the best work of either Kiarostami or Panahi, and he is not a lyricist like Makhmalbaf.

Farhadi came to the cinema from the theater (his college thesis was about the structural pauses and elisions in the works of Harold Pinter). He trained as a playwright and got his start writing radio plays and television scripts. He also works with a company of superb young actors. His manner of working is similar to that of the British master Mike Leigh (*Secrets & Lies* [1996]), with his scripts developed and shaped through painstaking and extensive rehearsals with his actors.

His third feature, *Fireworks Wednesday* (2006), was his first film to gain any significant traction in the West. *About Elly* (2009) played like an Iranian iteration of Michelangelo Antonioni's supreme masterpiece,

L'Avventura (1960), with its story about the unexplained disappearance of a young woman during a weekend retreat in the Caspian. Farhadi's greatest film, *A Separation* (2001), the Academy-award winner for best foreign language feature, used an unraveled marriage to explore with lacerating precision the patriarchal, harshly retaliatory treatment of women. *The Past* (2013), made in France, concerns the emotional and social consequences of exile. Like *About Elly* and *A Separation*, the slow-burning narrative uses a dramatic rupture as a means of introducing the larger network of characters.

With his seventh feature, *The Salesman*, Farhadi brings together his preoccupations and background details by intertwining the theater, marital discord, tortured masculinity, and political critique in his pungent and tense story about a married couple acting in a Tehran production of Arthur Miller's *Death of a Salesman* (1949) who watch their lives become irreversibly damaged in the aftermath of a frightening attack.

Farhadi works in a more sensationalist register than Kiarostami and Panahi. His style is more granular, composed of smaller parts that are fused together through incident and confrontation. *The Salesman* is a work shaped by dissonance. The film opens with images on the set of the theater adaptation framed by neon sign as the black fade signals the first of a series of violent disruptions. The movie's central couple, Emad (Shahab Hosseini) and Rana Etesami (Taraneh Alidoosti), who play Willy Loman and his wife Linda in the production, are forcibly evacuated from their home after their apartment building appears on the verge of collapsing. The structure remains standing though the serious structural damage, with gas leaks and massive cracks, causes them to seek alternate housing.

Babak (Babak Karimi), a member of the theater company, steps in with the offer of a somewhat dilapidated though spacious unit in a nearby apartment building. The apparently straightforward action is complicated by the behavior of the previous tenant. A mysterious (and never seen) woman with a young child, she refuses to collect the substantial personal belongings she left behind. Farhadi introduces a tone of low-key menace and confrontation, from the neighboring couple who warn Babak about being more selective about his tenants, Emad's contentious interaction with his (all-male) high school classroom and a claustrophobic cab ride with a disagreeable older woman.

The early, tense build up is predicated on the familiar, like Rana responding to the sound of the front door buzzer, believing it to be her husband. The idyll is shattered when Emad discovers a blood trail and signs of an apparent struggle and Rana gone missing. Emad tracks her to the emergency room of a local hospital, with medical personnel are attending to her blood-ravaged face. Emad learns that the intruder attacked her while she was in the shower.

The film is the closest Farhadi has come to making an outright thriller. It is a detective story that comes together sensationally in the sorrowful and devastating final movement. At his wife's insistence, Emad refuses to involve the police. He conducts his own amateur investigation after the attacker leaves behind two incriminating pieces of evidence, a cell phone and set of keys belonging to a truck parked nearby. *The Salesman* oscillates between two narrative tracks of Emad's search for the assailant contrasted against the personal repercussions of the attack, the vulnerability and increasing emotional withdrawal of Rana only intensifying his sense of shame and humiliation.

Miller's play is, with Tennessee Williams's *A Streetcar Named Desire* (1947) and Eugene O'Neill's *Long Day's Journey into Night* (1956), a foundational text of 20th century American theater. The discordance Farhadi works hard to achieve is developed through the cultural contrasts and parallels. In moving from hallucination, reverie, and a waking nightmare, Miller's play conjured an American dream illusory and tragic. *The Salesman* is the director's most political work, a denunciation of the repressive theocratic totalitarianism that throttled the best ideas of the revolution. (The reason Emad was delayed when his wife was attacked was he was negotiating with censors about retaining three scenes in the play.)

Emad is increasingly driven to the point of breakdown by his desire for vengeance, one he sees essential in his recovery of his personal honor. In one of the strongest scenes, during a performance of the play, Emad alters the dialogue to attack Babak on stage for what he believes is his colleague's complicity in the attack. Babak withheld information about the woman, revealed as a promiscuous entertainer of multiple acquaintances, or less euphemistically, a prostitute. Like *About Elly*, the movie becomes an inquisition into an unseen woman's sexuality. It makes for some riveting passages but also spotlights a weakness that also marred *A Separation* and *The Past*, movies that incorporated a woman's point of view without quite prioritizing it. For better and worse, the point of view here is virtually that of Emad alone.

The first part of *The Salesman* is a bit diffuse and too dependent upon narrative coincidence to advance the plot. The scenes with his students do not really lead anywhere, for instance. Farhadi is much more secure and confident in building toward a mesmerizing final showdown involving Emad and the mysterious man (Farid Sajjadi Hosseini) played out in the couple's stripped down, vacant original apartment. Farhadi is very good at imposing a restricted point of view, so that the action is perceived almost exclusively from Emad's perspective.

If Farhadi strains at times in establishing connections between the Miller play and his story, the associations come together sharply and painfully in this devastating final act. The signs that appear to implicate one young man actually lead to the actual culprit. Emad is both tormentor and aggressor, tearing apart the older man's confession until the man, like Willy Loman, is renounced and defeated. Emad is also damaged beyond repair, his hubris, arrogance, and own transgressions altering his relationship with Rana.

Shahab Hosseini, who won the best actor prize at Cannes, also worked with the director in *About Elly* and *A Separation*. Alidoosti is appearing in her fourth film by the director. Farhadi's skill with actors helps overcome his limitations as a writer. He is especially revealing and exciting working in compacted space, either the set of the production, the apartment or the closing passages.

Shahab Hosseini does exceptional work with his body and face, moving from aggrieved to stunned, his proud and defiant nature imploding moment to moment. Alidoosti is more interior, in the aftermath of the attack moving deeper and deeper until her every line is closed off, almost indecipherable. The two older men, Babak Karimi and Farid Sajjadi Hosseini, are also exceptional, their turns marked by pathos and pain.

The director's flair for melodrama appears in contradiction to the neo-realist strain of Iranian cinema embodied by Kiarostami. Through his choice of collaborators, Farhadi is an heir to the tradition indirectly.

The cinematographer of *The Salesman*, Hossein Jafarian also photographed Kiarostami's extraordinary *Through the Olive Trees* (1994), and Panahi's superb *Crimson Gold* (2003). Farhadi's visual style is direct and sharp, nicely attuned to the tumult and volatility. The production design of Keyvan Moghaddam is also impressive, particularly his conception of the Miller production to an Iranian context.

If there is a lingering weakness about the film, Farhadi needs to pivot more decisively from Emad to Rana, all too often privileging his range over her violation. Farhadi is a more protean talent than the major New Wave directors. *The Salesman* underscores his desire to say something new and interesting. Farhadi is at his most interesting when he is open-ended, like the ambiguous question of what exactly transpired between Rana and her attacker. The new work is not as euphoric and exciting as the director's best work. It is more raw and visceral, suggesting a potentially exciting new evolution, a shape of things to come.

Patrick Z. McGavin

CREDITS

Rana Etesami: Taraneh Alidoosti
Emad Etesami: Shahab Hosseini
Babak: Babak Karimi
Naser: Farid Sajjadi Hosseini
Sanam: Mina Sadati
Origin: United States
Language: Persian, English
Released: 2017
Production: Alexandre Mallet-Guy, Asghar Farhadi; released by Farhadi Film Production, Memento Films Production, arte France Cinema
Directed by: Asghar Farhadi
Written by: Asghar Farhadi
Cinematography by: Hossein Jafarian
Music by: Sattar Oraki
Editing: Hayedeh Safiyari
Art Direction: Keyvan Moghaddam
Costumes: Sara Samiee
MPAA rating: PG-13
Running time: 125 minutes

REVIEWS

Bradshaw, Peter. *Guardian*. May 21, 2016.
Camla, Giovanni Marchini. *Film Stage*. May 21, 2016.
Croll, Ben. *The Wrap*. May 22, 2016.
Gleiberman, Owen. *Variety*. May 21, 2016.
Hunter, Allan. *Screen International*. May 21, 2016.
Kiang, Jessica. *Playlist*. May 21, 2016.
Kurchak, Sarah. *Consequences of Sound*. September 10, 2016.
Robey, Tim. *Telegraph*. May 24, 2016.
Rosenbaum, Jonathan. *Chicago Reader*. October 13, 2016.
Young, Deborah. *Hollywood Reporter*. May 21, 2016.

QUOTES

Student: "How do people turn to cows?"
Emad: "Gradually!"

TRIVIA

The shooting was stopped due to the sudden death of Yadollah Najafi, the sound recorder in this project.

AWARDS

Oscars 2017: Foreign Film
Nominations:
Golden Globes 2017: Foreign Film

SAUSAGE PARTY

Macerated and educated.
—Movie tagline

Box Office: $97.7 Million

Sausage Party may be blatantly offensive, but that potential to offend is even greater if the viewer is unable to absorb the point the film makes about the need for human community-building outside the boundaries of rigid belief systems. So while this is a relentless barrage of sexual innuendo, stoner humor, and stereotyped characterizations, *Sausage Party*, as juvenile as it is, hardly registers as more objectionable than the societal divisions it mocks. The bottom line is this is a hysterical, often tasteless, movie that is likely to develop a cult following.

The Shopwell's supermarket is home to sentient grocery items that live under the mistaken impression that the humans who shop there are Gods. Thus, they believe that getting chosen to leave the store is a ticket to the "Great Beyond." The film actually opens with an ersatz song of praise that would be at home on any Christian radio station, with the food having no idea what truly happens after they are purchased.

Among these groceries is Frank (Seth Goldberg), a hotdog who lives a prepackaged life with his buddies Barry (Michael Cera) and Carl (Jonah Hill). Frank pines for Brenda (Kristen Wiig), a hotdog bun in a package nearby, but he is also far less sure of the Great Beyond than everyone else, especially after the appearance of a jar of Honey Mustard (Danny McBride) who has been returned to the store and shares the horrors that await them all. As Frank and Brenda are purchased, the jar commits suicide, but not before telling Frank to visit a bottle of booze named Firewater (Bill Hader) to learn the awful truth of the groceries universe. In the confusion following the suicide, Frank and Brenda leave the cart and are joined by Kareem (David Krumholtz) a lavash who clearly stands in for Muslims, and bagel Sammy (Edward Norton), a stand-in for the Jewish point of view. The three largest world religions accounted for, the film then introduces Douche (Nick Kroll), who is an actual Douche whose nozzle has been bent in the fracas. Douche blames Frank and swears revenge, setting off after the heroes.

Meanwhile, Frank has been meeting with Firewater, who not only confirms the rumors about the afterlife but reveals that it was he who invented the story of the "Great Beyond" to provide comfort to groceries on their way out the door. Needing proof so he can convince the grocery-world of the truth, Frank sets out for the freezer section. By this time, Carl and Barry and the other groceries have arrived and learned the terrifying truth first hand as a number of them, including Carl are violently killed, cooked, and eaten. Barry escapes and plans a return to Shopwell's, only to wind up in the shopping bag of a bath salts junkie who, after taking the drug, is able to see the groceries speak and move. The horrified junkie is decapitated in a kitchen accident before he can cook Barry, who carries the head back to Shopwell's on his own mission to awaken his fellow products.

Brenda has become frustrated by Frank's determination to upend the beliefs of grocery-kind and leaves him to his freezer quest. When Frank finds a cookbook, he shows everyone. But instead of the expected reaction, a large number of products choose not to believe rather than lose their comforting sense of purpose. But they change their minds when Barry appears with the head and everyone realizes the humans are not Gods, but can be killed. A plan hatches to prick the human shoppers in the store with bath salts laced toothpicks so that grocery/human communication can happen, but the humans completely panic at the sight of the talking groceries and a full-scale war ensues. Douche, who has been a few steps behind, comes out of the shadows to insert himself into a stockboy's anus and launches his own attack, only to be killed along with all of the other humans. Overtaken with joy at their victory, the groceries celebrate with a massive orgy which brings all of the items together able to accept one another's differences while celebrating their grocery-ness.

It is indeed surreal to watch an animated movie that combines the visual style of Pixar and more penis jokes than all of Seth Rogen's other movies combined. It also contains an astonishing number of ethnic stereotypes although they, and religion itself, are treated equally when it comes to the satirical aim. Rogen co-wrote the film with four others, all longtime creative partners who have filled in as producers and writers on his other projects. They are Evan Goldberg, who also gets a story credit with Rogen and Jonah Hill, along with Kyle Hunter, and Ariel Shaffir. The end result is absolutely bizarre but endlessly inventive and often hilarious in a pre-pubescent sort of way. Of course, pre-pubescents could never imagine a world this sexually over the top. Lesbian tacos, a talking douche, a used condom talking to Frank and company in the puddled gutter as a creamy streetlight glows. The orgy scene itself is breathtakingly encyclopedic. If there is a fetish for it, Rogen and his animators find a way bring it to the screen in a weirdly neutered, almost Ken and Barbie style. Still, it is difficult not to applaud the chutzpah it takes to make a Palestinian lavash and a Jewish bagel solve their conflicts by banging the hell out of each other.

Dave Canfield

CREDITS

Frank: Seth Rogen
Brenda: Kristen Wiig
Carl: Jonah Hill
Firewater/Tequila/El Guaco: Bill Hader
Barry: Michael Cera
Druggie: James Franco
Origin: United States
Language: English
Released: 2016
Production: Megan Ellison, Seth Rogen, Evan Goldberg, Conrad Vernon; released by Annapurna Pictures, Columbia Pictures Industries Inc., Point Grey Pictures
Directed by: Greg Tiernan; Conrad Vernon
Written by: Seth Rogen; Kyle Hunter; Ariel Shaffir; Evan Goldberg
Music by: Christopher Lennertz; Alan Menken
Sound: Geoffrey G. Rubay
Music Supervisor: Gabe Hilfer
Editing: Kevin Pavlovic
Art Direction: Kyle McQueen
Production Design: Kyle McQueen
MPAA rating: R
Running time: 89 minutes

REVIEWS

Braun, Liz. *Toronto Sun*. August 11, 2016.
Derakhshani, Tirdad. *Philadelphia Inquirer*. August 11, 2016.
Dujsik, Mark. *Mark Reviews Movies*. August 12, 2016.

Gire, Dann. *Chicago Daily Herald*. August 11, 2016.

Graham, Adam. *Detroit News*. August 11, 2016.

Lapin, Andrew. *NPR*. August 11, 2016.

Olsen, Alonso. *TheWrap*. August 11, 2016.

Rothkopf, Joshua. *TimeOut*. August 12, 2016.

Scott, A.O. *New York Times*. August 11, 2016.

Stewart, Sara. *New York Post*. August 11, 2016.

QUOTES

Gum: "I was stuck underneath the desk of a brilliant scientist."

TRIVIA

As of 2017, the movie is currently the highest-grossing R-rated animated film.

THE SECRET LIFE OF PETS

From the humans behind Despicable Me.
—Movie tagline

Box Office: $368.4 Million

The directness within the title for *The Secret Life of Pets* does not mislead. Its cutesy thesis is that, like the toys in Pixar's 1995 *Toy Story* (John Lasseter), everyone's pets live an active, social life when left alone during the day. Not only do they talk, but they have their own interests that human beings cannot understand through meows or barks. It is an idea that leads to some quaint visuals: a small white dog named Gidget (Jenny Slate) lives a primp life watching soap operas; a chubby tabby named Chloe (Lake Bell) wants to eat a big turkey high up in the fridge, and then finally reaches it; a posh poodle named Leonard headbangs to System of a Down. It is an amusing juxtaposition between a pet's silence and the personality one thinks they must not have, though not an extremely funny one. These images told viewers exactly what this movie would be like when they were included in a teaser, almost taking the form of a short film, over a year ago.

The Secret Life of Pets is another cynical enterprise from Illumination Entertainment, who previously ascended up the animation company ranks with films like *Despicable Me* (2010) and one of the most profitable spin-offs ever, *Minions* (2015). For such a successful company, they remain a candy factory when it comes to their stories, with easy scenarios fulfilled by shiny detail. It is telling that in the same year as *The Secret Life of Pets*, Illumination Entertainment also gave the world *Sing* (2016), which seeks to fulfill an animation audience's seemingly insatiable need to see computer-animated characters sing and dance.

The narrative for *The Secret Life of Pets* from writers Cinco Paul, Ken Daurio, and Brian Lynch inspires no deeper faith in craftiness. Louis C.K. voices a medium-sized terrier named Max, who in a sweet opening montage displays the love he has for his owner Katie (Ellie Kemper) and the space they share in a New York high-rise apartment. Their peace is challenged when a new dog, the super-sized, amiable shaggy dog Duke (Eric Stonestreet) is brought into the mix. Max cannot share the attention, and tries to find any way to get Duke out of the apartment, which brings an ugly narrative development—watching a selfish dog that viewers are meant to like then try to push out an animal that came from a shelter. When Max and Duke are rough-housing while at the park, they find themselves lost, and captured by animal control. When they escape after a devious bunny named Snowball (Kevin Hart) hijacks the truck with his crocodile and pig accomplice, Duke and Max witness an underground of other animals who have been rejected by owners. Meanwhile, Gidget enlists her various pet friends to journey across the city to rescue Duke and Max before they are scooped up by animal control.

The overt narrative borrowings of *Toy Story* would be passable were the story able to take on a life of its own. Instead, this "Pet Story" uses that familiarity as a symbol of how its narrative derives from the imagination of others, whether it is the baby talk that humans treat their furry friends with, easy animal jokes.

There is little wit about the characteristics of this pet world. Cats are selfish and slinky, dogs are eager and clumsy. When it comes to reversing expectations, it does so with one-note gags: the uptight poodle who head-bangs to System of a Dowb; white, fluffy rabbit Snowball is brought to life by a voice performance of Kevin Hart screaming into a microphone, and acts like a mafia boss 300 times his size. With the creation of these characters, even irony becomes a yawning expectation.

The Secret Life of Pets shows a lack of imagination even in the way characters interact with each other. Namely, violence is used as a type of resolution in a manner that is cringing but also boring, as if animators could not think beyond characters outsmarting each other than just beating each other up, as is the case with Gidget's ninja skills. Characters either hate each other or love each other, and fighting is the lazily-constructed bridge between those emotions.

Illumination projects often boast scope and color more than they do narrative wit, a tradition that is honored here. The animation for this endeavor is grade-A, with candy store detail to the environments inhabited by humans and adults alike. Skies are an optimistic, bright blue, trees are a warm orange, and sky-high apartment buildings are painted a lovely red. Architecture proves to be one of the safest bets with this movie, which paints a vivid setting of life in a metropolis.

As the concept of talking animals fails to make the film's pets any more compelling or interesting, there is a clear, *The Secret Life of Pets* brandishes a clear, almost stubborn allegiance to the idea of familiarity. It is not a movie that inspires any wonder about the world it is imagining. Rather, it tries to satiate viewers with images of their pets put into action and not just sleeping all day, but returning home before any conflict or true challenge should arise.

Nick Allen

CREDITS

Max: Louis C.K.
Duke: Eric Stonestreet
Snowball: Kevin Hart
Gidget: Jenny Slate
Katie: Ellie Kemper
Tiberius: Albert Brooks
Chloe: Lake Bell
Pops: Dana Carvey
Origin: United States
Language: English
Released: 2016
Production: Janet Healy, Christopher Meledandri; released by Illumination Entertainment, Universal Pictures Inc.
Directed by: Yarrow Cheney; Chris Renaud
Written by: Cinco Paul; Ken Daurio; Brian Lynch
Music by: Alexandre Desplat
Sound: David Acord
Editing: Ken Schretzmann
Art Direction: Colin Stimpson
Production Design: Eric Guillon
MPAA rating: PG
Running time: 87 minutes

REVIEWS

Chang, Justin. *Los Angeles Times.* July 7, 2016.
Clarke, Cath. *Time Out.* June 20, 2016.
Jones, J.R. *Chicago Reader.* July 7, 2016.
Lemire, Christy. *ChristyLemire.com.* July 26, 2016.
Morgenstern, Joe. *Wall Street Journal.* July 7, 2016.
Nicholson, Amy. *MTV.* July 8, 2016.
Rife, Katie. *The A.V. Club.* July 7, 2016.
Scott, A.O. *New York Times.* July 7, 2016.
Tobias, Scott. *NPR.* July 7, 2016.
Walsh, Katie. *Tribune News Service.* July 8, 2016.

QUOTES

Chloe: "Because she's a dog person, Max. And dog people do weird, inexplicable things. Like ... they get dogs instead of cats."

TRIVIA

At the party at Pops' place, the dog from the Minions short films makes a reappearance.

THE SHALLOWS

Not just another day at the beach.
—Movie tagline

Box Office: $55.1 Million

Steven Spielberg's *Jaws* (1975) was not the first movie to exploit audience fears of being chomped to bits by a man-eating shark—there was the Sam Fuller thriller *Shark* (1969), for example, and the creatures also popped up from time to time in James Bond movies in order to threaten the hero before snacking on a henchman or two—but it did so in such a spectacularly entertaining and exciting manner that it was difficult to imagine that anyone could possibly do anything with that particular subgenre that he had already done. Of course, that did not stop filmmakers eager to make a quick buck from making their own killer fish epics but in nearly every case—whether they were official sequels like *Jaws 2* (1978), which rejiggered the concept into a aquatic slasher movie with a shark as the mad killer stalking dumb teens, *Jaws 3-D* (1983), which tried to exploit a brief resurgence in 3-D to little effect, and *Jaws: The Revenge* (1987), which presumably bought Michael Caine a nice house, or cheesy rip-offs such as *The Last Shark* (1981), a film that so closely parroted the original *Jaws* that Spielberg successfully sued to keep it from being released in America, or the el cheapo items screened on the SyFy network such as *Mega Shark Vs. Giant Octopus* (2009) and the infamous *Sharknado* series—none of them came close to holding a candle to the Spielberg classic.

That said, there have been a couple of shark-based films that have broken through during that time but in those cases, the filmmakers offered audiences something more than a rehash of familiar material—the cheerfully ridiculous *Deep Blue Sea* (1999) has that crazy scene in which Samuel L. Jackson is attacked in a most unexpected manner and *Open Water* (2004) generated a lot of attention for actually dropping its actors in the water with real sharks. The sensationally effective *The Shallows* is another film that takes one of those premises that sounds so simple and obvious that you wonder why no one else ever came up with it before and then spends the next 90 minutes milking it for all that it is worth without ever resorting to overtly stealing from Spielberg. With its lean and unpretentious manner, it is pretty much a B-movie through and through but one that proves to be far more entertaining and satisfying than most of the expensive dim bulbs it is sharing space with at the multiplex.

Still suffering from the recent loss of her mother, medical student Nancy (Blake Lively) has dropped out of school and gone to Mexico with surfboard in tow in search of a secluded piece of beachfront where her mother used to ride the waves when she was younger. The locale is beautiful and she spends the day surfing alongside a couple of locals. At the end of the day, the other two go in but Nancy decides to take one last ride. This proves to be a bad idea because after she discovers the partially eaten carcass of a whale out there, she is about to make her last run when she is bitten on the leg by a shark. Despite her wound, she manages to swim to a rock roughly 200 yards from shore that is sticking out of the water because of the lowering tide. After stitching herself up utilizing her jewelry (a moment that should have even the hardiest of souls squirming in their seats), she realizes that the shark, whose feeding ground she has stumbled into, is not going away anytime soon and she has about 20 hours to figure out a way to get back to shore before the high tide comes in and submerges her perch.

As movie premises go, few in recent memory are as direct and to the point as *The Shallows*, so much so that it almost seems like a joke—*The Gossip Girl and the Sea*, as the more cynical of observers might dub it. However, screenwriter Anthony Jaswinski and director Jaume Collet-Serra (whose previous films include the berserk horror items *House of Wax* [2005] and *Orphan* [2009] and the Liam Neeson action vehicles *Unknown* [2011], *Non-Stop* [2013], and *Run All Night* [2014]) have taken it and transformed it into a stripped-down exercise in pure cinema of the kind that is rarely seen in an American pop cinema more concerned with establishing universes and setting up sequels than in telling a story. Although the story may sound crazy at first, Jaswinski takes pains to keep the gimmicks to an absolute minimum make everything seem relatively plausible (and mostly succeeds) and even when the film flirts with cutesiness when Nancy is joined on her rock by an injured seagull that she begins talking to and dubs "Steven" (Get it—Steven Seagull!), he doesn't overdo it. He also makes the smart decision not to transform the shark into some kind of increasingly implausible menace in the mold of the later *Jaws* sequels and knockoffs—it is just a shark that is following its biological imperative to eat something that entered his feeding ground. That does not make the creature any less fearsome, of course

and Collet-Serra does a wonderful job of milking the situation for all of the suspense that he possibly can and even uses the inescapable fact that viewers have almost certainly seen *Jaws* to his advantage by milking both the tension of the story and the expectations of audiences in scarily satisfying ways—the sequence going from the discovery of the whale to the shocking first glimpse of the shark is especially impressive in this regard.

The other secret weapon that *The Shallows* has in its arsenal is the performance by Blake Lively as Nancy. Look, there is almost no doubt that she was cast at least in part because of the undeniable fact that she looks great in the bikini and skintight surfing suit that constitutes her wardrobe for virtually the entire film. However, if that was all she had to offer, the film would be little more than an especially intense *Sports Illustrated* swimsuit issue photo shoot. Instead, she makes Nancy into a smart, likable, and compelling character that viewers are actually hoping avoids becoming fish food. A star on television through the beloved *Gossip Girl*, Lively has spent most of her film career so far in supporting roles but her work here is so striking, despite the genre trappings of the material and the skimpiness of her wardrobe, that it should help launch her into more lead roles in the future.

The Shallows has maybe two things that wind up working against it. The score by Marco Beltrami is nothing but a big "Meh!"—there was no way that he would possibly come up with something even close to the legendary music John Williams created for *Jaws* but he could have at least tried—and the final confrontation between Nancy and the shark is the moment when the film finally slips the surly bonds of plausibility and is resolved in a way that may inspire more snickers than shivers. Other than that, this is the kind of stylish and undeniably effective mid-level thriller that Hollywood used to churn out with some regularity. It is also one of the very few of this summer's crop of films that any sane person would want to see more than once. They will certainly have the time to do so because after watching *The Shallows*, any sane man will be steering clear of the beaches for the foreseeable future.

Peter Sobczynski

CREDITS

Nancy: Blake Lively
Carlos: Oscar Jaenada
Dad: Brett Cullen
Chloe: Sedona Legge
    Janelle Bailey
Origin: United States
Language: English, Spanish

Released: 2016

Production: Lynn Harris, Matti Leshem; released by Columbia Pictures Industries Inc.

Directed by: Jaume Collet-Serra

Written by: Anthony Jaswinski

Cinematography by: Flavio Martinez Labiano

Music by: Marco Beltrami

Editing: Joel Negron

Art Direction: Fiona Donovan

Costumes: Kym Barrett

Production Design: Hugh Bateup

MPAA rating: PG-13

Running time: 86 minutes

REVIEWS

Braun, Liz. *Toronto Sun.* June 23, 2016.

Chang, Justin. *Los Angeles Times.* June 23, 2016.

Debruge, Peter. *Variety.* June 23, 2016.

Kenny, Glenn. *New York Times.* June 23, 2016.

Lawson, Richard. *Vanity Fair.* June 23, 2016.

Lund, Carson. *Slant.* June 23, 2016.

McDonagh, Maitland. *Film Journal International.* June 23, 2016.

O'Sullivan, Michael. *Washington Post.* June 24, 2016.

Russo, Tom. *Boston Globe.* June 23, 2016.

Schaeffer, Stephen. *Boston Herald.* June 24, 2016.

QUOTES

Nancy: [to surfers] "GET OUT OF THE WATER, SHARK!"

Surfer #1 to Surfer #2: "It's okay ... no sharks come here."

TRIVIA

The movie was shot in part off the Gold Coast of Australia but other filming took place in a giant swimming pool.

SILENCE

Sometimes silence is the deadliest sound.
   —Movie tagline

Box Office: $7.1 Million

It took Martin Scorsese over two decades to get his vision of Shusaku Endo's 1966 novel *Silence* to the big screen, but it was worth the wait. *Silence* was already made as a film, a very good one by Masahiro Shinoda in 1971, but Scorsese had been trying to get his off the ground since at least the late 1990, when he mentioned it on the release of what is arguably his masterpiece, *GoodFellas*. Despite its centuries-old setting, this could be seen as Scorsese's most personal film. It is a story of faith tested and apostasy rewarded, that of a man who sees faithlessness all around him, including acts of extreme violence, but finds a way to hold on to his faith no matter the cost. Scorsese has said that he has read Endo's novel more than any other, returning to it as a source of inspiration. His respect for the source material is evident in every frame of this remarkable film, not only one of the best films of 2016 but one of the best of Scorsese's masterful career.

Silence opens with a scene of torture. A Jesuit priest in Japan named Cristovao Ferreira (Liam Neeson) is watching as his followers are being tortured. To stop the torture, he merely needs to renounce his faith. Scorsese then cuts to two of Ferreira's colleagues at St. Paul's College in Macau, learning of the news that their mentor has given up the church and now lives among the Japanese as an apostate. They refuse to believe such a claim, and Fathers Sebastiao Rodrigues (Andrew Garfield) and Francisco Garupe (Adam Driver) vow to travel to Japan to find Ferreira, and return him to Portugal.

To help guide them, the Fathers track down an alcoholic fisherman named Kichijiro (Yosuke Kubozuka), who has fled Japan after the death of his family. It is later revealed that Kichijiro gave into Japanese orders to apostatize, even though his family did not, and they were burned alive. He survived, but at what cost? And the pain has destroyed him, although he will regularly apostatize and betray his faith throughout the film in one of the story's most interesting threads thematically. He is a man who consistently denies his faith to save his life, but his safety is only temporary. It is both indicative of how fleeting denial of faith can be in terms of earthly rewards, and thematically consistent with the idea that Jesus gives him chance after chance, even after Kichijiro has turned his back on faith.

Before then, Kichijiro gets Rodrigues and Garupe to a seaside village called Tomogi, in which the Christian population is entirely underground, afraid of government spies who would inform on them if they even saw a rosary or a prayer in action. The Fathers help the religious people of the village maintain their faith, administering sacraments and guiding them, but their presence is eventually revealed. A man known as The Inquisitor (Issei Ogata) arrives, and tortures several of the villagers, including strapping three of them to crosses on the shore, where the tide will come in and drown them. The bodies are then burned, denying them a Christian burial. Rodrigues and Garupe see all of this from afar, unable to act. In this portion of the film comes one of the most resonant lines in terms of Scorsese's overall themes: "Surely he heard their prayers, but did he hear their screams?" This is a complex, dense examination of a silent, inactive God.

From here, the two men split up—Garupe goes to Hirado Island and Rodrigues travels to Goto Island, searching for Ferreira. It has been destroyed, but Rodrigues crosses paths with Kichijiro again, who betrays him to the local samurai. Rodrigues is taken to Nagasaki, where he is imprisoned with other Christians. The second half of *Silence* consists of a lot of torture of both Rodrigues and those who believe in him. Scorsese's approach is blunt and unforgiving. A beheading can happen in the middle of a conversation. A scene could cut to unimaginable torture, such as when people are hung upside down and barely cut, so the blood seeps down to their heads and to the ground barely below them. Rodrigues reunites with Garupe, but he has been captured as well, and dies trying to save three other prisoners, who have apostatized but are then killed anyway. Eventually, Rodrigues learns of the fate of Ferreira and has to make some tough decisions of his own.

By now, Scorsese has an all-star team of regular collaborators, all of whom bring their A-game to their friend's passion project. Jay Cocks, who co-wrote the script with Scorsese, has been the filmmaker's screenwriting partner for decades, earning Oscar nominations for his work on *The Age of Innocence* (1993) and *Gangs of New York* (2002). Cocks and Scorsese have made a film about faith that never feels preachy. It is about holding on to something that matters to you, but never feels designed to convert the unfaithful. Their script is delicate, nuanced, and remarkably subtle, working on multiple levels in that it can be read as an allegory for multiple faiths and beliefs.

Two of Scorsese's most common technical partners warrant acclaim here as well. One is a new collaborator—cinematographer Rodrigo Prieto, who earned the only Oscar nomination for *Silence*, reteaming with Scorsese after shooting *Wolf of Wall Street* (2013). Prieto has become one of the most essential cinematographers alive, also shooting *Argo* (2012), *Babel* (2006), *Brokeback Mountain* (2005), and many more. His work here is fluid and mesmerizing, turning his camera into an impartial observer, often coming around corners to reveal scenes of torture or natural beauty, but never feeling showy in the slightest. Thelma Schoonmaker, who has edited most of Scorsese's films and deserves as much credit for the filmmaker's style as anyone, does phenomenal work here as well, smoothly assembling a film with numerous speaking roles across multiple locations. There's a mesmerizing rhythm to *Silence* that would not be there with Schoonmaker.

As he so often has, Scorsese also draws fantastic performances from his cast. Neeson, Driver, and Ogata are stand-out, but the film belongs to Andrew Garfield, who has never been better than he is here, even in his 2016 Best Actor-nominated role in Mel Gibson's *Hack-saw Ridge*. That performance was very good, but seems to have won out over this one mostly because it's broader and showier. Much of what Garfield does here is internal, an observer to torture and someone going through a crisis of faith on the inside. What Garfield conveys with his body language and his eyes is breathtaking, and the entire film, as accomplished as it is technically, falls apart of Garfield is not as good as he is here.

Much was made of *Silence* "bombing" at the box office. However, this seems an odd self-fulfilling issue of expectations. Who on Earth expected a three-hour film about Jesuit priests being tortured to make waves at the box office? Comparing this film's take to a more accessible subject matter like the *Wolf of Wall Street* is just silly. It also had to go up against a wave of crowdpleasing Oscar fare like *Hidden Figures* (2016) and even the start of 2017 hits like *Split* (2017) and *XXX: The Return of Xander Cage* (2017). People also craved escapism near the end of 2016 and the beginning of 2017 given the tumultuous state of the world, and *Silence* most definitely is not escapism. It is a challenging, fantastic film, one that will find its audience over the years and decades to come. It deals with timeless themes and does so with masterful craftsmanship and attention to detail. And yet it also feels deeply human. One can sense that passion that Scorsese brought to every reading of the source material, and one wants to thank him for taking his time with such a personal project to get it this incredibly right.

Brian Tallerico

CREDITS

Rodrigues: Andrew Garfield
Garupe: Adam Driver
Ferreira: Liam Neeson
Interpreter: Tadanobu Asano
Father Valignano: Ciaran Hinds
Origin: United States
Language: English
Released: 2016
Production: Vittorio Cecchi Gori, Barbara De Fina, Randall Emmett, David Lee, Gastón Pavlovich, Emma Tillinger Koskoff, Irwin Winkler, Martin Scorsese; released by Cappa De Fina Productions, CatchPlay, Emmett/Furla/Oasis Films, Fábrica de Cine, SharpSword Films, Sikelia Productions, Waypoint Entertainment
Directed by: Martin Scorsese
Written by: Martin Scorsese; Jay Cocks
Cinematography by: Rodrigo Prieto
Music by: Kathryn Kluge; Kim Allen Kluge
Sound: Philip Stockton
Music Supervisor: Randall Poster; John Schaefer

Editing: Thelma Schoonmaker
Art Direction: Wen-Ying Huang
Costumes: Dante Ferretti
Production Design: Dante Ferretti
MPAA rating: R
Running time: 161 minutes

REVIEWS

Burr, Ty. *Boston Globe*. January 5, 2017.
Cataldo, Jesse. *Slant*. December 15, 2016.
Chang, Justin. *Los Angeles Times*. December 22, 2016.
Edelstein, David. *New York Magazine*. December 20, 2016.
McCarthy, Todd. *Hollywood Reporter*. December 10, 2016.
Nicholson, Amy. *MTV News*. January 21, 2017.
Roeper, Richard. *Chicago Sun-Times*. January 5, 2017.
Seitz, Matt Zoller. *RogerEbert.com*. December 27, 2016.
Stevens, Dana. *Slate*. December 27, 2016.
Zacharek, Stephanie. *Time*. December 22, 2016.

QUOTES

Ferreira: "There's a saying in here: 'Mountains and rivers can be moved but men's nature cannot be moved'."

TRIVIA

Adam Driver lost 50 pounds for the role—30 pounds before filming and 20 during filming.

AWARDS

Nominations:
Oscars 2016: Cinematog.

SING

Auditions begin 2016.
    —Movie tagline

Box Office: $267.7 Million

Before Garth Jennings's *Sing*'s barnyard karaoke animation begins in the theater, there are not the opening animations of Disney or Pixar. These are not the tactics or artistic ambitions of Illumination, the film's production company also behind this year's *The Secret Life of Pets* and 2015's annoying juggernaut *Minions*. Pre-sold advertisements replace pre-screening short films. A cover of Leonard Cohen's "Hallelujah" rings out slowly and drearily over a jittery collection of images that slowly reveal itself as an advertisement for the NFL's Thursday Night Football.

There was a corporate tie-in before the movie even began to roll. This is the new landscape of profitable

animated film, or at least that is the attitude *Sing* brings to the world of children's films: sell you on flash so its particular brand of flimsy fluff can rake in the massive profits by selling you on everything else. Looking at the proliferation of the Minions characters since their starring film makes it clear that the company's expertise lies in monetizing mediocrity. Keeping budgets relatively low and earning ludicrous returns (over a billion dollars for *Minions* and *The Secret Life of Pets* is following closely behind), the focus is on crafting something inescapable—something that cages parents in rather than invites children.

The film opens in much the same way. We zoom away from an opening musical drama, spinning to an audience of animals agape with wonder. Like Brian De Palma's *Dionysus in '69* (1970) sans split-screen and with rounded, cartoonish animals crowding its theater seats, *Sing* encourages its audience to think about audiences in general rather than the performance in front of them. That begins to make sense as the movie goes on, revealing the lack of substance, imagination, or fun in every facet of its filmmaking.

The ringleader of this charade is a koala enamored with show business, Buster Moon (voice of Matthew McConaughey, so chipper that his every line sounds like a talk show host who's just huffed something pleasant), that was gifted a theater by his hardworking father. His personal ineptitude fails to impact his career, as a steady stream of donors and bank-dodging (which makes no sense if the theater was a gift, but this is the type of kids movie that leaves the adults aimlessly considering the financial details of its background plot) keeps his personal entitlement to the performing arts afloat.

Moon plans a singing contest to generate interest in his dying business, apparently unaware that even the popular televised versions of singing contests have been replaced with the fake thrills of drivel like *Lip Sync Battle*. As Moon's schemes continue to go awry, *Sing* contains the same ethos as an animated version of that show. There's no reason for a carefully constructed entertainment commodity to risk anything less than star quality of either songs or performers. The film forgoes its competitive basis almost immediately, focusing on the whirlwind of circumstance and absurdity surround the lives of its animal-housed pop stars. There's a pig that never learned about birth control and is thus overrun by her twenty-odd children (voice of Reese Witherspoon), a punk porcupine who's pushed to pop music (Scarlett Johansson), a rodent Sinatra (Seth MacFarlane) that gets mixed up with the Bear Mob, a shy elephant (Tori Kelly), and an inexplicably British gorilla (Taron Egerton) who's both a getaway driver for his family's crime syndicate and a natural-born crooner. We learn about them all in a series of sloppily-written scenes without transitions between them, jumping all over the crime-ridden zoo-dystopia to see these sad animals who come to the competition purely for the mistyped prize money of $100,000. A few accidental extra zeroes tacked onto the end of a bottom line is the only reason for the film to exist, internally and externally.

Showing these characters with their personal tragedies drawn as thinly comic slapstick does not make viewers care about any of them. Its animation is technically proficient (especially some time lapse shots) but uninspired by its unambitious premise. The singing contest eventually crumbles into the dusty remains of an '80s movie plot revolving around a final blowout to save a beloved venue when Moon's ambitions accidentally destroy his father's theater. The film may not build up affection for its cast of characters, but its constant cuts to dancing animal children in the audience during the final concert performance underscore the film's true goal: wheedling its hand-clapping into the psyches of children everywhere so that Illumination's success can continue.

Jacob Oller

CREDITS

Buster Moon: Matthew McConaughey
Rosita: Reese Witherspoon
Mike: Seth MacFarlane
Ash: Scarlett Johansson
Eddie: John C. Reilly
Johnny: Taron Egerton
Meena: Tori Kelly
Origin: United States
Language: English
Released: 2016
Production: Janet Healy, Christopher Meledandri; released by Illumination Entertainment, Universal Pictures Inc.
Directed by: Garth Jennings
Written by: Garth Jennings
Music by: Joby Talbot
Sound: Dennis Leonard
Music Supervisor: JoJo Villanueva
Editing: Gregory Perler
Art Direction: François Moret
Production Design: Eric Guillon
MPAA rating: PG
Running time: 108 minutes

REVIEWS

Cerritos, Marco. *First Showing*. September 17, 2016.
Debruge, Peter. *Variety*. September 11, 2016.
Ellwood, Gregory. *Playlist*. September 12, 2016.

Felperin, Leslie. *Hollywood Reporter*. September 11, 2016.
Hoffman, Jordan. *The Guardian*. September 12, 2016.
Huls, Alexander. *RogerEbert.com*. September 17, 2016.
Pond, Steven. *The Wrap*. September 19, 2016.
Prentice, George. *Boise Weekly*. September 16, 2016.
Ryan, Mike. *Uproxx*. September 16, 2016.
Topel, Fred. *We Live Entertainment*. November 29, 2016.

QUOTES

Buster Moon: "Why aren't you rehearsing?"
Frog: "I'm through! They said I'm an intolerable egomaniac. I don't even know what that means!"

TRIVIA

This is the first Illumination Entertainment film not to feature any humans.

AWARDS

Nominations:

Golden Globes 2017: Animated Film, Song ("Faith")

SING STREET

Boy meets girl, girl unimpressed, boy starts band.
—Movie tagline

Box Office: $3.2 Million

In 2013, John Carney made a charming film called *Begin Again*, starring Mark Ruffalo and Keira Knightly. The original title of the film before it got changed by the Weinsteins was *Can A Song Save Your Life?* Film titles sometimes go through changes before release, so it is nothing unusual, but in this case, the film went from sounding interesting to sounding bland. Carney's follow-up film, *Sing Street*, never went through any such changes, but the title *Can A Song Save Your Life?* would fit for this film as well. *Sing Street* is about songs that change people's lives in terms of how they look at the world, how they choose to express themselves and the action they take with their lives that forever alter their trajectory. And this being 1985 when the film takes place, not only can a song change one's life, so can a music video on MTV.

Conor (Ferdia Walsh-Peelo) is a 15 year old in Dublin, Ireland, when music starts to change his life. He comes from a lower-middle-class family with parents who are on the verge of divorce. In order for the family to make ends meet financially, they transfer Conor to a cheaper school with priests of questionable morals and a school bully around every corner waiting to pounce on the new kid. Conor braves his first day at this school and does indeed get bullied by Barry (Ian Kenny), who tries to make every day for Conor a living hell. Back at home, his parents fight and his older brother acts as a sort of music mentor for Conor, who plays guitar and sings quietly in his room to pass the time while his parents argue.

One day at school, Conor notices a girl named Raphina (Lucy Boynton), who is around his age, but slightly older. She confidently stands by herself across the street. He strides over to her and strikes a conversation. She does not go to this school. She works as a professional model. For Conor, this is good news. He tells her he has a band and they are about to embark on their first-ever music video and they need a female model. She agrees, gives him her phone number and everything looks good. Conor then tells his friend Darren (Ben Carolan), "We need to start a band." With Darren by his side serving as a producer, they begin holding auditions for the best young, Dublin-based musicians they can find.

The first person they find ends up being the most advanced and prolific musician any teenager could ever hope to be. Eamon (Mark McKenna) can play just about every instrument imaginable and also has a quirky obsession with his pet rabbits. They recruit a keyboardist, and a bass-and-drum duo and, thus, begin their journey to create "futurist" rock. No nostalgia. They call themselves Sing Street, which is a play on words from their school name. Raphina shows up to the video shoot as planned and brings her make-up kit with her. Soon, she convinces the boys that they need to seriously change their physical appearance if they want to make an impact. Soon, the boys find themselves decked out in big jackets, mascara, and eyeshadow. The song Conor wrote for Raphina, "The Rhythm of a Model," is catchy and fun; the video, made with a VHS camcorder, fits the spirit just enough.

Conor's brother Brendon (Jack Reynor) says they are off to a great start and continues to give Conor lessons in being a true musical artist. Stay away from cover songs, learn to play your instruments, and the importance of a music video should never be discounted are just a few of the lessons Conor learns from his brother, who spends most of his time at home getting high and not motivating himself. Meanwhile, Conor and Raphina get closer as friends, but she already has a boyfriend. Brendan assures Conor that "no man who listens to Phil Collins can ever be much of a threat." More songs get written and recorded, all of them by Conor and Eamon, who end up embodying a kind of Lennon/McCartney-like authorship on the songs. Finally, the band gains enough confidence to try their first gig.

To hear the basic storyline for *Sing Street*, one would be led to believe that there exists little in the way of conflict or depth. True, *Sing Street* sometimes has the feel of a kind of happy-go-lucky musical, but the world in which these teenagers exist feels right and the personal conflicts they endure have more to do with outside forces, such as how and where their parents decide to live, that are beyond their control. Every day, they watch on television about how so many Irish have fled their homeland to live in England where there exists more of an opportunity for a secure living. Conor sees music as his one way out and Raphina sees modeling the same way. She claims to have a lot of experience, but she may still have a lot of learning to do. Conor, with each passing song, feels more ready and more confident in his ability to go to the next level.

Sing Street goes above and beyond in bringing to life the film's chosen time period. The fashions, from the over-sized coats with big shoulder pads to almost everything being in some form of denim, and the make-up, which gives the band members an appropriate amount of mid-80s androgyny, exist to bring out the best in the characters. Carney wisely never plays the '80s for laughs. There is no underlining how big the phones were or what kind of music had been popular back then. It adores its decade and its fashion and music choices, right down to the records that can be seen amongst Brendan's massive music collection. Sure, nobody listens to Soft Cell or Quarterflash anymore, but Brendan is never being made to look foolish for owning their records—this was 1985.

Carney's film would not succeed at all if the mostly unknown cast of real musicians did not have the acting chops necessary to make these characters believable and engaging. As Conor (later nicknamed "Cosmo"), Walsh-Peelo exudes confidence, charm, and a quality that would make anyone who feels uncool want to be more like him. His abilities as a musician, frontman, and teenage troublemaker bring to mind a young John Lennon, with a face that looks all-too-ready for stardom. As Raphina, Boynton exudes the same qualities, but while also nursing a wounded soul in slight need of a confidence boost from everyone around her. And as Brendan, Reynor is a perfectly fleshed-out character, where in any other movie he would mostly be seen as a buffoon. His relationship with Conor is perhaps the film's most important aspect as he not only wants Conor to succeed, he is envious of Conor's chances and it looms like a shadow over Brendan's own failures. Brendan's confession about all of this is one of the film's many highlights.

The main highlight for most people will, of course, be the music. *Sing Street*'s secret weapon is its soundtrack. Carney co-wrote many of the wonderful songs here, which sound like beautifully orchestrated pop with a youthful exuberance. Many will criticize that the teenagers here would never really sound this good unless they had practiced diligently for at least a year. But there exists a fantasy sequence in this film that lays such criticism to rest. *Sing Street* is a musical and the audience hears the music the way the musicians, especially Conor, hear it, Of course, it would never be this perfect. But the film is about one's need to escape from harsh realities through music and Carney has fashioned the music in a way that expresses that need. Lukas Moodysson made a film a few years prior called *We Are the Best* (2013) in which the teenagers in that film had no musical talent, but started a band anyway. *Sing Street* is about the band they probably saw themselves as when they started out.

Sing Street represents Carney's third outing as a director of musicals featuring down-to-earth characters who dream of making a living by making music. His break-out indie hit *Once* (2007) starred Glen Hansard and Marketa Irglova as two musicians and songwriters who had a life-changing friendship. *Begin Again*, with Knightly and Ruffalo, told the story of a former music exec and his chance encounter with an aspiring singer/songwriter. All three films are about collaboration and the need to bounce ideas off other people and what those other people can bring to a work of art. For *Sing Street*, Carney has collaborated with a winning group of musicians, songwriters, and actors to bring about what is surely one of the most joyous, funniest, and most rewarding films of 2016 with an ending that will make any teenager believe that he/she can take on the world and that a song can, in many ways, save one's life.

Collin Souter

CREDITS

Conor: Ferdia Walsh-Peelo
Robert: Aidan Gillen
Penny: Maria Doyle Kennedy
Brendan: Jack Reynor
Raphina: Lucy Boynton
Origin: United States
Language: English
Released: 2016
Production: Anthony Bregman, Kevin Scott Frakes, Christian Grass, Martina Niland, Raj Brinder Singh, Paul Trijbits, John Carney; released by FilmNation Entertainment, Likely Story
Directed by: John Carney
Written by: John Carney
Cinematography by: Yaron Orbach
Sound: Niall Brady

Music Supervisor: Becky Bentham
Editing: Andrew Marcus; Julian Ulrichs
Art Direction: Tamara Conboy
Costumes: Tiziana Corvisieri
Production Design: Alan MacDonald
MPAA rating: PG-13
Running time: 106 minutes

REVIEWS

Brody, Richard. *New York Post*. April 18, 2016.
Covert, Colin. *Star Tribune*. April 28, 2016.
Dowd, A.A. *The A.V. Club*. April 14, 2016.
Goodykoontz, Bill. *Arizona Republic*. April 28, 2016.
Hornaday, Ann. *Washington Post*. April 21, 2016.
Howell, Peter. *Toronto Star*. April 21, 2016.
Jones, J.R. *Chicago Reader*. April 21, 2016.
MacDonald, Moira. *Seattle Times*. April 28, 2016.
Rea, Stephen. *Philadelphia Enquirer*. April 22, 2016.
Walsh, Katie. *Los Angeles Times*. April 15, 2016.

QUOTES

Conor: "When you don't know someone, they're more interesting. They can be anything you want them to be. But when you know them, there's limits to them."

TRIVIA

The film premiered at the 2016 Sundance Film Festival.

AWARDS

Nominations:
Golden Globes 2017: Film—Mus./Comedy

SNOWDEN

You don't have to pick a side. But you will.
—Movie tagline

Box Office: $21.6 Million

In 2014, much of the Western world was spellbound by Laura Poitras' documentary *Citizenfour,* in which former CIA analyst Edward Snowden revealed in plain English that the US government was spying on its people. The computer specialist had learned something heinous about the surveillance practices his government was involved in and did something about it. Poitras, a Boston-born documentarian, flew to Hong Kong to meet with Snowden in secret while he disclosed that the government had been spying on free citizens under the guise of antiterrorism. Their intentions may have been pure at the outset of the project, but it morphed into preemptive paranoia. The US government wanted to spot terrorists before they became terrorists, which meant listening in on cellphone conversations, looking at Facebook pages and monitoring personal correspondence, all of which was illegal. The story of the United States' betrayal of its people's privacy wound up in *The Guardian* thanks to Snowden's expert testimony, and he has since lived in exile in Russia, unable to return to his home country.

Snowden has fascinated the world for many reasons since he opened up a permanent discussion on surveillance in America. He presented himself as a levelheaded, logical young man with a calm demeanor even as he was potentially marking himself for torture and death. What kind of new hero was this Edward Snowden? Oliver Stone, the famously self-medicated gonzo journalist-filmmaker intent on tearing off every Band-Aid America had ever placed over its self-inflicted wounds, decided he was the man to tell Snowden's story once and for all. The issue is that Snowden's story is a matter of very recent public record. Making it work dramatically evidently required a lot of heavy handed over-statement of the facts presented thus far because Stone ladles on the symbolism and metaphor like gravy on a particularly dry Thanksgiving Turkey. *Snowden* wants for many things, but emphasis and attempted immediacy are not among them.

Edward Snowden (Joseph Gordon-Levitt) is introduced to viewers in a hotel room in Hong Kong confessing to witnesses Glenn Greenwald (Zachary Quinto) and Laura Poitras (Melissa Leo) that he has information that will unseat most of the world. When the two journalists ask what led him to this moment, he recounts his history in minute detail. He starts with his time training for Special Forces after 9/11 galvanized him into trying to make a difference. Basic training was so intense that he broke both of his legs without realizing it and had to seek employment for the government in another field. He was quickly recruited into the CIA by Corbin O'Brian (Rhys Ifans), who saw in Snowden a fast learner and a naïve patriot. Both O'Brian and information/coding expert Hank Forrester (Nicolas Cage) give him a sense of purpose that he carries with him during the whole of his education. He outpaces his fellow recruits and finds himself in Geneva, Switzerland, assigned to computer network security for the CIA. While there, he orchestrates a sting operation with the help of a gung-ho field operative (Timothy Olyphant) and a fellow tech wizard named Gabriel (Ben Schnetzer) to blackmail a friendly banker (Bhasker Patel), just to see what his status and power mean in the real world. He does not like the feeling he gets when it means that the banker may have to surrender his freedom, so Snowden resigns and accepts work for Dell in Japan.

The real motivator behind Snowden's decisions during this portion of his life is his relationship to free-spirited artist Lindsay Mills (Shailene Woodley). It's her naked self-portraiture that makes him realize how vulnerable most citizens are to invasion of privacy. In Geneva, Gabriel shows him software that allows the US government to hack every webcam and cell phone if they decide there is reasonable doubt. This makes him morally queasy and drives him back into Lindsay's arms. Wanting to work out their differences and settle down, Edward and Lindsay move back to the States together. All seems idyllic until Edward starts displaying symptoms of epilepsy. His doctor suggests a warmer climate would be better for his health at the same time that O'Brian re-enters his life and fixes him a job working for a National Security Agency contractor called Booz Allen Hamilton. The job, coincidentally, is based in the NSA's Hawaii regional operations center, the perfect place for recuperation. It's there, greeted with images of drone pilots bombing people to dust in the Middle East, that he decides to take action and reclaim his self-respect. He gathers all the damning evidence he can fit on an external hard-drive, orchestrates an escape that leaves Lindsay and his co-workers looking innocent, and contacts Poitras. The rest, as they say, is history.

Snowden was at a unique disadvantage long before a single second of the movie had been shot. There is the fact that so much of Edward Snowden's story is widely known (thanks in no small part to Poitras' documentary) and that many people remember the revelations when they occurred in the pages of *The Guardian* or on CNN. It's difficult now to even say the word "Snowden" without thinking of hacked emails, hijacked webcams, and unlawful searches and seizures. Stone's attempt to humanize him through traditional Judeo-Christian dramatic shorthand was essentially unnecessary. Everyone who thinks Snowden is a traitor will not have their mind changed by learning of his medical history, or that his girlfriend took a job as a pole-dance fitness instructor to appease him. The film turns him into a hero by trying to make him look like an ordinary Joe. He was already ordinary in *Citizenfour*. Having Levitt put on a deeper voice and strain at playing a regular guy prone to outbursts of plot-specific conscience makes Snowden feel very much like a movie character, and much less like a man who took a stand. Stone's attempt to humanize him accidentally makes him unapproachable. It's easy to relate to the slightly awkward guy hiding under bed sheets to protect his passwords from prying eyes in *Citizenfour*. By casting him as a quasi-action hero, played by a movie star, he actually becomes less accessible and relatable.

Stone is also handicapped by his overcooked grammar. The same hyperactive mise-en-scene and

MTV-ready editing that made his tangent-heavy storytelling in *JFK* (1991) and *Nixon* (1995) so appealing and appropriately paranoid hobbles *Snowden*. Audiences are savvier than they were when Stone was establishing himself, thanks in part to his own work. Americans are now prepared to accept that their government is lying to them, so the moments of revelation that Stone banks on as dramatic catharsis can't possibly inspire the awe they are intended to. Anyone with a smart phone knows the government is spying on them because that information is on their Twitter and Facebook feeds 24 hours a day. Stone nevertheless treats that reveal with the same gravity he used to reserve for the conspiracy around the assassination of presidents and it just does not carry water. Snowden's "crimes" against the state are so fresh in the cultural memory they may as well have happened yesterday. Presenting the information as the arc of a traditional drama cannot possibly have the impact it's meant to.

Not helping matters is that Stone quite clearly took cues from a handful of recent would-be blockbusters and award winners. From Danny Boyle's *Steve Jobs* (2015), another technologically-minded biopic, he takes uncommon framing and meditative digital photography, courtesy of Boyle's regular cinematographer Anthony Dod Mantle. The film always looks stellar, thanks to Mantle's expressionistic angles, but *Snowden* never develops a visual personality of its own. The closest it comes is during a bravura sequence that tracks the flow of information when someone is suspected of terrorism. Stone also lifts liberally from David Fincher's *The Social Network* (2010), about the invention of Facebook, right down the rubbery synthesizer score by Craig Armstrong and Adam Peters, which apes Trent Reznor and Atticus Ross' work on the 2010 smash hit. Like *The Social Network*, *Snowden* focuses on an anti-social "nerd" with a knack for unlocking secrets via computer technology and finds himself a kind of public enemy on the other side of his portentous breakthrough. Stone is smart enough to understand that lifting that film's atmosphere will help audiences access and sympathize with Snowden as they did with Jesse Eisenberg's portrayal of Facebook founder Mark Zuckeberg. What he doesn't realize is that what made Fincher and screenwriter Aaron Sorkin's portrait of Zuckerberg so successful is that they played up the inherent contradictions and flaws in his personality.

It's easy to watch *The Social Network* (or for that matter *Steve Jobs*) and not know what to think about the protagonist. The same cannot be said of the title character of *Snowden*. Stone treats him like a saint on his way to canonization; treats his disease as a purely symbolic setback, evidence of his discomfort. Most offensively it treats his love for his girlfriend as a Rosetta Stone, as if trying to remain a good boyfriend is ultimately what forced him to release information on a global conspiracy. It invents characters like O'Brian (an amalgam of a few real government employees with whom Snowden had interactions, named after a character from George Orwell's *1984*) to make Snowden's awakening and conflict more tidy and centralized, rather than handle the more complex tangle of allegiances with which the young analyst was faced.

In short, the truth was too big, too unwieldy, and too complex for Stone, who tries to turn the most controversial act of whistleblowing of the 21st century into a simple hero's journey. When history looks back on Edward Snowden's acts, it will not look to Oliver Stone's too-pat version of events, less informative and only slightly more stylish than Snowden's own Wikipedia page, for clarification.

Scout Tafoya

CREDITS

Edward Snowden: Joseph Gordon-Levitt
Lindsay Mills: Shailene Woodley
Laura Poitras: Melissa Leo
Glenn Greenwald: Zachary Quinto
Ewen MacAskill: Tom Wilkinson
Hank Forrester: Nicolas Cage
Corbin O'Brian: Rhys Ifans
Origin: United States
Language: English
Released: 2016
Production: Moritz Borman, Eric Kopeloff, Philip Schulz-Deyle, Fernando Sulichin; released by Endgame Entertainment Inc., KrautPack Entertainment, Vendian Entertainment
Directed by: Oliver Stone
Written by: Oliver Stone; Kieran Fitzgerald
Cinematography by: Anthony Dod Mantle
Music by: Craig Armstrong; Adam Peters
Sound: Eric Hoehn; Wylie Stateman
Editing: Alex Marquez; Lee Percy
Art Direction: Adam O'Neill
Costumes: Bina Daigeler
Production Design: Mark Tildesley
MPAA rating: R
Running time: 134 minutes

REVIEWS

D'Angelo, Mike. *The A.V. Club.* September 14, 2016.
Ebiri, Bilge. *Village Voice.* September 14, 2016.
Edelstein, David. *New York Magazine.* September 17, 2016.
Ellwood, Gregory. *Playlist.* September 10, 2016.

Farber, Stephen. *Hollywood Reporter*. September 10, 2016.

Grierson, Tim. *Screen International*. September 10, 2016.

Phillips, Michael. *Chicago Tribune*. September 15, 2016.

Scott, A.O. *New York Times*. September 15, 2016.

Suzanne-Mayer, Dominick. *Consequence of Sound*. September 14, 2016.

Tallerico, Brian. *RogerEbert.com*. September 13, 2016.

QUOTES

Corbin O'Brian: "Bombs won't stop terrorism, brains will, and we don't have nearly enough of those. I'm gonna give you a shot, Snowden."

TRIVIA

To make sure the screenplay was not hacked or leaked, Oliver Stone wrote the script on a single computer with no Internet connection.

AWARDS

Nominations:

Golden Raspberries 2016: Worst Support. Actor (Cage)

SOUTHBOUND

No matter which road you choose, it's all going south.
—Movie tagline

Box Office: $23,665

Five interlocking stories explore themes of cosmic judgement and free will in this horror anthology. Unlike a lot of similar films, producer Brad Miska and his creative team offer a solid framing device and actually uses it to progress the narrative. The end result is a little loose and forgettable, but *Southbound* is easily in the very top tier of the recent spate of horror anthologies.

Each of the stories feature weary and sometimes bloodied travelers caught in an endless desert highway loop as their past and their destiny collide. The first story, "The Way Out," picks up midway, as two such bloodied and desperate men, Jack, (Matt Bettinelli-Olpin) and Mitch (Chad Villella), flee mysterious floating creatures. As they tear down the highway, a potential source of help looms; a dingy little gas station diner. But soon the pair realize they've been driven there by the creatures themselves, as their attempts to flee find them back where they started. Facing judgment, one man surrenders; the other, haunted by a photo of his daughter, finds himself chasing her specter, unable to save her from some awful fate, as his gaze is constantly drawn to an old man's mask on a table.

This segment is directed by Radio Silence, a creative collective whose members—Matt Bettinelli-Olpin, Justin Martinez, Tyler Gillett, and Chad Villella—are best known for their contribution to the *V/H/S* horror anthology. Matt Bettinelli-Olpin does the writing here, and also plays the part of Jack. "The Way Out" certainly has some things going for it. Most notably, the flying, scythe-bearing specters which make appearances throughout the film. Another nice touch throughout are the vocal cameos by Larry Fessenden, as an odd DJ/Evangelist whose store of consciousness ramblings about heaven and hell and the journey in-between offer gallows humor. As a narrative short though, "The Way Out" feels muddled and ambiguous. It only barely registers why the men are on the run. That said the setup does prove fruitful later on.

The next segment, "Siren," is easily the weakest. A female rock band breaks down on the side of the road where they are picked up by a very strange couple, the Kensingtons (Susan Burke and Davey Johnson), who offer to feed them and let them spend the night. While at the couple's house, a conversation between the bandmates takes place referencing the unnecessary death of Alex, a previous band member. At dinner that night, a disgusting mystery meatloaf is devoured by two of the girls, but the third, Sadie (Fabianne Therese), skips dinner, becoming increasingly alarmed by the odd situation. Soon, her bandmates are vomiting a blackish goo and refusing to leave. Later that night, Sadie wakes to find her bandmates gone. She leaves the house to search only to find them at a bonfire, being inducted into an occult sect. The robed figures, and her friends, give chase. She catches her foot in a bear trap and the ghost of Alex appears, saying, *Now we can all be together.* Terrified, Sadie runs into the night, down the road, quietly followed by one of the mysterious floating creatures from the first segment.

As directed and written by Roxanne Benjamin and co-written by Susan Burke there's little to like here. The chief issues are the ham-fisted writing and cartoonish performances of almost everyone involved. To be fair it would be difficult to imagine breathing too much life into the material. Fabianne Therese is fine as Sadie but has nothing good to work off. From the moment the girls find a bear trap in the backseat of the car, to the ultra-awkward dinner complete with a pair of creepy geek-guy twins, the viewer is likely to stop caring what happens to anyone dumb-enough not to leave the house. The revelation of the occult ceremony is really no revelation at all since the Kensingtons and the other dinner guests give numerous statements about being involved in a very strange religion.

Sadie runs right into a car accident herself, setting up "The Accident," directed and written by David

Bruckner. Lucas (Mather Zickel) hits Sadie in the middle of the road while distracted during a late-night drive home. Terrified, he wrestles with his conscience but gets out of the car and calls 911. Early into the call he realizes that the dispatcher somehow knows him by name. Instructed to drive to a nearby hospital he arrives only to find it completely abandoned. Both the dispatcher and an EMT tell him to stay on the line and direct him through a potentially lifesaving operation but Sadie dies. Beyond reason, Lucas frantically tries to escape the hospital as the voices laugh at him. Unable to leave, he answers his phone again, and the voices, surprisingly, agree with him as he cries "I don't deserve this!" They lead him to a locker room containing a shower and a change of clothes and then back out to the parking lot, where a duplicate of his car waits. A final message tells him not to worry and he speeds off into the night watched silently by one of the floating creatures.

This is easily the best segment of the film. Not only is the script tight, but the pacing and surreal atmosphere generated works wonders to suspend disbelief. In short, finding out just what is going to happen to Sadie and Lucas is made way more interesting than picking at minor shortcomings like the amount of time it takes Lucas to truly grasp that his situation is a supernatural one. Mather Zickel delivers a powerful performance in what is essentially a one-man showcase, hitting at the heart of just how difficult it is for all the characters in *Southbound* to sort through issues of moral culpability, what it means to seek forgiveness or offer penance, and exactly how fairness might play into the concept of cosmic judgment.

"Jailbreak," directed and co-written by Patrick Horvath and co-written by Dallas Hallam, is a little less effective but still works just fine. The mysterious dispatcher from the last segment watches Lucas drive away and walks into a bar where a poster for the girl band from segment two is on the wall. Another man (David Yow) follows from a distance and while the locals inside chat, he bursts through the door with a shotgun demanding to know where his sister is. Taking the bartender (Matt Peters) hostage, the man is led to a secret room where he finds his sister Jessie (Tipper Newtown) who refuses to leave. The man kills the bartender, kidnaps his sister, and drives off pursued by the locals who are, in reality, demons. When he leaves the highway his sister begs him to stop the car and explains that she lives in purgatory because she murdered their parents. Before he can start the car the demons take him as his sister drives away.

"Jailbreak" is a neat little exercise in exploring the nature of spiritual rescue. Can you force someone to accept it? What if that takes you to bad places? To be sure this is hardly presented as deep theology, but it is unnerving.

The last segment, "The Way In," directed by Radio Silence and written by Matt Bettinelli-Olpin, provides the backstory for the fate of characters in the first segment, "The Way Out." A young woman, Jem (Hassie Harrison) passes Jessie on the way back to her parents table. As Mom, Cait (Kater Beahan) and Dad, Daryl (Gerald Downey) talk over how lucky they all are to share a weekend before Jem leaves for college they are watched from the parking lot. After three masked men break into the family's vacation home Jem is able to hide. Meanwhile, one of the men tells Cait why they are there as Daryl begs for his family's life. The man says, "eye for an eye" and kills Cait in front of Daryl. When another of the men goes outside to investigate a noise, he is attacked by Jem, who is then told by the attackers to leave. They go back into the house and kill Daryl. As Daryl dies one of the men holds up a photo of a young girl that viewers will recognize from the first episode as a photo of Mitch's daughter. Removing their masks the two uninjured men are revealed to be Mitch and Jack. They grab their injured partner Shane (Damion Stephens) and attempt to leave, but are confronted by Jem. In the ensuing fight, they accidentally kill her and are immediately grief stricken that their revenge plot has ended so badly. Turning to leave they see the ground open up as the floating creatures grab Shane and drag him down to hell.

The film ends as Mitch and Jack are back on the road caught in the loop of purgatory, where they have the power to make choices, but must always suffer consequences at the hands of the creatures of cosmic judgment. The payoff is already pretty apparent by this time, but somehow continues to haunt. Almost none of the characters in *Southbound* is purely evil but the film does an effective job pointing out the ways in which they are far from perfectly good.

Dave Canfield

CREDITS

Mitch: Chad Villella
Jack: Matt Bettinelli-Olpin
Sutter: Kristina Pesic
Sadie: Fabianne Therese
Ava: Hannah Marks
Origin: United States
Language: English
Released: 2016
Production: Chris Harding, Brad Miska, Greg Newman, Roxanne Benjamin, Radio Silence
Directed by: Roxanne Benjamin; David Bruckner; Patrick Horvath; Radio Silence
Written by: Matt Bettinelli-Olpin; Roxanne Benjamin; David Bruckner; Patrick Horvath; Susan Burke; Dallas Richard Hallam

Cinematography by: Tarin Anderson; Tyler Gillett; Alexandre
  Naufel; Andrew Shulkind
Music by: The Gifted
Sound: Aaron Davies; Andrew Williams
Music Supervisor: Andrea von Foerster
Editing: Matt Bettinelli-Olpin; David Bruckner; Patrick
  Horvath; Tyler Gillett; Jason Eisener
Costumes: Dominique Dawson
Production Design: Jennifer Moller
MPAA rating: Unrated
Running time: 89 minutes

REVIEWS

Crump, Andy. *Paste Magazine*. February 5, 2016.
Goldstein, Gary. *Los Angeles Times*. February 4, 2016.
Gunslinger, Neil. *New York Times*. February 4, 2016.
Harvey, Dennis. *Variety*. February 5, 2016.
Hunter, Rob. *Film School Rejects*. September 29, 2015.
Jones, Alan. *Radio Times*. March 7, 2016.
Nemiroff, Perri. *Collider*. March 4, 2016.
Nordine, Michael. *Village Voice*. February 3, 2016.
Scheck, Frank. *Hollywood Reporter*. February 2, 2016.
Weinberg, Scott. *The Horrorshow*. February 8, 2016.

QUOTES

Lucas: "I'm in the middle of nowhere!"

TRIVIA

The tattoo on Jack's arm says "Only God Can Judge Me."

SOUTHSIDE WITH YOU

*In the summer of 1989, one first date would
  change history.*
  —Movie tagline

Box Office: $6.3 Million

How often are there movies in which characters are
given the freedom to just walk and talk? More specifically, how often do these films give voices to minority
characters at the center, allowing them to share their
perspectives? *Southside with You* is a miracle of a film,
and not just for making wonderful entertainment out of
Barack and Michelle Obama's first date.

Writer/director Richard Tanne's project works in
one part because it is bigger than even the future
President of the United States and the First Lady. In his
film, Barack Obama (Parker Sawyers) and Michelle
Robinson (Tika Sumpter) are relatable young professionals on a determined path. The two first met at a

corporate law firm, where Michelle worked as his adviser.
He had pursued her repeatedly for a chance to go out,
and she finally gave in.

But, because of their work conditions, Michelle
insists that this cannot be a "date." It would be inappropriate, and bad for her professional reputation, which
she has to fight for more than him. "I just got to work a
little harder to be taken seriously," she says, in Tika
Sumpter's straight-from-the-heart performance. Immediately, *Southside for You* takes on its richer concepts,
directly echoing how a modern call for diversity does
not mean only race: a man of the people like Barack
may be able to earn a high position and some sense of
respect, but a black woman like Michelle has to work
double-time "to be seen for who I am." The pressure of
this weighs on them throughout the story, with Tanne
making a sharp choice to make the charming, eloquent
Barack originally unaware of a woman's perspective.

Told through extended takes and expositional
dialogue, Tanne has a very confident vision, moving the
passages of his story along swiftly. Sawyers and Sumpter
have incredible chemistry, with neither impersonating
their true character as they touch upon family life, God,
Good Times, and more. *Southside with You* particularly
receives a great jolt of energy and sweetness from
Stephen James Taylor's score, which welcomes the viewers to this little story with a light, toe-tapping tone, and
guides them to a warm, romantic end.

Tanne has fun with the details of his true story.
There are some big laughs when Barack talks about how
some of his younger years went up in a "cloudy haze,"
or how he drives a jalopy with a hole in it. As for pointing towards the future, Tanne gives *Southside with You*
viewers a peek at President Barack Obama with a scene
in which he speaks to a small group of Altgeld Gardens
residents about a community center. Through a revelatory yet heartfelt speech (in which Sawyers nicely uses
Obama's inflections), one can see this character go from
member of the community to President of the United
States and back again.

Southside with You has a completely calm beauty as
it presents these lives. There is something so wonderful
about seeing two characters—who both talk about being
outsiders—simply share their pride and their lives. In
particular, a discussion about the two distancing
themselves from J.J. in "Good Times" as a stereotype has
a breathtaking pride to it, directly connecting to the
contemporary problem that writers only see people different from them in the form of a stereotype. When
Tanne then goes to a closeup of Barack, looking up in a
stoic but completely natural way, it has a gobsmacking
effect, without the presidential context.

A later scene wields a similar emotion, involving Barack and Michelle's venture to see Spike Lee's *Do the Right Thing* (1989). Tanne does not use this anticipated passage as just a reference to a genius film (and a helluva movie for a first date), but to show the two sides of Barack as a minority trying to communicate with a rich white man. His boss, also on a date at the movie by pure coincidence, asks Barack why "the delivery guy" throws the trash can at the window for Sal's Pizza. Barack explains it logistically, that Mookie was saving Sal's life, and that he knew Sal could collect insurance for damage to the store. When his boss leaves, Barack levels with Michelle, and the viewer, about why Mookie threw the trash can: he was angry, no doubt about that. (Spike Lee has always said that only white people question why Mookie did what he did.)

And yet that sweltering, deadly heat within Lee's artistic masterpiece is beautifully contrasted in Tanne's film with the presentation of an unjustly stigmatized part of America, the south side of Chicago. In the delicate beauty of Tanne's debut, this part of the city is refreshingly defined by pride and peace. This is just one of the film's many emotionally affecting details, as it offers a beautiful, down-to-earth romance in which the decades-later epilogue is but a mere bonus.

Nick Allen

CREDITS

Michelle Robinson: Tika Sumpter
Barack Obama: Parker Sawyers
Marian Robinson: Vanessa Bell Calloway
Fraser Robinson: Phillip Edward Van Lear
Janice: Taylar Fondren
Origin: United States
Language: English
Released: 2016
Production: Robert Teitel, Tika Sumpter, Richard Tanne; released by IM Global
Directed by: Richard Tanne
Written by: Richard Tanne
Cinematography by: Patrick Scola
Music by: Stephen James Taylor
Sound: Trevor Gates
Music Supervisor: David Schulhof
Editing: Evan Schiff
Art Direction: Adri Siriwatt
Costumes: Megan Spatz
Production Design: Lucio Seixas
MPAA rating: PG-13
Running time: 84 minutes

REVIEWS

Brody, Richard. *New Yorker.* August 22, 2016.
Chang, Justin. *Variety.* January 24, 2016.
Dargis, Manohla. *New York Times.* August 25, 2016.
Derakhshani, Tirdad. *Philadelphia Inquirer.* August 25, 2016.
Dowd, A.A. *The A.V. Club.* August 25, 2016.
MacDonald, Moira. *Seattle Times.* August 24, 2016.
Phillips, Michael. *Chicago Tribune.* August 24, 2016.
Pickett, Leah. *Chicago Reader.* September 1, 2016.
Stevens, Dana. *Slate.* August 26, 2016.
Zacharek, Stephanie. *Time.* August 24, 2016.

TRIVIA

The production was filmed in 15 days.

STAR TREK BEYOND

Box Office: $158.8 Million

There is a lot to like about this latest Star Trek film. It has perfect casting, great action sequences, and lots of witty banter, but like all lesser Star Trek films it takes no risks at all. It would hardly be fair to call the end result paint-by-the-numbers filmmaking, but it is also a vast overstatement to claim *Star Trek Beyond* advances the franchise beyond assuring there will be more Trek in the future. This is action-based storytelling, highly reminiscent of director J.J. Abrams solid TV writing, but offering mostly, emotional cliff notes and no real philosophical content for those whose love for Trek is based at least partially on its exploration of the deeper side of human nature.

The film opens on an amusing note with Captain James T. Kirk (Chris Pine) botching a diplomatic mission involving an obscure relic called the Abronath. The seemingly endless voyage of the USS Enterprise has made it difficult for him to maintain vision. As the ship arrives at the Yorktown Space Station for shore leave and supplies, Kirk interviews for promotion to the rank of Vice Admiral and Commanding Officer of Yorktown, recommending Spock take his place in the Captain's Chair. Meanwhile, Spock, already in turmoil from his breakup with Nyota Uhura (Zoe Saldana), hears from New Vulcan that his future self, Ambassador Spock has died.

Before any of this can be resolved, the Enterprise is sent on an emergency rescue operation to retrieve a drifting escape pod from an unknown nebula. There, they find Kalara (Lydia Wilson), who claims she escaped when her ship was stranded on a nearby planet. As Kirk and the rescue party attempt to locate Kalara's crew, the Enterprise is ambushed by an endlessly swarming cloud of smaller ships that tear it apart. The leader of the ambush, Krall (Idris Elba), and his soldiers board the stricken ship searching for the Abronath and kidnapping the remaining crew, as the saucer section of the Enterprise crash lands on the planet below.

The film continues with the crew largely separated from one another on the planet's surface. Uhura and Sulu (John Cho) are captured by Krall and taken back to his ship. Chekov (Anton Yelchin) and Kirk discover Kalara was in league with Krall. A wounded Spock (Zachary Quinto) and McCoy (Karl Urban) search for other survivors and begin an unlikely friendship. Only Scotty (Simon Pegg) is alone, though not for long. Shortly after landing in his own escape pod he meets Jaylah (Sofia Boutella), a warrior scavenger who has sworn vengeance on Krall after escaping his encampment and now lives in an abandoned Federation Starship, the USS Franklin.

The busyness all these relationships set in motion is handled mainly by giving the film over to a large number of action sequences. The special effects and action sequences overshadow everything, but it is a blast to watch the Enterprise going to battle with the swarm ships by using the frequency of the Beastie Boys' "Sabotage." The competency of the action is hardly surprising given that the director here is Justin Lin of the *Fast & Furious* franchise. He handles the action well but the script by Doug Jung and Simon Pegg goes into thoroughly predictable character arcs after the setup. The end result is a fun but not especially memorable story that could have formed the basis for any lesser Star Trek TV episode. It helps that the cast is pitch perfect here, continuing to embody the roles made famous by the original series. Everyone gets a "stand up and be counted moment." If the movie can be said to belong to any one character, then the obvious choice would be Jaylah, whose striking appearance and undeniable screen presence stand out in every scene. Sofia Boutella's powerful performance pulses with an alien life force. It's the one thing that stands out as truly "Trek" in the film. Viewers will instantly want to know more about her.

Idris Elba is worth a special mention as well. He makes for a dynamic antagonist in Krall, even though the design of his lizard-like creature makeup seems a tad uninspired. Said design does leave Elba plenty of room to emote and the actor makes good use of it, creating a strange sense of empathy long before the story reveals that Krall and his minions used to be human. Of course, the story also saddles Krall with a lackluster revenge plot and not even Elba can wring much emotion out of the cliché that has haunted the series villains repeatedly, most famously of course in *Star Trek II: The Wrath of Kahn* (1982). In fact, the instrument of Krall's revenge, the Abronath, which is revealed to be a bio-weapon, is a little too reminiscent of the Genesis project from *Kahn*. Ironic then that this film is much more fun than its predecessor, *Star Trek Into Darkness* (2013), which was essentially a remake of *Kahn*. Perhaps the series needs to branch out beyond its own history and boldly explore new stories and new plots before the audience, not just Kirk, starts to lose the wonderful vision started by creator Gene Roddenberry.

Dave Canfield

CREDITS

Captain Kirk: Chris Pine
Commander Spock: Zachary Quinto
Doctor McCoy: Karl Urban
Lieutenant Uhura: Zoe Saldana
Scotty: Simon Pegg
Sulu: John Cho
Chekov: Anton Yelchin
Krall: Idris Elba
Origin: United States
Language: English
Released: 2016
Production: J.J. J. Abrams, Bryan Burk, Roberto Orci; released by Paramount Pictures Corp., Skydance Productions
Directed by: Justin Lin
Written by: Simon Pegg; Doug Jung
Cinematography by: Stephen Windon
Music by: Michael Giacchino
Sound: Peter Brown
Editing: Greg D'Auria; Dylan Highsmith; Kelly Matsumoto; Steven Sprung
Art Direction: Don MacAulay
Costumes: Sanja Milkovic Hays
Production Design: Thomas E. Sanders
MPAA rating: PG-13
Running time: 122 minutes

REVIEWS

Anderson, Soren. *Seattle Times.* July 21, 2016.
Darling, Cary. *Fort Worth Star Telegram/DFW.com.* July 21, 2016.
Ebiri, Bilge. *Village Voice.* July 15, 2016.
Edelstein, David. *New York Magazine/Vulture.* July 21, 2016.
Gleiberman, Owen. *Variety.* July 15, 2016.
Grierson, Tim. *New Republic.* July 22, 2016.
Kohn, Eric. *IndieWire.* July 15, 2016.
Turan, Kenneth. *Los Angeles Times.* July 21, 2016.
Vishnevetsky, Ignatiy. *The A.V. Club.* July 22, 2016.
Willmore, Alison. *BuzzFeed News.* July 19, 2016.

QUOTES

Doctor 'Bones' McCoy: "We could be mauled to death by an interstellar monster."
Captain James T. Kirk: "That's the spirit, Bones."

TRIVIA

A month before the film's release, Anton Yelchin died in a freak vehicle accident. A dedication caption was added to the ending credits which read "For Anton."

AWARDS

Nominations:

Oscars 2016: Makeup

STORKS

A bundle of trouble is coming.
—Movie tagline

Box Office: $72.7 Million

Although the history books are not likely to remember it fondly due to weak box office receipts and its polarizing specific sense of humor, *Storks* is one of 2016's most original animated films. The screenplay comes from Nicholas Stoller, previously known for live-action, R-rated riffs on life stages of maturity like *Forgetting Sarah Marshall*, *Neighbors*, and 2016's *Neighbors 2: Sorority Rising*. Co-directed with Doug Sweetland, *Storks* is a film that enacts Stoller's creative catharsis into a zippy, clever story about the art of taking care of babies.

As the latest enterprise from the Warner Animation Group (who previously hit it big with 2014's *The Lego Movie*), Stoller loads his tale with adventures and goals, creating an experience that can be as busy narratively as it is visually. Set in a world where storks exist but have stopped delivering babies in order to become a new Amazon-like enterprise (named Cornerstore.com), it focuses on the goals of three characters. Junior (voiced by Andy Samberg) is a young upstart stork who dreams of getting a promotion from his malicious boss Hunter (Kelsey Grammer). The one task that stands in Junior's way is a human named Tulip (Katie Crown), who has been stranded as a former-stork baby since she was created by a machine that turns parents' letters of request into live human beings. For years, she has been an outsider in storks' mountaintop headquarters, but has never tried to leave to find her own home. Junior can't bring himself to fire Tulip from the headquarters, but makes her work in the now-vacant letters room, where she acts as security guard to an empty hall.

A journey between Tulip and Junior is set into action when Nate Gardner, a young boy in America (voiced by Anton Starkman) learns about the former stork service, and requests a little brother to play with, since his real estate company-owning parents (Henry and Sarah, voiced by Ty Burrell and Jennifer Aniston, respectively) are too busy to indulge his playful

imagination. In the mechanics of the world of *Storks*, Tulip throws Nate's letter into a previously-dormant contraption, and creates a baby that Junior needs to sneak out, while inspiring Tulip to find the family she was meant to meet decades ago.

Their adventure takes them though a healthy supply of amusing sequences, including a run-in with a large, crafty pack of wolves, led by the vocal talents of Keegan-Michael Key and Jordan Peele. In one of the movie's funniest running gags, they initially snarl about wanting to eat the baby, until they become enamored with its cuteness, turning them into puppy dogs with big eyes. As the movie's sense of humor goes, the wolf pack is also able to build a suspension bridge or submarine while chasing Tulip and Junior, leading to elaborate, detail visual gags.

As a screenwriter, Stoller's approach to the task of making an animated film for a wide audience, while using his specific sense of humor, makes for an ambitious spectacle itself. The venture is far from perfect, though, with various plot holes regarding the logic of the stork's world, and jokes that simply miss despite earnest intent. As *Storks* proves early on to adore its rampant quirkiness, it can be held back by simply not being as funny as it wants to be.

Storks has an approach to entertaining families and children especially that is distinctly less cynical than other animated tentpoles. Though it features babies prominently and often builds its jokes on the power that babies can have over adults, it is not an animated movie that talks down to viewers, whether children or adults. Jokes use concepts that might seem recognizable to kids, like the very idea of storks, but the Cornerstone.com enterprise is played up for its many Amazon parallels, making for clear-cut goofs on capitalism. These references are joined with high-concept jokes about taking care of babies, like when Tulip and Junior silently fight off a group of ninja penguins, all while trying to not wake the baby.

Especially with the subplot involving the Gardners, as the two parents learn to spend time with their son Nate and help him build a landing pad for the storks on their roof, the movie earns its heart by becoming about parenting. Ideas of caring for children, protecting them and indeed adoring them are given a lively send-up with screwball, slapstick influences. But it also makes *Storks* an anomaly, albeit a charming one. It is an animated comedy seemingly calibrated more for parents than children, especially with the quickness of its loaded dialogue, or the dry humor behind its many abrupt edits.

In one of the ways in which *Storks* more successfully challenges the standards for animated tentpoles, the characters are not mere vessels for celebrity voice acting. These are animated characters built on performances, focusing on the zippiness of vocal turns, as complemented by a focused amount of time to jokes. *Storks* garners a striking energy using longer takes and breathless passages from its voice cast of comedians, including Andy Samberg, Katie Crown, Keegan Michael-Key, and Jordan Peele. For example, Crown gives a live wire performance when amusing herself in the mail room, zipping between different characters in the same breath. It is the type of acting that makes performers like Kevin Hart a live-action marvel, but *Storks* is able to translate that into its unique entertainment.

Storks may not have proven an outward success for Warner Animation Group (its worldwide earnings of $179.8 million still pale compared to many other similarly-sized animated films of the year), but it stands as one of 2016's most singular passion projects. Along with making Stoller one of the more surprising filmmakers in mainstream comedy, it further challenges the belittling association that studio-backed animated films should be made primarily for children. *Storks* prevails artistically by reaching out to an animation film audience while thinking beyond baby talk.

Nick Allen

CREDITS

Junior: Andy Samberg
Tulip: Katie Crown
Hunter: Kelsey Grammer
Sarah Gardner: Jennifer Aniston
Henry Gardner: Ty Burrell
Origin: United States
Language: English
Released: 2016
Production: Brad Lewis, Nicholas Stoller; released by RatPac-Dune Entertainment, Stoller Global Solutions, Warner Bros. Animation
Directed by: Nicholas Stoller; Doug Sweetland
Written by: Nicholas Stoller
Cinematography by: Simon Dunsdon
Music by: Jeff Danna; Mychael Danna
Sound: Michael Babcock
Editing: John Venzon
Production Design: Paul Lasaine
MPAA rating: PG
Running time: 87 minutes

REVIEWS

Chang, Justin. *Los Angeles Times*. September 22, 2016.
Fear, David. *Rolling Stone*. September 23, 2016.
Genzlinger, Neil. *New York Times*. September 22, 2016.
Guzman, Rafer. *Newsday*. September 22, 2016.
Hartlaub, Peter. *San Francisco Chronicle*. September 21, 2016.
Lemire, Christy. *RogerEbert.com*. September 22, 2016.
Morgenstern, Joe. *Wall Street Journal*. September 22, 2016.
VanDenBurgh, Barbara. *Arizona Republic*. September 22, 2016.
Walsh, Katie. *Tribune News Service*. September 22, 2016.
Zacharek, Stephanie. *Time*. September 23, 2016.

QUOTES

Junior: "Orphan Tulip?"
Tulip: "Tulip is just fine; Orphan hurts my heart!"

TRIVIA

When a muscular wolf stands between walls of wolves in a split, it is a reference to a split actor Jean-Claude Van Damme did between two trucks in a commercial.

SUICIDE SQUAD

We need them bad.
—Movie tagline

Box Office: $325.1 Million

As the last big gun of the largely disappointing season, many people had been hoping that *Suicide Squad* would help redeem the cinematic summer of 2016 by standing the comic book genre on its head by offering a twisted take in which the villains were placed in the unlikely position of being the good guys for a change. Alas, it proves to be the final nail in the coffin for one of the grimmest moviegoing stretches in recent memory. This is a loud, ugly, ridiculously violent, and largely incomprehensible mess that thinks that it is bringing something new to the genre but which quickly falls into all of the old traps and a few new ones for bad measure thanks to its complete lack of excitement, wit, intriguing characters, or even a compelling justification for its own existence.

What the film does have in abundance, however, is exposition. Between introducing characters, explaining their backstories via flashbacks or monologues, revealing plans and uncovering secrets, it seems as if virtually every scene in the film has characters trying to explain things to each other and to those of us in the audience who might not have as much working knowledge in regards to the characters on display here as they might have with the likes of Batman or Superman. Taking place in the aftermath of *Batman vs. Superman: Dawn of Justice* (2016) with the world still mourning the loss of the Man of Steel with the government in the throes of a dilemma—what happens if the next "meta-human" to come along is more interested in destroying mankind than in protecting it. Well, you or I might suggest calling Batman or Wonder Woman but they are just so notoriously unreliable. No, according to federal agent Amanda Waller (Viola Davis), there is only one possible way to protect us from this potential threat—recruit a number of the most dangerous criminals in captivity to mold into a group that, not unlike *The Dirty Dozen* (1967), can channel their abilities at making mayhem toward good instead of evil. Seeing as how all of these would-be antiheroes are currently languishing in prison after being captured by the likes of Batman and other superheroes, you would think that you might lean toward getting help from the guys who put these bad guys away instead of springing them with the promise of knocking time off of their prison terms (hardly an inducement when you are already facing multiple life sentences as it is). Maybe the comic books offer a more plausible rationale for the formation of the team but based on what is presented here, the only takeaway to be had is that Amanda Waller is an idiot.

And who are these recruits that Waller wants to bring together to combat all-powerful evil with unimaginable powers? There is Deadshot (Will Smith), a crack-shot assassin who is now driven his desires to see his adorable moppet again and to kill Batman (played by Ben Affleck in a cameo that screams "contractual obligation') for having the audacity to have caught him. There is Harley Quinn (Margot Robbie), a one-time psychiatrist who was transformed by a certain green-haired patient into a seductive psychopath whose chief weapons include a baseball bat and hot pants and who also has a thing against Batman for capturing her. There is Captain Boomerang (Jai Courtney), who is essentially an Australian jewel thief who is really good at using boomerangs—seriously, that is his thing. There is El Diablo (Jay Fernandez), who actually has an amazing power—he can conjure up massive amounts of flame without flint or tinder—but who has not only renounced using his gifts but actually turned himself in in remorse for his misdeeds. There is Killer Croc (Adewale Akinnuoye-Agbaje), a scaly mutant who lives in a sewer-like cell and who is not unfamiliar with the taste of human flesh. There is Katana (Karen Fukuhara), a ninja who eventually turns up wielding a sword that harbors the souls of those that it has killed. There is Slipknot (Adam Beach), who is basically the Suicide Squad equivalent of Jimmy Carl Black. Finally, there is the Enchantress, a 7,000-year-old witch of unimaginable powers who has possessed the body of scientist June Moon (understandable considering that June is played by drop-dead gorgeous model/actress Cara Delevingne).

The Enchantress is already under the control of Waller—not only does she control June's heart metaphorically through a relationship with super-soldier Col. Rick Flagg (Joel Kinsman) but she also controls the Enchantress's actual heart that she uses as leverage to get the witch to do her bidding—and it is this success that inspires her plans for recruiting the others. Inevitably, her control over Enchantress goes sideways as she soon escapes, revives the spirit of her equally powerful and deadly brother, and begins wrecking havoc on Midway City by transforming residents into tar-faced foot soldiers while she puts together a weapon that, once completed, will presumably destroy the world or something like that. Our anti-heroes are dropped into action and eventually rally together to do battle with waves of the zombie-like soldiers before eventually going up against Enchantress. If that was not enough, Harley is hoping to use the chaos as a way of reuniting with her beloved Joker (Jared Leto), who is still out there causing his own brand of mayhem.

The superhero genre has gotten kind of stale in recent years but *Suicide Squad* fails so completely that it deserves to be put right alongside such previous all-out disasters as *Catwoman* (2004) and the recent attempts to reboot the *Spider-Man* and *Fantastic Four* franchises. Even if one is willing to ignore all the lapses of narrative logic on display—even by the standards of a comic book movie, little of what goes on makes any real sense—it does not matter because nothing else works. One major problem is the decision to turn the project over to writer/director David Ayer, best known for such gory and largely dreadful action films as *Sabotage* (2014) and *Fury* (2014). Left to his own devices, there is a possibility that he might have come up with something interesting or at least different but it quickly becomes evident that his only task is to make a film that will fit in thematically with *Man of Steel* (2013) and *Batman vs. Superman*—something dark and unpleasant and ridiculously violent that will still stick within the bounds of the all-important PG-13 rating—and it is not a good fit. The screenplay is terrible—the dialogue consists entirely of raw exposition, lame quips, and repeated references to how bad the main characters are, most of the characters are barely sketched in, and the villain is one of the lamest in memory. On the directing side, Ayer does evoke the mies-en-scene of Zach Snyder to a T—murky visuals, editing that reduces everything to a jittery blur, and long stretches where things become so confusing that it seems as if huge chunks of story were just yanked out at the last minute in order to make room for other moments included solely to set up future films in the DC universe that have nothing to do with this one.

Working within the confines of an ensemble cast for the first time in ages, Will Smith is a little less off-putting than he has been in many of his recent star vehicles but he is not served well by a script that works overtime to try to make him sympathetic despite his murderous ways. His former *Focus* (2015) co-star Margot

Robbie is a good choice to play Harley Quinn but she is also badly served by a screenplay that is far more interested in showing off her body than the depth of her Joker-inspired madness. Of their co-stars, Jay Hernandez comes off best as El Diablo because he has an actual character to play. By comparison, Cara Delevingne is good in her early scenes as June but becomes little more than a scantily-clad special effect later on, the charisma-free Jai Courtney even lamer than his boomerang-chucking character, and Viola Davis goes through her scenes clearly hoping that future audiences will just think that Angela Bassett played the part, as she did in the equally disastrous *Green Lantern* (2011). As for the much-hyped turn by Jared Leto as the Joker—a performance that, according to the hype, saw him going all Method while terrorizing his co-stars with "gifts" of live rats, dead pigs, and used condoms—it turns out to be a whole lot of nothing. Despite the mounds of publicity suggesting otherwise, his turn barely qualifies as a cameo—he is on the screen for maybe 7-8 minutes tops—and when he does actually turn up, the results are stunningly anticlimactic. Forget following in the footsteps of such former Jokers as Jack Nicholson and Heath Ledger—he is, at best, maybe slightly more menacing than Cesar Romero.

As a complete stand-alone enterprise—one not beholden to a screen universe or the commercial dictates of a PG-13 rating—*Suicide Squad* might have have struck a chord with audiences bored with the same-old, same-old in the same way that the overtly rude and crude *Deadpool* did. Unfortunately, corporate concerns clearly took precedence over artistic ones and the end result is a frustrating missed opportunity that is all the more irritating because it seemed like such a sure thing in theory. Done properly, this could have been the kind of late-summer surprise that moviegoers are usually praying for by the time August comes around. Instead, this is a movie where most viewers will come out of it A) arguing whether it was better or worse than *Batman vs. Superman* and B) realizing that the difference between the two is negligible at best.

Peter Sobczynski

CREDITS

Deadshot: Will Smith
The Joker: Jared Leto
Harley Quinn: Margot Robbie
Rick Flag: Joel Kinnaman
Amanda Waller: Viola Davis
Origin: United States
Language: English
Released: 2016

Production: Charles Roven, Richard Suckle; released by Atlas Entertainment, DC Comics Inc., DC Entertainment, Lin Pictures, Warner Bros. Entertainment Inc.
Directed by: David Ayer
Written by: David Ayer
Cinematography by: Roman Vasyanov
Music by: Steven Price
Sound: Richard King
Music Supervisor: Gabe Hilfer; Season Kent
Editing: John Gilroy
Art Direction: Brandt Gordon
Costumes: Kate Hawley
Production Design: Oliver Scholl
MPAA rating: PG-13
Running time: 123 minutes

REVIEWS

Clarke, Donald. *Irish Times*. August 2, 2016.
DeBruge, Peter. *Variety*. August 2, 2016.
Douglas, Edward. *New York Daily News*. August 2, 2016.
Duralde, Alonso. *TheWrap*. August 2, 2016.
Ebiri, Bilge. *Village Voice*. August 2, 2016.
Ehrlich, David. *IndieWire*. August 2, 2016.
Lawson, Richard. *Vanity Fair*. August 2, 2016.
McCarthy, Todd. *Hollywood Reporter*. August 2, 2016.
Truitt, Brian. *USA Today*. August 2, 2016.
Zacharek, Stephanie. *Time*. August 2, 2016.

QUOTES

Deadshot: "Stay evil, doll face."

TRIVIA

While working on the Joker's laugh, Jared Leto practiced different laughs in public to see which one made people the most uncomfortable.

AWARDS

Oscars 2016: Makeup
Nominations:
Golden Raspberries 2016: Worst Screenplay, Worst Support. Actor (Leto)

SULLY

The untold story behind the miracle on the Hudson.
—Movie tagline

Box Office: $125.1 Million

It must have seemed cruelly apropos when the stench of burning bird filled the cabin of US Airways Flight 1549 after its engines ingested Canada geese on

January 15, 2009, because 155 passengers upon the disabled plane were collectively sensing that their goose was probably also cooked. Luckily, venerable veteran Capt. Chesley "Sully" Sullenberger, along with First Officer Jeffrey Skiles, was already focused on confronting a problem on the fly that he had immediately recognized: a lack of sufficient thrust. Seconds later, there was cause for relief when the quick-witted Sullenberger finessed what now amounted to a 70-ton glider between the heavily-populated shores of the Hudson River for an improbably-death-free ditch. The triumphant touchdown, which was dubbed the "Miracle on the Hudson," provided much-need uplift amidst a deep economic recession, as well as lingering depression from the contrasting-apocalyptic aviation events of September 11, 2001, which had commenced out of the very same skies.

Akin to pilots, screenwriters are also in the business of transporting people who have purchased tickets and plunked down into seats. Similar to Sullenberger, Todd Komarnicki obviously determined that he faced a deficit in propulsive power when attempting to land the *Sully* contract, aiming to write a feature-length recounting of an event that only lasted 208 seconds (plus the swift, twenty-four-minute rescue) and was still fresh in everyone's mind after being exhaustively chronicled in the press. As a result, Komarnicki chose to add some (by all accounts but his own) drama-creating distortion, and this fictional embellishment to the feel-good facts created widely-reported, wholly-understandable bad feeling at the National Transportation Safety Board. Members of that well-respected, well-intentioned investigative body are portrayed here as snidely-skeptical, appallingly-unappreciative undercutters who were out to sully Sully (Tom Hanks), seeming to get a thrill as they grill him and Skiles (Aaron Eckhart). (Mike O'Malley's glaring, smirking killjoy is particularly unsubtle.) One gets the impression here that there were almost as many wet blankets present in the chilly environment of the NTSB meeting rooms as had been discarded upon the decks of the rescue boats that plucked hypothermic passengers off the submerging plane's wings.

It is as if the NTSB was almost hell-bent in trying to unjustly pin blame on straight-arrow Sullenberger while the rest of the world collectively clamored to justly pin a medal upon him. This addition of palpable, caricatured bureaucratic antagonism that left the NTSB quite taken aback is precisely what got someone to finally move forward with the dormant project. It piqued the interest of producer/director Clint Eastwood, who said that he had not known the NTSB had been "trying to paint the picture that he had done the wrong thing. They were kind of railroading him into (that) it was his fault, and that wasn't the case at all." No, it was indeed not the case that Sully had ever put those aboard at greater risk than they already were, especially when opt-

ing for a "forced water landing" instead of returning to LaGuardia or trying for New Jersey's Teterboro. However, it was also not the case that the Board was ever out to bring him down any more than the birds had been. "They are doing a very important job," Sullenberger had stipulated during script development, "and if, for editorial purposes, we want to make it more of a prosecutorial process," then he urged that real names be removed—yet another admirable act.

It is too bad that Komarnicki felt it necessary to "goose" the account along, because his script for *Sully* successfully gets one's attention with fascinating, true-to-life revelations about the angst in the aftermath of its pro-of-a-protagonist, a man who outwardly seems so contrastingly calm, cool, and collected. It is at least as engrossing as the IMAX iterations of the crisis and rush to rescue (its collective heroism captured with shiver-inducing desaturation) that Eastwood ironically examines from every possible angle like the NTSB. (The $60 million-budgeted film was a box office and critical success.) Some initial flight simulations during the investigation did show that Sullenberger could have landed safely at either aforementioned airport, but the NTSB then realized that they did not taking into account what was referred to as "the human factor": the test pilots always knew what was coming and turned toward predetermined destinations immediately. (The film gives both the epiphany and pressing of this game-changing point at the climax to Sullenberger in his own dramatic, exculpating defense.) That factor makes all the difference to the film, as well, as the it looks beyond the seemingly-superhuman achievement to reveal someone very human.

"Brace for impact," Sullenberger warns the passengers, but this production's focus is the subsequent one on him. Similar to the flight itself, there is quite a start near the start here, with a literal nightmare scenario of what might have been that jolts Sullenberger awake. "What the hell's the matter with you?" bellows a cab driver as a distracted Sully steps out into traffic, and viewers are already quite curious, as well. This man who strives for excellence is repeatedly shown jogging at night through the City that Never Sleeps as if he is afraid to do so himself, perhaps a physical manifestation of his eagerness to get away from both the dark deliberations going on within his own psyche and the questioning of the NTSB, as well as the unfamiliar onslaught of press attention and public adulation that obviously makes this unassuming man uncomfortable. Only limited comfort can be derived when reaching out through long-distance calls to his wife (Laura Linney, good for a performance given entirely on the phone). Sullenberger, who suffered from PTSD for weeks, has stated that he was anxious because everything was still so up in the air until his assertions that both engines were indeed useless could be scientifically corroborated in the NTSB's final report, something that takes days here but fifteen uncertain months in reality. Repeated shots emphasizing the steadiness of his grasp upon the stick are in stark juxtaposition to his subsequent unaccustomed feeling of not being in control, that the outcome—his professional reputation and future, as well as his family's prospective financial well-being—were now uncomfortably in the hands of others.

That the big-screen portrayal of Sullenberger wound up in Hanks' hands likely provided little trepidation, and the actor is well-cast as someone who modestly does the monumental, whose focused concern about doing his best comes from a bedrock sense of duty and decency. The first of those two is plainly and stirringly visible on Hanks' face as his character wades down the aisle of the sinking plane to make sure everyone has evacuated, in laudable line with the tradition of other captains imperiled upon the water who have been the last to disembark. The latter is plainly on display after being given the number he selflessly needed to hear: all who had been in his charge are accounted for and safe. Hank's Sullenberger is manifestly moved and grateful, eliciting identical feelings in the audience towards the inspiring hero.

So it is regrettable that this film able to bring tears to the eye also felt the need to give an unconvincing and undeserved black one to the NTSB. "There was no effort to crucify or embarrass him," insisted investigator Malcolm Brenner. Nevertheless, can it merely be an accident that a cross is seen prominently glowing amidst the enveloping darkness here above poor Sully's car just seconds after it first seems that the board is out to nail him?

David L. Boxerbaum

CREDITS

Chesley "Sully" Sullenberger: Tom Hanks
Jeff Skiles: Aaron Eckhart
Lorraine Sullenberger: Laura Linney
Jeff Kolodjay: Sam Huntington
Diane Higgins: Valerie Mahaffey
Origin: United States
Language: English
Released: 2016
Production: Frank Marshall, Tim Moore, Allyn Stewart, Clint Eastwood; released by FilmNation Entertainment, Flashlight Films, Kennedy/Marshall, Malpaso Productions, RatPac Entertainment, Village Roadshow Pictures, Warner Bros. Entertainment Inc.
Directed by: Clint Eastwood
Written by: Todd Komarnicki
Cinematography by: Tom Stern

Music by: Christian Jacob; Tierney Sutton Band
Sound: Bub Asman; Alan Robert Murray
Editing: Blu Murray
Art Direction: Kevin Ishioka
Costumes: Deborah Hopper
Production Design: James J. Murakami
MPAA rating: PG-13
Running time: 96 minutes

REVIEWS

Burr, Ty. *Boston Globe*. September 8, 2016.
Dargis, Manohla. *New York Times*. September 8, 2016.
Debruge, Peter. *Variety*. September 2, 2016.
Hornaday, Ann. *Washington Post*. September 8, 2016.
McCarthy, Todd. *Hollywood Reporter*. September 2, 2016.
Morgenstern, Joe. *Wall Street Journal*. September 8, 2016.
Nashawaty, Chris. *Entertainment Weekly*. September 2, 2016.
Rainer, Peter. *Christian Science Monitor*. September 9, 2016.
Roeper, Richard. *Chicago Sun-Times*. September 7, 2016.
Travers, Peter. *Rolling Stone*. September 8, 2016.

QUOTES

Carl Clark: "You know, it's been a while since New York had news this good. Especially with an airplane in it."

TRIVIA

This is the 35th film Clint Eastwood has directed.

AWARDS

Nominations:
Oscars 2016: Sound FX Editing

SUNSET SONG

An epic story of love, loss, and the land that inspired it all.
—Movie tagline

Box Office: $159,714

Although filmmaker Terrence Davies first announced an adaptation of *Sunset Song*, the 1932 novel by Lewis Grassic Gibbon that is cited as one of the key works of Scottish literature of the 20th century, as a potential follow-up to his screen version of *The House of Mirth* (2000), it would take another sixteen years before he was finally able to get it made. When a long gap like that occurs, there is always the possibility that a filmmaker may spend so much time directing it in their head that when they finally get a chance to actually make the film, it sometimes feels more like an afterthought than anything else. Although not without the occasional rough patches, Davies has not fallen into that particular trap here as the result is a well-made though occasionally awkward film that is jointly elevated by moments of stunning visual beauty and anchored by an unexpectedly powerful central performance from model-turned-actress Agyness Denn in the central role.

Spanning most of the 1910s and set in the fictional rural Scottish village of Kinraddie, the film follows the life of unassuming farmer's daughter Chris Guthrie (Denn), who is shown in the opening scenes to be smart, friendly, sensitive, and destined for a bright future. Standing in the way of this, alas, is her monstrous father, John (Peter Mullan), an autocratic brute who relentlessly beats her beloved brother and only real confidant, Will (Jack Greenlees), treats her long-suffering mother (Daniela Nardin) as little more than a baby-making machine, and demonstrates an interest in her modesty and chastity that feels somewhat less than fatherly. Chris' dreams of furthering her education are scuttled when, having been impregnated yet again by John just after having delivered twins with no small amount of difficulty, her mother decides to end her misery for good by poisoning herself and the twins. Following that tragedy, Will, unable to cope with his father's tyranny any longer, leaves home for good to make his way to Canada. To top it all off, John eventually succumbs to a stroke that renders him almost completely helpless and dependent on Chris before he finally passes.

With John's passing, things begin to look up a bit for Chris. Still tied emotionally to her family's land, she begins working the land herself and discovers that she has an aptitude for it after all. She also begins a shy and sweet romance with local farmer Ewan Tavendale (Kevin Guthrie) that eventually blossoms into a vision of marriage, motherhood, and sexuality far removed from the hideous bastardizations that she endured while growing up. For a while, everything seems to be going as well as can be for the couple but their happiness is eventually interrupted by the onset of World War I. Because to not do so would cause others to possibly look upon him as a coward, Ewan enlists, but when he returns home from training, the change between his former and current selves is immense. His formerly kind and loving nature has been transformed into something darker and uglier, and when the worried Chris calls him on it one night, he responds by attacking and raping her. Eventually, he goes off to the battlefield and when the inevitable happens, Chris is once again left to pick up the pieces and try to muster up the strength to go on.

Although *Sunset Song* might seem at first to be an odd subject for Terrence Davies to tackle based on the milieu of the narrative, it nevertheless finds him exploring certain themes that he has tackled in his past films. The dysfunctional family dynamic involving the brutish father, emotionally distraught mother, sensitive son, and the surprisingly resilient daughter in particular will remind some viewers of his masterpiece *Distant Voices, Still Lives* (1988). The difference between the two is that in the earlier film, those relationships were fleshed out a little more and the characters were given more depth. For example, the father figure in the earlier film, played by Pete Postlethwaite, was given moments that allowed us to see the pitiable man behind the blustering monster and evoked a genuine sense of sympathy for him. By comparison, aside from one moment in which he briefly fusses over his wife's corpse on their bed, there is precious little nuance to the depiction of John Guthrie.

That ties in with another aspect of the film that doesn't quite come off as well as it should have and that is the way in which Davies charts the passage of time and how it affects the characters. The stuff involving Ewan returning from military training a rage-filled brute in particular does not come off well because it is just not established very well. Granted, trying to streamline Gibbon's narrative to fit the parameters of a standard feature film would be a challenge for most people but considering how beautifully he transferred *The House of Mirth* from the page to the screen, what he has done here feels rough and unwieldy at some points.

And yet, while *Sunset Song* may suffer from the occasional dramatic stumble, it is such a stunner from a visual perspective that many people may not even notice. In order to properly convey the beauty and romance of the land that is so imperative to the story in general and Chris in particular, Davies and cinematographer Michael McDonough made the decision to shoot all of the film's exteriors in glorious 65mm and the results are glorious—Terrence Malick himself might weep with envy over some of the stunning imagery captured here.

The other knockout element of the film is the performance by Agyness Denn as Chris. While. The casting of the former model, who has only done a few small acting gigs in the past (including a fleeting appearance in *Clash of the Titans* [2010]) and who is not at all Scottish, in the part might sound insane on paper, her work here is simply amazing. Although she is not entirely convincing in the opening scenes—she looks several years older than her schoolgirl character is meant to be and it is a bit distracting—as the film goes on and her character grows in strength and resilience, so does Denn, and by the time she gets to the most dramatic moments of the story towards the end, Davies' instincts in casting her prove to have been correct. It is one of the standout acting performances of 2016.

Sunset Song is the best and most consistent thing that Davies has done in a while. The glories of the visual style and the Agyness Denn performance make it worth checking out even if it does not stand next to its masterful filmmaker's best. It may not be top-notch Davies, but considering that he is one of the most unique directorial voices working today, even a second-tier effort by him is ultimately a more valuable moviegoing experience than the best works that most other filmmakers could possibly muster.

Peter Sobczynski

CREDITS

John Guthrie: Peter Mullan
Chris Guthrie: Agyness Deyn
Reverend Gibbon: Mark Bonnar
Alex Mutch: Stuart Bowman
Uncle Tam: Ron Donachie
Origin: United States
Language: English
Released: 2016
Production: Roy Boulter, Sol Papadopoulos, Nicolas Steil; released by Hurricane Films
Directed by: Terence Davies
Written by: Terence Davies
Cinematography by: Michael McDonough
Music by: Gast Waltzing
Music Supervisor: Ian Neil
Editing: David Charap; Ruy Diaz
Art Direction: Margaret Horspool
Costumes: Uli Simon
Production Design: Andy Harris
MPAA rating: R
Running time: 135 minutes

REVIEWS

Anderson, Melissa. *Village Voice*. May 12, 2016.
Brody, Richard. *New Yorker*. May 15, 2016.
Debruge, Peter. *Variety*. October 15, 2015.
Ehrlich, David. *IndieWire*. May 11, 2016.
Holden, Stephen. *New York Times*. February 12, 2016.
Klawans, Stuart. *Nation*. May 4, 2016.
Linden, Sheri. *Los Angeles Times*. May 12, 2016.
Taylor, Ella. *NPR*. May 12, 2016.
Uhlich, Keith. *Slant*. September 16, 2015. .
Young, Deborah. *Hollywood Reporter*. October 15, 2015.

TRIVIA

Agyness Deyn's character's surname is Guthrie, which is the real surname of the actor who plays her husband.

SWISS ARMY MAN

We all need some body to lean on.
—Movie tagline

Box Office: $4.2 Million

It takes a certain artist to reinvent the way one thinks of a fart. That may be a blunt or bold statement, but it is the kind encouraged by the creativity within *Swiss Army Man*, a lovely and productively low-brow existential crisis from debut directors Dan Kwan and Daniel Scheinert (credited in their previous music videos as "Daniels"). It is a movie in full control of itself, whether one finds its whimsy or penchant for low-brow humor to be polarizing. And like very few movies can boast, it is original and unpredictable from start to finish, leading to the type of forward thinking that led to cinema's creation in the first place.

A tale of friendship, *Swiss Army Man* begins in a very lonely place. Paul Dano's character Hank has been isolated on an island for an untold amount of days, with the opening credits showing the viewer the various makeshift boats he made to carry his messages for help. Alone except for the crashes of the ocean, he opts to hang himself from a rock, overlooking the beach. His life is saved by a corpse later known as Manny (Daniel Radcliffe), who provides the first kind of contact. There is no communication from Manny, but there is rigor mortis, and plenty of flatulence. Soon enough, there is so much flatulence that Hank is able to ride Manny's body like a jet ski to land, a scientific anomaly that makes for a thrilling image, all while the voices of Manchester Orchestra clue viewers into a homemade saga that will be as inspiring as it is wild. Perfectly, the film's title arrives from outside of Radcliffe's bare butt while Dano's Hank screams with joy.

Now on land in what appears to be some west coast beach, Hank searches for people, but finds no one. Instead of leaving behind the body that got him to shore, he carries Manny like a mute, limp friend. There continue to be clues of campers and other human beings in the same Northwest woods that Hank and Manny travel through, but Hank is the only sign of life.

Progressively, by science that only Kwan and Scheinert understand but a viewer can appreciate, Manny starts to slowly speak, as if his brain were jump-started by Hank's affection for him. It excites and mystifies Hank, and makes him all the more useful. Progressively, Manny fulfills his title role, able to barf clean water from his mouth (which Hank uses to shower in one montage), or fire things from his mouth if placed inside. This is added to Manny's discovery of an erection, which has a mind of its own but also works as a compass. All the while, Manny remains a corpse, with a dead expression on his face, making for a bizarre and certainly memorable feat of physical acting from Radcliffe.

Aside from the fun that the movie's survival tale offers, it also goes inward to what Hank's life was like before he became so lost. This is the point where Kwan and Scheinert's attitude is crucial, as a main storyline about lost chances in life is both boyish and heartbreaking, and well under the writer/directors' control. A picture on Hank's iPhone of a young woman (Mary Elizabeth Winstead) becomes a type of catalyst for Hank and Manny to get back to the rest of the world, and find this person. Though it is soon revealed that this woman is not emotionally connected to Hank, nor did she even know the picture was being taken, Kwan and Scheinert's awareness of the innocence and ridiculousness of its characters remains pertinent. It is the rare movie that is able to show two young men fixated on the projections of a young woman, while not itself treating her as a mere objective.

The events of *Swiss Army Man* grip the viewer by going farther and farther than one might expect, with Hank's tale of trying to find another living soul taking unexpected turns as Manny becomes more sentient. As filmmakers, Kwan and Scheinert create sequences that seem clearly thought out, as in a bear attack that sends them into the sky after Manny's flatulence is used as a weapon, but just imagined with the same freedom in creativity. Part of the joy in watching the film is to see where it physically goes next, with either Manny's abilities or their venture through the woods.

There is a wondrous handmade quality to the film that fills its soul, but also threatens to take away some of its magic. Hank's penchant for creating things out in the woods goes from striking characteristic to Michel-Gondry-stealing pretty quickly, and is relied on for extended sequences. There is even one passage in which Hank recreates the bus that he used to see the woman from the picture everyday. Were the rest of the movie not so original with form or how it treats characters, it could be a possible twee death sentence. But as it stands here, though the visuals are nice, it makes for an uncharacteristically derivative attribute.

Attitude is a distinct spiritual quality within *Swiss Army Man*. Exchanges between Hank and Manny touch upon lasting and massive subjects, such as individuality, family, friendship, or why life is worth waking up for every day. But the movie does so with its own language, using discussions about masturbation, pooping, or even another person on the bus, and has the emotional acuity to connect deeply with its audience. That the film is unforgettable is a given from its first five minutes. But the power it has philosophically is one wholly earned.

Nick Allen

CREDITS

Hank: Paul Dano

Manny: Daniel Radcliffe
Sarah: Mary Elizabeth Winstead
Crissie: Antonia Ribero
Hank's Dad: Richard Gross
Origin: United States
Language: English
Released: 2016
Production: Miranda Bailey, Lawrence Inglee, Lauren Mann, Amanda Marshall, Eyal Rimmon, Jonathan Wang; released by Blackbird, Cold Iron Pictures
Directed by: Dan Kwan; Daniel Scheinert
Written by: Dan Kwan; Daniel Scheinert
Cinematography by: Larkin Seiple
Music by: Andy Hull; Robert McDowell
Sound: Brent Kiser
Editing: Matthew Hannam
Art Direction: David Duarte
Costumes: Stephani Lewis
Production Design: Jason Kisvarday
MPAA rating: R
Running time: 97 minutes

REVIEWS

Brody, Richard. *New Yorker*. June 20, 2016.
Catsoulis, Jeannette. *New York Times*. June 23, 2016.
Dowd, A.A. *The A.V. Club*. June 23, 2016.
Jones, J.R. *Chicago Reader*. July 8, 2016.
Merry, Stephanie. *Washington Post*. June 30, 2016.
Nicholson, Amy. *MTV*. June 24, 2016.
Rothkopf, Joshua. *Time Out*. June 24, 2016.
Seitz, Matt Zoller. *RogerEbert.com*. June 24, 2016.
Wolfe, April. *Village Voice*. June 22, 2016.
Zacharek, Stephanie. *Time*. June 16, 2016.

QUOTES

Manny: "Is this crying? I don't like it. It's wet and uncomfortable."

TRIVIA

Daniel Radcliffe promoted the film alongside a Manny doll, which attended interviews, conventions, and even a roller coaster ride.

AWARDS

Nominations:

Ind. Spirit 2017: Film Editing, First Feature

T

TEENAGE MUTANT NINJA TURTLES: OUT OF THE SHADOWS (TMNT 2)

Raise some shell.
—Movie tagline

Box Office: $82 Million

Teenage Mutant Ninja Turtles: Out of the Shadows is a significantly better film than its predecessor, 2014's *Teenage Mutant Ninja Turtles*. Does that mean that it's a good movie? Not at all. But it does mean that director Dave Green deserves credit for actually trying to find a tone that better suited his subject matter than the first Michael Bay-produced TMNT film. That movie, directed by Jonathan Liebesman, tried to shoehorn the Ninja Turtles, a children's pop culture mainstay, into a cookie-cutter, gritty, Jerry Bruckheimer-esque action movie plot. *Out of the Shadows,* on the other hand, actually tries to embrace the Turtles more cartoony roots, a decision that makes the sequel "fit" the Turtles concept better and ultimately makes the film more entertaining to watch, despite its many flaws.

Before fanboys raise any objections, yes, the Ninja Turtles do originally come from, admittedly, "gritty" roots. The original black-and-white TMNT comic books, created by Kevin Eastman and Peter Laird, are surprisingly violent, grim, and weird. That being said, for the past 30 years, the Teenage Mutant Ninja Turtles have become one of the most commoditized media properties, and the bulk of the TMNT empire has focused their attention on young children. There have

been several extremely popular cartoon series and toy lines over the past few decades, which definitely have cemented the Turtles as a children's property.

That's why the action movie tone of 2014's *Ninja Turtles* seemed like such a bad fit. Perhaps they were trying to appeal to the generation that grew up on (and aged out of) the Turtles, but the final product was too dour for children and too slapstick for adults. However, the sequel *Out of the Shadows* course-corrects by definitely shifting its focus more toward the cartoon audience. This is a very exaggerated vision of the Ninja Turtles that the screenwriters—Josh Appelbaum and André Nemec—have tried to make co-exist with the slick, Michael Bay world of the previous film. The end result is problematic to say the least, but, in a small victory, it does feel more like a Ninja Turtle movie than the studio's previous effort.

The story starts on a markedly silly note. Following the events of the first film, the Turtles—Leonardo, Donatello, Raphael, and Michelangelo—continue to fight crime in secret at the wish of Master Splinter. Thanks to their friendship with reporter April O'Neil (the bland, inappropriately sexualized-for-a-kid's-movie Megan Fox), the Turtles were able to give all of the credit for their very public defeat of the super-villain Shredder (Brian Tee) in the first movie to April's co-worker Vern Fenwick (Will Arnett). This plotline seems solely designed to give Arnett more opportunity to bring some humor into the film—a respite that is refreshing at first, but, like most of this film, quickly gets old.

While the Turtles brood about their life in the shadows (cue the title), a mad scientist named Baxter Stockman (played with a Jerry Lewis-esque abandon by

Tyler Perry) has constructed a teleportation device to help Shredder escape from prison. The Turtles try to prevent the escape—bringing them into contact with their soon-to-be ally, vigilante Casey Jones (Arrow's Stephen Amell, who delivers a certain "I'm just happy to be here" charm and not much else)—but Stockman is able to teleport away Shredder and two other prisoners, Bebop (Gary Anthony Williams) and Rocksteady (Stephen Farrelly).

This is the point where the story turns into a full-fledged Saturday morning cartoon. The teleportation goes haywire, sending Shredder and his unwitting new sidekicks into another dimension, where they meet Krang (voiced by Brad Garrett), an alien villain who looks like an anthropomorphic brain in a giant robot suit. Krang turns Bebop and Rocksteady into mutant animal hybrids, much like the Turtles, and tells Shredder to assemble three pieces of a long-lost machine that can help bridge the dimensional portal and allow him to conquer Earth. The Krang plot is pure camp—straight out of the "assemble the pieces" Weather Dominator storylines of the old *GI Joe* cartoon—but, regrettably, Green never takes the plunge and turns the movie into a pure cartoon kabuki fest.

Instead, the production team tries to create their own mutant hybrid. They attempt to breed together elements of a traditional Michael Bay film (filled with inch-deep characters, needless brooding, and stylized explosions) with a live-action cartoon throwback (that feels like it should take commercial breaks and end with a PSA about the dangers of petting unfamiliar dogs). The end result is, politely, a mess.

There are moments of fun thrown throughout the chaos. For every actor who appears to be having the time of their life hamming it up (Arnett, Perry), there's an actor like Laura Linney who shows up to make the audience wonder if she somehow stumbled into the wrong film. Unfortunately, Green, the screenwriters, and the production team simply fail to nail the tone of the piece. This should go without saying, but there is something inherently broad about a movie focused on Teenage Mutant Ninja Turtles. While a Turtles film should hit the hallmarks of the franchise—martial arts, pizza, the prerequisite Leonardo/Raphael tension—more than anything, it should wear its identity as a bold, self-aware piece of popcorn entertainment on its sleeve (or maybe its shell).

Teenage Mutant Ninja Turtles: Out of the Shadows makes an admirable attempt to move in that direction, but, in the end, it cannot escape the slick, too-cool-for-school, shallowness of the trademark Michael Bay style. It is an empty-headed action movie masquerading as a

Turtles adventure and kids, both current kids and children of the 1990s, can tell the difference.

Tom Burns

CREDITS

April O'Neil: Megan Fox
Vernon Fenwick: Will Arnett
Chief Vincent: Laura Linney
Casey Jones: Stephen Amell
Michelangelo: Noel Fisher
Donatello: Jeremy Howard
Leonardo: Pete Ploszek
Raphael: Alan Ritchson
Origin: United States
Language: English
Released: 2016
Production: Michael Bay, Andrew Form, Bradley Fuller, Scott Mednick, Galen Walker; released by Gama Entertainment Partners, Paramount Pictures Corp.
Directed by: Dave Green
Written by: Josh Appelbaum; Andre Nemec
Cinematography by: Lula Carvalho
Music by: Steve Jablonsky
Sound: Jason W. Jennings; Nancy Nugent
Editing: Bob Ducsay; Jim May
Art Direction: Miguel Lopez-Castillo
Costumes: Sarah Edwards
Production Design: Martin Laing
MPAA rating: PG-13
Running time: 112 minutes

REVIEWS

Andersen, Soren. *Seattle Times.* June 2, 2016.
Bowen, Chuck. *Slant.* June 3, 2016.
Coggan, Devan. *Entertainment Weekly.* June 2, 2016.
Douglas, Edward. *New York Daily News.* June 2, 2016.
Hassenger, Jesse. *The A.V. Club.* June 2, 2016.
McWeeny, Drew. *Hitfix.* June 2, 2016.
O'Sullivan, Michael. *Washington Post.* June 2, 2016.
Stewart, Sara. *New York Post.* June 2, 2016.
Zwecker, Bill. *Chicago Sun-Times.* June 2, 2016.

QUOTES

Michelangelo: [taps Krang suit] "I was expecting way worse."
[Krang pops out] Michelangelo: "It's like a chewed-up piece of gum, with a face!"

TRIVIA

The director of the film, Dave Green, has been a Teenage Mutant Turtle fan since childhood.

AWARDS

Nominations:

Golden Raspberries 2016: Worst Actress (Fox), Worst Sequel/Prequel

10 CLOVERFIELD LANE

Monsters come in many forms.
    —Movie tagline
Something is coming.
    —Movie tagline

Box Office: $72 Million

In a time when it seems nobody can cough on a movie set without it becoming instant public knowledge, a rare event was pulled off back in 2007. A secret project was launched by the production company of J.J. Abrams. So secret that audiences knew next-to-nothing about it save for the image of the Statue of Liberty's head being thrown down a city street before showings of *Transformers* (2007). Not even a title was presented. Just a date. Then on January 18, 2008, Matt Reeves' film was unleashed ushering in a whole new era of found footage horror efforts. Eight years later with the media more ferocious than ever, the Bad Robot team managed to do it again. They took a spec script called *The Cellar* and transformed it into what was called a "spiritual" follow-up to the first film. Despite having almost nothing in common with it but a name, that is an appropriate label for a film that keeps more than the spirit of *Cloverfield* (2008) alive.

The protagonist this time is Michelle (Mary Elizabeth Winstead) whom we first meet making a quick exit from her relationship. Packing everything into her car she leaves New Orleans and begins hearing scattered reports about city blackouts. In an instant, she crashes and wakes up chained in a room with just a mattress, medical supplies and, surprisingly, her things including her phone. When a man enters the locked room with food and even a key to free herself, he states unequivocally that he is "going to keep [her] alive." But for what purpose?

The man is named Howard (John Goodman) and he tells Michelle that there has been an attack. The nature of which is unknown but it appears to be the one that has been waiting to catch up with his paranoia his whole life. The underground bunker of his farmhouse is entirely of his own design. There is enough food to wait out whatever contamination the air may hold, a jukebox and movies to pass the time, and even some more company in the form of Emmett (John Gallagher Jr.) who works for Howard. Though their relationship is strained through Emmett's loose acceptance of his rules and blasé attitude of their predicament, he claims he witnessed the attack first hand.

For a film of this type to work a certain level of doubt has to be created within the audience to sustain the tension of the limited surroundings. After all there are only a few specific outcomes to Howard's story and it is important to keep everyone guessing while at the same time making them forget to even try. Much of this falls on the shoulders of Goodman who has risen to the short list of the most-reliable character actors out there. A most welcome addition to any cast no matter how small the role, Goodman for years seems to be just one scene away from an annual Best Supporting Actor nomination and Howard is one of his most fulfilling parts; a role that takes advantage of his folksy charm, authoritative yet approachable presence, and an underlying menace that can be ignited with the wrong word or glance. An initial dinner sequence masterfully takes advantage of Goodman playing with the growing discomfort toward his guests' behavior.

Though the mystery looms over what may or may not be outside these walls there exists an appreciation for the way Winstead and director Dan Trachtenberg are crafting a true female story of survival. Her character's past fills in a motivation for her determinism in the later scenes. The less known about why she had to leave so quickly in the opening moments provides also some fascinating blanks. There is an irony of being thrust from one possibly abusive relationship into the hands of another where the population may have dwindled but the power dynamic remains intact. Gauging the lingering threat level towards our injured heroine through suspense and uncertainty is a welcome counterpoint to the thrillers where women are bound and tortured at the hands of masked sadists.

10 Cloverfield Lane is economical in the way it is able to create suspense, making us clear of our surroundings and where the cracks are in the foundation. Goodman and Winstead create believable characters who behave not like movie stereotypes but problem solvers making the most out of an isolated world with the questions put in front of them. Winstead's casting also makes for a nice counterpoint to her role in the similarly Twilight Zone-themed *Faults* (2014) as a cult survivor restricted to a hotel room for deprogramming by a male specialist. Unlike the often ham-handed solutions to M. Night Shyamalan's slow burns of horror, the amped-up finale here fits perfectly within expectations and is a satisfying resolution to Michelle's journey. Every anthology series hits rough patches, but if the formula for a continued string of *Cloverfield* features needs to remain secret in the stale air of hype and pre-release spoilers, that may be worth locking ourselves away from the world for.

Erik Childress

CREDITS

Howard: John Goodman
Michelle: Mary Elizabeth Winstead
Emmett: John Gallagher, Jr.
Ben: Bradley Cooper (Voice)
Origin: United States
Language: English
Released: 2016
Production: J.J. Abrams, Lindsey Weber; Bad Robot Productions; released by Paramount Pictures Corp.
Directed by: Dan Trachtenberg
Written by: Josh Campbell; Matthew Stuecken; Damien Chazelle
Cinematography by: Jeff Cutter
Music by: Bear McCreary
Sound: Robert Stambler
Editing: Stefan Grube
Costumes: Meagan McLaughlin
Production Design: Ramsey Avery
MPAA rating: PG-13
Running time: 103 minutes

REVIEWS

Bell, Josh. *Las Vegas Weekly*. March 10, 2016.
Brody, Richard. *New Yorker*. March 14, 2016.
Dowd, A.A. *The AV Club*. March 10, 2016.
Edelstein, David. *New York Magazine/Vulture*. March 11, 2016.
Erbland, Kate. *IndieWire*. March 10, 2016.
Johanson, MaryAnn. *Flick Filosopher*. March 17, 2016.
Larsen, Josh. *LarsenOnFilm*. March 19, 2016.
Olson, J. *Cinemixtape*. April 7, 2016.
Snider, Eric D. *EricDSnider.com*. March 10, 2016.
Tobias, Scott. *NPR*. March 10, 2016.

QUOTES

Howard: "Crazy is building your ark after the flood has already come."

TRIVIA

During production, the name of the movie was kept from cast members to help preserve the secret as long as possible.

THINGS TO COME
(L'avenir)

Box Office: $388,140

The cinema of French director Mia Hansen-Løve is about the ecstasy of youth. Her accomplished and enthralling features limn the tumult and sometimes-contradictory actions of young people navigating the intricacies of adulthood. The films have a novelistic shape, each framed by a two or three-part structure and concerned with time, motion, and feeling with their intense, personal stories shaped around love, independence, or the need for self-expression.

The one-time protégé (and now partner) of French master Olivier Assayas (*Clouds of Sils Maria* [2014]), Hansen-Løve first caught attention with a small though important role of a beautiful schoolgirl carrying out a furtive affair with a much older novelist in Assayas's chamber drama, *Late August, Early September* (1998). She followed up with another part in the director's *Les destinées sentimentales* (2000) before embarking on her own shorts and larger projects.

Her films have displayed a striking natural talent and a poetic, rapturous ability at detailing the interior consciousness of young female consciousness, granting these women a jolting, lyrical quality in her very different work: Marie-Christine Fredrich in her frank debut, *All is Forgiven* (2007), Alice de Lencquesaing in her poised, ambitious *Father of My Children* (2009), and Lola Créton as the beautiful, infatuated Camille caught between two very different men in her autobiographically inflected *Goodbye, First Love* (2012). Her fourth film, *Eden* (2014), beautifully transmuted her family history into a vibrant cultural history with her kaleidoscopic and gracefully structured exploration of the French electronic music culture that fictionalized her brother's experiences. The movie's central character, Paul (Félix de Givry), describes his work as divided "between euphoria and melancholia," an apt description of the tonal range and plangent emotional currents.

Hansen-Løve's penetrating, lively new film, *Things to Come*, marks a departure in important ways in deepening her themes and ideas before taking off in important new directions. The protagonist, Nathalie Chazeaux, a university philosophy professor played by the great Isabelle Huppert, is older, more professionally established and financially secure than the characters of the director's other films. Nathalie's daily life, or moment-to-moment consciousness, is subject to the same whirlwind of emotions, private passion, and intellectual inquiry.

The movie is animated around a rupture, exploring the complicated aftermath of this accomplished and successful woman as her privileged existence is suddenly thrown out of balance by a series of personal and professional setbacks. As the English title underlines, in an echo of H.G. Wells' novel, *The Shape of Things to Come* (1933), the movie is about a woman confronting her fear of the unknown. (The movie's French title, *L'avenir*, is translated as "the future.")

At the start, Nathalie's existence is an idealized one, with a long-standing husband, Heinz (André Marcon), also a professor, and two accomplished children, a son and daughter approaching adulthood and ready to get on with their lives. She has recognition and cultural prestige as a public intellectual as the writer of a widely used textbook and the editor of a monograph series on philosophy. The idyll has cracks in the foundation, signaled right at the start as protesting students block Nathalie's entrance to her classroom. Her speech about Rousseau and democracy is hardly soothing. More problematic is the precarious emotional state of her mother Yvette (Édith Scob), a former model who now works as an occasional movie extra. The older woman now besieges Nathalie with attention-seeking phone calls and threats of suicide that leave her little option but place her mother in an assisted facility care.

"I'm lucky to be fulfilled intellectually," Nathalie says. It soon proves boldly insufficient. Her cool passion is soon interrupted by cataclysmic actions of loss, break up, and professional reversals. At the urging of his daughter, Heinz reveals his own secret, that he has been involved with another woman. The marketplace is just as withering and her textbook is discontinued. Nathalie's tense, exasperating exchanges with the marketing director at the publishing house are devastating, the fury of this accomplished woman running in hard opposition to the cruel dictates of commerce.

A woman alone, the suddenly unmoored Nathalie is deprived of her family history, her children gone and her estranged husband out of the picture (though not before he removed some of her priceless books that contained important work material). *Things to Come* is about her emotional reckoning. Her effort of reclaiming her life verges on the absurd, like a night spent at the movies, watching Abbas Kiarostami's elusive, cryptically beautiful *Certified Copy* (2011), another movie about marriage, as a stranger aggressively tries to pick her up.

The wild card is her former star student Fabien (Roman Kolinka). A skilled writer and thinker who contributed several essays and texts for her monograph series, he has forsaken his promising academic future to create with a group of French and German friends a radical commune on a tract of farmland in the French countryside. The exact nature of their friendship is left teasingly open. The suddenly available Nathalie must work out her feelings. Taking a trip to the visit Fabien and his friends, the stark opposition of her world is contrasted against the radical initiatives and bourgeois rejection the commune represents. The jolt of the new is a haunting one.

The conflicts, terrors, and fears dramatized in *Things to Come* are woven so beautifully and imperceptibly into the fabric and architecture of the film the emotional subtlety and range has a glancing and cumulative power that builds. The final exchange between Nathalie and Heinz, "I thought you'd love me forever," is absolutely heartbreaking. Another moment, when Natalie sees Heinz with his new companion, driving home her enforced solitude, is tinged with meaning.

The vulnerability and melancholy that Hansen-Løve captures is so tenderly arranged, the rhythm of understatement and release is not exactly cathartic but marks a deeper self-realization. Huppert is one of the two or three greatest actors currently working in the cinema. This performance, less showy and flamboyant than her work in Paul Verhoeven's *Elle* (2016), is restrained and muted though active and intense, emotionally believable and consistent with a woman whose very world is upended. Huppert's part is much different than the other actresses Hansen-Løve has showcased. The electric power and sensitivity is the same.

As a director, Hansen-Løve has shown a fluent and expressive watercolor style. The earlier work was shot primarily by Stephane Fontaine. Like *Eden*, the new film was shot by the superb Denis Lenoir, an important collaborator of Assayas. Lenoir also photographed *Late August, Early September*. His work tends toward the more fractured and elliptical. Hansen-Løve charts a complex visual progression, beginning in a radiant light before shifting to something darker, the fluid and tactile mobility of Lenoir's camerawork expressing her increasingly fractured and unsettled being.

The acting, writing, and direction fuse seamlessly. *Things to Come* is not a work of overstatement or declamation. The movie is quieter, subtle, and probing. Hansen-Løve shifts away from the ecstatic toward feelings, gestures, and actions harder to classify. The power and originality remain a force of nature.

Patrick Z. McGavin

CREDITS

Nathalie Chazeaux: Isabelle Huppert
Heinz: Andre Marcon
Fabien: Roman Kolinka
Yvette Lavastre: Edith Scob
Chloe: Sarah Le Picard
Origin: United States
Language: French, English, German
Released: 2016
Production: Charles Gillibert; released by CG Cinema
Directed by: Mia Hansen-Love

Written by: Mia Hansen-Love
Cinematography by: Denis Lenoir
Sound: Vincent Vatoux
Music Supervisor: Raphael Hamburger
Editing: Marion Monnier
Costumes: Rachel Raoult
Production Design: Anna Falgueres
MPAA rating: PG-13
Running time: 102 minutes

REVIEWS

Duralde, Alonso. *TheWrap.* December 2, 2016.
Ebari, Bilge. *Village Voice.* December 1, 2016.
Hornaday, Ann. *Washington Post.* December 8, 2016.
Keough, Peter. *Boston Globe.* December 8, 2016.
Lodge, Guy. *Variety.* February 15, 2016.
Morgenstern, Joe. *Wall Street Journal.* Dec 1, 2016.
Scott, A.O. *New York Times.* December 1, 2016.
Turan, Kenneth. *Los Angeles Times.* December 1, 2016.
Vishnevetsky, Ignatiy. *The A.V. Club.* November 30, 2016.
Stephanie Zacharek. *Time.* December 10, 2016.

TRIVIA

Writer/director Mia Hansen-Love based the film on her mother's life, so she asked her to approve the script. Her mother only changed one thing: the name of the cat, in order to respect her real cat's privacy.

13 HOURS: THE SECRET SOLDIERS OF BENGHAZI

When everything went wrong six men had the courage to do what was right.
—Movie tagline

Box Office: $52.8 Million

It's not difficult to understand why filmmaker Michael Bay is often the laughing stock of many cinephiles. His films are loud, crass, glossy, and bombastic and believable storylines typically fall by the wayside on lieu of "stuff that just looks cool." Say what you want about Bay but it's a fact that not only is the man a true auteur in almost every sense of the word, his films also make large amounts of money which is a truly rare thing to accomplish in the modern cinema landscape—a personal filmmaker making exactly the kind of film they want and finding success.

Bay's latest effort, *13 Hours: The Secret Soldiers of Benghazi*, is very much quintessential Bay in that it includes well-exercised Alpha-Males acting tough, oodles of explosions, and cross-cut editing so rapid fire there

should be a warning on this film in regards to people with epilepsy. But this is based on a true story (as was Bay's *Pain & Gain*, [2013]) and a quite divisive one at that in the way the film details a recent attack on an American embassy in Benghazi. As jingoistic and seemingly "right-wing" as Bay and his films tend to be, *13 Hours: The Secret Soldiers of Benghazi* is not only surprisingly even-handed—at least in terms of handling of subject matter—it's also a striking look at the confusion and almost laughable nature of the current occupation in the Middle East.

13 Hours: The Secret Soldiers of Benghazi opens with the introduction of military contractor Jack Silva (John Krasinski, best known as Jim on the television show *The Office*) who's new to Benghazi but an old hat at being a military-for-rent guy. He's picked up by longtime pal Tyrone "Rone" Woods (James Badge Dale) and their sassy male repartee takes immediate center stage. Bay loves to show the tough male camaraderie and in-the-know joking and belittling that goes on between old pals cut from the same rough-hewn cloth so much it's almost fetishized by the director. No sooner have the mutual insults started piling up when the duo finds themselves in trouble with the locals and they haven't even reached Benghazi yet.

Once they finally reach their outpost in Benghazi, more classic Bay-isms start clicking into place. There's Bob (David Costabile), the nebbish "man in charge" provided by "the establishment," whose by-the-book persona immediately clashes with Rone and his rough-and-tumble crew. There's Alexia (Sona Jillani), the tough but rather pushy woman who also seems to get in the way more than help. And let's not forget the ever-present Bay crew of dudes, too many to name but all of whom have a slick nickname ("Bub," "Tanto," "Oz," are just a few here), bulging biceps, and are seemingly always covered in sweat. It truly is a laughable standard from Bay but alas, the man knows what he, and evidently audiences at large, want to see.

Also comical is the buddy dialogue throughout the film that seems ripped from an '80s actioner, or better, from Max Fischer's Vietnam play in Wes Anderson's *Rushmore* (1998). Upon arriving in Benghazi and meeting The Boys one of them looks up tiredly and exclaims "welcome to Club Med." Other outdated bro-isms like "let's shake and bake" or "rock 'n roll!" drop out of characters' mouths with absolutely no sense of irony. But, in a way, all of these classic Bay moments and tropes almost add to a level of respect for the director. Bay is completely at ease and in his element with "these kinds" of films and it would be stretching the truth to say his films aren't typically pretty entertaining if not downright effective.

As *13 Hours: The Secret Soldiers of Benghazi* plays out, Jack and Rone become pretty likable. Yet everyone knows a major attack is coming and not everyone will survive. This, coupled with (by way of example) images Bay shows of Jack talking to his kids on Skype in the golden hour while an American flag gently blows in the desert heat are cinematic manipulations of the highest order, yet they are still beautifully framed, effective cinematic language. Same goes for his over-caffeinated editing, which, while at first jarring if not a bit confusing, almost always give way to some of the best action filmmaking ever committed to the screen. Bay knows how to direct huge action set pieces better than any Hollywood filmmaker working today and *13 Hours: The Secret Soldiers of Benghazi* has them by the truckload.

Somewhat surprisingly given its creator's politics, there is not really much of a political agenda in *13 Hours: The Secret Soldiers of Benghazi,* for better or worse. While right-wing extremists like to use the word "Benghazi" to mean some kind of massive liberal cover-up, Bay portrays the entire situation in the film as a massive failing of not just the governments in charge but also of the soldiers, contractors, and locally trained military who were supposed to help keep Libya a free state. It's now a failed state and an ISIL/ISIS stronghold because of these failures, which is clearly defined by the "FUBAR," to use the film's parlance, state of affairs in the Middle East and on display here.

When Bay is not luxuriating in dude-speak or making sure proper slow-motion editing technique is being used as soldiers run, scream, and fire weapons, he's showing audiences how America's presence in the Middle East is a half-baked operation at best where no one knows who is good or bad, including Americans and Middle Easterners. In classic films, good guys wore white, bad guys wore black. Here, everyone is dressed culturally casual; it's impossible for anyone to know what side any given person is on. Yet, at the end of the day (and at the end of the film's nearly two-and-a-half-hour running time), audiences do not want Michael Bay to be Michael Moore or Spike Lee and deliver a strong social message. They want to be entertained in the most garish, gory, butt-kicking American way ever, and by that standard, *13 Hours: The Secret Soldiers of Benghazi* and Michael Bay deliver.

Don R. Lewis

CREDITS

Jack Silva: John Krasinski
Tyrone "Rone" Woods: James Badge Dale
Kris "Tanto" Paronto: Pablo Schreiber
Dave "Boon" Benton: David Denman

John "Tig" Tiegen: Dominic Fumusa
Origin: United States
Language: English, Arabic
Released: 2016
Production: Erwin Stoff, Michael Bay; released by 3 Arts Entertainment, Latina Pictures
Directed by: Michael Bay
Written by: Chuck Hogan
Cinematography by: Dion Beebe
Music by: Lorne Balfe
Sound: Erik Aadahl; Ethan Van der Ryn
Editing: Pietro Scalia; Calvin Wimmer
Art Direction: Sebastian Schroder
Costumes: Deborah Lynn Scott
Production Design: Jeffrey Beecroft
MPAA rating: R
Running time: 144 minutes

REVIEWS

Andersen, Soren. *The Seattle Times.* January 14, 2016.
Berardinelli, James. *Reel Views.* January 17, 2016.
Dziemianowicz, Joe. *New York Daily News.* January 13, 2016.
Goble, Blake. *Consequence of Sound.* January 13, 2016.
Hoffman, Jordan. *The Guardian.* January 13, 2016.
Morgenstern, Joe. *Wall Street Journal.* January 14, 2016.
Rainer, Peter. *Christian Science Monitor.* January 15, 2016.
Robison, Tasha. *The Verge.* January 14, 2016.
Roeper, Richard. *Chicago Sun-Times.* January 14, 2016.
Travers, Peter. *Rolling Stone.* January 15, 2016.

QUOTES

Jack Silva: "You can't put a price on being able to live with yourself."

TRIVIA

John Krasinski dropped from 25 to 8 body fat in preparation for his role of Jack Silva.

TICKLED

It's not what you think.
—Movie tagline

Box Office: $613,956

While the consequence was certainly unintended and not really considered prior to overtaking the world's communication lines, the Internet has given near free reign to bullies, both anonymous as well as proudly hateful. Anyone can hide behind their keyboard with a fake moniker and say pretty much anything they want, repercussion free. And worse, with a simple mouse click that information is instantly accessible and distributable. The strange part of that sad and creepy way of living one's life (ie; as an "Internet Troll") is that almost everyone has use of the same tool these people are using and with some good old-fashioned legwork, it's not all that difficult to discover what sad little person is spreading lies and bullying people online. Yet it seems like rarely do people actually put work into casting a light on cowards who seek to destroy other people's lives anonymously. Luckily for fans of great storytelling, anti-bullying and documentaries about the bizarre, New Zealand filmmakers David Farrier and Dylan Reeve turn out to be exactly the wrong sort of people to mess with online.

Their film *Tickled* is a "stranger than fiction" tale that starts off as a silly whim but gets crazier by the minute. *Tickled* opens with the introduction of Farrier, who works at what seems to be the New Zealand version of Buzzfeed. It's his job to scour the Internet for off-the-wall stories that he can then investigate to present to his site's readers. In other words, he traffics in "clickbait." One day, he stumbles across a niche sport called "Competitive Endurance Tickling" on YouTube, and after some basic research, discovers a company called "Jane O'Brien Media" that runs ads for potential competitors to earn money as well as a free trip to Los Angeles, including a stay at a luxury hotel to "compete." Basically, a man (it's always men here) can send in a headshot and if selected get flown to L.A., treated to a stay in a nice hotel, fed lovely meals, and get paid to take part in a few hours of tickling from other men. As always, most things that seem too good to be true usually are.

After discovering the "sport" and how to get in contact with those running the competitions, Farrier fires off an email indicating his interest in doing a story for his popular site on the sport. He's almost immediately deluged with dismissive and then threatening emails basically saying to stay away from the company and their events. Farrier remains professional and cordial in his answers, but soon the emails from Jane O'Brien Media turn spiteful, personal, and anti-gay calling him out as "an active homosexual" amongst other slurs. While many people would simply then drop this idea from their list of potential stories, Farrier instead goes on the offensive and starts asking questions of former endurance tickling challenge participants. And like a loose thread on a sweater that once tugged causes a massive unraveling, *Tickled* only gets crazier the further along it goes. Farrier and viewers soon discover that there's much, much more to the already oddball story

than meets the eye, especially when it comes to what participants are being asked to do and worse, what happens if they don't comply.

Obviously, it would be incredibly bad form to dip even a toe into spoiler territory for a film as odd and ultimately shocking as *Tickled* so, that won't happen here. But it's important to note the doc is not only an intriguing watch for the sheer oddity of the story that builds into twists and turns few will see coming. *Tickled* also serves as an excellent reminder to viewers not only about exercising caution with personal information while online but as of the value of actual research journalism and how vital that can be to combat bullies of any ilk. Just as anyone can start a rumor or propagate hate online, a little digging can shed light on who this person is and where they work or go to school.

Fear of being outed as a person saying something awful can act as a powerful counter to make people think twice about saying it. Yet even saying that feels a bit moot in the case of *Tickled* as the only thing that can sometimes trump speaking truth to power is great big piles of money. This sad fact is something Farrier and Reeve discover as soon as their digging into Jane O'Brien Media starts yielding names, addresses, and tax information followed by a never-ending wave of legal threats. *Tickled* shows us the only thing worse than an average Internet bully is a rich one with a lot of free time.

Don R. Lewis

CREDITS

Himself: David Farrier
Himself: Dylan Reeve
Origin: United States
Language: English
Released: 2016
Production: Carthew Neal; released by Magnolia Pictures
Directed by: David Farrier; Dylan Reeve
Cinematography by: Dominic Fryer
Music by: Rodi Kirkcaldy; Florian Zwietnig
Editing: Simon Coldrick
MPAA rating: R
Running time: 92 minutes

REVIEWS

Brennan, Matt. *Slant.* June 12, 2016.
Dargis, Manhola. *New York Times.* June 16, 2016.
Harvey, Dennis. *Variety.* May 9, 2016.
Hornaday, Ann. *Washington Post.* June 30, 2016.
Lloyd, Kate. *Time Out London.* August 15, 2016.

Marshall, Lee. *Screen International.* May 9, 2016.
Morgenstern, Joe. *Wall Street Journal.* June 16, 2016.
Nashawaty, Chris. *Entertainment Weekly.* June 15, 2016.
Schindel, Daniel. *Film Stage.* May 9, 2016.
Walsh, Katie. *Playlist.* June 20, 2016.

TRIVIA

Several people from the film attended a screening and Q&A with Dylan Reeve. It was streamed live on Facebook and involved threats of criminal charges against the filmmakers by the film's subjects.

TONI ERDMANN

Box Office: $1.2 Million

The title figure of Maren Ade's exhilarating comedy *Toni Erdmann* is a court jester with an impudent wit and a devilishly high wire energy. His unpredictable fury makes everything around him volatile and almost impossible to fully anticipate. The ground trembles underneath him. He echoes C.L. Barber's description of Shakespeare's greatest comic invention, Falstaff, "a Lord of Misrule," his anarchic and devious wit streaked with a melancholy.

He has Falstaff's girth and shape, a shambling and hulking man who moves with the quickness and grace of a dancer. Erdmann is also, in a parallel of Falstaff's great soliloquy in *Henry IV, Part 1*, during the battle of Shrewsbury, a "counterfeit," the deliriously inventive and uproarious unpredictable alter ego of a German music schoolteacher named Winfried Conradi (Peter Simonischek).

He is also the combustive and soul-cleansing center of this freewheeling, unclassifiable, epic comedy. His straight-laced foil is his daughter, Ines (Sandra Hüller). She is a beautiful, ambitious, and tightly wound management consultant working in Bucharest. Fundamentally, the movie revolves around a question posed fairly early on: "Are you really a human?" The fun, daring, and excitement are in coming up with a proper response. The prickly dynamic of the central relationship achieves a heightened and complex emotional rhythm, beautiful, acrimonious, colorful, and unexpected. It carries the film aloft.

This is Ade's third feature and the first since her deeply accomplished, bruising break up drama, *Everyone Else* (2009). With Christian Petzold (*Phoenix* [2014]), Ade is the most significant figure of the Berlin School, the artistic movement of young German filmmakers who work in a sharply realist register. She displays an impeccable sense of timing and tone, always alert to the foibles and fears of her characters. The observational

humor is framed by painful moments of recognition. At 162 minutes, the movie is unusually long for a comedy, but little is wasted or overdone. In the wrong hands the movie would be deadly and interminable. *Toni Erdmann* is compulsively watchable, messy, heady, and always alive to nuance, feeling, and manners.

Opening and closing chapters in suburban Germany frame the movie. The merry prankster is introduced at the start as a deliveryman arrives with a package at his leafy suburban home. The apparently straightforward encounter with the postal worker yields the first of a series of quick change disguises that yields the flamboyant Toni, complete with his dime store fake teeth and elaborate black wig, wearing one handcuff (having just been released from jail for making "mail bombs"). Playing himself or his doppelganger, the man possesses a cruel, mocking wit that undermines the quotidian social discourse and acceptable norms of behavior, like dressing up his young students in ghoulish face paint during a celebration for a retiring teacher that turns into a mirthful, painful acknowledgement of the man's mortality. There are no boundaries with him, and people intuitively understand and respect that.

Ines also turns up at the start of a family gathering (her parents are now amicably divorced). She is there without quite being present; "always on the phone," observes one character. The party is in her honor, an early birthday acknowledgement, but she is preoccupied by her work. When her father begs to leave early, she hardly protests, promising only to Skype with him. Everything about her is seemingly controlled.

The movie is shot, by Patrick Orth, in widescreen. At first glance, the imagery is fairly direct and stripped down, but it is subtly amplified. Her uninflected style creates a tremendous emotional rapport, an intimate sense of listening in or watching over. Ade demonstrates right away a strong compositional line, always allowing her characters enough room to operate. She captures bodies in a constant state of movement and action. Especially good with time and space, Ade contrasts her protagonists beautifully: Winfried is open and ecstatic, Ines tight and withholding. The first significant dramatic rupture is a jump cut that inventively propels Winfried from his garden to the office lobby in Romania. In bringing together two discernable types, the practical joker and the cold businesswoman, the movie effectively splinters and juts off in multiple directions.

Winfried has turned up, without notice or warning, and invaded her carefully ordered space. Ines has been working in Bucharest advising an oil-company CEO, Henneberg (Michael Wittenborn), about carrying out a complex transaction that is going to result in the loss of hundreds of jobs. Eager to prove her competence in order to get a coveted Shanghai posting, Ines is deeply aware of the personal ramifications. Her job entails negotiating competing political, cultural, and social factions, entertaining the CEO's wife, going out for drinks or to a club, requiring a combination of discipline, finesse, and tact that seems the very antithesis of her father.

The father proves far more complex and implacable a figure than even Ines fully comprehends. If she regards him with a mixture of embarrassment and dread and is frustrated by his antics, his disarming, loose-limbed nature and capacity for surprise and wonder captures the imagination and interest of her business circle. A joke that should not work, his crack about hiring a "substitute daughter," to make up her absence, connects him temperamentally to the cold, dour Henneberg.

The other reason for the elastic and unruly aspect of the comedy is the normal lines of demarcation rarely apply. *Toni Erdmann* is not a film of hard exits and sharp lines. It is fluid, dense, and unpredictable. Ade justifies the running time in order to accommodate the expansiveness of her ideas. Winfried's apparent departure from the scene is simply a new avenue for Toni, the court jester, to take center stage. He does with relish and aplomb, wearing his outrageous outfit and adopted persona. The stylized fakery too easy to ignore, the movie is continually ambiguous about the extent everybody else is complicit in the joke.

Ade is one of the many European directors deeply influenced by the films of pioneering American independent John Cassavetes. The middle passages evoke the director's *A Woman Under the Influence* (1974), with Toni as a variant of Gena Rowlands's distressed housewife Mabel following her tense return home after being hospitalized. Presenting himself as either a freelance life coach or a German ambassador, he pushes moments, actions, scenes past the breakpoint, his performance like something out of Warhol, outrageous, discomfiting and finally surreal.

The movie unfolds in a series of transitory spaces of hotel rooms, business centers, restaurants, clubs, or Ines' sterile and impersonal corporate housing. In this very ephemeral world, this invented man fills a void even as he ruptures Ines' life. She ultimately surrenders, playing along with his extravagant performance, his panache and outrageousness helping illuminate the absurdity of the life she is heir to, the intercine corporate politics, sexual maneuvering, and cultural dislocation. Her own deeper revelation brings about two breathtaking set pieces that propel the movie into the peculiar and sublime.

This is the first significant exposure Hüller has ever received in this country, and the range and depth of her talent is something to behold. Working closely with Ade, she builds the part incrementally, starting off withholding and tense and then finding continually open pathways of exuberance and defiance. The first really big cathartic moment is her impromptu cover performance of Whitney Houston's "The Greatest Love of All," inside an intimate party she and her father have shown up. The other tonally daring moment is a long sequence inside her apartment. Governed around her ostensible birthday party, Ines transforms the scene her own performance art, a striking assertion of independence and sexual freedom that proves as hypnotic as it is fearless. The Austrian Simonischek is her equal. This is the work off a free man, subversive, funny, and giddy with possibility.

The movie is a deeply political work, directly and more subliminally (there is a fantastic scene between Winfried and one of the Romanian workers about to lost his job). Eager to escape from the dark shadows of the dictatorship of Nicolae Ceaucescu, the collective national portrait is a place desperate for a new identity. The great Romanian actor Vlad Ivanov, the back-alley abortionist in Cristian Mungiu's *Four Months, Three Weeks, Two Days* (2007), has a small, vital part and provides a sharp, telling context.

This film is markedly different from the masterpieces of New Romanian Cinema, like Cristi Puiu's *The Death of Mr. Lazarescu* (2006) and Corneliu Porumboiu's *Police, Adjective* (2009). Ade is a central figure in the modern European avant-garde as a director and a producer of films like Miguel Gomes' *Tabu* (2012), *Arabian Nights* (2015), and Ulrich Köhler's *Sleeping Sickness* (2011). These are iconoclastic films that challenge traditional orthodoxy of what narrative is. *Toni Erdmann* marks the fullest distillation of that aesthetic. It is dark, joyous and profound. The movie ends more or less where it started. Like the audience, nobody is the same after the experience.

Patrick Z. McGavin

CREDITS

Ines Conradi: Sandra Hüller
Winfried Conradi/Toni Erdmann: Peter Simonischek
Henneberg: Michael Wittenborn
Gerald: Thomas Loibl
Tim: Trystan Pütter
Origin: United States
Language: German, English, Romanian
Released: 2016
Production: Jonas Dornbach, Janine Jackowski, Michel Merkt, Maren Ade; released by Komplizen Film
Directed by: Maren Ade

Written by: Maren Ade
Cinematography by: Patrick Orth
Sound: Fabian Schmidt
Editing: Heike Parplies
Art Direction: Malina Ionescu
Costumes: Gitti Fuchs
Production Design: Silke Fischer
MPAA rating: R
Running time: 162 minutes

REVIEWS

Anderson, Melissa. *Village Voice.* December 21, 2016.
Chang, Justin. *Los Angeles Times.* December 22, 2016.
D'Angelo, Mike. *The A.V. Club.* December 20, 2016.
Kiang, Jessica. *Playlist.* May 19, 2016.
Edelstein, David. *New York Magazine.* December 21, 2016.
Lodge, Guy. *Variety.* May 19, 2016.
Morgenstern, Joe. *Wall Street Journal.* December 29, 2016.
Rainer, Peter. *Christian Science Monitor.* January 6, 2017.
Scott, A.O. *New York Times.* December 22, 2016.
Zacharek, Stephanie. *Time.* December 23, 2016.

QUOTES

Winfried Conradi alias Toni Erdmann: "You have to do this or that, but meanwhile life is just passing by."

TRIVIA

Writer/director Maren Ade discarded two days of footage after she felt she did not get what she needed.

AWARDS

Ind. Spirit 2017: Foreign Film

Nominations:

Oscars 2016: Foreign Film
British Acad. 2016: Foreign Film
Golden Globes 2017: Foreign Film

TOUCHED WITH FIRE
(Mania Days)

Box Office: $146,487

Touched with Fire takes on the lofty issues of mental illness and mostly reduces them to indie-film cliché. Carla (Katie Holmes) and Marco (Luke Kirby) are both intelligent artists dealing with the turmoil of bipolar disorder. The two of them meet in a psychiatric hospital and embark on a challenging romance filled with erratic (yet in the context of this rather simplistic film, also

somewhat predictable) behavior. Bipolar disorder is an undeniably complex illness that affects many, and writer/director/editor/composer Paul Dalio deserves some credit for seeking to depict it here. However, the film is frustrating in its treatment of manic episodes as shouting standoffs that would not be out of place in a soap opera, and its insistence that its two leads write florid and embarrassing poetry. Holmes' performance is strong, with her sweet face and voice standing in contrast to the anger roiling inside her. The most affecting scenes are those between Carla and her mother, Sara (Christine Lahti): in one early moment, Holmes projects tragic vulnerability as she begs her mother to give her some concrete answer as to when and why she turned out the way she did. Kirby never reaches the same emotional depths and mostly relies on reductive elements of mental illness performance: he shouts, he babbles about conspiracies, he does irrational things, but is not given a chance to be a more well-rounded character.

The film also plays fast and loose with the logistics of Carla and Marco's life together. After leaving the hospital the couple move in together, leaving the audience wondering how they were able to find an apartment and support themselves. Marco's father, George (Griffin Dunne), obliquely refers to his unseen wife's "sickness," and perhaps a scene or two of Marco and his mother, or a family flashback would add depth to his character. At times it seems Dalio is unsure what tone he wants to strike as the film vacillates between expository drama (as in nearly every scene featuring the couple and their parents) and whimsy. At the psych ward, Carla and Marco meet every night at 3 AM and the shadowy room highlighted by pops of color casts a dreamlike quality over the proceedings. In these scenes, where Carla and Marco talk about being from another planet, there is an element of authentic feeling missing from the rest of the film. While *Touched with Fire* ends on a hopeful note, this last scene of Carla and Marco reading their poetry together to an audience at a bookstore is too contrived. In the film's most aesthetically memorable moment, Marco discusses Van Gogh, and the way his mental illness ultimately inspired great art. The sky in *Starry Night* was painted the way Van Gogh saw it in his mind, and Marco feels this is something to celebrate. One night, when only Carla and Marco are awake, the walls of the psych ward pulse with the blue and yellow swirls of Van Gogh's iconic painting. It would be interesting to see what might happen if Dalio indulged more of these artistic impulses. The swirling walls nicely blend whimsy and sadness. They are inviting to look at, yet seen only by those who face a constant mental battle.

On some level, *Touched with Fire* earnestly wants to erase the stigma around mental illness, yet it falls into too many of the expected patterns to do so. The title of the film comes from a real-life book, *Touched with Fire: Manic-Depressive Illness and the Artistic Temperament*, written by Kay Redfield Jamison, a psychologist who herself has bipolar disorder. Marco values the book and uses its exploration of bipolar artists as a means of justifying going off his medication. Late in the film, Carla and Marco meet with Jamison, playing herself. The short scene feels oddly inert, as if Dalio felt he had to add a literal tribute to a text that inspired his story. Jamison talks about how medication has helped her, and while Carla comes away feeling inspired, and hoping Marco will feel the same, Marco reacts with incredulity and sees the psychologist as a sellout. The film's closing credits list a dedication to all the artists—Van Gogh, Emily Dickinson, and Lord Byron among them—who were presumed to have bipolar disorder and discussed in Jamison's book. This lofty dedication feels unearned, to say nothing of the dicey proposition of diagnosing those who are long dead. While *Touched with Fire* intermittently succeeds at showing bipolar struggles, it never reaches the heights of the artists referenced in the source material.

Abbey Bender

CREDITS

Carla: Katie Holmes
Marco: Luke Kirby
Sara: Christine Lahti
George: Griffin Dunne
Donald: Bruce Altman
Origin: United States
Language: English
Released: 2016
Production: Jeremy Alter, Jason Sokoloff, Kristina Nikolova; released by 40 Acres and a Mule Filmworks
Directed by: Paul Dalio
Written by: Paul Dalio
Cinematography by: Kristina Nikolova; Alexander Stanishev
Music by: Paul Dalio
Sound: Mac Smith
Editing: Paul Dalio; Lee Percy
Production Design: Kay Lee
MPAA rating: R
Running time: 106 minutes

REVIEWS

Ehrlich, David. *Rolling Stone*. February 12, 2016.
Hassenger, Jesse. *The A.V. Club*. February 11, 2016.
Holden, Stephen. *New York Times*. February 11, 2016.

Lapin, Andrew. *NPR*. February 11, 2016.
Leydon, Joe. *Variety*. March 20, 2015.
Merry, Stephanie. *Washington Post*. February 18, 2016.
Myers, Kimber. *IndieWire*. February 11, 2016.
Nakhnikian, Elise. *Slant*. February 8, 2016.
Walsh, Katie. *Los Angeles Times*. February 11, 2016.
Wloszczyna, Susan. *Roger Ebert*. February 12, 2016.

QUOTES

Marco: "Van Gogh. Top member of the Bipolar Club. You see this?"
Nurse Amy: "Yes, it's beautiful!"
Marco: "You know why?"
Nurse Amy: "Why?"
Marco: "Because it's the painting of the sky he saw from his sanitarium window when he was manic."
Nurse Amy: "Really?"
Marco: "Yeah. You don't believe me, go look it up."
Nurse Amy: "I believe you."
Marco: "Well, when you go out tonight, and you look at the sky and you see how dull it is, think about if you would've medicated Van Gogh!"

TRIVIA

The film is based on the life of director Paul Dalio.

TRIPLE 9

The code on the street is never black and white.
—Movie tagline

Box Office: $12.6 Million

John Hillcoat made it clear from his directorial debut, the harrowing dystopian prison drama *Ghosts...of the Civil Dead* (1988), that he was primarily interested in the dirty, violent things men do to other men—the hideous acts they perform to stay alive and how they become conditioned to believe them necessary. Through repetition and the constant threat of death, survival is confused with sometimes-mercenary thrill seeking. The men at the heart of *Triple 9* may once have gone into the business of robbery and murder to make ends meet, but they are now trapped by it. They would sooner dig a deeper grave than think about giving up the corrupted codes they live by.

Michael Atwood (Chiwetel Ejiofor) leads a gang of thieves with what Liam Neeson might call a "particular set of skills." Atwood and Russell Welch (Norman Reedus) are former guns-for-hire of the Blackwater school, while Franco Rodriguez and Marcus Belmont (Clifton Collins Jr. and Anthony Mackie) are current Atlanta detectives. Gabe (Aaron Paul), Russell's runty former addict brother, was a cop before he was dishonorably released from the force. Hillcoat introduces them doing one in a string of jobs they've been strong-armed into performing by the Russian mob, with tactical efficiency. Their usual contact, Vassili (Igor Komar), is in a Russian prison, so his wife Irina (Kate Winslet) has taken over and she's not interested in doing things the easy way. The criminal empire her husband lorded over was entirely too fussy and masculine for her, so she's clamping down and reorganizing. First step is squeezing Michael's gang harder than ever.

Irina wants evidence to get Vassili out of jail and is convinced there's enough of it in the closets and vaults of Atlanta's Russian mob contingent that can be stolen. Michael would say no but he got Irina's sister Elena (Gal Gadot) pregnant and their son is all the collateral Irina needs to keep him robbing banks for the rest of his life. Even so, she decides to further incentivize the crew by torturing Russell and leaving him for dead. Michael, Gabe, Franco, and Marcus all agree to the next robbery knowing what might happen if they don't. The question is how to hit the target, a homeland security outpost, without every police officer in Georgia rushing to the scene. Franco thinks killing a cop might distract local law enforcement long enough to get in and out with the goods. Marcus suggests his new partner Chris Allen (Casey Affleck), whose uncle Jeffrey (Woody Harrelson) is in charge of major crimes for the city. If Jeff hears Chris has been killed, he'd move heaven and earth to catch the guy who did it. The only real threat to the plan is Gabe's increasingly erratic conduct as his conscience starts acting up. With his brother dead, nothing holds him together and he returns to an old drug habit. But most troublingly he starts hanging around Chris Allen's house in an effort to let him know what his gang is planning.

As in previous Hillcoat films like *The Proposition* (2005) and *Lawless* (2012), *Triple 9* is over-reliant on tough guy clichés. The dialogue sounds cobbled together from dozens of hard-boiled cop movies and never quite feels like anything real crooks would say to each other. The performances go some of the way toward selling the patent falsity of the too-familiar scenario (Harrelson's unchecked overacting as drug-addled Uncle Jeff the exception) and it's clear screenwriter Matt Cook's addition of Homeland Security and Blackwater are attempts to pump some relevance into his old hat cops and robbers story. The problem is that they're two elements too many and in just trying to keep up with all the divergent threads, Hillcoat is already huffing and puffing when the final act kicks into gear.

Excluding a mid-film shoot out, Hillcoat and Cook can't line up the stakes properly. There are twists that are broadcasted from the first act and action set pieces with no real weight to them. A high-speed pursuit late in the film goes on entirely too long, especially given that the audience knows ahead of time how it will end. The robberies that Michael's crew stage meet with no meaningful resistance until they're well over and the audience's pulse will have stopped racing. Hillcoat relies heavily on machinery borrowed from other gangster movies and doesn't do enough with these old tropes to make them feel fresh. Blurring the lines between good and bad guys with badges and guns just isn't a novel enough idea to hang a movie on in 2016.

The moral schema Cook and Hillcoat draw up is all too easy to chart. Marcus seems perfectly ok with killing Chris until Chris saves his life during a stand off with a drug dealer. Gabe on the other hand is so bent out of shape at the idea of killing a cop that he frequently endangers his and Mike's lives to save Chris. Mike talks all the time about the familial bond he feels for his crew, until they're a threat to his son's life, at which point they're as expendable as any of the passersby they slaughter indiscriminately during their heists. These men think their bond keeps them above the law and invincible. Just as in *Lawless* and *The Proposition*, this film is populated by gunslingers who think they're superheroes, which doesn't make for terribly compelling drama. They only have one way to fall and Hillcoat makes sure the impact is fatal.

Everything the script tries to say with too-familiar tough guy talk, Hillcoat and cinematographer Nicolas Karakatsanis do a better job of showing. They splash deep crimson on a myriad of dark surfaces (bank paint bombs exploding on ski masks, blood on abattoir floor tiles, rotating beacon lights illuminating faces in shadow) to show how quickly and readily the souls of each character can be stained. Those pictures are worth a thousand words and *Triple 9* works best when it keeps its mouth shut. Images of Atlanta's mean streets filling up the margins around the plot are much more interesting than the sordid lives of men with guns. A streetwalker dancing on a dumpster, cops covered in paint thrown by outraged pedestrians, spilled beer on an abandoned stoop and a baby lying next to a pile of guns have a kind of poetry the rest of the film lacks. The passive images on the periphery of the action tell the story of *Triple 9* much more beautifully and much less laboriously than its characters.

Scout Tafoya

CREDITS

Michael Atwood: Chiwetel Ejiofor
Chris Allen: Casey Affleck

Marcus Belmont: Anthony Mackie
Jeffrey Allen: Woody Harrelson
Gabe Welch: Aaron Paul
Elena Vlaslov: Gal Gadot
Michelle Allen: Teresa Palmer
Russell Welch: Norman Reedus
Irina Vlaslov: Kate Winslet
Origin: United States
Language: English
Released: 2015
Production: Marc Butan, Bard Dorros, Anthony Katagas, Keith Redmon, Christopher Woodrow; released by Anonymous Content, Worldview Entertainment
Directed by: John Hillcoat
Written by: Matt Cook
Cinematography by: Nicolas Karakatsanis
Music by: Claudia Sarne; Bobby Krlic; Atticus Ross; Leopold Ross
Music Supervisor: Tracy McKnight
Editing: Dylan Tichenor
Costumes: Margot Wilson
Production Design: Tim Grimes
MPAA rating: R

REVIEWS

Burr, Ty. *Boston Globe*. February 25, 2016.
Dargis, Manohla. *New York Times*. February 25, 2016.
Duralde, Alonso. *TheWrap*. February 17, 2016.
McCarthy, Todd. *Hollywood Reporter*. February 17, 2016.
Morgenstern, Joe. *Wall Street Journal*. February 26, 2016.
Nashawaty, Chris. *Entertainment Weekly*. February 24, 2016.
Persall, Steve. *Tampa Bay Times*. February 25, 2016.
Scherstuhl, Alan. *Village Voice*. February 23, 2016.
Snydel, Michael. *The Film Stage*. February 26, 2016.
Tallerico, Brian. *RogerEbert.com*. February 25, 2016.

QUOTES

Jeffrey Allen: "Out here, there is no good and there is no bad. To survive out here, you've got to out monster the monster. Can you do that?"

TRIVIA

Norman Reedus and Aaron Paul have had roles on the AMC series *The Walking Dead* and *Breaking Bad,* respectively.

TROLLS

Find your happy place.
—Movie tagline

Box Office: $153.5 Million

There's a not-so-new trend sweeping animated films and it's becoming a bit overdone and more brazen of late: making fairly bad animated films that feature cute and cuddly creatures voiced by celebrities. Many of these films also use at least a quarter of their running time having their characters sing popular songs that may or may not fit the scene or the character but act as a Pavlovian Happy Chime to kids and adults alike. These songs also fill space where a well-thought-out plot should be. Yet plot is of no concern because these films are designed to do one thing and that's sell merchandise. As a result, many recent animated films are trifles at best, a waste of time at worst, and completely forgettable the moment the end credits roll. Recent examples of disposable animated films designed strictly for huge initial box office domination that live on, not in fond memory of being entertained, but rather in the toys, clothes, and backpacks in landfills and on playroom floors include *Minions* (2015), *The Secret Life of Pets* (2016), and *The Angry Birds Movie* (2016). *Trolls* (2016) is just the latest celebrity-anchored, product-driven movie.

As *Trolls* opens, viewers are introduced to the title characters, who are living a fairly terrifying existence as the number-one snack food of choice for a group of huge, ugly creatures called the Bergen. The Bergen are a grouchy group who firmly believe the only moment of happiness in their downtrodden lives is when they get to eat a troll. Meanwhile, the trolls spend their time "fiddling while Rome burns" by being overly happy, doling out positivity, hugging, and completely overcompensating for their impending doom with happiness as, they all know that a once-a-year occurrence called "Trollstice" is coming, and many of their troll brethren will be eaten. How long this has been going on for is never clearly defined but viewers are dropped into the story on the day when the trolls finally figure out that they can run away before Trollstice and live happily ever after somewhere else. So, they do. And the Bergen are then really unhappy.

From there, the film leaps forward several years as the trolls are back to their overly jovial selves, except one. Branch (Justin Timberlake) is a troll version of what humans call a prepper or survivalist and he goes against the troll societal grain by being incredibly grumpy. Always fearing the reemergence of the Bergen, Branch spends his days preparing for the day the Bergen find the trolls and what, with all the loud singing, dancing, and partying being lead by troll princess Poppy (Anna Kendrick) going on, the trolls are making it pretty easy to be rediscovered. Sure enough, this happens, and several key trolls are kidnapped, forcing polar opposites Branch and Poppy to join forces to find them.

Trolls is a mildly amusing film that, while clearly created to bring the oddball troll doll toys from the

1960s and '70s back to store shelves, has just enough odd moments to barely rise above the films noted earlier. One such highlight is the out-of-nowhere appearance of a character that looks like a cloud with legs. Described in the credits as merely "Cloud Guy" (voiced by Walt Dohrn) the character emerges at a key moment of the film and knows everything about heroes Poppy and Branch. How he knows what he knows and who he is never gets mentioned as no sooner has Cloud Guy stolen the film in his less than five minutes of screen time, then he disappears again only to show up later, as if the filmmakers realized the character served as a cheap (yet hilarious) plot device and he should be revisited to cover their tracks. And this is a pretty clear example of where *Trolls* fails as a film. Things just happen throughout with no explanation other than the plot needs them to happen.

Early in the film, a Bergen named Chef (Christine Baranski) is held accountable for the trolls escaping. How she is culpable is never divulged but the accusation is enough to move the plot in terms of her getting removed from the Bergen, which causes her to become obsessed with finding the trolls. There's other such unexplained moments in the film as well as motivations and characters. For example there's a troll who, when he passes wind, glitter comes out. No other troll has this "power" but it sure comes in handy at a certain point. Another troll looks like a camel for some reason, his hair is in dreadlocks and he's voiced by African-American comedian Ron Funches. The character apparently is only here to add a more racially diverse appearance to the cast of animated trolls as his limited dialogue is a riff on African-American slang. The most baffling occurrence in the film involves the trolls' famous hair. Here it's capable of power lifting, stretching to great lengths as well as camouflaging trolls when they are in trouble. These things just happen throughout the film with the only rhyme or reason being that the thing needs to happen. It's bad filmmaking and very bad writing, which in the end tips the film's hand in terms of why it was made; *Trolls* is not a film as much as it is a commercial for trolls merchandise.

Don R. Lewis

CREDITS

Princess Poppy: Anna Kendrick
Branch: Justin Timberlake
Bridget: Zooey Deschanel
King Gristle: Christopher Mintz-Plasse
Chef: Christine Baranski
Origin: United States
Language: English

Released: 2016
Production: Gina Shay; released by DreamWorks Animation L.L.C.
Directed by: Mike Mitchell
Written by: Jonathan Aibel; Glenn Berger
Cinematography by: Yong Duk Jhun
Music by: Christophe Beck
Sound: Erik Aadahl; Ethan Van der Ryn
Music Supervisor: Julianne Jordan; Julia Michels
Editing: Nick Fletcher
Art Direction: Timothy Lamb
Production Design: Kendal Cronkhite
MPAA rating: PG
Running time: 92 minutes

REVIEWS

Chang, Justin. *Los Angeles Times.* November 3, 2016.
Duralde, Alonso. *TheWrap.* October 8, 2016.
Greenblatt, Leah. *Entertainment Weekly.* November 3, 2016.
Hartlaub, Peter. *San Francisco Chronicle.* November 3, 2016.
Ihnat, Gwenn. *The A.V. Club.* November 2, 2016.
Lengel, Kerry. *Arizona Republic.* November 3, 2016.
Rizov, Vadim. *Village Voice.* November 2, 2016.
Savlov, Marc. *Austin Chronicle.* November 2, 2016.
Wloszczyna, Susan. *RogerEbert.com.* November 3, 2016.
Zwecker, Bill. *Chicago Sun-Times.* November 1, 2016.

QUOTES

Branch: "Why don't you try scrapbooking them to freedom?"
Poppy: "Solid burn, Branch."

TRIVIA

Branch refuses to sing in the movie. Ironically, his voice actor, Justin Timberlake, was the executive producer for the film's soundtrack.

AWARDS

Nominations:

Oscars 2016: Orig. Song Score and/or Adapt. ("Can't Stop the Feeling")
Golden Globes 2017: Song ("Can't Stop the Feeling")

20th CENTURY WOMEN

Box Office: $2.9 Million

Mike Mills shocked the world of independent film when he wrote and directed the stunning, heart-rending *Beginners* in 2010. The former skater and music video director had, almost overnight, become one of the most devastating talents on the American scene. His heart-on-the-sleeve, autobiographical writing style, pastel-heavy compositions, and way with actors announced a director who had synthesized the best of '70s filmmaking while also completely understanding and translating the ever-changing modern landscape his characters inhabit. Despite his protagonist's naïve and ironic worldview and too-hip job as a minimalist graphic designer, nothing in *Beginners* was too precious that its potent core couldn't shine through. Mills also had a secret weapon in Christopher Plummer, then 82 years old with a life of electric character work behind him, as the hero's dad, a thinly veiled version of Mills' own father. The role secured the lifer his first Academy Award. Whether or not Annette Bening is lauded in the same way for Mills' newest film, the similarly resplendent *20th Century Women* is beside the point. Her work is some of her best in a career made exclusively of highs, and Mills' place as one of the great actor/directors is assured. *20th Century Women* is even more well-rounded and focused a drama, without losing any of the shagginess that made *Beginners* so endearing. This time, the focus is on Mills' mother and the time in their lives when she made the biggest imprint on his development.

The setting is Santa Barbara in 1979. Dorothea Fields (Bening), 55 years old, lives in a big old house with her son Jamie (Lucas Jade Zumann), and boarders Abbie (Greta Gerwig) and William (Billy Crudup). Almost as permanent a fixture in the house is Jamie's best friend and crush Julie (Elle Fanning), who has taken to sneaking into Jamie's bedroom to sleep next to him, never allowing their relationship to grow sexual. She does this largely because she doesn't relate to her therapist mother (Allison Elliott) and stepsister (Olivia Hone) and feels inadequately equipped to support them. Jamie stays stuck on her even as she spends most of her time sleeping with boys she doesn't like, who don't respect her, which makes him angry and aloof. Dorothea has noticed this and other signs of his adolescent rebellion against the way they used to relate to each other and decides she is outmatched by puberty. Realizing that William, a carpenter and hippie, has nothing in common with Jamie, Dorothea turns to Abbie and Julie for help raising her son. She doesn't want them to take over for her, she just knows that Jamie will be himself around the two of them, and they may be able to offer him guidance he might actually listen to. Jamie is initially reluctant to take the extra mothering but he has begun to chafe so much under Dorothea's mix of over-parenting and under-sharing that he starts to think lessons in feminism and empathy from Julie and Abbie might be a welcome change of pace.

Mills' writing is defined by an empathetic exploration of humanity through material obsessions and addictions. He presents his characters first as a collection of their possessions and fetishes so that we recognize each when they appear in the narrative as a piece of a beautiful puzzle. When we start to separate the character from their possessions, we see who they really are. He did this as a somber internal monologue in *Beginners*, but in *20th Century Women* he uses his character's obsessions as a way to comment on the nature of personality itself. It's no accident that both Godfrey Reggio's landmark documentary *Koyaanisqatsi* or Jimmy Carter's "Crisis of Confidence" speech play a part in the film's third act. Both foretold a society reliant on goods instead of moral wellness or spiritual wholeness. Abbie's photography projects, wherein she takes pictures of all of her possessions and the events of her daily life (including trips to her doctor for information regarding the cervical cancer she inherited from her mother), are ways to straighten out the emotional whirlwind she too frequently finds herself at the mercy of. When you can recognize that the things around you only define who you have been and what you have been obsessed by, you begin to understand who you are and who you can be. Mills literalizes this through a beautiful and heartbreaking collection of confessions from the characters about who they become when the events of the movie are over. He also has Jamie relate to his mother via the signifiers of her upbringing. His constant refrain when anyone asks about her behavior is "She's from the depression."

Dorothea is the film's central mystery and also its beating heart. She shares only her material and external life with the people who share her home. Jamie inherited his place as the central figure in his mother's life only because she divorced her husband. So he now goes over the rise and fall of stocks with her every morning the way her ex-husband used to, something she confesses to William while casting about for connection in lieu of Jamie's presence. The cigarettes she smokes are a crutch and relic from her upbringing, one she won't admit are killing her. "When I started they weren't bad for you, they were just stylish," she offers when Julie tries to smoke one of her ever-present Salem cigarettes during a heart-to-heart. If she were to stop smoking (Bening should win an Oscar just for the way she smokes on screen), she'd lose a piece of the front that keeps her together. If any one piece of the puzzle came loose, she'd have to admit that she's lonely, something Jamie begs her to come to terms with. The film's big cathartic moment is not built around traditional signposts of love and affection or togetherness, but an acknowledgment of the limitations of stubborn individuality. All Dorothea wants is for Jamie to end up happier than she did, and all Jamie wants is for her to admit that she's as unhappy as he is. She clings to her emotional solitude like one of her cigarettes. She's worried what it might mean to give them up, just as she knows that it might eventually kill her. Dorothea Fields is, in short, one of the most uncompromisingly and honestly written female characters of the 21st century, a mix of Bogie, whom she idolizes, and Bacall.

Of course, the joys of this movie do not end with the writing or performances. Mills has a flair for a kind of American filmmaking that's heavy on montage and modest feats of trickery that somehow never feels like the lazy shorthand it ends up as in the hands of less generous directors. Mills' love for these characters and all their glaring contradictions is evident in every composition. His pastel palette and unobtrusive zooms and pans leave his actors room to breathe. Mills also dresses them realistically and modestly and knows how to capture them at their freest. So when he speeds up their actions or strands them wordlessly in montage, he's aiding their development by showing their existence as part of a continuum of social behavior. They merely exist in these montages, rather than learning or improving. That is all done very quietly in the moments of scripted conversation, but, the shots of his characters dancing are as telling and important to our understanding of them as any line of dialogue.

Mills and his cast have such a firm grip upon the characters in *20th Century Women* that they can express their inner life perhaps most clearly and honestly without speaking. Jamie's search for identity is told through his slight hesitance and uncertainty at losing control to music while Abbie's practiced nonchalance comes off as forced concentration while she writhes along to punk records in her bedroom. The film's most charming moment of discovery comes after Jamie is beaten up by a fellow skateboarder one day. Jamie tries to explain the mechanics of female orgasm (learned from Abbie and the feminist writing she gives him to study) to a boy bragging about having sex. That and his love of the Talking Heads over Black Flag earn him a black eye and a vandalized car. William and Dorothea try to understand the difference between the two bands following the act of vandalism and try dancing to both a Talking Heads song and a Black Flag song, attempting not to over-think either. William tries to get Dorothea to lose herself in the music and dance in his bizarre, arrhythmic fashion, learned from years living in a commune listening to hippie rock. Dorothea's style is more classical and she gives in to the music only after some coaxing. It's a beautiful moment of friendship and compromise between these two characters, but also a way for Dorothea to understand what her son is going through. Everything we need to know about these people can be found in the way they move to music and the way they attempt to navigate the intimate space of a dance floor together. As Dorothea asks while teaching William how to woo a woman through dance: "How are you going to get to know anyone way over there?" *20th Century Women* is full of characters viewers will want to get to know and who always break hearts when they leave.

Scout Tafoya

CREDITS

Dorothea: Annette Bening
Julie: Elle Fanning
Abbie: Greta Gerwig
William: Billy Crudup
Jamie: Lucas Jade Zumann
Origin: United States
Language: English
Released: 2017
Production: Anne Carey, Megan Ellison, Youree Henley; released by Annapurna Pictures, Archer Gray, Modern People
Directed by: Mike Mills
Written by: Mike Mills
Cinematography by: Sean Porter
Music by: Roger Neill
Sound: Frank Gaeta
Music Supervisor: Howard Paar
Editing: Leslie Jones
Costumes: Jennifer Johnson
Production Design: Chris Jones
MPAA rating: R
Running time: 119 minutes

REVIEWS

Anderson, Melissa. *Village Voice.* December 27, 2016.
Callahan, Dan. *The Wrap.* October 7, 2016.
Chang, Justin. *Los Angeles Times.* December 27, 2016.
Dowd, A.A. *The A.V. Club.* December 20, 2016.
Edelstein, David. *Vulture.* December 21, 2016.
Ellwood, Gregory. *Playlist.* October 7, 2016.
Grierson, Tim. *Screen International.* October 7, 2016.
Hoffman, Jordan. *Guardian.* October 7, 2016.
Macfarlane, Steve. *Slant.* October 13, 2016.
Newman, Nick. *Film Stage.* October 7, 2016.

TRIVIA

The house location was used for the exterior shots in the film adaptation of *Running with Scissors* (2006), also starring Annette Bening.

AWARDS

Nominations:

Oscars 2016: Orig. Screenplay
Golden Globes 2017: Actress--Mus./Comedy (Bening), Film--Mus./Comedy
Ind. Spirit 2017: Actress (Bening), Screenplay

THE WAILING
(Goksung)

The Wailing is a horror film that hangs in the air exactly in the way its title suggests, demanding not just to be remembered, but investigated and accounted for. It achieves this by crafting characters that are absolutely relatable in their virtues and vices but especially in their sufferings. At the same time, it provokes questions about not just the nature of good and evil but the balance of power in the dark universe it inhabits. Not for the faint of heart or those whose hearts are easily broken, *The Wailing* is one of the best horror films of the year and certainly one of the very best Korean horror films ever made.

In the small, South Korean village of Goksung people have begun rotting only to, finally, go mad and kill those closest to them. As the number of deaths starts to suggest a pattern, the villagers suspect a Japanese-speaking stranger (Jun Kunimura) who lives in the mountains outside of town. At first, the police are convinced wild mushrooms are to blame. But when bumbling-if-well-intentioned police officer Jong-goo (Kwak Do-won) meets a mysterious young woman Moo-myeong (Korean for "no name") (Chun Woo-hee) he becomes convinced of the stranger's connection to the case.

Further investigation uncovers a local hunter, who claims to have stumbled upon a naked, red-eyed, wild man in the mountain woods eating a deer. With the aid of a fellow officer and Japanese-speaking priest, Jong-goo journeys to the stranger's house where Jong-goo's colleague unearths a strange altar room filled with pictures and personal effects of all the infected and dead villagers. Before he can share this information, the old man's guard dog breaks free, attacking the priest and Jong-goo, who are saved when the old man arrives and calls off the dog. The men mutter apologies and quickly leave.

On the way home, the officer shares his findings, handing Jong-goo a child's shoe, taken from the altar. After realizing the shoe belongs to his own daughter Hyo-jin (Kim Hwan-hee), Jong-goo arrives home to discover her infected. Enraged, he races back to the stranger's house but discovers the evidence has been burned. In a fit, he destroys the altar room, kills the stranger's dog and demands he leave the village. The stranger stays and Hyo-jin becomes sicker, prompting Jong-Hoo's mother-in-law to hire an expensive but highly regarded shaman, Il-Gwang (Hwang Jung-min) to perform a ritual to banish the evil. Unable to watch his daughter suffer during the ritual, a desperate Jong-hoo stops it and gathers a group of friends to hunt the old man down.

Jong-goo is offered up as a unique hero. Clumsy, timid when his job demands strong action, Jong-goo is a laughingstock on the police force. His relationship with his wife is almost non-existent. Instead, he commits casual adultery in the back of a car with his neighbor, unaware his daughter is watching. These flaws are offset by his complete devotion to his daughter and his willingness to face down the evil destroying his village. Kwak Do-won delivers a performance that makes all these disparate elements seem part of one person. Besides the director's sure hand, he is the biggest asset here. Likewise, young actor Kim Hwan-hee, who moves effortlessly from normal little girl to someone oppressed and warped by wickedness, is remarkably strong. Jun Kunimura, as the stranger, is a marvelous cypher who could as easily be an agent of spiritual protection as a monster.

Writer/director Na Hong Jin, is best known for nail-biting thrillers, *The Chaser* (2008) and *The Yellow Sea* (2011). As excellent as those films are, *The Wailing* comes as a bit of a surprise, not because of how powerful it is but because of the virtuoso level of control the director maintains over its two hour and thirty-six minute runtime. The narrative seems to fly by, supported by, but never overwhelmed by the impressive and nightmarish set pieces that deliver the most intense jolts. One such set piece, the ritual in which Hyo-jin is ceremonially cut and burned by the whirling shaman as the stranger chants his own spell miles away, is so immersive that viewers are liable to be glad when it ends.

The director also takes great advantage of the small village location. Goksung seems to exist in its own world, apart from the rest of society. The people there seem trapped, hemmed in by the mountains and forest on every side and beaten down by the rains. The last forty minutes of the film reveals *The Wailing* to be not only a masterpiece of atmosphere and intricate plotting but a film seriously concerned both with why bad things happen to seemingly good people, and why evil seems so powerful in this world. This is epic horror delivered in the most intimate terms.

Unlike most occult thrillers *The Wailing* expands beyond the duality of supernatural good and evil. Na forces his human characters into believable but decidedly evil behavior in their battle against evil forces, even as he appeases the audience by slowly upping the ante of supernatural occurrence. This is a genre film, but one that reminds how its genre, in this case, horror, is something that goes beyond simple conventions and is connected, back to real life and moral agency. Good and evil only have the power that Na's characters give them. Luke 24:37-39 is quoted at the beginning of the film and strongly suggests the theme Na pursues here: "37 They were startled and frightened, thinking they saw a ghost. 38 He said to them, 'Why are you troubled, and why do doubts rise in your minds? 39 Look at my hands and my feet. It is I myself! Touch me and see; a ghost does not have flesh and bones, as you see I have.'" Na's characters fail to see their own flesh and blood, choosing instead to constantly search for evil outside themselves.

Dave Canfield

CREDITS

Jong-goo: Kwak Do-won
Il-Gwang: Hwang Jung-min
The Stranger: Jun Kunimura
The Woman of No Name: Chun Woo-hee
Hyo-jin: Kim Hwan-hee
Origin: South Korea, United States
Language: English, Korean
Released: 2016
Production: John Penotti; Side Mirror, 20th Century Fox; released by Well Go USA Entertainment
Directed by: Na Hong Jin
Written by: Na Hong Jin
Cinematography by: Kyung-Pyo Hong
Sound: Dong-Han Kim
Editing: Sun-min Kim
MPAA rating: Unrated
Running time: 156 minutes

REVIEWS

Bechervaise, Jason. *Screen International.* May 24, 2016.
Bowen, Chuck. *Slant.* May 25, 2016.
Chang, Justin. *Los Angeles Times.* June 2, 2016.
Conran, Pierce. *ScreenAnarchy.* May 13, 2016.
Crump, Andy. *Paste Magazine.* June 3, 2016.
Douglas, Edward. *Den of Geek.* June 1, 2016.
Dujsik, Mark. *Mark Reviews Movies.* June 3, 2016.
Kenny, Glenn. *New York Times.* June 20, 2016.
Nordine, Michael. *Village Voice.* June 1, 2016.
Young, Deborah. *Hollywood Reporter.* May 31, 2016.

QUOTES

Il-Gwang: "Not everything that moves, breathes, and talks is alive."

TRIVIA

The film was mainly based on folk religions in Korea.

WAR DOGS

Hustling their way to the American Dream.
   —Movie tagline

Box Office: $43 Million

Though it is a popular field of focus, no one has a specific idea on American twentysomething men quite like Todd Phillips, who has made an entire filmography of men unable to break from arrested development, despite their responsibilities or jobs. The director of *Old School* (2003) and *The Hangover* (2009) is a strong choice to adapt the Guy Lawson article (from *Rolling Stone*), about two twenty-somethings who combined their "bro" powers and started a type of all-American enterprise in the military weapons market. A fitting connection to this story is that these young men would be seeing Todd Phillips movies during the time of this setting, and probably idolizing the men they saw on screen.

With inspired casting, Phillips enlists Miles Teller and Jonah Hill to play the two men, who meet years after being best friends in junior high. Teller plays David Packouz, the viewer's surrogate into the story, introduced as a massage therapist failing to make it big by selling bed sheets to retirement homes. It is not until he reconnects with his friend Efraim Diveroli (Jonah Hill)—at a funeral of all places—that David understands that Efraim is deep within a highly profitable, and legal business.

In one of Phillips' most lasting comments, *War Dogs* frames the art of war as one of business, in which each soldier carries thousands of dollars on hand any given day, and the United States needs to procure those weapons and gear from independent contractors. Efraim has found his way into the market with his company, AEY, a Scarface poster over his desk like in a dorm room. Of course, Efraim's explanation to David about the process is heavily expositional, but comes with bro-speak that plays sincerely to their age: "I'm the fattest, most retarded kid," Efraim explains to David when contextualizing how AEY still has a shot against massive winners, similar to when their former classmates all received trophies for participation.

As Efraim guides David towards big paydays that involve buying from weapons distributors and winning bids chosen by the Pentagon, *War Dogs* maintains a key distance from its characters, observing them in the way that Martin Scorsese did with Jordan Belfort in *The Wolf of Wall Street* (2013), or Michael Bay did with his similar foray into the American dream, *Pain & Gain* (2013).

What starts as a dark comedy about boys in power then becomes a boring drama about being an adult, with Philips struggling to pinpoint what interests him so much in the story. As David and Efraim get more successful and their business reaches a peak deal, Philips is aesthetically stuck to present the process of how a massive deal imploded. His filmmaking reveals its limits, in which the cinematography is uninspired aside from a gray tint to the frigid setting of Albania, the setting of their biggest deal yet and inevitable downfall. The soundtrack proves a key weakness, using some of the most profoundly clichéd cues in American movies: a flying montage kicks off with Iggy Pop's "The Passenger," a Las Vegas scene prominently includes the explosive introductory horns of Dean Martin's "Ain't That a Kick

in the Head," and even the climax where everything collapses is accompanied with slow motion and The Who's "Behind Blue Eyes."

As the film reaches its first half, it is no coincidence that David's wife Iz, played by Ana de Armas, is disarmed from her power of opposition within the story, despite her albeit cheap usage to humanize David as a family man who needs to stop lying. The film's first half has her symbolizing a force of moral questioning, especially with relatives that are said to be in the war. But once David and Iz are shown inside a new beachside high-rise, she is muted, all the more obvious to how the movie drops its own interrogation of its subjects.

A bright light within this story is the chemistry between Teller and Hill, two actors who understand the male aggression and power they are working with. Teller is a strong fit for someone who could be roped into the macho success of selling guns, just as much as an original self-professed loser who gives massages. Coming off the high from his career-best performance in *The Wolf of Wall Street*, Hill is a sharp sell for the morally simple but emotionally complicated Efraim, with the actor endowing the character with a bizarre exhale of a cackle that provides levity throughout the movie.

Once known by its original article title, "Arms and the Dudes," Phillip's passion project becomes more of a missed opportunity, but by his own doing. His knowledge of what makes white men ridiculous keeps this story floating, especially as Hill's Efraim exemplifies a boyish selfishness by the movie's spectacular whiff of an ending. But the filmmaking here speaks for itself, showing that he continues to be a director with some ideas but is carried in great part by the people he enlists to embody them.

Nick Allen

CREDITS

Efraim Diveroli: Jonah Hill
David Packouz: Miles Teller
Iz Packouz: Ana de Armas
Ralph Slutsky: Kevin Pollak
Henry Girard: Bradley Cooper
Marlboro: Shaun Toub
Origin: United States
Language: English
Released: 2016
Production: Bradley Cooper, Mark Gordon, Todd Phillips; released by Green Hat Films, Joint Effort, The Mark Gordon Co.
Directed by: Todd Phillips
Written by: Todd Phillips; Stephen Chin; Jason Smilovic

Cinematography by: Lawrence Sher
Music by: Cliff Martinez
Sound: Cameron Frankley
Editing: Jeff Groth
Art Direction: Desma Murphy
Costumes: Michael Kaplan
Production Design: Bill Brzeski
MPAA rating: R
Running time: 114 minutes

REVIEWS

Bahr, Lindsay. *Associated Press*. August 17, 2016.
Brody, Richard. *New Yorker*. August 21, 2016.
Chang, Justin. *Los Angeles Times*. August 18, 2016.
Hornaday, Ann. *Washington Post*. August 18, 2016.
Jones, J.R. *Chicago Reader*. August 18, 2016.
Nicholson, Amy. *MTV*. August 20, 2016.
Seitz, Matt Zoller. *RogerEbert.com*. August 17, 2016.
VanDenBurgh, Barbara. *Arizona Republic*. August 18, 2016.
Vishnevetsky, Ignatiy. *The A.V. Club*. August 18, 2016.
Zacharaek, Stephanie. *Time*. August 18, 2016.

QUOTES

Efraim Diveroli: "Everyone's fighting over the same pie and ignoring the crumbs. I live off crumbs."

TRIVIA

The film is based on a true story.

AWARDS

Nominations:

Golden Globes 2017: Actor--Mus./Comedy (Hill)

WARCRAFT

> *Two worlds. One destiny.*
> —Movie tagline

Box Office: $47.4 Million

Duncan Jones' *Warcraft* is the type of imploding star that comes only a few times in a decade. More comparable to recent instant cult oddities like *John Carter* (2012) than the crop of lazy cash-in video game adaptations, it's a fascinating mess, but nowhere near the boondoggle that so many writers and fans alike have gleefully labeled it. It's a film that even with the built-in audience of one of the biggest video game franchises in the world, still feels entirely counterintuitive to megaplex success. And as such, there are numerous times where the film appears to only be preaching to the converted—a big budget adaptation where pieces of mythology dot every corner of the frame, but the tableaus are hardly ever gateways for new fans.

A game franchise with beginnings as a seminal real-time strategy series before expanding into a global phenomenon as an Massively Multiplayer Online game and card game, *Warcraft* doesn't just have the sterling expectations of the games, but the difficulty of presenting mountains of lore in a digestible package. From that viewpoint, the film is a failure and the rare fantasy story that would actually improve with more exposition dumps. But even when it fails, there's evidence of a valiant attempt, or at least, fragments of adventurous but unfulfilled ideas.

Jones and Charles Leavitt's screenplay tries to streamline the multitudinous dynamics of the game's world into two neatly oppositional factions—the humans and the orcs, who each have their own moral codes and social mores. There is a heavy quality slant towards the orc story for reasons related to both character development and a general vagueness in the human storyline. But, unusually for a film that metes out so few explanations, *Warcraft* is not afraid to repeatedly imply that there's also quite a bit happening off-screen, ranging from unarticulated motivations for major characters to unaddressed political in-fighting.

The main story is not easily summarized, but it revolves around a sorcerer named Gul'dan (Daniel Wu) who uses a dark magic called the fel to allow the orc race to use interdimensional portals to come to Azeroth, a planet where humans and many other fantasy species live. Upon arriving, the orcs immediately attack nearby settlements, drawing the attentions of the world, including the Stormwind Kingdom where the majority of the film's characters live.

From there, Jones' film divides the runtime between the inhabitants of the Stormwind Kingdom who are looking for a way to live peacefully or remove the orcs, and the orc camp, where Durotan (Toby Kebbell) and his clan have become increasingly suspicious of Gul'dan's motives and the true nature of the fel. The human's story is far less direct, focusing on Anduin (Travis Fimmel), a military commander, who teams up with a delinquent young mage named Khadgar (Ben Schnetzer) to find Medivh (Ben Foster), an ancient guardian of the land who has mysterious knowledge of the fel.

The best parts of the film inevitably have almost nothing to do with this convoluted main story, and are instead about the ways that different species interact with each other. At its best, the best analog for the orcs storyline may be the *Planet of the Apes* reboots in terms of both their reliance on CGI and the narrative concentration on primal but nuanced world views.

Durotan, in particular, provides the film with the closest thing to a soul in his complicated personal conflict between his inborn belief that violence is the only answer, and the need to cooperate with humans to help his people.

The human story, on the other hand, is plagued by a nearly universal sense of lethargy in both the performances and the listless storytelling. Fimmel brings a hopped-up energy to the human faction, but he's surrounded by actors whose characters seem defined more by their position than any dominant personality qualities.

The usually reliable Dominic Cooper brings a blandly noble essence to a superfluous role as the Stormwind king while the usually hyperactive Foster is deeply somnolent as the guardian and Schnetzer is firmly in the irritating sidekick niche. Garona (Paula Patton) a human/orc hybrid is the saving grace in the human storyline, bringing an intriguing tension as a character with allegiances to both sides. But it's undeniable that the film's pacing takes a hit nearly every time it returns to the humans.

And yet even with the numerous storytelling issues, there's something admirable about *Warcraft* and its ambitions to just go for it against any expectations of intimidating audiences, or looking cool. *Warcraft*'s visual style isn't the usual grimdark medieval milieu of an en vogue fantasy series like *Game of Thrones*.

The film is flamboyant with candy-colored creatures, ornate purple armors, and sorcery that's unabashedly artificial. And Jones and an army of visual effects specialists have rendered this world with an incredible level of detail and scale. Akin to the roving mouse in a strategy game, Jones regularly zooms out from an environment and switches to another set of characters, and while it's often jarring, it both deftly communicates the size of the world and the feel of a video game.

Warcraft isn't a success by traditional cinematic standards, and it's often a slog, but it's the work of a creator with a vision. That vision isn't always clear, and it's no doubt rough around the edges, but it's an ambitious failure that will be studied for decades to come.

Michael Snydel

CREDITS

Anduin Lothar: Travis Fimmel
Garona: Paula Patton
Medivh: Ben Foster
Llane Wrynn: Dominic Cooper
Durotan/Antonidas: Toby Kebbell
Gul'dan: Daniel Wu

Khadgar: Ben Schnetzer
Origin: United States
Language: English
Released: 2016
Production: Stuart Fenegan, Alex Gartner, Jon Jashni, Charles Roven, Thomas Tull; released by Atlas Entertainment, Legendary Pictures Films L.L.C.
Directed by: Duncan Jones
Written by: Duncan Jones; Charles Leavitt
Cinematography by: Simon Duggan
Music by: Ramin Djawadi
Sound: Wylie Stateman
Music Supervisor: Peter Afterman; Margaret Yen
Editing: Paul Hirsch
Art Direction: Helen Jarvis
Costumes: Mayes C. Rubeo
Production Design: Gavin Bocquet
MPAA rating: PG-13
Running time: 123 minutes

REVIEWS

Chang, Justin. *Los Angeles Times*. June 9, 2016.
Dargis, Manohla. *New York Times*. June 9, 2016.
Grierson, Tim. *Popular Mechanics*. June 8, 2016.
Lemire, Christy. *RogerEbert.com*. June 10, 2016.
Nicholson, Amy. *MTV*. June 8, 2016.
Robinson, Tasha. *Verge*. June 9, 2016.
Scherstuhl, Alan. *Village Voice*. June 8, 2016.
Sims, David. *Atlantic*. June 10, 2016.
VanDerWerff, Todd. *Vox*. June 11. 2016.
Zacharek, Stephanie. *Time*. June 9, 2016.

QUOTES

Anduin Lothar: "I've spent more time protecting my king, than my own son. Does that make me loyal, or a fool?"

TRIVIA

An Orcish dialect was created for the film.

THE WAVE
(Bolgen)

It was only a matter of time.
—Movie tagline

One of the best surprises in the refreshingly well-constructed *The Wave* is the realization that, apparently, other countries are now starting to make American-style disaster movies better than Americans. This Norwegian thriller is a big-budget, widescreen Irwin Allen-inspired catastrophe flick, but, unlike recent stateside films like

2012 (2009) or *San Andreas* (2015), it does not subject its audience to clumsy, cloying sentimentality, or cartoonish levels of CGI. This is a grounded, tense journey with thrills that feel more earned and emotionally honest than almost anything in Roland Emmerich's filmography. It's in no way a perfect film, but it's smarter and savvier than a movie about escaping a giant wave needed to be, which one has to appreciate.

The Wave was the highest grossing movie in Norway the year it was released (2015), which isn't a shock. There is something undeniably cinematic about watching a large-scale, almost-impossible-to-imagine spectacle unfold before your eyes, and director Roar Uthaug smartly staged the disaster imagery within a picturesque location that would appeal to both Norwegian audiences and anyone internationally who just enjoys watching pretty places "go boom." In this case, the locale destined to be destroyed is Geiranger, a popular tourist region known for its gorgeous mountains and lakes. However, Uthaug uses news footage in the film's opening to let us know that there's always a potential for danger, even in a place so beautiful.

Thanks to the tight crevasses between the mountains—and the resort towns at their base—the region is constantly on guard for landslides and avalanches. Not only could such a slide destroy a town, but when all that debris lands in the Geiranger's idyllic lakes, the laws of water displacement tell us that you're going to get one hell of a big wave (hence the title). But not just any wave, this is something akin to similar disaster movies like *The Impossible* (2012) or *Deep Impact* (1998). The only way the resort towns can guard against such disasters are with Geiranger's series of geological warning centers, which is where we meet our hero Kristian (Kristoffer Joner).

The set-up is pure *Dante's Peak* (1997). Kristian is the lone geologist who sees the signs that something terrible is headed towards Geiranger, and it's up to him to warn as many people as he can and try to escape with the people he loves. What distinguishes *The Wave* is how expertly Uthaug balances the rising tensions and audience expectations. Audiences know "the wave" is coming—it's the title of the movie—so, rather than trying to shock or surprise us, Uthaug instead just focuses on making sure the slow burn to destruction feels authentic and earned.

And, while the opening drags a bit, he's largely successful. We meet Kristian on his last day in Geiranger. He's preparing to move his family to a new town. His son and daughter are in the car with him, getting ready to board a ferry, while his wife Idun (Ane Dahl Torp) works her last few days at a local hotel. Quickly, however, Kristian begins to realize that something is not

right. He's convinced that the area is primed and ready for an avalanche and, at the last minute, he turns away from the ferry and heads back to the office to plead his case again.

While Kristian works on his skeptical supervisors, Idun and their children say farewell to their old house and wait for Kristian at the hotel. Of course, Kristian was right about his suspicions, verified by a helicopter trip to the base of the mountain range in question. Kristian (and the audience) get to watch the mountains shift and crack, the subsequent avalanche, and the origins of the titular wave. As mentioned, the first act could be leaner and fresher—Uthaug is playing with some extremely well-worn material here—but, when *The Wave* shifts into "survival mode," that's when it really begins to distinguish itself.

Kristian's family swiftly splits into two groups to give the action more scope. Kristian, his young daughter Julia, and family friend Anna head for higher ground in Kristian's car, while Idun helps evacuate the guests at the hotel and looks for their son Sondre (Jonas Hoff Oftebro), who's gone missing. It's a smart decision—one goes high, one goes low—that allows the filmmakers to really exploit different aspects of the oncoming tsunami in different ways.

And it's in those moments of survival where *The Wave* really shines. The overuse of CGI has robbed so many recent disaster thrillers of their weight. Nothing feels real. The danger is always at arm's length when any movie fan can easily tell that Dwayne Johnson is clearly running around a green-screen stage in Santa Monica rather than running away from a falling skyscraper. That's not to say that *The Wave* doesn't use any CGI (it does), but Uthaug's real achievement is finding ways to make the audience believe that his actors are truly in peril.

The ordeals that Kristian's family endure don't feel like cartoons. It looks like they are submerged in water and are scared as hell. While the director could have used more CGI to present more fantastic and over-the-top imagery, instead, Uthaug draws us in with claustrophobic moments in a car or in a narrow basement hallway. *The Wave* realizes that we've all seen bombastic disasters before, so it tries to show us the disaster less and make us feel it more. And it's a fairly successful strategy.

Is there anything revolutionary about *The Wave*? No. It's a movie about a really big wave. But it does remind us that big-budget spectacle can still be legitimately thrilling if it doesn't insult our intelligence while it tries to take our breath away.

Tom Burns

CREDITS

Kristian Eikjord: Kristoffer Joner
Idun Karlsen: Ane Dahl Torp
Sondre: Jonas Hoff Oftebro
Vibeke: Eili Harboe
Arvid Ovrebo: Fridtjov Saheim
Origin: Norway
Language: English, Norwegian
Released: 2015
Production: Are Heidenstrom, Martin Sundland; Fantefilm; released by Film Vast
Directed by: Roar Uthaug
Written by: John Kare Raake; Harald Rosenlow-Eeg
Cinematography by: John Christian Rosenlund
Music by: Magnus Beite
Sound: Christian Schaanning
Editing: Christian Siebenherz
Art Direction: Astrid Strom Astrup; Adrian Curelea
Costumes: Karen Fabritius Gram
Production Design: Lina Nordqvist
MPAA rating: R
Running time: 104 minutes

REVIEWS

D'Angelo, Mike. *The A.V. Club.* March 3, 2016.
Dargis, Manohla. *New York Times.* March 3, 2016.
Derakhshani, Tirdad. *Philadelphia Inquirer.* March 3, 2016.
Hartl, John. *Seattle Times.* March 3, 2016.
Morgenstern, Joe. *Wall Street Journal.* March 3, 2016.
Rainer, Peter. *Christian Science Monitor.* March 4, 2016.
Reed, Rex. *New York Observer.* March 3, 2016.
Rodriguez, Rene. *Miami Herald.* March 17, 2016.
Tallerico, Brian. *RogerEbert.com.* March 4, 2016.
Zacharek, Stephanie. *Time.* March 5, 2016.

TRIVIA

This film was the first disaster movie made in Norway and Scandinavia.

WEINER

Anthony Weiner was a young congressman on the cusp of higher office when a sexting scandal forced a humiliating resignation. Just two years later, he ran for Mayor of New York City, betting that his ideas would trump his indiscretions. He was wrong.
—Movie tagline

Box Office: $1.7 Million

If one was to compose a list of people who should never under any circumstances allow a documentary to be made about them and who should respond to any camera that comes their way by covering their face and running in the opposite direction, Anthony Weiner might not necessarily top it but he would certainly deserve a place in the top ten. With his astounding combination of ego, hubris, self-destructive tendencies, and not a single trace of sound judgment or self-awareness, this is a guy who is pretty much the textbook definition of the phrase "being your own worst enemy." And yet, demonstrating a lack of humility and foresight that even his most vociferous critics could not have possibly imagined that even he could possess, he nevertheless agreed to allow documentarians Josh Kriegman and Elyse Steinberg to follow him around for a film that he presumably hoped would help rehabilitate his tattered reputation. Not only did that not occur, the resulting film, *Weiner*, would prove to be the political equivalent of a hideous car accident that you can't help but continue to stare at in order to see how much grislier it could possibly get. If it had been produced entirely by his sworn enemies with the express point of destroying him in the most humiliating manner possible, the end result could not have been more damaging and embarrassing to him than this one.

Weiner, you will recall, was a congressman from New York City whose rise through the ranks of the Democratic party was brought to an abrupt halt when he was forced to resign from office after it came out that he was sending sexually explicit texts and photos to women he had met online that inevitably went public. Even more startling than this admission, in the eyes of many, was the fact that his then-pregnant wife, longtime Hillary Clinton aide Huma Abedin, decided to stick with him despite the embarrassing admissions. Faced with such a scandal—a silly one, to be sure, but one which suggests a colossal lack of judgment on someone's part—most people would be happy to simply fade from view but after spending a couple of years quietly trying to rehabilitate his reputation among his former constituents, Weiner decided in 2013 to make a run for mayor of New York City. Not only that, he invited Kriegman (a former aide) and Steinberg to tag along to document his campaign.

At first, it seems as if Weiner just might be able to pull off the seemingly impossible task—the steadily increasing crowds that he attracts appreciate his deft command of the key issues and respond angrily whenever his rival candidates or the media attempts to bring up his sordid past—but it isn't long before more salacious photos and texts emerge, all of which were sent after the initial scandal broke. Amazingly, Weiner thinks that he can somehow ride this one out and even enlists his wife, famous for her avoidance of the press, to not only help out with his campaign but to hold a press conference announcing that she will continue to stay by his side. While she responds to the gradually expanding scandal in the most cool and pragmatic ways imaginable (even advising another staffer about the dangers of leaving campaign headquarters, now swarming with photographers outside waiting for a shot of Weiner and/or Abedin, looking upset), Weiner responds to every new revelation (such as the revelation that his nom de tweet is the ridiculous "Carlos Danger") with increasing hostility towards everyone from the media to a guy in a bakery making snarky comments. To make matters worse, he is convinced that lashing out is just the ticket to turn around poll numbers that once had him leading the race but which have subsequently dropped to around 5% of the voters still in his corner. Perhaps he thinks that things cannot possibly get any worse, but as he soon discovers, they can and things do get worse as he spends his election night trying to dodge one of his textees, desperately trying to extend her fifteen minutes of fame.

For political junkies, this is pretty juicy stuff and Kriegman and Steinberg record it all with a fly on-the-wall approach that does adequately capture the combination of hectic intensity and grim futility of a political campaign in full self-destruct mode. Where the film fails, however, is the lack of curiosity that it demonstrates towards its subject and what it is that could possibly drive back to the same behavioral patterns that nearly destroyed him a couple of years earlier. At one point, we see him being interviewed by a cable news talking head who finally just blurts out an exasperated "What's wrong with you?" Inevitably, Weiner fumbles the question by snapping at his questioner in a way that makes him look unhinged (though he thinks he did great when he watches a tape of the confrontation later on) but the film might have been become something more than a political disaster movie if the filmmakers had pressed him on that very question themselves instead of giving him relative softballs that seem designed to engender otherwise unearned sympathy for a man who not only remains unrepentant for his behavior but seems confident that he can do anything and still somehow convince voters to stick with him. Even at the end, with his ambitions seemingly in tatters, he still does not appear to have learned anything from his experiences. (That would prove to be true as Weiner was caught once again sending questionable texts in the days leading up to the film's home video release.) At the very

end, Kriegman finally asks "Why have you let me film this?" and while the answer is illuminating in its opaqueness, it is ultimately too little too late.

Although she is never formally interviewed by the filmmakers, Huma Abedin proves to be the most fascinating and compelling character in the film, if only because her calm and collected nature stands in blessed relief to her husband's flailing at practically everyone but himself. On the one hand, she fully throws herself into Weiner's campaign because she knows the symbolic importance of her support in the eyes of voters and the media—she even finds herself calling donors to raise money for the campaign. As things progress and the revelations start coming out, her attitude becomes more complex as she goes back and forth between urging the other campaign staffers to keep up the hard work and regarding her husband with the kind of silent, eye-rolling disdain not seen since *The Office* went off the air. To be fair, she is trapped in an untenable position because any sign of marital discord will inevitably bring heat on her own boss at the time when she was beginning her presidential run. However, by the time the film ends, one wonders what exactly it would take to finally persuade her to leave her clueless and insanely narcissistic husband once and for all—of course, we would soon find out the answer to that particular question, but never mind.) Her perspective on these events might make for a follow-up film far more compelling but I suspect that she is just a little too smart and self-aware to ever allow that to happen. If only her husband took a page from her book—it might have resulted in a less interesting movie and he might still have a name and a career today.

Peter Sobczynski

CREDITS

Origin: United States

Language: English

Released: 2016

Production: Josh Kriegman, Elyse Steinberg; released by Motto Pictures

Directed by: Josh Kriegman; Elyse Steinberg

Written by: Josh Kriegman; Elyse Steinberg; Eli B. Despres

Cinematography by: Josh Kriegman

Music by: Jeff Beal

Sound: Tom Paul

Music Supervisor: Bruce Gilbert

Editing: Eli B. Despres

MPAA rating: R

Running time: 96 minutes

REVIEWS

Berkshire, Geoff. *Variety*. January 25, 2016.
DeFore, John. *Hollywood Reporter*. April 25, 2016.
Ebiri, Bilge. *Village Voice*. May 17, 2016.
Goldstein, Gary. *Los Angeles Times*. May 19, 2016.
Gray, Christopher. *Slant*. March 14, 2016.
Holden, Stephen. *New York Times*. May 19, 2016.
Hornaday, Ann. *Washington Post*. May 26, 2016.
Jenkins, Mark. *NPR*. May 20, 2016.
Klawans, Stuart. *Nation*. May 4, 2016.
Kohn, Eric. *IndieWire*. April 25, 2016.

QUOTES

Huma Abedin: "It's like living a nightmare."

TRIVIA

Anthony Weiner refused to endorse the film and said he did not intend to ever watch it.

AWARDS

Nominations:

British Acad. 2016: Feature Doc.
Directors Guild 2016: Documentary Director (Kriegman), Documentary Director (Steinberg)

WHEN THE BOUGH BREAKS

She's carrying more than just a secret.
—Movie tagline

Box Office: $29.7 Million

For three years now, Sony production company Screen Gems has catered a horror movie tradition that occurs on the second weekend of September, involving films that do not rely on the supernatural or even sequels. Films like *No Good Deed* (2014) and *The Perfect Guy* (2015) may appear insignificant with their TV-ready composition and lack of critic screenings, but the way they top the box office each opening weekend says otherwise. Other trends are curious too: These films are led by predominantly black casts, often with leads who have an awareness-claiming executive producer credit, and their scripts dance with the boundaries of passion and violent obsession. Unfailingly, they are polished productions of horrendous scripts that aim to seduce audiences with sexy, abusive stalkers.

The latest addition to this informal franchise is *When the Bough Breaks*, which boasts no good escapism

and a very imperfect sense of humanity. It is directed in large part by stimulating pieces: establishing shots of powerful skyscrapers or the interiors of a fancy home; close-ups of select PG-13 flesh. When it yearns for horror thrills, the "behind you!" beats are by-the-book. This would be fine if the story was not so hideous, this time replacing the violent masculinity of characters played previously by Idris Elba (*No Good Deed*) and Michael Ealy (*The Perfect Guy*) with the tale of a villainous pregnant woman seeking to destroy a marriage and their last hope at having a baby, all to see if the viewer has more taste than the film itself.

Steered by a wall-to-wall score that instructs the exact tone of a scene, *When the Bough Breaks* starts innocently enough, with a beautiful couple, John and Laura Taylor (Morris Chestnut and Regina Hall, respectively) who are trying to find the right surrogate mother. They have gone through three miscarriages and are on their last embryo. During the opening credits, they learn about Anna (Jaz Sinclair), a smiling young woman who loves the idea of having something that someone else wants. She has a shady fiancé, Mike (Theo Rossi), who helps her create the image of a nice young couple, so much that when Mike is arrested for beating Anna, she is invited to stay at the Taylors' beautiful New Orleans house, where an obsession suddenly flares within Anna. Anna is carrying their baby, but she wants to have John, too.

Despite the story's initially completely baffling but welcome focus on characters for a change, the movie is confused by the requirement of motivation, instead wanting to honor ideas of obsession while finding a way to get some dead body insert shots into the mix. A fun gap in all of this is the stated notion that the baby does not belong to the Taylors—ever, if Anna wishes—and it makes a pitch of Anna's mania essentially into that of a couple trying to snuff out the surrogate mother after failing to own her and then her baby. For these Screen Gems films that talk about personal boundaries, which are violated by evil, initially innocent people who take advantage of good will, now the viewer is meant to root for characters to take away a baby from a woman who is revealed to be a multi-foster home kid and survivor of sexual abuse. If she should get away from the couple with the baby without John somehow by her side, she is only entering a bleaker future with another life to take care of. The character trait of surrogate mother proves to be a terrible idea to create obsession with a person of close proximity; 2009's *Obsessed* (Steve Shill)—a Screen Gems movie too, starring Beyonce, Idris Elba, and an Ali Larter trying to get between them—does this much better by simply not overthinking its title.

Casting plays a key part in these films. It is not just in finding beautiful leads who make the experience go quicker but helping the viewer believe a smidgen of the hokum. In the case of *When the Bough Breaks*, Morris Chestnut and Regina Hall are excellent salespeople, imbuing sincerity into the characters and their progressively dumb actions, even going so far in the first act as to convince the audience that this drama will not eventually explode into a big ball of fire shortly after take-off. Hall, in particular, has a genuinely touching moment when she expresses the emotional pain of her miscarriages. "You start to hate your own body," she says, creating a sinking feeling in one's stomach this script does not deserve.

The wild card in the story is Jaz Sinclair, given an "and introducing" credit in the beginning. Her image of evil is made up of different attitudes, but it does not amount to a full character. She does not provide the believable shift from possibly innocent to possibly manipulated (by Mike) to then desperately obsessive. Her performance is oddly alien—literally, in that she tilts her head and observes John with the calculation of a Scarlett Johansson's extraterrestrial in *Under the Skin* (2013), the two of them robots seemingly trying to learn what is seductive. This is believably an editing fault in part—maybe there is a scene in which she bridges the different attitudes—but her character is not so much conflicted as cluttered.

Even with the cheapest of purposes, these Screen Gems projects are not just slick with their aesthetic, they are morally tasteless, which makes indulging in their campy tales all the more difficult. Previous installations featured abusive, obsessive men of intimidating physical presence, meant to be forbidden cocktails of sex and death—for the viewers, not for the characters who are decisions away from sexual assault or worse. Now the villain has changed genders and is treated like a bomb of which one don't know which wire to cut. Especially as it is stated out loud early on by John and Laura that perhaps Anna is just hormonal (they talk about her like she is a cat in heat), there is a bizarre connection to her aggressiveness involving those hormones, that of being violent and so procreant. By the force of sheer tastelessness, the movie succeeds in 1.) pregnant woman hormone-shaming and 2.) continuing the film series' aggressive lack of nuance, for the sake of letting psychos stimulate the audience and then get what is coming to them. While empathy is first to go in *When the Bough Breaks* and its Screen Gems predecessors, there is nothing good in its place.

Nick Allen

CREDITS

John Taylor: Morris Chestnut
Laura Taylor: Regina Hall
Anna Walsh: Jaz Sinclair
Todd Decker: Romany Malco
Mike Mitchell: Theo Rossi
Origin: United States
Language: English
Released: 2016
Production: Michael Lynne, Dylan Sellers, Robert Shaye; released by Screen Gems, Unique Features
Directed by: Jon Cassar
Written by: Jack Olsen
Cinematography by: David Moxness
Music by: John (Gianni) Frizzell
Sound: Steven Ticknor
Editing: Scott Powell
Costumes: Olivia Miles
Production Design: Chris Cornwell
MPAA rating: PG-13
Running time: 107 minutes

REVIEWS

Callahan, Dan. *TheWrap.* September 9, 2016.
Genzlinger, Neil. *New York Times.* September 9, 2016.
Goldstein, Gary. *Los Angeles Times.* September 9, 2016.
Hemphill, Jim. *Paste Magazine.* September 14, 2016.
Kupecki, Josh. *Austin Chronicle.* September 15, 2016.
Lane, Jim. *Sacramento News & Review.* September 15, 2016.
Leydon, Joe. *Variety.* September 9, 2016.
Linden, Sheri. *Hollywood Reporter.* September 10, 2016.
Orndorf, Brian. *Blu-ray.com.* September 9, 2016.
Rife, Katie. *The A.V. Club.* September 9, 2016.

TRIVIA

The three leads previously starred together in *Think Like A Man.*

WHISKEY TANGO FOXTROT

From the headlines to the front lines.
   —Movie tagline

Box Office: $23.1 Million

Journalists do not always have to make sense of the story they are covering. They just need to report the facts. This is especially true of those with the unenviable position on the outskirts of an armed conflict or a hostile region. Filmmakers, on the other hand, thrive on either having a point of view about their material or crafting a story with enough gray areas to allow the viewer to establish their own. Documentaries have often benefited from journalists offering a first-hand perspective from social issues at home to the battlefront abroad. Directors Glenn Ficarra and John Requa open the memoir-based *Whiskey Tango Foxtrot* with a party scene that quickly turns to confusion in the aftermath of yet another bombing in the Middle East. What starts as a grabbing statement similar to David O. Russell's opening to *Three Kings* (1999) devolves quickly into a metaphor for the film itself and its failed attempts to be the next *M*A*S*H* (1970) or *Good Morning, Vietnam* (1987).

During Operation Enduring Freedom, American journalist Kim Baker (Tina Fey) sees the opportunity to take an assignment in Afghanistan as a potential boost to her career. Though hardly a diva, the living conditions make her immediately regret her decision. One of her flatmates, BBC correspondent Tanya Vanderpoel (an underutilized Margot Robbie) helps make her a bit more at ease by making it clear that the women have as much power as the men, at least over their own bodies. Photographer Iain MacKelpie (Martin Freeman) is happy to take a pass at anyone within range and Marine General Hollanek (Billy Bob Thornton) would be happy if she stayed away from his troops to prevent her from enticing them to talk or otherwise.

With aid from her local fixer and translator, Fahim (Christopher Abbott), Kim begins to adapt to the surroundings as just another job. After catching her boyfriend with another woman, she feels no need to rush home and presses on. She develops a source in government official Ali Massoud Sadiq (Alfred Molina) whose flirtatious manner makes him just another man in the region. While observing American troops' role in winning hearts and minds (also referred to as "the two best places to shoot something,"), Kim discovers how Afghan women are willing to sabotage those efforts just to have a little time for themselves. After flashing forward a few years through numerous leads and stories that often lead to nothing, Kim asks the very pointed question, "How does this end," though she directs it to the wrong person and toward the wrong subject, just as the film does.

Based on the memoir by Kim Barker (changed to Baker for the film) called *The Taliban Shuffle: Strange Days in Afghanistan and Pakistan*, this is a film often in search of its own purpose and taking too many left turns for its own good to establish any momentum. It may be reflective of the everyday stumble to find a story that interests one's journalistic fervor that also matches a newsroom's desire back home to air it. So precisely what is the story here? Is it one woman's professional and personal growth in a boy's club that has often ignored the religious and political implications that have suppressed the women of that country? That would be a great place to begin and for a brief period Robert Carlock's screenplay feels ready to embrace that approach before backing off to remind audiences that Afghanistan is generally someplace they would rather not visit, never mind live. This is a foregone conclusion that every viewer has already accepted well before a gun is seen or the first foreign dialect is raised to shouting level.

"As much as people love the troops, they just don't want to watch them on the air anymore," Baker is told, which could have led to further indictments of corporate journalism but is merely an explanation as to why she did not get the big job she was hoping for. Another reason could be that Baker just is not that good of a reporter. She is barely that interesting of a character, beginning the film aloof enough to not know what she is getting herself into and ending by preparing the meal for a wounded soldier she believes she is responsible for. The veteran sums it up as best he can with a simplistic "what if" speech that sounds like Carlock studied Philip Seymour Hoffman's Zen master proverb from *Charlie Wilson's War* (2007), a film that expertly balanced the absurdity of war politics with the cost of the human suffering.

The casting of Tina Fey (who also produced the film) suggests that Barker's story contained enough irony for satiric purposes, a specialty of the multi-talented actress and writer going back to her days anchoring fake news on *Saturday Night Live*. An awkward sexual encounter may delight fans of *30 Rock*'s Liz Lemon and even her time in a full-body burqa inspires a humorous variation on the male gaze. But it is all left for naught as the film constantly downshifts into less-interesting storylines and feeble attempts to allow Fey the opportunity to play drama until everyone catches up to her initial assertion that she "doesn't have a good reason for being there."

Erik Childress

CREDITS

Kim Baker: Tina Fey
Tanya Vanderpoel: Margot Robbie
Iain MacKelpie: Martin Freeman
Ali Massoud Sadiq: Alfred Molina
General Hollanek: Billy Bob Thornton
Fahim Ahmadzai: Christopher Abbott
Origin: United States
Language: English
Released: 2016
Production: Tina Fey; Paramount Pictures Corp.; released by Little Stranger

Directed by: Glenn Ficarra; John Requa
Written by: Robert Carlock
Cinematography by: Xavier Perez Grobet
Music by: Nick Urata
Music Supervisor: Jason Ruder
Editing: Jan Kovac
Art Direction: Derek Jensen; Elise Viola
Costumes: Lisa Lovaas
Production Design: Beth Mickle
MPAA rating: R
Running time: 112 minutes

REVIEWS

Bell, Josh. *Las Vegas Weekly*. March 3, 2016.
Berardinelli, James. *ReelViews*. March 4, 2016.
Gire, Dann. *Daily Herald*. March 3, 2016.
Hornaday, Ann. *Washington Post*. March 3, 2016.
Minow, Nell. *Beliefnet*. March 3, 2016.
Nicholson, Amy. *MTV*. March 3, 2016.
O'Hehir, Andrew. *Salon.com*. March 3, 2016.
Renshaw, Scott. *Salt Lake City Weekly*. March 4, 2016.
Robinson, Tasha. *The Verge*. March 4, 2016.
Tobias, Scott. *NPR*. March 4, 2016.

QUOTES

Specialist Coughlin: "There's only so much any of us have any control of, good or bad. If you didn't learn that in Afghanistan, you were not paying attention."

TRIVIA

The title of the film is military phonetic alphabet for--and an allusion to--the abbreviation WTF.

WHY HIM?

Of all the guys his daughter could have chosen...
—Movie tagline

Box Office: $60.3 Million

A marriage at the center of your movie stirs a pot of potentially suppressed emotions and insecurities that makes for excellent comedy. When people are on edge, personae break down and pretense becomes a life raft. Our social fight-or-flight responses peak with those we love, because the most threatening thing most of us face in our lives is the danger of social failure and rejection. If one fails to live up to expectations, they will be alone. These psychologically morbid fears respond especially well to the lowest-brow humor.

Why Him? continues a theme found in *I Love You, Man* (2009) that director John Hamburg (also writer of

Meet the Parents [2000]) is so familiar with—that of approaching male relationships through a historically romantic Hollywood nucleus. Hamburg's circuitous route to his favorite topic (male insecurity) comes, like in *I Love You, Man,* in those confusing and hazy days pre-marriage.

When an enterprising healthcare student (Zoey Deutch, completely winning and still deserving of meatier roles since her supporting turn in the similarly punctuated *Everybody Wants Some!!* [2016] earlier this year) convinces her family to spend Christmas (another emotional prime time for comedy) with her boyfriend, the profane and inked Silicon Valley CEO Laird Mayhew (James Franco, at his most gleefully oily and unpretentious), the culture shock conducts like a blow dryer in a bathtub. Her father, the owner of a dying printing company (Bryan Cranston playing between his fatherly *Malcolm in the Middle* role and his put-upon, darker shade of *Breaking Bad* comedy), finds himself the focus of the most affection as Mayhew aims to propose with his blessing. An ultimatum is given and a quest is undertaken.

The worlds-colliding jokes come fast and often, starting with Franco's virtuosic swearing and unbridled enthusiasm for sexual candor. Few actors could handle this film's sheer wordcount of emphatic swearing while retaining an ounce of charm. Franco runs through a Holden Caulfield vocabulary like he's in *The Sound of Music,* arms wide and any filler words replaced by those with four letters. His infectious grin and bright eyes never hint at anger or guile, creating an inner juxtaposition as charmingly asymmetrical as the film's plot.

Cranston's initial shock, then growing frustration and defeatedness at his daughter's relationship choice, comes from a true place of empathetic cultural divide. There are commonalities beneath their sweater vest and tattoo-revealing tank top, but the difference between communication ethos is squeezed into its most dense concentration. A salesman, a smooth-talking pupil of Dale Carnegie, versus one of the programming new money who has never had an understanding of "professionalism" because he has had marketable skills since immaturity.

The divide is generational and, in some aspects, class-driven. Deutch's character slowly fades from the film, as her love is not contested by the pair (rightfully so, as the film makes its case for her autonomy late in the final act), and the possible father-son relationship comes to a head. Mayhew's childhood paternal lack created a void that his overbearing filterlessness yearns to fill, overperforming to impress Cranston's character like the foolish wooer in a typical romantic comedy. His love is not quite the opposite of Freudian (though the father-daughter sexual insecurity is certainly and cleverly present) but a more postmodern need, which, when siphoned through the strange world of the uber-rich (complete with deconstructed meals and a hilarious groundskeeper Gustav, played by Keegan-Michael Key), reveals a complex and deep well of humor.

Financial and carnal insecurities fit into jokes about sexual oversharing and technological ineptitude (especially with a bidet-equipped toilet that I swear has been recycled for a decade) while the set designers stuff every frame with an artistic gag. The film pops even when the camera is not ogling hilariously-labelled portraits of animals *in flagrante delicto*, with the modern architecture used to frame both its quietest conversations and rowdiest ragers inside the ever-present juxtaposition of Silicon Valley excess and Midwest conservatism.

The limited pop culture references and focus on its talented supporting players (especially the other family members, Megan Mullally as the mom and the wonderfully earnest Griffin Gluck as the little brother) give *Why Him?* a charm that does not bury its insight, beyond a closing cameo already meant as a bonding throwback to everyone's days as a romantic adolescent. While the film is not quite as nuanced or boundary-pushing as Hamburg's finest directorial effort, it's a continuation of the director's fascination with uncommon relationships in seemingly common comedic stories.

Jacob Oller

CREDITS

Laird Mayhew: James Franco
Ned Fleming: Bryan Cranston
Stephanie Fleming: Zoey Deutch
Barb Fleming: Megan Mullally
Lou Dunne: Cedric the Entertainer
Gustav: Keegan-Michael Key
Scotty Flemming: Griffin Gluck
Origin: United States
Language: English
Released: 2016
Production: Stuart Cornfeld, Dan Levine, Shawn Levy, Ben Stiller; released by Twentieth Century Fox Film Corp.; Red Hour Films, 21 Laps
Directed by: John Hamburg
Written by: John Hamburg; Ian Helfer
Cinematography by: Kris Kachikis
Music by: Theodore Shapiro
Sound: Andrew DeCristofaro
Music Supervisor: Liza Richardson
Editing: William Kerr
Art Direction: Gary Warshaw

Costumes: Leesa Evans
Production Design: Matthew Holt
MPAA rating: R
Running time: 111 minutes

REVIEWS

Catsoulis, Jeannette. *New York Times.* December 22, 2016.
Duralde, Alonso. *The Wrap.* December 12, 2016.
Ehrlich, David. *IndieWire.* December 12, 2016.
Hassenger, Jesse. *The A.V. Club.* December 19, 2016.
Jones, Preston. *Fort Worth Star-Telegram.* December 22, 2016.
Lapin, Andrew. *New York Magazine.* December 19, 2016.
Lemire, Christy. *RogerEbert.com.* December 20, 2016.
Pickett, Leah. *Chicago Reader.* December 22, 2016.
Walsh, Katie. *Tribune News Service.* December 16, 2016.
Wheeler, Brad. *Globe and Mail.* December 23, 2016.

QUOTES

Ned Fleming: "I mean, what in God's name is a double dicker?"

TRIVIA

The cast was encouraged to improvise; that led to 240 hours of film which was trimmed down to 90 minutes.

WIENER-DOG

Todd Solondz has made a career out of making great movies that nobody feels comfortable recommending. His films are designed to provoke, to haunt, and to make the audience feel uncomfortable in a way that can be off-putting, even to the most jaded film enthusiast. His films are purposely hard-to-love, often because of the nihilistic tone at their center. Characters react indifferently to tragedies, in which children and animals are not immune. At times, those same tragedies are looked at as an inevitability of life and they come with a feeling of hopelessness. Despite that, his films are mostly comedies, but there exists a feeling of dread throughout them that makes the laughter almost unbearable. Often, his films antagonize the audience to the point of walk-outs.

Wiener-Dog might be his most accessible movie yet, but that is only if one turns the film off just before the end credits, and even before that it can be hard to take. The ads and the poster have most certainly given the wrong impression to many filmgoers who paid admission believing they would see a humorous and quirky film about dog ownership. At times, the film plays with the notion of its audience getting a little too comfortable in their seats by setting up an unthinkable scenario or two and forcing the audience to react to it. Yes, the dog is cute and gets lots of screen time, but that will not in any way be the take-away from the experience. The film is designed to leave the viewer shaken, disturbed, and uncertain about whether or not to let their pet out of the house.

The film tells four separate stories, all of them connected by an adorable dachshund who goes from owner to owner. The film starts in a kennel, where she gets adopted by a father against the wishes of his wife. Dan (Tracy Letts) and Dina (Julie Delpy) have a boy named Remi (Keaton Nigel Cooke) who has a terminal illness. Dan gets him a dog and they immediately form a strong bond. Remi has many questions about death and the hard life dogs sometimes have. His mother does not mince words and tells him horrifying stories of dog rape and how death is a natural part of life. Remi's father talks to him about training a dog and how the dog's will must be broken in order for it to be properly house-trained.

The second story concerns two recurring characters from Solondz's most well-known film, *Welcome to the Dollhouse* (1996). Dawn Wiener (Greta Gerwig) is now a veterinarian and she steals the dachshund away just before she is about to be put to sleep. She runs into Brandon (Kieran Culkin), who is about to take a road trip to make amends with his family. Dawn feels an attraction to him, much as she did in *Dollhouse*, in spite of his off-putting creepiness. They make their way to his brother's house and Dawn learns of Brandon's difficult past with drugs and family members who have no idea what has happened in the past few years.

The third story concerns a film teacher named Dave Schmerz (Danny DeVito) who has been a faculty member at a prestigious film school for too many years now, but without tenure. His students have little interest in his screenwriting advice, and his health is failing. While trying to score a film deal for a screenplay he wrote, his job and reputation hang in the balance. The final story concerns a troubled young woman named Zoe (Zosia Mamet) and her artist friend named Fantasy (Michael James Shaw). Zoe visits her ailing grandmother Nana (Ellen Burstyn), who knows full well that Zoe needs money. Nana undergoes a bizarre existential moment of crisis, while dealing with the visit.

Each of these stories plays with the audience's expectations and puts the viewer through the mill during many key scenes. One moment focuses on a long stream of dog diarrhea for an interminable length while Clare de Lune plays in the background. Often, the dog does not play an active role in the story until the very end, at which time Solondz pulls the rug out from under the audience and forces the viewer to confront some harsh truths about human behavior. But Solondz also divides these four stories with an intermission sequence designed to put the viewer at ease before the inevitable tragedies that unfold later on. Those familiar with his work will know they are being had while the uninitiated will have no idea what to make of it, but will certainly find it adorable.

The unifying theme of the film is, of course, death. Mainly, the film concerns characters who are the victims of their own demise; people slowly killing themselves without even realizing it. The final moment in the film puts the capper on the idea that humans often live like many of God's creatures who neglect to look around for possible consequences for their actions and who lack the instinct to know better. Solondz makes his point clearly and in the only way he knows how: By confronting it head-on and without a filter. His nihilism has been a detriment to his films in the past (*Storytelling* [2001] is a prime example), but here it serves the themes in a way that makes it compelling and worthy of the audience's sympathy.

Solondz assembles one of his strongest ensemble casts along with cinematographer Ed Lachman, who gives the film his distinctly-tinted and carefully-framed visual look that perfectly complements Solondz's confrontational style and subject matter. DeVito, Culkin, and Burstyn give stand-out performances while Gerwig relies a little too heavily on being the typical indifferent and slump-shouldered Solondz archetype. With its dark and despairing outlook (and the darkest of all endings), *Wiener-Dog* has many uncomfortable laughs and cringe-worthy observations on human behavior. Like most of Solondz's work, though, one takes a big risk when sitting down to watch it.

Collin Souter

CREDITS

Remi: Keaton Nigel Cooke
Dan: Tracy Letts
Dina: Julie Delpy
Dawn Wiener: Greta Gerwig
Brandon: Kieran Culkin
Dave Schmerz: Danny DeVito
Zoe: Zosia Mamet
Fantasy: Michael James Shaw
Nana: Ellen Burstyn
Origin: United States
Language: English
Released: 2016
Production: Megan Ellison, Christine Vachon; released by Annapurna Pictures, Killer Films

Directed by: Todd Solondz
Written by: Todd Solondz
Cinematography by: Edward Lachman
Music by: James Lavino
Sound: Rich Bologna
Music Supervisor: Michael Hill
Editing: Kevin Messman
Costumes: Amela Baksic
Production Design: Akin McKenzie
MPAA rating: R
Running time: 88 minutes

REVIEWS

Chang, Justin. *Los Angeles Times*. June 23, 2016.
Hartl, John. *Seattle Times*. June 30, 2016.
Howell, Peter. *Toronto Star*. July 7, 2016.
Keough, Peter. *Boston Globe*. June 30, 2016.
Merry, Stephanie. *Washington Post*. June 30, 2016.
O'Malley, Sheila. *RogerEbert.com*. June 24, 2016.
Scott, A. O. *New York Times*. June 23, 2016.
Stalking, Allen. *New York Daily News*. June 24, 2016.
VanDenbergh, Barbara. *Arizona Republic*. July 7, 2016.
Wolfe, April. *Village Voice*. June 23, 2016.

TRIVIA

In less than a week, Keaton Nigel Cooke learned how to play "Clair De Lune" by Debussy on flute.

THE WILD LIFE
(Robinson Crusoe)

Adventure's in full swing!
—Movie tagline

Box Office: $8 Million

For parents who are looking for a film that they can deploy as a virtual babysitter to keep their young children occupied for ninety-one minutes without warping their fragile little minds with anything even slightly unsavory, *The Wild Life*, at least on the surface, would seem to fit the bill. It is rated PG for "mild action/peril and some rude humor" and rest assured that both the action/peril and the rude humor are as mild as can be. Moreover, it isn't especially loud, it isn't jam-packed with instantly-dated pop-culture references or current pop tunes and it is blessedly free of any jokes involving any of the ickier bodily functions. However, if one were looking at it solely in terms of what those kids might actually get out of it other than ninety-odd minutes of

distraction, that list would end up being as disturbingly empty as the movie itself. Here is a film that has absolutely nothing of value to offer viewers of any age—no excitement, wit, intelligence, style or any of the other elements that even the youngest viewers can still pick up on even if they don't quite understand what such things are as of yet—and it desecrates a perfectly viable piece of classic literature in the bargain. Not only would children be better off from a cultural perspective by staring at a blank screen for the same amount of time as this film lasts, they would probably be far more entertained by such a sight.

A question. When you read Daniel Defoe's *Robinson Crusoe* for the first time, did you think to yourself "Gee, this story of survival is pretty compelling but man, wouldn't it have been better if the whole thing had been told from the perspective of a talking parrot who dreams of leaving his isolated island in order to achieve his dream of finally seeing the outside world that he is positive is out there somewhere?" That is the hook for this particular take on the tale from the Belgian animation studio nWave, the home of such efforts as *Fly Me to the Moon 3D* (2008), *A Turtle's Tale: Sammy's Adventures* (2010), and *Thunder and the House of Magic* (2013). The real hero this time around is Mak (David Howard Thornton), a dreamer of a parrot who has grown disenchanted with living on a remote island with his perfectly content animal friends and yearns for some kind of concrete proof that there really is more to the world than the little patch that they are living upon. That proof finally washes up on shore one day in the form of a shipwreck containing neophyte seaman Crusoe (Yuri Lowenthal) and his faithful dog, Aynsley.

The other animals are terrified of these intruders and try to scare them away but eventually Mak is able to befriend the new arrivals and Crusoe even goes so far as to rename his new friend, Tuesday, a bit that will go over the heads of younger viewers and cause older ones to think "Ah, so that's how they are getting around that." The other animals eventually come around and before long, they are helping the all-thumbs Crusoe build the shelter and other amenities that will allow him to survive for the long haul. (Yes, the film does early on answer the question of why Crusoe doesn't simply eat the animals instead of banking on their potential construction skills.) Alas, a couple of especially nasty cats with a personal vendetta against Crusoe and Aynsley—don't ask—also survive the shipwreck and they try to mess things up for Crusoe and his new friends as well. Having been exiled from the island for a while, they, along with their equally vile progeny, mount a final attack that finds Crusoe and all the various animals fighting it out while sliding down a ginormous water slide-sized aqueduct while pandemonium reigns.

The idea of recounting a well-known story through the perspective of a hitherto unknown side character is not an unheard of--one in the annals of animated films, as anyone who saw the charming Disney short *Ben and Me* (1953) can attest, However, *The Wild Life* is a film that has so little to offer that reviewing it is almost impossible because there is barely anything of substance to discuss, either pro or con. The animation is utterly undistinguished—it is bright and colorful enough (especially if you avoid the 3D option) but there is not a single image that sticks out in the memory when it ends. The characters are just as slight and shabby—little more than composites of behavioral tics lifted wholesale from characters from Pixar movies—and the voice work by the no-name cast does precious little to give them any sense of life or ingenuity. The storyline is really terrible—even if you can somehow overlook the trashing of the original book, you are still left with a narrative where the jokes fall flat, the platitudes are utterly laughable, and incidents just happen without much rhyme, reason, or flow before the whole thing just ends abruptly, though probably not abruptly enough for most viewers.

Upon reflection, however, it should be noted that there are a couple of elements in the film that right-thinking parents might well object to exposing their children to, though most right-thinking parents will presumably be giving this one a wide berth in the first place. For starters, even though the film as a whole is as innocuous as can be, the aforementioned troublemaking cats are portrayed in an exceptionally nasty manner that might well prove to be too disturbing to younger or more sensitive viewers, especially if their families happen to have cats as pets. Not only are they portrayed as irretrievably mean and vicious throughout, they even, in the only legitimately surprising moment in the entire film (for all the wrong reasons), manage to flat-out kill Crusoe's loyal pet dog. Even more bizarrely, there is a sequence in which Crusoe attempts to figure out how to load and shoot a gun and when he is having problems, it actually shows him peering down the barrel of the loaded gun to try to figure out what is wrong. As anyone who has seen an Elmer Fudd cartoon can attest, this can be funny under the right circumstances but in a film aimed squarely at the youngest of viewers, such an inclusion comes across as dangerously irresponsible.

Demonstrating all the charm and artistic intent of a cheapo public domain DVD one might find for sale at the checkout line at Walgreens, *The Wild Life* is about as bottom-of-the-barrel as one can get when it comes to children's entertainment. Not only is it terrible in its own right, it is so devoid of entertainment value that it

could potentially put little kids off of movies and their potential to entertain and inform entirely. Although it did not become a box-office success by any means, the fact that such a thing could actually get a major release when a truly visionary animated film like *April and the Extraordinary World* (2015) is relegated to the art-house ghetto is too depressing to contemplate. One thing is for sure, when people get together to talk about the movies that they would like to have with them if they were ever stuck on a desert island, *The Wild Life* is unlike to be much of a factor.

Peter Sobczynski

CREDITS

Voice of Robinson Crusoe: Yuri Lowenthal
Voice of Mak/Tuesday: David Howard Thornton
Voice of Papagei Dienstag: Kaya Yanar
Voice of Tapir Rosie: Cindy aus Marzahn
Voice of Ziegenbock Zottel: Dieter Hallervorden
Origin: United States
Language: English, French, German
Released: 2016
Directed by: Vincent Kesteloot; Ben Stassen
Written by: Domonic Paris
Music by: Ramin Djawadi
MPAA rating: PG
Running time: 91 minutes

REVIEWS

Brady, Tara. *Irish Times.* August 8, 2016.
Debruge, Peter. *Variety.* March 27, 2016.
Hunter, Allan. *The List.* May 4, 2016.
Merry, Stephanie. *Washington Post.* September 9, 2016.
Mintzer, Jordan. *Hollywood Reporter.* March 31, 2016.
Orndorf, Brian. *Blu-ray.com.* September 8, 2016.
Puig, Claudia. *TheWrap.* September 8, 2016.
Russo, Tom. *Boston Globe.* September 8, 2016.
Stewart, Sara. *New York Post.* September 8, 2016.
Verongos, Helen T. *New York Times.* September 8, 2016.

TRIVIA

The film was originally released at a screening at Kings Dominion Parks.

THE WITCH
(The VVitch: A New-England Folktale)

Evil takes many forms.
—Movie tagline

Box Office: $25.1 Million

Its title seemingly augurs little more than a disposable genre exercise, but *The Witch* is a highly refined, slow-building work of primal tension, a chilly horror film that edges up to the supernatural but neither kowtows to convention nor tips into ridiculousness. The feature debut of writer/director Robert Eggers, the movie, a 17th-century period piece billed as a "New-England Folktale" in its title card, is instead characterized by genuine foreboding and a jagged emotionality—a representation and extension of the mortal stakes its God-fearing, ultra-religious characters feel. The end result is a mood piece that arrives at its scares seriously—not through jump-scare foley work or other emotional cattle-prodding, but the elongated evocation of unease and dread.

Rather improbably, distributor A24—who picked up the movie following its debut at the 2015 Sundance Film Festival—eschewed the seemingly smart, safe approach of a platform or limited market release, and opened *The Witch* wide, in more than 2,000 theaters in mid-February 2016. Its final theatrical domestic haul was more than $25 million, bolstered by an additional $14 million overseas—a not-inconsiderable sum for a work of mannered sophistication.

The film opens with William (Ralph Ineson), communally accused of blasphemy, being exiled from a Puritan plantation along with his entire family—wife Katherine (Kate Dickie), teenage daughter Thomasin (Anya Taylor-Joy), preteen son Caleb (Harvey Scrimshaw), young twins Mercy and Jonas (Ellie Grainger and Lucas Dawson), and baby Samuel. With an easy, unfussy economy, Eggers tracks the clan as they set up a new homestead on the edge of a forest with the family goat, Black Phillip, and prepare for harvest.

Unexplainable tragedy visits, however, when Samuel disappears from right in front of Thomasin while she is playing peek-a-boo with him. William assures the family it was a wolf that dragged Samuel away, but Thomasin is doubtful and Caleb additionally frets about the fate of his unbaptized younger brother's soul. Viewers, meanwhile, see glimpses of a grotesque witch from the nearby woods, performing bloody rituals. As more calamity befalls William's brood, the family comes unraveled.

After a fallow period in the late 1990s and stretching into the new millennium, the horror genre has experienced something of a rebirth recently, with franchises like *Paranormal Activity*, *Insidious*, and *Sinister* delivering steady earnings, and *The Conjuring* (2013) and its follow-up serving not only as reliable studio summer tentpoles (a prospect unthinkable a decade ago) but establishing lucrative spinoffs of their own. *The Witch*, however, is part of a steady, complementary stream of independent and arthouse horror, buoyed by

financiers who see in genre filmmaking a potential path to more lucrative returns.

Similar to Jennifer Kent's *The Babadook* (2014), Eggers' film for most of its running time relies more on psychological disquiet than gory shock, which no doubt accounts for its CinemaScore of "C-" amongst opening weekend theatrical filmgoers, primed as a younger, mainstream audience typically is for more desultory scares. And the film's dialogue is delivered exclusively in old-fashioned syntax ("Tis not easy to rise on a grey day—the devil holds fast your eyelids"), which requires additional considerable attention.

There is no denying, however, the quality and involving nature of *The Witch*'s construction. The colors of Linda Muir's extraordinarily detailed costumes match the muddy browns and greys of the outdoor locations of rural Ontario, in turn wonderfully captured by cinematographer Jarin Blaschke. Composer Mark Korven's music, with its choral-infused, thin marionette strings of stabbing trepidation, contributes mightily, and Eggers and editor Louise Ford also make smart use of insert shots and other creative, evocative editing techniques to help give off a continuing sense of lingering evil.

The Witch is basically about the dissolution of a family, gripped by fear and recrimination. Its religiosity is pervasive, but Eggers also thematically seems to flirt with commentary about man's relationship with unforgiving nature ("We will conquer this wilderness, it will not consume us," intones William at one point), and there is a clear through-line related to a fear or at least uneasiness with Thomasin's burgeoning sexuality, with Caleb stealing glances at his sister's cleavage. These elements feel somewhat incomplete, though, like they could be played up even further. Given the overall quality of its craftsmanship, one wishes for a few more turns of the narrative screw.

Still, Eggers has a gift with tone, and his movie touches moments of elemental dread. He proves himself a capable director of actors, too, abetted by a cast whose steadfast commitment and comfort with the sometimes unwieldy dialogue imbues *The Witch* with an unswerving authenticity. The deep, arresting bass of Ineson's voice lends the proceedings an almost archetypal, storybook quality, giving it sturdiness and form against the backdrop of a growing paranoia within the narrative. Taylor-Joy, meanwhile, is a major discovery, delivering the most vivid and noteworthy breakthrough turn by a young female performer since Elizabeth Olsen's debut in *Martha Marcy May Marlene* (2011). She plays Thomasin with an understated slyness and complexity.

The Witch is entirely a work of mood—like a held-down piano key or the bent, heavy note of an electric guitar. It will likely disappoint those used to and desirous of more conventionally plotted horror, rooted in grisly gore or at the very least scary faces emerging from the shadows. What distinguishes and elevates *The Witch*, though, is that it is open to interpretation, and utilizes a viewer's doubts and, indeed, belief system to reinforce the power of suggestion. Once one gets over the Old English and succumbs to its chilly vibe, there is unique reward to be found. For his follow-up, Eggers is reportedly next working on a remake of F.W. Murnau's classic silent film *Nosferatu* (1922), an undertaking for which he seems uniquely suited.

Brent Simon

CREDITS

Thomasin: Anya Taylor-Joy
William: Ralph Ineson
Katherine: Kate Dickie
Caleb: Harvey Scrimshaw
Mercy: Ellie Grainger
Jonas: Lucas Dawson
Origin: United States
Language: English
Released: 2016
Production: Daniel Bekerman, Lars Knudsen, Jodi Redmond, Rodrigo Teixeira, Jay Van Hoy; released by RT Features, Rooks Nest Entertainment
Directed by: Robert Eggers
Written by: Robert Eggers
Cinematography by: Jarin Blaschke

Music by: Mark Korven
Editing: Louise Ford
Costumes: Linda Muir
Production Design: Craig Lathrop
MPAA rating: R
Running time: 92 minutes

REVIEWS

Abele, Robert. *Los Angeles Times*. February 18, 2016.
Cataldo, Jesse. *Slant*. February 15, 2016.
Chang, Justin. *Variety*. January 26, 2015.
Dargis, Manohla. *New York Times*. February 18, 2016.
Ehrlich, David. *Slate*. February 18, 2016.
Lane, Anthony. *New Yorker*. February 29, 2016.
Morgenstern, Joe. *Wall Street Journal*. February 18, 2016.
Sacks, Ethan. *New York Daily News*. February 17, 2016.
Scherstuhl, Alan. *Village Voice*. February 16, 2016.
Toppman, Lawrence. *Charlotte Observer*. February 17, 2016.

QUOTES

William: "We will conquer this wilderness. It will not consume us."

TRIVIA

The film was shot mostly with available and natural light.

AWARDS

Ind. Spirit 2017: First Feature, First Screenplay

X-Z

X-MEN: APOCALYPSE

Only the strong will survive.
—Movie tagline

Box Office: $155.4 Million

Superhero films are as ubiquitous to summer as a heat wave and equally varied in how much a person can handle. While partisan bickering about which movies are "the best" amongst mega-fans of various comic companies has become the norm, it's fair to say that the very best superhero movies of the past decade have been created by Marvel under the Disney umbrella. They seem to be always pushing new angles, introducing characters in exciting ways and satisfying audiences just enough so that they will line up for more every few months. The same cannot be said for DC Comics films or the Marvel Comics films to which 20th Century Fox has the rights.

X-Men: Apocalypse is one of those Marvel titles owned by Fox (along with *Fantastic Four*), and while the Marvel/Disney films seem to actually be following a money-minting plan of execution mapped out for the next twenty years, the Marvel/Fox movies seem to be spinning their wheels. Fox just cannot seem to get *Fantastic Four*) to be what they (and, everyone else) want it to be and while fans of the *X-Men* comics have been treated to good to great adaptations (*X-Men 2* [2003], *X-Men: Days of Future Past* [2011]), the latest installment, *X-Men: Apocalypse,* feels like a reboot mixed with an origin story created to lead to more plots and stories already depicted recently.

Like previous films, *X-Men: Apocalypse* features Michael Fassbender as the wishy-washy and troubled Magneto/Erik Lehnsherr and James McAvoy as the equally troubled and persistently martyred Professor Charles Xavier. Professor X refuses to believe his former friend is truly "bad," and, eventually in each film, Magneto proves him right. Sort of. Sometimes each of them form a posse of mutants and fight each other; other times they form a posse of mutants and fight together against a greater evil. Typically, it occurs within the same film.

This time around, Bryan Singer introduces a new Scott Summers/Cyclops in young Tye Sheridan, who has recently discovered his mutant power of shooting a powerful laser-like beam out of his eyes. There is also a new Jean Grey/Phoenix in Sophie Turner, who is also learning more about her mutant power of telekinesis. Again, fans who have ever read any *X-Men* comics or seen the original films know that these two will eventually fall in love as Jean's powers grow even more powerful until true romantic tragedy strikes the couple as well as the X-Men. It is truly a sad and well-told story in the comics. It's also one already adapted in this franchise. As for a villain, this time the evil is mutant patient zero Apocalypse (Oscar Isaac), who has been alive since early Egyptians ruled the earth.

As Apocalypse is brought out of his centuries deep slumber, he gets right back into the swing of things as a megalomaniacal demi-God hell-bent on ruling the world. Thus, he sets forth to recruit the four most powerful mutants to help him weed out the weak, but what he settles for is apparently the most convenient ones in franchise newbie Psylocke (Olivia Munn) whose power is a purple sword/whip thing and Angel (Ben Hardy) who has really big wings. Apocalypse also stumbles upon a rebooted and recast Storm (she can control the weather) in Alexandra Shipp. The newly formed baddie group seeks out Erik Lehnsherr, who has recently lost his wife and child to a freak accident thus reigniting his Magneto character who enjoys doing very bad things by controlling and shaping metal. One thing the *X-Men* movies can really do is remind you how many things in daily life contain metal.

X-Men: Apocalypse contains subplots of romance, longing, leaving, and fighting, but it all feels like a boring and lazy rehash. The CGI here also looks incredibly cheap and phony. As a longtime fan of the source material and the rich tapestry of characters, stories, and allegories therein, it's almost painful to say all these negative things. There's truly no reason for boring or mediocre *X-Men* movies yet Fox can't seem to get a grasp on what makes the X-Men so popular. *X-Men: Apocalypse* certainly is not a complete travesty but it's sheer mediocrity makes it a frustrating and dull experience.

Don R. Lewis

CREDITS

Professor Charles Xavier: James McAvoy
Erik Lehnsherr/Magneto: Michael Fassbender
Raven/Mystique: Jennifer Lawrence
Hank McCoy/Beast: Nicholas Hoult
En Sabah Nur/Apocalypse: Oscar Isaac
Scott Summers/Cyclops: Tye Sheridan
Jean Grey: Sophie Turner
Psylocke: Olivia Munn
Angel: Ben Hardy
Storm: Alexandra Shipp
Origin: United States
Language: English, Polish, German, Arabic
Released: 2016
Production: Hutch Parker, Lauren Shuler Donner, Bryan Singer, Simon Kinberg; released by Twentieth Century Fox Film Corp.
Directed by: Bryan Singer
Written by: Simon Kinberg
Cinematography by: Newton Thomas (Tom) Sigel
Music by: John Ottman
Sound: Craig Berkey; John A. Larsen
Editing: John Ottman; Michael Louis Hill
Art Direction: Michele Laliberte
Costumes: Louise Mingenbach
Production Design: Grant Major
MPAA rating: PG-13
Running time: 144 minutes

REVIEWS

Anderson, John. *Time.* May 26, 2016.
Bastien, Angelica Jade. *RogerEbert.com.* May 23, 2016.
Douglas, Edward. *New York Daily News.* May 9, 2016.
Ebiri, Bilge. *Village Voice.* May 9, 2016.
Edelstein, David. *New York Magazine/Vulture.* May 26, 2016.
McCarthy, Todd. *Hollywood Reporter.* May 9, 2016.
Morgenstern, Joe. *Wall Street Journal.* May 26, 2016.
Roeper, Richard. *Chicago Sun-Times.* May 25, 2016.
Roffman, Michael. *Consequence of Sound.* May 10, 2016.
Stewart, Sara. *New York Post.* May 26, 2016.

QUOTES

Apocalypse: "Everything they've built will fall! And from the ashes of their world, we'll build a better one!"

TRIVIA

The dog at the X-Mansion is Tauntaun, the pet dog of director Bryan Singer.

YOGA HOSERS

Do your 'wurst.
    —Movie tagline

Make no mistake about it, *Yoga Hosers* is a very, very bad film. It's moronic, slap dash, cheap-looking, and barely holds together as an actual "film." In fact, it's nearly a total waste of time. To a casual, sober moviegoer, the film should be avoided at all costs. For those willing to suffer, the film does allow one a chance to think about the relationship of art to an audience as well as the crossroad of art and commerce.

Written and directed by indie film stalwart Kevin Smith, *Yoga Hosers* (2016) is the story of two Canadian high school best friends named Colleen Collette (Lily-Rose Depp, daughter of Johnny Depp) and Colleen McKenzie (Harley Quinn Smith, daughter of Kevin Smith) who play in a band and work at a convenience store called "Eh-2-Zed." If the store's name seems misspelled or wrong here, it's not. Rather it's one of endless jokes about Canadian accents that proliferate the film, each one less funny and more dated than the rest. Much like the protagonists in Smith's excellent debut feature *Clerks* (1994), the Colleens hate their miserable counter-jockey jobs yet it remains unclear why they feel the need to work at the store when both are not even sixteen years old yet and live at home, rent free.

Since what remains of the plot is simply too thin and dumb to really delve into, the basic story is that at school, the girls learn of a much-hushed Canadian Nazi sympathizer group from the 1940s, which had amongst its ranks a mad scientist named Andronicus Arcane (Ralph Garman). When the Canadian Nazi group fell apart, Arcane disappeared and was never found. Ironically, this story comes into play just as several murders are taking place around town and, sure enough, the culprit turns out to be tiny Nazi bratwursts called "Bratzi's" (who are all played by Smith...and there's a lot of them), which are tiny, poorly constructed CGI bratwursts in Nazi uniforms who crawl into people's rectums and kill them. Why they do this and what it has to do with Nazis, Canada or, well, anything, is never explained.

Not only is this whole idea as childishly moronic as it sounds, Smith's level of creativity surrounding them is beyond lazy, and includes such lackadaisical touches as their only dialogue being the German word "wunderbar" (which means "wonderful" so that makes no sense) and some extraordinarily cheap-looking CGI. Of its many faults, *Yoga Hosers* and Smith's need to traffic in indolent, redundant spoken words are perhaps the biggest annoyance here. Every character pronounces "about" as "aboot" because, you know, that's what Canadians say.

It would be easy to count the myriad ways *Yoga Hosers* is barely a film and a near total disaster but, why bother? Slamming this film is akin to beating up an invalid or a person incapable of defending themselves. Rather, smart viewers might enjoy pulling back the curtain on this cinematic debacle and hone in on what Smith might actually be trying to express.

Fans or followers of Smith's career know he never fully got over the low audience turnout and general critical dismissal of his most personal film to date, *Jersey Girl* (2004). Since that time, he's continued to whine about the film's reception (often, self-effacingly) and continues making films to varying success both financially and critically. But as a veteran artist, Smith has still never learned to accept critical dismissal. While constantly bemoaning "haters" who dislike his work, Smith eventually did a smart thing in that he focused in on growing his solid, supportive, niche audience by embarking on lengthy, live, almost stand-up comedy performances, as well as launching a popular podcasting network called "Smodcast." This has given Smith a nepotistic support group that feeds him creatively, as well as financially, and has encouraged him to embark on his most recent and extremely off-brand features *Red State* (2011), a kind of horror/thriller and *Tusk* (2014), a body horror film that is nearly as unwatchable as *Yoga Hosers*.

This tapping into his fans and a niche audience who are willing to buy whatever he's selling is brilliant. Yet, at the same time, with "efforts" like *Yoga Hosers*, one can't help but think he's taking advantage of his devotees. This film is barely even trying to be anything more than a trifle or marijuana-induced living dream from Smith, and since he clearly does not care about his art, why should anyone else?

Thus, the intersection of art and commerce can be an intriguing context by which to examine *Yoga Hosers*. For instance, almost every artist in any medium wishes to exist in a functional creative vortex where they are free to bring their ideas to life and present them to the public for consumption and reaction. Yet, does every whim of the artist need to be seen and consumed by the public? Smith has developed a strategy and a supportive enough base to help him see his visions come to life in actual movie theaters, but when something is this halfhearted, cheap and poorly made, does it need to populate theaters? Why not sell it directly to fans and spare others the misery of paying for garbage? It's all a tricky conundrum and for a filmmaker as clever and affable as Smith, one should expect much more than a scant plot populated by friends the filmmaker has acquired through his privilege of being a once well thought of filmmaker (Johnny Depp, Justin Long, Tony Hale, and Natasha Lyonne all have bit parts in *Yoga Hosers*) and take more time to create something lasting and meaningful at best, entertaining at least.

Don R. Lewis

CREDITS

Colleen Collette: Lily-Rose Depp
Colleen McKenzie: Harley Quinn Smith
Guy Lapointe: Johnny Depp
Ichabod: Adam Brody
Bob Collette: Tony Hale
Andronicus Arcane: Ralph Garman
Origin: United States
Language: English
Released: 2016
Production: Elizabeth Destro, Jordan Monsanto, Jennifer Schwalbach Smith; released by Abbolita Productions, Destro Films, Invincible Pictures, Smodcast Pictures, StarStream Media
Directed by: Kevin Smith
Written by: Kevin Smith
Cinematography by: James Laxton
Music by: Christopher Drake
Sound: Tony Lamberti; Kelly Oxford
Music Supervisor: Bruce Gilbert
Editing: Kevin Smith
Art Direction: Brett McKenzie
Costumes: Carol Beadle

Production Design: Cabot McMullen
MPAA rating: PG-13
Running time: 88 minutes

REVIEWS

Chang, Justin. *Variety*. February 1, 2016.
DeFore, John. *Hollywood Reporter*. February 1, 2016.
Dowd, A.A. *The A.V. Club*. August 31, 2016.
Ebiri, Bilge. *New York Magazine (Vulture)*. February 1, 2016.
Fink, John. *Film Stage*. February 1, 2016.
Fischer, Russ. *Playlist*. February 1, 2016.
Fujishima, Kenji. *Slant*. August 31, 2016.
Smith, Nigel M. *Guardian*. February 1, 2016.
Suzanne-Mayer, Dominick. *Consequence of Sound*. February 1, 2016.
Vonder Haar, Pete. *Village Voice*. August 30, 2016.

QUOTES

Colleen McKenzie and Colleen Collette: "Sorry aboot that."

TRIVIA

Lily-Rose Depp is real-life best friends with Harley Quinn Smtih. They met at the Hollywood Schoolhouse in Kindergarten.

THE YOUNG MESSIAH

Discover the savior when he was a child.
—Movie tagline

Box Office: $6.5 Million

The Young Messiah is an unfashionably earnest and religious film of the sort that feels meant to be shown at Sunday schools. Based on Anne Rice's novel *Christ the Lord: Out of Egypt* the film follows Jesus as a seven-year-old boy as he journeys from Egypt to Nazareth with his family. Along the way he interacts with fellow children, rabbis, and non-believers, and shows his supernatural abilities. It's a dramatized overview of biblical events that provides a tidy guide to Jesus as a child in a rather bland visual style.

It is strange to think that *The Young Messiah* was released this year. While there is always a cottage industry of faith-based films, something like *The Young Messiah* vaguely recalls the biblical epics of the 1950s, though it doesn't rely on campy spectacle (perhaps if it did, it would be more interesting). Overall, it's meant to present religious history in a family friendly fashion. There's a bit of swords-and-sandals fighting, but most of the film is focused on the child's journey. Adam Greaves-Neal, with his tousled hair and innocent yet wise delivery makes for an appealing messiah, and embodying such a role as a child is no easy task. Curiously, most of the performers have distractingly British sounding accents, and at one point when a character says "Well, he's not dead now," it's hard not to suppress a chuckle while thinking of Monty Python. The dialogue is about what one might expect from this type of picture—it frequently seems overly simplified and expository. "God is your father," says Mary, and of course this wouldn't be a Jesus movie without someone saying, "It's a miracle." It's more interesting to see Jesus' moments of vulnerability, as when he shyly asks, "Am I dangerous?" he is, after all, a young boy just trying to come to terms with who he is and what he is capable of. So many artistic depictions of Jesus show him as a baby or an adult, so *The Young Messiah* takes a relatively novel approach.

While the decision to depict Jesus' childhood is interesting, the aesthetic often is not. The costumes and makeup tend to look a bit cheap, and don't really convey an ancient style. Of course, this is a challenge with any film set during this time, but one might wish for more inspired visuals. There are some nice images of the desert setting, but many of the interiors feel drab and one outdoor scene relies far too heavily on lens flares as a means of conveying mysticism. The score feels similarly nondescript. The film is unlikely to inspire a non-religious audience, and it doesn't have the powerful aesthetic of many biblical films. It ends up existing in a strange grey area: an inspiring biblical epic in theory that never truly becomes epic or inspiring.

The most memorable scene in *The Young Messiah* comes late in the film. Jesus and Mary recline under a tree. The setting is sun-dappled and pastoral, and as Jesus and Mary cuddle, she observes, "You're getting so big we won't be able to do this much longer." This moment, which feels like it could take place between any mother and child, is a poignant respite in a film which too often feels muddled. This is the scene where Mary explains Jesus' birth as best she can. The story's been told so many times before—in paintings, music, films, books, etc.—and while *The Young Messiah* might not necessarily bring anything new to the table, it finds sweetness in a scene that presents Jesus and Mary as just a mother and child lounging outside on a nice day. Sara Lazzaro brings an appropriate maternal serenity to the role of Mary. Joseph (Vincent Walsh), who with his curly hair and beard almost looks more 1970s than ancient, is less distinctive. The bond between Jesus and Mary is the most interesting thing on display here. When Mary tells Jesus who he is and how he's special, he says, "I think I'm here just to be alive." The film gives us a modest chance to watch him come to terms with this as he performs miracles but is just a boy. While *The Young Messiah* ultimately does not contribute much to the canon of religious films, it does show some of Mary and Joseph's anxieties and Jesus' earnest curiosity about who he is. Who knows...the Sunday school students might enjoy it, though it's just as likely they'll end up bored.

Abbey Bender

CREDITS

Jesus: Adam Greaves-Neal
Mary: Sara Lazzaro
Joseph: Vincent Walsh
Herod: Jonathan Bailey
Severus: Sean Bean
Origin: United States
Language: English
Released: 2016
Production: Chris Columbus, Tracey K. Price, Michael Barrathan, Mark Radcliffe, Mark W. Shaw; 1492 Pictures, CJ Entertainment, Hyde Park International, Ocean Blue Entertainment; released by Focus Features.
Directed by: Cyrus Nowrasteh
Written by: Cyrus Nowrasteh; Betsy Giffen Nowrasteh
Cinematography by: Joel Ransom
Music by: John Debney
Sound: Ethan Beigel
Editing: Geoffrey Rowland
Art Direction: Domenico Sica
Costumes: Stefano De Nardis
Production Design: Francesco Frigeri
MPAA rating: PG-13
Running time: 111 minutes

REVIEWS

Hoffman, Jordan. *The Guardian.* March 11, 2016.
Holub, Christian. *Entertainment Weekly.* March 14, 2016.
Lemire, Christy. *Roger Ebert.com.* March 11, 2016.
Murray, Noel. *Los Angeles Times.* March 11, 2016.
Prigge, Matt. *Metro.* March 11, 2016.
Schager, Nick. *Variety.* March 11, 2016.
Uhlich, Keith. *Hollywood Reporter.* March 11, 2016.
Vishnevetsky, Ignatiy. *The A.V. Club.* March 11, 2016.
Webster, Andy. *New York Times.* March 13, 2016.
White, Dave. *The Wrap.* March 11, 2016.

QUOTES

Joseph: "I know you have many questions. But you need to let them sleep in your heart for now. Why? Because your questions are the questions of a child. But the answers are the answers for a man. That is one bridge I cannot build. I don't know how. But God can, and we must trust him."
Jesus: "I do. I trust him for everything."

TRIVIA

In the Bible, Jesus performed miracles when he reached adulthood in Nazareth. His first miracle was transforming water into wine.

ZOOLANDER 2

Flowers, nature's own little supermodels.
   —Movie tagline

Box Office: $28.8 Million

"It just doesn't hold up, does it?" asks a character late in multi-hyphenate Ben Stiller's feeble, fashion-world comedy. In theory the character is referring to some element of his diabolical scheme, but coming three-quarters of the way into *Zoolander 2*, it feels and plays like a shrugging, apologetic admission of unpreparedness and inferiority for the film as a whole. Stiller's endeavor, of course, is a follow-up to *Zoolander* (2001), a male model comedy that, premiering two weeks after the September 11 terrorist attacks, somewhat withered on the commercial vine upon release, grossing $45 million domestically before finding an especially devoted cult following on home video, powered by memes that celebrated its willful thickheadedness and oddball throwaway one-liners.

Fifteen years later, *Zoolander 2* collapses under the weight of its own smugness, and a deep, deep roster of mostly self-congratulatory celebrity cameos that do little more than reinforce the fame of its participants. At once labored and ill-thought out, the film never finds a convincing narrative path, losing itself in a thicket of half-baked ideas that do not fit together. *Zoolander 2* was released on February 12, where it served as a theatrical chew-toy for weekend competitor *Deadpool*, limping to just under $29 million overall in the United States during its run, and eventually banking another $27 million internationally.

The film opens with Interpol agent Valentina Valencia (Penelope Cruz) working to solve a string of murders of pop stars. Meanwhile, a three-minute credits sequence recaps the life of hermitic isolation that former top model Derek Zoolander (Stiller) has led ever since the "Center For Kids Who Can't Read Good" he built at the end of the previous film collapsed, killing his wife Matilda (Christine Taylor). Having subsequently lost custody of his son Derek Jr. (Cyrus Arnold), Derek has retired and become estranged from friend and fellow model Hansel McDonald (Owen Wilson), whose face was also scarred in the aforementioned accident.

Valentina's investigation unearths a shared, signature look in all of the victims—the same look Derek once

427

used to sell a line of bottled water called "Aqua Vitae." This connects to an elaborate mythology having to do with a sort of Illuminati of the fashion world, as explained by Sting (yes, the singer). In the most practical terms, however, this just means that as Derek also reconnects with his son, he and Hansel cast their lot with Valentina, and find themselves again at odds with Derek's old nemesis, demented designer Jacobim Mugatu (Will Ferrell), who blows into the movie more than one hour into the proceedings and injects it with a brief burst of wild, loose-limbed life.

A perverse repertory programmer might one day deliver a double-bill of 2016's big-screen fashion world commentary in the form of *Zoolander 2* and *The Neon Demon*, though the two movies could scarcely be more different in tone and content. The sort of jokes that Stiller and his three credited co-screenwriters (old collaborators John Hamburg and Justin Theroux, and new hired hand Nicholas Stoller) seem to think are the most outrageous—commitment-phobic Hansel trading in one eclectic group of orgy partners for another—are undercut by Stiller's unwillingness as a filmmaker to really go for broke, in the manner that Sacha Baron Cohen so often has in his movies.

In some respects, this movie, stylized in unintentionally prophetic fashion as *Zoolander No. 2* on posters, seems almost doomed from the start. Drake Sather, the co-writer of the original film and the man Stiller himself calls the creator of Derek Zoolander, committed suicide in 2004, thus robbing Stiller of an important collaborator. More pointedly, at the time of its release, *Zoolander* felt fresh in its caricature and weirdness. This sequel arrives at a time when short-form comedy is more popular than ever, with Vine stars and YouTube content creators commanding large millennial audiences, and Funny or Die churning out consistently trenchant satirical sketches.

Big-screen comedies consequently need to be tack-sharp in their narrative construction, or at the very least have the advantage of appealing, well-sketched characters. *Zoolander 2* feels clammy and desperate, however. Part of what made the character funny in the first film was that he was not just a simpleton, but that Derek had a flintiness to match his unearned confidence. It worked for some of the same reasons that the nerd petulance of *Napoleon Dynamite* (2004) was so richly entertaining—because it was a marginalized character with a confused disdain for anyone who would get in his way.

With Derek thrown off his game and lacking a consistent foil in *Zoolander 2*, the character becomes merely a vessel for whatever sort of different wan silliness any given scenario dictates. Ergo, when Stiller finds himself painted into a corner (of at least partially his

own making), he throws in gag riffs using audio cues of old Wham! and Frankie Goes to Hollywood songs. This is textbook laziness.

More broadly, though, gone from *Zoolander 2* is its previously held absurdist, anything-goes sensibility, as well as the stinging, prescient satire that lampooned the fetishization of poverty in something like Mugatu's "Derelicte" collection, celebrating homelessness. Whereas the original movie offered a sincere tip of the cap to fashion's creativity but also took hearty if straight-faced aim at its excesses, Stiller's follow-up takes the edge off at almost every turn. It is polite, even in its fleeting moments of rudeness. It is a work which first and foremost attempts to make the inhabitants of its fashion-world setting comfortable, and locate laughs secondarily.

Cinematographer Dan Mindel shoots a pretty frame, and production designer Jeff Mann and costume designer Leesa Evans also earn every bit of their salaries with colorful work. As far as the performances, young Arnold, as Derek Jr., is quite solid, but it is again Ferrell who manages to steal the movie with his scenes as Mugatu.

Of all the cameos, Benedict Cumberbatch scores most definitively, as a gender-vague model known simply as All. It is a well-crafted joke and scene ("All is not defined by binary constructs"), perhaps the movie's finest. But Cumberbatch also plays the character perfectly, delivering a performance at once haughty and mysterious; when he/she disappears, one wishes they could follow All off into another movie. Most of the other walk-throughs (no doubt receiving an assist in their booking by way of a location shoot at Rome's Cinecitta Studios) find participants playing themselves, so once the amusement of this face-spotting wears off, *Zoolander 2* is just killing time.

Brent Simon

CREDITS

Derek: Ben Stiller
Hansel: Owen Wilson
Matilda: Christine Taylor
Valentina Valencia: Penelope Cruz
Jacobim Mugatu: Will Ferrell
Alexanya Atoz: Kristen Wiig
All: Benedict Cumberbatch
Derek Jr.: Cyrus Arnold
Origin: United States
Language: English, Italian
Released: 2016
Production: Stuart Cornfeld, Scott Rudin, Clayton Townsend, Ben Stiller; released by Red Hour Films, Scott Rudin Productions

Directed by: Ben Stiller
Written by: Ben Stiller; Justin Theroux; Nicholas Stoller; John Hamburg
Cinematography by: Dan(iel) Mindel
Music by: Theodore Shapiro
Sound: Craig Henighan
Music Supervisor: George Drakoulias
Editing: Greg Hayden
Costumes: Leesa Evans
Production Design: Jeff Mann
MPAA rating: PG-13
Running time: 102 minutes

REVIEWS

Graham, Adam. *Detroit News*. February 11, 2016.
Heaton, Michael. *Cleveland Plain Dealer*. February 12, 2016.
Howell, Peter. *Toronto Star*. February 11, 2016.
Morgenstern, Joe. *Wall Street Journal*. February 11, 2016.
Schindel, Dan. *Film Stage*. February 10, 2016.
Smith, Kyle. *New York Post*. February 11, 2016.
Tobias, Scott. *NPR*. February 11, 2016.
Turan, Kenneth. *Los Angeles Times*. February 11, 2016.
VanDenburgh, Barbara. *Arizona Republic*. February 11, 2016.
Wheat, Alynda. *People*. February 11, 2016.

QUOTES

Derek Zoolander: "I'm going to retire, withdraw from public life, and become a hermit crab."

TRIVIA

Ben Stiller, Owen Wilson, and Will Ferrell are all left-handed.

AWARDS

Golden Raspberries 2016: Worst Actress--Supporting (Wiig)
Nominations:
Golden Raspberries 2016: Worst Actor (Stiller), Worst Director (Stiller), Worst Picture, Worst Sequel/Prequel, Worst Support. Actor (Ferrell), Worst Support. Actor (Wilson)

ZOOTOPIA
(Zootropolis)

Welcome to the urban jungle.
—Movie tagline

Box Office: $341.3 Million

The period that begins roughly with 2010's *Tangled* will be remembered as the era when Disney Animation Studios pulled out all the stops to beat their sister company Pixar at its own game. From the hook-laden girl power anthems of *Frozen* (2013) to the superhero-based, zeitgeist-courting *Big Hero 6* (2014), Disney seemed intent during this period to put the digi-mation dynamos in their place. *Zootopia* is an interesting addition to the new Disney canon in that it returns to their old standby of focusing on talking, anthropomorphic animals, which is how the company made a name for itself in the first place, but places them in a very modern discussion of race and political corruption. *Zootopia*'s reference points may be lost on the young kids who will undoubtedly get a kick out of its top-notch jokes and animation, but the message of acceptance is pitched at just the right level of sophistication that kids can understand.

Ever since she was a kid, rabbit Judy Hopps (voiced by Ginnifer Goodwin) has been an overachiever. We meet her while she's acting in a school play, hamming up a death scene to describe that the reason animals live in harmony is that predators lost their killer instinct many years ago. Harmony now reigns supreme in the animal kingdom. This truce between carnivores and herbivores means that anyone is free to take part in the animals' system of government. Even so, when Judy tells her parents (Bonnie Hunt and Don Lake) that she wants to be a police officer, she's met with trepidation. She may be qualified and honorable and have fierce self-determination, but it's a big world out there for a little rabbit. All their handwringing about her safety just makes her more dead set on becoming a cop, to the point that she graduates top of her class from the academy. The only thing left to do is actual police work.

Within minutes of arriving in Zootopia, the metropolis where most of these animals go about their business, Judy finds herself in a cramped apartment with loud neighbors and assigned to a traffic detail, because her gruff commanding officer, Chief Bogo (Idris Elba), does not think she is capable of handling real challenges. She sets out to prove him wrong and to make herself indispensable, but this only lands her in more trouble. She catches a thieving weasel (Alan Tudyk) who first runs amok through a rodent town but Bogo does not think the produce he stole was worth the scene she caused in apprehending him. All this is frustrating enough, but when she catches a fox named Nick Wilde (Jason Bateman) in the middle of a con but can't find evidence enough to book him, it seems like the final straw. She's disappointed and Bogo would certainly love an excuse to get the rabbit off his police force but they are both stuck when a missing person's case comes to their attention.

A grieving otter (Octavia Spencer) says her husband went missing days ago and the police have not found any leads. Judy steps up to take the case and the deputy mayor, Ms. Bellweather (Jenny Slate) overhears her. It was Ms. Bellweather's idea to start letting herbivores onto the police force in the first place, even if the mayor (J.K. Simmons) took credit for it, so she's naturally thrilled that Judy is taking initiative. Bogo gives Judy forty-eight hours to find the missing person, one Emmett Otterton, and unfortunately the only lead she has brings her right back to Nick Wilde. Between Judy's go-getter's dedication and Wilde's underworld ties and fecklessness, the case looks to be as good as solved. The issue becomes muddier when the mayor himself appears to be tied up in the many other missing person's cases that have wracked Zootopia the last few months.

The film's McGuffin is something that turns animals back into their uncivilized, pre-domesticated state. The missing otter is discovered to be nearly feral, which doesn't comfort his bereaved wife. The film plays its hand perhaps a little too late in the game with this turn of events, because then it can only expend one-third of its running time on its central theme: in short, don't judge a book by its cover. Just because only predators have at one point been savage and violent, doesn't mean that all predators are in danger of returning to their primal state. Judy learns this too late and offends Nick with her naïve response to the discovery. Soon, no predators in Zootopia are able to find work, including her biggest champion at work, a chubby, fun-loving jungle cat receptionist named Clawhauser (Nate Torrence). Judy's idealism sparks something akin to class war, with predators turned into a feared and hated other. When it's discovered that the government is behind this plot, it should surprise no one. Writers/directors Byron Howard, Jared Bush, and Phil Johnston, (and their numerous co-writers) make no bones about what they are throwing darts at with their furry allegory. Right down to a *Breaking Bad* reference (which is strictly for the adults in the room), this is a movie ripped out of 2016's headlines. It's more than a little radical for a movie featuring a dancing gazelle with the voice of Shakira to be about government officials trying to incite a race war, even if the film does posit a utopian finish with all the proper people behind bars and the vague hope of a better system. It's not perfect, but it's certainly more political than *Finding Dory* (2016) or *Monsters University* (2014).

Thankfully, the movie that transpires around this progressive agenda is also something worth celebrating. The animation is breathtaking, all shiny, round, and full of voluptuous detail. The animal world is as adorable as one could hope for, down to the tiniest detail, literally. The ways in which the film showcases the lowliest rodent are hugely clever and most adorable. The chase scene through the tiny town is a goofy highlight, as is a rodent kingpin (Maurice LaMarche) modeled on Marlon Brando's performance in *The Godfather* (1974). *Zootopia* is cute even at its most dire or frightening, as the chemistry between Judy and Nick never ceases to endear. The film's villains all turn about to be a little too cute for their own good, but as a measure against too many children in the audience being traumatized, it's more than forgivable. With any luck, kids will look back on this movie as the start of their unconscious liberalism and unconditional love for their fellow man. Failing that, it will still be good fun for the whole family a hundred years from now.

Scout Tafoya

CREDITS

Judy Hopps: Ginnifer Goodwin (Voice)
Nick Wilde: Jason Bateman (Voice)
Mrs. Otterton: Octavia Spencer
Mayor Lionheart: J.K. Simmons
Mr. Big: Maurice La Marche
Duke Weaselton: Alan Tudyk
Bonnie Hopps: Bonnie Hunt (Voice)
Stu Hopps: Don Lake
Chief Bogo: Idris Elba (Voice)
Bellwether: Jenny Slate (Voice)
Clawhauser: Nate Torrence (Voice)
Origin: United States
Language: English
Released: 2016
Production: Clark Spencer; The Walt Disney Studios; released by Walt Disney Animation Studios
Directed by: Byron Howard; Rich Moore
Written by: Byron Howard; Rich Moore; Jared Bush; Josie Trinidad; Jim Reardon; Phil Johnston; Jennifer Lee; Dan Fogelman
Music by: Michael Giacchino
Sound: Addison Teague
Music Supervisor: Tom MacDougall
Editing: Jeremy Milton; Fabienne Rawley
Art Direction: Matthias Lechner
Production Design: David Goetz
MPAA rating: PG
Running time: 108 minutes

REVIEWS

Chaney, Jen. *Washington Post*. March 3, 2016.
Genzlinger, Neil. *New York Times*. March 3, 2016.
Goldstein, Gary. *Los Angeles Times*. March 3, 2016.
Lane, Anthony. *New Yorker*. March 7, 2016.
McWeeny, Drew. *Hitfix*. March 1, 2016.
Rechtshaffen, Michael. *Hollywood Reporter*. February 12, 2016.

Roeper, Richard. *Chicago Sun-Times*. March 2, 2016.

Seitz, Matt Zoller. *RogerEbert.com*. March 5, 2016.

Suzanne-Mayer, Dominick. *Consequence of Sound*. March 5, 2016.

Zacharek, Stephanie. *Time*. March 5, 2016.

QUOTES

Chief Bogo: "Life isn't some cartoon musical where you sing a little song and all your insipid dreams magically come true. So let it go."

TRIVIA

Chief Bogo's name is based on the Swahili word for buffalo: mbogo.

AWARDS

Oscars 2016: Animated Film

Golden Globes 2017: Animated Film

Nominations:

British Acad. 2016: Animated Film

List of Awards

Academy Awards

Film: *Moonlight*

Animated Film: *Zootopia*

Director: Damien Chazelle (*La La Land*)

Actor: Casey Affleck (*Manchester by the Sea*)

Actress: Emma Stone (*La La Land*)

Supporting Actor: Mahershala Ali (*Moonlight*)

Supporting Actress: Viola Davis (*Fences*)

Original Screenplay: Kenneth Lonergan (*Manchester by the Sea*)

Adapted Screenplay: Barry Jenkins, Tarell Alvin McCraney (*Moonlight*)

Cinematography: Linus Sandgren (*La La Land*)

Editing: John Gilbert (*Hacksaw Ridge*)

Production Design: David Wasco, Sandy Reynolds-Wasco (*La La Land*)

Visual Effects: Robert Legato, Adam Valdez, Andrew R. Jones, Dan Lemmon (*The Jungle Book*)

Sound Mixing: Kevin O'Connell, Andy Wright, Robert Mackenzie, Peter Grace (*Hacksaw Ridge*)

Sound Editing: Sylvain Bellemare (*Arrival*)

Makeup: Alessandro Bertolazzi, Giorgio Gregorini, Christopher Nelson (*Suicide Squad*)

Costume Design: Colleen Atwood (*Fantastic Beasts and Where to Find Them*)

Original Score: Justin Hurwitz (*La La Land*)

Original Song: "City of Stars" (Justin Hurwitz, Benj Pasek, Justin Paul *La La Land*)

Foreign Language Film: *The Salesman*

British Academy of Film & Television Awards

Film: *La La Land*

Animated Film: *Kubo and the Two Strings*

Outstanding British Film: *I, Daniel Blake*

Director: Damien Chazelle (*La La Land*)

Actor: Casey Affleck (*Manchester by the Sea*)

Actress: Emma Stone (*La La Land*)

Supporting Actor: Dev Patel (*Lion*)

Supporting Actress: Viola Davis (*Fences*)

Original Screenplay: Kenneth Londergan (*Manchester by the Sea*)

Adapted Screenplay: Luke Davies (*Lion*)

Editing: John Gilbert (*Hacksaw Ridge*)

Cinematography: Linus Sandgren (*La La Land*)

Production Design: Stuart Craig, Anna Pinnock (*Fantastic Beasts and Where to Find Them*)

Costume Design: Madeline Fontaine (*Jackie*)

Makeup: J. Roy Helland, Daniel Phillips (*Florence Foster Jenkins*)

Sound: Claude La Haye, Bernard Gariépy Strobl, Sylvain Bellemare (*Arrival*)

Visual Effects: Robert Legato, Dan Lemmon, Andrew R. Jones, Adam Valdez (*The Jungle Book*)

Music: Justin Hurwitz (*La La Land*)

John Schlesinger Britannia Award for Excellence in Directing: Ang Lee (*Billy Lynn's Long Halftime Walk*)

Directors Guild of America Awards

Outstanding Directorial Achievement in Motion Pictures: Damien Chazelle (*La La Land*)

Outstanding Directorial Achievement of a First-Time Feature Film Director in Motion Pictures: Garth Davis (*Lion*)

Golden Globes

Film, Drama: *Moonlight*

Film, Musical or Comedy: *La La Land*

Animated Film: *Zootopia*

Director: Damien Chazelle (*La La Land*)

Actor, Drama: Casey Affleck (*Manchester by the Sea*)

Actor, Musical or Comedy: Ryan Gosling (*La La Land*)

Actress, Drama: Isabelle Huppert (*Elle*)

Actress, Musical or Comedy: Emma Stone (*La La Land*)

Supporting Actor: Aaron Taylor-Johnson (*Nocturnal Animals*)

Supporting Actress: Viola Davis (*Fences*)

Screenplay: Damien Chazelle (*La La Land*)

Score: Justin Hurwitz (*La La Land*)

Song: "City of Stars" (Justin Hurwitz, Benj Pasek, Justin Paul *La La Land*)

Foreign Language Film: *Elle*

Golden Raspberry Awards

Worst Supporting Actor: Jesse Eisenberg (*Batman vs. Superman: Dawn of Justice*)

Worst Supporting Actress: Kristen Wiig (*Zoolander 2*)

Worst Screenplay: Chris Terrio, David S. Goyer (*Batman vs. Superman: Dawn of Justice*)

Worst Screen Combo: Ben Affleck, Henry Cavill (*Batman vs. Superman: Dawn of Justice*)

Worst Prequel, Remake, Rip-Off or Sequel: (*Batman vs. Superman: Dawn of Justice*)

Redeemer Award: Mel Gibson (*Hacksaw Ridge*)

Independent Spirit Awards

Film: *Moonlight*

First Film: *The Witch*

Director: Barry Jenkins (*Moonlight*)

Actor: Casey Affleck (*Manchester by the Sea*)

Actress: Isabelle Huppert (*Elle*)

Supporting Actor: Ben Foster (*Hell or High Water*)

Supporting Actress: Molly Shannon (*Other People*)

Screenplay: *Moonlight*

First Screenplay: *The Witch*

Cinematography: *Moonlight*

Editing: *Moonlight*

Foreign Film: *Toni Erdmann*

Robert Altman Award: *Moonlight*

John Cassavetes Award: *Krisha*

Someone to Watch Award: Anna Rose Holmer (*The Fits*)

Screen Actors Guild Awards

Actor: Denzel Washington (*Fences*)

Actress: Emma Stone (*La La Land*)

Supporting Actor: Mahershala Ali (*Moonlight*)

Supporting Actress: Viola Davis (*Fences*)

Ensemble Cast: *Hidden Figures*

Stunt Ensemble: *Hacksaw Ridge*

Writers Guild of America Awards

Original Screenplay: Barry Jenkins, Tarell Alvin McCraney (*Moonlight*)

Adapted Screenplay: Eric Heisserer, Ted Chiang (*Arrival*)

Obituaries

Edward Albee (March 12, 1928-September 16, 2016). Three-time Pulitzer Prize-winning playwright Edward Albee is best known for his acclaimed play *Who's Afraid of Virginia Woolf?* (1962), which won the Tony Award for Best Play in 1963 and was adapted into a feature film, directed by Mike Nichols and starring Elizabeth Taylor and Richard Burton, in 1966. Albee's first play was *The Zoo Story*, which he wrote in 1958 over the course of three weeks (the play, a disturbing two-hander about two men on a park bench, has been adapted for television multiple times), and he would win the Pulitzer Prize for Drama award for his plays *A Delicate Balance* (1966), *Seascape* (1975), and *Three Tall Women* (1991). With proceeds from his best-known work, he established the Edward F. Albee Foundation in 1967, which continues to fund the endeavors of writers and visual artists, and he served as a guest instructor at various universities throughout the United States. Albee died on September 16, 2016, at the age of 88 at his home in Montauk, New York, after a brief illness.

Muhammad Ali (January 17, 1942-June 3, 2016). He was known as "the Greatest," and Muhammad Ali proved the nickname multiple times over, inside and outside the boxing ring. Ali was born Cassius Marcellus Clay, Jr. in Louisville, Kentucky, where he was raised and began training for boxing at the age of 12. At the age of 18, he won the gold medal at the 1960 Summer Olympics in the lightweight division. A few months later, on October 29, he made his professional boxing debut and would go undefeated in the ring for his next 30 fights, winning the title of world champion in the heavyweight division from the World Boxing Council—a title he would successfully defend 19 times over the course of his career—and the World Boxing Association, which he defended ten times. Ali was a political activist during the civil rights movement. He converted to Islam and changed his name in 1964, shortly after winning the WBC title, and he was suspended from professional boxing after refusing induction into the armed services during the Vietnam War. The legal battle

over his protest would reach the Supreme Court, where his 1967 conviction on a felony draft evasion charge was overturned by unanimous decision. Ali retired from boxing in 1981 and was diagnosed with Parkinson's disease in 1984. He still made public appearances, although limited, including lighting the Olympic cauldron at the 1996 Summer Olympics, a 2002 appearance before Congress to push for increased funding for Parkinson's disease, and bearing the Olympic flag at the 2012 Summer Olympics. Ali has been the subject of multiple documentaries (*When We Were Kings* [1996], *The Trials of Muhammad Ali* [2013], and *I Am Ali* [2014]), as well as the subject of Michael Mann's 2001 narrative feature *Ali*, in which Will Smith played the pugilist. Ali died in Scottsdale, Arizona, on June 3, 2016, at the age of 74.

Alexis Arquette (July 28, 1969-September 11, 2016). An actress known for her work in independent film, Alexis Arquette, herself transgender, was also an outspoken supporter of transgender issues and people. Arquette's first credited film role was as Georgette, a transgender sex worker, in *Last Exit to Brooklyn* (1989), an adaptation of Hubert Selby, Jr.'s controversial 1964 novel. She also appeared in *Threesome* (1994) and *Pulp Fiction* (1994), and Arquette played a Boy George-serenading player in *The Wedding Singer* (1998). Arquette was part of a Hollywood family that included actor siblings Rosanna, Richmond, Patricia, and David Arquette. A documentary about her sex reassignment surgery in 2006, entitled *Alexis Arquette: She's My Brother*, premiered at the Tribeca Film Festival in 2007. On September 11, 2016, Arquette at the age of 47 of cardiac arrest caused by complications from HIV, which she lived with for almost three decades.

Hector Babenco (February 7, 1946-July 13, 2016). Academy Award-nominated director Hector Babenco was born in Argentina and had a career that included work in his homeland, Brazil, and the United States. He came to international attention with his 1981 narrative film *Pixote*, which followed the lives of abandoned children on the streets of Sao Paulo. Babenco was the first Latin American director to receive an Academy Award nomination for Best Director with *Kiss of the Spider Woman* (1985), an adaptation of Manuel Puig's novel. His final film *My Hindu Friend* (2016), about a director near death after being diagnosed with cancer (Babenco himself was a cancer survivor), was released in March of 2016. Babenco died four months later, on July 13, at the age of 70.

Kenny Baker (August 24, 1934-August 13, 2016). Best known as the actor inside R2-D2 in seven of the *Star Wars* films, Kenny Baker began his acting career in the theater and the circus. While working with Jack Purvis in a comedy act called the Minitones, filmmaker George Lucas chose the 3-foot-8-inch Baker to play the plucky sidekick robot in *Star Wars* (1977). In addition to the role of R2-D2, Baker appeared in *Flash Gordon* (1980), *The Elephant Man* (1980), and *Time Bandits* (1981), as well as roles in *Amadeus* (1984) and *Labyrinth* (1986). Baker died at the age of 81 on August 13, 2016.

David Bowie (January 8, 1947-January 10, 2016). One of the most unique and well-regarded figures of popular music, David Bowie had a music career that spanned over five decades and an acting career that went for more than four decades. Bowie, born David Robert Jones in south London, had a life-long love of music. He formed his first band at 15, and after a handful of unsuccessful record attempts in the 1960s (under the, at the time, confusing names Davie Jones and Davy Jones), the singer chose his professional stage name. His song "Space Oddity," released just before the launch of the Apollo 11, made it to the UK charts in 1969. Bowie's real rise began in 1972, when he adopted the stage persona Ziggy Stardust, with the release of his album *The Rise and Fall of Ziggy Stardust and the Spiders from Mars*, especially the earlier release of the single "Starman." Bowie "retired" the persona the next year, and the rest of his music career was one of constant, stylistic evolution from soul and funk to German-influenced abstraction, from popular rock to electronic. While creating some of the era's most revolutionary music, Bowie also maintained a steady career of film acting. His first significant role was in Nicolas Roeg's *The Man Who Fell to Earth* (1976), in which he played an alien who comes to Earth to return water to his dying planet. In 1983, he had starring roles in Tony Scott's *The Hunger* and Nagisa Oshima's *Merry Christmas, Mr. Lawrence*. His other notable appearances in films include the roles of the Goblin King in Jim Henson's *Labyrinth* (1986), Pontius Pilate in Martin Scorsese's *The Last Temptation of Christ* (1988), Andy Warhol in Julian Schnabel's *Basquiat* (1996), and Nikola Tesla in Christopher Nolan's *The Prestige* (2006). Bowie, the father of film director Duncan Jones, continued working until the end of his life. His final album *Blackstar* was released two days before his death from liver cancer on January 10, 2016. He was 69 years old.

Tony Burton (March 23, 1937-February 25, 2016). Along with the *Rocky* franchise's stars Sylvester Stallone and Burt Young, Tony Burton was the only actor to appear in every entry in the series. In high school, Burton was an accomplished athlete, competing in boxing and football. After a short boxing career, Burton spent three and a half years in prison for robbery. While there, he learned about theater through a workshop and began working with theater companies in Los Angeles after serving his time. Burton began working in television before landing two significant 1976 film roles: as a prisoner in John Carpenter's *Assault on Precinct 13* and as a trainer in *Rocky*. Tony "Duke" Evers, the character from the latter film, would appear in the film's subsequent five sequels. Burton died of complications from pneumonia at the age of 78 on February 25, 2016.

Charmian Carr (December 27, 1942-September 17, 2016). Before being cast in *The Sound of Music* (1965), Charmian Carr (born Charmian Anne Farnon) was a high school athlete with no vocal training or acting experience. She played Liesl Von Trapp, the eldest daughter, in that film adaptation of the Broadway musical. In 1966, Carr appeared in the television anthology series *ABC Stage 67* in a musical by Stephen Sondheim. A year later, she married and retired from show business. In addition to writing two books, she was the mother of two daughters, grandmother of two grandchildren, and owned an interior design firm. Carr died of complications from dementia at the age of 73 on September 17, 2016.

William Christopher (October 20, 1932-December 31, 2016). Best known for playing Father Mulcahy on *M*A*S*H* (1972-1983) and its short-lived spinoff *After MASH* (1983-1985), William Christopher began his acting career on the stage in off-Broadway productions. Following his Broadway debut, he moved to Los Angeles and had appearances on various television series, before landing the role of the kindly Catholic priest on *M*A*S*H*. Christopher had some small roles in feature films and continued to act in television and on the stage throughout his life. The actor also did philanthropic work to raise awareness of autism. Christopher died of cancer on December 31, 2016, at the age of 84.

Michael Cimino (February 3, 1939-July 2, 2016). A filmmaker of contemporary critical controversy and modern critical reevaluation, Michael Cimino's second film was *The Deer Hunter* (1978), a critical and award darling that won five Academy Awards, including Best Picture and Best Director. His career after that film never matched its success. Cimino received bachelor's and master's degrees in painting from Yale University and became a successful television commercial director in New York City. He moved to Los Angeles in 1971 to start a career in screenwriting, and his screenplay for *Thunderbolt and Lightfoot* (1974), his debut film, caught the attention of Clint Eastwood. After the success of his first two features, Cimino had total control over his third film *Heaven's Gate* (1980), an ambitious epic Western. The film was met with universal criticial panning and did so poorly at the box office, after its final cost came in multiple times over budget, that United Artists, the studio that backed the production, was put up for sale by its parent company. The filmmaker would go on to direct four additional features, all critical and financial disappointments. In recent years, *Heaven's Gate* has undergone a critical reassessment, leading to a 2012 DVD and Blu-ray release of the film's director's cut by the Criterion Collection. Cimino, aged 77, died of heart failure at his Los Angeles home on July 2, 2016.

Leonard Cohen (September 21, 1934-November 7, 2016). A singer and songwriter whose music is a staple of film and television soundtracks, Leonard Cohen began as a poet and novelist, not releasing his first album until the age of 33. Known for his deep, resonant voice and soulful lyrics, Cohen released 14 studio albums between 1967 and 2016. His association with film soundtracks began when director Robert Altman included three songs from Cohen's first album *Songs of Leonard Cohen* (1967) in *McCabe & Mrs. Miller* (1971). In regular rotation on soundtracks are "Everybody Knows" (from *I'm Your Man* [1988]), "Waiting for the Miracle" (from *The Future* [1992]), and "Hallelujah" (from *Various Positions* [1984]), his most famous song, which has been covered by hundreds of artists. Cohen appeared in a few films and was the subject of four documentaries, one of which (*Leonard Cohen: Bird on a Wire*, following the artist on his 1972 20-city European tour) was believed to be lost after its 1974 premiere, until a DVD was released in 2010. His final album *You Want It Darker* was released in 2016, three weeks before his death on November 7, 2016, at the age of 82.

Pat Conroy (October 26, 1945-March 4, 2016). An author greatly influenced by his upbringing, Pat Conroy's work was influenced by his life as a "military brat," who often moved during his youth on account of his father's military service. Conroy wrote novels and memoirs. Four of those novels were adapted into feature films, and the cinematic adaptations of *The Great Santini* (1979) and *The Prince of Tides* (1991) were nominated for multiple Academy Awards (Conroy was nominated for co-writing the screenplay of the latter). At the age of 70, Conroy died on March 4, 2016, of pancreatic cancer.

Gloria DeHaven (July 23, 1925-July 30, 2016). An actress who began her film career working with Charlie Chaplin in *Modern Times* (1936), Gloria DeHaven was a contract star for Metro-Goldwyn-Mayer. The daughter of actor/director Carter DeHaven and actress Flora Parker DeHaven, the actress portrayed her mother in the 1950 musical *Three Little Words*, starring Fred Astaire. DeHaven was also a professional singer, appeared on numerous television shows, and performed on Broadway. In 1960, she was given a star on the Hollywood Walk of Fame. DeHaven's final film was *Out to Sea* (1997), in which she played the love interest of Jack Lemmon's character. DeHaven died in hospice care at the age of 91 on July 30, 2016.

Larry Drake (February 21, 1949-March 17, 2016). Larry Drake played the role of Benny Stulwicz on *L.A. Law*—a role for which he would win two consecutive Primetime Emmy Awards, from 1987 until the end of the show in 1994. He played mobster Robert G. Durant in Sam Raimi's *Darkman* (1990) and the film's 1995 direct-to-video sequel *Darkman II: The Return of Durant*. Drake voiced the character Pops on the animated series *Johnny Bravo*, and he appeared in multiple movies and television shows. At the age of 67, the actor died of blood cancer on March 17, 2016.

Patty Duke (December 14, 1946-March 29, 2016). At the age of 16, Patty Duke won the Academy Award for Best Supporting Actress for playing Helen Keller in the 1962 film *The Miracle Worker*, a role she originated at the age of 12 in the 1959 Broadway production. Duke played "identical cousins" on *The Patty Duke Show* (1963-1966), which was created for her. During the mid-to-late-1960s, she had

a successful singing career. To break into adult roles, Duke starred in *Valley of the Dolls* (1967) and *Me, Natalie* (1969). She returned to television throughout the 1970s and 1980s. In 1982, she was diagnosed with bipolar disorder, a fact she revealed in her 1987 autobiography *Call Me Anna*. The book was adapted for television in 1990, with Duke playing herself. She became an advocate on issues of mental health; following her death, Duke's son, actor Sean Astin, started a crowdfunding campaign to raise money for mental health in her name. She was the second woman to serve as president of the Screen Actors Guild, and her career in film and television continued through the 1990s and 2000s. Duke died of sepsis at the age of 69 on March 29, 2016.

Ronit Elkabetz (November 27, 1964-April 19, 2016). Israeli actress and filmmaker Ronit Elkabetz came to international attention with her starring role in *Late Marriage* (2001) and her final film *Gett: The Trial of Viviane Amsalem* (2014), which she starred in and co-wrote and co-directed with her younger brother Shlomi. The 2014 film was the third of a triptych of films (following *To Take a Wife* [2004] and *Shiva* [2008]) about the life of the eponymous character. Elkabetz began her career as a model but became an acclaimed actor, earning three Ophir Awards for acting from the Israeli Academy of Film and Television, and filmmaker, receiving an Ophir nomination for *Shiva*, which she also co-directed with her brother. Living in both Tel Aviv and Paris, Elkabetz also worked in the French film industry, and in 2010, she received a lifetime achievement Ophir Award. Elkabetz died of cancer on April 19, 2016, at the age of 51.

Fyvush Finkel (October 9, 1922-August 14, 2016). Before an acting career on Broadway, off-Broadway, television, and film, Fyvush Finkel had a near four-decade career, beginning at the age of nine, in Yiddish theaters. He made his Broadway debut in the original 1964 production of *Fiddler on the Roof*. He would later play the show's lead role during the national tour. Finkel made appearances in small roles on television, but it was his performance as an attorney in Sidney Lumet's *Q & A* (1990) that would land him the role of Douglas Wambaugh, a public defender, on David E. Kelley's television drama *Picket Fences* (1992-1996). He won an Emmy Award for his performance on the show in 1994. He also appeared in Oliver Stone's *Nixon* (1995) and Joel and Ethan Coen's *A Serious Man* (2009). Finkel died following heart problems at the age of 93 on August 14, 2016.

Carrie Fisher (October 21, 1956-December 27, 2016). Born into entertainment-world royalty, Carrie Fisher became famous for playing a princess in a galaxy far, far away. The daughter of actress/singer Debbie Reynolds and singer/actor Eddie Fisher, Fisher first appeared on the Broadway stage in a 1973 revival of *Irene*, which starred her mother. Her film debut came in 1975's *Shampoo*, but it was her role as Princess (later, General) Leia in *Star Wars* (1977) and its two sequels that made her a star. She also appeared in *The Blues Brothers* (1980) and Woody Allen's *Hannah and Her Sisters* (1986). In addition to her acting career, Fisher was a novelist, memoirist, and screenwriter. She wrote the screenplay for *Postcards from the Edge* (1990), adapted from her semi-autobiographical 1987 novel of the same name, which was a fictionalized account of her drug addiction and relationship with her mother. Fisher was frank and public about her issues with addiction and mental illness. Her 2006 one-woman play *Wishful Drinking*, which she adapted into a 2008 book, discussed her personal life and career with often-sardonic humor. Fisher continued to act in film and on television, reprising her role of Leia in *Star Wars: The Force Awakens* (2015) and completing her performance in the role in that film's 2017 follow-up. In addition to her famous parents, Fisher was sister to director/producer Todd Fisher, half-sister to actresses Joely Fisher and Tricia Leigh Fisher, and mother to actress Billie Lourd. Four days after suffering a medical emergency during a flight, Fisher died of cardiac arrest at the age of 60 on December 27, 2016. Her mother died the following day.

Bernard Fox (May 11, 1927-December 14, 2016). Part of an acting family, Bernard Fox resumed his childhood career after serving in the Royal Navy during World War II. He is best known for playing Dr. Bombay on *Bewitched* (1964-1972) and Colonel Crittendon on *Hogan's Heroes* (1965-1971), although he also had roles in two films about the sinking of the RMS *Titanic*: an uncredited role in 1958's *A Night to Remember* and as Archibald Gracie IV in James Cameron's *Titanic* (1997). Fox appeared in numerous television shows and films between 1956 and 2004. He died on December 14, 2016, at the age of 89 of heart failure.

Glenn Frey (November 6, 1948-January 18, 2016). Glenn Frey was a founding member of and lead singer for the band the Eagles, which he and Don Henley formed 1971. The band became almost as famous for their 1980 break-up and 1994 reunion as it did for a series of hit songs, including Frey-led "Take It Easy," "Tequila Sunrise," "Lyin' Eyes," and "Heartache Tonight." During his post-Eagles solo career, Frey recorded "The Heat Is On" for the soundtrack of *Beverly Hills Cop* (1984), "You Belong to the City" for the television series *Miami Vice* (1984-1989), "Flip City" for *Ghostbusters II* (1989), and "Part of Me, Part of You" for *Thelma & Louise* (1991). He guest starred on various television series, including *Miami Vice*, and appeared in the films *Let's Get Harry* (1986) and *Jerry Maguire* (1996). While recovering from surgery, which resulted from complications from medication for rheumatoid arthritis, Frey died at the age of 67 on January 18, 2016.

Zsa Zsa Gabor (February 6, 1917-December 18, 2016). Before becoming an iconic Hungarian-American actress and socialite, Zsa Zsa Gabor was Sari Gabor, the middle of three daughters in a Jewish family. In 1934, Gabor's talents as a singer were discovered by tenor Richard Tauber in Vienna in 1934; two years later, Gabor was crowned Miss Hungary. From there, she built a career on her powerful presence, co-writing a novel in 1944 with Victoria Wolf titled *Every Man for Himself*, which is said to have been inspired in part by her own life. As for a career on the silver screen, her filmography was eclectic, ranging from *Touch of Evil* (Orson Welles, 1958) to Chuck Russell's *A Nightmare on Elm Street: Dream Warriors* (1987) and beyond. She was a regular on television shows, with hosts that included Milton Berle, Jack Paar, Howard Stern, and Joan Rivers. Gabor led an iconic life, both on screens and off of them. She passed away at the age of 99 from cardiac arrest on December 18, 2016.

George Gaynes (May 3, 1917-February 15, 2016). Born George Jongejans, actor, voice artist, comedy performer, and theatrical actor George Gaynes was born in Finland in 1917. He served during World War II as a translator, given the multilingual abilities he had learned being born to a Russian artist mother and a Dutch businessman father. A career as an actor took off when he started acting on Broadway in 1946, and becoming an American citizen in 1948. George became a presence in the world of film and television in the early '60s, appearing in the likes of *The Way We Were* (Sydney Pollack, 1973), *Tootsie* (Sydney Pollack, 1982) and Louis Malle's *Vanya on 42nd Street* (1994). He also had a big part in the *Police Academy* movies, and on the show *Punky Brewster*. His last on-screen performance happening in 2003, Gaynes passed away at the age of 98 at his home in North Bend, Washington, on February 15, 2016.

Ron Glass (July 10, 1945-November 25, 2016). American actor Ron Glass (born Ronald Earle Glass) knew that he wanted to be an actor when attending college at the University of Evansville, after having grown up in the same Indiana town. His acting career was mostly on the stage, but his TV career started in 1972 when he appeared on an episode of *Sanford and Son,* with appearances on *Hawaii Five-O*, *All in the Family*, and *Barney Miller* following shortly after. Glass enjoyed a few roles in films like 1995's *Houseguest* (Randall Miller), but had his largest role arguably in the 2005 Joss Whedon film *Serenity*, a feature based on the series *Firefly* which Glass also appeared in. Glass died on November 25, 2016, of respiratory failure at the age of 71.

Tammy Grimes (January 30, 1934-October 30, 2016). Tammy Lee Grimes was born in Lynn, Massachusetts, the daughter of a spiritualist mother and a farmer father. In her lifetime she developed a memorable presence on the stage with a speaking voice that was famously compared to a buzz saw, starting her stage career in 1955. Throughout her time in theater, she became a mainstay of Noel Coward's productions, including having the lead role in Coward's 1959 Broadway production of *Look After Lulu!* The year after, she won the Tony Award for Best Featured Actress in a Musical for her work in *The Unsinkable Molly Brown*, a musical comedy. Grimes' career on the silver screen started in 1967 with the comedy *Three Bites of the Apple* (Alvin Ganzer), and then appearances in various films like *America* (Robert Downey Sr., 1986) and *High Art* (Lisa Cholodenko, 1998). Grimes was inducted into the American Theater Hall of Fame in 2003, and in 2007 had her own one-woman show, the acclaimed *An Evening with Miss Tammy Grimes*. Grimes passed away on October 30, 2016, at the age of 82 in Englewood, New Jersey.

Dan Haggerty (November 19, 1942-January 15, 2016). Actor Dan Haggerty grew up in a family that ran its own small wild-animal attraction, where he helped train a black bear that performed tricks. His experience with animals got him onto the sets of various productions, where he worked as either a stunt man or an animal trainer. He even assisted in building motorcycles for the iconic road movie *Easy Rider* (Dennis Hopper, 1969). This wisdom of the outdoors, productions, and acting coalesced into his most iconic role, the nature-inclined title character of the 1974

Richard Friedenberg film *The Life and Times of Grizzly Adams*. The role would be so famous that it would spawn a TV show of the same name in which he played the character in both the show and the TV movies that followed. Haggerty enjoyed various other appearances in TV and film after that success. He passed away on January 15, 2016, at the age of 73 from spinal cancer.

Guy Hamilton (September 16, 1922-April 20, 2016). Film director Guy Hamilton was born Mervyn Ian Guy Hamilton in Paris, France, to British parents. After attending school in England, Hamilton was first exposed to the film industry when working as a clapperboard boy in Nice in 1938, before serving time in World War II and eventually receiving the Distinguished Service Cross. Not long after the war, Hamilton worked as assistant director on some Carol Reed productions, including 1948's *The Fallen Idol* and 1949's *The Third Man*. After making his debut as a feature director in 1952 with the mystery film *The Ringer*, Hamilton made a career for himself of helming pictures mostly of the war variety, until he fell into the gig to direct fictional secret agent James Bond. Hamilton directed four Bond movies throughout his career: *Goldfinger* (1964), *Diamonds Are Forever* (1971), *Live and Let Die* (1973), and *The Man with the Golden Gun* (1974). Hamilton directed other pictures of note including war film *Force 10 from Navarone* (1978, starring Harrison Ford) and *Remo Williams: The Adventure Begins* (1985, starring Fred Ward). Hamilton's last directed film was 1989's *Try This One for Size*. Hamilton died on April 20, 2016, at the age of 93 in Majorca, Spain.

Curtis Hanson (March 24, 1945-September 20, 2016). Born Curtis Lee Hanson in Reno, Nevada, the future Oscar winner was the son of a real estate agent and teacher, growing up in Los Angeles. After dropping out of high school, Hanson took on a different education when he worked as a freelance photographer and editor for *Cinema* magazine, a road that would lead him to writing and directing. Hanson started filmmaking under the wing of iconic B-movie producer Roger Corman, who produced Hanson's first script, *The Dunwich Horror* in 1970 (Daniel Haller). Hanson made his directorial debut with the 1973 film *Sweet Kill*, a Corman production that Hanson also wrote. Hanson's career would then expand beyond B-movies to larger budgets and numerous genres, including the 1997 noir film *L.A. Confidential,* for which he won the Oscar for Best Adapted Screenplay (shared with Brian Helgeland). Hanson then directed the likes of *Wonder Boys* (2000), *8 Mile* (2002), and *In Her Shoes* (2005), proving his range as a director for various projects that relied on more than just its stars' power. Hanson retired from work after 2012's *Chasing Mavericks*, and died of natural causes on September 20, 2016, at the age of 71 in his home in Hollywood Hills, California.

Florence Henderson (February 14, 1934-November 24, 2016). Entertainment was in the blood of American actress and singer Florence Henderson, was born on Valentine's Day into a large family in a small Indiana town. Taught to sing by her mother at a very young age, Henderson soon took her career as a performer from singing at grocery stores to performing in Broadway musicals. Her most iconic turn as an actress came in 1969, when a career of various TV

performances led her to the role of matriarch Carol Brady on *The Brady Bunch,* a role that she had for the show's five-year run and would be cherished for the rest of her life. She made her film debut in 1970 in the operetta adaptation *Song of Norway* (Andrew L. Stone), but would not appear in many movies after. She did, however, enjoy many appearances in both TV and film playing herself, her iconic nature preceding her as an American talent everyone could love. Henderson died on November 24, 2016, at the age of 82 in Los Angeles, California, of heart failure.

Michael Herr (April 13, 1940-June 23, 2016). Born Michael David Herr, American writer and war correspondent Michael Herr made his way into the film world by his unique perspective, which would inform in particular two of the greatest films of all time. After writing the book *Dispatches* in 1977, which Truman Capote said was the best book to have been written about the Vietnam War, Herr was enlisted to work on the narration for Francis Ford Coppola's epic *Apocalypse Now* (1979). In 1987, Herr co-wrote the screenplay for *Full Metal Jacket* with director Stanley Kubrick and Gustav Hasford, receiving an Oscar nomination. Their collaboration on that film would lead to a professional relationship, in which Herr wrote various pieces for *Vanity Fair* about Kubrick, which later became a small, very personal biography named *Kubrick.* Herr died in Delhi, New York, at the age of 76 on June 23, 2016.

Steven Hill (February 22, 1922-August 23, 2016). Born Solomon Krakovsky to Russian Jewish immigrant parents, Steven Hill made breakout as an actor in 1950 when he co-starred opposite Hedy Lamarr in *A Lady Without Passport* (Joseph H. Lewis). That role launched a career of B-movies, which then got him to a big starring role in the 1966 series *Mission: Impossible*. However, due to his Orthodox Jewish faith and his desire to observe the Sabbath, he was fired from the show after one season for not working Saturdays, which caused him to disappear from acting until the '80s. He then co-starred in films like Claudia Weill's 1980 project *It's My Turn* (opposite Michael Douglas, Jill Clayburgh, and Charles Grodin) and *Yentl* (Barbara Streisand, 1983). Hill returned to TV to play a long-lasting role on *Law & Order,* as a district attorney who led with integrity, not unlike Hill himself. Hill passed away on August 23, 2016, at the age of 94 in New York.

Arthur Hiller (November 22, 1923-August 17, 2016). Canadian-American television and film director Arthur Hiller was born into a life of entertainment, the son of two Jewish parents in Edmonton that loved putting on small theater productions for their Jewish community. Along with developing a love for music and literature at a young age, Hiller started his career of directing in Canada, working on shows like *Alfred Hitchcock Presents, Gunsmoke* and *Playhouse 90.* Hiller made his debut as a film director with 1957's *The Careless Years.* He had a critical success of note a few films later with *The Americanization of Emily* (1964), one of two collaborations he did with screenwriter Paddy Chayefsky. Hiller had his most successful film in 1970 with *Love Story,* starring Ryan O'Neal and Ali MacGraw as two young lovers in a romantic tragedy, which earned Hiller the Oscar nomination for Best Director. The next year, Hiller made *The Hospital* starring George C. Scott, which earned writer Paddy Chayefsky an Oscar for

Best Original Screenplay. Hiller collaborated with another famous writer, Neil Simon, in two back-to-back successes: 1970's *The Out-of-Towners* and 1971's *Plaza Suite*, which boasted Hiller's gift for smooth direction in complicated scenes of comedy. This very reputation, along with the projects that could prove it hit after hit, helped him earn the stature of President of the Directors Guild of America from 1989 to 1993 and President of the Academy of Motion Picture Arts and Sciences from 1993 to 1997, along with the Jean Hersholt Humanitarian Award in 2002. Hiller also served as a member of the National Film Preservation Board of the Library of Congress from 1989-2005. At the age of 92, Hiller died of natural causes in Los Angeles, California.

Ken Howard (March 28, 1944-March 23, 2016). Kenneth Joseph Howard was an American actor whose career was filled with and bookended by acclaim, starting with the Tony Award he received in 1970 for his part in the production of *Child's Play*. Soon after, he starred as Thomas Jefferson in the Broadway production of *1776*, and then reprised the role for the 1972 film directed by Peter H. Hunt. One of his best-known roles was as basketball coach Ken Reeves on the television drama *The White Shadow*. After years of TV and film roles, Howard wrote a book in 2003 based on dramatic courses that he taught at Harvard University, *Act Natural: How to Speak to Any Audience*. Six years later, Howard received an Emmy Award for his work opposite Jessica Lange in the 2009 HBO adaptation of *Grey Gardens*. In the same year, he was elected National President of the Screen Actors Guild, serving until 2012. Howard died at the age of 71 in Valencia, California, on March 23, 2016.

David Huddleston (September 17, 1930-August 2, 2016). Born David William Huddleston in Vinton, Virginia, the Emmy Award nominee and notable character actor enjoyed a prolific career. He appeared on a large amount of TV shows in the 1960s and '70s after starting an acting career in 1968, programs that included *Gunsmoke, Bonanza, The Waltons, The Mary Tyler Moore Show, Hawaii Five-O, Charlie's Angels* and *Sanford and Son*. Perhaps no role of his was more iconic than playing the title tycoon of the Coen brothers' 1998 film *The Big Lebowski*, which used his large, commanding presence for some of its most pivotal scenes. Huddleston appeared on the stage and on the screen until 2009. He passed away from heart and kidney disease on August 2, 2016, in Santa Fe, New Mexico.

Anne Jackson (September 3, 1925-April 12, 2016). Anna Jane "Anne" Jackson was born in Millvale, Pennsylvania. After studying acting in New York at the Neighborhood Playhouse and The Actor's Studio, she made her Broadway debut in 1945, beginning a career of theater performances that included productions of *Summer and Smoke, The Waltz of the Toreadors*, and *Lost in Yonkers*. Her first role in film was in 1950, with the Bernard Vorhaus drama *So Young, So Bad*, leading to a filmography that included work on Arthur Hiller's *The Tiger Makes Out* (1967) and Stanley Kubrick's *The Shining* (1980). Jackson also appeared on various television shows that ranged from *Gunsmoke* to *Law & Order*. Jackson shared her knowledge of the craft when later

teaching at the Herbert Berghof Studio in New York City. She passed away at the age of 90 in her Manhattan home on April 12, 2016.

Marvin Kaplan (January 24, 1927-August 25, 2016). Marvin Wilbur Kaplan was born in Brooklyn, New York, a location that greatly informed the unique presence he brought to the screen. The stocky, bespectacled, and thick-accented actor was discovered on the stage by Katharine Hepburn, who had him make his first on-screen role in a small part in 1949's *Adam's Rib* (George Cukor). Kaplan would then lend his voice to the likes of the cartoon series *Top Cat* and *Garfield*, while making appearances in films like *It's a Mad, Mad, Mad, Mad World* (Stanley Kramer, 1963) and Gary Nelson's *Freaky Friday* (1976). As a creative, Kaplan was a member of Theatre West, the oldest continually operating theater company in Los Angeles, performing in many plays and also being known as an accomplished playwright. Kaplan died on August 25, 2016, at the age of 89 of natural causes.

George Kennedy (February 18, 1925-February 28, 2016). George Harris Kennedy Jr. was born into a show business family in New York City, his father a musician and orchestra leader, his mother a ballet dancer. He made his debut on stage at the age of two for a production of *Bringing Up Father*, and had his first notable on-screen role as a military advisor in the TV sitcom *The Phil Silvers Show*. From there he had a career as an actor that included more than 200 film and TV appearances, which included an Oscar-winning performance for *Cool Hand Luke* (Stuart Rosenberg, 1967) opposite Paul Newman. He also appeared in all four of the *Airport* films as one of the main characters, and in two pictures opposite Clint Eastwood, *Thunderbolt and Lightfoot* (Michael Cimino, 1974) and *The Eiger Sanction* (Clint Eastwood, 1975). On television, Kennedy appeared in such shows as *The Blue Knight* and *Dallas*, the latter in which he had a role that lasted from 1988 to the show's end in 1991. Kennedy received a star on the Hollywood Walk of Fame for his work in movies, and in 2011 wrote an autobiography titled *Trust Me*. Kennedy passed away on February 28, 2016, at the age of 91 in Middleton, Idaho.

Abbas Kiarostami (June 22, 1940-July 4, 2016). Iranian filmmaker Abbas Kiarostami achieved his cinematic legacy by being one of the leading directors of his nation, having directed 40 films, shorts, and documentaries in his lifetime. Of particular note was his gorgeous 1990 film *Close-Up*—which blended fact and fiction in a way that still inspires filmmakers to this day—1997's *A Taste of Cherry* and 1999's *The Wind Will Carry Us*. His films, and his artistry as a poet, photographer, painter, illustrator, and graphic designer made him a key part of the Iranian New Wave. Kiarostami's work received acclaim throughout his life, creating an audience that was truly international, while making films that were at the same time unmistakably of Persian inspiration. Kiarostami died at the age of 76 in Paris, France, on July 4, 2016.

Burt Kwouk (July 18, 1930-May 24, 2016). Herbert Tsangtse "Burt" Kwouk was born in England but grew up in Shanghai and was then college educated in Brunswick, Maine. His career as an actor started in 1957 with the film *Windom's Way* (Ronald Neame), but took off when he became known for playing Cato Fong, the reoccurring manservant of character Inspector Clouseau in the *Pink Panther* movies. Kwouk built a career out of appearing in television and film, often when an Asian character was specifically required, as when he played a Chinese expert named Mr. Ling in Guy Hamilton's *Goldfinger* (1964), or a Japanese general in another James Bond movie, *You Only Live Twice* (Lewis Gilbert, 1967). His career later involved voice acting for video games, audio theater, and television commercials. Kwouk died on May 24, 2016, in Hampstead, London, England, at the age of 85 from cancer.

Harper Lee (April 28, 1926-February 19, 2016). Nelle Harper Lee was raised in Monroeville, Alabama, a life experience that would influence the future author's best-selling book, *To Kill a Mockingbird*. Published in 1960, the novel won a Pulitzer Prize and inspired an Oscar-winning adaptation from director Robert Mulligan, starring Gregory Peck. Lee led a very private life after the book's release, in spite of the acclaim always bestowed on the novel and the multiple adaptations that were made from it. She was awarded the Presidential Medal of Freedom by U.S. President George W. Bush in 2007, and the 2010 National Medal of Arts by U.S. President Barack Obama. Lee passed away on February 19, 2016, at the age of 89.

Herschell Gordon Lewis (June 15, 1926-September 26, 2016). American filmmaker Herschell Gordon Lewis became known as the "Godfather of Gore" for his pioneering of the "splatter" subgenre in horror. Born in Pittsburgh and raised in Chicago, Lewis worked with the needs of audience when he started working on TV ads and teaching graduate classes on advertising. This led to a savviness that came in handy when Lewis started directing his own movies, blood-soaked and sex-filled ventures that would lure audiences who adored the exploitation. His legacy started arguably with the 1963 film *Blood Feast*, which is said to be the first "gore" film of its kind. After making a batch of more films, including 1967's *A Taste of Blood* and *The Gruesome Twosome* of the same year, Lewis took a long break from directing in 1972. He then went on to work in advertising and copywriting, of which he wrote many books about in the 1980s. Lewis returned to directing in 2002 with *Blood Feast 2: All U Can Eat*, while enjoying status as cult icon who had changed the game on violence and sex in cinema. Lewis died at the age of of 90 in Fort Lauderdale, Florida, on September 26, 2016.

Garry Marshall (November 13, 1934-July 19, 2016). Although his work in both television and feature films rarely received rave reviews from critics, Marshall's generally feel-good entertainments more often than not found great favor with the public and even launched the careers of more than a few unknowns into superstardom. Born in the Bronx in 1934 to a father who directed industrial films and a mother who was a dance instructor, Marshall attended college at Northwestern University and broke into the entertainment industry by writing jokes for the Jack Parr incarnation of *The Tonight Show*, He then partnered up with Jerry Belson and wrote for such programs as *The Dick Van Dyke Show* and *The Joey Bishop Show* before setting off to produce their own programs, the most notable of which was a TV spinoff of Neil Simon's *The Odd Couple*. Splitting with Belson, Marshall continued to develop shows for

television and came up with three of the biggest programs of the 1970s with *Happy Days*, *Laverne & Shirley* (which co-starred his sister Penny) and *Mork & Mindy* (which brought instant fame to its star, a then-unknown comedian named Robin Williams). In the Eighties, he shifted his focus to film, making his directorial debut with the soap opera spoof *Young Doctors in Love* (1982). He received strong reviews for his next two films, the nostalgic *The Flamingo Kid* (1984) and the comedy/drama *Nothing in Common* (1986). He followed those up with the romantic farce *Overboard* (1987) and the melodrama hit *Beaches* (1988) before striking gold with the modern-day Cinderella story *Pretty Woman* (1990), which recharged the waning career of Richard Gere and made a superstar out of Julia Roberts. The next decade saw a number of less successful films, an adaptation of the play *Frankie & Johnny* (1991), a bizarrely bad comedic take on Anne Rice's serious S&M-tinged novel *Exit to Eden* (1994), the forgettable *Dear God* (1996), and the mawkish *The Other Sister* (1999) before regaining his audience by reuniting with Roberts and Gere for *Runaway Bride* (1999). He then went back to the contemporary fairy tale well with *The Princess Diaries* (2001) and not only had a hit but made a star out of newcomer Anne Hathaway. Over the next few years, he would make the innocuous Kate Hudson vehicle *Raising Helen* (2004), the inevitable *The Princess Diaries 2* (2004), and *Georgia Rule* (2007), a dark melodrama that was overshadowed by the behind-the-scenes misbehavior of star Lindsay Lohan. He would conclude his directing career with a trio of multi-story films that centered around major holidays and included most current members of SAG in their sprawling casts: *Valentine's Day* (2010), *New Year's Eve* (2011), and *Mother's Day* (2016). He also made the occasional appearance in front of the camera, most notably as an incredulous casino manager in Albert Brooks' *Lost in America* (1985), and his gravelly voice and garrulous manner also kept him in demand as a voice artist in cartoons such as *The Simpsons*. He passed away on July 19, 2016, a few weeks after the release of *Mother's Day*, of complications from pneumonia following a stroke.

Michael Massee (September 1, 1952-October 20, 2016). Although his odd and somewhat sinister look would make him a familiar face to moviegoers and a favorite of directors like David Fincher and David Lynch, Massee's biggest claim to fame would prove to be his unfortunate connection to one of Hollywood's most infamous set tragedies. Born in Kansas City, Missouri, in 1952, Massee had only one previous screen credit, *My Father is Coming* (1991), when he was hired to play a key supporting role as one of the bad guys in *The Crow* (1994). For a scene in which his character was supposed to fire a gun at star Brandon Lee, Massee was handed a gun that had been improperly loaded with a full power blank and which also contain a bullet from an earlier shot that had gotten stuck in the barrel. When Massee fired the gun, the blank forced the bullet out and hit Lee in the lower spine and he would die of his injuries the next day. Although cleared of any wrongdoing, Massee considered leaving the business for good but soon returned to the industry and appeared over the next couple of years in such films as *Sahara* (1995), *Seven* (1995), *Tales from the Hood* (1995), *One Fine Day* (1996), *The Game*

(1997), *The End of Violence* (1997), *Lost Highway* (1997), and *Amistad* (1997). In later years, he would turn up frequently on television on such shows as *The X-Files*, *Murder One*, *24*, *Carnivale*, and *Alias* and in films like *Catwoman* (2004), *The Amazing Spider-Man* (2012), and *The Amazing Spider-Man 2* (2014). He died on October 20, 2016, in Los Angeles, California, of complications from cancer.

Michele Morgan (February 29, 1920-December 20, 2016). One of the last survivors of the Golden Age of filmmaking, both in Europe and the United States, Morgan was 15 when she left her home in the suburbs of Paris, France, to make it as an actress, funding her lessons by working as an extra. She would get her big break a couple of years later when she was cast as the female lead in *Gribouille* (1937) and would soon appear in other films such as *Le Quai des brunes* (1938) and *Remorques* (1941). In 1940, she fled to the United States before the Nazis landed in France and attempted to make a go of it there. Although she appeared in films like *Joan of Paris* (1942), *Higher and Higher* (1943), and *Passage to Marseilles* (1944), her U.S. career was most notable for a part that she did not get, the role of Ilsa in *Casablanca* (1942) that she was considered for before it went to Ingrid Bergman. After the war concluded, she returned to Europe and appeared in films steadily for the next two decades, including *La Symphone Pastoral* (1946)—for which she received the first Best Actress award presented by the Cannes Film Festival—*The Fallen Idol* (1948), *Here in the Beauty* (1949), *Obsession* (1954), and *Napoleon* (1954). After making *Diary of an Innocent Boy* (1967), she largely retired from films aside from the occasional cameo role, the last being in *Everybody's Fine* (1990), and spent the following years painting and writing her autobiography, *With These Eyes*, which was published in 1977. Among the awards bestowed upon her, she received the Legion d'Honneur in 1967, an honorary Cesar in 1992, and a Career Golden Lion from the Venice Film Festival in 1996. She passed away on December 20, 2016, in France from natural causes.

Bill Nunn (October 20, 1953-September 24, 2016). Best known for his films with Spike Lee and later for his appearances in the first Spider-Man franchise, Bill Nunn was born in Pittsburgh in 1953 and attended Morehouse College, where Lee was one of his classmates. Although his first film role was an uncredited bit part in *Sharky's Machine* (1981), Nunn's first major part came when he co-starred in Lee's musical drama *School Daze* (1988), the first of a series of collaborations with Lee that would also include his portrayal of Radio Raheem in the landmark *Do the Right Thing* (1989) and turns in *Mo' Better Blues* (1990) and *He Got Game* (1998). Throughout the Nineties, he turned up in a number of popular films, including *New Jack City* (1991), *Regarding Henry* (1991), *Sister Act* (1992), *The Last Seduction* (1994), and *Kiss the Girls* (1997). He later appeared as James "Robbie" Robertson in the smash hit *Spider-Man* (2002) and the sequels *Spider-Man 2* and *Spider-Man 3* (2007); he was also seen in films such as *Idlewild* (2006) and made numerous stage appearances, including the lead role in a production of *Fences*. Nunn passed away on September 24, 2016, after a battle with leukemia; he was 62.

Hugh O'Brian (April 19, 1925-September 5, 2016). Although he became an actor largely as the result of a fluke encounter, O'Brian would nevertheless go on to a long career that would see him become one of the biggest stars in the early years of television. Born Hugh Charles Krampe in Rochester, New York, he dropped out of the University of Cincinnati in 1942 to join the Marines and after serving there, he moved to Los Angeles to study law. While dating an actress, he attended a rehearsal of a play she was in and when one of the actors didn't show, the director, Ida Lupino, asked him to read the lines and was so impressed by his work that she cast him in the role instead. Later, Lupino would cast him in a film she was directing, *Never Fear* (1949), and this would lead to a contract with Universal Studios. For the next few years, he appeared in a number of films, mostly B westerns but also in such classics as *D.O.A.* (1949) and *There's No Business Like Show Business* (1954), and also turned up regularly on television. In 1955, he signed on to play the lead role in *The Life & Legend of Wyatt Earp*, an adult-oriented Western series that would run for more than 200 episodes before leaving the air in 1961 and which would earn him a Emmy nomination for Best Actor in 1957. After the end of the series, he divided his career between appearances in television shows, including *Alfred Hitchcock Presents*, *Perry Mason*, *Charlie's Angels*, *Police Story*, and *Fantasy Island* and films such as *Come Fly with Me* (1963), *Ten Little Indians* (1965), *Assassination in Rome* (1965), *The Shootist* (1976)—where he became the last man John Wayne killed on screen—*Killer Force* (1976), *Game of Death* (1979), *Twins* (1988), and *Wyatt Earp: Return to Tombstone* (1994). O'Brian died on September 5, 2016, in Beverly Hills, California, of natural causes.

Jon Polito (December 29, 1950-September 1, 2016). Best known for his appearances in numerous films by the Coen Brothers, Polito's explosive personality made him a favorite character actor on film and television who often played either cops or crooks. Born in Philadelphia in 1950, Polito attended college at Villanova, where he studied theater, and made his first Broadway appearance at the age of 26 when he was hired as Kenneth McMillan's understudy for the original run of David Mamet's *American Buffalo*. He made his television debut in 1981 with a supporting role on the short-lived period drama *The Gangster Chronicles* and also appeared on such acclaimed shows as *Crime Story* and *Homicide*. On the big screen, he had small roles in films such as *C.H.U.D.* (1984), *Remo Williams: The Adventure Begins* (1985), *Compromising Positions* (1985), *Highlander* (1986), and *Critical Condition* (1987) before taking on the scene-stealing role of gangster Johnny Caspar in the Coens' gangster epic *Miller's Crossing* (1990), the beginning of a collaboration that would see Polito working with them again on *Barton Fink* (1991), *The Hudsucker Proxy* (1994), *The Big Lebowski* (1998), and *The Man Who Wasn't There* (2001). Outside of his work with the Coens, Polito turned up in a number of other films, including *The Freshman* (1990), *The Rocketeer* (1991), *Blankman* (1994), *The Crow* (1994), *The Tailor of Panama* (2001), *The Singing Detective* (2003), *Flags of our Fathers* (2006), *American Gangster* (2007), *Atlas Shrugged: Part 1 (2011)*, *Gangster Squad*

(2013), and *Big Eyes* (2014). Polito died in California on September 1, 2016, of complications from multiple myeloma.

Prince (June 7, 1958-April 21, 2016). Although justifiably famous as one of the most prodigiously talented singer/songwriters of his era as well as one of its most electrifying performers, Prince Rogers Nelson also made occasional forays into the world of film with equally striking results. Born in Minneapolis in 1958, the musical prodigy signed his first record contract at the age of 18 and his first five albums, culminating with the smash hit *1999*, won him a steadily expanding fan base for his blend of funk, rock, and soul. Like other pop stars before him, Hollywood beckoned to sign him up for what they presumably thought would be a quickie movie meant to exploit both his popularity and that of the newly emerging force known as MTV. Instead, the resulting film, *Purple Rain* (1984), was a dark and semi-autobiographical psychodrama driven by his undeniable magnetism and the power of the soundtrack that he composed and performed with his band, The Revolution, that included such hits as "When Doves Cry," "Let's Go Crazy," and the title tune. Both the album and the film were enormous hits, even earning Prince an Oscar for Original Song Score, and Hollywood then clamored for a followup. Instead of giving them *Purple Rain 2*, Prince came up with a strange Thirties-influenced fantasy titled *Under the Cherry Moon* (1986) in which he played a gigolo on the French Riviera who fell in love with a spoiled heiress (Kristen Scott Thomas). The film, which Prince also directed, was a flop though the soundtrack album, *Parade*, was more successful. He returned to the director's chair with *Sign O' the Times* (1988), a concert film chronicling a 1987 European tour promoting the album of the same name. His last major excursion into filmmaking came with *Graffiti Bridge* (1990), a mystical semi-sequel to *Purple Rain* that did not come close to approaching the original in terms of popularity. Prince's other major foray into cinema came when he was approached to compose songs for the soundtrack to the blockbuster superhero film *Batman* (1989) that helped contribute to the popularity of that film. In subsequent years, he would contribute the occasional song to films as varied as *Showgirls* (1995) and *Happy Feet* (2006) and made highly publicized appearances on episodes of *Muppets Tonight* and *New Girl*. Prince passed away from what was determined to be a fentanyl overdose at his Paisley Park mansion and studio on April 21, 2016, at the age of 57.

Nancy Reagan (July 6, 1921-March 6, 2016). Although she only made eleven feature films during her relatively brief screen career, the former Anne Francis Robbins would nevertheless become one of the most famous women in the world thanks to her marriage to fellow actor, one-time co-star, and future U.S. President Ronald Reagan. Born in New York in 1921, she attended Smith College and upon graduating in 1943, she decided to follow in the footsteps of her mother, radio actress Edith Prescott Luckett, by pursuing a career in acting. She landed a supporting role in the 1946 Broadway musical *Lute Song* and was eventually signed to a contract with MGM and made her screen debut in *Portrait of Jennie* (1948). Over the next few years, she appeared in such films as *The Doctor and the Girl* (1949),

East Side, West Side (1949), *Shadow on the Wall* (1950), *The Next Voice You Hear...* (1950), *Night Into Morning* (1950), *It's a Big Country* (1951), *Talk About Strangers* (1952), and *Shadow in the Sky* (1952). In 1952, she married Reagan and the next year saw her appear in one of her best-known films, the cult horror favorite *Donovan's Brain* (1953). Her next film, *Hellcats of the Navy* (1956), was her only feature film appearance with Reagan (though they appeared together in episodes of television shows such as *Zane Grey Theatre*, *Wagon Train*, and *The Tall Man*) and her next screen appearance in *Crash Landing* (1958) would prove to be her last. Nearly four decades later, she almost came out of retirement when Albert Brooks offered her the part of the cheerfully off-putting title character in his comedy *Mother* (1996) but declined in order to care for her husband, who was in the grips of Alzheimer's disease. Reagan died on March 6, 2016, in Bel-Air, California, at the age of 94 from congestive heart failure.

Debbie Reynolds (April 1, 1932-December 28, 2016). Whether it was the stage, the screen, or the recording studio, there was hardly an artistic field that Debbie Reynolds went into that she failed to triumph at during her long and celebrated career. Born in El Paso, Texas, in 1932, her family moved to Burbank, California, in 1939 and when she turned 16, she won a beauty contest and was named Miss Burbank. This brought her to the attention of talent scouts from both Warner Brothers and MGM and while she initially went with the former, she moved to MGM when Warner Brothers began phasing out the production of musicals. She made her screen debut with a bit part in *June Bride* (1948) and was noticed two years later when her performance in *Three Little Words* (1950) earned her a Golden Globe nomination for New Star of the Year and *Two Weeks in Love* (1950) earned her a gold record for her recording of the song "Aba Daba Honeymoon" (1950). She would then achieve screen immortality for her performance as ambitious starlet Kathy Selden in *Singin' in the Rain* (1952), the film generally considered to be the greatest screen musical of all time. For the next two decades, she was a regular screen presence whose credits included such titles as *I Love Melvin* (1953), *The Tender Trap* (1955), *The Catered Affair* (1956), *Tammy and the Bachelor* (1957), *Say One for Me* (1959), *How the West was Won* (1962), an Oscar and Golden Globe-nominated turn in *The Unsinkable Molly Brown* (1964), and *The Singing Nun* (1966). She then began to shift from films into television and stage work, both on Broadway, where she received a Tony nomination for *Irene* in 1975, and in cabaret with only occasional screen appearances such as *What's the Matter with Helen?* (1971) and supplying the voice of the benevolent spider in an animated version of *Charlotte's Web* (1973). She began her screen comeback with an appearance in Oliver Stone's war drama *Heaven & Earth* (1993) and received raves for her performance in the title role in Albert Brooks' *Mother* (1996). In later years, she appeared in such films as *In & Out* (1997), *Connie & Carla* (2004), *One for the Money* (2012), and as Liberace's mother in *Behind the Candelabra* (2013), as well as TV shows ranging from *Will & Grace* to *Rugrats*. In 2014, she received the SAG Lifetime Achievement Award and the next year was presented with the Jean Hersholt Humanitarian Award at the Academy Awards. She passed away on December 28, 2016, from a stroke, one day after the unexpected passing of her daughter, actress/writer Carrie Fisher, with whom she appeared in the documentary *Bright Lights* (2016).

Alan Rickman (February 21, 1946-January 14, 2016). Although one of the most celebrated actors of his time, the London-born Rickman originally studied graphic design and had even begun his own firm when a long-standing interest in theater led him to audition for the Royal Academy of Dramatic Arts at the relatively late age of 26. He passed and then began appearing on the stage and on television in England, first attracting attention in the United States with his performance in the Broadway version of the classic novel *Les Liasons Dangereuses* in 1987. A year later, he made his screen debut as a slick Euro-criminal going up against lone wolf cop Bruce Willis in the confines of a 40-story building in *Die Hard* (1988), which became an instant action classic that made him one of the most iconic screen villains of all time. Instead of simply being pigeonholed as a baddie, Rickman embarked on an eclectic career that saw him playing a wide variety of characters in films such as *The January Man* (1989), *Truly Madly Deeply* (1990), another scene-stealing villain in *Robin Hood: Prince of Thieves* (1991), *Closet Land* (1991), *Bob Roberts* (1992), *Sense & Sensibility* (1995), a television movie of *Rasputin* that earned him an Emmy and a Golden Globe, *Galaxy Quest* (1999), and *Dogma* (1999). He then took on the role of the dour Professor Severus Snape in *Harry Potter & the Sorcerer's Stone* (2001), the enormously successful screen adaptation of the J. K. Rowling bestseller and reprised the role through the seven subsequent films in the series that concluded with *Harry Potter & the Deathly Hollows: Part II* (2011). When not haunting the halls of Hogwarts, he appeared in films like *Love Actually* (2003), *Perfume: The Story of a Murderer* (2006), *Sweeney Todd: The Demon Barber of Fleet Street* (2007), *Alice in Wonderland* (2010), *Lee Daniels' The Butler* (2013), *Eye in the Sky* (2015), and *Alice Through the Looking Glass* (2016). In addition to his acting work, he also wrote and directed the films *The Winter Guest* (1997) and *A Little Chaos* (2014). Rickman passed away in London, England, on January 14, 2016, at the age of 69 from pancreatic cancer.

Jacques Rivette (March 1, 1928-January 29, 2016). One of the leading lights of what would become known as the French New Wave, Rivette went from being a film buff to a film critic before becoming one of his country's most celebrated filmmakers. Born in Rousen in 1928, he was interested in film from a young age and at 20 made his first short film, inspired by the works of Jean Cocteau. He soon moved to Paris and became a familiar face at local cinema clubs and Henri Langlois' famed Cinematheque Francaise along with such fellow obsessives as Francois Truffaut, Jean-Luc Godard, Eric Rohmer, and Claude Chabrol. In 1953, he was hired as a critic for the esteemed *Cahiers du Cinema* and professed a fascination with American films that was radical for the times. He then became the first of his group to cross over to begin production on a feature film, though his debut, *Paris Belong to Us* (1961), would not debut until after Truffaut and Godard had released their initial efforts. His next film, *The Nun* (1966), engendered a tremendous amount of controversy and faced a ban by the

Minister of Information before finally debuting to acclaim at the Cannes Film Festival. Unhappy with his experience on that film, he took on a new style that embraced the political turmoil of the times, improvisational theater techniques, elements of fantasy, and extended running times to create sprawling narratives. His first efforts with this style resulted in the highly acclaimed works *Out 1: Don't Touch Me* (1970), which clocked in at around 13 hours, and *Celine and Julie Go Boating* (1974), which ran for a comparatively svelte three hours. He would continue this approach for the next decade or so in films like *Duelle* (1976), *Merry-Go-Round* (1983), and *Love on the Ground* (1984), before switching to a more direct style of storytelling with *Gang of Four* (1989). He achieved his greatest critical and commercial success with *La Belle Noiseuse* (1991), a spellbinding four-hour-long look at the creative process centering on the relationship between a retired artist (Michel Piccoli), his former muse (Jane Birkin), and the young woman (Emmanuelle Beart) who unexpectedly reignites his artistic drive. His subsequent films became more eclectic, including the biopic *Joan the Maiden* (1994), the musical *Up Down Fragile* (1995), the screwball comedy *Va Savoir* (2001), the Balzac adaptation *The Duchess of Langeais* (2007), and the drama *Around a Small Mountain* (2009). That would prove to be his last film as he was already beginning to show the signs of the Alzheimer's disease that would lead to his death on January 29, 2016, at the age of 87.

Doris Roberts (November 4, 1925-April 17, 2016). Although she will be best remembered for her considerable television work, Doris Roberts also made a number of big-screen appearances throughout her long career, including a few titles that went on to become cult favorites. Born in St. Louis in 1925, she soon moved to the Bronx with her mother and maternal grandparents. She began working in television in 1951 and was soon appearing regularly on shows such as *Studio One*, *The Naked City*, *Way Out*, *Ben Casey*, and *The Defenders*. She made her screen debut as a mean co-worker of Carroll Baker in the indie drama *Something Wild* (1961) and over the next decade, she turned up in small roles in *Barefoot in the Park* (1967), *Divorce, American Style* (1967), *No Way to Treat a Lady* (1968), *The Honeymoon Killers* (1970), *Little Murders* (1971), *A New Leaf* (1971), and *The Heartbreak Kid* (1972). For the next few years, she worked mostly in television, appearing in episodes of *All in the Family*, *Barney Miller*, *Soap*, and *St. Elsewhere*, for which she won her first Emmy award before landing a supporting role on *Remington Steele*. She also appeared during this time in such films as *National Lampoon's Christmas Vacation* (1989), *Used People* (1992), and *The Grass Harp* (1995) before achieving her greatest success, not to mention four additional Emmys, as Ray Romano's overbearing mother on the long-running sitcom *Everybody Loves Raymond*. When that show left the air, she continued to make guest appearances in a number of television shows, including *Law & Order: Criminal Intent*, *The Middle*, *Grey's Anatomy*, and *Desperate Housewives*. Roberts passed away at the age of 90 on April 17, 2016, after having suffered a stroke.

Andrew Sachs (April 7, 1930-November 23, 2016). Although Sachs would work in film, television, radio, and the stage throughout his career, he would become most famous for his performance as the hilariously clueless waiter Manuel in the classic British sitcom *Fawlty Towers*. Born in Berlin in 1930, he and his family fled Germany in 1938 and wound up living in London. While studying shipping management in school, Sachs did some occasional voice work for BBC radio and later decided to pursue acting full-time, first on the stage and then on television and film, making his big-screen debut in *The Night We Dropped a Clanker* (1959). In the Seventies, he appeared in films like *Hitler, The Last Ten Days* (1973), *Frightmare* (1974), *Robin Hood Jr.* (1975), *Are You Being Served?* (1977), and *Revenge of the Pink Panther* (1978), but achieved his greatest stardom on *Fawlty Towers*, which ran in 1975 and 1979 and which is often cited as one of the funniest shows ever produced for television. In later years, he continued working on the stage and television, made appearances in *History of the World, Part I* (1981), *Consuming Passions* (1988), *Nowhere in Africa* (2001), *Quartet* (2012), and *Alice Through the Looking Glass* (2016), and published *I Knew Nothing: The Autobiography* in 2015. Sachs died in London, England, at the age of 86 on November 23, 2016, from vascular dementia.

Theresa Saldana (August 20, 1954-June 6, 2016). Born in Brooklyn in 1954, Saldana began taking acting lessons when she was 12 and worked on the stage before making her screen debut in *Nunzio* (1978). Over the next couple of years, she appeared in such films as *I Wanna Hold Your Hand* (1978), *Home Movies* (1980), and *Defiance* (1980), and played Joe Pesci's wife in *Raging Bull* (1980). Her promising career was derailed in 1982 when a drifter who had become obsessed with her after seeing her in *Defiance* and *Raging Bull* and had been stalking her for a while stabbed her ten times and nearly killed her. After four hours of emergency surgery and four months in the hospital, she recovered and eventually played herself in the made-for-TV movie *Victims for Victims: The Theresa Saldana Story*. She then appeared in the Charles Bronson film *The Evil That Men Do* (1984) but began to focus mostly on television work, making appearances on shows such as *The Twilight Zone, Matlock, MacGyver*, and *Hunter* (where she appeared in a loose recreation of her own case) before being cast in the long-running drama *The Commish* in 1991. When that show went off the air in 1996, she appeared on such programs as *Law & Order, All My Children*, and *The Bernie Mac Show* and made her final screen appearance in the film *Gang Warz* (2004). She also spent a good deal of her time working with victims' advocacy groups and also told her story in the 1986 memoir *Beyond Survival*. Saldana died on June 6, 2016, of pneumonia at the age of 61.

William Schallert (July 6, 1922-May 8, 2016). Although best known for his role as the ever-understanding father on the much-loved sitcom *The Patty Duke Show* and his election to the presidency of the Screen Actors Guild in 1979, Schallert amassed a long line of film and television credits throughout his career. Born in Los Angeles in 1922, he studied acting at the University of Southern California until he left school in order to serve in World War II. After returning to the States, he founded the Circle Theater along with Sydney Chaplin and in 1948, he starred in a production of *Rain* directed by Sydney's father, Charles. He made his screen debut with a tiny part in *This Reckless Moment* (1949) and turned up in a number of supporting roles over the next decade or so, including turns in such favorites as *The Man from Planet X* (1951), *Them* (1954), *The Gunslinger* (1956), *The Incredible Shrinking Man* (1957), *The Tarnished Angels* (1957), and *Pillow Talk* (1959), while also appearing in episodes of *The Twilight Zone, Gunsmoke*, and *Perry Mason*, among many other shows. Following the run of *The Patty Duke Show*, he turned up on episodes of *Star Trek, Get Smart*, and *The Partridge Family* and was seen on the big screen in *In the Heat of the Night* (1967), *Will Penny* (1968), *Colossus: The Forbin Project* (1970), and *Charley Varrick* (1973). In 1979, he was elected to a two-year term as president of SAG and when it concluded, returned to acting, most notably in a string of films with Joe Dante, who used him in *Twilight Zone, the Movie* (1983), *Innerspace* (1987), and *Matinee* (1993). He also made appearances in episodes of *How I Met Your Mother, Desperate Housewives, According to Jim, True Blood*, and *Bag of Bones* before he was forced into retirement by the onset of peripheral neuropathy. He passed away at his home in Pacific Palisades, California, on May 8, 2016, at the age of 93.

Angus Scrimm (August 19, 1926-January 9, 2016). Although this Kansas City native did not appear in his first movie until the age of 47, his imposing height and creepy demeanor made him a favorite with horror film fans around the world. Born in Kansas City, he first worked as a journalist and served as a writer and editor for such publications as *TV Guide*, the *Los Angeles Herald-Examiner* and *Cinema*. During this time, he also worked for Capitol Records as a writer of liner notes, including such albums as the Beatles' first American release, *Meet the Beatles*, and *Korngold: The Classic Erich Wolfgang Korngold*, a 1974 release that won him a Grammy for his efforts. Always interested in acting, Scrimm made his first appearance in a film in an uncredited bit in *The Severed Arm* (1973) and followed that up with small roles in *Sweet Kill* (1973), *Scream Bloody Murder* (1973), and *Jim, the World's Greatest* (1976). It was on that film that he met the then-17-year-old co-director Don Coscarelli, who befriended the actor and offered him a part in his next film, a gory horror film in which he would play a super-creepy mortician harboring a shocking secret involving the corpses that come his way. The film was *Phantasm* (1979) and it became an instant cult hit that spawned four sequels, *Phantasm II* (1988), *Phantasm III, Lord of the Dead* (1994), *Phantasm IV: Oblivion* (1998), and *Phantasm: Ravager* (2016), and made Scrimm into an instant genre icon with his performance as the character known only as the Tall Man. In between those films, he appeared in a number of low-budget, B-horror films, often playing off of his Tall Man persona, became a fixture on the sci-fi/fantasy/horror circuit, and had his biggest exposure as an actor with his recurring role on the TV series *Alias*. Scrimm passed away in Los Angeles, California, at the age of 89 from natural causes on January 9, 2016.

Peter Shaffer (May 15, 1926-June 6, 2016). One of the most acclaimed playwrights of his era, Shaffer was born in 1926 in Liverpool, England; his twin brother, Anthony, would also go on to acclaim as a writer as well. After attending Trinity College, Shaffer worked at a number of odd jobs before developing his literary talents. His first play, *The Salt Land,* was produced by the BBC in 1954 and he first achieved international acclaim in 1958 with *Five Finger Exercise.* Over the years, a number of his plays would be adapted to the screen, starting with *Five Finger Exercise* (1962) and *The Royal Hunt of the Sun* (1969). Shaffer then began adapting his own plays to the screen, beginning with *The Public Eye* (1973) and then with his Oscar-nominated screenplay for his Tony-winning drama *Equus* (1977). His most famous work was *Amadeus,* a place based on the contentious relationship between Wolfgang Amadeus Mozart and court composer Antonio Salieri that won the Tony for Best Play in 1979 and was the basis of a hit 1984 screen adaptation that swept that year's Oscars, including one for Shaffer for Adapted Screenplay, and introduced the works of Mozart to a new audience. Over the years, Shaffer received numerous accolades for his work and in 2007, he was inducted into the American Theatre Hall of Fame. Shaffer passed away in Ireland on June 6, 2016, at the age of 90.

Garry Shandling (November 29, 1949-March 24, 2016). One of the most celebrated comedians of his time, Shandling had already made a name for himself, first as a stand-up comedian and then as the creator of two long-running series that helped to revolutionize television comedy, long before he stepped in front of a movie camera for the first time. Born in Chicago in 1949, Shandling and his family soon moved to Arizona, where he attended college at the University of Arizona. After graduating, he went out to Los Angeles and worked at an ad agency for a while before writing scripts for the hit sitcoms *Sanford & Son* and *Welcome Back, Kotter.* In 1977, he was in a bad car wreck and while recovering, he decided to finally take a chance on making it as a stand-up comedian. His dry humor struck a chord with audiences and he soon became a frequent guest host for Johnny Carson during his absences from *The Tonight Show.* He then went on to produce two consecutive hit series for cable, the meta-sitcom *It's Garry Shandling's Show* in 1985 and 1992's *The Larry Sanders Show* which captured the behind-the-scenes madness that went into producing a late-night talk show. The two shows would earn Shandling a combined total of 19 Emmy nominations over the years and eventually attracted the interest of Hollywood. Following a brief bit in *The Night We Never Met* (1993), he made his first real big-screen appearances in Warren Beatty's remake of *Love Affair* (1994) and the ensemble comedy *Mixed Nuts* (1994) and then moved to drama with *Hurlyburly* (1998). He wrote, produced, and starred in the sci-fi sex comedy *What Planet Are You From?* (2000) and reteamed with Beatty in the romantic farce *Town & Country* (2001). Those two films were major flops, the latter remains one of the biggest movie losers of all time, and pretty much ended his attempts to make it as a movie star, though he would make brief appearances in the superhero epics *Iron Man 2* (2010) and *Captain America: The Winter Soldier* (2014). His biggest film success came through contributing his voice to the family oriented hits *Doctor Dolittle* (1998), *Over the Hedge* (2006), and *The Jungle Book* (2016). The latter film debuted in theaters a few weeks after his surprising death from a heart attack in Los Angeles, California, on March 24, 2016, at the age of 66.

Douglas Slocombe (February 10, 1913-February 22, 2016). Born in London in 1913, Slocombe originally started out as a photojournalist for such publications as *Life* and *Paris Match* in the years before World War II. After serving in the war as a newsreel cameraman, he went to work for England's Ealing Studios, originally as a camera operator but eventually graduating to cinematographer on the horror classic *Dead of Night* (1945). For years, he served as a house cinematographer for the studio, with credits including such classics as *Kind Hearts and Coronets* (1949), *The Man in the White Suit* (1951), and *The Lavender Hill Mob* (1951), before leaving to work on projects of his own choosing, both in England and the United States and covering a wide variety of genres. Among his more notable efforts in the Sixties were *Circus of Horrors* (1960), *Freud* (1962), *The L-Shaped Room* (1962), *The Servant* (1963), which earned him the first of three BAFTA Awards, *The Blue Max* (1966), *Fathom* (1967), *The Fearless Vampire Killers* (1967), *The Lion in Winter* (1968), and *The Italian Job* (1969). In the next decade, he received the first of three Oscar nominations with *Travels with My Aunt* (1972) and also worked on *Jesus Christ, Superstar* (1973), *The Great Gatsby* (1974), which won him his second BAFTA prize, *Rollerball* (1975), and *Julia* (1977), for which he scored his third BAFTA and his second Oscar nomination. He received his last Oscar nomination for his work on *Raiders of the Lost Ark* (1981) and also shot *Never Say Never Again* (1983), *Indiana Jones and the Temple of Doom* (1984), *Water* (1985), and *Lady Jane* (1986) before retiring after completing work on his final project, *Indiana Jones and the Last Crusade* (1989). Slocombe died from injuries following a fall on February 22, 2016, a few days after his 103rd birthday.

Liz Smith (December 11, 1921-December 24, 2016). Born Betty Gleadle in Scunthorpe, Lincolnshire, England, the woman who would become known as Liz Smith will be best remembered for her BAFTA-winning role in *A Private Function* (1984). After a relatively tough life, including a mother who died when she was two and a father who left shortly thereafter, Smith became an actress late, not having a career breakthrough until she was 49, appearing in Mike Leigh's first film *Bleak Moments* (1971). While she was primarily a TV actress in the 1970s and '80s, Smith did make some memorable film appearances, including roles in *Trail of the Pink Panther* (1982) and *Apartment Zero* (1988). She remained active in film and television through the '00s, deep into her eighties. She passed away on December 24, 2016, at the age of 95 and is survived by two children from a marriage to Jack Thomas in the 1940s and '50s.

Bud Spencer (October 31, 1929-June 27, 2016). Born Carlo Pedersoli, this Italian actor will be most remembered for his collaborations with film partner Terence Hill, with whom he appeared in, produced, and directed more than 20 films. Born in Naples, Pedersoli was first a professional swimmer, playing water polo for the Rome team and becoming the first Italian to swim the 100m freestyle in less than a minute in 1950. He even participated in the 1952 and 1956 Summer Olympics on the Italian team. As a lot of athletes are prone to doing, he turned his fame in one field into an attempt at a film career. He was basically an extra in the classic *Quo Vadis* (1951), but his life changed in 1960 when he married Maria Amato, the daughter of the famous producer Giuseppe Amato. His film career picked up and it was when he met Mario Girotti (who would change his name to Terence Hill) on the set of *God Forgives...I Don't!* (1967) that everything changed. Their names were deemed too Italian for the Western genre, so they were changed, Bud Spencer taking his pseudonym from Budweiser beer and the actor Spencer Tracy, two undeniably American institutions. He passed away on June 27, 2016, at the age of 86.

Vanity (January 4, 1959-February 15, 2016). Denise Katrina Matthews would change her name to Vanity, after the all-girl trio she fronted called Vanity 6, and parlay her sexuality and screen presence into a small career as a model and actress. Vanity lived many lives in her too-short six decades on Earth, working as a beauty pageant queen, dancer, actress, model, and eventually even as an evangelical spokesperson, disowning the sexually provocative nature of her '80s fame. Vanity actually had a small role under a different stage name (D.D. Winters) in 1980 when she appeared in *Terror Train,* and she was renamed Vanity by the singer and actor Prince, to whom she was romantically linked and who asked her to be the lead singer of the group he was forming, Vanity 6. They only recorded one album, but Vanity released two albums on her own in the '80s. As for film, Vanity appeared in a number of movies, including *The Last Dragon* (1985), *52 Pick-Up* (1986), *Action Jackson* (1988), and *Kiss of Death* (1997). She was 57 when she passed away on February 15, 2016.

Peter Vaughan (April 4, 1923-December 6, 2016). Born Peter Ewart Ohm in Shropshire, the man who would become Peter Vaughan served in the Second World War, not even appearing as an actor until his late 30s, becoming far more famous in his much-older age on HBO's *Game of Thrones*. That role came a half-century after his first major role, second-billed to Frank Sinatra in *The Naked Runner* (1967), a film mostly and wisely forgotten by history. Other big roles over the rest of his career would follow, including a pair of films from Terry Gilliam, *Time Bandits* (1981) and *Brazil* (1985), and he was set to star in one of the failed iterations of the director's *The Man Who Killed Don Quixote*. Other major films included *Eyewitness* (1970), *Straw Dogs* (1971), *The French Lieutenant's Woman* (1981), *Mountains of the Moon* (1990), and, most notably, as Sir Anthony Hopkins' father in James Ivory's *The Remains of the Day* (1993). He would memorably play Maester Aemon in HBO's Emmy Award-winning drama *Game of Thrones*. He passed away at the age of 93 on December 6, 2016.

Robert Vaughn (November 22, 1932-November 11, 2016). The man who would play one of the most suave spies in espionage history— Napoleon Solo—on the TV series *The Man from U.N.C.L.E.* was born in New York, New York, to a family of actors. His father was a radio actor and his mother was a stage actress. However, Vaughn tried to leave the family business, going to school for journalism, before finally giving in to his genetics and going into theater. He made his TV debut in 1955, and it was not long before he was making waves, appearing in *The Young Philadelphians* (1959), and earning an Oscar and Golden Globe nomina-

tion for his trouble. His fame skyrocketed from there, especially after a major role in the massive hit *The Magnificent Seven* (1960). He segued to TV success for the bulk of the '60s, and then moved seamlessly right back to major films, appearing in 1968's *Bullitt* (1968) for which he was nominated for a BAFTA for Best Supporting Actor. Things slowed down a bit from there, but he worked consistently in television, and appeared in *The Towering Inferno* (1974), *Battle Beyond the Stars* (1980), *Superman III* (1983), and *The Delta Force* (1986). Later in life, he would essentially mock his own suave persona in comedies like *Joe's Apartment* (1996), *BASEketball* (1998), and *Pootie Tang* (2001). He would also appear in a regretful number of straight-to-video movies in the 1990s and '00s. He passed away on November 11, 2016, from leukemia days before his 84th birthday.

Abe Vigoda (February 24, 1921-January 26, 2016). American actor Abraham Charles Vigoda may always be best remembered as Phil Fish on the TV series *Barney Miller* and its spin-off *Fish* but he also had a notable film career, particularly as Salvatore Tessio in the Best Picture-winning *The Godfather* (1972). Perhaps surprisingly given his less-than-typical looks for an actor, Vigoda was a Broadway star in the '60s, but he got the role of Tessio after an open audition and nothing would be the same. He became something of a cameo king, popping up in comedies like *Look Who's Talking* (1989), *Joe Versus the Volcano* (1990), *North* (1994), and many more. He gained a unique level of notoriety as the regular subject of death hoaxes, particularly after he basically retired and Conan O'Brien started a bit in which he tried to find Vigoda, mostly to prove he was still alive. After finding him, Vigoda became something of a regular face on Conan's show. He died of natural causes on January 26, 2016, at the age of 94. We think.

Andrzej Wajda (March 6, 1926-October 9, 2016). One of the godfathers of Polish cinema, Andrzej Witold Wajda was the Recipient of an Honorary Oscar, an Honorary Golden Lion Award, and saw four of his films nominated for Best Foreign Language Film: *The Promised Land* (1975), *The Maids of Wilko* (1979), *Man of Iron* (1981), and *Katyn* (2007). Perhaps more essential to world cinema than even those films was Wajda's trilogy of war works: *A Generation* (1954), *Kanal* (1956), and *Ashes and Diamonds* (1958). He worked all the way up to his death, well into his 80s, releasing a film posthumously in 2017 (*Afterimage*). He may not be the household name of other international auteurs but his impact cannot be understated. In 1990, he was only the third director to get a lifetime achievement award from the European Film Awards, after Federico Fellini and Ingmar Bergman. Ten years later, the Academy Awards followed suit with a similar award. Wajda passed away on October 9, 2016, at the age of 90.

Margaret Whitton (November 30, 1949-December 4, 2016). New York actress Margaret Whitton made her Broadway debut in 1982 but it was the film work she did in the latter part of that decade and the early part of the next one for which she will be most remembered, typically in broad comedies of the day like her roles in the Michael J. Fox hit *The Secret of My Success*, the cult comedy classic *Major League* (1989), and its sequel. Other notable film credits of Whitton's career include *The Best of Times* (1986), *The Man*

Without a Face (1993), and *9½ Weeks* (1986). When the film roles dried up, she returned to the stage, and even served as president of an independent film company called Tashtego Films. She passed away at the age of 67 on December 4, 2016.

Gene Wilder (June 11, 1933-August 29, 2016). Few faces will forever be associated with film comedy history as much as Gene Wilder's. It's in the same pantheon as Charlie Chaplin or Groucho Marx's. He was a legend, gone too soon. Born Jerome Silberman in Milwaukee, Wisconsin, Wilder's life will forever be defined by three comedic partnerships, that with his wife Gilda Radner, his writer/director Mel Brooks, and his co-star Richard Pryor. And those don't even include the role for which most people first know Gene Wilder, as Willy Wonka in *Willy Wonka & the Chocolate Factory* (1971). Wilder reportedly became entranced with acting at the age of eleven, moving on to study communication and theatre arts at the University of Iowa. He worked in theater in college and shortly thereafter, having his life changed forever when he played a leading role on stage in *Mother Courage and Her Children* in 1963 opposite Anne Bancroft, who introduced Wilder to her boyfriend, Mel Brooks. At the time, Brooks was working on a script called *Springtime For Hitler*, which would become *The Producers* (1968), for which Wilder was nominated for a Best Supporting Actor Oscar (and Brooks would win). Wilder would parlay this success into Willy Wonka and working with Woody Allen (*Everything You Always Wanted to Know About Sex* (*But Were Afraid to Ask)* [1972]), but it was 1974 when everything would change. While Wilder was working on his script for *Young Frankenstein* (1974), he got a call that Brooks also needed him to star in *Blazing Saddles* (1974). The one-two punch of those films is still one of the most impressive in history. The next year he was sent a script for a film set to star someone who was almost in *Blazing Saddles*, Richard Pryor. The movie was eventually called *Silver Streak* (1976), and it began a comedy partnership that was a box office and (mostly) critical smash. Other notable credits include *Stir Crazy* (1980), *The Woman in Red* (1984), and *Another You* (1991), which would be his final film. He would appear in TV shows after that, including a memorable guest spot on *Will & Grace*, but his career was over far too early. There were rumors of a comeback when he passed from complications due to Alzheimer's disease on August 29, 2016, at the age of 83.

Anton Yelchin (March 11, 1989-June 19, 2016). This wonderful young actor was just getting started when his rising star was snuffed out at way-too-early an age after a horrible accident involving his Jeep pinning him against his mailbox. He may be best remembered as Pavel Chekov in the string of *Star Trek* films released in the 2000s, but he was really starting to put together an incredibly diverse array of characters in independent cinema, including the 2016 hit *Green Room* and *Thoroughbred* (2017), one of his final roles. Born in Russia but emigrating at a young age, Yelchin had an amazing ability to feel genuine in every moment in which he performed. His loss is a great one. Notable film credits include *Hearts in Atlantis* (2001),

Alpha Dog (2006), *Star Trek* (2009), *Terminator Salvation* (2009), *Like Crazy* (2011), *The Beaver* (2011), *Fright Night* (2011), and *Only Lovers Left Alive* (2013). He passed away on June 19, 2016, at the age of 27.

Alan Young (November 19, 1919-May 19, 2016). The actor who played Wilbur Post from the classic TV show *Mister Ed* lived almost a century and travelled far from his roots in the U.K. to a Hollywood life. The man who *TV Guide* once called "The Charlie Chaplin of Television" also starred in his own variety/comedy show in the 1940s and '50s, winning two Emmy Awards for it. Young never quite had the fame in film that he had in TV, but he appeared in a number of Walt Disney Productions and one of the most notable versions of *The Time Machine* (1960). Other popular credits include *The Cat from Outer Space* (1978), the voice of Scrooge McDuck in *Mickey's Christmas Carol* (1983), *The Great Mouse Detective* (1986), and *Alice Through the Looking Glass* (1987). Young would voice Scrooge several times in television and films, often straight-to-video. He did a lot of voice work late in life, doing several characters on *The Smurfs, Alvin and the Chipmunks, DuckTales,* and more. He passed away at the age of 96 on May 19, 2016.

Vilmos Zsigmond (June 16, 1930-January 1, 2016). A survey in 2003 of the International Cinematographers Guild named Hungarian Vilmos Zsigmond one of the ten most influential cinematographers of all time. After moving to the United States and becoming a citizen, Zsigmond worked in low-budget filmmaking as a young man, before getting his break when Robert Altman hired him to shoot *McCabe & Mrs. Miller* (1970). From that point on, he was one of the most important visual artists of arguably the most important era in film history, working with Altman again, John Boorman, Brian De Palma, Michael Cimino, Richard Donner, Steven Spielberg, George Miller, Woody Allen, and more. The auteurs of the '70s get a lot of credit for defining it, but Zsigmond is the throughline connecting a lot of these filmmakers. Notable credits include *Deliverance* (1972), *The Long Goodbye* (1973), *The Sugarland Express* (1974), *Close Encounters of the Third Kind* (1977, for which he won the Oscar), *The Deer Hunter* (1978), *Heaven's Gate* (1980), *Blow Out* (1981), *The Witches of Eastwick* (1987), and *The Black Dahlia* (2006). He was 85 when he passed away on January 1, 2016.

Andrzej Zulawski (November 22, 1940-February 17, 2016). An essential part of Poland's film history, Zulwaski carved his own way in film history, making controversial, un-commercial works his entire career. He challenged audience expectations and earned a loyal following by being true only to himself. Zulawski started his career as an assistant to another essential Polish filmmaker who passed in 2016, Andrzej Wajda. His early films were so controversial that they were often banned in Poland, so Zulawski moved to France, where he made films for the majority of his career. He was also a novelist. Notable films include *The Devil* (1972), *Possession* (1981), *On the Silver Globe* (1988), *Boris Godunov* (1989), and *Cosmos* (2016). He passed away on February 17, 2016, at the age of 75.

Selected Film Books of 2016

Arnold, Jeremy and Robert Osborne. *Turner Classic Movies: The Essentials: 52 Must-See Movies and Why They Matter,* Running Press, 2016. The author picks only 52 essential films, one a week for young, new film lovers unfamiliar with the canon of movie history. The choices may be obvious but it's a solid starter, especially for movie fans born after 1990.

Ayoade, Richard. *Ayoade on Ayoade: A Cinematic Odyssey,* Faber & Faber, 2016. The star of television's cult hit *The IT Crowd* and films such as *The Watch* (2012), as well as the director of *Submarine* (2010) and *The Double* (2012) offers a playful semi-autobiography in which the multi-talented star interviews himself.

Barrymore, Drew. *Wildflower,* Dutton, 2016. A household name from a very early age, the multi-talented star offers her autobiography.

Barsam, Richard and Dave Monahan. *Looking at Movies* (Fifth Edition), W.W. Norton & Company, 2016. The hit reference book authored by film studies professors from Hunter College and the University of North Carolina gets a 2016 update. The purpose is there right on the cover: "An introduction to film."

Bergestrom, Signe. *Suicide Squad: Behind the Scenes with the Worst Heroes Ever,* Harper Design, 2016. An illustrated book that offers fans details on the making of one of the biggest box office hits of the year in David Ayer's action blockbuster.

Bernard, Sheila Curran. *Documentary Storytelling: Creative Nonfiction on Screen,* Focal Press, 2016. An award-winning filmmaker and writer who taught at Princeton University offers her insight into how to make a documentary. She's won Emmy and Peabody Awards, so she's worth listening to.

Bingen, Steven. *Paramount: City of Dreams,* Taylor Trade Publishing, 2016. The story of the golden era of one of Hollywood's most formative and influential studios is documented in this coffee table book that offers stills and anecdotes from the days when the Paramount backlot was one of the most important places to be in the world.

Block, Paula M. and Terry J. Erdmann. *Labyrinth: The Ultimate Visual History,* Insight Editions, 2016. The definitive history of the beloved Jim Henson film on its 30th anniversary.

Bogle, Donald. *Toms, Coons, Mulattoes, Mammies, and Bucks: An Interpretive History of Blacks in American Films, Updated and Expanded 5th Edition,* Bloomsbury Academic, 2016. One of the most noted black-cinema historians expands on his influential and widely cited book about the history of racist caricatures and depictions of race in cinema for a new edition.

Bordwell, David and Kristin Thompson. *Film Art: An Introduction,* McGraw-Hill Education, 2016. Two of the most important film studies professors of all time update their influential reference book for an eleventh edition.

Bozzacchi, Gianni and Joey Tayler. *My Life in Focus: A Photographer's Journey with Elizabeth Taylor and the Hollywood Jet Set,* University Press of Kentucky, 2016. The author accepted an assignment to be a set photographer on *The Comedians* (1967) and it changed his life. His skill set caught the eye of the film's star, Elizabeth Taylor, and he became her personal photographer as her star continued to rise. He tells the story of their time together.

Braudy, Leo and Marshall Cohen. *Film Theory and Criticism: Introductory Readings,* Oxford University Press, 2016. Hyped as the most-used book in film studies classes in the history of such a thing, this definitive reference volume gets an update in its latest edition.

Brooks, Mel and Judd Apatow. *Young Frankenstein: A Mel Brooks Book: The Story of the Making of the Film,* Black Dog & Leventhal, 2016. The writer/director of arguably the best comedy of all time offers his stories about its production, including never-before-seen stills and original interviews.

Brown, Blain. *Cinematography: Theory and Practice: Image Making for Cinematographers and Directors,* Focal Press, 2016. The third edition of one of the most essential volumes when it comes to understanding visual composition, along with the various camera styles available for cinematographers today.

Castle, Alison. *The Stanley Kubrick Archives,* TASCHEN America LLC, 2016. The King of the coffee table books goes DEEP with this 846-page volume on the history of one of film's most notable auteurs. The massive gift set includes more than 1,500 stills, essays, articles, and even an audio CD of an interview with Kubrick. The first print run even included a 12-frame film strip from a 70mm print of *2001: A Space Odyssey* (1968).

Coppola, Francis Ford. *The Godfather Notebook,* Regan Arts, 2016. This film lover's dream was billed as the most definitive book on the making of *The Godfather* (1972) in history, including the filmmaker's detailed notes and annotations while the masterpiece was in production. Including exclusive photographs, the idea is to recreate Coppola's notebook that he used while in production on a movie that would change film history.

Cranston, Bryan. *A Life in Parts,* Scribner, 2016. The Oscar-nominated and Emmy-winning star of *Breaking Bad* (2008-2013), *Trumbo* (2015), and *The Infiltrator* (2016) finally gets around to writing his memoir.

Cumming, Alan. *You Gotta Get Bigger Dreams: My Life in Stories and Pictures,* Rizzoli Ex Libris, 2016. The star of *The Good Wife* (2010-2016), and dozens of films and plays, is one of the most entertaining men in Hollywood, and he offers another volume of stories and anecdotes from his life.

Darcy, Jen. *Disney Villains: Delightfully Evil: The Creation - The Inspiration - The Fascination,* Disney Editions, 2016. A look at the long history of iconic villains in Disney and Pixar films, including rare concept art and photographs that detail how these characters came to life.

Darlington, Tenaya and Andre Darlington. *Turner Classic Movies: Movie Night Menus: Dinner and Drink Recipes Inspired by the Films We Love,* Running Press, 2016. The people behind the brilliant programming at the increasingly popular TCM offer up culinary treats to tie in with your favorite movie marathon.

Dice, Mark. *The Illuminati in Hollywood: Celebrities, Conspiracies, and Secret Societies in Pop Culture and the Entertainment Industry,* The Resistance Manifesto, 2016. A "writer" behind several books on secret societies and conspiracies throws some fuel on the nonsense fire that is the idea that there's a secret group or club that runs Hollywood.

DK. *Star Wars: Complete Locations,* DK, 2016. The title pretty much says it all—these are illustrated guides to the locations of the Star Wars franchise. Every time you think there's not a side of this film series yet to be covered, something new gets released.

Dyer, Jay. *Esoteric Hollywood: Sex, Cults and Symbols in Film,* Trine Day, 2016. A collection of essays about philosophy, religion, symbolism, and geopolitics in film. It claims to offer insight into "the secret meanings of cinema." It's about time.

Edward, Gavin. *The Tao of Bill Murray: Real-Life Stories of Joy, Enlightenment, and Party Crashing,* Random House, 2016. Not so much a typical biography but a series of anecdotes and stories about the notoriously eccentric star of *Ghostbusters* (1984), *Rushmore* (1998), *Lost in Translation* (2003), and so many more beloved films.

Egan, Joseph. *The Purple Diaries: Mary Astor and the Most Sensational Hollywood Scandal of the 1930s,* Diversion Publishing, 2016. One of the Golden Age of Hollywood's most notable scandals gets the analysis it deserves. When Mary Astor and Dr. Franklyn Thorpe got into a heated custody battle, it was her diary (which kept the secrets of some of Hollywood's biggest names) that threatened to derail an entire industry.

Floyd-Thomas, Juan M. and Stacey M. Floyd-Thomas. *The Altars Where We Worship: The Religious Significance of Popular Culture,* Westminster John Knox Press, 2016. The writers look at how much pop culture has taken a place in society of worship and admiration that used to only be occupied by religious institutions and leaders.

Furniss, Maureen. *A New History of Animation,* Thames & Hudson, 2016. This volume by an animation history professor at California Institute of the Arts purports to cover the entire history of animation, including various forms from around the world.

Gale. *VideoHound's Golden Movie Retriever 2017: The Complete Guide to Movies on VHS, DVD, and Hi-def Formats,* Gale Research Inc., 2016. The most definitive and complete guide available for capsule film reviews approaches almost 2,000 pages in its latest, comprehensive edition.

Goldberg, Aaron H. and 2Faced Design. *The Disney Story: Chronicling the Man, the Mouse and the Parks,* Quaker Scribe, 2016. A decade-by-decade look at arguably the most influential and important company in entertainment history from the debut of Mickey Mouse in 1928 through to the opening of Shanghai Disneyland in 2016. How has this company stayed on top for so long?

Gordon, Shep. *They Call Me Supermensch: A Backstage Pass to the Amazing Worlds of Film, Food, and Rock 'n' Roll,* Anthony Bourdain/Ecco, 2016. A memoir of one of the power players in music and film, a man who worked with some of the biggest names in Hollywood, including Bette Davis, Raquel Welch, Groucho Marx, Sylvester Stallone, and many more. His story was featured in the documentary of the same name from 2013.

Griffin, Kathy. *Kathy Griffin's Celebrity Run-Ins: My A-Z Index,* Flatiron, 2016. The latest from the red carpet staple and New Year's Eve co-host includes an alphabetized compendium of anecdotes from her most entertaining celebrity encounters.

Gross, Edward and Mark A. Altman. *The Fifty-Year Mission: The Complete, Uncensored, Unauthorized Oral History of Star Trek: The First 25 Years,* Thomas Dunne Books, 2016. Another book that purports to offer the "unauthorized, uncensored, and unbelievable true story" behind the history of one of the most popular sci-fi franchises of all time.

Harman, Ken and Spoke Gallery. *Wes Anderson Collection: Bad Dads: Art Inspired by the Films of Wes Anderson,* Harry N. Abrams, 2016. The latest in a series of coffee table books about one of the modern era's most beloved filmmakers focused on the best artwork from "Bad Dads," an exhibition of art inspired by the films of Wes Anderson that takes place every year in San Francisco, and features work by more than 400 artists.

Haynes, Emily and Travis Knight. *The Art of Kubo and the Two Strings,* Chronicle Books, 2016. LAIKA, the Academy Award-nominated company who gave the world *Coraline* (2009), *ParaNorman* (2012), and *The Boxtrolls* (2014) have made arguably their best film to date in the magical *Kubo and the Two Strings*. Here's how it was made.

Hedren, Tippi. *Tippi: A Memoir,* William Morrow, 2016. The legendary star offers her life history, with an emphasis on her relationship with Alfred Hitchcock on the sets of *The Birds* (1963) and *Marnie* (1964). The actress even accuses Hitch of abuse, a claim that made this book rather controversial. She also offers some insight into the strange production of *Roar* (1981), one of the most dangerous shoots of all time.

Henson, Taraji P. and Denene Miller. *Around the Way Girl: A Memoir,* Atria/37 INK, 2016. The star of the FOX hit *Empire* and the Best Picture nominee *Hidden Figures* (2016) offers her story.

Hidalgo, Pablo and Simon Beecroft. *Star Wars Character Encyclopedia, Updated and Expanded,* DK Children, 2016. It's a Star Wars World, we just live in it. Yet another book that purports to offer details on all the characters of the Lucasfilm franchise.

Hidalgo, Pablo. *Star Wars Propaganda: A History of Persuasive Art in the Galaxy,* Harper Design, 2016. One of the writers of several books aimed at Star Wars fans, primarily children, imagines a world of propaganda posters including images of the Stormtroopers and Darth Vader that might exist in the universe of the films.

Isackes, Richard M. and Karen L. Maness. *The Art of the Hollywood Backdrop,* Regan Arts, 2016. Long before the era of CGI, the Hollywood backdrop was the way to transport viewers to magical places around the world.

Johnson, Jacob. *Marvel's Doctor Strange: The Art of the Movie,* Marvel, 2016. The coffee table book assembly line continues with the latest gift offering for the latest Marvel flick, the sorta-successful *Doctor Strange,* starring Benedict Cumberbatch, Chiwetel Ejiofor, and Tilda Swinton. Expect the standards-stills, interviews, etc.

Jones, Brian Jay. *George Lucas: A Life,* Little, Brown and Company, 2016. How did one man change feature films forever? The biographer of Jim Henson turns to another magic man in this story of the life of George Lucas, which focuses on his work on the *Star Wars* saga.

Julius, Jessica and Maggie Malone. *The Art of Moana,* Chronicle Books, 2016. The hit Disney film gets the coffee table book art treatment with stills, concept art, and details about the making of the film starring Dwayne Johnson, and with songs written by Lin-Manuel Miranda.

Julius, Jessica and John Lasseter. *The Art of Zootopia,* Chronicle Books, 2016. One of the most successful films of the year gets the art book treatment with this thick volume filled with stills, concept art, and details about the making of the hit movie featuring voice work by Ginnifer Goodwin and Jason Bateman.

Kaling, Mindy. *Why Not Me?* Three Rivers Press, 2016. The film and movie star, best known for her own series *The Mindy Project* and her stint on NBC's *The Office,* goes the autobiography route with this story of her life.

Kendrick, Anna. *Scrappy Little Nobody,* Touchstone, 2016. The Oscar-nominated star of *Up in the Air* and *Pitch Perfect,* among many others, offers her life story in the latest celebrity autobiography.

Kothenschulte, Daniel and John Lasseter. *The Walt Disney Film Archives: The Animated Movies 1921-1968,* Taschen America. The king of the expensive coffee table book strikes again with this $200, 600-page volume that offers a detailed history of the formative years of the Walt Disney company and their foundational work in the field of animated film.

Lasseter, John and Steve Pilcher. *The Art of Finding Dory,* Chronicle Books, 2016. Disney/Pixar's massive summer blockbuster sequel gets the art book treatment in this competent volume for animation fans and movie lovers.

Levy, Lawrence. *To Pixar and Beyond: My Unlikely Journey with Steve Jobs to Make Entertainment History,* Houghton Mifflin Harcourt, 2016. This Silicon Valley lawyer was hired by Steve Jobs in 1994 to be the CFO and member of the Office of the President of Pixar Animation. The rest was history. He offers it to you now for your reading pleasure.

LucasFilm Ltd and Josh Kushins. *The Art of Rogue One: A Star Wars Story,* Harry N. Abrams, 2016. The first official Star Wars spin-off film was also the highest-grossing release of 2016. It gets a solid art book with stills, production details, and interviews.

Macdonald, Norm. *Based on a True Story: A Memoir,* Spiegel & Grau, 2016. The writer/star of *Saturday Night Live* and regular stand-up comedian offers an atypical book from a comedy star in that it's more of a series of short stories or unique anecdotes than a traditional comedy book.

Matzen, Robert and Leonard Maltin. *Mission: Jimmy Stewart and the Fight for Europe,* Paladin Communications, 2016. Not a lot of people know that the legendary everyman movie star was also a war hero, enlisting in March of 1941 and rising from private to colonel, while serving in 20 World War II combat missions. This book with a foreword by Leonard Maltin details Jimmy Stewart's time in country.

Mckee, Robert. *Dialogue: The Art of Verbal Action for Page, Stage, and Screen,* Twelve, 2016. The king of advice for screenwriters returns with another advisory volume on how to write dialogue for film.

McQuarrie, Ralph and Brandon Alinger. *Star Wars Art: Ralph McQuarrie,* Harry N. Abrams, 2016. The "most iconic artist in the history of Star Wars" gets his own art book in this heavy tome that details how McQuarrie worked with Lucas on the design of Darth Vader, C-3PO, R2-D2, and so much more of the most influential film universe in history.

Miller, James Andrew. *Powerhouse: The Untold Story of Hollywood's Creative Artists Agency,* Custom House, 2016. The agents of CAA have been power players behind the scenes in Hollywood for almost half a century now. A great book for those interested in understanding how agents work with studios and producers to make movie magic even possible.

Myers, Mike. *Canada,* Doubleday Canada, 2016. The star of *Saturday Night Live* and feature films offers a biography that focuses on his love for his home country.

Nathan, Ian. *Inside the Magic: The Making of Fantastic Beasts and Where to Find Them,* Harper Design, 2016. The spin-off of the Harry Potter universe gets an affordable making-of volume that works more as a fans-only companion to the hit film than a coffee table book.

Nesteroff, Kilph. *The Comedians: Drunks, Thieves, Scoundrels and the History of American Comedy,* Grove Press, 2016. The title pretty much says it all, and this book promises a history of American comedy from the Marx Brothers to Milton Berle to George Carlin to Eddie Murphy to Louis CK.

Power, Dermot. *The Art of the Film: Fantastic Beasts and Where to Find Them,* Harper Design, 2016. A traditional coffee table book for the hit Warner Brothers spin-off of the Harry Potter franchise starring Eddie Redmayne.

Revenson, Jody. *Harry Potter: The Artifact Vault,* Harper Design, 2016. There will be no aspect of the Harry Potter films and books that does not get its own spin-off volume for hardcore fans of the series. This one focuses on the "artifacts" of the film universe, focusing on the design of potion bottles, brooms, maps, etc.

Salisbury, Mark. *The Case of Beasts: Explore the Film Wizardry of Fantastic Beasts and Where to Find Them,* Harper Design, 2016. Another volume on the latest offshoot of the Harry Potter series from a writer from *Premiere Magazine*. This one is pretty standard making-of material, but a little less unwieldy than a traditional coffee table "Art of the Film" book.

Schumer, Amy. *The Girl with the Lower Back Tattoo,* Gallery Books, 2016. The star of *Trainwreck* (2015) authors another comedy book that offers her brand of personal storytelling that's unapologetic and self-effacing at the same time.

Seitz, Matt Zoller. *The Oliver Stone Experience,* Harry N. Abrams, 2016. The Oscar-winning writer and director offers a self-guided tour through his own history, working in conjunction with the Pulitzer Prize-nominated editor of RogerEbert.com to offer a detailed, illustrated view of a career.

Shatner, William and David Fisher. *Leonard: My Fifty-Year Friendship with a Remarkable Man,* Thomas Dunne Books, 2016. The star of the *Star Trek* franchise and legendary actor offers his take on being friends with the man who played Spock, Leonard Nimoy.

Smith, Dave. *Disney A to Z: The Official Encyclopedia* (Fifth Edition), Disney Editions, 2016. This massive tome (900 pages) offers a full history of the entire company and has been updated for its latest edition. It was written by the chief archivist for Disney for more than 40 years.

Sorel, Edward. *Mary Astor's Purple Diary: The Great American Sex Scandal of 1936,* Liveright, 2016. The second of two

2016 books about the Mary Astor scandal is reportedly the better of the two, reimagined and told through the style of a comic book by a legendary cartoonist with more 75 color illustrations.

Squire, Jason E. *The Movie Business Book,* Focal Press, 2016. The associate professor of practice at the USC School of Cinematic Arts offers his advice on how to break into and survive in the shark-filled waters of the movie business.

Sunstein, Cass R. *The World According to Star Wars,* Dey Street Books, 2016. More of a fan-based approach to the series, the author offers his theories as to why Star Wars has endured while other franchises have faded from memory.

Toombs, Ariel Teal and Colt Baird Toombs. *Rowdy: The Roddy Piper Story,* Random House Canada, 2016. The wrestler who had a brief flirtation with movie stardom when he appeared in John Carpenter's fantastic *They Live* (1988) gets the biography treatment from a fan and wrestling expert. It started as an autobiography before Piper's fatal heart attack in 2015.

Vieira, Mark A. *Into the Dark: The Hidden World of Film Noir, 1941-1950,* Running Press, 2016. The author is a photographer and writer who specializes in Hollywood history and offers his insight into the height of the noir genre during and just after World War II.

Wagner, Robert and Scott Eyman. *I Loved Her in the Movies: Memories of Hollywood's Legendary Actresses,* Viking, 2016. The legendary star of stage and screen offers his stories of working with some of Hollywood's most prominent leading ladies, including Joan Crawford, Bette Davis, Marilyn Monroe, Glenn Close, and the two he married, Natalie Wood and Jill St. John, among others.

Wall, Mick. *Prince: Purple Reign,* Trapeze, 2016. The UK's best-known rock writer offers his take on the life of the musician and movie star Prince, released somewhat suspiciously quickly after his untimely death.

Williams-Paisley, Kimberly. *Where the Light Gets In: Losing My Mother Only to Find Her Again,* Crown Archetype, 2016. The star of the *Father of the Bride* films and friend of actor Michael J. Fox, who offers a foreword, tells her story of her mother's rare form of dementia, and how it changed both of their lives.

Wills, David. *Audrey: The 50s,* Dey Street Books, 2016. A volume of photographs of one of Audrey Hepburn's most popular and influential periods, the 1950s, an era in which she defined stardom and set fashion trends. Photographs from the set of *Roman Holiday* (1953), *Sabrina* (1954), and *Funny Face* (1957) are included.

Wilson, Mara. *Where Am I Now?: True Stories of Girlhood and Accidental Fame,* Penguin Books, 2016. The child star of *Mrs. Doubtfire* (1993), *Miracle on 34th Street* (1994), and *Matilda* (1996) left Hollywood behind when she got older. She offers an autobiography on how she survived life as a child star to become a writer and playwright in adulthood.

Zahed, Ramin. *The Art of the Iron Giant,* Insight Editions, 2016. Almost two decades after its release, *The Iron Giant* (1999) is as popular as ever, finally getting the art making-of book that it's always deserved.

Director Index

Marc Abraham
I Saw the Light

Ross Adam
The Lovers & the Despot

Maren Ade
Toni Erdmann

Ben Affleck (1972-)
Live by Night

Alexandre Aja (1978-)
The 9th Life of Louis Drax

Woody Allen (1935-)
Café Society

Pedro Almodovar (1951-)
Julieta

Fede Alvarez (1978-)
Don't Breathe

Andrea Arnold
American Honey

Peter Atencio (1983-)
Keanu

Jacques Audiard (1952-)
Dheepan

David Ayer (1972-)
Suicide Squad

Jason Bateman (1969-)
The Family Fang

Noah Baumbach (1969-)
De Palma

Michael Bay (1965-)
13 Hours: The Secret Soldiers of
Benghazi

Juan Antonio Bayona (1975-)
A Monster Calls

Warren Beatty (1937-)
Rules Don't Apply

Enrique Begne
Compadres

Timur Bekmambetov
Ben-Hur

William Brent Bell
The Boy

Roxanne Benjamin
Southbound

Peter Berg (1964-)
Deepwater Horizon
Patriots Day

Shane Black (1961-)
The Nice Guys

J. Blakeson
The 5th Wave

James Bobin
Alice Through the Looking Glass

David Bruckner
Southbound

Bryan Buckley
The Bronze

Robert Budreau
Born to Be Blue

Tim Burton (1960-)
Miss Peregrine's Home for Peculiar Children

Paco Cabezas
Mr. Right

Robert Cannan
The Lovers & the Despot

Alessandro Carloni
Kung Fu Panda 3

John Carney
Sing Street

Steve Carr
Middle School: The Worst Years
of My Life

D.J. Caruso (1965-)
The Disappointments Room

Jon Cassar (1958-)
When the Bough Breaks

Damien Chazelle (1985-)
La La Land

Don Cheadle (1964-)
Miles Ahead

Yarrow Cheney
The Secret Life of Pets

Stephen Chiau (1962-)
See Stephen (Chiau) Chow

Stephen (Chiau) Chow (1962-)
The Mermaid

Jon M. Chu
Now You See Me 2

Derek Cianfrance
The Light Between Oceans

Jericca Cleland
Ratchet & Clank

Ron Clements (1953-)
Moana

Ethan Coen (1957-)
Hail, Caesar!

Joel Coen (1954-)
Hail, Caesar!

Jaume Collet-Serra (1974-)
The Shallows

Harold Cronk
God's Not Dead 2

Jonas Cuaron
Desierto

Paul Dalio
Touched With Fire

Terence Davies (1945-)
Sunset Song

Garth Davis
Lion

James DeMonaco (1968-)
The Purge: Election Year

Scott Derrickson
Doctor Strange

Christian Desmares
April and the Extraordinary
World

Arnaud Desplechin (1960-)
My Golden Days

Christian Ditter
How to Be Single

Michael Dudok de Wit (1953-)
The Red Turtle

Clint Eastwood (1930-)
Sully

Gareth Edwards
Rogue One: A Star Wars Story

Robert Eggers
The Witch

Atom Egoyan (1960-)
Remember

Franck Ekinci
April and the Extraordinary
World

Sean Ellis (1970-)
Anthropoid

Roland Emmerich (1955-)
Independence Day: Resurgence

Ben Falcone
The Boss

Asghar Farhadi (1972-)
The Salesman

David Farrier
Tickled

Jon Favreau (1966-)
The Jungle Book

Paul Feig (1962-)
Ghostbusters

Jeff Feuerzeig
Author: The JT LeRoy Story

Glenn Ficarra
Whiskey Tango Foxtrot

Mike Flanagan (1978-)
Ouija: Origin of Evil

Dexter Fletcher (1966-)
Eddie the Eagle

Anne Fontaine (1959-)
The Innocents

Tom Ford
Nocturnal Animals

Jodie Foster (1963-)
Money Monster

David Frankel (1959-)
Collateral Beauty

Stephen Frears (1941-)
Florence Foster Jenkins

Kelly Fremon
See also Kelly Fremon Craig

Kelly Fremon Craig
The Edge of Seventeen

Antoine Fuqua (1966-)
The Magnificent Seven

Brad Furman
The Infiltrator

Laura Gabbert
City of Gold

Dennis Gansel (1973-)
Mechanic: Resurrection

Rodrigo Garcia (1959-)
Last Days in the Desert

Mel Gibson (1956-)
Hacksaw Ridge

Craig Gillespie
The Finest Hours

Sophie Goodhart
My Blind Brother

Josh Gordon
Office Christmas Party

Michael Grandage
Genius

Dave Green
Teenage Mutant Ninja Turtles:
Out of the Shadows

Robert Greene (1976-)
Kate Plays Christine

Paul Greengrass (1955-)
Jason Bourne

Ciro Guerra
Embrace of the Serpent

John Hamburg (1970-)
Why Him?

Mia Hansen-Love (1981-)
Things to Come

Chad Hartigan
Morris from America

Stewart Hendler
Max Steel

Werner Herzog (1942-)
Lo and Behold: Reveries of the
Connected World

Jared Hess (1979-)
Masterminds

John Hillcoat (1961-)
Triple 9

Anna Rose Holmer
The Fits

Gavin Hood (1963-)
Eye in the Sky

Stephen Hopkins (1958-)
Race

Patrick Horvath
Southbound

Mamoru Hosoda
The Boy and the Beast

Byron Howard
Zootopia

Ron Howard (1954-)
Inferno

Matt Hullum
Lazer Team

Mick Jackson (1943-)
Denial

Jonathan Jakubowicz
Hands of Stone

Jim Jarmusch (1953-)
Paterson

Barry Jenkins
    Moonlight

Garth Jennings (1972-)
    Sing

Zhangke Jia
    Mountains May Depart

Kirsten Johnson (1965-)
    Cameraperson

Liza Johnson
    Elvis & Nixon

Duncan Jones
    Warcraft

Kirk Jones
    My Big Fat Greek Wedding 2

Henry Joost
    Nerve

Ross Katz
    The Choice

Clay Kaytis
    The Angry Birds Movie

Chris Kelly
    Other People

Vincent Kesteloot
    The Wild Life

Travis Knight
    Kubo and the Two Strings

John Krasinski (1979-)
    The Hollars

Josh Kriegman
    Weiner

Justin Kurzel
    Assassin's Creed

Karyn Kusama (1968-)
    The Invitation

Dan Kwan
    Swiss Army Man

Yorgos Lanthimos
    The Lobster

Pablo Larrain
    The Club
    Jackie
    Neruda

Ang Lee (1954-)
    Billy Lynn's Long Halftime Walk

Malcolm Lee (1970-)
    Barbershop: The Next Cut

Louis Leterrier (1973-)
    The Brothers Grimsby

Justin Lin
    Star Trek Beyond

Richard Linklater (1960-)
    Everybody Wants Some!!

Ken Loach (1936-)
    I, Daniel Blake

Kenneth Lonergan (1963-)
    Manchester by the Sea

David Lowery
    Pete's Dragon

Jon Lucas
    Bad Moms

David Mackenzie (1966-)
    Hell or High Water

Angus MacLane
    Finding Dory

John Madden (1949-)
    Miss Sloane

Sharon Maguire (1960-)
    Bridget Jones's Baby

Terrence Malick (1943-)
    Knight of Cups

Garry Marshall (1934-2016)
    Mother's Day

Dan Mazer (1971-)
    Dirty Grandpa

Ewan McGregor (1971-)
    American Pastoral

Greg McLean
    The Darkness

Theodore (Ted) Melfi
    Hidden Figures

Meera Menon
    Equity

Rebecca Miller (1962-)
    Maggie's Plan

Tim Miller
    Deadpool

Mike Mills (1966-)
    20th Century Women

Mike Mitchell
    Trolls

Rich Moore
    Zootopia

Scott Moore
    Bad Moms

Jocelyn Moorhouse (1960-)
    The Dressmaker

Greg Mottola (1964-)
    Keeping Up with the Joneses

Kevin Munroe
    Ratchet & Clank

Toni Myers
    A Beautiful Planet

Hong-jin Na
    The Wailing

Mira Nair (1957-)
    Queen of Katwe

Ilya Naishuller
    Hardcore Henry

Babak Najafi
    London Has Fallen

Andrew Neel
    Goat

Jeff Nichols (1978-)
    Loving
    Midnight Special

Cedric Nicolas-Troyan
    The Huntsman: Winter's War

Cyrus Nowrasteh (1956-)
    The Young Messiah

Gavin O'Connor
    The Accountant
    Jane Got a Gun

Mark Osborne
    The Little Prince

Jake Paltrow
    De Palma

Chan-wook Park (1963-)
    The Handmaiden

Nate Parker (1979-)
    The Birth of a Nation

Tyler Perry (1969-)
    Boo! A Madea Halloween

Nicolas Pesce (1990-)
    The Eyes of My Mother

Todd Phillips (1970-)
    War Dogs

Alex Proyas (1965-)
    Gods of Egypt

Dylan Reeve
    Tickled

Nicolas Winding Refn (1970-)
    The Neon Demon

Kelly Reichardt
    Certain Women

Screenwriter Index

Efthymis Filippou
  The Lobster

Kieran Fitzgerald
  Snowden

T.J. Fixman
  Ratchet & Clank

Josh Flanagan
  Lazer Team

Mike Flanagan (1978-)
  Ouija: Origin of Evil

Dan Fogelman
  Zootopia

Anne Fontaine (1959-)
  The Innocents

Tom Ford
  Nocturnal Animals

Amy Fox
  Equity

Dana Fox
  How to Be Single

Kelly Fremon
  See also *Kelly Fremon Craig*

Kelly Fremon Craig
  The Edge of Seventeen

Anthony Frewin
  Anthropoid

Chi Keung Fung
  The Mermaid

Ellen Brown Furman
  The Infiltrator

Laura Gabbert
  City of Gold

Mateo Garcia
  Desierto

Rodrigo Garcia (1959-)
  Last Days in the Desert

Tony Gilroy (1956-)
  Rogue One: A Star Wars Story

Evan Goldberg
  Sausage Party

Evan Goldberg (1982-)
  Neighbors 2: Sorority Rising

Jane Goldman (1970-)
  Miss Peregrine's Home for Peculiar Children

Malcolm T. Goldman
  Norm of the North

Akiva Goldsman (1962-)
  The 5th Wave

Sophie Goodhart
  My Blind Brother

David S. Goyer (1965-)
  Batman *vs.* Superman: Dawn of Justice

Susannah Grant (1963-)
  The 5th Wave

David Gordon Green (1975-)
  Goat

Robert Greene (1976-)
  Kate Plays Christine

Paul Greengrass (1955-)
  Jason Bourne

Christian Gudegast
  London Has Fallen

Ciro Guerra
  Embrace of the Serpent

Marc Haimes
  Kubo and the Two Strings

Toby Halbrooks
  Pete's Dragon

Dallas Hallam
  See *Dallas Richard Hallam*

Dallas Richard Hallam
  Southbound

John Hamburg (1970-)
  Why Him?
  Zoolander 2

Mia Hansen-Love (1981-)
  Things to Come

Gary Hardwick
  The Perfect Match

David Hare (1947-)
  Denial

Kevin Hart (1979-)
  Kevin Hart: What Now?

Chad Hartigan
  Morris from America

Phil Hay
  The Invitation
  Ride Along 2

Carey Hayes (1961-)
  The Conjuring 2

Chad Hayes (1961-)
  The Conjuring 2

Eric Heisserer
  Arrival
  Lights Out

Ian Helfer
  Why Him?

Marshall Herskovitz (1952-)
  Jack Reacher: Never Go Back

Werner Herzog (1942-)
  Lo and Behold: Reveries of the Connected World

Guy Hibbert
  Eye in the Sky

Tom Hines
  Mother's Day

Miu-Kei Ho
  The Mermaid

Chuck Hogan
  13 Hours: The Secret Soldiers of Benghazi

Kara Holden
  Middle School: The Worst Years of My Life

Anna Rose Holmer
  The Fits

Patrick Horvath
  Southbound

Mamoru Hosoda
  The Boy and the Beast

Byron Howard
  Zootopia

Jeff Howard
  Ouija: Origin of Evil

Matt Hullum
  Lazer Team

Kyle Hunter
  Sausage Party

Jonathan Jakubowicz
  Hands of Stone

Jim Jarmusch (1953-)
  Paterson

Anthony Jaswinski
  The Shallows

Barry Jenkins
  Moonlight

Garth Jennings (1972-)
  Sing

Zhangke Jia
  Mountains May Depart

David Leslie Johnson
  The Conjuring 2

Eric Johnson
  The Finest Hours

Phil Johnston
  The Brothers Grimsby
  Zootopia

Ti West (1980-)
  In a Valley of Violence
William Wheeler
  Queen of Katwe
Kennilworthy Whisp (1965-)
  See J. K. Rowling
Kennilworthy Kathleen Whisp
  (1965-)
  See J. K. Rowling
August Wilson
  Fences
Caleb Wilson
  Nine Lives

Erin Cressida Wilson (1964-)
  The Girl on the Train
Michael J. Wilson
  Ice Age: Collision Course
Alice Winocour
  Disorder
Edmond Wong
  Ip Man 3
James A. Woods (1979-)
  Independence Day: Resurgence
Linda Woolverton (1959-)
  Alice Through the Looking Glass
Nicolas Wright
  Independence Day: Resurgence

Marcin Wrona
  Demon
Christopher Yost (1973-)
  Max Steel
Ben Younger (1972-)
  Bleed for This
Mauricio Zacharias
  Little Men
Joshua Zetumer
  Patriots Day
Edward Zwick (1952-)
  Jack Reacher: Never Go Back

Cinematographer Index

Editor Index

Art Director Index

Music Director Index

Michael Andrews
    Dirty Grandpa
    Neighbors 2: Sorority Rising

Craig Armstrong (1959-)
    Bridget Jones's Baby
    Me Before You
    Snowden

Lorne Balfe
    13 Hours: The Secret Soldiers of
      Benghazi

Tierney Sutton Band
    Sully

Rocque Banos
    Risen

Roque Banos (1968-)
    Don't Breathe

Lesley Barber (1968-)
    Manchester by the Sea

Jeff Beal (1963-)
    Weiner

Christophe Beck (1972-)
    Trolls

Magnus Beite
    The Wave

Marco Beltrami (1966-)
    Ben-Hur
    Gods of Egypt
    The Shallows

Danny Bensi
    The Fits
    Last Days in the Desert

Volker Bertelmann
    Lion

Joseph Bishara
    The Conjuring 2
    The Other Side of the Door

Brooke Blair
    Green Room

Will Blair
    Green Room

David Braid
    Born to Be Blue

Nicholas Britell
    Free State of Jones
    Moonlight

David Buckley
    The Brothers Grimsby
    Jason Bourne
    The Nice Guys

Lukasz Pawel Buda
    Hunt for the Wilderpeople

Carter Burwell (1955-)
    The Family Fang
    The Finest Hours

Carlos Cabezas
    The Club

Jeff Cardoni
    Middle School: The Worst Years
      of My Life
    Mike and Dave Need Wedding
      Dates

Nick Cave (1957-)
    Hell or High Water

Darya Charusha
    Hardcore Henry

Stanley Clarke (1951-)
    Barbershop: The Next Cut

Erran Baron Cohen
    The Brothers Grimsby

Matthew Compton
    Popstar: Never Stop Never Stop-
      ping

Adam Cork
    Genius

Paul Dalio
    Touched With Fire

Jeff Danna (1964-)
    Billy Lynn's Long Halftime Walk
    Storks

Mychael Danna (1958-)
    Billy Lynn's Long Halftime Walk
    Remember
    Storks

John Debney (1956-)
    Ice Age: Collision Course
    The Jungle Book
    Mother's Day
    The Young Messiah

Rebecca Delannet
    The Little Prince

Alexandre Desplat (1961-)
    American Pastoral
    Florence Foster Jenkins
    The Light Between Oceans
    The Secret Life of Pets

Keegan DeWitt
    Kate Plays Christine
    Morris from America
Ramin Djawadi (1974-)
    Warcraft
    The Wild Life
Jim Dooley
    Fifty Shades of Black
Christopher Drake
    Yoga Hosers
Anne Dudley (1956-)
    Elle
Fil Eisler
    How to Be Single
Danny Elfman (1953-)
    Alice Through the Looking Glass
    The Girl on the Train
Warren Ellis
    Hell or High Water
Micky Erbe
    A Beautiful Planet
Benjamin Esdraffo
    Love & Friendship
Kurt Farquhar
    The Perfect Match
Sven Faulconer
    Blood Father
Andrew Feltenstein
    The Bronze
George Fenton (1950-)
    I, Daniel Blake
Ola Flottum
    Louder Than Bombs
Opetaia Foa'i
    Moana
Robin Foster
    Anthropoid
Marcello De Francisci
    Jane Got a Gun
Simon Franglen
    The Magnificent Seven
John (Gianni) Frizzell (1966-)
    When the Bough Breaks
Evgueni Galperine
    Nine Lives
Sacha Galperine
    Nine Lives
Lisa Gerrard (1961-)
    Jane Got a Gun

Michael Giacchino (1967-)
    Doctor Strange
    Rogue One: A Star Wars Story
    Star Trek Beyond
    Zootopia
The Gifted
    Southbound
Robert Glasper
    Miles Ahead
Ludwig Goransson (1984-)
    Central Intelligence
Jeff Grace
    Certain Women
    In a Valley of Violence
Harry Gregson-Williams (1961-)
    Live by Night
Rupert Gregson-Williams (1966-)
    Hacksaw Ridge
    The Legend of Tarzan
Valentin Hadjadj
    April and the Extraordinary
        World
Chris Hajian
    The Infiltrator
Nathan Halpern
    The Lovers & the Despot
Yoshihiro Hanno
    Mountains May Depart
Daniel Hart
    Pete's Dragon
Richard Harvey (1953-)
    The Little Prince
Alex Heffes (1971-)
    Queen of Katwe
Paul Hepker
    Eye in the Sky
Gregoire Hetzel
    The Innocents
    My Golden Days
Michael Higham
    Miss Peregrine's Home for Pecu-
        liar Children
Dickon Hinchliffe (1967-)
    Little Men
David Hirschfelder (1960-)
    The Dressmaker
Tom Holkenborg (1967-)
    See Junkie XL
Julia Holter
    Bleed for This

James Horner (1953-)
    The Magnificent Seven
Katsu Hoshi
    Only Yesterday
James Newton Howard (1951-)
    Fantastic Beasts and Where to
        Find Them
    The Huntsman: Winter's War
Fuhua Huang
    The Mermaid
Andy Hull
    Swiss Army Man
Ian Hultquist
    The First Monday in May
    My Blind Brother
Sofia Hultquist
    The First Monday in May
Justin Hurwitz
    La La Land
Alberto Iglesias (1955-)
    Julieta
Mark Isham (1951-)
    The Accountant
    Mechanic: Resurrection
    Papa: Hemingway in Cuba
Nicolas Jaar
    Dheepan
Steve Jablonsky (1970-)
    Deepwater Horizon
    Keanu
    Teenage Mutant Ninja Turtles:
        Out of the Shadows
Henry Jackman (1974-)
    The Birth of a Nation
    Captain America: Civil War
    The 5th Wave
    Jack Reacher: Never Go Back
Christian Jacob
    Sully
Jim Jarmusch (1953-)
    Paterson
Yeong-wook Jo
    The Handmaiden
Johann Johannsson
    Arrival
Bobby Johnston (1967-)
    City of Gold
Samuel Jones
    Equity

Junkie XL (1967-)
  Batman *vs.* Superman: Dawn of
    Justice
  Deadpool

Saunder Jurriaans
  The Fits
  Last Days in the Desert

Federico Jusid
  Neruda

Kenji Kawai (1957-)
  Ip Man 3

Brian H. Kim
  Hello, My Name is Doris

Rodi Kirkcaldy
  Tickled

Johnny Klimek (1962-)
  The Darkness
  A Hologram for the King

Harald Kloser (1956-)
  Independence Day: Resurgence

Kathryn Kluge
  Silence

Kim Allen Kluge
  Silence

Todor Kobakov (1978-)
  Born to Be Blue

Mark Korven
  The Witch

Abel Korzeniowski
  Nocturnal Animals

Mike Kourtzer
  My Golden Days

Bobby Krlic
  Triple 9

Jed Kurzel
  Assassin's Creed

Nathan Lanier
  Max Steel

James Lavino
  Wiener-Dog

Joann Le Blanc
  The Little Prince

Yoann Lemoine
  See Woodkid

Christopher Lennertz (1972-)
  Bad Moms
  The Boss
  My Big Fat Greek Wedding 2
  Ride Along 2
  Sausage Party

Mica Levi
  Jackie

Mike Levy
  Disorder

Dominic Lewis
  Money Monster

Nascuy Linares
  Embrace of the Serpent

Carter Logan
  Paterson

Ariel Loh
  The Eyes of My Mother

Steve London (1970-)
  Born to Be Blue

Marcin Macuk
  Demon

Mark Mancina (1957-)
  Moana

Clint Mansell (1963-)
  High-Rise

Matthew Margeson
  Eddie the Eagle
  Miss Peregrine's Home for Pecu-
    liar Children

Dario Marianelli (1963-)
  Kubo and the Two Strings

Alexis Marsh
  Equity

Cliff Martinez (1954-)
  The Neon Demon
  War Dogs

Bear McCreary
  10 Cloverfield Lane

Bear McCreary (1979-)
  The Boy
  The Forest

Robert McDowell
  Swiss Army Man

Stephen McKeon
  Norm of the North

Alan Menken (1949-)
  Sausage Party

Angelo Milli (1975-)
  Hands of Stone

Arjan Miranda
  Goat

Lin-Manuel Miranda
  Moana

Jake Monaco
  Keeping Up with the Joneses

Trevor Morris (1970-)
  London Has Fallen

Will Musser
  God's Not Dead 2

John Nau
  The Bronze

Roger Neill (1963-)
  20th Century Women

Thomas Newman (1955-)
  Finding Dory
  Passengers

The Newton Brothers
  Ouija: Origin of Evil

Dustin O'Halloran
  Lion

Sattar Oraki
  The Salesman

Atli Orvarsson
  The Edge of Seventeen

John Ottman (1964-)
  The Nice Guys
  X-Men: Apocalypse

John Paesano
  Almost Christmas

Krzysztof Penderecki (1933-)
  Demon

Heitor Pereira
  The Angry Birds Movie

Laurent Perez Del Mar (1974-)
  The Red Turtle

Adam Peters
  Snowden

Rachel Portman (1960-)
  Race

Randall Poster
  The Bronze

John Powell (1963-)
  Jason Bourne

Keith Power
  Criminal

Steven Price
  Suicide Squad

Trent Reznor (1965-)
  Patriots Day

Max Richter
  Miss Sloane

Josh Ritter (1976-)
  The Hollars

Michael Rohatyn
  Maggie's Plan

Atticus Ross
   Patriots Day
   Triple 9

Elvin Ross
   Boo! A Madea Halloween

Leopold Ross
   Triple 9

RZA
   Meet the Blacks

Jonathan Sadoff
   The Meddler

Claudia Sarne
   Triple 9

Samuel Scott
   Hunt for the Wilderpeople

Theodore Shapiro (1971-)
   Central Intelligence
   Collateral Beauty
   Ghostbusters
   The Invitation
   Office Christmas Party
   Why Him?
   Zoolander 2

Ed Shearmur (1966-)
   Elvis & Nixon

Howard Shore (1946-)
   Denial

Carlo Siliotto (1950-)
   Miracles From Heaven

Alan Silvestri (1950-)
   Allied

Rob Simonsen (1978-)
   Nerve

Maribeth Solomon
   A Beautiful Planet

Alex Somers
   Captain Fantastic

Squrl
   Paterson

Masakatsu Takagi
   The Boy and the Beast

Joby Talbot (1971-)
   Sing

Stephen James Taylor
   Southside with You

Hanan Townshend
   Knight of Cups

Joseph Trapanese
   Allegiant

Tom Tykwer (1965-)
   A Hologram for the King

Brian Tyler
   Criminal
   The Disappointments Room
   Now You See Me 2

Nick Urata
   Whiskey Tango Foxtrot

Joan Valent
   Compadres

Fernando Velazquez
   A Monster Calls
   Pride and Prejudice and Zombies

Jay Wadley
   Indignation

Benjamin Wallfisch
   Hidden Figures
   Lights Out

Gast Waltzing (1956-)
   Sunset Song

Thomas Wander
   Independence Day: Resurgence

Julian Wass
   Other People

Patrick Watson
   The 9th Life of Louis Drax

Conrad Wedde
   Hunt for the Wilderpeople

Walter Werzowa (1960-)
   Author: The JT LeRoy Story

Nathan Whitehead
   Keanu
   The Purge: Election Year

Jeff Williams
   Lazer Team

John Williams (1932-)
   The BFG

Pharrell Williams (1973-)
   Hidden Figures

Adam Wingard (1982-)
   Blair Witch

David Wingo
   Loving
   Midnight Special

Evan Wise
   Ratchet & Clank

Woodkid
   Desierto

Lyle Workman (1957-)
   Bad Santa 2

Geoff Zanelli (1974-)
   Masterminds

Marcelo Zarvos
   The Choice
   Fences
   Our Kind of Traitor

Wendy Zheng
   The Mermaid

Aaron Zigman
   I Saw the Light
   Mr. Right

Hans Zimmer (1957-)
   Batman *vs.* Superman: Dawn of
      Justice
   Hidden Figures
   Inferno
   Kung Fu Panda 3
   The Little Prince

Florian Zwietnig
   Tickled

Performer Index

Christopher Abbott
  Whiskey Tango Foxtrot

Barkhad Abdi
  Eye in the Sky

Amy Adams (1974-)
  Arrival
  Batman *vs.* Superman: Dawn of
    Justice
  Nocturnal Animals

Jovan Adepo
  Fences

Ben Affleck (1972-)
  The Accountant
  Batman *vs.* Superman: Dawn of
    Justice
  Live by Night

Casey Affleck (1975-)
  The Finest Hours
  Manchester by the Sea
  Triple 9

Diana Agostini
  The Eyes of My Mother

Riz Ahmed (1982-)
  Jason Bourne

Jessica Alba (1981-)
  Mechanic: Resurrection

Laura Albert
  Author: The JT LeRoy Story

Mahershala Ali (1974-)
  Free State of Jones
  Moonlight

Taraneh Alidoosti
  The Salesman

Keith Allen (1953-)
  Eddie the Eagle

Marcelo Alonso
  The Club

Bruce Altman (1955-)
  Touched With Fire

Joe Alwyn (1991-)
  Billy Lynn's Long Halftime Walk

Mathieu Amalric (1965-)
  My Golden Days

Robbie Amell (1988-)
  Nine Lives

Stephen Amell (1981-)
  Teenage Mutant Ninja Turtles:
    Out of the Shadows

Ella Anderson
  The Boss

Jennifer Aniston (1969-)
  Mother's Day
  Office Christmas Party
  Storks

Jesuthasan Antonythasan
  Dheepan

Maude Apatow (1997-)
  Other People

Christina Applegate (1971-)
  Bad Moms

Olivia Grace Applegate
  Krisha

Bryn Apprill
  The Boy and the Beast

Nina Arianda (1984-)
  Florence Foster Jenkins

Ana de Armas (1988-)
  Hands of Stone

Will Arnett (1970-)
  Teenage Mutant Ninja Turtles:
    Out of the Shadows

Zackary Arthur
  The 5th Wave

Tadanobu Asano (1973-)
  Silence

Cindy aus Marzahn
  The Wild Life

Kevin Bacon (1958-)
  The Darkness
  Patriots Day

Janelle Bailey
  The Shallows

Jonathan Bailey
  The Young Messiah

Alec Baldwin (1958-)
  Rules Don't Apply

Christian Bale (1974-)
  Knight of Cups

Caitriona Balfe (1979-)
  Money Monster

Ellie Bamber
  Pride and Prejudice and Zombies

Adam Brody (1980-)
  Yoga Hosers

Josh Brolin (1968-)
  Hail, Caesar!

Albert Brooks (1947-)
  Finding Dory
  The Secret Life of Pets

Caleb Brown
  Mother's Day

Tuwatchai Buawat
  Cemetery of Splendor

Billy Burke (1966-)
  Lights Out

Makyla Burnam
  The Fits

Burnie Burns
  Lazer Team

Ty Burrell (1967-)
  Storks

Danny Burstein (1964-)
  Indignation

Gerard Butler (1969-)
  Gods of Egypt
  London Has Fallen

Asa Butterfield (1997-)
  Miss Peregrine's Home for Peculiar Children

Agata Buzek (1976-)
  The Innocents

Gabriel Byrne (1950-)
  Louder Than Bombs

Rose Byrne (1979-)
  The Meddler
  Neighbors 2: Sorority Rising

Nicolas Cage (1964-)
  Snowden

Sarah Wayne Callies (1977-)
  The Other Side of the Door

Vanessa Bell Calloway (1957-)
  Southside with You

Maria Canals-Barrera
  God's Not Dead 2

Lizzy Caplan (1982-)
  Allied

Steve Carell (1962-)
  Café Society

Jerrod Carmichael
  The Meddler

Helena Bonham Carter (1966-)
  Alice Through the Looking Glass

Dana Carvey (1955-)
  The Secret Life of Pets

Vincent Cassel (1966-)
  Jason Bourne

Bryan Casserly
  Krisha

Kyle Cassie (1976-)
  Deadpool

Alfredo Castro
  The Club

Diego Catano
  Desierto

Henry Cavill (1983-)
  Batman *vs.* Superman: Dawn of Justice

Cedric the Entertainer (1964-)
  Barbershop: The Next Cut
  Why Him?

Michael Cera (1988-)
  Sausage Party

Petcharat Chaiburi
  Cemetery of Splendor

Kyle Chandler (1965-)
  Manchester by the Sea

Sylvia Chang (1953-)
  Mountains May Depart

Omar Chaparro
  Compadres

Jessica Chastain (1981-)
  The Huntsman: Winter's War
  Miss Sloane

Don Cheadle (1964-)
  Kevin Hart: What Now?
  Miles Ahead

Morris Chestnut (1969-)
  When the Bough Breaks

John Cho (1972-)
  Star Trek Beyond

Sarita Choudhury (1966-)
  A Hologram for the King

Luci Christian
  The Boy and the Beast

Markees Christmas
  Morris from America

Woo-hee Chun
  The Wailing

Sam Claflin (1986-)
  Me Before You

Morfydd Clark
  Love & Friendship

Emilia Clarke (1987-)
  Me Before You

Jemaine Clement (1974-)
  The BFG
  Moana

Florence Clery
  The Light Between Oceans

George Clooney (1961-)
  Hail, Caesar!
  Money Monster

Lauren Cohan (1982-)
  The Boy

Gary Cole (1957-)
  The Bronze

Joe Cole
  Green Room

Lily Collins (1989-)
  Rules Don't Apply

Olivia Colman (1974-)
  The Lobster

Condor (1963-)
  See Kevin D. Mitnick

Jennifer Connelly (1970-)
  American Pastoral

Anne Consigny (1963-)
  Elle

Keaton Nigel Cooke
  Wiener-Dog

Bradley Cooper (1975-)
  10 Cloverfield Lane (*V*)
  War Dogs

Chris Cooper (1951-)
  Demolition

Dennis Cooper
  Author: The JT LeRoy Story

Dominic Cooper (1978-)
  Warcraft

Sharlto Copley (1973-)
  Hardcore Henry
  The Hollars

John Corbett
  My Big Fat Greek Wedding 2

Emayatzy Corinealdi
  Miles Ahead

Nikolaj Coster-Waldau (1970-)
  Gods of Egypt

Kevin Costner (1955-)
  Criminal
  Hidden Figures

Devin Druid
Louder Than Bombs
Dinara Drukarova (1976-)
My Golden Days
Colton Dunn
Lazer Team
Griffin Dunne (1955-)
Touched With Fire
Kirsten Dunst (1982-)
Hidden Figures
Midnight Special
Shariff Earp
Moonlight
Courtney Eaton
Gods of Egypt
Aaron Eckhart (1968-)
Bleed for This
Sully
Joel Edgerton (1974-)
Jane Got a Gun
Loving
Midnight Special
Virginie Efira (1977-)
Elle
Zac Efron (1987-)
Dirty Grandpa
Mike and Dave Need Wedding
Dates
Neighbors 2: Sorority Rising
Taron Egerton
Eddie the Eagle
Sing
Jennifer Ehle (1969-)
Little Men
Alden Ehrenreich (1989-)
Hail, Caesar!
Rules Don't Apply
Jesse Eisenberg (1983-)
Batman *vs.* Superman: Dawn of
Justice
Café Society
Louder Than Bombs
Now You See Me 2
Chiwetel Ejiofor (1977-)
Doctor Strange
Triple 9
Carmen Ejogo (1973-)
Born to Be Blue
Idris Elba (1972-)
The Jungle Book
Star Trek Beyond
Zootopia (*V*)

Erick Elias
Compadres
Kimberly Elise (1971-)
Almost Christmas
Noah Emmerich (1965-)
Jane Got a Gun
Linda Emond (1959-)
Indignation
Edvin Endresen
Eddie the Eagle
Mike Epps (1970-)
Fifty Shades of Black
Meet the Blacks
Omar Epps (1973-)
Almost Christmas
Yousef Erakat (1990-)
Boo! A Madea Halloween
Zaïd Errougui-Demonsant
Disorder
Lauren Esposito
The Conjuring 2
Choi Eun-hee
The Lovers & the Despot
Chris Evans (1981-)
Captain America: Civil War
Luke Evans (1979-)
The Girl on the Train
High-Rise
Rupert Evans (1976-)
American Pastoral
Rupert Evans (1977-)
The Boy
Eve (1978-)
Barbershop: The Next Cut
Rupert Everett (1959-)
Miss Peregrine's Home for Pecu-
liar Children
Tracey Fairaway
A Hologram for the King
Krisha Fairchild
Krisha
Donald Adeosun Faison (1974-)
The Perfect Match
Dakota Fanning (1994-)
American Pastoral
Elle Fanning (1998-)
Live by Night
The Neon Demon
20th Century Women
Courtney Fansler
Miracles From Heaven

Golshifteh Farahani (1983-)
Paterson
Robert Farias
The Club
Taissa Farmiga (1994-)
In a Valley of Violence
Vera Farmiga (1973-)
The Conjuring 2
Colin Farrell (1976-)
Fantastic Beasts and Where to
Find Them
The Lobster
David Farrier
Tickled
Michael Fassbender (1977-)
Assassin's Creed
The Light Between Oceans
X-Men: Apocalypse
Oakes Fegley
Pete's Dragon
Tom Felton (1987-)
Risen
Rebecca Ferguson
Florence Foster Jenkins
The Girl on the Train
Alison Fernandez
Only Yesterday
Will Ferrell (1968-)
Zoolander 2
Tina Fey (1970-)
Whiskey Tango Foxtrot
Sally Field (1946-)
Hello, My Name is Doris
Joseph Fiennes (1970-)
Risen
Ralph Fiennes (1962-)
Hail, Caesar!
Kubo and the Two Strings
Travis Fimmel (1979-)
Maggie's Plan
Warcraft
Colin Firth (1960-)
Bridget Jones's Baby
Genius
Peter Firth (1953-)
Risen
Laurence Fishburne (1961-)
Passengers

Isla Fisher (1976-)
   The Brothers Grimsby
   Keeping Up with the Joneses
   Nocturnal Animals

Noel Fisher (1984-)
   Teenage Mutant Ninja Turtles:
      Out of the Shadows

Danny Flaherty
   Goat

Dan Fogler (1976-)
   Fantastic Beasts and Where to
      Find Them

Taylar Fondren
   Southside with You

Ben Foster (1980-)
   The Finest Hours
   Hell or High Water
   Warcraft

Megan Fox (1986-)
   Teenage Mutant Ninja Turtles:
      Out of the Shadows

Mackenzie Foy (2000-)
   The Little Prince

Sean Francis
   Remember

Dave Franco (1985-)
   Nerve
   Now You See Me 2

James Franco (1978-)
   The Little Prince
   Sausage Party
   Why Him?

James Edward Franco (1978-)
   See James Franco

Gavin Free
   Lazer Team

Martin Freeman (1971-)
   Whiskey Tango Foxtrot

Morgan Freeman (1937-)
   Ben-Hur
   London Has Fallen

Nick Frost (1972-)
   The Huntsman: Winter's War

Lucy Fry
   The Darkness

Dominic Fumusa (1969-)
   13 Hours: The Secret Soldiers of
      Benghazi

Josh Gad (1981-)
   The Angry Birds Movie

Sarah Gadon (1987-)
   Indignation
   The 9th Life of Louis Drax

Gal Gadot (1985-)
   Batman *vs.* Superman: Dawn of
      Justice
   Keeping Up with the Joneses
   Triple 9

Zach Galifianakis (1969-)
   Keeping Up with the Joneses
   Masterminds

John Gallagher, Jr. (1984-)
   10 Cloverfield Lane

John Galliano (1960-)
   The First Monday in May

Andy Garcia (1956-)
   Max Steel
   Passengers

Paulina Garcia
   Little Men

Cecile Garcia-Fogel
   My Golden Days

Manuel Garcia-Rulfo (1981-)
   The Magnificent Seven

Virginia Gardner
   Goat

Andrew Garfield (1983-)
   Hacksaw Ridge
   Silence

Jennifer Garner (1972-)
   Miracles From Heaven
   Nine Lives

Jean-Paul Gaultier (1952-)
   The First Monday in May

Anna Geislerova (1976-)
   Anthropoid

Greta Gerwig (1983-)
   Jackie
   Maggie's Plan
   20th Century Women
   Wiener-Dog

Paul Giamatti (1967-)
   Ratchet & Clank

Panio Gianopoulos
   Author: The JT LeRoy Story

Lauren Gibson
   The Fits

Mel Gibson (1956-)
   Blood Father

Karen Gillan (1987-)
   In a Valley of Violence

Aidan Gillen (1968-)
   Sing Street

Robin Givens (1964-)
   God's Not Dead 2

Lily Gladstone
   Certain Women

Brendan Gleeson (1955-)
   Assassin's Creed
   Live by Night

Danny Glover (1946-)
   Almost Christmas

Griffin Gluck (2000-)
   Middle School: The Worst Years
      of My Life

Karl Glusman
   The Neon Demon

Luis Gnecco
   Neruda

Jeff Goldblum (1952-)
   Independence Day: Resurgence

Matthew Goode (1978-)
   Allied

John Goodman (1952-)
   Patriots Day
   10 Cloverfield Lane

Ginnifer Goodwin (1978-)
   Zootopia (*V*)

Joseph Gordon-Levitt (1981-)
   Snowden

Eli Goree
   Race

Ryan Gosling (1980-)
   La La Land
   The Nice Guys

Olivier Gourmet (1963-)
   April and the Extraordinary
      World

Andrzej Grabowski
   Demon

Maggie Grace (1983-)
   The Choice

Heather Graham (1970-)
   Norm of the North

Lauren Graham (1967-)
   Middle School: The Worst Years
      of My Life

Ellie Grainger
   The Witch

Holliday Grainger (1988-)
   The Finest Hours

Kelsey Grammer (1954-)
Storks

Dario Grandinetti (1959-)
Julieta

Hugh Grant (1960-)
Florence Foster Jenkins

Daniel Grao
Julieta

Susan Gray
Last Days in the Desert

Adam Greaves-Neal
The Young Messiah

Eva Green (1980-)
Miss Peregrine's Home for Peculiar Children

Janet-Laine Green (1951-)
Born to Be Blue

Max Greenfield (1980-)
Hello, My Name is Doris

Frank Grillo (1965-)
The Purge: Election Year

Marc-André Grondin (1984-)
April and the Extraordinary World

Richard Gross
Swiss Army Man

Patrick Güldenberg
Morris from America

Anna Gunn (1968-)
Equity

Diego Muñoz
Neruda

Emilio Gutierrez-Caba (1942-)
Neruda

Ryan Guzman (1987-)
Everybody Wants Some!!

Jake Gyllenhaal (1980-)
Demolition
Nocturnal Animals

Jung-woo Ha (1978-)
The Handmaiden

Tiffany Haddish (1980-)
Keanu

Bill Hader (1978-)
The Angry Birds Movie
Sausage Party

Kathryn Hahn (1973-)
Bad Moms
Captain Fantastic

Tony Hale (1970-)
Yoga Hosers

Jackie Earle Haley (1961-)
The Birth of a Nation
London Has Fallen

Rebecca Hall (1982-)
The BFG

Regina Hall (1970-)
Barbershop: The Next Cut
When the Bough Breaks

Dieter Hallervorden
The Wild Life

Jon Hamm (1971-)
Keeping Up with the Joneses

Armie Hammer (1986-)
The Birth of a Nation

Paul Hamy
Disorder

Colin Hanks (1977-)
Elvis & Nixon

Tom Hanks (1956-)
A Hologram for the King
Inferno
Sully

Eili Harboe
The Wave

Diana Hardcastle
The Boy

William Jackson Harper (1980-)
Paterson

Woody Harrelson (1962-)
The Edge of Seventeen
Now You See Me 2
Triple 9

Jared Harris (1961-)
Allied
Certain Women

Naomie Harris (1976-)
Collateral Beauty
Moonlight
Our Kind of Traitor

Kevin Hart (1979-)
Central Intelligence
Kevin Hart: What Now?
Ride Along 2
The Secret Life of Pets

Melissa Joan Hart (1976-)
God's Not Dead 2

Jo Hartley
Eddie the Eagle

Maddie Hasson
I Saw the Light

Anne Hathaway (1982-)
Alice Through the Looking Glass

Kali Hawk
Fifty Shades of Black
The Perfect Match

Ethan Hawke (1971-)
Born to Be Blue
In a Valley of Violence
Maggie's Plan
The Magnificent Seven

Holland Hayes
Kate Plays Christine

Sam Hazeldine (1972-)
Mechanic: Resurrection

Bella Heathcote (1987-)
The Neon Demon
Pride and Prejudice and Zombies

Lucas Hedges
Manchester by the Sea

Garrett Hedlund (1984-)
Billy Lynn's Long Halftime Walk

Miles Heizer (1994-)
Nerve

Simon Helberg (1980-)
Florence Foster Jenkins

Brad Heller
God's Not Dead 2

Ed Helms (1974-)
Kevin Hart: What Now?

Chris Hemsworth (1983-)
Ghostbusters
The Huntsman: Winter's War

Liam Hemsworth (1990-)
The Dressmaker
Independence Day: Resurgence

Zulay Henao (1979-)
Meet the Blacks

Martin Henderson (1974-)
Miracles From Heaven

Stephen Henderson (1949-)
Fences

Christina Hendricks (1975-)
Bad Santa 2

Barry (Shabaka) Henley (1954-)
Paterson

Taraji P. Henson (1970-)
Hidden Figures

Katarzyna Herman
Demon

Callie Hernandez
Blair Witch

Patrick Heusinger
  Jack Reacher: Never Go Back
Alex Hibbert
  Moonlight
Alondra Hidalgo
  Desierto
Tom Hiddleston (1981-)
  High-Rise
  I Saw the Light
John Michael Higgins (1963-)
  Almost Christmas
Royalty Hightower
  The Fits
Jonah Hill (1983-)
  Sausage Party
  War Dogs
Ciaran Hinds (1953-)
  Bleed for This
  Last Days in the Desert
  Silence
Aldis Hodge (1986-)
  Jack Reacher: Never Go Back
Edwin Hodge (1985-)
  The Purge: Election Year
Tyler Hoechlin (1987-)
  Everybody Wants Some!!
Dustin Hoffman (1937-)
  Kung Fu Panda 3
Anders Holm
  How to Be Single
Arielle Holmes
  American Honey
Katie Holmes (1978-)
  Touched With Fire
Russell Hornsby (1974-)
  Fences
Farid Sajjadi Hosseini
  The Salesman
Shahab Hosseini (1974-)
  The Salesman
Julianne Hough (1988-)
  Dirty Grandpa
Nicholas Hoult (1989-)
  X-Men: Apocalypse
Djimon Hounsou (1964-)
  The Legend of Tarzan
Rachel House (1971-)
  Hunt for the Wilderpeople
  Moana
Bryce Dallas Howard (1981-)
  Pete's Dragon

Kate Hudson (1979-)
  Deepwater Horizon
  Mother's Day
Michiel Huisman (1981-)
  The Invitation
Sandra Hüller (1978-)
  Toni Erdmann
Lynn Hung
  Ip Man 3
Sam Huntington (1982-)
  Sully
Isabelle Huppert (1953-)
  Elle
  Louder Than Bombs
  Things to Come
John Hurt (1940-)
  Jackie
Jack Huston (1982-)
  Ben-Hur
Jung-min Hwang
  The Wailing
Ice Cube (1969-)
  Barbershop: The Next Cut
  Ride Along 2
Ralph Ineson
  The Witch
Marin Ireland
  The Family Fang
Jeremy Irons (1948-)
  Assassin's Creed
  High-Rise
Oscar Isaac (1980-)
  X-Men: Apocalypse
Hugh Jackman (1968-)
  Eddie the Eagle
Samuel L. Jackson (1948-)
  The Legend of Tarzan
  Miss Peregrine's Home for Peculiar Children
Oscar Jaenada
  The Shallows
Lily James (1989-)
  Pride and Prejudice and Zombies
Stephan James (1993-)
  Race
Theo James (1984-)
  Allegiant
Allison Janney (1959-)
  Miss Peregrine's Home for Peculiar Children

Eve Jihan Jeffers (1978-)
  See Eve
Richard Jenkins (1947-)
  The Hollars
Terrence Jenkins (1982-)
  The Perfect Match
Blake Jenner
  The Edge of Seventeen
  Everybody Wants Some!!
Ken Jeong (1969-)
  Norm of the North
Hector Jimenez (1973-)
  Compadres
Jin-woong Jo (1976-)
  The Handmaiden
Scarlett Johansson (1984-)
  Captain America: Civil War
  Hail, Caesar!
  Sing
Dave Johns
  I, Daniel Blake
Aaron Johnson (1990-)
  See Aaron Taylor-Johnson
Dakota Johnson (1989-)
  How to Be Single
Dwayne 'The Rock' Johnson (1972-)
  Central Intelligence
  Moana
Kirsten Johnson (1965-)
  Cameraperson
Duncan Joiner
  The Disappointments Room
Angelina Jolie (1975-)
  Kung Fu Panda 3
Nick Jonas (1992-)
  Goat
Kristoffer Joner (1972-)
  The Wave
Cherry Jones (1956-)
  I Saw the Light
Felicity Jones (1983-)
  Inferno
  A Monster Calls
  Rogue One: A Star Wars Story
Gemma Jones (1942-)
  Bridget Jones's Baby
Leslie Jones (1967-)
  Ghostbusters
  Masterminds
Michael Jones
  Lazer Team

Toby Jones (1966-)
Anthropoid

Tommy Lee Jones (1946-)
Criminal
Jason Bourne
Mechanic: Resurrection

Carla Juri
Morris from America

Martin Kabanza
Queen of Katwe

Babak Karimi
The Salesman

Philippe Katerine (1968-)
April and the Extraordinary
World

David Kaye (1964-)
Ratchet & Clank

Zoe Kazan (1983-)
My Blind Brother

Toby Kebbell (1982-)
Ben-Hur
A Monster Calls
Warcraft

Lina Keller
Morris from America

Brett Kelly (1993-)
Bad Santa 2

Minka Kelly (1980-)
Papa: Hemingway in Cuba

Tori Kelly (1992-)
Sing

Victoria Loren Kelly (1992-)
See Tori Kelly

Ellie Kemper (1980-)
The Secret Life of Pets

Anna Kendrick (1985-)
The Accountant
The Hollars
Mike and Dave Need Wedding
Dates
Mr. Right
Trolls

Riley Keough (1989-)
American Honey

Keegan Michael Key (1971-)
Keanu

Irrfan Khan (1967-)
Inferno

Nicole Kidman (1966-)
The Family Fang
Genius
Lion

Ben Kingsley (1943-)
The Jungle Book

Joel Kinnaman (1979-)
Suicide Squad

Greg Kinnear (1963-)
Little Men

Taylor Kinney (1981-)
The Forest

Luke Kirby (1978-)
Touched With Fire

Vanessa Kirby (1989-)
Me Before You

Keira Knightley (1985-)
Collateral Beauty

Johnny Knoxville (1971-)
Elvis & Nixon

Sidse Babett Knudsen
A Hologram for the King
Inferno

Roman Kolinka (1986-)
Things to Come

Danila Kozlovsky (1985-)
Hardcore Henry

John Krasinski (1979-)
The Hollars
13 Hours: The Secret Soldiers of
Benghazi

Lawrence Krauss
Lo and Behold: Reveries of the
Connected World

Nick Kroll (1978-)
Loving
My Blind Brother

Diane Kruger (1976-)
Disorder
The Infiltrator

David Krumholtz (1978-)
I Saw the Light

Michelle Krusiec (1974-)
The Invitation

Agata Kulesza (1971-)
The Innocents

Joanna Kulig (1982-)
The Innocents

Jun Kunimura (1955-)
The Wailing

Mila Kunis (1983-)
Bad Moms

Do Won Kwak
The Wailing

Taryn Kyaze
Queen of Katwe

Shia LaBeouf (1986-)
American Honey

Tyler Labine (1978-)
The Boss

Laurent Lafitte (1973-)
Elle

Karl Lagerfeld (1933-)
The First Monday in May

Christine Lahti (1950-)
Touched With Fire

Martin Landau (1928-)
Remember

Diane Lane (1965-)
Batman *vs.* Superman: Dawn of
Justice

Sasha Lane (1995-)
American Honey

Stephen Lang (1952-)
Don't Breathe

Frank Langella (1938-)
Captain Fantastic

Bouli Lanners (1965-)
April and the Extraordinary
World

Oona Laurence
Pete's Dragon

Jude Law (1972-)
Genius

Jennifer Lawrence (1990-)
A Beautiful Planet
Passengers
X-Men: Apocalypse

Sara Lazzaro
The Young Messiah

Charlotte Le Bon
Anthropoid

Denis Leary (1957-)
Ice Age: Collision Course

Abbey Lee
The Neon Demon

Byung-hun Lee (1970-)
The Magnificent Seven

John Legend (1978-)
La La Land

Sedona Legge
The Shallows

James LeGros (1962-)
Certain Women

John Leguizamo (1964-)
    Ice Age: Collision Course
    The Infiltrator

Melissa Leo (1960-)
    London Has Fallen
    Snowden

Sarah Le Picard
    Things to Come

Logan Lerman (1992-)
    Indignation

Jared Leto (1971-)
    Suicide Squad

Tracy Letts (1965-)
    Indignation
    Wiener-Dog

Ted Levine (1957-)
    Bleed for This

Hope Levy (1966-)
    Only Yesterday

Jane Levy (1989-)
    Don't Breathe

Damian Lewis (1971-)
    Our Kind of Traitor

Judah Lewis
    Demolition

Juliette Lewis (1973-)
    Nerve

Jing Dong Liang
    Mountains May Depart

Lil Duval
    Meet the Blacks

Jelly Lin
    The Mermaid

Laura Linney (1964-)
    Genius
    Sully
    Teenage Mutant Ninja Turtles:
        Out of the Shadows

John Lithgow (1945-)
    Miss Sloane

Blake Lively (1987-)
    Café Society
    The Shallows

Ron Livingston (1967-)
    The 5th Wave

Thomas Loibl
    Toni Erdmann

McCaul Lombardi
    American Honey

Banlop Lomnoi
    Cemetery of Splendor

Aiden Longworth (2004-)
    The 9th Life of Louis Drax

Gabriela Lopez
    The 5th Wave

Jennifer Lopez (1970-)
    Ice Age: Collision Course

Louis C.K. (1967-)
    The Secret Life of Pets

Aiden Lovekamp
    The Invitation

Patrice Lovely
    Boo! A Madea Halloween

Jack Lowden (1990-)
    Denial

Diego Luna (1979-)
    Blood Father
    Rogue One: A Star Wars Story

Zhixiang Luo
    The Mermaid

Vincent Macaigne
    The Innocents

Lewis MacDougall (2002-)
    A Monster Calls

Seth MacFarlane (1973-)
    Sing

Eoin Macken
    The Forest

David Mackey
    Kate Plays Christine

Anthony Mackie (1978-)
    Captain America: Civil War
    Triple 9

William H. Macy (1950-)
    Blood Father

Kika Magalhaes
    The Eyes of My Mother

Valerie Mahaffey (1953-)
    Sully

Romany Malco (1968-)
    Almost Christmas
    When the Bough Breaks

John Malkovich (1953-)
    Deepwater Horizon

Jena Malone (1984-)
    The Neon Demon

Louis Mandylor (1966-)
    My Big Fat Greek Wedding 2

Leslie Mann (1972-)
    How to Be Single

Jason Mantzoukas
    Dirty Grandpa

Rooney Mara (1985-)
    Kubo and the Two Strings
    Lion

Andre Marcon (1948-)
    Things to Come

Mark Margolis (1939-)
    My Big Fat Greek Wedding 2

Hannah Marks (1993-)
    Southbound

Logan Marshall-Green (1976-)
    The Invitation

Margo Martindale (1951-)
    The Hollars

Gugu Mbatha-Raw (1983-)
    Free State of Jones
    Miss Sloane

Rachel McAdams (1978-)
    Doctor Strange
    The Little Prince

James McAvoy (1979-)
    X-Men: Apocalypse

Danny McBride (1976-)
    The Angry Birds Movie

Melissa McCarthy (1970-)
    The Boss
    Ghostbusters

Matthew McConaughey (1969-)
    Free State of Jones
    Kubo and the Two Strings
    Sing

James Allen McCune
    Blair Witch

Ewan McGregor (1971-)
    American Pastoral
    Jane Got a Gun
    Last Days in the Desert
    Miles Ahead
    Our Kind of Traitor

Stephen McHattie (1947-)
    Born to Be Blue

Dylan McKiernan
    I, Daniel Blake

Kate McKinnon (1984-)
    Ghostbusters
    Masterminds
    Office Christmas Party

Wendi McLendon-Covey (1969-)
    Hello, My Name is Doris

Gerald McRaney (1947-)
    The Disappointments Room
Emily Meade (1989-)
    Nerve
Tim Meadows (1961-)
    Popstar: Never Stop Never Stopping
Colm Meaney (1953-)
    Norm of the North
Ben Mendelsohn (1969-)
    Rogue One: A Star Wars Story
Chris Messina (1974-)
    Live by Night
Method Man (1971-)
    Keanu
    Paterson
David Meunier (1973-)
    Kevin Hart: What Now?
Eimer Ni Mhaoldomhnaigh
    Love & Friendship
Thomas Middleditch
    The Bronze
Yauenku Migue
    Embrace of the Serpent
Mads Mikkelsen (1965-)
    Doctor Strange
Penelope Ann Miller (1964-)
    The Birth of a Nation
Sienna Miller (1981-)
    High-Rise
    Live by Night
T.J. Miller (1981-)
    Office Christmas Party
Ming Na (1963-)
    The Darkness
Dylan Minnette
    Don't Breathe
Da'Sean Minor
    The Fits
Christopher Mintz-Plasse (1989-)
    Trolls
Ilyena Vasilievna Mironov (1945-)
    See Helen Mirren
Dame Helen Mirren (1945-)
    See Helen Mirren
Helen Mirren (1945-)
    Collateral Beauty
    Eye in the Sky
Elizabeth Mitchell (1970-)
    The Purge: Election Year

Radha Mitchell (1973-)
    The Darkness
Shay Mitchell (1987-)
    Mother's Day
Kevin D. Mitnick (1963-)
    Lo and Behold: Reveries of the Connected World
Kevin David Mitnick (1963-)
    See Kevin D. Mitnick
Gretchen Mol (1972-)
    Manchester by the Sea
Alfred Molina (1953-)
    Little Men
    Whiskey Tango Foxtrot
Jordi Molla (1968-)
    Criminal
Janelle Monáe (1985-)
    Hidden Figures
Michelle Monaghan (1976-)
    Patriots Day
Maika Monroe
    Independence Day: Resurgence
Julianne Moore (1960-)
    Maggie's Plan
Mercedes Moran (1955-)
    Neruda
Chloe Grace Moretz (1997-)
    The 5th Wave
    Neighbors 2: Sorority Rising
Jeffrey Dean Morgan (1966-)
    Desierto
Joey Morgan
    Compadres
Erin Moriarty
    Blood Father
Jennifer (Jenny) Morrison (1979-)
    The Darkness
Temuera Morrison (1960-)
    Moana
Viggo Mortensen (1958-)
    Captain Fantastic
Elisabeth (Elissabeth, Elizabeth, Liz) Moss (1982-)
    High-Rise
Anson Mount (1973-)
    Mr. Right
Megan Mullally (1958-)
    Why Him?
Peter Mullan (1959-)
    Sunset Song

Olivia Munn (1980-)
    Office Christmas Party
    Ride Along 2
Cillian Murphy (1976-)
    Anthropoid
Bill Murray (1950-)
    The Jungle Book
Jenn Murray
    Love & Friendship
Elon Musk
    Lo and Behold: Reveries of the Connected World
Madina Nalwanga
    Queen of Katwe
Paul Nazak
    The Eyes of My Mother
Alexis Neblett
    The Fits
Liam Neeson (1952-)
    A Monster Calls
    Silence
Ruth Negga (1982-)
    Loving
Sam Neill (1947-)
    Hunt for the Wilderpeople
Tioreore Ngatai-Melbourne
    Hunt for the Wilderpeople
Danielle Nicolet
    Central Intelligence
Bill Nighy (1949-)
    Norm of the North
Alexa Nisenson
    Middle School: The Worst Years of My Life
Jeremy Northam (1961-)
    Eye in the Sky
    Our Kind of Traitor
Edward Norton (1969-)
    Collateral Beauty
Jim Norton (1938-)
    The Boy
Lupita Nyong'o (1983-)
    The Jungle Book
    Queen of Katwe
Dylan O'Brien (1991-)
    Deepwater Horizon
Mark O'Brien (1984-)
    Arrival
Jack O'Connell (1990-)
    Money Monster

John C. Reilly (1965-)
The Lobster
Sing

Alysia Reiner (1970-)
Equity

Jeremy Renner (1971-)
Arrival

Callum Keith Rennie (1960-)
Born to Be Blue

Ryan Reynolds (1976-)
Criminal
Deadpool

Jack Reynor
Sing Street

Trevante Rhodes
Moonlight

Monica Rial
The Boy and the Beast

Antonia Ribero
Swiss Army Man

Giovanni Ribisi (1974-)
Papa: Hemingway in Cuba

Angourie Rice
The Nice Guys

Haley Lu Richardson (1995-)
The Bronze
The Edge of Seventeen

Joely Richardson (1965-)
Papa: Hemingway in Cuba

Alan Rickman (1946-2016)
Eye in the Sky

Daisy Ridley (1992-)
Only Yesterday

Peter Riegert (1947-)
American Pastoral

Charlotte Riley (1981-)
London Has Fallen

Sam Riley (1980-)
Pride and Prejudice and Zombies

Daniel Robb (1929-)
See Christopher Plummer

Margot Robbie (1990-)
The Legend of Tarzan
Suicide Squad
Whiskey Tango Foxtrot

Emma Roberts (1991-)
Nerve

Julia Roberts (1967-)
Money Monster
Mother's Day

Kim Roberts
Remember

Craig Robinson (1971-)
Morris from America

Nick Robinson
The 5th Wave

Wes Robinson (1983-)
Blair Witch

Jean Rochefort (1930-)
April and the Extraordinary
World

Rock, The (1972-)
See Dwayne 'The Rock' Johnson

Sam Rockwell (1968-)
Mr. Right

Gina Rodriguez
Deepwater Horizon

Seth Rogen (1982-)
Neighbors 2: Sorority Rising
Sausage Party

Kylie Rogers
Miracles From Heaven

Hayden Rolence
Finding Dory

Ray Romano (1957-)
Ice Age: Collision Course

Stephen (Steve) Root (1951-)
Hello, My Name is Doris
Mike and Dave Need Wedding
Dates

Sofia Rosinsky
The Other Side of the Door

Theo Rossi
When the Bough Breaks

Tim Roth (1961-)
Hardcore Henry
Mr. Right

Vincent Rottiers (1986-)
Dheepan

Lou Roy-Lecollinet
My Golden Days

Paul Rudd (1969-)
The Little Prince

Maya Rudolph (1972-)
The Angry Birds Movie
Maggie's Plan

Jarinpattra Rueangram
Cemetery of Splendor

Mark Ruffalo (1967-)
Now You See Me 2

James Russell
The Boy

Keri Russell (1976-)
Free State of Jones

Kurt Russell (1951-)
Deepwater Horizon

Wyatt Russell (986-)
Everybody Wants Some!!

Amy Ryan (1968-)
Central Intelligence
Louder Than Bombs

Winona Ryder (1971-)
Author: The JT LeRoy Story

Mark Rylance (1960-)
The BFG

Mina Sadati
The Salesman

Katey Sagal (1954-)
Bleed for This

Fridtjov Saheim
The Wave

Noriko Sakura
The Forest

Zoe Saldana (1978-)
Live by Night
Star Trek Beyond

Andy Samberg (1978-)
Popstar: Never Stop Never Stop-
ping
Storks

Ashton Sanders
Moonlight

Shin Sang-ok
The Lovers & the Despot

Rodrigo Santoro (1975-)
Ben-Hur
Jane Got a Gun

Susan Sarandon (1946-)
The Meddler

Peter Sarsgaard (1971-)
Jackie

Parker Sawyers
Southside with You

Akiva Schaffer
Popstar: Never Stop Never Stopping

Rob Schneider (1963-)
Norm of the North

Ben Schnetzer
Goat

Matthias Schoenaerts (1977-)
  Disorder
Pablo Schreiber (1978-)
  13 Hours: The Secret Soldiers of
    Benghazi
Tomasz Schuchardt
  Demon
Matthias Schweighofer
  The Wild Life
Edith Scob (1937-)
  Things to Come
Adam Scott (1973-)
  My Blind Brother
Andrew Scott (1976-)
  Denial
Brandon Scott
  Blair Witch
Harvey Scrimshaw
  The Witch
Kyra Sedgwick (1965-)
  The Edge of Seventeen
Martin Sensmeier
  The Magnificent Seven
Neel Sethi
  The Jungle Book
Lea Seydoux (1985-)
  The Lobster
Jane Seymour (1951-)
  Fifty Shades of Black
Briana Shann
  I, Daniel Blake
Michael Shannon (1974-)
  Elvis & Nixon
  Loving
  Midnight Special
  Nocturnal Animals
Molly Shannon (1964-)
  Other People
Brighton Sharbino
  Miracles From Heaven
Alia Shawkat (1989-)
  Green Room
Michael Sheen (1969-)
  Passengers
Stephanie Sheh
  Only Yesterday
Kate Lyn Sheil
  Kate Plays Christine
Sam Shepard (1943-)
  Midnight Special

Tye Sheridan (1996-)
  Last Days in the Desert
Trey Edward Shults
  Krisha
Maggie Siff
  The 5th Wave
Sarah Silverman (1970-)
  Popstar: Never Stop Never Stop-
    ping
J.K. Simmons (1955-)
  The Accountant
  Kung Fu Panda 3
  La La Land
  The Meddler
  Patriots Day
Peter Simonischek (1946-)
  Toni Erdmann
Jaz Sinclair
  When the Bough Breaks
Bryan Singer (1966-)
  X-Men: Apocalypse
Jeremy Sisto (1974-)
  The Other Side of the Door
Alexander Skarsgard (1976-)
  The Legend of Tarzan
Stellan Skarsgard (1951-)
  Our Kind of Traitor
Ed Skrein
  Deadpool
Jenny Slate (1982-)
  My Blind Brother
  The Secret Life of Pets
  Zootopia (V)
Amanda Smith
  Remember
Harley Quinn Smith (1999-)
  Yoga Hosers
Will Smith (1968-)
  Collateral Beauty
  Suicide Squad
Cobie Smulders (1982-)
  Jack Reacher: Never Go Back
Sarah Snook
  The Dressmaker
Karan Soni
  Deadpool
Joseph Julian Soria
  The Purge: Election Year
Kevin Spacey (1959-)
  Elvis & Nixon
  Nine Lives

Timothy Spall (1957-)
  Denial
Adrian Sparks
  Papa: Hemingway in Cuba
Octavia Spencer (1970-)
  Allegiant
  Hidden Figures
Brandon Spink
  Mother's Day
Samantha Spiro
  Me Before You
Hayley Squires
  I, Daniel Blake
Kalieaswari Srinivasan
  Dheepan
Sebastian Stan (1982-)
  The Bronze
  Captain America: Civil War
Keith Stanfield (1991-)
  Miles Ahead
Lakeith Lee Stanfield (1991-)
  See Keith Stanfield
Jason Statham (1967-)
  Mechanic: Resurrection
Hailee Steinfeld (1996-)
  The Edge of Seventeen
Kristen Stewart (1990-)
  Billy Lynn's Long Halftime Walk
  Café Society
  Certain Women
Julia Stiles (1981-)
  Jason Bourne
Ben Stiller (1965-)
  Zoolander 2
Emma Stone (1988-)
  La La Land
Eric Stonestreet (1971-)
  The Secret Life of Pets
Meryl Streep (1949-)
  Florence Foster Jenkins
Juston Street
  Everybody Wants Some!!
Cecily Strong
  The Meddler
Mark Strong (1963-)
  The Brothers Grimsby
  Miss Sloane
Michael Stuhlbarg (1968-)
  Arrival
  Miss Sloane

Emma Suarez (1964-)
Julieta

Jason Sudeikis (1975-)
The Angry Birds Movie
Masterminds
Race

Alison Sudol (1984-)
Fantastic Beasts and Where to
Find Them

Tika Sumpter (1980-)
Ride Along 2
Southside with You

John Swasey
The Boy and the Beast

Tilda Swinton (1960-)
Doctor Strange

Omar Sy (1978-)
Inferno

Talia Tabin
My Blind Brother

Jorma Taccone (1977-)
Popstar: Never Stop Never Stopping

George Takei (1940-)
Kubo and the Two Strings

Patrick Tam (1968-)
Ip Man 3

Jeffrey Tambor (1944-)
The Accountant

Theo Taplitz
Little Men

Buck Taylor (1938-)
Hell or High Water

Christine Taylor (1971-)
Zoolander 2

James Arnold Taylor (1969-)
Ratchet & Clank

Aaron Taylor-Johnson (1990-)
Nocturnal Animals

Anya Taylor-Joy
The Witch

Miles Teller (1987-)
Allegiant
Bleed for This
War Dogs

Fabianne Therese
Southbound

Charlize Theron (1975-)
The Huntsman: Winter's War
Kubo and the Two Strings

Justin Theroux (1971-)
The Girl on the Train

Henry Thomas (1971-)
Ouija: Origin of Evil

Sarah Megan Thomas
Equity

Sean Patrick Thomas (1970-)
Barbershop: The Next Cut

Emma Thompson (1959-)
Bridget Jones's Baby

Jack Thompson (1940-)
The Light Between Oceans

Bella Thorne (1997-)
Boo! A Madea Halloween

Billy Bob Thornton (1955-)
Bad Santa 2
Whiskey Tango Foxtrot

David Howard Thornton
The Wild Life

Sebastian Thrun
Lo and Behold: Reveries of the
Connected World

Brenton Thwaites (1989-)
Gods of Egypt

Lucas Till (1990-)
The Disappointments Room

Justin Timberlake (1981-)
Trolls

Itay Tiran
Demon

Ane Dahl Torp (1975-)
The Wave

Nate Torrence (1977-)
Zootopia (V)

Nilbio Torres
Embrace of the Serpent

Shaun Toub (1963-)
Papa: Hemingway in Cuba
War Dogs

Stanley Townsend
Florence Foster Jenkins

John Travolta (1954-)
In a Valley of Violence

Hark Tsui
The Mermaid

Chris Tucker (1971-)
Billy Lynn's Long Halftime Walk

Alan Tudyk (1971-)
Rogue One: A Star Wars Story

Michael G. Tyson (1966-)
See Mike Tyson

Mike Tyson (1966-)
Ip Man 3

Adriana Ugarte
Julieta

Karl Urban (1972-)
Star Trek Beyond

Usher (1978-)
See Usher Raymond

Jessie T. Usher
Independence Day: Resurgence

Jaime Vadell
The Club

Eric Vale
The Boy and the Beast

Carice van Houten (1976-)
Race

Phillip Edward Van Lear
Southside with You

Courtney B. Vance (1960-)
Office Christmas Party

Nia Vardalos (1962-)
My Big Fat Greek Wedding 2

Vince Vaughn (1970-)
Hacksaw Ridge

Yul Vazquez
The Infiltrator

Cassie Ventura
The Perfect Match

Alicia Vikander (1988-)
Jason Bourne
The Light Between Oceans

Ana Villafane
Max Steel

Chad Villella
Southbound

Claudine Vinasithamby
Dheepan

Terry Virts
A Beautiful Planet

Stephanie Vogt
The Forest

Mark Wahlberg (1971-)
Deepwater Horizon
Patriots Day

Christopher Walken (1943-)
The Family Fang
Nine Lives

Subject Index

Action-Adventure

Allied
April and the Extraordinary
　World
Assassin's Creed
The BFG
The Boy and the Beast
Captain America: Civil War
Deadpool
Desierto
Doctor Strange
Fantastic Beasts and Where to
　Find Them
The 5th Wave
The Finest Hours
Gods of Egypt
Hardcore Henry
The Huntsman: Winter's War
Independence Day: Resurgence
Inferno
Ip Man 3
Jack Reacher: Never Go Back
The Jungle Book
Kubo and the Two Strings
The Legend of Tarzan
London Has Fallen
The Magnificent Seven
Max Steel
Moana
Now You See Me 2
Passengers
Pete's Dragon
Pride and Prejudice and Zombies
Ratchet & Clank
Risen

Rogue One: A Star Wars Story
The Secret Life of Pets
Sully
Teenage Mutant Ninja Turtles:
　Out of the Shadows
13 Hours: The Secret Soldiers of
　Benghazi
Trolls
Warcraft
X-Men: Apocalypse

Action-Comedy

The Angry Birds Movie
Bad Santa 2
Central Intelligence
Ghostbusters
Keeping Up with the Joneses
Kung Fu Panda 3
Masterminds
Mike and Dave Need Wedding
　Dates
Mr. Right
The Nice Guys
Ride Along 2
Sausage Party
Storks
War Dogs
Yoga Hosers

Adapted from a Book

Alice Through the Looking Glass
Allegiant
American Pastoral
Ben-Hur
The BFG

Billy Lynn's Long Halftime Walk
Denial
The Dressmaker
Elle
Fantastic Beasts and Where to
　Find Them
The Girl on the Train
The Handmaiden
Hidden Figures
High-Rise
Hunt for the Wilderpeople
Indignation
Inferno
The Jungle Book
The Legend of Tarzan
The Light Between Oceans
Lion
The Little Prince
Live by Night
Love & Friendship
Middle School: The Worst Years
　of My Life
Miss Peregrine's Home for Pecu-
　liar Children
The 9th Life of Louis Drax
Nocturnal Animals
Our Kind of Traitor
Queen of Katwe
Silence
Sully
Sunset Song
13 Hours: The Secret Soldiers of
　Benghazi
Whiskey Tango Foxtrot
The Young Messiah

Diseases or Illness

The Hollars
The 9th Life of Louis Drax

Divorce

Nocturnal Animals
Things to Come

Doctors

Doctor Strange
The 9th Life of Louis Drax

Doctors or Nurses

High-Rise

Documentary Films

Author: The JT LeRoy Story
A Beautiful Planet
Cameraperson
De Palma
The First Monday in May
Kate Plays Christine
Lo and Behold: Reveries of the
    Connected World
The Lovers & the Despot
Tickled
Weiner

Dogs

Wiener-Dog

Dragons

Pete's Dragon

Drama

Allied
American Honey
American Pastoral
Arrival
Billy Lynn's Long Halftime Walk
The Birth of a Nation
Bleed for This
Certain Women
The Choice
The Club
Collateral Beauty
Deepwater Horizon
Demolition
Denial
Dheepan
The Dressmaker
Elle
Embrace of the Serpent
The Eyes of My Mother
Fences

The Finest Hours
The Fits
Florence Foster Jenkins
Free State of Jones
Genius
Goat
God's Not Dead 2
The Handmaiden
Hands of Stone
Hidden Figures
High-Rise
I, Daniel Blake
The Innocents
Ip Man 3
Julieta
Last Days in the Desert
The Light Between Oceans
Lion
Little Men
Louder Than Bombs
Loving
Manchester by the Sea
Me Before You
Midnight Special
Miss Sloane
A Monster Calls
Moonlight
Morris from America
Mountains May Depart
Nocturnal Animals
Only Yesterday
Other People
Papa: Hemingway in Cuba
Passengers
Patriots Day
Queen of Katwe
Race
Risen
Rules Don't Apply
The Salesman
The Shallows
Silence
Sing Street
Snowden
Sully
Sunset Song
Things to Come
13 Hours: The Secret Soldiers of
    Benghazi
Touched With Fire
Triple 9
War Dogs
When the Bough Breaks

Drugs

Blood Father

The Infiltrator
Keanu
Office Christmas Party
Ride Along 2

Education or Schooling

God's Not Dead 2
Indignation
Middle School: The Worst Years
    of My Life

Entertainment Industry

Florence Foster Jenkins
Nerve

Epic Battles

Ben-Hur

Escapes

The Lovers & the Despot

Ethics & Morals

The Light Between Oceans

Etiquette

Mike and Dave Need Wedding
    Dates

Europe

Anthropoid
Inferno

Family

Alice Through the Looking Glass
Captain Fantastic
The Darkness
Demolition
Dheepan
The Family Fang
Finding Dory
The Huntsman: Winter's War
The Light Between Oceans
Lights Out
Louder Than Bombs
Manchester by the Sea
Mother's Day
Mountains May Depart
Pride and Prejudice and Zombies

Family Comedy

Nine Lives
Sing

Family Drama

American Pastoral
Ben-Hur

Little Men
The Little Prince
Neighbors 2: Sorority Rising
Pete's Dragon
Popstar: Never Stop Never Stopping
Ratchet & Clank
The Secret Life of Pets
Swiss Army Man
War Dogs
Zoolander 2

Fugitives
Hell or High Water
Neruda
Snowden

Funerals
Captain Fantastic

Games
Nerve

Germany
Morris from America

Ghosts or Spirits
Boo! A Madea Halloween
The Darkness
Demon
The Disappointments Room
Ghostbusters
Lights Out
Ouija: Origin of Evil

Giants
The BFG

Gifted Children
Midnight Special
Miss Peregrine's Home for Peculiar Children

Great Britain
Denial
Eddie the Eagle
I, Daniel Blake
The Legend of Tarzan
Me Before You
Our Kind of Traitor
Pride and Prejudice and Zombies

Gymnastics
The Bronze

Hackers
Snowden

Handicapped
Me Before You

Hawaii
Mike and Dave Need Wedding Dates

Heists
Bad Santa 2
Don't Breathe
Hell or High Water
Masterminds
Triple 9

High School
The Edge of Seventeen
Nerve

High School Reunions
Central Intelligence

Holidays
Mother's Day

Holocaust
Anthropoid
Denial

Homosexuality
The Handmaiden
Moonlight

Horror
Blair Witch
The Boy
The Conjuring 2
The Darkness
The Disappointments Room
The Eyes of My Mother
The Forest
Green Room
The Neon Demon
The Other Side of the Door
Ouija: Origin of Evil
Pride and Prejudice and Zombies
Southbound
The Witch

Horror Comedy
Boo! A Madea Halloween

Horse Racing
Ben-Hur

Hospitals or Medicine
The Hollars
The 9th Life of Louis Drax

Hostages
Mechanic: Resurrection
Money Monster

Hotels or Motels
The Lobster

Hunting
Desierto

Immigration
Desierto
Morris from America

India
Lion
The Other Side of the Door

Infants
The Light Between Oceans
Storks

Intelligence Service Agencies
The Accountant
Allied
Anthropoid
Central Intelligence
Criminal
Jason Bourne
Keeping Up with the Joneses
Our Kind of Traitor
Snowden
Suicide Squad

International Relations
Central Intelligence
Our Kind of Traitor
War Dogs

Interracial Affairs
The Birth of a Nation
Hidden Figures
Loving
Morris from America

Interviews
Lo and Behold: Reveries of the Connected World
The Lovers & the Despot

Romance

Allied
The Choice
The Dressmaker
Everybody Wants Some!!
The Handmaiden
How to Be Single
The Huntsman: Winter's War
La La Land
The Lobster
Love & Friendship
Loving
Maggie's Plan
Me Before You
The Meddler
Mountains May Depart
Mr. Right
Only Yesterday
Passengers
Rules Don't Apply
Sing Street
Southside with You
Touched With Fire

Romantic Comedy

Bridget Jones's Baby
My Blind Brother

Roommates

The Secret Life of Pets

Russia/USSR

Hardcore Henry
Our Kind of Traitor

Salespeople

American Honey

Satire or Parody

The Lobster

Science Fiction

Arrival
Assassin's Creed
Captain America: Civil War
Doctor Strange
The 5th Wave
Hardcore Henry
Independence Day: Resurgence
Max Steel
Midnight Special
Miss Peregrine's Home for Peculiar Children
Passengers
Rogue One: A Star Wars Story
Southbound

Teenage Mutant Ninja Turtles: Out of the Shadows
X-Men: Apocalypse

Science or Scientists

April and the Extraordinary World
Embrace of the Serpent
Lo and Behold: Reveries of the Connected World

Scotland

Sunset Song

Screwball Comedy

Masterminds

Security Guards

Disorder
Masterminds

Sex or Sexuality

The Choice
Fifty Shades of Black
The Handmaiden

Sexual Abuse

The Club

Shipwrecked

The Red Turtle

Sibling Rivalry

Ben-Hur
My Blind Brother
Office Christmas Party

Singles

Bridget Jones's Baby
How to Be Single

Slavery

Ben-Hur
The Birth of a Nation
Free State of Jones
The Lovers & the Despot

Slice of Life

The Secret Life of Pets

South America

The Club
Embrace of the Serpent
The Infiltrator

Space Exploration or Outer Space

A Beautiful Planet
Hidden Figures
Passengers
Star Trek Beyond

Spain

Julieta

Spies and Espionage

Allied
Anthropoid
Jason Bourne
Keeping Up with the Joneses
Our Kind of Traitor
Snowden

Sports

Everybody Wants Some!!
Fences
Hands of Stone
My Blind Brother
Race

Star Wars Saga

Rogue One: A Star Wars Story

Storytelling

The Little Prince

Suburban Dystopia

Keeping Up with the Joneses

Suicide

Kate Plays Christine
Swiss Army Man

Super Heroes

Captain America: Civil War
Deadpool
Doctor Strange
Max Steel
Suicide Squad

Surfing

The Shallows

Survival

Blood Father
The Purge: Election Year
The Red Turtle

Teaching or Teachers

Things to Come

Teamwork

Hidden Figures
Middle School: The Worst Years
    of My Life
Nerve
Now You See Me 2
The Secret Life of Pets

Technology

Lo and Behold: Reveries of the
    Connected World
Nerve

Television

Kate Plays Christine
Money Monster

Terrorism

American Pastoral
Criminal
Patriots Day

Texas

Hell or High Water

Thrillers

The Accountant
Anthropoid
Deepwater Horizon
Demon
Disorder
Don't Breathe
Elle
The Girl on the Train
Green Room
The Handmaiden
Inferno
Miss Sloane
The 9th Life of Louis Drax
Nocturnal Animals
The Salesman
The Shallows
Snowden
When the Bough Breaks

Time Travel

Alice Through the Looking Glass
Doctor Strange
Miss Peregrine's Home for Pecu-
    liar Children

Tokyo

Only Yesterday

Torrid Love Scenes

The Handmaiden

Trains

The Girl on the Train

Treasure Hunt

Don't Breathe

True Crime

The Infiltrator
Masterminds
Neruda
Patriots Day
Snowden

True Stories

Anthropoid
The Birth of a Nation
Bleed for This
Denial
The Disappointments Room
Hacksaw Ridge
Hidden Figures
The Innocents
Jackie
Lion
The Lovers & the Despot
Loving
Papa: Hemingway in Cuba
Queen of Katwe
Sully
War Dogs

Twins

The Forest

UFOs

Arrival

Unexplained Phenomena

The 9th Life of Louis Drax

United States Armed Forces

Billy Lynn's Long Halftime Walk
Hacksaw Ridge

Unusual Partnerships

The BFG
The Boy and the Beast
Max Steel
Trolls

Vacations

The Darkness
Dirty Grandpa

Veterans

Disorder

Veterinarians

The Choice

Vietnam War

American Pastoral

Vigilantes

Desierto
The Purge: Election Year

War Between the Sexes

Mike and Dave Need Wedding
    Dates

War: General

Billy Lynn's Long Halftime Walk
Dheepan
High-Rise
Independence Day: Resurgence
Rogue One: A Star Wars Story
13 Hours: The Secret Soldiers of
    Benghazi
War Dogs
Warcraft

Washington, D.C.

Miss Sloane

Weddings

Demon
Mike and Dave Need Wedding
    Dates

Westerns

Hell or High Water
In a Valley of Violence
The Magnificent Seven

Wilderness Areas

Captain Fantastic

Witchcraft

Blair Witch

The Witch

Women

Bad Moms

The Boss

Certain Women

Equity

Hidden Figures

Mother's Day

The Neon Demon

Women of Substance

Arrival

Certain Women

Elle

Hidden Figures

Jackie

Moana

World War Two

Allied

Anthropoid

Hacksaw Ridge

The Innocents

Writers

Author: The JT LeRoy Story

Genius

Papa: Hemingway in Cuba

Touched With Fire

Yoga

Yoga Hosers

Zombies

Boo! A Madea Halloween

Pride and Prejudice and Zombies

Title Index

This cumulative index is an alphabetical list of all films covered in the volumes of the *Magill's Cinema Annual*. Film titles are indexed on a word-by-word basis, including articles and prepositions. English leading articles (A, An, The) are ignored, as are foreign leading articles (El, Il, La, Las, Le, Les, Los). Acronyms appear alphabetically as if regular words. Common abbreviations in titles file as if they are spelled out. Proper names in titles are alphabetized beginning with the individual's first name. Titles with numbers are alphabetized as if the numbers were spelled out. When numeric titles gather in close proximity to each other, the titles will be arranged in a low-to-high numeric sequence. Films reviewed in this volume are cited in bold; films reviewed in past volumes are cited with the *Annual* year in which the review was published. Original and alternate titles are cross-referenced to the American release title. Titles of retrospective films are followed by the year, in brackets, of their original release.

A

A corps perdu. *See* Straight for the Heart.

A. I.: Artificial Intelligence 2002

A la Mode (Fausto) 1995

A Lot Like Love 2006

A Ma Soeur. *See* Fat Girl.

A nos amours 1984

Abandon 2003

ABCD 2002

ABCs of Death, The 2014

Abduction 2012

Abgeschminkt! *See* Making Up!.

About a Boy 2003

About Adam 2002

About Elly 2016

About Last Night... 1986

About Last Night (2015) 2015

About Schmidt 2003

About Time 2014

Above the Law 1988

Above the Rim 1995

Abraham Lincoln: Vampire Hunter 2013

Abrazos rotos, Los. *See* Broken Embraces.

Abre Los Ojos. *See* Open Your Eyes.

Abril Despedacado. *See* Behind the Sun.

Absence of Malice 1981

Absolute Beginners 1986

Absolute Power 1997

Absolution 1988

Abyss, The 1989

Accepted 2007

Accidental Tourist, The 1988

Accompanist, The 1993

Accordeur de tremblements de terre, L'. *See* Piano Tuner of Earthquakes, The.

Accountant, The 2017

Accused, The 1988

Ace in the Hole [1951] 1986, 1991

Ace Ventura: Pet Detective 1995

Ace Ventura: When Nature Calls 1996

Aces: Iron Eagle III 1992

Acid House, The 2000

Acqua e sapone. *See* Water and Soap.

Across the Tracks 1991

Across the Universe 2008

Act of Killing, The 2014

Act of Valor 2013

Acting on Impulse 1995

Action Jackson 1988

Actress 1988

Adam 2010

Adam Sandler's 8 Crazy Nights 2003

Adam's Rib [1950] 1992

Adaptation 2003

Addams Family, The 1991

Addams Family Values 1993

Addicted 2015

Addicted to Love 1997

Alive 1993

Alive and Kicking 1997

All About My Mother 2000

All About Steve 2010

All About the Benjamins 2003

All Dogs Go to Heaven 1989

All Dogs Go to Heaven II 1996

All Good Things 2011

All I Desire [1953] 1987

All I Want for Christmas 1991

All is Lost 2014

All of Me 1984

All or Nothing 2003

All Over Me 1997

All Quiet on the Western Front [1930] 1985

All the King's Men 2007

All the Light in the Sky 2014

All the Little Animals 2000

All the Pretty Horses 2001

All the Rage. *See* It's the Rage.

All the Real Girls 2004

All the Right Moves 1983

All the Vermeers in New York 1992

All's Fair 1989

All-American High 1987

Allan Quatermain and the Lost City of Gold 1987

Allegiant 2017

Alley Cat 1984

Allied 2017

Alligator Eyes 1990

Allnighter, The 1987

Almost an Angel 1990

Almost Christmas 2017

Almost Famous 2001

Almost Heroes 1999

Almost You 1985

Aloha 2016

Aloha Summer 1988

Alone. *See* Solas.

Alone in the Dark 2006

Alone with Her 2008

Along Came a Spider 2002

Along Came Polly 2005

Alpha and Omega 2011

Alpha Dog 2008

Alphabet City 1983

Alpine Fire 1987

Altars of the World [1976] 1985

Alvin and the Chipmunks 2008

Alvin and the Chipmunks: Chipwrecked 2012

Alvin and the Chipmunks: Road Chip 2016

Alvin and the Chipmunks: The Squeakquel 2010

Always (Jaglom) 1985

Always (Spielberg) 1989

Amadeus 1984, 1985

Amanda 1989

Amantes. *See* Lovers.

Amantes del Circulo Polar, Los. *See* Lovers of the Arctic Circle, The.

Amantes pasajeros, Los. *See* I'm So Excited.

Amants du Pont Neuf, Les 1995

Amateur 1995

Amateur, The 1982

Amazing Grace 2008

Amazing Grace and Chuck 1987

Amazing Panda Adventure, The 1995

Amazing Spider-Man, The 2013

Amazing Spider-Man 2, The 2015

Amazon Women on the Moon 1987

Ambition 1991

Amelia 2010

Amelie 2002

Amen 2004

America 1986

American, The 2011

American Anthem 1986

American Beauty 2000

American Blue Note 1991

American Buffalo 1996

American Carol, An 2009

American Chai 2003

American Cyborg: Steel Warrior 1995

American Desi 2002

American Dream 1992

American Dreamer 1984

American Dreamz 2007

American Fabulous 1992

American Flyers 1985

American Friends 1993

American Gangster 2008

American Gothic 1988

American Haunting, An 2007

American Heart 1993

American History X 1999

American Honey 2017

American Hustle 2014

American in Paris, An [1951] 1985

American Justice 1986

American Me 1992

American Movie 2000

American Ninja 1984, 1991

American Ninja 1985

American Ninja II 1987

American Ninja III 1989

American Outlaws 2002

American Pastoral 2017

American Pie 2000

American Pie 2 2002

American Pop 1981

American President, The 1995

American Psycho 2001

American Reunion 2013

American Rhapsody, An 2002

American Sniper 2015

American Stories 1989

American Splendor 2004

American Summer, An 1991

American Taboo 1984, 1991

American Tail, An 1986

American Tail: Fievel Goes West, An 1991

American Teen 2009

American Ultra 2016

American Wedding 2004

American Werewolf in London, An 1981

American Werewolf in Paris, An 1997

American Women. *See* The Closer You Get.

America's Sweethearts 2002

April and the Extraordinary World 2017

April Fool's Day 1986

April Is a Deadly Month 1987

Apt Pupil 1999

Aquamarine 2007

Arabian Knight, 1995

Arachnophobia 1990

Ararat 2003

Arashi Ga Oka 1988

Arbitrage 2013

Arch of Triumph [1948] 1983

Archangel 1995

Architecture of Doom, The 1992

Are We Done Yet? 2008

Are We Officially Dating? *See* That Awkward Moment.

Are We There Yet? 2006

Argent, L' 1984

Argo 2013

Aria 1988

Ariel 1990

Arlington Road 2000

Armageddon 1999

Armageddon, The. *See* Warlock.

Armed and Dangerous 1986

Armed Response 1986

Armee des ombres, L'. *See* Army of Shadows.

Armored 2010

Army in the Shadows. *See* Army of Shadows.

Army of Darkness 1993

Army of Shadows 2007

Around the Bend 2005

Around the World in 80 Days 2005

Arrangement, The [1969] 1985

Aristocrats, The 2006

Arrival 2017

Arrival, The 1996

Art Blakey 1988

Art Deco Detective 1995

Art of Cinematography, The. *See* Visions of Light.

Art of Getting By, The 2012

Art of War, The 2001

Art School Confidential 2007

Artemisia 1999

Arthur 1981

Arthur 2012

Arthur Christmas 2012

Arthur II 1988

Arthur and the Invisibles 2008

Arthur Newman 2014

Arthur's Hallowed Ground 1986

Article 99 1992

Artist, The 2012

As Above, So Below 2015

As Good As It Gets 1997

Ashes of Time Redux 2009

Ashik Kerib 1988

Ask the Dust 2007

Aspen Extreme 1993

Assassin, The 2016

Assassination 1987

Assassination of Jesse James by the Coward Robert Ford, The 2008

Assassination of Richard Nixon, The 2006

Assassination Tango 2004

Assassins 1995

Assasin's Creed 2017

Assault, The 1986

Assault of the Killer Bimbos 1988

Assault on Precinct 13 2006

Assignment, The, 1997

Associate, The 1996

Astonished 1989

Astro Boy 2010

Astronaut Farmer, The 2008

Astronaut's Wife, The 2000

Asya's Happiness 1988

Asylum 2006

At Any Price 2014

At Close Range 1986

At First Sight 2000

At Play in the Fields of the Lord 1991

Atame. *See* Tie Me Up! Tie Me Down!.

Atanarjuat, the Fast Runner 2002

A-Team, The 2011

Atentado, El. *See* Attack, The.

ATL 2007

Atlantic City 1981

Atlantis 1995

Atlantis: The Lost Empire 2002

Atlas Shrugged: Part 1 2012

Atlas Shrugged II: The Strike 2013

Atonement 2008

Atraves da Janela. *See* Through the Window.

Attack, The 2014

Attack the Block 2012

Attention Bandits. *See* Warning Bandits.

Au Revoir les Enfants 1987

Auf der anderen Seite. *See* Edge of Heaven, The.

August 1996

August: Osage County 2014

August Rush 2008

August 32nd on Earth 1999

Aura, The 2007

Austenland 2014

Austin Powers in Goldmember 2003

Austin Powers: International Man of Mystery, 1997

Austin Powers: The Spy Who Shagged Me 2000

Australia 2009

Author! Author! 1981

Author: The JT Leroy Story 2017

Auto Focus 2003

Autumn in New York 2001

Autumn Tale 2000

Avalon (Anderson) 1988

Avalon (Levinson) 1990

Avanti [1972] 1986

Avatar 2010

Avengers: Age of Ultron 2016

Avengers, The 1999

Avengers, The 2013

Avenging Angel 1985

Avenging Force 1986

Aventure Malgache 1995

Avenue Montaigne 2008

Aviator, The (Miller) 1985

Bari, Al. *See* Innocent, The.

Barjo 1993

Bark! 2003

Barney's Great Adventure 1999

Barney's Version 2011

Barnyard 2007

Bartleby 2003

Barton Fink 1991

BASEketball 1999

Bashu, the Little Stranger 1990

Basic 2004

Basic Instinct 1992

Basic Instinct 2 2007

Basileus Quartet 1984

Basket, The 2001

Basket Case II 1990

Basket Case III: The Progeny 1992

Basketball Diaries, The 1995

Basquiat 1996

Bastille 1985

Bat 21 1988

Batkid Begins 2016

Batman [1989] 1995

Batman and Robin 1997

Batman Begins 2006

Batman Forever 1995

Batman: Mask of the Phantasm 1993

Batman Returns 1992

Batman vs. Superman 2017

Bats 2000

Battement d'Aniles du Papillon, Le, *See* Happenstance.

Batteries Not Included 1987

Battle for Terra 2010

Battle in Seattle 2009

Battle: Los Angeles 2012

Battle of Shaker Heights, The 2004

Battle of the Year 2014

Battlefield Earth 2001

Battleship 2013

Battlestruck 1982

Baule les Pins, La. *See* C'est la vie.

Baxter, The 2006

Bay, The 2013

Be Cool 2006

Be Kind Rewind 2009

Beach 1985

Beach, The 2001

Beach Girls, The 1982

Beaches 1988

Bean 1997

Beans of Egypt, Maine, The 1995

Bears 2015

Beast, The 1988

Beast in the Heart, The. *See* Don't Tell.

Bear, The (Annaud) 1989

Bear, The (Sarafian) 1984

Beast Within, The 1982

Beastly 2012

Beastmaster, The 1982

Beastmaster II 1991

Beasts of No Nation 2016

Beasts of the Southern Wild 2013

Beat, The 1987

Beat Generation-An American Dream, The 1987

Beat Street 1984

Beating Heart, A 1992

Beating of the Butterfly's Wings, The *See* Happenstance.

Beats, Rhymes & Life: The Travels of a Tribe Called Quest 2012

Beau Mariage, Le 1982

Beau Pere 1981

Beau Travail 2001

Beaufort 2009

Beaumarchais: The Scoundrel 1997

Beautician and the Beast, The 1997

Beautiful 2001

Beautiful Boy 2012

Beautiful Creatures 2002

Beautiful Creatures 2014

Beautiful Dreamers 1991

Beautiful Girls 1996

Beautiful Mind 2002

Beautiful People 2001

Beautiful Planet, A 2017

Beautiful Thing 1996

Beauty and the Beast 1991

Beauty Shop 2006

Beaver, The 2012

Beavis and Butt-head Do America 1996

Bebe's Kids 1992

Bebes. *See* Babies.

Because I Said So 2008

Because of Winn-Dixie 2006

Becky Sharp [1935] 1981

Becoming Colette 1992

Becoming Jane 2008

Bed and Breakfast 1992

Bed of Roses 1996

Bedazzled 2001

Bedroom Eyes 1986

Bedroom Window, The 1987

Bedtime for Bonzo [1951] 1983

Bedtime Stories 2009

Bee Movie 2008

Bee Season 2006

Beefcake 2000

Beerfest 2007

Beethoven 1992

Beethoven's Second 1993

Beetlejuice 1988

Before and After 1996

Before I Go to Sleep 2015

Before Midnight 2014

Before Night Falls 2001

Before Sunrise 1995

Before Sunset 2005

Before the Devil Knows You're Dead 2008

Before the Rain 1995

Before We Go 2016

Begin Again 2015

Beginners 2012

Begotten 1995

Beguiled, The [1971] 1982

Behind Enemy Lines 2002

Behind the Sun 2002

Beijing Bicycle 2003

Being at Home with Claude 1993

Being Flynn 2013

Being Human 1995

Being John Malkovich 2000

Bowfinger 2000

Box, The 2010

Box of Moonlight 1997

Boxer, The 1997

Boxer and Death, The 1988

Boxing Helena 1993

Boxtrolls, The 2015

Boy, The 2017

Boy and the Beast, The 2017

Boy in Blue, The 1986

Boy in the Striped Pajamas, The 2009

Boy Next Door, The 2016

Boy Who Could Fly, The 1986

Boy Who Cried Bitch, The 1991

Boyfriend School, The. *See* Don't Tell Her It's Me.

Boyfriends 1997

Boyfriends and Girlfriends 1988

Boyhood 2015

Boynton Beach Bereavement Club, The. *See* Boynton Beach Club, The.

Boynton Beach Club, The 2007

Boys 1996

Boys, The 1985

Boys and Girls 2001

Boys Are Back, The 2010

Boys Don't Cry 2000

Boys from Brazil, The [1978] 1985

Boys Next Door, The 1986

Boys on the Side 1995

Boyz N the Hood 1991

Bra Boys 2009

Braddock 1988

Brady Bunch Movie, The 1995

Brady's Escape 1984

Brain Damage 1988

Brain Dead 1990

Brain Donors 1995

Brainstorm 1983

Bram Stoker's Dracula 1992

Branches of the Tree, The 1995

Brand New Day. *See* Love Happens.

Brand Upon the Brain! 2008

Brandon Teena Story, The 2000

Brassed Off 1997

Brat. *See* Brother.

Bratz 2008

Brave 2013

Brave One, The 2008

Brave Little Toaster, The 1987

Braveheart 1995

Brazil 1985

Breach 2008

Bread and Roses 2002

Bread and Salt 1995

Bread and Tulips 2002

Bread, My Sweet, The 2004

Break of Dawn 1988

Break-Up, The 2007

Breakdown 1997

Breakfast Club, The 1985

Breakfast of Champions 2000

Breakfast on Pluto 2006

Breakin' 1984

Breakin' All the Rules 2005

Breaking and Entering 2008

Breaking In 1989

Breaking the Rules 1992

Breaking the Sound Barrier. *See* Sound Barrier, The.

Breaking the Waves 1996

Breakin' II: Electric Boogaloo 1984

Breaking Up 1997

Breath of Life, A 1993

Breathing Room 1996

Breathless 1983

Brenda Starr 1992

Brendan and the Secret of Kells. *See* Secret of Kells, The.

Brewster McCloud [1970] 1985

Brewster's Millions 1985

Brian Wilson: I Just Wasn't Made for These Times 1995

Brick 2007

Brick Mansions 2015

Bride, The 1985

Bride and Prejudice 2006

Bride of Chucky 1999

Bride of Re-Animator 1991

Bride of the Wind 2002

Bride Wars 2010

Bride with White Hair, The 1995

Brideshead Revisited 2009

Bridesmaid, The 2007

Bridesmaids 2012

Bridge of San Luis Rey, The [1929] 1981

Bridge of San Luis Rey, The 2006

Bridge of Spies 2016

Bridge on the River Kwai, The [1957] 1990

Bridget Jones's Baby 2017

Bridge to Terabithia 2008

Bridges of Madison County, The 1995

Bridget Jones: The Edge of Reason 2005

Bridget Jones's Diary 2002

Brief Encounter [1946] 1990

Brief History of Time, A 1992

Bright Angel 1991

Bright Lights, Big City 1988

Bright Star 2010

Bright Young Things 2005

Brighton Beach Memoirs 1986

Brimstone and Treacle 1982

Bring It On 2001

Bring on the Night 1985

Bringing Down the House 2004

Bringing Out the Dead 2000

Brittania Hospital 1983

Broadcast News 1987

Broadway Damage 1999

Broadway Danny Rose 1984

Brodre. *See* Brothers.

Brokeback Mountain 2006

Brokedown Palace 2000

Broken April. *See* Behind the Sun.

Broken Arrow 1996

Broken Blossoms [1919] 1984

Broken City 2014

Broken Embraces 2010

Broken English 1997

Broken Flowers 2006

Broken Hearts Club, The 2001

Broken Lizard's Club Dread. *See* Club Dread.

Broken Rainbow 1985

Broken Vessels 1999

Broken Wings 2005

Bronson 2010

Bronx Tale, A 1993

Bronze, The 2017

Brooklyn 2016

Brooklyn Castle 2013

Brooklyn's Finest 2011

Brother (Balabanov) 1999

Brother (Kitano) 2001

Brother Bear 2004

Brother from Another Planet, The 1984

Brother of Sleep 1996

Brotherhood of the Wolf 2003

Brothers 2006

Brothers 2010

Brothers, The 2002

Brothers Bloom, The 2010

Brothers Grimm, The 2006

Brothers Grimsby, The 2017

Brother's Keeper 1993

Brother's Kiss, A 1997

Brothers McMullen, The 1995

Brothers Solomon, The 2008

Brown Bunny, The 2005

Brown Sugar 2003

Browning Version, The 1995

Bruce Almighty 2004

Bruce Lee Story, The. *See* Dragon.

Brüno 2010

Bu-Su 1988

Bubba Ho-Tep 2004

Bubble 2007

Bubble Boy 2002

Buche, La [2000] 2001

Buck 2012

Bucket List, The 2009

Buckminster Fuller: Thinking Out Loud 1996

Bucky Larson: Born to Be a Star 2012

Buddy 1997

Buddy Boy 2001

Buddy Buddy 1981

Buddy System, The 1984

Buena Vista Social Club, The 2000

Buffalo 66 1999

Buffalo Soldiers 2004

Buffy the Vampire Slayer 1992

Bug 2008

Bug's Life, A 1999

Bugsy 1991

Building Bombs 1995

Bull Durham 1988

Bulldog Drummond [1929] 1982

Bullet to the Head 2014

Bulletproof (Carver) 1988

Bulletproof (Dickerson) 1996

Bulletproof Heart 1995

Bulletproof Monk 2004

Bullets Over Broadway 1995

Bullhead 2013

Bullies 1986

Bullshot 1985

Bully 2002

Bully 2013

Bully Project, The. *See* Bully.

Bulworth 1999

Bum Rap 1988

'Burbs, The 1989

Burglar 1987

Burglar, The 1988

Buried 2011

Buried on Sunday 1995

Burke and Hare 2012

Burke and Wills 1987

Burlesque 2011

Burn After Reading 2009

Burnin' Love 1987

Burning Plain, The 2010

Burning Secret 1988

Burnt 2016

Burnt by the Sun 1995

Bushwhacked 1995

Business of Fancydancing, The 2003

Business of Strangers, The 2002

Busted Up 1987

Buster 1988

But I'm a Cheerleader 2001

Butcher Boy, The 1999

Butcher's Wife, The 1991

Butler, The. *See* Lee Daniels' The Butler.

Butter 2013

Butterfield 8 [1960] 1993

Butterflies 1988

Butterfly 2003

Butterfly Effect 2005

Buy and Cell 1988

Buying Time 1989

By Design 1982

By the Sea 2016

By the Sword 1993

Bye Bye Blue Bird 2001

Bye Bye Blues 1990

Bye Bye, Love 1995

Byzantium 2014

C

Cabaret Balkan 2000

Cabeza de Vaca 1992

Cabin Boy 1988

Cabin Fever 2004

Cabin in the Woods, The 2013

Cabinet of Dr. Ramirez, The 1995

Cable Guy, The 1996

Cache 2007

Cactus 1986

Caddie [1976] 1982

Caddyshack II 1988

Cadence 1991

Cadillac Man 1990

Cadillac Records 2009

Cafe Ole 2001

Cafe Society 1997

Cafe Society 2017

Cage 1989

Cage aux folles III, La 1986

Cage/Cunningham 1995

Caged Fury 1984

Cairo Time 2011

Cake 2016

Cal 1984

Calendar 1995

Calendar Girl 1993

Calendar Girls 2004

Calhoun. *See* Nightstick.

Call, The 2014

Call Me 1988

Calle 54 2002

Caller, The 1987

Calling the Shots 1988

Came a Hot Friday 1985

Cameraperson 2017

Cameron's Closet 1989

Camilla 1995

Camille Claudel 1988, 1989

Camorra 1986

Camp 2004

Camp at Thiaroye, The 1990

Camp Nowhere 1995

Campaign, The 2013

Campanadas a medianoche. *See* Falstaff.

Campus Man 1987

Can She Bake a Cherry Pie? 1983

Canadian Bacon 1995

Can't Buy Me Love 1987

Can't Hardly Wait 1999

Candy Mountain 1988

Candyman 1992

Candyman II: Farewell to the Flesh 1995

Cannery Row 1982

Cannonball Run II 1984

Canone Inverso. *See* Making Love.

Cantante, El 2008

Canyons, The 2014

Cape Fear 1991

Capitalism: A Love Story 2010

Capitano, Il 1995

Capote 2006

Captain America: Civil War 2017

Captain America: The First Avenger 2012

Captain Corelli's Mandolin 2002

Captain Fantastic 2017

Captain Phillips 2014

Captain Ron 1992

Captive 2016

Captive Hearts 1987

Captive in the Land, A 1995

Captives 1996

Captivity 2008

Capturing the Friedmans 2004

Car 54, Where Are You? 1995

Caramel 2009

Carandiru 2005

Caravaggio 1986

Cardinal, The [1963] 1986

Care Bears Adventure in Wonderland, The 1987

Care Bears Movie, The 1985

Care Bears Movie II 1986

Career Girls 1997

Career Opportunities 1991

Careful He Might Hear You 1984

Carlito's Way 1993

Carlos 2011

Carmen 1983

Carnage 2004

Carnage 2012

Carne, La 1995

Caro Diario 1995

Carol 2016

Carpenter, The 1988

Carpool 1996

Carrie 2014

Carried Away 1996

Carriers Are Waiting, The 2001

Carrington 1995

Cars 2007

Cars 2 2012

Casa de los Babys 2004

Casa de mi Padre 2013

Casa in bilico, Una. *See* Tottering Lives.

Casanova 2006

Case 39 2011

Casino 1995

Casino Jack 2011

Casino Jack and the United States of Money 2011

Casino Royale 2007

Casper 1995

Cassandra's Dream 2009

Cast Away 2001

Castle, The 2000

Casual Sex? 1988

Casualties of War 1989

Cat on a Hot Tin Roof [1958] 1993

Cat People [1942] 1981, 1982

Catacombs 1988

Catch a Fire 2007

Catch and Release 2008

Catch Me If You Can 1989

Catch Me If You Can (Spielberg) 2003

Catch That Kid 2005

Catfish 2011

Catfish in Black Bean Sauce 2001

Cats & Dogs 2002

Cats & Dogs: The Revenge of Kitty Galore 2011

Cats Don't Dance 1997

Cat's Meow, The 2003

Cattle Annie and Little Britches 1981

Catwoman 2005

Caught 1996

Caught Up 1999

Calvary 2015

Camp X-Ray 2015

Can a Song Save Your Life? *See* Begin Again.

Captain America: The Winter Soldier 2015

Captive, The 2015

Cave, The 2006

Cave Girl 1985

Cave of Forgotten Dreams 2012

Caveman's Valentine, The 2002

CB4 1993

Cease Fire 1985

Cecil B. Demented 2001

Cedar Rapids 2012

Celebrity 1999

Celeste 1982

Celeste & Jesse Forever 2013

Celestial Clockwork 1996

Cell, The 2001

Cellular 2005

Celluloid Closet, The 1996

Connection, The 2016

Connie and Carla 2005

Consenting Adults 1992

Conspiracy Theory 1997

Conspirator, The 2012

Conspirators of Pleasure 1997

Constant Gardener, The 2006

Constantine 2006

Consuming Passions 1988

Contact 1997

Contagion 2012

Conte d'Automne. *See* Autumn Tale.

Conte de Noël, Un. *See* Christmas Tale, A.

Conte de printemps. *See* Tale of Springtime, A.

Conte d'Hiver. *See* Tale of Winter, A.

Contender, The 2001

Continental Divide 1981

Contraband 2013

Control 2008

Control Room 2005

Convent, The 1995

Conviction 2011

Convicts 1991

Convincer, The. *See* Thin Ice.

Convoyeurs Attendent, Les. *See* The Carriers Are Waiting.

Coogan's Bluff [1968] 1982

Cook, the Thief, His Wife, and Her Lover, The 1990

Cookie 1989

Cookie's Fortune 2000

Cookout, The 2005

Cool as Ice 1991

Cool Dry Place, A 2000

Cool Runnings 1993

Cool School, The 2009

Cool World 1992

Cooler, The 2004

Cop 1987

Cop and a Half 1993

Cop Land 1997

Cop Out 2011

Copie conforme. *See* Certified Copy.

Cops and Robbersons 1995

Copycat 1995

Coraline 2010

Core, The 2004

Coriolanus 2012

Corky Romano 2002

Corporation, The 2005

Corpse Bride. *See* Tim Burton's Corpse Bride.

Corrina, Corrina 1995

Corruptor, The 2000

Cosi 1997

Cosi Ridevano. *See* Way We Laughed, The.

Cosmic Eye, The 1986

Cosmopolis 2013

Cotton Club, The 1984

Couch Trip, The 1988

Counselor, The 2014

Count of Monte Cristo, The 2003

Countdown to Zero 2011

Counterfeiters, The 2009

Country 1984

Country Bears, The 2003

Country Life 1995

Country of My Skull. *See* In My Country.

Country Strong 2011

Coup de foudre. *See* Entre nous.

Coup de torchon 1982

Coupe de Ville 1990

Couples Retreat 2010

Courage Mountain 1990

Courage of Lassie [1946] 1993

Courage Under Fire 1996

Courageous 2012

Courier, The 1988

Cours Toujours. *See* Dad On the Run.

Cousin Bette 1999

Cousin Bobby 1992

Cousins 1989

Cove, The 2010

Covenant, The 2007

Cover Girl 1985

Coverup 1988

Cowboy [1958] 1981

Cowboy Way, The 1995

Cowboys & Aliens 2012

Cowboys Don't Cry 1988

Coyote Ugly 2001

CQ 2003

Crabe Dans la Tete, Un. *See* Soft Shell Man.

Crack House 1989

Crack in the Mirror 1988

Crackdown. *See* To Die Standing.

Crackers 1984

Cradle 2 the Grave 2004

Cradle Will Rock 2000

Craft, The 1996

Crank 2007

Crank: High Voltage 2010

Crash (Cronenberg) 1997

Crash (Haggis) 2006

Crawlspace 1986

Crazies, The 2011

crazy/beautiful 2002

Crazy Family, The 1986

Crazy Heart 2010

Crazy in Alabama 2000

Crazy Love 2008

Crazy Moon 1988

Crazy People 1990

Crazy, Stupid, Love 2012

Creation 2011

Creator 1985

Creature 2012

Creature from the Black Lagoon, The [1954] 1981

Creed 2016

Creepozoids 1987

Creepshow 1982

Creepshow II 1987

Crew, The 2001

Crime + Punishment in Suburbia 2001

Crime of Father Amaro, The 2003

Crimes and Misdemeanors 1989

Crimes of Passion 1984

Crimes of the Heart 1986

Criminal 2005

Criminal 2017

Criminal Law 1988, 1989

Criminal Lovers 2004

Crimson Peak 2016

Crimson Tide 1995

Crisscross 1992

Critical Care 1997

Critical Condition 1987

Critters 1986

Critters II 1988

Crna macka, beli macor. *See* Black Cat, White Cat.

"Crocodile" Dundee 1986

"Crocodile" Dundee II 1988

"Crocodile" Dundee in Los Angeles 2002

Crocodile Hunter: Collision Course, The 2003

Cronos 1995

Croods, The 2014

Crooked Hearts 1991

Crooklyn 1995

Cropsey 2011

Cross Country 1983

Cross Creek 1983

Cross My Heart 1987

Crossed Tracks. *See* Roman de gare.

Crossing Delancey 1988

Crossing Guard, The 1995

Crossing Over 2010

Crossing the Bridge 1992

Crossover Dreams 1985

Crossroads 1986

Crossroads 2003

Crouching Tiger, Hidden Dragon 2001

Croupier [1997] 2001

Crow: City of Angels, The 1996

Crow, The 1995

Crucible, The 1996

Crude Oasis, The 1995

Cruel Intentions 2000

Cruel Story of Youth [1960] 1984

Crumb 1995

Crush (Maclean) 1993

Crush (McKay) 2003

Crush, The (Shapiro) 1993

Crusoe 1988

Cry Baby Killers, The [1957]

Cry Freedom 1987

Cry in the Dark, A 1988

Cry in the Wild, The 1990

Cry, the Beloved Country 1995

Cry Wolf [1947] 1986

Cry_Wolf 2006

Cry-Baby 1990

Crying Game, The 1992

Crystal Fairy & the Magical Cactus 2014

Crystal Heart 1987

Crystalstone 1988

Cuban Fury 2015

Cucaracha, La 2000

Cuckoo, The 2004

Cujo 1983

Cup, The 2001

Cup Final 1992

Curdled 1996

Cure, The 1995

Cure in Orange, The 1987

Curious Case of Benjamin Button, The 2009

Curious George 2007

Curly Sue 1991

Current Events 1990

Curse of the Golden Flower 2007

Curse of the Jade Scorpion, The 2002

Curse of the Pink Panther 1983

Cursed 2006

Curtains 1983

Cut and Run 1986

Cutthroat Island 1995

Cutting Edge, The 1992

Cyborg 1989

Cyclo 1996

Cyclone 1987

Cyrano de Bergerac 1990

Cyrus 2011

Czlowiek z Marmuru. *See* Man of Marble.

Czlowiek z Zelaza. *See* Man of Iron.

D

D Train, The 2016

Da 1988

Da Vinci Code, The 2007

Dabba. *See* Lunchbox, The.

Dad 1989

Dad On the Run 2002

Daddy and the Muscle Academy 1995

Daddy Day Camp 2008

Daddy Day Care 2004

Daddy Nostalgia 1991

Daddy's Boys 1988

Daddy's Dyin' 1990

Daddy's Home 2016

Daddy's Little Girls 2008

Dadetown 1996

Daffy Duck's Quackbusters 1988

Dai zong shi, Yi. *See* Grandmaster, The.

Dakhtaran-e Khorshid. *See* Daughters of the Sun.

Dakota 1988

Dallas Buyers Club 2014

Damage 1992

Damned in the U.S.A. 1992

Damned United, The 2010

Damsels in Distress 2013

Dan in Real Life 2008

Dance Flick 2010

Dance Maker, The 2000

Dance of the Damned 1989

Dance with a Stranger 1985

Dance with Me 1999

Dancer in the Dark 2001

Dancer, Texas Pop. 81 1999

Dancer Upstairs, The 2004

Dancers 1987

Dances with Wolves 1990

Dancing at Lughnasa 1999

Dancing in the Dark 1986

Dangerous Beauty 1999

Dangerous Game (Ferrara) 1995

Dangerous Game (Hopkins) 1988

Dangerous Ground 1997

Dangerous Liaisons 1988

Dangerous Lives of Altar Boys, The 2003

Dangerous Love 1988

Dangerous Method, A 2012

Dangerous Minds 1995

Dangerous Moves 1985

Dangerous Woman, A 1993

Dangerously Close 1986

Daniel 1983

Danish Girl, The 2016

Danny Boy 1984

Danny Collins 2016

Danny Deckchair 2005

Danny the Dog. *See* Unleashed.

Dante's Peak 1997

Danton 1983

Danzon 1992

Darbareye Elly. *See* About Elly.

Daredevil 2004

Darfur Now 2008

Darjeeling Limited, The 2008

Dark Backward, The 1991

Dark Before Dawn 1988

Dark Blue 2004

Dark Blue World 2002

Dark City

Dark Crystal, The 1982

Dark Days 2001

Dark Eyes 1987

Dark Half, The 1993

Dark Horse 2013

Dark Knight, The 2009

Dark Knight Rises, The 2013

Dark Obsession 1991

Dark of the Night 1986

Dark Places 2016

Dark Shadows 2013

Dark Skies 2014

Dark Star [1975] 1985

Dark Water 2006

Dark Wind, The 1995

Darkest Hour, The 2012

Darkman 1990

Darkness 2005

Darkness, The 2017

Darkness, Darkness. *See* South of Reno.

Darkness Falls 2004

Darling Companion 2013

D.A.R.Y.L. 1985

Date Movie 2007

Date Night 2011

Date with an Angel 1987

Daughter of the Nile 1988

Daughters of the Dust 1992

Daughters of the Sun 2001

Dauntaun Herozu. *See* Hope and Pain.

Dave 1993

Dave Chappelle's Block Party 2007

Dawn of the Dead 2005

Dawn of the Planet of the Apes 2015

Day After Tomorrow, The 2005

Day I Became a Woman, The 2002

Day in October, A 1992

Day of the Dead 1985

Day the Earth Stood Still, The 2009

Daybreakers 2011

Dayereh. *See* Circle, The.

Daylight 1996

Days of Glory 2008

Days of Thunder 1990

Days of Wine and Roses [1962] 1988

Daytrippers, The 1997

Dazed and Confused 1993

D.C. Cab 1983

De Eso No Se Habla. *See* I Don't Want to Talk About It.

De-Lovely 2005

De Palma 2017

De Poolse Bruid. *See* Polish Bride, The.

Dead, The 1987

Dead Again 1991

Dead Alive 1993

Dead Bang 1989

Dead Calm 1989

Dead Heat 1988

Dead Man 1996

Dead Man Down 2014

Dead Man on Campus 1999

Dead Man Walking 1995

Dead Man's Curve 2000

Dead Men Don't Wear Plaid 1982

Dead of Winter 1987

Dead Poets Society 1989

Dead Pool, The 1988

Dead Presidents 1995

Dead Ringers 1988

Dead Silence 2008

Dead Snow 2010

Dead Space 1991

Dead Women in Lingerie 1991

Dead Zone, The 1983

Dead-end Drive-in 1986

Deadfall 1995

Deadfall 2013

Deadline 1987

Deadly Eyes 1982

Deadly Friend 1986

Deadly Illusion 1987

Deadly Intent 1988

Deadpool 2017

Deal, The 2006

Deal of the Century 1983

Dealers 1989

Dear American 1987

Dear Diary. *See* Caro Diario.

Dear Frankie 2006

Dear God 1996

Dear John 2011

Dear White People 2015

Death and the Maiden 1995

Death at a Funeral 2008

Death at a Funeral 2011

Death Becomes Her 1992

Death Before Dishonor 1987

Death of a Soldier 1986

Death of an Angel 1986

Death of Mario Ricci, The 1985

Death of Mr. Lazarescu, The 2007

Death Proof. *See* Grindhouse.

Death Race 2009

Death Sentence 2008

Death to Smoochy 2003

Dr. Seuss' Horton Hears a Who! 2009

Dr. Seuss' How the Grinch Stole Christmas 2001

Dr. Seuss' The Cat in the Hat 2004

Dr. Seuss' The Lorax 2013

Dr. Sleep. *See* Close Your Eyes.

Dr. T and the Women 2001

Doctor Zhivago [1965] 1990

Do-Deca-Pentahlon, The 2013

Dodgeball: A True Underdog Story 2005

Dog of Flanders, A 2000

Dog Park 2000

Dogfight 1991

Dogma 2000

Dogtooth 2011

Dogville 2005

Doin' Time on Planet Earth 1988

Dolls 1987

Dolls 2006

Dolly Dearest 1992

Dolly In. *See* Travelling Avant.

Dolores Claiborne 1995

Dolphin Tale 2012

Dolphin Tale 2 2015

Dom Hemingway 2015

Domestic Disturbance 2002

Dominick and Eugene 1988

Dominion: Prequel to the Exorcist 2006

Domino 2006

Don Jon 2014

Don Jon's Addiction. *See* Don Jon.

Don Juan DeMarco 1995

Don Juan, My Love 1991

Don McKay 2011

Dona Herlinda and Her Son 1986

Donkey Who Drank the Moon, The 1988

Donna della luna, La. *See* Woman in the Moon.

Donnie Brasco 1997

Donnie Darko 2003

Donny's Boy. *See* That's My Boy.

Don't Be a Menace to South Central While Drinking Your Juice in the Hood 1996

Don't Be Afraid of the Dark 2012

Don't Breathe 2017

Don't Come Knocking 2007

Don't Cry, It's Only Thunder 1982

Don't Move 2006

Don't Say a Word 2002

Don't Tell 2007

Don't Tell Her It's Me 1990

Don't Tell Mom the Babysitter's Dead 1991

Don't Tempt Me! *See* No News from God.

Don't Touch the Axe. *See* Duchess of Langeais, The.

Doom 2006

Doom Generation, The 1995

Doomsday 2009

Door in the Floor, The 2005

Door to Door 1984

Doors, The 1991

Dopamine 2004

Dope 2016

Doppia ora, La. *See* Double Hour, The.

Dorm That Dripped Blood, The 1983

Dorothy and Alan at Norma Place 1981

Double, The 2012

Double, The 2015

Double Dragon 1995

Double Edge 1992

Double Happiness 1995

Double Hour, The 2012

Double Impact 1991

Double Indemnity [1944] 1981, 1986, 1987

Double Jeopardy 2000

Double Life of Veronique, The 1991

Double Take 2002

Double Team 1997

Double Threat 1993

Double Trouble 1992

Double Vie de Veronique, La. *See* Double Life of Veronique, The.

Doublure, La. *See* Valet, The.

Doubt 2009

Doug's First Movie 2000

Down and Out in Beverly Hills 1986

Down by Law 1986

Down in the Delta 1999

Down in the Valley 2007

Down Periscope 1996

Down Terrace 2011

Down the Hill. *See* Footnote.

Down to Earth 2002

Down to You 2001

Down Twisted 1987

Down With Love 2004

Downfall 2006

Downtown 1990

Dracula. *See* Bram Stoker's Dracula.

Dracula: Dead and Loving It 1995

Dracula 2001. *See* Wes Craven Presents: Dracula 2001.

Dracula Untold 2015

Draft Day 2015

Drag Me to Hell 2010

Dragnet 1987

Dragon 1993

Dragon Chow 1988

Dragonball: Evolution 2010

Dragonfly 2003

Dragonheart 1996

Dragonslayer 1981

Draughtsman's Contract, The 1983

Dream a Little Dream 1989

Dream Demon 1988

Dream for an Insomniac 1999

Dream House 2012

Dream Lover (Kazan) 1986

Dream Lover (Pakula) 1995

Dream of Light 1995

Dream Team, The 1989

Dream With the Fishes 1997

Dreamcatcher 2004

Dreamchild 1985

Dreamer: Inspired by a True Story 2006

Dreamers, The 2005

Dreamgirls 2007

Dreamlife of Angels, The 2000

Dreams. *See* Akira Kurosawa's Dreams.

Dreams with Sharp Teeth 2009

Dreamscape 1984

Dredd 2013

Drei Sterne. *See* Mostly Martha.

Dresser, The 1983

Dressmaker, The 1988

Dressmaker, The 2017

Drifter, The 1988

Drifting 1984

Drillbit Taylor 2009

Drinking Buddies 2014

Drive 1992

Drive 2012

Drive Angry 2012

Drive Me Crazy 2000

Driven 2002

Driving Miss Daisy 1989

Drop, The 2015

Drole de Felix. *See* Adventures of Felix, The.

Drop Dead Fred 1991

Drop Dead Gorgeous 2000

DROP Squad 1995

Drop Zone 1995

Drowning by Numbers 1988

Drowning Mona 2001

Drug War 2014

Drugstore Cowboy 1989

Drumline 2003

Drunks 1997

Dry Cleaning 2000

Dry White Season, A 1989

D3: The Mighty Ducks 1996

Duchess, The 2009

Duchess of Langeais, The 2009

Duck Season 2007

Ducktales, the Movie 1990

Dude, Where's My Car? 2001

Dudes 1987

Dudley Do-Right 2000

Due Date 2011

Duel in the Sun [1946] 1982, 1989

Duet for One 1986

Duets 2001

DUFF, The 2016

D.U.I. 1987

Duke of Burgundy, The 2016

Dukes of Hazzard, The 2006

Dulcy [1923] 1981

Duma 2006

Dumb and Dumber 1995

Dumb and Dumber To 2015

Dumb and Dumberer: When Harry Met Lloyd 2004

Dummy 2004

Dune 1984

Dungeons & Dragons 2001

Dunston Checks In 1996

Duolou Tianshi. *See* Fallen Angels.

Duplex 2004

Duplicity 2010

Dust Devil: The Final Cut 1995

Dutch 1991

Duva satt pa en gren och funerade pa tillvaron, En. *See* Pigeon Sat on a Branch Reflecting on Existence, A.

Dying Gaul, The 2006

Dying Young 1991

Dylan Dog: Dead of Night 2012

E

E la nave va. *See* And the Ship Sails On.

Eagle, The 2012

Eagle Eye 2009

Eagle vs. Shark 2008

Earth 2001

Earth 2010

Earth Girls Are Easy 1989

Earth to Echo 2015

Earthling, The 1981

East, The 2014

East Is East 2001

East is Red, The 1995

Eastern Promises 2008

East-West 2002

Easy A 2011

Easy Money 1983

Easy Virtue 2010

Eat a Bowl of Tea 1989

Eat and Run 1986

Eat Drink Man Woman 1995

Eat Pray Love 2011

Eat the Rich 1988

Eating 1990

Eating Raoul 1982

Ebro Runs Dry, The 1993

Echo Park 1986

Echoes 1983

Echoes of Paradise 1989

Eclipse, The 2011

Ed 1996

Ed and His Dead Mother 1993

Ed Wood 1995

Eddie 1996

Eddie and the Cruisers 1983

Eddie and the Cruisers II 1989

Eddie the Eagle 2017

Eddie Macon's Run 1983

Eddie Murphy Raw 1987

Eden 1999

Eden 2016

Edes Emma, Draga Bobe: Vazlatok, Aktok. *See* Sweet Emma, Dear Bobe: Sketches, Nudes.

Edge, The 1997

Edge of Darkness 2011

Edge of Heaven, The 2009

Edge of Sanity 1989

Edge of Seventeen 2000

Edge of Seventeen, The 2017

Edge of Tomorrow 2015

Edith and Marcel 1984

Edith's Diary 1986

Ed's Next Move 1996

Edtv 2000

Educating Rita 1983

Education, An 2010

Education of Little Tree, The 1997

Edukators, The 2006

Edward Scissorhands 1990

Edward II 1992

Ernest Saves Christmas 1988

Ernest Scared Stupid 1991

Eros 2006

Erotique 1995

Escanaba in da Moonlight 2002

Escape Artist, The 1982

Escape from Alcatraz [1979] 1982

Escape from L.A. 1996

Escape from New York 1981

Escape From Planet Earth 2014

Escape from Safehaven 1989

Escape From Tomorrow 2014

Escape Plan 2014

Escape 2000 1983

Escobar: Paradise Lost 2016

Escort, The. *See* Scorta, La.

Especially on Sunday 1993

Esperame en el cielo. *See* Wait for Me in Heaven.

Espinazo de Diablo, El. *See* Devil's Backbone, The.

Est-Ouest. *See* East-West.

Esther Kahn 2003

Et maintenant on va ou? *See* Where Do We Go Now?

E.T.: The Extra-Terrestrial 1982

Etat sauvage, L' [1978] 1990

Ete prochain, L'. *See* Next Summer.

Eternal Sunshine of the Spotless Mind 2005

Eternity and a Day 2000

Ethan Frome 1993

Etoile du nord 1983

Eu Tu Eles. *See* Me You Them.

Eulogy 2005

Eulogy of Love. *See* In Praise of Love.

Eureka 1985

Eureka 2002

Europa 1995

Europa, Europa 1991

Europa Report 2014

Eurotrip 2005

Evan Almighty 2008

Eve of Destruction 1991

Evelyn 2003

Even Cowgirls Get the Blues 1995

Evening 2008

Evening Star 1996

Event Horizon 1997

Events Leading Up to My Death, The 1995

Ever After: A Cinderella Story 1999

Everest 2016

Everlasting Piece, An 2002

Everlasting Secret Family, The 1989

Every Breath 1995

Every Little Step 2010

Every Man for Himself [1979] 1981

Every Time We Say Goodbye 1986

Everybody Wants Some!! 2017

Everybody Wins 1990

Everybody's All-American 1988

Everybody's Famous! 2002

Everybody's Fine 1991

Everybody's Fine 2010

Everyone Says I Love You 1996

Everyone's Hero 2007

Everything is Illuminated 2006

Everything Must Go 2012

Every Thing Will Be Fine 2016

Eve's Bayou 1997

Evil Dead 2014

Evil Dead, The 1983

Evil Dead II 1987

Evil That Men Do, The 1984

Evil Under the Sun 1982

Evil Woman. *See* Saving Silverman.

Evita 1996

Evolution 2002

Ex Machina 2016

Excalibur 1981

Excess Baggage 1997

Exchange Lifeguards 1995

Execution Protocol, The 1995

Executive Decision 1996

Exiles, The 2009

eXistenZ 2000

Exit Through the Gift Shop 2011

Exit to Eden 1995

Exit Wounds 2002

Exodus: Gods and Kings 2015

Exorcism of Emily Rose, The 2006

Exorcist: The Beginning 2005

Exorcist III, The 1990

Exorcist, The [1973] 2001

Exotica 1995

Expendables, The 2011

Expendables 3, The 2015

Expendables 2, The 2013

Experience Preferred...but Not Essential 1983

Experimenter 2016

Explorers 1985

Exposed 1983

Express, The 2009

Extract 2010

Extramuros 1995

Extraordinary Measures 2011

Extreme Measures 1996

Extreme Ops 2003

Extreme Prejudice 1987

Extremely Loud and Incredibly Close 2012

Extremities 1986

Eye for an Eye, An 1996

Eye in the Sky 2017

Eye of God 1997

Eye of the Beholder 2001

Eye of the Needle 1981

Eye of the Tiger, The 1986

Eye, The 2009

Eyes of My Mother, The 2017

Eyes of Tammy Faye, The 2001

Eyes Wide Shut 2000

F

F/X 1986

F/X II 1991

Fabulous Baker Boys, The 1989

Fabulous Destiny of Amelie Poulain, The. *See* Amelie.

Face/Off 1997

Faces of Women 1987

Facing Windows 2005

Factory Girl 2008

Factotum 2007

Faculty, The 1999

FernGully: The Last Rainforest 1992

Ferris Bueller's Day Off 1986

Festival Express 2005

Festival in Cannes 2003

Feud, The 1990

Fever 1988

Fever Pitch 1985

Fever Pitch 2000

Fever Pitch 2006

Few Days with Me, A 1988

Few Good Men, A 1992

Fido 2008

Field, The 1990

Field in England, A 2015

Field of Dreams 1989

Fierce Creatures 1997

15 Minutes 2002

Fifth Element, The 1997

Fifth Estate, The 2014

5th Wave, The 2017

50 First Dates 2005

51st State, The. *See* Formula 51.

54 1999

50/50 2012

Fifty-Fifty 1993

56 Up 2014

Fifty Shades of Black 2017

Fifty Shades of Grey 2016

Fifty-two Pick-up 1986

Fight Club 2000

Fighter 2002

Fighter, The 2011

Fighting 2010

Fighting Back 1982

Fighting Temptations, The 2004

Fill the Void 2014

Fille coupée en deux, La. *See* Girl Cut in Two, A.

Fille du RER, La. *See* Girl on the Train, The.

Filles ne Savent pas Nager, Les. *See* Girls Can't Swim.

Filly Brown 2014

Film Socialisme 2012

Film Unfinished, A 2011

Fils, Le. *See* Son, The.

Filth 2015

Filth and the Fury, The 2001

Fin aout debut septembre. *See* Late August, Early September.

Final Analysis 1992

Final Approach 1991

Final Cut 2005

Final Destination 2001

Final Destination, The 2010

Final Destination: Death Trip 3D. *See* Final Destination, The.

Final Destination 2 2004

Final Destination 3 2007

Final Destination 4. *See* Final Destination, The.

Final Destination 5 2012

Final Fantasy: The Spirits Within 2002

Final Friday, The. *See* Jason Goes to Hell.

Final Girls, The 2016

Final Option, The 1983

Final Sacrifice, The. *See* Children of the Corn II.

Final Season 1988

Final Season, The 2008

Find Me Guilty 2007

Finders Keepers 1984

Finding Dory 2017

Finding Forrester 2001

Finding Nemo 2004

Finding Neverland 2005

Finding Vivian Maier 2015

Fine Mess, A 1986

Fine Romance, A 1992

Finest Hours, The 2017

Finestra di Fronte, La. *See* Facing Windows.

Finzan 1995

Fiorile 1995

Fire and Ice (Bakshi) 1983

Fire and Ice (Bogner) 1987

Fire Birds 1990

Fire Down Below 1997

Fire from the Mountain 1987

Fire in Sky 1993

Fire This Time, The 1995

Fire Walk with Me. *See* Twin Peaks: Fire Walk with Me.

Fire with Fire 1986

Fired Up! 2010

Fireflies in the Garden 2012

Firefox 1982

Firehead 1991

Firelight 1999

Firemen's Bell, The [1967] 1985

Fireproof 2009

Firestorm 1999

Firewalker 1986

Firewall 2007

Fireworks 1999

Fires of Kuwait 1995

Firm, The 1993

First Blood 1982

First Daughter 2005

First Descent 2006

First Kid 1996

First Knight 1995

First Love, Last Rites 1999

First Monday in May, The 2017

First Monday in October 1981

First Name, Carmen 1984

First Position 2013

First Power, The 1990

First Saturday in May, The 2009

First Sunday 2009

First Wives Club, The 1996

Firstborn 1984

Fish Called Wanda, A 1988

Fish Tank 2011

Fisher King, The 1991

Fistfighter 1989

Fits, The 2017

Fitzcarraldo 1982

Five Corners 1987

Five Days One Summer 1982

Five Graves to Cairo [1943] 1986

Five Heartbeats, The 1991

(500) Days of Summer 2010

Five Minutes of Heaven 2010

Five Senses, The 2001

Five-Year Engagement, The 2013

Four Days in September 1999

Four Feathers, The 2003

Four Friends 1981

Four Lions 2011

4 Little Girls 1997

4 luni, 3 saptâmani si 2 zile. *See* 4 Months, 3 Weeks and 2 Days.

4 Months, 3 Weeks and 2 Days 2009

Four Rooms 1995

Four Seasons, The 1981

Four Weddings and a Funeral 1995

1492: Conquest of Paradise 1992

1408 2008

Fourth Kind, The 2010

4th Man, The 1984

Fourth Protocol, The 1987

Fourth War, The 1990

Fox and the Hound, The 1981

Foxcatcher 2015

Foxfire 1996

Foxtrap 1986

Fracture 2008

Frailty 2003

Frances 1982

Frances Ha 2014

Frank 2015

Frank and Ollie 1995

Frank Miller's Sin City. *See* Sin City.

Frank Miller's Sin City: A Dame to Kill For. *See* Sin City: A Dame to Kill For.

Frankenhooker 1990

Frankenstein. *See* Mary Shelley's Frankenstein.

Frankenstein Unbound. *See* Roger Corman's Frankenstein Unbound.

Frankenweenie 2013

Frankie & Alice 2011

Frankie and Johnny 1991

Frankie Starlight 1995

Frantic 1988

Fraternity Vacation 1985

Frauds 1995

Freaked 1993

Freakonomics 2011

Freaky Friday 2004

Fred Claus 2008

Freddie as F.R.O.7 1992

Freddy Got Fingered 2002

Freddy vs. Jason 2004

Freddy's Dead 1991

Free and Easy 1989

Free Birds 2014

Free Enterprise 2000

Free Radicals 2005

Free Ride 1986

Free State of Jones 2017

Free Willy 1993

Free Willy II: The Adventure Home 1995

Free Willy III: The Rescue 1997

Freebie, The 2011

Freedom On My Mind 1995

Freedom Writers 2008

Freedomland 2007

Freeheld 2016

Freejack 1992

Freeway 1988

Freeway 1996

Freeze—Die—Come to Life 1995

French, La. *See* Connection, The.

French Connection, The [1971] 1982

French Kiss 1995

French Lesson 1986

French Lieutenant's Woman, The 1981

French Twist 1996

Frequency 2001

Fresh 1995

Fresh Horses 1988

Freshman, The 1990

Freud [1962] 1983

Frida 2003

Friday 1995

Friday After Next 2003

Friday Night 2004

Friday Night Lights 2005

Friday the 13th 2010

Friday the 13th, Part III 1982

Friday the 13th, Part IV 1984

Friday the 13th, Part VI 1986

Friday the 13th Part VII 1988

Friday the 13th Part VIII 1989

Fried Green Tomatoes 1991

Friend of the Deceased, A 1999

Friends & Lovers 2000

Friends With Benefits 2012

Friends with Kids 2013

Friends with Money 2007

Fright Night 1985

Fright Night 2012

Frighteners, The 1996

Fringe Dwellers, The 1987

From Beyond 1986

From Dusk Till Dawn 1996

From Hell 2002

From Hollywood to Deadwood 1988

From Paris With Love 2011

From Prada to Nada 2012

From Swastikas to Jim Crow 2001

From the Hip 1987

From Up on Poppy Hill 2014

Front, The [1976] 1985

Frosh: Nine Months in a Freshman Dorm 1995

Frost/Nixon 2009

Frozen 2011

Frozen 2014

Frozen Assets 1992

Frozen River 2009

Fruhlingssinfonie. *See* Spring Symphony.

Fruit Machine, The 1988

Fruitvale Station 2014

Fu-zung cen. *See* Hibiscus Town.

Fucking Amal. *See* Show Me Love.

Fugitive, The 1993

Full Blast 2001

Full Frontal 2003

Full Metal Jacket 1987

Full Monty, The 1997

Full Moon in Paris 1984

Full Moon in the Blue Water 1988

Full of It 2008

Fun Down There 1989

Fun Size 2013

Good Bye Cruel World 1984

Good Bye, Lenin! 2005

Good Day to Die Hard, A 2014

Good Deeds. *See* Tyler Perry's Good Deeds.

Good Dinosaur, The 2016

Good Evening, Mr. Wallenberg 1995

Good German, The 2007

Good Girl, The 2003

Good Hair 2010

Good Kill 2016

Good Luck Chuck 2008

Good Man in Africa, A 1995

Good Marriage, A. *See* Beau Mariage, Le.

Good Morning, Babylon 1987

Good Morning, Vietnam 1987

Good Mother, The 1988

Good Night, and Good Luck 2006

Good Old Fashioned Orgy, A 2012

Good Shepherd, The 2007

Good Son, The 1993

Good, the Bad, the Weird, The 2011

Good Thief, The 2004

Good Weather, But Stormy Late This Afternoon 1987

Good Will Hunting 1997

Good Woman, A 2007

Good Woman of Bangkok, The 1992

Good Work. *See* Beau Travail.

Good Year, A 2007

Goodbye, Children. *See* Au Revoir les Enfants.

Goodbye Lover 2000

Goodbye, New York 1985

Goodbye People, The 1986

Goodbye Solo 2010

Goodbye to Language 2015

GoodFellas 1990

Goods: Live Hard, Sell Hard, The 2010

Goods: The Don Ready Story, The. *See* Goods: Live Hard, Sell Hard, The.

Goofy Movie, A 1995

Goon 2013

Goonies, The 1985

Goosebumps 2016

Gordy 1995

Gorillas in the Mist 1988

Gorky Park 1983

Gorky Triology, The. *See* Among People.

Gosford Park 2002

Gospel 1984

Gospel According to Vic 1986

Gossip 2001

Gossip (Nutley) 2003

Gost 1988

Gotcha! 1985

Gothic 1987

Gothika 2004

Gout des Autres, Le. *See* Taste of Others, The.

Gouttes d'Eau sur Pierres Brulantes. *See* Water Drops on Burning Rocks.

Governess 1999

Goya in Bordeaux 2001

Grace Is Gone 2008

Grace of My Heart 1996

Grace Quigley 1985

Gracie 2008

Graffiti Bridge 1990

Gran Fiesta, La 1987

Gran Torino 2009

Grand Bleu, Le. *See* Big Blue, The (Besson).

Grand Budapest Hotel, The 2015

Grand Canyon 1991

Grand Canyon: The Hidden Secrets 1987

Grand Chemin, Le. *See* Grand Highway, The.

Grand Highway, The 1988

Grand Illusion, The 2000

Grand Isle 1995

Grand Piano 2015

Grand Seduction, The 2015

Grande bellezza, La. *See* Great Beauty, The.

Grande Cocomero, Il. *See* Great Pumpkin, The.

Grandfather, The 2000

Grandma 2016

Grandma's Boy 2007

Grandmaster, The 2014

Grandview, U.S.A. 1984

Grass Harp, The 1996

Gravesend 1997

Graveyard Shift. *See* Stephen King's Graveyard Shift.

Gravity 2014

Gray Matters 2008

Gray's Anatomy 1997

Grease [1978] 1997

Grease II 1982

Great Balls of Fire! 1989

Great Barrier Reef, The 1990

Great Beauty, The 2014

Great Buck Howard, The 2010

Great Day In Harlem, A 1995

Great Debaters, The 2008

Great Expectations 1999

Great Gatsby, The 2014

Great Mouse Detective, The 1986

Great Muppet Caper, The 1981

Great Outdoors, The 1988

Great Pumpkin, The 1993

Great Raid, The 2006

Great Wall, A 1986

Great White Hype, The 1996

Greatest, The 2011

Greatest Game Ever Played, The 2006

Greatest Movie Ever Sold, The. *See* POM Wonderful Presents: The Greatest Movie Ever Sold.

Greedy 1995

Green Card 1990

Green Desert 2001

Green Hornet, The 2012

Green Inferno, The 2016

Green Lantern 2012

Green Mile, The 2000

Green Room 2017

Green Zone 2011

Greenberg 2011

Greenfingers 2002

Greenhouse, The 1996

Gregory's Girl 1982

Gremlins 1984

Gremlins II 1990

Grey, The 2013

Grey Fox, The 1983

Grey Zone, The 2003

Greystoke 1984

Gridlock'd 1988

Grief 1995

Grievous Bodily Harm 1988

Grifters, The 1990

Grim Prairie Tales 1990

Grind 2004

Grindhouse 2008

Gringo 1985

Grizzly Man 2006

Grizzly Mountain 1997

Groomsmen, The 2007

Groove 2001

Gross Anatomy 1989

Grosse Fatigue 1995

Grosse Pointe Blank 1997

Ground Truth, The 2008

Ground Zero 1987, 1988

Groundhog Day 1993

Grown Ups 2011

Grown Ups 2 2014

Grudge, The 2005

Grudge 2, The 2007

Grumpier Old Men 1995

Grumpy Old Men 1993

Grudge Match 2014

Grune Wuste. *See* Green Desert.

Guard, The 2012

Guardian, The 1990

Guardian, The 2007

Guardians of the Galaxy 2015

Guarding Tess 1995

Guatanamera 1997

Guelwaar 1995

Guerre du Feu, La. *See* Quest for Fire.

Guess Who 2006

Guess Who's Coming to Dinner? [1967] 1992

Guest, The 1984

Guest, The 2015

Guests of Hotel Astoria, The 1989

Gui lai. *See* Coming Home.

Guilt Trip, The 2013

Guilty as Charged 1992

Guilty as Sin 1993

Guilty by Suspicion 1991

Guinevere 2000

Gulliver's Travels 2011

Gummo 1997

Gun in Betty Lou's Handbag, The 1992

Gun Shy 2001

Gunbus. *See* Sky Bandits.

Guncrazy 1993

Gunfighter, The [1950] 1989

Gung Ho 1986

Gunman, The 2016

Gunmen 1995

Gunner Palace 2006

Guru, The 2004

Guy Named Joe, A [1943] 1981

Guy Thing, A 2004

Guys, The 2003

Gwendoline 1984

Gwoemul. *See* Host, The.

Gyakufunsha Kazoku. *See* Crazy Family, The.

Gymkata 1985

H

H. M. Pulham, Esq. [1941] 1981

Hable con Ella. *See* Talk to Her.

Hackers 1995

Hacksaw Ridge 2017

Hadesae: The Final Incident 1992

Hadley's Rebellion 1984

Haevnen. *See* In a Better World.

Hail, Caesar! 2017

Hail Mary 1985

Hairdresser's Husband, The 1992

Hairspray 1988

Hairspray 2008

Haizi wang. *See* King of the Children.

Hak hap. *See* Black Mask

Hak mau. *See* Black Cat.

Half-Baked 1999

Half Moon Street 1986

Half of Heaven 1988

Halfmoon 1996

Hall of Fire [1941] 1986

Halloween (Zombie) 2008

Halloween II 2010

Halloween III: Season of the Witch 1982

Halloween IV 1988

Halloween V 1989

Halloween VI: the Curse of Michael Myers 1995

Halloween H20 1999

Halloween: Resurrection 2003

Hall Pass 2012

Hamburger 1986

Hamburger Hill 1987

Hamlet (Zeffirelli) 1990

Hamlet (Branagh) 1996

Hamlet (Almereyda) 2001

Hamlet 2 2009

Hammett 1983

Hana-Bi. *See* Fireworks.

Hancock 2009

Hand That Rocks the Cradle, The 1992

Handful of Dust, A 1988

Handmaid's Tale, The 1990

Handmaiden, The 2017

Hands of Stone 2017

Hangfire 1991

Hanging Garden, The 1999

Hanging Up 2001

Hangin' with the Homeboys 1991

Hangover, The 2010

Hangover Part III, The 2014

Hangover Part II, The 2012

Hanky Panky 1982

Hanna 2012

Hanna K. 1983

Hannah and Her Sisters 1986

Hannah Arendt 2014

Hannah Montana: The Movie 2010

Hannibal 2002

Hannibal Rising 2008

Hanoi Hilton, The 1987

Hans Christian Andersen's Thumbelina 1995

Hansel and Gretel 1987

Hansel & Gretel: Witch Hunters 2014

Hanussen 1988, 1989

Happening, The 2009

Happenstance 2002

Happily Ever After 1993

Happily Ever After 2006

Happily N'Ever After 2008

Happiness 1999

Happy Accidents 2002

Happy Christmas 2015

Happy End 2001

Happy Endings 2006

Happy Feet 2007

Happy Feet Two 2012

Happy '49 1987

Happy Gilmore 1996

Happy Hour 1987

Happy New Year 1987

Happy, Texas 2000

Happy Times 2003

Happy Together 1990

Happy Together 1997

Happy Valley 2015

Happy-Go-Lucky 2009

Happythankyoumoreplease 2012

Hard Candy 2007

Hard Choices 1986

Hard Core Logo 1999

Hard Eight 1997

Hard Hunted 1995

Hard Promises 1992

Hard Rain 1999

Hard Target 1993

Hard Ticket to Hawaii 1987

Hard Times 1988

Hard to Hold 1984

Hard to Kill 1990

Hard Traveling 1986

Hard Way, The (Badham) 1991

Hard Way, The (Sherman) 1984

Hard Word, The 2004

Hardball 2002

Hardbodies 1984

Hardbodies II 1986

Hardcore Henry 2017

Hardware 1990

Harlem Nights 1989

Harley Davidson and the Marlboro Man 1991

Harmonists, The 2000

Harold & Kumar Escape from Guantanamo Bay 2009

Harold & Kumar Go to White Castle 2005

Harriet Craig [1950] 1984

Harriet the Spy 1996

Harrison's Flowers 2003

Harry and Son 1984

Harry and the Hendersons 1987

Harry Brown 2011

Harry, He's Here to Help. *See* With a Friend Like Harry.

Harry Potter and the Chamber of Secrets 2003

Harry Potter and the Deathly Hallows: Part 1 2011

Harry Potter and the Deathly Hallows: Part 2 2012

Harry Potter and the Goblet of Fire 2006

Harry Potter and the Half-Blood Prince 2010

Harry Potter and the Order of the Phoenix 2008

Harry Potter and the Prisoner of Azkaban 2005

Harry Potter and the Sorcerer's Stone 2002

Harry, Un Ami Qui Vous Veut du Bien. *See* With a Friend Like Harry.

Hart's War 2003

Harvard Man 2003

Harvest, The 1995

Hasty Heart, The [1949] 1987

Hatchet Man, The [1932] 1982

Hatchet II 2011

Hateful Eight, The 2016

Hateship Loveship 2015

Hatouna Mehuheret. *See* Late Marriage.

Haunted Honeymoon 1986

Haunted House, A 2014

Haunted House 2, A 2015

Haunted Mansion, The 2004

Haunted Summer 1988

Haunting, The 2000

Haunting in Connecticut, The 2010

Hauru no ugoku shiro. *See* Howl's Moving Castle.

Haute tension. *See* High Tension.

Hav Plenty 1999

Havana 1990

Hawk, The 1995

Hawks 1988

Haywire 2013

He Got Game 1999

He Liu. *See* River, The.

He Loves Me…He Loves Me Not 2004

He Named Me Malala 2016

He Said, She Said 1991

Head Above Water 1997

Head in the Clouds 2005

Head Office 1986

Head of State 2004

Head On 2000

Head-On 2006

Head Over Heels 2002

Headhunters 2013

Heads or Tails 1983

Hear My Song 1991

Hear No Evil 1993

Hearat Shulayim. *See* Footnote.

Hearing Voices 1991

Heart 1987

Heart and Souls 1993

Heart Condition 1990

Heart in Winter, A. *See* Coeur en hiver, Un.

Heart Like a Wheel 1983

Heart of a Stag 1984

Heart of Dixie 1989

Heart of Midnight 1989

Heart of the Game, The 2007

Heartaches 1982

Heartbreak Hotel 1988

Heartbreak Kid, The [1972] 1986

Heartbreak Kid, The (Farrelly/Farrelly) 2008

Heartbreak Ridge 1986

Heartbreaker 1983

Heartbreakers 2002

Heartburn 1986

Heartland 1981

Hearts in Atlantis 2002

Hearts of Darkness: A Filmmaker's Apocalypse 1992

Hearts of Fire 1987

Heat 1987

Heat (Mann) 1995

Heat, The 2014

Heat and Dust 1984

Heat of Desire 1984

Heathcliff 1986

Heathers 1989

Heatwave 1983

Heaven (Keaton) 1987

Heaven (Tykwer) 2003

Heaven and Earth (Kadokawa) 1991

Heaven and Earth (Stone) 1993

Heaven Help Us 1985

Heaven Is for Real 2015

Heaven Knows What 2016

Heaven's Gate 1981

Heaven's Prisoners 1996

Heavenly Bodies 1984

Heavenly Creatures 1995

Heavenly Kid, The 1985

Heavy 1996

Heavyweights 1995

Hecate 1984

Hedwig and the Angry Inch 2002

Heidi Fleiss: Hollywood Madame 1996

Heights 2006

Heist, The 2002

Helas Pour Moi 1995

Held Up 2001

Hell High 1989

Hell or High Water 2017

Hell Ride 2009

Hellbent 1989

Hellbound 1988

Hellboy 2005

Hellboy II: The Golden Army 2009

Heller Wahn. *See* Sheer Madness.

Hellion 2015

Hello Again 1987

Hello, Dolly! [1969] 1986

Hello I Must Be Going 2013

Hello Mary Lou 1987

Hello, My Name is Doris 2017

Hellraiser 1987

Hellraiser III: Hell on Earth 1992

Hellraiser IV: Bloodline 1996

Help, The 2012

Henna 1991

Henri Langlois: The Phantom of the Cinematheque 2006

Henry 1990

Henry and June 1990

Henry IV 1985

Henry V 1989

Henry Fool 1999

Henry Poole in Here 2009

Her 2014

Her Alibi 1989

Her Name Is Lisa 1987

Herbes folles, Les. *See* Wild Grass.

Herbie: Fully Loaded 2006

Hercules 1983

Hercules 2015

Hercules II 1985

Herdsmen of the Sun 1995

Here Come the Littles 1985

Here Comes the Boom 2013

Here On Earth 2001

Hereafter 2011

Here's to Life 2002

Hero 1992

Hero 2004

Hero 2005

Hero and the Terror 1988

Hesher 2012

He's Just Not That Into You 2010

He's My Girl 1987

Hey Arnold! The Movie 2003

Hexed 1993

Hibiscus Town 1988

Hidalgo 2005

Hidden. *See* Cache.

Hidden, The 1987

Hidden Agenda 1990

Hidden Hawaii 1995

Hidden Figures 2017

Hide and Seek 2006

Hideaway 1995

Hideous Kinky 2000

Hiding Out 1987

Hifazaat. *See* In Custody.

High Art 1999

High Crimes 2003

High Fidelity 2001

High Heels 1991

High Heels and Low Lives 2002

High Hopes 1988, 1989

High Lonesome: The Story of Bluegrass Music 258

High-Rise 2017

High Risk 1995

High Road to China 1983

High School 2013

High School High 1996

High School Musical 3: Senior Year 2009

High Season 1988

High Spirits 1988

High Tension 2006

High Tide 1987

Higher Ground 2012

Higher Learning 1995

Highlander 1986

Highlander 2: The Quickening 1991

Highlander 3: The Final Dimension 1995

Highlander: Endgame 2001

Highway Patrolman 1995

Highway 61 1992

Highway to Hell 1992

Hijacking, A 2014

Horseman on the Roof, The 1996

Horton Hears a Who! *See* Dr. Seuss' Horton Hears a Who!

Host, The 2008

Host, The 2014

Hostage 2006

Hostel 2007

Hostel: Part II 2008

Hot Chick, The 2003

Hot Dog...The Movie 1984

Hot Fuzz 2008

Hot Pursuit 1987

Hot Pursuit 2016

Hot Rod 2008

Hot Shots! 1991

Hot Shots! Part Deux 1993

Hot Spot, The 1990

Hot to Trot 1988

Hot Tub Time Machine 2011

Hot Tub Time Machine 2 2016

Hotel Colonial 1987

Hotel De Love 1997

Hotel for Dogs 2010

Hotel New Hampshire, The 1984

Hotel Rwanda 2005

Hotel Terminus 1988

Hotel Transylvania 2013

Hotel Transylvania 2 2016

Hotshot 1987

Hottest State, The 2008

Hound of the Baskervilles, The 1981

Hours, The 2003

Hours and Times, The 1992

House 1986

House II 1987

House Arrest 1996

House at the End of the Street 2013

House Bunny, The 2009

House of Cards 1993

House of D 2006

House of Flying Daggers 2005

House of Fools 2004

House of Games 1987

House of Luk 2001

House of Mirth 2002

House of 1,000 Corpses 2004

House of Sand and Fog 2004

House of the Devil, The 2010

House of the Spirits, The 1995

House of Wax 2006

House of Yes, The 1997

House on Carroll Street, The 1988

House on Haunted Hill 2000

House on Limb, A. *See* Tottering Lives.

House on Sorority Row, The. *See* Sorority Row.

House Party 1990

House Party II 1991

House Party III 1995

House Where Evil Dwells, The 1982

Houseboat [1958] 1986

Houseguest 1995

Household Saints 1993

Householder, The 1984

Housekeeper, A 2004

Housekeeper, The 1987

Housekeeping 1987

Housesitter 1992

How Do You Know 2011

How I Got into College 1989

How I Killed My Father 2004

How I Live Now 2014

How She Move 2009

How Stella Got Her Groove Back 1999

How to Be Single 2017

How to Deal 2004

How to Eat Fried Worms 2007

How to Get Ahead in Advertising 1989

How to Get the Man's Foot Outta Your Ass. *See* Baadasssss!

How to Lose a Guy in 10 Days 2004

How to Lose Friends & Alienate People 2009

How to Make an American Quilt 1995

How to Make Love to a Negro Without Getting Tired 1990

How to Survive a Plague 2013

How to Train Your Dragon 2011

How to Train Your Dragon 2 2015

Howard the Duck 1986

Howard's End 1992

Howl 2011

Howling, The 1981

Howling III, The. *See* Marsupials, The.

Howl's Moving Castle 2006

Hsi Yen. *See* Wedding Banquet, The.

Hsimeng Jensheng. *See* Puppetmaster, The.

H2: Halloween 2. *See* Halloween II.

Hudson Hawk 1991

Hudsucker Proxy, The 1995

Hugh Hefner: Once Upon a Time 1992

Hugo 2012

Hugo Pool 1997

Huit Femmes. *See* 8 Women.

Hulk 2004

Human Centipede: First Sequence, The 2011

Human Centipede II (Full Sequence), The 2012

Human Nature 2003

Human Resources 2002

Human Shield, The 1992

Human Stain, The 2004

Humongous 1982

Humpday 2010

Hunchback of Notre Dame, The 1996

Hundred-Foot Journey, The 2015

Hungarian Fairy Tale, A 1989

Hunger, The 1983

Hunger Games, The 2013

Hunger Games: Catching Fire, The 2014

Hunger Games: Mockingjay—Part 1, The 2015

Hunger Games: Mockingjay—Part 2, The 2016

Hungry Feeling, A 1988

Hungry Hearts 2016

Hunk 1987

Hunt, The 2014

Hunt for Red October, The 1990

Illtown 1999

Illuminata 2000

Illusionist, The 2007

Illusionist, The 2011

Illustrious Energy 1988

Ils se Marient et Eurent Beaucoup D'Enfants. *See* Happily Ever After.

I'm Dancing as Fast as I Can 1982

I'm Going Home 2003

I'm No Angel [1933] 1984

I'm Not There 2008

I'm Not Rappaport 1997

I'm So Excited 2014

I'm Still Here 2011

I'm the One That I Want 2001

Imagemaker, The 1986

Imaginarium of Doctor Parnassus, The 2010

Imaginary Crimes 1995

Imaginary Heroes 2006

Imagine 1988

Imagine Me & You 2007

Imagine That 2010

Imitation Game, The 2015

Immediate Family 1989

Immigrant, The 2015

Immortal Beloved 1995

Immortals 2012

Imperative 1985

Importance of Being Earnest, The 1995

Importance of Being Earnest, The (Parker) 2003

Imported Bridegroom, The 1991

Impossible, The 2013

Imposter, The 2013

Impostor 2003

Impostors 1999

Impromptu 1991

Impulse (Baker) 1984

Impulse (Locke) 1990

In a Better World 2012

In a Shallow Grave 1988

In a Valley of Violence 2017

In a World... 2014

In America 2004

In and Out 1997

In Bloom. *See* Life Before Her Eyes, The.

In Bruges 2009

In Country 1989

In Crowd, The 2001

In Custody 1995

In Dangerous Company 1988

In Darkness 2013

In Dreams 2000

In Fashion. *See* A la Mode.

In God's Hands 1999

In Good Company 2006

In Her Shoes 2006

In-Laws, The 2004

In Love and War 1997

In My Country 2006

In Our Hands 1983

In Praise of Love 2003

In Secret 2015

In the Army Now 1995

In the Bedroom 2002

In the Company of Men 1997

In the Cut 2004

In the Heat of Passion 1992

In the Heat of the Night [1967] 1992

In the Heart of the Sea 2016

In the Land of Blood and Honey 2012

In the Land of the Deaf 1995

In the Land of Women 2008

In the Line of Fire 1993

In the Loop 2010

In the Mirror of Maya Deren 2004

In the Mood 1987

In the Mood for Love 2002

In the Mouth of Madness 1995

In the Name of the Father 1993

In the Name of the King: A Dungeon Seige Tale 2009

In the Realms of the Unreal 2006

In the Shadow of Kilimanjaro 1986

In the Shadow of the Moon 2008

In the Shadow of the Stars 1992

In the Soup 1992

In the Spirit 1990

In the Valley of Elah 2008

In This World 2004

In Time 2012

In Too Deep 2000

In Weiter Ferne, So Nah! *See* Faraway, So Close.

Incendies 2012

Inception 2011

Inchon 1982

Incident at Oglala 1992

Incident at Raven's Gate 1988

Incognito 1999

Inconvenient Truth, An 2007

Incredible Burt Wonderstone, The 2014

Incredible Hulk, The 2009

Incredible Journey, The. *See* Homeward Bound.

Incredibles, The 2005

Incredibly True Adventures of Two Girls in Love, The 1995

Incubus, The 1982

Indecent Proposal 1993

Independence Day 1996

Independence Day: Resurgence 2017

Indian in the Cupboard, The 1995

Indian Runner, The 1991

Indian Summer 1993

Indiana Jones and the Kingdom of the Crystal Skull 2009

Indiana Jones and the Last Crusade 1989

Indiana Jones and the Temple of Doom 1984

Indigènes. *See* Days of Glory.

Indignation 2017

Indochine 1992

Inevitable Grace 1995

Infamous 2007

Infernal Affairs 2005

Inferno 2017

Infiltrator, The 2017

Infinitely Polar Bear 2016

Infinity 1991

Infinity (Broderick) 1996

It's Pat 1995

It's the Rage 2001

Ivan and Abraham 1995

I've Heard the Mermaids Singing 1987

I've Loved You So Long 2009

J

J. Edgar 2012

Jack 1996

Jack and His Friends 1993

Jack and Jill 2012

Jack and Sarah 1996

Jack Frost 1999

Jack Goes Boating 2011

Jack Reacher 2013

Jack Reacher: Never Go Back 2017

Jack Ryan: Shadow Recruit 2015

Jack the Bear 1993

Jack the Giant Slayer 2014

Jackal, The 1997

Jackass Number Two 2007

Jackass Presents: Bad Grandpa 2014

Jackass 3D 2011

Jacket, The 2006

Jackie 2017

Jackie Brown 1997

Jackie Chan's First Strike 1997

Jacknife 1989

Jackpot 2002

Jack's Back 1988

Jacob 1988

Jacob's Ladder 1990

Jacquot of Nantes 1993

Jade 1995

Jafar Panahi's Taxi 2016

Jagged Edge 1985

Jagten. *See* Hunt, The.

J'ai epouse une ombre. *See* I Married a Shadow.

Jailhouse Rock [1957] 1986

Jake Speed 1986

Jakob the Liar 2000

James and the Giant Peach 1996

James Cameron's Sanctum. *See* Sanctum.

James' Journey to Jerusalem 2005

James Joyce's Women 1985

James White 2016

Jamon, Jamon 1993

Jane Austen Book Club, The 2008

Jane Eyre 1996

Jane Eyre 2012

Jane Got a Gun 2017

January Man, The 1989

Japanese Story 2005

Jarhead 2006

Jason Bourne 2017

Jason Goes to Hell 1993

Jason X 2003

Jason's Lyric 1995

Jawbreaker 2000

Jaws: The Revenge 1987

Jaws 3-D 1983

Jay and Silent Bob Strike Back 2002

Jazzman 1984

Je Rentre a la Maison. *See* I'm Going Home.

Je tu il elle [1974] 1985

Je vous salue, Marie. *See* Hail Mary.

Jean de Florette 1987

Jeanne Dielman, 23 Quai du Commerce, 1080 Bruxelles [1976] 1981

Jeepers Creepers 2002

Jeepers Creepers 2 2004

Jeff, Who Lives at Home 2013

Jefferson in Paris 1995

Jeffrey 1995

Jekyll and Hyde…Together Again 1982

Jem and the Holograms 2016

Jennifer Eight 1992

Jennifer's Body 2010

Jerky Boys 1995

Jerome 2001

Jerry Maguire 1996

Jersey Boys 2015

Jersey Girl 2005

Jerusalem 1996

Jessabelle 2015

Jesus of Montreal 1989

Jesus' Son 2000

Jet Lag 2004

Jet Li's Fearless 2007

Jetsons 1990

Jeune et Jolie. *See* Young and Beautiful.

Jewel of the Nile, The 1985

JFK 1991

Jigsaw Man, The 1984

Jim and Piraterna Blom. *See* Jim and the Pirates.

Jim and the Pirates 1987

Jiminy Glick in Lalawood 2006

Jimmy Hollywood 1995

Jimmy Neutron: Boy Genius 2002

Jimmy the Kid 1983

Jindabyne 2008

Jingle All the Way 1996

Jinxed 1982

Jiro Dreams of Sushi 2013

Jit 1995

Jo-Jo at the Gate of Lions 1995

Jo Jo Dancer, Your Life Is Calling 1986

Joan the Mad. *See* Mad Love.

Joan Rivers: A Piece of Work 2011

Jobs 2014

Jocks 1987

Jodaelye Nader az Simin. *See* Separation, A.

Jodorowsky's Dune 2015

Joe 2015

Joe Dirt 2002

Joe Gould's Secret 2001

Joe Somebody 2002

Joe the King 2000

Joe Versus the Volcano 1990

Joe's Apartment 1996

Joey 1985

Joey Takes a Cab 1991

John and the Missus 1987

John Carpenter's Ghosts of Mars 2002

John Carpenter's The Ward. *See* Ward, The.

John Carpenter's Vampires 1999

John Carter 2013

Karate Kid: Part III, The 1989

Kari-gurashi no Arietti. *See* Secret World of Arrietty, The.

Kate & Leopold 2002

Kate Plays Christine 2017

Katy Perry: Part of Me 2013

Kazaam 1996

Kaze tachinu. *See* Wind Rises, The.

Kazoku. *See* Where Spring Comes Late.

Keanu 2017

Keep, The 1983

Keep the River On Your Right: A Modern Cannibal Tale 2002

Keep the Lights On 2013

Keeping Mum 2007

Keeping Room, The 2016

Keeping the Faith 2001

Keeping Up with the Joneses 2017

Keeping Up with the Steins 2007

Kerouac, the Movie 1985

Kevin Hart: Let Me Explain 2014

Kevin Hart: What Now? 2017

Key Exchange 1985

Keys of the Kingdom, The [1944] 1989

Keys to Tulsa 1997

Khuda Gawah. *See* God Is My Witness.

Kick-Ass 2011

Kick-Ass 2 2014

Kickboxer 1989

Kickboxer II 1991

Kicked in the Head 1997

Kickin' It Old Skool 2008

Kicking and Screaming (Baumbach) 1995

Kicking & Screaming 2006

Kid, The. *See* Vie en Rose, La.

Kid & I, The 2006

Kid Brother, The 1987

Kid Colter 1985

Kid in King Arthur's Court, A 1995

Kid Stays in the Picture, The 2003

Kid with a Bike, The 2013

Kidnapped 1987

Kids 1995

Kids Are All Right, The 2011

Kids in the Hall: Brain Candy, The 1996

Kids in America. *See* Take Me Home Tonight.

Kika 1995

Kikujiro 2001

Kill Bill: Vol. 1 2004

Kill Bill: Vol. 2 2005

Kill List 2013

Kill Me Again 1989

Kill Me Later 2002

Kill the Irishman 2012

Kill the Messenger 2015

Kill Your Darlings 2014

Kill-Off, The 1990

Killer Elite 2012

Killer Image 1992

Killer Inside Me, The 2011

Killer Instinct 1995

Killer Joe 2013

Killer Klowns from Outer Space 1988

Killer of Sheep 2008

Killer Party 1986

Killers 2011

Killing Affair, A 1988

Klling Fields, The 1984

Killing Floor, The 1995

Killing of a Chinese Bookie, The [1976] 1986

Killing of John Lennon, The 2009

Killing Them Softly 2013

Killing Time 1999

Killing Time, The, 1987

Killing Zoe 1995

Killpoint 1984

Killshot 2010

Kindergarten Cop 1990

Kindred, The 1987

King, The 2007

King Arthur 2005

King and I, The 2000

King David 1985

King Is Alive, The 2002

King Is Dancing, The 2002

King James Version 1988

King Kong [1933] 1981

King Kong 2006

King Kong Lives 1986

King Lear 1987

King of Comedy, The 1983

King of Jazz [1930] 1985

King of Kong: A Fistful of Quarters, The 2008

King of Masks, The 2000

King of New York 1990

King of the Children 1988

King of the Hill 1993

King Ralph 1991

King Solomon's Mines 1985

Kingdom, Part 2, The 1999

Kingdom, The 1995

Kingdom, The 2008

Kingdom Come 2002

Kingdom of Heaven 2006

Kingpin 1996

Kings and Queen 2006

Kings of Summer, The 2014

King's Ransom 2006

King's Speech, The 2011

Kingsman: The Secret Service 2016

Kinjite 1989

Kinky Boots 2007

Kinsey 2005

Kipperbang 1984

Kippur 2001

Kirk Cameron's Saving Christmas. *See* Saving Christmas.

Kiss Before Dying, A 1991

Kiss Daddy Good Night 1987

Kiss Kiss Bang Bang 2006

Kiss Me a Killer 1991

Kiss Me Goodbye 1982

Kiss Me, Guido 1997

Kiss Me, Stupid [1964] 1986

Kiss of Death 1995

Kiss of the Dragon 2002

Kiss of the Spider Woman 1985

Kiss or Kill 1997

Kiss, The 1988

Liquid Sky 1983

Lisa 1990

Listen to Me 1989

Listen Up 1990

Listen Up Philip 2015

Little Big League 1995

Little Bit of Heaven, A 2013

Little Black Book 2005

Little Boy 2016

Little Buddha 1995

Little Children 2007

Little Devil, the 1988

Little Dorrit 1988

Little Drummer Girl, The 1984

Little Fockers 2011

Little Giants 1995

Little Indian, Big City 1996

Little Jerk 1985

Little Man 2007

Little Man Tate 1991

Little Men 1999

Little Men 2017

Little Mermaid, The 1989

Little Miss Sunshine 2007

Little Monsters 1989

Little Nemo: Adventures in Slumberland 1992

Little Nicky 2001

Little Nikita 1988

Little Noises 1992

Little Odessa 1995

Little Prince, The 2017

Little Princess, A 1995

Little Rascals, The 1995

Little Secrets 1995

Little Secrets (Treu) 2003

Little Sex, A 1982

Little Shop of Horrors [1960] 1986

Little Stiff, A 1995

Little Sweetheart 1988

Little Thief, The 1989

Little Vampire, The 2001

Little Vegas 1990

Little Vera 1989

Little Voice 1999

Little Women [1933] 1982

Little Women 1995

Live By Night 2017

Live Die Repeat: Edge of Tomorrow. *See* Edge of Tomorrow.

Live Flesh 1999

Live Free or Die Hard 2008

Live Nude Girls 1995

Live Virgin 2001

Lives of Others, The 2008

Livin' Large 1991

Living Daylights, The 1987

Living End, The 1992

Living in Oblivion 1995

Living on Tokyo Time 1987

Living Out Loud 1999

Living Proof: HIV and the Pursuit of Happiness 1995

L'ivresse du pouvoir. *See* Comedy of Power.

Lizzie McGuire Movie, The 2004

Ljuset Haller Mig Sallskap. *See* Light Keeps Me Company.

Lo and Behold 2017

Lo sono l'amore. *See* I Am Love.

Loaded 1996

Lobster, The 2017

Local Hero 1983

Locke 2015

Lock, Stock, and Two Smoking Barrels 2000

Lock Up 1989

Lockout 2013

Locusts, The 1997

Lodz Ghetto 1989

Loft, The 2016

Lola 1982

Lola La Loca 1988

Lola Rennt. *See* Run, Lola, Run.

Lola Versus 2013

Lolita 1999

London Has Fallen 2017

London Kills Me 1992

Lone Ranger, The 2014

Lone Runner, The 1988

Lone Star 1996

Lone Survivor 2014

Lone Wolf McQuade 1983

Lonely Guy, The 1984

Lonely Hearts (Cox) 1983

Lonely Hearts (Lane) 1995

Lonely in America 1991

Lonely Lady, The 1983

Lonely Passion of Judith Hearne, The 1987

Lonesome Jim 2007

Long Day Closes, The 1993

Long Dimanche de Fiancailles, Un. *See* Very Long Engagement, A.

Long Good Friday, The 1982

Long Gray Line, The [1955] 1981

Long Kiss Goodnight, The 1996

Long Live the Lady! 1988

Long, Long Trailer, The [1954] 1986

Long Lost Friend, The. *See* Apprentice to Murder.

Long Walk Home, The 1990

Long Way Home, The 1999

Long Weekend, The 1990

Longest Ride, The 2016

Longest Yard, The 2006

Longshot, The 1986

Longshots, The 2009

Longtime Companion 1990

Look at Me 2006

Look of Silence, The 2016

Look Who's Talking 1989

Look Who's Talking Now 1993

Look Who's Talking Too 1990

Lookin' to Get Out 1982

Looking for Comedy in the Muslim World 2007

Looking for Richard 1996

Lookout, The 2008

Looney Tunes: Back in Action 2004

Loong Boonmee raluek chat. *See* Uncle Boonmee Who Can Recall His Past Lives.

Looper 2013

Loophole 1986

Loose Cannons 1990

Loose Connections 1988

Loose Screws 1986

L'ora di religione: Il sorriso di mia madre. *See* My Mother's Smile.

Lorax, The. *See* Dr. Seuss' The Lorax.

Lord of Illusions 1995

Lord of the Flies 1990

Lord of the Rings: The Fellowship of the Ring 2002

Lord of the Rings: The Return of the King 2004

Lord of the Rings: The Two Towers 2003

Lord of War 2006

Lords of Discipline, The 1983

Lords of Dogtown 2006

Lords of the Deep 1989

Lords of Salem, The 2014

Lore 2014

Lorenzo's Oil 1992

Loser 2001

Losers, The 2011

Losin' It 1983

Losing Isaiah 1995

Loss of a Teardrop Diamond, The 2010

Loss of Sexual Innocence 2000

Lost and Delirious 2002

Lost and Found 2000

Lost Angels 1989

Lost Boys, The 1987

Lost City, The 2007

Lost Highway 1997

Lost in America 1985

Lost in La Mancha 2004

Lost in Siberia 1991

Lost in Space 1999

Lost in Translation 2004

Lost in Yonkers. *See* Neil Simon's Lost in Yonkers.

Lost Moment, The [1947] 1982

Lost Prophet 1995

Lost River 2016

Lost Souls 2001

Lost Weekend, The [1945] 1986

Lost Words, The 1995

Lost World, The 1997

Lottery Ticket 2011

Lou, Pat, and Joe D 1988

Louder Than a Bomb 2012

Louder Than Bombs 2017

Louis Bluie 1985

Louis Prima: The Wildest 2001

Loulou 1981

Love Actually 2004

Love Affair 1995

Love After Love 1995

Love Always 1997

Love and a .45 1995

Love and Basketball 2001

Love and Death in Long Island 1999

Love & Friendship 2017

Love and Human Remains 1995

Love & Mercy 2016

Love and Murder 1991

Love and Other Catastrophes 1997

Love and Other Drugs 2011

Love & Sex 2001

Love at Large 1990

Love Child, The 1988

Love Child: A True Story 1982

Love Come Down 2002

Love Crimes 1992

Love Don't Cost a Thing 2004

Love Field 1992

Love Guru, The 2009

Love Happens 2010

Love in Germany, A 1984

Love in the Afternoon [1957] 1986

Love in the Time of Cholera 2008

Love in the Time of Money 2003

Love Is a Dog from Hell 1988

Love is All You Need 2014

Love Is Strange 2015

Love Is the Devil 1999

love jones 1997

Love/Juice 2001

Love Letter, The 2000

Love Letters 1984

Love Liza 2004

Love Potion #9 1992

Love Ranch 2011

Love Serenade 1997

Love Song for Bobby Long, A 2006

Love Songs 2009

Love Stinks 2000

Love Story, A. *See* Bound and Gagged.

Love Streams 1984

Love the Coopers 2016

Love the Hard Way 2004

Love, the Magician. *See* Amor brujo, El.

Love! Valour! Compassion! 1997

Love Walked In 1999

Love Without Pity 1991

Lovelace 2014

Loveless, The 1984, 1986

Lovelines 1984

Lovely & Amazing 2003

Lovely Bones, The 2010

Lover, The 1992

Loverboy 1989

Loverboy 2007

Lovers 1992

Lovers of the Arctic Circle, The 2000

Lovers on the Bridge 2000

Lovers and the Despot, The 2017

Love's a Bitch. *See* Amores Perros.

Love's Labour's Lost 2001

Loves of a Blonde [1965] 1985

Lovesick 1983

Loving 2017

Loving Jezebel 2001

Low Blow 1986

Low Down, The 2002

Low Down Dirty Shame, A 1995

Low Life, The 1996

Lucas 1986

Lucia, Lucia 2004

Lucia y el Sexo. *See* Sex and Lucia.

Lucie Aubrac 2000

Luckiest Man in the World, The 1989

Lucky Break 2003

Lucky Number Slevin 2007

Lucky Numbers 2001

Lucky One, The 2013

Marvel's The Avengers. *See* Avengers, The.

Marvin & Tige 1983

Marvin's Room 1996

Mary and Max 2010

Mary Reilly 1996

Mary Shelley's Frankenstein 1995

Masala 1993

Mask 1985

Mask, The 1995

Mask of the Phantasm. *See* Batman: Mask of the Phantasm.

Mask of Zorro, The 1999

Masked and Anonymous 2004

Masque of the Red Death 1989

Masquerade 1988

Mass Appeal 1985

Massa'ot James Be'eretz Hakodesh. *See* James' Journey to Jerusalem.

Master, The 2013

Master and Commander: The Far Side of the World 2004

Master of Disguise 2003

Master of the Crimson Armor. *See* Promise, The.

Masterminds 1997

Masterminds 2017

Masters of the Universe 1987

Matador, The 2007

Match Point 2006

Matchmaker, The 1997

Matchstick Men 2004

Material Girls 2007

Matewan 1987

Matilda 1996

Matinee 1993

Matrix, The 2000

Matrix Reloaded, The 2004

Matrix Revolutions, The 2004

Matter of Struggle, A 1985

Matter of Taste, A 2002

Maurice 1987

Maverick 1995

Max 2003

Max 2016

Max Dugan Returns 1983

Max Keeble's Big Move 2002

Max Payne 2009

Max Steel 2017

Maxie 1985

Maximum Overdrive 1986

Maximum Risk 1996

May Fools 1990

Maybe Baby 2002

Maybe…Maybe Not 1996

Maze Runner, The 2015

Maze Runner: The Scorch Trials 2016

McBain 1991

McFarland USA 2016

McHale's Navy 1997

Me and Earl and the Dying Girl 2016

Me and Isaac Newton 2001

Me and My Gal [1932] 1982

Me and Orson Welles 2010

Me and the Kid 1993

Me and Veronica 1995

Me and You 2015

Me and You and Everyone We Know 2006

Me Before You 2017

Me, Myself & Irene 2001

Me Myself I 2001

Me Without You 2003

Me You Them 2002

Mean Creek 2005

Mean Girls 2005

Mean Season, The 1985

Meatballs II 1984

Meatballs III 1987

Meatballs IV 1992

Mechanic, The 2012

Mechanic: Resurrection 2017

Medallion, The 2004

Meddler, The 2017

Medicine Man 1992

Mediterraneo 1992

Meek's Cutoff 2012

Meet Dave 2009

Meet Joe Black 1999

Meet John Doe [1941] 1982

Meet the Applegates 1991

Meet the Blacks 2017

Meet the Browns. *See* Tyler Perry's Meet the Browns.

Meet the Deedles 1999

Meet the Fockers 2005

Meet the Hollowheads 1989

Meet the Parents 2001

Meet the Robinsons 2008

Meet the Spartans 2009

Meet Wally Sparks 1997

Meeting Venus 1991

Megaforce 1982

Megamind 2011

Mein Liebster Feind. *See* My Best Fiend.

Melancholia 2012

Melinda and Melinda 2006

Melvin and Howard 1981

Memento 2002

Memoirs of a Geisha 2006

Memoirs of a Madman 1995

Memoirs of a River 1992

Memoirs of an Invisible Man 1992

Memories of Me 1988

Memphis Belle 1990

Men 1986

Men 1999

Men at Work 1990

Men Don't Leave 1990

Men in Black 1997

Men in Black II 2003

Men in Black 3 2013

Men in Tights. *See* Robin Hood.

Men of Honor 2001

Men of Respect 1991

Men Who Stare at Goats, The 2010

Men with Brooms 2003

Men with Guns 1999

Men, Women & Children 2015

Menace II Society 1993

Ménage 1986

Men's Club, The 1986

Mephisto 1981

Mercenary Fighters 1988

Merchant of Venice, The 2006

Merci pour le Chocolat 2003

Mercury Rising 1999

Mermaid, The 2017

Mermaids 1990

Merry Christmas. *See* Joyeux Noel.

Merry Christmas, Mr. Lawrence 1983

Merry War, A 1999

Mesrine 2011

Mesrine: Killer Instinct. *See* Mesrine.

Mesrine: Public Enemy #1. *See* Mesrine.

Message in a Bottle 2000

Messenger, The 1987

Messenger, The 2010

Messenger: Joan of Arc, The 2000

Messenger of Death 1988

Messengers, The 2008

Metallica: Some Kind of Monster 2005

Metallica Through the Never 2014

Metalstorm: The Destruction of Jarred-Syn 1983

Metamorphosis: The Alien Factor 1995

Meteor Man, The 1993

Metro 1997

Metroland 2000

Metropolitan 1990

Mexican, The 2002

Mi Vida Loca 1995

Mia Eoniotita ke Mia Mers. *See* Eternity and a Day.

Miami Blues 1990

Miami Rhapsody 1995

Miami Vice 2007

Michael 1996

Michael Clayton 2008

Michael Collins 1996

Michael Jackson's This Is It 2010

Mickey Blue Eyes 2000

Micki & Maude 1984

Micmacs 2011

Microcosmos 1996

Midan, Al. *See* Square, The.

Middle Men 2011

Middle of Nowhere 2013

Middle School: The Worst Years of My Life 2017

Midnight (Leisen) 1986

Midnight (Vane) 1989

Midnight Clear, A 1992

Midnight Crossing 1988

Midnight in the Garden of Good and Evil 1997

Midnight in Paris 2012

Midnight Run 1988

Midnight Special 2017

Midsummer Night's Sex Comedy, A 1982

Midwinter's Tale, A 1996

Mies Vailla Menneisyytta. *See* Man Without a Past, The.

Mifune 2001

Mighty, The 1999

Mighty Aphrodite 1995

Mighty Ducks, The 1992

Mighty Heart, A 2008

Mighty Joe Young 1999

Mighty Macs, The 2012

Mighty Morphin Power Rangers: The Movie 1995

Mighty Quinn, The 1989

Mighty Wind, A 2004

Mike and Dave Need Wedding Dates 2017

Mike's Murder 1984

Mikey and Nicky 1984

Milagro Beanfield War, The 1988

Mildred Pierce [1945] 1986

Miles Ahead 2017

Miles from Home 1988

Milk 2009

Milk and Honey 1989

Milk & Honey 2006

Milk Money 1995

Millennium 1989

Millennium Mambo 2003

Miller's Crossing 1990

Million Dollar Arm 2015

Million Dollar Baby 2005

Million Dollar Hotel, The 2002

Million Dollar Mystery 1987

Million to Juan, A 1995

Million Ways to Die In the West, A 2015

Millions 2006

Mimic 1997

Mina Tannenbaum 1995

Mindhunters 2006

Mindwalk 1991

Minions 2016

Ministry of Vengeance 1989

Minner. *See* Men.

Minority Report 2003

Minotaur 1995

Minus Man, The 2000

Mio Viaggio in Italia. *See* My Voyage to Italy.

Miracle 2005

Miracle, The 1991

Miracle at St. Anna 2009

Miracle Mile 1988, 1989

Miracle on 34th Street 1995

Miracle Woman, The (1931) 1982

Miracles From Heaven 2017

Miral 2012

Mirror, The 2000

Mirror Has Two Faces, The 1996

Mirror Mirror 2013

Mirrors 2009

Misadventures of Mr. Wilt, The 1990

Mischief 1985

Miserables, The 1995

Miserables, The 1999

Misery 1990

Misfits, The [1961] 1983

Mishima 1985

Misma luna, La. *See* Under the Same Moon.

Misplaced 1995

Misplaced 1989

Miss Congeniality 2001

Miss Congeniality 2: Armed and Fabulous 2006

Miss Firecracker 1989

Miss March 2010

Miss Mary 1986

Miss Mona 1987

Miss...or Myth? 1987

Miss Peregrine's Home for Peculiar Children 2017

Miss Pettigrew Lives for a Day 2009

Miss Potter 2008

Miss Sloane 2017

Miss You Already 2016

Missing 1982, 1988

Missing, The 2004

Missing in Action, 1984

Missing in Action II 1985

Mission, The (Joffe) 1986

Mission, The (Sayyad) 1983

Mission: Impossible 1996

Mission: Impossible—Ghost Protocol 2012

Mission: Impossible Rogue Nation 2016

Mission: Impossible 2 2001

Mission: Impossible III 2007

Mission to Mars 2001

Missionary, The 1982

Mississippi Burning 1988

Mississippi Grind 2016

Mississippi Masala 1992

Mist, The 2008

Mr. and Mrs. Bridge 1990

Mr. & Mrs. Smith 2006

Mr. Baseball 1992

Mr. Bean's Holiday 2008

Mr. Brooks 2008

Mr. Death: The Rise and Fall of Fred A. Leuchter, Jr. 2000

Mr. Deeds 2003

Mr. Deeds Goes to Town [1936] 1982

Mr. Destiny 1990

Mr. Frost 1990

Mr. Holland's Opus 1995

Mr. Holmes 2016

Mr. Jealousy 1999

Mister Johnson 1991

Mr. Jones 1993

Mr. Love 1986

Mr. Magoo 1997

Mr. Magorium's Wonder Emporium 2008

Mr. Mom 1983

Mr. Nanny 1993

Mr. Nice Guy 1999

Mr. North 1988

Mr. Payback 1995

Mr. Peabody & Sherman 2015

Mr. Popper's Penguins 2012

Mr. Right 2017

Mister Roberts [1955] 1988

Mr. Saturday Night 1992

Mr. Smith Goes to Washington [1939] 1982

Mr. 3000 2005

Mr. Turner 2015

Mr. Wonderful 1993

Mr. Woodcock 2008

Mr. Write 1995

Mr. Wrong 1996

Mistress 1992

Mrs. Brown 1997

Mrs. Dalloway 1999

Mrs. Doubtfire 1993

Mrs. Henderson Presents 2006

Mrs. Palfrey at the Claremont 2007

Mrs. Parker and the Vicious Circle 1995

Mrs. Soffel 1984

Mrs. Winterbourne 1996

Mistress America 2016

Misunderstood 1984

Mit Liv som Hund. *See* My Life as a Dog.

Mitad del cielo, La. *See* Half of Heaven.

Mixed Blood 1985

Mixed Nuts 1995

Mo' Better Blues 1990

Mo' Money 1992

Moana 2017

Moartea domnului Lazarescu. *See* Death of Mr. Lazarescu, The.

Mobsters 1991

Mod Squad, The 2000

Modern Girls 1986

Modern Romance 1981

Moderns, The 1988

Mogan Do. *See* Infernal Affairs.

Mois d'avril sont meurtriers, Les. *See* April Is a Deadly Month.

Moitie Gauche du Frigo, La. *See* Left Hand Side of the Fridge, The.

Moll Flanders 1996

Molly 2000

Mom and Dad Save the World 1992

Môme, La. *See* Vie en Rose, La.

Mommie Dearest 1981

Moms' Night Out 2015

Mon bel Amour, Ma Dechirure. *See* My True Love, My Wound.

Mon meilleur ami. *See* My Best Friend.

Mona Lisa 1986

Mona Lisa Smile 2004

Mondays in the Sun 2004

Mondo New York 1988

Mondovino 2006

Money for Nothing 1993

Money Man 1995

Money Monster 2017

Money Pit, The 1986

Money Talks 1997

Money Train 1995

Money Tree, The 1992

Moneyball 2012

Mongol 2009

Mongolian Tale, A 1997

Monkey Kingdom 2016

Monkey Shines 1988

Monkey Trouble 1995

Monkeybone 2002

Monsieur Hire 1990

Monsieur Ibrahim 2004

Monsieur Lazhar 2013

Monsieur N 2006

Monsignor 1982

Monsoon Wedding 2003

Monster 2004

Monster, The 1996

Monster House 2007

Monster in a Box 1992

Monster Calls, A 2017

Monster-in-Law 2006

Monster in the Closet 1987

Monster Squad, The 1987

Monsters 2011

Monster's Ball 2002

Monsters, Inc. 2002

Monsters University 2014

Monsters vs. Aliens 2010

Montana Run 1992

Monte Carlo 2012

Montenegro 1981

Month by the Lake, A 1995

Month in the Country, A 1987

Monty Python's The Meaning of Life 1983

Monument Ave. 1999

Monuments Men, The 2015

Mood Indigo 2015

Moolaade 2005

Moon 2010

Moon in the Gutter 1983

Moon Over Broadway 1999

Moon over Parador 1988

Moon Shadow [1995] 2001

Moonlight 2017

Moonlight and Valentino 1995

Moonlight Mile 2003

Moonlighting 1982

Moonrise Kingdom 2013

Moonstruck 1987

More Than A Game 2010

Morgan Stewart's Coming Home 1987

Moriarty. *See* Sherlock Holmes.

Morning After, The 1986

Morning Glory 1993

Morning Glory 2011

Morons from Outer Space 1985

Morris From America 2017

Mort de Mario Ricci, La. *See* Death of Mario Ricci, The.

Mortal Instruments: City of Bones, The 2014

Mortal Kombat 1995

Mortal Kombat II: Annihilation 1997

Mortal Thoughts 1991

Mortdecai 2016

Mortuary Academy 1988

Morvern Callar 2003

Mosca addio. *See* Moscow Farewell.

Moscow Farewell 1987

Moscow on the Hudson 1984

Mosquito Coast, The 1986

Most Dangerous Game, The [1932] 1985

Most Dangerous Man in America: Daniel Ellsberg and the Pentagon Papers, The 2011

Most Fertile Man in Ireland, The 2002

Most Violent Year, A 2015

Most Wanted 1997

Most Wanted Man, A 2015

Mostly Martha 2003

Mother 1996

Mother 2011

Mother, The 2005

Mother and Child 2011

Mother Lode 1983

Mother Night 1996

Mother Teresa 1986

Motherhood 2010

Mothering Heart, The [1913] 1984

Mother's Boys 1995

Mother's Day 2017

Mothman Prophecies, The 2003

Motorama 1993

Motorcycle Diaries, The 2005

Moulin Rouge 2002

Mountain Gorillas 1995

Mountains May Depart 2017

Mountains of Moon 1990

Mountaintop Motel Massacre 1986

Mouse Hunt 1997

Mouth to Mouth 1997

Movers and Shakers 1985

Movie 43 2014

Moving 1988

Moving the Mountain 1995

Moving Violations 1985

MS One: Maximum Security. *See* Lockout.

Much Ado About Nothing 1993

Much Ado About Nothing 2014

Mud 2014

Mui du du Xanh. *See* Scent of Green Papaya, The.

Mujeres al borde de un ataque de nervios. *See* Women on the Verge of a Nervous Breakdown.

Mulan 1999

Mulholland Drive 2002

Mulholland Falls 1996

Multiplicity 1996

Mumford 2000

Mummy, The 2000

Mummy Returns, The 2002

Mummy: Tomb of the Dragon Emperor, The 2009

Munchie 1995

Munchies 1987

Munich 2006

Muppets, The 2012

Muppet Christmas Carol, The 1992

Muppets from Space 2000

Muppet Treasure Island 1996

Muppets Most Wanted 2015

Muppets Take Manhattan, The 1984

Mur, Le. *See* Wall, The.

Murder at 1600 1997

Murder by Numbers 2003

Murder in the First 1995

Murder One 1988

Murderball 2006

Murderous Maids 2003

Muriel's Wedding 1995

Murphy's Law 1986

Murphy's Romance 1985

Muscle Shoals 2014

Muse, The 2000

Muses Orphelines, Les. *See* Orphan Muses, The.

Museum Hours 2014

Music and Lyrics 2008

Music Box 1989

Music for the Movies: Bernard Herrmann 1995

Music From Another Room 1999

Music of Chance, The 1993

Music of the Heart 2000

Music Tells You, The 1995

Musime si Pomahat. *See* Divided We Fall.

Musketeer, The 2002

Must Love Dogs 2006

Mustang: The Hidden Kingdom 1995

Musuko. *See* My Sons.

Mutant on the Bounty 1989

Mute Witness 1995

Mutiny on the Bounty [1962] 1984

My African Adventure 1987

My All American 2016

My American Cousin 1986

My Apprenticeship. *See* Among People.

My Architect 2005

My Baby's Daddy 2005

My Beautiful Laundrette 1986

My Best Fiend 2000

My Best Friend 2008

My Best Friend Is a Vampire 1988

My Best Friend's Girl 1984

My Best Friend's Girl 2009

My Best Friend's Wedding 1997

My Big Fat Greek Wedding 2003

My Big Fat Greek Wedding 2 2017

My Blind Brother 2017

My Bloody Valentine 3D 2010

My Blue Heaven 1990

My Blueberry Nights 2009

My Boss's Daughter 2004

My Boyfriend's Back 1993

My Chauffeur 1986

My Cousin Rachel [1952] 1981

My Cousin Vinny 1992

My Crazy Life. *See* Mi Vida Loca.

My Dark Lady 1987

My Demon Lover 1987

My Dinner with Andre 1981

My Family (Mi Familia) 1995

My Father Is Coming 1992

My Father, the Hero 1995

My Father's Angel 2002

My Father's Glory 1991

My Favorite Martian 2000

My Favorite Season 1996

My Favorite Year 1982

My Fellow Americans 1996

My First Mister 2002

My First Wife 1985

My Foolish Heart (1949) 1983

My Giant 1999

My Girl 1991

My Girl II 1995

My Golden Days 2017

My Heroes Have Always Been Cowboys 1991

My Idiot Brother. *See* Our Idiot Brother.

My Left Foot 1989

My Life 1993

My Life and Times with Antonin Artaud 1996

My Life as a Dog [1985] 1987

My Life in Pink. *See* Ma Vie en Rose.

My Life in Ruins 2010

My Life So Far 2000

My Life Without Me 2004

My Life's in Turnaround 1995

My Little Pony 1986

My Mom's a Werewolf 1989

My Mother's Castle 1991

My Mother's Courage

My Mother's Smile 2006

My Name is Joe 2000

My Neighbor Totoro 1993

My New Gun 1992

My New Partner 1985

My Old Lady 2015

My One and Only 2010

My Other Husband 1985

My Own Private Idaho 1991

My Reputation [1946] 1984, 1986

My Science Project 1985

My Sister's Keeper 2010

My Son, My Son, What Have Ye Done 2011

My Son the Fanatic 2000

My Sons 1995

My Soul to Take 2011

My Stepmother Is an Alien 1988

My Summer of Love 2006

My Super Ex-Girlfriend 2007

My Sweet Little Village 1986

My True Love, My Wound 1987

My Tutor 1983

My Twentieth Century 1990

My Uncle's Legacy 1990

My Voyage to Italy 2003

My Week With Marilyn 2012

My Wife Is an Actress 2003

Mysterious Skin 2006

Mystery, Alaska 2000

Mystery Date 1991

Mystery of Alexina, The 1986

Mystery of Rampo 1995

Mystery of the Wax Museum [1933] 1986

Mystery Men 2000

Mystery Science Theater 3000: The Movie 1996

Mystery Train 1989

Mystic Masseur, The 2003

Mystic Pizza 1988

Mystic River 2004

Myth of Fingerprints, The 1998

N

Nacho Libre 2007

Nader and Simin, a Separation. *See* Separation, A.

Nadine 1987

Nadja 1995

Naked 1993

Naked Cage, The 1986

Naked Gun, The 1988

Naked Gun 2 1/2, The 1991

Naked Gun 33 1/3: The Final Insult 1995

Naked in New York 1995

Naked Lunch 1991

Name of the Rose, The 1986

Namesake, The 2008

Nana, La. *See* Maid, The.

Night and the City 1992

Night at the Museum 2007

Night at the Museum: Battle of the Smithsonian 2010

Night at the Museum: Secret of the Tomb 2015

Night at the Roxbury, A 1999

Night Before, The 2016

Night Catches Us 2011

Night Crossing 1982

Night Falls on Manhattan 1997

Night Friend 1988

Night Game 1989

Night in Heaven, A 1983

Night in the Life of Jimmy Reardon, A 1988

Night Listener, The 2007

'night, Mother 1986

Night Moves 2015

Night of the Comet 1984

Night of the Creeps 1986

Night of the Demons II 1995

Night of the Hunter, The [1955] 1982

Night of the Iguana, The [1964] 1983

Night of the Living Dead 1990

Night of the Pencils, The 1987

Night of the Shooting Stars, The 1983

Night on Earth 1992

Night Patrol 1985

Night Shift 1982

Night Song [1947] 1981

Night Visitor 1989

Night Watch 2007

Night We Never Met, The 1993

Nightbreed 1990

Nightcap. *See* Merci pour le Chocolat.

Nightcrawler 2015

Nightfall 1988

Nightflyers 1987

Nighthawks 1981

Nighthawks II. *See* Strip Jack Naked.

Nightmare at Shadow Woods 1987

Nightmare Before Christmas, The 1993

Nightmare on Elm Street, A 2011

Nightmare on Elm Street, A 1984

Nightmare on Elm Street: II, A 1985

Nightmare on Elm Street: III, A 1987

Nightmare on Elm Street: IV, A 1988

Nightmare on Elm Street: V, A 1989

Nightmare, The 2016

Nightmares III 1984

Nights in Rodanthe 2009

Nightsongs 1991

Nightstick 1987

Nightwatch 1999

Nil by Mouth 1999

Nim's Island 2009

9 2010

Nine 2010

9 1/2 Weeks 1986

9 Deaths of the Ninja 1985

Nine Lives 2017

Nine Months 1995

Nine Queens 2003

976-EVIL 1989

1918 1985

1969 1988

1990: The Bronx Warriors 1983

1991: The Year Punk Broke 1995

Ninety Days 1986

99 Homes 2016

Ninja Assassin 2010

Ninja Turf 1986

Ninotchka [1939] 1986

Ninth Gate, The 2001

9th Life of Louis Drax, The 2017

Nixon 1995

No 1999

No 2014

No Country for Old Men 2008

No End in Sight 2008

No Escape 1995

No Escape 2016

No Fear, No Die 1995

No Good Deed 2015

No Holds Barred 1989

No Looking Back 1999

No Man of Her Own [1949] 1986

No Man's Land 1987

No Man's Land 2002

No Mercy 1986

No News from God 2003

No Picnic 1987

No Reservations 2008

No Retreat, No Surrender 1986

No Retreat, No Surrender II 1989

No Secrets 1991

No Small Affair 1984

No Strings Attached 2012

No Such Thing 2003

No Way Out 1987, 1992

Noah 2015

Nobody Loves Me 1996

Nobody Walks 2013

Nobody's Fool (Benton) 1995

Nobody's Fool (Purcell) 1986

Nobody's Perfect 1990

Noce en Galilee. *See* Wedding in Galilee, A.

Noche de los lapices, La. *See* Night of the Pencils, The.

Nochnoi Dozor. *See* Night Watch.

Nocturnal Animals 2017

Noel 2005

Noises Off 1992

Nomads 1986

Non ti muovere. *See* Don't Move.

Non-Stop 2015

Nora 2002

Norbit 2008

Nordwand. *See* North Face.

Norm of the North 2017

Normal Life 1996

Norte, El 1983

North 1995

North Country 2006

North Face 2011

North Shore 1987

North Star, The [1943] 1982

Northfork 2004

Nostalgia 1984

On the Road 2013
On the Town [1949] 1985
On Valentine's Day 1986
Once 2008
Once Around 1991
Once Bitten 1985
Once More 1988
Once Were Warriors 1995
Once Upon a Crime 1992
Once Upon A Forest 1993
Once Upon a Time in America 1984
Once Upon a Time in Anatolia 2013
Once Upon a Time in Mexico 2004
Once Upon a Time in the Midlands 2004
Once Upon a Time...When We Were Colored 1996
Once We Were Dreamers 1987
Ondine 2011
One 2001
One, The 2002
One and a Two, A. *See* Yi Yi.
One Crazy Summer 1986
One Day 2012
One Day in September 2001
One Direction: This Is Us 2014
One False Move 1992
One Fine Day 1996
One Flew over the Cuckoo's Nest [1975] 1985, 1991
One for the Money 2013
One from the Heart 1982
One Good Cop 1991
One Hour Photo 2003
101 Dalmatians 1996
101 Reykjavik 2002
102 Dalmatians 2001
187 1997
112th and Central 1993
127 Hours 2011
One I Love, The 2015
One Magic Christmas 1985
One Missed Call 2009
One More Saturday 1986
One More Tomorrow [1946] 1986
One Nation Under God 1995

One Night at McCool's 2002
One Night Stand 1997
One Shot. *See* Jack Reacher.
One Tough Cop 1999
One True Thing 1999
Onegin 2000
Ong Bak: The Beginning. *See* Ong Bak 2.
Ong Bak 2 2010
Onimaru. *See* Arashi Ga Oka.
Only Emptiness Remains 1985
Only God Forgives 2014
Only Lovers Left Alive 2015
Only the Lonely 1991
Only the Strong 1993
Only the Strong Survive 2004
Only Thrill, The 1999
Only When I Laugh 1981
Only You 1995
Only Yesterday 2017
Open Doors 1991
Open Range 2004
Open Season 2007
Open Water 2005
Open Your Eyes 2000
Opening Night 1988
Opera 1987
Operation Condor 1997
Operation Dumbo Drop 1995
Opportunists, The 2001
Opportunity Knocks 1990
Opposite of Sex, The 1999
Opposite Sex, The 1993
Orange County 2003
Orchestra Seats. *See* Avenue Montaigne.
Ordeal by Innocence 1985
Order, The 2004
Orfanato, El. *See* Orphanage, The.
Orgazmo 1999
Original Gangstas 1996
Original Kings of Comedy, The 2001
Original Sin 2002
Orlando 1993
Orphan 2010

Orphan Muses, The 2002
Orphanage, The 2009
Orphans 1987
Orphans of the Storm 1984
Osama 2005
Oscar 1991
Oscar & Lucinda 1997
Osmosis Jones 2002
Ososhiki. *See* Funeral, The.
Osterman Weekend, The 1983
Otac Na Sluzbenom Putu. *See* When Father Was Away on Business.
Otello 1986
Othello 1995
Other Boleyn Girl, The 2009
Other Guys, The 2011
Other People 2017
Other People's Money 1991
Other Side of the Door, The 2017
Other Side of Heaven, The 2003
Other Sister, The 2000
Other Voices, Other Rooms 1997
Other Woman, The 2015
Others, The 2002
Ouija 2015
Ouija 2 2017
Our Brand is Crisis 2016
Our Family Wedding 2011
Our Idiot Brother 2012
Our Kind of Traitor 2017
Our Lady of the Assassins 2002
Our Relations [1936] 1985
Our Song 2002
Out Cold 1989
Out for Justice 1991
Out in the World. *See* Among People.
Out of Africa 1985
Out of Bounds 1986
Out of Control 1985
Out of Life. *See* Hors la Vie.
Out of Order 1985
Out of Sight 1999
Out of Sync 1995
Out of the Dark 1989
Out of the Furnace 2014

Past, The 2014

Pastime 1991

Patch Adams 1999

Patch of Blue, A [1965] 1986

Paterson 2017

Pathfinder 1990

Pathfinder 2008

Pathology 2009

Paths of Glory [1957] 1991

Patinoire, La. *See* Ice Rink, The.

Patriot, The 2001

Patriot Games 1992

Patriots Day 2017

Patsy, The 1985

Patti Rocks 1987

Patty Hearst 1988

Paul 2012

Paul Blart: Mall Cop 2010

Paul Blart: Mall Cop 2 2016

Paul Bowles: The Complete Outsider 1995

Paulie 1999

Pauline a la plage. *See* Pauline at the Beach.

Pauline and Paulette 2003

Pauline at the Beach 1983

Paura e amore. *See* Three Sisters.

Pavilion of Women 2002

Pawn Sacrifice 2016

Pay It Forward 2001

Payback 2000

Paycheck 2004

PCU 1995

Peace, Love, & Misunderstanding 2013

Peace, Propaganda & The Promised Land 2006

Peaceful Air of the West 1995

Peacemaker, The 1997

Peanuts Movie, The 2016

Pearl Harbor 2002

Pearl Jam Twenty 2012

Pebble and the Penguin, The 1995

Pecker 1999

Peeples 2014

Pee-wee's Big Adventure 1985

Peggy Sue Got Married 1986

Pelican Brief, The 1993

Pelle Erobreren. *See* Pelle the Conqueror.

Pelle the Conquered 1988

Pelle the Conqueror 1987

Penelope 2009

Penguins of Madagascar 2015

Penitent, The 1988

Penitentiary II 1982

Penitentiary III 1987

Penn and Teller Get Killed 1989

Pennies from Heaven 1981

People I Know 2004

People Like Us 2013

People on Sunday [1929] 1986

People Under the Stairs, The 1991

People vs. George Lucas, The 2012

People vs. Larry Flynt, The 1996

Pepi, Luci, Bom 1992

Percy Jackson & the Olympians: The Lightning Thief 2011

Percy Jackson: Sea of Monsters 2014

Perez Family, The 1995

Perfect 1985

Perfect Candidate, A 1996

Perfect Getaway, A 2010

Perfect Guy, The 2016

Perfect Host, The 2012

Perfect Man, The 2006

Perfect Match, The 1987

Perfect Match, The 2017

Perfect Model, The 1989

Perfect Murder, A 1999

Perfect Murder, The 1988

Perfect Score, The 2005

Perfect Son, The 2002

Perfect Storm, The 2001

Perfect Stranger 2008

Perfect Weapon, The 1991

Perfect World, A 1993

Perfectly Normal 1991

Perfume: The Story of a Murderer 2008

Perhaps Some Other Time 1992

Peril 1985

Peril en la demeure. *See* Peril.

Perks of Being a Wallflower, The 2013

Permanent Midnight 1999

Permanent Record 1988

Persepolis 2009

Personal Best 1982

Personal Choice 1989

Personal Services 1987

Personal Velocity 2003

Personals, The 1983

Persuasion 1995

Pervola, Sporen in die Sneeuw. *See* Tracks in the Snow.

Pest, The 1997

Pet Sematary 1989

Pet Sematary II 1992

Pete Kelly's Blues [1955] 1982

Peter Ibbetson [1935] 1985

Peter Pan 2004

Peter Von Scholten 1987

Peter's Friends 1992

Pete's Dragon 2017

Petit, Con. *See* Little Jerk.

Petite Bande, Le 1984

Petite Veleuse, La. *See* Little Thief, The.

Peyote Road, The 1995

Phantasm II 1988

Phantom 2014

Phantom, The 1996

Phantom of the Opera, The (Little) 1989

Phantom of the Opera, The (Schumacher) 2005

Phantoms 1999

Phar Lap 1984

Phat Beach 1996

Phat Girlz 2007

Phenomenon 1996

Philadelphia 1993

Philadelphia Experiment, The 1984

Philadelphia Experiment II, The 1995

Philomena 2014

Phobia 1988

Phoenix 2016

Rachel Getting Married 2009
Rachel Papers, The 1989
Rachel River 1987
Racing Stripes 2006
Racing with the Moon 1984
Radio 2004
Radio Days 1987
Radio Flyer 1992
Radioland Murders 1995
Radium City 1987
Rage: Carrie 2 2000
Rage in Harlem, A 1991
Rage of Honor 1987
Raggedy Man 1981
Raggedy Rawney, The 1988
Raging Angels 1995
Raging Fury. See Hell High.
Ragtime 1981
Raid: Berandal, The. See Raid 2, The.
Raid: Redemption, The 2013
Raid 2, The 2015
Raiders of the Lost Ark 1981
Railway Man, The 2015
Rain 2003
Rain. See Baran.
Rain Killer, The 1990
Rain Man 1988
Rain Without Thunder 1993
Rainbow Brite and the Star Stealer
   1985
Rainbow, The 1989
Raining Stones 1995
Raintree County [1957] 1993
Rainy Day Friends 1985
Raise the Red Lantern 1992
Raise Your Voice 2005
Raisin in the Sun, A [1961] 1992
Raising Arizona 1987
Raising Cain 1992
Raising Helen 2005
Raising Victor Vargas 2004
Rambling Rose 1991
Rambo 2009
Rambo: First Blood Part II 1985
Rambo III 1988

Ramona 1995
Ramona and Beezus 2011
Rampage 1987, 1992
Rampart 2012
Ran 1985
Random Hearts 2000
Rango 2012
Ransom 1996
Rapa Nui 1995
Rapid Fire 1992
Rappin' 1985
Rapture, The 1991
Raspad 1992
Rasputin [1975] 1985
Rat Race 2002
Ratatouille 2008
Ratboy 1986
Ratchet & Clank 2017
Rat's Tale, A 1999
Ratcatcher 2001
Rate It X 1986
Raven, The 2013
Ravenous 2000
Raw Deal 1986
Rawhead Rex 1987
Ray 2005
Rayon vert, Le. See Summer.
Razorback 1985
Razor's Edge, The 1984
Re-Animator 1985
Read My Lips 2003
Reader, The 1988, 1989
Reader, The 2009
Ready to Rumble 2001
Ready to Wear 1995
Real Blonde, The 1999
Real Genius 1985
Real McCoy, The 1993
Real Men 1987
Real Steel 2012
Real Women Have Curves 2003
Reality 2014
Reality Bites 1995
Reaping, The 2008
Rear Window [1954] 2001

Reason to Believe, A 1995
Rebel 1986
Rebelle. See War Witch.
Rebound 2006
[Rec] 2 2011
Reckless 1984
Reckless 1995
Reckless Kelly 1995
Reckoning, The 2005
Recruit, The 2004
Recruits 1986
Red 1995
RED 2011
Red Army 2016
Red Cliff 2010
Red Corner 1997
Red Dawn 1984
Red Dawn 2013
Red Dragon 2003
Red Eye 2006
Red Firecracker, Green Firecracker
   1995
Red Heat 1988
Red Hill 2011
Red Hook Summer 2013
Red Lights 2013
Red Planet 2001
Red Riding Hood 2012
Red Riding Trilogy, The 2011
Red Riding: 1980. See Red Riding
   Trilogy, The.
Red Riding: 1983. See Red Riding
   Trilogy, The.
Red Riding: 1974. See Red Riding
   Trilogy, The.
Red Road 2008
Red Rock West 1995
Red Scorpion 1989
Red Sonja 1985
Red Sorghum 1988
Red State 2012
Red Surf 1990
Red Tails 2013
Red Turtle, The 2017
RED 2 2014
Red Violin, The 1999

Sapphires, The 2014

Sara 1995

Saraband 2006

Sarafina! 1992

Satan 1995

Satisfaction 1988

Saturday Night at the Palace 1987

Saturday Night, Sunday Morning: The Travels of Gatemouth Moore 1995

Saul fia. *See* Son of Saul.

Sausage Party 2017

Sauve qui peut (La Vie). *See* Every Man for Himself.

Savage Beach 1989

Savage Island 1985

Savage Nights 1995

Savages 2013

Savages, The 2008

Savannah Smiles 1983

Save the Last Dance 2002

Save the Tiger [1973] 1988

Saved! 2005

Saving Christmas 2015

Saving Grace (Young) 1986

Saving Grace (Cole) 2001

Saving Mr. Banks 2014

Saving Private Ryan 1999

Saving Silverman 2002

Savior 1999

Saw 2005

Saw V 2009

Saw IV 2008

Saw VI 2010

Saw III 2007

Saw 3D: The Final Chapter 2011

Saw II 2006

Say Anything 1989

Say It Isn't So 2002

Say Yes 1986

Scandal 1989

Scandalous 1984

Scanner Darkly, A 2007

Scanners III: The Takeover 1995

Scaphandre et le papillon, Le. *See* Diving Bell and the Butterfly, The.

Scarface 1983

Scarlet Letter, The [1926] 1982, 1984

Scarlet Letter, The 1995

Scarlet Street [1946] 1982

Scary Movie 2001

Scary Movie 2 2002

Scary Movie 3 2004

Scary Movie 4 2007

Scary Movie 5 2014

Scavengers 1988

Scenes from a Mall 1991

Scenes from the Class Struggle in Beverly Hills 1989

Scent of a Woman 1992

Scent of Green Papaya, The (Mui du du Xanh) 1995

Scherzo del destino agguato dietro l'angelo come un brigante di strada. *See* Joke of Destiny, A.

Schindler's List 1993

Schizo 2006

Schizopolis 1997

School Daze 1988

School for Scoundrels 2007

School of Flesh, 432

School of Rock 2004

School Spirit 1985

School Ties 1992

Schtonk 1995

Schultze Gets the Blues 2006

Science des reves, La. *See* Science of Sleep, The.

Science of Sleep, The 2007

Scissors 1991

Scooby-Doo 2003

Scooby-Doo 2: Monsters Unleashed 2005

Scoop 2007

Scorched. *See* Incendies.

Scorchers 1995

Score, The 2002

Scorpion 1986

Scorpion King, The 2003

Scorta, La 1995

Scotland, PA 2003

Scott Pilgrim vs. the World 2011

Scout, The 1995

Scout's Guide to the Zombie Apocalypse 2016

Scream 1996

Scream 4 2012

Scream 2 1997

Scream 3 2001

Scream of Stone 1995

Screamers 1996

Screwed 2001

Scrooged 1988

Se, jie. *See* Lust, Caution.

Sea Inside, The 2005

Sea of Love 1989

Sea Wolves, The 1982

Seabiscuit 2004

Search and Destroy 1995

Search for Signs of Intelligent Life in the Universe, The 1991

Searching for Bobby Fischer 1993

Searching for Sugar Man 2013

Season of Dreams 1987

Season of Fear 1989

Season of Men, The 2003

Season of the Witch 2012

Seasons 1995

Second Best 1995

Second Best Exotic Marigold Hotel, The 2016

Second Chance, The 2007

Second Sight 1989

Second Skin 2003

Second Thoughts 1983

Secondhand Lions 2004

Secret Admirer 1985

Secret Garden, The 1993

Secret in Their Eyes, The 2011

Secret in Their Eyes 2016

Secret Life of Bees, The 2009

Secret Life of Pets, The 2017

Secret Life of Walter Mitty, The [1947] 1985

Secret Life of Walter Mitty, The 2014

Secret Lives of Dentists, The 2004

Secret Love, Hidden Faces. *See* Ju Dou.

Sharky's Machine 1981

Sharma and Beyond 1986

Shatterbrain. *See* Resurrected, The.

Shattered 1991

Shattered Glass 2004

Shaun of the Dead 2005

Shaun the Sheep Movie 2016

Shaunglong Hui. *See* Twin Dragons.

Shawshank Redemption, The 1995

She Hate Me 2005

She Must Be Seeing Things 1987

Sherrybaby 2007

She-Devil 1989

Sheena 1984

Sheer Madness 1985

Shelf Life 1995

Sheltering Sky, The 1990

Sherlock Holmes [1922] 1982

Sherlock Holmes 2010

Sherlock Holmes: A Game of Shadows 2012

Sherman's March 1986

She's All That 2000

She's De Lovely. *See* De-Lovely.

She's Funny That Way 2016

She's Gotta Have It 1986

She's Having a Baby 1988

She's Out of Control 1989

She's Out of My League 2011

She's So Lovely 1997

She's the Man 2007

She's the One 1996

Shi. *See* Poetry.

Shiloh 2: Shiloh Season 2000

Shimian Maifu. *See* House of Flying Daggers.

Shine 1996

Shine a Light 2009

Shining, The [1980]

Shining Through 1992

Shipping News, The 2002

Shipwrecked 1991

Shiqisuide Danche. *See* Beijing Bicycle.

Shirley Valentine 1989

Shiza. *See* Shizo.

Shoah 1985

Shock to the System, A 1990

Shocker 1989

Shomerei Ha'saf. *See* Gatekeepers, The.

Shoot 'Em Up 2008

Shoot the Moon 1982

Shoot to Kill 1988

Shooter 2008

Shooting, The [1966] 1995

Shooting Dogs. *See* Beyond the Gates.

Shooting Fish 1999

Shooting Party, The 1985

Shootist, The [1976] 1982

Shopgirl 2006

Short Circuit 1986

Short Circuit II 1988

Short Cuts 1993

Short Film About Love, A 1995

Short Term 12 2014

Short Time 1990

Shorts: The Adventures of the Wishing Rock 2010

Shot, The 1996

Shout 1991

Show, The 1995

Show Me Love 2000

Show of Force, A 1990

Showdown in Little Tokyo 1991

Shower, The 2001

Showgirls 1995

Showtime 2003

Shrek 2002

Shrek Forever After 2011

Shrek the Third 2008

Shrek 2 2005

Shrimp on the Barbie, The 1990

Shutter 2009

Shutter Island 2011

Shvitz, The. *See* New York in Short: The Shvitz and Let's Fall in Love.

Shy People 1987

Siberiade 1982

Sibling Rivalry 1990

Sicario 2016

Sicilian, The 1987

Sick: The Life and Death of Bob Flanagan, Supermasochist 1997

Sicko 2008

Sid and Nancy 1986

Side by Side 2013

Side Effects 2014

Side Out 1990

Sidekicks 1993

Sidewalk Stories 1989

Sidewalks of New York, The 2002

Sideways 2005

Siege, The 1999

Siesta 1987

Sightseers 2014

Sign o' the Times 1987

Sign of the Cross, The [1932] 1984

Signal Seven 1986

Signal, The 2015

Signs 2003

Signs & Wonders 2002

Signs of Life 1989

Silence 2017

Silence, The 2001

Silence After the Shot, The. *See* Legend of Rita, The.

Silence at Bethany, The 1988

Silence of the Lambs, The 1991

Silence, The 2014

Silencer, The 1995

Silent Fall 1995

Silent Hill 2007

Silent Hill: Revelation 3D 2013

Silent Madness, The 1984

Silent House 2013

Silent Night 1988

Silent Night, Deadly Night 1984

Silent Night, Deadly Night II 1987

Silent Night, Deadly Night III 1989

Silent Rage 1982

Silent Tongue 1995

Silent Touch, The 1995

Silent Victim 1995

Silk Road, The 1992

Silkwood 1983

Silver City (Sayles) 2005

Silver City (Turkiewicz) 1985

Silver Linings Playbook 2013

Silverado 1985

Simon Birch 1999

Simon Magnus 2002

Simon the Magician 2001

Simone 2003

Simpatico 2000

Simple Men 1992

Simple Plan, A 1999

Simple Twist of Fate, A 1995

Simple Wish, A 1997

Simply Irresistible 2000

Simpsons Movie, The 2008

Sin City 2006

Sin City: A Dame to Kill For 2015

Sin Nombre 2010

Sin Noticias de Dios. *See* No News from God.

Sinbad: Legend of the Seven Seas 2004

Since Otar Left 2005

Sincerely Charlotte 1986

Sinful Life, A 1989

Sing 1989

Sing 2017

Sing Street 2017

Singin' in the Rain [1952] 1985

Singing Detective, The 2004

Singing the Blues in Red 1988

Single Man, A 2010

Single Moms' Club, The. *See* Tyler Perry's The Single Moms' Club.

Single Shot, A 2014

Single White Female 1992

Singles 1992

Sinister 2013

Sinister 2 2016

Sioux City 1995

Sirens 1995

Sister Act 1992

Sister Act II 1993

Sister, My Sister 1995

Sister, Sister 1987

Sisterhood of the Traveling Pants, The 2006

Sisterhood of the Traveling Pants 2, The 2009

Sisters 2016

Sisters. *See* Some Girls.

Sitcom 2000

Sitter, The 2012

Siu lam juk kau. *See* Shaolin Soccer.

Siulam Chukkau. *See* Shaolin Soccer.

Six Days, Seven Nights 1999

Six Days, Six Nights 1995

Six Degrees of Separation 1993

Six Pack 1982

Six-String Samurai 1999

Six Ways to Sunday 2000

Six Weeks 1982

16 Blocks 2007

Sixteen Candles 1984

Sixteen Days of Glory 1986

Sixth Day, The 2001

Sixth Man, The 1997

Sixth Sense, The 2000

Sixty Glorious Years [1938] 1983

'68 1987

Skeleton Key, The 2006

Skeleton Twins, The 2015

Ski Country 1984

Ski Patrol 1990

Skin Deep 1989

Skin I Live In, The 2012

Skins 2003

Skinwalkers 2008

Skipped Parts 2002

Skulls, The 2001

Sky Bandits 1986

Sky Blue 2006

Sky Captain and the World of Tomorrow 2005

Sky High 2006

Sky of Our Childhood, The 1988

Skyfall 2013

Skyline 1984

Skyline 2011

Slacker 1991

Slackers 2003

Slam 1997

Slam Dance 1987

Slap Shot [1977] 1981

Slapstick 1984

Slate, Wyn, and Me 1987

Slave Coast. *See* Cobra Verde.

Slave Girls from Beyond Infinity 1987

Slaves of New York 1989

Slaves to the Underground 1997

Slayground 1984

SLC Punk 2000

Sleazy Uncle, The 1991

Sleep With Me 1995

Sleepers 1996

Sleeping Beauty 2012

Sleeping with Other People 2016

Sleeping with the Enemy 1991

Sleepless in Seattle 1993

Sleepover 2005

Sleepwalk with Me 2013

Sleepwalkers. *See* Stephen King's Sleepwalkers.

Sleepwalking 2009

Sleepy Hollow 2000

Sleepy Time Gal, The 2002

Sleuth 2008

Sliding Doors 1999

Sling Blade 1996

Slingshot, The 1995

Slipping Down Life, A 2005

Slither 2007

Sliver 1993

Slow Burn 2008

Slow West 2016

Slugs 1988

Slumdog Millionaire 2009

Slums of Beverly Hills 1999

Small Faces 1996

Small Soldiers 1999

Small Time Crooks 2001

Small Wonders 1996

Smart People 2009

Smash Palace 1982

Smashed 2013

Smell of Camphor, Fragrance of Jasmine 2001

Smile Like Yours, A 1997

Smiling Fish and Goat on Fire 2001

Smilla's Sense of Snow 1997

Smithereens 1982, 1985

Smoke 1995

Smoke Signals 1999

Smokey and the Bandit, Part 3 1983

Smokin' Aces 2008

Smoking/No Smoking [1995] 2001

Smooth Talk 1985

Smurfs, The 2012

Smurfs 2, The 2014

Smurfs and the Magic Flute, The 1983

Snake Eyes 1999

Snake Eyes. *See* Dangerous Game.

Snakes on a Plane 2007

Snapper, The 1993

Snatch 2002

Sneakers 1992

Sniper 1993

Snitch 2014

Snow Angels 2009

Snow Day 2001

Snow Dogs 2003

Snow Falling in Cedars 2000

Snow Flower and the Secret Fan 2012

Snow White. *See* Mirror Mirror.

Snow White and the Huntsman 2013

Snowden 2017

Snowpiercer 2015

Snows of Kilimanjaro, The [1952] 1982

S.O.B. 1981

So I Married an Axe Murderer 1993

Soapdish 1991

Sobibor, October 14, 1943, 4 p.m. 2002

Social Network, The 2011

Society 1992

Sofie 1993

Soft Fruit 2001

Soft Shell Man 2003

Softly Softly 1985

Sokhout. *See* Silence, The.

Sol del Membrillo, El. *See* Dream of Light.

Solarbabies 1986

Solaris 2003

Solas 2001

Soldier 1999

Soldier, The 1982

Soldier's Daughter Never Cries, A 1999

Soldier's Story, A 1984

Soldier's Tale, A 1988

Solid Gold Cadillac, The [1956] 1984

Solitary Man 2011

Solo 1996

Soloist, The 2010

Solomon and Gaenor 2001

Some Girls 1988

Some Kind of Hero 1982

Some Kind of Wonderful 1987

Some Like It Hot [1959] 1986, 1988

Some Mother's Son 1996

Someone Else's America 1996

Someone Like You 2002

Someone to Love 1987, 1988

Someone to Watch Over Me 1987

Somersault 2007

Something Borrowed 2012

Something in the Air 2014

Something New 2007

Something to Do with the Wall 1995

Something to Talk About 1995

Something Wicked This Way Comes 1983

Something Wild 1986

Something Within Me 1995

Something's Gotta Give 2004

Somewhere 2011

Sommersby 1993

Son, The 2003

Son of Darkness: To Die For II 1995

Son of God 2015

Son of No One, The 2012

Son of Rambow 2009

Son of Saul 2016

Son of the Bride 2003

Son of the Mask 2006

Son of the Pink Panther 1993

Son-in-Law 1993

Sonatine 1999

Song for Marion. *See* Unfinished Song.

Song for Martin 2003

Songcatcher 2001

Songwriter 1984

Sonny 2003

Sonny Boy 1990

Sons 1989

Sons of Steel 1988

Son's Room, The 2002

Sontagsbarn. *See* Sunday's Children.

Sophie's Choice 1982

Sorcerer's Apprentice, The 2011

Sorority Babes in the Slimeball Bowl-o-Rama 1988

Sorority Boys 2003

Sorority House Massacre 1987

Sorority Row 2010

Soshite chichi ni naru. *See* Like Father, Like Son.

Sotto Sotto. *See* Softly Softly.

Soul Food 1997

Soul Kitchen 2011

Soul Man 1986

Soul Men 2009

Soul Plane 2005

Soul Power 2010

Soul Surfer 2012

Soul Survivors 2002

Sound Barrier, The [1952] 1984, 1990

Sound City 2014

Sound of My Voice, The 2013

Sound of Thunder, A 2006

Sour Grapes 1999

Source, The 2000

Source Code 2012

Soursweet 1988

Sous le Sable. *See* Under the Sand.

Sous le Soleil de Satan. *See* Under the Sun of Satan.

Star Trek V: The Final Frontier 1989

Star Trek VI: The Undiscovered Country 1991

Star Trek: First Contact 1996

Star Trek: Generations 1995

Star Trek: Insurrection 1999

Star Trek: Nemesis 2003

Star Trek: The Motion Picture [1979] 1986

Star Wars: Episode I—The Phantom Menace 2000

Star Wars: Episode II—Attack of the Clones 2003

Star Wars: Episode III—Revenge of the Sith 2006

Star Wars: Episode IV—A New Hope [1977] 1997

Star Wars: Episode VII—The Force Awakens. *See* Star Wars: The Force Awakens.

Star Wars: The Clone Wars 2009

Star Wars: The Force Awakens 2016

Starchaser 1985

Stardom 2001

Stardust 2008

Stardust Memories [1980] 1984

Stargate 1995

Starman 1984

Starred Up 2015

Stars and Bars 1988

Stars Fell on Henrietta, The 1995

Starship Troopers 1997

Starsky & Hutch 2005

Starstruck 1982

Starter for 10 2008

Startup.com 2002

State and Main 2001

State of Grace 1990

State of Play 2010

State of Things, The 1983

Statement, The 2004

Stateside 2005

Station, The 1992

Station Agent, The 2004

Stay 2006

Stay Alive 2007

Stay Tuned 1992

Staying Alive 1983

Staying Together 1989

Steal America 1992

Steal Big, Steal Little 1995

Stealing Beauty 1996

Stealing Harvard 2003

Stealing Heaven 1988

Stealing Home 1988

Stealth 2006

Steamboy 2006

Steaming 1986

Steel 1997

Steel Magnolias 1989

Steele Justice 1987

Stella 1990

Stella Dallas [1937] 1987

Step Brothers 2009

Step Into Liquid 2004

Step Up 2007

Step Up: All In 2015

Step Up Revolution 2013

Step Up 3D 2011

Step Up 2 the Streets 2009

Stepfather, The 1987

Stepfather, The 2010

Stepfather II 1989

Stepford Wives, The 2005

Stephanie Daley 2008

Stephen King's Cat's Eye 1985

Stephen King's Children of the Corn 1984

Stephen King's Graveyard Shift 1990

Stephen King's Silver Bullet 1985

Stephen King's Sleepwalkers 1992

Stephen King's The Night Flier 1999

Stephen King's Thinner 1996

Stepmom 1999

Stepping Out 1991

Steve Jobs 2016

Stick 1985

Stick, The 1988

Stick It 2007

Sticky Fingers 1988

Stigmata 2000

Still Alice 2015

Still Crazy 1999

Still Mine 2014

Still of the Night 1982

Stille Nach Dem Schuss, Die. *See* Legend of Rita, The.

Sting II, The 1983

Stir Crazy [1980] 1992

Stir of Echoes 2000

Stitches 1985

Stoker 2014

Stolen Life, A [1946] 1986

Stolen Summer 2003

Stomp the Yard 2008

Stone 2011

Stone Boy, The 1984

Stone Cold 1991

Stone Reader 2004

Stonewall 1996

Stonewall 2016

Stoning of Soraya M., The 2010

Stop Making Sense 1984

Stop! Or My Mom Will Shoot 1992

Stop-Loss 2009

Stories from the Kronen 1995

Stories We Tell 2014

Storks 2017

Stormy Monday 1988

Story of Qiu Ju, The 1993

Story of the Weeping Camel, The 2005

Story of Us, The 2000

Story of Women 1989

Story of Xinghau, The 1995

Storytelling 2003

Storyville 1992

Straight for the Heart 1990

Straight Out of Brooklyn 1991

Straight Outta Compton 2016

Straight Story, The 2000

Straight Talk 1992

Straight to Hell 1987

Strange Brew 1983

Strange Days 1995

Strange Invaders 1983

Strange Love of Martha Ivers, The [1946] 1991

Thelonious Monk 1988

Then She Found Me 2009

Theory of Everything, The 2015

Theory of Flight, The 1999

There Goes My Baby 1995

There Goes the Neighborhood 1995

There Will Be Blood 2008

There's Nothing Out There 1992

There's Something About Mary 1999

Therese. *See* In Secret.

Theremin: An Electronic Odyssey 1995

They All Laughed 1981

They Call Me Bruce 1982

They Drive by Night [1940] 1982

They Live 1988

They Live by Night [1949] 1981

They Might Be Giants [1971] 1982

They Still Call Me Bruce 1987

They Won't Believe Me [1947] 1987

They're Playing with Fire 1984

Thiassos, O. *See* Traveling Players, The.

Thief 1981

Thief, The 1999

Thief of Hearts 1984

Thieves 1996

Thin Blue Line, The 1988

Thin Ice 2013

Thin Line Between Love and Hate, A 1996

Thin Red Line, The 1999

Thing, The 1982

Thing, The 2012

Thing Called Love, The 1995

Things Are Tough All Over 1982

Things Change 1988

Things to Come 2017

Things to Do in Denver When You're Dead 1995

Things We Lost in the Fire 2008

Think Big 1990

Think Like a Man 2013

Think Like a Man Too 2015

Third Person 2015

Third World Cop 2001

Thirst 2010

Thirteen 2004

13 Assassins 2012

Thirteen Conversations About One Thing 2003

Thirteen Days 2001

Thirteen Ghosts 2003

13 Going On 30 2005

13 Hours 2017

Thirtieth Floor, The 2000

Thirtieth Warrior, The 2000

30 Days of Night 2008

30 Minutes or Less 2012

35 Shots of Rum 2011

Thirty Two Short Films About Glenn Gould 1995

Thirty-five Up 1992

37, 2 le Matin. *See* Betty Blue.

Thirty-six Fillette 1988

33, The 2016

This Boy's Life 1993

This Christmas 2008

This Is Elvis 1981

This Is 40 2013

This is My Father 2000

This is My Life 1992

This Is Spinal Tap 1984

This Is It. *See* Michael Jackson's This Is It.

This Is the End 2014

This Is Where I Leave You 2015

This Means War 2013

This Must Be the Place 2013

This Side of the Truth. *See* Invention of Lying, The.

This World, Then the Fireworks 1997

Thomas and the Magic Railroad 2001

Thomas Crown Affair, The 2000

Thomas in Love 2002

Thor 2012

Thor: The Dark World 2014

Those Who Love Me Can Take the Train 2000

Thou Shalt Not Kill 1988

Thousand Acres, A 1997

Thousand Pieces of Gold 1991

Thousand Words, A 2013

Thrashin' 1986

Three Amigos 1986

Three Brothers 1982

Three Burials of Melquiades Estrada, The 2007

3 Days to Kill 2015

Three...Extremes 2006

3:15 1986

Three for the Road 1987

Three Fugitives 1989

300 2008

360 2013

300: Rise of an Empire 2015

3-Iron 2006

Three Kinds of Heat 1987

Three Kings 2000

Three Lives & Only One Death 1996

Three Madeleines, The 2001

Three Men and a Baby 1987

Three Men and a Cradle 1986

Three Men and a Little Lady 1990

Three Monkeys 2010

Three Musketeers, The 1993

Three Musketeers, The 2012

Three Ninjas Kick Back 1995

Three Ninjas 1992

Three O'Clock High 1987

Three of Hearts 1993

Three Seasons 2000

Three Sisters 1988

Three Stooges, The 2013

3 Strikes 2001

3:10 to Yuma 2008

3000 Miles to Graceland 2002

Three to Get Ready 1988

Three to Tango 2000

Three Wishes 1995

Threesome 1995

Threshold 1983

Through the Eyes of the Children. *See* 112th and Central.

Through the Olive Trees 1995

Through the Wire 1990

Through the Window 2001

Throw Momma from the Train 1987

Thumbelina. *See* Hans Christian Andersen's Thumbelina.

Thumbsucker 2006

Thunder Alley 1986

Thunderbirds 2005

Thunderheart 1992

THX 1138 [1971] 1984

Thy Kingdom Come…Thy Will Be Done 1988

Tian di ying xiong. *See* Warriors of Heaven and Earth.

Tian Yu. *See* Xiu Xiu: The Sent Down Girl.

Tian zhu ding. *See* Touch of Sin, A.

Ticket to Ride. *See* Post Grad.

Tickled 2017

Tideland 2007

Tie Me Up! Tie Me Down! 1990

Tie That Binds, The 1995

Tieta of Agreste 2000

Tiger Warsaw 1988

Tigerland 2002

Tiger's Tale, A 1987

Tigger Movie, The 2001

Tightrope 1984

Til' There Was You 1997

Till Human Voices Wake Us 2004

Tillman Story, The 2011

Tillsammans. *See* Together.

Tim and Eric's Billion Dollar Movie 2013

Tim Burton's Corpse Bride 2006

Timbuktu 2016

Time After Time 1983

Time and Tide 2002

Time Bandits 1981

Time Code 2001

Time for Drunken Horses, A 2001

Time Indefinite 1995

Time Machine, The (Pal) [1960] 1983

Time Machine, The (Wells) 2003

Time of Destiny, A 1988

Time of Favor 2002

Time of the Gypsies 1990

Time Out 2003

Time Out of Mind 2016

Time Regained 2001

Time to Die, A 1991

Time to Kill, A 1996

Time to Leave 2007

Time Traveler's Wife, The 2010

Time Will Tell 1992

Timebomb 1992

Timecop 1995

Timeline 2004

Timerider 1983

Timothy Leary's Dead 1997

Tin Cup 1996

Tin Men 1987

Tinker Tailor Soldier Spy 2012

Titan A.E. 2001

Titanic 1997

Tito and Me 1993

Titus 2000

TMNT 2008

To Be or Not to Be 1983

To Begin Again. *See* Volver a empezar.

To Die For 1989

To Die For 1995

To Die Standing (Crackdown) 1995

To Do List, The 2014

To Gillian on Her 37th Birthday 1996

To Kill a Mockingbird [1962] 1989

To Kill a Priest 1988

To Live 1995

To Live and Die in L.A. 1985, 1986

To Protect Mother Earth 1990

To Render a Life 1995

To Return. *See* Volver.

To Rome with Love 2013

To Sir with Love [1967] 1992

To Sleep with Anger 1990

To the Wonder 2014

To Wong Foo, Thanks for Everything! Julie Newmar 1995

Todo Sobre Mi Madre. *See* All About My Mother.

Together 2002

Together 2004

Tokyo Pop 1988

Tokyo-Ga 1985

Tom and Huck 1995

Tom and Jerry 1993

Tom & Viv 1995

Tomb Raider. *See* Lara Croft: Tomb Raider.

Tomboy 1985

Tombstone 1993

Tomcats 2002

Tommy Boy 1995

Tomorrow [1972] 1983

Tomorrowland 2016

Tomorrow Never Dies 1997

Tomorrow's a Killer. *See* Prettykill.

Toni Erdmann 2017

Too Beautiful for You 1990

Too Hot to Handle [1938] 1983

Too Much 1987

Too Much Sleep 2002

Too Much Sun 1991

Too Outrageous! 1987

Too Scared to Scream 1985

Too Soon to Love [1960]

Tooth Fairy 2011

Tootsie 1982

Top Dog 1995

Top Five 2015

Top Gun 1986

Top of the Food Chain 2002

Top Secret 1984

Topio stin omichi. *See* Landscape in the Mist.

Topsy-Turvy 2000

Tora-San Goes to Viena 1989

Torajiro Kamone Uta. *See* Foster Daddy, Tora!

Torch Song Trilogy 1988

Torinoi lo, A. *See* Turin Horse, The.

Torment 1986

Torn Apart 1990

Torn Curtain [1966] 1984

Torque 2005

Torrents of Spring 1990

Tortilla Soup 2002

Total Eclipse 1995

Total Recall 1990

Total Recall 2013

Totally F***ed Up 1995

Toto le heros. *See* Toto the Hero.

Toto the Hero 1992

Tottering Lives 1988

Touch 1997

Touch and Go 1986

Touch of a Stranger 1990

Touch of Evil [1958] 1999

Touch of Larceny, A [1959] 1986

Touch of Sin, A 2014

Touch the Sound 2006

Touched with Fire 2017

Touching the Void 2005

Touchy Feely 2014

Tough Enough 1983

Tough Guys 1986

Tough Guys Don't Dance 1987

Tougher than Leather 1988

Touki-Bouki 1995

Tourist, The 2011

Tous les matins du monde 1992

Toward the Within 1995

Tower Heist 2012

Town, The 2011

Town and Country 2002

Town is Quiet, The 2002

Toxic Avenger, The 1986

Toxic Avenger, Part II, The 1989

Toxic Avenger, Part III, The 1989

Toy, The 1982

Toy Soldiers (Fisher) 1984

Toy Soldiers (Petrie) 1991

Toy Story 1995

Toy Story 3 2011

Toy Story 2 2000

Toys 1992

Trace, The 1984

Trance 2014

Traces of Red 1992

Track 1988

Tracks 2015

Tracks in the Snow 1986

Trade 2008

Trade Winds [1939] 1982

Trading Hearts 1988

Trading Mom 1995

Trading Places 1983

Traffic 2001

Tragedia di un umo ridiculo. *See* Tragedy of a Ridiculous Man.

Tragedy of a Ridiculous Man 1982

Trail of the Lonesome Pine, The. *See* Waiting for the Moon.

Trail of the Pink Panther 1982

Train de Vie. *See* Train of Life.

Train of Life 2000

Training Day 2002

Trainspotting 1996

Trainwreck 2016

Traitor 2009

Trancers 1985

Transamerica 2006

Transcendence 2015

Transformers 2008

Transformers, The 1986

Transformers: Age of Extinction 2015

Transformers: Dark of the Moon 2012

Transformers 4. *See* Transformers: Age of Extinction.

Transformers: Revenge of the Fallen 2010

Transporter Refueled, The 2016

Transporter 3 2009

Transporter 2 2006

Transsiberian 2009

Transylvania 6-5000 1985

Trapped 2003

Trapped in Paradise 1995

Traps 1995

Traveling Players, The [1974] 1990

Traveller 1997

Travelling Avant 1987

Travelling North 1987

Traviata, La 1982

Tre fratelli. *See* Three Brothers.

Treasure Island 2001

Treasure of the Four Crowns 1983

Treasure of the Sierra Madre, The [1948] 1983

Treasure Planet 2003

Tree of Life, The 2012

Trees Lounge 1996

Trekkies 2000

Tremors 1990

Trenchcoat 1983

Trespass 1992

Trespass 2012

Trial, The 1995

Trial and Error 1997

Trial by Jury 1995

Tribe, The 2016

Tribulations of Balthasar Kober, The 1988

Trick 2000

Trick or Treat 1986

Trigger Effect, The 1996

Trilogia: To Livadi pou dakryzei. *See* Weeping Meadow.

Trilogy: After the Life, The 2005

Trilogy: An Amazing Couple, The 2005

Trilogy: On the Run, The 2005

Trilogy: Weeping Meadow, The. *See* Weeping Meadow.

Trip, The 2012

Trip to Bountiful, A [1953] 1982

Trip to Bountiful, The 1985

Trip to Italy, The 2015

Triple 9 2017

Triplets of Belleville, The 2004

Trippin' 2000

Trishna 2013

Tristan & Isolde 2007

Tristram Shandy: A Cock and Bull Story 2007

Triumph of Love, The 2003

Triumph of the Spirit 1989

Trixie 2001

Trmavomodry Svet. *See* Dark Blue World.

Trois Couleurs: Blanc. *See* White.

Trois Couleurs: Bleu. *See* Blue.

Trois Couleurs: Rouge. *See* Red.

Trois Hommes et un couffin. *See* Three Men and a Cradle.

Trojan Eddie 1997

Trol Hunter, The. *See* Trollhunter.

Troll 1986

Trollhunter 2012

Trolljegeren. *See* Trollhunter.

Trolls 2017

Trolosa. *See* Faithless.

TRON 1982

TRON: Legacy 2011

Troop Beverly Hills 1989

Trop belle pour toi. *See* Too Beautiful for You.

Tropic Thunder 2009

Tropical Rainforest 1992

Trouble at the Royal Rose. *See* Trouble with Spies, The.

Trouble Bound 1995

Trouble in Mind 1985

Trouble with Dick, The 1987

Trouble with Spies, The 1987

Trouble with the Curve 2013

Troubles We've Seen: A History of Journalism in Wartime, The 2006

Troublesome Creek: A Midwestern 1997

Trout, The 1983

Troy 2005

Truce, The 1999

Trucker 2010

True Believer 1989

True Blood 1989

True Colors 1991

True Confessions 1981

True Crime 2000

True Grit 2011

True Heart Susie [1919] 1984

True Identity 1991

True Lies 1995

True Love 1989

True Romance 1993

True Stories 1986

True Story 2016

Truite, La. *See* Trout, The.

Truly, Madly, Deeply 1991

Truman Show, The 1999

Trumbo 2016

Trumpet of the Swan, The 2002

Trust 1991

Trust 2012

Trust Me 1989

Trust the Man 2007

Trusting Beatrice 1993

Truth 2016

Truth About Cats & Dogs, The 1996

Truth About Charlie, The 2003

Truth or Consequences: N.M., 1997

Truth or Dare 1991

Tsotsi 2007

Tuck Everlasting 2003

Tucker 1988

Tucker & Dale vs. Evil 2012

Tuff Turf 1985

Tully 2004

Tumbleweeds 2000

Tune, The 1992

Tune in Tomorrow… 1990

Tunel, El. *See* Tunnel, The.

Tunnel, The 1988

Turandot Project, The 2002

Turbo 2014

Turbo: A Power Rangers Movie, 1997

Turbulence, 1997

Turin Horse, The 2013

Turist. *See* Force Majeure.

Turistas 2007

Turk 182 1985

Turn It Up 2001

Turner and Hooch 1989

Turning Paige 2003

Turtle Beach 1995

Turtle Diary 1985, 1986

Turtles are Back…In Time, The. *See* Teenage Mutant Ninja Turtles III.

Tusk 2015

Tuxedo, The 2003

TV Set, The 2008

Twelfth Night 1996

Twelve 2011

Twelve Monkeys 1995

Twelve O'Clock High [1949] 1989

12 Rounds 2010

12 Years a Slave 2014

Twenty Bucks 1993

20 Dates 2000

28 Weeks Later 2008

20 Feet from Stardom 2014

20th Century Women 2017

25th Hour 2003

24 Hour Party People 2003

24 Hours. *See* Trapped.

21 & Over 2014

21 Grams 2004

TwentyFourSeven 1999

24 Hour Woman 2000

28 Days 2001

28 Days Later 2004

28 Up 1985

2046 2006

Twenty-ninth Street 1991

Twenty-one 1991

21 Jump Street 2013

20,000 Days on Earth 2015

2012 2010

21 2009

27 Dresses 2009

22 Jump Street 2015

Twice Dead 1988

Twice in a Lifetime 1985

Twice upon a Time 1983

Twilight 1999

Twilight 2009

Twilight of the Cockroaches 1990

Twilight of the Ice Nymphs 1999

Twilight Saga: Breaking Dawn, Part 1, The 2012

Twilight Saga: Breaking Dawn, Part 2, The 2013

Twilight Saga: Eclipse, The 2011

Twilight Saga: New Moon, The 2010

Twilight Samurai, The 2005

Twilight Zone: The Movie 1983

Twin Dragons 2000

Twin Falls Idaho 2000

Twin Peaks: Fire Walk with Me 1992

Victor/Victoria 1982

Victory 1981

Victory. *See* Vincere.

Videodrome 1983

Vie Apres l'Amour, La. *See* Life After Love.

Vie continue, La 1982

Vie d'Adele, La. *See* Blue is the Warmest Color.

Vie de Boheme, La 1995

Vie en Rose, La 2008

Vie est rien d'autre, La. *See* Life and Nothing But.

Vie est un long fleuve tranquille, La. *See* Life Is a Long Quiet River.

Vie Promise, La. *See* Promised Life, The.

Vierde Man, De. *See* 4th Man, The.

View from the Top 2004

View to a Kill, A 1985

Village, The 2005

Village of the Damned 1995

Ville est Tranquille, La. *See* Town is Quiet, The.

Vince Vaughn's Wild West Comedy Show: 30 Days & 30 Nights— Hollywood to the Heartland 2009

Vincent and Theo 1990

Vincere 2011

Violets Are Blue 1986

Violins Came with the Americans, The 1987

Violon Rouge, Le. *See* Red Violin, The.

Viper 1988

Virgen de los Sicanos, La. *See* Our Lady of the Assassins.

Virgin Queen of St. Francis High, The 1987

Virgin Suicides, The 2001

Virtuosity 1995

Virus 2000

Vision Quest 1985

Visions of Light 1993

Visions of the Spirit 1988

Visit, The 2002

Visit, The 2016

Visiting Hours 1982

Visitor, The 2009

Visitor, The. *See* Ghost.

Vital Signs 1990

Volcano 1997

Volere, Volare 1992

Volunteers 1985

Volver 2007

Volver a empezar 1982

Vor. *See* Thief, The.

Vow, The 2013

Voyage du ballon rouge, Le. *See* Flight of the Red Balloon.

Voyager 1992

Voyages 2002

Voyeur 1995

Vroom 1988

Vulture, The 1985

Vzlomshik. *See* Burglar, The.

W

W. 2009

Wackness, The 2009

Waco: The Rules of Engagement 1997

Wag the Dog 1997

Wagner 1983

Wagons East! 1995

Wah-Wah 2007

Wailing, The 2017

Waist Deep 2007

Wait for Me in Heaven 1990

Wait Until Spring, Bandini 1990

Waiting… 2006

Waiting for Gavrilov 1983

Waiting for Guffman 1997

Waiting for 'Superman' 2011

Waiting for the Light 1990

Waiting for the Moon 1987

Waiting to Exhale 1995

Waitress 1982

Waitress (Shelly) 2008

Waking Life 2002

Waking Ned Devine 1999

Waking the Dead 2001

Walk, The 2016

Walk Among the Tombstones, A 2015

Walk Hard: The Dewey Cox Story 2008

Walk in the Clouds, A 1995

Walk in the Woods, A 2016

Walk Like a Man 1987

Walk on the Moon, A 1987

Walk on the Moon, A (Goldwyn) 2000

Walk the Line 2006

Walk to Remember, A 2003

Walker 1987

Walking and Talking 1996

Walking After Midnight 1988

Walking Dead, The 1995

Walking Tall 2005

Walking with Dinosaurs 3D 2014

Wall, The 1986

Wall Street 1987

Wallace & Gromit: The Curse of the Were-Rabbit 2006

WALL-E 2009

Wall Street: Money Never Sleeps 2011

Waltz Across Texas 1983

Waltz with Bashir 2009

Wandafuru raifu. *See* After Life.

Wanderlust 2013

Wannsee Conference, The 1987

Wannseekonferenz, Die. *See* Wannsee Conference, The.

Wanted 2009

Wanted: Dead or Alive 1987

War 1988

War (Arwell) 2008

War, The 1995

War Against the Indians 1995

War and Love 1985

War at Home, The 1997

War Dogs 2017

War Horse 2012

War, Inc. 2009

War of the Buttons 1995

War of the Roses, The 1989

War of the Worlds 2006

What Dreams May Come 1999

What Happened to Kerouse? 1986

What Happened Was... 1995

What Happens in Vegas 2009

What If 2015

What Just Happened 2009

What Lies Beneath 2001

What Maisie Knew 2014

What Planet Are You From? 2001

What the (Bleep) Do We Know? 2005

What Time Is It There? 2002

What to Expect When You're Expecting 2013

What We Do in the Shadows 2016

What Women Want 2001

Whatever 1999

Whatever It Takes (Demchuk) 1986

Whatever It Takes (Raynr) 2001

Whatever Works 2010

What's Cooking? 2001

What's Eating Gilbert Grape 1993

What's Love Got To Do With It 1993

What's the Worst That Could Happen? 2002

What's Your Number? 2012

When a Man Loves a Woman 1995

When a Stranger Calls 2007

When Brendan Met Trudy 2002

When Did You Last See Your Father? 2009

When Father Was Away on Business 1985

When Harry Met Sally 1989

When in Rome 2011

When Love Comes 2000

When Nature Calls 1985

When Night is Falling 1995

When the Bough Breaks 2017

When the Cat's Away 1997

When the Game Stands Tall 2015

When the Party's Over 1993

When the Whales Came 1989

When the Wind Blows 1987

When We Were Kings 1997

When Will I Be Loved 2005

Where Angels Fear to Tread 1992

Where Are the Children? 1986

Where Do We Go Now? 2013

Where Spring Comes Late 1988

Where the Boys are '84 1984

Where the Day Takes You 1992

Where the Green Ants Dream 1985

Where the Heart Is (Boorman) 1990

Where the Heart Is (Williams) 2001

Where the Heart Roams 1987

Where the Money Is 2001

Where the Outback Ends 1988

Where the River Runs Black 1986

Where The Rivers Flow North 1995

Where the Truth Lies 2006

Where the Wild Things Are 2010

Where to Invade Next 2016

Wherever You Are 1988

While We're Young 2016

While You Were Sleeping 1995

Whip It 2010

Whiplash 2015

Whiskey Tango Foxtrot 2017

Whispers in the Dark 1992

Whistle Blower, The 1987

Whistleblower, The 2012

White 1995

White Badge 1995

White Balloon, The 1996

White Bird in a Blizzard 2015

White Boys 2000

White Chicks 2005

White Countess, The 2006

White Dog 1995

White Fang 1991

White Fang II: Myth of the White Wolf 1995

White Girl, The 1990

White God 2016

White House Down 2014

White Hunter, Black Heart 1990

White Man's Burden 1995

White Material 2011

White Men Can't Jump 1992

White Mischief 1988

White Nights 1985

White Noise 2006

White of the Eye 1987, 1988

White Oleander 2003

White Palace 1990

White Ribbon, The 2010

White Rose, The 1983

White Sands 1992

White Sister, The [1923] 1982

White Squall 1996

White Trash 1992

White Winter Heat 1987

Whiteout 2010

Who Framed Roger Rabbit 1988

Who Killed the Electric Car? 2007

Who Killed Vincent Chin? 1988

Who Knows? *See* Va Savoir.

Who Shot Pat? 1992

Whole Nine Yards, The 2001

Whole Ten Yards, The 2005

Whole Wide World, The 1997

Whoopee Boys, The 1986

Whore 1991

Who's Afraid of Virginia Wolf? [1966] 1993

Who's Harry Crumb? 1989

Who's That Girl 1987

Who's the Man? 1993

Whose Life Is It Anyway? 1981

Why Did I Get Married? 2008

Why Did I Get Married Too? 2011

Why Do Fools Fall In Love 1999

Why Has Bodhi-Dharma Left for the East? 1995

Why Him? 2017

Why Me? 1990

Why We Fight 2007

Wicked Lady, The 1983

Wicked Stepmother 1989

Wicker Man, The [1974] 1985

Wicker Man, The 2007

Wicker Park 2005

Wide Awake 1999

Wide Sargasso Sea 1993

Widow of Saint-Pierre, The 2002

Widows' Peak 1995

Wiener-Dog 2017

Wife, The 1996

Wigstock: the Movie 1995

Wilbur Wants to Kill Himself 2005

Wild 2015

Wild, The 2007

Wild America 1997

Wild at Heart 1990

Wild Bill 1995

Wild Bunch, The [1969] 1995

Wild Duck, The 1985

Wild Geese II 1985

Wild Grass 2011

Wild Hearts Can't Be Broken 1991

Wild Hogs 2008

Wild Horses 1984

Wild Life, The 1984

Wild Life, The 2017

Wild Man Blues 1999

Wild Orchid 1990

Wild Orchid II: Two Shades of Blue 1992

Wild Pair, The 1987

Wild Parrots of Telegraph Hill, The 2006

Wild Reeds 1995

Wild Tales 2016

Wild Thing 1987

Wild Things 1999

Wild Thornberrys Movie, The 2003

Wild West 1993

Wild West Comedy Show. *See* Vince Vaughn's Wild West Comedy Show: 30 Days & 30 Nights— Hollywood to the Heartland.

Wild Wild West 2000

Wildcats 1986

Wilde 1999

Wilder Napalm 1993

Wildfire 1988

Willard 2004

William Shakespeare's A Midsummer's Night Dream 2000

William Shakespeare's Romeo & Juliet 1996

William Shakespeare's The Merchant of Venice. *See* Merchant of Venice, The.

Willow 1988

Wilt. *See* Misadventures of Mr. Wilt, The.

Wimbledon 2005

Win. *See* Vincere.

Win a Date with Tad Hamilton 2005

Win Win 2012

Wind 1992

Wind, The [1928] 1984

Wind in the Willows, The 1997

Wind Rises, The 2014

Wind the Shakes the Barley, The 2008

Wind Will Carry Us, The 2001

Window Shopping 1995

Window to Paris 1995

Windtalkers 2003

Windy City 1984

Wing Commanders 2000

Winged Migration 2004

Wings of Desire 1988

Wings of the Dove 1997

Winner, The 1997

Winners, The 2000

Winners Take All 1987

Winnie the Pooh 2012

Winslow Boy, The 2000

Winter Guest, The 1997

Winter Meeting [1948] 1986

Winter of Our Dreams 1982

Winter on Fire: Ukraine's Fight for Freedom 2016

Winter Passing 2007

Winter People 1989

Winter Sleep 2015

Winter Solstice 2006

Winter Tan, A 1988

Winter War, The. *See* Talvison.

Winter's Bone 2011

Winter's Tale 2015

Wiping the Tears of Seven Generations 1995

Wired 1989

Wired to Kill 1986

Wirey Spindell 2001

Wisdom 1986

Wise Guys 1986

Wisecracks 1992

Wish I Was Here 2015

Wish You Were Here 1987

Wishmaster 1997

Witch, The 2017

Witchboard 1987

Witches, The 1990

Witches of Eastwick, The 1987

With a Friend Like Harry 2002

With Friends Like These... 2006

With Honors 1995

With Love to the Person Next to Me 1987

Withnail and I 1987

Without a Clue 1988

Without a Paddle 2005

Without a Trace 1983

Without Evidence 1996

Without Limits 1999

Without You I'm Nothing 1990

Witless Protection 2009

Witness 1985

Witness for the Prosecution 1986

Witness to a Killing 1987

Witnesses, The 2009

Wittgenstein 1995

Wizard, The 1989

Wizard of Loneliness, The 1988

Wizard of Oz, The [1939], 1999

Wo De Fu Qin Mu Qin. *See* Road Home, The.

Wo Die Gruenen Ameisen Traeumen. *See* Where the Green Ants Dream.

Wo Hu Zang Long. *See* Crouching Tiger, Hidden Dragon.

Wolf 1995

Wolf of Wall Street, The 2014

Wolfen 1981

Wolfman, The 2011

Wolfpack, The 2016

Wolverine, The 2014